Dictionary of Anonymous and Pseudonymous English Literature

Dictionary
OF
Anonymous and Pseudonymous English Literature

(SAMUEL HALKETT AND JOHN LAING)

NEW AND ENLARGED EDITION

BY

DR JAMES KENNEDY
LIBRARIAN, NEW COLLEGE, EDINBURGH

W. A. SMITH AND A. F. JOHNSON
PRINTED BOOKS DEPARTMENT, BRITISH MUSEUM

VOLUME THREE

HASKELL HOUSE PUBLISHERS LTD.
Publishers of Scarce Scholarly Books
NEW YORK. N. Y. 10012
1971

First Published 1926-1934

HASKELL HOUSE PUBLISHERS LTD.
Publishers of Scarce Scholarly Books
280 LAFAYETTE STREET
NEW YORK, N. Y. 10012

Library of Congress Catalog Card Number: 72-171232

Standard Book Number 8383-1245-4

Printed in the United States of America

A Dictionary of the

Anonymous and Pseudonymous Literature of Great Britain

H

H.M.S. —— By "Klaxon" [Commander John Graham Bower, D.S.O.]. 8vo. Pp. 355. [*Camb. Univ. Lib.*] Edinburgh, 1918

H.M.S. Anonymous. By "Taffrail" [Henry Taprell Dorling]. 8vo. Pp. 320. [*Lit. Year Book.*] London, 1919

H. N. Oxenham; recollections of an old friend; reprinted from the *Manchester Guardian.* [Signed: Vicesimus, *i.e.* J. Oakley.] 8vo. Pp. 29. [*Brit. Mus.*] Manchester, 1888

HADES, or the house of many mansions; with prolegomena and episode (extracted from part six of unpublished miscellanies): a serious rhyme, for the new year. By the author of *Lines upon the death of Wellington* [Charles Hancock]. 8vo. [*Nat. Lib. of Scot.*] Taunton [1853]

HADES; or, the invisible world. By the author of *The destiny of the human race* [Henry Dunn]. 8vo. London [1868]

HADOW of Shaws. [A novel.] By Theo Douglas [Mrs H. D. Everett]. 8vo. Pp. 310. [*Lit. Year Book.*] London, 1913

HAGAR. By Stephen Yorke [Mary Linskill]. 8vo. [*Lit. Year Book.*] London, 1887

HAGAR. By the author of *St Olave's*, etc. [Eliza Tabor, *later* Mrs Stephenson]. 8vo. 3 vols. [*Brit. Mus.*] London, 1870

HAGAR; or, Scripture facts concerning marriage, especially in regard to polygamy, concubinage, divorce. . . . By M. D. [Mercer Davies]. 8vo. Pp. viii. 206. [*Brit. Mus.*] London, 1881

HAGARENE. By the author of *Guy Livingstone* [George Alfred Lawrence]. 8vo. 3 vols. [*Camb. Univ. Lib.*] London, 1874

HAGGARD (the) side; being essays in fiction. By the author of *Times and days* [John H. Balfour-Browne]. 8vo. [*Amer. Cat.*] London, 1903

HAGLEY; a descriptive poem. [By Rev. Thomas Maurice.] 4to. [*Gent. Mag.* xciv. i. 468.] London, 1777

HAIR powder; a plaintive epistle to Mr Pitt. By Peter Pindar, Esq. [John Wolcot, M.D.]. To which is added Frogmore fête, an ode for music, for the first of April. A new edition. 4to. Pp. 35. [*D. N. B.* vol. 62, p. 293.] London, 1795

HAL; the story of a clodhopper. By Rev. Peter Pennot [William M. F. Round]. 12mo. [Kirk's *Supp.*] Boston, 1880

HALESWORTH (the) Dunciad; a satire on pedantry, addressed to [Rev. John Dennant] the censor of the stages. [By John Hugman.] 8vo. [*Brit. Mus.*] Halesworth, 1808

HALF a dozen songs. By Brittannicus [Thomas Brittain]. 8vo. [Sutton's *Lanc. Authors.*] Manchester, 1846

HALF a hero; a novel. By Anthony Hope [Sir Anthony Hope Hawkins]. 8vo. [*Lit. Year Book.*] London, 1894

HALF a truth. [A novel.] By Rita [Mrs W. Desmond Humphreys, *née* Eliza M. J. Gollan]. 8vo. [*Lit. Year Book.*] London, 1911

HALF brothers. [A tale.] By Hesba Stretton [Sarah Smith]. 8vo. Pp. 192. London [1906]

See the note to *Alone in London.*

HALF round the world; or, among the uncivilised. By Oliver Optic [William T. Adams]. 12mo. Pp. 364. [Kirk's *Supp.*] Boston, 1896

HALF (a) year at Brounckton. By Margaret Sidney [Mrs Harriet Mulford Lothrop]. 8vo. [Kirk's *Supp.*] Boston, 1881

HALF-A-DOZEN housekeepers; a story for girls in half-a-dozen chapters. By Kate Douglas Wiggin [Mrs George Christopher Riggs]. 8vo. Pp. 162. London, 1903

HALF-A-DOZEN songs. By Brittannicus [Thomas Brittain]. 4to. Pp. 12. Manchester, private print [1846]

HALF-AND-HALF; a poem, with two shorter pieces. [By James Henry, M.D.] 8vo. [O'Donoghue's *Poets of Ireland.*] Dresden [1853]

HALF-AND-HALF (a) tragedy; scenes in black and white. By Ascott R. Hope [Ascott Robert Hope Moncrieff]. 8vo. Pp. 348. [*Brit. Mus.*] London, 1913

HALF-CASTE (the); an old Governor's story; and other tales. By the author of *John Halifax, Gentleman* [Mrs Craik, *née* Dinah M. Mulock]. 8vo. Edinburgh, 1897

HALF-CENTURY'S (a) personal reminiscences of New Zealand and Garden of South Africa. By Strickland [C— Strickland Mackie]. 8vo. Pp. 78. [Mendelssohn's *South Afr. Bibl.*] London [1902?]

HALF-HOURS in story-land. By Lynde Palmer [Mrs Mary L. Peebles]. 12mo. [Cushing's *Init. and Pseud.* i. 224.] Troy, New York, 1889

HALF-HOURS with an old golfer. By "Calamo currente" [James M'Hardy]. 8vo. Pp. 192. London, 1895

HALF-HOURS with Free-thinkers; edited by "Iconoclast" [Charles Bradlaugh]. 8vo. [*Brit. Mus.*] London, 1858

HALF-HOURS with Old Humphrey [George Mogridge]. 12mo. Pp. iv. 356. [*Brit. Mus.*] London [1849]

HALF-HOURS with the microscope. [By Edwin Lankaster.] . . . illustrated by F. West. 8vo. [*Brit. Mus.*] London [1859]

HALF-LENGTH portraits. [Biographical essays.] By Gibson Craig [James Hain Friswell]. 8vo. Pp. vii. 304. London, 1876

HALF-PAY (the) officer; or, memoirs of Charles Chanceley. [By John Heriot.] 8vo. 3 vols. [*Biog. Dict.* 1816.] London, 1788

HALF-PAY (the) officers; a comedy; as it is acted by His Majesty's servants. [By Charles Molloy.] Second edition. 12mo. Pp. v. 79. [Baker's *Biog. Dram.*] London, 1720

HALF-SMART (the) set. [A novel.] By Florence Warden [Florence Alice Price, *later* Mrs George E. James]. 8vo. London, 1908

HALF-TEXT history: chronicles of school-life. By Ascott Robert Hope [Ascott Robert Hope Moncrieff]. 12mo. Pp. 336. [*Lit. Year Book.*] New York, 1897

HALF-TINTS; or, table d'hôte and drawing-room. [By Addison Perle Russell.] 8vo. [Kirk's *Supp.*] New York, 1867

HALIFAX and its gibbet-law placed in a true light; with a description of the town, the nature of the soil, the temper and disposition of the people, the antiquity of its customary law, and the reasonableness thereof. [By Dr Samuel Midgley.] 8vo. Pp. 96. [Turner's *Halifax Books.*] Halifax [1701]

"The real author of this book was Dr Samuel Midgley, a practitioner in physic, who wrote it for his support while in Halifax Jail for debt, where he died in 1695. His poverty prevented his printing it; and John Bentley, parish clerk of Halifax (under whose name this volume is generally known, and who signs the dedication) claimed the honour of it after his death."—Upcott. See further *The History of the famous town of Halifax* . . ., which is really the second edition.

HALL (the) in the grove. [A tale.] By Pansy [Mrs Isabella Alden, *née* Macdonald]. 8vo. Pp. 429. Boston [1890]

HALL (the) of Lawford Hall; records of an Essex House and its proprietors, from the Saxon times to the reign of Henry VIII. [By Francis Morgan Nichols.] 4to. [Gross's *Sources and Lit. of Eng. Hist.*] London, 1891

HALLELUJAH; or, certain hymns composed out of Scripture to celebrate some special and publick occasions. By W. B. [William Barton], M.A. . . . 8vo. Pp. 52. [*Brit. Mus.*] London, 1651

The name of the author is shown in an acrostic at the end of the volume.

HALLET (the) family; a story. . . . By Aunt Friendly [Mrs Sarah S. Baker]. 12mo. [Kirk's *Supp.*] Edinburgh, 1863

HALLETTS (the): a country town chronicle. By Leslie Keith [Grace Leslie Keith Johnston]. 8vo. 3 vols. [*Brit. Mus.*] London, 1891

HALLOWEEN; a romaunt: with lays meditative and devotional. . . . [By Arthur Cleveland Coxe, D.D.] 12mo. [Kirk's *Suppl.*] Philadelphia, 1869

HALT! Who goes there? By the author of *Aunt Sarah and the War* [Wilfrid Magnell]. 8vo. Pp. 94. [*Brit. Mus.*] London, 1916

The third impression omits "Halt" from the title.

HAMARTIA; an inquiry into the nature and origin of evil. [By Rev. John W. Farquhar.] 8vo. Pp. 48. London, 1878

HAMILTON King; or, the smuggler and the dwarf. By the old sailor, author of *Tough yarns*, etc. [Matthew Henry Barker]. 12mo. 3 vols. [*Brit. Mus.*] London, 1839

HAMILTON versus Mill. [By Thomas Collyns Simon.] Parts I., II. 8vo. Edinburgh, 1866-67

HAMILTON (the) wedding; a humourous poem on the marriage of Lady Susan. . . . By the author of *Field sports* [Captain William Hamilton Maxwell]. 8vo. [*Brit. Mus.*] London, 1833

HAMILTONIAD (the); or, the effects of discord: an original poem. . . . By a young gentleman of Philadelphia [Joseph R. Hopkins]. 8vo. [Cushing's *Init. and Pseud.* ii. 157.] Philadelphia, 1804

HAMILTONS (the) or the new æra. By the author of *Mothers and daughters* [Mrs Gore, *née* Catherine Grace F. Moody]. 12mo. 3 vols. London, 1834

HAMLET, and As you like it; a specimen of a new edition of Shakespeare. [By Thomas Caldecott and William Crowe, LL.D.] 8vo. [Lowndes' *Bibl. Man.*] London, 1819

HAMLET travestie; in three acts, with annotations by Dr Johnston and George Stevens Esq. and other commentators. [By John Poole.] Fourth edition. 12mo. [Watt's *Bibl. Brit.*] London, 1811

HAMMERS (the) of hate. [A novel.] By Guy Thorne [Cyril A. E. Ranger-Gull]. 8vo. Pp. 256. London, 1919

HAMMOND'S hard lines. By Skelton Kuppord [J. Adams]. 8vo. Pp. 223. London [1895]

HAMON and Catar; or, the two races: a tale. [By Charles Mitchell Charles.] 8vo. [*Nat. Lib. of Scot.*] London, 1851

HAMPDEN in the nineteenth century; or, colloquies on the errors and improvement of society. [By John Minter Morgan.] 8vo. 2 vols. London, 1834

A third (supplementary) volume was published in 1837.

HAMPERED; or, the Hollister family and their trials. By Nellie Graham [Mrs Annie Dunning, *née* Ketchum]. 12mo. [Kirk's *Supp.*] New York, 1884

HAMPTON heights; or, the spinster's ward. By Caleb Starbuck [E. C. Godwin]. 8vo. [Cushing's *Init. and Pseud.* ii. 140.] New York, 1856

HAMSTEAD Heath; a comedy, as it was acted at the Theatre Royal in Drury Lane. By the author of *The yeoman of Kent* [Thomas Baker]. 4to. Pp. 56. [Baker's *Biog. Dram.*] London, 1706

HANBURY Mills; a study of contrasts. By the author of *Lady Betty* [Christabel Rose Coleridge]. With original illustrations, by H. W. Petherick. 8vo. Pp. x. 464. [*Nat. Lib. of Scot.*] London [1872]

HAND in hand; verses by a mother and daughter [Mrs Alice Kipling and Mrs A. M. Fleming]. 8vo. Pp. viii. 122. [*Brit. Mus.*] London, 1902

HAND (the) of destiny; from the German of Ossip Schubin [Lola Kirschner]. 12mo. New York, 1892

HAND (the) of God; a fragment: and other poems. [By Edward Swaine.] 8vo. Pp. xi. 174. [Dobell's *Private Prints*, p. 174.] Hanley, 1839

Presentation copy, with name filled in by the author.

HAND (the) with the keys. By "Fleeta" [Kate W. Hamilton]. 12mo. [*Amer. Cat.*] Philadelphia, 1890

HAND (a) without a wedding-ring. [A novel.] By Bertha M. Clay [Charlotte M. Braeme]. 8vo. London, 1898

HANDBOOK (a) and history of Sidmouth, from the Triassic period up to "Now." By ארטש [Peter Orlando Hutchinson]. 8vo. Pp. 28. [*Brit. Mus.*] London [1885]

HANDBOOK and index to the principal Acts of Assembly of the Free Church of Scotland. . . . [By Rev. Thomas Cochrane.] 12mo. [*New Coll. Lib.*] Edinburgh, 1869

HAND-BOOK (a) for emigrants to New Zealand; being a digest of the most recent and authentic intelligence respecting Auckland, the capital of the colony. [By Thomas S. Forsaith.] 12mo. London, 1856

The 6th edition, 1857, has the author's name.

HAND-BOOK (a) for holidays spent in and near London. Edited by Felix Summerly, Esq., author of *Handbooks for Hampton Court and the National Gallery* [Sir Henry Cole]. 12mo. Pp. 62. [*D. N. B.* vol. 11, p. 269.] London, 1842

HANDBOOK (the) for New Zealand; consisting of the most recent information. Compiled by a late Magistrate of the Colony. . . . [Edward Jerningham Wakefield]. 12mo. Pp. viii., 493. [Collier's *New Zeal. Lit.* p. 48.] London, 1848

HANDBOOK for School Trustees; a manual of school officers, teachers, and parents in the State of New York. [By H. Brownell.] 8vo. Pp. 64. [*Brit. Mus.*] Syracuse, N.Y., 1886

HANDBOOK for the architecture, sculptures, tombs, and decorations of Westminster Abbey. By Felix Summerly [Sir Henry Cole]. 12mo. [*D. N. B.* vol. 11, p. 269.] London, 1842

HAND-BOOK (a) for the architecture, tapestries, paintings, gardens, and grounds of Hampton Court. By Felix Summerly, Esq. [Sir Henry Cole]. With embellishments engraved on wood by ladies. 12mo. [*D. N. B.* vol. 11, p. 269.] London, 1841

HAND-BOOK (a) for the churches; or an argument in a nutshell about the things of the church, addressed to the children of the kingdom. By a labourer for peace [Jane Ogilvie]. 12mo. Edinburgh, 1840

HANDBOOK for the city of Canterbury, its historical associations, and works of art. By Felix Summerly [Sir Henry Cole]. 8vo. [*D. N. B.* vol. 11, p. 269.] London, 1833

HAND-BOOK for the National Gallery; containing 1. A numerical catalogue of the pictures, and remarks. 2. Alphabetical list of the painters, their chronology, their schools, and references to their pictures. By Felix Summerly; author of *Hand-books for Westminster Abbey*, *Hampton Court*, etc. [Sir Henry Cole]. Fourth edition. 12mo. No pagination. [*D. N. B.* vol. 11, p. 269.] London, 1843

HANDBOOK (a) for the stranger in Philadelphia. By a Philadelphian [W. Williams]. 8vo. [Cushing's *Init. and Pseud.* i. 229.] Philadelphia, 1849

HANDBOOK for the study and discussion of Popery, with special reference to its political relations. By a layman [George M'Gibbon]. 8vo. 2 vols. Edinburgh, 1868

HANDBOOK for Torquay and its neighbourhood; with the natural history of the district. [By E. Croydon.] 8vo. Pp. vii., 293. Torquay, 1854

HANDBOOK (a) for tourists in Yorkshire, and complete history of the county. . . . By W. W. [William Wheater]. 4to. 2 vols. [*Brit. Mus.*] Leeds, 1891

HANDBOOK for travellers in Central Italy, including the Papal States, Rome, and the cities of Etruria. [By Octavian Blewitt.] 12mo. [*Edin. Univ. Lib.*] London, 1843

Many later editions, revised.

HAND-BOOK (a) for travellers in Denmark, Norway, Sweden, and Russia. [By John Murray.] 12mo. [*Athen. Cat.* p. 218.] London, 1839

HANDBOOK (a) for travellers in Devon and Cornwall. [By Thomas Clifton Paris.] With maps. 8vo. [Boase and Courtney's *Bibl. Corn.* ii. 423.] London, 1850

HANDBOOK for travellers in Greece. . . . [By Sir George Ferguson Bowen.] Fourth edition, revised and enlarged. 8vo. [*Brit. Mus.*] London, 1872

HANDBOOK (a) for travellers in India, Burma, and Ceylon. . . . Eighth edition. . . . [By Herbert Charles Fanshawe.] 8vo. Pp. cxvi., 530. [*Brit. Mus.*] London, 1911

HANDBOOK (a) for travellers in Kent and Sussex, etc. [By Richard John King.] 12mo. [*Brit. Mus.*] London, 1858

HANDBOOK for travellers in Spain and readers at home, describing the country and cities, natives, manners, antiquities, religion. . . . [By Richard Ford.] 2 vols. 12mo. [*Brit. Mus.*] London [1845]

HANDBOOK (a) for travellers in Surrey, Hampshire, and the Isle of Wight. [By Richard John King.] 8vo. [*Brit. Mus.*] London, 1858

HAND-BOOK (a) for travellers in Switzerland, and the Alps of Savoy and Piedmont. . . . [The second part was written by William Brockedon.] 12mo. [*D. N. B.* vol. 6, p. 371.] London, 1838

The eighteenth edition was edited by W. A. B. C., *i.e.* William A. B. Coolidge.

HANDBOOK (a) for travellers in Syria and Palestine; including an account of the geography, history, antiquities, and inhabitants of these countries, the peninsula of Sinai, Edom, and the Syrian desert; with detailed descriptions of Jerusalem, Petra, Damascus, and Palmyra. Maps and plans. [By John Leech Porter, D.D., LL.D.] 12mo. 2 parts. London, 1858

The edition of 1868 has the author's name.

HANDBOOK for visitors to Chelsea Hospital. . . . [Signed: J. D., *i.e.* John Dowling.] New edition. 8vo. Pp. 62. [*Brit. Mus.*] London, 1885

HANDBOOK (a) for visitors to Oxford. [By John Henry Parker.] 8vo. [*D. N. B.* vol. 43, p. 251.] Oxford, 1847

HANDBOOK (the) for Youghal; containing an account of St Mary's Collegiate Church . . . and the monastery of St John's; with the historical annals of the town. [By Samuel Hayman.] 8vo. [*Brit. Mus.*] Youghal, 1852

HANDBOOK for young sportsmen. By Will Wildwood [Frederick Eugene Pond]. 8vo. [Kirk's *Supp.*] Cincinnati, 1876

HANDBOOK of American literature—historical, biographical, and critical. [By Margaret E. Foster.] 8vo. Pp. xiv. 319. [*Brit. Mus.*] Edinburgh [1848]

Ascribed also to Joseph Gostick.

HANDBOOK (a) of angling; teaching fly-fishing, trolling, bottom-fishing, and salmon-fishing; with the natural history of river fish, and the best modes of catching them. By Ephemera, of *Bell's Life in London* [Edward Fitzgibbon]. 8vo. [*Brit. Mus.*] London, 1847

HANDBOOK of anonymous and pseudonymous literature. . . . By Frederick Marchmont [Hugh Arthur Torriano]. 8vo. Pp. 164. [Supp. to Lowndes' *Bibl. Man.*] London, 1902

HAND-BOOK (the) of astrology; by which every question of the future, on which the mind is anxious, may be truly answered. By Zadkiel Tao Sze, author of the *Grammar of astrology*, etc. [Lieut. Richard James Morrison, R.N.]. 12mo. Vol. I. London, 1861

Vol. II., with a somewhat different title, was published in 1863.

HANDBOOK of British East Africa, including Zanzibar, Uganda, and the territory of the Imperial British East Africa Company. . . . [By Capt. Hubert John Foster, R.E.] 8vo. Pp. 176. [*Brit. Mus.*] London, 1893

HAND-BOOK of Chatsworth and Hardwick. [By William Spencer Cavendish, Duke of Devonshire.] 4to. Pp. 233. [*Martin's Cat.*] London [1844]

Written in the form of a letter to the author's sister, the Countess Granville.

HANDBOOK of curative mesmerism. [By David Pae.] 12mo. Edinburgh, 1854

HANDBOOK of fictitious names; being a guide to authors, chiefly in the lighter literature of the XIXth century, who have written under assumed names; and to literary forgers, impostors, plagiarists, and imitators. . . . By Olphar Hamst [Ralph Thomas], Esq. 8vo. London, 1868

HANDBOOK of Greek lace-making. [By Julia Herschel.] 8vo. London, 1870

HANDBOOK of gymnastics. By George Forrest, Esq., M.A. [Rev. John George Wood, M.A.]. 8vo. [Allibone's *Dict.*] London, 1858

HANDBOOK (the) of Hastings, St Leonards, and their neighbourhood. [By Mary M. Howard.] 8vo. Hastings, 1845

An edition of 1893 has the author's name.

HANDBOOK of music and musicians. By C. Herman [Otto Ebel]. Fifth edition, enlarged. 8vo. [*Amer. Cat.*] New York, 1902

HANDBOOK (a) of Nantucket; an historical sketch, with notes. [By John H. Folger]. 8vo. [Kirk's *Supp.*] Nantucket, Mass., 1874

HANDBOOK (a) of Newport and Rhode Island. By the author of *Pen and ink sketches*, etc. [John Ross Dix]. 12mo. Pp. xii. 170. [*Brit. Mus.*] Newport, R. I. 1852

Signed: J. R. D.

HANDBOOK of painting: the German, Flemish, Dutch, Spanish, and French schools. Partly translated from the German of Kugler by a lady [Mrs Margaret Hutton]. 8vo. [*Brit. Mus.*] London, 1854

HANDBOOK (a) of Rome and its environs. . . . [By Octavian Blewitt.] 12mo. [*Brit. Mus.*] London, 1867

HANDBOOK of South Australia. [By John Fairfax Conigrave.] 8vo. [*Brit. Mus.*] London, 1886

HANDBOOK (a) of swimming and skating. By George Forrest, Esq., M.A. [Rev. John George Wood, M.A.], author of *The playground*; editor of *Every boy's book*, etc. 8vo. Pp. 61. [*Bibliographer*, vol. 4, p. 20.] London, 1858

HAND-BOOK (the) of swindling. By the late Captain Barabbas Whitefeather [Douglas William Jerrold]; edited by John Jackdaw. 8vo. [*Brit. Mus.*] London, 1839

HAND-BOOK of the Bengal Presidency; with an account of Calcutta city. . . . [By Lieut. Edward B. Eastwick.] 8vo. [*Calc. Imp. Lib.*] London, 1882

HAND-BOOK of the Bombay Presidency. [By Edward B. Eastwick.] Second edition. 8vo. [*Calc. Imp. Lib.*] London, 1881

HANDBOOK of the ecclesiastical, educational, medical, charitable, and provident institutions of Aberdeen. [By G. Milne.] 8vo. [Mitchell & Cash's *Scot. Top.* ii. 18.] Aberdeen, 1883

HAND-BOOK (a) of the history of painting, from the age of Constantine the Great to the present time. By Franz Theodor Kugler. Translated from the German by a lady [Mrs Margaret Hutton]. Part I. The Italian schools of painting. 12mo. [*Brit. Mus.*] London, 1842

HANDBOOK (a) of the history of painting. . . . By F. T. Kugler. Part II. The German, Flemish, and Dutch schools of painting; translated from the German by a lady [Mrs Margaret Hutton]. 12mo. [*Brit. Mus.*] London, 1846

HANDBOOK of the law and practice in the County Courts. [By Richard George Clarke.] 8vo. Pp. 148. [*Brit. Mus.*] London [1879]

HANDBOOK of the Madras Presidency; with a notice of the Overland route to India. [By Edward B. Eastwick.] Second edition. 8vo. [*Calc. Imp. Lib.*] London, 1879

HANDBOOK of the united parishes of Colvend and Southwick. [By W. R. MacDiarmid.] 8vo. [Scott's *Fasti*, second ed., i. 262.] Dumfries, 1873

A second edition appeared in 1895.

HAND-BOOK (the) of Toronto; containing its climate, geology, natural history, educational institutions. . . . By a member of the Press [G. P. Ure]. 8vo. Pp. 272. [Cushing's *Init. and Pseud.*] Toronto, 1858

HANDBOOK (a) of Warwickshire. [Edited by H. M. Cundall.] 8vo. [*Brit. Mus.*] London, 1899

Signed: H. M. C.

HANDBOOK of young artists and amateurs in oil painting. By an American artist [Laughton Osborn]. 8vo. [Cushing's *Init. and Pseud.* i. 13.] New York, 1845

HAND-BOOK on gold and silver. By an Indian official [R. H. Hollingbery]. [*Lib. Journ.* iii. 199.] London, 1878

HANDBOOK (the) to Battle Abbey; to which is added a description of Battle Church. By the author of *Gleanings respecting Battle and its Abbey* [F. W. Ticehurst]. Fourth edition. 12mo. [Anderson's *Brit. Top.*] Battle [1840]

HANDBOOK to Christian and ecclesiastical Rome. By M. A. R. T. and H. M. [M. A. R. Tuker and Hope Malleson]. 8vo. [*Brit. Mus.*] London, 1900

HANDBOOK (a) to Hereford Cathedral. By R. J. K. [Richard John King]. 8vo. [*Brit. Mus.*] London, 1864

HANDBOOK (a) to Lisdoonvarna and its vicinity. . . . [Signed: P. D. *i.e.* Philip Dwyer.] 8vo. Pp. 86. [*Brit. Mus.*] Dublin, 1876

HANDBOOK (a) to Rosslyn and Hawthornden. By Cuthbert Bede [Rev. Edward Bradley]. 12mo. [*D. N. B.* First Supp. vol. 1, p. 257.] Edinburgh [1864]

HANDBOOK to St Albans. [By Richard John King.] 8vo. London, 1877

HANDBOOK to the Cathedrals of England; St Paul's [in London. By Henry Hart Milman, D.D.]. 8vo. Pp. 286. London, 1879

HANDBOOK to the Cornwall railway, from Plymouth to Penzance and Falmouth. [By Joseph Polsue.] 12mo. Pp. 100. [Boase and Courtney's *Bibl. Corn.*] Truro [1865]

HANDBOOK to the desk, office, and platform. . . . [By Charles Vines.] 8vo. 3 parts. [*Brit. Mus.*] London [1872]

HANDBOOK (a) to the Guildhall, and the various offices of the Corporation of London. [By Abraham Harvey.] Second edition. 8vo. [Anderson's *Brit. Top.*] London, 1862

HANDBOOK to Thurso, and guide to the County of Caithness. [By John R. Russell.] 8vo. [Mowat's *Bibl. of Caithness*, p. 81.] Thurso [1875]

HANDBOOKS of elementary art. . . . By N. d'Anvers [Mrs Nancy Bell, *née* Meugens]. 8vo. [*Lit. Year Book.*] London, 1883

HANDFUL (a) of honesty; or, Cato in English verse. . . . By J. P. [John Penkethman], lover of learning. 8vo. [*D. N. B.* vol. 44, p. 302.] London, 1623

HANDFUL (a) of Irish bog lilies. [Poems.] By "Maureen" [Maura Garvery]. 8vo. [O'Donoghue's *Poets of Ireland.*] Dublin, 1910

HANDFUL (a) of rebels; escapades of five young Pickles. By Raymond Jacberns [Georgina M. Selby Ash]. 8vo. Pp. 272. [*Lit. Year Book.*] London, 1901

HANDFUL (a) of stories. By Ascott R. Hope [Ascott Robert Hope Moncrieff]. 8vo. Pp. 128. [*Lit. Year Book.*] London [1886]

HANDICAPPED; a collection of tales. By Marion Harland [Mary Virginia Hawes, *later* Mrs Terhune]. 8vo. [Kirk's *Supp.*] New York, 1881

HANDKERCHIEFE (a) for loyal mourners, groaning for the bloody murther of K. Chas. By T. W. [Thomas Warmstry, D.D.]. 4to. London, 1659

HANDLEY Cross; or, the Spa hunt: a sporting tale. By the author of *Jorrocks' jaunts and jollities*, etc. [Robert Smith Surtees]. 12mo. 3 vols. [*Brit. Mus.*] London, 1843

HANDLING (the) of words. By Vernon Lee [Violet Paget]. 8vo. London, 1923

HANDLING the hog, from start to finish. By "Westerner" [John P. Donovan]. 8vo. Pp. 150 [*Amer. Cat.*] New York [1910]

HANDLIST (a) of the works of John Evelyn, author of *Sylva*, and of books connected with him: compiled by G. L. K. [Geoffrey Langdon Keynes] and A. T. B. [Augustus Theodore Bartholomew]. 8vo. [*Camb. Univ. Lib.*] 8vo. Cambridge, 1916

Only 25 copies printed.

HANDLIST of what is believed to be the largest collection in the world of editions of The Imitation of Thomas à Kempis. [By Walter A. Copinger.] 8vo. Pp. 98. Private print [1908]

The collection was presented in 1922 by Mr James Byrne to Harvard University.

HANDMAID (the) to the arts; teaching, I. A perfect knowledge of the materia pictoria. . . . II. The several devices employed for the more easily and accurately making designs from nature, or depicted representations. . . . III. The various manners of gilding, silvering, and bronzing. . . . [By Robert Dossie.] 8vo. Pp. xxiv. 469. [*Bodl.*] London, 1758

A second edition was published in 1764 (2 vols.).

HANDS (the) at Whist. By "Aquarius" [Lowis d'Aguilar Jackson]. 8vo. Pp. 64. [*Brit. Mus.*] London, 1884

HANDS (the) of God; or King David's choice: a sermon. By T. S. [Thomas Swadlin], D.D. 4to. [Thomason's *Coll. of Tracts*, i. 620.] London, 1648

HANDWRITING (the) on the wall. [A novel.] By R. O. Chipperfield [Isabel Egenton Ostrander]. 8vo. Pp. 255. [*Brit. Mus.*] London [1925]

HANDY (the) book of games for gentlemen; billiards, bagatelle, backgammon, chess, draughts, whist, cribbage, écarté, picquet, etc. By Captain Crawley [George Frederick Pardon]. 8vo. Pp. xii., 563. [*Brit. Mus.*] London [1860]

HANDY book of Kent; with map. [By Edward Smith.] 8vo. [Anderson's *Brit. Top.*] London, 1873

HANDY book of medical information and advice; containing a brief account of the nature and treatment of common diseases. . . . By a physician [James Warburton Begbie, M.D.]. 8vo. London [1859]

Later editions give the author's name.

HANDY (the) book of shopkeeping; or shopkeeper's guide: designed to give stability to the interests of the shopkeeper, by instructing him how to place his business upon a secure foundation. By the author of *Enquire within upon everything* [Robert Kemp Philp]. Fifteenth thousand. 8vo. Pp. 96. London, 1866

HANDY (a) guide to dry-fly fishing. By Cotswold Isys, M.A. [Rev. R. H. Glover]. 8vo. Pp. 34. London, 1895

HANDY (a) guide to the fishing in the neighbourhood of Bath. . . . By Piscator [—— Hiskey]. 8vo. [Green's *Bibl. Somers.* i. 410]. Bath, 1882

HANDY (a) guide to the small debt courts of Scotland. . . . with the forms used in these courts. By the author of *A treatise on bills of exchange* [Robert Thomson, advocate]. 8vo. Pp. 48. [*Nat. Lib. of Scot.*] Edinburgh, N.D.

HANDY (the) guide-book to Dunfermline. . . . [By Harry Blyth, newspaper editor.] 8vo. [Beveridge's *Bibl. of Dunfermline.*] Cupar-Fife [1881]

HANDY guide-book to the Japanese Islands; with maps and plans. [By F. W. Seton Kerr.] 8vo. Pp. xi. 157. [*Brit. Mus.*] Hong-Kong [1888]

HANDY (the) horse book; or, practical instructions in driving, riding, and the general care and management of horses. By a cavalry officer [Captain Maurice Hartland Mahon]. 12mo. Pp. x. 145. [*Brit. Mus.*] Edinburgh, 1865

Preface signed: Magenta.

HANKY Panky; a book of conjuring tricks. By the author of *The secret out* [Wiljálba Frikell]. 8vo. [*Brit. Mus.*] London [1872]

HANNAH. By the author of *John Halifax, gentleman, etc.* [Dinah Maria Mulock, later Mrs Craik]. 8vo. 2 vols. London, 1872

HANNAH Hewit; or, the female Crusoe; being the history of a woman of uncommon mental and personal accomplishments, who after a variety of extraordinary and interesting adventures in almost every station of life, from splendid prosperity to abject adversity, was cast away in the Grosvenor East-Indiaman, and became for three years the sole inhabitant of an island in the South Sea. Supposed to be written by herself. [By Charles Dibden.] 12mo. 3 vols. [*D. N. B.* vol. 15, p. 5.] London [1792]

HANNAH Jane. By Petroleum V. Nasby [David Ross Locke]. 4to. [Kirk's *Supp.*] Boston, 1886

HANNAH Jarne; a story. By the author of *Mr Greysmith* [Mary E. Hullah]. 8vo. [*Brit. Mus.*] London, 1885

HANNAH Lake; or, the lost five minutes. [By Mary Charlotte Phillpotts, later Mrs Herbert.] 8vo. Pp. 47. [Boase and Courtney's *Bibl. Corn.* ii. 486.] London [1865]

HANNIBAL; a drama, in two parts, each in five acts and in verse. [By Louisa C. Shore.] 8vo. Pp. vi. 259. [*Brit. Mus.*] London, 1861

HANNIBAL at the gates; or, the progress of Jacobitism. With the present danger of the Pretender. [By Daniel Defoe?] 8vo. [Wilson's *Life of Defoe.*] London, 1712

HANNIBAL'S passage of the Alps. By a member of the University of Cambridge [Professor Henry Lawes Long]. 8vo. Pp. viii. 155. [D. Laing.] London, 1830

HANS Breitmann's party; with other ballads. [By Charles Godfrey Leland.] 8vo. [*Brit. Mus.*] London [1868]

HANS of Iceland. [By Victor Hugo.] 8vo. London, 1825

HANWELL Rectory. [By James Alexander Emerton.] 12mo. [*Brit. Mus.*] London [1847]

HAPLESS (the) lovers; or, Shechem and Dinah. [By Mrs M. Place.] 8vo. [Cushing's *Anon.*] Portland [Maine] 1830

HAPPENINGS (the) of Jill. By "Iota," author of *A Yellow Aster*, *A Quaker Grandmother*, etc. [Mrs Mannington Caffyn]. 8vo. [*Brit. Mus.*] London, 1901

HAPPINESS. [A novel.] By John Travers [Mrs G. H. Bell]. 8vo. Pp. 282. [*Lit. Year Book.*] London, 1916

HAPPINESS; a characteristic poem: written by a Gentleman of Newcastle-upon-Tyne in Old England [Isaac Thompson]. 8vo. [Evans' *Amer. Bibl.* vol. 5, p. 78.] Philadelphia, 1774

HAPPINESS; an epistle [in verse] to a friend. [By Charles Collignon.] 4to. Cambridge, 1763

HAPPINESS (the) of a religious state. . . . Written in Latin by Father Hierome Platus, of the Societie of Jesus; divided into three bookes, and now translated into English by H. M. [Henry More, S.J.]. 4to. Pp. 613. [Gillow's *Bibl. Dict.*] N.P., 1632

HAPPINESS (the) of dead clergymen, provided they die in the Lord; a funeral sermon preached in the L—gh K—k of Gl—g—w, on the death of the C—m—tee which sat there. By the R—v—d D— T— [William Thom, M.A., minister of Govan]. 8vo. *N. and Q.* 1856, p. 475.] Glasgow, 1769

HAPPINESS (the) of heaven. By a Father of the Society of Jesus [Florentin J. Boudreaux]. 12mo. Pp. viii. 372. [Sommervogel's *Dictionnaire.*] Baltimore, 1871

HAPPY (the) choice. [By Matilda Rickman.] 8vo. Pp. 16. [*Supp. to Smith's Cat. of Friends' Books*, p. 283.] Gloucester [1872]

HAPPY (the) Christian. By an unknown Christian [Albert Ernest Richardson]. 8vo. Pp. 146. [*Brit. Mus.*] London [1922]

HAPPY (the) courtezan; or, the prude demolish'd: an epistle from the celebrated Mrs C—— P—— [Constantia Phillips], to the angelick Signior Far—n—le [Faranelle]. Fol. Pp. 20. [*Bodl.*] London, 1735

HAPPY (the) dawn of a new reign. By Stepniak [Sergie Michaelovitch Kravchinsky]. 8vo. [*Lit. Year Book.*] London, 1905

HAPPY (a) day; a family farce. By Richard—Henry [Richard Butler, and Henry Chace Newton]. 8vo. Pp. 164. [*Brit. Mus.*] London [1894]

HAPPY days. [By George Clement Boase.] 8vo. N.P., N.D

HAPPY (a) family. By B. M. Bower [Bertha W. Sinclair]. 8vo. [*Amer. Cat.*] Chicago, 1910

HAPPY (the) future state of England; or, a discourse by way of letter to the late Earl of Anglesey, vindicating him from the reflections of an affidavit published by the House of Commons, A°. 1680. [Signed: P. P. *i.e.* Sir Peter Pett.] Fol. [Watt's *Bibl. Brit.*] London, 1688

Republished (anonymously in 1689) as "A discourse of the growth of England in populousness and trade. . . ."

HAPPY-GO-LUCKY. By Ian Hay [John Hay Beith, M.A.]. 8vo. Pp. 334. [*Lit. Year Book.*] Edinburgh, 1913

HAPPY-GO-LUCKY. [A tale.] By Ismay Thorn [Edith Caroline Pollock]. 8vo. Pp. 191. [Kirk's *Supp.*] London [1894]

HAPPY (the) home. By the author of *Life in Earnest* [James Hamilton, D.D.]. 12mo. London, 1855

Afterwards included in his collected works.

HAPPY home stories for boys. By Aunt Hattie [Mrs Harriet Newell Baker, *née* Woods]. 12mo. [Kirk's *Supp.*] Boston, 1871

HAPPY home stories for girls. By Aunt Hattie [Mrs Harriet Newell Baker, *née* Woods]. 8vo. [Kirk's *Supp.*] Boston, 1871

HAPPY horses. By Miss Teerius [Mrs Frederick Horner]. 8vo. London, N.D.

HAPPY hours at Wynford Grange; a story for children. By Cuthbert Bede [Rev. Edward Bradley, B.A.]. 8vo. [*D. N. B.* First Supp. vol. 1, p. 251.] London, 1859

HAPPY hours; or, affection's whispers: miscellaneous poems, domestic and social. By C. A. R. [Catherine Anne Rowland]. 8vo. [*Brit. Mus.*] London, 1861

HAPPY ignorance; or, church and state: a religious adventure. With notes by the editors. [By John Penrose, M.A.] 8vo. Pp. 214. [Boase and Courtney's *Bibl. Corn.* ii. 458.] London, 1847

HAPPY (the) interview; or, long look'd for, found out at last: a plain narrative; giving an account, how Common-sense, having withdrawn himself in disgust from the public view, was, after the indefatigable search and enquiries of his friend Plain Honesty, found out, in his retirement, under the direction of Truth. [By Rev. John Lindsay.] 12mo. [Lathbury's *Hist. of Nonjurors*, pp. 399-400.] London, 1756

HAPPY (the) man's shirt; and the Magic Cap; imitated from the Italian of G. B. Casti [by John Payne Collier]. Pp. 16. London, 1850

HAPPY memories of twenty years; in memoriam B. C. S. By L. S. [Mrs Lilian Spender]. 8vo. [Green's *Bibl. Somers.* i. 453.] Bath, 1881

HAPPY (a) mothers' meeting; and other addresses for mothers. By the author of *A letter for you* [Mrs Jane M. King]. 8vo. Pp. 199. [*Brit. Mus.*] London, 1901

Signed: J. M. K.

HAPPY (a) night. By William J. Patmore [William J. Patmore Clarke]. 8vo. [*Amer. Cat.*] New York, 1908

HAPPY (the) place; a novel, translated from the French [of G. de Bremond] by a Person of Quality. 12mo. [Arber's *Term Cat.* i. 524.] London, 1676

HAPPY (the) six. By Penn Shirley [Sarah J. Clarke]. 8vo. Pp. 171. Boston [1897]

HAPPY (the) Union of England and Holland. [By John Evelyn, junr. ?] 4to. London, 1689

HAPPY (the) Vanners. [A novel.] By Keble Howard [John Keble Bell]. 8vo. [*Lond. Lib. Cat.*] London, 1911

HAPPY (the) wanderer; and other verse. By Percy Hemingway [William Percy Addleshaw]. 8vo. Pp. vii. 75. [*Brit. Mus.*] London, 1896

HAPS and mishaps of a tour in Europe. By Grace Greenwood [Sarah Jane Clarke, later Mrs Leander K. Lippincott]. 12mo. Pp. viii. 372. [Kirk's *Supp.*] London, 1854

HARBINGER (the); a May gift. [Three parts. Part I. by Park Benjamin, Part II. by Oliver Wendell Holmes, and Part III. by Osborne Sargent.] 8vo. Pp. vi. 96. [Ives' *Bibl. of Holmes.*] Boston, 1833

HARBINGERS (the) of the Reformation; or, a biographical sketch of Wickliffe, Hus, and Jerome. By the author of the *History of the Reformation* [William Sime]. 12mo. Pp. xii. 191. [*Brit. Mus.*] Edinburgh, 1827

HARBOROVVE (an) for faithfoll and trevve svbiectes, agaynst the late blowne blaste [by John Knox] concerninge the gouernmēt of VVemen, wherein be confuted all such reasons as a straunger of late made in that behalfe, with a briefe exhortation to obedience. Anno. M.D. LIX. [By John Aylmer, D.D., Bishop of London.] 4to. [*Christie-Miller Cat.*]
At Strasborowe the 26. of Aprill. [1559]

HARBOUR (the) bar; a tale of Scottish life. [By Mrs Grace Prestwich.] 8vo. 2 vols. [*Bodl.*] London, 1847

HARCOURT. [A novel.] By Gabrielli [Mrs Mary Meeke]. 8vo. 4 vols. [*D. N. B.* vol. 37, p. 210.] London, 1799

HARD (a) bit of road. [A story.] By Raymond Jacberns [Georgina M. Selby Ash]. 8vo. [*Lit. Year Book.*] Paisley, 1908

HARD (the) case of a country vicar, in respect of small tythes. By a country vicar [William Sharpe, M.A., of Holmest, Dorset]. 8vo. Pp. 62. [Mayo's *Bibl. Dors.* p. 278.] London [1776]

HARD (a) heart; from the German of Golo Kaimund [Georg Dannenburg]. 8vo. [*Amer. Cat.*] Philadelphia, 1884

HARD maple. [A tale. By Anna B. Warner.] 8vo. [*Nat. Lib. of Scot.*] London, 1868

HARD (a) nut to crack, or a word in season to Mr Bulteel. By a member of the Church of God at Oxford [William Palmer, M.A., of Worcester College]. Third edition. 8vo. [*Bodl.*] Oxford, 1832

HARD Pan. [By Miss Geraldine Bonner.] 8vo. San Francisco, 1900

HARD questions; the doubts and difficulties of a teaching parson [Rev. C. Newman]. 8vo. Pp. 160. London, 1912

HARD (the) sum, and other stories. By Aunt Hattie [Mrs Harriet Newell Baker, *née* Woods]. 8vo. [Kirk's *Supp.*] Cincinnati, 1870

HARDER than steel. By Guy Thorne [Cyril A. E. Ranger-Gull]. 8vo. Pp. 217. [*Brit. Mus.*] London, 1919

HARDNESS; or, the uncle. [By Captain Charles Knox.] 12mo. 3 vols. [*Nat. Lib. of Scot.*] London, 1841

HARDSHIPS (the) occasioned by the oaths to the present government considered and argued. By a well-wisher to his country [—— Reynolds, a Dissenter]. 8vo. [Darling's *Cyclop. Bibl.*] London, 1716

HARDSHIPS (the) of publishing. [By William Heinemann.] 4to. London, private print, 1893

HARDY (a) Norseman; a novel. By Edna Lyall [Ada Ellen Bayley]. 8vo. [*Lit. Year Book.*] London, 1854

HARDY Knute; a fragment. [Verse. By Elizabeth, Lady Wardlaw.] Fol. [*Brit. Mus.*] Edinburgh, 1719

HARDY-ON-THE-HILL. [A novel.] By M. E. Francis [Mrs Francis Blundell, *née* Sweetman]. 8vo. Pp. 334. London, 1908

HARILEH; a romance of modern Central Asia. By "Ganpat" [Martin Louis Alan Gompertz]. 8vo. Pp. xiv. 342. [*Brit. Mus.*] Edinburgh, 1923

HARKYOLOGY. Mr T. Smitheram's account of the sayings of the Cambrian Archæological Association. [By Thomas Hingston Harvey.] 16mo. [*Brit. Mus.*] Truro, 1862

HARLEIAN (the) miscellany; or, a collection of scarce, curious, and entertaining pamphlets and tracts, as well in manuscript as in print, found in the late Earl of Oxford's library: interspersed with historical, political, and critical notes. With a table of the contents, and an alphabetical index. [By William Oldys.] 4to. 8 vols. London, 1744-1746

HARLEQUIN Blue Beard, the Great Bashaw. . . . A new . . . pantomime. By the author of *Harlequin Hogarth*, etc. [John Maddison Morton]. 8vo. Pp. 18. [*Brit. Mus.*] London, 1855

HARLEQUIN eggs. [A book for the young.] By Ismay Thorn [Edith Caroline Pollock]. 4to. London, 1884

HARLEQUIN Hydaspes; or, the Greshamite: a mock opera. [Three acts, prose and verse. By Mrs Aubert.] 8vo. [Baker's *Biog. Dram.*] London, 1719

HARLEQUIN Sorcerer; with the Loves of Pluto and Proserpine: as performed at the Theatre-Royal in Covent-Garden. [By Lewis Theobald.] 8vo. Pp. 23. [Baker's *Biog. Dram.*] London, 1752

HARLEQUIN-HORACE; or, the art of modern poetry. [By Rev. James Miller.] 8vo. Pp. 59. [Baker's *Biog. Dram.*] London, 1731

HARLINGHAM (the) case. By Florence Warden [Florence Alice Price, later Mrs George E. James]. 8vo. Pp. 304. [*Brit. Mus.*] London [1918]

HARLOW'S ideal; and other stories. By Mrs Forrester [Mrs Bridges]. 8vo. Pp. 319. [*Amer. Cat.*] London, 1896

HARMEN Pols. [A Dutch story.] By Maarten Maartens [Joost M. W. Van der Poorten-Schwartz]. 8vo. London, 1910

HARMLESS (the) traytor self-condemned; in a sermon at the Cathedral Church of Ely, Jan. 30. Aaron's rod in vigour; a visitation sermon before . . . Edward, Lord Bishop of Norwich, at Ipswich in Suffolk, preached by L.W.[Lawrence Womock], D.D., A.D.S. 4to. London, 1676

HARMONIA. [A novel. By Mary Allan-Olney.] 8vo. 3 vols. [*London Lib. Cat.*] London, 1887

HARMONIA; a chronicle. By Henry Hayes [Mrs Ellen Olney Kirk]. 12mo. [Kirk's *Supp.*] New York, 1888

HARMONIA Musarum; containing Nugæ Cantabrigenses, Florilegium sanctæ aspirationis, and Anthologia borealis et australis. Edited by Alumnus Cantabrigensis [T. Forster?]. 12mo. [*Brit. Mus.*] Bruges, 1843

Preface signed: T. F. Not published.

HARMONIA trigonometrica; or, a short treatise of trigonometry; wherein the harmony between plane and spherical trigonometry is clearly exhibited, and thereby all the difficulties and perplexities of the latter are entirely removed. . . . . [By Henry Owen, D.D.] 4to. [*Bodl.*] London, 1748

HARMONY (the) between the old and present Nonconformists' principles, in relation to the terms of conformity, displayed, with respect both to clergy and people: with the history of the original of the English Liturgy, and some letters between Lord Cecyl and Archbishop Whitgift. [By Stephen Lobb.] 4to. Pp. viii. 96. London, 1682

HARMONY (a) in Christianity; being an answer to Mr Tho. Chubb's book, entitled, The true Gospel of Jesus Christ. . . . By a sufferer for truth [Ebenezer Hewlett]. 8vo. [*Camb. Univ. Lib.*] London, 1738

Also attributed, with reserve, to Caleb Fleming.

HARMONY in religion . . . [By Thadeus O'Malley.] 8vo. Dublin, 1872

HARMONY (a) of Anglican doctrine with the doctrine of the Catholic and Apostolic Church of the East; being the longer Russian catechism, with an appendix, consisting of notes and extracts from Scottish and Anglican authorities. . . . [Edited by the Rev. William Palmer, M.A., of Magdalen College, Oxford.] 8vo. Pp. xvi. 260. [*D. N. B.* vol. 43, p. 168.] Aberdeen, 1746

HARMONY (the) of birds; a poem. [By John Skelton.] 12mo. [*Bibliographer*, v. 14.] London [*c.* 1550]

Reprinted for the Percy Society, with introduction and notes [by John Payne Collier].

HARMONY (the) of Christian faith and Christian character. [By John Abercrombie, M.D.] 12mo. Pp. 87. Edinburgh, 1835

Afterwards published with the author's name.

HARMONY (the) of divinity and law, in a discourse [on Prov. xxx. 31] about not resisting of soveraigne princes. [By George Hickes, D.D.] 4to. Pp. 96. [*Bodl.*] London, 1684

HARMONY (the) of interests, agricultural, manufacturing, and commercial. [By Henry C. Carey.] 8vo. 3 parts. [Sabin's *Dictionary*.] [Philadelphia, 1849-50]

HARMONY (the) of natural and positive divine laws. [By Walter Charleton, M.D., Physician to Charles II.] 8vo. [*Camb. Univ. Lib.*] London, 1682

HARMONY (the) of the Bible with facts; addressed to young men. By a lay member of the Church of Scotland [Alan Stevenson]. 8vo. Pp. 47. Edinburgh, 1867

HARMONY (the) of the comprehensible world. [By Sir Richard Rawlinson Vyvyan.] 8vo. 2 vols. [*D. N. B.* vol. 58, p. 400.] London, 1842

HARMONY (an) of the Confessions of the Faith of the Christian and Reformed Churches of Europe, in the name of the Churches of France and Belgia, submitted to the judgement of all other Churches. Newlie translated out of [the] Latine [of —— Salnar]. Also the Confession of the Church of Scotland. 8vo. [*Brit. Mus.*] Cambridge, 1586

HARMONY (the) of the four evangelists; or the history of Jesus Christ from the four evangelists, in one continued history. [Attributed to Sir Matthew Hale.] Fol. [Darling's *Cyclop. Bibl.*] London, 1720

HARMONY (the) of the four Gospels, wherein the different manner of relating the facts by each Evangelist is exemplify'd. . . . With the history of the Acts of the Apostles. [By Sir Edward Harley, M.P.] 8vo. Pp. lxxix. 456. [*D. N. B.* vol. 24, p. 394.] London, 1733

HARMONY (a) of the Gospels; being a comparative view of the different statements of the four evangelists; showing where they agree, where they vary, and where any are silent. . . . [By William Benning.] 12mo. Pp. 387. [Horne's *Introduction*, v. 161.] London, 1836

HARMONY (the) of the Holy Gospels digested into one history, according to the order of time; done originally by [John Austin] the author of the *Devotions by way of Offices* [adapted for use by Protestants and] publish'd by Dr [George] Hicks: reformed and improved by James Bonnel. 8vo. London, 1705

See also, "Devotions; First part. . . ."

HARMONY (the) of the religious life. By Fra Arminio [Herman J. Heuser]. 8vo. [*Amer. Cat.*] New York, 1904

HARMONY (the) of the truth, an absolute confutation of all infidelity; addressed to Mr L——y [Theophilus Lindsey], on the publication of the Sequel to the Apology: being chiefly a comment on or illustration of the author's Reply to the author of the Remarks on a Scriptural confutation of the Apology; with some strictures on the Critical and London Reviewers, by way of preface. [By William Burgh.] 8vo. Pp. 55. [*Nat. Lib. of Scot.*] London, 1776

HARNESS as it has been, as it is, and as it should be. . . . By John Philipson. With remarks on traction, and the use of the Cape cart, by Nimshivich [Septimus Berdmore]; also an appendix by the same author. 8vo. Pp. vii. 80. [*Brit. Mus.*] Newcastle-upon-Tyne, 1882

HAROLD; a tragedy. [By Thomas Hopkins.] 8vo. Manchester, 1843

HAROLD; and other stories. [By Fanny Bent.] 8vo. Philadelphia, 1866

HAROLD Erle; a biography [in verse]. By the author of *The story of a life* [Colonel Moyle Sherer]. 12mo. London [1824?]

HAROLD Hartley; a tale. By A. L. O. E. [A Lady of England, *i.e.* Charlotte M. Tucker]. 12mo. Edinburgh, 1885

HAROLD Leicester; or, the latter days of Henry VII.: an historical romance. [By C. C. Anderson.] 8vo. 2 vols. [*Brit. Mus.*] London, 1858

HAROLD; or, a day in feudal times: a tragedy. By T. H. [Thomas Hollins]. 8vo. Pp. 43. Manchester, 1843

HAROLD Saxon; a story of the Church and the world. By Alan Muir [Rev. Hayes Robinson]. 8vo. 3 vols. [*Lond. Lib. Cat.*] London, 1880

HAROLD the dauntless; a poem, in six cantos. By the author of *The Bridal of Triermain* [Sir Walter Scott, Bart.]. 8vo. Pp. 199. Edinburgh, 1817

HAROLD, the last of the Saxon kings. By the author of *Rienzi* [Edward George Earle Lytton Bulwer-Lytton, Baron Lytton]. 12mo. 3 vols. London, 1848

Dedicatory epistle signed: E. B. L.

HAROLD'S bride; a tale. By A. L. O. E. [A Lady Of England, *i.e.* Charlotte M. Tucker]. 8vo. Pp. xiii. 226. London, 1888

HARP (the) and the plow. By the "Peasant bard" [Josiah D. Canning]. 8vo. [Kirk's *Supp.*] Greenfield, Mass., 1852

HARP (the) of a thousand strings; or, laughter for a lifetime. . . . By Spavery [Samuel P. Avery]. 8vo. [Kirk's *Supp.*] New York, 1868

HARP (the) of Delaware. By the Milford bard [Dr John Lofland]. 8vo. [Cushing's *Init. and Pseud.* i. 484.] Baltimore, 1840

HARP (the) of Innisfail; a poem, with notes: and other poems. By D. S. L. [Denis Shine Lawlor]. 8vo. [O'Donoghue's *Poets of Ireland.*] Dublin, 1829

HARP (the) of life; a novel. By Elizabeth Godfrey [Jessie Bedford]. 8vo. Pp. 338. London, 1900

HARP (the) of life. [A novel.] By Alan St Aubyn [Mrs Francis Marshall]. 8vo. Pp. 318. [*Lit. Year Book.*] London, 1908

HARP (the) of Renfrewshire; a collection of songs and other poetical pieces (many of which are original), accompanied with notes. . . . [By William Motherwell.] 12mo. Pp. 532. Paisley, 1819

HARP (the) of St Hilda; a poem. [By Richard Winter.] 8vo. Pp. 36. [Smale's *Whitby Authors*, p. 52.] Whitby, 1814

The author's name is given in a later edition.

HARP (the) of Salem. [Hymns and a few Psalm-versions.] By a lady [Mrs —— Reid]. 8vo. Edinburgh, 1827

HARP (the) of the desert; containing the Battle of Algiers, with other pieces in verse. By Ismael Fitzadam, formerly able seaman on board the —— Frigate [John Macker]. [O'Donoghue's *Poets of Ireland.*] London, 1818

HARP (the) of the willows. By Elvira [Mrs Judith Grant Perkins]. 8vo. [Cushing's *Init. and Pseud.* i. 89.] Boston, 1858

HARRIETTE Clifford. [A tale. By Mary Grylls.] 8vo. Pp. 111. [*Brit. Mus.*] London [1862]

HARRINGTONS (the) at home. [A tale.] By Ismay Thorn [Edith Caroline Pollock]. 8vo. Pp. 112. London [1894]

HARRISES (the); being an extract from the common-place book of Alexander Smith the elder. [By George Robert Gleig]. 8vo. 3 vols. [*Nat. Lib. of Scot.*] London, 1870

HARROW recollections. By an old Harrovian [Sir Douglas Straight]. 8vo. Pp. viii. 124. London, 1867

Preface signed: Sidney Daryl, *pseud.* of Sir Douglas Straight.

HARRY. [Verse.] By the author of *Mrs Jerningham's journal* [Mrs Hart, *née* Fanny Wheeler]. 8vo. Pp. 145. [*Brit. Mus.*] New York, 1877

HARRY Ambler . . . By Sidney Marlow [Paschal Heston Coggins, lawyer]. 8vo. Philadelphia, 1891

HARRY and Archie; or, first and last communion. [By Edward Monro, M.A.] [Darling's *Cyclop. Bibl.*] 8vo. Two parts. London [1848, 1849]

HARRY and Willie. [Verse.] By the author of *Creation* [Mary B. Tuckey]. 16mo. [*Brit. Mus.*] Dublin, 1844

HARRY Calverley; a novel. By the author of *Cecil Hyde* [Sir Martin Archer Shee]. 12mo. 3 vols. [*Camb. Univ. Lib.*] London, 1835

HARRY Disney; an autobiography: edited [but rather written] by Atholl de Walden [Alexander Charles Ewald]. 8vo. 3 vols. [*Brit. Mus.*] London, 1871

HARRY Escombe; a tale of adventure in Peru. By Harry Collingwood [William Joseph Cosens Lancaster]. 8vo. [*Lit. Year Book.*] London, 1909

HARRY Fludyer at Cambridge; a series of family letters. [By Rudolf C. Lehmann.] 8vo. London, 1890

An edition of 1904 has the author's name.

HARRY Hawkins's H book; shewing how he learned to aspirate his H's. [By Mrs Ellen Anne Shove Eccles.] 12mo. [*Brit. Mus.*] London, 1857

HARRY Muir; a story of Scottish life. By the author of *Passages in the life of Mrs Margaret Maitland*, etc. [Mrs Margaret O. Oliphant, *née* Wilson]. 8vo. 3 vols. London, 1853

HARRY Mustifer; or, a few years on the road: miscellaneous poems. [By Daniel Puseley, literateur and philanthropist.] 8vo. [*D. N. B.* vol. 47, p. 53.] London, 1847

HARRY Preston; or, "To him that overcometh": a story for boys. By the author of *Ellen Mansell*, etc. [Harriet Waters Preston]. 8vo. [*Brit. Mus.*] London [1878]

HARRY Russell; a Rockland College boy. By "Cuthbert" [J. E. Copus]. 8vo. [*Amer. Cat.*] New York, 1903

HARRY White his humour, so neare as may be set forth by M. P. [Martin Parker].

In which is exprest,
Both earnest and jest:
Let honest men buy,
And knaves let it lye;
This is not for them,
Who vertue contemne.

8vo. No pag. B. L. [*Bodl.*] London, N.D.

Reprinted in "The Literature of the sixteenth and seventeenth centuries, illustrated by reprints of very rare tracts," edited by James Orchard Halliwell, Esq., F.R.S. London: for private circulation only. 1851. 4to.

HARTFORD in the olden time; its first thirty years. By Scaeva [Isaac William Stuart]. 8vo. [Cushing's *Init. and Pseud.* i. 261.] [Hartford, Conn.] 1853

HARTLEY (the) brothers; or, the Knights of Saint John. By A. L. O. E. [A Lady of England, *i.e.* Charlotte M. Tucker]. 8vo. Pp. xiii. 226. London, 1889

HARTWELL (the) farm. By Laura Caxton [Lizzie B. Comins]. 8vo. [Kirk's *Supp.*] Boston, 1876

HARUM Scarum, a poor relation. [A novel.] By Esmé Stuart [Amélie Claire Leroy]. 8vo. Pp. 284. [*Brit. Mus.*] London, 1896

HARUM Scarum married. By Esmé Stuart [Amélie Claire Leroy]. 8vo. Pp. 302. [*Brit. Mus.*] London, 1918

Previously published with the title *Two Troubadours.*

HARUM Scarum's fortune. [A novel.] By Esmé Stuart [Amélie Claire Leroy]. 8vo. Pp. vi. 312. London [1915]

HARVEST (the); and other poems. By E. P. [E. Porter]. 8vo. [*Brit. Mus.*] Saxmundham, 1848

HARVEST. [A novel.] By John Strange Winter [Mrs Arthur Stannard, *née* Henrietta E. V. Palmer]. 8vo. London, 1889

HARVEST (the) crowned; a thanksgiving sermon, 1st Oct. 1854. [By Rev. Adam Batty.] 8vo. [*W.*] London, 1854

HARVEST (the) festival, and other poems. By F. S. H. [F. S. Hill]. 12mo. [*Brit. Mus.*] Boston, 1826

HARVEST gleanings and gathered fragments [in verse]. By Marianne Farningham [Marianne Hearne, of Farningham]. 8vo. Pp. 215. [*Brit. Mus.*] London, 1906

HARVEST (the) home; a domestic romance. By the author of *Fatherless Fanny* [Clara Reeve]. 8vo. [*Brit. Mus.*] London [1852]

HARVEST home; being the summe of certain sermons upon Job 5. 26, one whereof was preached at the funeral of Mr Ob. Musson, an aged godly minister of the gospel in the Royally Licensed rooms in Coventry; the other since continued upon the subject. By J. B. [John Bryan], D.D., late pastor of the Holy Trinity in that ancient and honourable city. The first part. . . . 4to. Pp. 60. [*W.*] London, 1674

Left unfinished.

HARVEST (the) of a quiet eye; leisure thoughts for busy lives. By the author of *My study chair*, etc. [Rev. John Richard Vernon, M.A.]. 8vo. Pp. xiv. 301. [*Brit. Mus.*] London [1867]

Appeared previously in The Leisure Hour and Sunday at Home.

HARVEST (the) of the city, and the workers of to-day. . . . By Pearl Fisher [Thomas Paul]. 8vo. Pp. viii. 252. [*Brit. Mus.*] London [1884]

HARVEST (a) of thorns. By Arrah Leigh [Mrs H. C. Hoffman]. 8vo. New York, 1885

HAS Marischal College, in New Aberdeen, the power of conferring Degrees in Divinity, Law, and Medicine? [By David Thomson.] 8vo. Pp. 52. [Anderson's *Aberdeen Univ. Bibl.* p. 462.] Aberdeen, 1850

HASCHISCH; a story. By Thorold King [Charles Gatchell]. 8vo. Chicago, 1888

HASELRIGGE. By Amica religionis [Mrs H. M. Dodge]. 8vo. Utica, N. Y., 1827

HASTE to the rescue: or, work while it is day. By Mrs C. W. [Mrs Julia Bainbridge Wightman]. 8vo. [*Brit. Mus.*] London, 1859 and 1871

Similar works by the same writer are *Annals of the rescued* and *Arrest the destroyer's march.*

HASTINGS (the) guide. . . . To which is added some account of the Cinque Ports and of the Battle of Hastings. The second edition. By an inhabitant [I. Still]. 8vo. [*Brit. Mus.*] London, 1794

Several other editions followed.

HASTINGS, past and present; with notices of the most remarkable places in the neighbourhood; and an appendix, containing a list of books relating to the district and other supplementary matter. By the author of *Brampton Rectory*, and other works [Mary Matilda Howard]. 8vo. [*Brit. Mus.*] Hastings, 1855

HASTINIAD (the); a heroick poem. [By Elizabeth Ryves?] 8vo. [*Brit. Mus.*] London, 1785

HASTY productions. [By Horace Walpole]. 4to. Pp. 88. Norwich, 1791

In the Rt. Hon. Thos. Grenville's copy in the British Museum is the following note—"Only 25 copies were printed, some of which were burnt by his executor, Mrs Damer. They might all have gone to the fire, for they are sad trash." Mr Martin in his Catalogue of privately printed books declines to believe that Horace Walpole wrote this work, and says, "Mr Grenville's authority on bibliography is so great, that it is almost presumptuous to dispute it; but I cannot help thinking that these 'productions' were the work of his eccentric nephew, George, Earl of Orford, who died in 1791."

HASTY pudding (the); a poem in three cantos, written at Chambery, in Savoy, January, 1793 [by Joel Barlow]: together with the Ruling passion, by Robert T. Paine, Jun., Esq. 12mo. Hallowell, U.S.A., 1815

Published with the author's name, New York, 1827, 12mo.

HASTY (a) sketch of the conduct of the four Commissioners . . . with a concise state of the case of the four regiments. [By Sir Francis Baring.] 8vo. Pp. 32. London, 1788

HASTY (the) wedding; or, the intriguing squire: a comedy. [By Charles Shadwell.] 8vo. [*Brit. Mus.*] London, 1717

HATCHIE, the guardian slave; or, the heiress of Bellevue: a tale of the Mississippi and the South-West. By Warren T. Ashton [William Taylor Adams]. 8vo. [Kirk's *Supp.*] Boston, 1853

HATE (the) of man. [A novel.] By Headon Hill [Francis Edward Grainger]. 12mo. [*Amer. Cat.*] London, 1917

HAU Kiou Choaan; or, the pleasing history: a translation from the Chinese language, to which are added, I. The argument or story of a Chinese play. II. A collection of Chinese proverbs, and III. Fragments of Chinese poetry [by James Wilkinson]. With notes [by Dr Percy, Bishop of Dromore]. 12mo. 4 vols. [*W.*] London, 1761-74

HAUD immemor; a few personal recollections of Mr Thackeray in Philadelphia. By W. B. R. [William Bradford Reed]. 8vo. [Cushing's *Init. and Pseud.* i. 264.] Philadelphia, 1864

HAUNTED (the) bridge; or, the man who married a ghost. By the author of *Dr Rondeau*, etc. [William E. A. Axon]. 8vo. [*Brit. Mus.*] Manchester [1870]

HAUNTED (the) castle; a Norman romance. [By George Walker, a bookseller.] 12mo. 2 vols. [*Biog. Dict.*, 1816.] 1794

HAUNTED (the) farmer; or, the ghost of the granary: a tale applicable to the times. [By Rev. Robert Sadler.] 8vo. [*Brit. Mus.*] Chippenham, 1800

HAUNTED hearts; a tale of New Jersey. By the author of *The lamplighter* [Maria S. Cummins]. New edition. 8vo. Pp. viii. 342. London, 1868

HAUNTED (the) housemaid; or, the villain of the velvet veskit. By a member of the Dramatic Lunatic Asylum [Crosbie Ward, Esq.]. 8vo. Christchurch, New Zealand, 1865

HAUNTED (a) life. By Bertha M. Clay [Charlotte M. Braeme]. 12mo. New York, 1887

HAUNTED (the) mine. By Harry Castlemon [Charles A. Fosdick]. 8vo. [*Amer. Cat.*] Philadelphia, 1902

HAUNTED (the) pool. By George Sand [Madame Amandine L. A. Dudevant]. 8vo. Pp. 117. Boston, 1892

HAUNTED (the) priory; or, the fortunes of the house of Rayo: a romance. . . . [By Stephen Cullen.] 12mo. Pp. 262. [*Brit. Mus.*] Dublin, 1794

HAUNTED (the) room; a tale. By A. L. O. E., author of *The Spanish Cavalier*, etc. [Charlotte Maria Tucker]. 8vo. Pp. 341. London, 1876

HAUNTED (the) shore. [A novel.] By Morice Gerard [John Jessop Teague]. 8vo. Pp. 283. [*Brit. Mus.*] London, 1918

HAUNTED (the) tower; a comic opera, in three acts: as it is performed at the Theatre-Royal, Crow Street. [By James Cobb.] 12mo. Pp. 54. [Baker's *Biog. Dram.*] Dublin, 1793

HAUNTED (the) Tower; or, the adventures of Sir Egbert de Rothsay. [By Charles Giberne.] 12mo. [*Brit. Mus.*] London, 1822

HAUNTED (the) vintage. [A novel.] By Marjorie Bowen [Gabrielle Vere Campbell, later Madame Long]. 8vo. Pp. 320. [*Lond. Lib. Cat.*] London, 1920

HAUNTING (the) of Low Fennel; a novel. By Sax Rohmer [John Sarsfield Ward]. 8vo. Pp. 252. London, 1920

HAUNTINGS; fantastic stories. By Vernon Lee [Violet Paget]. 8vo. Pp. 250. [*Lond. Lib. Cat.*] London, 1906

HAUNTS of ancient peace. [Poems.] By the author of *The garden that I love*, etc. [Alfred Austin]. 8vo. London, 1902

HAVE at you all; or, the Drury-Lane Journal. By Madame Roxana Termagant; address'd to Sir Alexander Drawcansir, author of the *Covent-Garden Journal*. [By Bonnell Thornton.] 8vo. Pp. 286. London, 1752

xii. numbers, the 12th being misprinted 13.

HAVE we a revelation from God? Being a review of Professor W. R. Smith's article "Bible" in the *Encyclopædia Britannica*, ninth edition. [By John Nelson Darby. Reprinted, by permission, from the *Bible Witness and Review*.] 8vo. Pp. 96. London, 1877

HAVE we any "Word of God?" By the author of *Is the Bible true?* [Robert Benton Seeley]. 8vo. [*D. N. B.* vol. 51, p. 193.] London [1864]

HAVE you any fear of death? By C. P. M. [Christopher Parr Male]. 8vo. [*Brit. Mus.*] Birmingham, 1851

HAVEN (the) and the home. By the author of *Memorials of Captain Hedley Vicars* [Catherine Marsh]. 12mo. Pp. 62. London, 1860

HAVEN (the) finding art; or, the way to find any haven or place at sea by the latitude and variation; lately published in the Dutch, French, and Latine tongues . . . and now translated into English. . . . [by Robert Barker]. 4to. Pp. 27. [Watt's *Bibl. Brit.*] London, 1599

HAVEN (a) of rest, and Dr Pertwee's poor patients. By the author of *Episodes in an obscure life* [Rev. Richard Rowe]. 8vo. [*Brit. Mus.*] London, 1878

HAVEN (the) of rest, and the voyage to it; an allegorical narrative. [By James Clark of Taunton.] 8vo. [Green's *Bibl. Somers.* ii. 472.] Taunton, 1872

HAVEN (the); or, some of Christ's words of peace in the New Testament: a devotional text book for every evening. By the author of *Morning and Night Watches* [John Ross Macduff, D.D.]. 12mo. Pp. 75. London, N.D.

HAVEN (the) under the hill. [A novel.] By Stephen Yorke [Mary Linskill]. 8vo. 3 vols. [*Lond. Lib. Cat.*] London, 1886

HAWBUCK Grange; or, the sporting adventures of Thomas Scott, Esq. By the author of *Handley Cross; or, the Spa hunt*, etc. [Robert Smith Surtees]. With eight illustrations by Phiz [Hablot K. Browne]. 8vo. Pp. 329. [*Nat. Lib. of Scot.*] London, 1847

HAW-HO-NOO; or, records of a tourist. [By Charles Lanman.] 8vo. [Allibone's *Dict.*] Philadelphia, 1851

HAWKERS (the) and street-dealers of the north of England manufacturing districts, including Quack Doctors, Cheap Johns, Booksellers by hand, Bookstall Keepers, etc. . . . By Felix Folio [John Page]. Second edition. 12mo. Pp. 140. [*Manch. Free Lib.*] Manchester, 1858

HAWKEYES. [By Robert J. Burdette.] 12mo. [Kirk's *Supp.*] New York, 1879

HAWKHERST; a sketch of its history and antiquities, upon the plan suggested in the Gentleman's Magazine for procuring parochial histories throughout England. [By David Jennings, of Hawkherst.] 4to. [Nichols' *Lit. Anec.* ix. 123.] 1792

HAWKIE; the autobiography of a gangrel; edited [or rather written] by John Strathesk [John Tod, of Lasswade]. 12mo. [*Brit. Mus.*] Edinburgh, 1888

HAWKING, hunting, and fishing, with the true measures of blowing; newly corrected and amended, 1586. [Attributed to Dame Juliana Bernes.] 4to. B. L. [*Brit. Mus.*] London, 1586

HAWKING, hunting, fowling, and fishing, with the true measures of blowing. . . . Now newly collected by W. G. [William Gryndall] Faulkener. 4to. [Westwood's *Bibl. Pisc.*] London, 1596

Another edition of the preceding.

HAWKS (the) of Hawk-Hollow; a tradition of Pennsylvania. . . . [By Robert Montgomery Bird, M.D.] 8vo. [Allibone's *Dict.*] Philadelphia, 1835

HAWKSTONE; a tale of and for England in 184-. [By Elizabeth Missing Sewell.] 8vo. 2 vols. London, 1845

HAWKSTONE (the) Bow-meeting [in verse] By the author of the *Moore Country* [Rowland E. E. Warburton]. 8vo. [*Brit. Mus.*] Chester, 1835

HAWKSVIEW; a family history of our own times. By Holme Lee, author of *Sylvan Holt's daughter*, etc. [Harriet Parr]. 8vo. Pp. 323. [*Lit. Year Book.*] London, 1859

HAWTHORNE ballads. By Alice Hawthorne [Septimus Winner]. 8vo. [Cushing's *Init. and Pseud.* i. 127.] Philadelphia, 1850

HAWTHORNE blossoms. By Emily Hawthorne [Emily Thornton Charles]. 8vo. [Cushing's *Init. and Pseud.* i. 127.] Philadelphia, 1876

HAZARD (the) of a death-bed repentance, fairly argued, from the late remorse of W[illiam] late D[uke] of D[evonshire]; with serious reflections on his adulterous life, on his living so long in a known sin, on that Latin epitaph he order'd to be set on the tomb-stone of Miss Campion, and upon his seeming penitence in his last sickness. . . . [By John Dunton.] 8vo. Pp. vi. 63. [*Brit. Mus.*] London, 1708

HAZARD (the) of the die. [A novel.] By Averil Beaumont [Mrs Margaret Hunt]. 8vo. 3 vols. [*Lit. Year Book.*] London, 1878

HAZARD (the) of the ill. By George Egerton [Mrs Egerton Clairmonte, *née* Gertrude Dunn]. 8vo. [*Lit. Year Book.*] London, 1896

HAZEL bloom. By Pitresia Peters [Julia Carter Aldrich]. 8vo. [*Amer. Cat.*] New York, 1899

HAZEL Combe; or, the golden rule. By the author of *Recommended to mercy* [Mrs M. C. Houstoun]. Second edition. 8vo. 3 vols. [*Brit. Mus.*] London, 1863

HAZEL Grafton; an Irish tale. By Coragh Travers [May S. Crawford]. 8vo. Pp. 350. [S. J. Brown's *Ireland in fiction.*] London, 1911

HE. By the authors of *It*, *Bess*, *King Solomon's Wives* [Andrew Lang and Walter Herries Pollock]. 8vo. Pp. 119. [*Brit. Mus.*] London, 1887

A burlesque imitation of H. Rider Haggard's *She*.

HE and I. By the author of *Annals of a baby* [Mrs Sarah Bridges Stebbins]. 8vo. [Kirk's *Supp.*] New York, 1877

HE and She. By Paul E. de Musset. Translated from the French by E. Tristan and G. F. Monkshood [W. J. Clarke]. 8vo. [*Brit. Mus.*] London, 1910

HE [*sic*] begynneth an interlocucyon, with an argument, betwyxt man and woman, whiche of them could prove to be most excellēt. [Translated from the French of Guillaume Alexis.] 4to. No pagination. B. L. [*Brit. Mus.*] [London, *c.* 1525]

HE for God only. By "Iota" [Mrs Mannington Caffyn]. 8vo. London, 1903

HE giveth songs. . . . Religious lyrics. By A. E. H. [Anna Elizabeth Hamilton] and others. 8vo. Dublin, 1885

HE restoreth my soul. By A. H. W. [A. H. Wigmore]. 8vo. London, 1910

HE shall come again. By an unknown Christian [Albert Ernest Richardson]. 8vo. Pp. 168. [*Brit. Mus.*] London [1922]

HE that overcometh; a novel. By Berkley Aikin [Fanny Aikin Kortwright]. 8vo. 2 vols. London, 1876

HE went for a soldier; a novel. By John Strange Winter [Mrs Arthur Stannard, *née* Henrietta E. V. Palmer]. 8vo. London, 1890

HE wou'd if he cou'd; or, an old fool worse than any: a burletta, as it is performed at the Theatre Royal in Drury-Lane. [By Isaac Bickerstaffe.] 8vo. Pp. 27. [Baker's *Biog. Dram.*] London, 1771

HEAD and hand; or, thought and action in reference to success and happiness. By the author of *Elements of physical science* [Rev. Robert W. Fraser, M.A.]. 8vo. London [1865]

HEAD (the) and heart enlisted against Popery, under the banner of Christian faith; a prize essay, designed for Sabbath School teachers and scholars. [By Thulia Susannah Henderson, afterwards Mrs Engall.] 8vo. [*Brit. Mus.*] London [1852]

HEAD (the) of Medusa. By George Fleming, author of *A Nile novel* [Julia Constance Fletcher]. 8vo. 3 vols. [*Lond. Lib. Cat.*] London, 1880

HEAD (the) of Nile; or, the turnings and windings of the factions since Sixty, in a dialogue between Whigg and Barnaby. [By Thomas Baker.] 4to. Pp. 44. [Wood's *Fasti Oxon.* ii. 362.] London, 1681

HEAD (the) of the family; a novel. By the author of *Olive* [Dinah Maria Mulock, later Mrs Craik]. 8vo. 3 vols. London, 1852

HEAD (the) of the firm. By F. G. Trafford [Mrs Charlotte Eliza Lawson Riddell]. 8vo. [*D. N. B.*, Second Supp. vol. 3, p. 193.] New York, 1892

HEADLONG Hall. [By Thomas Love Peacock.] Second edition. 12mo. [*Brit. Mus.*] London, 1816

HEAD-PIECE (the); or, phrenology opposed to divine revelation. By James the Less [Rev. James Everett, Wesleyan]. 8vo. Pp. 114. [Osborn's *Method. Lit.* p. 100.] London, 1828

HEAD-PIECES and tail pieces. [Stories.] By a travelling artist [Leitch Ritchie]. 12mo. [*Brit. Mus.*] London, 1826

HEADQUARTER (the) recruit; and other stories. By Richard Dehan [Clotilde I. M. Graves]. 8vo. Pp. ix. 368. [*Brit. Mus.*] London, 1913

HEADS of a course of lectures in divinity. [By John Randolph, D.D.] 8vo. Pp. 16. [*D. N. B.* vol. 47, p. 275.] [Oxford? 1784]

HEADS (the) of a course of lectures on experimental philosophy. [By William Samuel Powell, D.D.] 8vo. [*Brit. Mus.*] Cambridge, 1746

HEADS of a recent discussion between a learned doctor in divinity and the author of *Commentaries on the Principia of Sir Isaac Newton.* [By J. M. F. Wright, M.A.] 8vo. London, 1847

HEADS of agreement assented to by the united ministers in and about London, formerly called Presbyterian and Congregational. [Mainly drawn up by John Howe.] 4to. London, 1691

The Union lasted in London for less than four years, but continued longer in other parts of England.

HEADS of all fashions; being, a plaine desection or definition of diverse, and sundry sorts of heads, butting, jetting, or pointing at vulgar opinion; and allegorically shewing the diversities of religion in those distempered times. . . . [By John Taylor, the water-poet.] 4to. Pp. 8. [Lowndes' *Bibl. Man.*] London, 1642

HEADS of ancient history, from the deluge to the partition of Alexander's empire. [By Hudson Gurney, of Keswick Hall, Norwich.] 12mo. [Martin's *Cat.*] London, 1814

HEADS of lectures for the use of the highest class of Students in Humanity in the University of Edinburgh. [By John Hill, LL.D., Professor.] 8vo. Pp. 60. Edinburgh, 1780

HEADS of objections to the Marriage Affinity Bill. [By Robert Smith Candlish, D.D.] 8vo. [*New Coll. Lib.*] Edinburgh [186-]

HEADS of the lectures on rhetorick and belles lettres, in the University of Edinburgh, 1767. [By Hugh Blair, D.D., Professor.] 12mo. [*Edin. Univ. Lib.*] Edinburgh [1767]

HEADS (the) of the people. By Paul Prendergast [Douglas William Jerrold]. 8vo. [Cushing's *Init. and Pseud.* i. 238.] London, 1825

HEADS of Mpongwe grammar. . . . By a late Missionary, Gaboon, West Africa [Rev. John Leighton Wilson]. 8vo. [*Brit. Mus.*] London, 1879

HEADSMAN (the); or, the abbaye des Vignerons: a tale. By the author of *The bravo*, etc. [James Fenimore Cooper]. 12mo. 3 vols. London, 1833

HEALERS (the). [A novel.] By Maarten Maartens [Joost M. W. van der Poorten-Schwartz]. 8vo. Pp. 386. [*Brit. Mus.*] London, 1906

HEALING (the) art. . . . [By William Henry Davenport Adams.] 8vo. London, 1887

See note to "The Amazon . . ."

HEALING (the) art the right hand of the Church; or, practical medicine an essential element in the Christian system. By Therapeutes [David Brodie, M.D.]. 8vo. [*Nat. Lib. of Scot.*] Edinburgh, 1859

HEALING (the) attempt; being a representation of the government of the Church of England, according to the judgment of her Bishops, unto the end of Q. Elizabeth's reign. . . . [Signed: J. H. *i.e.* John Humphrey.] 4to. Pp. 84. [*Brit. Mus.*] London, 1689

HEALING (the) attempt [by John Humphrey] examined and submitted to the Parliament and Convocation, whether it be healing or hurtful to the peace of the Church. [By Thomas Long, B.D.] 4to. London, 1689

HEALING (the) paper; or, a Catholick receipt for union between the moderate Bishop, & sober Non-conformist, maugre all the aversation of the unpeaceable. By a follower of peace, and lover of sincerity [John Humphrey]. 4to. [*Brit. Mus.*] London, 1678

HEALING (a) question propounded and resolved upon occasion of the late publique call to humiliation. [By Sir Henry Vane, junior.] 4to. [Thomason's *Coll. of Tracts*, ii. 148 and 158.] London, 1656

HEALTH; a poem, shewing how to keep and preserve it in a sane and sound state: to which is annex'd, the Doctor's decade. By Darby Dawne [Edward Baynard, M.D.]. 8vo. Pp. iv. 46. [*D. N. B.* vol. 3, p. 453.] London [1716]

This popular work, containing medical advice in homely form, ran through at least ten editions (1716-64), in which the latter portion of the title varies. The pseudonym has sometimes been misprinted as "Dabry Dawne" and "Darby Downe."

HEALTH, and the laws of health. [By J. Barker.] 8vo. [*Brit. Mus.*] London [1863]

HEALTH resorts of the Mediterranean and Italy. By an invalid in search of health [David Duncan, of Cardiff]. 8vo. Cardiff, 1880

HEALTH (a) to the gentlemanly profession of serving men; or, the serving mans comfort: with other thinges not impertinent to the premisses, as well pleasant as profitable to the courteous reader. [By Jervis or Gervase Markham.] No pag. B. L. 4to. [*Bodl.*] London, 1598

HEAR the Church! A word for all. By a doctor of divinity, but not of Oxford [Thomas Raffles, D.D.]. 8vo. [*D. N. B.* vol. 47, p. 161.] London, 1839

This pamphlet exposed the unwisdom of Dr Walter Farquhar Hook in taking a mere fragment of Scripture and misapplying the three words (Matt. 13-17) as the basis of a pulpit discourse. [*D. N. B.* vol. 27, p. 277.]

HEAR the other side. [By Charles King Whipple.] 8vo. [Cushing's *Anon.*] Boston, 1871

HEAR then the verdict; and other poems. By Lorin Ludlow [James Louis Daymude]. 12mo. [*Amer. Cat.*] Boston, 1903

HEART and cross. By the author of *Margaret Maitland*, etc. [Mrs Margaret Oliphant]. 8vo. London, 1863

HEART (the) and its difficulties. By A. Lindsay [Thomas Bowick]. 8vo. [*Brit. Mus.*] London, 1902

HEART and sword. [A novel.] By John Strange Winter [Mrs Arthur Stannard, *née* Henrietta E. V. Palmer]. 8vo. London, 1908

HEART echoes; a book of poems. By Nellie A. Man [Helen A. Manville]. 8vo. [Cushing's *Init. and Pseud.* ii. 494.] New York, 1874

HEART echoes. By Meta [Mrs Mary Lewis]. 8vo. [Cushing's *Init. and Pseud.* ii. 193.] Baltimore, 1873

HEART lines; poems. By Hezekiah Jones' wife [Frank A. van Denburg]. 8vo. [*Amer. Cat.*] Boston, 1904

HEART melodies, and life lights [in verse]. By A. M. H. [Amelia Matilda Hull]. 12mo. [Kirk's *Supp.*] London, 1864

HEART melodies of an aged pilgrim. By the author of *Only a servant* [John B. Bishop, banker]. 8vo. Pp. viii. 164. Edinburgh, 1891

HEART (the) of a child; being passages from the early life of Sally Snape, Lady Kidderminster. By Frank Danby [Mrs Julia Frankau]. 8vo. Pp. 388. [*Lit. Year Book.*] London, 1920

HEART (the) of a girl. [A novel.] By Florence Warden [Florence Alice Price, later Mrs George E. James]. 8vo. Pp. 338. London, 1903

HEART (the) of a heretic; being a human document on the search for spiritual truth. [By Sydney Hallifax, of Berkhamstead.] 8vo. Pp. ix. 327. [Lewis Evans' *Collection of Hertfordshire Books*, p. 11.] London, 1903

HEART (the) of a hero. [A novel.] By Morice Gerard [Rev. John Jessop Teague, M.A.]. 8vo. Pp. 226. London, 1913

HEART (the) of a rose; a narrative drama. By William Mara Bell [William Marabell]. 8vo. [*Amer. Cat.*] New York, 1906

HEART (the) of Babylon. By Deas Cromarty [Mrs Robert A. Watson, *née* Elizabeth Sophia Fletcher], author of *A high little world.* 8vo. Pp. vi. 298. London [1900]

HEART (a) of darkness. By Joseph Conrad [Joseph Conrad Korzeniowski]. 8vo. [*Lit. Year Book.*] London, 1910

HEART (the) of Erin; an Irish story of to-day. By E. Owens Blackburne [Elizabeth Owens Blackburne Casey]. 8vo. 3 vols. [S. J. Brown's *Ireland in fiction.*] London, 1882

HEART (the) of Hindustan. [A novel.] By Edmund White [James Blythe Patton]. 8vo. Pp. 374. London, 1910

HEART (the) of life. By Pierre de Coulevain [Mademoiselle — Favre]; translated from the French. 8vo. Pp. 376. London, 1912

HEART (the) of Maureen. [A novel.] By John Strange Winter [Mrs Arthur Stannard, *née* Henrietta E. V. Palmer]. 8vo. Pp. 311. London, 1910

HEART (the) of Mid-lothian; a romantic national drama, founded on the popular tale [by Sir Walter Scott By Daniel Terry]. . . . 8vo. Pp. 66. [*Brit. Mus.*] Edinburgh, 1823

HEART (the) of O Hana San. [A drama.] By Clive Holland [Charles J. Hankinson]. 8vo. [*Lond. Lib. Cat.*] London, 1902

HEART (the) of Princess Osra. [A novel.] By Anthony Hope [Sir Anthony Hope Hawkins]. 8vo. London, 1902

HEART (a) of steel. [A novel.] By Christian Reid [Mrs James M. Tiernan, *née* Frances Fisher]. 8vo. [Kirk's *Supp.*] New York, 1883

HEART (the) of the moor. By Beatrice Chase [Olive Katherine Parr]. 8vo. Pp. 324. [*Lit. Year Book.*] London, 1914

HEART (the) of the weed. [By Mrs L. C. Berry.] 8vo. Boston, 1886

Wrongly ascribed to Mrs Thomas Sargeant.

HEART of the west. [A collection of short stories.] By O. Henry [William Sydney Porter]. 8vo. [*Brit. Mus.*] London, 1920

HEART (the) of toil. [Stories of struggle in Illinois and Iowa.] By Octave Thanet [Alice French]. 8vo. [*Amer. Cat.*] New York, 1898

HEART (a) on fire; a novel. By the author of *Recommended to Mercy* [Mrs M. C. Houstoun]. 8vo. 3 vols. [*Brit. Mus.*] London, 1887

HEART (the) opened by Christ; or, the conditions of a troubled soul that could find no true rest, peace, comfort, nor satisfaction in anything below the divine power and glory of God. . . . Written in the year 1654, in the third moneth, commonly called May, by R. F. [Richard Farnworth]. [Smith's *Cat. of Friends' Books.*] N.P., N.D.

HEART or head. By Philip Wharton, one of the authors of *The wits and beaux of society* [John Cockburn Thomson]. 8vo. 2 vols. [*Nat. Lib. of Scot.*] London, 1864

HEART to heart; hymns. By the author of *The old, old story* [Katherine Hankey]. 12mo. Pp. 80. London, 1874

HEART to heart talks mit Dinkelspiel. [By George V. Hobart.] 8vo. [*Amer. Cat.*] New York, 1900

HEART tones, and other poems. By D. O'Kelly Branden [Rev. Dominic Brennan]. 12mo. Pp. 168. Buffalo, N. Y., 1897

HEART treasure; or, a treatise tending to fill and furnish the head and heart of every Christian with soul-inriching treasure. . . . By O. H. [Oliver Heywood]. 12mo. [Calamy's *Nonconf. Mem.* Palmer's ed. iii. 435.] London, 1670

HEART wins; The Australian aunt; and other stories. By Mrs Alexander [Annie French, later Mrs Alexander Hector]. 8vo. [*Lit. Year Book.*] London, 1890

HEARTACHE, and the old woman Izergil. . . . By Maksim Gor'ky [Aleksyei Maksimovich Pyeshkov]; translated from the Russian. . . . 8vo. Pp. 94. London, 1906

HEARTH ghosts. By the author of *Gilbert Rugge*, etc. [Henry Jackson]. 8vo. [*Nat. Lib. of Scot.*] London, 1871

HEARTHRUG farces. By Alan Muir [Rev. Hayes Robinson]. 8vo. [*Lond. Lib. Cat.*] London [1883]

HEARTS and hands. By Christian Reid [Frances C. Fisher, later Mrs James N. Tiernan]. 8vo. [Kirk's *Supp.*] New York, 1875

HEARTS are trumps; a novel. By Sarah Tytler [Henrietta Keddie]. 8vo. [*Lit. Year Book.*] London, 1904

HEART'S (a) bitterness. By Bertha M. Clay [Charlotte M. Braeme]. 8vo. Pp. 277. New York, 1889

HEARTS courageous. [Lyric poems.] By John Oxenham [William Arthur Dunkerley]. 8vo. Pp. 88. [*Lit. Year Book.*] London, 1918

HEART'S delight. By E. W. A. [Mrs Elizabeth Winslow Allerdice]. 8vo. [*Lib. Journ.* iv. 457.] New York, 1879

HEART'S (a) idol. By Bertha M. Clay [Charlotte M. Braeme]. 8vo. Pp. 225. New York [1889]

HEARTS in exile. By John Oxenham [William Arthur Dunkerley]. 8vo. Pp. 312. [*Lit. Year Book.*] London, 1904

HEARTS in mortmain; and Cornelia. [Tales. By Margaret Sandbach.] 8vo. Pp. 458. [*Brit. Mus.*] London, 1850

HEART'S mystery; being a story in three periods. By Ralph Strode [Ralph Strauss]. 8vo. Pp. 315. [*Brit. Mus.*] Private print, 1903

HEARTS of gold. [A novel.] By Leslie Keith [Grace Leslie Keith Johnston]. 8vo. [*Lit. Year Book.*] London, 1906

HEARTS (the) of men. By Henry Fielding [Henry Fielding Hall]. 3rd edition. 8vo. Pp. 320. [*Lond. Lib. Cat.*] London, 1904

HEARTS (the) of steel; an Irish historical tale of the last century. By the author of *The Wilderness*, etc. [James MacHenry, M.D.]. 8vo. 3 vols. [*D. N. B.* vol. 35, p. 108.] London, 1825

Wrongly attributed to Thomas Berkeley Greaves. Another edition was issued at Philadelphia in 1826.

HEARTS of Wales; an old romance. By Allen Raine [Mrs Benyon Puddicombe, *née* Annie A. Ellis]. 8vo. Pp. 347. [*Lit. Year Book.*] London, 1905

HEART'S (the) guest. [Poems.] By Barton Grey [George Herbert Sass]. 8vo. [*Amer. Cat.*] Charleston, S.C., 1904

HEARTS triumphant. [A tale.] By W. Scott King [Rev. William Kingscote Greenland]. 8vo. Pp. 256. [*Lit. Year Book.*] London, 1915

HEARTS win; and other stories. By Mrs Alexander [Mrs Alexander Hector, *née* Annie French]. 8vo. New York, 1890

HEARTS-EASE in heart-trouble; or, a sovereign remedy against all trouble of heart that Christ's disciples are subject to, under all kinds of afflictions in this life: prescribed by the great Physician the Lord Jesus Christ. . . . By J. B., a servant of Jesus Christ [James Bardwood, Nonconformist]. Second edition. 12mo. Pp. 190. [Brown's *Life of Bunyan*, p. 448; Vinable's *Life of John Bunyan, Bibl. Appendix.*] London, 1691

Wrongly ascribed to John Bunyan.

HEARTSEASE; or, the brother's wife. By the author of *The heir of Redclyffe* [Charlotte Mary Yonge]. 8vo. London, 1854

HEATHEN England, and what to do for it; being a description of the . . . godless majority of the English nation . . . [Signed: Geo. R., *i.e.* George S. Railton.] 8vo. [*Brit. Mus.*] London, 1877

HEATHENS (the) divinity set upon the heads of all called Christians that say they had not known that there had been a God, or a Christ, unless the Scriptures had declared it to them. G. F. [George Fox]. 4to. [Smith's *Cat. of Friends' Books*, i. 672.] Printed 167⅔

HEATHER. [A novel.] By John Trevena [Ernest George Henham]. 8vo. Pp. 486. [*Lond. Lib. Cat.*] London, 1908

HEATHER and harebell. [Songs and lyrics.] By John Arbory [John Macfarlane]. 8vo. Montreal, 1891

HEATHER belles; a modern Highland story. By Sigma [Rev. John Sinclair, M.P.]. 8vo. Pp. 248. [Mowat's *Bibl. of Caithness.*] Edinburgh, 1886

HEATHER (a) holiday. By May Wynne [Mabel Wynne Knowles]. 8vo. Pp. 203. London, 1922

HEATHER mixture. [A novel.] By Klaxon [Capt. John Graham Bower, R.N.]. 8vo. Pp. 308. London, 1922

HEATHER (a) mixture. [A story of the Scottish Highlands.] By Morice Gerard [John Jessop Teague, M.A.]. 8vo. Pp. 320. [*Brit. Mus.*] London, 1914

HEATH-HOUSE (the) stories. [By Mrs Gertrude Parsons, *née* Hext.] 12mo. [Boase and Courtney's *Bibl. Corn.* ii. 426.] London [*c.* 1865]

HEATHSIDE farm; a tale of country life: edited by the author of *Emilia Wyndham*, etc. [Mrs Anne Marsh-Caldwell]. 12mo. 2 vols. [*D. N. B.* vol. 36, p. 219.] London, 1863

HEAUTONPARNUMENOS; or, a treatise of self-denyall. Intended for the pulpit. . . . [By Thomas Hooker.] 4to. [*M'Alpin Coll. Cat.*] London, 1646

HEAVEN; a manual for the heirs of heaven, designed for the satisfaction of the inquisitive as well as for assistance to the devout: also, on angels and their ministry. [By Robert Weaver, Congregationalist minister.] 12mo. London, 1837

HEAVEN and earth; a mystery. [By George Gordon Noel Byron, Lord Byron.] 12mo. Pp. 35. [*Brit. Mus.*] London, 1823

HEAVEN open to all men; or a theological treatise wherein it is solidly prov'd by Scripture and reason that all men shall be saved. . . . [By Pierre Cappé.] Translated from the French. 8vo. Pp. xxviii. 115. London, 1743

Replies written include "A candid examination . . ." [by Bp. W. Abernethy-Drummond], "A short answer . . ." [by Vincent Perronet], and "A dialogue between the gallows and a freethinker . . ."

HEAVEN opened; or, a brief and plain discovery of the riches of Gods covenant of grace: being the third part of Vindiciae pietatis. By R. A. [Richard Alleine]. 8vo. Pp. 312. [*New Coll. Lib.*; Green's *Bibl. Somers.* ii. 107.] London, 1666

HEAVEN our home; we have no Saviour but Jesus, and no home but heaven. [By William Branks, minister at Torphichen.] 8vo. Pp. xiii. 274. [*Nat. Lib. of Scot.*] Edinburgh, 1861

HEAVEN upon earth. [Essays on economic and social subjects.] By a Polish exile [L. D. H. Zabranhi]. 8vo. Edinburgh, 1848

HEAVEN upon earth; or, the best friend in the worst times. . . . By J. J. [James Janeway, M.A., Nonconformist minister ejected from Kirsall, Hertfordshire]. 8vo. [Palmer's ed. of Calamy's *Nonconf. Mem.* iii. 512.] London, 1667

HEAVENLY aspirations; or, streams from the fountain of life. By the author of *The faithful witness*, etc. [John Ross Macduff, D.D.]. 12mo. Pp. 155. London [1885]

HEAVENLY (a) child, born and brought up with difficulty; or, Satan defeated by a safe-guarding Majesty. Drawn up by T. J. [Timothy Jordan, Nonconformist vicar, ejected from Eckington, in Worcestershire]. 8vo. [Palmer's ed. of Calamy's *Nonconf. Mem.* iii. 392.] London, 1659

HEAVENLY dew-drops; or, good thoughts for all readers. . . . [Signed: W. T. *i.e.* William Thoseby.] 8vo. [*Brit. Mus.*] London [1869]

HEAVENLY (a) diurnall, Glory be to God on high, peace on earth, good will towards men. It was good news, is, and ever will be; or the long expected returne of the many publike and private humiliations of the people of God. . . . By J. B. [Jonathan Blackwell]. 4to. London, 1644

"He was mad at ye time and put into Bedlam; about a year after, he was out again."—MS. note in contemporary hand in the British Museum copy. "A tract of propositions and arguments addressed to the Parliament for the allowing of payment of just debts due by delinquents to be made out of their forfeited estates."—*Cat. Lond. Inst.* ii. 482.

HEAVENLY love and earthly echoes. By a Glasgow merchant [Henry K. Wood]. . . . 8vo. Glasgow, 1870

HEAVENLY (the) twins. [A novel.] By Sarah Grand [Mrs David C. MacFall, *née* Frances Elizabeth Clark]. 8vo. 3 vols. [*Brit. Mus.*] London, 1894

HEAVEN'S gate; a story of the Forest of Dean. By Lawrence Severn [Ada M. Trotter]. 8vo. [*Lib. Journ.* xii. 89.] Boston, 1886

HEAVENS glory, and hells horror; or, the parable of Dives and Lazarus opened and applyed: wherein the everlasting joy of the saints and the endless torments of the wicked are discovered. . . . By J. H. a servant of Jesus Christ [John Hart]. 8vo. No pagination. B. L. [*Bodl.*] London, 1678

HEAVENS of brass. [A novel.] By W. Scott King [Rev. William Kingscote Greenland]. 8vo. Pp. 280. [*Lit. Year Book.*] London, 1899

HEAVENWARD led; or, the two bequests. By Jane R. Sommers [Cornelia Jones]. 12mo. [Kirk's *Supp.*] Philadelphia, 1870

HEAVY laden. By Ilse Frapan [Ilse Levien]. Translated by Mrs Macdonell. 8vo. [*Brit. Mus.*] London, 1892

HEAVY (a) reckoning; a novel. By E. Werner [Elizabeth Bürstenbinder]. Translated from the German. 8vo. 3 vols. London, 1890

HEBREW children; poetic illustrations of Biblical characters. [By Mary Pyper.] 8vo. [*Brit. Mus.*] London, 1858

HEBREW elements; or, a practical introduction to the reading of the Hebrew Scriptures. . . . [By Thomas Burgess, D.D., Bishop of St David's.] 8vo. Pp. xli. 80. [*Aberdeen Pub. Lib.*] London, 1807

Part I. of the author's *Hebrew Reader*. Advertisement signed: T. St. D.

HEBREW heroes; a tale founded on Jewish history. By A. L. O. E., author of *The triumph over Midian*, etc. [Charlotte M. Tucker]. 8vo. Pp. 336. London, 1875

HEBREW lyrics; transfusing the pious spirit of the divine psalmist into devout exercises of prayer praise and thanksgiving. By an octogenarian [Hans Busk, sen.]. 8vo. Pp. xxiv. 483. London, 1859

Attributed also to Walter Savage Landor.

HEBREW (the) maiden. [By Clara Reeve?] 8vo. [*Brit. Mus.*] London, 1840

HEBREW (the) martyrs. [By John Waddington, D.D.] 8vo. London, 1844

HEBREW (the) migration from Egypt. [By John Baker S. Greene, LL.B., M.B. (T.C.D.)] 8vo. London, 1879

The author's name is given in the second edition, 1883.

HEBREW root-book; or, the principal roots in the Hebrew Scriptures of the Old Testament. . . . [By Robert Young, of Edinburgh.] 12mo. [*Brit. Mus.*] Edinburgh [1855]

HECTOR; a dramatic poem [in five acts]. [By Richard Shepherd, D.D., archdeacon of Bedford.] 4to. [*Brit. Mus.*] London, 1770

HECTOR; a tragedy, in five acts. By J. Ch. J. Luce de Lancifal. Translated by E. M. [Edward Mangin]. 8vo. [Green's *Bibl. Somers.* i. 334.] Bath, 1810

HECTOR; a tragic cento. [By John Galt.] 8vo. [*Brit. Mus.*] London, 1814

HECTOR Lennox. By Howe Benning [Mary H. Henry]. 8vo. [*Lib. Journ.* iv. 457.] New York, 1879

HECTORS (the); or, the false challenge: a comedy. . . . [By Edmund Prestwich?] 4to. Pp. 68. [*Brit. Mus.*] London, 1656

HECUBA; a tragedy acted at the Theatre Royal in Drury Lane. [By Richard West, Lord Chancellor of Ireland.] 4to. [*D. N. B.* vol. 60, p. 338.] London, 1726

This drama is different from the following.

HECUBA; a tragedy [in three acts and in verse]; as it is acted at the Theatre Royal in Drury-Lane. [By John Delap, D.D.] 8vo. Pp. 81. *D. N. B.* vol. 14, p. 312.] London, 1762

HECUBA (the) of Euripides; the text closely rendered, and the most difficult words parsed and explained. By a first-class man of Balliol College, Oxford [Thomas Nash]. 8vo. Pp. vi. 58. [*Bodl.*] Oxford, 1869

HEDGE (a) fence [and other tales]. By Pansy [Isabella Macdonald, later Mrs Alden]. 8vo. Pp. 120. [Haynes' *Pseud.*] London, 1903

HEDGEROW and byeway. By J. E. [J— Ellis]. 12mo. London, 1918

HEDWIG in England. By the author of *Marcia in Germany* [Sybil Spottiswoode]. 8vo. Pp. 286. [*Lond. Lib. Cat.*] London, 1909

HE-GOATS (the) horn broken; or, innocency elevated against insolency and impudent falshood, in answer to two books against the . . . Quakers. . . . By a witness of Christ. . . . G. W. [George Whithead]. 4to. [Smith's *Cat. of Friends' Books.*] London, 1660

HEIDELBERG and the way thither. By Nil [H. J. Whitling]. 8vo. [*Preface to his "Pictures from Nuremburg."*] London, 1845

HEIDELBERG (the) Catechism; the German text, with a revised translation and introduction [by Alexander Smellie, D.D.]. 12mo. Pp. lxxxviii. 101. London, 1900

HEIDELBERG; its princes and its palaces. By Elizabeth Godfrey [Jessie Bedford]. 8vo. [*Lond. Lib. Cat.*] New York, 1907

HEIDENMAUER (the); or, the Benedictines: a legend of the Rhine. By the author of *The pilot* [James Fenimore Cooper]. 8vo. 3 vols. [Allibone's *Dict.*] London, 1832

HEIGH-HO for a husband! A comedy as performed at the Theatre Royal in the Hay-market. [By F. G. Waldron.] 8vo. [Baker's *Biog. Dram.*] London, 1794

HEIGHTS and depths. By Mollie Myrtle [Mrs Agnes Hill?]. 8vo. Chicago, 1871

HEIR (the). By Sydney C. Grier [Hilda C. Gregg]. 8vo. Pp. 356. [*Lit. Year Book.*] Edinburgh, 1906

HEIR (the) apparent; or, the life of Commodus the son and successor of the good M. Aurelius Antoninus, emperor of Rome: translated from the Greek of Herodian, with preface adapted to the present times [by Rev. Richard Graves]. 8vo. [Green's *Bibl. Somers.* ii. 445.] London, 1789

HEIR at law (the), and other tales. By "Waters" [William Russell]. 8vo. [*Nat. Lib. of Scot.*] London [1861]

HEIR (the) expectant. [A novel.] By the author of *Raymond's heroine* [Isabella Harwood]. 8vo. 3 vols. [*Brit. Mus.*] London, 1870

HEIR (the) of Ardennan; a story of domestic life in Scotland. By the author of *Anne Dysart* [Christiana Jane Douglas]. 8vo. 3 vols. [*Camb. Univ. Lib.*] London, 1852

HEIR of Cholmeley's Dene. [By Harriet Eleanor Phillimore.] [*Lib. Journ.* iii. 310.] London, 1878

HEIR (the) of Elmdale. By the author of *Their road to fortune* [Mrs M. C. Houston]. 8vo. London, 1888

HEIR (the) of Glendornie. [By William Robbie.] 8vo. [Robertson's *Aberdeen Bibl.*] Aberdeen, 1880

HEIR (the) of Linne. [A poetical drama.] By Ross Neil [Isabella Harwood]. 8vo. [*Lond. Lib. Cat.*] London, 1879

HEIR (the) of Mordaunt. By the author of *Adelaide* [Miss Cathcart]. 12mo. 3 vols. [*Nat. Lib. of Scot.*] London, 1835

HEIR (the) of Redclyffe. By the author of *The two guardians*, etc. [Charlotte Mary Yonge.] 8vo. 2 vols. London, 1853

HEIR (the) of Selwood; or, three epochs of a life. By the authoress of *Mothers and daughters*, etc. [Mrs Catherine G. F. Gore]. 12mo. 3 vols. London, 1838

HEIRESS (the), a novel. [By Ellen Pickering.] 12mo. 3 vols. [*Brit. Mus.*] London, 1833

HEIRESS (the); from the French of Henry Gréville [Madame Alice Marie C. F. Durand]. 8vo. [Haynes' *Pseud.*] New York, 1892

HEIRESS (the) of Densley Wold. [A novel.] By Florence Warden [Florence Alice Price, later Mrs George E. James]. 8vo. Pp. 348. London, 1907

HEIRESS (the) of Haughton; or, the mother's secret. By the author of *Emilia Wyndham*, etc. [Mrs Anne Marsh-Caldwell]. 8vo. 3 vols. [*D. N. B.* vol. 36, p. 219.] London, 1855

HEIRESS (the) of Hilldrop. By Bertha M. Clay [Charlotte M. Braeme]. 12mo. New York, 1886

HEIRESS of the Blackburnfoot; a tale of rural Scottish life. [By Miss Urquhart.] 8vo. [*Nat. Lib. of Scot.*] London, 1866

HEIRS (the) of Blackridge Manor; a tale of the past and present. By Diana Butler [Mrs Henrietta E. Tindal.] 8vo. 3 vols. [*Brit. Mus.*] London, 1856

HEIRS of the royal house of Baliol. [By Alexander Sinclair.] Pp. 15. [*Brit. Mus.*] Edinburgh, private print [1870?]

HELD by the enemy; a novel of love and war. [By Henry Llewellyn Williams]; founded, by special permission, on the popular play of W. Gillette. 8vo. Pp. 63. London [1889]

HELD in bondage; or, Granville De Vigne: a tale of the day. By Ouida [Louise de la Ramée]. 8vo. 3 vols. [*Lit. Year Book.*] London, 1863

HELDERBERGIA; or, the apotheosis of the heroes of the antirent war. [Verse. By Henry R. Schoolcraft.] 8vo. Pp. 54. [Sabin's *Dictionary.*] Albany, 1855

HELEN. By Oswald Valentine [Oswald Sickert]. 8vo. New York, 1894

HELEN Alliston. By the author of *Elizabeth's Children* [Margaret Westrup, later Mrs Sydney Stacey]. 8vo. Pp. 352. London, 1904

HELEN and her cousins; or, two months at Ashfield Rectory. [By Mary Grylls.] 8vo. Pp. 175. [*Brit. Mus.*] London [1863]

HELEN and Olga; a Russian tale. By the author of *Mary Powell* [Anne Manning]. 8vo. Pp. iv. 304. London, 1857

HELEN Cameron; from grub to butterfly. By the author of *Mary Stanley; or, the secret ones* [—— Stallybrass]. 8vo. 3 vols. London, 1872

HELEN Charteris; a novel. [By Harriet Ward.] 12mo. 3 vols. [*Nat. Lib. of Scot.*] London, 1848

HELEN Courtney's promise. [A tale. By Caroline Howard Gilman, later Mrs Jervey.] 8vo. Boston, 1872

HELEN Davenant. [A novel.] By Violet Fane [Mrs Singleton, later Lady Mary Montgomerie Currie]. 8vo. 2 vols. [*Lond. Lib. Cat.*] London, 1889

HELEN Egerton; or, for conscience' sake. By Marie Cezinski [Mrs H. A. Steinhauer]. 12mo. [*Lib. Journ.* iv. 457.] Philadelphia, 1873

HELEN Fleetwood. By Charlotte Elizabeth [Mrs Charlotte Elizabeth Tonna]. 8vo. Pp. vi. 448. London, 1841

HELEN Gardner's wedding-day. By Marion Harland [Mary Virginia Hawes, later Mrs Terhune]. 12mo. [Kirk's *Supp.*] New York, 1867

HELEN Heath; or, the triumph of a faithful mother. . . . [By Clara A. Willard.] 12mo. Boston, 1859

HELEN Leslie; or, a little leaven. . . . By Darley Dale [Francesca M. Steele]. 8vo. Pp. 192. [*Lit. Year Book.*] London [1879]

HELEN Leslie; or, truth and error. By "Adeline" [Emily Frances Adeline Sergeant]. 12mo. [*D. N. B.* Second Supp. vol. 3, p. 291.] London, 1848

HELEN Morton's trial. . . . By Cousin Alice [Mrs Alice Haven, *née* Bradley Neal]. 12mo. [Cushing's *Init. and Pseud.* i. 10.] New York, 1852

HELEN of four gates. By an ex-mill girl [Ethel Holdsworth]. 8vo. [*Lit. Year Book.*] London, 1916

HELEN of Glenross; a novel. By the author of *Historic tales* [H. Martin]. 12mo. 4 vols. [Lowndes' *Bibl. Man.* p. 2325]. London, 1801

HELEN of the glen. [A tale of the Covenanters. By Robert Pollok.] [*D. N. B.* vol. 46, p. 70.] Glasgow, 1824

HELEN Sinclair; a novel. By a lady [Elizabeth Isabella Spence]. 12mo. 2 vols. [*Mon. Rev.* xxix. 99.] London, 1799

HELEN the historian. By "Pansy" [Mrs Isabella (Macdonald) Alden]. 12mo. Boston, 1891

HELEN Treveryan; or, the ruling race. [A novel.] By John Roy [Sir Henry Mortimer Durand]. 8vo. 3 vols. [*Calc. Imp. Lib.*] London, 1892

HELENA'S dower; or, a troublesome ward. By Eglanton Thorne [Emily Charlton]. 8vo. Pp. 318. [*Brit. Mus.*] London, 1907

HELENA'S household; a tale of Rome in the first century. [By James De Mille.] 12mo. New York, 1867

Reprinted Edinburgh, 1868, also anonymously.

HELENA'S love-story. By Guy Thorne [Cyril A. E. Ranger-Gull]. 8vo. Pp. 316. [*Lit. Year Book.*] London, 1906

HELENE. [A poem. By John Henry Mackay.] 8vo. Pp. 133. [*Brit. Mus.*] Zürich, 1888

HELEN'S babies; with some account of their ways. . . . By their latest victim, Uncle Harry [John Habberton]. 8vo. Pp. 183. [*Brit. Mus.*] Glasgow, 1877

HELEN'S fault; a tale for the young. . . . [By Mrs Anne Marsh, later Marsh-Caldwell.] 8vo. [*D. N. B.* vol. 36, p. 219.] London, 1853

HELEN'S secret; or, little by little. By Darley Dale [Francesca M. Steele]. 12mo. [*Lit. Year Book.*] London, 1882

HELEN'S trouble. [A tale. By Margaret Punnett, later Mrs Butlin.] 12mo. Pp. 118. London [1869]

HELGA; a tale in verse [relating to Shetland]. By Reinhold Fuchs; translated from the German by K. I. [Katherine Irvine]. 12mo. Pp. 47. Lerwick, 1897

HELIANTHUS; a romance of modern Europe. By Ouida [Louise de la Ramée]. 8vo. [*Lit. Year Book.*] London, 1908

HELICAL gears. By a foreman pattern-maker [Joseph G. Horner]. 8vo. [*Amer. Cat.*] London, 1893

HELIOCENTRIC astrology; or, essentials of astronomy and solar mentality. . . . By Yarmo Vedra [Holmes Whittier Merton]. 8vo. Pp. xii. 265. Philadephia [1899]

HELICONUNDRUMS. [Poems. By William James Linton.] 8vo. Pp. 91. [*Brit. Mus.*] London [1892]

HELIGOLAND; or, reminiscences of childhood. . . . By M. L'E. [Miss M. L'Estrange]. Fifth edition. 8vo. [*Brit. Mus.*] London, 1851

HELIODORA; and other poems. By H. D. [Hilda Doolittle.] 8vo. Pp. 127. [*Brit. Mus.*] London, 1924

HELIONDÉ; or, adventures in the sun. [By Sydney Whiting.] 8vo. Pp. xiv. 424. [*Athenæum Cat.*] London, 1855

HELIOTROPE (the); or, pilgrim in pursuit of health. [By William Beattie, M.D.] 8vo. Pp. 80, 96. London, 1833

HELL. [By Joseph Barker.] 8vo. [*Brit. Mus.*] London [1863]

HELL. By "Bricktop" [George G. Small]. 4to. [Cushing's *Init. and Pseud.* i. 39.] New York, 1878

HELL illuminated; or, Sancy's Roman Catholic confession. . . . [A satire; translated from the French of T. A. d'Aubigné.] 8vo. [*Brit. Mus.*] London, 1679

The same work was re-issued in 1686, but with a new title-page and other slight changes. See "The Catholick confession of Monsieur de Sancy. . . ."

HELL open'd; or, the infernal sin of murther punished: being a true relation of the poysoning of a whole family in Plymouth, and the punishment of the malefactors. By J. Q. [John Quicke], minister of the Gospel. 8vo. [Davidson's *Bibl. Devon.* p. 39.] London, 1676

HELL upon earth; or, the bard and the demon: a romaunt. [By Francis Edward Stainforth.] 8vo. London, 1877

HELL'S broke loose. [The argument, signed: S. R. *i.e.* Samuel Rowlands.] 4to. London, 1605

Reprinted by the Hunterian Club, 1872.

HELOISE; or, the siege of Rhodes: a legendary tale. By the author of *Maria, or the generous rustic* [George Monck Berkeley]. 8vo. London, 1788

HELOISE; or, the unrevealed secret. By Talvi [Thérèse Albertine Louise Von Jacob, later Mrs Robinson]. 8vo. [Cushing's *Init. and Pseud.* i. 280.] New York, 1850

HELOT and hero; sundry developments of love and war: a novel. By E. Livingston Prescott [Edith Katherine Spicer-Jay]. 8vo. Pp. 412. [*Lit. Year Book.*] London, 1899

HELP and comfort for the sick poor. By the author of *Sickness, its trials and blessings* [Priscilla Maurice]. 8vo. Pp. iv. 78. London, 1853

HELP (a) for the use of parents and sponsors. . . . By J. R. W. [John Rowland West]. 8vo. [*Brit. Mus.*] London, 1855

HELP (a) to English history, containing a succession of all the kings of England, the English, Saxons, and the Britains; the kings and princes of Wales, the kings and lords of Man, and the Isle of Wight. . . . By Robt. Hall, Gent. [Peter Heylin]. 12mo. Pp. 379. [Moule's *Bibl. Herald.* p. 124.] London, 1641

The second edition, 1652, has the author's name.

HELP (a) to the performance of the plain yet neglected duty of self-examination. [By Mrs R. C. Brackenbury, of Raithby Hall, Lincolnshire.] 12mo. London, 1829

HELP (a) to the study of the Scriptures. . . . By a Churchman [Rev. Edward Bickersteth, rector of Watton]. 8vo. [*Brit. Mus.*] London, 1814

HELP (a) to young clergymen, in reading and preaching in the congregation of the church. By Presbyterus [Robert Hussey, of Christ Church]. 12mo. Pp. iv. 119. [*Gent. Mag.* Jan. 1857, p. 111.] Oxford, 1839

HELPE (a) to discourse, or a misselanny of seriousnesse, with merriment . . . now the seventh time published and much inlarged. By the former authors W. B. [W. Basse] and E. P. [E. Philips]. 12mo. 3 parts. [*Brit. Mus.*] London, 1628

HELPES to humiliation. By R. B. [Robert Bolton]. 8vo. [*Brit. Mus.*] Oxford, 1631

HELPS for every hour [By George Mogridge.] 12mo. [*Brit. Mus.*] London, 1846

HELPS over hard places. . . . By Lynde Palmer [Mary Louisa Parmlee, later Mrs A. Peebles]. 8vo. [Cushing's *Init. and Pseud.* i. 224.] New York, 1862

HELPS to a holy Lent. . . . By F. D. H. [Rev. Frederic Dan Huntington]. 8vo. [Cushing's *Init. and Pseud.* i. 123.] New York, 1872

HELPS to the study of the Bible; with a general index, dictionary of proper names, and concordance. [By Rev. James Wood, of Edinburgh.] 8vo. London [1890]

HELPS to the young in their efforts at self-guidance. [By William Ellis.] Edited by Rev. W. Jowitt, M.A. 8vo. [*Brit. Mus.*] London, 1872

HELTER Skelter; or, the devil upon two sticks: a comedy, as it is spitefully acted between High-Church and Low-Church, in most taverns about London. By the author of *All men mad*, etc. [Edward Ward]. 4to. Pp. 27. [*Bodl.*] London, 1704

HEMPFIELD; a novel. By David Grayson [Ray Stannard Baker]. 8vo. Pp. ix. 335. [*Amer. Cat.*] New York, 1915

HEN-PECKED (the) husband; a novel. By the author of *The M.P.'s wife* [Lady Harriet Anne Scott, *née* Shanks]. 12mo. 3 vols. [*Nat. Lib. of Scot.*] London, 1847

HENRI Quatre; or, the lays of the League. [By J. H. Mancur.] 8vo. [Cushing's *Anon.*] Philadelphia, 1833

HENRIADE (the); an epic poem by Voltaire, translated into English rhyme, with historical and critical notes by a lady [the Countess of Charleville]. 4to. [O'Donoghue's *Poets of Ireland.*] Dublin, 1797

HENRIADE; an epick poem by François M. A. de Voltaire, translated from the French into English blank verse: to which are now added the argument to each canto, and large notes, historical and critical [by John Lockman]. . . . 8vo. [*Brit. Mus.*] London, 1732

HENRIETTA. By the author of *The Female Quixotte* [Charlotte Lennox, *née* Ramsay]. 12mo. 2 vols. London, 1758

"By Charlotte Lennox."—MS. note in the handwriting of Dyce.

HENRIETTA Temple, a love story. By the author of *Vivian Grey* [Benjamin Disraeli, later Earl of Beaconsfield]. 12mo. 3 vols. London, 1837

HENRIETTA'S wish; or, domineering: a tale. By the author of *Scenes and characters*, etc. [Charlotte Mary Yonge]. 8vo. Pp. 299. London, 1850

HENRY. [A novel.] By the author of *Arundel* [Richard Cumberland, LL.D.]. 12mo. 4 vols. [*Brit. Mus.*] London, 1795

HENRY; a novel. By the author of *The Cypher; or, the world as it goes* [P. Littlejohn]. 12mo. [*Crit. Rev.* ix. 475; xxxi. 355.] London, 1793

HENRY and Bessie. [By Elizabeth Payson, later Mrs Prentiss.] 8vo. [Kirk's *Supp.*] New York, 1855

HENRY and Emma; a new poetical interlude, altered from Prior's Nut-brown maid, with additions, and a new air and chorus (the music by Dr Arne). . . . [By Henry Bate.] 8vo. [Baker's *Biog. Dram.*] London, 1774

HENRY and Frances; a novel. [By Richard and Elizabeth Griffith.] 12mo. London [1766]

HENRY and Isabella; or, a traite through life. By the author of *Caroline; or, the diversities of fortune* [Mrs Anne Hughes]. 12mo. 4 vols. [*Biog. Dict.* 1816.] London, 1788

HENRY Arden. By Charles Martel [Thomas Delf]. 8vo. [*Brit. Mus.*] London, 1866

HENRY Dunbar; the story of an outcast. By the author of *Lady Audley's secret*, etc. [Mary Elizabeth Braddon, later Mrs John Maxwell]. 8vo. 3 vols. London, 1864

HENRY VIII. and his court. By Louise Mühlbach [Mrs Clara Müller Mundt]. 8vo. New York, 1887

HENRY Holbeach, student in life and philosophy; a narrative and a discussion. [By William Brighty Rands.] Second edition. 8vo. 2 vols. [*Brit. Mus.*] London, 1866

HENRY Irving, actor and manager; a criticism of a critic's [William Archer's] criticism. By an Irvingite [Francis Albert Marshall]. 8vo. [*Brit. Mus.*] London, 1883

HENRY Irving in England and America, 1883-84. By Frederic Daly [Lewis Frederick Austin, private secretary to Sir Henry]. 8vo. [*Lib. Journ.* ix. 127.] London, 1884

HENRY James. By Rebecca West [Cecily Fairfield]. 8vo. Pp. 127. [*Brit. Mus.*] London, 1916

"Writers of the day."

HENRY James; an appreciation. By Joseph Conrad [Joseph Conrad Korzeniowski]. 8vo. [*Brit. Mus.*] Private print, 1919

HENRY M. Stanley; the story of his life, from his birth in 1841 to his discovery of Livingstone in 1871. . . . By Cadwalader Rowlands [J. F. Roberts]. 8vo. London, 1872

HENRY, Lord Darnley; a tragedy, in five acts. [By Robert Brown.] [Inglis' *Dramatic writers*, p. 21.] Edinburgh [1823?]

HENRY Masterton; or, the adventures of a young cavalier. By the author of *Richelieu* [George P. R. James]. 12mo. 3 vols. [*Brit. Mus.*] London, 1832

HENRY Morgan; or, the sower and the seed. By M. H. [Matilda Horsburgh]. 8vo. [*Nat. Lib. of Scot.*] Edinburgh, 1863

HENRY of Navarre; a Huguenot romance. By May Wynne [Mabel Wynne Knowles]. 8vo. [*Lit. Year Book.*] London, 1909

HENRY St Clair; a tale of the persecution [of Covenanters] in Scotland; and the Martyr of Freedom. [Both in verse. By John Montgomerie Bell, Sheriff of Kincardine.] 8vo. Pp. viii. 112. Edinburgh, 1833

Information from a personal friend.

HENRY Schultze; a tale. [By Eaton Stannard Barrett?] 8vo. London, 1821

HENRY Standon. By D'Arcy Drew [St George Jackson Mivart, Ph.D., M.D.]. 8vo. 3 vols. [F. Boase's *Mod. Eng. Biog.*] London, 1894

Re-issued in 1900 with the author's name and a different title—*Castle and manor*.

HENRY the Second, King of England; with the death of Rosamond: a tragedy, acted at the Theatre-Royal by their Majesties servants. [By John Bancroft.] 4to. [Baker's *Biog. Dram.*] London, 1693

HENRY Worthington, idealist. By Elizabeth Hastings [Margaret Sherwood]. 8vo. London, 1899

HENRY'S first history of England. . . . By the author of *Home and its duties*, etc. [Mrs J. Werner Laurie]. 12mo. [*Brit. Mus.*] London [1868]

HEN'S (a) party. [By Mrs —— Tulloch.] 8vo. [Robertson's *Aberd. Bibl.*] Aberdeen, N.D.

HENWIFE (the). [By Mrs —— Fergusson Blair.] 8vo. Edinburgh, 1861

Attributed also to Mrs Elsington Blair, later Mrs Arbuthnot.

HEPSWORTH (the) millions ; a novel. By Christian Lys [Percy James Brebner]. 8vo. Pp. 470. [*Lit. Year Book.*] London, 1898

HEPTALOGIA (the) ; or, the Seven against sense : a cap with seven bells. [By Algernon Charles Swinburne.] 8vo. [*D. N. B.* Second Supp. vol. 3, p. 463.] London, 1880

A burlesque directed against seven contemporaries.

HER associate members. [A tale.] By "Pansy" [Mrs Isabella (Macdonald) Alden]. 8vo. Pp. viii. 261. London, 1891

HER celestial husband. [A novel.] By Daniel Woodroffe [Mrs J. C. Woods]. 8vo. Pp. 226. [*Brit. Mus.*] London, 1901

HER day of service. By Edward Garrett [Mrs John Mayo, *née* Isabella Fyvie]. 8vo. Pp. 256. [*Lit. Year Book.*] Edinburgh, 1894

HER dearest foe ; a novel. By Mrs Alexander [Mrs Alexander Hector, *née* Annie French]. 8vo. 3 vols. [*Brit. Mus.*] London, 1876

HER father's inheritance. By Crona Temple [Miss Corfield]. 8vo. London, 1881

HER father's soul. [A novel.] By Lucas Cleeve [Mrs Howard Kingscote, *née* Adelina G. I. Wolff]. 8vo. [*Lit. Year Book.*] London, 1907

HER friend's lover. By Sophie May [Rebecca Sophia Clarke]. 8vo. [*Amer. Cat.*] Boston, 1892

HER gentle deeds. [A tale.] By Sarah Tytler [Henrietta Keddie]. 8vo. Pp. viii. 344. London, 1886

HER girlhood's lover. By Bertha M. Clay [Charlotte M. Braeme]. 12mo. New York, 1893

HER Grace at bay. By Headon Hill [Francis Edward Grainger]. 8vo. Pp. 158. [*Brit. Mus.*] London, 1910

HER happy thoughts. By P. J. Stahl [Peter Jules Hetzel]. 8vo. [Cushing's *Init. and Pseud.* i. 273.] Boston, 1887

HER husband's country. [A novel.] By the author of *Marcia in Germany* [Sybil Spottiswoode]. 8vo. [*Lond. Lib. Cat.*] London, 1910

HER husband's friend. By Albert Ross [Linn Boyd Porter]. 8vo. [*Amer. Cat.*] New York, 1891

HER Ladyship's income. [A novel.] By Lorin Kaye [Lorin G. Lothrop, and F. Konstam]. 8vo. Pp. 344. London, 1896

HER last stake. By Norman Stuart [Mrs Bartle Teeling, *née* —— Lane-Clarke]. London, N.D.

HER Majesty's prerogative in Ireland . . . in answer to . . . the Case of the City of Dublin. . . . [By Joseph Trapp, D.D.] 8vo. Pp. 53. [*Brit. Mus.*] London, 1712

HER Majesty's reasons for creating the Electoral Prince of Hanover a Peer of this realm ; or, the preamble of his patent as Duke of Cambridge in Latin and English : with remarks upon the same. [By John Toland.] 4to. [*Nat. Lib. of Scot.*] London, 1712

HER martyrdom. By Bertha M. Clay [Charlotte M. Braeme]. 12mo. New York, 1885

HER measure ; a novel. By Curtis Yorke [Mrs W. S. Richmond Lee, *née* —— Jex-Long]. 8vo. Pp. 328. [*Lond. Lib. Cat.*] London, 1915

HER memory ; a novel. By Maarten Maartens [Joost M. W. van der Poorten-Schwartz]. 8vo. Pp. 286. [*Brit. Mus.*] London, 1898

HER Most Gracious Majesty the Queen [Victoria]. . . . By Sarah Tytler [Henrietta Keddie]. 4to. 3 vols. London, 1897

HER mother's sin. By Bertha M. Clay [Charlotte M. Braeme]. 12mo. New York, 1887

HER object in life. [A novel.] By Edward Garrett [Mrs John Mayo, *née* Isabella Fyvie]. 8vo. [*Lit. Year Book.*] London [1884]

HER one ambition. [A novel.] By Rowland Grey [Miss Lilian Rowland Brown]. 4to. [*Lit. Year Book.*] London, 1890

HER only brother. [A novel.] By A. Heimburg [Martha Behrens] ; translated from the German. . . . 8vo. Pp. 406. New York, 1889

HER only sin. By Bertha M. Clay [Charlotte M. Braeme]. 8vo. New York, 1892

HER only son. By the author of *Jessica's first prayer* [Sarah Smith]. 12mo. Pp. 109. Glasgow, 1887

See the note to *Alone in London*.

HER own counsel ; a novel. By the author of *Dr Edith Romney* [Anne Elliot]. 8vo. 3 vols. [*Lond. Lib. Cat.*] London, 1889

HER own way. [A story.] By Eglanton Thorne [Emily Charlton]. 8vo. Pp. 260. [*Brit. Mus.*] London, 1906

HER part; a novel of real life. By A. N. Mount Rose [Alexander Hay Japp, LL.D.] 8vo. Pp. vii. 301. [*Brit. Mus.*] London, 1899

HER picture. [By Philip Gilbert Hamerton.] 8vo. London, 1882

HER point of view. [A novel.] By G. M. Robins [Mrs Louis Baillie-Reynolds]. 8vo. [*Lit. Year Book.*] London, 1896

HER Prairie Knight. [A novel.] . . . By B. M. Bower [Bertrand Muzzy Sinclair]. 8vo. [*Amer. Cat.*] New York, 1907

HER price. [A story.] By Tom Cooke [John William Southern]. 8vo. Pp. 108. [*Brit. Mus.*] London [1881]

HER Royal Highness Woman. By Max O'Rell [Paul Blouet]. 8vo. Pp. 108. [*Brit. Mus.*] London, 1901

HER second love. By Bertha M. Clay [Charlotte M. Braeme]. 12mo. New York, 1887

HER Serene Highness; a novel. By John Graham [David Graham Phillips]. 8vo. London, 1902

HER son; a novel. By E. Werner [Elizabeth Bürstenbinder]; translated from the German by Christina Tyrrell. 8vo. 3 vols. London, 1887

HER splendid sin. [A novel.] By Headon Hill [Frank E. Grainger]. 8vo. [*Lond. Lib. Cat.*] London, 1908

HER title of honour. By Holme Lee, author of *Kathie Brande*, etc. [Harriet Parr]. 8vo. Pp. 282. London, 1871

Reprinted from *The People's Magazine.*

HER waiting heart. By Louisa Capsadell [Mrs E. H. Hammond]. 8vo. [Cushing's *Init. and Pseud.* i. 50.] New York, 1875

HER wedding day. [A novel.] By Marion Harland [Mary Virginia Hawes, later Mrs Terhune]. 8vo. Pp. 224. [Kirk's *Supp.*] London [1883]

HER week's amusement. [A novel.] By the author of *Phyllis* [Mrs Margaret Argles, later Hungerford]. 8vo. Pp. 300. [*Brit. Mus.*] London, 1886

HER wild oats; a novel. By John Bickerdyke [Charles H. Cook]. 8vo. [*Lit. Year Book.*] London, 1898

HERACLITUS ridens; or, a discourse between jest and earnest, where many a true word is spoken in opposition to all libellers against the government. [By Thomas Flatman.] Fol. [*Bodl.*] London, 1681-82

This work consists of 82 numbers, containing 2 pages each. Number 1 appeared on Tuesday, February 6. 1681. Number 82 appeared on Tuesday, August 22, 1682. The title of all the numbers except the first is "Heraclitus ridens: or a dialogue between jest and earnest, concerning the times."

HERACLITUS ridens redivivus; or, a dialogue between Harry and Roger [L'Estrange] concerning the times. [By Thomas Brown.] 4to. [*D. N. B.* vol. 33, p. 126.] Oxford, 1688

HERALD (the) of the future; or, essays on politics, religion, etc. By one of the many [George Frederick Manlay]. 8vo. Pp. 39. [*Manch. Free Lib.*] Manchester, 1839

HERALD (the) of truth; or, friend of religion, literature, and science. [By Benjamin Wood.] 8vo. [Smith's *Cat. of Friends' Books*, ii. 953.] Liverpool, 1828-29

HERALDIC anomalies; or, rank confusion in our orders of precedence: with disquisitions, moral, philosophical, and historical, on all the existing orders of society. By it matters not *who* [Edward Nares, D.D.]. 2 vols. 8vo. [*D. N. B.* vol. 40, p. 91.] London, 1823

HERALDIC (the) calendar; a list of the nobility and gentry whose arms are registered and pedigrees recorded in the Herald's office in Ireland. [By William Skey.] 8vo. [*Brit. Mus.*] Dublin, 1846

HERALDIC miscellanies; consisting of the lives of Sir William Dugdale, Garter, and Gregory King, Esq., Windsor Herald, written by themselves; with an exact copy of the third part of *The Boke of St Albans*, first printed in 1486. [Edited by James Dallaway.] 4to. Pp. 112. N.P. [1793]

HERALDRY of Smith in Scotland. . . . [By Francis Montagu Smith.] 4to. [*Brit. Mus.*] London, 1873

HERB (the) o' Grace; a monthly miscellany. [Edited by Laurence Hope, *i.e.* Adela Nicolson.] 8vo. 2 vols. London, 1901-2

HERB (the) of the field; reprinted from "Chapters on flowers," in the *Magazine for the young*. By the author of *The kings of England*, etc. [Charlotte Mary Yonge]. 8vo. London, 1853

HERBAL (an) for the Bible; containing a plaine and familiar exposition of such similitudes, parables, and metaphors, bothe in the olde Testament and the newe, as are borrowed and taken from herbs, plants, trees, fruits and simples by observation of their vertues, qualities, natures, properties, operations and effects. . . . Drawen [out of Levinus Lemnius] into English by Thomas Newton. 8vo. Pp. 287. [*W.*] London, 1587

HERBERT Lacy. By the author of *Granby* [Thomas Henry Lister]. 12mo. 3 vols. London, 1828

HERBERT Spencer on socialism; a reply. By Frank Fairman [Theodore R. Wright]. 8vo. [*Gladstone Lib. Cat.* (*Lib. Club*).] London, 1884

HERBERT Vanlennert. [A novel.] By Charles Francis Keary [H. Ogram Matuce]. 8vo. [*Lond. Lib. Cat.*] London, 1896

HERBERTS (the). By the author of *Elphinstone* [Alfred Butler]. 12mo. 3 vols. [*Camb. Univ. Lib.*] London, 1842

HERBERT'S holidays; a tale. . . . [By Margaret Agnes Colville, later Mrs Paul.] 12mo. [*Nat. Lib. of Scot.*] London, 1860

HERB-MOON (the); a fantasia. By John Oliver Hobbes [Mrs Reginald Walpole Craigie, *née* Pearl M. T. Richards]. 8vo. [*Brit. Mus.*] London, 1896

HERBS (the) of Medea; a five-pointed leaf from the tree Ygdrasil. By Theophila North [Dorothea Hollins]. 12mo. London, 1904

HERCULES; a musical drama. [By Rev. Thomas Broughton.] 8vo. [*Brit. Mus.*] London, 1745

[HERE all may see, that] justice and judgement is to rule; and the power of God, without respecting mens persons, or observing the worlds complements; and sheweth how the pure religion keeps out from the spots of the world. . . . [Signed: G. F. *i.e.* George Fox.] 4to. London, 1656

HERE and there; an album of adventures. By Ascott R. Hope [Ascott Robert Hope Moncrieff]. 8vo. Pp. 340. [*Lit. Year Book.*] London, 1910

HERE and there in England; including a pilgrimage to Stratford-upon-Avon. By a Fellow of the Society of Antiquaries of Scotland [John Dick]. 8vo. Pp. ii. 224. [*Nat. Lib. of Scot.*] London, 1871

HERE and there lyrics. By E. A. N. [Ernest Alfred Newton]. 8vo. Pp. xv. 67 Liverpool, 1894

HERE and there memories. By H. R. N. [John J. Dunne]. 8vo. London, 1896

HERE and there, over the water; being cullings in a trip to the Netherlands. . . . By Omnium Gatherum. Drawn and written by M. E. [M. Egerton], Esq. 4to. Pp. 34. [*Brit. Mus.*] London, 1825

HERE are several queries put forth in print for all, or any of you whose names are here under written (and likewise for them at Cambridge and Oxford, who are there teaching and training of such up to practice such things as you your selves are now acting in, or any other of your Societies that will answer the same), and return your answer in print, to the view and satisfaction of many people; who are now questioning whether any of all your practises do proceed from the true Foundation. . . . G[eorge] F[ox]. 4to. [Smith's *Cat. of Friends' Books*, i. 354.] London, 1657

HERE beginneth a right fruteful mater; hathe to name the boke of surueyinge and improuementes. [By Sir John Fitzherbert]. 8vo. Ff. 54. B. L. [Macdonald's *Agricultural writers.*] Londini, 1523

Wrongly attributed to Sir Anthony Fitzherbert, the author's brother.

HERE begynneth a deuout treatyse in Englysshe called the Pylgrimage of perfection. [By William Bonde.] 4to. 2 vols. B. L. [*Book prices current*, 1921.] Richarde Pynson [London], 1526

Another edition (1521) begins thus: "A devout treatyse . . . called the Pilgrymage of perfeccyon."

HERE begynneth a lytel treatyse called, The contraverse bytwene a lover and a jaye. [By Thomas Feylde.] London, printed by Wynken de Worde, N.D.

Reprinted by the Roxburghe Club, London, 1918.

HERE begynneth a lytell treatyse named the bowge of courte. [Colophon.] Thus endeth the bowge of courte. [By John Skelton.] 4to. B. L. Emprynted at Westmynster. By me Wynkyn the Worde. N.D.

HERE begynneth a newe tracte or treatyse moost pfytable for all husbade men, and very frutefull for all other persones to rede, newly correcte, and amended by the auctour [Sir John Fitzherbert], with dyverse other thynges added thereunto. 4to. B. L. [Macdonald's *Agricultural writers*, p. 13.] London [1523?]

Wrongly attributed to Sir Anthony Fitzherbert, the author's brother. See also *The booke of husbandry*.

HERE begynneth the complaynte of them that ben to late maryed. [By Robert Copland.] 4to. 8 leaves. B. L. [Colophon:] Here endeth the complaynt of to late maryed. [*Christie-Miller Cat.*] London [1535?]

See also "A complaynt of them that be to soone maryed."

HERE begynneth the lyfe of Saynt Radegunde. [By Henry Bradshaw.] [Verse.] 4to. B. L. [*Christie-Miller Cat.*]
London, Rycharde Pynson [1521 ?]

HERE begynneth the seyng of urynes, of all the coloures that urynes be of, and the medycynes annexed to every uryne: very necessary for every man to knowe. [By —— Lloyd.] Here endeth the boke of seynge of waters. 12mo. 32 leaves unpaged. [*W.*]
Imprynted by me Robert Wyer, [London, *c.* 1530]

HERE begynneth ye temple of glas. [By John Lydgate.] 4to. [*Nat. Lib. of Scot.*] Wynkyn de Worde, 1500

No title-page.

Wrongly attributed to Stephen Hawes. See, also, an earlier edition, printed by Caxton, under *The temple of glass.*

HERE endith a compendiouse treetise dyalogue, etc. *See* Compendiouse (a) treetise, etc.

HERE is declared the manner of the naming of children in the old time, without a priest sprinkling them with water, which now is, and hath been in these times; yet they have the Scriptures, but shews their contrary walking to Scripture. . . . Given forth by G. F. [George Fox]. 4to. London, 1658

HERE you may see what was the true honour amongst the Jewes, to magistrates, kings, fathers, mothers, masters, dames, and old men; which did not use the putting off the hat, nor scraping backwards the foot; and what was the honour they forbade. . . . [Signed: G. F. *i.e.* George Fox.] 4to.
London, 1660

HEREDITARY right exemplified; or, a letter of condolence from Mr E—d C—l [Edmund Curll]. 8vo.
London, 1728

HEREDITARY (the) right of the crown of England asserted; the history of the succession since the Conquest clear'd; and the true English constitution vindicated from the misrepresentation of Dr Higden's View and defence. Wherein some mistakes also of our common historians are rectify'd. By a gentleman [Rev. George Harbin]. Fol. London, 1713

"The introduction to this book was wrote by the Rev. Mr Theophilus Downes, M.A. fellow of Baliol college, ejected from his fellowship in 1690. The book itself the labour of the Rev. Mr George Harbin, M.A. of . . . college, in Cambridge, and chaplain to Dr Turner, the deprived bishop of Ely, with whom he suffered, tho' the Rev. Mr Hilkiah Bedford, formerly fellow of St John's college, in Cambridge, and rector of Wittering, in Northamptonshire (of both which he was deprived) corrected the press, and suffered as editor and author."—Bliss, *Reliquiæ Hearnianæ*, i. 387.

This evoked replies from John Asgill and several anonymous writers.

HEREDITY; being a village dialogue on some causes of degeneracy in our race. By a Protestant clergyman [E. Wyat-Edgell]. 8vo. [*Brit. Mus.*]
London, 1878

HEREFORD (the) guide; containing a concise history of the city of Hereford; a description of its public buildings, episcopal see, cathedral, parochial churches, and other interesting particulars relating to the place; also an account of the principal seats and remarkable places in the neighbourhood. . . . [By William Jenkins Rees.] Second edition. 12mo. [Allen's *Bibl. Heref.*] Hereford, 1808

The first edition appeared in 1806.

HEREFORD orchards, a pattern for all England; written in an epistolary address to Samuel Hartlib, Esq. By I. B. [John Beale]. 8vo. [*Brit. Mus.*]
London, 1724

First printed in 1657.

HEREFORDSHIRE glossary. [By Sir George Cornewall Lewis.] 8vo. [Bliss' *Cat.* p. 177.] 1839

HERESIES (the) of the Christian Church; dedicated to all the religious denominations of the world: containing a new biography of Jesus, founded on Scripture, with criticisms on the characters of his associates. . . . By the author of *The Jesus of history and tradition identified* [George Solomon]. 8vo. Pp. vi. 226. London, 1896

HERESY (the) of a professional one-man ministry, and a claim for the priesthood of believers, and the free exercise of spiritual gifts. . . . By Compaginator [Prof. George Bush, of New York]. Third edition. 8vo. Pp. 102. [*Manch. Free Lib.*]
Manchester, 1866

First published in Philadelphia, 1857, under the title of "The origin of priesthood and clergy . . ."

HERESY (the) of teetotalism; in the light of Scripture, science and legislation. By Eglanton Thorne [Emily Charlton]. 8vo. Pp. 340.
London, 1903

HERETICKES, sectaries, and schismaticks discovered to be the Antichrist yet remaining, and the enemies of the peace of this kingdome; the question rightly stated and debated; with a hint about Ordination and the Covenant. [By John Elligson, of Easington.] 4to. Pp. 32. [Whitley's *Bapt. Bibl.* i. 32.] London, 1647

HERITAGE (the). [A novel.] By Sydney C. Grier [Hilda C. Gregg]. 8vo. [*Lit. Year Book.*] Edinburgh, 1917

HERITAGE (the) of Langdale. [A novel.] By Mrs Alexander [Mrs Alexander Hector, *née* Annie French]. 8vo. [*Brit. Mus.*] London, 1894

HERMÆOLOGIUM; or, an essay at the rationality of the art of speaking. . . . By B. J. [Basset Jones, M.D.]. 8vo. [Watt's *Bibl. Brit.*] London, 1659

HERMAN and Dorothea; translated from the hexameters of Göthe [by William Whewell, D.D.]. 12mo. [*Camb. Univ. Lib.*] [Cambridge, 1839]

HERMAN; and other stories. By the author of *Stepping heavenward* [Mrs Elizabeth Prentiss, *née* Payson]. 8vo. Pp. 252. [Kirk's *Supp.*] London, 1902

HERMAN; or, the little preacher: Little threads, and the story Lizzie told. By the author of *The flower of the family*, etc. [Mrs Elizabeth Prentiss]. 8vo. [Kirk's *Supp.*] London, 1874

HERMAN; or, young knighthood. . . . By E. Foxton [Sarah Hammond Palfrey]. 8vo. [Cushing's *Init. and Pseud.* i. 104.] Boston, 1866

HERMANN. [A love-story.] By E. Werner [Elizabeth Bürstenbinder]; translated from the German. 8vo. New York, 1879

HERMETICAL (the) triumph; or, the victorious philosophical stone: a treatise more compleat and intelligible than any has been yet, concerning the hermetical mystery. Translated from the French [of A. T. de Limojon (Sieur de Saint-Didier)]. . . . 8vo. Pp. xvi. 147. [Barbier's *Dictionnaire*, iv. col. 838.] London, 1723

The author's name is concealed in a Latin anagram "Dives—sicut—ardens, S * * *."

HERMIA SUYDAM. By Frank Lin [Mrs Gertrude Franklin Atherton]. 8vo. [*Amer. Cat.*] New York, 1889

HERMILDA in Palestine; the first canto and part of the second: with other poems. [By Edward Hovell Thurlow, Baron Thurlow.] 4to. [*Brit. Mus.*] London, 1812

HERMINIUS; a romance. By J. E. S. [James Carnegie, Earl of Southesk]. 8vo. Pp. 228. [*Nat. Lib. of Scot.*] Edinburgh, 1862

HERMINIUS and Espasia; a tragedy, as it was acted at the Theatre in Edinburgh. [By Charles Hart.] 8vo. [Baker's *Biog. Dram.*] Edinburgh, 1754

Robert Hart, according to Dr David Laing; or *Samuel* Hart, according to another.

HERMIPPUS redivivus; or, the sage's triumph over old age and the grave: wherein a method is laid down for prolonging the life and vigour of man. . . . [By John Henry Cohausen; translated by John Campbell, LL.D.] Third edition. 8vo. Pp. viii. 248. [*Dyce Cat.* i. 191.] London, 1771

The first edition was published in 1743.

HERMIT (the); a novel. [By Lady —— Atkyns.] 12mo. 2 vols. London, 1769

HERMIT (the); a poem. [By Thomas Parnell, D.D.] 12mo. [*Brit. Mus.*] N.P. [1720?]

HERMIT (the) abroad. By the author of *The Hermit in London*, and *Hermit in the country* [Capt. Felix M'Donough]. 8vo. [*Brit. Mus.*] London, 1823

HERMIT (the) in Edinburgh; or, sketches of manners and real characters and scenes in the drama of life. [By Capt. Felix M'Donough.] 12mo. 3 vols. London, 1824

HERMIT (the) in London; or, sketches of English manners. [By Capt. Felix M'Donough.] 12mo. 3 vols. [*Gent. Mag.* June, 1836, p. 672.] London, 1819

HERMIT (the) in the country; or, sketches of English manners. [By Capt. Felix M'Donough.] 12mo. 4 vols. London, 1820

A new edition, in three volumes, was published in 1823, with the title, "The hermit in the country; or, sketches of British manners."

HERMIT (the) in Van Diemen's Land. By Simon Stukeley [—— Wills]. 8vo. [*Brit. Mus.*] Hobart, 1829

HERMIT (the) of Dumpton Cave; or, devotedness to God and usefulness to man exemplified in the old age of J. C. Petit . . . [By Mrs Elizabeth Strutt.] 12mo. [*Brit. Mus.*] London, 1828

HERMIT (the) of Eskdaleside, with other poems. By I. A. M. [Mrs I. A. Merryweather]. Second edition. 12mo. Pp. 136. [Smales' *Whitby Authors*, p. 152.] Whitby, 1833

HERMIT (the) of Powis; a ballad romance of the olden times. [By David Grant, teacher.] 8vo. Pp. 12. Aberdeen, 1862

HERMIT (the) of Snowdon; or, memoirs of Albert and Lavinia, taken from a faithful copy of the original manuscript which was found in the hermitage of the late Rev. Dr L. and Mr ——, in the year 17—. [By Elizabeth Ryves.] 8vo. [Disraeli's *Calamities of authors*, ed. 1859, p. 109.] London, 1789

HERMIT (the) of the Pyrenees, and other miscellaneous poems. By Rednaxela [Hon. Mrs Cropper]. 8vo. Pp. x. 126. London, 1858

HERMIT (the) of Warkworth; a Northumbrian ballad: in three fits or cantos. [By Thomas Percy, D.D., Bishop of Dromore.] 4to. Pp. 52. [*D. N. B.* vol. 44, p. 439.] London, 1771

HERMIT (the); or, the unparalled [*sic*] sufferings and surprising adventures of Mr Philip Quarll, an Englishman, who was lately discovered by Mr Dorrington . . . upon an uninhabited island in the South Sea. . . . [The preface signed: P. L. *i.e.* Peter Longueville.] 8vo. Pp. xi. 264. [*The Library*, ii. 187.] Westminster, 1727

See also "The English hermit. . . ."

HERMITAGE (the); a British story. [By William Hutchinson.] 12mo. [Nichols' *Lit. Illust.* i. 423.] 1772

HERMIT'S (the) apprentice. . . . By Ascott R. Hope [Ascott Robert Hope Moncrieff]. 8vo. Pp. 219. [*Lit. Year Book.*] Edinburgh, 1886

HERMIT'S (the) dell; from the diary of a penciller [Henry C. Wetmore]. 8vo. [Cushing's *Init. and Pseud.* i. 227.] New York, 1854

HERMIT'S (a) idea that the stars are the homes of the heavenly hosts. [By John Stow.] 4to. [Cushing's *Init. and Pseud.* ii. 73.] London, 1862

HERMIT'S (a) tale, recorded by his own hand, and found in his cell. By the author of *The recess* [Sophia Lee]. 4to. London, 1787

The recess is not anonymous.

HERMSPRONG; or, man as he is not: a novel. By the author of *Man as he is* [Robert Bage]. 12mo. 3 vols. London, 1796

HERNANDO. [A novel.] By Owen Hall [H. H. Lusk]. 8vo. Pp. 400. [*Lond. Lib. Cat.*] London, 1902

HERO (a); Philip's book. By the author of *Olive*, *John Halifax*, etc. [Dinah Maria Mulock, later Mrs Craik]. 12mo. London, 1858

HERO and heroine; the story of a first year at school. By Ascott R. Hope [Ascott Robert Hope Moncrieff]. 8vo. Pp. 356. London, 1912

HERO and Leander; a burletta. . . . [By Isaac Jackman.] 8vo. [*Brit. Mus.*] London [1787]

HERO and Leander; a poem, by Musaeus: translated from the Greek [by Edward Taylor]. 4to. Pp. 28. [O'Donoghue's *Poets of Ireland.*] Glasgow, 1783

HERO and Leander; a poem: from the Greek of Musaeus. [Translated, with notes, by Edward Burnaby Greene.] 4to. [Lowndes' *Bibl. Man.*] London, 1773

Preface signed: E. B. G.

HERO and Leander, in burlesque. [By William Wycherley.] 8vo. Pp. 84. [*Bodl.*] London, 1669

HERO (the) in man. By A. E. [George William Russell]. 4to. [*Brit. Mus.*] London [1909]

HERO (a) of a hundred fights. By Sarah Tytler, author of *Papers for thoughtful girls*, etc. [Henrietta Keddie]. 8vo. Pp. vi. 345. London, 1881

HERO (a) of Pigeon Camp. By Martha James [Mrs Martha Claire MacGowan Doyle]. 8vo. [*Amer. Cat.*] Boston, 1908

HERO (a) of the pen; a novel. By E. Werner [Elizabeth Bürstenbinder]; from the German by S. Phillips. 8vo. 2 vols. London, 1878

HERO (the) of Urbino. By May Wynne [Mabel Wynne Knowles]. 8vo. Pp. 318. [*Lit. Year Book.*] London, 1914

HEROD and Mariamne; a tragedy: acted at the Duke's Theatre. [By Samuel Pordage.] 4to. Pp. 65. [Baker's *Biog. Dram.*] London, 1674

Elkanah Settle, whose name is attached to the dedication to Elizabeth, Duchess of Albemarle, was the publisher.

HEROD and Pilate reconciled; or, a late dialogue betwixt an Independent and a Malignant [upon the return of Charles I. to Homeby. A political satire in verse. By Robin Bostock.] 4to. [Thomason's *Coll. of Tracts*, i. 499.] London [1647]

The following is a continuation or second part.

HEROD and Pilate reconciled; a new dialogue betwixt a Malignant and an Independent. [By Robin Bostock.] 4to. [Thomason's *Coll. of Tracts*, i. 509.] London [1647]

HEROE (the) of Lorenzo; or, the way to eminencie and perfection: a piece of serious Spanish wit, originally in that language written [by Balthasar Gracian], and in English by Sir John Skeffington Kt. and Barronet. 12mo. [Graesse's *Trésor de livres rares.*] London, 1652

Balthasar Gracian published his works under the name of his brother Lorenzo.

HEROES (the) and battles of the American Revolution; or, thrilling stories . . . of that eventful period. By a veteran soldier [John Frost]. 12mo. Pp. 252. [Sabin's *Dictionary*.] Philadelphia, 1845

HEROES everywhere! By an Officer of the Bengal Staff Corps [Lieut. Colonel C. I. McDowell]; read at the Soldiers' Institute, Poona. 8vo. Pp. 37. Bombay, 1863

HEROES in homespun. By Ascott R. Hope [Ascott Robert Hope Moncrieff]. 8vo. [*Lit. Year Book.*] London, 1894

HEROES of American discovery. By N. D'Anvers [Mrs Nancy R. E. Bell, *née* Meugens]. 8vo. [*Brit. Mus.*] London, 1885

HEROES (the) of Asgard and the giants of Jötunheim; or, the week and its story. By the author of *Mia and Charlie*, and her sister [Annie and Eliza Keary]. 8vo. London, 1857

HEROES of discovery in Africa. By N. D'Anvers [Mrs Nancy R. E. Bell, *née* Meugens]. 8vo. [*Brit. Mus.*] London, 1900

HEROES of invention and discovery. . . . [By Robert Cochrane.] 8vo. [*Brit. Mus.*] London, 1879

HEROES of North African discovery. By Mrs N. D'Anvers [Nancy R. E. Bell, *née* Meugens]. 8vo. [*Brit. Mus.*] London, 1886

HEROES of South African discovery. By N. D'Anvers [Mrs Nancy R. E. Bell, *née* Meugens]. 8vo. London, 1878

HEROES of the desert; lives of Moffat and Livingstone. By the author of *Mary Powell* [Anne Manning, later Mrs Rathbone]. 8vo. London, 1875

HEROES of the Empire; deeds of valour on Britain's scroll of glory. By John Lea [John Lea Bricknell]. 4to. [*Brit. Mus.*] London [1916]

HEROES of the mine. By the author of *English hearts and English hands* [Catherine M. Marsh] and L. E. O'R. 12mo. Pp. 111. London [1877]

HEROES (the) of young America. By Ascott R. Hope, author of *A peck of troubles*, etc. [Ascott Robert Hope Moncrieff]. With maps and illustrations. 8vo. Pp. ix. 318. London, 1877

HEROES, philosophers, and courtiers of the time of Louis XVI. By the author of the *Secret history of the court of France under Louis XV* [Mrs Annie Emma Challice]. 8vo. 2 vols. [*Camb. Univ. Lib.*] London, 1863

Wrongly ascribed to Dr Challice.

HEROIC (an) address in prose to the Rev. Richard Watson [afterwards Bishop of Llandaff] on his late discourse to the clergy of the Archdeaconry of Ely. [By Thomas James Mathias.] 8vo. [*D. N. B.* vol. 37, p. 48.] London, 1780

HEROIC (an) answer [in verse], from Richard Twiss, Esq., F.R.S., at Rotterdam, to Donna Teresa Pinna y Ruiz, of Murcia. [By William Preston.] 8vo. [O'Donoghue's *Poets of Ireland.*] Dublin, 1776

Wrongly attributed to Leonard Macnally.

HEROIC (an) epistle from Donna Teresa Pinna y Ruiz, of Murcia, to Richard Twiss, Esq., F.R.S.; with several explanatory notes, written by himself. [By William Preston.] Third edition. 8vo. Dublin, 1776

A satire; wrongly assigned to L. Macnally.

HEROIC (an) epistle from Mons. Vestris, Sen., in England, to Mademoiselle Heinel in France; with notes. [By John Nott, M.D.] 4to. 1781

In a list of Dr Nott's works given in *Gent. Mag.* xcv. ii. 566, the title is given thus—"Heroic epistle in verse, from Mons. Vestris, in London, to Madm. Heimel in France." The above title is taken from *Mon. Rev.* lxv. 236.

HEROIC epistle from Serjeant Bradshaw, in the shades, to John Dunning, Esq. [By Sir James Bland Burges.] 4to. [Upcott and Shoberl's *Biog. Dict.* p. 47.] London, 1780

HEROIC (an) epistle [in verse] from the quadruple obelisk in the Market Place to the New Exchange [in Manchester. By Joseph Aston]. 8vo. Pp. 24. [*Brit. Mus.*] Manchester, 1809

HEROIC epistle of Mr Manly . . . to Mr Pinchbeck. [By William Preston, M.A., barrister.] 8vo. [O'Donoghue's *Poets of Ireland.*] Dublin, 1775

HEROIC (an) epistle to George Edmund Howard, from George Faulkner [Robert Jephson, Irish M.P.]. 8vo. [*Camb. Univ. Lib.*] Dublin, 1771

HEROIC (an) epistle to Mr Winsor, patentee of the gaslights. [By William Gifford.] 4to. London, 1808

HEROIC (an) epistle to Sir James Wright. [By William Combe.] 4to. [*D. N. B.* vol. 2, p. 433.] 1778

HEROIC (an) epistle to Sir William Chambers, Knight, Comptroller general of his Majesty's works, and author of a late Dissertation on Oriental gardening; enriched with explanatory notes, chiefly extracted from that elaborate performance. [By the Rev. William Mason, assisted by Horace Walpole.] 4to. Pp. 16. [Mason's *Satirical Poems*, ed. Paget Toynbee, 1926.] London, 1773

HEROIC (an) epistle to the noble author of the Duchess of Devonshire's cow; a poem. [By William Combe.] 4to. Pp. iv. 15. [*D. N. B.* vol. 2, p. 433.] London, 1777

HEROIC (an) epistle [in verse] to the Rev. R. Watson, enriched with elaborate notes. . . . [By Thomas James Mathias.] 4to. [*Brit. Mus.*] London, 1780

HEROIC (an) epistle to the Right Honourable the Lord Craven, on his delivering the following sentence at the county meeting at Abingdon, on Tuesday, November 7, 1775. "I will have it known there is respect due to a Lord." [By William Combe.] 4to. [*Bodl.*] London, 1775

HEROIC (the) musqueteer; or, the female warrior; a true history, very delightful and full of pleasant adventures in the campagnes of 1676, 1677. [By —— de Prechac.] Translated out of French. 12mo. [Arber's *Term Cat.* i. 524.] London, 1678

HEROIC (an) poem, in six books. [By Richard Owen, of Cambridge.] 4to. London, 1757

HEROIC (an) postscript to the public, occasioned by their favourable reception of a late heroic epistle to Sir William Chambers, Knt., etc. By the author of that Epistle [William Mason]. 4to. Pp. 41. London, 1774

HEROIC (an) sinner, and the pilgrim spinster. By Gorham Silva [Elizabeth Lawrence]. 8vo. New York, 1893

HEROICK epistle from Hamet the Moor, slippermaker in London, to the Emperor of Morocco; with an apology for publication, address'd to the Lutheran and Calvinistical embassadors. [By —— Fielding, son of Henry.] 4to. Pp. 31. [*Bodl.*] London, 1780

HEROINE (the) of Chelton School; a book for girls. By May Wynne [Mabel Wynne Knowles]. 8vo. [*Lit. Year Book.*] London, 1920

HEROINE (the) of love; a musical piece, in three acts. [By —— Robertson.] 8vo. [Baker's *Biog. Dram.* iii. 474.] York, 1778

HEROINE (the) of the Peninsula; or, Clara Matilda of Seville. By the author of *The Hermit in London* and other popular works [Capt. Felix M'Donough]. 12mo. 2 vols. London, 1826

HEROINES in obscurity; a second series of "Papers for thoughtful girls." By the author of *Papers for thoughtful girls* [Henrietta Keddie]. 8vo. Pp. 397. London, 1871

HEROINES (the) of a schoolroom; a sequel to *The Thistles of Mount Cedar*. By Ursula Tannerforst [Emily Tilghman]. 8vo. [*Amer. Cat.*] Philadelphia, 1907

HEROINES of our time; being sketches of the lives of eminent women, with examples of their benevolent works, truthful lives, and noble deeds. [By Joseph Johnson.] 8vo. [*Manch. Free Lib. Cat.* p. 373.] London [1860]

HEROINES of the household. By the author of *The heavenward path*, etc. [William Wilson, M.A.]. With illustrations by M. Ellen Edwards. 8vo. Pp. 299. [*Bodl.*] London [1864]

HERONRY (the); a tale. By "Scrutator" [K. W. Horlock]. 12mo. [*Nat. Lib. of Scot.*] London, 1864

HERRE followythe a lamyntabill tragedye, ful of concytete myrthe, yclepede, a mirroure fore magystrattis, baylyes, councylloures, and crafftessmenne: conteynynge the ryghte dolorose, tragycalle, and deinge speeches offe somme herretoeforre famose rueleres. . . . [By Alexander Jamieson, bookseller.] 8vo. Pp. 22.

Impryntede atte the costes and chargys offe mi moste woorthye patroune, his worchyppe Aldyrmanne Thornne=Backke, be me Ihone Daye, atte the signne of the Guse and Grydyrone, neare untoe the Change House, Fysshe Strete. Reprinted in the modern tongue, for W. M'William, High Street, Edinburgh. 1819.

HERRINGS (a) tayle; contayning a poetical fiction of divers matters worthie the reading. [By Richard Carew.] 4to. 18 leaves. [*Brit. Mus.*] London, 1598

HERVEIANA; or, graphic and literary sketches of the life and writings of the Rev. James Hervey. [By John Cole, bookseller.] 8vo. Scarborough, 1822

Contemporary attestation.

HERWALD de Wake; or, the two apostates: a romance. [By Hewson Clark.] 12mo. 3 vols. [*Bodl.*] London, 1823

HE'S a lunatic; a farce. By Felix Dale [Herman Charles Merivale, B.A.]. 8vo. London, 1867

HE'S much to blame; a comedy in five acts, as performed at the Theatre Royal, Covent Garden. [By Thomas Holcroft.] 8vo. Pp. 96. [Baker's *Biog. Dram.*] London, 1798

HESPERIDES; the occupations, relaxations, and aspirations of life. By Launcelot Cross [Frank Carr, timber merchant]. 8vo. Pp. iv. 485. [*Lond. Lib. Cat.*] London, 1883

HESPERIA; a poem. [By Richard Henry Wilde.] 8vo. [O'Donoghue's *Poets of Ireland.*] Boston, Mass., 1867

This poem was edited by the author's son, William C. Wilde. The half-title runs: "Hesperia; a fragment, by the late Fitzhugh De Lancy."

HESPERI—neso—graphia; or, a description of the Western Isle [Ireland]; in eight cantos. By W. M. [William Moffet, really Walter-Jones]. 12mo. [O'Donoghue's *Poets of Ireland.*] Dublin, 1724

Another edition was published at Monaghan in 1814. See also "The history of Ireland, in verse. . . ."

HESPERUS; and other poems. By Louis Barnaval [Charles De Kay]. 8vo. [Cushing's *Init. and Pseud.* i. 30.] New York, 1880

HESTER and I; or, beware of worldliness. By Mrs Manners [Mrs Cornelia H. Richards]. 8vo. Pp. 211. [*Brit. Mus.*] London, 1861

HESTER; and other New England stories. By Margaret Sidney [Mrs Harriet Mulford Lothrop]. 8vo. [Kirk's *Supp.*] Boston, 1886

HESTER Kirkton. [By Mrs Katherine S. MacQuoid, the author of *A bad beginning.*]. 8vo. 2 vols. [*Brit. Mus.*] London, 1874

HESTER Morley's promise. By Hesba Stretton [Sarah Smith]. 8vo. Pp. 526. London, 1898

See the note to "Alone in London."

HESTER redeemed. By Guy Thorne [Cyril A. E. Ranger-Gull]. 8vo. Pp. 312. [*Brit. Mus.*] London, 1917

HESTER, the bride of the island. [A novel. By Sylvester Blackmore Beckett.] 8vo. [Cushing's *Anon.*] Portland [Maine] 1860

HESTER'S happy summer. [A tale. By Mary Ellen Atkinson.] 8vo. [Cushing's *Anon.*] Boston, 1875

HESTER'S history; a novel. [By Rosa Mulholland, Lady Gilbert.] (Reprinted from *All the year round.*) 8vo. 2 vols. [*Camb. Univ. Lib.*] London, 1869

HESTER'S sacrifice. By the author of *St Olave's*, etc. [Eliza Tabor, later Mrs Stephenson]. 8vo. 3 vols. London, 1866

HESTER'S venture. [A novel.] By the author of *The Atelier du Lys* [Margaret Roberts]. 8vo. 2 vols. [*Brit. Mus.*] London, 1887

HETTY Wesley. By Q. [Sir Arthur T. Quiller-Couch]. A new edition. 8vo. Pp. 277. Bristol, 1908

HETTY'S strange story. [By Mrs Helen M. Jackson.] 8vo. [Cushing's *Anon.*] Boston, 1877

HEXAMETRICAL experiments; or, a version of four of Virgil's Pastorals. . . . [By James Blundell, M.D.] 4to. Pp. xi. 92. [*Brit. Mus.*] London, 1838

HEXAPLA Jacobœa; a specimen of loyalty towards His present Majesty, James the II. . . . in six pieces. By [Edward Wetenhall] an Irish Protestant Bishop [of Cork and Rosse]. 12mo. [*D. N. B.* vol. 60, p. 383.] Dublin, 1686

"HEY for Cavaliers." [A novel.] By May Wynne [Mabel Wynne Knowles]. 8vo. Pp. 314. London, 1912

HEZEKIAH, King of Judah; or, invasion repulsed, and peace restored: a sacred drama of national application at this awful crisis. Inscribed to the most noble the Marchioness of Stafford. [By William Allen, Warden of Dulwich College.] 8vo. [Nichols' *Lit. Anec.* ix. 205.] 1798

HEZEKIAH; or, brief lessons on Church truths. . . . By C. S. [Charles Stanley, Plymouthist in Sheffield]. 8vo. London [1879]

HEZEKIAH, the king; or, the city defended by God. By Mildred Duff and Noel Hope [Sarah L. Morewood]. 8vo. Pp. 101. [*Brit. Mus.*] London [1911]

HEZEKIAH'S kortship. By Hezekiah Jones' wife [Frank A. Van Denburg]. 8vo. [*Amer. Cat.*] Boston, 1904

HEZEKIAH'S return of praise for his recovery. [A sermon on Isaiah 38, 17-19]. By A. L. [Adam Litleton, D.D.]. 4to. [*Brit. Mus.*] London, 1668

HIATUS; the void in modern education, its cause, and antidote. By Outis [John Lucas Tupper]. 8vo. [*Brit. Mus.*] London, 1869

HIAWATHA; the story of the Iroquois sage, in prose and verse. [By Benjamin Franklin Da Costa, D.D.] 8vo. New York, 1873

HIBERNIA curiosa; a letter from [John Bush] a gentleman in Dublin to his friend, at Dover, giving a general view of the manners, dispositions, trade, agriculture, and curiosities of the inhabitants of Ireland. 8vo. [Watt's *Bibl. Brit.*] London [1767]

HIBERNIA freed; a tragedy as it is acted at the Theatre-Royal in Lincoln's-Inn-Fields. [By Captain William Phillips.] 8vo. Pp. 57. [Baker's *Biog. Dram.* i. 571.] London, 1722

HIBERNIAN (the) patriot; being a collection of the Drapier's Letters to the people of Ireland, concerning Mr Wood's brass half-pence; together with considerations on the attempts made to pass that coin, and reasons for the people of Ireland's refusing it: to which are added, poems and songs relating to the same subject. [By Jonathan Swift, D.D.] 8vo. Pp. 264. [*Bodl.*] Dublin: reprinted, London, 1730

HIBERNICUS'S letters; or, a philosophical miscellany, containing essays . . . with original poems and translations; written by several hands in Dublin [chiefly James Arbuckle, though Francis Hutchison, Samuel Boyse, and the poet Parnell made a few contributions]. Second edition. 8vo. [*D. N. B.* vol. 2, p. 59.] London, 1734

This collection of papers, which first appeared in a Dublin journal, came to be known under the pen-name of the main contributor.

HIDDEN depths. [By Felicia M. F. Skene.] 8vo. 2 vols. [*D. N. B.* First Supp. vol. 3, p. 347.] Edinburgh, 1866

Though in the form of a novel, this work depicts many scenes actually witnessed by the writer. It was republished in 1886 with her name, and a longer title, "Hidden depths; a story of cruel wrong" (London, pp. xii. 243).

HIDDEN (the) gift; and other poems. By Kalamos [M. M. Wilson]. 8vo. Pp. 156. London, 1908

HIDDEN (the) life of the soul; from the French [of Jean Nicolas Grou] by the author of *A Dominican Artist* [Henrietta L. Farrer, later Mrs Sidney Lear]. 8vo. Pp. xvi. 256. London, 1870

HIDDEN links; or, the schoolfellows: a tale. [By Charles Francis Liddell.] 12mo. 3 vols. London, 1857

HIDDEN (the) path. By Marion Harland [Mary Virginia Hawes, later Mrs Terhune]. 12mo. [Allibone's *Dict.*] New York, 1855

HIDDEN paths. [A novel.] By W. Scott King [Rev. William Kingscote Greenland]. 8vo. Pp. 223. [*Lit. Year Book.*] London, 1920

HIDDEN (the) power; a tale illustrative of youthful influence. By the author of *The lamp of life*, etc. [Fanny Elizabeth Bunnett]. 8vo. [*Nat. Lib. of Scot.*] London, 1857

HIDDEN saints; life of Sœur Marie, the workwoman of Liege. By the author of *Wild Times* [Cecilia Mary Caddell]. 8vo. [*Brit. Mus.*] London, 1869

HIDDEN (the) sin; a novel. [By Frances Browne.] 8vo. 3 vols. [*Brit. Mus.*] London, 1866

HIDDEN (the) submarine; or, the plot that failed. By Clive Holland [Charles J. Hankinson]. 8vo. Pp. 320. [*Lond. Lib. Cat.*] London, 1917

HIDDEN talent. By Faith Latimer [Mrs John A. Miller]. 8vo. [Cushing's *Init. and Pseud.* i. 186.] New York, 1884

HIDDEN treasure. By Clara Vance [Mrs Mary Andrews Denison]. 8vo. [Cushing's *Init. and Pseud.* i. 292.] Boston, 1877

HIDDEN (the) treasure; and other tales. By M. H. [Matilda Horsburgh]. 8vo. Edinburgh, 1869

HIDDEN (the) treasure; or, the value and excellence of holy Mass: with a practical and devout method of hearing it with profit. By the blessed Leonard [Casanuovo] of Port Maurice. Translated from the Italian at the particular instance of [Thomas Grant] the Bishop of Southwark: with an introduction by his lordship. 12mo. [*W.*] Edinburgh, 1855

HIDDEN (the) treasures of Egypt; a romance. By Robert Eustace [E. Rawlins]. 8vo. Pp. xxxii. 352. [*Brit. Mus.*] London [1925]

HIDDEN (the) victim. By Headon Hill [Frank E. Grainger]. 8vo. Pp. 320. [*Lond. Lib. Cat.*] London, 1907

HIERO; or, the condition of royalty: a conversation. From the Greek of Xenophon, by the translator of Antoninus's *Meditations* [Rev. Richard Graves]. 8vo. Pp. 138. [Green's *Bibl. Somers.* ii. 445.] Bath, 1793

HIEROCLES upon the Golden verses of the Pythagoreans; translated immediately out of the Greek into English [by John Norris]. 8vo. 27 leaves, unpaged, and pp. 166. London, 1682

HIEROGLYPHIC tales. [By Horace Walpole, Earl of Orford.] 8vo. Pp. ix. 50. Strawberry-Hill, 1785

"Only six copies of this were printed, besides the revised copy."—MS. note in the Dyce copy.

HIEROMANIA (the); a poem. [By Thomas Iwymmer Champneys.] 8vo. Pp. 54. [Green's *Bibl. Somers.* ii. 227.] [Frome] 1808

HIERON'S last farewell; a sermon preached at Modbvry in Devon, at the funerall of . . . Master Samvel Hieron, sometimes preacher there. By I. B. [John Barlow]. 4to. Pp. 33. [Dredge's *Devon Bibl.* p. 89.] London, 1618

HIGH altars; the battle-fields of France and Flanders as I saw them. By John Oxenham [William Arthur Dunkerley]. 12mo. Pp. 78. London, 1918

HIGH Church. [By Frederick William Robinson.] 8vo. 2 vols. [*Brit. Mus.*] London, 1860

HIGH (the) Church address to Dr Henry Sacheverell, for the great service he has done the established Church and nation; wherein is shewn the justice of the proceedings of those gentlemen who have encouraged the pulling down and destroying those nurseries of schism, the Presbyterian meeting-houses. . . . [By Daniel Defoe.] 8vo. [Wilson's *Life of Defoe.*] London, 1710

HIGH Church displayed; being a complete history of the affair of Dr Sacheverell. [By John Toland.] 8vo. [*Camb. Mod. Hist.* vol. 5, p. 859.] London, 1711

HIGH (the) Church legion; or, the memorial examin'd: being, a new test of moderation, as 'tis recommended to all that love the Church of England, and the constitution. [By Daniel Defoe.] 4to. Pp. vi. 21. [Wilson's *Life of Defoe.*] London, 1705

HIGH Church; or, Audi alteram partem. By H. H. A. S. [Hely Hutchinson A. Smith]. 8vo. Pp. 124. [*Brit. Mus.*] London, 1873

HIGH Church politics; being an appeal to the friends of the British constitution against the principles of High Churchmen, as exemplified in the opposition to the Repeal of the Test Laws and in the Riots at Birmingham. [By C. Heywood.] 8vo. Birmingham, 1792

From a MS. note on Messrs Harding's copy. Attributed also to Joseph Priestly.

HIGH (the) court of justice; or, Cromwels new slaughter-house in England: with the authority that constituted and ordained it, arraigned, convicted and condemned, for usurpation, treason, tyranny, theft and murther: being the third part of the *History of Independency*, written by the same authour [Clement Walker]. 4to. [*D. N. B.* vol. 59, p. 48.]

Printed Anno Domini 1651. In the second year of the States liberty, and the peoples slavery.

HIGH (the) estate of service. [By Isabella Cowan.] 8vo. Pp. 98. Edinburgh, 1887

The second edition, 1898, bears the author's name.

HIGH life below stairs; a farce of two acts, as it is performed at the Theatre-Royal in Drury-Lane. [By Rev. James Townley, M.A.] 8vo. Pp. 54. [Baker's *Biog. Dram.*] London, 1759

Wrongly ascribed to David Garrick.

HIGH life in New York. By Jonathan Slick, Esq., of Weathersfield, Connecticut [Mrs Ann Sophia Stephens]. 8vo. [Cushing's *Init. and Pseud.* ii. 138.] Philadelphia, 1854

HIGH life; or, the history of Miss Faulkland. [By Henry Higgs.] 8vo. 2 vols. [*Lond. Lib. Cat.*] London, 1768

HIGH lights. [By Caroline Leslie Whitney, later Mrs Field.] 8vo. Boston, 1886

HIGH (a) little world, and what happened there. By Deas Cromarty [Mrs R. A. Watson, *née* Elizabeth S. Fletcher]. 8vo. [*Lit. Year Book.*] London, 1896

HIGH (the) Old Court of Impeachment. By P. E. R. Simmons [De Witt Clinton Cooley]. 8vo. [Kirk's *Supp.* i. 382.] St Paul, Minnesota, 1878

HIGH (the) price of food, butcher-meat, meal, and bread-stuffs, etc., stated and illustrated. . . . By a Writer to the Signet [Alexander Kennedy]. 8vo. Edinburgh [1860]

Signed: A. K.

HIGH stakes. [A novel.] By Laurence L. Lynch [Emma M. Murdoch, later Mrs F. M. Van Deventer]. New edition. 8vo. Pp. 424. [*Brit. Mus.*] London, 1901

HIGHER aspects of Spiritualism. By M. A., Oxon. [Rev. William Stainton Moses]. 8vo. [*Brit. Mus.*] London, 1879

HIGHER criticism principles and practice; an appeal to members of all Christian Churches, regarding the questions raised by Professor [William Robertson] Smith's article "Bible," and others in the . . . *Encyclopædia Britannica*. . . . By a layman [James Barnhill]. 8vo. Pp. 35. [*New Coll. Lib.*] Glasgow, 1877

HIGHER law; a romance. By the author of *The pilgrim and the shrine* [Edward Maitland, B.A.]. 8vo. 3 vols. [*Nat. Lib. of Scot.*] London, 1870

A revised edition appeared in 1871.

HIGHEST references. [A novel.] By Florence Warden [Florence Alice Price, later Mrs George E. James]. 8vo. Pp. 236. London [1892]

HIGH-FLOWN episcopal and priestly claims freely examined; in a dialogue betwixt a country gentleman and a country vicar; wherein church-authority, confirmation, absolution, the burial of the dead, the power of Bishops to give the Holy Ghost, and of priests to forgive sins . . . are particularly considered. . . . [By Rev. Micaiah Towgood.] 8vo. [*D. N. B.* vol. 57, p. 94.] London, 1737

HIGH-FLYER'S (the) guide [in rearing pigeons]; or, how to breed and train tipplers, tumblers, rollers, cumulets, and cross-breeds. [By G. Smith.] 8vo. Nottingham, 1890

HIGH-GERMAN (the) doctor, with many additions and alterations; to which is added, a large explanatory index. [By Philip Horneck.] 12mo. 2 vols. [Lowndes' *Bibl. Man.*] London, 1719

This paper commenced on Tuesday, 4th May 1714, was published twice a week, and having attained 100 numbers, expired on 12th May 1715.

HIGHLAND (the) Gentleman's Magazine, for January, 1751. The first after jubilee year. [By John Campbell, LL.D.] 8vo. London, 1751

HIGHLAND lassies; or, the Roua Pass: a new edition. By Erick Mackenzie [Mrs Millicent Grogan]. 12mo. London, 1862

HIGHLAND legends and fugitive pieces of original poetry, with translations from the Gaelic and vice versa. By "Glenmore" [Donald Shaw]. 8vo. Pp. 204. [*Nat. Lib. of Scot.*] Edinburgh, 1859

HIGHLAND Mary; a novel. By the author of *The foundling of Glenthorn*, etc. [Alexander Balfour]. 12mo. 4 vols. [*Camb. Univ. Lib.*] London, 1826

HIGHLAND (a) memory. By an old Colonial [Kenneth M. Cameron]. 8vo. [*Brit. Mus.*] London, 1892

HIGHLAND (the) rogue; or, the memorable actions of the celebrated Robert MacGregor, commonly called Rob Roy: containing a genuine account of his education, grandeur, and sudden misfortune. . . . [By Daniel Defoe.] 8vo. [*Brit. Mus.*] London, 1723

HIGHLAND (the) shepherd. By the author of *Sheep-farmers and drovers* [William Robertson, Sheriff of Argyll]. 8vo. Pp. 64. [*D. Laing.*] Edinburgh, 1867

HIGHLAND (the) smugglers. By the author of *Adventures of a Kuzzilbash*, etc. [James Baillie Fraser]. 12mo. 3 vols. [*Bodl.*] London, 1832

HIGHLAND tales and songs. [By Robert Buchanan.] 8vo. Pp. 72. [*D. Laing.*] Glasgow, 1817

HIGHLAND (the) Watch Tower; or the sons of Glenalvon: a romance. By the author of *Fatherless Fanny* [Clara Reeve]. 8vo. London, 1842

The authorship has been questioned.

HIGHLANDER (the); a poem: in six cantos. [By James Macpherson.] 12mo. Pp. 82. Edinburgh, 1758

"This poem is a curiosity, being the first production of James Macpherson, Esq. author of Ossian, Historian, & Translator of Homer."—MS. note by Isaac Reed.

HIGHLANDERS (the); a tale. By the author of *The Hermit in London* [Captain Felix MacDonogh]. 12mo. 3 vols. [*Brit. Mus.*] London, 1824

HIGHWAY (the) of sorrow at the close of the nineteenth century. By Hesba Stretton [Sarah Smith]. 8vo. Pp. 440. London, 1897

See the note to "Alone in London."

HIGHWAY (the) to heaven; its hindrances and helps. By Austin Clare [Miss W. M. James]. 8vo. Pp. 216. [*Lit. Year Book.*] London, 1892

HIGHWAYMEN (the) of Wiltshire; or, a narrative of . . . divers freebooters and smugglers in this and the adjoining counties. [By James Waylen.] 12mo. [*Brit. Mus.*] Devises [1845]

HIGH-WAYS and by-ways; or tales of the roadside, picked up in the French provinces. By a walking gentleman [Thomas Colley Grattan]. Second edition. 8vo. 2 vols. [*Camb. Univ. Lib.*] London, 1823

HIGH-WAYS & dry-ways; or, the Britannia and Conway tubular bridges. By the author of *Stokers and Pokers* [Sir Francis Bond Head]. 8vo. Pp. 83. London, 1849

HIKE and the aeroplane. By Tom Graham [Sinclair Lewis]. 8vo. Pp. 275. [*Amer. Cat.*] New York [1912]

HILARIA; the festive board. [By Captain —— Morris.] 8vo. London, 1798

HILARY'S career. [A novel.] By Parry Truscott [Katharine Edith Spicer-Jay]. 8vo. Pp. 310. [*Lit. Year Book.*] London, 1913

HILARY'S folly. [A tale.] By Bertha M. Clay [Charlotte M. Braeme]. 12mo. New York, 1887

HILDA among the broken gods. By the author of *Olrig Grange* [Walter Chalmers Smith, D.D.]. 8vo. Glasgow, 1878

HILDA and I; a story of three lovers. [By Mrs Elizabeth Dundas Benjamin.] 8vo. [Kirk's *Supp.*] New York, 1880

HILDA; or, the old seat of Council. By Skelton Yorke [Margaret Plues]. 8vo. London, 1868

HILDEGARDE; or, He leadeth. By Ernest Gilmore [Mrs Helen H. Farley]. 8vo. [Cushing's *Init. and Pseud.* i. 117.] New York, 1889

HILLIAD (the); an epic poem, to which are prefixed . . . prolegomena and notes . . . of . . . Martinus Macularius [Christopher Smart]. 4to. [*Brit. Mus.*] London, 1753

A satire on Sir John Hill.

HILLINGDON Hall; or, the cockney squire: a tale of country life. By the author of *Handley Cross*, etc. [Robert Smith Surtees]. 12mo. 3 vols. [*Brit. Mus.*] London, 1888

HILLS and plains; a very old story. [By Theobald Mathew.] 8vo. 2 vols. London, 1861

HILLS (the) of hell; and other poems. By Desmond Mountjoy [W. M. Chapman Houston]. 8vo. Pp. 40. [O'Donoghue's *Poets of Ireland.*] London, 1911

HILLS (the) of Rual; and other stories. By Fiona Macleod [William Sharp]. Fol. Pp. 100. [*Lit. Year Book.*] London, 1921

HILLS (the) of the Shatemuc. By the author of *The wide, wide world* [Susan Warner]. 8vo. Pp. iv. 514. London, 1856

HILL-SIDE (the); illustrations of some of the simplest terms used in logic. By the author of *Mary Powell* [Anne Manning, later Mrs Rathbone]. 12mo. Pp. iv. 89. [*Brit. Mus.*] London [1854]

HILLSIDE rhymes; chiefly of Manorhead, Manor Water, and district. [By John Veitch, LL.D., Professor in Glasgow University.] 8vo. Pp. 123. Glasgow, 1872

HILTON Castle in olden days; a legendary tale, in four cantos. [By John Fawcett.] 8vo. Sunderland, 1830

HINC illae lachrymæ; or, the impietie of impunitie: containing a short demonstration of the originall of all the grand grievances. By a faithfull friend to the truth, and a servant to all loyall and religious Presbyterian Members of Parliament [John Gaudeny, D.D.?]. 4to. London, 1647

HIND (the) and the panther; a poem: in three parts. [By John Dryden.] 4to. Pp. 145. [*Brit. Mus.*] London, 1687

HIND (the) and the panther transvers'd to the story of the country-mouse and the city-mouse. [By Matthew Prior and Charles Montague, Earl of Halifax.] 4to. Pp. 36. [*Bodl.*] London, 1687

In the composition of this piece, Prior seems to have had by far the greater share. —*See* Scott's edition of Dryden's Works, vol. i. p. 330.

HIND (a) let loose; or, an historical representation of the testimonies of the Church of Scotland, for the interest of Christ, with the true state thereof in all its periods. . . . By a lover of true liberty [Alexander Shields, minister of St Andrews]. 8vo. 1687

HINDEE story-teller; or, entertaining expositor of the Roman, Persian, and Nagree characters . . . in their application to the Hindoostanee language. By the author of the *Hindoostanee dictionary*, etc. [John Borthwick Gilchrist]. 8vo. 2 vols. [*Edin. Univ. Lib.*] Calcutta, 1802-3

HINDERERS (the); a story of the present time. By Edna Lyall [Ada Ellen Bayly]. 8vo. Pp. 179. [*Lit. Year Book.*] London, 1902

HINDU (the) examiner of the true religion; or, dialogues on religious matters between a Catholic priest and a Hindu. By a missionary apostolic [T. A. M. Gambier]. 8vo. Pp. xviii. 305. [*Brit. Mus.*] Mangalore, 1889

HINDU (the) pantheon. [By Edward Moor.] 8vo. [Black's *Gypsy Bibl.* p. 1237.] London, 1832

HINDU women; with glimpses into their life and zenanas. By H. Ll. [Rev. Henry Lloyd]. 8vo. Pp. 143. [*Brit. Mus.*] London, 1882

HINTS addressed to card parties. [By John Coakley Lettsom, M.D.] 8vo. [Smith's *Cat. of Friends' Books*, i. 77; ii. 105.] London, 1798

HINTS addressed to the small holders and peasantry of Ireland on . . . health, temperance, morals, etc. By Martin Doyle [Rev. William Hickey]. 8vo. Pp. 92. [*Lit. Year Book.*] Dublin, 1839

HINTS and essays, theological and moral, intended briefly to expose the corrupt principles of Calvinism, and briefly to offer other principles better corresponding with reason and Scripture. . . . By a layman [John Hollis]. 12mo. [*Bibl. Parriana*, p. 56.] 1775

HINTS and reflections for railway travellers and others; or, a journey to the phalanx. By Minor Hugo [Luke Hansard ?]. 8vo. 3 vols. [*Camb. Univ. Lib.*] London, 1843

HINTS, chiefly Scriptural, respecting regeneration. [By Richard Phillips.] 8vo. [Smith's *Cat. of Friends' Books*, ii. 408.] London, 1808

The author's name appears in the second edition, 1809.

HINTS, &c.; submitted to the serious attention of the clergy, nobility and gentry, *newly* associated. By a layman, a friend to the true principles of the constitution, in Church and State and to religious and civil liberty [Augustus Henry Fitzroy, 3d Duke of Grafton]. Fourth edition, revised, with additions. 8vo. [*Queen's Coll. Cat.* pp. 111, 811.] London, 1790

HINTS for a reform, particularly in the Gambling Clubs. By a Member of Parliament [James Duff, second Earl of Fife]. 8vo. Pp. 24. London, 1784

HINTS for a specific plan for an abolition of the slave trade. . . . [By James White.] 8vo. [*Brit. Mus.*] London, 1788

HINTS for a system of education for a female orphan-house. . . . By Eubante [—— Walker]. 8vo. [*Brit. Mus.*] Dublin, 1793

HINTS for an argument against the reception of a petition by either House of Parliament, from the Presbyteries of Scotland, unless sanctioned by the approbation of the General Assembly. By a barrister [John Joseph Dillon, of Lincoln's Inn]. 8vo. [*New Coll. Lib.*] N.P., March 2, 1813

A private paper, not published.

HINTS for an index to our historical records preserved in MS. in the archives of Parliament, in the offices of state, by corporations of all sorts, in public libraries and in private collections, at home, in the colonies, in India, and in foreign countries; with a specimen of such an index, submitted to the Right Honourable the Master of the Rolls. [By Saxe Bannister, M.A.] 8vo. [*Bodl.*]

No title-page.

HINTS for Eton masters. By W. J. [William Johnson, later William Cory]. 8vo. Pp. 32. [*Brit. Mus.*] London, 1898

HINTS for Oxford; containing I. Hints prefatory. II. Hints to freshmen. III. On debt and duns. IV. On studies and reading for the schools. V. Amusements. VI. On college parties and conversation. [By John Campbell, B.A.] 8vo. Pp. 74. [*Bodl.*] Oxford, 1823

HINTS for pedestrians. By Medicus [George Bott Churchill Watson]. 8vo. [Cushing's *Init. and Pseud.* i. 186.] London, 1842

HINTS for promoting a bee society. [By John Coakley Lettsom, M.D.] [A wood-cut of a bee-hive.] 8vo. [Nichols' *Lit. Anec.* ix. 186.] London, 1796

HINTS for the considerate; how should the members and adherents of the Free Church conduct themselves towards the Establishment and those adhering to it? [By Rev. James W. Taylor.] 8vo. [*New Coll. Lib.*] Perth, 1844

HINTS for the "Evidences of Spiritualism." By M. P. [John Delaware Lewis]. 8vo. Pp. vii. 119. [*Brit. Mus.*] London, 1872

HINTS for the hunting-field. By the Master of the Cleveland hounds [W. H. A. Wharton]. 12mo. Pp. 19. [*Brit. Mus.*] London, 1897

HINTS for the improvement of early education and nursery discipline. [By Louisa Hoare.] 12mo. [Smith's *Cat. of Friends' Books*, i. 955.] London, 1819

HINTS for the small farmers of Ireland. By Martin Doyle [Rev. William Hickey, M.A.]. 12mo. Dublin, 1830

HINTS for the table; or, the economy of good living: with a few words on wines. [By John Timbs.] 8vo. [*Lond. Lib. Cat.*] London, 1859

HINTS for the use of Highland tenants and cottagers. By a proprietor [Sir Francis Mackenzie, Bart.]. 8vo. Inverness, 1838

In Gaelic and English.

HINTS from a lawyer. [By Edgar A. Spencer.] 8vo. [*Lib. Journ.* xiv. 59.] New York, 1888

HINTS from a minister [Rev. Sir James Stonhouse, M.D.] to a curate [Rev. Thomas Stedman]. 8vo. [*D. N. B.* vol. 54, p. 418.] London [1760?]

HINTS from my arm-chair. By C. B. N. [C. B. Newnham]. 8vo. [Green's *Bibl. Somers.* i. 370.] Bath [1879]

HINTS of the glory of Christ; on Canticles v. 10 to 16. By A. D. [Anne Dutton]. 8vo. London, 1748

HINTS on advocacy, as to opening a case . . . examples of reply, peroration, etc. By a barrister [Richard Harris]. Second edition. 8vo. Pp. 296. [*Brit. Mus.*] London, 1879

HINTS on agriculture, adapted to a midland county. [By Cornelius Tongue.] 8vo. [*Bodl.*] London, 1855

HINTS on agriculture, relative to profitable draining and manuring, etc. By "Cecil" [Cornelius Tongue]. 8vo. [Haynes' *Pseud.*] London, 1858

HINTS on angling, with suggestions for angling excursions in France and Belgium; to which are appended some brief notices of the English, Scottish, and Irish waters. By Palmer Hackle, Esq. [Robert Blakey]. 8vo. Pp. xvi. 339. [*Camb. Univ. Lib.*] London, 1846

A later edition (1898), with an abbreviated title, gives the author's name and a memoir; also notes by "Red Spinner" [William Senior].

HINTS on banking. By a New Yorker [John MacVickar, D.D.]. 8vo. [Cushing's *Init. and Pseud.* i. 203.] New York, 1827

HINTS on dress. By an American woman [Helen C. Smith]. 8vo. [Cushing's *Init. and Pseud.* i. 14.] New York, 1872

HINTS on emigration to Upper Canada, addressed to the lower classes in Great Britain and Ireland. By Martin Doyle [Rev. William Hickey, M.A.]. 12mo. Dublin, 1831

HINTS on etiquette and the usages of society. By Ἄγωγος [Charles William Day]. 8vo. [Cushing's *Init. and Pseud.* i. 7.] New York, 1843

HINTS on federation. By an elector [Albert Sturt]. 8vo. Sydney, N.S.W., 1898

HINTS on horsemanship, to a nephew and niece; or, common sense and common errors in common riding. By an officer of the household brigade of cavalry [Colonel George Greenwood]. 8vo. Pp. 105. [*Nat. Lib. of Scot.*] London, 1839

HINTS on house-building. By Tom Cringle [William Walker]. 8vo. Manchester [1870?]

HINTS on human conduct in various relations. [By James Welsh.] 8vo. Edinburgh, 1834

HINTS on husbandry. By D. C. [D. Coatsworth], late of Yarm. 8vo. Stockton, 1806

HINTS on life, and how to rise in society. By C. B. C., Amicus [Charles Barwell Coles]. 8vo. London, 1845

HINTS on longevity. [By Sir John Sinclair, Bart.] 4to. [Courtney's *Secrets*, p. 26.] [London, 1802]

HINTS on prophecy. [By George Montagu, Duke of Manchester.] 8vo. London, 1830

HINTS on rural residences. [By Nicholas Carlisle, F.S.A.] 4to. Pp. 107. [*W.*; Martin's *Cat.*] London, 1825

HINTS on the formation and management of Sunday schools. [By Thomas Hartwell Horne.] 12mo. London, 1807

From a list of his works in the handwriting of the author.

HINTS on the formation of a plan for the safe and effective revival of the Professorial system in Oxford. By a resident Member of Convocation [Archibald Campbell Tait, afterwards Archbishop of Canterbury]. 8vo. Pp. vii. 46. Oxford, 1839

HINTS on the formation of gardens and pleasure grounds; with designs in various styles of rural embellishment. . . . [By John Claudius.] 4to. [*Brit. Mus.*] London, 1812

HINTS on the improvement of day schools. [By Mrs Maria B. Howard?] 8vo. London, 1827

HINTS on the instruction of youth. [By William Fell, teacher.] 8vo. [*D. N. B.* vol. 18, p. 300.] Manchester, 1798

HINTS on the ordinance of a Gospel ministry. By a friend to order in the Church [Rev. Robert Culbertson, of Leith]. 8vo. Edinburgh, 1800

HINTS on the principles of a constitutional police; in observations on "A letter [by Henry Cockburn] to the inhabitants of Edinburgh on the new police-bill." [By J. Simpson.] 8vo. [*W.*; *Brit. Mus.*] Edinburgh, 1822

HINTS on the propriety of establishing a typographical society in Newcastle-upon-Tyne. [By John Trotter Brockett.] 12mo. Pp. 8. [*W.*] Private print, Newcastle, 1818

HINTS on the service for the visitation of the sick. [By Priscilla Maurice.] 8vo. Pp. iv. 74. [*Bodl.*] London, 1845

HINTS on the topography of Wiltshire; queries submitted to the consideration of the nobility, etc., of the County of Wilts, with a view to promote a general history of the County. [By Sir Richard Colt Hoare, Bart.] 8vo. [*W.*; Martin's *Cat.*] Salisbury, 1818

HINTS on toleration, in five essays for the consideration of Viscount Sidmouth and the dissenters. [By P. Broxbourne.] 8vo. London, 1810

HINTS on vegetation, and questions regarding the nature and principles thereof; addressed to farmers, nurserymen, and gardeners. [By Sir John Sinclair.] 4to. Pp. 22. [*Brit. Mus.*] London, 1796

HINTS on village nursing. By E. A. E. [E. A. Eminson]. 8vo. [*Bodl.*] London, 1885

HINTS on wages, the corn-laws, high and low prices, paper-money, and banking; arising from a consideration of three Lectures on the cost of obtaining money, and on some effects of private and government paper-money, delivered before the University of Oxford, by Nassau William Senior, A.M. . . . By a British merchant [J. H. Renny]. 8vo. Pp. x. 332. [*Edin. Univ. Lib.*] London, 1832

HINTS respecting the chlorosis of boarding-schools. By the author of *Hints respecting the distresses of the poor* [John Coakley Lettsom, M.D.]. 8vo. [Nichols' *Lit. Anec.* ix. 186.] London, 1795

HINTS respecting the distresses of the poor. [By John Coakley Lettsom, M.D.] 8vo. [Nichols' *Lit. Anec.* ix. 186.] 1795

HINTS respecting the improvement of the education of candidates for the Degree of Doctor of Medicine in the University of Edinburgh. By a Graduate of King's College, Aberdeen [John Thomson, M.D.]. 8vo. Edinburgh, 1874

Information from a friend of the author.

HINTS respecting wills and testaments. [By John Coakley Lettsom, M.D.] 8vo. [Smith's *Cat. of Friends' Books*, i. 76.] London, 1796

HINTS to a curate for the management of a parish. [By Rev. Sir James Stonhouse, M.D.] Second edition. 12mo. [Darling's *Cyclop. Bibl.*] London, 1776

HINTS to all ranks. [By Hannah More.] 12mo. [*Brit. Mus.*] London, 1795

HINTS to anglers; or, the art of angling epitomised, in verse, with explanatory notes. By T. F. S. [T. F. Salter] an old piscator, containing his directions for making ground baits, pastes, etc. 8vo. Pp. 13. [Westwood and Satchell's *Pisc. Bibl.*] London, 1808

HINTS to freshmen at the University of Cambridge. [By Philip Stanhope Dodd, M.A.] Third edition. 8vo. Pp. 56. [*Camb. Univ. Lib.*] London, 1807

HINTS to freshmen in the University of Oxford. [By Samuel Reynolds Hole, D.D., Dean of Rochester.] 8vo. [*Brit. Mus.*] Oxford, 1847

HINTS to horse-keepers. By Frank Forester [Henry William Herbert]. 8vo. [Cushing's *Init. and Pseud.* i. 104.] New York, 1859

HINTS to horsemen; shewing how to make money by horses. By Harry Hieover, author of *Table talk and stable talk*, etc. [Charles Bindley]. 8vo. London, 1856

HINTS to J. Nollekens, Esq., R.A. [in verse] on his modelling a bust of Lord G——le. [By James Sayers.] 4to. [*Brit. Mus.*] London, 1808

HINTS to masters and mistresses respecting female servants. [By John Coakley Lettsom, M.D.] 8vo. [*Brit. Mus.*] London, 1800

HINTS to medical students on a future life. [By Rev. Henry John Todd, D.D.] 8vo. [*D. N. B.* vol. 56, p. 429.] York, 1823

HINTS to my countrymen. By an American [Theodore Sedgwick]. 8vo. Pp. v. 216. [*Brit. Mus.*] New York, 1826

HINTS to servants; being a poetical and modernized version of Dean Swift's "Directions to servants." By an upper servant [John Jones]. London, 1843

HINTS to small [Irish] holders on planting and on cattle. By Martin Doyle [Rev. William Hickey, M.A.]. 8vo. [*Lit. Year Book.*] Dublin, 1830

HINTS to sportsmen on guns and shooting. . . . By "Stonehenge" [John Henry Walsh]. 8vo. [*Brit. Mus.*] London, 1858

HINTS to stammerers. By a minute philosopher [Rev. Charles Kingsley]. Reprinted from *Fraser's Magazine*, 1859. 8vo. [*Brit. Mus.*] London, 1864

Signed: C. K.

The same work appeared with a different title, "The irrationale of speech."

HINTS to strolling parsons, and a word or two respectfully addressed to the people of New Kilpatrick. By one of themselves [A. Dunlop, of Clobar]. 8vo. Glasgow, 1843

HINTS to Sunday-school teachers. By a pastor [Rev. Thomas Bayley Fox]. 8vo. [Cushing's *Init. and Pseud.* ii. 118.] Boston, 1840

HINTS to the Age of Reason. By a member of the Rotula [Edward Athenry Whyte]. 8vo. [Upcott and Shoberl's *Biog. Dict.* p. 384.] Dublin, N.D.

HINTS to the bearers of walking sticks and umbrellas. [By John Shute Duncan.] Illustrated by six engravings. 8vo. Pp. 32. [*Manch. Free Lib.* p. 207.] London, 1808

HINTS to the legislature and to the nation on the provisions, character and defects of the Imprisonment for Debt Bill . . . 1838. [By Sir Francis Myers.] London, 1838

Contemporary attestation.

HINTS to the people of England for the year 1793. [By Charles Edward de Coetlogon, M.A.] 8vo. [*D. N. B.* vol. 11, p. 214.] London, 1792

HINTS to the public and the legislature, on the nature and effect of evangelical preaching. By a barrister [James Sedgwick]. 8vo. [*Gent. Mag.* April 1851, p. 436.] London, 1812

The above is the general title-page to the five parts, of which the work consists, when bound together in one volume: of these five parts, the first and second appeared in 1808, the third in 1809, the fourth in 1810, and the fifth in 1812.

HINTS to travellers in Italy. By R. C. H. [Sir Richard Colt Hoare]. 12mo. London, 1815

HINTS to witnesses in the courts of justice. By a barrister [Barron Field]. 8vo. [*Brit. Mus.*] London, 1815

HINTS to young generals. . . . By an old soldier [General John Armstrong]. 8vo. [Sabin's *Dictionary.*] Kingston, 1812

HINTS to young ministers; designed more particularly for the use of those educated at Hoxton academy. By T. W. [Rev. Thomas Wilson]. 8vo. [*Brit. Mus.*] London, 1802

HINTS towards an attempt to reduce the poor-rate; or, at least, to prevent its further increase. [By Sir William Elias Taunton.] 8vo. [*Gent. Mag.* lxxxix. i. 539.] Oxford, 1819

HINTS towards an improved system of taxation, extending to all persons in exact proportion to their property. . . . [By Richard Watson, D.D., Bishop of Llandaff.] 8vo. London, 1798

HINTS towards forming the character of a young princess. [By Hannah More.] 8vo. 2 vols. [*D. N. B.* vol. 38, p. 419.] London, 1805

HINTS towards the investigation of the nature, cause, and cure of the rabies canina. . . . [By Thomas Percival, M.D.] 8vo. [*Brit. Mus.*] London [1789]

HINTS upon hats. By Clio [Thomas Clio Rickman, bookseller]. 8vo. [*Brit. Mus.*] London, 1803

HINTS upon the question of jury trial, as applicable to the proceedings in the Court of Session. [By Sir Ilay Campbell.] 8vo. [*Nat. Lib. of Scot.*] London, 1809

ΙΠΠ-ΑΝΘΡΩΠΟΣ; or, an ironicall expostulation with death and fate, for the losse of the late Lord Mayor of London; who on Friday October 27, 1648, expired together with his office; and both he and his bay-horse di'd o'th' sullens; whereunto is annexed an epitaph both on Mayor and horse. Also a dialogicall brief discourse held Octob. 29, between Col. Rainsborough and Charon, at their meeting; composed by Philanar and Misostratus, two London-apprentices once incounter'd last yeer for their loyalty. [By John Taylor, the Water Poet.] 4to. Pp. 10. [*D. N. B.* vol. 55, p. 437.] 1648

HIRELL; a novel. By the author of *Abel Drake's wife* [John Saunders]. 8vo. 3 vols. [*Brit. Mus.*] London, 1869

HIS besetting sin; a novel. By the author of *Recommended to mercy* [Mrs Houstoun, *née* Margaret C. Jones]. 8vo. [*Brit. Mus.*] London, 1888

HIS child friend. By the author of *The Cheveley novels*, etc. [Valentine Durrant]. 8vo. Pp. 272. [*Brit. Mus.*] London, 1886

HIS cousin Adair. [A novel.] By Gordon Roy [Helen Wallace]. 8vo. 3 vols. Edinburgh, 1891

HIS Excellency's English Governess. By Sydney C. Grier [Hilda Gregg]. 8vo. Pp. vi. 367. [*Brit. Mus.*] Edinburgh, 1896

HIS familiar foe; the story of the degrading inheritance of Captain Robert Ducie. . . . [A novel.] By E. Livingston Prescott [Edith K. Spicer-Jay]. 8vo. Pp. 358. [*Lit. Year Book.*] London, 1901

HIS fault or hers? By the author of *A high little world, and what happened there* [Mrs Robert A. Watson, *née* Elizabeth S. Fletcher]. 8vo. Pp. 288. London, 1897

HIS first brief; a comedietta. By Sidney Daryl [Sir Douglas Straight]. 8vo. [*Lit. Year Book.*] London, 1870

HIS first charge. By Faye Huntington [Mrs Isabella H. Foster]. 8vo. Pp. 308. [Cushing's *Init. and Pseud.* i. 134.] Boston [1897]

HIS fortunate grace. By Frank Lin [Mrs Gertrude Franklin Atherton]. 12mo. Pp. 210. [*Amer. Cat.*] New York, 1897

HIS foster sister. By Albert Ross [Linn Boyd Porter]. [*Amer. Cat.*] New York [1885?]

HIS great self. By Marion Harland [Mary Virginia Hawes, later Mrs Terhune]. 8vo. Pp. 355. [Kirk's *Supp.*] London, 1892

HIS heart of oak. By Bertha M. Clay [Charlotte M. Braeme]. 8vo. London, 1881

HIS heart to win; a novel. By Curtis Yorke [Mrs S. W. Richmond Lee]. 8vo. [*Lit. Year Book.*] London, 1899

HIS heart's desire. [A novel. By Mrs J. F. Kirk, *née* Ellen Warner Olney.] 8vo. [Kirk's *Supp.*] Philadelphia, 1878

HIS Highnesse the Lord-Protector protected in his accepting, or if you will have it so, in his assuming, the Protectorship, as is here cautioned. . . . By S. H., Senior [Rev. Samuel Hunton]. 4to. [*Cat. Lond. Inst.* ii. 466.] London, 1654

HIS idol. [A novel. By Richard Burleigh Kimball, LL.D.] 8vo. New York, 1880

HIS Italian wife; a novel. By Lucas Cleeve [Mrs Howard Kingscote, *née* Adelina G. I. Wolff]. 8vo. [*Lit. Year Book.*] London, 1902

HIS last stake. [A novel.] By Shirley Smith [Ella J. Curtis]. 8vo. 3 vols. [*Brit. Mus.*] London, 1878

HIS letters. By Julien Gordon [Mrs Julie Van Rensselaer Cruger]. 8vo. Pp. 280. [*Brit. Mus.*] New York [1892]

HIS life's magnet. By Baynton Foster [Theodora C. Elmslie]. 8vo. [*Brit. Mus.*] London, 1896

HIS little mother; and other tales and sketches. By the author of *John Halifax, gentleman*, etc. [Dinah Maria Mulock, later Mrs Craik]. 8vo. Pp. 336. London, 1881

HIS little Royal Highness. By Ruth Ogden [Mrs Frances Otis Ide]. 8vo. [*Amer. Cat.*] New York, 1898

HIS Majesties concessions to the Bill of Abolition of Archbishops and Bishops, &c., stated and considered. [By Richard Visces.] 4to. [*Brit. Mus.*] London, 1648

His Majesties [William III.] most gracious speech to both Houses of Parliament, with additions and explications; directed to the House of Commons by the freeborn people of England. [By Thomas Wagstaffe, A.M.] 4to. [*Bodl.*]

No title-page.

HIS Maiesties [Charles I.] passing through the Scots armie, etc. [Edited by John Trotter Brockett.] 8vo. Newcastle, 1820

Reprinted from the original issued in 1641. Preface signed: J. T. B.

HIS Majesties propriety and dominion on the Brittish seas asserted; together with a true account of the Neatherlanders insupportable insolencies and injuries they have committed, and the inestimable benefits they have gained in their fishing on the English seas. . . . [By Robert Clavel.] 8vo. [*W.*] London, 1665

Dedicatory Epistle signed: R. C.

HIS Majesty Baby, and some common people. By Ian Maclaren [John Watson, D.D.]. 8vo. Pp. 260. London, 1902

HIS Majesty, Myself. [By Wm. Munford Baker, D.D.] 8vo. [Cushing's *Anon.*] Boston, 1880

HIS Majesty's [Charles II.] declaration defended, in a letter to a friend; being an answer to a seditious pamphlet, called A letter from a person of quality to his friend; concerning the Kings late declaration touching the reasons which moved him to dissolve the two last Parliaments at Westminster and Oxford. [By John Dryden.] Fol. Pp. 20. London, 1681

HIS Majesty's [George I.] government vindicated from the false representations of the Tory-party; in two conversations. [By James Tyrrell.] 8vo. [*Brit. Mus.*] Nottingham, 1716

HIS mother's book. By H. F. E. [Evelyn Everett Green]. 8vo. Pp. 192. [*Brit. Mus.*] London [1883]

HIS neighbour's landmark. By "Alien" [Mrs L. A. Baker]. 8vo. Pp. 320. [*Lit. Year Book.*] London, 1907

HIS own image; a novel. By Alan Dale [Alfred J. Cohen]. 8vo. [*Amer. Cat.*] New York, 1905

HIS private character. By Albert Ross [Linn Boyd Porter]. 8vo. [*Amer. Cat.*] New York, 1889

HIS reverence the Rector. [A novel.] By Sarah Tytler [Henrietta Keddie]. 8vo. Pp. 316. London, 1905

HIS second campaign. [A novel. By Maurice Thompson.] 8vo. [Cushing's *Anon.*] Boston, 1883

HIS triumph. By Clara Vance [Mrs Mary Andrews Denison]. 8vo. [Cushing's *Init. and Pseud.* i. 292.] Boston, 1883

HIS vanished star. By Charles Egbert Craddock [Mary Noailles Murfree]. 8vo. [Kirk's *Supp.*] Boston, 1894

HIS verses. R. G. G. [R. G. Gordon]. 8vo. Pp. 59. [*Brit. Mus.*] Bombay, 1917

HIS way and her will. By A. X. [Fannie Aymar Mathews]. 8vo. [*Amer. Cat.*] Chicago, 1888

HIS wife's judgment. By Bertha M. Clay [Charlotte M. Braeme]. 8vo. Pp. 264. New York, 1889

HIS wife's soul. [A novel.] By Ernest Wilding [Joseph Fitzgerald Molloy]. 8vo. 3 vols. [O'Donoghue's *Poets of Ireland.*] London, 1893

HIS word of honor. By Ernst Werner [Elizabeth Bürstenbinder]; from the German. 8vo. New York, 1890

HISTORIA Anglorum; or, an help to English history, containing a succession of all the Kings of England, the English, the Saxon, and the British; the Kings and Princes of Wales, the Kings and Lords of Man, and of the Isle of Wight; as also all the Dukes, Marquisses, Earls, and Bishops. . . . By Robert Hall [Peter Heylin, D.D.]. 12mo. [Watt's *Bibl. Brit.*] London, 1641

Reprinted with the author's name in 1670, 1675, and afterwards enlarged.

HISTORIA Anglo-Scotica; or, an impartial history of all that happened between the Kings and Kingdoms of England and Scotland, from the beginning of William the Conqueror to the reign of Queen Elizabeth: with a prefatory dedication. Translated from an original manuscript by James Drake, M.D. [or rather wholly written by Drake himself]. 8vo. [Watt's *Bibl. Brit.*] London, 1703

HISTORIA histrionica; an historical account of the English stage, shewing the ancient use, improvement, and perfection of dramatick representations in this nation: in a dialogue of plays and players. [By James Wright.] 4to. Pp. 32. [Lowndes' *Bibl. Man.*] London, 1699

HISTORIA litteraria; or, an exact and early account of the most valuable books published in the several parts of Europe. No. II. [By Archibald Bower.] 8vo. [Lowndes' *Bibl. Man.* p. 1074.] London, 1730

No. II. of a work in four volumes, edited by Bower, which was commenced in 1730, and closed in 1733, or early in 1734.

HISTORIA mundi; or, Mercator's atlas. . . . Written by Judocus Hondy in Latin, and Englished by W. S. [Wye Saltonstall]. Fol. London, 1635

HISTORIA sacra, or the holy history; giving an exact and comprehensive account of all the feasts and fasts of the Church of England, with their various etymologies and appellations, and the true reasons and grounds of their celebrations. . . . [By Thomas Brodrick.] Second edition. 8vo. [*W.*; *Brit. Mus.*] London, 1720

HISTORIAN (the) unmask'd; or, some reflections on the late History of passive-obedience [by Abednego Seller]: wherein the doctrine of passive-obedience and non-resistance is truly stated and asserted. By one of those divines, whom the historian hath reflected upon in that book . . . [Thomas Long]. 4to. [Arber's *Term Cat.* ii. 616.] London, 1689

HISTORIANS (the) guide, or Englands remembrancer; being a summary account of all the actions, exploits, sieges, etc., and other remarkable passages that hath happened in his Majesties dominions, from the year 1600 until the year 1679. The second edition. . . . [By Samuel Clarke, minister of St Bennett Finck.] 12mo. Pp. 126. [*Bodl.*] London, 1679

A continuation was written by Benjamin Smithurst.

HISTORIANS of the first French Revolution. [By Edward Edwards, Librarian in Manchester.] 8vo. [*Brit. Mus.*] Manchester, 1849

Extract from *The British Quarterly.*

HISTORIC certainties respecting the early history of America, developed in a critical examination of the book of the chronicles of the land of Ecnarf [France]. By Rev. Aristarchus Newlight, Phil. Dr of the University of Giessen; corresponding member of the Theophilanthropic and Pantisocratical Societies of Leipsig; late Professor of all religions in several distinguished academies at home and abroad, etc. [William Fitzgerald, D.D.]. 8vo. Pp. 62. London, 1851

An ironical pamphlet, wrongly attributed to Archbishop Whately, who wrote a similar brochure previously; see "Historic doubts . . ." below.

HISTORIC (the) character of the Pentateuch vindicated; a reply to Bishop Colenso. [By George Warington.] 8vo. 2 vols. [Kirk's *Supp.*] London, 1863-4

HISTORIC (an) defence of experimental religion; in which the doctrine of divine influences is supported by the authority of Scripture and the experience of the wisest and best men. . . . [Preface signed: T. W. *i.e.* Thomas Williams, editor of the Evangelical Magazine.] 8vo. 2 vols. [*Brit. Mus.*] London, 1795

HISTORIC doubts relative to Napoleon Buonaparte. [By Richard Whately, D.D.] 8vo. London, 1819

Cf. "Historic certainties . . ." above.

HISTORIC (the) literature of Ireland; an essay on the publications of the Irish Archæological Society. [By Sir John T. Gilbert.] 8vo. Dublin, 1851

HISTORIC memoir on the French Revolution; to which are annexed strictures on the "Reflections" of the Right Hon. Edward Burke. [By William Belsham.] 8vo. [Watt's *Bibl. Brit.*] London, 1791

HISTORIC memorials of Coldstream Abbey, Berwickshire; collected by a Delver in antiquity [William B. D. D. Turnbull, D.D.]: containing a translation of the Chartulary, as preserved in the Macfarlane and Harleian MSS. . . . 8vo. Pp. 120. 1850

HISTORIC (an) sketch of Cowane's Hospital, Stirling. By a member of the Guildry [James Shirra]. 8vo. Stirling, 1867

HISTORICAL (an) account, and defence, of the canon of the New Testament; in answer to [Toland's] Amyntor. [By Stephen Nye.] 8vo. [Darling's *Cyclop. Bibl.*] London, 1700

HISTORICAL (an) account and description of the city of Moscow. . . . By I. A. M. S. [Ivan A. M. Sulkowski]. 8vo. Pp. 47. London, 1873

HISTORICAL (an) account of a degradation of gold made by an anti-elixir; a strange chemical narrative. [By the Hon. Robert Boyle.] 4to. [*Brit. Mus.*] London, 1698

HISTORICAL (an) account of all the voyages round the world performed by English navigators. [The first two volumes were compiled by David Henry; the third and fourth by another hand; to which, in 1775, Mr Henry added a fifth, containing Capt. Cook's voyage in the *Resolution*; and in 1786, a sixth, containing the last voyage of Capt. Cook.] 8vo. 4 vols. [*Gent. Mag.* June 1792, p. 579.] 1774

HISTORICAL (an) account of Christ Church, Boston. By the Rector [Rev. Asa Eaton]. 8vo. Boston, 1824

HISTORICAL (an) account of comprehension, and toleration, from the old Puritan to the new Latitudinarian; with their continued projects and designs, in opposition to our more orthodox Establishment. By the author of *The Dutch way of toleration* [Rev. William Baron]. 2 parts. 4to. Pp. 88. [*Edin. Univ. Lib.*] London, 1705-6

HISTORICAL (a) account of his Majesty's visit to Scotland. [By Robert Mudie.] 8vo. Pp. 336. [*Nat. Lib. of Scot.*] Edinburgh, 1822

HISTORICAL (an) account of some things relating to the nature of the English government, and the conceptions which our fore-fathers had of it; with some inferences thence made for the satisfaction of those who scruple the Oath of Allegiance to King William and Queen Mary. [By Daniel Whitby.] 4to. Pp. 60. [Watt's *Bibl. Brit.*] London, 1690

HISTORICAL account of Stoke Park, London. [By John Penn, LL.D.] 8vo. [*Brit. Mus.*] London, 1813

HISTORICAL (an) account of Sturbridge, Bury, and the most famous Friars. . . . [By Charles Caraccioli?] 8vo. [Bowes' *Cat. of Camb. Books.*] Cambridge [*c.* 1767]

HISTORICAL (an) account of the advantages that have accru'd to England by the succession of the illustrious house of Hanover. [By Mathias Earbery.] 8vo. 2 parts. London, 1722

HISTORICAL (an) account of the antient rights and power of the Parliament of Scotland; humbly offer'd to the consideration of the Estates, when they come to settle limitations for the next successor. . . . [By George Ridpath.] 8vo. Pp. xxxii. 160. [*Nat. Lib. of Scot.*] N.P. 1703

Attributed also to Andrew Fletcher of Saltoun. [*Lincoln's Inn Cat.*]

HISTORICAL (an) account of the antiquities in the Cathedral Church of . . . Lincoln. . . . [By Edward James Willson.] 8vo. [*Brit. Mus.*] Lincoln [1771]

HISTORICAL (an) account of the antiquity and unity of the Britanick Church; continued from the conversion of these islands to the Christian faith by St Augustine, to this present time. By a presbyter of the Church of England [Samuel Grascome]. 4to. Pp. 110. [*Bodl.*] London, 1692

The epistle to the reader signed: S. G.

HISTORICAL (an) account of the bitter sufferings and melancholly circumstances of the Episcopal Church in Scotland, under the barbarous usage and bloody persecution of the Presbyterian Church government; with an essay on the nature and necessity of a toleration in the North of Britain. [By Daniel Defoe.] 8vo. [Lee's *Life of Defoe.*] Edinburgh, 1707

HISTORICAL (an) account of the Charter-House, compiled from the works of Hearne, and Bearcroft, Harleian, Cottonian, and private manuscripts, and from other authentic sources. By a Carthusian [Robert Smythe]. 4to. [*Camb. Hist. of Eng. Lit.* vol. 14, p. 597.] London, 1808

HISTORICAL (an) account of the curiosities of London and Westminster. [By David Henry.] 12mo. [*Brit. Mus.*] London, 1759

HISTORICAL (an) account of the expedition against the Ohio Indians, in the year 1764, under the command of Henry Bouquet, Esq., Colonel of Foot, and now Brigadier General in America. . . . Published from authentic documents, by a lover of his country [Rev. William Smith, D.D., of Philadelphia]. 4to. [*Christie-Miller Cat.*] Philadelphia, printed: London, reprinted, 1766

Attributed by Rich (*Bibl. Amer.* i. 151) to Thomas Hutchins: but said by Field (*Essay towards an Indian bibliography*, p. 368) to have been written by William Smith, on the authority of a letter from the author.

HISTORICAL (an) account of the heresie denying the Godhead of Christ. [By Lancelot Addison, D.D.] 12mo. [*Nat. Lib. of Scot.*] London, 1696

The title really begins with two Greek words, Χριστὸς αὐτόθεος.

HISTORICAL (an) account of the laws against the Roman-Catholics of England. [By Daniel O'Connell.] 8vo. Pp. 51. [*Bodl.*] London, 1811

Said on the title-page to be by Mr Butler and Mr Jerningham.

HISTORICAL (an) account of the life and reign of David King of Israel, interspersed with various conjectures, digressions, and disquisitions; in which (among other things) Mr Bayle's criticisms upon the conduct and character of that Prince, are fully considered. By the author of *Revelation examin'd with candour* [Patrick Delany, D.D.]. 8vo. 3 vols. [Darling's *Cyclop. Bibl.*] London, 1740-2

HISTORICAL (an) account of the lives and writings of our most considerable English poets, whether epick, lyrick, elegiack, epigrammatists, etc. [By Giles Jacob.] 8vo. 2 vols. London, 1724

Vol. II. has the following title:—"The poetical register: or, the lives and characters of the English dramatick poets." Each volume has a separate dedication, signed: G. J. Two earlier editions (1719 and 1723) appeared with the title, "The poetical register: or, the lives and characters of all the English poets." See "The Poetical Register . . ."

HISTORICAL account of the noble family of Kennedy, Marquess of Ailsa and Earl of Cassillis, with notices of some of the principal cadets thereof. [By David Cowan.] 4to. Pp. 98. Edinburgh, 1849

HISTORICAL (an) account of the oaths and subscriptions required in the University of Cambridge, on matriculation, and of all persons who proceed M.A. [By Gilbert Ainslie, D.D.] 8vo. Pp. 70. [Bartholomew's *Cat. of Camb. Books.*] Cambridge, 1833

HISTORICAL (an) account of the origin, progress, and present state of Bethlem Hospital, founded by Henry the Eighth, for the cure of lunatics. . . . [By Thomas Bowen.] 4to. [*Camb. Univ. Lib.*] London, 1783

HISTORICAL (an) account of the original and nature as well as the law of devises and revocations. By a late learned judge [Sir Geoffrey Gilbert]. 8vo. [*Brit. Mus.*] London, 1739

HISTORICAL (an) account of the plague at Marseilles in 1720. . . . [By Jean B. Bertrand, a physician]; translated from the original French by John Soame, M.D. 8vo. [*New Coll. Lib.*] London, 1724

A different translation ("An historical relation of the plague . . .") was published in 1805, bearing the name of the author and that of the translator, Anne Plumptre.

HISTORICAL (an) account of the privileges of the College of Justice. [By Walter Ross, W.S.] 4to. Pp. 129. [*Nat. Lib. of Scot.*] [Edinburgh, 1778?]

HISTORICAL (a) account of the rights and priviledges of the Royal College of Physicians and of the Incorporation of Chirurgions in Edinburgh. . . . [By William Eccles, M.D.] 4to. [*Edin. Univ. Lib.*] [Edinburgh] 1707

HISTORICAL (an) account of the rights of elections of the several counties, cities, and boroughs of Great Britain, collected from public records and the Journals of Parliament, to the year one thousand seven hundred and fifty-four. By a late Member of Parliament [for Minehead, Thomas Carew]. Fol. 2 parts. [Green's *Bibl. Somers.* ii. 220.] London, 1755

HISTORICAL (an) account of the rise and growth of the West India Colonies, and of the great advantages they are to England, in respect of trade. [By Dalby Thomas.] 4to. [Arber's *Term Cat.* ii. 616.] London, 1690

HISTORICAL (an) account of the rise and progress of the colonies of South Carolina and Georgia. [By Alexander Hewatt.] 8vo. 2 vols. [Rich's *Bibl. Amer.* i. 273.] London, 1779

HISTORICAL account of the rise . . . of the canal navigation in Pennsylvania. [By Robert Morris.] 8vo. [Sabin's *Dictionary.*] Philadelphia, 1795

HISTORICAL (an) account of the Royal Hospital for Seamen at Greenwich. [By Rev. John Cooke, M.A., and Rev. John Maule, M.A., chaplains.] 4to. Pp. 158. London, 1789

HISTORICAL (an) account of the Seceders; in a letter to . . . chosen Member of the ensuing General Assembly from a real friend to the Church of Scotland [Rev. John Brown, of Haddington]. 8vo. [*New Coll. Lib.*] Edinburgh, 1766

HISTORICAL (an) account of the settlement and possession of Bombay by the English East India Company, and of the rise and progress of the war with the Mahratta nation. [By Samuel Pechel.] 8vo. Pp. 341. [*Brit. Mus.*] London, 1781

Never published: only a few copies were given away by the author.

HISTORICAL (an) account of the several attempts for a further reformation of the establish'd Church. By the author of the *Essay for allaying the animosities amongst British Protestants* [John Platts]. 8vo. Pp. 46. [Darling's *Cyclop. Bibl.*] London, 1716

HISTORICAL account of the substances which have been used to describe events, and to convey ideas; from the earliest date to the invention of paper. Printed on the first useful paper manufactured soley [*sic*] from straw. [By Matthias Koops, Esq.] 8vo. Pp. 91. London, 1800

Dedicated to George III.; and the dedication in the copy in the British Museum is signed in MS. with the author's name.

The second edition (London, 1801) has the author's name.

HISTORICAL (an) account of the town and parish of Nantwich; with a particular relation of the remarkable siege it sustained, in the grand rebellion, in 1643. [By Joseph Partridge.] 8vo. Pp. 88. [Cooke's *Bibl. Cestr.*] Shrewsbury, 1774

HISTORICAL (an) account of the town of Lancaster. . . . [By C. Clark, printer.] 8vo. [*Brit. Mus.*] Lancaster, 1807

HISTORICAL (a) and architectural description of Corfe Castle. By a near resident [John Brown]. 8vo. Pp. ii. 75. [Mayo's *Bibl. Dors.* p. 138.] Poole, 1839

HISTORICAL (an) and architectural notice of the gate tower of the ancient cemetery of St Edmund, known as the Norman tower, St Edmund's Bury. [By Samuel Timms.] 8vo. [*Brit. Mus.*] London, 1846

HISTORICAL (an) and chronological deduction of the origin of commerce, from the earliest accounts; containing an history of the great commercial interests of the British Empire. . . , [By Adam Anderson.] Carefully revised, corrected, and continued to the present time [by William Combe]. 4to. 4 vols. [*W.*] London, 1787-9

HISTORICAL and commercial sketches of Washington and its environs . . . its prominent places and people. . . . . [By E. E. Barton.] 8vo. Pp. xvi. 272. Washington, 1884

HISTORICAL (an) and critical account of Hugh Peters; after the manner of Mr Bayle. [By William Harris, D.D.] 4to. [*D. N. B.* vol. 25, p. 287.] London, 1751; reprinted 1818

HISTORICAL (an) and critical account of the life and writings of the ever-memorable Mr John Hales, Fellow of Eton College, and Canon of Windsor, being a specimen of an historical and critical English dictionary. [By Pierre Des Maizeaux.] 8vo. Pp. xii. 96. [*Nat. Lib. of Scot.*] London, 1719

HISTORICAL (an) and critical account of the lives and writings of the living authors of Great Britain; wherein their respective merits are discussed with the utmost candour and impartiality. [Signed: W. R. *i.e.* William Rider, B.A.] 8vo. Pp. 34. [*Bodl.*] London, 1762

HISTORICAL (an) and critical enquiry into the evidence produced by the Earls of Murray and Morton, against Mary Queen of Scots; with an examination of the Rev. Dr Robertson's Dissertation, and Mr Hume's History, with respect to that evidence. [By William Tytler, W.S.] 8vo. [*Nat. Lib. of Scot.*] Edinburgh, 1860

HISTORICAL (an) and critical essay on the life and character of Petrarch; with a translation of a few of his sonnets. Illustrated with portraits and engravings. [By Alexander Fraser Tytler, Lord Woodhouselee.] 8vo. Pp. vii. 269. [*Brit. Mus.*] Edinburgh, 1810

This is a new edition of the "Essay on the life and character of Petrarch," *q.v.*

HISTORICAL (an) and critical essay, on the thirty-nine Articles of the Church of England; wherein it is demonstrated that this clause, "The Church has power to decree rites and ceremonies, and autority [*sic*] in controversies of faith," inserted in the 20th Article, is not a part of the Articles, as they were established by Act of Parliament in the 13th of Eliz. or agreed on by the Convocations of 1562 and 1571. [By Anthony Collins.] 8vo. [*Brit. Mus.*] London, 1724

HISTORICAL (an) and critical essay on the true rise of nobility, political and civil; from the first ages of the world thro the Jewish, Grecian, Roman commonwealths, etc. down to this present time. . . . [By Maurice Shelton, of Barningham Hall, Norfolk.] 8vo. [Lowndes' *Bibl. Man.* p. 1694.] London, 1718

Sometimes found with titles attributing the authorship to Rev. John Randall, of Guilford.

HISTORICAL (an) and critical review of the civil wars in Ireland, from the reign of Queen Elizabeth to the settlement under King William, from authentic materials; with the state of the Irish Catholics, from that settlement to the relaxation of the Popery laws, in the year 1768. [By John Curry, M.D.] 4to. London, 1775

The second edition (2 vols. London, 1786, 8vo.) has the author's name. The above is a second edition of "Historical memoirs of the Irish rebellion, &c." (See below.)

HISTORICAL (an) and descriptive account of Blackpool, Lytham, and Southport. By a popular writer [P. Whittlo]. 8vo. Manchester, N.D.

HISTORICAL (an) and descriptive account of Iceland, Greenland, and the Faroe islands; with illustrations of their natural history. [By James Nicoll.] Maps by Wright, and engravings by Jackson and Bruce. 8vo. Pp. 416. [*Nat. Lib. of Scot.*] Edinburgh, 1840

Edinburgh Cabinet Library, vol. xxviii.

HISTORICAL (an) and descriptive account of the Royal Hospital and the Royal Military Asylum at Chelsea; to which is prefixed an account of King James's College at Chelsea: embellished with engravings. . . . [By Thomas Faulkner.] 12mo. Pp. 115. [*Upcott*, ii. 593.] London, 1805

HISTORICAL (an) and descriptive account of the town and castle of Warwick, and of the neighbouring spa of Leamington. . . . [By Rev. William Field.] 8vo. [*Upcott.*] Warwick, 1815

Signed: W. F.
Another edition, with modified title, appeared in 1817.

HISTORICAL and descriptive anecdotes of steam-engines, and of their inventors and improvers. By Robert Stuart [Robert Meikleham]. 8vo. 2 vols. [*Brit. Mus.*] London, 1829

The pagination is continuous.

HISTORICAL and descriptive delineations of London and Westminster. . . . [By Joseph Nightingale.] 8vo. London, 1814

HISTORICAL (an) and genealogical account of the Bethunes of the island of Sky. [By Rev. Thomas Whyte, minister of Liberton.] 8vo. [Lowndes' *Bibl. Man.* p. 2913.] Edinburgh, Private print, 1778

HISTORICAL (an) and genealogical account of the clan Maclean, from its first settlement at Castle Duart, in the Isle of Mull, to the present period, with pedigree. By a Seneachie [J. C. Sinclair]. 8vo. Pp. xvi. 362. [Mitchell and Cash's *Scot. Top.* i. 69.] London, 1838

Attributed also to Lachlan Maclean.

HISTORICAL (an) and genealogical account of the noble family of Greville to the time of Francis, the present Earl Brooke and Earl of Warwick, including the history and succession of the several Earls of Warwick since the Norman conquest; and some account of Warwick castle. [By Joseph Edmondson.] 8vo. [*Upcott*, ii. 1267.] London, 1766

HISTORICAL and legal examination of part of the decision of the Supreme Court of the United States in the Fred Scott case. . . . By the author of the *Thirty years' view* [Thomas Hart Benton]. 8vo. [*Brit. Mus.*] New York, 1858

HISTORICAL and literary account of the Formularies, Confessions of Faith, or Symbolic Books, of the Roman Catholic, Greek, and principal Protestant Churches. By the author of the *Horæ Biblicæ* [Charles Butler]. 8vo. [*W.*; Lowndes' *Brit. Lib.*] London, 1816

HISTORICAL and literary tour of a foreigner in England and Scotland. [From the French of Amédée Pichot.] 8vo. 2 vols. [*Brit. Mus.*] London, 1825

HISTORICAL and miscellaneous questions for the use of young people. [By Miss Magnall.] 12mo. [*Mon. Rev.* xxxix. 96.]. London, 1802

Ascribed by Watt to Michael Magnall.

HISTORICAL and philosophical memoirs of Pius VI., and of his pontificate: containing particulars concerning his private life, the causes that led to the subversion of the papal throne, and the Roman Revolution. [By Jean-François Bourgoing.] Translated from the French. 8vo. 2 vols. [*Mendham Collection Cat.* (*Supp.*), p. 4.] London, 1799

HISTORICAL (an) & philosophical sketch of the discoveries & settlements of the Europeans in Northern & Western Africa, at the close of the eighteenth century. [By John Leyden.] 8vo. [*Brit. Mus.*] Edinburgh, 1799

HISTORICAL and political reflections on the rise and progress of the American rebellion; in which the causes of that rebellion are pointed out, and the policy and necessity of offering to the Americans a system of government founded in the principles of the British constitution, are clearly demonstrated. By the author of *Letters to a nobleman, on the conduct of the American War* [Joseph Galloway]. 8vo. Pp. 145. [Rich's *Bibl. Amer.* i. 287.] London, 1780

HISTORICAL and political remarks upon the tariff of the Commercial Treaty; with preliminary observations. [By Rev. Alexander C. Schomberg.] 8vo. Pp. 170. [Harding's *Cat.*] London, 1787

HISTORICAL (an) and political view of the Decan, including a sketch of the extent and revenue of the Mysorean dominions, as possessed by the Tippoo Sultaun, to the . . . commencement of the present war in 1790. [By Jonathan Scott, LL.D.] 4to. [*Brit. Mus.*] London, 1790

HISTORICAL (an) and political view of the present and ancient state of the Colony of Surinam, in South America. . . . By a person who lived there ten years [Philippe Firmin. Translated from the French]. 8vo. [*Christie-Miller Cat.*] London, 1781

HISTORICAL and practical sermons for Lent and Easter. [By Rev. Edw. Monro, M.A.] 12mo. Oxford, 1858

HISTORICAL and practical sermons on the sufferings and resurrection of our Lord. By one of the authors of *Tracts for Christian seasons* [Rev. Edward Monro, M.A.]. 12mo. 2 vols. Oxford, 1860

HISTORICAL (an) and rational inquiry into the necessity of an uninterrupted succession of diocesan bishops (superior by divine right to presbyters) as necessary to the conveyance of the ministerial office and the validity of ordinances in the Church. . . [By John Platts.] 8vo. Pp. 113. [*Bodl.*] London, 1719

HISTORICAL (an) and topographical account of the town of Woburn; also a concise genealogy of the House of Russell, and memoir of Francis, Duke of Bedford. [By Stephen Dodd.] 8vo. [*Lond. Lib. Cat.*] Woburn, 1818

HISTORICAL and traditional sketches of Highland families, and of the Highlands. By an Inverness centenarian [J. Maclean]. 8vo. Dingwall, 1848

HISTORICAL and traditional tales, in prose and verse, connected with the South of Scotland. [By —— Nicholson.] 8vo. Kirkcudbright, 1843

HISTORICAL (the) and unrevealed memoirs of the political and private life of Napoleon Buonaparte; serving as an illustration of the manuscript of St Helena; from 1781 to 1798. [By Mademoiselle R. d'Ancemont.] 12mo. Pp. 172. [*Bodl.*] London, 1819

HISTORICAL anecdotes of heraldry and chivalry, tending to shew the origin of many English and foreign coats of arms, circumstances and customs. Illustrated with engravings. [Generally ascribed to Mrs Susannah Dobson.] 4to. [Lowndes' *Bibl. Man.* p. 1047.] Worcester [1796]

HISTORICAL anecdotes of the Charterhouse. By a Carthusian [James Smyth]. 4to. [Watt's *Bibl. Brit.*] London, 1808

HISTORICAL applications, and occasional meditations upon several subjects, newly reprinted with additions. Written by a person of honour [George Berkeley, Earl of Berkeley]. 8vo. Pp. 186. [Park's *Walpole*, iii. 337.] London, 1680

The first edition was published in 1670. The Dedication to the Lady Harmonia (supposed to be Mary, Countess of Warwick) is signed: Constans.

HISTORICAL charades. By the author of *Letters from Madras* [Julia Charlotte Maitland]. 8vo. Pp. 240. [*Bodl.*] London, 1847

HISTORICAL (the) charters and constitutional documents of the City of London; with an introduction and notes. By an antiquary [Walter De Gray Birch]. 4to. [*Brit. Mus.*] London, 1884

HISTORICAL collections concerning Church affairs; in which it is shew'd, from the ancient Church historians, Fathers, and other ecclesiastical writers, that the right to dispose of bishops, purely in relation to their spiritual charges, in their respective districts, was believed to be subjected in the clergy alone, as a separate independent body from the lay power, during the reigns of Constantine and Constantius, the two first Christian Emperors. . . . By a presbyter of the Church of England [Simon Lowth, a Nonjuror]. 4to. [*D. N. B.* vol. 34, p. 216.] London, 1696

HISTORICAL collections, concerning district-successions, and deprivations, during the three first centuries of the Church; in which it is shew'd, from the Church history, Fathers, Councils, and ecclesiastical writers of that time, that the right to place and remove bishops, purely as to their spiritual charges in their respective districts, was then vested in the Catholick bishops only. . . . By a presbyter of the Church of England [Simon Lowth, a Nonjuror]. 8vo. [*D. N. B.* vol. 34, p. 216.] London, 1713

HISTORICAL collections, out of several grave Protestant historians, concerning changes of religion, and the strange confusions following; in the reigns of King Henry the Eighth, King Edward the Sixth, Queen Mary, and Queen Elizabeth. . . . [By George Touchet, a Benedictine monk.] 8vo. Pp. 438. [*N. and Q.* 1860, p. 388; Jones' *Peck*, ii. 271.] London, 1686

HISTORICAL collections [with notes] regarding the Royal Burgh and the parish of Kinghorn. Compiled by G. W. B. [G. W. Ballingall]. 8vo. Pp. 40. Kirkcaldy, 1893

HISTORICAL collections relating the originals, conversions, and revolutions of the inhabitants of Great Britain to the Norman conquest, in a continued discourse. . . . [By Thomas Salmon, jun., M.A.] 8vo. Pp. 451. [*Nat. Lib. of Scot.*] London, 1706

HISTORICAL collections relative to the town of Belfast, from the earliest period to the Union with Great Britain. [By Henry Joy.] 8vo. [*Camb. Univ. Lib.*] Belfast, 1817

HISTORICAL conversations for young persons; containing I. The history of Malta and of the Knights of St John; II. The history of Poland. By Mrs Markham, author of the *Histories of England and France* [Mrs Elizabeth Penrose, *née* Cartwright]. 12mo. Pp. 395. [*D. N. B.* vol. 44, p. 342.] London, 1836

The author took her pseudonym from the village in which her early years were spent.

HISTORICAL curiosities relating to St Margaret's Church, Westminster. [Signed: J. R. *i.e.* John Rickman.] 8vo. [Anderson's *Brit. Top.*] London, 1837

HISTORICAL description of Dunimarle and its antiquities. By J. T. [John Todd, newspaper editor]. Pp. 20. [Beveridge's *Dunf. Bibl.*] Dunfermline [1890]

HISTORICAL description of the Kingdom of Macasar in the East Indies; in three books. [By Nicolas Gervaise.] Translated from the French. 12mo. London, 1701

HISTORICAL (an) description of the Metropolitical Church of Christ, Canterbury; containing an account of its antiquities, and of its accidents and improvements since its first establishment. [By John Burnby, attorney of Cambridge.] 8vo. [Smith's *Bibl. Cant.* p. 133.] Canterbury, 1772

A second, enlarged edition appeared in 1783.

HISTORICAL description of the monastery and chapel-royal of Holyrood House. [By Charles Mackie.] 12mo. Edinburgh, 1829

HISTORICAL (an) description of the Tower of London and its curiosities. . . . [Originally prepared by David Henry.] 8vo. Pp. iv. 60. [*Manch. Free Lib.*] London, 1803

HISTORICAL (a) description of the village, castle, and chapel of Farley, Hungerford, in the County of Somerset. . . . By J. J. [John Edward Jackson, rector of Leigh Delamere]. 8vo. [Green's *Bibl. Somers.* ii. 523.] Bath, 1829

HISTORICAL (an) discourse concerning the necessity of the ministers intention in administring the sacraments. [By Peter Allix, D.D.] 4to. Pp. 68. [*Brit. Mus.*] London, 1688

HISTORICAL (an) discourse of the uniformity of the government of England. The first part; from the first times till the reign of Edward the third. [By Nathaniel Bacon.] 4to. [*D. N. B.* vol. 2, p. 364.] London, 1647

The author's name appears on the title-page of the "Continuation" published in 1651. An edition of Part I, published in 1665, was suppressed; in 1676, when another edition was prepared, the printer was prosecuted but fled from the country.

HISTORICAL (an) dissertation concerning the antiquity of the English constitution. [By Gilbert Stuart, LL.D.] 8vo. [*Brit. Mus.*] Edinburgh, 1768

HISTORICAL (an) dissertation on idolatrous corruptions in religion from the beginning of the world; and of the methods taken by Divine Providence in reforming them. . . . [By Arthur Young, LL.D.] 8vo. 2 vols. [Darling's *Cyclop. Bibl.*] London, 1734

HISTORICAL (an) enquiry into the unchangeable character of a war in Spain. [By Richard Ford.] 8vo. Pp. 76. [*D. N. B.* vol. 19, p. 422.] London, 1837

HISTORICAL epitome of the Old and New Testaments, in which the events are arranged according to chronological order. By a member of the Church of England [—— Case]. 12mo. [*Camb. Univ. Lib.*] London, 1820

HISTORICAL (an) essay on Mr [Joseph] Addison. [By Thomas Tyers, of the Middle Temple.] 8vo. Pp. 96. [*Camb. Univ. Lib.*] London, 1783

HISTORICAL (an) essay on the English constitution; or, an impartial inquiry into the elective power of the people, from the first establishment of the Saxons in this kingdom: wherein the right of Parliament to tax our distant provinces is explained and justified . . . [By Allan Ramsay, Junr.] 8vo. [*Nat. Lib. of Scot.*] London, 1771

HISTORICAL essay on the origin of printing, translated from the French of M. de la Serna Santander [by Thomas Hodgson]. 8vo. Newcastle, 1819

HISTORICAL (an) essay on the temporal power of the Popes; translated from the French [of J. E. A. Gosselin]. 8vo. 2 vols. London, 1825

HISTORICAL (an) essay on the Thirty-nine Articles of the Church of England, etc. *See* "Historical (an) and critical essay," etc.

HISTORICAL (an) essay upon the ballance of civil power in England, from its first conquest by the Anglo-Saxons, to the time of the Revolution; in which is introduced a new dissertation upon parties. . . . [By Samuel Squire, Bishop of St David's.] 8vo. Pp. 96. [*Bodl.; D. N. B.* vol. 53, p. 440.] London, 1748

HISTORICAL (an) essay upon the loyalty of Presbyterians in Great Britain and Ireland from the Reformation to this present year 1713; . . . and an answer given to the calumnies of their accusers, and particularly to two late pamphlets [by William Tisdal, D.D.], viz. 1. A sample of true-blew Presbyterian loyalty, etc. 2. The conduct of the Dissenters in Ireland, etc. [By James Kirkpatrick, M.D., D.D.] 4to. Pp. xv. 574. [*D. N. B.* vol. 31, p. 221.] N.P. Private print, 1713

HISTORICAL (the) ethnic, and philological arguments in favour of British identity with the lost Ten Tribes of Israel, clearly stated. . . . By Philo-Israel [—— Bird]. 8vo. Pp. 16. London, 1879

HISTORICAL (an) examination of the authority of General Councils; shewing the false dealing that hath been used in the publishing of them, and the difference among the Papists themselves about their number. [By Rev. Robert Jenkin.] 4to. Pp. 76. [*Brit. Mus.*] London, 1688

HISTORICAL fragments of the Mogul empire of the Morattoes and of the English concerns in Indostan, from the year 1659. [By Robert Orme.] 8vo. Pp. 234, 173. [*Brit. Mus.*] London, 1782

HISTORICAL fragments relative to Scotish affairs from 1635 to 1664. [Edited by James Maidment.] 8vo. Edinburgh, 1833

HISTORICAL (an) game of the Romans. . . . [By Jehoshaphat Aspin.] 8vo. London, 1805

HISTORICAL (an), geographical, and statistical history of Candia, or ancient Crete. By the American Minister at Paris [Lewis Cass]. 8vo. [Cushing's *Init. and Pseud.* ii. 7.] Richmond, Va., 1839

HISTORICAL gossip about golf and golfers. By a golfer [George Robb]. 4to. Edinburgh, 1863

HISTORICAL (an) guide to Great Yarmouth, in Norfolk; with the most remarkable events recorded of that town, and an accurate sketch of the estuary Hierus, with the towns bordering thereon, as taken A.D. 1000. [By George William Manby.] 8vo. Pp. 68. [*Bodl.*] Yarmouth, 1806

The author's name is given in a MS. note by Dawson Turner.

HISTORICAL illustrations of the origin and progress of the passions, and their influence on the conduct of mankind; with some subordinate sketches of human nature and human life. [By Samuel Walter Burgess.] 8vo. 2 vols. [*N. and Q.* 21st Feb. 1863, p. 154.] London, 1825

Another edition was issued in 1828.

HISTORICAL law-tracts. [By Henry Home, Lord Kames.] 8vo. 2 vols. [*Nat. Lib. of Scot.*] Edinburgh, 1758

HISTORICAL life of Joanna of Sicily, Queen of Naples and Countess of Provence; with correlative details of the literature and manners of Italy and Provence in the thirteenth and fourteenth centuries. [By Frances Moore.] 8vo. 2 vols. [*Brit. Mus.*] London, 1824

HISTORICAL, literary, and artistical travels in Italy; a complete and methodical guide for travellers and artists. By M. Valery [Antoine Claude Pasquin]. Translated . . . from the second corrected and improved edition. . . . 8vo. [*Brit. Mus.*] Paris, 1842

HISTORICAL manual of the South Church in Andover, Mass.; August 1859. [By George Mooar.] 8vo. Pp. 200. Andover [Mass.] 1859

Preface signed : G. M.

HISTORICAL (a) memoir of Frà Dolcino and his times; being an account of a general struggle for ecclesiastical reform, and of an anti-heretical crusade in Italy, in the early part of the fourteenth century. By L. Mariotti [Antonio Gallenga], author of *Italy, past and present.* 8vo. [*Edin. Univ. Lib.*] London, 1853

HISTORICAL (an) memoir of the first year of the reign of Frederic William II. King of Prussia . . . By the Count de Hertzberg, Minister of State, Curator and Member of the Academy. Translated from the French [by Joseph Towers, LL.D.]. 8vo. [*Mon. Rev.* lxxviii. 534.] 1788

HISTORICAL (an) memoir on Italian tragedy, from the earliest period to the present time; illustrated with specimens and analyses of the most celebrated tragedies. . . . By a member of the Arcadian Society of Rome [Joseph Cooper Walker]. 4to. [Watt's *Bibl. Brit.*] London, 1799

HISTORICAL memoires on the reigns of Queen Elizabeth and King James. [By Francis Osborne.] 12mo. [*Brit. Mus.*] London, 1658

HISTORICAL memoirs of religious dissensions, addressed to the seventeenth Parliament of Great Britain. [By Rev. Jeremiah Trist, M.A.] 8vo. Pp. 99. London, 1790

The second edition, 1791, has the author's name.

HISTORICAL memoirs of [F. M. Arouet de Voltaire] the author of the *Henriade*, with some original pieces; to which are added genuine letters of Mr de Voltaire, taken from his own minutes. Translated from the French [of J. L. Wagnière]. 8vo. [*Brit. Mus.*] London, 1777

HISTORICAL memoirs of the House of Vernon. [By Thomas Stapleton.] 4to. [*D. N. B.* vol. 54, p. 104.] London [1855]

Unfinished; ends at p. 115.

HISTORICAL memoirs of the Irish Rebellion, in the year 1641; extracted from Parliamentary journals, state-acts, and the most eminent Protestant historians. . . . In a letter to Walter Harris, Esq. [By John Curry, M.D.] 8vo. [*D. N. B.* vol. 13, p. 343.] London, 1767

Republished under the title, "Historical and critical review of the civil wars in Ireland, etc.," *q.v.*

HISTORICAL memoirs of the life and writings of the late Rev. William Dodd, from his entrance at Clare Hall, Cambridge, in 1745, to his fatal exit at Tyburn, June 27, 1777. [By Isaac Reed.] 12mo. [*W.; D. N. B.* vol. 15, p. 157.] London [1777]

HISTORICAL memoranda, charters, documents, and extracts, from the records of the Corporation and books of the Coopers' Company, London, 1396-1848. [By James Francis Firth.] 8vo. Private print, 1848

HISTORICAL memorials concerning the Provincial Councils of the Scottish Clergy. . . . [By Sir David Dalrymple, Lord Hailes.] 4to. [*Nat. Lib. of Scot.*] Edinburgh, 1769

HISTORICAL memorials of John Knox. [By Rev. John Aiton, D.D.] 8vo. Leith, 1831

HISTORICAL memorials of Presbyterianism in Newcastle-upon-Tyne. By an Episcopalian [Thomas George Bell]. 8vo. Pp. vi. 107. Newcastle, 1847

HISTORICAL narration of certain events that took place in the Kingdom of Great Britain in the month of July, in the year of our Lord 1553. Written by P. V. [P. M. Vermigli; translated by J. B. Inglis and edited by J. P. Bergeau]. 8vo. [*Brit. Mus.*] London, 1865

HISTORICAL (an) narration of the life and death of our Lord Jesus Christ. [By Abraham Woodhead.] 4to. [*Brit. Mus.*] Oxford, 1685

HISTORICAL narrative of the horrid plot and conspiracy of Titus Oates, called the Popish Plot. [By William Eusebius Andrews, a Romanist.] 8vo. [Gillow's *Bibl. Dict.*] London, 1816

HISTORICAL notes and other literary materials now first collected towards the formation of a systematic bibliographical description of mediæval illuminated manuscripts of Hours, Offices, and other books of devotion. . . . [By Richard Thomson, Librarian.] 8vo. [*Brit. Mus.*] London, 1858

HISTORICAL notes and reminiscences of Cupar. [By George Innes, journalist.] 8vo. Pp. viii. 149. Cupar-Fife, 1884

Reprinted from the *Fife Herald.*

HISTORICAL notes on the Libraries of the Universities of Aberdeen. By P. J. A. [Peter J. Anderson, LL.B.]. 8vo. [*Aberd. Univ. Lib.*] Aberdeen, 1893

HISTORICAL notes on the Rajghal Plateau, Benares, etc. [Signed: A. C. *i.e.* Sir Aucland Colvin.] 4to. [*Calc. Imp. Lib.*] Lucknow, 1887

HISTORICAL notice of the church of St Mary Magdalene, Gedney. [By J. A. Atkinson.] 8vo. [Guppy and Vines' *Cat. of Archit. Works.*] Lincoln, 1897

HISTORICAL notices concerning some of the peculiar tenets of the Church of Rome. [By the Hon. Arthur Philip Perceval.] 12mo. [*Bodl.*] London, 1836

HISTORICAL notices of Edward and William Christian, two characters in *Peveril of the Peak.* [By Lieut.-Col. Mark Wilks.] 8vo. Pp. 42. [Harrison's *Bibl. Monensis*, p. 107.] London, 1823

HISTORICAL notices of Free St Stephen's Church, Edinburgh. [By Rev. Edward Thomson, M.A.] 8vo. [*New Coll. Lib.*] Edinburgh, 1888

HISTORICAL notices of psalmody, extracted from the *Christian Observer* for October 1847. [By Thomas Hartwell Horne, D.D.] 8vo. [Horne's *Reminiscences*, p. 163.] London, 1847

HISTORICAL notices of the New North Religious Society in . . . Boston. . . . [By Ephraim Eliot, M.A.] 8vo. [Sabin's *Dictionary.*] Boston [1852]

HISTORICAL notices of the parish of Withyham in the county of Sussex, with a description of the church and Sackville chapel. [Dedication signed R. W. SW.: *i.e.* Reginald Windsor Sackville-West, rector of Withyham.] 4to. Pp. viii. 100. London, 1857

HISTORICAL novels. By Louise Mühlbach [Mrs Clara Müller Mundt]. 8vo. [*Amer. Cat.*] New York, 1893

HISTORICAL observations upon the reigns of Edward I. II. III. and Richard II.; with remarks upon their faithful counsellors and false favourites. Written by a person of honour [George Savile, Marquis of Halifax, or Sir Robert Howard]. 8vo. Pp. 196. London, 1689

This work was republished in 1690 with the title of "The history of the reigns of Edward and Richard II., written by Sir R. Howard." But Walpole, in his Royal and noble authors, ascribes it to G. Savile, Marquis of Halifax; and in the Bodleian copy, the author's name is given as Savile, in the handwriting of Wood, who says that the work was published about the beginning of Feb. 1688.

HISTORICAL (an) outline of the Greek Revolution. [By W. Martin Leake.] With a map. 8vo. Pp. 75. [*Sig. Lib.*] London, 1825

HISTORICAL outlines of political Catholicism. [By William Bullen.] 8vo. [*Lond. Lib. Cat.*] London, 1853

HISTORICAL parallels. [By Arthur Thomas Malkin.] 8vo. 2 vols. [*Nat. Lib. of Scot.*] London, 1831-5

Knight's Library of Entertaining Knowledge.

HISTORICAL (an) plea for ecclesiastical and educational unity; or, the Westminster Assembly and its standards,—what these have done for Scotland, and what they may yet do for unity among evangelical Churches. . . . [By James W. Taylor, D.D., of Flisk.] 8vo. Pp. 45. [*New Coll. Lib.*] London, 1854

HISTORICAL questions exhibited in the *Morning Chronicle*, in January 1818; enlarged, corrected, and improved. [By Sir Philip Francis.] 8vo. [*Bodl.*] London, 1818

HISTORICAL (the) reason why. English history. . . . By the author of *The reason why* [Robert Kemp Philp]. 8vo. Pp. xvi. 318. [Boase and Courtney's *Bibl. Corn.* ii. 493.] London [1859]

HISTORICAL record of the 81st Regiment, or Loyal Lincoln Volunteers (Second Battalion Loyal North Lancashire); containing an account of the formation of the Regiment in 1793, and of its subsequent services to 1872. [By S. Rogers.] 8vo. Gibraltar, 1872

HISTORICAL record of the Honourable East India Company's First Madras European Regiment. . . . By a Staff-Officer [General James George Smith Neill]. 8vo. [*Brit. Mus.*] London, 1843

HISTORICAL records of the Third; or, King's own regiment of Light Dragoons, from the year 1685 to the present time. [By William James Downes.] 12mo. Glasgow, 1833

Attributed also to R. Cannon.

HISTORICAL (the) register for the year 1736; as it is acted at the New Theatre in the Hay-Market; to which is added a very merry tragedy, called Eurydice hiss'd, or, a word to the wise. Both written by the author of Pasquin [Henry Fielding]. . . . 8vo. Pp. 48. [Baker's *Biog. Dram.*] London [1737]

HISTORICAL (an) relation of the Conspiracy of John Lewis, Count de Fieschi, against the city and republick of Genoua, in the year 1547. [By A. Mascardi. Done into English by the Hon. H. Hare.] 8vo. 2 vols. [*Brit. Mus.*] Edinburgh, 1886

HISTORICAL (an) relation of the late General Assembly, held at Edinburgh, from Octob. 16. to Nov. 13. in the year 1690. In a letter from a person in Edinburgh [John Cockburn, D.D.] to his friend in London. 4to. [*Nat. Lib. of Scot.*] London, 1691

This was followed by "A continuation of the Historical relation . . ."

HISTORICAL remarks and anecdotes on the Castle of the Bastille; translated from the French [of Brossais du Perray, and edited by J. Howard]. 8vo. [*Brit. Mus.*] London, 1780

See another edition below.

HISTORICAL remarks and observations upon the ancient and present state of London and Westminster. . . . By R. B. [Richard Burton, *i.e.* Nathaniel Crouch]. Fifth edition. 12mo. Pp. 156. London, 1703

Several other editions followed. See the note to "Admirable curiosities. . . ."

HISTORICAL remarks on the Castle of the Bastille; with curious and entertaining anecdotes of that fortress. . . . Translated from the French [of Brossais du Perray]. 8vo. London, 1789

See another edition above.

HISTORICAL remarks on the second volume of Bishop Burnet's History of his own time; or, a critical review of the most extraordinary passages therein contained. By Philalethes [Matthias Earbery]. 8vo. London, 1734

HISTORICAL remarks on the taxation of free states, in a series of letters to a friend. [By Sir William Meredith, Bart.] 4to. Pp. 88. [M'Culloch's *Lit. of Pol. Econ.* p. 90.] London, 1778

Not more than thirty copies were printed.

HISTORICAL researches into the politics, intercourse and trade of the Carthaginians, Ethiopians and Egyptians. By A. H. L. Heeren. . . . Translated from the German [by D. A. Talboys]. 8vo. 2 vols. Oxford, 1832

HISTORICAL researches into the politics, intercourse and trade of the principal nations of antiquity. By A. H. L. Heeren. . . . Translated from the German [by D. A. Talboys]. 8vo. 3 vols. Oxford, 1833

HISTORICAL retrospect of the Wiltshire Regiment. . . . [Signed: H. M. C. *i.e.* Harry Molyneux Carter.] 8vo. Pp. 12. [*Brit. Mus.*] Aldershot [1899]

HISTORICAL reveries [in verse]. By a Suffolk villager [Sarah Wilkinson]. 12mo. [*Brit. Mus.*] Sudbury, 1839

HISTORICAL reveries. . . . [By Rev. Charles Alexander Johns, F.L.S.] 8vo. [Cushing's *Anon.*] London, 1851

HISTORICAL (an) review of the constitution and government of Pensylvania, from its origin; so far as regards the several points of controversy, which have, from time to time, arisen between the several governors of that province, and their several assemblies: founded on authentic documents. [By Benjamin Franklin?] 8vo. Pp. viii. 464. [Smith's *Bibl. Anti-Quaker.* p. 42.; Rich's *Bibl. Amer.* i. 128.] London, 1759

Commonly attributed to Franklin, and printed in Sparke's edition of his works, but he disowned it in a letter to Hume.

HISTORICAL (an) rhapsody on Mr [Alexander] Pope. By the editor of the *Political conferences* [Thomas Tyers]. Second edition, corrected and enlarged. 8vo. Pp. xi. 143. [Nichol's *Lit. Anec.* viii. 95.] London, 1782

HISTORICAL (an) romance of the wars between the mighty giant Gallieno [Louis XIV. of France] and the great Knight Nasonius [William III. of Great Britain] and his associates. [By John Sergeant.] 4to. Pp. 90. Dublin, 1694

HISTORICAL sketch and essay on the resources of Montana. . . . [By H. N. Maguire and Henry Horr.] 8vo. [Cushing's *Anon.*] Helena, 1868

HISTORICAL sketch and laws of the Royal College of Physicians of Edinburgh, from its institution to December 1865. [By Alexander Wood, M.D.] 8vo. Pp. 136. [*Nat. Lib. of Scot.*] Edinburgh, 1867

HISTORICAL sketch, illustrative of the law, civil and ecclesiastical, relative to Church patronage in Scotland. [By Alexander Peterkin.] 8vo. Edinburgh, 1833

HISTORICAL sketch of Armenia and the Armenians, in ancient and modern times, with special reference to the present crisis. By an old Indian [Rev. William Stephen, minister at Kelty]. 8vo. Pp. viii. 200. London, 1896

Authorship personally acknowledged by the writer.

HISTORICAL sketch of educational movements preceding the formation of the National Public School Association. [By William Edward Hickson.] Reprinted from *The Westminster Review.* 8vo. Pp. 30. [*D. N. B.* vol. 26, p. 362.] London, 1851

HISTORICAL (an) sketch of Gibraltar; with an account of the siege which that fortress stood against the combined forces of France and Spain. . . . [By John Heriot.] 8vo. Pp. viii. 148. [*Manch. Free Lib.*] London, 1792

HISTORICAL (an) sketch of Sanscrit literature, with copious bibliographical notices of Sanscrit works and translations. From the German of [Friedrich] Adelung, with numerous additions and corrections [by D. A. Talboys]. 8vo. Pp. 234. Oxford, 1832

HISTORICAL (an) sketch of the African Mission of the Protestant Episcopal Church of the United States of America. [By Lizzie Rose Foster.] 8vo. [Cushing's *Anon.*] New York, 1884

HISTORICAL (an) sketch of the American Sunday School Union. . . . [By Frederick Adolphus Packard, LL.D.] 8vo. [Cushing's *Anon.*] Philadelphia, 1865

HISTORICAL sketch of the Bank of England; with an examination of the question as to the prolongation of the exclusive privileges of that establishment. [By John R. M'Culloch.] 8vo. Pp. 77. London, 1831

Authorship acknowledged in his "Handbook to the Literature of Political Economy."

HISTORICAL (a) sketch of the Brooklyn Ferry. By a Director [Henry E. Pierrepont]. 8vo. Brooklyn, 1879

HISTORICAL (an) sketch of the Church and Missions of the United Brethren, commonly called Moravian. . . . [By Edward H. Reichel.] 8vo. Bethlehem, Pennsylvania, 1848

HISTORICAL (an) sketch of the English translations of the Bible. By a member of the Massachusetts Bible Society [Abiel Holmes, D.D.]. 8vo. [Cushing's *Init. and Pseud.* ii. 98.] Boston, 1815

HISTORICAL (an) sketch of the explaining-away system of interpretation adopted by Romanists and by Romanising Tractarians; extracted from *The Church of England Quarterly Review* for January 1842. [By Thomas Hartwell Horne, D.D.] 8vo. London, 1842

From a chronological list of the author's works appended to his "Reminiscences."

HISTORICAL (an) sketch of the last years of the reign of Gustavus the fourth Adolphus, King of Sweden, including a narrative of the late Revolution. . . . [By Gustave, Baron de Wetterstedt.] Translated from the Swedish. 8vo. London, 1812

HISTORICAL sketch of the Middlesex Canal. . . . [By Caleb Eddy.] 8vo. [Cushing's *Anon.*] Boston, 1843

HISTORICAL sketch of the origin, progress, and wants of Illinois College. . . . [By Thomas Baldwin.] 8vo. [Cushing's *Anon.*] New York, 1832

HISTORICAL sketch of the origin of English prose literature, and of its progress till the reign of James the First. [By William Gray, of Magdalen College.] 8vo. Pp. 107. [*Bodl.*] Oxford, 1832

HISTORICAL (an) sketch of the paper money issued by Pennsylvania; together with a complete list of all the dates, issues, amounts, etc. [Signed: H. P. junr. *i.e.* Henry Phillipps.] 8vo. [*Brit. Mus.*] Philadelphia, 1862

HISTORICAL (an) sketch of the Presbyterian Church in New Castle, Delaware. By the pastor [John Boswell Spotswood, D.D.]. 8vo. [Kirk's *Supp.*] Philadelphia, 1859

HISTORICAL (an) sketch of the princes of India, stipendiary, subsidiary, protected, tributary and feudatory; with a sketch of the origin and progress of the British power in India. By an officer in the service of the Honourable East India Company [John Clunes]. 8vo. Edinburgh, 1833

HISTORICAL sketch of the rise and progress of the science of political economy. [By John R. M'Culloch.] 8vo. Pp. 96. Edinburgh, 1826

HISTORICAL (a) sketch of the Woodside water supply [for Aberdeen. By D. Ferrier]. 8vo. [Robertson's *Aberd. Bibl.*] Aberdeen, N.D.

HISTORICAL sketches and recreations. By J. A. G. Barton [Shoshee Chunder Dutt]. 8vo. 2 vols. [*Lond. Lib. Cat.*] London, 1879

HISTORICAL sketches, chiefly relating to the early settlement of Friends at Falls, in Bucks County, Penna. By G. W. B. [George W. Brown, M.D.]. 8vo. Pp. 24. Philadelphia, 1881

HISTORICAL sketches of Montrose, ancient and modern. Illustrated. [By W. N. Strachan.] 8vo. Pp. 56. Montrose, 1879

HISTORICAL sketches of the Church and parish of Fowlis Easter. [By James Stuart.] 8vo. Dundee, 1865

HISTORICAL sketches of the old painters. By the authoress of *Three experiments of living* [Mrs Hannah F. Lee]. 8vo. [*Brit. Mus.*] Bristol [1840]

HISTORICAL sketches of the ten miles square forming the District of Columbia. . . . [By Jonathan Elliott.] 8vo. [Cushing's *Anon.*] Washington, 1830

HISTORICAL sketches of towns in Plymouth and Barnstable Counties, Massachusetts. [By Dean Dudley.] 8vo. [Cushing's *Anon.*] Boston, 1873

HISTORICAL sketches on some interesting discoveries. [By William Dickson.] First published in the *Philosophical Magazine*. 8vo. Private print, London, 1804

HISTORICAL sketches; or, the spirit of orthodoxy. . . . [By Rev. Joseph Field, M.A.] 8vo. [Cushing's *Anon.*] Springfield [Mass.], 1823

HISTORICAL souvenir of the Crystal Palace. By Austin Fryers [William Edward Clery]. 8vo. [*Brit. Mus.*] London, 1901

HISTORICAL summary of the several attacks that have been made upon the city of New York. . . . [By Samuel L. Mitchell, LL.D.] 8vo. [Cushing's *Anon.*] New York, 1812

HISTORICAL survey of the character of Napoleon Buonaparte, founded on his own words and actions: forming an introduction to the Secret Memoirs by one who never quitted him for fifteen years. [By Charles Doris.] Translated from the sixth Paris edition. 12mo. [*Brit. Mus.*] London, 1815

HISTORICAL (an) survey of the County of Cornwall. . . . [By W. Penaluna.] 12mo. 2 vols. Helston, 1838

HISTORICAL tales for young Protestants. By J. H. C. [J. H. Crosse]. 12mo. London, 1883

HISTORICAL tales of the wars of Scotland; and of the Border raids, forays and conflicts. [By John Parker Lawson, M.A.] 8vo. 2 vols. [*Nat. Lib. of Scot.*] Edinburgh, 1839

HISTORICAL (the) tragedy of Macbeth (written originally by Shakespear), newly adapted to the stage, with alterations, as performed at the theatre in Edinburgh. [By John Lee.] 8vo. Pp. 92. [Baker's *Biog. Dram.* i. 447; iii. 3.] Edinburgh, 1753

HISTORICAL (an) treatise, written by an author of *The communion of the Church of Rome, touching transubstantiation;* wherein is made appear, that according to the principles of that Church, the doctrine cannot be an article of faith. [Translated from the French of the Abbé Louis Dufour de Longuerne by William Wake, Archbishop of Canterbury.] 4to. Pp. viii. 73. [Barbier's *Dictionnaire; Biog. Brit.*] London, 1687

HISTORICAL (an) view of Christianity, containing select passages from Scripture. [By —— Bernard.] 4to. Pp. 140. London, 1806

HISTORICAL view of plans for the government of British India, and regulation of trade to the East Indies; and outlines of a plan of foreign government, of commercial oeconomy, and of domestic administration, for the Asiatic interests of Great Britain. [By John Bruce.] 4to. [*Nat. Lib. of Scot.*] London, 1793

Ascribed also to H. Dundas, Lord Melville. [*Athen. Cat.* (*Second* Supp.) p. 95.]

HISTORICAL (an) view of the constitution and government of Pennsylvania, from its origin; founded on authentic documents. [By Benjamin Franklin.] 8vo. [*Brit. Mus.*] Philadelphia, 1759

Republished at Philadelphia in 1812, with the author's name and a modified title.

HISTORICAL (an) view of the controversy concerning an intermediate state and the separate existence of the soul between death and the general resurrection, deduced from the beginning of the Protestant Reformation, to the present times. . . . [By Francis Blackburne.] 8vo. Pp. lvii. 127. [*D. N. B.* vol. 5, p. 122.] London, 1765

A second, and greatly enlarged, edition was published in 1772.

HISTORICAL (an) view of the Court of Exchequer, and of the King's revenues there answered. By a late learned Judge [Sir Geoffrey or Jeffrey Gilbert]. 8vo. [Watt's *Bibl. Brit.*] Savoy, 1738

HISTORICAL (an) view of the French Revolution, from the assembling of the States General in . . . 1789 to . . . 1795. . . . [By M. Angus.] 8vo. Newcastle-upon-Tyne, 1796

HISTORICAL view of the languages and literature of the Slavic nations; with a sketch of their popular poetry. By Talvi [Thérèse Albertine Louise von Jakob, afterwards Mrs Robinson]. With a preface by [her husband] Edward Robinson, D.D., LL.D. author of *Biblical researches in Palestine*, etc. 8vo. Pp. xv. 412. New York, 1850

"Talvi" is a word formed of the initials of the author's maiden name.

HISTORICAL (an) view of the revolutions of Portugal, since the close of the Peninsular war ; exhibiting a full account of the events which have led to the present state of that country. By an eye-witness [Capt. John Murray Browne]. 8vo. [*Gent. Mag.* xcix. i. 604.] [London] 1827

HISTORICAL (an) view of the state of Church Patronage in Scotland ; with a summary of the arguments advanced in support of the various plans proposed for removing the evils of the present system. [By John Wilson, D.D., Stirling.] 8vo. Pp. 45. [Scott's *Fasti.*] Edinburgh, 1833

HISTORICAL vindication of the Church of England in point of schism, as it stands separated from the Roman and reformed by Queen Elizabeth. [By Sir Roger Twysden.] 4to. [Watt's *Bibl. Brit.*] London, 1657

HISTORICAL (an) vindication of "The naked Gospel" [written by Dr Arthur Bury], recommended to the University of Oxford. [By Jean Le Clerc.] 4to. [*D. N. B.* vol. 8, p. 22.] [London] 1690

See the note to "The naked Gospel."

HISTORICALL (an) description of the most famous kingdomes and commonweales in the worlde, translated [from the Italian of Giovanni Botero, by R. I. *i.e.* Robert Johnson]. . . . 4to. Pp. 268. [*Brit. Mus.*] London, 1603

The title of the edition of 1601 begins "The worlde, or an historicall description. . . ." See also "Relations of the most famous kingdomes. . . ."

HISTORICALS for young folks. By Oro Noque [Bessie C. Blakeman]. 8vo. [Cushing's *Init. and Pseud.* ii. 106.] Boston, 1874

HISTORICO - THEOLOGICAL (an) criticism of "The Pope and the [Vatican] Council, by Janus" [Dr Johann J. I. von Döllinger]. By Anti-Janus [Phil. Hergenröther, D.D.]. 8vo. [*Amer. Cat.*] New York, 1871

HISTORIE (the) and life of King James the Sext. Written towards the latter part of the sixteenth century. [Edited by Malcolm Laing.] 8vo. [*W.* ; Lowndes' *Bibl. Man.*] Edinburgh, 1804

HISTORIE (the) and life of King James the Sext ; being an account of the affairs of Scotland from the year 1566 to the year 1596, with a short continuation to the year 1617. [By John Colville, Bannatyne Club.] 4to. Pp. xxii. 446. Edinburgh, 1825

HISTORIE and policie re-viewed in the heroick transactions of Oliver, late Lord Protector, from his cradle to his tomb. . . . [By H. Dawbeny.] 8vo. Pp. 306. [*W.* ; Lowndes' *Bibl. Man.*, p. 604.] London, 1659

HISTORIE (the) of Aurelio and of Isabell, daughter of the kinge of Schotlande, nyewly translatede in foure languages, Frenche, Italien, Spanishe and Inglishe. [By Jean de Flores.] 8vo. [*W.* ; Lowndes' *Bibl. Man.*] Anuers, 1556

HISTORIE (the) of Cambria, now called Wales ; a part of the most famous Yland of Brytaine, written in the Brytish language above two hundreth yeares past. [By Caradoc of Llancarvan.] Translated . . . by H. Lhoyd, gentleman. . . . 4to. B. L. [*Brit. Mus.*] London [1584]

HISTORIE (the) of England ; the first booke. . . . By Philomathes [Henoch Clapham]. 4to. [*Camb. Univ. Lib.*] London, 1602

HISTORIE (the) of Episcopacie. By Theophilus Churchman [Peter Heylin, D.D.]. 4to. 2 parts. [*Bodl.*] London, 1642

HISTORIE (the) of Great Britannie, declaring the successe of times and affaires in that iland, from the Romans first entrance vntill the raigne of Egbert, the West-Saxon Prince ; who reduced the severall principalities of the Saxons and English into a monarchie, and changed the name of Britannie into England. [By John Clapham.] 4to. Pp. 302. [Bliss' *Cat.* ; Lowndes' *Bibl. Man.*, p. 273.] London, 1606

Ascribed also to George Salteren.

HISTORIE (the) of Italie, a boke excedyng profitable to be redde ; because it intreateth of the astate of many and diuers common weales, how thei have ben and now be governed. [By William Thomas, native of Wales, educated at Oxford.] [Hart's *Index Purg. Angl.* p. 4.] [London] 1549

HISTORIE (ye) of Leadenhall [market]. By J. L. D. [James Lewis Dowling]. 12mo. [Anderson's *Brit. Top.*] London [1877]

HISTORIE (the) of Orlando Fvrioso, one of the twelve Peeres of France ; as it was playd before the Queenes Maiestie. [By Robert Greene.] 4to. No pagination. [*Bodl.*] London, 1599

"Written by Robert Greene."—MS. note.

HISTORIE (the) of Scotland during the minority of King James ; written in Latine by Robert Johnston, done into English by T. M. [Thomas Middleton]. 12mo. Pp. 164. [*W.* ; Lowndes' *Bibl. Man.*] London, 1646

HISTORIE (the) of the Baron of Petfoddils, quha was wirriet by his awin catt. [A poem. Signed: W. D. *i.e.* W. Duncan.] 12mo. Pp. 13. Abirdene, 1839

HISTORIE (the) of the Civill Warres of France, written in Italian by H. C. Davila; translated out of the original [by Charles Cotterell and William Aylesbury]. Fol. 2 parts. [*Brit. Mus.*] London, 1647-8

HISTORIE of the discoverie and conquest of the East Indias. By Hernan Lopez de Castaneda; translated by N. L. [Nicholas Lichfield], Gentleman. 4to. [*Christie-Miller Cat.*] London, 1582

HISTORIE (the) of the great and mightie kingdome of China, and the situation thereof; togither with the great riches, huge citties, politike governement, and rare inventions in the same; translated out of Spanish [of Juan Gonçalez de Mendoza] by R[obert] Parke. 4to. [*W.*] London, 1588

HISTORIE (the) of the life and death of Mary Stuart, Queene of Scotland. By William Stranguage [William Udall]. Fol. London, 1624

The edition of 1635 gives the author's name.

HISTORIE (the) of the most renowned and victorious Princesse Elizabeth, late Queene of England; contayning all the important and remarkeable passages of state both at home and abroad, during her long and prosperous raigne. . . . [By William Camden. In four books.] Fol. [*Bodl.*] London, 1630

HISTORIE (the) of the perfect-cursed-blessed man. By J. F. [Joseph Fletcher] Master of Arts, etc. 4to. [Lowndes' *Bibl. Man.*] London, 1629

HISTORIE (the) of the trovbles of Hvngarie; containing the pitifull losse and ruine of that kingdome, and the warres happened there in that time, betweene the Christians and Turkes. By Mart. Fvmee, Lord of Genille, Knight of the Kings Order. Newly translated out of French into English by R. C. [Rooke Churche], Gentleman. Fol. Pp. 392. [*New Coll. Lib.*] London, 1600

HISTORIE (the) of the uniting of the kingdom of Portugall to the crowne of Castill, containing the last warres of the Portugals against the Moores of Africke, the end of the house of Portugall and change of that government. . . . [Translated from the Italian of Girolamo Conestaggio, or Joannes de Silva.] Fol. Pp. 324. [*W.*] London, 1600

Dedication to 'Henry Earle of Southampton' signed: Edw. Blount.

HISTORIES of noble British families, with biographical notices of the most distinguished individuals in each; illustrated by their armorial bearings, portraits, monuments, seals, etc. [By Henry Drummond, M.P.] Fol. 2 vols. [*Athen. Cat.* (*Second Supp.*) p. 41.] London, 1846

HISTORIES (the) of the most famous and worthy cronographer Polybius; discoursing of the warres betwxt thei Romanes and the Carthginienses. . . . Englished by C. W. [Christopher Watson, M.A.] . . . 8vo. [*D. N. B.* vol. 60, p. 3.] London, 1568

HISTORIETTES; or, tales of Continental life. By the author of *The English in Italy* [Constantine Henry Phipps, Marquis of Normanby]. 8vo. 3 vols. [*Brit. Mus.*] London, 1827

HISTORY (the) and adventures of an atom. [By Tobias George Smollett.] 12mo. 2 vols. London, 1769

The advertisement from the publisher to the reader is signed: S. Etherington.

HISTORY (the) and adventures of Gil Blas. [By Alain René Le Sage. Translated from the French by Tobias G. Smollett.] 12mo. 4 vols. [*Brit. Mus.*] Edinburgh, 1771

The titles of other editions vary: "The adventures of Gil Blas of Santillane," 1749, "The history of Gil Blas," 1732.

HISTORY (the) and analysis of the Common Law of England. Written by a learned hand [Sir Matthew Hale]. 8vo. [*D. N. B.* vol. 24, p. 23.] London, 1713

HISTORY (the) and analysis of the supposed automaton chess-player of . . . Kempelen . . . [By Gamaliel Bradford, M.D.] 8vo. Boston, 1826

HISTORY (the) and annals of Blackley and neighbourhood. By P. Wentworth [Peter Hall]. 4to. Middleton, 1892

HISTORY (the) and antiquities of Barnwall Abbey, and of Sturbridge Fair. [By J. Nichols.] 4to. [Bartholomew's *Camb. Books*, p. 19.] London, 1786

A later edition, with varied title, was published in 1806.

HISTORY (the) and antiquities of Carlisle, with account of the castles, gentlemen's seats, and antiquities, and memoirs of eminent men. [By Samuel Jefferson.] 8vo. [*Athen. Cat.* (*Second Supp.*) p. 74.] London, 1838

HISTORY (the) and antiquities of Colchester Castle. [By John Horace Round.] 8vo. Colchester, 1882

HISTORY (the) and antiquities of Glastonbury. [By Richard Rawlinson.] To which are added, (1) the endowment and orders of Sherrington's Chantry, founded in Saint Paul's Church, London. (2) Dr Plot's letter to the Earl of Arlington concerning Thelford: to all which pieces (never before printed) a preface is prefix'd, and an appendix subjoyn'd by the publisher, Thomas Hearne, M.A. [By Charles Eyston.] 8vo. Pp. xciii. 366. [*Bodl.*] Oxford, 1722

See Hearne's Coll., vol. 83. pp. 130 and 153. See also the author's letter to Mr H., dated Oct. 23. 1719.

HISTORY (the) and antiquities of Gloucestershire; comprising the topography, antiquities, curiosities, produce, trade, and manufactures of that county . . . [Partly based on the work of Sir Robert Atkyns, but with supplementary material added from other sources, or supplied by the editor and printer, Samuel Rudder.] Fol. [Watt's *Bibl. Brit.*] Cirencester, 1779

HISTORY (the) and antiquities of Horsham. By the author of *Juvenile researches* [Howard Dudley]. 8vo. Pp. 80. [Anderson's *Brit. Top.*] London, 1836

HISTORY (the) and antiquities of Kiddington. [By Thomas Warton.] Third edition. 8vo. [W. D. Macray's *Cat.*] London, 1815

HISTORY and antiquities of Newbury and its environs, including twenty-eight parishes situate in the county of Berks; also a catalogue of plants, found in the neighbourhood. [By Edward Whitaker Gray.] 8vo. Pp. 352. Speenhamland, 1839

HISTORY (the) and antiquities of Pleshy, in the county of Essex [Preface signed: R. G. *i.e.* Richard Gough.] 4to. [Anderson's *Brit. Top.*] London, 1803

HISTORY (the) and antiquities of Rochester and its environs; to which is added, a description of the towns, villages, gentlemen's seats, and ancient buildings, situate on, or near the road from London to Margate, Deal, and Dover. [Begun by William Shrubsole, but much increased by Rev. Samuel Denne.] 8vo. Pp. xiv. 353. [Nichols' *Lit. Anec.*] Rochester, 1772

A second edition, published in 1817, was enlarged by W. Wildash.

HISTORY (the) and antiquities of Scotland, from the earliest accounts to the death of James I., anno 1437, by Mr [William] Maitland; and from that period to the accession of James VI. to the crown of England, anno 1603, by another hand [Thomas Grainger, M.D.]. Fol. 2 vols. [Mitchell and Cash's *Scot. Top.*] London, 1757

HISTORY (the) and antiquities of the ancient villa of Wheatfield, in the county of Suffolk. [By John Clubbe, rector of Wheatfield.] 4to. [*D. N. B.* vol. 11, p. 136.] London, 1758

A burlesque imitation, frequently reprinted, of P. Morant's "History of Colchester."

HISTORY (the) and antiquities of the cathedral church of Rochester; containing I. The local statutes of that church. II. The inscriptions upon the monuments, tombs, and grave-stones. III. An account of the bishops, priors, deans, and arch-deacons. IV. An appendix of monumental inscriptions in the cathedral church of Canterbury, supplementary to Mr Somner's and Mr Batteley's accounts of that church. V. Some original papers, relating to the church and diocese of Rochester. [By Richard Rawlinson, LL.D., Non-juring Bishop.] 8vo. Pp. 242. London, 1717

"This publication has been ascribed to John Lewis, but it is generally understood to have been written by Dr Richard Rawlinson."—Upcott.

HISTORY (the) and antiquities of the cathedral-church of Salisbury, and the Abbey-church of Bath. [By Richard Rawlinson, LL.D.] 8vo. Pp. xvi. 351. London, 1719

HISTORY (the) and antiquities of the Cathedral of Hereford. [By James Norris Brewer.] 8vo. Hereford [1815]

HISTORY (the) and antiquities of the city and cathedral church of Hereford; containing an account of all the inscriptions, epitaphs, etc. upon the tombs, monuments, and grave-stones. . . . [By Richard Rawlinson, LL.D.] 8vo. [*Brit. Mus.*] London, 1717

HISTORY (the) and antiquities of the city of York from its origin to the present times. [By William Combe?] 12mo. 3 vols. [*Brit. Mus.*] York, 1785

HISTORY (the) and antiquities of the four Inns of Court; namely, the Inner Temple, Middle Temple, Lincoln's Inn, and Gray's Inn; and of the nine Inns of Chancery; . . . containing every particular circumstance relative to each of them, comprized in the well-known and justly celebrated work, written by Sir William Dugdale, and published in folio in the years 1666, 1671, and 1680, under the title of Origines Juridiciales, etc. . . . [By Timothy Cunningham.] 8vo. Pp. xx. 251. [*Lincoln's Inn Cat.*] London, 1780

In a MS. note, nearly contemporary, on the copy in the King's Library, British Museum, this work is attributed to John Rayner.

HISTORY (the) and antiquities of the parish and Church of St Michael, Crooked Lane [London]. . . . [By William Herbert, librarian.] 8vo. [*Brit. Mus.*] London [1831]

HISTORY (the) and antiquities of the parish of Lambeth, in the County of Surrey; including biographical anecdotes of several eminent persons. . . . [By John Nichols.] 4to. [*W.; Upcott.*] London, 1786

HISTORY (the) and antiquities of the town and borough of Reading in Berkshire; with some notices of the most considerable places in the same county. [By John Doran.] 12mo. Reading, 1835

Issued in 1836 with the author's name.

HISTORY and antiquities of the town of Ludlow and its ancient castle; lives of the Lord Presidents, accounts of seats and villages, etc. [By Thomas Wright.] 12mo. Ludlow, 1822

HISTORY (the) and antiquities of Westminster Abbey. . . . [By Edward Wedlake Brayling.] 4to. [*Brit. Mus.*] London, 1856

HISTORY (the) and antiquities of Winchester . . . together with the charters, laws, customs . . . and privileges of that ancient city. [By Thomas Warton.] 12mo. 2 vols. Winton, 1773

Attributed also to J. Wavell and —— Porter; it is possible that both were engaged on the work under the encouragement and supervision of Dr Richard Rawlinson. [Watt's *Bibl. Brit.*]

HISTORY (the) and antiquities of Windsor Castle, and the Royal college and chapel of St George: with the institution, laws, and ceremonies of the most noble order of the Garter. . . . [By Joseph Pote.] 4to. [*Upcott*, i. 15.] Eton, 1749

HISTORY and antiquities relative to the origin of government, beginning of laws, antiquities of our laws in England, etc. Extracted from Dugdale's Origines. [By Timothy Cunningham.] 8vo. [*Lincoln's Inn Cat.*] London, 1780

HISTORY (the) and character of St Paul, examined; in a letter to Theophilus, a Christian friend: occasioned by [Lord Lyttelton's] "Observations on the conversion and apostleship of St Paul." . . . [By Peter Annet.] 8vo. [*D. N. B.* vol. 2, p. 9.] London [1742?]

HISTORY (the) and chronology of the fabulous ages considered, particularly with regard to the two ancient deities Bacchus and Hercules. By a member of the Society of Antiquaries in London [Francis Wise, B.D., F.S.A.]. 4to. Oxford, 1764

HISTORY (a) and defence of Magna Charta; containing a copy of the original Charta at large, the Bill of Rights, etc., an essay on Parliaments, describing their origin in England, etc. [By Samuel Johnson, Rector of Corringham.] 8vo. London, 1769

The second edition, 1772, has the author's name.

HISTORY (the) and description of Ashby-de-la-Zouch . . . with excursions in the neighbourhood. [By Edward Mammatt.] 8vo. [Anderson's *Brit. Top.*] London, 1852

HISTORY (the) and description of Colchester, (the Camulodunum of the Britains, and the first Roman colony in Britain;) with an account of the antiquities of that most ancient borough. [By Joseph or Benjamin Strutt.] 8vo. 2 vols. [*Upcott*, i. 234.] Colchester, 1803

HISTORY (the) and description of fossil fuel—the collieries and coal trade of Great Britain. By the author of *Manufactures in metal* in the Cabinet Cyclopædia [John Holland]. 8vo. [M'Culloch's *Lit. of Pol. Econ.* p. 230.] London, 1841

HISTORY and description of Moscow. [By Joseph Sulkowski.] 8vo. [Cushing's *Anon.*] London, 1813

HISTORY and description of the Great Western Railway. [By George Thomas Clark, civil engineer.] 8vo. London, 1846

HISTORY and description of the Isle of Man; its history, laws, customs, etc. [By George Waldron.] Second edition. 12mo. [Harrison's *Bibl. Monensis.*] London, 1744

HISTORY and description of the restored parish Church of Saint Mary, Wymeswold, Leicestershire. [By Henry Alford, D.D.] 8vo. Pp. 29. [*Bodl.*] London [1846]

HISTORY and description of the town and borough of Ipswich, including the villages and country seats in its vicinity. . . . [By G. R. Clarke.] 4to. Pp. 504. [*Manch. Free Lib.*] Ipswich [1830]

HISTORY and description of the skeleton of a new sperm whale lately set out in the Australian Museum. . . . [By William S. Macleay.] 8vo. [*Brit. Mus.*] Sydney, 1851

HISTORY (a) and description of the town of Inverness. [By George Cameron.] 8vo. [P. J. Anderson's *Inverness Bibl.* p. 120.] Inverness, 1847

HISTORY (the) and fate of sacrilege. By Sir Henry Spelman. Edited, in part from two MSS., revised and corrected, with a continuation, large additions and an introductory essay, by two priests of the Church of England [John Mason Neale and Joseph Haskoll]. 8vo. Pp. clxix. 367. [*N. and Q.* 1881, pp. 109, 138, 178.] London, 1846

Another edition was issued in 1895.

HISTORY and geography of Wales, for the young. By an owner of Welsh land [Miss A. J. Harding, of Banbury]. 8vo. London [1888]

HISTORY and life of a pilgrim. By G. W. [R. G. Noble]. 8vo. [*Brit. Mus.*] Dublin, 1753

HISTORY and life of Robert Blake. . . . Written by a gentleman bred in the family [John Oldmixon]. 8vo. [*D. N. B.* vol. 42, p. 115.] London, 1740

HISTORY (the) and management of the East-India Company, from its origin in 1600 to the present times. Volume the first, containing the affairs of the Carnatic. . . . [By James Macpherson, M.D.] 4to. [*Brit. Mus.*] London, 1779

No more published.

HISTORY and policy of the native land-laws of New Zealand, from 1840 to 1886. [By Patrick Stirling Maclean.] 8vo. Pp. 88. [Collier's *Literature of New Zealand*, p. 159.] Napier, N.Z., 1886

HISTORY (the) and present state of Virginia, in four parts. I. The history of the first settlement of Virginia, and the government thereof, to the present time. II. The natural productions and conveniences of the country, suited to trade and improvement. III. The native Indians, their religion, laws, and customs, in war and peace. IV. The present state of the country, as to the polity of the government, and the improvements of the land. By a native and inhabitant of the place [Robert Beverley]. 8vo. [*Nat. Lib. of Scot.*] London, 1705

The title of the second edition [1722] begins "The history of Virginia . . ." (See below.)

HISTORY (the) and principles of the first constituted Presbytery of Relief; founded in consequence of the Law of Patronage, by the late Reverend Messrs Gillespie and Boston. . . . [By Rev. David Galletly.] 8vo. Pp. 42. Edinburgh, 1795

HISTORY and progress of education. By Philobiblius [Linus Pierpont Brockett, M.D.]. 8vo. [Cushing's *Init. and Pseud.* i. 232.] New York, 1859

HISTORY (the) and reasons of the dependency of Ireland upon the Imperial Crown of the Kingdom of England. . . . [By William Attwood.] 8vo. [Arber's *Term Cat.* iii. 687.] London, 1698

HISTORY (the) and records of the Elephant Club. . . . By Knight Russ-Ockside [Mortimer M. Thompson]. 8vo. [Cushing's *Init. and Pseud.* i. 568.] New York, 1856

HISTORY (the) and scenery of Fife and Kinross. By the author of *Bygone days in our village* [Jean L. Watson]. 8vo. [*Nat. Lib. of Scot.*] Edinburgh, 1875

HISTORY (the) and scenery of Peeblesshire. [By Jean L. Watson.] 8vo. [Mitchell and Cash's *Scot. Top.*] Edinburgh, 1874

HISTORY and statutes of the Royal Infirmary of Edinburgh. [By John Stedman, M.D.] 4to. [Laing's *Cat.* 1828.] Edinburgh, 1778

HISTORY (the) and survey of the cities of London and Westminster. . . . By a gentleman of the Inner Temple [John Mottley]. 8vo. [*D. N. B.* vol. 39, p. 198.] London, 1753

Previously published in 1736 (4to) with the title "An accurate survey of the cities of London and Westminster, and borough of Southwark. . . ." By Robert Seymour, Esq.

HISTORY (the) and teaching of the English Church; a lecture. . . . [By —— Dunlop.] 8vo. Pp. 34. [Smales' *Whitby Authors.*] Whitby, 1856

HISTORY (the) and the mystery of Good Friday. [By Rev. Robert Robinson, Baptist minister.] 8vo. [*Brit. Mus.*] London, 1777

At least ten editions were printed.

HISTORY (the) and traditions of Upper Annandale. By Agnes Marchmont [Mrs —— Marshall]. 8vo. Paisley, 1901

HISTORY, constitution, rules of discipline, and confession of faith of the Calvinistic Methodists in Wales. [Translated by David Davies, of Castle Green.] 8vo. London, 1827

HISTORY for teachers. By Mary Blake [Mrs Mary N. Blakeslee]. 8vo. [*Lib. Journ.* xiii. 28.] [Boston, 1880]

HISTORY in all ages. [By Rev. Edward Parsons, Halifax, Yorks.] 8vo. London, 1830

HISTORY is on our side; a vindication, from the evidence of historians, of the thesis that Israel is found in Britain: a lecture delivered in . . . Bath. . . . By "Oxonian" [Rev. W. M. H. Milner, M.A.]. 8vo. London, 1888

HISTORY (a) military and municipal of the ancient borough of Devizes and subordinately of the entire Hundred of Potterne and Cannings. . . . [By Henry Bull?] 8vo. [*Brit. Mus.*] London, 1859

HISTORY (the) of a Church and a warming-pan; written for the benefit of the Associators and Reformers of the age for ecclesiastical reform. [By James Montgomery.] 8vo. Pp. 56. London, 1793

Signed: J. M. G.

HISTORY (the) of a clergyman's widow and her young family. [By Barbara Hoole, later Mrs Hofland.] 12mo. London, 1812

HISTORY (the) of a corporation of servants, discovered a few years ago in the interior parts of South America; containing some very surprising events and extraordinary characters. [By John Witherspoon, D.D.] 4to. Pp. 76. [*D. N. B.* vol. 62, p. 272.] Glasgow, 1765

A satirical exposure of the evils of ecclesiasticism, first, in earlier times, and later in the Church of Scotland.

HISTORY (the) of a flirt; related by herself. [By Lady Charlotte Maria Bury.] 8vo. 3 vols. London, 1840

HISTORY of a French louse; or, the spy of a new species, in France and England; containing a description of the most remarkable personages in those kingdoms: giving a key to the chief events of the year 1779 and those which are to happen in 1780. [By —— Delauney.] Translated from the fourth edition of the revised and corrected Paris copy. 8vo. Pp. iv. 123. [Quérard's *La France littéraire.*] London, 1779

HISTORY of a great industry; twenty-one years of trawling. [By William Pyper.] 8vo. Dundee, 1903

HISTORY (the) of a merchant's widow. By the author of *The officer's widow* [Barbara Hoole, later Mrs Hofland]. 12mo. [*Brit. Mus.*] London, 1823

HISTORY (the) of a needle. . . . By A. L. O. E. [Charlotte M. Tucker]. 12mo. London, 1857

HISTORY (the) of a pilgrim; with some account of the shrine to which he journeyed. [By R. G. Noble.] 8vo. London [1861]

HISTORY (the) of a pocket Prayer-Book, written by itself. [Signed: B. D. *i.e.* Benjamin Dorr.] Parts 1-5. 12mo. [Corns and Sparke's *Unf. Books*, p. 72.] London [1854]

HISTORY (the) of a sandal-wood box written by itself; a tale for youth. [By Mrs Henry Glassford Bell.] 4to. Pp. 60. [Glasgow, N.D.]

Not printed for publication.

HISTORY (the) of a savage girl, caught in the woods of Champagne; newly translated from the French of Madame H—t [Hacquet]. 12mo. [Barbier's *Dictionnaire.*] London, 1784

HISTORY of a six weeks' tour through a part of France, Switzerland, Germany, and Holland; with letters descriptive of a sail round the lake of Geneva, and of the glaciers of Chamouni. [By Percy Bysshe Shelley and Mary W. Shelley.] 12mo. Pp. vi. 183. [*Dyce Cat.* ii. 296; Courtney's *Secrets*, p. 59.] London, 1817

HISTORY (the) of a woman of quality; or, the adventures of Lady Frail. By an impartial hand [Sir John Hill]. 8vo. Pp. xii. 227. [*Brit. Mus.*] London, 1751

HISTORY of a world of immortals without a God; translated from an unpublished manuscript in the library of a continental University. By Antares Skorpios [Jane Barlow]. 12mo. [*Quinn Sale Cat.*] Dublin, 1891

HISTORY (the) of addresses. By one very near a kin to the author of the *Tale of a tub* [John Oldmixon]. Part I. 8vo. Pp. 244. [*Brit. Mus.*] London, 1709

HISTORY (the) of addresses; with remarks serious and comical: in which regard is had to all such as have been presented since the impeachment of Dr Sacheverell. Part II. By the author of the first [John Oldmixon]. 8vo. Pp. iv. 358. London, 1711

HISTORY (a) of Africa. By the author of *Conversations on chronology* [Mrs Jane Marcet]. 12mo. London, 1830

HISTORY (the) of Alcidalis and Zelida; a tale of the fourteenth century. [By Vincent Voiture.] 8vo. Pp. 95. Printed at Strawberry Hill, 1789

Probably a translation of a French work by Voiture, published at London in 1678, with a new title. In the appendix to Lowndes' *Bibl. Man.* (ed. Bohn), p. 240, the imprint is said to be fictitious. The work is not included in Martin's list of books printed at Strawberry Hill.

HISTORY (the) of Alicia Montague. By the author of *Clarinda Cathcart* [Mrs Jane Marshall]. 12mo. 2 vols. [Baker's *Biog. Dram.*] London, 1767

Watt gives the name as Jean Marishall.

HISTORY of all the real & threatened invasions of England. [By Charles Knight.] 8vo. London, 1794

HISTORY (the) of America. . . . Extracted from the American edition of the Encyclopædia. [By Jendidiah Morse.] 12mo. [Sabin's *Dictionary.*] Philadelphia, 1790

HISTORY (the) of an Irish family; in which the unspeakable advantages of a virtuous education in the formation of the human character are strikingly exemplified. . . . [By Mrs Beatrice Grant.] 12mo. Pp. 192. [Couper's *Millers of Haddington*, p. 297.] Haddington, 1822

HISTORY (the) of an officer's widow and her young family. [By Barbara Hoole, later Mrs Hofland.] 12mo. London, 1809

HISTORY (the) of an old lady [*i.e.* the City of London] and her family. [By Paul Whitehead.] 8vo. London, 1754

HISTORY of ancient America. By Count Joannes [George Jones]. [Cushing's *Init. and Pseud.* i. 142.] New York, 1843

HISTORY (the) of ancient Greece, from the earliest times till it became a Roman Province. [Translated from the French of Pons Augustin Alletz, by W. Robertson.] 12mo. Edinburgh, 1768

Later editions give the names.

HISTORY (the) of ancient Paganism, as delivered by Eusebius, etc., with critical and historical notes; shewing, first, its origin, progress, decay and revival, thro' a misconstrued Christianity; and, secondly, a Phœnician and Egyptian chronology, from the first man, down to the first Olympiad, agreeable to the Scripture accounts. . . [By Francis Mason, or Masson.] 8vo. Pp. vii. 128. [*Bodl.*] London, 1743

HISTORY (the) of Andrew Dunn, an Irish Catholic. [By J. Kelly.] 8vo. Pp. 40. [*Brit. Mus.*] London, 1830

HISTORY (a) of antient ceremonies; containing an account of their rise and growth, their first entrance into the Church, and their gradual advancement to superstition therein. [By —— Martin, pastor of the French Church in London.] 12mo. London, 1669

Written originally in French and translated by John Wilson. [*Macalpin Coll. Cat.*]

HISTORY (the) of Antonio and Mellida. The first part, as it hath beene sundry times acted, by the children of Paules. Written by I. M. [John Marston]. 4to. No pagination. [Baker's *Biog. Dram.*] London, 1602

HISTORY (the) of Appian of Alexandria, in two parts: the first, consisting of the Punick, Syrian, Parthian, Mithridatick, Illyrian, Spanish, and Hannibalick, wars; the second, containing five books of the civil wars of Rome. Made English by J. D. [John Davies, of Kidwelly]. Fol. Pp. 251, 273. [Arber's *Term Cat.* iii. 379]. London, 1679

HISTORY (the) of Arsaces, Prince of Betlis. By the editor of *Chrysal* [Charles Johnston]. 12mo. 2 vols. [*Dyce Cat.*] Dublin, 1775-1774

HISTORY (a) of Australia. By Vindex [George William Rusden]. 8vo. 3 vols. [*Lond. Lib. Cat.*] London, 1883

HISTORY (the) of Ayder Ali Khan Nabob-Bahader; or, new memoirs concerning the East Indies; with historical notes by M. M. D. L. T. [M. Maître de la Tour], General of ten thousand men in the army of the Mogol Empire. . . . 8vo. 2 vols. [*Brit. Mus.*] Dublin, 1774

HISTORY (the) of banks. . . . [By Richard Hildreth.] 12mo. [Cushing's *Anon.*] Boston, 1837

HISTORY (the) of Baptism; or, one faith, one baptism, in the several editions thereof under Noah, Moses, Christ. . . . By J. St N. [John St Nicholas, minister at Lutterworth]. 8vo. [Arber's *Term Cat.* i. 309.] London, 1678

HISTORY of Barthomley [in Cheshire], in letters from a former Rector [Rev. Edward Hinchliffe, M.A.] to his eldest son. 8vo. Pp. viii. 370. [Simms' *Bibl. Staff.* p. 226.] London, 1856

Rigidly suppressed.

HISTORY (the) of Belfast. [By George Benn.] 8vo. [*Brit. Mus.*] London, 1823

HISTORY (the) of Betty Barnes. [A novel. By Sarah Fielding ?.] 8vo. 2 vols. London, 1753

HISTORY of Boston [Mass.] from 1630 to 1856 . . . [By Isaac Smith Homans, jun.] 8vo. [Cushing's *Anon.*] Boston, 1856

HISTORY (the) of Cales passion; or, as some will by-name it, the miss-taking of Cales; presented in vindication of the sufferers, to forwarne the future. By G. T. [George Tooke]. 4to. [*Brit. Mus.*] London, 1652

HISTORY (a) of Campbell County, Kentucky . . . [By Mary K. Jones.] 8vo. [Cushing's *Anon.*] Newport, Kentucky, 1876

HISTORY (the) of Carausius; or, an examination of what has been advanced on that subject by Genebrier and Dr Stukeley. [By Richard Gough.] 4to. [Nichol's *Lit. Anec.* vi. 271.] London, 1762

HISTORY (the) of Cataline's Conspiracy; with the four Orations of Cicero: to which are added notes and illustrations. By George Frederic Sydney [Sir Henry Seton Steuart, Bart.]. 8vo. [*D. N. B.* vol. 54, p. 227.] London, 1795

HISTORY (the) of Champaign County, Ohio. [By J. W. Ogden.] 8vo. Pp. 922. [*Brit. Mus.*] Chicago, 1881

HISTORY (the) of Ceylon from the earliest period to the year 1815. . . . By Philalethes, A.M. Oxon. [Robert Fellowes, D.D., LL.D.]. To which is subjoined, Robert Knox's Historical relation of the island, with an account of his captivity during a period of near twenty years. . . . 4to. [*Camb. Univ. Lib.*] London, 1817

Attributed also to Rev. G. Bissett.

HISTORY (the) of Charles XII., King of Sweden; in eight books. [Translated from the French of Voltaire, by Andrew Henderson, M.A.] 4to. Pp. 163. [*Brit. Mus.*] London, 1734

HISTORY (the) of Charles Wentworth, Esq., in a series of letters, interspersed with a variety of important reflections calculated to improve morality, and promote the oeconomy of human life. [By A. Bancroft.] 12mo. 3 vols. [Watt's *Bibl. Brit.*] London, 1770

HISTORY (a) of Chelsworth in Suffolk. By H. E. A. [Sir Henry Edmund Austen]. 8vo. Ipswich, 1850

HISTORY (the) of Cheltenham and its environs; including an inquiry into the nature and properties of the mineral waters, etc. and a concise view of the county of Glocester. [By Thomas Frognall Dibdin.] 8vo. [*Upcott*, i. 270.] Cheltenham, 1803

The dedication and the preface are signed "H. Ruff," the publisher.

HISTORY (the) of chess, together with short and plain instructions, by which any one may easily play at it without the help of a teacher. [By Robert Lambe, vicar of Norham.] 8vo. Pp. 148. [*Bodl.*] London, 1765

HISTORY (the) of Chesterfield, with particulars of the hamlets contiguous to the town, and descriptive accounts of Chatsworth, Hardwick, and Bolsover Castle. [By Rev. George Hall, with additions.] 8vo. Pp. vi. 504. [*Brit. Mus.*] London, 1839

Attributed also to Thomas Ford.

HISTORY (the) of Christian altars. [By J. H. Collison.] 8vo. Cambridge, 1847

Attributed also to J. H. Crosse.

HISTORY (a) of Christian names. By the author of *The heir of Redclyffe*, etc. [Charlotte Mary Yonge]. 8vo. 2 vols. London, 1863

HISTORY (the) of Christina Alessandra, Queen of Swedland . . . [By John Burbury.] 12mo. [*Camb. Univ. Lib.*] London, 1658

HISTORY of Churcher's College, Petersfield, Hants; with a sketch of the life of the founder, and a report of the case in the High Court of Chancery between the trustees and several of the inhabitants of Petersfield. [By Nathaniel Atcheson.] 8vo. [*Lincoln's Inn Cat.*] London, 1823

HISTORY (a) of Congress . . . 1789-1793. [By John Agg.] 8vo. [*Brit. Mus.*] Philadelphia, 1834

HISTORY (the) of Cornelia; a novel. [By Mrs Sarah Scott.] 12mo. [Brydges' *Cens. Lit.* iv. 292.] London, 1750

HISTORY (the) of Croesus, king of Lydia, in 4 parts; containing observations, I. On the antient notion of destiny. II. On dreams. III. On the origin and credit of oracles. IV. And the principles upon which their responses were defended against any attack. [By Walter Anderson, D.D.] 12mo. Pp. xxiv. 211. [*Brit. Mus.*] Edinburgh, 1755

HISTORY (the) of Crowland Abbey, digested from the materials collected by Mr Gough, and published in quarto in 1783 and 1797; including an abstract of the observations of Mr Essex respecting the ancient and present state of the Abbey, and the origin and use of the triangular bridge. [By Benjamin Holdich.] . . . 8vo. Pp. 198. [*W.; Upcott*, i. 641.] Stamford, 1816

HISTORY of Cuba; or, notes of a traveller in the Tropics. [By Maturin Murray Ballou.] 8vo. [Cushing's *Init. and Pseud.* i. 286.] Boston, 1854

HISTORY (the) of Cutchacutchoo. [By John Wilson Croker.] 12mo. Pp. 22. [*Bodl.*] Dublin, 1805

HISTORY (the) of democracy in the United States of America. . . . [By Nahum Capen.] 8vo. [Cushing's *Anon.*] Boston, 1852

HISTORY (the) of Don Francisco de Miranda's attempt to effect a revolution in South America. By an officer under that General [Henry Adams Bullard]. 8vo. [Sabin's *Dictionary.*] Boston, 1808

HISTORY (the) of Dorastus and Fawnia, daughter and heir to the King of Bohemia; profitable to youth, to avoid other wanton pastimes. . . . By R. G. [Robert Greene]. 8vo. [Arber's *Term. Cat.* iii. 430.] London, 1704

HISTORY of Dorchester, Mass. [By Ebenezer Clapp, junr.] 8vo. [Cushing's *Anon.*] Boston, 1859

HISTORY (the) of Dublin, New Hampshire. . . . [By Levi Washburn Leonard, D.D.] 8vo. [Cushing's *Anon.*] Boston, 1855

HISTORY (a) of duelling in all countries; translated [by Richard Hengist Horne] from the French. 12mo. [Thimm's *Bibl. of the Art of Fence*, p. 88.] N.P., N.D.

HISTORY (the) of Edward, Prince of Wales, commonly termed the Black Prince, eldest son of King Edward the Third; with a short view of the reigns of Edward I., Edward II., and Edward III. and a summary account of the institution of the Order of the Garter. [By Alexander Bicknell.] 8vo. [*D. N. B.* vol. 5, p. 9.] London, 1776

HISTORY (the) of Emily Montagu. By the author of *Lady Juliana Mandeville* [Frances Brooke, *née* Moore]. 12mo. 4 vols. London, 1769

HISTORY of England . . . [In verse. By William L. Hunter.] 4to. [*Brit. Mus.*] New York, 1867

HISTORY (the) of England. The first book, declaring the state of the isle of Britain under the Roman empire. [By John Clapham.] 4to. Pp. 116. [*Harleian Miscellany*, vii. 1.] London, 1602

HISTORY (the) of England, abridged from Hume. By the author of the *Abridgement of Mr Gibbon's Roman History* [Rev. Charles Hereford]. 8vo. [Lowndes' *Bibl. Man.*] London, 1795

HISTORY of England and France under the House of Lancaster; with an introductory view of the early reformation. [By Henry Brougham, Lord Brougham and Vaux.] 8vo. [*D. N. B.* vol. 6, p. 457.] London, 1852

HISTORY (the) of England during the reign of George the Third. [By James Robins, under the name of Robert Scott.] 6 vols. [*Gent. Mag.* 1836, p. 665.] London, 1820-4

HISTORY (the) of England during the reigns of K. William, Q. Anne, and K. George I.; with an introductory review of the reigns of the Royal Brothers, Charles and James; in which are to be found the seeds of the Revolution. By a lover of truth and liberty [James Ralph, assisted by Lord Melcombe]. Fol. Pp. iv. 1078. [*Brit. Mus.*] London, 1744

The introductory review of the reigns of Charles and James occupies the whole of the work. The second volume, containing the history of the reigns of William, Anne, and George I. appeared in 1746.

HISTORY (the) of England, during the reigns of the royal house of Stuart, wherein the errors of the late histories are discover'd and corrected; with proper reflections, and several original letters from King Charles II., King James II., Oliver Cromwell, etc.: as also Lord Saville's famous forged letter of invitation, which brought the Scots into England in the year 1640, and gave occasion to the beginning of the Civil Wars; this letter being never before publish'd, led the Earl of Clarendon, Bishop Burnet, Mr Echard, Dr Welwood, and other writers, into egregious mistakes upon this head. . . . By the author of the *Critical history of England* [John Oldmixon]. Fol. Pp. xxi. 803. [*Brit. Mus.*] London, 1730

HISTORY (a) of England for family use and the upper classes of schools. By the author of *An introduction to the history of England*, etc. [Augusta Theodosia Drane]. 8vo. [*Brit. Mus.*] London, 1864

HISTORY (the) of England, for the use of schools and young persons. By Edward Baldwin, Esq., author of the *History of Rome*, and *History of Greece, on a similar plan*, etc. [William Godwin]. A new edition, . . . 12mo. Pp. viii. 184. [Lowndes' *Bibl. Man.* p. 906.] London, 1854

HISTORY (the) of England, from the earliest accounts to . . . George II., including the History of Scotland and Ireland. By an impartial hand [Isaac Kimber]. 8vo. [*Brit. Mus.*] London, 1746

HISTORY (a) of England, from the earliest times to the year eighteen hundred and fifty-eight. By James White [John Hill Burton, LL.D.]. 8vo. [*D. N. B.* vol. 8, p. 10.] London, 1860

HISTORY (a) of England, from the first invasion by the Romans to the 14th year of the reign of Queen Victoria; with conversations at the end of each chapter. By Mrs Markham [Mrs Elizabeth Penrose]. For the use of young persons. New and revised edition. 12mo. Pp. viii. 581. London, 1853

The authoress took her pseudonym from the village of Markham, where her early years were spent. She composed a similar "History of France": see below.

HISTORY (an) of England, in a series of letters from a nobleman to his son. [By Oliver Goldsmith.] 12mo. 2 vols. [*D. N. B.* vol. 22, p. 94.] London, 1764

This work was at first ascribed to the Earl of Orrery, to Lord Lyttelton, and to the Earl of Chesterfield.

HISTORY (a) of England, in which it is intended to consider men and events on Christian principles. By a clergyman of the Church of England [Henry Walter]. 12mo. 2 vols. [*Brit. Mus.*] London, 1828-39

HISTORY (the) of England under the House of Stuart, including the Commonwealth, 1603-88. [By Robert Vaughan, D.D.] 8vo. [*Brit. Mus.*] London, 1840

HISTORY (a) of Europe during the middle ages. [By Samuel Astley Dunham, LL.D.] 8vo. 4 vols. [*Brit. Mus.*] London, 1833, 1834

Lardner's Cabinet Cyclopædia.

HISTORY of Epsom; with a description of the origin of horse-racing and of Epsom races, and an account of the mineral waters; with an appendix containing a botanical survey. By an inhabitant [Henry Pownall]. 8vo. [*Reform Club Cat.*] Epsom, 1825

HISTORY of Erie County, Pennsylvania. By Fanchon [Mrs Laura M. Sanford]. 8vo. [Cushing's *Init. and Pseud.* i. 98.] Philadelphia, 1862

HISTORY (the) of faction, alias hypocrisy, alias moderation, from its first rise down to its present toleration in these kingdoms; wherein its original and increase are set forth, its several contrivances to subvert the Church and State apparently detected, and the steps it has made towards getting into the supream power from the Reformation to the rising of the last Parliament, are consider'd. [By Col. Sackville Tufton.] 8vo. [*Brit. Mus.*] London, 1705

Ascribed also to Charles Leslie.

HISTORY (the) of Fairford church, in Gloucestershire. [By Samuel Rudder.] 8vo. No pagination. [*Bodl.*] Cirencester, 1765

HISTORY (the) of Faringdon, and the neighbouring towns & seats in Berkshire. By a society of gentlemen. [By John Stone, organist of Faringdon.] 8vo. Pp. iv. 164. [*Bodl.*] Faringdon, 1798

HISTORY (the) of Father La Chaise, Jesuit, and Confessor to Lewis XIV., present King of France; discovering the secret intrigues by him carried on, as well in the Court of England as in all the Courts of Europe. . . . [By P. Le Noble]; made English from the French original. 12mo. [Arber's *Term Cat.* ii. 616.] London, 1693

HISTORY (a) of Ford Abbey, Dorsetshire, late in the county of Devon. [By Mrs M. Allen.] 12mo. Pp. iv. 98. [Davidson's *Bibl. Devon.* p. 34.] London, 1846

HISTORY (the) of France from the earliest times, to the accession of Louis XVI., with notes critical and explanatory. By John Gifford [John Richards Green]. 4to. 4 vols. [*D.N.B.* vol. 21, p. 305.] London, 1793

HISTORY (a) of France, from the earliest times to the establishment of the Second Empire in 1852. [By W. Henley Jarvis.] 8vo. [*New Coll. Lib.*] London, 1862

HISTORY (a) of France, from the earliest times to 1848. By James White [John Hill Burton]. 8vo. [*D. N. B.* vol. 8, p. 10] Edinburgh, 1859

HISTORY (the) of France, from the first establishment of that monarchy to the present Revolution. [By Rev. Charles Hereford.] 8vo. 3 vols. [Lowndes' *Bibl. Man.*] London, 1790

Attributed also to Rev. John Adams. [Watt's *Bibl. Brit.*]

HISTORY (a) of France, with conversations at the end of each chapter. By Mrs Markham, author of the *History of England* [Mrs Elizabeth Penrose]. 12mo. 2 vols. London, 1827

See the note to her "History of England." See also below, "History of Germany."

HISTORY (the) of Francis-Eugene, Prince of Savoy . . . compiled from the best authorities. By an English officer who served under his Highness in the last war with France [John Banks]. 12mo. [*Brit. Mus.*] London, 1741

A second edition, corrected, was issued in 1742.

HISTORY (the) of Freemasonry, drawn from authentic sources of information; with an account of the Grand Lodge of Scotland, from its institution in 1736, to the present time. . . . [By Sir David Brewster.] 8vo. Pp. xx. 340. [*N. and Q.* May 1863, p. 366.] Edinburgh, 1804

Dedication signed: Alex. Lawrie.

HISTORY of Galloway, from the earliest period; with appendixes. [By Rev. William Mackenzie, of Comrie.] 8vo. 2 vols. [Mitchell and Cash's *Scot. Top.*] Kirkcudbright, 1841

HISTORY of Genghizcan the Great, first Emperor of the antient Moguls and Tartars. By François Petis de la Croix. Translated from the French [by P. Audin]. 12mo. [*Brit. Mus.*] London, 1722

HISTORY of George Godfrey; written by himself. [By Thomas Gaspey.] 12mo. 3 vols. [*Camb. Univ. Lib.*] London, 1828

HISTORY of Germany from the invasion of Germany by Marius to the battle of Leipzic, 1813; on the plan of Mrs Markham's [Mrs Elizabeth Penrose's] histories. [By Robert Bateman Paul, M.A.] 8vo. Pp. xii. 480. [Boase and Courtney's *Bibl. Corn.* ii. 432.] London, 1847

Introduction signed: R. B. P.

HISTORY (a) of Gibraltar and its sieges. [By Frederick George Stephens.] 4to. [*Brit. Mus.*] London, 1870

HISTORY (the) of Gil Blas.—See "The history and adventures of Gil Blas."

HISTORY (the) of Giles Gingerbread. By Tom Trip [Giles Jones]. 8vo. [Cushing's *Init. and Pseud.* i. 287.] New York, 1880

HISTORY (the) of Great and Little Bolton. [By John Brown, of Bolton, a literary worker.] 8vo. Parts 1-17. Pp. 398. Manchester [1825]

No more published.

HISTORY (the) of Great Yarmouth; collected from antient records and other authentic materials. [By Rev. Charles Parkin, M.A.] 8vo. Pp. 416. [*Upcott.*] London, 1776

HISTORY (the) of Greece. [By John Rigaud, B.D.] Published under the direction of the Committee of general literature and education, appointed by the Society for promoting Christian knowledge. 12mo. Pp. iv. 184. [*Bodl.*] London, 1846

HISTORY of Greece; from the earliest records of that country to the time in which it was reduced to a Roman province, for the use of schools and young persons. By Edward Baldwin, author of *The history of Rome*, etc. [William Godwin]. A new edition, revised and improved, with questions, by W. S. Kenny. . . . 12mo. Pp. xii. 222. [Lowndes' *Bibl. Man.* p. 906.] London, 1862

HISTORY of Greece from the earliest times to its final subjection to Rome. [By Arthur Thomas Malkin.] Published under the superintendence of the Society for the diffusion of useful knowledge. 8vo. Pp. 288. [*Nat. Lib. of Scot.*] London, 1829

HISTORY (the) of Gustavus Ericson, king of Sweden; with an introductory history of Sweden, from the middle of the twelfth century. By Henry Augustus Raymond, Esq. [Mrs Sarah Scott]. 8vo. [Brydges' *Cens. Lit.* iv. 266.] London, 1761

HISTORY (the) of Herbert Lake. By the author of *Anne Dysart*, etc. [Christiana Jane Douglas, later Mrs Davies]. 12mo. 3 vols. [*Nat. Lib. of Scot.*] London, 1854

HISTORY (the) of Henry IV., surnamed the Great, King of France and Navarre; written by [Hardouin, de Perefixe] the Bishop of Rodez, and made English by J. D. [John Davies, of Kidwelly]. 8vo. [Arber's *Term Cat.* i. 524.] London, 1672

An earlier edition was published in 1663. The translation has also been attributed to John Dauncy.

HISTORY (the) of hereditary-right; wherein its indefeasibleness, and all other such late doctrines, concerning the absolute power of princes, and the unlimited obedience of subjects are fully and finally determin'd, by the Scripture standard of divine right. [By Robert Fleming, junr.] 8vo. Pp. 156. [Wilson's *Hist. of Diss. Ch.* ii. 483.] London [1711]

Both the preface and the book itself are signed: F. T., being the first letter of Fleming and the last of Robert.

HISTORY (the) of his sacred majesty Charles the II., king of England, Scotland, France, and Ireland, Defender of the faith, etc. Begun from the murder of his royal father of happy memory, and continued to this present year, 1660. By a person of quality [John Dauncy]. 12mo. Pp. 260. [*Bodl.*] London, 1660

Epistle dedicatory signed: I. D.

"Hen. Foulis of Linc. Coll. use to tell me yt John Dauncy of Putney, near London, aged 21, was ye Author of this book."—MS. note in the handwriting of Wood.

HISTORY (the) of Howden Church [in Yorkshire. By James Savage]. 8vo. [Anderson's *Brit. Top.*] Howden, 1799

HISTORY (the) of Huntingdon from the earliest to the present times; with an appendix containing the Charter of Charles I. under which the borough is now governed. [By Robert Carruthers, Master of Huntingdon Grammar School.] 8vo. Pp. ix. 338. [*N. and Q.* Jan. 1866, p. 33.] Huntingdon, 1824

Signed: R. C.

HISTORY (a) of Hurstpierpoint. . . . By a native, a minor [William Smith Ellis]. 12mo. Pp. iv. 74. [*Brit. Mus.*] Brighton, 1837

HISTORY (the) of Hyder Shah, alias Hyder Ali Khan Bahadur; or, new memoirs concerning the East Indies, with historical notes. By M. M. D. L. T. [Monsieur Le Maître de la Tour] . . . Translated from the French. . . . 8vo. [*Calc. Imp. Lib.*] Calcutta, 1848

HISTORY (the) of Ilium or Troy, including the adjacent country, and the opposite coast of the Chersonesus of Thrace. By the author of *Travels in Asia Minor and Greece* [Richard Chandler, D.D.]. 4to. Pp. xvii. 167. [*Camb. Univ. Lib.*] London, 1802

HISTORY (the) of Independency, with the rise, growth, and practices of that powerfull and restlesse faction. [By Clement Walker.] 4to. Pp. 79. [Dexter's *Cong. Bibl.*] 1648

See "Relations and observations," "Anarchia Anglicana," "The High Court of Justice," and the next title.

HISTORY (the) of Independency, with the rise, growth, and practices of that powerfull and restlesse faction. The fourth and last part. Continued from the death of his late majesty, King Charles the First of happy memory, till the deaths of the chief of that Juncto. By T. M. Esquire, a lover of his king and country [Clement Walker]. 4to. Pp. 132. London, 1660

The four parts form "The compleat history of Independency."

HISTORY (the) of infamous imposters; or, the lives and actions of several notorious counterfeits, who, from the most abject and meanest of the people, have usurped the titles of Emperours, Kings, and Princes. [By J. B. de Rocoles.] 8vo. [Arber's *Term Cat.* i. 524.] London, 1682

HISTORY (the) of ingratitude, or a second part of Ancient precedents for modern facts. [By Sir Thomas Burnet, son of Bishop Burnet.] 8vo. Pp. 37. [*Queen's Coll. Cat.* p. 80.] 1712

HISTORY (the) of inland navigations, particularly those of the Duke of Bridgwater and the intended one by Earl Gower. [By James Brindley.] 8vo. [*Brit. Mus.*] London, 1766

HISTORY (the) of Ireland in verse; or, a description of the Western Isle, in eight cantos. By J. K. [William Moffat]. 12mo. [O'Donoghue's *Poets of Ireland.*] Dublin [1750?]

This is a later edition of "Hesperi-nesographia . . ." (1724): see above.

Wrongly attributed to Walter Jones, B.A.

HISTORY (a) of Irish Presbyterians. [By James Seaton Reid, D.D.] 12mo. Belfast, 1811

HISTORY (the) of Isaac Jenkins, and of the sickness of Sarah, his wife, and their three children. [By Thomas Beddoes.] 12mo. [*Brit. Mus.*] Madeley, 1792

HISTORY (the) of Jack Connor. [By Peter Chaigneau.] 12mo. 2 vols. [*N. and Q.* 2 Jan. 1864, p. 11.] Dublin, 1752

HISTORY (the) of Jamaica; a general survey of the antient and modern state of that island: with reflections on its situation, settlements, inhabitants, climate, products, commerce, laws, and government. [By Edward Long.] 4to. 3 vols. [Sabin's *Dictionary.*] London, 1774

HISTORY (the) of James Lovegrove, Esq. [By James Ridley.] 12mo. 2 vols. [Watt's *Bibl. Brit.*; *Mon. Rev.* xxiv. 352.] 1761

HISTORY of Japan, in words of one syllable. By Hazel Shepard [Helen Ainslie Smith]. 8vo. [Cushing's *Init. and Pseud.* ii. 137.] London, 1887

HISTORY (the) of Jemmy and Jenny Jessamy. By the author of *The history of Betsy Thoughtless* [Mrs Eliza Heywood, *née* Fowler]. 12mo. 3 vols. [Watt's *Bibl. Brit.*] London, 1753

HISTORY of Job, in language adapted to children. By the author of *Peep of Day* [Mrs Farell Lee Mortimer]. 12mo. London [1880?]

HISTORY (the) of John Bull and his three sons; written for the amusement and instruction of their numerous families and dependents, and addressed to all the gentle and simple readers in these dominions. By Peter Bullcalf [Joseph Storrs Fry]. 8vo. [Smith's *Cat. of Friends' Books*, i. 820.] London, 1819

HISTORY (the) of John Bull the Clothier. [By the Rev. Jeremy Belknap, D.D.] 8vo. Boston, 1790

HISTORY (the) of John [Churchill], Duke of Marlborough . . . including a more exact narrative of the late war than has ever yet appeared. . . . By the author of the *History of Prince Eugene* [John Banks]. 12mo. London, 1741

HISTORY (the) of John Gilpin, how he went farther than he intended, and came home safe at last. [A ballad. By William Cowper.] 16mo. Pp. 16. [*Brit. Mus.*] London [1784]

Other anonymous editions were entitled "The diverting history of John Gilpin . . ."; "Gilpin's rig . . ."; "John Gilpin's journey . . ."; and "The journey of John Gilpin . . ."

HISTORY (the) of John Juniper, Esq., alias Juniper Jack; containing the birth, parentage, and education, life, adventures, and character of that most wonderful and surprizing gentleman. By the editor of *The adventures of a guinea* [Charles Johnston]. 12mo. 3 vols. London, 1781

HISTORY (the) of Johnny Quae Genus, the little foundling of the late Dr Syntax; a poem. By the author of the *Three tours* [William Combe]. 8vo. Pp. 259. [*Brit. Mus.*] London, 1822

HISTORY (the) of Joseph; a poem, in eight books. By the author of *Friendship in death* [Mrs Elizabeth Rowe, *née* Singer]. 8vo. Pp. 82. London, 1736

HISTORY (the) of Joseph consider'd; or, the moral philosopher vindicated against Mr Samuel Chandler's Defence of the prime ministry and character of Joseph: occasionally interspersed with moral reflexions on important subjects. By Mencius Philalethes [Peter Annet]. 8vo. Pp. iv. 118. [Lowndes' *Bibl. Man.* p. 48.] London, 1744

HISTORY (the) of Joseph in verse; in six dialogues. [By John Ryland.] 12mo. [Whitley's *Bapt. Bibl.*] London, 1824

HISTORY (the) of Joseph; or, a continuation of *Scripture stories.* [By Helen Plumptre.] Second edition. 12mo. Pp. viii. 239. [*Brit. Mus.*] London, 1822

HISTORY of Joshua . . ., a continuation of *Scripture stories.* [By Helen Plumptre.] 12mo. [*Brit. Mus.*] London, 1848

HISTORY (the) of Josiah. By the author of *Gideon* [Lady Harriet Howard]. 8vo. [*Brit. Mus.*] London, 1842

HISTORY of Julius Cæsar. [By Napoleon III., Emperor of the French. Translated by T. Wright.] 8vo. 2 vols. [*Ryland's Lib. Cat.*] London [1865-6]

HISTORY of Kamtschatka, and the Kurilski Islands [by Stepan P. Krascheninnikoff]; translated from the Russian by James Grieve. 4to. [Edwards' *Cat.*] Glocester, 1764

HISTORY of Keighley, past and present . . . [By Richard Holmes.] 8vo. York, 1858

HISTORY (the) of King William the Third. [By Abel Boyer.] 8vo. 3 vols. [*Brit. Mus.*] London, 1702

HISTORY (the) of Kington. By a member of the Mechanics' Institute [Richard Parry]. 8vo. Kington, 1845

HISTORY (the) of Lady Julia Mandeville. By the translator of Lady Catesby's letters [Frances Brooke, *née* Moore]. Third edition. 12mo. 2 vols. [Watt's *Bibl. Brit.*] Dublin, 1775

HISTORY of Leicester, from the time of the Romans to the end of the seventeenth century. [By James Thomson.] 8vo. Leicester, 1859

HISTORY (the) of Leonora Meadowson. By the author of *Betsy Thoughtless* [Mrs Eliza Heywood]. 12mo. 2 vols. London, 1788

HISTORY (the) of Liberton. [By Rev. George M'Guffie, Presbyterian minister at Etal, in Northumberland.] 12mo. Edinburgh [1860]

HISTORY (the) of Lincoln; containing an account of the antiquities, edifices, trade, and customs of that ancient city. . . . [By Edward James Willson.] 4to. [*D. N. B.* vol. 62, p. 53.] Lincoln, 1816

HISTORY (the) of Lincoln; with an appendix, containing a list of the members returned to serve in Parliament, as also of the mayors and sheriffs of the city. [By Adam Stark.] 12mo. Lincoln, 1810

HISTORY (the) of little Davy's new hat. By R. B. [Robert Bloomfield]. 12mo. [*Brit. Mus.*] London, 1815

Other editions give the author's full name.

HISTORY (the) of little Henry and his bearer. [By Mary Martha Butt, later Mrs Sherwood.] 12mo. [*Brit. Mus.*] London, 1832

HISTORY (the) of Liverpool from the earliest authenticated period down to the present time. . . . [By John Corry.] 4to. [O'Donoghue's *Poets of Ireland.*] Liverpool, 1810

HISTORY of London and its environs. . . . [By John Stockdale.] 4to. London, 1796-8

Published in parts, issued at intervals.

HISTORY (the) of Lothian Road United Free Church congregation. [Preface signed: A. H. M. *i.e.* Alexander H. Mitchell.] 8vo. Pp. viii. 208. [*New Coll. Lib.*] Edinburgh, 1911

HISTORY (the) of Lucy Clare. . . . By the author of *Susan Gray*, etc. [Mary Martha Butt, later Mrs Sherwood]. 12mo. Wellington [Salop], 1815

See also "Lucy Clare; and the babes in the basket." (Edinburgh, 1882.)

HISTORY (a) of Madeira; with a series of twenty-seven coloured engravings, illustrative of the costumes, manners, and occupations of the inhabitants of that island. [By William Combe?] Fol. Pp. v. 118. [*Gent. Mag.* 1852, p. 467.] London, 1821

HISTORY (the) of magic; including a clear and concise exposition of its procedure, its rites, and its mysteries. By Elphias Lévi [Alphonse Louis Constant]; translated from the French by A. E. Waite. 8vo. Pp. 572. [*Brit. Mus.*] London, 1913

HISTORY (the) of Manon Lescaut and the Chevalier de Grieux. [By Antoine F. Prevost d'Exiles.] Translated from the French. 12mo. [Watt's *Bibl. Brit.*] Dublin, 1767

HISTORY (the) of maritime and inland discovery. [By William Desborough Cooley.] 8vo. 3 vols. [M'Culloch's *Lit. of Pol. Econ.* p. 151.] London, 1830

Lardner's *Cabinet Cyclopædia.*

HISTORY (the) of Martin; being a proper sequel to "The tale of a tub": with a digression concerning the nature, usefulness, and necessity of wars and quarrels. By the Rev. D—n S—t [Jonathan Swift, D.D.]. To which is added, a dialogue between A— P—e, Esq.; and Mr C—s C—ffe, poets, in St James's Park. 8vo. Pp. 24. London, 1742

HISTORY (the) of Mary Prince, a West Indian slave. [By George Pringle.] 8vo. Pp. 44. London, 1831

HISTORY (the) of Matthew Wald. [By John Gibson Lockhart.] 8vo. Pp. 386. [*Nat. Lib. of Scot.*] Edinburgh, 1824

HISTORY (the) of Mecklenburgh, from the first settlement of the Vandals in that country to the present time; including a period of about three thousand years. [By Mrs Sarah Scott.] 8vo. [Brydges' *Cens. Lit.* iv. 292.] London, 1762

HISTORY (the) of Michael Kemp, the happy farmer's lad. [By Anne Woodrooffe.] 12mo. [Green's *Bibl. Somers.* i. 587.] Bath, 1819

HISTORY (the) of Miss Betsy Thoughtless. [By Mrs Eliza Heywood.] 12mo. 4 vols. [Watt's *Bibl. Brit.*] London, 1751

HISTORY (the) of Miss Clarinda Cathcart, and Miss Fanny Renton. [By Mrs Jane Marshall.] 12mo. 2 vols. [Baker's *Biog. Dram.*] London, 1765

HISTORY (the) of Miss Sally Sable. By the author of *Memoirs of a Scotch family* [Mrs Woodfin]. 12mo. 2 vols. [Watt's *Bibl. Brit.*] London, 1757

HISTORY (the) of missions in China. [By Sarah Tuttle.] 8vo. Boston, 1841

HISTORY (the) of moderation; or, the life, death and resurrection of moderation: together with her nativity, country, pedigree, kindred, character, friends, and also her enemies. Written by Hesychius Pamphilus, and now faithfully translated out of the original. [By Richard Brathwayt.] 8vo. Pp. 143. [*Bodl.*] London, 1669

Dedication and Epistle to the reader signed: N. S. The work has been declared "a pretended translation from the work of an imaginary author."

HISTORY (the) of modern Europe; with an account of the decline and fall of the Roman Empire, and a view of the progress of society from the 5th to the 18th century: in a series of letters from a nobleman to his son. [By William Russell, LL.D.] 8vo. 2 vols. London, 1779

Pt. ii., 1648-1763, 8vo, 3 vols., appeared under Dr Russell's name in 1784. He projected a third part (1763-83) but did not complete it. The work has been frequently reprinted, with continuations.

HISTORY (the) of Montanism. By a lay-gentleman [Francis Lee, M.D.]. 8vo. [Darling's *Cyclop. Bibl.; D. N. B.* vol. 32, p. 352.] London, 1709

Part (pp. 73-352) of a work which bears the title—"The spirit of enthusiasm exorcised: in a sermon preach'd before the university of Oxford, &c. The fourth edition, much enlarg'd. By George Hickes, D.D. With two discourses occasioned by the New Prophets pretensions to inspiration and miracles: the first, the History of Montanism, by a lay-gentleman; the other, the new pretenders to prophecy examin'd. By N. Spinckes, a presbyter of the Church of England. London, 1709," 8vo.

HISTORY (the) of Mother Shipton; containing an account of her strange and unnatural conception, her birth, life, actions and death; the correspondence she held with the devil, and many strange and wonderful things perform'd by her: together with all the predictions and prophecies that have been made by her, and since fulfilled from the reign of King Henry the VII. to the third year of the late deceased sovereign lady Queen Ann. . . . [By Richard Head.] Pp. 20. [*Bodl.*] N.P., N.D.

See also "The life and death of Mother Shipton."

HISTORY (the) of Mr John Welsh, minister of the gospel at Aire. [By James Kirkton, minister at Edinburgh.] 4to. Pp. 34. [Wodrow's *Correspondence*, iii. 175.] Edinburgh, 1703

HISTORY (the) of Mr Loveill; a novel. [By Sir John Hill, M.D.] 8vo. London [1760?]

HISTORY (an) of Muhammedanism; comprising the life and character of the Arabian prophet. . . . [By Charles Mills.] 8vo. [*Calc. Imp. Lib.*] London, 1817

HISTORY (the) of my pets. By Grace Greenwood [Sarah Jane Clarke, later Mrs Lippincott]. 8vo. Pp. 84. London, 1853

Reprinted at New York, 1890.

HISTORY (the) of Napoleon. . . . By Richard Henry (or Hengist) Horne [assisted by Miss Mary Gillies]. 8vo. 2 vols. London, 1841

HISTORY (the) of Napoleon Buonaparte. [By John Gibson Lockhart.] With engravings on steel and wood. 8vo. 2 vols. [*Nat. Lib. of Scot.*] London, 1829

HISTORY (the) of Ned Evans; a tale of the times. [By Mrs Jane West.] 8vo. 2 vols. Dublin [1796]

HISTORY (a) of New England, from the English planting in the yeere 1628, until the yeere 1652; declaring the forme of their government, civill, military, and ecclesiastique; their wars with the Indians, their troubles with the Gortonists, and other heretiques; their manner of gathering of churches, the commodities of the country, and description of the principall towns and havens, with the great encouragements to increase trade betwixt them and old England. . . . [By Capt. Edward Johnson.] 4to. Pp. 245. [*Bodl.*] London, 1654

The address to the reader is signed: T. H. Wrongly attributed to Sir F. Gorges.

HISTORY (the) of New South Wales. [By J. O'Hara.] 8vo. [*Brit. Mus.*] London, 1817

HISTORY (a) of New York, from the beginning of the world to the end of the Dutch dynasty; containing, among many surprising and curious matters, the unutterable ponderings of Walter the Doubter, the disastrous projects of William the Testy, and the chivalric achievements of Peter the Headstrong, the three Dutch governors of New Amsterdam; being the only authentic history of the times that ever hath been published. By Diedrich Knickerbocker, author of *The Sketch Book* [Washington Irving]. A new edition. 8vo. Pp. 520. London, 1820

HISTORY of nonconformity in Warminster. [Dedication signed: H. M. G. *i.e.* Henry Mayo Gunn.] 8vo. Pp. 68. [*Olphar Hamst*, p. 59.] London, 1853

HISTORY (a) of North-Allerton, in the county of York. . . . [By Thomas Langdale.] Second edition. 12mo. Northallerton, 1813

HISTORY (the) of Nourjahad. By the editor of *Sidney Bidulph* [Mrs Frances Sheridan, *née* Chamberlaine]. 8vo. Pp. 244. [Baker's *Biog. Dram.*] London, 1767

HISTORY (the) of Oliver Cromwel; being an impartial account of all the battles, sieges, and other military atchievements, wherein he was ingaged, in England, Scotland and Ireland; and likewise, of his civil administrations while he had the supream government of these three kingdoms, till his death, relating only matters of fact, without reflection or observation. By R. B. [Richard Burton, really Nathaniel Crouch]. 12mo. Pp. 180. [*Bodl.*] London, 1692

HISTORY (the) of Ophelia. Published by the author of *David Simple* [Sarah Fielding]. 12mo. 2 vols. London, 1760

HISTORY (the) of oracles, and the cheats of the Pagan priest [by Bernard Le Bovier de Fontonelle]; made English, in two parts. [Signed: A. B. *i.e.* Mrs Aphra Behn.] 12mo. London, 1688

For a reply, see above, "An answer to Mr de Fontonelle's history. . . ."

HISTORY (the) of Oswestry from the earliest period; its antiquities and customs; with a short account of the neighbourhood; collected from various authors, with much original information. [By William Price.] 8vo. [*Upcott*, iii. 1143.] Oswestry [1815]

HISTORY (the) of our B. Lady of Loreto. [Translated from the Latin of O. Torsellino by T. P. *i.e.* Thomas Price.] 8vo. [*Brit. Mus.*] London, 1608

HISTORY (the) of our customs, aids, subsidies, national debts, and taxes, from William the Conqueror, to the present year 1761. Part I. [-IV.] [By Timothy Cunningham.] 8vo. London, 1761

The third edition (1778) has the author's name.

HISTORY (the) of our national debts and taxes, from the year 1688 to the present year 1751. [By George Gordon.] 8vo. 4 parts. [Harding's *Cat.*] London, 1751-3

HISTORY of our own times. By the author of *The court and times of Frederick the Great* [Thomas Campbell, the poet]. 12mo. 2 vols. [Corns and Sparkes' *Unf. Books*, p. 45.] London, 1843

HISTORY (the) of our Reserve Forces, with suggestions for their organisation as a real Army of Reserve. . . . By a Militia Officer [George Alfred Raikes]. 8vo. [*Brit. Mus.*] London, 1870

HISTORY (the) of our Saviour Jesus Christ, related in the words of Scripture; containing, in order of time, all the events and discourses recorded in the four evangelists: with some short notes for the help of ordinary readers. [By John Locke.] 8vo. [*Crit. Rev.* lv. 474.] London, 1705

HISTORY (the) of Paddy Blake and Kathleen O'More; a tale [with songs and poems interspersed]. By a country gentleman [Edward Houston Caulfield]. 8vo. [O'Donoghue's *Poets of Ireland.*] Dungannon, 1847

HISTORY (a) of paper; its genesis and its revelations. [By Joseph E. A. Smith.] 4to. Holyoke, U.S.A., 1882

HISTORY (the) of Parismus, Prince of Bohemia . . . to which is added, The adventures and travels of Parismenos. [By Emanuel Forde.] 12mo. [*Brit. Mus.*] London [1790?]

Earlier editions bear different titles: "Of the famous and pleasant history of Parismus . . ." (1680?); "The famous and pleasant history of Parismus" (1680); "The most famous . . . history of Parismus" (1696).

HISTORY (the) of passive obedience since the Reformation. [By Abednego Seller.] 4to. Pp. 147. [*Bodl.*] Amsterdam, 1689

This was followed by "A continuation of the History. . . ."

HISTORY (a) of Penrith. [By J. Walker.] 8vo. Pp. viii. 235. [*Brit. Mus.*] Penrith, 1858

HISTORY (a) of pews . . . with an appendix containing a report on the statistics of pews. [By John Mason Neale, D.D.] Third edition. 8vo. Pp. viii. 103. [*D. N. B.*, vol. 40, p. 146.] Cambridge, 1843

HISTORY (a) of Philadelphia; with a notice of the villages in the vicinity. . . . [By Daniel Bowen.] 8vo. [Cushing's *Anon.*] Philadelphia, 1839

HISTORY (the) of Pithole. By "Crocus" [Charles C. Leonard]. 8vo. Pp. 106. [Cushing's *Init. and Pseud.* i. 71.] Pithole City, Penn., 1867

HISTORY (the) of Poland. [By Samuel Astley Dunham.] 8vo. Pp. xix. 324. [*Brit. Mus.*] London, 1831

HISTORY (the) of Poland, from its origin as a nation to the commencement of the year 1795; to which is prefixed, an accurate account of the geography and government of that country, and the customs and manners of its inhabitants. [By Stephen Jones.] Pp. vii. 518. [Watt's *Bibl. Brit.*] Dublin, 1795

HISTORY (the) of Polindor and Flostella; with other poems. By J. H. [Sir John Harington]. 8vo. [Green's *Bibl. Somers.* ii. 469.] London, 1651

HISTORY (the) of Polybius, the Megalopolitan; containing a general account of the transactions of the world and principally of the Roman people during the first and second Punick wars, etc. Translated by Sir H. S. [Henry Shears]. To which is added, a Character of Polybius and his writings, by Mr Dryden. 8vo. 3 vols. [*W.*] London, 1693-8

HISTORY (the) of Pompey the Little; or, the life and adventures of a lap-dog. [By Francis Coventry.] 12mo. [Green's *Bibl. Somers.* i. 126.] London, 1751

HISTORY (the) of Popedom; containing the rise, progress, and decay thereof. . . . By Samuel von Pufendorf. Translated into English by J. C. [John Chamberlayne]. 8vo. [*Camb. Univ. Lib.*] London, 1691

HISTORY (the) of Prince Titi; a royal allegory. Translated [from the French of H. Cordonnier de Saint-Hyacinthe] by a Lady [the Hon. Mrs Eliza Stanley]. 12mo. [Barbier's *Dictionnaire;* Quaritch's *Cat.*] London, 1736

This was followed by "Ismenia and the Prince," and next by "Pausanias and Aurora."

HISTORY (the) of progress in Great Britain. By the author of *Enquire within* [Robert Kemp Philp]. 8vo. 2 vols. [*Brit. Mus.*] London, 1866

HISTORY (the) of Pudica [Miss Sotherton], a lady of N—rf—lk; with an account of her five lovers; viz. Dick Merryfellow, Count Antiquary [Mr Earle], Young Squire Fog [Mr Hare, Jun.], of Dumplin-Hall, Jack Shadwell of the Lodge [Mr Buxton], and Miles Dinglebob, of Popgun-hall, Esq. [Mr Branthwait]; together with Miss Pudica's sense of the word Eclaircissement, and an epithalamium on her nuptials, by Tom Tenor, clerk of the parish. To the tune of "Green grow the rushes o'." By William Honeycomb, Esq. [Richard Gardiner]. 8vo. Pp. 99. [*Memoirs of Richard Gardiner*, p. 22; *Lond. Lib. Cat.*] London, 1754

HISTORY (the) of religion. By an impartial hand [Rev. James Murray]. 8vo. 4 vols. [Lowndes' *Bibl. Man.* p. 2070.] London, 1764

HISTORY (the) of religion, as it has been managed by priestcraft. By a person of quality [Sir Robert Howard]. 12mo. Pp. xxiii. 120. [Watt's *Bibl. Brit.*] London, 1694

HISTORY of revivals of religion in the British isles, especially in Scotland. By the author of the *Memoir of the Rev. M. Bruen* [Mrs Mary Grey Lundie Duncan]. 8vo. Pp. ii. 406. [*New Coll. Lib.*] Edinburgh, 1836

HISTORY (the) of Rhedi, the hermit of Mount Ararat; an oriental tale. [By Rev. Wm. Duff, M.A.] 12mo. [*Calc. Imp. Lib.*] London, 1773

HISTORY (the) of Richard Potter, a sailor and prisoner in Newgate, tried at the Old Baily . . . sentenced to death for attempting to receive 30 sh. prize money due to another. [By Alexander Cruden.] 12mo. [Watt's *Bibl. Brit.*] London, 1763

HISTORY (the) of Richmond, in the County of York; including a description of the Castle, Friary, Easeby-Abbey, and other remains of antiquity in the neighbourhood. [By Christopher Clarkson.] 12mo. Pp. 436. Richmond, 1814

A later edition (1821) bears the author's name.

HISTORY (the) of Rock County, Wisconsin . . . also, History of Wisconsin. [By C. Willshire Butterfield.] 8vo. Pp. iv. 897. Chicago, 1879

HISTORY of Rome. [By David Masson, LL.D.] 8vo. [*D. N. B.* Second Supp. vol. 2, p. 585.] Edinburgh, 1848

Chambers's Educational Course.

HISTORY of Rome. [By Robert Bell.] 8vo. 2 vols. London, 1833-5

Lardner's *Cabinet Cyclopædia.*

HISTORY of Rome, from the building of the city to the ruin of the republic; for the use of schools and young persons. By Edward Baldwin [William Godwin], author of *The history of Greece*, etc. 12mo. London, 1809

HISTORY (the) of Rome, from the foundation of the city by Romulus, to the death of Marcus Antoninus. . . . By the author of the *History of France* [Rev. Charles Hereford]. 8vo. [Lowndes' *Bibl. Man.*] London, 1792

Ascribed also to Rev. John Adams. [Watt's *Bibl. Brit.*]

HISTORY (a) of Russia. [By Robert Bell.] 12mo. 3 vols. [*Brit. Mus.*] London, 1835-8

Lardner's *Cabinet Cyclopædia.*

HISTORY of Russia, in words of one syllable. By Hazel Shepard [Helen Ainslie Smith]. 8vo. [Cushing's *Init. and Pseud.* ii. 137.] London, 1887

HISTORY (the) of St Andrews. [By William Barclay David Donald Turnbull. Reprinted from the *Dublin Review.*] 8vo. Pp. 16. N.P. [1844]

HISTORY (the) of St Dominic; with a sketch of the Dominican Order. [By Augusta Theodosia Drane.] 8vo. [*Brit. Mus.*] London, 1857

HISTORY (the) of S. Elizabeth, daughter of the King of Hungary; according to sundry authours who have authentically written her life. . . . By H. A. [Henry Hawkins, S.J.]. 12mo. [*Brit. Mus.*] [Paris] 1632

HISTORY (a) of Sammy's bed, not of down, nor a turn down, though it turned out down at last. Drawn by himself [Charles Hawker, of the Ordnance Office]. 8vo. [*W.*] London, 1857

HISTORY (the) of Sandford and Merton; a work intended for the use of children. [By Thomas Day.] The fifth edition, corrected. 12mo. 3 vols. London, 1710

HISTORY (the) of Scotch-presbytery; being an epitome of *The hind let loose* by Mr Shields. With a preface by a presbyter of the Church of Scotland [Alexander Monro, D.D.]. 4to. Pp. 55. London, 1697

HISTORY (the) of Scotland and Ireland. By R. B. [Richard Burton, really Nathaniel Crouch]. 12mo. London, 1685

On the authorship see the note to "Admirable curiosities."

HISTORY of Scotland, from Fergus to the Union; to which is added an account of the Rebellion in 1715. By J. W. [James Wallace, M.D.]. 8vo. [*Nat. Lib. of Scot.*] Dublin, 1724

HISTORY (a) of shipwrecks and disasters at sea, from the most authentic source. [Translated from the French of J. de Perthes.] 18mo. 2 vols. [Sabin's *Dictionary.*] London, 1833

HISTORY (a) of Shrewsbury. [By Hugh Owen and J. B. Blakeway.] 4to. 2 vols. [Gross's *Sources of English History.*] London, 1825

HISTORY (the) of sign-boards, from the earliest times to the present day. By Jacob Larwood [H. D. J. van Schevichaven] and John Camden Hotten. 8vo. Pp. xii. 536. [*N. and Q.* 4th Dec. 1920.] London, 1866

"Larwood" has been attributed to L. R. Sadler and to L. R. Wood.

Another edition was issued in 1900.

HISTORY (the) of sin and heresie attempted; from the first war that they rais'd in heaven, through their various successes and progress upon earth; to the final victory over them, and their eternal condemnation in hell. . . . [By Charles Leslie.] 4to. Pp. 60. [Smith's *Anti-Quak.* p. 271.] London, 1698

HISTORY (the) of Sir Charles Grandison, in a series of letters published from the originals, by the editor of *Pamela* and *Clarissa* [Samuel Richardson]; to the last of which is added, an historical and characteristical index. . . . 12mo. 7 vols. London, 1754

HISTORY (the) of Sr. Francis Drake, exprest by instrumentall and vocall musick, and by art of perspective in scenes, etc. The first part; represented daily at the cockpit in Drury-Lane at three after-noon punctually. [By Sir William Davenant.] 4to. Pp. 39. [*Brit. Mus.*] London, 1659

HISTORY (the) of Sir George Ellison. [By Sarah Scott.] 12mo. 2 vols. [Brydges' *Cens. Lit.* iv. 292.] London, 1766

HISTORY (the) of Sir John Perrott, Knight of the Bath, and Lord Lieutenant of Ireland. [Published from the original MS., written about the latter end of the reign of Q. Elizabeth, by Richard Rawlinson.] 8vo. [*W.*] London, 1728

HISTORY (the) of Sir Richard Calmady. [A novel.] By Lucas Malet [Mrs St Leger Harrison, *née* Mary Kingsley]. 8vo. [*Lit. Year Book.*] London, 1901

HISTORY (the) of Sir Thomas Thumb. By the author of *The heir of Redclyffe*, etc. [Charlotte Mary Yonge]. 8vo. Edinburgh, 1855

HISTORY (the) of Sir William Harrington; written some years since [by Thomas Hull], and revised and corrected by the late Mr Richardson: now first published. 12mo. 4 vols. [*Brit. Mus.*] London, 1771

Another edition was published in 1797.

HISTORY (the) of Spain and Portugal. [By Samuel Astley Dunham, LL.D.] 8vo. 5 vols. [*Brit. Mus.*] London, 1832-3

Lardner's *Cabinet Cyclopædia.*

HISTORY (the) of Spain and Portugal, from B.C. 1000 to A.D. 1814. [By Mrs William Busk.] [*Brit. Mus.*] 12mo. London, 1833

HISTORY (the) of Spain, from the establishment of the colony of Gades by the Phœnicians, to the death of Ferdinand, surnamed the Sage. By the author of the *History of France* [Rev. Charles Hereford]. 8vo. 3 vols. [Lowndes' *Bibl. Man.*] London, 1793

Ascribed also to Rev. J. Adams. [Watt's *Bibl. Brit.*]

HISTORY (the) of Sunday. By the author of *Time and faith* [William E. Hickson]. 8vo. [*D. N. B.* vol. 26, p. 362.] London [1857]

HISTORY (the) of Susan Gray, as related by a clergyman, and designed for the benefit of young women when going on service. [By Mrs Mary Martha Sherwood, *née* Butt.] 12mo. [Courtney's *Secrets*, p. 51.] London, 1802

HISTORY (the) of Switzerland. [By Thomas Colley Grattan.] 8vo. [*D. N. B.* vol. 22, p. 426.] London, 1825

HISTORY (the) of Switzerland. [By John Wilson.] 12mo. [*W.*] London, 1832

Lardner's *Cabinet Cyclopædia.*

HISTORY (the) of that famous preacher, Friar Gerund de Campazos, otherwise Gerund Zotes. [By Father Joseph Francis de l'Isla.] Translated from the Spanish [by Thomas Nugent, LL.D.]. 8vo. 2 vols. London, 1772

Written to cast ridicule on the itinerant Spanish preachers.

HISTORY (the) of the Abbey Church of St Peter's, Westminster, its antiquities and monuments. [By R. Ackerman.] 4to. 2 vols. London, 1812

Attributed also to William Combe.

HISTORY (the) of the abbey, palace, and chapel-royal of Holyrood house; including a description of the buildings as they now exist. . . . Second edition. [By Charles Mackie.] 8vo. Pp. 118. Edinburgh, 1821

HISTORY (the) of the administration of Cardinal Ximenes, great Minister of State in Spain. [By M. Baudier.] 8vo. [Arber's *Term Cat.* i. 524.] London, 1670

HISTORY (the) of the adventures of Arthur O'Bradley. [By John Potter, musician.] 12mo. 2 vols. [*Brit. Mus.*] London, 1769

HISTORY (the) of the adventures of Joseph Andrews and his friend Mr Abraham Adams; written in imitation of the manner of Cervantes. [By Henry Fielding.] Second edition, revised and corrected. 12mo. 2 vols. [*Brit. Mus.*] London, 1742

In a few editions, the title is abbreviated, as "The history of Joseph Andrews."

HISTORY (a) of the American mission to the Pawnee Indians. . . . [By Sarah Tuttle.] 8vo. [Cushing's *Anon.*] Boston, 1839

HISTORY (a) of the American Revolution. [By Rev. William Shepherd.] 8vo. [*Brit. Mus.*] London [1830]

Library of Useful Knowledge.

HISTORY (a) of the ancient and present state of the town of Liverpool. [By T. Wallace.] 8vo. London, 1795

HISTORY (a) of the ancient town of Shaftesbury, from the founder, Alfred the Great; partly selected from Tutchins. . . . [By Thomas Adams.] 8vo. [Mayo's *Bibl. Dors.*] Sherborne [1808]

HISTORY (the) of the antient town of Cirencester, in two parts; illustrated with plates. [By Samuel Rudder, printer.] Second edition. 8vo. [Hyatt and Bazeley's *Bibl. of Gloucest. Lit.*] Cirencester, 1800

Another edition was issued in 1842.

HISTORY (the) of the Apostles Creed; with critical observations on its several articles. Second edition. [By Peter King, Lord Chancellor, Baron Ockham.] 8vo. Pp. 415. [*D. N. B.* vol. 31, p. 144.] London, 1703

HISTORY (a) of the art of engraving in mezzotinto, from its origin to the present times, including an account of the works of the earliest artists. [By James Chelsum, D.D.] 12mo. [Lowndes' *Bibl. Man.*] Winchester, 1786

HISTORY (the) of the art of printing, containing an account of its invention and progress in Europe . . . and a preface by the publisher [James Watson. Translated from the French of Jean de la Caille]. 8vo. Pp. 24, xlviii. 64. [W. J. Couper's *Watson's preface.*] Edinburgh, 1713

HISTORY (the) of the Athenian Society, for the resolving all nice and curious questions. By a gentleman who got secret intelligence of their whole proceedings. By L. R. [Charles Gildon]. . . . Fol. [*Camb. Univ. Lib.*] London [1693?]

HISTORY of the Azores, or Western Islands; containing an account of the government, laws, and religion, the manners, ceremonies, and character of the inhabitants, and demonstrating the importance of these valuable Islands to the British Empire. [Signed: T. A., Captain Light Dragoons, *i.e.* Capt. Thomas Ashe.] 4to. [*N. and Q.* Oct. 1868, p. 341.] London, 1813

HISTORY (the) of the Bastile; with a concise account of the late Revolution in France. . . . [By Quintin Craufurd.] 8vo. [*D. N. B.* vol. 13, p. 90.] London, 1798

HISTORY of the Basutus of South Africa. By the Special Commissioner of the Cape Argus [Joseph Miller Orpen]. 12mo. Cape Town, 1857

HISTORY (the) of the Bible; translated from the French [of David Martin] by R. G. [Richard Gough] jnr. in 1746. Fol. Pp. 612. [Martin's *Cat.*] London, 1747

HISTORY (the) of the Bohemian persecutions, from the beginning of their conversion to Christianity in the year 894 to the year 1632, Ferdinand the 2 of Austria, reigning. . . . [By Joh. Amos Comenius.] 12mo. Pp. 385. London, 1650

A translation from the similarly anonymous Latin original issued in 1648. "Comenius" is a Latinized form of Komensky.

HISTORY (a) of the Boston Dispensary. Compiled by one of the Board of Managers [William Richards Lawrence, M.D.]. 8vo. [Cushing's *Init. and Pseud.* i. 216.] Boston, 1859

HISTORY (the) of the Buccaneers of America. . . . New edition, with some introductory notices of piracies on the coast of New England to . . . 1724. [By Alexander Olivier Exquemelin. With an introduction by Samuel G. Drake.] 8vo. [*Brit. Mus.*] Boston, 1853

Many other editions bear the author's name.

HISTORY (the) of the Buchan railway contest. By Peter Caput [R. Grant]. 8vo. Aberdeen, 1858

HISTORY (the) of the campagnes in 1548 and 1549; being an exact account of the martial expeditions perform'd in those days by the Scots and French on the one side, and by the English and their foreign auxiliaries on the other. Done in French, under the title of, The Scots war, etc. by Monsieur Beague [*sic*], a French gentleman. Printed at Paris in the year 1556. With an introductory preface by the translator [Patrick Abercromby]. 8vo. Pp. lxxi. 128. [Watt's *Bibl. Brit.*] 1707

"The Preface was written by Mr Crawford, our historiographer, now dead. The translator lies in saying it was his owne, but poor Crawford was dead."—MS. note in Dr David Laing's copy.

HISTORY of the campaign of the British, Dutch, Hanoverian, and Brunswick armies under the Duke of Wellington. . . . By C. de M. [Carl de Müffling]. 8vo. [*Brit. Mus.*] London, 1816

HISTORY (the) of the Caribby-Islands, viz. Barbados, St Christophers, St Vincents, Martinico, Dominico, Barbouthos, Monserrat, Mevis, Antego, etc. in all xxviii. In two books, the first containing the natural, the second the moral history of those islands. . . . With a Caribbean-vocabulary. [By Charles Cæsar de Rochefort.] Rendered into English by John Davies of Kidwelly. Fol. Pp. 376. [Barbier's *Dictionnaire.*] London, 1666

Abeille says the true author is Louis de Poincy.

HISTORY (the) of the castle and town of Knaresbrough; with remarks on Spofforth, Rippon, Aldborough, Boroughbridge, Ribston, etc. [By Ely Hargrove.] 8vo. [Anderson's *Brit. Top.*] Knaresbrough, 1769

The third edition, published in 1782, has the author's name.

HISTORY (the) of the Cathedral Church of Durham. [By Christopher Hunter.] Second edition. 12mo. [*Brit. Mus.*] Durham [1733]

HISTORY (the) of the Chancery; relating to the judicial power of that court, and the rights of the masters. [By Samuel Burroughs.] 12mo. [*Brit. Mus.*] London, 1726

HISTORY (a) of the Christian Church, from the first till the nineteenth century. [By William Sime.] 12mo. [*New Coll. Lib.*] Edinburgh, 1829

HISTORY of the Christmas festival, the new year, and their peculiar customs. [By George Newcomb.] 12mo. Pp. 72. [*Bodl.*] Westminster, 1843

Presentation copy from the author.

HISTORY of the church and parish of St Cuthbert, or West Kirk of Edinburgh. By the author of the *Histories of the Reformation, Christian Church,* etc. [William Sime]. 12mo. [*Nat. Lib. of Scot.*] Edinburgh, 1829

HISTORY (the) of the Church from the beginning of the world to A.D. 1718; compendiously written by Lewis Ellis Dupin. Translated [by Thomas Fenton], according to the third Paris edition, revised, enlarged, and put into a new method by the author. Third edition. 12mo. 4 vols. [*Brit. Mus.*] London, 1724

HISTORY (the) of the Church, in respect both to its ancient and present condition: to which is added, a continuation of the same. . . . By one called an High-Churchman [Charles Leslie]. 4to. [*Brit. Mus.*] London, 1706

HISTORY of the Church of Christ, previous to the Reformation . . . chiefly . . . during the Early and Middle Ages. [Based on the work of Joseph and Isaac Milner, by George Stokes, who added notes and recast vol. 6.] 8vo. 6 vols. London [1833?]

HISTORY (the) of the Church of Crosthwaite, in Cumberland. [By Henry Manders.] 8vo. London, 1853

HISTORY (the) of the Church of Great Britain, from the birth of our Saviour until the year of our Lord, 1667; with an exact succession of the Bishops, and the memorable acts of many of them: together with an addition of all the English Cardinals, and the several orders of the English monks, friars, and nuns, in former ages. [By William Geaves.] 4to. Pp. 457. [*Bodl.*] London, 1675

Ascribed also to George Geeves and to William Gearing.

HISTORY (the) of the Church of Japan; written originally in French by M. l'abbé de Talon [Jean Crasset] and now translated into English by N. N. [—— Webb]. 4to. 2 vols. [*Camb. Univ. Lib.*] London, 1705-7

HISTORY (a) of the Church of St Mary the Virgin [in Oxford], from Domesday to the installation of the late Duke of Wellington, Chancellor of the University. [By Edmund S. Ffoulkes.] 8vo. Oxford, 1892

HISTORY of the church, parish, and manor of Howden. [By Thomas Clarke.] 8vo. Pp. 88. [Boyne's *Yorkshire Library*, p. 171.] Howden, 1850

HISTORY (a) of the churches in England and Scotland, from the Reformation to this present time. By a clergyman [James Murray]. 8vo. 3 vols. [*Sig. Lib.*] Newcastle-upon-Tyne, 1771

HISTORY of the churches of New Bedford. [By Jessie Fillmore Kelley.] 8vo. New Bedford, 1869

HISTORY of the city of Aberdeen. [By John Moir.] 8vo. [J. F. K. Johnstone's *Bibl.*] Edinburgh, 1825

HISTORY of the city of Adrian [in Michigan. By Richard L. Bonner]. 8vo. Adrian, Mich., 1874

HISTORY of the city of Chester from its foundation to the present time. . . . With an account of parochial and other charities. [Dedication signed: I. M. B. P. *i.e.* I. M. B. Pigott.] 8vo. Pp. iii. 334. [*Brit. Mus.*] Chester, 1815

HISTORY of the city of Denver . . . containing a history of the State of Colorado. [By W. B. Vickers.] 8vo. [Cushing's *Anon.*] Chicago, 1880

HISTORY of the city of New York. [Compiled] by David T. Valentine [William I. Paulding]. 8vo. New York, 1853

HISTORY (the) of the Civil War in America, Vol. I.; comprehending the campaigns of 1775, 1776, and 1777. By an officer of the army [Capt. Hall]. 8vo. [Rich's *Bibl. Amer.* i. 283.] London, 1780

No more published.

HISTORY (the) of the Civil War [in England], in verse. [By Samuel Daniell.] 12mo. N.P. 1717

HISTORY (the) of the civil wars in Germany, from the year 1630 to 1635; also, genuine memoirs of the wars of England, in the unhappy reign of Charles the First; containing the whole history of those miserable times, until the king lost his head on the scaffold, in the memorable year 1648. Written by a Shropshire gentleman. . . . [By Daniel Defoe.] 8vo. Pp. vii. 376. Newark, 1782

Edited by E. Staveley, and is generally known as "Memoirs of a Cavalier. . . ."

HISTORY (the) of the Civil Wars of England, from . . . 1640 to 1660. By T. H. [Thomas Hobbes]. 12mo. Pp. 286. [*Brit. Mus.*] London, 1679

The edition of 1680 begins "Behemoth . . ."

HISTORY (the) of the College of Bonhommes, at Ashbridge, in the County of Buckingham, founded in the year 1276 by Edmund, Earl of Cornwall; compiled from original records. [By Rev. Henry John Todd, M.A.] Private print, N.P. 1823

HISTORY (the) of the Colleges of Winchester, Eton, and Westminster; with the Charter-House, the schools of St Paul's, Merchant Taylors, Harrow, and Rugby, and the Free-school of Christ's Hospital. [By William Combe?] 4to. London, 1816

HISTORY (a) of the colonisation of America. By Talvi [Thérèse A. L. Von Jacob, wife of Professor Edward Robinson]. 8vo. 7 vols. [Cushing's *Init. and Pseud.* i. 280.] London, 1851

The initials of the author's name form her pseudonym.

HISTORY of the colonization of the free states of antiquity, applied to the present contest between Great Britain and her American colonies; with reflections concerning the future settlement of these colonies. [By William Barron, Professor in St Andrews.] 4to. [M'Culloch's *Lit. of Pol. Econ.* p. 90.] London, 1777

HISTORY of the common law of England; written by a learned hand [Sir Matthew Hale]. 8vo. [*Brit. Mus.*] London, 1713

A posthumous work, somewhat fragmentary.

HISTORY (the) of the consecration of altars, temples, and churches; shewing the various forms of it among Jews, heathens, and Christians. . . . Written by the author of *Moderation, a virtue* [Rev. James Owen]. 8vo. [Arber's *Term Cat.* iii. 687.] London, 1706

HISTORY (an) of the constancy of nature; wherein, by comparing the latter age with the former, it is maintained that the world doth not decay universally. . . . By John Jonston, of Poland: translated from the Latin [by John Rowland?]. 8vo. [*Brit. Mus.*] London, 1657

See also, "An History of the wonderful things of nature. . . ."

HISTORY (the) of the Convocation of the prelates and clergy of the province of Canterbury, summon'd to meet at the cathedral church of St Paul, London, on February 6, 1700; faithfully drawn from the journal of the upper, and from the narrative and minutes of the lower-house. [By White Kennett, D.D.] 4to. Pp. xxxii. 264. [*Bodl.*] London, 1702

HISTORY (the) of the Consulate and the Empire of Napoleon. By Mons. Thiers. . . . Translated from the Paris edition [by Cyrus Redding]. 8vo. 2 vols. [*D. N. B.* vol. 47, p. 371.] London, 1846-48

HISTORY (the) of the Cophites, commonly called Jacobites, under the dominion of the Turk and Abyssin Emperor. By Josephus Abudacnus; done into English from the original Latin by Sir E. S. [Edward Sadleir]. 4to. [Arber's *Term Cat.*] London, 1693

See also "The history of the Jacobites . . ."

HISTORY (an) of the Corporation and Test Acts, with an investigation of their importance. . . . By C. L. [Capell Lofft, sen.]. 8vo. [*D. N. B.* vol. 34, p. 70.] Bury, 1790

HISTORY (the) of the Countess of Delwyn. By the author of *David Simple* [Sarah Fielding]. 12mo. 2 vols. [Green's *Bibl. Somers.* i. 184.] Bath, 1759

HISTORY (a) of the County of Berkshire, Massachusetts; in two parts. . . . By gentlemen in the County, Clergymen [chiefly Rev. David D. Field, D.D., and Rev. Chester Dewey], and laymen. 12mo. Pp. 468. Pittsfield, 1829

HISTORY (the) of the County of Lincoln from the earliest period to the present time. By the author of the *Histories of London, Yorkshire*, etc. [Thomas Allen], assisted by several gentlemen residing in the County. . . . 4to. 2 vols. [Anderson's *Brit. Top.*] London, 1834

The first part appeared at Leeds in 1830, with a different title, and with the author's name.

HISTORY (the) of the Court of the King of China; out of the French [of M. Baudier]; translated by A. A. 12mo. Pp. 102. London, 1682

HISTORY of the Covenanters of Scotland. By the author of the *Histories of the Reformation, Christian Church*, etc. [William Sime]. 12mo. 2 vols. [*Nat. Lib. of Scot.*] Edinburgh, 1830

HISTORY (the) of the Creation, contained in the first chapter of Genesis [Gen. i. 1 to ii. 3] explained and proved to be in complete harmony with the discoveries of geology. . . . [By William Parker.] 8vo. Pp. 78. London, Private print, 1853

HISTORY of the Crown Inn. [By John Arbuthnot, M.D.] 8vo. London [1716?]

A political pamphlet directed against the British government in the early reign of George I.

See also "An Appendix to the History of the Crown Inn," "The present state of the Crown Inn," and "A Supplement to the History of the Crown Inn."

HISTORY (the) of the damnable Popish Plot in its various branches & progress; published for the satisfaction of the present and future ages. By the authors of the *Weekly pacquet of advice from Rome* [Henry Care, and —— Robinson]. 8vo. [Arber's *Term Cat.* i. 525.] London, 1680

HISTORY (a) of the decline and fall of the British Empire. By Edwarda Gibbon [Charles J. Stone]. 8vo. Auckland, 2884 [*i.e.* 1884]

HISTORY (the) of the Desertion [of the throne by James II.]; or an account of all the publick affairs in England, from the beginning of September 1688 to the twelfth of February following: with an answer to a piece [by Jeremy Collier] call'd "The Desertion discussed, in a letter to a country gentleman." By a person of quality [Edmund Bohun]. 4to. 2 parts. Pp. 176. [*D. N. B.* vol. 5, p. 307.] London, 1689

HISTORY of the discovery of America. By a citizen of Connecticut [James Steward, D.D.]. 8vo. [Cushing's *Init. and Pseud.* i. 58.] Norwich, Conn., 1810

The name here given is that of the real author; but the work bears that of Henry Turnbull on the title-page.

HISTORY of the district of Craven, Yorkshire. [By Rev. William Carr, B.D.] 12mo. [*Brit. Mus.*] London, 1824

HISTORY (a) of the doctrine of the Deity of Jesus Christ. By Albert Réville. Translated from the French [by Anne Swaine]. 8vo. [*Brit. Mus.*] London, 1870

HISTORY (a) of the Dreyfus case, from the arrest of Captain Dreyfus in October 1894, up to the flight of Esterhazy in September 1898. By George Barlow [James Hinton]. 8vo. Pp. xi. 480. [*Lit. Year Book.*] London, 1899

See above: "Dreyfus, the prisoner."

HISTORY of the early Church, from the first preaching of the Gospel to the council of Nicea; for the use of young persons. By the author of *Amy Herbert* [Elizabeth Missing Sewell]. 12mo. Pp. viii. 385. London, 1859

HISTORY (the) of the English & Scotch presbytery; wherein is discovered their designes and practises for the subversion of government in Church and State. Written in French, by an eminent divine of the Reformed Church [Peter Du Moulin, D.D., jun.] and now Englished [by Matthew Playford, minister of Stanmore, Middlesex]. Pp. 56. 324. Villa Franca [London], 1659

The following MS. note on the title-page of the second edition, in the handwriting of Thomas Rud, librarian in the Cathedral Church of Durham, throws light on the authorship. "The French original is dedicated to Charles 2ᵈ by the Author, M. F., perhaps Molineus Filius, Peter the son of Peter, D.D. and præbendary of Canterbury, who writ *Regii sanguinis clamor ad coelum.* Ant. Wood (Ath. Oxon. V. 1. p. last) makes Dʳ Basire to be the author of it, but yᵉ Dʳˢ son, John B. never heard his father speak of it. Yᵉ book was writ abᵗ 1650 v. p. 203. Du Moulin in yᵉ pref. to yᵉ 2ᵈ book of his Lat. poems, says he writ *Gallica Diatriba justi voluminis* in defence of the Church & states yˢ in yᵉ book."

The authorship has also been ascribed to Isaac Basire, and to John Bramhall, Bishop of Derry.

HISTORY (a) of the English Church, from its foundation to the reign of Queen Mary. . . . By M. C. S. [Mary Charlotte Stapley]. 8vo. [*Brit. Mus.*] Oxford, 1869

Later editions give the full name of the writer. See also "A short history of the English Church. . . ."

HISTORY (the) of the English College at Doway, from its first foundation in 1568 to the present time. . . . By R. C. [Hugh Tootell, alias Charles Dodd], chaplain to an English regiment that march'd in upon its surrendering to the Allies. 8vo. [Gillow's *Bibl. Dict.* iii. 484.] London, 1713

This pamphlet was an attack on the English Jesuits, for whom a reply was made [by Thomas Hunter] in "A modest defence . . . against R. C.'s 'History of Doway,'" to which, in turn, Tootell published "The secret policy of the English Society of Jesus discovered . . ." (see below); Hunter, in response, wrote "An answer," which, however, was not published.

HISTORY (the) of the English Revolution, by Lord Macaulay. By Wykeham Frederick [Frederick Gale, solicitor]. 8vo. London, 1867

HISTORY (the) of the English stage, from the Restauration to the present time; including the lives, characters, and amours of the most eminent actors and actresses. . . . By Mr Thomas Betterton. [By William Oldys.] 8vo. [Lowndes' *Bibl. Man.* p. 166; *N. and Q.*, Feb. 1869, p. 168.] London, 1741

Partly collected from Betterton's papers.

HISTORY (the) of the ever renowned Knight Don Quixote de la Mancha; containing his many wonderful and admirable atchievements and adventures; with the pleasant humours of his trusty Squire, Sancha Pancha: being very comical and diverting. [By Miguel de Cervantes; translated from the Spanish.] 4to. [*Brit. Mus.*] London [1680?]

An abridgment. Several English translations have been published: the titles of some are indicated under "The delightful history of Don Quixote. . . ."

HISTORY (the) of the excellence and decline of the constitution, religion, laws, manners, and genius of the Sumatrans; and of the restoration thereof in the reign of Amurath the Third. [By John Shebbeare, M.D.] 8vo. [Watt's *Bibl. Brit.*] London, 1760

HISTORY (the) of the execrable Irish Rebellion, trac'd from many preceding acts to the grand eruption the 23. of October 1641, and thence pursued to the Act of Settlement 1662. [By Edmund Borlase.] Fol. [*D. N. B.* vol. 5, p. 397.] London, 1680

According to Ant. à Wood, much of this book is taken from another, entitled, *The Irish rebellion* (Lond. 1646, 4to), written by Sir John Temple, Knt.

HISTORY (the) of the Factory movement, from the year 1802 to the enactment of the Ten Hours' Bill in 1847. By Alfred [Rev. Samuel Kydd]. 8vo. 2 vols. [*Brit. Mus.*; J. S. Turner's *Halifax Books*, p. 195.] London, 1857

HISTORY (the) of the famous and passionate love between a fair noble Parisian lady and a beautiful young singing-man; an heroic poem, in two cantos. [By John Crowne.] 4to. [*Christie-Miller Cat.*] London, 1692

HISTORY of the famous city of York, and of its magnificent cathedral; also an account of St Mary's Abbey and other antient religious houses. . . . By T. G. [Thomas Gent, printer]. 12mo. York, 1730

HISTORY (the) of the famous Edict of Nantes; containing an account of all the persecutions that have been in France from its first publication. . . . Printed first in French, by the authority of the States of Holland and West-Friezland, and now translated into English, with Her Majesties royal privilege. [The author of the original work, printed at Delft, 1693, 95, and consisting of five volumes, was Elie Benoist, who signs the Epistle dedicatory, B. M. A. D. *i.e.* Benoist, minister at Delft. The translation is by —— Cooke, who signs the Epistle dedicatory to the Queen.] 4to. Vols. I., II. [*Brit. Mus.*] London, 1694

No more issued.

HISTORY (the) of the famous town of Halifax in Yorkshire; being a description thereof: their manufactures and trade: of the nobility, gentry, and other eminent persons born and inhabiting thereabout: with a true account of their ancient odd customary gibbet law. . . . [By Samuel Midgley, M.D.] 12mo. [J. S. Turner's *Halifax Books.*] London, 1712

The second edition of "Halifax and its gibbet-law placed in a true light. . . ." London, 1708. See above.

HISTORY (a) of the female Jockey Club. [By Charles Pigott.] 8vo. London, 1794

In some editions, the title begins: "The Female Jockey Club; or, a sketch of the manners of the age."

HISTORY (a) of the First Bushmen's Club in Australia. [By William Hugo.] 8vo. Adelaide, 1872

HISTORY (the) of the five Indian nations depending on the Province of New York in America. [By Cadwallader Colton.] 12mo. Pp. xvii. 119. [Evans' *Amer. Bibl.* i. 367.] New-York, 1727

HISTORY (the) of the five wise philosophers; or, the wonderful relation of the life of Jehosaphat the Hermit, son of Avenerio, King of Barma in India; the manner of his conversion to the Christian faith, and the horrid persecutions he suffered for the same; with the miracles he wrought. . . . By H. P. [Henry Parsons], Gent. 12mo. [Arber's *Term Cat.* iii. 375.] London, 1671

An abridged translation of a work attributed to St John of Damascus. Later editions, 1703 and 1711, appeared under the initials N. H., those of the editor N. Herrick.

HISTORY (the) of the Flagellants, or the advantages of discipline; being a paraphrase and commentary on the Historia Flagellantium of the Abbé Boileau, Doctor of the Sorbonne, Canon of the Holy Chapel etc. By somebody who is not Doctor of the Sorbonne [John Louis Delolme]. 4to. Pp. 340. [*Brit. Mus.*] London [1777]

HISTORY (the) of the Fleet Street House; a report of sixteen years. [By George Jacob Holyoake.] 8vo. [*Brit. Mus.*] London, 1856

HISTORY (a) of the foundations in Manchester of Christ's College, Chetham's Hospital, the Free Grammar School, and the ancient parish Church. [By Dr S. Hibbert Ware, J. Palmer, and W. R. Whatton.] 4to. London, 1834-48

HISTORY (the) of the French prophets; their pretended revelations, false prophecies, and hypocritical behaviour on that account; with the many bloody murders . . . and other villanies committed by them, under cover of religion, in the Sevennes. . . . [Written in French by the Abbé Jean Baptiste Louvreleuil, and published at Avignon in 1704.] 12mo. Pp. 225. London, 1709

HISTORY of the General Council and General Assembly of the Leeward Islands, with the condition of the slaves through their settlements. [By Clement Cairnes.] 8vo. St Christopher, 1804

HISTORY of the gentle craft, showing what famous men have been shoemakers in former ages, with their worthy deeds. . . . [By Thomas Deloney.] 12mo. [Arber's *Term Cat.* iii. 342.] London, 1737

Other editions bear a different title; see "The pleasant history of the gentle craft. . . ."

HISTORY (the) of the grand rebellion; containing, the most remarkable transactions from the beginning of the reign of King Charles I. to the happy Restoration: together with the impartial characters of the most famous and infamous persons, for and against the monarchy: digested into verse. Illustrated with about a hundred heads of the worthy Royalists and other principal actors, drawn from the original paintings of Vandike, An. More, Dobson, Cor. Johnson, and other eminent painters. . . . [By Edward Ward.] 8vo. 3 vols. [*Brit. Mus.*] London, 1713

HISTORY (the) of the Grand Visiers, Mahomet and Achmet Copragli; of the three last Grand Signiors, their Sultanas and chief favourites; with the most secret intrigues of the Seraglio: besides several other particulars of the wars of Dalmatia, Transylvania, Hungary, Candia, and Poland. [By F. de Chassepol.] Englished by John Evelyn, junior. 8vo. [Arber's *Term Cat.* i. 524.] London, 1677

HISTORY (a) of the Grange movement, the farmers' war against monopolies. By Edward Winslow Martin [James Dabney MacCabe]. 8vo. [*Lib. Journ.* viii. 111.] Chicago, 1873

HISTORY (the) of the Great Plague in London, in the year 1665; containing observations and memorials of the most remarkable occurrences, both public and private, that happened during that dreadful period. By a citizen who lived the whole time in London. To which is added, a journal of the plague at Marseilles, in the year 1720. [By Daniel Defoe.] 8vo. Pp. 380. London, 1754

For the first edition, see below "A journal of the plague year. . . ."

HISTORY (a) of the Great Western Railway. . . . By G. A. Sekon [G. A. Nokes]. 8vo. London, 1895

HISTORY (the) of the Gunpowder-treason, collected from approved authors, as well Popish as Protestant. [By John Williams, D.D., Bishop of Chichester.] 4to. [*Bodl.*] London, 1678

For another edition 1681, see "The history of the powder-treason. . . ."

HISTORY (the) of the Harlequinade. [A translation of part of "Masques et bouffons."] By Maurice Sand [Maurice Dudevant]. 8vo. 2 vols. [*Brit. Mus.*] London, 1915

HISTORY (a) of the harp. By Mr Aptommas [—— Thomas, the harpist]. 8vo. [*Amer. Cat.*] New York, 1864

HISTORY (a) of the Hebrew monarchy from the administration of Samuel to the Babylonish captivity. [By Francis William Newman.] 8vo. Pp. vii. 370. [*D. N. B.* First Supp. vol. 3, p. 222.] London, 1847

HISTORY (the) of the Honourable Edward Mortimer. By a lady [Albinia Gwynn]. 12mo. 2 vols. [*Mon. Rev.* lxxxiii. 465.] London, 1785

HISTORY (the) of the Honourable Mrs Rosemont and Sir Henry Cardigan, in a series of letters. [By Miss Elliott.] 8vo. 2 vols. [*European Mag.* iii. 365.] London, 1781

HISTORY (the) of the House of Esté, from the time of Forrestus until the death of Alphonsus the last Duke of Ferrara; with an account of the pretended devolution of that Dutchy unjustly usurped by Clement VIII.: wherein likewise the most considerable revolutions of Italy from the year 452 to the year 1598 are briefly touched. [By James Craufurd.] 8vo. Pp. 291. [*Nat. Lib. of Scot.*] London, 1681

Ascribed also to David Craufurd of Drumsoy.

HISTORY (the) of the House of Orange; or, a brief relation of the glorious and magnanimous atchievements of His Majesties renowned predecessors, and likewise of his own heroick actions till the late wonderful Revolution: together with the history of William and Mary, King and Queen of England, Scotland, France and Ireland, etc. . . . By R. B. [Richard Burton, *i.e.* Nathaniel Crouch]. 12mo. Pp. 186. [*Bodl.*] London, 1693

See the note to "Admirable curiosities. . . ."

HISTORY (the) of the House of Stanley, from the Conquest to the death of the Right Honourable Edward, Earl of Derby, in 1776; containing a genealogical and historical account of that illustrious house: to which is added a complete history of the Isle of Man. . . . [By John Seacombe.] 8vo. [*Brit. Mus.*] Manchester, 1821

HISTORY (a) of the Huguenots; or, the Protestant Reformation in France. By the author of *Father Darcy*, *Other men's tales*, etc. [Mrs Anne Marsh-Caldwell]. 8vo. 2 vols. [*D. N. B.* vol. 36, p. 219.] London, 1847

HISTORY (the) of the human œconomy. By a member of the Royal College of Physicians in London [Whitlock Nicholl, M.D., of Ludlow, Salop]. 8vo. Pp. 19. London, N. D.

No title-page.

HISTORY of the Hundred of Rowell [otherwise Rothwell]. By Paul Cypher [Hans Busk]. 12mo. Rowell [1850?]

HISTORY of the Imperiall Estate of the Grand Seigneurs; translated out of French by E. G. S. A. [Edward Grimston]. 4to. [*Christie-Miller Cat.*] London, 1635

HISTORY (the) of the incorporated towns and parishes of Gravesend and Milton, in the County of Kent. . . . [By Robert Pocock, printer.] 4to. [Watt's *Bibl. Brit.*] Gravesend, 1797

HISTORY (a) of the Indian revolt, and of the expeditions to Persia, China and Japan, 1856-7-8. . . . [Preface signed "G. D." *i.e.* George Dodd.] 8vo. Pp. viii. 634. London, 1859

HISTORY (a) of the Indian Wars with the first settlers of the United States. . . . [By Daniel C. Sanders.] 16mo. Pp. 319. [*Brit. Mus.*] Montpelier, Vt., 1812

HISTORY (the) of the Indulgence; showing its rise, conveyance, progress and acceptance: together with a demonstration of the unlawfulness thereof, and an answer to contrary objections: as also a vindication of such as scruple to hear the Indulged. By a Presbyterian [John Brown, minister of Wamphray]. 4to. Pp. 162. [*Nat. Lib. of Scot.*] 1678

Reprinted at Kilmarnock, 1783, in "Faithful witness-bearing exemplified; a collection . . ." [edited by John Howie of Lochgoin].

HISTORY (a) of the Inquisition. . . . [By James Browne, LL.D.] 8vo. [*D. N. B.* vol. 7, p. 49.] Edinburgh [1815?]

HISTORY (the) of the Inquisition as it is exercised at Goa, giving an account of the horrid cruelties which are exercised therein; written in French by the ingenious Monsieur [Claude] Dellon, who laboured five years under those severities, with an account of his deliverance. Translated into English [by Henry Wharton]. 4to. Pp. 70. [Watt's *Bibl. Brit.*] London, 1688

A new translation [by Richard Garland] was published in 1815.

HISTORY of the Inquisition, from its establishment to the present time; with an account of its procedure, and narratives of its victims. [By Charles H. Davie.] 12mo. [*Mendham Collection Cat.* p. 92.] Liverpool, 1850

HISTORY (the) of the Inquisition of Spain. By Don Juan Nellerto [Juan Antonio Llorente]. London, 1827

HISTORY (the) of the Inquisitions, including the secret transactions of those horrible tribunals. [By John Joseph Stockdale.] 4to. [*Brit. Mus.*] London, 1810

HISTORY (a) of the island of Anglesey, from its first invasion by the Romans until finally acceded to the Crown of England . . . serving as a supplement to Rowland's "Mona antiqua restaurata." To which are also added, Memoirs of Owen Glendowr . . . [By Nicholas Owen, M.A.] 4to. [*N. and Q.* Nov. 1865, p. 437.] London, 1775

Ascribed also to J. Thomas. [*Nat. Lib. of Scot.*]

HISTORY (a) of the Island of Dominica; containing a description of its situation, extent, climate . . . [By Thomas Atwood, chief-judge in Dominica.] 8vo. [*D. N. B.* vol. 2, p. 242.] London, 1791

HISTORY (the) of the Island of St Domingo, from its first discovery by Columbus to the present period. [By Sir James Baskett?] 8vo. [Sabin's *Dictionary*.] London, 1818

HISTORY (the) of the Isle of Wight. [By Sir Richard Wolsley.] 4to. [Anderson's *Brit. Top.*] London, 1781

HISTORY (the) of the Isle of Wight. [By Richard Warner.] 8vo. [Anderson's *Brit. Top.*] Southampton, 1795

HISTORY (a) of the Isle of Wight, from the earliest times, both ancient and modern. [By John Albin.] 8vo. Newport, 1794

Later editions bear the author's name.

HISTORY (the) of the Italian Peninsula. . . . [By Adolphus Lance.] 8vo. [*Brit. Mus.*] London [1859]

HISTORY (the) of the Jacobites of Ægypt, Lybia, and Neubia, etc.; their origine, ceremonies, laws, and customs. To which is added, some account of the Jacobites in England: done by E. S. [Sir Edward Sadleir], Baronet. 8vo. [Arber's *Term. Cat.* ii. 380.] London, 1691

See also "The history of the Cophites. . ."

HISTORY (a) of the Jesuits; to which is prefixed a reply to Mr Dallas's Defence of that Order. [By John Poynder.] 8vo. 2 vols. [*Brit. Mus.*] London, 1816

HISTORY (the) of the Jews. [By Henry Hart Milman, D.D.] 12mo. 3 vols. [*D. N. B.* vol. 38, p. 37.] London, 1829

Improved editions were issued in 1863 and 1867. See "A Letter to the Rev. Henry Hart Milman . . ."

HISTORY (the) of the Jews, from the call of Abraham to the birth of Christ. [By George Stokes.] 12mo. 2 vols. London, 1841

HISTORY (the) of the Jews, from the taking of Jerusalem by Titus to the present time; comprising a narrative of their wanderings, persecutions, commercial enterprises, and literary exertions: with an account of the various efforts made for their conversion. [By James A. Huie.] 8vo. [Huie's *History of Missions.*] Edinburgh, 1840

HISTORY of the Jews of all ages. . . By the author of *History in all ages* [Rev. Edward Parsons]. 12mo. London, 1835

HISTORY of the Judicial or Adawlut system in Bengal. [By General Sir George Leith, Judge Advocate-General in Madras.] 8vo. Madras, 1820

HISTORY of the Kentish petition. [By Daniel Defoe.] 4to. [Wilson's *Life of Defoe.*] London, 1701

HISTORY (the) of the Kingdom of Ireland; being an account of all the battles, sieges and other considerable transactions, both civil and military, during the late wars there, till the entire reduction of that countrey by the victorious arms of our most gracious soveraign, King William. To which is prefixed, a brief relation of the ancient inhabitants, and first conquest of that nation by King Henry II. By R. B. [Richard Burton, *i.e.* Nathaniel Crouch]. 12mo. Pp. 188. [*Bodl.*] London, 1693

See the note to "Admirable curiosities. . ."

HISTORY (the) of the Kingdom of Scotland, from Fergus the first king, to the commencement of the union of the two kingdoms of Scotland and England, in the sixth year of the reign of our late sovereign Queen Anne, Anno 1707; wherein several mistakes of Buchanan, and other of the common writers of the history of Scotland, are refuted. By J. W. [James Wallace], M.D. 4to. [*Nat. Lib. of Scot.*] Dublin, 1724

HISTORY (the) of the Kingdoms of Scotland and Ireland. . . . By R. B. [Richard Burton, *i.e.* Nathaniel Crouch]. 12mo. Pp. 233. [*Brit. Mus.*] London, 1685

See note to "Admirable curiosities. . . ."

HISTORY (the) of the Kings Majesties affairs in Scotland, under the conduct of the most Honourable James, Marques of Montrose, Earle of Kincardin, etc. and Generall Governour of that kingdome, in the years 1644, 1645, & 1646. [Translated from the Latin of George Wishart, Bishop of Edinburgh.] 4to. Pp. 112. N.P., 1648

An edition, with full bibliography, is given in Murdoch and Simpson's "Deeds of Montrose" (1893).

HISTORY (the) of the last Parliament began at Westminster, the tenth day of February, in the twelfth year of the reign of King William, An. Dom. 1700. [By James Drake, M.D.] To which is added, the Short defence of the last Parliament, etc. by the same author. Second edition. 8vo. Pp. 212. [*Brit. Mus.*] London, 1702

HISTORY (a) of the last sessions of Parliament; addressed to the . . . Earl of Charlemont. By a member of the Sub-Committee of Convention [William Bruce]. 8vo. [*Brit. Mus.*] Dublin, 1784

Signed "Gracchus."

HISTORY (the) of the late conspiracy against the King [William III.] and the nation: with a particular account of the Lancashire Plot. . . . [By Jacques Abbadie.] 8vo. Pp. 197. London, 1696

The French original ("Histoire de la dernière conjuration . . .") was also published anonymously. [Brunet.]

HISTORY of the late contest for the County of Bedford; from the notes of a Freeholder [William Astell, M.P.]. 8vo. Pp. 87. [*Brit. Mus.*] London, 1827

HISTORY (the) of the late English Rebellion, deduced from its first flame in 1640, and continued to the quenching thereof by His Majesties happy Restauration, 1660. By W. Y. [William Younger]. To which is added, Fundamentum patriae; or, Englands settlement: being a view of the state affairs in this kingdom since His Majesties Restauration, to the year 1663. 8vo. Pp. 84. London, 1665

HISTORY (a) of the late important period, from the beginning of His Majesty's illness to the settlement of the executive government and the appointment of a Regent. . . . [By Rev. Louis Dutens.] 8vo. Pp. 543. [*Brit. Mus.*] London, 1789

HISTORY (the) of the late Minority in Parliament during the years 1762, 1763, 1764, and 1765. [By John Almon.] 8vo. Pp. 332. [*Brit. Mus.*] London, 1766

Other anonymous prints previously published (in 1764) on the same subject are "A defence of the Minority . . ." [by Chas. Townsend], "A defence of the Majority..." [by Chas. Lloyd], and "A reply to the Defence of the Majority . . ." [by Sir W. Meredith.]

See also the note to "The history of the minority . . ."

HISTORY (an) of the late Revolution in Sweden, which happened on the 19th of August, 1772; containing, in three parts, the abuses, and the banishment of liberty in that kingdom. Written by a gentleman who was a Swede [George Stahlberg]. 8vo. [*Nat. Lib. of Scot.*] Edinburgh, 1776

HISTORY of the late Revolution in the Dutch Republic. [By George Ellis.] 4to. [Martin's *Cat.*] [London] 1789

HISTORY (the) of the late war in Germany, between the King of Prussia and the Empress of Germany, and her allies. . . . By a General Officer who served several campaigns in the Austrian army [General Henry Lloyd]. 4to. [*Brit. Mus.*] London, 1766

HISTORY (the) of the life and adventures of Mr Duncan Campbell, a gentleman, who, tho' deaf and dumb, writes down any stranger's name at first sight, with their future contingencies of fortune. . . . [By Daniel Defoe.] 8vo. [Wilson's *Life of Defoe*, p. 171.] London, 1720

HISTORY (the) of the life and death of Sr. Thomas More, Lord High Chancellor of England, in King Henry the Eight's time. Collected by J. H. [John Hoddesdon], Gent. 12mo. Pp. 190. London, 1662

The edition published at London, 1652, 8vo, has the dedication signed: J. Hoddesdon.

HISTORY (the) of the life and reign of Mary Queen of Scots, and Dowager of France; extracted from original records, and writers of credit. [By Dr Samuel Jebb.] 8vo. [*W.*] London, 1725

HISTORY (the) of the life and reign of the Czar Peter the Great. [By John Banks.] 8vo. Pp. 346. [*Brit. Mus.*] London, 1740

HISTORY (a) of the life and reign of William III., introduced with a brief account of the history and genealogy of his family. By the author of the *Critical review of the life of Oliver Cromwell* [John Banks]. 12mo. [*Brit. Mus.*] London, 1744

HISTORY (the) of the life and times of Cardinal Wolsey, Prime Minister of Henry VIII., in which are interspersed the lives . . . of the most eminent persons. . . . [By Joseph Grove.] 8vo. 4 vols. [*Camb. Univ. Lib.*] London, 1742-4

HISTORY (the) of the life of Cardinal [Richard] Pole. [By Thomas Phillips.] 8vo. 2 vols. [*D. N. B.* vol. 45, p. 215.] Oxford, 1764

The second edition (London, 1767) gives the author's name.

HISTORY (the) of the life of Catherine de Medicis, Queen Mother and Regent of France; or, the exact pattern of the French King's policy. [Taken partly from the work of Henri Estienne.] 8vo. [Arber's *Term Cat.* ii. 424, 616.] London, 1692

HISTORY (the) of the life of our Lord Jesus Christ; newly and faithfully translated from the fifth edition of the French. By W. C. [William Crathorne, Romish priest]. 8vo. [Gillow's *Bibl. Dict.* i. 587.] London, 1739

HISTORY of the life of the Duke of Espernon. [By Guillaume Girard.] Englished by C. Cotton. Fol. [*W.*] London, 1670

HISTORY (the) of the life of William Pitt, Earl of Chatham. [By William Godwin.] 8vo. Pp. xv. 302. [*Brit. Mus.*] London, 1783

HISTORY of the life, reign, and death of Edward II. king of England, and Lord of Ireland; with the rise and fall of his great favourites, Gaveston and the Spencers. Written by E. F. [Henry Cary, first Lord Viscount Falkland] in the year 1627; and printed verbatim from the original. Fol. Pp. 176. [*Bodl.*] London, 1680

HISTORY of the lives and reigns of the Kings of Scotland, from Fergus the First, and continued to the Union. By an impartial hand [Richard Rowlands]. 4to. Dublin, 1722

Attributed also to William Duncan. [*Brit. Mus.*]

HISTORY of the lives of English divines who were most zealous in promoting the Reformation. By R. B. [Richard Burton, *i.e.* Nathaniel Crouch]. 12mo. London, 1709

See the note to "Admirable curiosities."

HISTORY (the) of the Mahometan Empire in Spain; containing a general history of the Arabs, their institutions, conquests, literature, arts, sciences, and manners, to the expulsion of the Moors. [By J. Shakespear and Thomas H. Horne.] 4to. [*Calc. Imp. Lib.*] London, 1816

HISTORY of the man after God's own heart. [By Archibald Campbell, son of Dr Archibald Campbell, Professor of Church History in the University of St Andrews.] 8vo. Pp. xxvi. 107. [*N. and Q.* 1855, p. 204, 205.] London, 1764

This work has been ascribed also to Peter Annet, to John Noorthouck, and to —— Huet.

HISTORY (a) of the military transactions of the British nation in Indostan, from the year 1745; to which is prefixed a Dissertation on the establishments made by Mahomedan conquerors in Indostan. [By Robert Orme.] 4to. London, 1763

The narrative ends with the year 1755. A second volume, in two parts, continuing the history to 1761, was published in 1778.

HISTORY (the) of the Minority [in the House of Commons], during the years 1762, 1763, 1764, and 1765; exhibiting the conduct, principles, and views of that party. [By John Almon.] The fourth impression. Pp. xii. 332. [*D. N. B.* vol. i. p. 341.] London, 1765

Reprinted, with some additions, in 1766.

The first impression consisted of only twelve copies, privately printed in 1765; the second impression, a very large one, in which there were several additions, was published at the beginning of June, 1766; the third impression, likewise large, was printed about the middle of the same month; the fourth impression, which was still larger, appeared about the latter end of the succeeding July.

Among several pamphlets issued during the political controversy traced in this narrative, reference may be made to "A defence of the Minority . . ." [by Charles Townshend], and "A defence of the Majority . . ." [by Charles Lloyd]. See above (in vol. ii.).

HISTORY (the) of the moderne Protestant divines; containing their parents, countries, education, lives, etc. . . . Faithfully translated out of the Latine [of J. Verheiden and R. Holland], by D. L. [Donald Lupton]. 8vo. Pp. 364. [*Brit. Mus.*] London, 1637

HISTORY (the) of the most remarkable life, and extraordinary adventures of the truly honourable Colonel Jacque, vulgarly called Colonel Jack, who was born a gentleman, put apprentice to a pick-pocket, flourished six-and-twenty years a thief, and was then kidnapped to Virginia; came back a merchant; . . . was made Colonel, is now at the head of his regiment in the service of the Czarina, fighting against the Turks, completing a life of wonders, and resolves to die a General. Written by the author of *Robinson Crusoe* [Daniel Defoe]. 8vo. [Wilson's *Life of Defoe.*] London, 1722

HISTORY (the) of the most Serene House of Brunswick-Lunenburgh, in all the branches thereof, from its origin, to the death of Queen Anne . . . [Dedication signed: D. J. *i.e.* David Jones.] Second edition. 8vo. Pp. 496. [*Brit. Mus.*] London, 1716

HISTORY (the) of the most unfortunate Prince, King Edward II., with choice political observations on him, and his unhappy favourites, Gaveston and Spencer. . . . [By Edward Fannant?] 8vo. [*Brit. Mus.*] London, 1680

See also "The history of the life, reign and death of Edward II. . . ."

HISTORY of the mutiny at Spithead and the Nore; with an enquiry into its origin and treatment: and suggestions for the prevention of future discontent in the Royal Navy. [By William Johnson Neale.] 8vo. Pp. xii. 415. [*Brit. Mus.*] London, 1842

No. lxxx. of the Family Library.

HISTORY (the) of the negotiation of the Ambassadors sent to the Duke of Savoy by the Protestants of Switzerland, concerning the Vaudois. [By Antoine Teissier]; translated from the original. 4to. [Arber's *Term Cat.* ii. 617.] London, 1690

HISTORY (a) of the nine worthies of the world. By Robert [or Richard] Burton [Nathaniel Crouch]. 12mo. [*Brit. Mus.*] London, 1687

Later editions in 1713, 1727, etc. See the note to "Admirable curiosities. . . ."

HISTORY (the) of the office of Stadtholder, from its origin to the present times. Translated from the original [of the Abbé Raynal] published at the Hague [in 1747]. 8vo. [Barbier's *Dictionnaire.*] London, 1787

See below, the title of an earlier edition (1749), "The history of the Stadtholdership."

HISTORY (the) of the Old Testament, extracted out of Sacred Scripture and writings of the Fathers. . . . Translated from the works of . . . le Sieur de Royaumont [rather Nicolas Fontaine] by J. Coughen, and supervised by Anthony Hornelk and other orthodox divines. . . . [Also] The History of the New Testament. . . . Fol. 2 vols. [*Brit. Mus.*] London, 1690, 1688

Other editions followed, with varying titles. The original has with less reason been attributed to L. J. Le Maitre de Sacy.

HISTORY of the oracles and the cheats of the pagan priests. [By Bernard le Bovier de Fontenelle, who borrowed from Anthony Van Dale. The translation from the French was made by Mrs Aphra Behn.] 8vo. [Darling's *Cyclop. Bibl.*; Arber's *Term Cat.* ii. 617.] London, 1688

HISTORY (the) of the origin, progress, and termination of the American War. By Charles Stedman [William Thomson, LL.D.]. 8vo. London, 1794

HISTORY (the) of the original and progress of ecclesiastical revenues; wherein is handled according to the laws, both ancient and modern, whatsoever concerns matters beneficial, the regale, investitures, nominations and other rights attributed to princes. Written in French by a learned priest [Richard Simon], and now done into English. 8vo. [Watt's *Bibl. Brit.*] London, 1685

The author published the work at Frankfort (1684, and 1709) under the pseudonym Jerome à Costa.

HISTORY (the) of the parish and abbey of Hayles, in Gloucestershire; proposed as a specimen of a new history of that county. [By Samuel Rudder, printer.] Fol. Pp. 12. [*Bodl.*] [Cirencester] 1768

HISTORY (a) of the parish church of All Saints, Hereford. By A. L. O. H. [William Collins, of Hereford]. 8vo. Pp. 28. Hereford, 1909

HISTORY (the) of the parishes of Whiteford and Holywell. [By Thomas Pennant.] 4to. Pp. 328. [W. D. Macray's *Cat.*] London, 1796

HISTORY (a) of the Parliament of Great Britain, from the death of Queen Anne to the death of King George the First. [By John Almon.] 8vo. [*D. N. B.* vol. 1, p. 341.] London, 1764

HISTORY (the) of the Picts; containing an account of their original, language, manners, government, religion, bounds and limits of their kingdom. . . . [By Henry Maule, of Melgum?] 8vo. Pp. 97. Edinburgh, 1706

The advertisement says—"The author of this history is not so certainly known; some name Sir James Balfour Lyon, King at arms in K. Charles I. time, for the author of it, because the original manuscript in the Lawyers Library at Edinburgh seems to be the same hand with his annals, which unquestionablie is an autograph. But others more probably think that Henry Maule of Melgum is the author, since he subscribes his name to the copy of verses which is subjoyned to this."

HISTORY (a) of the Picts' or Romano-British Wall, and of the Roman stations and Vallum; with an account of their present state, taken during a pilgrimage along that part of the Island, June 1849. . . . [By Richard Abbatt.] 8vo. [*Brit. Mus.*] London, 1849

HISTORY (the) of the Pilgrims; or, the . . . story of the first settlers of New England. By a grandfather [Joseph Sylvester Clark]. 8vo. [Cushing's *Init. and Pseud.* ii. 67.] Boston, 1848

HISTORY of the political connection between England and Ireland, from the reign of Henry II. to the present time. [By William Barron, professor in the University of St Andrews.] 4to. [*Brit. Mus.*] London, 1780

HISTORY of the political life and public services, as a senator and as a statesman, of the Right Honourable Charles James Fox, one of his Majesty's principal Secretaries of State. [By Rev. John Moir.] 8vo. [*European Mag.* iv. 126.] London, 1783

Ascribed also to Dr French Lawrence. [*Bibl. Parriana*, p. 401.]

HISTORY (a) of the political life of the Right Honourable William Pitt; including some account of the times in which he lived. By John Gifford, Esq. [John Richards Green]. 4to. 3 vols. [*Brit. Mus.*] London, 1809

HISTORY (the) of the Powder-treason; with a vindication of the proceedings, and matters relating thereunto, from the exceptions made against it, and more particularly of late years by the author of the Catholick Apologie and others. . . . [By John Williams, Bishop of Chichester.] 4to. [*D. N. B.* vol. 61, p. 421.] London, 1681

For an earlier edition, see "The history of the Gunpowder-treason. . . ."

HISTORY (the) of the [English] Prayer-book. By the author of *One year* [Francis Mary Peard]. 8vo. Pp. iv. 187. [*Brit. Mus.*] London [1870]

HISTORY of the Prayer-book of the Church of England. [By Rev. Edward Berens.] 12mo. [*Brit. Mus.*] London, 1841

HISTORY (the) of the present Parliament and Convocation; with the debates at large relating to the conduct of the war abroad, the mismanagements of the ministry at home. . . . [Signed: W. P. *i.e.* William Pittis.] 8vo. [*Brit. Mus.*] London, 1711

HISTORY of the Press-Yard; or, a brief account of the customs and occurrences that are put in practice, and to be met with in that antient repository of living bodies, called His Majesty's Gaol of Newgate. [By Daniel Defoe.] 8vo. [Wilson's *Life of Defoe.*] London, 1717

HISTORY (the) of the principal discoveries and improvements in the several arts and sciences; particularly the great branches of commerce, navigation, and plantation in all parts of the known world. [By Daniel Defoe.] 8vo. Pp. viii. 312. [*Athen. Cat.* (*Supp.*), p. 46.] London, 1727

HISTORY of the principal states of Europe, from the peace of Utrecht. [By Lord John, later Earl Russell.] 8vo. 2 vols. [*Athen. Cat.* p. 271.] London, 1826

HISTORY (the) of the Principality of Wales. By R. B. [Richard Burton, *i.e.* Nathaniel Crouch]. 12mo. [*Brit. Mus.*] London, 1695

See the note to "Admirable curiosities. . . ."

HISTORY (the) of the proceedings in the case of Margaret, commonly called Peg, only lawful sister to John Bull, Esq. [By Adam Ferguson, LL.D.] 8vo. Pp. 192. [*D. N. B.* vol. 18, p. 337.] London, 1761

A political pamphlet.

HISTORY (the) of the public opening of the grand sea-front scheme at Weston-super-Mare. By Cock-Robin [Henry Lucas Bean]. 8vo. Weston-super-Mare, 1885

HISTORY (a) of the Punjab, and of the rise, progress, and condition of the sect and nation of the Sikhs; founded on the work of Captain W. Murray. [By James Prinsep.] 8vo. 2 vols. London, 1846

Attributed also to Thomas Thornton [Cushing].

HISTORY (the) of the quarrels of Pope Paul V. with the State of Venice; in seven books. [By Father Paul, *i.e.* Paolo Sarpi.] Faithfully translated out of the Italian, and compared with the French copie [by C. Potter]. 4to. Pp. xx. 435. [*Brit. Mus.*] London, 1626

Preface signed: C. P.

HISTORY (a) of the Rebellion in Ireland, in the year 1798 . . . containing an impartial account of the proceedings of the Irish Revolutionists, from the year 1782 till the suppression of the Rebellion. . . . [By Rev. James Gordon, vicar of Barragh, in Ireland.] 8vo. [Watt's *Bibl. Brit.*] London, 1801

HISTORY (a) of the Rebellion in Scotland in 1745-46. [Verse. By Dougald Graham.] New edition. 12mo. Pp. 168. [*A. Jervise.*] Aberdeen, 1850

HISTORY (the) of the Rebellion in 1745 and 1746; extracted from the *Scots Magazine*: with an appendix containing an account of the trials of the rebels, the Pretender's and his son's declarations, &c. [By Francis Douglas, bookseller.] 12mo. [*Nat. Lib. of Scot.*] Aberdeen, 1755

HISTORY (the) of the Rebellion, 1745 and 1746; containing a full account of its rise, progress and extinction; the character of the Highlanders, and their chieftains; all the declarations of the Pretender, and the journal of his marches through England, as published by himself. . . . By an impartial hand, who was an eye-witness to most of the facts [Andrew Henderson, M.A.]. 8vo. Pp. 204. [Fishwick's *Lancashire Library*, p. 304.] Edinburgh, 1748

HISTORY (the) of the Reformation and other ecclesiastical transactions in and about the Low-Countries, from the beginning of the eighth century down to the famous Synod of Dort, inclusive. . . . By the Reverend and learned Mr Gerard Brandt, late professor of divinity, and minister to the Protestant Remonstrants at Amsterdam. Faithfully translated from the original Low-Dutch [by John Chamberlayne]. Fol. 4 vols. [*W.*] London, 1720-3

HISTORY of the Reformation in Aberdeen. [By Joseph Robertson, LL.D.] 8vo. [Robertson's *Aberd. Bibl.*] London, 1887

HISTORY of the Reformation in the principal countries of Europe. [By William Sime.] 12mo. 2 vols. Edinburgh, 1829

Attributed also to Alexander Bower [Cushing].

HISTORY (the) of the reigns of Henry the Seventh, Henry the Eighth, Edward the Sixth and Queen Mary; the first written by the Right Honourable Francis [Bacon] Lord Verulam, Viscount St Alban; the other three by . . . Francis Godwyn, Lord Bishop of Hereford. [Translated by Morgan Godwyn, son of the Bishop.] Fol. [*W.*] London, 1676

HISTORY (the) of the remarkable life of John Sheppard; containing a particular account of his many robberies and escapes, etc. . . . [By Daniel Defoe.] [Lee's *Life of Defoe*, p. 224.] [London] 1724

HISTORY (a) of the revolt of Ali Bey, against the Ottoman Porte, including an account of the form of government of Egypt; together with a description of Grand Cairo, and of several celebrated places in Egypt, Palestine, and Syria: to which are added, a short account of the present state of the Christians who are subjects to the Turkish government, and the journal of a gentleman who travelled from Aleppo to Bassora. By S. L., Κοσμοπολίτης [S. Lusignan]. 8vo. Pp. xii. 259. [*Bodl.*] London, 1783

HISTORY (the) of the revolutions in Portugal. . . . By René Aubert de Vertot. . . . Translated from the French [by John Hughes]. 12mo. [*D. N. B.* vol. 28, p. 180.] London, 1712

HISTORY (the) of the revolutions of Portugal from the foundations of that kingdom to the year 1667. [By Thomas Carte.] With letters of Sir Robert Southwell, during his embassy there, to the Duke of Ormond. 8vo. [*Brit. Mus.*] London, 1740

HISTORY (a) of the ridiculous extravagancies of Monsieur Oufle; occasion'd by his reading books treating of magick . . . witches . . . spectres . . . dreams, etc. Written originally in French by the Abbot B— [Laurent Bordelon] and now translated into English. 8vo. Pp. 312. [*Brit. Mus.*] London, 1711

HISTORY (a) of the rise and progress of Middlesborough. . . . By Landor Praed [George Jacob Holyoake]. Reprinted, revised, and enlarged from the *Newcastle Daily Chronicle.* 8vo. Pp. 28. [*Brit. Mus.*] Newcastle-upon-Tyne, 1863

HISTORY (the) of the rise and progress of the Civil Wars in England, from the year 1625 to 1660; written in Latine in three parts: the two first by Dr George Bates . . . the third part, with a continuation to the year 1670, by Thomas Skinner, M.D. Made English. To which is added a preface and several original papers; by a person of quality [Archibald Lovell, M.A.]. 8vo. Second edition. London, 1688

Variations in the title occur in the edition of 1685.

HISTORY of the rise and progress of the naval power of England, interspersed with various important notices relative to the French marine. . . . Translated from an original work [by Guill. Emm. Jos. Guilhem de Clermont Lodève, Baron de Sainte Croix] in French, by Thomas Evanson White. 8vo. Pp. 420. London, 1802

HISTORY (an) of the River Thames. [By William Combe.] 4to. 2 vols. [*Gent. Mag.* May 1852, p. 468.] London, 1794-6

HISTORY of the Roman or Civil Law, shewing its origin and progress; how and when the several parts of it were first compiled. . . . Translated from the French of Claude de Ferrier by J. B. [John Beaver], Esq. 8vo. [Watt's *Bibl. Brit.*] London, 1724

HISTORY (the) of the royal abbey of Bec, near Rouen, in Normandy. By Dom. John Bourget, Benedictine monk of the congregation of St Maur in the said House, and Fellow of the Society of Antiquaries of London. Translated from the French [by Andrew Collée Ducarel, LL.D.]. 12mo. [*W.*] London, 1779

HISTORY of the Royal Berkshire Militia (now Third Battalion, Royal Berks Regiment). [By Emma E. Thoyts.] 8vo. Reading, 1897

Note by a local friend.

HISTORY of the royal malady [of George III.]. . . . With a variety of entertaining anecdotes. . . . By a page of the presence [Philip Withers]. 8vo. [*Brit. Mus.*] London, 1789

HISTORY (the) of the Russian Empire, from its foundation to the death of the . . . Empress Catherine. [By John Mottley.] 8vo. 2 vols. [*Brit. Mus.*] London, 1757

HISTORY (the) of the Russian Revolution to Brest-Litovsk. By Leo Trotsky [Leiba D. Bronshtein]. 8vo. Pp. 149. [*Brit. Mus.*] London, 1919

HISTORY (a) of the Scottish people from the earliest times to . . . 1887. [By the Rev. Thomas Thomson; continued by Charles Annandale.] 8vo. [*Brit. Mus.*] London [1894]

HISTORY of the secret societies of the army, and of the military conspiracies which had for their object the destruction of the government of Bonaparte. [By Charles Nodier.] Translated from the French. 8vo. Pp. xvi. 236. London, 1815

HISTORY (a) of the sect of Maharajas or Valla Bhacharyas in Western India. [By Karsandas Mulji.] With an exhaustive appendix [by Ralph T. H. Griffith]. . . . 8vo. London, 1865

HISTORY of the session 1852-3; a Parliamentary retrospect. [By Edward Michael Whitty.] 8vo. Pp. 222. [*Brit. Mus.*] London, 1854

HISTORY of the Sevarites or Sevarambi, a nation inhabiting part of the third continent called Terra Australis Incognita. Translated from the French [of Denis Vairasse]. 8vo. [Watt's *Bibl. Brit.*] London, 1675

A second part was published in 1679. The work is fictitious.

HISTORY (a) of the siege of Chester during the Civil Wars in the time of King Charles I. [By John Broster.] 8vo. [*Brit. Mus.*] Chester [1790]

HISTORY of the siege of Delhi. By an officer who served there [William Wotherspoon Ireland, M.D.]; with a sketch of the leading events in the Punjaub connected with the great rebellion of 1857. 12mo. Pp. xii. 331. [*Nat. Lib. of Scot.*] Edinburgh, 1861

HISTORY (the) of the Spanish school of painting; to which is appended an historical sketch of the rise and progress of the art of miniature illumination. By the author of *Travels through Sicily and the Lipari Islands*, the *History of the Azores*, and the *History of various styles of architecture* [Captain Edward Boid]. 8vo. Pp. ii. 199. [*W.*] London, 1843

HISTORY (the) of the Stadtholdership, from its origine to the present time. Written by a Frenchman [l'Abbé Thomas Guillaume François Raynal] and translated by an Englishman. With notes by the translator. 8vo. London, 1749

A later edition (1787) differs slightly in the title: "The history of the office of Stadtholder."

HISTORY of the Standard Bank of South Africa. [By George Thomas Amphlett.] 4to. Glasgow, 1914

HISTORY (the) of the steam-engine, from the second century before the Christian era to the time of the Great Exhibition. [Signed: R. W. *i.e.* Robert Wallace, M.A., mathematician.] 12mo. [*Brit. Mus.*] London, 1852

HISTORY (the) of the Temperance movement in Scotland, with special reference to its legislative aspect. [By David Lewis, J.P.] 8vo. Pp. 345. Edinburgh [1851]

HISTORY (the) of the thorn tree and bush, from the earliest time; in which is clearly shewn the descent of Her Majesty [Queen Victoria] and her Anglo-Saxon people from the half-tribe of Ephraim. . . . By Theta [William Thorn, M.D.]. 12mo. Pp. viii. 182. [*Brit. Mus.*] Edinburgh, private print, 1862

HISTORY (the) of the Test Act; in which the mistakes in some late writings against it are rectified, and the importance of it to the Church explain'd. [By Thomas Sherlock, D.D.] 8vo. Pp. 31. [*Bodl.*] London, 1732

Ascribed also to Edmund Gibson, Bishop of London.

HISTORY of the three late famous impostors, viz. Padre Ottomano . . . Mahomed Bei . . . and Sabatai Levi; with a brief account of the present war between the Turk and the Venetian: together with the cause of the final extirpation . . . of the Jews out of the Empire of Persia. [By John Evelyn.] 8vo. [*Brit. Mus.*] In the Savoy, 1669

HISTORY (the) of the town and parish of Halifax, containing a description of the town, the nature of the soil, etc.; . . . also, the unparalleled tragedies committed by Sir John Eland of Eland, and his grand antagonists. . . . [By Rev. —— Nelson.] 8vo. Pp. 650. [Boyne's *Yorkshire Lib.* pp. 94, 95; Turner's *Hal. Books.*] Halifax, N.D.

The portion of the work relating to Sir John Eland and his antagonists has a separate title, extends to 70 pages, and is dated 1789. Some copies of the entire work have the date 1789.

HISTORY (a) of the town and parish of Leeds; compiled from various authors: to which are added a history of Kirkstall Abbey and a Leeds directory for 1798. [By John Ryley.] 12mo. Leeds [1798]

HISTORY (a) of the town of Belfast, with an accurate account of its former and present state. . . . [By George Benn.] 8vo. Pp. 298. [*Camb. Univ. Lib.*] Belfast, 1823

HISTORY of the town of Houlton (Maine), from 1804 to 1883. [By George H. Gilman.] Haverhill, Mass., 1884

HISTORY (the) of the Treaty of Nimeguen; with remarks on the interest of Europe in relation to that affair: translated out of French [of Luc. Courchetet d'Esnans]. 8vo. London, 1681

HISTORY (the) of the Triumvirates; the first that of Julius Cæsar, Pompey, and Crassus; the second that of Augustus, Anthony, and Lepidus. . . . Written originally in French [by Citri De La Guette], and made English by Tho. Otway. . . . 8vo. 2 vols. [*Manch. Free Lib.*] London, 1686

The pagination is continuous.

HISTORY (the) of the tryall of chevalry; with the life and death of Cavaliero Dicke Bowyer. [A play, in verse. By William Wager.] 4to. [*Brit. Mus.*] London, 1605

HISTORY (the) of the twelve Cæsars, Emperors of Rome. By Suetonius. Newly translated into English [by Andrew Marvell]. 8vo. [*Brit. Mus.*] London, 1672

HISTORY (the) of the two late kings, Charles the Second and James the Second; . . . together with a relation of the happy Revolution, and the accession of their present majesties, King William and Queen Mary, to the throne, Feb. 13. 168⅞. By R. B. [Richard Burton, *i.e.* Nathaniel Crouch]. 12mo. Pp. 180. [*Bodl.*] London, 1693

See the note to "Admirable curiosities."

HISTORY of the Union between the Presbyterian and Congregational ministers, in and about London; and the causes of the breach of it. [By Rev. Richard Taylor.] 4to. Pp. iv. 27. London, 1698

HISTORY (the) of the United States for 1796, including a variety of interesting particulars relative to the Federal Government previous to that period. [By James Thomson Callender.] 8vo. Pp. viii. 312. [Sabin's *Dictionary*.] Philadelphia, 1797

HISTORY of the United States, from their first settlement as colonies to the close of the War with Great Britain in 1815. [By Salma Hale.] 8vo. Pp. 467. [*Brit. Mus.*] New York, 1826

HISTORY of the United States: No. 1, or Uncle Philip's conversations . . . about Virginia. [By Francis Lister Hawkes.] 12mo. [Allibone's *Dict.*] New York, 1840

HISTORY of the United States of America. . . . By a Citizen of Massachusetts [Charles Prentiss]. Second edition. 12mo. Pp. 276. [Sabin's *Dictionary*.] Keene, N.H., 1821

HISTORY of the University of Cambridge; its colleges, halls, and public buildings. [By William Combe.] 4to. 2 vols. [*Brit. Mus.*] London, 1815

HISTORY (a) of the University of Oxford. [By Frederick Shoberl.] Fol. [*Brit. Mus.*] London, 1814

HISTORY (the) of the University of Oxford, from the death of William the Conqueror to the demise of Queen Elizabeth. [By Sir John Pechell.] 4to. Pp. 264. Oxford, 1773

HISTORY (a) of the University of Oxford, its colleges, halls, and public buildings. [By William Combe.] 4to. 2 vols. [*Brit. Mus.*] London, 1814

HISTORY (the) of the University of Oxford, to the death of William the Conqueror. [By Sir John Pechell.] 8vo. Pp. 32. [*Brit. Mus.*] Oxford, 1772

HISTORY (the) of the valourous and witty Knight-Errant, Don Quixote, of the Mancha. [By Miguel de Cervantes Saavedra.] Translated out of the Spanish [by John Shelton]. Fol. London, 1652

HISTORY (the) of the variations of the Protestant Churches. By Jacques Benigne Bossuet, Bishop of Condom and Meaux; translated from the French [by Levinius Brown, S.J.]. 8vo. 2 vols. [*De Backer.*] Antwerp, 1742

HISTORY (a) of the Waldenses, from the earliest period to the present time. [By William Sime.] 8vo. [Allibone's *Dict.*] Edinburgh, 1829

HISTORY (a) of the war between the King of Prussia and the Empress of Germany and her allies. By a General Officer who made several campaigns with the Austrians [Henry Lloyd]. 8vo. [*Brit. Mus.*] London, 1766

HISTORY (the) of the war in America between Great Britain and her colonies from its commencement to the end of the year 1778 . . . [By Patrick Gordon.] 8vo. 3 vols. [Sabin's *Dictionary*.] Dublin, 1779-85

Vol. 3 continues the work to 1783.

HISTORY (a) of the war in the north [of New Zealand] against the Chief Heke, in the year 1845; told by an old Chief of the Ngapuhi tribe. By Pakeha Maori [Frederick Edward Maning]. 8vo. Pp. 113. [Collier's *New Zeal. Lit.* p. 85.] Auckland, 1864

HISTORY (the) of the War of Cyprus; written originally in Latin [by Antonio Maria Graziani, and translated from the Latin by Robert Midgley]. 8vo. Pp. 370. [*Brit. Mus.*] London, 1687

HISTORY (the) of the warr of Ireland from 1641 to 1653. By a British officer, of the regiment of Sir John Clottworthy. Edited with preface, notes, and appendix, by E. G. [Rev. Edmund Ignatius Hogan, S.J.]. 8vo. Pp. xvi. 160. Dublin, 1873

HISTORY of the wars of his present Majesty Charles XII. King of Sweden; from his first landing in Denmark, to his return from Turkey to Pomerania. By a Scots gentleman, in the Swedish service [Daniel Defoe]. 8vo. Pp. 400. London, 1715

—— With a continuation to his death. Second edition. [Lee's *Defoe*, p. 169.] 1720

HISTORY (the) of the Western world. [By Henry Fergus.] The United States. 8vo. 2 vols. [*Brit. Mus.*] London, 1830, 1832

Lardner's Cyclopædia.

HISTORY (a) of the Westminster election [of Fox, Hood, and Wray], containing every material occurrence from the 1st of April to the 17th of May, 1784. By lovers of truth and justice [J. Hartley and another]. . . . 4to. London, 1784

HISTORY (the) of the Whiggish Plot. [By John Turner?] Fol. London, 1684

HISTORY (a) of the witches of Renfrewshire. [By J. Millar, schoolmaster in Beith.] A new edition. . . . 8vo. Pp. xxv. 219. Paisley, 1877

HISTORY (the) of the wonderful Don Ignatius de Loyola, founder of the Order of the Jesuits; with an account of the establishment and government of that Order. Translated from the French [of Hercule Rasiel de Selva, *i.e.* Pasquier Quesnel, or Charles Gabriel Porée]. 12mo. 2 vols. [*Brit. Mus.*] London, 1754

HISTORY (a) of the wonderful things of nature; wherein are contained the wonders of the heavens, elements, meteors. . . . By Johannes Jonston; rendered [from Latin] into English by a person of quality [John Rowland]. Fol. London, 1657

See also "An history of the constancy of Nature. . . ."

HISTORY (the) of the Workhouse or Poor's Hospital of Aberdeen from 1739 to 1818. . . . By A. W. [Alexander Walker]. 8vo. Pp. 60. [Robertson's *Aberd. Bibl.*] Aberdeen, 1885

HISTORY (the) of Thirsk; including an account of its . . . castle, Topliffe, Bieland and Rievalx Abbeys . . . With biographical notices of eminent men. [By J. B. Jefferson.] 8vo. Pp. viii. 180. [*Manch. Free Lib.* p. 368.] Thirsk, 1821

HISTORY (the) of Tim Higgins, the Cottage Visitor. [By Abigail Roberts, of Mountrath, Ireland.] 12mo. Pp. 182. [*Supp.* to Smith's *Cat. of Friends' Books*, p. 16.] Dublin, 1823

HISTORY (the) of Timur-Bec, known by the name of Tamerlain the Great, Emperor of the Moguls and Tartars; written in Persian by Charefeddin Ali . . . translated into French by Petis de la Croix . . . now faithfully render'd into English [by John Darby]. 8vo. 2 vols. Pp. xxxi. 542, 428. [*Brit. Mus.*] London, 1723

HISTORY (the) of tithes, patriarchal, levitical, Catholic, and Protestant; with . . . suggestions for abolishing tithes, and supporting the clergy without them. By Biblicus [Rev. William Thorn]. 8vo. [Cushing's *Init. and Pseud.* i. 35.] London, 1831

A second edition, enlarged, was published during the same year.

HISTORY (the) of Tom Fool. [By George Alexander Stevens.] 12mo. 2 vols. [Baker's *Biog. Dram.*] London, 1760

HISTORY (the) of Tom Rigby. [By John Chater.] 12mo. 3 vols. [Wilson's *Hist. of Diss. Ch.* iii. 112.] London, 1773

HISTORY of Toussant Louverture. [By M. D. Stephens, Esq.] 8vo. London, 1814

Another edition of "Buonaparte in the West Indies."

HISTORY (the) of travayle in the West and East Indies, and other countryes lying eyther way towards the fruitfull and ryche Moluccaes . . . with a discourse of the North-West Passage; gathered in parte and done into Englyshe [from the Latin of Peter Martyr] by Richard Eden: newly set in order, augmented and finished by Richard Willes. Sm 4to. B. L. [*Christie-Miller Cat.*] London, 1577

HISTORY of Vigo County, Indiana; with biographical selections. [Compiled by H. C. Bradsby.] 4to. Pp. xiv. 1080. Chicago, 1891

HISTORY (the) of Virginia, in four parts. I. The history of the first settlement of Virginia, and the government thereof to the year 1706. II. The natural productions and conveniences of the country suited to trade and improvement. III. The native Indians, their religion, laws, and customs, in war and peace. IV. The present state of the country as to the polity of the government, and improvements of the land, the 10th of June, 1720. By a native inhabitant of the place [Robert Beverly]. The second edition, revis'd and enlarg'd by the author. 8vo. Pp. 308. [*Christie-Miller Cat.*] London, 1722

The first edition (1705) has a fuller title: "The history and present state of Virginia...." (See above.)

HISTORY (the) of Wales; containing some interesting facts concerning the existence of a Welsh tribe among the aborigines of America: arranged as a catechism for young persons. By a lady of the Principality of Wales [Eliza Constantia Campbell]. 8vo. Pp. 80. [*Brit. Mus.*] Shrewsbury, 1833

HISTORY (a) of Wednesbury, in the county of Stafford; compiled from various authentic sources, both ancient and modern; and embracing an account of the coal and iron trade. [By John Nock Bagnall, Esquire of West Bromwich.] 8vo. Pp. xi. 182. [*Bodl.*] Wolverhampton, 1854

HISTORY of West Calder. . . . By a native [William Cochrane Learmouth]. 8vo. Pp. xviii. 268, xxxiii. [*Brit. Mus.*] Edinburgh, 1885

HISTORY (the) of White's. [By William Biggs Boulton.] 4to. 2 vols. [*Brit. Mus.*] London, 1892

HISTORY (a) of Wimborne Minster; the Collegiate Church of Saint Cuthberga and King's Free Chapel at Wimborne. [By Charles Mayo, M.A.] 8vo. Pp. 143. [Mayo's *Bibl. Dors.* p. 263.] London, 1860

HISTORY (a) of William III. [By Walter Harris.] 8vo. 4 vols. [*D. N. B.* vol. 25, p. 26.] Dublin, 1747

As this edition was issued by the bookseller in a curtailed form, against the wishes of the author, the latter published the work in full, with his name, at London (folio, 1749), under the title "The history of the life and reign of William-Henry, Prince of Nassau and Orange, King of England. . . ."

HISTORY (the), opinions, and present legal position of the English Presbyterians. [By Rev. Thomas Falconer.] 8vo. Pp. 181. [*Brit. Mus.*] London, 1834

HISTORY (a) or description, general and circumstantial, of Burghley House, the seat of the Right Honorable the Earl of Exeter. [By J. Horne.] 8vo. Pp. vii. 206. [*Nat. Lib. of Scot.*] Shrewsbury, 1797

HISTORY (the), or present state of Sweden; in a letter to Sir J[acob] B[ancks], by birth a Swede, but naturaliz'd, and a M[embe]r of the present P[arliamen]t; concerning the late Minehead doctrine, which was establish'd by a certain Free Parliament of Sweden, to the utter enslaving of that kingdom. [By William Benson.] 4to. [*Trin. Coll. Dub. Lib.* p. 265.] London, 1711

See "A letter to Sir J. B., etc."

HISTORY travestied in the first memorial tablet erected [to Dean Hannay] in the Great Kirk of Edinburgh since its restoration. By Metropolitan [Rev. Ranald Macpherson]. 8vo. [*New Coll. Lib.*] Edinburgh [1880]

HISTORYE (the) of the Bermudaes. By John Smith, Governor of Virginia [but really written by Captain Nathaniel Butler]. 8vo. Pp. xii. 327. [*Brit. Mus.*] London, 1882

HISTRIO-MASTIX; or, the player whipt. [Ascribed to John Marston.] 4to. [*Pollard and Redgrave.*] London, 1610

HISTRIOMASTIX; or, the untrussing of the Drury Lane Squad. By Peregrine Prynne [J. Cahnac]. 8vo. London, 1819

HISTRIONADE (the), or theatrical tribunal; a poem in two parts. By Marmaduke Myrtle [Thomas Dermody]. 8vo. [O'Donoghue's *Poets of Ireland.*] London, 1802

HISTRIONIC epistles. [By Rt. Hon. John Wilson Criker.] 12mo. [*Brit. Mus.*] Dublin, 1801

HITCHINGBROOKE. [By Edward George Henry Montagu, eighth Earl of Sandwich.] 4to. Private print, 1910

HITHER and thither; songs and verses. By the author of *Times and days* [John H. Balfour Browne]. 8vo. London, 1903

HITS and dashes; or, a medley of sketches and scraps. . . . By Cymon [Frederick Thomas Sowerby]. 8vo. [Cushing's *Init. and Pseud.* i. 72.] Boston, 1851

HITS at American whims, and hints for home use. By Carl and Cauty Carl [Frederick William Sawyer]. 8vo. [Cushing's *Init. and Pseud.* i. 50.] Boston, 1860

HIVE (the) and its wonders. [By J. H. Cross.] Revised [and enlarged] edition. 8vo. Pp. 124. London [1881]

The first edition appeared at Edinburgh [1852]. 12mo.

H. MORE. By Marion Harland [Mary Virginia Hawes, later Mrs Terhune]. 8vo. [Kirk's *Supp.*] New York, 1900

HO! for Elfland. By Alice Kingsbury [Alice Kingsbury Cooley]. 8vo. [Kirk's *Supp.*] San Francisco, 1877

HOBBLEDEHOYS. [A tale.] By Raymond Jacberns [Georgina Selby Ash]. 8vo. London, 1899

HOBBY-HORSE (the); a characteristical satire on the times: printed from a manuscript found among the papers of a late deceased satirist. [By John Potter.] 4to. [*European Mag.*] London, 1767

HOBBY horses. [By Miss — Winford.] Read at Batheaston. 4to. Bath, 1780

HOBOMOK; a tale of early times. By an American [Mrs Lydia Maria Child]. 8vo. [Cushing's *Init. and Pseud.* i. 13.] Boston, 1824

HOBSON'S horse-load of letters; or a president for epistles; the first booke, being a most exact method for men, of what qualitie soeuer, how to indight according to the forme of these times, whether it be for serious negotiations, priuate businesses, amorous accomplyment, wanton merryment, or the defence of honor and reputation. . . . [Dedication signed: G. M. *i.e.* Gervase Markham.] 4to. No pagination. London, 1613

HOCHELAGA; or, England in the New World. [By Major George D. Warburton.] Edited by Eliot Warburton, Esq. 12mo. 2 vols. London, 1846

HOCKEN and Hunken; a tale of Troy. By "Q" [Sir Arthur Thomas Quiller-Couch]. 8vo. Pp. vi. 370. Edinburgh, 1912

HOG (the). Compiled by a father [William Lee]. 12mo. Wisconsin, 1823

HOGAN, M.P.; a novel. [By May Laffan, later Mrs Hartley.] 8vo. 3 vols. [*Brit. Mus.*] London, 1876

HOGLANDIAE descriptio, or description of Hampshire; a mock heroic poem: with an English translation. [By Thomas Richards.] 8vo. [Gilbert and Godwin's *Bibl. Hanton.* p. 56.] London, 1719

Dedication signed: M. G. C.

HOGMAN'S (the) vindication from some aspersion lately cast upon him, relating to matters in difference touching the relief of the poor of Mile-end Old-town in the parish of Stepney; also some arguments to shew both how the poor are increased, and the means to prevent it for the future. [By E. Elderton.] 4to. [Arber's *Term. Cat.* iii. 687.] London, 1702

HOITY Toity; the good little fellow. By Charles Camden [Richard Rowe, journalist]. 8vo. London, 1873

HOLDEN with the cords. [A novel.] By Mrs W. M. L. Jay [Mrs Julia L. M. Woodruff]. 8vo. [*Lit. Year Book.*] London, 1891

HOLE (a) and corner marriage. [A novel.] By Florence Warden [Florence Alice Price, later Mrs George E. James]. 8vo. Pp. 316. London, 1902

HOLE (the) in the bag, and other stories. By Kruna [Mrs Julia P. Ballard]. 8vo. [Cushing's *Init. and Pseud.* i. 159.] New York, 1877

HOLE (a) in the coat. By Charles Eddy [Charles E. Rose]. 8vo. London, 1907

HOLE (the) in the pocket. By Aunt Hattie [Mrs Harriet Newell Baker, *née* Woods]. 12mo. [Haynes' *Pseud.*] Boston, 1866

HOLE (the) of the pit. [A novel.] By Adrian Ross [Arthur Reid Ropes, M.A.]. 8vo. Pp. 308. [*Lit. Year Book.*] London, 1914

HOLIDAY (a) chaplet of stories. By A. L. O. E., author of *The silver casket*, etc. [Charlotte Maria Tucker]. 8vo. Pp. 222. London, 1867

HOLIDAY excursions of a naturalist; forming a guide-book to the natural history of the inland and the littoral. [By Robert Garner, F.L.S.] 8vo. Pp. viii. 375. [*Brit. Mus.*] London, 1867

HOLIDAY haunts on the west coast of Clare, Ireland. By H. B. H. [H. B. Harris]. 8vo. Pp. 87. [*Brit. Mus.*] Limerick, 1891

HOLIDAY (a) in North Uist. [By William Carmichael Mackintosh, Professor in St Andrews.] 8vo. [P. J. Anderson's *Inverness Bibl.* p. 204.] London, 1865

HOLIDAY (a) in Norway; or, sights and scenes in Norseland. By "Viator" [Rev. Thos. Boston Johnstone, D.D.]. 8vo. Bolton (Lancashire), 1884

HOLIDAY (the) keepsake. By Peter Parley [William Martin]. 8vo. London, 1865

Attributed also to —— Tegg, son of Thomas Tegg, publisher.

HOLIDAY (a); or, Mima and her friends: an entirely original Christmas extravaganza. By Sir Charles Rockingham [Philippe F. A. de Rohan-Chabot, Count de Jarnac]. 8vo. Pp. 40. [*Brit. Mus.*] Worksop, 1866

HOLIDAY (a) queen. [A story for children.] By Elsie Jeannette Oxenham [Elsie Jeannette Dunkerley]. 8vo. Pp. 346. [*Brit. Mus.*] London [1910]

HOLIDAY rambles in ordinary places. By a wife with her husband [Richard Holt Hutton, LL.D.]. Republished from the *Spectator*. 8vo. [*London Quart. Rev.* Oct. 1918, p. 218.] London, 1877

HOLIDAY (the) round. [A series of humorous sketches, from *Punch*.] By A. A. M. [A. A. Milne]. 8vo. London, 1912

HOLIDAY songs. By Mrs Alexander [Annie French, later Mrs Hector]. Scot's music by Lady Arthur Hill. 8vo. London, 1884

HOLIDAY tales and conversations. By the author of *Eastern Hospitals* [Frances Magdalen Taylor]. 12mo. London, 1861

HOLIDAY (the) task; an occasional magazine of contributions by the pupils of Whitminster Grammar-school. [By Ascott Robert Hope Moncrieff.] 8vo. [*Lit. Year Book.*] Edinburgh, 1875

HOLIDAY trips; in extempore doggerel. . . . [By Sir William Symonds.] 12mo. [*Brit. Mus.*] London, private print, 1847

HOLIDAYS at home. By Margaret Vandergrift [Margaret Thomson Janvier]. 8vo. [Cushing's *Init. and Pseud.* i. 292.] Philadelphia [1880?]

HOLIDAYS at Newhall. By the author of *The boys of Highfield*. [H. Frederick Charles]. 12mo. Pp. 128. London [1880]

Ascribed also to C. F. Higginson.

HOLIDAYS at the cottage, or a visit to Aunt Susan. [By Marion Eliza Weir.] 8vo. [*Nat. Lib. of Scot.*] Edinburgh, 1856

HOLIDAYS in the far North. By Finlay A. M'E. [M'Ewen]. 8vo. Sheffield, 1875

HOLINESS (the) of the human body. [Subscribed: A. P. F. *i.e.* Alexander Penrose Forbes, D.C.L.] [*Brit. Mus.*] London, 1853

HOLINESS; or, the legend of St George: a tale from Spenser's Faerie Queene. By a mother [Mrs —— Peabody]. 8vo. [Cushing's *Init. and Pseud.* ii. 103.] Boston, 1836

HOLLAND-TIDE; or, Munster popular tales. [By Gerald Griffin.] 12mo. Pp. 378. [*Brit. Mus.*] London, 1827

HOLLINGBOURNE, 1851. [Verses, signed: L. T. *i.e.* Mrs L. Thomas.] 16mo. Pp. 13. [*Brit. Mus.*] Maidstone, 1881

HOLLOAS from the hills; a book of hunting verses. . . . By "Teviotdale" [Thomas Scott Anderson, M.D., Selkirk]. 8vo. Edinburgh [1880?]

HOLLY. [A novel.] By "Nomad" [Adèle Crafton-Smith]. 8vo. 2 vols. [*Lond. Lib. Cat.*] London, 1891

HOLLY and ivy for Christmas holidays. [Verse.] By Anthony Evergreen [Rev. John O'Rourke, Canon]. 8vo. [O'Donoghue's *Poets of Ireland.*] Dublin [1875?]

HOLLY (the) branch. By Harriet Annie [Harriet Annie Wilkins]. 8vo. Pp. 140. [Cushing's *Init. and Pseud.* i. 126.] Hamilton, Canada West, 1851

HOLY altar and sacrifice explained, in some familiar dialogues on the Mass. . . . By P—B., O.S.F. [P. Baker, Franciscan monk]. 12mo. [*Brit. Mus.*] London, 1768

An abridgment of the author's "Liturgical discourse of the Holy sacrifice of the Mass. . . ."

HOLY (the) angels. . . . [By George Morris.] 8vo. [*Brit. Mus.*] London, 1868

HOLY baptism; prayers, meditations, and select passages on the sacrament of baptism, with the baptismal offices according to the use of the English Church. [Introduction signed: H. E. M. *i.e.* Henry Edward Manning, D.D.] 12mo. Pp. 248. London, 1844

HOLY (the) Bible; containing the Authorised Version of the Old and New Testaments, with twenty thousand emendations. [By John Tricker Conquest, M.D.] 8vo. [*Brit. Mus.*] London, 1841

HOLY (the) Catholic Church of Christ delineated in her faith and practice, agreeable to the Word of God and sound reason. . . . By a minister of the Established Church [John Mill]. 8vo. Pp. 341. [*Scot. Hist. Soc. Publications*, vol. iii.] Edinburgh, 1773

HOLY (the) childhood of our Blessed Lord; meditations for a month. By the author of *Tales of Kirkbeck* [Henrietta Louisa Farrer, later Mrs Sidney Lear]. 8vo. Pp. viii. 80. London, 1860

HOLY (the) city and the light therein. [By Thomas Lake Harris.] 8vo. N.P. 1880

HOLY (the) Communion and eucharistical office. [By Rev. Joshua Lingard.] 12mo. [*Brit. Mus.*]
Manchester, 1843

HOLY (the) court, in five tomes. The first treating of motives which should excite men of quality to Christian perfection; the second, of the prelate, souldier, statesman and lady; the third, of maxims of Christianity against prophaness . . . ; the fourth, containing the command of reason over the passions; the fifth, containing the lives of the most famous and illustrious courtiers taken both out of the Old and New Testament, and other modern authors. Written in French by Nicholas Caussin; translated into English by Sr. T. H. [Thomas Hawkins] and others. Fourth edition. Fol. [*W.*] London, 1678

Dedicated to Henrietta Maria, Queen-Mother of Great Britain. The first volume appeared originally in 1626 at Paris.

HOLY David and his old English translators clear'd; containing, I. Directions for the more devout use of the Psalms, and a short historical account of the translation and translators. II. The Psalter or Psalms of David, after the translation of the Great Bible. . . . III. A general defence of this old translation. [By Rev. John Johnson, M.A., a Nonjuror.] 8vo. [W. L. Taylor's *Cat. of Psalm Versions*, p. 59.]
London, 1706

A second edition was published in 1709, with the author's name.

HOLY (the) Eastern Church; a popular outline of its history, doctrines, liturgies, and vestments. By a priest of the English Church [John Mason Neale, D.D.]. The preface by the Rev. [R. F.] Littledale. Second edition. 4to. Pp. xi. 102. London, 1873

HOLY (the) ideots contemplations on divine love, rendered into English [from the Latin of Gertrude More] by W. K. B. [Sir Walter Kirkham Blount, Bart.] of Sodington. 12mo.
Paris, 1669

HOLY (the) Inquisition; wherein is represented what is the religion of the Church of Rome; and how they are dealt with that dissent from it. [Epistle dedicatory signed: L. B. *i.e.* Luke de Beaulieu.] 8vo. Pp. 272.
London, 1681

"By ye Reverd Mr Luke Beaulieu, who honourd me wth this booke 1695."—MS. note by Barlow in the Bodleian copy.

HOLY Island monastery; a legend of the fourteenth century. [By G. Clark.] 8vo. [Green's *Bibl. Somers.* ii. 493.]
Bridgwater, N.D.

HOLY (the) isle; a legend of Bardsey Abbey. By Ignatius, O. S. B. [Joseph Leycester Lyne]. Dedicated without permission, to Lord Newborough, and to the Rev. Hugh Roberts, vicar of Aberdaron, Carnarvonshire. 8vo. Pp. 56. London, 1870

HOLY (an) kiss of peace, sent from the seed of life, greeting all the lambs and little ones with a tender salutation. . . . [Signed: W. S. *i.e.* William Smith, of Besthorp.] 4to. [*Brit. Mus.*]
London, 1660

HOLY (the) land; being sketches of the Jews, and of the land of Palestine: compiled from the best sources. [By Rev. Andrew Redman Bonar.] 8vo. [*Nat. Lib. of Scot.*] London, 1844

HOLY (a) life here, the only way to eternal life hereafter; or, a discourse grounded on these words, The weapons of our warfare, 2. Cor. 10. 4. . . . By R. S. [Richard Stanwix], B.D. 8vo. Pp. 300. [Watt's *Bibl. Brit.*]
London, 1652

The author's name is in the handwriting of Barlow, who received a presentation copy.

HOLY (the) life of Gregory Lopez, a Spanish hermite in the West Indies. By Father Francis Losa; done out of Spanish [by Abraham Woodhead]. Second edition. 8vo. [*D. N. B.* vol. 62, p. 400.] London, 1675

HOLY (the) life of Mons. de Renty, a late nobleman of France. . . . Written in French by John Baptist S. Jure, and faithfully translated into English by E. S. [Edward Sheldon], Gent. 8vo. Pp. 347. [*D. N. B.* vol. 52, p. 23.] London, 1658

HOLY meditations for every day; compiled and edited by B. E. B. [B. E. Bishop] from ancient and modern writers. 8vo. London [1867]

HOLY (the) oblation. . . . By an Anglo-Catholic priest [Edward Burton, D.D.]. 8vo. [*Brit. Mus.*] London, 1848

HOLY of holies. [Poems.] Confessions of an Anarchist [John E. Barlas]. 8vo. Pp. 47. [*Brit. Mus.*]
Chelmsford, 1887

HOLY (the) of holies unveiled; an explanation of theosophic figures and scriptural emblems. Written by Philadelphus [Joanna Southcote]. 8vo.
London [1814]

HOLY (the) Order; or, Fraternity of the Mourners in Sion: whereunto is added Songs in the night, or cheerfulnesse under affliction. By J. H., B. N. [Joseph Hall, Bishop of Norwich]. 8vo. 2 parts. [*Brit. Mus.*]
London, 1655

Sometimes wrongly attributed to John Hieron, M.A.

HOLY Orders; the tragedy of a quiet life. [A novel.] By Marie Corelli [Caroline Cody]. 8vo. Pp. viii. 520. [*Brit. Mus.*] London, 1908

HOLY pictures of the mysticall figures of the most holy Sacrifice and Sacrament of the Eucharist, set forth in French by Lewis Richome . . . Translated . . . by C. A. [Christopher Anderton]. 4to. Pp. 300. [*The Library*, Sept. 1926.] [Birchley Hall] 1619

HOLY (the) practises of a devine lover, or the sainctly ideots deuotions. [By David Baker, in religion Augustine Baker.] 12mo. [*Camb. Univ. Lib.*] Paris, 1657

HOLY (the) sacrament explained. [By Edmund Gibson, Bishop of London.] 8vo. [Watt's *Bibl. Brit.*] London, 1705

HOLY (the) Scriptures from scandals are cleared; or an answer to a book set forth by the baptizers; to wit, Henry Hagger and Thomas Pollard, entituled, The Holy Scriptures clearing itself of scandals; . . . Written by a servant of the Lord, in the 6th moneth, 1655. By R. F. [Richard Farnworth]. 4to. Pp. 60. [Smith's *Cat. of Friends' Books*, i. 589.] London, 1655

HOLY (the) sinner; a tractate meditated on some passages of the storie of the penitent woman in the Pharisees house. By W. H. [W. Hodgson]. 12mo. [Hazlitt.] Printed for Andrew Crooke in Paules Churchyard, 1639.

HOLY (the) Spirit the author of immortality; or immortality a peculiar grace of the Gospel, no natural ingredient of the soul: proved from the Holy Scriptures and Fathers, against Mr Clarke's bold assertion of the soul's natural immortality. . . . By a Presbyter of the Church of England [Joseph Pitts]. 8vo. [Arber's *Term Cat.* iii. 687.] London, 1707

HOLY (the) supper, and its administering mediums [in the New Jerusalem Church]. By a Deacon [Francis Black]. 8vo. Pp. xi. 49. [*Brit. Mus.*] London, 1894

HOLY (the) table, name and thing, more anciently, properly, and literally used under the New Testament, then that of an altar; written long ago by a minister in Lincolnshire, in answer to D. Coal, a judicious divine of Q. Maries dayes [but really in reply to Peter Heylin's treatise, "A coale from the altar. . . ." By John Williams, D.D., Bishop of Lincoln, afterwards Archbishop of Canterbury.] 4to. Pp. 238. [*Brit. Mus.*] Lincoln, 1637

Two other issues in the same year differ merely in their titles.

HOLY things for holy men. . . . By S. S. [Samuel Shaw, M.A.] minister of the Gospel. 12mo. London, 1658

HOLY thoughts on a God made man; or, the mysterious Trinity prov'd: also reasons given, that the wise Creator fram'd not the universal all, only for the benefit of this earthly globe, but likewise for many other worlds. . . . By the author of the *Meditations of a divine soul* [Charles Povey]. 8vo. Pp. 560. [*N. and Q.* 1859, p. 115.] London, 1704

HOLY Tonga. By "The Vagabond" [Thomas Julian]. 8vo. Melbourne [1890?]

HOLY Week in Jerusalem in the fourth century; being a translation [by M. L. M'Clure] of the portion of the Peregrinatio Etheriae (Silviae) printed in Mgr. Duchesne's Christian Worship. 8vo. [*Brit. Mus.*] London, 1905

HOLY (the) year; or, hymns for Sundays and holy days, and for other occasions. [Of the 200 hymns, 117 are by the editor, Christopher Wordsworth, D.D., Bishop of Lincoln.] 8vo. Pp. xl. 351. [Julian's *Dict. of Hymnology.*] London, 1862

HOLY zeal against sin shewn to be an acceptable and seasonable duty; in a sermon preached at Lynn Regis in Dorsetshire, Sept. the 4th, 1700, at a Quarterly Lecture appointed for the promoting the reformation of manners. By J. E. [John England], minister of the gospel. 8vo. [Arber's *Term Cat.* iii. 282.] London, 1701

HOLYROOD (the) annual. By the author of *Angus Graeme* [Sophie F. F. Veitch]. 8vo. Paisley, 1884-5

HOMBURG (a) story. By Gordon Seymour [Charles Waldstein, later Sir Charles Walston]. 8vo. Pp. 166. [*Brit. Mus.*] London, 1897

HOME. [A novel. By George Agnew Chamberlain, U.S. Consul at Delagoa Bay.] 8vo. pp. 334. London, 1914

HOME. [A poem.] By the author of *Emmanuel* [Miss E. Colthurst]; with explanatory notes. 12mo. [O'Donoghue's *Poets of Ireland.*] Cork, 1836

HOME; a novel. [By Margaret Cullen.] 12mo. 5 vols. [Watt's *Bibl. Brit.*] London, 1802

HOME; a poem. [By John Boyd Greenshields, Advocate.] 8vo. Pp. 248. [*N. and Q.* 1859, p. 114.] Edinburgh, 1806

Ascribed also to Ann Cuthbert Knight.

HOME amusements. By M. E. W. S. [Margaret Elizabeth Wilson, later Mrs Sherwood]. 8vo. [Cushing's *Init. and Pseud.* i. 257.] New York, 1881

HOME (the) and age of the Avesta. Translated from the German of Emil J. von Dillon [by T. A. Walsh]. 8vo. [*Calc. Imp. Lib.*] Bombay, 1887

HOME, and home papers. By Christopher Crowfield [Mrs Harriet Beecher Stowe]. 8vo. [Cushing's *Init. and Pseud.* i. 71.] Boston, 1875

HOME and its duties; a practical manual of domestic economy for schools and families. . . . [By Mrs J. Werner Laurie.] New edition. 8vo. [*Brit. Mus.*] London [1870]

HOME and school; a story for school girls: a sequel to *The Snowball Society*. [By Mary Bramston.] 12mo. London [1883]

HOME as found. By the author of *Homeward bound* [James Fenimore Cooper]. 12mo. 2 vols. [*Brit. Mus.*] Philadelphia, 1838

HOME ballads. By Nilla [Mrs Abby Carter, *née* Allin]. 12mo. [Cushing's *Init. and Pseud.* i. 204.] New York, 1849

HOME (the) circle. By A. S. P. [Ann S. Paschall]. [Cushing's *Init. and Pseud.* i. 221.] Philadelphia, 18—

HOME defence. By an old Adjutant [James F. Macpherson]. 8vo. Edinburgh, 1900

HOME discipline, or thoughts on the origin and exercise of domestic authority; with an appendix. By a mother and the mistress of a family [Adelaide Sophia Kilvert]. 8vo. Pp. xv. 160. London, 1841

The author's name is given in the second edition.

HOME education. By the author of *Natural history of enthusiasm* [Isaac Taylor, of Ongar, the younger]. Fourth edition. 8vo. Pp. x. 429. London, 1842

The preface is signed: I. T. The first edition appeared in 1837.

HOME fetters. [A tale.] By Raymond Jacberns [Georgina Selby Ash]. 8vo. Pp. 224. [*Lit. Year Book.*] London, 1904

HOME gymnastics for young and old. By L. Hoffmann [Angelo John Lewis]. 8vo. [*Lit. Year Book.*] London, 1892

HOME (the) hymn-book. [By Miss H. P. Hawkins.] 12mo. London, N.D.

HOME in South Africa. By a plain woman, author of *Alone among the Zulus*, etc. [Charlotte Barter]. 8vo. Pp. 158. London [1867]

HOME (a) in the sea; or, the adventures of Philip Brusque, designed to shew the nature and advantages of government. By the author of *Peter Parley's tales* [Samuel Griswold Goodrich]. 12mo. [*Brit. Mus.*] Philadelphia, 1845

HOME (the) kitchen; a collection of practical and inexpensive receipts. By Marion Harland [Mary Virginia Hawes, later Mrs Terhune]. 8vo. Pp. 276. [Kirk's *Supp.*] London, 1884

HOME lessons on the old paths; or, conversations on the [Westminster] Shorter Catechism. By M. T. S. [Mary Thomson Symington]. 8vo. Pp. vi. 288. [*Brit. Mus.*] Paisley, 1878

HOME (the) library. By Arthur Penn [James Brander Matthews]. 12mo. Pp. 154. [Cushing's *Init. and Pseud.* i. 227.] New York, 1883

HOME life in Russia [a translation of "Dead souls"]. By a Russian noble [Nikolai V. Gogol]. Revised by the editor of *Revelations of Siberia* [Krystn Lach Szyrma]. 12mo. 2 vols. [*Brit. Mus.*] London, 1854

HOME life under the Stuarts, 1603-1649. By Elizabeth Godfrey [Jessie Bedford]. 8vo. [*Camb. Univ. Lib.*] London, 1903

This was followed by "Social life under the Stuarts."

HOME life with Herbert Spencer. By "Two" [the Misses —— Baker]. 8vo. Bristol, 1906

The material supplied by the Misses Baker was edited by A. G. L. Rogers.

HOME memories, and other poems. By L. B. L. [Lydia Bosworth Lees]. 8vo. N.P. 1873

HOME (the) of the Bible. By Marion Harland [Mrs Mary V. A. Terhune, *née* Hawes]. 8vo. [Kirk's *Supp.*] New York, 1895

HOME (the) of the dragon; a Tonquinese idyll. By Anna Catharina [Lillie Rebek]. 8vo. London, 1893

Pseudonym Library.

HOME (the) of the mutineers. [By T. B. Murray?] 16mo. Pp. 342. [Sabin's *Dictionary*.] Philadelphia, 1854

HOME (the) of to-day. By a woman who keeps one [Mrs Catherine Masters]. 8vo. Pp. 420. London, 1916

HOME plays for ladies. [I. Lina and Gertrude; or, the Swiss chalet: a drama, in one act. II. Choosing a bride; a comedy, in one act. III. My daughter's daughter; a comedy, in one act. IV. A wonderful cure; a farce, in one act. V. My aunt's heiress; a comedy, in one act. All by Katherine Lacy.] 8vo. London [*c.* 1865]

Published in parts.

HOME portraiture for amateur photographers. By Richard Penlake [Percy R. Salmon]. 8vo. [*Lit. Year Book.*] London, 1899

HOME reminiscences. By E. S. C. [Elizabeth Susan Abbot, Baroness Colchester]. 8vo. [*Brit. Mus.*] London, 1861

HOME rule and Imperial Parliament. By E. Vannin [S. F. Page]. 8vo. [*Gladstone Lib. Cat.*] London, 1886

HOME scenes and heart studies. By G. A. [Grace Aguilar]. 8vo. [Cushing's *Init. and Pseud.* i. 3.] London, 1852

HOME scenes during the Rebellion [of Southern States against the Northern]. By Eiggam Strebor [Maggie Roberts]. 8vo. [*Lib. Journ.* v. 153.] New York, 1875

HOME songs. . . . [By Mrs Postlethwaite.] 12mo. London [1850?]

HOME sounds; from the German of E. Werner [Elizabeth Bürstenbinder]. 12mo. [*Amer. Cat.*] New York, 1888

HOME sunshine; or, the Gordons. By "Cousin Kate" [Catherine Douglas Bell]. 12mo. [Haynes' *Pseud.*] Edinburgh, 1859

HOME, sweet home; a novel. By F. G. Trafford [Mrs Charlotte E. L. Riddell]. 8vo. 3 vols. [*Lond. Lib. Cat.*] London, 1873

HOME tales, founded on fact. By the author of *Charlie Burton*, etc. [Jane Alice Sargant]. 12mo. 8 parts. London, 1853-61

HOME they brought her warrior dead; an "In Memoriam" to the late Prince Imperial of France. By Julian Home [Edward Richard Christie]. 8vo. Pp. 200. London [1880]

HOME thoughts. By "C." [Mrs James F. Cox]. 8vo. [*Amer. Cat.*] New York, 1902

HOME thoughts for mothers and mothers' meetings. [By Jane Ellice Hopkins.] 8vo. London, 1869

HOME (the) treasury of books, pictures, toys. . . . By Felix Summerly [Sir Henry Cole, K.C.B.]. 8vo. [*D. N. B.* vol. 11, p. 269.] London, 1844

HOME-BREAKERS (the). By a looker-on [J. S. Stainton]. 8vo. Pp. 348. London, 1913

HOMELY hints from the fireside. [By Henrietta Wilson.] 12mo. Edinburgh, 1859

HOMELY hints to Sunday-school teachers. By Ephraim Holding [George Mogridge]. 8vo. [Cushing's *Init. and Pseud.* i. 131.] London, 1843

HOMELY musings. By a rustic maiden [Miss —— Stevenson]. 8vo. Pp. 115. [*Nat. Lib. of Scot.*] Kilmarnock, 1870

HOMELY talks about homely things. By Marianne Farningham [Mary Anne Hearne, of Farningham]. 8vo. Pp. vi. 207. London, 1886

HOMELY talks with young men, on the young men of the Bible. . . . By the author of *Joined to an idol* [Mrs Morgan Morgan]. 8vo. Pp. x. 314. [*Brit. Mus.*] London, 1885

HOMEMADE stories. By Ascott R. Hope [Ascott Robert Hope Moncrieff]. 8vo. London, 18—

HOMER a la mode; a mock poem upon the first and second books of Homer's Iliad. [By James, second and last Viscount Scudamore.] 8vo. [*N. and Q.* 1867, p. 297.] Oxford, 1665

HOMER and Virgil not to be compar'd with the two Arthurs. [By Sir Richard Blackmore.] 12mo. Pp. xii. 165. [*Dyce Cat.* i. 97.] London, 1700

HOMER the Second's Bulliad; a satire of the South African campaign. By John Gwynne [A. L. Peticolas]. [*Amer. Cat.*] Milwaukee, 1900

HOMER travestie; being a new translation of the four first books of the Iliad. By Cotton Junior [Thomas Bridges]. 12mo. Pp. 231. [*Brit. Mus.*] London, 1762

A translation of Books I. to XII. by the same writer bears a different title ("A burlesque translation of Homer"): see Vol. I. p. 261.

HOMERIDES; or, a letter to Mr Pope, occasion'd by his intended translation of Homer. By Sir Iliad Doggrel [Thomas Burnet, D.D., in conjunction with George Ducket]. 8vo. Pp. 30. [*D. N. B.* vol. 7, p. 241.] London, 1715

The former of the two writers is sometimes said to have been Sir Thomas Burnet. The title of an edition issued in 1716 is slightly different: "Homerides, or Homer's first book moderniz'd."

HOMER'S Battle of the frogs and mice; with the remarks of Zoilus: to which is prefix'd, the life of the said Zoilus. [By Thomas Parnell, D.D.] 8vo. 21 leaves unpaged, pp. 42. [*N. and Q.* 1858, p. 395.] London, 1717

HOMER'S Iliad, faithfully rendered in Homeric verse, from the original Greek. By Philhellen Etonensis [Lancelot Shadwell, of St John's College, Cambridge. Books I. to IX.]. 8vo. [Cushing's *Init. and Pseud.* ii. 280.] London, 1844-5

Each book is in separate covers; but only I. and II. are anonymous, the author's name being given on the covers of III. to IX.

HOME-RULE (the) and ultramontane alliance. By Scrutator [W. R. Ancketill.] 8vo. Pp. 14. [*Brit. Mus.*] Belfast, 1875

HOME-SPUN; or, five-and-twenty years ago. By Thomas Lackland [George Canning Hill]. 8vo. [Cushing's *Init. and Pseud.* i. 160.] New York, 1867

HOME-SPUN stories. "By Cherith" [Fanny Surtees]. 12mo. [*Lib. Journ.* v. 120.] London, 1877

HOMESTEAD (the); embracing observations and reflections on America and Ireland, on the writer's return from the United States. . . . By Cecil [Charles Edward Fisher]. 8vo. [Cushing's *Init. and Pseud.* i. 53.] London, 1862

HOMEWARD bound; or, Jack Wilson's return from sea. [By Matilda Mary Pollard.] 12mo. Pp. 94. [Boase and Courtney's *Bibl. Corn.* ii. 505.] London [1872]

HOMEWARD bound; or, the chase: a tale of the sea. By the author of *The Pilot*, etc. [James F. Cooper]. 12mo. 2 vols. [*Brit. Mus.*] Philadelphia, 1842

HOMEWARD; songs by the way. By A. E. [George William Russell]. 8vo. [O'Donoghue's *Poets of Ireland.*] Dublin, 1894

HOMEWARD (the) voyage; a book of adventure for boys. By Harvey Collingwood [William J. C. Lancaster]. 8vo. Pp. 384. [*Lit. Year Book.*] London, 1897

HOME-WHIST; an easy guide to correct play. By "Five of Clubs" [Richard Anthony Proctor]. 12mo. [*Brit. Mus.*] London, 1885

HOMILETICAL aids for the Christian Year. By a clergyman [Rev. Edward Wynne, D.D.]. 8vo. London, 1875

HOMILIES for Holy Days and seasons commemorative of our Lord and Saviour Jesus Christ, from Advent to Whitsuntide inclusive; translated from the writings of the Saints, with biographical notices of the writers. [Preface signed: F. O. *i.e.* Rev. Frederick Oakeley.] 8vo. [*Brit. Mus.*] London, 1842

HOMO *v.* Darwin; an examination of Darwin's Descent of man. [By William Penman Lyon, B.A.] 8vo. [F. Boase's *Mod. Eng. Biog.* vol. vi.] London, 1872

HOMŒOPATHIC hand-book, and guide to the domestic use of the medicines. [By Charles Tuckett.] 8vo. [*Brit. Mus.*] London, 1859

HOMOSELLE; a tale. [By Mrs Mary F. Tiernan, *née* Spear.] 12mo. Boston, 1881

HON. (the) Miss Ferrard. [A novel.] By the author of *Hogan, M.P.* [May Laffan, later Mrs Hartley]. 8vo. 3 vols. [*Brit. Mus.*] London, 1881

HONEST and earnest. By Neil Forrest [Mrs Cornelia Floyd]. 12mo. [Cushing's *Init. and Pseud.* ii. 429.] New York, 1873

HONEST (an) answer to the late published Apologie for private preaching; wherein is justly refuted their mad forms of doctrine. . . . With an objection to their common-plea of divine inspiration. . . . By J. T. [John Taylor]. 8vo. Pp. 8. [Whitley's *Bapt. Bibl.* i. 33.] London, 1648

HONEST apprehensions; or, the unbiassed, and sincere confession of faith of a plain, honest lay-man [Edward King, F.R.S., F.A.S.]. 8vo. Pp. 80. [Darling's *Cyclop. Bibl.*] London, 1803

HONEST counsaile; a merrie fitte of a poeticall furie: good to read, better to follow. [In verse. Dedication and preface signed: N. B. *i.e.* Nicholas Breton.] 4to. [*Brit. Mus.*] London, 1605

HONEST (the) ghost; or, a voice from the vault. [By Richard Brathwayt.] 8vo. Pp. 332. [*D. N. B.* vol. 6, p. 234.] London, 1658

HONEST (the) man; or, the art to please in Court. By Nicolas Faret. Translated into English by E. G. [Edward Grimstone]. 12mo. [*Brit. Mus.*] London, 1632

HONEST (an) man's reasons for declining to take any part in the new administration; in a letter to the Marquis of —— [Rockingham. By Charles Lloyd, private secretary to Richard Grenville Temple, first Earl Temple]. 8vo. [*Cat. Lond. Inst.* ii. 13.] London, 1765

In *Bibl. Parriana*, p. 671, this work is entered thus, "An honest man's [Charles Townsend, Dii boni, an honest man!] reasons," etc.

HONEST (the) man's speech. [By Eaton Stannard.] 8vo. [*Brit. Mus.*] Dublin, 1749

The speech was delivered in the Irish House of Commons, on the prosecution of C. Lucas.

HONEST (the) soldier; a comedy in five acts. [By John Henry Colls.] 8vo. [Baker's *Biog. Dram.*] 1805

HONESTY. [A novel.] By M. E. Francis [Mrs Francis Blundell, *née* Margaret E. Sweetman]. 8vo. Pp. 320. London, 1912

HONESTY in distress, but reliev'd by no party; a tragedy, as it is basely acted by Her Majesty's subjects upon God's stage, the world. [By Edward Ward.] 4to. Pp. 30. [*Bodl.*] London, 1705

HONESTY the best policy; or, the hop blossoms. . . . By the author of *The basket of flowers* [John Christoph von Schmid]. 12mo. London, 1853

HONESTY'S best policy; or, penitence the sum of prudence. [By Marchamont Needham.] 4to. London [1678?]

Contemporary attestation.

HONEY and gall; poems. By Cupid Jones [Frank S. Saltus, journalist]. 12mo. Pp. 231. [Cushing's *Init. and Pseud.* i. 143.] Philadelphia, 1873

HONEY (the) bee. [By Alexander Harvey.] 8vo. [Aberdeen] 1868

HONEY bee. By Anatole France [Jacques Anatole Thibault]; translated from the French by Mrs John Lane. 4to. Pp. 186. London, 1911

HONEY out of the rock, flowing to little children, that they may know to refuse the evil and chuse the good: certain select hymns for the use of such, taken from the excellent Mr Isaac Watts. . . . [By Cotton Mather.] With 3 pages of "The Body of divinity versify'd" by another hand [C. M.]. 12mo. Pp. 24. [*Book prices current*, 1921.] Boston, 1715

HONEYMOON'S (a) eclipse. By Sarah Tytler [Henrietta Keddie]. 8vo. Pp. viii. 272. [*Brit. Mus.*] London, 1899

HONEYSUCKLE cottage. By H. N. W. B. [Mrs Harriet Newell Baker, *née* Woods]. 8vo. [Kirk's *Supp.*] Boston, 1870

HONG-KONG to London; or, our new road home from China. By the author of *A reminiscence of Canton* [P. G. Laurie]. 8vo. [*Brit. Mus.*] London, 1872

Preface signed: P. G. L.

HONOR d'Evrel. By Barbara Yechton [Lydia Farrington Krausé]. 8vo. [*Amer. Cat.*] New York, 1903

HONOR May. [By Mary Bartol.] 12mo. [Cushing's *Anon.*] Boston, 1866

HONOR (the) of the University of Oxford defended against the illiberal aspersions of E. B. [Edmund Burke], Esq. . . . Translated from the original Latin of E. B. [Edward Bentham], D.D. 8vo. [*Brit. Mus.*] London [1781?]

HONOR Ormthwaite. By the author of *Lady Jean's vagaries* [Henrietta Keddie]. 8vo. Pp. 332. London, 1896

HONOR redivivus; or, the analysis of honor and armory, with many useful and necessary additions, and supply'd with the names and titles of honour of the present Nobility of England. . . . [By Matthew Carter.] 12mo. [Arber's *Term Cat.* i. 525.] London, 1692

HONORABLE (the) Britons; a poem. [By John Barlow.] 8vo. Dorchester, 1798

HONORABLE (the) Club. By Lynde Palmer [Mary Louise Parmlee, later Mrs A. Peebles]. 8vo. [Cushing's *Init. and Pseud.* i. 224.] New York, 1867

HONORABLE (the) Mrs Moonlight. [A novel.] By Onoto Watanna [Mrs Winnifred Eaton Babcock]. 8vo. Pp. 184. London, 1912

HON^BLE. Mrs Vereker. [A novel. By Mrs Margaret (Hamilton) Argles, later Mrs Hungerford.] 8vo. 2 vols. [*Brit. Mus.*] London, 1888

HONORABLE (the), pleasant and rare conceited Historie of Palmendos, sonne to the famous Prince Palmerin d'Oliua: translated out of French by A. M. [Anthony Munday]. 4to. [*Christie-Miller Cat.*] London, 1589

HONORIA; or, the day of All Souls: a poem, with other poetical pieces. [By Edward Jerningham.] 4to. Pp. 29. [*Bodl.*] London, 1782

HONORIA'S patchwork. [By Mercedes Macandrew.] 8vo. [*Brit. Mus.*] London, 1904

HONORS fame in triumph riding; or, the life and death of the late Honorable Earle of Essex. [Epistle dedicatorie signed: R. P. *i.e.* Robert Pricket.] 8vo. No pagination. [*Bodl.*] London, 1604

HONOUR; a poem inscribed to the Right Honble the Lord Viscount Lonsdale. [By John Brown, D.D.] 4to. [*W.*] London, 1743

HONOUR! A tale. [By Eliza Peake.] 12mo. London, 1844

HONOUR (the) and dishonour of agriculture; translated from the Spanish [of Father R. G. Feijoo] by a farmer in Cheshire. [Edited, if not translated, by Benjamin Stillingfleet.] 8vo. [Nichols' *Lit. Anec.* ii. 336.] London, 1760

HONOUR (the) and justice of the present Parliament, and of their Commissioners of enquiry, vindicated from the calumnies and misrepresentations contained in a late pamphlet [by Sir David Dalrymple, Lord Hailes], entituled, The laws and judicatures of Scotland vindicated, etc. In a letter to the author. [By Patrick Haldane, advocate.] 8vo. [*Camb. Univ. Lib.*] Edinburgh, 1718

The author's name in the handwriting of Dr David Laing.

HONOVR in his perfection; or, a treatise in commendation of the vertues and renowned vertuous vndertakings of the illvstrious and heroicall Princes Henry, Earle of Oxenford, Henry, Earle of Southampton, Robert, Earle of Essex: and the euer praiseworthy and much honoured Lord, Robert Bartve, Lord Willoughby of Eresby; with a briefe chronology of theirs and their auncestours actions: and to the eternall memory of all that follow them now, or will imitate them hereafter, especially those three noble instances, the Lord Wriouthesley, the Lord Delaware and the Lord Mountioy. [Dedication signed: G. M. *i.e.* Gervase Markham.] 4to. [*W.*; Lowndes' *Bibl. Man.*] London, 1624

HONOUR is my guide. By Jeanie Hering [Mrs Adams Acton]. 8vo. London, 1886

HONOUR (the) of chivalry; or, the famous and delectable history of Don Bellianis of Greece [written in Spanish by Geronimo Fernandez: translated by J. Shirley]. 4to. [Arber's *Term Cat.* i. 525.] London, 1672

Various other editions were published.

HONOUR (the) of the school. By May Wynne [Mabel Wynne Knowles]. 8vo. Pp. 299. [*Lit. Year Book.*] London, 1918

HONOUR (the) of Christ. By Graham Hope [Jessie Hope]. 8vo. Pp. 349. [*Lit. Year Book.*] London, 1908

HONOUR (the) of the Seals; or, memoirs of the noble family of Talbot: with the Life of Lord Chancellor Talbot. [By Dr Johnston, of Pontefract.] 8vo. [Martin's *Cat.*] N.P. 1737

HONOUR (the) of the taylors; or, the famous and renowned history of Sir John Hawkwood, knight; containing his many rare and singular adventures, witty exploits, heroic atchievements, and noble performances, relating to love & arms, in many lands: in the series of which history are contained likewise the no less famous actions and enterprizes of others of the same art and mystery. . . . [By William Winstanley.] 4to. Pp. 60. [*Bodl.*] London, 1687

HONOURABLE (the) Jim. By Baroness Orczy [Mrs —— Montague Barstow]. 8vo. [*Lond. Lib. Cat.*] London, 1924

HONOURABLE (the) Peggy. [A novel.] By G. B. Lancaster [Edith Lyttleton]. 8vo. Pp. 438. [*Lond. Lib. Cat.*] London, 1911

HONOURABLE (the) prentice; or, this taylor is a man: shewed in the life and death of Sir John Hawkewood, sometime prentice of London; interlaced with the famous history of the noble Fitzwalter, Lord of Woodham in Essex, and of the poisoning of his faire daughter; also of the merry customes of Dunmow, where any one may freely haue a gammon of bacon, that repents not marriage in a yeere and a day: whereunto is annexed the most lamentable murther of Robert Hall at the high altar in Westminster Abbey. [By William Vallans.] 4to. Pp. 38. [*Bodl.*] London, 1615

Reprinted under the title, "Three ancient and curious histories."

HONOURS academie; or, the famous pastorall of the faire shepheardesse Iulietta. By Nicolas de Montreux: done into English by R. T. [Robert Toft], gentleman. Fol. [*Christie-Miller Cat.*] London, 1610

HONOUR'S fetters. [A novel.] By May Wynne [Mabel Wynne Knowles]. 8vo. Pp. 288. London, 1911

HONOURS (the) of the Lords Spiritual asserted; and their priviledges to vote in capital cases in Parliament maintained by reason and precedents: collected out of the Records of the Tower and the Journals of the House of Lords. [By Thomas Hunt.] Fol. Pp. 32. [Moule's *Bibl. Herald.*; Clarke's *Law Cat.*] London, 1679

Ascribed also to Thomas Frankland.

HONOURS (the) of the table; or, rules of behaviour during meals: with the whole art of carving. By the author of *Principles of politeness* [John Trusler, LL.D.]. 12mo. [*Brit. Mus.*] London, 1788

Several later editions have the author's name.

HOOK (a) in the nose of Leviathan. [By Henry James Prince.] 8vo. Pp. 40. [*Brit. Mus.*] Bridgwater, 1877

Signed: B.

HOOP-PETTICOAT (the); an heroi-comical poem, in two books. By Mr Gay [Captain John Durant de Breval, M.A.]. Third edition. 8vo. Pp. vii. 39. London, 1720

The second edition was published in 1716 under the title of "The petticoat," etc.

HOOPS into spinning-wheels; a tragicomedy, written by a gentleman in Gloucestershire [John Blanch]. 4to. Pp. 39. [*Bodl.*] Gloucester, 1725

The epistle dedicatory is signed: J. B.

HOORAY!!! The royal visit and St Patrick's ruction. [Verse.] By Barney Bradey [William Theodore Parkes, journalist]. 8vo. [O'Donoghue's *Poets of Ireland.*] Dublin, 1868

HOOSIER (the) doctor; a medicated story. By Karl Kringle [J. P. Buckner]. 8vo. [Cushing's *Init. and Pseud.* ii. 83.] Columbus, Ohio, 1881

HOPE and rest; or, the hills of the Shatemuc. By Elizabeth Wetherell [Susan Warner]. 8vo. Pp. 437. [*Brit. Mus.*] London [1890]

HOPE Campbell; or, know thyself. By Cousin Kate [Catherine Douglas Bell]. 8vo. [Haynes' *Pseud.*] Edinburgh [1854]

HOPE evermore; or, some thing to do. . . . [By Mrs Yorick Smythies, *née* Gordon.] 8vo. [*Nat. Lib. of Scot.*] London, 1860

HOPE Leslie; or, early times in the Massachusetts. By the author of *Redwood* [Catherine Maria Sedgwick]. 12mo. 3 vols. [*Nat. Lib. of Scot.*] London, 1828

HOPE Loring; a novel. By Lilian Bell [Mrs A. H. Bogue]. 8vo. [*Amer. Cat.*] Boston, 1902

HOPE Meredith. By the author of *St Olave's*, etc. [Eliza Tabor, later Mrs Stephenson]. 8vo. 3 vols. London, 1874

HOPE (the) of peace, by laying open such doubts and manifest untruthes as are divulged by the Archpriest [George Blackwell] in his Letter or Answere to the bookes which were published by the Priestes. [Signed: J. B. *i.e.* John Bennett.] 4to. [*Brit. Mus.*] Franckford, 1601

HOPE (the) of the faythful, declarying brefely and clearlye the Resurreccion of our Lorde Jesus Chryst past, and of our true essēcial bodyes to come. . . . [By Otho Werdmüller *or* Wermüller. Translated by Miles Coverdale.] 16mo. [*Brit. Mus.*] N. P. [*c.* 1555]

HOPE (the) of the Katzekopfs, or the sorrows of selfishness; a fairy tale. By William Churne, of Staffordshire [Rev. Francis Edward Paget]. 12mo. Pp. xv. 211. [*Bodl.*] Rugeley, 1844

The author's name is given in the second edition, 1846.

HOPE Reed's upper windows. [A tale.] By Howe Benning [Mrs Mary H. Henry]. 8vo. Pp. 255. [*Brit. Mus.*] London [1887]

HOPE the hermit; a romance of Borrowdale. By Edna Lyall [Ada Ellen Bayly]. 8vo. Pp. 156. [*Lit. Year Book.*] London, 1920

HOPEFULL (a) way to cure that horrid sinne of swearing; or, an help to save swearers, if willing to be saved: being an offer or message from Him whom they so daringly and audaciously provoke; also a curb against cursing. [By Richard Young, or Younge, of Roxwell, Essex.] 8vo. [*Brit. Mus.*] London, 1652

HOPES and fears; or, scenes from the life of a spinster. By the author of *The heir of Redclyffe*, etc. [Charlotte Mary Yonge]. 8vo. 2 vols. London, 1860

HOPES (the) of the Church of God as revealed in prophecy. . . . By J. N. D. [John Nelson Darby]. London, 1867

HORACE at the University of Athens. [By Sir George Otto Trevelyan.] Second edition. 8vo. Pp. 68. [Bowes' *Cat. of Camb. Books.*] Cambridge, 1862

HORACE Harwood; a tale. By the author of *The Curate of West Norton* [George Robert Wynne]. 8vo. [*Brit. Mus.*] London [1873]

HORACE in homespun; a series of Scottish pastorals. By Hugh Haliburton, shepherd of the Ochils [James Logie Robertson, M.A.]: with preface, notes, and glossary by J. L. Robertson. 4to. Pp. xi. 100. Edinburgh, 1886

HORACE in London; consisting of imitations of the first two books of the Odes of Horace. By the authors of *Rejected addresses, or the new theatrum poetarum* [Horace and James Smith]. 12mo. Pp. xi. 173. London, 1813

HORACE in New York. [By Isaac Starr Clason.] 12mo. [Sabin's *Dictionary.*] Boston, 1826

HORACE on the links. . . . By C. J. B. [Charles James Billson] and P. S. W. [P. S. Ward]; with notes from Horace Hutchinson's writings. 8vo. Pp. 100. London, 1903

HORACE'S Art of poetry, translated into English verse. By A Graduate of Cambridge [Rev. Charles Nesfield, M.A.]. 8vo. London, 1854

HORACE'S Epistle to the Pisos, on the art of poetry; translated into English verse [by John Stedman, M.D.]. 8vo. [Laing's *Cat.*] Edinburgh, 1784

HORACE'S first satire modernized, and addressed to Jacob Henriques. [By George Canning, of the Middle Temple.] 4to. Pp. 27. [*Bodl.*] London, 1762

HORÆ canonicæ; or, devotions for the seven stated hours of prayer. [By Rev. Fred. Oakeley, M.A.] 12mo. London, 1841

HORÆ Icenæ; being the lucubrations of a winter's evening, on the result of the general election, 1835. By Publicus Severus [Sir John Joseph Dillon]. 8vo. Pp. viii. 75. Private print, N.P., N.D.

The author's name in the handwriting of Dawson Turner, to whom a copy was presented.

HORÆ momenta Cravenæ; or, the Craven dialect, exemplified in two dialogues, between Farmer Giles and his neighbour Bridget: to which is annexed a copious glossary. By a native of Craven [William Carr, B.D., of Magdalen College, Oxford]. 8vo. Pp. 125. [*Bodl.*] London, 1824

The second edition (1828) is entitled "The dialect of Craven," *q.v.*

HORÆ poeticæ. [By Charles Burton, D.D., Manchester.] 8vo. [*Manch. Free Lib.*] Glasgow, private print [1826]

HORÆ poeticæ. By J. G. M. [John Gray M'Kendrick, M.D.]. 8vo. Pp. 124. Glasgow, 1904

HORÆ poeticæ; or, poems, with notes. By a retired physician [Disney Alexander]. 8vo. [*Brit. Mus.*] London, 1837

HORÆ Romanæ; or, an attempt to elucidate St Paul's Epistle to the Romans, by an original translation, explanatory notes, and new divisions. By Clericus [Robert Cox]. 8vo. [*Brit. Mus.*] London, 1823

HORÆ solitariæ; or, essays upon the names and titles of Jesus Christ. [By Ambrose Serle.] 8vo. 2 vols. [*Brit. Mus.*] London, 1804

HORÆ subsecivæ; observations and discourses. [By Grey Brydges, Lord Chandos.] 8vo. Pp. 542. [Park's *Walpole*, ii. 184; Brydges' *Cens. Lit.* vi. 192.] London, 1620

Ascribed by Wood to Gilbert Cavendish.

HORÆ subsecivæ; or, a treatise shewing the original grounds, reasons, and provocations necessitating our sanguinary laws against Papists made in the daies of Q. Elizabeth, and the gradations by which they ascended unto that severity; and shewing that no Papist hath been executed in England on the single account of his religion, either in the daies of Edw. 6, Q. Elizabeth, K. James, Car. I. or Car. 2., though multitudes of Protestants were, in the daies of H. 8. and Q. Mary. By D. W. Esq; [William Denton, M.D.]. 4to. Pp. 90. [*D. N. B.* vol. 14, p. 381.] London, 1664

HORÆ viaticæ; the author, Mela Britannicus [Charles Kelsall]. 12mo. Pp. vi. 412. [*Royal Institution Cat.*] London, 1836

HORARY astrology. By Raphael [R. C. Smith]. 12mo. London, 1883

Attributed also to J. Palmer.

HORATIAN (the) canons of friendship; being the third satire of the first book of Horace imitated. . . . By Ebenezer Pentweazle, of Truro in the county of Cornwall, Esq. [Christopher Smart]. 4to. London, 1750

HORATIAN metres, attempted in English. By C. C. [Charles Chorley]. 8vo. [Boase and Courtney's *Bibl. Corn.*] Truro, 1867

HORATIAN (an) ode to the King's most excellent Majesty, June 22nd 1911. [By Austin Dobson.] 8vo. Pp. 4. [*Dobson Bibl.* 1925] Private print, 1911

HORATII (the); a tragedy. [By Ichabod H. Wright.] 8vo. Pp. vi. 86. [*Nat. Lib. of Scot.*] London, 1846

HORATIO and Amanda; a poem. By a young lady [Mary Julia Young]. 4to. [*Brit. Mus.*] London, 1777

HORATIO Nelson, England's sailor hero. By Mardale [Richard H. Holme, of Newcastle]. 8vo. London, 1905

HORATIUS. Epistolæ; English translation and notes, and two dissertations on the provinces of the drama and poetical imitation. [By Richard Hurd, D.D.] 12mo. 2 vols. [*D. N. B.*] Cambridge, 1757

HORE (le) di recreatione; or, the pleasant historie of Albino and Bellama. . . . To which is added Il Insonio insonadado, or a sleeping-waking dreame. . . . By N. W. [N. Whiting], Master in Arts of Queenes Colledge in Cambridge. [In verse.] 12mo. [*Brit. Mus.*] London, 1637

See another edition beginning "The most pleasante historie of Albino and Bellama" . . . 1639.

HORINDIAD (the); a poem, in three books. [By John Ricketts.] 12mo. [*J. Maidment.*] N.P. 1770

HORN (the) exalted; or roome for cuckolds: being a treatise concerning the reason and original of the word cuckold, and why such are said to wear horns. . . . [By George Rogers, M.D.?] 8vo. London, 1661

HOROLOGICAL dialogues; in three parts: shewing the nature, use, and right managing of clocks and watches; with an appendix containing Mr Oughtred's method for calculating of numbers: the whole being a work very necessary for all that make use of these kind of movements. By J. S. [John Smith], clock-maker. 8vo. Pp. 120. London, 1675

HORRIDA bella; an impeachment of the war system. [By William Catchpool.] 12mo. London, 1889

HORRIDA hystrix, satyricon Castoreanum; quod ex schedis manuscriptis deprompsit civis Beverlacensis [Robert Mackenzie Beverley]. 8vo. Pp. lxv. 61. [*Brit. Mus.*] Villæ Regis, 1826

The introduction is in English.

HORRORS (the) of bribery; a penitential epistle [in verse] from Philip Hamlin, tinman to the Right Hon. H. Addington, Prime Minister. . . . Edited [but rather written] by Peter Pindar, Esq. [John Wolcot, M.D.]. 4to. Pp. 26. [*Brit. Mus.*] London, 1802

HORSE (the). By William Youatt (reprinted from "Knight's Store of knowledge"); a new edition, re-edited and revised, with observations on breeding cavalry horses, by Cecil, author of *The stud farm*, etc. [Cornelius Tongue]. 12mo. [*W.*] London, 1855

See an earlier edition (1840) below.

HORSE (the) and his rider; an anecdotic medley. By Thormanby [W. W. Dixon]. 8vo. Pp. vi. 302. [*Lond. Lib. Cat.*] London, 1888

HORSE and horsemanship of the United States and British Provinces. By Frank Forester [Henry William Herbert]. 8vo. 2 vols. [*Lit. Year Book.*] New York, 1857

HORSE (the) and the hound; their various uses and treatment, including practical instructions in horsemanship, and a treatise on horse-dealing. By Nimrod [Charles James Apperley]. 8vo. Pp. viii. 524. [Haynes' *Pseud.*] Edinburgh, 1842

HORSE flesh for the Observator; being a comment on Gusman, ch. 4, v. 5, held forth at Sam's Coffee House. By T. D., B.D., chaplain to the Inferiour Clergies Guide [John Phillips, nephew of John Milton]. 4to. [*Brit. Mus.*] London, 1682

HORSE (the) Guards; by the two mounted sentries. [By Lieutenant-Colonel John Josiah Hort.] With twelve coloured illustrations. 8vo. Pp. viii. 104. London, 1850

HORSE (the); with a treatise on draught, and a copious index. [By William Youatt.] 8vo. [*Brit. Mus.*] London, 1840

Library of Useful Knowledge. See a later edition (1855) above.

HORSE-HOING (the) husbandry; or, an essay on the principles of tillage and vegetation: a method of introducing a sort of vineyard culture into the corn-fields. By I. T. [Jethro Tull]. Fol. [*Brit. Mus.*] London, 1733

In an earlier edition (1731), the title begins "The new horse-houghing husbandry. . . ."

HORSES and hounds; a practical treatise on their management. By "Scrutator" [K. W. Horlock]. Illustrated by Harrison Weir. 8vo. Pp. xii. 302. [*Brit. Mus.*] London, 1855

HORSES and roads; or, how to keep a horse sound on his legs. . . . By Free Lance [J. T. Denny]. 8vo. Pp. xii. 229. London, 1880

HORSES I have known; with stories about them. By G. G. [Henry George Harper]. 8vo. Pp. 224. [*Lit. Year Book.*] London, 1905

HORSE'S (a) tale. By Mark Twain [Samuel Langhorne Clemens]. 8vo. [*Lit. Year Book.*] London, 1907

HORSES; their rational treatment, causes of their deterioration and premature decay. . . . By Amateur [G. R. Walker]. 8vo. Pp. 70. [*Brit. Mus.*] London, 1865

HORSE-SHOE Robinson; a tale of the Tory ascendency. By the author of *Swallow Barn* [John Pendleton Kennedy]. 12mo. 3 vols. [*Nat. Lib. of Scot.*] London, 1835

Incorrectly attributed to J. K. Paulding.

HORSE-SHOE nails; or, new ideas on old subjects. By Minor Hugo [Luke Hansard?]. 12mo. [*Camb. Univ. Lib.*] London, 1843

HORSHAM; its history and antiquities. [By Miss D. Hurst.] 8vo. [*Brit. Mus.*] London, 1868

HORTENSE; from the German of Wilhelm Heimburg [Bertha Behrens]. 8vo. Chicago, 1891

HORTUS Anglicus; or, the modern English garden: containing a familiar description of all the plants which are cultivated in the climate of Great Britain, either for use or ornament, and of a selection from the established favourites of the stove and greenhouse. . . . By the author of *The British botanist* [Stephen Clarke]. 12mo. 2 vols. [*Brit. Mus.*] London, 1822

HORTUS vitæ; or, the hanging gardens: moralising essays. By Vernon Lee [Violet Paget]. 8vo. [*Lit. Year Book.*] London, 1904

HOSANNAH to the Son of David; or, a testimony to the Lord's Christ, offering itself indifferently to all persons, though more especially intended for the people who pass under the name of Quakers; wherein not so much the detecting of their persons, as the reclaiming the tenderhearted among them from the error of their way, is modestly endeavoured. . . . By a lover of truth and peace [John Jackson]. 4to. Pp. 176. [Smith's *Bibl. Anti-Quak.* pp. 11, 247.] London, 1657

HOSPITAL days. [By Jane Stuart Woolsey.] 8vo. Pp. 182. [*Brit. Mus.*] New York, 1870

HOSPITAL days [during the Great War]. By Platoon Commander [Arthur Hobart Mills]. 8vo. Pp. 187. [*Brit. Mus.*] London, 1916

HOSPITAL (an) for fools; a dramatic fable, as it is acted at the Theatre-Royal, by His Majesty's servants. [By Rev. James Miller.] The musick by Mr Arne. Sung by Mrs Clive. 8vo. [Baker's *Biog. Dram.*] London, 1739

HOSPITALL (the) of incurable fooles, erected in English as neere the first Italian model [of Tommaso Garzoni] . . . as the unskilfull hand of an ignorant architect could devise. 4to. [*Brit. Mus.*] London, 1600

HOSPITALLARIA; or, a synopsis of the rise, exploits, privileges, insignia, etc. of the . . Order of Knights Hospitallers of Saint John of Jerusalem; with a brief account of the Sixth or British Branch. [By Sir Richard Brown, Bart.] 8vo. [*Brit. Mus.*] London, 1837.

HOSPITALS and sisterhoods. [By Mary Stanley.] Second edition. 12mo. Pp. viii. 156. [*Brit. Mus.*] London, 1855

HOSPITALS, large and small; with hints on legislative self-provision. [By George Cordwent, M.D.] 8vo. Taunton, 1879

HOSTAGES to fortune; a novel. By the author of *Lady Audley's secret*, etc. [Mary Elizabeth Braddon, later Mrs Maxwell]. 8vo. 3 vols. [*Brit. Mus.*] London, 1875

HOT pressed doctors outwitted; or, who's afraid? By Hugo de la Loy [Hugh Leslie]. 8vo. Edinburgh, 1808

HOT water as a remedy. . . . By J. M. [John Butler, M.D.]. 8vo. [*Brit. Mus.*] New York [1887]

HOT (the) water cure. [By Adam Blenkinsop, M.D.] 8vo. London, 1846

HOTCH-POT. By "Umbra" [Charles Cavendish Clifford, M.P.]. 8vo. Pp. 151. [*Brit. Mus.*] Edinburgh, 1866

Another edition appeared in 1867, with the following addition to the title:—An old dish with new materials.

HOTCH-POTCH; or, the food of pilgrims climbing towards the light. By Modern Hermit [John Bentley]. 8vo. Pp. ix. 171. [*Brit. Mus.*] Sunderland, 1894

HÔTEL d'Angleterre; and other stories. By Lanol Falconer [Mary Elizabeth Hawker]. 8vo. [*Brit. Mus.*] London, 1891

HÔTEL (the) du petit St Jean; a Gascon story. [By Charlotte Louisa Hawkins Dempster.] 8vo. Pp. viii. 315. [*Nat. Lib. of Scot.*] London, 1869

HOUGHAM Church, Kent; its architectural history as told by its stones to the vicar. [Signed: C. A. M. *i.e.* Charles Arthur Molony.] 8vo. [*Brit. Mus.*] London, 1878

HOUNDS, gentlemen, please. By Maintop [W. B. Forbes]. 8vo. [*Amer. Cat.*] New York, 1910

HOUP-LA; a tale. By John Strange Winter [Mrs Henrietta E. V. Stannard, *née* Palmer]. 8vo. London, 1885

HOUR (the) before the dawn; an appeal to men. [By Mrs Josephine E. Butler.] 8vo. Pp. 111. [*Brit. Mus.*] London, 1876

HOUR (an) in His Majesty's gaol of Newgate. . . . [By Sir James Williams.] Third edition. 12mo. [*Brit. Mus.*] London [1820]

HOUR (the) of beauty; songs and poems. By Fiona Macleod [William Sharp]. 8vo. Pp. xii. 110. [*Amer. Cat.*] Portland, Maine, 1907

HOUR (an) with Miss Streatov. By "Pansy" [Mrs Isabella Alden, *née* Macdonald]. 8vo. [*Lit. Year Book.*] Boston, 1884

HOUR (an) with the children. By Mrs L. L. Worth [Mrs Mary Wolcott Ellsworth]. 12mo. [Cushing's *Init. and Pseud.* i. 309.] Boston, 1866

HOURES of recreation, or after dinners; which may aptly be called The garden of pleasure; containing most pleasant tales, worthy deedes and wittie sayings, of noble princes & learned philosophers; with their morals, no less delectable than profitable. [By Ludovico Guicciardini.] Done firste out of Italian into Englishe by James Sandford, Gent., and now by him newly perused, corrected and enlarged. . . . 8vo. 2 parts. B. L. [*Brit. Mus.*] London, 1576

The first edition, 1573, was entitled, "The garden of pleasure. . . ."

HOUR-GLASS (the) mystery. [A novel.] By Headon Hill [Frank E. Grainger]. 8vo. Pp. 320. [*Lond. Lib. Cat.*] London, 1913

HOURS (the); being prayers for the third, sixth and ninth hours. [By Arthur H. D. Acland-Troyte.] 12mo. [*Brit. Mus.*] London, 1841

HOURS in the picture gallery of Thirlestone House, Cheltenham; being a catalogue with critical and descriptive notices of some of the principal paintings in Lord Northwick's collection. [By Henry Davies?] New edition. 8vo. [*Brit. Mus.*] Cheltenham, 1846

Signed: H. D.

HOURS of idleness; poems, original and translated. By a noble author [Lord Byron]. 12mo. Pp. 183. [*Brit. Mus.*] London, 1822

HOURS of leisure; poems. [By S. B. Ritchie.] 8vo. [O'Donoghue's *Poets of Ireland.*] [Belfast, 1880?]

HOURS of quiet thought. . . . By M. W. [John M. Whitelaw]. 8vo. London, 1865

HOURS of rest; or, Sabbath-thoughts for Sabbath-days. By the author of *The protoplast* [Mrs E. C. E. Baillie, *née* Lattor]. 8vo. Pp. iv. 315. [*Brit. Mus.*] London, 1867

HOURS of solitude; a collection of original poems, now first published. By Charlotte Dacre [Mrs Byrne], better known by the name of Rosa Matilda. 8vo. 2 vols. London, 1805

HOURS of solitude; or, poetical recreations of a bachelor. By T.V. [T. Veasey?]. 12mo. [*Brit. Mus.*] London, 1851

HOURS of sorrow cheered and comforted; poems by C. E., author of *Hymns for a week*, etc. [Charlotte Elliott]. Sixth edition. 8vo. Pp. viii. 178. [*Camb. Univ. Lib.*] London, 1863

For an earlier edition, see the following entry.

HOURS of sorrow; or, thoughts in verse, chiefly adapted to seasons of sickness . . . [By Charlotte Elliott.] Third edition. 12mo. London, 1844

Presentation copy from the author.

HOURS of sun and shade; reveries in prose and verse, with translations from various European languages. By Viscount Percy V. G. de Montgomery [James Hickman]. 8vo. [*Brit. Mus.*] London, 1856

HOURS of thought. [By William M'Combie.] 8vo. Pp. 176. Edinburgh, 1835

Later editions give the author's name.

HOURS with John Darby. [By James E. Garretson, M.D.] 12mo. [Kirk's *Supp.*] Philadelphia, 1876

HOURS with the first falling leaves. [Verse. By Kenelm Henry Digby.] 8vo. N.P., N.D.

Other copies bear the author's name, and a date (1868).

HOUSE beautiful; or, the Bible museum. By A. L. O. E., authoress of *The shepherd of Bethlehem*, etc. [Charlotte Maria Tucker]. 8vo. Pp. 243. London, 1877

HOUSE (the) by the churchyard. [A novel.] By Charles de Cresseron [Joseph Sheridan Le Fanu]. 8vo. [Baker's *Guide to the best fiction*, p. 232.] London, 1863

HOUSE (the) by the river; a novel. By Florence Warden [Florence Alice Price, later Mrs George E. James]. 8vo. Pp. 314. [*Brit. Mus.*] London, 1905

HOUSE (the) by the works; a novel. By the author of *The occupations of a retired life* [Isabella Fyvie, later Mrs John R. Mayo]. 8vo. 2 vols. [*Brit. Mus.*] London, 1879

HOUSE (the) called Hurrish; a novel. By "Rita" [Mrs W. Desmond Humphreys, *née* Eliza M. J. Gollan]. 8vo. [*Brit. Mus.*] London, 1909

HOUSE (the) in town; a sequel to *Opportunities*. By the author of *The wide wide world* [Susan Warner]. 8vo. Pp. 204. London, 1871

HOUSE (the) of Commons for the people. [By Henry Wait Hall.] 8vo. [Shune's *Bath Books*, p. 96.] 1856

HOUSE (the) of Commons on stimulants. By the author of *Study and stimulants* [Alfred Arthur Reade]. 8vo. Pp. 23. [*Brit. Mus.*] London, 1885

HOUSE (the) of correction; or, certayne satyricall epigrams, written by I. H. [probably John Heath], Gent. Together with a few characters called Par Pari, or, like to like, quoth the devill to the collier. 8vo. [Lowndes' *Bibl. Man.* p. 964.] London, 1619

HOUSE (the) of danger. By Guy Thorne [Cyril A. E. Ranger-Gull]. 8vo. Pp. 256. [*Brit. Mus.*] London, 1920

HOUSE (the) of dreams. [By Rev. William James Dawson.] 8vo. London, 1897

The fifth edition, 1901, has the author's name.

HOUSE (the) of Elmore; a family history. [By Frederick William Robinson.] 8vo. 3 vols. [*Brit. Mus.*] London, 1855

HOUSE (the) of fulfilment. By George M. Martin [Mrs Atwood R. Martin]. 12mo. [*Amer. Cat.*] New York, 1904

HOUSE (the) of grass. By Cousin Annie [Annie Maria Barnes]. 8vo. Pp. 336. [*Amer. Cat.*] Nashville, Tenn., 1893

HOUSE (the) of hidden treasure; a novel. By Maxwell Gray [Mary Gleed Tuttiett]. 8vo. Pp. 367. [*Lit. Year Book.*] London, 1898

HOUSE (the) of Israel; Scripture story from the birth of Isaac to the death of Jacob. By the author of *The wide wide world* [Susan Warner]. New edition. 8vo. Pp. 360. [*Brit. Mus.*] London, 1903

HOUSE (the) of Joseph in England. By a watcher [Mrs —— Worsley?]. 12mo. [*Brit. Mus.*] London, 1881

HOUSE (the) of quiet; an autobiography, edited [but rather written] by J. T. [Arthur Christopher Benson]. 4to. Pp. 243. [*Lond. Lib. Cat.*] London, 1904

HOUSE (the) of Raby; or, our Lady of darkness. [By Jane M. Winnard, later Mrs Hoop.] 8vo. 3 vols. London, 1854

HOUSE (the) of reform that Jack built and The political advertiser. [Two squibs. By William Hone?] 8vo. [*Brit. Mus.*] London [1832]

For another edition, see "The Tories' Refuge for the destitute. . . ."

HOUSE (the) of the misty star. By the author of *The lady of the decoration* [F. Little]. 8vo. Pp. 296. [*Amer. Cat.*] London, 1915

HOUSE (the) of the strange woman. By F. Norreys Connell [Conal O'Connell O'Riordan]. 8vo. [O'Donoghue's *Poets of Ireland.*] London, 1895

HOUSE (the) of Usna. [A play.] By Fiona Macleod [William Sharp]. 8vo. [*Lit. Year Book.*] New York, 1903

HOUSE (the) of wisdom. The house of the sons of the Prophets. An house of exquisite enquiry, and of deep research; where the mind of Jehovah Ælohim in the holy Scriptures of truth, in the original words and phrases, and their proper significancy, is diligently studied, faithfully compared, and aptly put together, for the further promoting, and higher advancing of Scripture-knowledges, of all useful arts, and profitable sciences; in the one book of books, the word of Christ, copied out, and commented upon, in created beings. . . . [By Francis Bampfield.] Fol. Pp. 30. [*D. N. B.* vol. 3, p. 101.] London, 1681

The Hebrew title is—

בֵּית חָכְמוֹת. בֵּית בְּנֵי הַנְּבִיאִים. בֵּית הַמִּדְרָשׁ.

HOUSE (the) of Yorke. . . . By M. A. T. [Mary Agnes Tincker]. 8vo. [Cushing's *Init. and Pseud.* i. 279.] New York, 1872

HOUSE (the) on the marsh. By Florence Warden [Mrs George E. James, *née* Florence Alice Price]. 8vo. London, 1905

HOUSE (the) on the moor. By the author of *Margaret Maitland*, etc. [Mrs Margaret O. Oliphant]. 8vo. 3 vols. London, 1861

HOUSE (the) on the rock. By the author of *The dream chintz*, *A trap to catch a sunbeam*, etc. [Matilda Anne Planché, afterwards Mrs Mackarness]. 12mo. London, 1852

HOUSE (the) on the sunless side. By Florence Warden [Florence Alice Price, later Mrs George E. James]. 8vo. Pp. 20. London, 1899

HOUSE (the) on wheels; or, far from home. From the French of Madame de Stolz [Countess Fanny de Bégon], by N. D'Anvers [Mrs Nancy Bell, *née* Meugens]. 8vo. [*Brit. Mus.*] London, 1874

HOUSE (the) opposite. By "Rita" [Mrs W. Desmond Humphreys, *née* Eliza M. J. Gollan]. 8vo. Pp. 303. [*Brit. Mus.*] London, 1912

HOUSE (the) party; a novel. By "Ouida" [Louise de la Ramée]. 8vo. [*Lit. Year Book.*] London, 1886

HOUSE (the) that baby built. By the author of *The fight at Dame Europa's school* [Henry William Pullen, M.A.]. 8vo. Pp. 259. [*Brit. Mus.*] Salisbury, 1874

HOUSE (the) that Jack built. By Annan Dale [Rev. James Wesley Johnstone, Wesleyan]. 8vo. [*Method. Who's Who.*] New York, 1898

HOUSE (the) that Jack built. By "Fleeta" [Kate W. Hamilton]. 8vo. [*Amer. Cat.*] Philadelphia, 1880

HOUSE (the) that Tweed built. [By William James Linton.] 8vo. Cambridge, Mass. [1871]

HOUSE (the), the garden, and the steeple; a collection of old mottoes. [By Arthur Lee Humphreys.] 8vo. Pp. 88. [*Brit. Mus.*] London, 1907

Signed: A. L. H.

HOUSE (a) with a history. By Florence Warden [Florence Alice Price, later Mrs George E. James]. 8vo. Pp. 310. London, 1901

HOUSE (the) with the golden windows. By J. E. Buckrose [Mrs Falconer Jameson]. 8vo. Pp. 318. [*Lond. Lib. Cat.*] London, 1921

HOUSE (the) with the green shutters. By George Douglas [George Douglas Brown, B.A.]. 8vo. [Baker's *Guide to the best fiction*, p. 204.] London, 1901

HOUSE-BOAT (the) boys. By Harry Castlemon [Charles Austin Fosdick]. 8vo. [Cushing's *Init. and Pseud.* i. 52.] New York, 1896

HOUSEFUL (a) of girls. By Sarah Tytler [Henrietta Keddie]. 8vo. Pp. viii. 408. [*Lit. Year Book.*] London, 1889

HOUSEHOLD (the) angel in disguise. By Madeline Leslie [Mrs Harriet Baker, *née* Woods]. 8vo. Pp. 319. [*Brit. Mus.*] London [1883]

HOUSEHOLD expenses, for one year, of Philip, third Lord Wharton. [Edited by W. C. Trevelyan.] 4to. [Martin's *Cat.*] Newcastle-on-Tyne, 1829

HOUSEHOLD happiness, and how to secure it. By Old Chatty Cheerful [William Martin]. 12mo. [Haynes' *Pseud.*] Norwich, 1866

HOUSEHOLD (the) of Bouverie; or, the elixir of gold: a romance. By a Southern lady [Mrs Catherine Ann Warfield, *née* Ware]. 8vo. [Cushing's *Init. and Pseud.* i. 271.] New York, 1860

HOUSEHOLD (the) of Sir Thos. More. By the author of *Mary Powell* [Anne Manning]. Libellus a Margareta More, quindecim annos nata, Chelseiæ inceptvs. 8vo. Pp. 275. London [1851]

HOUSEHOLD puzzle. By Pansy [Mrs Isabella Alden, *née* Macdonald]. 8vo. Pp. 319. London, 1889

HOUSEHOLD (the) Robinson Crusoe . . . [With an introductory memoir signed: W. H. D. A. *i.e.* W. H. Davenport Adams.] 8vo. [*Brit. Mus.*] London, 1871

HOUSEHOLD stories from the land of Hofer; or, popular myths of Tirol, including the Rose-garden of King Lareyn. By the author of *Patrañas; or, Spanish stories*, etc. [Rachel Henriette Busk]. 8vo. Pp. iv. 420. [*Brit. Mus.*] London, 1871

HOUSEKEEPER'S (the) friend. By J. W. B. [Jane W. Buckingham]. 8vo. [Cushing's *Init. and Pseud.* ii. 13.] Zanesville, Ohio, 1876

HOUSE-ROOM. [A novel.] By Ida Wild [Mrs Meynell Plasson]. 8vo. Pp. 313. London, 1916

HOUSES for town and country. By William Herbert [Herbert David Croly]. 8vo. [*Amer. Cat.*] New York, 1907

HOUSEWIFE'S (the) reason why; affording to the manager of household affairs intelligible reasons for the various duties she has to superintend or perform. . . . Tenth thousand. By the author of *The reason why—General science*, etc. [Robert Kemp Philp]. 8vo. Pp. xlii. 352. [Boase and Courtney's *Bibl. Corn.* ii. 493.] London [1857[

HOVEDEN, V.C. [A novel.] By W. S. Gregg [Frances Mabel Robinson]. 8vo. 3 vols. London, 1891

HOVERERS (the); a tale. By Lucas Cleeve [Mrs Adelina Georgina Isabella Kingscote, *née* Wolff]. 8vo. Pp. 304. [*Lit. Year Book.*] London, 1908

HOW a penny became a thousand pounds. [By Robert Kemp Philp.] 8vo. Pp. 96. [Boase and Courtney's *Bibl. Corn.* ii. 492.] London, 1856

HOW about Fiji? or, annexation *versus* non-annexation; with a sketch of the group. [By James Herman de Ricci.] 8vo. Pp. 81. [*Col. Inst. Lib.*] London, 1874

HOW an innocent man was sent to prison. [By Walter Wren.] 12mo. Reading [1877]

HOW armies fight. By "Ubique" [General F. G. Guggisberg]. 8vo. Pp. 490. [*Lit. Year Book.*] London, 1914

The earlier edition (1902) is entitled "Modern Warfare."

HOW Bennie did it. By Mat Merchant [W. S. Wood]. 8vo. [Cushing's *Init. and Pseud.* i. 192.] Portland, Maine, 1874

HOW can bank paper be best protected from fraudulent imitation? [By Rev. John Davies.] Fol. Pp. 4. [*Brit. Mus.*] [London, 1822]

HOW can paper money increase the wealth of a nation? [By John Twells, banker.] 8vo. [*Brit. Mus.*] London, 1867

HOW can the Church educate the people? . . . A letter addressed to the . . . Archbishop of Canterbury. By a member of the National Society [G. F. Mathison]. 8vo. Pp. iii. 131. [*Brit. Mus.*] London, 1844

HOW Charlie helped his mother. By Ruth Buck [Mrs Joseph Lamb]. 8vo. [*Nat. Lib. of Scot.*] London [1861]

HOW China ought to be governed. By John Coming [Archibald Lamont]. 8vo. Pp. 182. London, 1914

HOW Cynthia went a-maying; a romance of long ago, wherein the siege of Wardour Castle is truly chronicled. By Christopher Hare [Mrs Marion Andrews]. 8vo. Pp. 266. [*Lond. Lib. Cat.*] London, 1901

HOW do you like it? or, dried rose leaves. By S. E. S. C. [Sophy Emily Stewart Clark]. 8vo. N.P., N.D.

HOW Donald kept faith. By "Fleeta" [Kate W. Hamilton]. 8vo. [*Amer. Cat.*] Philadelphia, 1900

HOW England saved Europe; the story of the Great War (1792-1815). By Vedette [Rev. William Henry Fitchett]. 8vo. 4 vols. [*Lond. Lib. Cat.*] London, 1899

HOW I became a Unitarian. . . . By a clergyman of the Protestant Episcopal Church [Rev. G. W. Hyer]. 8vo. [Cushing's *Init. and Pseud.* i. 163.] Boston, 1852

HOW I came to be Governor of the Island of Cacona. By the Hon. Francis Thistleton, late Governor of the Island of Cacona [William Henry Fleet]. 8vo. Montreal, 1853

HOW I cured my craving for drink. By one who twice suffered from delirium tremens [Ferguson Sumerville Dalkeith]. 8vo. Glasgow, 1885

HOW I escaped . . . [By W. H. Parkins.] 8vo. [*Brit. Mus.*] London, 1894

HOW I made money at home with the incubator, bees, etc. By John's wife [Hunter M'Culloch]. 8vo. [*Lib. Journ.* xv. 222.] Philadelphia, 1884

HOW I managed and improved my estate. . . . [By Coventry K. D. Patmore.] 8vo. [*Lond. Lib. Cat.*] London, 1886

HOW I managed my house on £200 a year. By a lady [Mrs Millicent Whiteside Cook]. 12mo. [Cushing's *Init. and Pseud.* i. 161.] London [1880?]

HOW I tamed Mrs Cruiser. By Benedict Cruiser. Edited [but really written] by George Augustus Sala. 8vo. London, 1858

HOW I won over fifty prizes in Weekly Periodicals. . . . By J. E. S. [J. E. Sorrel]. 8vo. London, 1900

HOW is the cholera propagated? The question considered, and some facts stated. By an American physician [Patrick Macaulay, M.D.]. 8vo. [Cushing's *Init. and Pseud.* i. 14.] London, 1831

HOW is the Queen's Government to be carried on? The problem solved by the restoration of the Privy Council. [By Stewart Erkine Rolland.] 8vo. [*Brit. Mus.*] London, 1866

HOW it came about. By Nellie Grahame [Mrs Annie Ketchum Dunning]. 12mo. Cushing's *Init. and Pseud.* i. 119.] Philadelphia, 1884

HOW little Katie knocked at the door of heaven. By Aunt Fanny [Mrs Fanny Barrow]. 8vo. [Cushing's *Init. and Pseud.* ii. 58.] London, 1864

HOW little Winks took his friends to see the Cambridge Anatomical Museum. . . . [By T. W. Ricardo.] 8vo. Pp. 20. [Bowes' *Cat. of Camb. Books.*] Cambridge, 1882

HOW Louis defended his arbour; and how Aleck wanted part of Constantine's lake. Fifth thousand. [By Samuel Norwood.] 8vo. Pp. 27. [*F. Madan.*] London [1871]

Said to have appeared first under the title of "Account of the fight around the arbour of Louis in Dame Europa's School."

HOW Marjory helped. By Martha Caroll [Martha Brooks]. 12mo. [Cushing's *Init. and Pseud.* i. 151.] Boston, 1874

HOW not to do it; a manual for the awkward squad; or a handbook of directions written for the instruction of raw recruits in our rifle volunteer regiments. By one of themselves [Robert Michael Ballantyne]. With illustrations. 8vo. Edinburgh, 1859

HOW Paul's penny became a pound. By the author of *Dick and his donkey* [Mrs C. E. Bowen]. 4to. [*Brit. Mus.*] London [1866]

HOW Peter's pound became a penny. [By Mrs C. E. Bowen.] 4to. [*Brit. Mus.*] London [1866]

HOW she came into the kingdom; a romance. [Dedication signed: C. M. C. *i.e.* Charlotte Moore Clark.] 8vo. [*Brit. Mus.*] London, 1878

HOW should we keep Whitsun-week? [By Willoughby T. Balfour.] 8vo. [*Brit. Mus.*] London [1869]

HOW soldiers fight. By F. Norreys Connell [Conal O'Connell O'Riordan]. 8vo. [O'Donoghue's *Poets of Ireland.*] London, 1899

HOW the children raised the wind. By Edna Lyell [Ada Ellen Bayly]. 8vo. [*Lit. Year Book.*] London, 1895

HOW the dreams came true. By the author of *When the swallows come again* [Mabel Fitzroy Wilson]. 8vo. London, 1901

HOW the French took Algiers; or the Janissary's slave: from the German of Wilhelm Oertel [W. O. Horn]. 8vo. [Kirk's *Supp.*] Edinburgh, 1881

HOW the ground of temptation is in the heart of the creature. [By James Nayler.] 4to. [Smith's *Cat. of Friends' Books*, i. 37.; ii. 230.] N.P. [1662]

HOW the parish of Debach borrowed £400, and refused to pay it all back. [By Ralph Thomas.] 8vo. London, 1879

HOW the rain-sprites were freed. By Davida Coit [Vida D. Scudder]. 8vo. [Kirk's *Supp.*] New York, 1885

HOW they got the land; or, the origin, nature, and incidence of the land-tax. By Aliquis [Alexander Robertson, of Dundonnachie]. 8vo. [*Brit. Mus.*] London, 1892

HOW they went to Europe. By Margaret Sidney [Mrs Harriet Mulford Lothrop]. 8vo. [Kirk's *Supp.*] Boston, 1885

HOW they were caught in a trap; a tale of France in 1802. By Esmé Stuart [Miss Amélie Claire Leroy]. 8vo. [*Lond. Lib. Cat.*] London, 1880

HOW things went wrong. [A tale.] By Raymond Jacberns [Georgina Selby Ash]. 8vo. Pp. 252. [*Lit. Year Book.*] London, 1905

HOW to attract the birds; and other talks about bird-neighbors. By Neltje Blanchan [Mrs Nellie B. Doubleday]. 8vo. [*Amer. Cat.*] New York, 1902

HOW to be a hero. By E. E. L. [E. Elizabeth Lay]. 8vo. [Kirk's *Supp.*] Baltimore, 1875

HOW to be happy. By Grace Gold [Mrs Maria Frink]. Sixth edition, revised. 8vo. [*Amer. Cat.*] Valparaiso, Ind., 1901

HOW to be happy though civil. By the author of *How to be happy though married* [Rev. Edward John Hardy, M.A.]. 8vo. [*Brit. Mus.*] London, 1909

HOW to be happy though married. By a Graduate of the University of Matrimony [Rev. Edward John Hardy, M.A.]. 8vo. [*Lond. Lib. Cat.*] London, 1885

HOW to be witty; or, old saws with new teeth. By Irwin Longman [Ingersoll Lockwood]. 12mo. New York, 1886

HOW to become an author; information regarding choice of subjects. . . . By Prince Hiland [Hiland Bertie Merrill]. 8vo. [*Amer. Cat.*] New York, 1904

HOW to build or buy a country cottage. By "Home Counties" [J. W. Robertson Scott]. 8vo. [*Brit. Mus.*] London, 1905

HOW to build ships; an essay upon the weakness of large iron steamships. By a seaman [Samuel P. Griffin]. 8vo. New York, 1876

HOW to buy a horse; with hints on shoeing and stable management. By Pelagius [F. J. Morgan]. 12mo. Pp. xii. 132. [*Brit. Mus.*] London, 1896

Some later editions give the author's name.

HOW to capture and govern Gibraltar; a vindication of civil government against the attacks of the Ex-Governor, Sir Robert William Gardiner, in his secret and unlicensed report. . . . [By Charles Blake.] 8vo. [*Brit. Mus.*] London, 1856

HOW to choose a good milk-cow, etc. Translated from the French of J. H. Magne [by Henry Beveridge, advocate, Ingievar]. 8vo. Glasgow, 1853

HOW to do it. By Nellie Grahame [Mrs Annie Dunning, *née* Ketchum]. 12mo. [Cushing's *Init. and Pseud.* i. 119.] Philadelphia, 1884

HOW to dress on £15 a year as a lady. By a lady [Mrs Millicent Whiteside Cook]. 8vo. Pp. 129. [*Brit. Mus.*] London, 1874

HOW to economize like a lady. By the author of *How to dress on fifteen pounds a year* [Mrs Millicent Whiteside Cook]. 8vo. Pp. 192. [*Brit. Mus.*] London [1874]

HOW to estimate the true worth of a picture. . . . By an old critic [Frederick T. Mott]. 12mo. Pp. 23. [*Brit. Mus.*] London, 1882

HOW to get a farm and where to find one. . . . [By Edmund Morris.] 8vo. Pp. 345. [Sabin's *Dictionary.*] New York, 1864

HOW to get fat; or, the means of preserving the medium between leanness and obesity. By a London physician [Edward Smith, M.D.]. 8vo. Pp. 29. [*Nat. Lib. of Scot.*] London, 1865

HOW to get married. By the author of *How to be happy though married* [Rev. Edward John Hardy, M.A.]. 8vo. [*Brit. Mus.*] London, 1909

HOW to get married although a woman; or, the art of pleasing men. By "a young widow" [Irene W. Hartt]. 8vo. [*Brit. Mus.*] London, 1895

HOW to get out of Newgate. By one who has done it, and can do it again [Sir Francis Cowley Burnand]. 8vo. Pp. 32. [*Brit. Mus.*] London [1873]

HOW to get rich! Written for poor men and young beginners of life. By their affectionate friend, Uncle Ben [Daniel F. Tyler]. 8vo. [Cushing's *Init. and Pseud.* ii. 17.] New York, 1872

HOW to get up a children's play. By Maggie Browne [Margaret Hamer, afterwards Mrs Andrewes]. 8vo. London, 1903

HOW to keep a cat in health. By two friends of the race—Mrs Ellis Walton [Mrs F. Percy Cotton] and Mr G. J. R. Ouseley. 8vo. London, 1901

HOW to keep a dog in the city. [By Thomas Wesley Mills.] 8vo. [*Amer. Cat.*] New York, 1891

HOW to keep books; the tradesman's guide to bookkeeping. By a practical man [J. Stuart, newspaper editor]. 8vo. [*Brit. Mus.*] Swansea [1896]

HOW to know the ducks, geese, and swans. By Owen Nox [Charles Barney Cory]. 8vo. Pp. 92. [*Amer. Cat.*] Boston, 1897

HOW to know the shore-birds (limicolæ) of North America (south of Greenland and Alaska) . . . By Owen Nox [Charles Barney Cory]. 8vo. Pp. 89. [*Amer. Cat.*] Boston, 1897

HOW to learn the Morse alphabet in half an hour. By the author of *International correspondence by means of numbers* [Charles Stewart, M.A.]. 8vo. [*Brit. Mus.*] London, 1876

HOW to live the victorious life. By an unknown Christian [Albert Ernest Richardson]. 8vo. Pp. 143. [*Brit. Mus.*] London [1921]

HOW to make a Saint; or, the process of canonization in the Church of England. By the Prig [Thomas Longueville]. 12mo. [*Brit. Mus.*] London, 1887

HOW to make home healthy. By the author of *The teacher's companion* [Robert Nelson Collins]. 12mo. London [1855]

HOW to make home unhealthy. [By Henry Morley.] Reprinted from the *Examiner.* 12mo. Pp. 82. [*Brit. Mus.*] London, 1850

HOW to make money from poultry. By the author of *Eggs all the year round* [W. Powell Owen]. 8vo. Pp. 116. [*Brit. Mus.*] London [1919]

HOW to make money in a country hotel. By Charles Martyn [J. Elliott Lane]. 8vo. [*Amer. Cat.*] New York, 1904

HOW to meet the difficulties of the Bible. [By Rev. Robert Tuck, B.A.] 8vo. [*Brit. Mus.*] London, 1896

HOW to nurse sick children. [By Charles West, M.D.] 8vo. London, 1854

Later editions bear the author's name.

HOW to obtain capital . . . without security, free from interest and never repayable. [By W. P. M. Black.] 8vo. [*Brit. Mus.*] London, 1896

HOW to pass 90 per cent. and earn "Excellent." By one who does it [Alfonzo Gardiner]. 8vo. [*Brit. Mus.*] Manchester, 1886

HOW to play base-ball. By Connie Mack [Cornelius M'Gillicuddy]. 8vo. [*Amer. Cat.*] Philadelphia, 1903

HOW to play Bridge. By Badsworth [Lindsay Lister]. 8vo. [*Amer. Cat.*] London, 1900

HOW to play Whist; with the laws and etiquette. . . . By "Five of Clubs" [Richard Anthony Proctor]. 8vo. [*Brit. Mus.*] London, 1885

HOW to prepare dishes of fishes; with hints about sauces and seasonings. By Jenny Wren [Jane Atkinson]. 8vo. [Cushing's *Init. and Pseud.* i. 310.] London [1888]

HOW to print and publish a book. . . . [By William Thorn Warren.] 8vo. Pp. 39. [*Brit. Mus.*] London, 1890

HOW to punch the bag. . . . By Young Corbett [W. H. Rothwell]. 8vo. [*Amer. Cat.*] New York, 1904

HOW to read the future from tea-leaves. Translated from the Chinese by Mandra [Miss J. M. Mason]. 8vo. Pp. 15. [*Brit. Mus.*] Stamford, 1925

HOW to rise in the world, to respectability, independence, and usefulness. By Old Chatty Cheerful [William Martin]. 12mo. [*Brit. Mus.*] London [1861]

HOW to row. [By Thomas Jones Derington.] 8vo. [*Brit. Mus.*] Oxford, 1870

HOW to see the English Lakes. [By Mrs Bitha Lloyd, *née* Fox.] 8vo. Pp. 110. [Kirk's *Supp.*] London [1858]

HOW to settle the church-rate question. [By Augustus Kerr Bozzi Granville, M.A.] 8vo. London [1856]

HOW to shy her; or, a peep at the moors: a comedy, in five acts. [By Alexander Dunlop.] 8vo. Glasgow, 1828

HOW to study the Old Testament. . . . By S. M. A. [Mrs Susan M. Alexander]. 8vo. [Cushing's *Init. and Pseud.* ii. 3.] New York, 1873

HOW to teach geography; an introduction to "Glimpses of the globe." [By John Richard Blackiston.] 8vo. Pp. 42. London [1886]

HOW to tell a story, and other essays. By Mark Twain [Samuel L. Clemens]. 8vo. Pp. 233. [*Brit. Mus.*] New York, 1897

HOW to train up a parent in the way he should go; from "Sermons out of Church." By the author of *John Halifax, gentleman* [Dinah Maria Mulock, later Mrs Craik]. 8vo. Pp. 43. [*Brit. Mus.*] London, 1913

HOW to use a camera. By Clive Holland [Charles J. Hankinson]. 8vo. Pp. 132. [*Lond. Lib. Cat.*] London, 1908

HOW to win at Auction Bridge. By "Cut Cavendish" [Edwin Anthony]. 8vo. Pp. 194. [*Lit. Year Book.*] London, 1914

HOW to win love; or, Rhoda's lesson. By the author of *John Halifax, gentleman* [Dinah Maria Mulock, later Mrs Craik]. 8vo. Pp. 91. [*Brit. Mus.*] London [1883]

HOW to write a good play. By Frank Archer [Frank Bishop Arnold]. 8vo. Pp. xi. 224. [*Brit. Mus.*] London, 1920

HOW to write a novel. By a novelist [Emily Foster]. 8vo. London, 1887

HOW Tom and Dorothy made and kept a Christian home. By Margaret Sidney [Mrs Harriett Mulford Lothrop, *née* Stone]. 8vo. [Kirk's *Supp.*] Boston, 1894

HOW Tommy saved the barn. By James Otis [James Otis Kaler]. 8vo. Pp. 87. [Kirk's *Supp.*] New York [1895]

HOW two girls tried farming. By Dorothea Alice Shepherd [Mrs Ella Pratt, *née* Farnam]. 8vo. [*Lib. Journ.* iv. 457.] Boston, 1879

HOW we did them in seventeen days! To wit, Belgium, the Rhine, Switzerland and France; described and illustrated by one of ourselves [Richard Marrack, solicitor], aided . . . by the other [Rev. E. G. Harvey]. 8vo. Pp. 68. [Boase and Courtney's *Bibl. Corn.*] Truro [1875]

HOW we educate our officers; the latest warrant for the regulation of the Army Competitive Examinations. By the author of *The Franco-German War; its causes and immediate effects* [John Tecklenborough]. 8vo. Pp. vi. 170. [*Brit. Mus.*] London, 1884

Ascribed also to Henry Naidley.

HOW we manage at our Board, and "The Hoose." [By Alex. Walker and Wm. Forsyth.] 8vo. [Robertson's *Aberd. Bibl.*] Aberdeen, 1881

HOW we raised our baby. [By Jerome Walker, M.D.] With an introduction by the author of *Helen's babies* [John Habberton]. 12mo. [Kirk's *Supp.*] New York, 1877

HOW we spent the autumn; or, wanderings in Britanny. By the authoresses of *The timely retreat* [Madeleine A. W. Dunlop and Rosalind H. W. Dunlop]. 8vo. London, 1860

HOW we spent the summer; or, a voyage en zigzag in Switzerland and Tyrol. . . . [By Elizabeth Tuckett.] Second edition. Obl. fol. [*Brit. Mus.*] London, 1871

HOW we went to Rome in 1857. By C. F. M. [Caroline Fuller Maitland]. 8vo. Pp. 103. [*Brit. Mus.*] London, private print, 1892

HOW Willie became a hero; a tale for boys. By the author of *Clary's confirmation* [Frances E. Reade]. 8vo. [Kirk's *Supp.*] London [1881]

HOWETOON; records of a Scottish village [Kirriemuir]. By a residenter [Alan Reid]. 8vo. Pp. 193. [Mitchell and Cash's *Scot. Top.*] Paisley [1895]

HOYDEN (the); a novel. By the author of *The Duchess* [Mrs Margaret Argles, later Mrs Hungerford]. 8vo. Pp. 313. [*Amer. Cat.*] New York, 1893

HOYLE made familiar; being a companion to the card-table. . . . By Eidrah Trebor [Robert Hardie]. 12mo. London, 1830

H.R.H. the Prince of Wales. [By Mrs Lowndes, *née* Marie Belloc.] 8vo. London, 1898

HUBBLE (the) Shue. By Miss Carstairs. [Edited by William H. Logan, with a preface by James Maidment.] 12mo. [*W.*; Martin's *Cat.*] [1835]

HUBERT, or, the orphans of St Madelaine; a legend [in verse] of the persecuted Vaudois. By a clergyman's daughter [Frances Lydia Bingham]. 8vo. Pp. iv. 75. [Sparke's *Bibl. Bolt.* p. 24.] Bolton, 1845

HUBERT'S wife; a story for you. By Minnie Mary Lee [Mrs Julia Amand Wood, *née* Sargent]. 12mo. [Cushing's *Init. and Pseud.*] New York, 1884

HUDIBRAS: the first part; written in the time of the late wars. [By Samuel Butler.] 8vo. Pp. 125. London, 1663

—— The second part. By the author of the first [Samuel Butler]. 8vo. Pp. 125. London, 1664

These two parts are the author's editions. For an account of the various editions of the three parts, see Bohn's *Lowndes*, p. 334 *et seq.*

HUDIBRAS redivivus; or, a burlesque poem on the times. [By Edward Ward.] 4to. 2 vols. [*Bodl.*] London, 1705-7

Each volume contains 12 parts.

HUE (a) and cry after the false prophets and deceivers of our age; and a discovery of them by their works and fruits, and who they are in this age that follow the same spirit, and act the same things as did the false prophets in former generations. [Signed: E. B. *i.e.* Edward Burrough.] 4to. [*Bodl.*] London, 1661

HUE (an) and cry after the fundamental lawes and liberties of England, occasionally written upon the stealing of one of the grand assertors of them out of Newgate, by a party of men on horseback, pretending themselves to be souldiers, raised and paid by the people of England (not for the subversion but) the preservation of the said lawes and liberties &c. . . . By a well-wisher to the saints now reigning on earth, had they had the patience to have staid till the people had chose them, or that Christ the King of Saints above . . . had setled the government upon them [John Lilburne]. 4to. Pp. 8. [Thomason's *Coll. of Tracts*, ii. 38.]

Europe, printed in the year of Melodious Discord, to the tune of the Cross and the Harp when the servants are princes and the masters are slaves. [London, 1653] Signed: Anonimus.

HUGH; a romance. By the author of *Annie Jennings* [Leslie Gore]. 12mo. 2 vols. [*Nat. Lib. of Scot.*] London, 1871

HUGH Crichton's romance. By the author of *Lady Betty*, etc. [Christabel Rose Coleridge]. 8vo. 3 vols. [*Camb. Univ. Lib.*] London, 1875

HUGO Blanc, the artist; a tale of practical and ideal life. By an artist [Lester A. Roberts]. 8vo. [Cushing's *Init. and Pseud.* i. 20.] New York, 1867

HUGO Grotius's Second part of the Truth of Christian religion; or the confutation of Paganism, Judaism, and Mahumetism: translated from the Latin by C. B. [Clement Barksdale], a divine of the Church of England. . . . 8vo. [Arber's *Term Cat.* ii. 587.] London, 1696

HUGUENOT (the) family. By Sarah Tytler, author of *Citoyenne Jacqueline*, etc. [Henrietta Keddie]. 8vo. 3 vols. London, 1867

HUGUENOTS (the) in France and America. By the author of *Three experiments of living* [Mrs Hannah F. Lee]. 12mo. [*Brit. Mus.*] London, 1843

HUIA'S homeland; and other verses. By Roslyn [—— Sinclair]. 8vo. London, 1897

HULS pillar of providence erected; or, the providentiall columne, setting out heavens care for deliverance of that people . . . from the bloud-sucking cavaliers who had for six weeks closely besieged them. By T. C. [Thomas Coleman], minister of God's word. 4to. Pp. 60. [*Bibl. Lind.*] London, 1644

HULSE House; a novel. By the author of *Anne Grey* [Hon. Harriet Cradock, *née* Lister]. 12mo. 2 vols. [*Bodl.*] London, 1860

HUMAN authority, in matters of faith, repugnant to Christian charity; illustrated in two discourses on Matth. xxiii. 8. With a prefatory address, explaining the particular occasion of offering them to the public. By the author of an *Essay on the justice of God* [—— Haslet]. 8vo. Pp. xxii. 57. [*Bodl.*] London, 1774

HUMAN (the) cobweb; a romance of Old Peking. By B. L. Putnam Weale [Bertram Len Simpson]. 8vo. Pp. 446. [*Brit. Mus.*] London, 1910

HUMAN (the) complex; essays. By Charles Granville [Francis Charles Granville Egerton, Earl of Ellesmere]. 8vo. Pp. 85. [*Brit. Mus.*] London, 1910

HUMAN documents; lives re-written by the Holy Spirit. By Lionel North [G. J. H. Northcroft]. 8vo. Pp. 270. [*Lit. Year Book.*] London, 1909

HUMAN happiness; a poem . . . with several other miscellaneous poems . . . [By Giles Jacob.] 8vo. [*Brit. Mus.*] London, 1721

Signed: G. J.

HUMAN nature in its four-fold state of primitive integrity, entire depravation, begun recovery, and consummate happiness or misery . . . in several practical discourses. By a minister of the Gospel in the Church of Scotland [Thomas Boston, of Ettrick]. 8vo. Pp. 634. Edinburgh, 1720

Later editions have the author's name.

HUMAN nature surveyed by philosophy and revelation, in two essays. I. Philosophical reflections on an important question. II. Essay on the dignity of human nature. With aphorisms and indexes to both essays. By a gentleman [Andrew Wilson, M.D.]. 8vo. Pp. iv. 164. [Orme's *Bibl. Bib.* p. 471.] London, 1758

HUMAN ordure, botanically considered; the first essay, of the kind, ever published in the world. By Dr S—t [Jonathan Swift, D.D.]. 8vo. [*Bodl.*] Printed at Dublin; reprinted at London, 1733

HUMAN passions delineated; in figures droll, satyrical and humorous. By Timothy Bobbin [John Collier]. Fol. [*Brit. Mus.*] Manchester, 1773

In a later edition (London, 1810, 4to) the title begins, "The passions humorously delineated. . . ."

HUMAN (the) quest; being some thoughts . . . on the art of happiness. By Sarah Grand [Mrs Francis E. M'Fall, *née* —— Clark]. 8vo. [*Lond. Lib. Cat.*] London, 1900

HUMAN (the) soul revealed. By "Minerva Vickers" [William Norman Wilson]. 8vo. London, 1907

HUMAN sympathy; a collection of rough blocks of verse. By "one of those who loves his fellow men" [Edmund Ryley Eckersley, solicitor]. Pp. 68. [Sparke's *Bibl. Bolt.*] Bolton [Lancs] private print, 1887.

HUMAN (the) touch. By "Sapper" [Cyril M'Neile]. 8vo. Pp. 298. [*Lit. Year Book.*] London, 1918

HUMAN (the) touch of sympathy. By J. E. [J. Ellis]. 12mo. London, 1916

HUMAN (the) tragedy. By Anatole France [Jacques Anatole Thibaut]; translated by Alfred Allinson. 4to. Pp. 146. London, 1919

HUMANE industry; or, a history of most manual arts, deducing the original, progress, and improvement of them: furnished with variety of instances and examples, shewing forth the excellency of humane wit. [By Thomas Powell, D.D.] 8vo. Pp. 188. [*Brit. Mus.*] London, 1661

HUMANE life; or, a second part of the Enquiry after happiness. By the author of *Practical Christianity* [Richard Lucas, D.D.]. The third edition. 8vo. Pp. 258. [*Bodl.*] London, 1696

HUMANE prudence; or, the art by which a man may raise himself and fortune to grandeur. By A. B. [William de Britaine]. 12mo. Pp. 141. [*Bodl.*] London, 1680

HUMANITY; or, the cause of the creatures advocated: a poem, for young persons. By the author of *Nugæ sacræ*, etc. [William Ball]. 8vo. [Smith's *Cat. of Friends' Books*, p. 96.] London, 1828

HUMANITY; or, the rights of nature: a poem, in two books. By the author of *Sympathy* [Samuel Jackson Pratt]. 4to. [*Brit. Mus.*] London, 1788

HUMBLE (the) address of the people of Great-Britain to His Majesty. [By J. Woodhouse.] 8vo. [*Nat. Lib. of Scot.*] London, 1763

HUMBLE (a) address to the Churches of Christ, not to forsake the assembling themselves together. [By Benjamin Wallin.] 8vo. [Whitley's *Bapt. Bibl.* i. 120.] London, 1750

HUMBLE (an) address to the clergy of England, recommending a method for the more speedy augmentation of the income of their indigent brethren. . . . [By the Rev.——Hutchinson, of Holywell, Hunts.] 8vo. Pp. 31. [Bartholomew's *Camb. Books.*] London, 1764

HUMBLE (an) address to the Commissioners appointed to judge of all performances relating to the longitude; wherein it is demonstrated, from Mr Flamsteed's observations, that by Sir I. Newton's theory of the moon, as it is now freed from some errors of the press, the longitude may be found by land and sea, either night or day, when the moon is visible, and in proper weather, within very few miles of certainty. By R. W. [Robert Wright]. 4to. [*W.*] London, 1728

HUMBLE (an) address to the knights, citizens, and burgesses elected to represent the Commons of Great Britain in the ensuing Parliament. By a freeholder [William Pulteney, Earl of Bath]. 8vo. London, 1734

HUMBLE advice to the Conforming and Non-conforming ministers and people, how to behave themselves under the present liberty. By the author of *Toleration not to be abused* [Francis Fullwood, D.D.]. 8vo. [*Brit. Mus.*] London, 1672

HUMBLE (the) and modest inquiry concerning the right and power of electing and calling ministers to vacant churches, finished; in two parts. The first being the history of settlements for the space of ninety years, from the establishing of the Reformation, anno 1560, down to the abolishing of the patronages, anno 1649 . . . the second being an account of the poor and wretched defence of the pretended divine right of the people, made by some who stile themselves Protesters against the Assembly 1732, in a pamphlet [by Sir Thomas Gordon, and others], intituled The mutual negative to parish and Presbytery in the election of a minister. By the author of the *Humble and modest inquiry* [George Logan, A.M.]. 8vo. Pp. 153. [*New Coll. Lib.*] Edinburgh, 1733

HUMBLE (an) apology for Christian orthodoxy. [By Patrick Delany, D.D.] 8vo. Pp. xvi. 44. [*Brit. Mus.; D. N. B.* vol. 14, p. 311.] London, 1761

Incorrectly ascribed to Robert Clayton, Bishop of Clogher.

HUMBLE (an) apology for St Paul, and the other apostles; or, a vindication of them and their doxologies from the charge of heresy. By Cornelius Paets [Arthur Ashley Sykes, D.D.]. 8vo. [Disney's *Memoir of Sykes*, p. xv.] London, 1719

HUMBLE (a) attempt at scurrility, in imitation of those great masters of the art, the Rev. Dr S—th [Smith], the Rev. Dr Al—n [Allison], the Rev. Mr Ew—n [Ewing], the Rev. D. J. D—ve [Dove], and the heroic J—n D—n [John Dickinson], Esq. . . . By Jack Retort, student in scurrility [William Franklin]. 8vo. Quilsilvania [Pennsylvania], 1765

Written by a son of Dr Benjamin Franklin in defence of his father.

HUMBLE (the) attempt of a layman towards a confutation of Mr H. Mayo's pamphlet, call'd, The Scripture doctrine of Baptism, etc. . . . By Philalethes [Thomas Randall]. 8vo. [Whitley's *Bapt. Bibl.* i. 107.] London, 1767

HUMBLE (an) attempt to form a system of conjugal morality; the substance of six discourses to young people. [By Joseph Fawcett.] 8vo. Manchester, 1787

HUMBLE attempt to investigate and defend the Scripture doctrine concerning the Father, the Son, and the Holy Spirit; to which is added observations concerning the mediation of Jesus Christ. . . . [By James Purves.] 8vo. [Evans' *Amer. Bibl.* vol. 7, p. 259.] Philadelphia, 1788

HUMBLE (the) Christian. By the author of *The Primitive Church in its Episcopacy* [Rev. Robert Armitage]. 12mo. [*Brit. Mus.*] London, 1846

HUMBLE (an) desired union between prerogative and priviledge. . . . [By John Taylor, the Water-poet.] 4to. [*Ashley Lib.*] London, 1642

HUMBLE (an) enquiry into the nature of the dependency of the American Colonies upon the Parliament of Great Britain. By a freeholder of South Carolina [Rev. John J. Zubly]. 4to. [Evans' *Amer. Bibl.* vol. 4, p. 212.] [Charleston, So. Carolina?] 1769

HUMBLE (an) essay on Christian Baptism. [By Rev. Daniel Taylor, Baptist Minister.] 12mo. Pp. 70. [Whitley's *Bapt. Bibl.* i. 188.] Leeds, 1768

HUMBLE (an) essay toward the settlement of peace and truth in the Church, as a certain foundation of lasting union. [By Sir Edward Harley.] 4to. [*D. N. B.* vol. 24, p. 393.] London, 1681

HUMBLE (an) examination of a printed abstract of the answers [by John Williams, Abp. of York] to nine reasons of the House of Commons, against the votes of Bishops in Parliament. [By Cornelius Burges.] Printed by order of a Committee of the Honourable House of Commons, now assembled in Parliament. 4to. Pp. 77. [Thomason's *Coll. of Tracts*, i. 22.] London, 1641

The same work as a "Vindication of the nine reasons, etc.," *q.v.*

HUMBLE (an) inquiry into the Scripture-account of Jesus Christ; or, a short argument concerning his deity and glory, according to the Gospel. [By Thomas Emlyn.] 4to. Pp. 30. [*Bodl.*] N.P. 1702

HUMBLE (an) motion to the Parliament of England concerning the advancement of learning; and reformation of the Universities. By J. H. [John Hall, of Durham]. 4to. Pp. 47. [*Camb. Univ. Lib.*] London, 1651

HVMBLE (an) motion vvith svbmission vnto the Right Honorable LL. of Hir Maiesties Privie Covnsell. VVherein is laid open to be considered, how necessarie it were for the good of this lande, and the Queenes Majesties safety, that ecclesiasticall discipline were reformed after the worde of God: and how easily there might be provision for a learned ministery. [By John Penry.] 4to. Pp. 111. [Strype's *Life of Whitgift*, p. 348; Dexter's *Cong. Bibl.; D. N. B.* vol. 44, p. 348.] Anno 1590

This was preceded by another anonymous work from the same writer, entitled "A treatise wherein is manifestlie proved . . ." See below.

HVMBLE motives for association to maintaine religion established; published as an antidote against the pestilent treatises of secular priests. [By William Bradshaw.] 8vo. [*D. N. B.* vol. 6, p. 184; *Nat. Lib. of Scot.*] N.P. 1601

Attributed also, with little reason, to Thomas Digges.

HUMBLE (an) petition for a birth; addressed to the inhabitants of Glasgow. By a rhymer [Thomas Bell]. 12mo. [*Brit. Mus.*] Glasgow, 1809

HUMBLE (the) petition of the Freethinkers to the Rt. Hon. P—p E—l of H—k, L—d H—h C—r of G—t B—n, setting forth their right of patronage in a certain book, called The divine L—n of M—s demonstrated, etc., and praying to be restored to the same. [By Benjamin Newton.] 8vo. [*Brit. Mus.*] London, 1756

HUMBLE pleadings for the good old way; or, a plain representation of the rise, grounds and manner of several contendings of the Reverend Mr John Hepburn (minister of the Gospel at Orr in Galloway) and his adherents (a considerable body of people, in the South and West) against many sins and defections in the Establishment and proceedings of the Church and State of Scotland, about and since the Revolution. In two parts. . . . [By Gavin Mitchell.] 12mo. Pp. 252. [Wodrow's *Corresp.* ii. 268.] N.P. 1713

Wrongly attributed to John Hepburn.

HUMBLE (an) proposal for parochial reformation, by restoring Rural Deans and Chapters, according to the ancient way of the Church; commended to the consideration of all Conformists and Dissenters as the best way to peace and unity. By J. M. [James Metford], Presbyter of the Church of England. 4to. Pp. 140. [Arber's *Term Cat.* iii. 479.] London, 1705

HUMBLE (an) proposal for the relief of debtors, and speedy payment of their creditors. [By Sir T. Culpeper, jun.] 4to. [*Manch. Free Lib.*] London, 1671

HUMBLE (an) proposal to the people of England, for the encrease of their trade, and encouragement of their manufactures; whether the present uncertainty of affairs issues in peace or war. By the author of the *Compleat tradesman* [Daniel Defoe]. 8vo. Pp. 59. London, 1729

HUMBLE proposals for the relief, encouragement, security, and happiness of the loyal, courageous seamen of England in their lives and payment. . . . [By William Hodges.] 4to. [Quaritch's *Cat.*] London, 1695

HUMBLE (the) proposals of sundry learned and pious divines within this kingdome; concerning the Engagement, intended to be imposed on them for their subscriptions. [By Edward Reynolds, D.D., senior.] 4to. [*Bodl.; D. N. B.* vol. 48, p. 41.] London, 1650

The author's name in the handwriting of Barlow.

HUMBLE (an) remonstrance concerning some additional confirmations of the Kingdom of Christ to be in its succession 1697. . . . [By Thomas Beverley.] 4to. [*Brit. Mus.*] [London, 1690]

HUMBLE (an) remonstrance to His Majesty [Charles I.] against the tax of ship-money imposed, laying open the illegalitie, abuse, and inconvenience thereof. [By William Prynne.] 4to. [*Brit. Mus.*] [London] 1641

HUMBLE (an) remonstrance to the High Court of Parliament. By a dutifull sonne of the Church [Joseph Hall, D.D., Bishop of Norwich]. 4to. Pp. 43. [*Brit. Mus.*] London, 1640

HUMBLE (an) remonstrance to the Members of the House of Commons. By a native Roman Catholic prelate [Rev. John Milner, D.D.]. 8vo. [Gillows' *Bibl. Dict.*] London, 1816

HUMBLE (a) tribute to . . . Justice Shee. [In verse. By John Davis.] 12mo. [London, private print] 1864

HUMBLE (a) tribute to the memory of Mr Abram Rumney, late master of the grammar school in Alnwick. By a friend of his age [—— Dawson]. 8vo. Alnwick, 1794

The Dedication is signed "Euphemon."

HUMBLING recollections of my ministry. By a clergyman of the Established Church [Rev. —— Peel]. 8vo. Pp. 45. London, 1842

HUMBUG; a poem. [By W. Elliott.] 8vo. London, 1826

HUMILIATIONS followed with deliverances. . . . With an appendix containing a narrative . . . relating to the captivity and deliverance of Hannah Swarton. [By Cotton Mather.] 12mo. Pp. 72. [*G. Brinley's American Library.*] [Boston, 1697]

HUMILITY; a poetical essay. [By George Burgess.] 8vo. Peterborough, 1792

HUMOROUS (the) adventures of Tom Trevail, related in the pure unadulterated vernacular [of Cornwall]. By A. C. I. G. [A Cornishman In Gloucestershire, *i.e.* John White, bookseller]. Part I. 8vo. Pp. 20. [Boase and Courtney's *Bibl. Corn.*] Stroud, 1872

HUMOROUS ethics; or, an attempt to cure the vices and follies, by a method entirely new: in five plays, as they are now acting to the life, at the great theatre, by his Majesty's company of comedians. [By Dr Phanuel Bacon, of Magdalen College, Oxford.] 8vo. [*D.N.B.*, vol. 2, p. 372.] London, 1758

HUMOROUS (the) lieutenant; or, generous enemies: a comedy, as it is now acted by his Majesties servants, at the Theatre-Royal in Drury-Lane. [By John Fletcher.] 4to. Pp. 68. [*Bodl.*] London, 1697

Ascribed also to Beaumont and Fletcher. [Baker's *Biog. Dram.*]

HUMOROUS (the) miscellany; or, riddles [in verse] for the beaux. . . . By E. B. [Elizabeth Boyd]. 4to. Pp. 32. [*Brit. Mus.*] London, 1733

HUMOROUS (the) quarrel; or, the battle of the grey beards: a farce, as it is acted at Mr Davis's theatrical booth on the Bowling-Green, during the time of Southwark Fair. [By Israel Pottinger.] 8vo. Pp. 30. [Baker's *Biog. Dram.*] London [1761]

HUMOROUS sketches and addresses. By Prof. J. Q. Smith [John P. Burt]. 8vo. Dubuque, Indiana, 1879

HUMORSOME rhymes, respictfully dedicated to Oor twa Squads, Dundee Harbour. [By Archibald Henry Rea.] 12mo. Pp. 24. Dundee [*c.* 1890]

HUMOUR (the) and pathos of Anglo-Indian life. . . . Edited [but rather written] by J. E. Mayer. 8vo. Pp. 277. [*Brit. Mus.*] London, 1895

HUMOUR (the) of the age; a comedy, as it is acted at the Theatre-Royal in Drury-Lane by his Majesty's servants. [By Thomas Baker.] 4to. Pp. 65. [Baker's *Biog. Dram.*] London, 1701

HUMOURIST (the); being essays upon several subjects, viz. News-writers; enthusiasm; the spleen; country entertainments; love; the history of Miss Manage; ambition and pride; idleness; fickleness of human nature; prejudice; witchcraft; ghosts and apparitions; the weather. . . . By the author of the *Apology for Parson Alberoni*, etc. [Thomas Gordon]. 8vo. Pp. xxx. 240. [*Bodl.*] London, 1720

A second volume was issued in 1725.

HUMOURS (the) of a coffee-house; a comedy, as it is dayly acted by Levy, a recruiting officer; Hazard, a gamester; Bite, a sharper, etc. Note. These persons are introduc'd only as occasion serves. [By Edward Ward.] 4to. [Baker's *Biog. Dram.*] London, 1707

HUMOURS (the) of Cynicus. [By J. Martin Anderson.] 4to. [*Brit. Mus.*] London, 1892

HUMOURS (the) of Glenbruar. By Fergus Mackenzie [Rev. James Anderson, of Dyce, Aberdeen]. 8vo. [Robertson's *Aberd. Bibl.*] London [1893]

HUMOURS (the) of Oxford; a comedy, as it is acted at the Theatre-Royal by His Majesty's servants. By a gentleman of Wadham-College [Rev. James Miller]. 8vo. Pp. 80. [Baker's *Biog. Dram.*] London, 1730

HUMOURS (the) of the Fleet; an humerous descriptive poem: written by a gentleman of the College, under the following heads, viz: I. His being arrested for debt, and hurried away by those horrid merciless fellows the bailiffs to the spunging-house. II. His not liking the exorbitant demands of that place, is by a Habeas Corpus brought over to the Fleet prison. III. His being receiv'd by the turn-key, is introduc'd to a proper place, in order (as they term it) to paint his face, to prevent his making an escape, in disguise through the Jigg. IV. The merry scene between the prisoner, the chamberlain, the chum and the cook. . . . [By W. Paget.] 8vo. London, 1749

HUMOURS of the Law. By Jacob Larwood [L. R. R. Sadler]. 8vo. [*Lond. Lib. Cat.*] London, 1903

HUMOURS ordinarie; where a man may be verie merrie and exceeding well used for his sixpence. [By Samuel Rowlands.] 4to. Pp. 85. [Hart's *Index Expurg. Angl.* p. 47.] London [1601]

This title was substituted by the publisher for "The letting of humours blood . . ." (1600), as an order had been issued that the book should be burnt; the original title was restored, however, in the edition of 1611.

HUNDRED (the) and ten considerations of Signior John Valdesso, treating of those things which are most profitable, most necessary and most perfect in our Christian profession. Written in Spanish, brought out of Italy by Vergerius, and first set forth in Italian at Basil by Cœlius Secundus Curio, anno. 1550, afterward translated into French, and printed at Lions 1563, and again at Paris 1565, and now translated out of the Italian copy into English, with notes [by Nicholas Ferrar]. 8vo. Pp. 356. [Madan's *Oxford Books*, i. 211.] Oxford, 1638

On the leaf before p. 1, is "a copy of a letter written by Mr George Herbert to his friend the Translator of this book," dated from "Bemmorton, Sept. 29." The translator of this work, Nicholas Ferrar, was the celebrated founder of the Protestant Nunnery at Little Gidden, and the friend of Herbert. In Walton's *Life of Herbert* there is an account both of Ferrar and of Valdesso, which concludes with these words: "This account of John Valdesso I received from a friend that had it from the mouth of Mr Ferrar. And the reader may note, that in this retirement John Valdesso, writ his Hundred and ten considerations, and many other treatises of worth, which want a second Mr Ferrar to procure and translate them."

HUNDRED (a) meditations on the love of God. By Robert Southwell. . . . [Really translated from the Spanish of Diego de Estella.] 12mo. Pp. xix. 538. [*Brit. Mus.*] London, 1873

HUNDRED (the) wonders of the world, and of the three kingdoms of nature; described according to the best and latest authorities. By the Rev. C. C. Clarke [Sir Richard Phillips]. Eighth edition. 12mo. [*Brit. Mus.*] London, 1820

See *Bibliographer*, vol. 4.

HUNDRED (a) years later; Burns under the light of the Higher Criticism. [By William Gifford.] 8vo. Edinburgh, 1897

HUNGARIAN (the) controversy; an exposure of the falsifications and perversions of the slanderers of Hungary. By R. C. [Robert Carter]. 8vo. [Kirk's *Supp.*] Boston, 1852

HUNGARIAN (the) rebellion; or, an historical relation of the late wicked practises of the three Counts, Nadasti, Serini, and Frangipani: tending to subvert the Government of His present Imperial Majesty in Hungary, and introduce the Mahometan. . . . Translated into English by P. A. [Philip Ayres], Gent. 8vo. [Arber's *Term Cat.* i. 110.] London, 1672

HUNGARIAN tales. By the author of *The lettre de cachet* [Mrs Catherine G. F. Gore]. 8vo. 3 vols. London, 1829

HUNGARY; its constitution and its catastrophe. By Corvinus [Travers Twiss, D.C.L.]. 8vo. [*D.N.B.* vol. 57, p. 394.] London, 1850

HUNGER. By Knut Hamsun. Translated from the Danish by George Egerton [Mrs Mary C. Clairmonte]. 8vo. [*Brit. Mus.*] London, 1899

HUNGER; a Dublin story. By James Esse [James Stephens]. 8vo. Pp. 32. [Williams' *Bibl. of Stephens.*] Dublin, 1918

HUNGER and revolution. By the author of *Daily bread* [Johann Lhotsky]. 8vo. Pp. 38. [*Brit. Mus.*] London [1843]

Written against the Corn Laws.

HUNGER (the); being realities of the famine years in Ireland, 1845-48. By Merry Andrew [Mrs Mildred H. G. Gordon-Dill]. 8vo. Pp. 436. [S. J. Brown's *Ireland in fiction.*] London, 1910

HUNT (a) cup; or, Loyalty before all! A novelette. By Wat. Bradwood [Walter Bradford Woodgate]. 8vo. [*Lond. Lib. Cat.*] London, 1873

HUNT the slipper. By Jane Wardle [Oliver Madox Hueffer]. 8vo. London [*c.* 1910]

HUNTED down. [A detective story.] By J. M'Govan [William C. Honeyman]. 8vo. [*Brit. Mus.*] London, 1900

HUNTER (the); a discourse of horsemanship. [By Gerard Langbaine, the younger.] 12mo. [*Brit. Mus.*] Oxford, 1685

HUNTERIAN (the) oration (February 14. 1851) that would have been delivered by a member of the College of Surgeons, of London, if permission had been granted to him by the president and council. . . . [By Edward Crisp, M.D.] From the London Medical Examiner, March 1851. 8vo. [*W.*] [London] 1851

No title-page.

HUNTER'S (a) experiences in the Southern States of America. By "The Ranger" [Captain —— Flack]. 8vo. [Cushing's *Init. and Pseud.* i. 247.] London, 1866

HUNTERS (the) of Kentucky; or, the trials and toils of traders and trappers during an expedition to the Rocky Mountains. . . . [By Benjamin Bilson.] 8vo. Pp. 100. [Sabin's *Dictionary.*] New York, 1847

HUNTIAD (the); being a speech delivered at the Guildhall, November 4th; done into English, and into verse. [By Bishop Samuel Butler, D.D.] 4to. Pp. xiii. 40. Shrewsbury, 1806

An election squib.

HUNTING and fishing in Florida. . . . By Owen Nox [Charles Barney Cory]. 8vo. Boston, 1896

HUNTING bits. By "Phiz" [Hablot Knight Browne]. obl. fol. [*Brit. Mus.*] London [1862]

HUNTING (the) counties of England. . . . A guide to hunting men. By Brooksby [Edward Pennell Elmhirst]. 8vo. [*Brit. Mus.*] London, 1878

HUNTING (the) grounds of the old world. By *The old Shekarry*, H. A. L. [Henry Astbury Leverson]. First series. Second edition. 8vo. Pp. xii. 520. [*Lit. Year Book.*] London, 1860

HUNTING (the) of Badlewe; a dramatic tale. By J. H. Craig, of Douglas, Esq. [James Hogg, the Ettrick shepherd]. 8vo. Pp. viii. 131. [*Nat. Lib. of Scot.*] London, 1814

HUNTING (the) of the foxes from New-Market and Tiploe-Heaths to White-hall, by five small beagles . . . (late of the armie); or the Grandie-Deceivers unmasked. . . . [By John Lilburne.] 4to. [*Brit. Mus.*] [London, *c.* 1649]

HUNTING (the) of the Snark; an agony in eight fits. By Lewis Carroll [Rev. Charles L. Dodgson, M.A.]. 8vo. [*Brit. Mus.*] London, 1876

HUNTING reminiscences; comprising memoirs of masters of hounds; notices of the crack riders; and characteristics of the hunting countries of England. By Nimrod [Charles James Apperley]. Illustrated by Wildrake, Henderson, and Alken. 8vo. [*Brit. Mus.*] London, 1843

HUNTING songs, ballads, etc. By R. E. E. W——, Esq. [Rowland Eyles Egerton Warburton]. With illustrations. 8vo. Pp. 47. [*Brit. Mus.*] Chester, 1834

HUNTING tours. By "Nimrod" [Charles James Apperley]; interspersed with characteristic anecdotes, sayings and doings of sporting men. . . . 8vo. [*Brit. Mus.*] London, 1909

HUNTING tours; descriptive of various fashionable countries and establishments, with anecdotes of masters of hounds and others connected with fox hunting. By "Cecil" [Cornelius Tongue]. 12mo. Pp. xiii. 439. [*Bodl.*] London, 1864

HUNTING (the) Vicar and the Commissioners; or, the woodcock and the snipe. By Abednego [Rev. Jacob Stanley, Wesleyan minister]. 8vo. Pp. 30. Stockport, 1820

HUNTING with the Eskimos. By Harry Whitney [Patrick Kennedy, bookseller in Ireland]. 8vo. Pp. 468. London, 1910

HUNTING-FIELD (the). By Harry Hieover, author of *The stud*, etc. [Charles Bindley]. 8vo. [*Lit. Year Book.*] London, 1850

HUNT-ROOM stories and yachting yarns. By the author of *Across country*, etc. [Elim H. D'Avigdor]. 8vo. [*Brit. Mus.*] London, 1884

HUNTYNG (the) and fyndyng out of the Romyshe foxe, which more then seuen yeares hath bene hyd among the bisshoppes of Englonde, after that the kynges hyghnes had commanded hym to be dryuen owt of hys realme. By William Wraghton [William Turner, M.D.]. 8vo. No pagination. [Lowndes' *Brit. Lib.*] Basyll, 1543

HURDCOTT. [A novel.] By John Ayscough [Monsignor Francis Bickerstaffe-Drew]. 8vo. Pp. 400. [*Lit. Year Book.*] London, 1911

HURRAH! The Fleet! [Verse]. By William Scribble [William Smyth, comedian and journalist]. 8vo. [O'Donoghue's *Poets of Ireland.*] Dublin, 1863

HURRICANE (the); a poem. By an eye-witness [Edward Burt]; also, historical notices of St Domingo. 8vo. [*Lond. Lib. Cat.*] Bath, 1844

HURRICANE (a) in petticoats; a novel. By Leslie Keith [Grace Leslie Keith Johnston]. 8vo. 3 vols. [*Lit. Year Book.*] London, 1889

HURST-CAREWE; a tale of two Christmases. By H. E. S. [Harriette Elizabeth Streatfield]. 8vo. Pp. xvi. 192. [*Brit. Mus.*] London, 1882

HURSTWOOD; a tale of the year 1715. [By Rev. John Harvey Ashworth, M.A.] 12mo. 3 vols. [F. Boase's *Mod. Brit. Biog.* i. col. 98.] London, 1823

HUSBAND (the); in answer to the Wife. [By Mrs Eliza Haywood.] 12mo. Pp. v. 279. [*D. N. B.* vol. 21, p. 315.] London, 1756

HUSBAND (the) and the lover; an historical and moral romance. [By Alicia Tindal Palmer.] 12mo. 3 vols. [*Biog. Dict.* 1816.] London, 1809

HUSBAND and wife; a novel. By Marie Connor [Mrs Robert Leighton]. 8vo. 3 vols. London, 1888

HUSBAND (a) of no importance. [A novel.] "By Rita" [Eliza M. J. Gollan, later Mrs Otto von Booth, *next* Mrs W. Desmond Humphreys]. 8vo. [*Lit. Year Book.*] London, 1894

HUSBANDMAN'S (the) instructor, or countryman's guide. . . . By A. S. [Adam Speed]. 12mo. [Watt's *Bibl. Brit.*] London [1697]

HUSBANDMAN'S (the) manual; directing him how to improve the several actions of his calling, and the most usual occurrences of his life, to the glory of God and the benefit of his soul. The fourth edition, corrected and enlarged. Written by a minister in the country, for the use of his parishioners [Edward Welchman, M.A.]. 12mo. Pp. 60. [*Brit. Mus.*] London, 1707

Address to his parishioners signed: E. W.

HUSBANDS and homes. By Marion Harland [Mrs Mary V. H. Terhune]. 8vo. [Kirk's *Supp.*] New York, 1892

HUSH! A novel. By Curtis Yorke [Mrs W. S. Richmond Lee]. 8vo. [*Lond. Lib. Cat.*] London, 1895

HUSH money; a life drama. By Boswell Butt [Charles Henry Ross]. 8vo. [Cushing's *Init. and Pseud.* i. 43.] London, 1875

HUSSAR (the). [A novel.] By the author of *The subaltern* [George Robert Gleig]. 8vo. 2 vols. [*Brit. Mus.*] London, 1837

HUSTLED history. . . . By the authors of *Wisdom while you wait*, etc. [Edward V. Lucas and Charles L. Graves]. 8vo. London, 1908

HUT (the) and the castle; a romance. By the author of *The romance of the Pyrenees*, etc. [Catherine Cuthbertson]. 12mo. 4 vols. [*N. and Q.* 1922, p. 225.] London, 1823

HYACINTH. [A novel.] By George A. Birmingham [James Owen Hannay, D.D.]. 8vo. [*Lit. Year Book.*] London, 1906

HYACINTH O'Gara, Honor Delany, Irish priests and English landlords. By the author of *Mothers and sons* [George Brittaine]. New edition. 8vo. [*Brit. Mus.*] London, 1839

HYACINTHE; or, the contrast. By the authoress of *Alice Seymour* [Mrs Elizabeth Caroline Grey]. 8vo. Pp. 260. [*Bodl.*] London, 1835

HYDE Marston; or, a sportsman's life. By Craven [Capt. John William Carleton]. 12mo. 3 vols. [*Nat. Lib. of Scot.*] London, 1844

HYGEIAN (the) treatment of the . . . diseases of India. [By James Morison, hygeist.] 8vo. [*Brit. Mus.*] London, 1836

HYGIASTICON; or, the right course of preserving life and health unto extream old age; together with soundnesse and integritie of the senses, judgement, and memorie. Written in Latine by Leonard Lessius, and now done into English [by Nicholas Ferrar]. 12mo. Pp. 210. Cambridge, 1634

Contains also "A treatise of temperance and sobrietie; written by Lud. Cornarus, translated into English by Mr George Herbert," pp. 46. "A discourse translated out of Italian, that a spare diet is better then a splendid and sumptuous. A paradox," pp. 47-70.

In Peckard's *Life of Nicholas Ferrar*, 8vo, 1790, p. 216, it is stated that Ferrar translated the Hygiasticon and sent the manuscript to Herbert, who returned it to him with his own translation of Cornaro, from which the above is printed; but in the preface "To the Reader," which is signed: T. S. [Thomas Sheppard ?] is the following sentence,—"They requested from me the translation of it into English, whereupon hath ensued what you shall now receive."

In 1742, a new translation was published by Timothy Smith; as the initials of this translator are the same as those of the edition of 1634, they are apt to be confounded, but they are quite distinct translations. [*W.*]

HYLAS; a lament. [By Sir William D. Geddes.] 8vo. N.P. [1883]

HYLTON House and its inmates; a novel. By the author of *The hen-pecked husband*, etc. [Lady Muriel Anne Scott, *née* Shanks]. 12mo. London, 1850

HYMEN. [Poems.] By H. D. [Hilda Doolittle, Mrs Richard Aldington]. 8vo. Pp. 48. [*Brit. Mus.*] London, 1921

HYMENÆAN (an) essay; or, an epithalamy upon the royall match of his most excellent majesty Charles the Second, with the most illustrious Katharine, Infanta of Portvgall. 1662. By J. D. [John Drope, M.A.]. 4to. [*Bodl.*] 1662

The author's name in the handwriting of Wood.

HYMENS praeludia, or Loves masterpiece; being that so much admired romance intituled Cleopatra. Written originally in the French [by Gauthier de Costes, Sieur de la Calprenède]; rendered into English by Robert Loveday. Fol. 2 vols. [Arber's *Term Cat.* i. 521.] London, 1674

An earlier translation [by John Coles] was published in 1658; Loveday's version was reprinted in 1736.

HYMN (a) ["Glory to Thee, whose lofty state"]. [By Rev. Richard Greswell.] 8vo. Pp. 27. [*Athen. Cat.* p. 135.] [Oxford, 1834]

HYMN for saints' days, and other hymns. By a layman [Horatio Nelson, third Lord Nelson]. 12mo. London, 1864

HYMN music adapted to all the peculiar metres in the United Presbyterian Hymn Book; including a collection of Doxologies and 54 Chants by the best composers: intended as a supplement to *Scottish Psalmody*. Edited by a member of the United Presbyterian Synod [Rev. William Thomson, of Slateford]. Revised and enlarged edition. 12mo. Edinburgh, 1870

The first edition was published in 1857.

HYMN (a) of praise for the abundant harvest of 1796. By L. [Hannah More]. 12mo. [*Brit. Mus.*] London [1796]

HYMN (the) question. By a layman [of the Reformed Presbyterian Church, *i.e.* Matthew S. Tait]. 12mo. Pp. 32. Edinburgh, 1868

HYMN to Miss Laurence in the pump-room at Bath. [By J. Hall-Stevenson.] Fol. London, 1755

HYMN (a) to peace; occasion'd, by the two Houses joining in one address to the Queen. By the author of *The true-born English-man* [Daniel Defoe]. 8vo. London, 1709

HYMN (an) to the Creator of the world; the thoughts taken chiefly from Psalm civ. To which is added, in prose, an idea of the Creator from his works. [By James Burgh.] Second edition. 8vo. Pp. 44. [Darling's *Cyclop. Bibl.*] London, 1750

HYMN (a) to the mob. [By Daniel Defoe.] 8vo. Pp. vi. 40. [Wilson's *Life of Defoe.*] London, 1715

HYMN (a) to the pillory. [By Daniel Defoe.] 4to. Pp. 24. [Wilson's *Life of Defoe.*] London, 1703

HYMN to the power of harmony; humbly inscribed to the Right Honourable the Earl of Bute. [By John Callander of Craigforth.] 4to. Pp. 25. Edinburgh, 1763

HYMN (an) to the Redeemer. [By William Godwin.] Fol. Pp. 12. [*Brit. Mus.*] London, 1813

HYMN (a) to Tybourn; being a sequel to the *Hymn to the pillory.* [By Daniel Defoe.] 4to. [Arber's *Term Cat.* iii. 687.] London, 1703

HYMNAL (a) for use in the English Church. [By Rev. Fraser Henry Murray, M.A.] 12mo. London, 1852

HYMNAL (a) for use in the English Church, with accompanying tunes; also supplement. By J. G. [J. Grey]. 8vo. London, 1866

HYMNAL (the) noted. [By John Mason Neale, D.D.] 12mo. Part I. [Julian's *Dict.*] London, 1885

HYMNAL suited for the services of the Church [of England], together with a selection of introits. [By Rev. George R. Prynne, M.A.] 12mo. Pp. 364. [Julian's *Dict.*] London, 1866

HYMNARIUM Anglicanum; or, the ancient hymns translated from the Salisbury Breviary and fitted for the tunes. [By Thomas Doubleday.] 12mo. Pp. xviii. 66. London, 1844

HYMNES (the) and songs of the Church, diuided into two parts. The first part comprehends the canonicall hymnes, and such parcels of Holy Scripture, as may properly be sung, with some other ancient songs and creeds. The second part consists of spirituall songs, appropriated to the seuerall times and occasions obseruable in the Church of England. Translated and composed by G. VV. [George Wither]. 8vo. Pp. 218. London, 1623

HYMNS. [By C. Fawcett.] 12mo. Birmingham, 1858

HYMNS. By A. M. H. [Amelia Matilda Hull]. 12mo. [*Brit. Mus.*] London, 1850

HYMNS. By a minister [Rev. John Howard Hinton, M.A.]. 12mo. Pp. 84. [Julian's *Dict.*] London, 1833

HYMNS. By a physician [John Gardner, M.D.]. 12mo. [*Brit. Mus.*] London, 1872

HYMNS. By C. F. [Christina Forsyth]. 12mo. [Julian's *Dict.*] London, 1861

HYMNS. By F. R. S. [Francis Reginald Statham]. 12mo. Pp. 54. Edinburgh, 1872

HYMNS; a supplement to Watts. By G. B. [George Burder]. Second edition. 12mo. Coventry, 1787

HYMNS ancient and modern tested by Holy Scripture and the Articles of the Church of England. By a layman [W. H. Tucker]. 8vo. [*Brit. Mus.*] London [1886]

HYMNS and anthems. [By Rev. William Johnson Fox.] 12mo. [*Brit. Mus.*] London, 1845

HYMNS and anthems . . . a companion to the suppressed Prayer-book of Bishop Torry. [By Robert Campbell.] 12mo. [Julian's *Dict.*] London, 1850

HYMNS and devotional verses. [By George Burden Bubier.] 12mo. Pp. 47. [Julian's *Dict.*] Birmingham, 1867

HYMNS and devotions in honour of the Virgin Mother of good counsel; edited [and really written] by [John A. Nowlan], the Rev. Guardian of the Shrine, St Augustine's, and St John's, John Street, Dublin. 8vo. Dublin, 1885

HYMNS and meditations. By A. L. W. [Anna Letitia Waring]. 12mo. Pp. 125. [*Brit. Mus.*] London, 1850

HYMNS and miscellaneous poems. [By John Taylor.] 8vo. [Julian's *Dict.*] London, 1818

Another edition was issued in 1863.

HYMNS and poems. By A. L. O. E., author of *The triumph over Midian*, &c. [Charlotte Maria Tucker]. 8vo. Pp. 158. London, 1868

HYMNS and poems for the sick and suffering. [Edited by Thomas Vincent Fosbery, M.A., vicar of St Giles, Reading.] 12mo. Pp. 47, 460. London, 1844

Preface signed: T. V. F.

HYMNS and poems, on various occasions. By a member of the Protestant Episcopal Church [William Duke]. 12mo. Pp. 90. [Evans' *Amer. Bibl.* vol. 8, p. 25.] Baltimore, 1790

HYMNS and poetry for infant and juvenile schools. [By Mrs H. Mayo.] Fifth edition. 12mo. London, 1853

HYMNS and sacred lyrics, in three parts. By "Constantius" [Joseph Cottle]. 12mo. Pp. xxvi. 468. [Julian's *Dict.*] London, 1826

HYMNS and sacred poems of noted and admired authors. Edited by M. L. B. [Mabel Louisa Barnes]. 8vo. London, 1865

HYMNS and sacred songs, for Sunday Schools and social worship; in two parts. I. Hymns and songs for childhood and youth. II. Hymns for general purposes, especially for elder scholars, teachers, etc. [Edited by George Burden Bubier.] 12mo. Pp. 256. [*W.*] Manchester, 1855

Preface signed: B.

HYMNS and scenes of childhood; or a sponsor's gift. [By Jane Euphemia Leeson.] 12mo. Pp. viii. 195. [Julian's *Dict.*] London, 1842

HYMNS and sketches in verse. By the author of *Tales of the great and brave*, etc. [Margaret Fraser Tytler]. 12mo. Pp. xi. 224. [*Brit. Mus.*] London, 1840

HYMNS and songs, for the Church of man. By Munullog [Robert Jones Derfel]. 12mo. Manchester [1893]

HYMNS and spiritual songs. [By William Batty, Inghamite preacher.] 12mo. Kendal, 1773

HYMNS and spiritual songs, collected from various authors; to which are added [original] hymns of instruction. [By John Johnson, of Reading.] 12mo. Reading, 1783

HYMNS and spiritual songs, intended for the use of real Christians of all denominations. [By Charles Wesley.] Third edition. 12mo. Pp. viii. 124. [*Bodl.*] London, 1754

HYMNS and spiritual songs on several subjects. By the author of *Dissenters no schismatics* [Jeremiah Hunt, D.D.]. 12mo. London, 1715

HYMNS and spiritual songs, on several subjects; to which is added, The marriage-supper of the Lamb, a poem. [By John Hoy, the bookseller.] 8vo. Pp. 144. Edinburgh, 1774

Wrongly attributed to the Duke of Roxburghe.

HYMNS and spiritual songs; recreations of a rural pastor [John Wakefield]. 8vo. Pp. 32. [Julian's *Dict.*] Much Wenlock [1888]

HYMNS and thoughts in verse; series I. and II. By E. A. W. [Eliza Ann Walker], author of *Memoir of W. F. Clarke*. 8vo. Pp. xiii. 168. [*Brit. Mus.*] London, 1887

An earlier edition (of part i.) appeared in 1864.

HYMNS and thoughts on religion. By Novalis [Friedrich Leopold von Hardenberg]. With a biographical sketch. . . . Translated by William Hastie. 8vo. Edinburgh, 1888

HYMNS and verses. By G. T. [Rev. Godfrey Thring, B.A., Rector of Alford and Hornblotton]. 12mo. Pp. 161. [Julian's *Dict.*] London, 1874

HYMNS, anthems and introits, adapted to the ecclesiastical year, for the parish Church of St Andrew, Enfield. Revised edition. [By Alfred Bowen Evans, D.D.] 12mo. Pp. 72. Enfield, 1858

HYMNS arranged for the Sundays and holy-days of the Church of England. [By John Rowland West.] 8vo. London, 1855

HYMNS by the Rev. Caesar Malan, of Geneva, translated into English verse [by Rev. Ingram Cobbin, M.A.]. 12mo. Pp. iv. 142. [Julian's *Dict.*] London, 1825

HYMNS composed for the use of the [Moravian] Brethren. [By Count Nicholas Lewis Zinzendorf]. 12mo. [London] 1719

HYMNS descriptive and devotional. . . . By the author of *Hymns for little children* [Cecil Frances Humphreys, later Mrs Alexander]. 12mo. [*Brit. Mus.*] London, 1858

HYMNS for Ascension-day. [By Charles Wesley.] 12mo. Pp. 12. [*Bodl.*] London, 1753

HYMNS for children, on the Lord's Prayer. [By Mrs Harriet Mozley, sister of Cardinal Newman.] 12mo. Pp. 57. Derby, 1837

HYMNS for enquirers after Jesus. [By Dr Gifford.] 12mo. London, 1766

HYMNS for little children. By the author of *The Lord of the forest*, etc. [Mrs Cecil Frances Alexander, *née* Humphreys]. Sixth edition. 12mo. Pp. 72. [*D. N. B.* First Supp. vol. 1, p. 31.] London, 1853

Dedication signed: C. F. H.

HYMNS for morning, evening, and midnight. By the author of the *Manual of prayers for the use of scholars at Winchester School* [Thomas Kerr, afterwards Bishop]. 12mo. [Julian's *Dict.*] London, 1699

HYMNS for our Lord's resurrection. [By Charles Wesley.] 12mo. Pp. 23. [*Bodl.*] London, 1754

HYMNS for private devotions, selected and original. [By Mrs Colquhoun, *née* Frances S. Fuller-Maitland.] 12mo. [*Brit. Mus.*] London, 1827

HYMNS for public worship. [By James Yates.] 12mo. London, 1835

HYMNS for public worship and private devotion, original, and translated from the German. [By Rev. Arthur Tozer Russell, M.A., for the benefit of the London German Hospital, Dalston.] 8vo. [Julian's *Dict.*] London, 1848

HYMNS for St Saviour's, Clapham, [By Rev. W. E. Green.] 8vo. 1865

HYMNS for special services. [By John Ellerton, M.A.] 12mo. Chester, 1869

HYMNS for Sunday schools. [By Rev. John Buckworth.] 12mo. [Julian's *Dict.*] London, 1814

HYMNS for the Church of England. Third edition, revised and enlarged. [By Rev. Thomas Darling, who included some original hymns.] 12mo. London, 1857

Later editions give the author's name.

HYMNS for the cottage. By C. W. [Charlotte White]. 12mo. [*Brit. Mus.*] London, 1840

HYMNS for the Feasts [in the Catholic Apostolic Church. By Edmund Wigglesworth]. 12mo. 1878

HYMNS for the festival of the Sunday school of the first parish, Cambridge, Mass. By the pastor [William Newell]. 12mo. Cambridge, Mass., 1860

HYMNS for the household of faith, and lays of the Better Land. . . . Second edition, considerably enlarged. [By Mrs J. Williamson.] 8vo. [*Brit. Mus.*] London, 1867

HYMNS for the little ones. [By Mrs —— Dunsterville.] 12mo. Pp. 94. London [1880?]

HYMNS for the nativity of our Lord. [By Charles Wesley.] Fourth edition. 12mo. Pp. 24. [*Bodl.*] Bristol, 1750

HYMNS for the poor of the Flock. [Compiled by Sir Edward Denny, who added original hymns.] 12mo. Pp. xxiv. 337, 84. [Julian's *Dict.*] London [1841]

HYMNS for the principal festivals of the Church. . . . [By Richard Edmonds, jun.] [*Brit. Mus.*] London, 1857

HYMNS for the public worship of the Church. [By Rev. E. Wackerbath.] 12mo. London, 1849

HYMNS for the service of the Church. [By Joseph Oldknow, D.D.] 12mo. Birmingham [*c.* 1850]

HYMNS for the service of the King. [By Rev. Ethelbert William Bullinger, D.D.] 12mo. London, 1881

HYMNS for the services of the Church. [By Rev. H. Pearson.] 12mo. London, 1863

HYMNS for the sick. [By John Mason Neale, D.D.] 12mo. Pp. 59. [*Bodl.*] Cambridge, 1843

HYMNS for the use of the Birmingham Oratory. [By John Henry Newman, D.D.] 12mo. [*D. N. B.* vol. 40, p. 349.] Dublin, 1854

HYMNS for the use of the schools and congregation of St Wilfrid's, Staffordshire. By F. W. F. [Frederick William Faber, D.D.]. 12mo. [Julian's *Dict.*] London, 1849

HYMNS for the use of Unitarian Christians. [By Lant Carpenter.] 12mo. Bristol, 1831

HYMNS for the watch-night. [By Charles Wesley.] 12mo. Pp. 12. [*Bodl.*] N.P., N.D.

HYMNS for the week, and hymns for the seasons. Translated from the Latin [by Henry Copeland?]. 8vo. Pp. xxiii. 183. [*Nat. Lib. of Scot.*] London, 1848

Ascribed also to William John Copeland. [Bliss' *Cat.*]

HYMNS for the year 1756. [By Charles Wesley.] Second edition. 12mo. Pp. 24. [*Bodl.*] Bristol, N.D.

HYMNS for those that seek and those that have redemption. [By Charles Wesley.] 8vo. [Bliss' *Cat.* 329.] Bristol, 1755

HYMNS for times of trouble and persecution. [By Charles and John Wesley]. 12mo. Pp. 47. London, 1744

HYMNS for villagers, chiefly on rural subjects. By Aliquis [Thomas Beck]. 12mo. Pp. 72. London, 1821

HYMNS for young persons. [Preface signed: R. H. *i.e.* Rev. Richard Harvey, M.A.] Second edition. 12mo. Pp. 118. [*Brit. Mus.*] London, 1837

HYMNS from the land of Luther. [Translated by Jane Borthwick and Mrs E. Findlater.] 12mo. London, 1862

HYMNS, home, Harvard. By M. C. S. [Mary Crowinshield, later Mrs Sparks]. 8vo. [*Lib. Journ.* viii. 155.] Boston, 1883

HYMNS in prose for children. [By Mrs Anna Letitia Barbauld.] Sixth edition. 12mo. [Julian's *Dict.*] London, 1794

HYMNS intended to help the communion of saints. [By Mary Bowley, later Mrs Peters.] 12mo. [Julian's *Dict.*] London, 1847

HYMNS of life and love. [By W. J. Jupp.] 12mo. Newport, Isle of Wight, 1898

HYMNS (the) of Orpheus, translated from the original Greek; with a preliminary dissertation on the life and theology of Orpheus. [By Thomas Taylor.] 8vo. [*Brit. Mus.*] London, 1792

HYMNS of praise, prayer, and devout meditation. By Josiah Conder. Prepared for publication by the author [and edited with a preface, by E. R. C. *i.e.* Eustace R. Conder]. 12mo. Pp. 217. [*Brit. Mus.*] London, 1856

HYMNS of the ages. Compiled by C. S. W. [Mrs Cardine Snowden Guild, *née* Whitmarsh] and A. E. G. [Mrs Anne E. Guild]. Boston, 1865

HYMNS of the Catholic Church; compiled from various sources. [By J. Colles, D.D.] 12mo. Stratford-upon-Avon, 1853

HYMNS of the Church militant. Compiled by the author of *The wide, wide world* [Susan Warner]. London [*c.* 1860]

HYMNS of the Church Universal, in two parts: I. The spirit of the Psalms; II. General hymns, with prefaces, annotations, and indexes. [By John Rylands.] 8vo. Manchester, private print, 1885

HYMNS of the holy feast. [By Caroline Sellon.] 12mo. London [1859]

HYMNS of the Reformation, by Dr Martin Luther and others, from the German; to which is added his life, translated from the original Latin of Philip Melancthon. By the author of *The pastor's legacy* [Henrietta Joan Fry]. 12mo. Pp. 231. [Smith's *Cat. of Friends' Books*, i. 816.] London, 1845

HYMNS of the Two-in-one, for bridal worship of the new life. By Chrysanthea, Chrysantheus [Mrs Lily C. Harris, and Thomas Lake Harris]. 8vo. Pp. 48. Salem-on-Erie, 1876

HYMNS on God's everlasting love; in two parts. [By Charles Wesley.] Second edition. 12mo. Pp. 84. [*Bodl.*] London, 1756

HYMNS on the Catechism [Signed: I. W. *i.e.* Isaac Williams, B.D.] Third edition. 12mo. Pp. 128. [*Brit. Mus.*] London, 1851

HYMNS on the Litany. By A. C. [Ada Cambridge, afterwards Cross]. 8vo. [Julian's *Dict.*] London, 1865

HYMNS on the Psalms. By the author of *The Book of Psalms of David the King and Prophet* [Edward Falkener]. 8vo. Pp. xvi. 127. London, 1878

HYMNS on various subjects. By the author of the *Essay on the happiness of the life to come* [Jane Bowdler]. 8vo. [Green's *Bibl. Somers.* i. 273.] Bath, 1806

HYMNS; or, the voice of the Bride: to which is appended a Catena Aurea or golden chain of Scripture passages referring to the coming of the Lord. [By Henry James Prince.] 8vo. Pp. 84. [*Brit. Mus.*] London, 1886

Signed: B.

HYMNS, original and select. [By Richard Phillips.] 12mo. 1880

HYMNS reprinted from "The Antiphone and Grael." [By the Rev. G. H. Palmer.] 12mo. London, 1882

HYMNS, selected and original. . . . Compiled by J. P. C. [John Peele Clapham]. 12mo. [Julian's *Dict.*] London, 1833

HYMNS, selected from various authors, and chiefly intended for the instruction of young persons. [By Priscilla Gurney.] 12mo. [Smith's *Cat. of Friends' Books*, i. 896.] London, 1818

HYMNS to the goddess; from the Tantra and other Shâstra, and the Stotras of Shangkarâchâryya, with introduction and commentary. Translated from the Sanskrit by Arthur and Ellen Avalon [Sir John and Ellen Woodroffe]. 8vo. London, 1913

HYMNS to the Supreme Being, in imitation of the Eastern songs. [By Edward King.] 8vo. Pp. vii. 168. [Taylor's *Coll. of Psalm-versions*, p. 157.] London, 1780

Later editions (some surreptitious) bear the author's name.

HYMNS translated from the Parisian Breviary. By the author of *The cathedral* [Rev. Isaac Williams, B.D.]. 12mo. Pp. viii. 352. [Julian's *Dict.*] London, 1839

HYMNS translated or imitated from the German; to which is prefixed . . . an account of the origin of the Lutheran hymns. By a clergyman [George Walker, D.D., minister at Kinnell]. 8vo. Pp. 116. [Julian's *Dict.*] London, 1860

HYMNS written in the time of the tumults, June 1780. [By John and Charles Wesley.] 8vo. Pp. 19. [*Brit. Mus.*] Bristol, 1780

HYMN-TUNES of the oratory, Birmingham. [By John Henry Newman, D.D.] 12mo. Private print, 1860

HYP (the) doctor. By Jonadab Swift, M.D. [John Henley]. 8vo. [*Brit. Mus.*] London, 1730

HYPATIA; or, the history of a most beautiful, most vertuous, most learned, and every way accomplish'd lady; who was torn to pieces by the clergy of Alexandria, to gratify the pride, emulation, and cruelty of their archbishop, commonly but undeservedly stiled St Cyril. [By John Toland.] 8vo. [*Bodl.*] London, 1753

Reprinted from Tetradymus.

HYPERCRITIC (the). [A reply to articles in the *Monthly Reviews*. By James Elphinstone.] 8vo. [*Brit. Mus.*] London, 1783

HYPERCRITICISM exposed; in a letter addressed to the readers of *The Quarterly Review*, respecting an article in the xivth number of that publication [by Octavius Gilchrist], professing to be an examen of Mr Stephen Jones's edition of the *Biographia dramatica*, lately published. By a friend to candour and truth [Stephen Jones]. 8vo. London, 1812

The following note is in the British Museum copy—"Probably the very rarest of modern pamphlets—its existence denied over and over again by dramatic booksellers and collectors."

HYPERION; a romance. By the author of *Outre-mer* [Henry Wadsworth Longfellow]. 8vo. 2 vols. [*Brit. Mus.*] New York, 1839

HYPER-TRACTARIANISM; being a letter addressed to [Archibald Campbell Tait] the Lord Bishop of London. By the author of *Philip Paternoster; a Tractarian love-story* [Henry Nutcombe Oxenham]. 8vo. [*Brit. Mus.*] London, 1859

HYPNEROTOMACHIA; the strife of Loue, in a dream. By Francesco Colonna. [A condensed translation of the Latin original printed at Venice in 1499. Dedication signed: R. D., probably R. Dallington.] 4to. [*Christie-Miller Cat.*] London, 1592

HYPNOTISM explained and discussed. By Silas Thorn [James Clark, M.A.]. 8vo. Pp. 40. Leeds, 1890

HYPOCRISY detestable and dangerous; four sermons. [By James Oswald, D.D.] 8vo. Pp. 51. [*New Coll. Lib.*] Glasgow, 1791

HYPOCRISY unmasked; or, a short inquiry into the religious complaints of our American Colonies. [By Samuel Johnson, LL.D.] 12mo. Pp. 24. London, 1776

HYPOCRISY unveiled, and calumny detected; in a review of *Blackwood's Magazine*. [By Macvey Napier, advocate.] Fourth edition; with appendix. 8vo. Pp. 55. [*Nat. Lib. of Scot.*] Edinburgh, 1818

Wrongly ascribed to James Grahame, advocate.

HYPOCRITE (the). [A tale. By Cyril A. E. Ranger-Gull.] 8vo. Pp. viii. 167. London, 1898

HYPOCRITE (the); a comedy, as it is performed at the Theatre Royal in Drury-Lane. Taken from Molière and Cibber, by the author of the alterations of the *Plain-dealer* [Isaac Bickerstaffe]. 8vo. [Baker's *Biog. Dram.*] London, 1769

HYPOCRITE (the); or, sketches of American society. By Æsop [Mrs Lillie Devereux Blake]. 8vo. New York, 1874

HYPOCRITES (the) vnmasking; or, a cleare discovery of the grosse hypocrisy of the officers and agitators in the army, concerning their pretended forwardnesse, and reall syncere desires to relieve Ireland, with the obstruction whereof they falsely charge some of the 11 impeached members, (who cordially advanced it) in the 6, 7, 8, 9, 10, 11, 12, 13, & 14 articles of their most false and scandalous charge. . . . [By William Prynne.] 4to. London, 1647

HYPOCRITICAL (the) nation described in a sermon [on Zach. 7:5] preached at St Maries in Cambridge upon the day of publick fasting. [By Simon Patrick, Bishop of Ely.] With an epistle prefixed. . . . 4to. [*Brit. Mus.*] London, 1657

HYPOLITUS, Earl of Douglas; containing memoirs of the Court of Scotland; with the secret history of MackBeth of Scotland. [Translated from the French of Marie Catherine La Mothe, Countess d'Aulnoy.] 12mo. [*Lond. Lib. Cat.*] London, 1708

HYPONOIA; or, thoughts on a spiritual understanding . . . of the Apocalypse. [By John R. Hurd.] 8vo. [Cushing's *Anon.*] New York, 1844

HYPOTHESIS concerning the formation and generation of spiritual and material beings. [By R. Casway.] 8vo. London, 1748

HYSSOP; a novel. By James Prior [James Prior Kirk]. 8vo. Pp. 310. London, 1904

I

I. D. B.; or, the adventures of Solomon Davis on the diamond fields [in South Africa] and elsewhere. By W. T. E. [W. T. Eady]. 8vo. Pp. vi. 344. [Mendelsohn's *South Afr. Bibl.* i. 507.] London, 1887

I. Y.; an Imperial Yeoman at war. By "The Corporal" [P. E. Boddington]. London, 1901

"I BELIEVE"; and other essays. By Guy Thorne [Cyril Arthur Edward Ranger-Gull]. 8vo. Pp. 320. [*Lit. Year Book.*] London, 1907

I BELIEVE in the Holy Ghost; a book of daily devotion. [Preface signed: C. M. T. *i.e.* C. M. Tatham.] 8vo. Pp. 126. London [1891]

I GO a-marketing. By Henrietta [Henrietta Sowle]. 8vo. [*Amer. Cat.*] Boston, 1900

I HAVE lived and loved. [A novel.] By Mrs Forrester [Mrs —— Bridges]. 8vo. 3 vols. [*Amer. Cat.*] London, 1883

I, JOHN Bale. By Thomas Bennet [Thomas Munro]. 8vo. Pp. viii. 203. Paisley, 1917

Private information.

I LOVED her once; a novel. By John Strange Winter [Mrs Arthur Stannard, *née* Henrietta E. V. Palmer]. 8vo. Pp. 118. [*Lit. Year Book.*] London, 1896

I MARRIED a wife; a novel. By John Strange Winter [Mrs Arthur Stannard, *née* Henrietta E. V. Palmer]. 8vo. London, 1895

I MUST keep the chimes going; a story of real life. [By Emily Steele Elliott.] 8vo. London, 1869

I MUST keep this feast. By a Glasgow merchant [Henry K. Wood]. 8vo. Edinburgh, 1870

I PRAY you be not angry, for I will make you merry; a pleasant and merry dialogue, betweene two trauellers, as they met on the highway. [By Nicholas Breton.] 4to. No pagination. B. L. [*Bodl.*] London, 1624

I SAW three ships; and other winter tales. By Q. [Sir Arthur T. Quiller-Couch]. 8vo. Pp. 304. [*Lit. Year Book.*] London, 1892

I SAYS, says I; a novel. By Thinks-I-to-myself [Edward Nares]. Second edition, corrected. 12mo. 2 vols. [*Bodl.*] London, 1812

I TOLD you so; or, an autobiography. By Mrs T. Narcisse Doutney [Harriet G. Storer]. 8vo. [Cushing's *Init. and Pseud.* i. 83.] Cambridge, Mass., 18 . .

"I TOO." By Beelzebub [Henry Newton Goodrich]. 8vo. Pp. 108. [*Brit. Mus.*] London, 1856

I, TOO; a novel, in two books. By Mrs Gerard Ford [Mrs Vevey Stockley]. 8vo. Pp. 299. London, 1892

I WATCHED the heavens; a poem. By V. author of *IX. poems* [Mrs Archer Clive, *née* Caroline Wrigley]. 8vo. Pp. 58. [*Bodl.*] London, 1842

I WILL maintain. [A novel.] By Marjorie Bowen [Gabrielle Vere Campbell, afterwards Long]. 8vo. Pp. 538. [*Lond. Lib. Cat.*] London, 1910

I WILL repay; a romance. By Baroness Orczy [Mrs Montague Barstow]. 8vo. Pp. 326. [*Lit. Year Book.*] London, 1907

I WONDER; essays for the young people. By the author of *Confessio medici* [Stephen Paget, M.D.]. 8vo. [*Brit. Mus.*] London, 1911

I WOULD and would not. [The Address to the reader signed: B. N. *i.e.* Nicholas Breton.] 4to. [*Christie-Miller Cat.*] London, 1614

IA. By Q. [Sir Arthur Thomas Quiller-Couch]. 8vo. Pp. 224. [*Lit. Year Book.*] London, 1896

IADES. By a descendant [Isabella Clifford]. 8vo. Pp. 105. [Dobell's *Private prints*, p. 233.] Venice, private print, N.D.

IBERIA; with an invocation to the patriots of Spain: a poem. To which is added, War; an ode. By "Falkland" [M. Glanville]. Second edition. 8vo. Pp. 16. London, 1812

IBERIA'S crisis; a fragment of an epic poem, in three parts. [By Henry Gally Knight.] 8vo. [*Brit. Mus.*] London, 1809

IBIS ad Cæsarem; or, a submissive appearance before Cæsar: in answer to Mr Mountague's Appeale, in the points of Arminianisme and Popery, maintained and defended by him against the Church of England, 1626. [By John Yates.] 4to. [Leslie's *Cat.* 1849.] London, 1626

ICARUS. By the author of *A jaunt in a junk* [Sir Ian S. M. Hamilton]. 8vo. [*Brit. Mus.*] London, 1885

ICE-BOUND (the) ship and the dream. By W. H. [William Horsnell]. 8vo. [Cushing's *Init. and Pseud.* i. 124.] Montreal, 1860

ICELAND (an) fisherman. [A novel.] By Pierre Loti [Capt. Louis M. J. Viand]; translated from the French. 8vo. [*Lond. Lib. Cat.*] New York, 1896

ICELANDIC notes. By W. F. [Daniel Willard Fiske, Ph.D.]. 8vo. [Cushing's *Init. and Pseud.* i. 57.] Berlin, 1880

ICHABOD. [A lament for the death of Cardinal Wiseman. By Robert Stephen Hawker, M.A.] 8vo. [*Brit. Mus.*] London, 1865

Signed: Karn-idzek.

ICHABOD; or, the five groans of the Church prudently foreseeing and passionately bewailing her second fall. . . . [By Thomas Kerr, D.D.] 4to. [*Brit. Mus.; D. N. B.* vol. 30, p. 403.] Cambridge, 1663

Though the authorship has been called in question, there is no other writer than the Bishop of Bath to whom the work can with greater probability be ascribed. It was reissued anonymously in 1689 as "Lachrymae ecclesiarum . . ." and in 1711, with Kerr's name, as "Expostulatoria, or the complaints of the Church of England . . ."; and again in 1737 as "The Church of England's complaints. . . ."

ICONOCLASTES; or, a hammer to break down all invented images, image-makers and image-worshippers; shewing how contrary they are both to the law and the gospel. [Signed: G. F. *i.e.* George Fox.] 4to. Pp. 28. N.P., 1671

"I'D be a butterfly"; a ballad. . . . The words and melody by T. H. B. [Thomas Haynes Bayly]. Fol. London [1827]

I'D choose to be a daisy. [By Miss D. Aston.] 8vo. London [1860?]

IDA Lee; or, the child of the wreck. [A novel.] By Fairfax Balfour [Watts Phillips]. 8vo. London, 1864

IDA May; a story of things actual and possible. By Mary Langdon [Mary H. Pike]. Edited by an English clergyman. 8vo. Pp. 323. [*Brit. Mus.*] London, 1854

Attributed also to Sydney A. Story. Several other editions followed.

IDA Nicolari. By Eglanton Thorne [Emily Charlton]. 8vo. Pp. 320. London [1886]

IDA Wilmot. By Aunt Abbie [Abby Skinner]. 8vo. [Cushing's *Init. and Pseud.* i. 5.] Boston, 1866

IDALIA; a romance. By Ouida, author of *Strathmore*, etc. [Louise de la Ramée]. 8vo. 3 vols. London, 1867

IDEA (the) of a nation. By Chanel [Arthur Edward Clery]. 8vo. Pp. 76. [*Brit. Mus.*] Dublin, 1907

IDEA (the) of a patriot king. [By Henry Saint John, Viscount Bolingbroke.] 8vo. [*Brit. Mus.*] [London, 1743]

IDEA (the) of Christian love; being a translation, at the instance of Mr Waller, of a Latin sermon upon John xiii. 34-35, preach'd by Mr Edward Young, prebend of Salisbury. With a large paraphrase on Mr Waller's poem of Divine love. . . . [By William Atwood.] 8vo. [*N. and Q.* 1852, p. 226.] London, 1688

IDEA (an) of the present state of France, and of the consequences of the events passing in that kingdom. By the author of *The example of France a warning to Britain* [Arthur Young, F.R.S.]. Second edition, with additions. 8vo. [*Brit. Mus.*] London, 1795

IDEAL (the) home and its problems. By Hallie Killick [Mrs Eustace Miles]. 8vo. London, 1911

IDEAL (the) man. By a philokalist [Felix Paul Wierzbicki]. 8vo. Boston, 1842

IDEAL (the) of man. By Arthur Lovell [David Arthur Lovell-Williams]. 8vo. Pp. vi. 250. [*Lit. Year Book.*] London, 1891

IDEAL physical culture; truth about the strong man. By Apollo [William Bankier]. 8vo. Pp. 140. London, 1900

IDEALA. By Sarah Grand [Mrs D. C. M'Fall, *née* Frances Elizabeth Clark]. 8vo. [*Lond. Lib. Cat.*] Warrington, 1890

IDEAS for rustic furniture, proper for garden seats, summer-houses, hermitages, cottages. . . . [By William Wrighte, architect.] 8vo. [*Brit. Mus.*] London [1790?]

IDEAS on prophecy; being a sequel to *The gold-headed image.* By Minor Hugo [Luke Hansard?]. 8vo. [*Camb. Univ. Lib.*] London, 1845

IDEAS, opinions, and facts. [By Thomas Ballantyne.] 8vo. [*Brit. Mus.*] London, 1865

"IDENTITY" (the) exchange; a story. By R. Andom [Alfred W. Barrett]. 8vo. [*Lit. Year Book.*] London, 1902

IDENTITY (the) of Junius, with a distinguished living character [Sir Philip Francis] established. [By John Taylor, publisher.] 8vo. [*Nat. Lib. of Scot.*] London, 1816

IDENTITY (the) of Popery and Tractarianism; observations extracted from the *Christian's Monthly Magazine and Universal Review* for April, 1844. [By Thomas Hartwell Horne.] 8vo. [*Reminiscences of T. H. Horne*, p. 154.] London, 1844

IDENTITY (the) of Romanism and Paganism. By the author of *The worship of the dead* [John Garnier]. 8vo. Pp. 120. [*Brit. Mus.*] London, 1914

IDES (the) of March. By G. M. Robins [Mrs Louis Baillie Reynolds]. 8vo. Pp. 328. [*Lit. Year Book.*] London, 1900

IDIOTS (the). By Joseph Conrad [Joseph Conrad Korzeniowski]. 8vo. Pp. 55. [*Brit. Mus.*] New York [1920]

IDLE (an) farthing. [A novel.] By Esmé Stuart [Amélie Claire Leroy]. New edition. 8vo. [*Lond. Lib. Cat.*] London, 1895

IDLE hours. [Verse.] By Shingawn [Harry Quilter, M.A., Cambridge]. 8vo. London, 1872

IDLE musings; essays in social mosaic. By E. Conder Gray [Alexander Hay Japp]. 8vo. Pp. vi. 316. [*D. N. B.* Second Supp. vol. 3, p. 363.] London, 1890

IDLE tales. By F. G. Trafford [Mrs Charlotte E. L. Riddell]. 8vo. [*Lond. Lib. Cat.*] New York, 1892

IDLE thoughts of a lazy girl. By Jenny Wren [Jane Atkinson]. Seventh edition. 8vo. [Cushing's *Init. and Pseud.* i. 310.] London, 1891

IDLEHURST. [A novel.] By John Halsham [G. Forrester Scott]. 8vo. London, 1898

IDLENESS and industry; or, the story of Jem Preston. [By Maria Edgeworth.] 8vo. [*Brit. Mus.*] London [1860]

IDLENESS (the) of business; a satyr, addressed to one who said, "A man sheweth his spirit, industry, and parts, by his love of business." [By William Wycherley.] 8vo. [Arber's *Term Cat.* iii. 687.] London, 1706

IDLER (the). By the author of *The Rambler* [Samuel Johnson, LL.D.]. With additional essays. 12mo. 2 vols. Fifth edition. London, 1796

IDOL (the) of the clownes; or, insurrection of Wat the Tyler, with his fellow Kings of the Commons, against the English Church, the King, the lawes, nobility and gentry. . . . Anno 1381. [By John Cleveland.] 12mo. [Smith's *Bibl. Cant.*] London, 1654

Reprinted under the title of "The rustick rampant."

IDOLATERS ruine and Englands triumph; or, the meditations of a maimed souldier. By W. W. [William Whitfeild]. 4to. [Thomason's *Coll. of Tracts*, i. 357.] London, 1645

IDOLS in the heart; a tale. By A. L. O. E., authoress of *The giant killer*, etc. [Charlotte M. Tucker]. 8vo. Pp. 302. London, 1860

IDOL'S (an) passion. [A novel.] By Irene Osgood [Mrs Robert Harborough Sherard]. 8vo. New York, 1906

IDOL-SHRINE (the); or, the origin, history, and worship of the great temple of Jagannáth. By the author of *Orissa, the garden of superstition and idolatry* [Colonel W. F. B. Lawrie]. 8vo. Pp. 45. [*Bodl.*] London, 1851

Preface signed: W. F. B. L.

IDONE; or, incidents in the life of a dreamer. [By James Henry Laurence Archer.] 8vo. [*Brit. Mus.*] London, 1852

IDSTONE (the) papers; a series of articles and desultory observations on sport and things in general. By "Idstone" [Rev. Thomas Pearce] of *The Field.* 8vo. [*Lit. Year Book.*] London, 1872

IDWAL; a poem, with notes. [By Peter Bayley.] 8vo. [*Brit. Mus.*] London, 1824

IDYL (an) of the Alps. By the author of *Mary Powell* [Anne Manning, later Mrs Rathbone]. 8vo. [*Brit. Mus.*] London, 1876

IDYL (an) of the primitive Church. By Nathan [Nathan C. Kouns]. 8vo. [*Amer. Cat.*] New York, 1884

IDYLL (an) of All fools' day. By Ingraham Lovell [Mrs Josephine D. D. Bacon]. 8vo. [*Amer. Cat.*] New York, 1908

IDYLL (the) of the White Lotus. By M. C. [Mabel Collins, later Mrs Cook], Fellow of the Theosophical Society. 8vo. Pp. 141. [*Brit. Mus.*] London, 1884

IDYLLIA. [Twenty-five poems.] By the author of *Thysia* [Morton Luce]. 8vo. Pp. 39. London, 1911

IDYLLS of other days. By George Umber [William Findlay, M.D.]. 8vo. [*Mitchell Library.*] Glasgow, 1896

IDYLLS of Rosehill. By Ramsay Guthrie [Rev. John G. Bowran]. 8vo. Pp. 162. [*Meth. Who's Who.*] London, 1901

IDYLLS of Spain; varnished pictures of travels in the Peninsula. By Rowland Thirlmere [John Walker]. 8vo. Pp. 228. [*Lond. Lib. Cat.*] London, 1897

IDYLLS of Yorkshire. [Ten stories.] By Hubert Cloudesley [John Wrigglesworth]. 8vo. Pp. iv. 292. Elland [1890?]

IDYLS of battle, and poems of the Rebellion. By Howard Glyndon [Mrs Laura Catherine Scaring, *née* Redden]. 8vo. [Kirk's *Supp.*] New York, 1864

IDYLS of the months; poems and drawings. By Aunt May [Mrs Mary A. Lathbury]. 4to. [Haynes' *Pseud.*] New York, 1885

ΙΗΣΟΥ, its usage and sense in Holy Scripture. By Herman Heinfetter [Frederick Parker]. 12mo. London, 1844

ΙΗΣΟΥΣ. ΚΥΡΙΟΣ; their usage and sense in Holy Scripture. By Herman Heinfetter [Frederick Parker], author of *Rules for ascertaining the sense conveyed in ancient Greek manuscripts.* Second edition. 12mo. Pp. 72. London, 1857

IF; a nightmare on the conditional mood. By the authors of *Wisdom while you wait* [Edward V. Lucas, and Charles L. Graves]. 8vo. London, 1908

IF Britain is to live. By Norman Angell [Ralph Norman Angell Lane]. 8vo. [*Lond. Lib. Cat.*] London, 1922

IF the Gospel narratives are mythical—what then? [By John Taylor Brown, LL.D.] 8vo. Pp. viii. 82. [*Nat. Lib. of Scot.*] Edinburgh, 1869

IF ye fulfil the royal law. By A. H. W. [A. H. Wigmore]. 8vo. London, 1916

IF you know not me, you know no bodie; or, the troubles of Queene Elizabeth. [By Thomas Heywood.] 4to. No pagination. [*Pollard and Redgrave.*] London, 1605

IGNATIUS his conclave; or his inthronization in a late election in hell: wherein many things are mingled by way of satyr, concerning the disposition of Iesuits, the creation of a new hell, the establishing of a church in the moone. There is also added an apology for Iesuites. . . . Translated out of Latine. [By John Donne, D.D.] 12mo. Pp. 143. [*Camb. Univ. Lib.*] London, 1611

An edition, with the author's name, was printed at London in 1653, and forms part of a volume by Dr Donne entitled, "Paradoxes, problems, essayes, characters. . . ." London, 1652.

IGNATIUS Loyola, and the early Jesuits. By Stewart Rose [Countess of Buchan—Caroline Rose Erskine]. 8vo. [*Lond. Lib. Cat.*] London, 1870

IGNATIUS [Joseph Leycester Lyne], monk of the order of S. Benedict, by virtue of vows of obedience to the holy rule of S. Benedict, to the Reverend Father Darby, Catholic priest of the diocese of Manchester, ministering in the church under the invocation of S. Luke the Evangelist, in the city of Manchester. 8vo. Pp. 32. Manchester, N.D.

IGNORAMUS; a comedy. Written in Latine by George Ruggle: translated into English by R. C. [Robert Codrington]. 4to. [*Brit. Mus.*] London, 1662

IGNORAMUS (the) justices; being an answer to the order of Sessions at Hicks's-Hall, bearing date the 13th of January, 1681: wherein it plainly appears, the said order is against law; also a short account of all the Acts that relate to Protestant Dissenters at this day in force against them, which will appear only two, viz. the Act made in the 22 year of this king, intituled, An Act against Conventicles: the other, called, The Oxford Act, or Five Mile Act, made in the 17 of this king. . . . By Drawde Rekatihw [Edward Whitaker]. 4to. London, 1681

IGNORANTIA scientifica; a brief essay on man's not knowing his time . . . upon a special and mournful occasion [the death of Samuel Hirst. By Cotton Mather]. 8vo. Pp. 24. [*G. Brinley's Amer. Lib.*] Boston, 1727

IGNOTA febris; fevers mistaken, in doctrine and practice: shewing how they assurge, and whereon they depend: hinting the proper means of allay and extinction; adapt to the true notion thereof. By E. M. [Everard Maynwaring] Med. D. 4to. [*Bodl.*] [London, 1691]

ILDERIM; a Syrian tale, in four cantos. [By Henry Gally Knight.] 8vo. Pp. 74. [*Bodl.*] London, 1816

ILE (the) of Gulls; as it hath been often acted in the Black Fryars by the children of the Revels. [By John Day.] 4to. [*Pollard and Redgrave.*] London, 1633

ILIAD (the) of Homer [Book I. only], faithfully rendered in Homeric verse from the original Greek. By Philhellen Etonensis [Lancelot Shadwall]. 8vo. Pp. 20. London, 1844

Books I. to IX. were afterwards published (1844-45) with the translator's name.

ILKA, the captive maiden; and other stories. By S. G. [Selina Gaye], author of *All's well that ends well*, etc. 8vo. Pp. 128. London, 1905

ILL (the) effects of animosities among Protestants in England detected. . . . [By Gilbert Burnet, D.D.] 4to. Pp. 23. [*Brit. Mus.*] N.P. 1688

I'LL ne'er consent. . . . By Dolores Marbourg [Mrs Mary S. Hoke Bacon]. 8vo. New York, 1888

I'LL try. [A story for girls.] By Mrs Madeleine Leslie [Harriette Newell Baker]. 12mo. [Kirk's *Supp.*] Boston [1870?]

ILLEGITIMACY, and the influence of seasons upon conduct. By Albert Tracy [Albert Loffingwell]. 8vo. London, 1892

ILL-MATCHED (an) pair; the story of a marriage of convenience. . . . By Austin Clare [Miss W. M. James]. 8vo. Pp. 242. [*Brit. Mus.*] London [1896]

ILL-REGULATED (an) mind. [A novel.] By Katharine Wylde [Helen Hester Colvill]. 8vo. [*Camb. Univ. Lib.*] Edinburgh, 1885

ILL-TEMPERED (the) cousin; a novel. By Florentine [Mrs Minto Elliot, *née* Frances Dickinson]. 8vo. 2 vols. London, 1885

ILLUMINATED (the) Psalter. [By Rev. Peter Southmead Glubb, B.D.] 4to. [Boase and Courtney's *Bibl. Corn.*] [1870]

ILLUSION; a romance of modern Egypt. By E. Livingston Prescott Edith Katherine Spicer-Jay]. 8vo. Pp. viii. 301. [*Lond. Lib. Cat.*] London, 1899

ILLUSTRATED (the) book of patience games. By Professor L. Hoffmann [Angelo John Lewis]. 8vo. [*Lit. Year Book.*] London, 1900

ILLUSTRATED (the) fly-fishers text book. By Theophilus South, Gent. [Edward Chitty, barrister-at-law]. 8vo. [Westwood and Satchell's *Bibl. Pisc.*] London, 1841

ILLUSTRATED guide to Cardiff and its neighbourhood. [By Arthur Mee.] 8vo. Cardiff, 1897

ILLUSTRATED (the) handbook and visitor's guide to Redcar, with a historical and descriptive narration of places of interest suitable for rambles. . . . [By John Richard Walbran.] Also remarks on sea air, bathing, etc., by a surgeon. 12mo. Pp. 115. [Boyne's *Yorkshire Library*, p. 193.] Redcar, 1850

ILLUSTRATED handbook to St John's Church — Old Cathedral — Calcutta. [By E. W. Madge.] 8vo. [*Calc. Imp. Lib.*] Calcutta, 1909

ILLUSTRATED historical sketches. By Annie Myrtle [Annie Myrtle Chester]. 12mo. London, 1877

ILLUSTRATED (an) history of Ireland, from the earliest period. By F. M. C. (in monogram) [Frances Mary Cusack]. With historical illustrations by Henry Doyle. 8vo. Pp. xxiv. 581. London, 1868

ILLUSTRATED (an) itinerary of the County of Lancaster. [By Cyrus Redding, aided by Dr John R. Beard and W. C. Taylor.] 8vo. Pp. 238. lviii. [*Brit. Mus.*] London, 1842

ILLUSTRATED (an) record of important events in the annals of Europe during the years 1812, 1813, 1814, and 1815. [By Thomas Hartwell Horne.] Fol. London, 1815

From a list of his works in the handwriting of the author.

ILLUSTRATION of Mr Daniel Neal's History of the Puritans, in the article of Peter Smart, A.M., Prebendary of Durham, prosecuted for preaching a vile sermon in the Cathedral there. [By Christopher Hunter, physician and antiquary of Durham.] 8vo. [Leslie's *Cat.* 1850, p. 124.] 1736

ILLUSTRATION (an) of the Holy Scriptures by notes and explications on the Old and New Testament, the observations of the most learned men applied, and such new notes added as will greatly explain the nature and spirit of the Holy Scriptures, shew the gracious design of God in every part of them, etc. [By Robert Goadby.] Sixth edition. Fol. 3 vols. [Darling's *Cyclop. Bibl.*] London, 1759-70

ILLUSTRATION (an) of the present critical state of the Synod of Ulster; in three letters. . . . By a Presbyter [Rev. Henry Henry]. 8vo. Pp. 28. Belfast, 1802

ILLUSTRATION (an) of the wisdom and equity of an indulgent providence, in a similar treatment of all creatures on this globe, wherein the nature and ground of happiness, and also the origin of evil, are carefully examined and represented. [By Rev. John Edmonds.] 8vo. [Darling's *Cyclop. Bibl.*] London, 1761

ILLUSTRATIONS of a poetical character; in six tales: with other poems. [By Robert Pearce Gillies.] Second edition, corrected and enlarged. 8vo. Pp. 255. [*Nat. Lib. of Scot.*] Edinburgh, 1816

ILLUSTRATIONS of baptismal fonts. [By Thomas Combe]; with an introduction by F. A. Paley, M.A., Honorary Secretary of the Cambridge Camden Society. 8vo. No pagination. [*Bodl.*] London, 1844

ILLUSTRATIONS of British Hawk moths, and their larvæ. [By Theodore Johnson.] 8vo. 1874-6

ILLUSTRATIONS of eating, displaying the omnivorous character of man, and exhibiting the natives of various countries at feeding-time. By a Beefeater [George Vasey]. 8vo. Pp. 88. [*Manch. Free Lib.*] London, 1847

ILLUSTRATIONS of faith; eight plain sermons. By one of the writers of the *Tracts for the Christian Seasons* [Edward Monro]. 8vo. [*Brit. Mus.*] London, 1862

ILLUSTRATIONS of Hogarth; *i.e.* Hogarth illustrated from passages in authors he never read, and could not understand. [By Edmund Ferrers, rector of Cheriton, Hants.] 8vo. Pp. 55. London, 1816

The second edition is entitled "Clavis Hogarthiana," etc., *q.v.*

ILLUSTRATIONS of human life. By the author of *Tremaine* and *De Vere* [Robert Plumer Ward]. 12mo. 3 vols. London, 1837

The preface is signed: R. P. W.

ILLUSTRATIONS of [Free] Masonry. By one of the Fraternity [Captain William Morgan]. 8vo. New York, 1826

ILLUSTRATIONS of Mr Hume's Essay concerning liberty and necessity; in answer to Dr Gregory of Edinburgh. By a Necessitarian [John Allen, M.D.]. 8vo. [*Nat. Lib. of Scot.*] London, 1795

ILLUSTRATIONS of Northern antiquities, from the earlier Teutonic and Scandinavian romances; being an abstract of the Book of heroes and Nibelungen Lay: with translations from the Old German, Danish, Swedish, and Icelandish languages, with notes and dissertations. [By Henry Weber and Robert Jamieson.] 4to. [*Brit. Mus.*] Edinburgh, 1814

ILLUSTRATIONS of Parables. By A. L. O. E. [A Lady Of England, *i.e.* Charlotte M. Tucker]. 8vo. Edinburgh, 1861

ILLUSTRATIONS of prophecy; in the course of which are elucidated many predictions which occur in Isaiah, or Daniel, in the writings of the Evangelists, or the book of Revelation; and which are thought to foretell, among other great events, a Revolution in France, favourable to the interests of mankind, the overthrow of the papal power, and of ecclesiastical tyranny, the downfall of civil despotism, and the subsequent melioration of the state of the world. . . . [By Rev. Joseph Lomas Towers.] 8vo. 2 vols. [Orme's *Bibl. Bib.*] London, 1796

ILLUSTRATIONS of Scripture. By an animal painter; with notes by a Naturalist [James Wilson]. Fol. [*Brit. Mus.*] Edinburgh [1855]

Signed: J. W.

ILLUSTRATIONS of Scripture; the Hebrew converts; and other poems. By S. S. [Sarah Sheppard]. 12mo. [*Bodl.*] London, 1837

ILLUSTRATIONS of the Anglo-French coinage; taken from the cabinet of a Fellow of the Antiquarian Societies of London, and Scotland; of the Royal Societies of France, Normandy, and many others, British as well as foreign. [By Lieut.-Gen. George Robert Ainslie.] 4to. Pp. x. 167. London, 1830

The author's name is on a copy presented by him to a friend.

ILLUSTRATIONS of the doctrine, principles, and practice of the Church of England. [Preface signed: F. M. *i.e.* Rev. Frederick Martin.] 8vo. Pp. 203. London, 1840

ILLUSTRATIONS of the history and practice of the Thugs, and notices of some of the proceedings of the Government of India for the suppression of the crime of Thuggee. [By Edward Thornton, of the East India House.] 8vo. Pp. 475. [*Calc. Imp. Lib.*] London, 1837

ILLUSTRATIONS of the manners and expences of antient times in England, in the fifteenth, sixteenth, and seventeenth centuries; deduced from the accompts of churchwardens and other authentic documents. . . . [Preface signed: J. N. *i.e.* John Nichols.] 4to. [*Brit. Mus.*] London, 1797

Attributed also to Samuel Pegge.

ILLUSTRATIONS of the site and neighbourhood of the new Post-office, [London], comprehending antiquarian notices of St Martin's-le-Grand; with an account of the ancient Mourning Bush tavern and others. [By William Herbert, Librarian.] 8vo. [*Univ. Art. Cat.* p. 1641.] London, 1830

ILLUSTRATIVE replies, in the form of essays, to questions proposed by Bishop Maish to candidates for Holy orders. [By Nath. Ogle.] 8vo. [Lowndes' *Brit. Lib.* p. 814.] London, 1821

ILLUSTRATIVE views of the metropolitan Cathedral Church of Canterbury . . . with historical descriptions . . . [By William Woolnoth.] 4to. Pp. 58. [*Brit. Mus.*] Canterbury, 1836

ILLUSTRATOR (the) illustrated. By the author of the *Curiosities of literature* [Isaac D'Israeli]. 8vo. Pp. 85. London, 1838

ILLUSTRIOUS (the) and renown'd history of the seven famous champions of Christendom. [By Richard Johnson.] 12mo. Pp. 162. [*Brit. Mus.*] London, 1719

ILLUSTRIOUS Irishwomen; being memoirs of some of the most noted Irishwomen, from the earliest ages to the present century. By E. Owens Blackburne, author of *A woman scorned*, etc. [Elizabeth Owens Blackburne Casey]. 8vo. 2 vols. [*Brit. Mus.*] London, 1877

ILLUSTRIOUS women who have distinguished themselves for virtue, piety, and benevolence. [Signed: G. F. P. *i.e.* George Frederick Pardon.] 8vo. [*Brit. Mus.*] London [1868]

"I'M fur 'im; solid for Mulhooly." A sketch of municipal politics. . . . [By Rufus Edmunds Shapley.] 8vo. Philadelphia, 1881

IMAGE (the) breakers. By Gertrude Dix [Mrs —— Nicol]. 8vo. [*Lond. Lib. Cat.*] London, 1900

IMAGE (the) of bothe churches, Hierusalem and Babel, unitie and confusion, obedienc and sedition. By P. D. M. [Matthew Pattenson, or Patison, Doct. Med.]. 8vo. [Dodd's *Ch. Hist.*] Torney, 1623

The second edition was published in London, 1653, under the title, "Jerusalem and Babel; or the image of both churches."

IMAGE (the) of the beast; shewing what a conformist the Church of Rome is to the pagan. By T. D. [Thomas De Laune]. 8vo. [*New Coll. Lib.*] London, 1712

IMAGE (the) of war; a sporting autobiography. By "Snaffle" [Robert Dunkin]. 8vo. Pp. 428. Edinburgh, 1914

IMAGERY (the) of foreign travel; or, descriptive extracts from Scenes and impressions in Egypt, India, etc. Selected and republished by the author [Major Moyle Sherer]. 12mo. London, 1838

IMAGES (the) of the antients, particularly those in the University of Oxford. . . . A poem. By a tradesman [George Smith Green]. 8vo. Oxford, 1758

IMAGINARY conversation between Mr Herbert Spencer and a poet in a railway carriage. [By William Joseph Ibbett.] 8vo. Pp. 4. [*Brit. Mus.*] [Epsom, 1888]

Signed: Antaeus.

IMAGINARY (an) conversation between W. Shakespeare and his friend H. Wriothesly, Earl of Southampton. . . . [Signed: W. G. D. *i.e.* William Giles Dix.] 8vo. Boston, 1844

IMAGINARY conversation. Solon and Peisistratus. [By Walter Savage Landor.] 8vo. Pp. 12. [*Ashley Library.*] Private print, 1832

IMAGINARY dialogues in Cambridge. By the author of *Experiences of a convict* [John Frederick Mortlock]. 8vo. London, 1866

IMAGINARY interviews with composers. By Gerald Cumberland [Fred. C. Kenyon]. 8vo. Pp. 332. London [1909]

IMAGINATION; a poem. [By Louisa Frances Poulter.] 8vo. [*Brit. Mus.*] London, 1820

An edition, with other poems added, was issued in 1841.

IMAGINATION and its wonders. By Arthur Lovell [David Arthur Lovell Williams]. 8vo. Pp. 202. London, 1899

IMAGINATIONS and reveries. [Essays.] By A. E. [George William Russell]. 8vo. Pp. 268. [*Brit. Mus.*] Dublin, 1915

IMAGO saeculi; the image of the age, represented in four characters, viz. the ambitious statesman; insatiable miser; atheisticall gallant; factious schismatick: to which is added a Pindarique elegie on the most learned, and famous physitian, Dr Willis. By the same authour, N. W. [N. West]. 8vo. [Lowndes' *Bibl. Man.* p. 2877.] Oxford, 1676

Attributed also to N. Williams.

IMAUDDEEN; and other poems. By E. A. W. [Mrs Edward Ashley Walker]. 8vo. London, 1872

IMELDA; or, retribution: a romance of Kilkee. By J. B. S. [Rev. J. B. M'Govern of Chorlton, Manchester]. 8vo. [S. J. Brown's *Ireland in fiction.*] London, 1883

IMITATION (an) of Horace's first Epistle, written and printed at Trinity College, Cambridge, in 1793. [By Rev. Charles Valentine Le Grice, M.A.] 8vo. [*Brit. Mus.*] Truro, 1850

IMITATION (an) of Horace's 16th Epode. [By Sir E. Turner.] Fol. [*Bodl.*] London, 1739

IMITATION (an) of the new way of writing, introduc'd by the learned Mr Asgill; humbly offer'd to his admirers. [By Simon Ockley.] 8vo. [*Bodl.*] London, 1712

IMITATION (the) or following of Christ, and the contemning of worldly vanities; at the first written by Thomas Kempise [Thomas Hamaercken, or Hämmerlein, now generally known as Thomas à Kempis], a Dutchman: amended and polished by Sebastianus Castalis, an Italian [rather Sébastien Châteillon, the French Reformer], and Englished by E. H. [Edward Hake]. 8vo. [Watt's *Bibl. Brit.*] London, 1567

The translator omitted what he deemed "not good Scripture." Other anonymous translations are "The folowing of Christ, translated out of Latin. . . . [By Richard Whitford] (1556.)" — "The imitation of Jesus Christ; in four books; translated into English [by Richard Challoner] . . . N.P. 1706"—"The Christians pattern . . . 1668."

IMITATIONS of celebrated authors; or imaginary rejected articles. [By Peter George Patmore.] Fourth edition. 8vo. [*Brit. Mus.*] London, 1844

IMITATIONS of some of the Epigrams of Martial. [By N. B. Halhed.] In four parts. Latin and English. 4to. London, 1793-4

Each part has a separate title-page and pagination.

"These imitations are by N. B. Halhed (Sheridan's coadjutor in translating Aristænetus). He died insane."—MS. note in the handwriting of Dyce.

IMMANUEL; or, a discovery of true religion as it imports a living principle in the minds of men, grounded upon Christ's discourse with the Samaritaness. . . . By S. S. [Samuel Shaw]. 12mo. [*Brit. Mus.*] London, 1667

IMMANUEL'S Land, and other [poetical] pieces. By A. R. C. [Mrs Annie Ross Cousin, *née* Cundell]. 8vo. Pp. 267. London, 1876

IMMEDIATE (an) and effectual mode of raising the rental of landed property of England, and rendering Great Britain independent of other nations for a supply of corn. [By John Claudius Loudon, a Scotch farmer.] 8vo. Pp. 157. [*Manch. Free Lib.* p. 424.] London, 1808

IMMEDIATE (the) necessity of building a Lazaretto for a regular quarantine after the Italian manner to avoid the plague, and to preserve private property from the plunderers of wrecks upon the British coast. . . . [By Joseph Cawthorne?] 4to. [*Brit. Mus.*] London, 1768

IMMEDIATE, not gradual abolition; or, an inquiry into the shortest, safest, and most effectual means of getting rid of West-Indian slavery. [By Elizabeth Heyrick.] 8vo. [Smith's *Cat. of Friends' Books*, i. 93.] London, 1824

IMMEDIATE revelation; being a brief view of the dealings of God with man in all ages, showing the universal and immediate agency of the Holy Spirit under different dispensations; and that the Christian is especially authorized to expect immediate communications of the divine will. [By Henry Callaway.] 12mo. [Smith's *Cat. of Friends' Books*, ii. 375.] London, 1841

IMMINENT dangers to the free institutions of the United States, through foreign immigrations and the present state of the naturalization laws; a series of numbers originally published in the New-York Journal of Commerce. Revised and corrected, with additions. By an American [Samuel F. B. Morse]. 8vo. [Cushing's *Init. and Pseud.* i. 137.] New York, 1835

IMMORALITY (the) of prophane swearing demonstrated; in a new method. . . . Dedicated to modern Deists and Christians. By a lover of his country [Caleb Fleming]. 8vo. [*Bodl.*] London [1746]

IMMORALITY (the) of The moral philosopher; being an answer to a book [by Dr Thomas Morgan] lately published, entitled The moral philosopher. [By Joseph Hallet.] 8vo. Pp. 72. [*Gent. Mag.* vii. 374.] London, 1737

IMMORTAL (the) hour; a drama. By Fiona Macleod [William Sharp]. 4to. [*Amer. Cat.*] Portland, Me., 1907

IMMORTAL (the) manhood. By "Koresh" [Cyrus R. Teed]. 8vo. [*Amer. Cat.*] Chicago, 1903

IMMORTALITY. . . . By T. [William Henry Trenwith]. 8vo. [Cushing's *Init. and Pseud.* i. 278.] New York, 1878

IMMORTALITY in harmony with man's nature and experience. By Thomas Brevior [Thomas Shorter]. 8vo. [Boase's *Mod. Brit. Biog.* vol. 6, col. 554.] London, 1875

IMMORTALITY (the) of the soul. [By W. J. Curzon Siggers.] 8vo. Brisbane, 1890

IMMORTALITY (the) of the soul; a poem. Book the first. Translated from the Latin [of Isaac Hawkins Browne, by John Byrom]. . . . 4to. Pp. 31. [*Bibliographer*, vol. 4, p. 1507.] London, 1754

IMMORTALITY (the) of the soule; the excellencie of Christ Jesus treated on. . . . By T. H. [Rev. Thomas Hooker, of Hartford, Connecticut]. 4to. Pp. 21. [Sabin's *Dict.*] London, 1645

IMMORTALITY or annihilation? The question of a future state discussed and decided by the arguments of reason. [A translation, from the German, of Part I. of an anonymous work "Elpizon" by Ch. Friedrich Sintenis.] 8vo. Pp. x. 260. London, 1827

IMMORTALITY; or, the consolation of human life: a monody. [By Thomas Denton.] 4to. Pp. 20. [*Brit. Mus.*] London, 1754

IMMORTALITY preternatural to human souls; the gift of Jesus Christ, collated by the Holy Spirit in baptism; proved to be a catholick doctrine by the universal consent of the Holy Fathers of the first four centuries; being a vindication of Mr Dodwell against that part of Mr Clark's Answer which concerns the Fathers. . . . By a presbyter of the Church of England [Joseph Pitts]. 8vo. Pp. 271. [*Brit. Mus.*] London, 1708

IMMUTABLE (the) laws of nature in relation to God's providence. By a layman [Thomas Stevenson, engineer]. 12mo. Pp. 65. Edinburgh, 1868

IMPARITY among pastors, the government of the Church by divine institution; as maintain'd in an extemporary debate by an Episcopal divine against one of the Presbyterian perswasion. [By John Hay, D.D.] 4to. N.P., 1703

IMPARTIAL (an) account of Lieut.-Col. Bradstreet's expedition to Fort Frontenac; to which are added, a few reflections on the conduct of that enterprise. . . . By a Volunteer on the Expedition [John Bradstreet]. 8vo. Pp. 60. [Sabin's *Dict.*] London, 1759

IMPARTIAL (an) account of the affairs of Scotland, from the death of King James V. to the tragical exit of the Earl of Murray, Regent of Scotland; wherein, besides other material passages of State not hitherto published, is the Scotch Embassy to Queen Elizabeth, to declare her successor; with the learned arguments on that head. Written by an eminent hand [George Buchanan]. 8vo. [Watt's *Bibl. Brit.*] London, 1705

IMPARTIAL (an) account of the conduct of the Excise towards the breweries in Scotland, particularly in Edinburgh; pointing out the beneficial effects of the new mode of survey, by which several thousand pounds per annum have been already added to the revenue in the Edinburgh collection, and by which, if generally adopted through Scotland, many thousands more might be annually put into the Exchequer. . . . [By Hugh Bell, brewer.] 8vo. Pp. 85. [*Manch. Free Lib.*] Edinburgh, 1791

IMPARTIAL (an) account of the late expedition against St Augustine under General Oglethorpe. [By James Edward Oglethorpe.] 8vo. [*Camb. Hist. of Amer. Lit.* i. 376.] London, 1742

IMPARTIAL (an) account of the trial of F. S. for publishing Tom Ticklefoot . . . [By Francis Smith.] 8vo. Pp. 8. [Whitley's *Bapt. Bibl.* i. 112.] London, 1680

IMPARTIAL (an) by-stander's review of the controversy concerning the wardenship of Winchester College. [By John Speed, M.D.] 8vo. [*Nat. Lib. of Scot.*] London, 1759

Signed: Statutophilus.

IMPARTIAL (an) consideration of those speeches, which pass under the name of the five Jesuits, lately executed,—viz. Mr Whitehead, Mr Harcourt, Mr Gawen, Mr Turner, and Mr Fennick: in which it is proved, that according to their principles, they not only might, but also ought, to die after that manner, with solemn protestations of their innocency. [By John Williams, D.D.] Fol. [*Bodl.*] London, 1679

IMPARTIAL (an) enquiry into the causes of rebellion and civil war in this kingdom, in an examination of Dr Kennett's sermon, Jan. 31. 170¾; and vindication of the royal martyr. [By Mrs Mary Astell.] 4to. Pp. 64. [Arber's *Term Cat.* iii. 687.] London, 1704

IMPARTIAL (an) enquiry into the causes of the present fears and dangers of the government; being a discourse between a Lord-Lieutenant and one of his deputies for raising the Militia. [By Henry Booth, Earl of Warrington.] 4to. London, 1692

IMPARTIAL (an) enquiry into the existence and nature of God; being a modest essay towards a more intelligible account of the Divine perfections: with remarks on several authors both ancient and modern. . . . By S. C. [Samuel Colliber]. 8vo. [*Brit. Mus.*] London, 1718

IMPARTIAL (an) enquiry into the moral character of Jesus Christ; wherein he is considered as a philosopher: in a letter to a friend. [By George Turnbull, LL.D.] 8vo. Pp. 64. [Darling's *Cyclop. Bibl.*] London, 1740

Signed: Philalethes.

IMPARTIAL (an) enquiry into the state and utility of the Province of Georgia. [By Benjamin Martyn, Secretary to the Colonising Trustees.] 8vo. [Sabin's *Dict.*] London, 1741

IMPARTIAL (an) examination of the Bishop of Lincoln's and Norwich's speeches at the opening of the second article of Dr Sacheverell's impeachment. [By Edmund Curll.] 8vo. [*Brit. Mus.*] London, 1710

IMPARTIAL (an) historical narrative of . . . events which have taken place in this country . . . from the year 1816 to 1823. . . . Illustrated. [By Robert Bowyer.] Fol. [*Brit. Mus.*] London, 1823

IMPARTIAL (an) history of the late war. [By John Almon.] 12mo. [Watt's *Bibl. Brit.*] London, 1763

IMPARTIAL (an) history of the life and actions of Peter Alexovitz, the present Czar of Muscovy; from his birth down to this present time: giving an account of his travels and transactions in the several courts of Europe. . . . Written by a British officer in the service of the Czar. [By Daniel Defoe.] 8vo. Pp. 420. [Lee's *Life of Defoe*, p. 216.] London, 1723

IMPARTIAL (an) history of the town and county of Newcastle upon Tyne and its vicinity; comprehending an account of its origin, population, coal, coasting, and foreign trade. . . . [By Rev. John Baillie.] 8vo. [*Upcott*, ii. 1039.] Newcastle upon Tyne, 1801

IMPARTIAL (the) inquirer; being a candid examination of the conduct of [James Madison] the President of the United States, in execution of the powers vested in him by the Act of Congress of May 1, 1810: to which is added, some reflections upon the invasion of the Spanish territory of West Florida. By a citizen of Massachusetts [John Lowell]. 8vo. [*Brit. Mus.*] [Boston?] 1811

IMPARTIAL (an) inquiry into the benefits and damages arising to the nation from the present very great use of low-priced spirituous liquors; with proper estimates thereupon, and some considerations humbly offered for preventing the introduction of foreign spirits not paying the duties. By J. T., of Bristol [Josiah Tucker, D.D.]. . . . 8vo. Pp. 33. [*Brit. Mus.*] London, 1751

IMPARTIAL (an) inquiry into the order and government setled by Christ and his apostles in the church. [By Simon Couper, curate at Dunfermline.] 4to. Pp. 39. Edinburgh, 1704

IMPARTIAL (an) narrative of the reduction of Belleisle; containing a detail of the military operations, and every interesting anecdote since the first landing of our forces on the island to the surrender of the citadel of Palais: in a series of letters written by an officer, employed on the expedition [William Smith]. 8vo. Pp. 48. [*Bodl.*] London, 1761

IMPARTIAL reflections on the present situation of the Queen of France. By a friend to humanity [Mrs Mary Robinson, *née* Darby]. 8vo. [*D. N. B.* vol. 49, p. 32.] London, 1791

IMPARTIAL reflections upon Dr [Gilbert] Burnet's posthumous History. By Philalethes [Matthias Earbery]. 8vo. Pp. 109. [*Camb. Univ. Lib.*] London, 1724

IMPARTIAL (an) relation of some last parish transactions at Newark; containing a full and circumstantial answer to a late libel, entituled Remarks on a book entituled An account of the donations to the parish of Newark. [By —— Heron.] 8vo. Pp. 256. [*Upcott*, iii. 1490.] N.P. 1751

IMPARTIAL (an) relation of the first rise and cause of the recent differences in publick affairs in the Province of North Carolina, and of the past tumults and riots that lately happened in that province. . . . [By Herman Husband.] 12mo. Pp. 104. [Evans' *Amer. Bibl.* vol. 4, p. 231.] N.P. 1770

IMPARTIAL relation of the military operations in Ireland, in consequence of the landing of French troops, August 1798. By an officer who served under Marquis Cornwallis [Lieutenant General Sir Herbert Taylor]. 8vo. Pp. 72. London, 1799

IMPARTIAL (an) relation of the whole proceedings against St Mary Magdalen Colledge in Oxon, in the year of our Lord 1687; containing only matters of fact as they occurred. [By Henry Fairfax.] 4to. Pp. 42. [*Bodl.*] N.P. 1688

"Published in Oxon about the beginning of Feb. 1687."—MS. note by Wood. A second edition, "to which is added the most remarkable passages, omitted in the former, by reason of the severity of the press; collected by a Fellow of the said College," was published at London, in 1689. Also ascribed to Dr C. Aldworth [*Mendham Collection Cat.* p. 3], and to John Hough, Bishop of Worcester [*Nat. Lib. of Scot.*].

IMPARTIAL remarks upon Dr Freind's Account of the Earl of Peterborow's conduct in Spain chiefly since the raising the siege of Barcelona, 1706. [By Dr Richard Kingston, preacher of S. James, Clerkenwell.] 8vo. [*N. and Q.* 1862, p. 470.] London, 1707

IMPARTIAL remarks upon the Preface of Dr Warburton, in which he has taken uncommon liberties with the character of Dr Taylor. [By John Taylor, LL.D.] 8vo. [Watt's *Bibl. Brit.*] N.P. 1758

IMPARTIAL review of the controversy concerning moral and positive duties, etc. [By N. Nichols.] 8vo. [Leslie's *Cat.* 1843.] London, 1731

IMPARTIAL thoughts upon the nature of the human soul, and some passages concerning it in the writings of Mr Hobbes and Mr Collier. . . . By a divine of the Church of England [Rev. Francis Gregory]. 4to. London, 1704

IMPARTIAL (an) view of the state of religion in Penzance and its vicinity. By Vindicator [Rev. William Woodis Harvey]. 8vo. Pp. 58. Penzance, 1824

IMPARTIALIST (the) satyre that ever was seen, that speaks truth without fear, or flattry, or spleen; read as you list, commend it, or come mend it, the man that pen'd it, did with Finis end it. [By John Taylor, the water-poet.] 4to. Pp. 8. London, 1652

The original edition. "That it was written by Taylor, I have no doubt."—MS. note in the handwriting of Dyce.

IMPARTIALL (an) disquisition, how far conquest gives the conqueror a title. [By —— Gatford.] 4to. [*Bodl.*] N.P., N.D.

This has no separate title-page. It is an abstract of a treatise written by Mr Ghest, a learned and pious Suffolk divine, when the usurpers over Charles the martyr pretended a title by conquest.

IMPATIENT Griselda; a comedy in resolved discords. By Laurence North [James D. Symon]. 8vo. Pp. viii. 9. London, 1911

IMPEACHMENT (the), or Great Britain's charge against the present M—y [Ministry], Sir Roger Bold, the L— C—lay, and Dr S—ll [Sacheverell]; with the names of those credible persons that are able to prove . . . the whole impeachment . . . . By the unknown author of *Neck or nothing* [John Dunton]. 4to. Pp. 44. [*Manch. Free Lib.*] London [1710]

IMPECUNIOUS (an) lady. By Mrs Forrester [Mrs —— Bridges]. 8vo. Pp. 136. London, 1888

IMPERATOR et Rex; William II. of Germany. By the author of *The martyrdom of an Empress* [Margaret Cunliffe Owen]. 8vo. London, 1904

IMPERFECT hints towards a new edition of Shakespeare, written chiefly in the year 1782. [By Samuel Felton.] Two parts. 4to. London, 1787-8

IMPERFECT (an) pourtraicture of his sacred majesty Charles the II. . . . Written by a loyal subject, who most religiously affirms, se non diversas spes, sed incolumitatem Cæsaris simpliciter spectare [Walter Charleton, M.D.]. 4to. Pp. 23. [*Bodl.*] London, 1661

IMPERIA; a story from the Court of Austria. By Octavia Hensel [Mary A. I. Seymour]. 8vo. New York, 1892

IMPERIAL (the) epistle from Kien Long, Emperor of China, to George the Third, King of Great Britain, etc. in the year 1794; transmitted from the Emperor, and presented to his Britannick Majesty by his Excellency the Right Honourable George Earl Macartney of the Kingdom of Ireland, K.B., ambassador extraordinary and plenipotentiary to the Emperor of China in the years 1792, 1793, and 1794; translated into English verse from the original Chinese poetry, with notes. . . . [By Thomas James Mathias.] The third edition. 8vo. Pp. viii. 32. [*Dyce Cat.* ii. 66.] London, 1797

IMPERIAL India; letters from the East. By John Oliver Hobbes [Mrs Reginald Walpole Craigie, *née* Pearl Teresa Richards]. 8vo. London, 1903

IMPERIAL (an) manifesto; and other poems. By Mahaba [John Abraham]. 8vo. Pp. 32. Liskeard, 1872

IMPERIAL poems. By J. R. [James Rae]. 8vo. London [1888]

IMPERIAL ritual of magic, including full instruction in the genuine Kaballa, the making of talismans and amulets. . . . By Pythagoras, 38 [Reuben S. Clymer, D.D.]. 8vo. Pp. 200. [*Amer. Cat.*] Allentown, Pa., 1909

IMPERIAL strategy. By the Military Correspondent of *The Times* [Lieut. Colonel Charles A'Court Repington]. 8vo. Pp. xii. 376. London, 1906

IMPERIAL (the) tragedy; taken out of a Latin play, and very much altered by a gentleman for his own diversion, who, on the importunity of his friends, has consented to have it published, but without his name. . . . [By Sir William Killigrew.] Fol. Pp. 51. [*Bodl.*] London, 1669

IMPERIALE; a tragedy. [By Sir Ralph Freeman.] 4to. [*N. and Q.* 1867, p. 5.] London, 1655

IMPERIUM pelagi; a naval lyrick: written in imitation of Pindar's spirit, occasion'd by his Majesty's return, Sept. 1729, and the succeeding peace. [By Edward Young, LL.D.] 8vo. Pp. 60. [*Nat. Lib. of Scot.*] London, 1730

IMPERSONALITY (the) of the Holy Ghost; an humble endeavour to refute the opinion that God and his Spirit are two distinct persons. [By John Marston, Baptist Minister.] 8vo. [*Brit. Mus.*] London, 1787

IMPERTINENCE (the) and imposture of modern antiquaries display'd; or, a refutation of the Rev. Mr Wise's letter to Dr Mead, concerning the White horse, and other antiquities in Berkshire: in a familiar letter to a friend. By Philalethes Rusticus [probably William Asplin, vicar of Banbury]. 4to. [Nichols' *Lit. Anec.* v. 527.] London [1739]

IMPERTINENT (the) lovers; or, a coquet at her wit's end: a comedy, acted at the Theatre-Royal in Drury-Lane. . . . By a citizen of London [Francis Hawling]. 8vo. [Baker's *Biog. Dram.*] London, 1723

IMPERTINENT (the); or, a visit to the Court. By an eminent hand [Alexander Pope]. 8vo. [*Ashley Library.*] London, 1733

IMPETUS; an address to the members of the Wesleyan Methodist Association. . . . By a local preacher [William Henry Rodd]. 8vo. London, 1844

IMPIETY and superstition expos'd; a poetical essay: with a discourse by way of preface, wherein is discovered the original of deism, libertinism and superstition, the three great enemies of religion. And of the present ceremonies of the Church of Rome, draw'n partly from the old abolish'd Jewish oeconomy, and partly from the pagan rites, invented by Numa Pompilius, etc. By W. B. [William Brown] Gent. 4to. [Watt's *Bibl. Brit.*] Edinburgh, 1710

IMPOLICY and injustice of imprisoning O'Connell; demonstrated to Sir Robert Peel. By the author of *Ireland and its rulers since* 1829 [Daniel Owen Madden]. 8vo. Pp. 43. London, 1844

IMPORTANCE (the) and advantage of Cape Breton truly stated and impartially considered: taken principally from Charlevoix's Nouvelle France [by Sir William Pepperell]. 8vo. Pp. viii. 156. [*Brit. Mus.*] London, 1746

Ascribed also to William Bollan.

IMPORTANCE (the) of Canada considered; in two letters to a Noble Lord. [By Lieut. Charles Lee.] 8vo. Pp. iv. 38. London, 1761

IMPORTANCE (the) of effectually supporting the Royal African Company of England impartially consider'd; shewing that a free and open trade to Africa, and the support and preservation of the British colonies and plantations in America, depend upon maintaining the forts and settlements, rights and privileges belonging to that corporation against the encroachments of the French, and all other foreign rivals in that trade . . . in a letter to a Member of the House of Commons. [By —— Hays.] 4to. [*W.*] London, 1744

The following note by Francis Hargrave is taken from the copy in the British Museum —"I am informed, that this tract was written by Mr Hays, deputy governor of the African Company, from materials supplied by the directors and from the company's p[rivate?] papers."

IMPORTANCE (the) of gaining and preserving the friendship of the Indians of the Six Nations to the British interest considered. [By Archibald Kennedy.] 8vo. Pp. 46. [*Brit. Mus.*] London, 1752

IMPORTANCE (the) of Rabbinical learning; or, the advantage of understanding the rites, customs, usages, phraseology, etc. of the Talmudists, considered; with some remarks on their ænigmatical and sublime method of instruction, occasion'd by Mr John Gill's preface to his learned comment on the New Testament. [By John Dove.] 8vo. [Darling's *Cyclop. Bibl.*] London, 1746

The author was a learned layman, generally known to his contemporaries as "the Hebrew tailor."

IMPORTANCE (the) of the colonies of North America, and the interest of Great Britain, with regard to them, considered; together with remarks on the stamp duty. [By William Bollan.] 4to. Pp. 16. [Rich's *Bibl. Amer.* i. 153.] London, 1766

IMPORTANCE (the) of the Cowgate-bridge [in Edinburgh] . . . considered. [By James Brown, architect.] 8vo. [*Bodl.*] Edinburgh, 1775

IMPORTANCE (the) of the Guardian considered, in a second letter to the Bailiff of Stockbridge. By a friend of Mr St—le [Jonathan Swift, D.D.]. 8vo. [*Bodl.*] London, 1713

IMPORTANT considerations for the people of this Kingdom [of Great Britain and Ireland. By William Cobbett, M.P.]. 8vo. [*Brit. Mus.*] London, 1803

IMPORTANT considerations, which ovght to move all trve and sovnd Catholikes who are not wholly iesuited, to acknowledge without all equiuocations, ambiguities, or shiftings, that the proceedings of her Maiesty [Queen Elizabeth], and of the state with them, since the beginning of her Highnesse raigne, haue bene both mild and mercifull. Published by sundry of vs, the secular priests, in dislike of many treatises, letters, and reports. . . . [By William Watson, secular priest.] 4to. Pp. 25, 43. [*D. N. B.* vol. 60, p. 43; T. G. Law's *Arch-priest controversy*, published by the Camden Society.] 1601

The Epistle is signed: W. W.

IMPORTANT facts regarding the East-India Company's affairs in Bengal, from the year 1752 to 1760; this treatise contains an exact state of the Company's revenues in that settlement; with copies of several very interesting letters; shewing particularly the real causes which drew on the Presidency of Bengal the dreadful catastrophe of the year 1756; and vindicating the character of Mr Holwell from many scandalous aspersions unjustly thrown out against him, in an anonymous pamphlet, published March 6th, 1764, intitled, Reflections on the present state of our East-India affairs. [By John Zephaniah Holwell.] 4to. Pp. 135. [*Nat. Lib. of Scot.*] London, 1764

IMPORTANT (an) inquiry; or the nature of a church reformation fully considered: wherein is shown that the late pretended Reformation was groundless in the attempt, and defective in the execution. [By Sebastian Redford, S.J.] 8vo. Pp. 412. London, 1758

IMPORTANT proposals for national and universal peace, on a plan both just and new; with some remarks concerning the Catholic claims; vigorous war in Spain, and strenuous objections urged against hasty revocation of the orders in Council. By a real lover of freedom [William P. Russel]. 8vo. London, 1812

See his work entitled *The counsellor.*

IMPORTANT questions affecting the existence of the Roman Catholic Church in England; or an answer to a letter published by Cardinal Wiseman in the Parisian "Univers" against some articles of the "Ami de la religion." . . . By a Roman Catholic [Hardinge F. Ivers]. 8vo. [*Brit. Mus.*] London, 1854

IMPORTANT questions of state, law, justice and prudence, both civil and religious, upon the late revolutions and present state of these nations. By Socrates Christianus [Edward Stephens]. 4to. [*Brit. Mus.*] London, 1689

IMPORTANT trial by Jury; total abstinence against moderation. [Signed: G. J. F. *i.e.* George Jarvis Foster.] 8vo. [*Brit. Mus.*] London [1889]

IMPORTANT truths in simple verse. [Signed: S. W. P. *i.e.* Samuel William Partridge.] 8vo. [*Brit. Mus.*] London, 1841

IMPOSSIBILITIES. By Israfel [Miss —— Hudson]. 8vo. London, 1898

IMPOSSIBILITY (the) of witchcraft further demonstrated, both from Scripture and reason; wherein several texts of Scripture relating to witches are prov'd to be falsely translated; with some cursory remarks on two trifling pamphlets in defence of the existence of witches. By the author of *The impossibility of witchcraft* [Francis Bragge]. 8vo. Pp. xv. 30. [*Nat. Lib. of Scot.*] London, 1712

In order of issue, the following treatise preceded.

IMPOSSIBILITY (the) of witchcraft; plainly proving, from Scripture and reason, that there never was a witch; and that it is both irrational and impious to believe that there ever was. In which the depositions against Jane Wenham, lately try'd and condemned for a witch, at Hertford, are confuted and exposed. [By Francis Bragge.] The second edition. 8vo. Pp. 36. [*Nat. Lib. of Scot.*] London, 1712

IMPOSSIBLE (an) husband. [A novel.] By Florence Warden [Florence Alice Price, later Mrs George E. James]. 8vo. London, 1904

IMPOSSIBLE (the) lover. By Ben Bolt [Rev. Ottwell Binns]. 8vo. Pp. 254. [*Lit. Year Book.*] London, 1921

IMPOSTER (the) detected; or, a review of some of the writings of "Peter Porcupine" [William Cobbett]. By Timothy Tickletoby [Samuel F. Bradford]. 8vo. [Cushing's *Init. and Pseud.* i. 283.] Philadelphia, 1796

IMPOSTOR (the); or, born without a conscience. By the author of *Anti-Coningsby* [William North]. 8vo. 3 vols. [*Camb. Univ. Lib.*] London, 1845

IMPOSTURE (the) defeated; or, a trick to cheat the devil. [A comedy, in five acts and in prose. By George Powell.] 4to. [*Brit. Mus.*] London, 1698

IMPRESS of seaman; considerations on its legality, policy and operation applicable to the motion intended to be made in the House of Commons on Friday 12th May 1786 by William Pulteney, Esq. [By Lieut. J. Mackenzie.] 8vo. Pp. 51. London, 1786

The writer acknowledged authorship in a manuscript dedication attached to a presentation copy.

IMPRESSIONS. By Pierre Loti [Julien Viaud, Lieut. in the French Navy]; translated, with an introduction, by H. James. 8vo. Pp. 189. London, 1898

IMPRESSIONS and opinions. By Walter Lecky [William A. M'Dermott]. 8vo. New York, 1898

IMPRESSIONS of Germany. By an American lady [Mrs M. Griffin]. 8vo. [Cushing's *Init. and Pseud.* i. 14.] Dresden, private print [1866]

IMPRESSIONS of Ireland and the Irish. By the author of *Random recollections of the Lords and Commons*, etc. [James Grant, journalist]. 12mo. 2 vols. [*Camb. Univ. Lib.*] London, 1844

IMPRESSIONS of Rome, Florence, and Turin. By the author of *Amy Herbert* [Elizabeth Missing Sewell]. 8vo. Pp. xii. 330. [*Brit. Mus.*] London, 1862

IMPRESSIONS of the Ammergau Passion-play. By an Oxonian [Rev. Henry Scott Holland, M.A.]. 8vo. London, 1870

IMPRESSIONS of the heart, relative to the nature and excellence of genuine religion. [By Lady Janet Colquhoun.] Second edition. 8vo. [*Nat. Lib. of Scot.*] Edinburgh, 1834

IMPRESSIONS of the West and South during a six weeks' holiday. [Signed: W. K. *i.e.* William Kingsford, LL.D.] 8vo. Pp. 84. [*Brit. Mus.*] Toronto, 1858

IMPRESSIONS of Theophrastus Such. By George Eliot [Marian Evans, later Mrs Cross]. 8vo. Pp. 357. [*Brit. Mus.*] Edinburgh, 1879

IMPROVED whist. Part I., Whist with swabbers restored. Part II., Common whist improved. By Aquarius [Lowis d'Aguilar Jackson]. 8vo. Pp. 92. [*Brit. Mus.*] London, 1890

IMPROVEMENTS in the microscope. [By Cornelius Varley.] 8vo. [*Brit. Mus.*] London, 1832

IMPROVISATIONS from the spirit. [Verses.] By J. J. G. W. [James John Garth Wilkinson], of St John's Wood. 8vo. London, 1857

IMPROVISATRICE (the); and other poems. By L. E. L. [Letitia Elizabeth Landon, afterwards Mrs M'Lean]. Third edition. 8vo. Pp. viii. 326. [*Lond. Lib. Cat.*] London, 1824

On the engraved title-page, it is said to be a new edition, and is dated 1825.

IN a Dak bungalow; a collection of short tales. By J. A. N. [John Renton Denning]. 8vo. Pp. 70. [*Brit. Mus.*] Madras, 1895

IN a German pension. By Katherine Mansfield [Kathleen Beauchamp, afterwards Mrs J. Middleton Murry]. 8vo. Pp. 251. [*Who's Who in Lit.*] London [1911]

IN a north country village. By M. E. Francis [Margaret E. Sweetman, later Mrs Francis Blundell]. 8vo. [*Lit. Year Book.*] London, 1893

IN a steamer chair; and other stories. By Luke Sharp [Robert Barr]. 8vo. [*Lit. Year Book.*] London, 1892

IN a winter city; a sketch. By Ouida, author of *Puck*, etc. [Louise de la Ramée]. 8vo. Pp. 389. [*Lit. Year Book.*] London, 1876

IN accordance with the evidence. [A novel.] By Oliver Onions [George Oliver]. 8vo. Pp. 298. [*Brit. Mus.*] London, 1912

IN Afrikanderland and the Land of Ophir; being notes and sketches in political, social, and financial South Africa. [By F. Edmund Garrett.] 8vo. Pp. 99. [Mendelssohn's *South Afr. Bibl.* i. 589.] London, 1891

IN and out of Florence; a new introduction to a well-known city. By Max Vernon [Vernon Lyman Kellogg]. 8vo. [*Amer. Cat.*] New York, 1910

IN and out. [A book for the young.] By Ismay Thorne [Edith Caroline Pollock]. 4to. London, 1884

IN bad company; and other stories. By Rolf Boldrewood [Thomas Alexander Browne]. 8vo. Pp. 522. [*Lond. Lib. Cat.*] London, 1901

IN brief authority. [A novel.] By F. Anstey [Thomas Anstey Guthrie]. 8vo. Pp. 413. [*Lit. Year Book.*] London, 1915

IN camphor. [Poems. By R. Blanche Woodyear.] 8vo. Pp. 101. New York, 1895

IN chimney corners; merry tales of Irish folk-lore. By Mac [Seumas MacManus]. 8vo. [S. J. Brown's *Ireland in fiction.*] London, 1899

IN Christ's service. . . . By Edward Garrett [Isabella Fyvie, later Mrs John R. Mayo]. 8vo. [*Brit. Mus.*] London, 1887

IN Clarissa's day; a novel. By Sarah Tytler [Miss Henrietta Keddie]. 8vo. [*Lit. Year Book.*] London, 1903

IN Cupid's net. By Bertha M. Clay [Mrs Charlotte M. Braeme, *née* Law]. 8vo. New York, 1885

IN cure of her soul. By "J. S. of Dale" [Frederick Jesup Stimson]. 8vo. [*Amer. Cat.*] New York, 1906

IN darkest London; a story of the Salvation Army. By John Law [Miss M. E. Harkness]. 8vo. [*Lit. Year Book.*] London [1890]

IN deep abyss. By Georges Ohnet [Gorges Hénot]. Translated from the French by Fred. Rothwell. 8vo. Pp. 327. [*Brit. Mus.*] London, 1910

IN double harness. By Anthony Hope [Sir Anthony Hope Hawkins]. 8vo. [*Lit. Year Book.*] London, 1904

IN doubt. By Tom Clifton [Alfred F. Robbins]. 8vo. London, 1878

IN durance vile; and other stories. By the author of *Molly Bawn* [Margaret W. Hamilton, later Mrs Argles, then Mrs Hungerford]. 8vo. 3 vols. [*Brit. Mus.*] London, 1889

IN duty bound. By the author of *Mark Warren*, etc. [Isa Craig, afterwards Mrs Knox]. 8vo. London [1881]

IN earnest; or, Edith Palmer's motto. By Faye Huntington [Mrs Isabella H. Foster]. 8vo. [Kirk's *Supp.*] Philadelphia, 1869

IN evening lights. By Marianne Farningham [Mary Anne Hearne, of Farningham]. 8vo. Pp. 116. [*Brit. Mus.*] London, 1897

IN exchange for a soul. By Stephen Yorke [Mary Linskill]. [*Lond. Lib. Cat.*] London, 188—

IN Fairy-fane. [Verses.] By "Chanticleer" [G. F. Joy]. 8vo. Pp. 82. [*Brit. Mus.*] London [1913]

IN fear of a throne. . . . By R. Andom [Alfred W. Barrett]. 8vo. Pp. 323. [*Brit. Mus.*] London, 1911

IN festo dedicationis; and other poems. [By Susanna Neale.] 12mo. 4 parts. London, 1864

IN forest and jungle; or, adventures with wild beasts. By Ascott R. Hope [Ascott Robert Hope Moncrieff]. 8vo. London, 1891

IN furthest Ind. By Sydney C. Grier [Hilda C. Gregg]. 8vo. [*Lit. Year Book.*] London, 1900

IN Glenoran; a story. By M. B. Fife [Margaret M. Black]. 8vo. Edinburgh, 1888

IN golden shackles; a novel. By Alien [Mrs L. A. Baker]. 8vo. [*Lit. Year Book.*] London, 1899

IN Happy Hollow. By Max Adeler [Richard Heber Clark]. 8vo. [*Brit. Mus.*] London, 1903

IN her earliest youth; a novel. By "Tasma" [Jessie Huybers, later Mrs Fraser, then Madame Auguste Couvrier]. 8vo. 3 vols. [*Lond. Lib. Cat.*] London, 1890

IN herself complete; a novel. By Frances Harrod [Frances Forbes Robertson]. 8vo. London, 1898

IN his grasp. By Esmé Stuart [Amélie Claire Leroy]. 8vo. [*Lond. Lib. Cat.*] London, 1887

IN His name; the story of the Waldenses, seven hundred years ago. By Col. F. Ingham [Edward Everett Hale]. 8vo. [Cushing's *Init. and Pseud.* i. 137.] Boston, 1888

IN his own image. [A novel.] By Frederick Baron Corvo [Frederick William S. A. Rolfe]. 8vo. Pp. 432. London, 1901

IN Kedar's tents; a novel. By Henry Seton Merriman [Hugh Stowell Scott]. 8vo. Pp. 340. [*Lond. Lib. Cat.*] London, 1895

IN life's afternoon; and other stories. By Curtis Yorke [Mrs W. S. Richmond Lee, *née* —— Jex Long]. 8vo. Pp. 292. [*Lond. Lib. Cat.*] London, 1903

IN life's garden; poems. By Una [A. Macdonald]. 8vo. London, 1911
Presentation copy from the author.

IN London town; a novel. By Katharine Lee [Mrs Katharine Lee Jenner, *née* Rawlings]. 8vo. 3 vols. [*Brit. Mus.*] London, 1884

IN London's fields; a story of the lights and shadows of a child's life. By Eglanton Thorne [Emily Charlton]. 8vo. Pp. 188. London [1884]

IN love's crucible. [A novel.] By Bertha M. Clay [Mrs Charlotte M. Braeme, *née* Law]. 8vo. London [1896]

IN Maremma; a story. By Ouida [Louise de La Ramée]. 8vo. 3 vols. London, 1882

IN memoriam. [By Alfred, Lord Tennyson.] 8vo. [Wise's *Bibl. of Tennyson.*] London, 1850
A tribute to Arthur Hallam.

IN memoriam, Edward Hall Jackson, F.R.H.S., 1838-1923. [Signed: R. W. G. *i.e.* Richard Wm. Goulding.] 8vo. Pp. 8. [*Brit. Mus.*] [Louth, 1923]

IN memoriam; Garfield, and other poems. [By R. Bell.] 8vo. London, 1887

IN memoriam; Sidney H. Lear. [By H. P. Lear.] 4to. Pp. 202. Private print, 1868

IN memoriam. The burial of the Burials Bill. . . . By a county magistrate [Rev. Francis O. Morris, B.A.]. 8vo. London, 1890

IN memoriam; the Rev. W. Leeves, author of the air of "Auld Robin Gray," with a few notices of other members of his family. [By Mrs Anna Maria Moon, *née* Elsdale.] Pp. xxiv. 220. [Brighton] private print, 1873

IN memory of the Right Honourable John, Earl of Strathmore, kill'd at the Battle of Sheriffmuir, November the 13th, 1715. [Verse. By William Merton, Regent in Marischal College, Aberdeen.] 4to. Pp. 8. [*London Mercury*, v. 406.] N.P. [1716]

IN Mr Knox's country. . . . By Edith Œone Somerville and Martin Ross [Violet Martin]. 8vo. Pp. vii. 311. [*Brit. Mus.*] London, 1915

IN my city garden. By George Umber [William Findlay, M.D., Dennistoun]. 8vo. Pp. 229. [*Brit. Mus.*] Paisley, 1895

IN Oban town; a novel. [By Campbell MacKellar.] 8vo. Pp. 440. [*Brit. Mus.*] Paisley, 1896

IN old New York. By Ivory Black [Thomas Allibone Janvier]. 8vo. New York, 1894

IN old Quinnebasset. By Sophie May [Rebecca Sophia Clarke]. 8vo. [*Lit. Year Book.*] Boston, 1892

IN one town. By the author of *Anchor watch yarns* [Edmund Downey]. 8vo. 2 vols. [*Lit. Year Book.*] London, 1886

IN our county; stories of old Virginia life. By Marion Harland [Mrs Mary Terhune, *née* Hawes]. 8vo. [Kirk's *Supp.*] New York, 1902

IN our midst; the letter of Callicrates to Dione, Queen of the Xanthians, concerning England and the English, A.D. 1902. [Edited, or rather written] by William Thomas Stead; with illustrations. 8vo. [*Calc. Imp. Lib.*] London, 1903

IN palace and in faubourg. By C. J. G. [Caroline J. Freeland]. 8vo. Pp. 462. London, 1889

IN peril on the sea. By the author of *In the Northern mists* [Montagu Thomas Hainsselin]. 8vo. London, 1918

IN Piccadilly; a novel. By Benjamin Swift [William Romaine Paterson]. 8vo. [*Lit. Year Book.*] London, 1903

IN prison and out. By Hesba Stretton, author of *Jessica's first prayer*, etc. [Sarah Smith]. 8vo. Pp. vii. 208. London, 1880

See the note to "Alone in London."

IN pursuit of Priscilla. By Childe Harold [Elizabeth Salisbury Field]. 8vo. [*Amer. Cat.*] Philadelphia, 1907

IN quarters; chronicles of the 25th, the Black Horse, Dragoons. [A novel.] By John Strange Winter [Mrs Arthur Stannard, *née* Henrietta E. V. Palmer]. 8vo. Pp. 197. London, 1885

IN remembrance of the Hon. Sir George Rose, etc. By G. W. B. [G. W. Bell]. 8vo. London, 1877

IN royal service. By M. C. Ramsay [Mary Ramsay Calder]. 8vo. [*Lit. Year Book.*] London, 1912

IN St Dominic's country [viz. Languedoc]. By Catherine Mary Antony [Catherine Mary Antony Woodcock]. 8vo. Pp. xxiv. 316. [*Brit. Mus.*] London, 1912

IN Scottish fields. By Hugh Haliburton [James Logie Robertson]. 8vo. [*Lond. Lib. Cat.*] London, 1890

IN search of the truth. By Aunt Amy [Marion Pritchard]. 8vo. London, 1878

IN spirit and in truth; an essay on the ritual of the New Testament. [By Rev. Thomas E. Bridgett.] 8vo. Pp. vii. 341. London, 1869

IN spite of all. [A novel.] By Edna Lyall [Ada Ellen Bayly]. 8vo. [*Lit. Year Book.*] London, 1901

IN spite of herself. [A novel.] By Leslie Keith [Grace Leslie Keith Johnston]. 8vo. 3 vols. [*Brit. Mus.*] London, 1892

IN Stella's shadow. [A novel.] By Albert Ross [Linn Boyd Porter]. 8vo. [*Lit. Year Book.*] New York, 1892

IN sunny lands; out-door life in Hassan and Cuba. By William Drysdale [William Drysdale Crawford]. 4to. New York, 1885

IN sunny Switzerland; a story of six weeks. By Rowland Grey [Lilian K. Rowland Brown]. 8vo. Pp. 274. [*Lond. Lib. Cat.*] London, 1884

IN tent and bungalow. By the author of *Indian idylls* [Edith E. Cuthell]. 8vo. [*Lit. Year Book.*] London, 1892

IN the Alsatian mountains; a tour in the Vosges. By Katharine Lee [Mrs Katharine Lee Jenner, *née* Rawlings]. 8vo. [*Lond. Lib. Cat.*] London, 1883

IN the border country. By Ingraham Lovell [Mrs Josephine D. D. Bacon]. 8vo. [*Amer. Cat.*] New York, 1909

IN the Celtic past. [Sketches in prose.] By Ethna Carbery [Mrs Anna Macmanus, *née* Johnston]. 8vo. Pp. 120. [S. J. Brown's *Ireland in fiction.*] Dublin, 1904

IN the Central Provinces; or, sketches in prose and verse, descriptive of scenes and manners in the Central Provinces of India. By "Pekin" [Louis Kossuth Lawrie]. 8vo. Allahabad, 1881

IN the city; a story of Old Paris. [By Deborah Alcock.] 8vo. [*Lond. Lib. Cat.*] London, 1880

IN the clouds. [A novel.] By Charles Egbert Craddock [Mary Noailles Murfree]. 8vo. [Kirk's *Supp.*] London, 1894

IN the Counsellor's house. By Eugenie Marlitt [Eugenie John]; translated from the German by A. Wood. 8vo. 3 vols. [*Lond. Lib. Cat.*] London, 1876

Another translation (1877) has the title "At the Councillor's."

IN the dark. [A novel.] By Esmé Stuart [Amélie Claire Leroy]. 8vo. Pp. 340. [*Lond. Lib. Cat.*] London, 1899

IN the days of Drake. By a son of the soil [Joseph Smith Fletcher]. 8vo. Pp. 248. [*Amer. Cat.*] New York, 1897

IN the days of Luther; or, the fate of Castle Löwengard. . . . By Esmé Stuart [Amélie Claire Leroy]. 8vo. Pp. vi. 400. [*Lond. Lib. Cat.*] London, 1890

IN the dead of night; a novel. [By Thomas Wilkinson Speight.] 8vo. [*Brit. Mus.*] London, 1878

IN the depths of the sea; a tale. By Old Boomerang [John Richard Houlding]. 8vo. Pp. 378. [*Lit. Year Book.*] London, 1885

IN the Derbyshire Highlands. By "Strephon" [Edward Bradbury]. 8vo. [*Lit. Year Book.*] Buxton, 1881

IN the desert; a story of the Church under the Cross. By the author of *The Spanish brothers*, etc. [Deborah Alcock]. 8vo. London [1879]

IN the eagle's talon. By Sheppard Stevens [Mrs William C. Stevens]. 8vo. [*Amer. Cat.*] Boston, 1902

IN the face of night; a novel. By Dick Donovan [Joyce E. P. Muddock]. 8vo. Pp. 318. [*Brit. Mus.*] London, 1908

IN the face of the world. [A novel.] By Alan St Aubyn [Miss Frances Marshall]. 8vo. 2 vols. [*Lit. Year Book.*] London, 1894

IN the fairy's garden; verses. By John Lea [John Lea Bricknell]. 4to. [*Brit. Mus.*] London [1917]

IN the fir wood. E. V. B. [Eleanor Vere Boyle]. Illustrated with eight photographs by Cundall & Fleming. 8vo. Pp. 32. London, 1866

IN the fire; and other fancies. By Effie Johnson [Mrs Euphemia Johnson Richmond]. 8vo. Pp. 148. [*Lond. Lib. Cat.*] London, 1892

IN the Force; or, revelations by a private policeman; edited [but rather written] by Samuel Bracebridge Hemyng. 8vo. Pp. 120. [*Brit. Mus.*] London [1884]

IN the fort. [A tale.] By Sarah Tytler [Henrietta Keddie]. 8vo. Pp. 276. [*Lit. Year Book.*] London, 1886

IN the gloaming. . . . [By Meta Orred.] 8vo. [*Brit. Mus.*] London, 1886

IN the golden days. By Edna Lyall [Ada Ellen Bayly]. 8vo. [*Lit. Year Book.*] London, 1889

IN the green leaf and the sere. By a son of the marshes [Denham Jordan]. Edited by J. A. Owen. 8vo. [*Lond. Lib. Cat.*] London, 1896

IN the Green Park. [A novel.] By F. Norreys Connell [Conal O'Connell O'Riordan]. 8vo. [O'Donoghue's *Poets of Ireland.*] London, 1894

IN the grip of the law. [Tales.] By Dick Donovan [Joyce E. P. Muddock]. 8vo. Pp. 313. [*Brit. Mus.*] London, 1892

IN the grip of the Terror in Hungary. By Lumen [John Samuels]. 8vo. Pp. 40. [*Brit. Mus.*] London [1919]

IN the heart of the Bitter-Root Mountains; the story of the Carlin hunting-party. . . . By Heclawa [A. L. Artman Himmelwright]. 8vo. Pp. 259. New York, 1895

IN the heart of the storm; a tale of modern chivalry. By Maxwell Gray [Mary Gleed Tuttiett]. 8vo. Pp. 394. [*Lond. Lib. Cat.*] London, 1916

IN the hills; and other views: a book of frivolous verse. By Dum-Dum [Colonel John Kendal, R.E.]. 8vo. [*Lit. Year Book.*] London, 1903

IN the hollow of his hand. By Hesba Stretton [Sarah Smith]. 8vo. Pp. 191. London [1897]

See the note to "Alone in London."

IN the land of extremes. By Marie Cottrell [Mrs M. R. Harlan]. [*Amer. Cat.*] New York, 1909

IN the land of make-believe. [Poems.] By Olive Verte, author of *A sunset idyll, and other poems* [Mrs Mary M. Paine]. 8vo. Pp. 60. London, 1901

IN the land of the Brora; or camp-life and sport in Dalmatia and Herzegovina, 1894-1896. By "Snaffle" [Robert Dunkin]. 8vo. Pp. viii. 406. [*Brit. Mus.*] London, 1897

IN the land of the mosques and minarets [Algeria and Tunis]. By Francis Miltoun [Milburg Francisco Mansfield]. 8vo. [*Amer. Cat.*] Boston, 1908

IN the light of the XXth century. By Innominatus [Edward Heneage Dering]. 8vo. London, 1886

IN the market-place; a novel. By Jane Valentine [Nellie J. Meeker]. 8vo. [*Amer. Cat.*] New York, 1901

IN the matter of the Stowe scandal; Lord Byron's defence. [In verse. By Henry Savile Clarke.] 4to. [*Brit. Mus.*] London, 1869

IN the meshes. By Christine Mackenzie [Miss Annie Duffell]. 8vo. [Cushing's *Init. and Pseud.* i. 181.] Philadelphia, 1877

IN the midst of alarms. By Luke Sharp [Robert Barr]. 8vo. [*Lit. Year Book.*] London, 1894

IN the mountains. By the author of *Elizabeth and her German garden* [Countess von Arnim, afterwards Countess Russell]. 8vo. Pp. 278. London, 1923

IN the name of time; a tragedy. By Michael Field [Katharine Harris Bradley and Edith Emma Cooper]. 8vo. Pp. 93. [*Brit. Mus.*] London, 1919

IN the northern mists; a Grand Fleet chaplain's note-book. [By Montagu Thomas Hainsselin.] 8vo. Pp. 242. [*Lond. Lib. Cat.*] London, 1918

IN the olden time. [A novel.] By the author of *The Atelier du Lys*, etc. [Margaret Roberts]. 8vo. 2 vols. [*Brit. Mus.*] London, 1883

IN the poverty year. By Marian Douglas [Annie Douglas Green Robinson]. 8vo. [*Amer. Cat.*] New York, 1901

IN the Queen's service. [A novel.] By Dick Donovan [Joyce E. P. Muddock]. 8vo. [*Lit. Year Book.*] London, 190—

IN the ranks. . . . [A novel. By Henry Llewellyn Williams.] 8vo. [*Brit. Mus.*] London [1886]

IN the rapids; a romance. By Gerald Hart [Thomas J. Irving]. 8vo. [Cushing's *Init. and Pseud.* i. 127.] Boston, 1875

IN the rat-trap. [A novel.] By Daniel Woodroffe [Mrs Mary Woods]. 8vo. [*Amer. Cat.*] London, 1912

IN the saddle. By Oliver Optic [William Taylor Adams]. 8vo. Pp. 451. [Kirk's *Supp.*] Boston, 1895

IN the same regiment; and other stories. By John Strange Winter [Mrs Arthur Stannard, *née* Henrietta E. V. Palmer]. 8vo. Pp. 110. London, 1898

IN the Schillingscourt; from the German of E. Marlitt [Eugenia John]. 8vo. Pp. 488. Chicago, 1895

IN the shadow of God; sketches of life in France during the eighteenth century. By the author of *The Spanish brothers*, etc. [Deborah Alcock]. 8vo. Pp. viii. 372. [*Brit. Mus.*] London, 1877

IN the shadow of Islam. By Demetra Vaka [Mrs Kenneth Brown]. 8vo. London, 1911

IN the shadow of the purple. [A novel.] By George Gilbert [Miss —— Arthur]. 8vo. London, 1902

IN the silver age; essays—"that is, dispersed meditations." By Holme Lee, author of *Maude Talbot*, etc. [Harriet Parr]. 8vo. 2 vols. [*Brit. Mus.*] London, 1864

IN the smoke of war; a story of civil strife. By Tom Cobbleigh [Walter Raymond]. 8vo. Pp. 234. [*Lit. Year Book.*] New York, 1895

IN the straits of time; a romance of Old France. By Christopher Hake [Mrs Marion Andrews]. 8vo. Pp. 320. [*Lond. Lib. Cat.*] London, 1904

IN the "Stranger People's" country. By Charles Egbert Craddock [Mary Noailles Murfree]. 8vo. [Kirk's *Supp.*] London, 1891

IN the "Sunbeam," R.Y.S. (to Bombay and Tiurrachee) . . . 1913-1914. [By Thomas, Earl Brassey.] 8vo. Pp. 28. [*Brit. Mus.*] Private print [1914]

IN the sweet west country. By Alan St Aubyn [Mrs Frances Marshall]. 8vo. [*Lit. Year Book.*] London, 1895

IN the Temple. By Faith Latimer [Mrs John A. Miller]. 8vo. [Cushing's *Init. and Pseud.* i. 166.] New York, 1884

IN the Tennessee mountains. By Charles Egbert Craddock [Mary Noailles Murfree]. 8vo. [Kirk's *Supp.*] London, 1884

IN the three zones. [Three stories.] By J. S., of Dale [Frederick Jesup Stimson]. 8vo. Pp. 204. [*Lond. Lib. Cat.*] New York, 1893

IN the track of a storm. [A tale of convict life.] By Owen Hall [H. H. Lusk]. 8vo. London, 1896

IN the tropics. By a settler in Santo Domingo [Joseph Warren Fabens]. 8vo. [Cushing's *Init. and Pseud.* i. 265.] New York, 1863

IN the Tsar's dominions. [A tale.] By Le Voleur [Rose N. Carey]. 8vo. Pp. 408. London, 1899

IN the Union Army. By a nurse and spy [S. Emma E. Edmonds]. 8vo. [Cushing's *Init. and Pseud.* i. 206.] Hartford [Conn.] 1865

IN the valley of Havilah. By Frederick Thickstun [Frederick Thickstun Clark]. 8vo. New York, 1890

IN the Valley of Stars there is a Tower of Silence. By Smara Khamara [Frederick Hadland Davis]. 8vo. [*Lit. Who's Who.*] London [*c.* 1910]

IN the valleys of South Down. [A novel.] By "Athene" [Miss S. M. Harris]. 8vo. Pp. viii. 155. Belfast, 1898

IN the Veldt [of South Africa]. By Harley [Alfred P. Hillier, B.A., M.D.]. 8vo. Pp. 112. [*Brit. Mus.*] London, 1894

IN the vortex; a Latin Quarter romance. By Clive Holland [Charles J. Hankinson]. 8vo. Pp. 356. [*Lond. Lib. Cat.*] London, 1912

IN the web of war. By Francis Prevost [Henry Francis Prevost Battersby]. 8vo. [*Lit. Year Book.*] London, 1900

IN the West Countrie. By the author of *Queenie* [May Crommelin]. 8vo. 3 vols. [*Brit. Mus.*] London, 1883

IN the woods, and out; and other stories. By Pansy [Mrs Isabella Alden, *née* Macdonald]. 8vo. Pp. 256. Boston [1895]

IN the world. [An autobiography.] By Maxim Gorki [Aleksyei Maksimovitch Pyeshkov]; translated by Mrs G. M. Foakes. 8vo. Pp. v. 464. [*Brit. Mus.*] London, 1916

IN the world of bewilderment; a novel. By John Travers [Mrs G. H. Bell]. 8vo. Pp. 308. [*Lit. Year Book.*] London, 1912

IN the world of mimes; a novel. By Lewis Melville [Lewis S. Benjamin]. 8vo. Pp. 320. [*Lit. Year Book.*] London, 1902

IN troubled times. [A novel.] By A. S. C. Wallis [Miss Adèle Opzoomer]; translated from the Dutch by E. J. Irving. 8vo. Pp. 592. London, 1902

IN vain. By Heraclitus Grey [Charles Marshall]. 8vo. 3 vols. [Cushing's *Init. and Pseud.* i. 120.] London, 1868

IN vinculis; or, the prisoner of war. By a Virginia Confederate [A. M. Keiley]. 8vo. [Kirk's *Supp.*] New York, 1866

INCA (an) queen; or, lost in Peru. . . . By J. Evelyn [E. J. Bowen]. 8vo. Pp. 314. London, 1891

INCARNATE (the) Word; an exposition of the first eighteen verses of St John's gospel; with two introductory discourses. By a Protestant layman [Willett L. Adye]. Pp. 117. London, 1857

INCENDIARY (the) corrected; or, injured virtue and honesty defended: a satyric poem; being an answer to . . . . The Bouseliad [by John Colls]. . . . . By Phils [Rev. Joseph Proud]. 8vo. Norwich, 1786

INCENSE and ritualism in the Church of England; their use vindicated. . . . By a South Australian lay reader [C. W. Scott]. 8vo. Adelaide, 1873

INCENSE for the golden altar; a mode of partaking of or assisting at Holy Communion, according to the Liturgy of the Scottish [Episcopal] Church; newly compiled. [By Henry Humble.] 12mo. Pp. xv. 204. [*New Coll. Lib.*] Aberdeen, 1865

INCHCAPE (the) bell; or, the sea-rover's fate: a metrical legend. [By John Bremnar.] 12mo. Pp. 10. [*And. Jervise.*] Arbroath, 1846

INCHCOLM, Aberdour, North Rona, Sula Sgeir: a sketch addressed to J. Y., Minster Yard, Lincoln. [By Thomas S. Muir.] 8vo. [Edinburgh, 1872]

Signed: Unda. Twenty-five copies privately printed.

INCHIQUIN the Jesuit's letters, during a late residence in the United States: being a fragment of a correspondence accidentally discovered in Europe. . . . [By Charles Jared Ingersoll.] 8vo. [Cushing's *Init. and Pseud.*] New York, 1810

INCIDENTAL poems. By the rustic bard [Robert Dinsmoor]. 8vo. [Cushing's *Init. and Pseud.* i. 255.] Haverhill, Mass., 1828

INCIDENTS in my Sunday school life. By Lillie Montfort [Eliza Mumford]. 8vo. London, 1873

INCIDENTS in the life of a slave girl. By Linda Brent [Mrs Harriet Jacobs]. 8vo. [Cushing's *Init. and Pseud.* i. 39.] Boston, 1861

INCIDENTS in the lives of good men. By E. A. A. [Mrs Elizabeth Allen Annable Needham]. 8vo. [Cushing's *Init. and Pseud.* i. 3.] Boston, 1865

INCIDENTS of personal experience. . . . By a minister of the Gospel [Rev. Herman Snow]. Boston, 1852

INCIDENTS of the Apostolic age in Britain. [By Jefferys Taylor.] 8vo. London, 1844

INCIDENTS of travel in Egypt, Arabia Petræa, and the Holy Land. By an American [John Lloyd Stephens]. 8vo. [*Brit. Mus.*] New York, 1837

INCIDENTS of travel in Greece, Turkey, Russia, and Poland. By the author of *Incidents of travel in Egypt, Arabia Petræa, and the Holy Land* [John Lloyd Stephens]. With a map and engravings. 12mo. 2 vols. [*Bodl.*] London, 1838

INCIDENTS of youthful life; or, the true history of William Langley. [By William Beloe.] 8vo. [*Brit. Mus.*] London, 1798

INCLE and Yarico; a tragedy, of three acts, as it was intended to have been performed at the Theatre-Royal, in Covent-Garden. By the author of *The city farce*, etc. [—— Wedderburn, a journeyman printer]. 8vo. [Baker's *Biog. Dram.*] London, 1742

INCOGNITA; or, love and duty reconcil'd: a novel. [By William Congreve.] 8vo. Pp. 75. [*Biog. Brit.* iv. 69.] London, 1700

INCOME (the) tax fathered; as also the mode of raising the supplies, without funding. . . . [By George Edwards, M.D.] 8vo. [*Lond. Lib. Cat.*] London [1799?]

INCOME tax; to pay or not? By the ex-Crown Surveyor of the Income Tax Enquiry Office [J. J. Hitchings]. 8vo. Pp. 70. [*Brit. Mus.*] London [1890]

INCOMPARABLE (the) game of chess. . . . Translated from the Italian of Dr Ercolo Dal Rio [but rather of D. Ponziani, known as the "Anonimo Modenese"] by J. S. Bingham, Esq. . . . 8vo. Pp. xv. 340. [*Manch. Free Lib.*] London, 1820

INCOMPLETE (an) Etonian. [A novel.] By Frank Danby [Mrs Julia Frankau]. 8vo. [*Lond. Lib. Cat.*] London, 1909

INCONSISTENCY of several passages in Doctor Watt's hymns with Scripture, and with each other. [By Ralph Eddowes.] 8vo. [*Brit. Mus.*] London, 1808

INCONVENIENCIES (the) of toleration; or, an answer to a late book [by David Jenkins], intituled, A proposition made to the King and Parliament, for the safety and happiness of the King and kingdom. [By Thomas Tomkins, chaplain to the Archbishop of Canterbury.] 4to. [Green's *Bibl. Somers.* ii. 502.] London, 1667

INCORRIGIBLE (the) twins. By D'Esterre [Lily Young]. 8vo. Pp. 104. London, 1904

INCREASE (the) of faith. [By William Lee, Glasgow University.] 8vo. Pp. xii. 238. Edinburgh, 1868

The author's name appears in the second edition.

INCREASE (the) of manufactures . . . commerce, and finance; with the extension of civil liberty proposed in regulations for the interest of money. [By William Playfair.] 4to. Pp. 122. [*Brit. Mus.*] London, 1785

INCUMBENT (the) of Axhill; a sequel to the *Chorister Brothers*. [By Mrs Disney Leith.] 8vo. [*Brit. Mus.*] London, 1885

INCUMBERED Estates (Ireland) Bill; objections by the Irish attorneys and solicitors; and answers by a member of the English Bar [John Hodgkin]. 8vo. London, 1849

INDECORVM; or a briefe treatise vpon one of Salomons Prouerbs. Chap. ii. 22; wherein is shewed how ill beseeming all common gifts and worldly blessings are to all such, as are not furnished with some answerable measure, of spirituall and saving grace. [By Stephen Egerton.] 8vo. [*Bodl.*] London, 1613

INDELICATE (the) duellist. [A novel.] By Irene Osgood [Irene Harvey, later Mrs R. H. Sherard]. 8vo. Pp. 218. London, 1914

INDEPENDENCE (the) of Great Britain as the first of maritime powers essential to neutrality; and the existence of France, in its present state, incompatible with the prosperity and preservation of all European nations. [By Rev. Edward Hankin, M.D.] 8vo. Pp. 42. [Watt's *Bibl. Brit.*] London, 1804

INDEPENDENCE (the) of the Church of Scotland. [By James Lillie.] 8vo. Edinburgh, 1838

INDEPENDENCIE Gods veritie; or, the necessitie of toleration: unto which is added the chief principles of the government of Independent Churches. Written by J. G. [John Goodwin], B.D. 8vo. London, 1647

INDEPENDENCIE no schisme; or, an answer to a scandalous book, entituled, The schismatick sifted, written by M. J. Vicars; which may serve also for a reply to Master Edwards his Gangrene. . . . By M. N., Med. Pr. [Marchamont Nedham, Medical Practitioner]. 4to. [*Brit. Mus.*] London, 1646

INDEPENDENT (the); a novel. [By George Monck Berkeley.] 8vo. 2 vols. [*Edin. Univ. Lib.*] London, 1774

Attributed also to Andrew Macdonald.

INDEPENDENT (the) credenda in theology, accompanied by annotations and explanatory observations. . . . By a country gentleman [Edward Day]. 8vo. Pp. 60. [Eddy's *Universalism in America*, ii. 522.] Baltimore, 1832

INDEPENDENT (the) Whig. [By Thomas Gordon.] 8vo. London, 1721

This work was originally published in numbers, the first of which appeared on Wednesday, 20 January 1719-20, and the fifty-third and last on Wednesday, 4 January 1720-21.

INDEPENDENT'S (the) loyalty; or, the most barbarous plot (to murther His sacred Majestie) very fully discovered: with a cleere and perfect answer, to the Lord Wharton's evasions. [By Richard Osborne?] 4to. [*Brit. Mus.*] 1648

INDEX Biblicus multijugus; or, a table to the Holy Scripture, wherein each of the books, chapters, and divers matters are distinguished and epitomized. . . . [By Leonard Hoare.] 8vo. London, 1672

This abridged title is that of the second edition; the following is that of the first edition.

INDEX Biblicus; or, the historical Books of the Holy Scripture abridged: with each book, chapter and sum of diverse matter distinguished, and a chronology to every eminent epocha of time superadded. . . . [Signed: L. H. *i.e.* Leonard Hoare.] 8vo. [*Brit. Mus.*] London, 1668

INDEX librorum prohibitorum; being notes, bio- biblio- icono-graphical and critical on curious and uncommon books. By Pisanus Fraxi [Henry Spencer Ashbee]. 8vo. London, private print, 1877

INDEX materiæ medicæ; or, a catalogue of simple medicines that are fit to be used in the practice of physick and surgery. . . . [By James Douglas, M.D.] 4to. [*Brit. Mus.*] London, 1724

INDEX (an) to [Tennyson's] In Memoriam. [By Rev. Charles L. Dodgson.] 8vo. [Wise's *Bibl. of Tennyson.*] London, 1862

INDEX (an) to mankind; or, maxims selected from wits of all nations. . . . By Mrs Mary Midnight [John Newbery]. 8vo. [*D. N. B.* vol. 40, p. 312.] London, 1751

INDEX (an) to the anatomical, medical, chirurgical and physiological papers contained in the transactions of the Royal Society of London, from the commencement of that work to the end of the year 1813, chronologically and alphabetically arranged. [By James Briggs.] 4to. [*W.*] Westminster, 1814

INDEX (an) to the Bible. By the late J. N. D. [John Nelson Darby]. 8vo. London [1887]

INDEX to the Bible, in which the various subjects which occur in Scripture are alphabetically arranged. . . . [By Joseph Priestley, LL.D.] 8vo. [*D. N. B.*, vol. 46, p. 368.] Philadelphia, 1804

Reprinted in London (1805, 1811, 1812): wrongly attributed to Rev. —— Simeon.

INDEX to the Heralds' Visitations in the British Museum. [By Sir Nicholas Harris Nicolas.] 8vo. [*D. N. B.* vol. 40, p. 41.] London, 1823

INDEX (an) to the History of English poetry by Thomas Warton, B.D., Fellow of Trinity College, Oxford, and of the Society of Antiquaries, and late Professor of poetry in the University of Oxford. [By William Fillingham, of the Temple.] 4to. [*Bodl.*] London, 1806

The index to each volume has a separate pagination.

INDEX (an) to the persons, places, and subjects occurring in the Holy Scriptures. [By Benjamin Vincent.] 12mo. [*W.*] London, 1848

INDEX (an) to the Records, with directions to the several places where they are to be found: and short explanations of the different kinds of Rolls, Writs, &c. To which is added, a list of the Latin sir-names, and names of places, as they are written in the old Records, explained by the modern names. . . . [By Sir Joseph Ayloff.] 8vo. Pp. 182. London, 1739

Attributed also to —— Strachey.

INDEX (an) to the sermons published since the Restoration; pointing out the texts in the order they lie in the Bible, shewing the occasion on which they were preached, and directing to the volume and page where they occur. [By Sampson Letsome, M.A.] 8vo. Pp. 96. [*Bodl.*] London, 1734

INDEX villaris; or, an exact register, alphabetically digested, of all the cities, market-towns, parishes, villages, etc. in England and Wales. [By John Adams.] Fol. Pp. 419. [*Brit. Mus.*] London, 1690

INDIA. By Pierre Loti [Louis M. Julien Viaud]; translated from the French. . . . 8vo. Pp. 290. London, 1906

INDIA; a poem, in four cantos. [By —— Cotes, Captain in the Indian Army.] 8vo. Pp. x. 106. Newcastle, 1812

INDIA; its dangers, as considered in 1856. By a retired officer [Colonel N. Alves]; with last words. 8vo. [*Calc. Imp. Lib.*] Jersey, 1859

INDIA; its history, religions, and government. . . . [By Rev. Geo. Gould, Baptist minister.] 8vo. London, 1858

INDIA, past and present; with minor essays. By Shoshee Chunder Dutt [otherwise Sasi Chandra Datt, *i.e.* James A. G. Barton]. 8vo. [*Lond. Lib. Cat.*] London, 1880

INDIA, pictorial and descriptive. By the author of *The Mediterranean illustrated* [William H. Davenport Adams]. 4to. Pp. 271. [*Brit. Mus.*] London, 1888

INDIA seventy years ago. By the nephew of an East India Director [Augustus Bosanquet]. 8vo. Pp. viii. 311. [*Brit. Mus.*] London, 1881

INDIA since the mutiny. [By George Smith, LL.D., C.I.E.] 8vo. Serampore, 1874

INDIAN (the) Alps, and how we crossed them; being a narrative of two years' residence in the Eastern Himalaya, and two months' tour into the Interior. By a Lady Pioneer [Mrs Nirva Elizabeth Mazuchelli]. 4to. [*Lond. Lib. Cat.*] London, 1876

INDIAN (the) amateur dairy-farm. . . . With a chapter on bees and their treatment in India. By "Landolicus" [W. Landale]. 8vo. [*Calc. Imp. Lib.*] Calcutta, 1895

INDIAN Buddhism. [Signed: J. M. *i.e.* John Muir, D.C.L.] 8vo. [*Bodl.*] N.P., N.D.

INDIAN (the) chief. [A tale.] By Henley L. Arden [Henrietta Knight]. 8vo. Pp. 64. [*Brit. Mus.*] London, 1883

INDIAN (the) chief; a story of the Revolution. By Gustave Aimard [Ollivier Gloux. Translated from the French by Sir F. C. Lascelles Wraxall, Bart.]. 8vo. [*Brit. Mus.*] London, 1861

INDIAN (the) cottage; translated from the French [of Jacques H. B. de Saint-Pierre, by Edward Augustus Kendall]. 12mo. Pp. 132. [*Brit. Mus.*] London, 1791

Two different translations appeared in 1797 and 1879.

INDIAN (the) convert; a poem. By the author of *Under the Arches*, etc. [Mrs Sarah B. Hancock]. 8vo. [Green's *Bibl. Somers.* i. 122.] Bath [1873]

INDIAN dialogues; or, side-lights on the administration of justice in the North-Western Provinces, India. By a friend of India [R. C. Saunders]. 8vo. [*Calc. Imp. Lib.*] London, 1899

INDIAN dialogues, for their instruction in that great service of Christ, in calling home their country-men to the knowledge of God, and of themselves, and of Jesus Christ. [Dedication signed: J. E. *i.e.* John Eliot, missionary to the North American Indians.] 8vo. Pp. 81. [*Bodl.*] Cambridge, 1671

INDIAN (an) district [viz. Gouda, in Oudh]. By a District Officer [F. Barrow]. 8vo. Pp. xi. 97. [*Brit. Mus.*] Allahabad, 1895

INDIAN (the) exchange, shewing the enormous loss to India yearly, and the remedy to be applied. By W. H. O. [W. H. Owen]. 8vo. Pp. 22. [*Brit. Mus.*] Exeter, 1879

INDIAN (an) gem; a novel. By Alan St Aubyn [Mrs Frances Marshall]. 8vo. Pp. 316. [*Lond. Lib. Cat.*] London, 1904

INDIAN love. [Poems.] By Laurence Hope [Mrs Adela Violet Nicolson, *née* Cory]. 8vo. [*Lond. Lib. Cat.*] London, 1905

INDIAN love-letters. By Ellis Martin [Mrs Marah Ellis Martin Ryan]. 8vo. [*Amer. Cat.*] Chicago, 1907

INDIAN nullification of the unconstitutional laws of Massachusetts relative to the Marshpee Tribe; or, the pretended riot explained. By William Apes. [Really by William Joseph Snelling.] 12mo. [Sabin's *Dictionary.*] Boston, 1835

INDIAN railways and their probable results; with maps, and an appendix containing statistics of internal and external commerce of India. By an old Indian Postmaster [Sir William Patrick Andrew]. Third edition. 8vo. [*Brit. Mus.*] London, 1848

INDIAN railways as connected with the power and stability of the British Empire in the East, the development of its resources, and the civilization of its people. . . . By an old Indian Postmaster [Sir William Patrick Andrew]. 8vo. [*Brit. Mus.*] London, 1846

INDIAN (the) religions; or, the results of the mysterious Buddhism. By an Indian missionary [Hargrave Jennings]. 12mo. [*Brit. Mus.*] London, 1858

INDIAN (the) sceptic confuted, and Brahmin frauds exposed; in a series of letters addressed to the . . . Episcopal bench. By the author of *Indian antiquities* [Thomas Maurice]. 8vo. [*Brit. Mus.*] London, 1813

This is a later edition of "Brahminical fraud detected. . . ." (1812).

INDIAN (the) scout; a story of the Aztec city. By Gustave Aimard [Ollivier Gloux. Translated from the French by Sir F. C. Lascelles Wraxall]. 8vo. London, 1876

INDIAN snapshots. By John Law [Miss M. E. Harkness]. Third edition. 8vo. Madras, 1912

INDIAN (the) tribes of the United States; their history, antiquities, customs, religion, arts, language, traditions, oral legends, and myths. [By Henry R. Schoolcraft]; edited by F. S. Drake. 4to. 2 vols. Philadelphia, 1884

INDIAN (the) uncle. By Leslie Keith [Grace Leslie Keith Johnston]. 8vo. Pp. vi. 340. [*Brit. Mus.*] London, 1887

INDIAN (the) wrestler. [A novel. By Henry Llewellyn Williams.] 8vo. [*Brit. Mus.*] London [1890]

INDIAN zoology. [Coloured plates, with descriptive letterpress by Thomas Pennant.] Fol. [*Brit. Mus.*] [London, 1769]

INDIANA. [A story of love and marriage]. By George Sand [Madame Amandine L. A. Dudevant]; translated from the French. 8vo. Philadelphia, 1850

INDIANE primer. . . . The Indian primer, or the first book, by which children may know truely to read the Indian language. [By John Eliot.] And Milk for babes (by John Cotton) [translated into Massachusetts-Indian by Grindal Rawson]. Massachusetts-Indian and English. 12mo. 84 leaves. [*Christie-Miller Cat.*] Boston, 1720

INDIANS (the); a tragedy, performed at the Theatre-Royal, Richmond. [By William Richardson, Professor of Humanity, Glasgow.] 8vo. Pp. 81. [Baker's *Biog. Dram.*] London, 1790

INDIANS (the) of North America. [By George Mogridge.] 16mo. [*Brit. Mus.*] London [1843?]

INDIANS (the) [of North America]; their manners and customs. By Robin Rustler [John Maclean]. 8vo. Pp. 350. Toronto, 1889

INDIANS (the) of New England. . . . By a citizen of Middletown, Conn. [Joseph Barratt]. 8vo. [Cushing's *Init. and Pseud.* ii. 31.] Middletown, 1851

INDICTMENT (the), trial, and sentence of Mess. T—s K—r [Thomas Kerr], A—w B—n [Andrew Brown], and R—t M—n [Robert Morton], before the Associate Synod, at the instance of the Rev. Mr Adam Gib. By a gentleman of the law [Andrew Moir, Secession minister, Selkirk]. 8vo. Pp. viii. 106. [*New Coll. Lib.*] Edinburgh, 1768

INDIFFERENCE in disputes recommended by a Pantheist [John Toland?] to an orthodox friend. 8vo. London, 1705

INDIGNANT rhymes, addressed to the electoral body at large. By an ill-used candidate [George John Cayley]. 12mo. [*Brit. Mus.*] London, 1859

INDIRECT taxation a robbery of the poor. By the author of the *Catechism on the corn laws* [General T. Perronet Thompson]. 4to. [*D. N. B.* vol. 56, p. 225.] Bradford, 1863

INDISCREET (an) chronicle from the Pacific. By Putnam Weale [Bertram Lenox Simpson]. 8vo. Pp. 310. London, 1923

INDISCREET letters from Peking; being the notes of an eye-witness, which set forth in some detail, from day to day, the real story of the siege and sack of a distressed capital in 1900—the year of great tribulation: edited by B. L. Putnam Weale [Bertram Lenox Simpson]. 8vo. Pp. 322. [*Lond. Lib. Cat.*] London, 1907

INDISCRETION (the) of Gladys. [A novel.] By Lucas Cleeve [Mrs Howard Kingscote, *née* Adelina G. I. Wolff]. 8vo. [*Brit. Mus.*] London, 1903

INDISCRETION (the) of the Duchess. By Anthony Hope [Sir Anthony Hope Hawkins]. 8vo. Pp. 316. [*Lit. Year Book.*] London, 1917

INDISPENSIBLE (the) obligation of ministring expresly and manifestly the great necessaries of publick worship proved, by Scripture arguments, the liturgies of the Universal Church, &c. [in answer to Dr Thomas Brett]; with supplement of further proofs, and supplement continued. [By Rev. Roger Laurence.] 8vo. [Darling's *Cyclop. Bibl.*] London, 1732-34

INDISSOLUBLE (the) knot; a veiled tragedy of the conventions; in six chapters. By Charles Granville [Francis Charles Granville Egerton, third Earl of Ellesmere]. 8vo. Pp. 210. London, 1908

INDIVIDUAL liberty,—legal, moral, and licentious; in which the political fallacies of J. S. Mill's Essay "On liberty" are pointed out. By Index [George Vasey]. 8vo. [*Brit. Mus.*] London, 1867

INDIVIDUALISTS (the); Cain and Artème: a strange companion . . . by Maksim Gor'ky [Aleksyei Maksimovich Pyeshkov]. . . . Translated from the Russian. 8vo. Pp. 111. [*Brit. Mus.*] London, 1906

INDO-ANGLIAN literature. [By Sir Edward Buck, Secretary to the Government of India.] 8vo. Calcutta, 1883

Certification by a friend of the author.

INDO—Burma—China railway connections a pressing necessity. . . . [By John Ogilvy Hay.] 8vo. London, 1888

Signed: Old Arakan.

INDOLENCE; a poem. By the author of *Almida* [Mrs Dorothea Celisia, *née* Mallet]. 4to. Pp. 23. [Baker's *Biog. Dram.*] London, 1772

INDULGENCE and toleration considered; in a letter unto a person of honour. [By John Owen, D.D.] 4to. London, 1667

Reprinted in the author's collected works.

INDULGENCE not justified; being a continuation of the Discourse of toleration: in answer to the arguments of a late book [by Dr John Owen], entituled A peace-offering, or plea for indulgence: and to the cavils of another [by John Corbet], call'd The second discourse of the religion in England. [By Richard Perrinchief.] 4to. [*Brit. Mus.*] London, 1668

INDUSTRIAL (the) and social position of women in the middle and lower ranks. [By John Duguid Milne.] 8vo. [*Brit. Mus.*] London, 1857

A revised edition, giving the author's name, was issued in 1870.

INDUSTRIAL (the) arts; historical sketches, with numerous illustrations. [By Rev. William Maskell, M.A.] 8vo. [*D. N. B.* vol. 36, p. 414.] London, 1876

INDUSTRIAL explorings in and around London. By Robert Andom [Alfred Walter Barrett]. 8vo. [*Lit. Year Book.*] London, 1895

INDUSTRY and idleness; a moral contrast. By the author of *A memoir of B. B. Woodward* [Frederick Bolingbroke Ribbans]. 12mo. [*Brit. Mus.*] London, 1877

INEBRIETY. [A satire. By George Crabbe.] 4to. [Courtney's *Secrets*, p. 122.] Ipswich, 1775

INEFFICACY (the) of preaching; or, government the best instructor: being an attempt to prove, in the testimony of past ages, and the experience of the present, how little either poets, historians, philosophers or divines, have ever contributed to the reformation of mankind. . . . Translated from the original of a celebrated French author [L'Abbé Gabriel F. Coyer]. 8vo. London, 1771

INEFFICACY (the) of satire; a poem. [By Rev. Philip Parsons.] 4to. [*Gent. Mag.* lxxxii. 2. 292.] London, 1766

INEZ; a tragedy. [By Charles Symmons, D.D.] 8vo. Pp. vi. 124. [Baker's *Biog. Dram.*] London, 1796

INEZ; or, the bride of Portugal. [A poetical drama.] By Ross Neil [Isabella Harwood]. 8vo. [*Lond. Lib. Cat.*] London, 1871

INFALLIBILITY (the), dignity, and excellency of humane judgment; being a new art of reasoning, and discovering truth. . . . [By —— Lyons.] 8vo. [*Brit. Mus.*] London, 1719

A new and enlarged edition (1721) bears the title "The infallibility of humane judgment . . ."

INFALLIBILITY (the) of the Pope; a lecture. By the author of *The Oxford undergraduate of fifty years ago*, &c. [Thomas William Marshall]. 8vo. Pp. 39. [*Bodl.*] London, 1873

INFALLIBILITY (the) of the Roman Catholick Church and her miracles, defended against Dr Stillingfleets cavils, unworthily made publick in two late books, the one called, An answer to several treatises, &c., the other, a Vindication of the Protestant grounds of faith, against the pretence of infallibility in the Roman Church &c. By E. W. [Edward Worsley]. The first part. 8vo. [Dodd's *Ch. Hist.* iii. 314.] Antwerp, 1674

The second part will be found under "A discourse concerning miracles," etc.

INFALLIBLE (the) astrologer; or, Mr Silvester Partridge's prophesie and predictions. . . . [By Edward Ward and Thomas Brown.] Fol. London, 1700-1

INFALLIBLE (an) scheme to pay the publick debt of this nation in six months; humbly offered to the consideration of the present P—t. By D—n S—t [Jonathan Swift, D.D., Dean of St Patrick's]. 8vo. Dublin, printed; London, reprinted, 1732

INFALLIBLE (an) way to contentment in the midst of publick and private calamities; to which is added, encouragement against the fear of fire and poverty, evil tidings, and death itself. By the author of *The devout Communicant* [Abednego Seller]. 8vo. [Arber's *Term Cat.* iii. 164.] London, 1699

Other editions were published, earlier and later, with varying titles.

INFANCY; or, the economy of nature: a poem. [By Walter Paterson.] 8vo. Edinburgh, 1816

INFANT baptism. . . . By a clergyman [Rev. James Edward Dalton]. 8vo. Cambridge, 1841

INFANT baptism, and the first query thereupon; whether all parents, how notorious soever for their deboysery, are privileged upon account of their own baptism, to present their infants thereunto. The negative is here maintained. [By Hezekiah Woodward.] 4to. Pp. 38. [*Trin. Coll. Dub. Cat.* p. 193.] London, 1656

INFANT baptism defended; from Scripture, antiquity, and reason. [By —— Shepherd, of Bath Chapel.] 12mo. [*Bodl.*] Bath, 1773

INFANT baptism of Christ's appointment. . . . By S. P. [Samuel Petto] minister of the gospel. 12mo. [Whitley's *Bapt. Bibl.* i. 120.] London, 1687

INFANT baptism vindicated. . . . By a clergyman of the Church of England [John Graham]. 8vo. [*Brit. Mus.*] York, 1803

INFANT baptism vindicated. . . . By the apologist [David Huntington]. 8vo. [Cushing's *Init. and Pseud.* ii. 8.] New London, Conn., 1789

INFANT (the) class. By Sara J. Timanus [Mrs Wilbar F. Crafts]. 8vo. [Cushing's *Init. and Pseud.* ii. 145.] Chicago, 1870

INFANT institutes, part the first; or, a nurserical essay on the poetry, lyric and allegorical, of the earlier ages. With an appendix. [By Rev. Baptist Noel Turner.] 8vo. Pp. 69. [*Gent. Mag.* xcvi. ii. 468.] London, 1791

INFANT morality displayed in Miss Rose's address to the impartial admirers of theatrical merit. [Signed: E. D. F. *i.e.* Mrs E. D. Franchett.] 4to. [*Brit. Mus.*] London [1774]

INFANT salvation considered; a discourse. By the author of *Holiday exercises* [Samuel Blair]. 8vo. [*Brit. Mus.*] London, 1840

INFANT salvation; an essay to prove the salvation of all who die in infancy. . . . [By Thomas Williams.] Second edition. 8vo. London, 1803

INFANT schools. [By Mathew Carey.] Philadelphia, 1829-31

INFANT sprinkling is not Christian Baptism. [By Bourne Hall Draper.] 8vo. Pp. 83. London, 1837

INFANT treatment under two years of age. [By Mrs Louisa M. Barwell.] 8vo. [*Brit. Mus.*] Edinburgh, 1836

INFANTICIDE; its prevention and cure. [By Joseph Smith Hill.] 8vo. [*Brit. Mus.*] [London, 1866]

INFANTRY (the) exercise of the United States Army; abridged for the use of the Militia of the United States. [By Paraclete Potter.] Third edition. 12mo. Pp. 156. [Sabin's *Dictionary.*] Poughkeepsie, 1819

INFANTRY tactics and modern weapons; a tactical and psychological study. . . . Translated from the German . . . by P. H. [Percy Holland]. 8vo. Allahabad, 1897

INFANTS' (the) advocate; or, the minister's address to parents to bring their children to Church baptism. [By Henry Gandy, Nonjuring Bishop.] 8vo. [Whitley's *Bapt. Bibl.* i. 143.] London, 1712

INFANT'S (the) decalogue; or, a metrical version of the Ten Commandments. By M. A. C. [Mary Ann Cursham]. 12mo. [*Brit. Mus.*] Derby, 1836

INFANT'S (the) guide to spelling and reading. [By Mr and Mrs Crofton Croker.] 12mo. Pp. 31. [*W.*; Martin's *Cat.*] London, 1834

Only six copies privately printed for the use of their son.

INFATUATION (an). By "Gyp" [Sibylle Gabrielle Marie Antoinette, Comtesse de Martel de Janville]; from the French. . . . 8vo. Pp. 199. [*Lit. Year Book.*] New York [1895]

INFERNAL conferences; or, dialogues of devils. By the listener [Rev. John Macgowan]. 12mo. 2 vols. [Wilson's *Hist. of Diss. Ch.* i. 453.] London, 1772

INFERNAL (the) observator; or, the quickning dead. [By Luke de Beaulieu.] 8vo. [*D. N. B.* vol. 4, p. 52.] London, 1684

Wood states that this work was originally written in French.

INFERNO (the) of Dante; translated [by Charles Rogers, F.R.S.]. 4to. [*D. N. B.* vol. 49, p. 115.] London, private print, 1782

INFIDEL (the) father. By the author of *A tale of the times*, etc. [Mrs Jane West]. 12mo. 3 vols. London, 1802

INFIDELITY extirpated; or, Mirabaud's System of nature analyzed. [By Leon Kenworthy.] 12mo. Manchester, 1853

INFIDELITY unmasked; or, the confutation of a booke published by Mr William Chillingworth under this title The religion of Protestants a safe way to salvation. [By Edward Knott, alias Nich. Smith, alias Matthew Wilson, the latter being his real name.] 4to. Pp. 94. [Wood's *Athen. Oxon.* iii. 181.] Printed in Gant, 1652

INFLATION; an argument in its favour. By T. H. C. [T. H. Carter]. 8vo. N.P., 1876

INFLUENCE; a moral tale. By a lady [Charlotte Anley]. 12mo. London, 1822

The writer's name is given in later editions.

INFLUENCE (the) of Italian works of imagination on the same class of compositions in England. [By Arthur H. Hallam.] 8vo. Pp. 29. Cambridge, 1831

INFLUENCE (the) of language and companions; an address.... By H. N. [Miss H. Nokes]. 12mo. [*Brit. Mus.*] London, 1889

INFLUENCE (the) of local attachment with respect to home; a poem. [By Richard Polwhele.] 8vo. Pp. 68. [*Brit. Mus.*] London, 1796

INFLUENCE (the) of slavery on the white population. By a former resident of Slave States [Mrs L. J. Barker]. 8vo. [Cushing's *Init. and Pseud.* i. 104.] New York, 1880

INFLUENCE (the) of the [Roman] Catholic doctrines on the emancipation of slaves. By a member of the Sodality of the B. V. Mary [Rev. James Fitton]. 8vo. [Cushing's *Init. and Pseud.* i. 191.] Boston, 1863

INFLUENCE (the) of the ministry at large in the city of Boston. By a spectator, C. A. B. [Cyrus Augustus Bartol]. 8vo. [Cushing's *Init. and Pseud.* i. 272.] Boston, 1836

INFLUENCE of the zodiac upon human life. By Eleanor Kirk [Mrs Ellen Maria E. Ames]. 8vo. [Cushing's *Init. and Pseud.* i. 156.] Brooklyn, 1894

INFLUENCE (the) of Welsh tradition on the literature of Germany, France, and Scandinavia. By San-Marte [Albert Schultz]. 8vo. [Cushing's *Init. and Pseud.* i. 260.] Llandovery, 1841

INFLUENCE (the) of women on society; a rhapsody in verse. [By Thomas Atkinson.] 4to. [*Brit. Mus.*] Glasgow, 1824

INFLUENCE; or, the evil genius. By the author of *A trap to catch a sunbeam* [Matilda Anne Planché, later Mrs Mackarness]. 8vo. [*Brit. Mus.*] London, 1853

INFLUENCES (the) of democracy on liberty, property, and the happiness of society considered. By an American [Fisher Ames]. 8vo. [Cushing's *Init. and Pseud.* i. 13.] London, 1835

INFORMACON for pylgrymes vnto the Holy Londe. [By John Moreson.] 4to. [Lowndes' *Bibl. Man.*] London [1498?]

INFORMATION and direction to such persons as are inclined to America, more especially those related to the province of Pennsylvania. [By William Penn.] Fol. [Smith's *Cat. of Friends' Books*, i. 42; ii. 302.] N.P., N.D.

Not included in Penn's works.

INFORMATION for authors; hints and suggestions concerning all kinds of literary work. By Eleanor Kirk [Mrs Eleanor Ames]. 8vo. New York, private print, 1888

INFORMATION (an) to all good Christians within the kingdome of England, from the noblemen, barrons, barrows, ministers, and commons of the kingdome of Scotland, for vindicating their intentions and actions from the unjust callumnies of their enemies. [By John Durie.] 4to. Pp. 13. Edinburgh, 1639

Durie spent most of his time and talents in endeavouring to effect a union of all the Protestant Churches.

INFORMATION upon the ... cold water cure of Germany.... By a Bostonian [John Henry Gray]. 8vo. [Cushing's *Init. and Pseud.* ii. 19.] Boston, 1844

INFORMATION wanted; and other sketches. By Mark Twain [Samuel Langhorne Clemens]. 8vo. Pp. 143. London [1876]

INFORMATORY (an) vindication of a poor, wasted, misrepresented, remnant of the suffering, anti-popish, anti-prelatick, anti-erastian, anti-sectarian, true Presbyterian Church of Christ in Scotland united together in a general correspondence. By way of reply to various accusations, in letters, informations, and conferences, given forth against them. [By James Renwick, and Alex. Shiels, conjointly writing at Leadhills in 1678.] 12mo. Pp. 278. [J. Dodds' *The fifty years' struggle of the Scottish Covenanters*, 1638-1688, p. 302.] 1707

Between pp. 232 and 233 are inserted 12 unpaged leaves, containing "The declaration, &c. Published at Sanquhair." The first edition was published in 1687.

INFORMER'S (the) doom; or, an amazing and seasonable letter from Utopia, directed to the man in the moon: giving a full ... account of ... enemies that ... molest all kingdoms ... throughout the Christian world. [By John Dunton.] 8vo. Pp. 160. [*Brit. Mus.*] London, 1683

Signed: Philagathus.

INGELHEIM. [A novel.] By the author of *Miss Molly* [Beatrice May Butt]. 8vo. 3 vols. [*Brit. Mus.*] Edinburgh, 1892

INGEMISCO. [A novel.] By "Fadette" [Marian Colhoun Legaré Reeves]. 8vo. [Cushing's *Init. and Pseud.* i. 98.] New York, 1867

Attributed also to Mrs Minnie Reeves Rodney.

INGENIOUS (the) and diverting letters of the Lady ——'s travels into Spain; describing the devotions, nunneries, humour, customs, laws, militia, trade, diet and recreations of that people, . . . and country. [By Marie Catharine Jumelle de Berneville, Countess d'Aulnoy.] The seventh edition, with the addition of a letter of the state of Spain as it was in the year 1700, by an English gentleman. 8vo. Pp. 4, 296. [Arber's *Term. Cat.* iii. 578.] London, 1708

INGENUE; or, the death of Marat; a romance. By the author of *Monte Christo* [Alexandre Dumas Davy de la Pailleterie, the elder]; translated from the French. 8vo. [*Brit. Mus.*] London [1859]

INGHAM (the) papers. By Colonel Frederic Ingham [Edward Everett Hale]. 8vo. [Cushing's *Init. and Pseud.* i. 137.] Boston, 1869

INGLEDEW House. By Bertha M. Clay [Charlotte M. Braeme, *née* Law]. 8vo. New York, 1884

INGLENOOK; a story for children. By Carrie Carleton [Mrs Mary Wright, *née* Booth]. 8vo. [Cushing's *Init. and Pseud.* i. 50.] New York, 1868

INGLESIDE. By Barbara Yechton [Lyda Farrington Krausé]. 8vo. New York, 1893

INGLESIDE; or, without Christ, and with Him. By Mrs Madeline Leslie [Mrs Harriet N. Baker]. 8vo. Pp. 443. [Kirk's *Supp.*] London, 1886

INGOLDSBY (the) legends; or mirth and marvels. By Thomas Ingoldsby, Esquire [Richard Harris Barham]. 8vo. London, 1840

—— Second series. Third edition. 8vo. London, 1842

—— Third series. 12mo. [*Brit. Mus.*] London, 1847

INGOLDSBY (the) letters, in reply to the Bishops in Convocation and in the House of Lords, on the revision of the Book of Common Prayer. [By James Hildyard, B.D., rector of Ingoldsby.] Third edition. 8vo. 2 vols. [*Brit. Mus.*] London, 1862

INGOLDSBY (the) lyrics. By Thomas Ingoldsby [Richard Harris Barham]; edited by his son. 8vo. Pp. xii. 308. [*Brit. Mus.*] London, 1881

INGOMAR, the son of the desert; a drama. By Friedrich Halm [Freiherr von Münch-Bellinghausen]. 8vo. [*W.*] Denbigh, 1849

INGRAM Place; a novel. By a Cape Colonist [May Byrne]. 8vo. 2 vols. [Cushing's *Init. and Pseud.* i. 50.] London, 1874

INGRATE'S (the) gift; a dramatic poem, in five acts. [By Robert W. Jameson, W.S.] 12mo. [*Nat. Lib. of Scot.*] Edinburgh, 1830

INHERITANCE (the). By the author of *Marriage* [Susan Edmonstone Ferrier]. 8vo. 3 vols. [*D. N. B.* vol. 18, p. 391.] Edinburgh, 1824

INHERITANCE (the) of evil; or, the consequence of marrying a deceased wife's sister. [By Felicia M. F. Skene.] 12mo. London, 1849

INHERITOR and economist; a poem. [By Sir Samuel Ferguson, LL.D.] 8vo. [O'Donoghue's *Poets of Ireland.*] Dublin, 1849

INHERITORS (the); an extravagant story. By Joseph Conrad [Joseph Conrad Korzeniowski] and Ford M. Hueffer. 8vo. [*Lit. Year Book.*] London, 1901

INIQUITY display'd; or the Settlement of the Kingdom of Ireland, commonly call'd The Act of Settlement . . . laid open. . . . [By Nicholas French, Roman Catholic Bishop of Fearns.] 4to. Pp. 70. [*Brit. Mus.*] [London] 1704

This is a reprint, with additions, of "A narrative of the [Earl of Clarendon's] Settlement" (1688).

INITIALS (the); a novel. [By the Baroness J. Tautphœus.] 12mo. 3 vols. London, 1850

INJUR'D innocence; a tragedy. [By Fettiplace Bellers.] [*D. N. B.* vol. 4, p. 190.] London, 1732

INJURED (the) islanders; or, the influence of art upon the happiness of nature. [A poem. By Samuel Wallis, Commander in R.N.] 4to. Pp. 28. [Boase and Courtney's *Bibl. Corn.*] London, 1799

INJURED (an) Queen; Caroline of Brunswick. By Lewis Melville [Lewis Samuel Benjamin]. 8vo. 2 vols. [*Lit. Year Book.*] London, 1912

INKLE and Yarico. See "Incle," etc.

INK-SLINGER (the). [A novel.] By Rita [Eliza M. J. Gollan, later Mrs W. Desmond Humphreys]. 8vo. [*Lit. Year Book.*] London, 1914

INN (the) by the shore; a novel. By Florence Warden [Florence Alice Price, later Mrs Geo. E. James]. 8vo. Pp. 292. London, 1901

INNER and outer Ireland. By A. E. [George W. Russell]. 8vo. Pp. 27. [*Brit. Mus.*] London, 1921

INNER (the) life; hymns on the "Imitation of Christ," by Thomas à Kempis. . . . By the author of *Thoughts from a girl's life*, etc. [Miss L. F. M. Phillips]. 12mo. Pp. 103. Oxford, 1871

INNER (the) life of Lady Georgiana Fullerton; with notes of retreat and diary. [By Frances Margaret Taylor.] 8vo. Pp. xi. 399. [*Brit. Mus.*] London [1899]

INNER (the) life; or, the joys of my father's house. By a wayfaring man [Clinton G. Gilroy]. 8vo. [Kirk's *Supp.*] Philadelphia, 1865

INNISHEENY. By George A. Birmingham [James Owen Hannay, D.D.], author of *Spanish gold.* 8vo. Pp. 228. [*Lit. Year Book.*] London, 1920

INNOCENCY (the) and conscientiousness of the Quakers asserted and cleared from the evil surmises, false aspersions, and unrighteous suggestions of Judge Kealing expressed in his speech . . . in the Old Baily. . . . By W. S. [William Smith, of Besthorp]. 4to. [Smith's *Cat. of Friends' Books*]. London, 1664

INNOCENCY and truth triumphing together; or, the latter part of an answer to a discourse by William Prynne, called, A full reply to certaine briefe observations . . . about Church government. [By John Goodwin.] 4to. Pp. 99. [Thomason's *Coll. of Tracts*, i. 355.] London, 1645

INNOCENCY cleared from lyes; in answer or reply to some particular things: which them, who are scornfully called Quakers, are charged with in a book intituled, Malice stript and whipt, &c. . . . J[ohn] B[owater?] 4to. Pp. 20. [*M'Alpin Coll. Cat.*] London, 1658

INNOCENCY (the) of error, asserted and vindicated; in a letter to —— ——. By Eugenius Philalethes [Arthur Ashley Sykes, D.D.]. The second edition, corrected; with a preface in answer to the Remarks, &c. lately made upon it. 8vo. [Disney's *Memoir of Sykes*, p. xi.] London, 1715

INNOCENCY (the) of the righteous seed of God cleared from all slanderous tongues. [By Richard Hubberthorne.] 8vo. [Thomason's *Coll. of Tracts*, ii. 119.] London, 1655

INNOCENCY with her open face presented by way of apology for the book entituled, The sandy foundation shaken, to all serious and enquiring persons, particularly the inhabitants of the city of London. By W. P. J. [William Penn]. 8vo. 1669

INNOCENT; her fancy and his fact: a novel. By Marie Corelli [Caroline Cody]. 8vo. Pp. vii. 432. [*Brit. Mus.*] London [1914]

INNOCENT (an) impostor; and other stories. By Maxwell Gray [Mary Gleed Tuttiett]. 8vo. Pp. 266. [*Lond. Lib. Cat.*] London, 1893

INNOCENT (an) maiden; a story. By Theo. Gift [Mrs Theodora Boulger, *neé* Havers]. 8vo. [*Lit. Year Book.*] London, 1884

INNOCENT masqueraders. [A novel.] By Sarah Tytler [Henrietta Keddie]. 8vo. London, 1907

INNOCENT (the) usurper; or, the death of the Lady Jane Grey: a tragedy. Written by J. B. [John Banks]. 4to. [Arber's *Term Cat.* ii. 511.] London, 1694

INNOCENT (the) vindicated; or, those falsely called Arrians defended, by a few plain texts of Scripture, from the wicked aspersions of uncharitable men, who think themselves infallible, and are wise above what is written. [By —— Drake, a tailor.] 8vo. [Darling's *Cyclop. Bibl.*] Exon, 1718

Attributed also to James Peirce.

INNOCENTS (the); a sacred drama. Ocean and the earthquake at Aleppo: poems. [By Mrs Edwin Toby Caulfield.] 8vo. [Green's *Bibl. Somers.* i. 96.] Bath, 1824

INNOCENTS (the) abroad; or, "humours" from the latest lectures of Mark Twain, author of *Pleasure trip on the Continent*, etc. [Samuel L. Clemens]. 8vo. London [1872]

INNOCENTS (the) at home. By Mark Twain, author of *The celebrated jumping frog* [Samuel L. Clemens]. 8vo. Pp. 224. London [1872]

INNOCENTS no saints; or, a paire of spectacles for a dark-sighted Quaker: whereby, if he be not wilfully blind, he may discern truth from lies. Being a rejoynder to a paper lately published, intituled, Innocency cleared from lies. . . . By E. D. [Edward Dodd]. 4to. Pp. 20. [Smith's *Anti-Quakeriana*, p. 152.] London, 1658

INNOVATIONS (the) in the Established Church, considered with special reference to re-union. By a Presbyter [Rev. Ernest Thoyts]. 8vo. Edinburgh, 1885

INNOVATIONS; where will they end. By Thistle [Louisa Macdonnell, of Glengarry]. 8vo. Edinburgh, 1880

INOCULATION de bon sens; the inoculation of good sense: an estimate of the present manners of the French nation. [By Nicolas Joseph Sélis.] French and English. 8vo. [*Brit. Mus.*] London, 1761

INOCULATOR (the); a comedy in three acts [and in prose]. (Poems on several occasions.) The Cottagers; an opera in three acts [and in prose, with songs. By George Saville Carey]. 8vo. [*Brit. Mus.*] London, 1766

INQUIRER (the) after truth. [By Rev. Daniel Baxter Langley.] 8vo. [Kirk's *Supp.*] London, 1854

INQUIRIES into the causes of our miseries. . . . [By Hezekiah Woodward.] 4to. [*D. N. B.* vol. 62, p. 422.] [London] 1644

The first of five parts intended to have been issued: it was secretly printed. The second was seized while in the press: the others were never written.

INQUIRIES into the effects of fermented liquors. By a Water Drinker [Basil Montagu, barrister]. 8vo. [Upcott and Shoberl's *Biog. Dict.* p. 238.] London, 1814

INQUIRIES occasioned by an Address of the General Association of New Hampshire on the doctrine of the Trinity. [By Rev. Leonard Worcester.] [Sprague's *Annals*, ii. 458.] 1812

Signed: Cephas.

INQUIRING (the) parishioner; or, the plan of salvation briefly explained. By a clergyman [Beauchamp W. Stannus]. 12mo. [*Bodl.*] London, N.D.

INQUIRY (an) as to the armorial insignia of the city of Glasgow. [By Andrew MacGeorge.] 4to. Glasgow, private print, 1866

INQUIRY (an) concerning a plan of a literary corespondence. [By John Chambers, D.D., minister of Elie, and Hary Spens, D.D., minister of Wemyss.] 8vo. Edinburgh, 1751

INQUIRY (an) concerning the author of the Letters of Junius, with reference to the Memoirs by a celebrated literary and political character [Richard Glover, author of *Leonidas*. By Richard Duppa, B.C.L.]. 8vo. Pp. iv. 114. London, 1814

INQUIRY (an) concerning the cause of the pestilence, and the diseases in fleets and armies. In three parts. With an appendix, containing some facts taken from history, the works of physicians, etc., relating to the subject. [By Alexander Bruce.] 8vo. Edinburgh, 1759

A MS. note in the Nat. Lib. of Scot. copy of *Mon. Rev.*, xxi. p. 201, states that the author was a leather merchant in Edinburgh.

INQUIRY (an) concerning the principles in the constitution of human nature, which are the causes of moral evil. By a layman [David Rowland, solicitor]. 8vo. [*Brit. Mus.*] London, 1856

INQUIRY (an) concerning virtue and happiness; in a letter to a friend. [By Philip Glover.] 8vo. [Wilson's *Hist. of Diss. Ch.* i. 124.] London, 1751

INQUIRY (an) concerning virtue, in two discourses. . . . [By Anthony Ashley Cooper, third Earl of Shaftesbury.] 8vo. Pp. 199. [*Brit. Mus.*] London, 1699

INQUIRY (an), historical and critical, into the evidence against Mary, Queen of Scots; and an examination of the histories of Dr Robertson and Mr Hume, with respect to that evidence. [By William Tytler, W.S.] Third edition. 8vo. Pp. xiv. 385. Edinburgh, 1772

INQUIRY (an) into religion, and the use of reason in reference to it. By a lay-hand [Sir Richard Cox]. 8vo. Pp. 219. [*Bodl.*] London, 1711

Entered also under "Enquiry," etc.; but the above is the correct title.

INQUIRY (an) into some of the principal monopolies (especially those of salt and opium) of the East India Company. [By John Crawfurd.] 8vo. [M'Culloch's *Lit. of Pol. Econ.* p. 111.] London, 1830

INQUIRY (an) into some parts of Christian doctrine and practice, having relation more especially to the Society of Friends; with an appendix. [By Edward Ash, M.D.] 12mo. [Smith's *Cat. of Friends' Books*, i. 105, 134.] London, 1841

INQUIRY (an) into the alleged justice and necessity of the war with Russia; in which the theories of statesmen, and the claims of our Mahommedan allies are contrasted with the lessons of history and the wants and sufferings of our own fellow countrymen. By an English landowner [Sir Arthur Hallam Elton]. 12mo. Pp. 123. [*W.*] London, 1855

INQUIRY (an) into the alleged tendency of the separation of convicts, one from the other, to produce disease and derangement. By a citizen of Pennsylvania [Frederick Adolphus Packard]. 8vo. [Cushing's *Init. and Pseud.* i. 39.] Philadelphia, 1849

INQUIRY (an) into the antient Greek game, supposed to have been invented by Palamedes, antecedent to the siege of Troy; with reasons for believing the same to have been known from remote antiquity in China, and progressively improved into the Chinese, Indian, Persian, and European chess. . . . [By James Christie.] 4to. [*D. N. B.* vol. 10, p. 284.] London, 1801

INQUIRY into the causes and remedies of the late and present scarcity and high prices of provisions, in a letter to the Right Hon. Earl Spencer, K.G. . . . [By Sir Gilbert Blane, Bart., M.D.] 8vo. Pp. 71. London, 1800

INQUIRY (an) into the causes of popular discontents in Ireland. By an Irish country gentleman [William Parnell]. 8vo. Pp. 74. [*Brit. Mus.*] London, 1804

A reprint in 1805 begins, "An enquiry . . ."

INQUIRY (an) into the causes which have retarded . . . the Southern States. . . . By a Carolinian [Daniel R. Goodloe]. 8vo. [Cushing's *Init. and Pseud.* ii. 27.] Washington, 1846

INQUIRY (an) into the causes which obstructed the Reformation, and have hitherto prevented its progress . . . [By Philip Bendlowes.] 8vo. Pp. 53. [*Brit. Mus.*] London, 1768

INQUIRY (an) into the commercial position of Great Britain . . . By a Manchester man [Richard Burn]. 8vo. [Kirk's *Supp.*] Manchester [1869]

INQUIRY (an) into the conduct of Lord Pigot from his arrival at Fort St George to his expedition to Tanjore. . . . [By Andrew Stuart?] 4to. Pp. 217. [*Brit. Mus.*] [London] 1778

INQUIRY (an) into the connection between the present price of provisions and the size of farms; with remarks on population as affected thereby; to which are added, proposals for preventing future scarcity. By a farmer [John Arbuthnot, of Mitcham]. 8vo. [*Brit. Mus.*] London, 1773

INQUIRY (an) into the constitution, government, & practices of the Churches of Christ, planted by his Apostles; containing strictures on Principal Campbell's Ecclesiastical history; Mr Malthus on population; Mr J. A. Haldane's View of social worship; . . . in a series of letters. By Simplex [John Young] to Philophilos. 8vo. Pp. xii. 451. Edinburgh, 1808

INQUIRY into the decline of salmon fisheries. [By Alexander Jopp.] 8vo. [Robertson's *Aberd. Bibl.*] Aberdeen, 1860

INQUIRY (an) into the difference of style observable in ancient glass paintings, especially in England; with hints on glass painting. By an amateur [Charles Winston]. Part I. Text. Part II. Plates. 8vo. Oxford, 1847

The second edition, 1867, gives the author's name.

INQUIRY into the doctrines lately promulgated concerning Juries, Libels, etc., upon the principles of the law and the constitution. [By John Dunning, Lord Ashburnham.] 8vo. [*D. N. B.* vol. 16, p. 215.] London, 1764

INQUIRY (an) into the early history of Greek sculpture. By the late J. C. [James Christie]. 4to. London, 1833

INQUIRY (an) into the effects of our foreign carrying trade upon the agriculture, morals, and population of the country. By Columella [Clement Clarke Moore, LL.D.]. 8vo. [Cushing's *Init. and Pseud.* i. 65.] New York, 1806

INQUIRY (an) into the effects of putting a stop to the African slave trade, and of granting liberty to the slaves in the British sugar colonies. By the author of the *Essay on the treatment and conversion of African slaves in the British West Indies* [Rev. James Ramsay]. 8vo. [*Brit. Mus.*] London, 1784

This humanitarian clergyman published several other pamphlets, with his name, all urging abolition of the slave-trade. See also "Cursory remarks . . ."

INQUIRY (an) into the expediency of applying the principles of colonial policy to the government of India, and of effecting an essential change in its landed tenures and consequently in the character of its inhabitants. [By Major Gavin Young.] 8vo. Pp. xvi. 382. [M'Culloch's *Lit. of Pol. Econ.* p. 109.] London, 1822

INQUIRY (an) into the genealogy and present state of the ancient Scottish surnames; with an account of the Macdonalds, MacNeills, MacLeods, etc. [By Peter Buchan.] 8vo. Edinburgh, 1819

INQUIRY (an) into the general state of the profession of physic, and of the several departments of which it is composed . . . [By Edward Barlow, M.D.] 8vo. [*Edin. Univ. Lib.*] Edinburgh, 1818

INQUIRY (an) into the grounds and nature of the several species of ratiocination; in which the argument made use of in the philosophical essays of D. Hume, Esq., is occasionally taken notice of. By A. G. O. T. U. O. C. [A gentleman of the University of Cambridge, Owen Manning, B.D.]. 8vo. [Nichol's *Lit. Anec.* ix. 751.] Cambridge, 1754

INQUIRY (an) into the history and influence of the Lichfield Waters. [By Dr —— Rawson.] 8vo. Lichfield, 1840

INQUIRY (an) into the influence of the excessive use of spirituous liquors in producing crime, disease, and poverty in Ireland. [By Charles Haliday, M.R.I.A.] 8vo. Dublin, 1830

INQUIRY (an) into the legal method of suppressing riots; with a constitutional plan of future defence. [By Sir William Jones.] 8vo. [Watt's *Bibl. Brit.*] London, 1780

INQUIRY (an) into the long-continued depression in the cotton trade. By a cotton manufacturer [William Hoyle]. 8vo. [*D. N. B.* vol. 28, p. 133.] London, 1869

INQUIRY (an) into the manner in which the different wars in Europe have commenced, during the last two centuries; to which are added the authorities upon the nature of a modern declaration. By the author of the *History and foundation of the law of nations in Europe* [Robert Ward, of the Inner Temple?]. 8vo. [*Brit. Mus.*] London, 1805

INQUIRY (an) into the manner of creating peers. [By Richard West, Lord Chancellor of Ireland.] 8vo. Pp. 74. [*Brit. Mus.*] London, 1719

INQUIRY (an) into the miscarriages of the four last years reign; wherein it appears, by sixty-five articles, that a scheme was laid to raise the grandeur of France and Spain, break the confederacy, make a separate peace, destroy the establish'd Church, sink the trade of the nation, betray the Queen, and bring in the Pretender. [By Charles Povey.] 8vo. [*Brit. Mus.*] London, 1714

INQUIRY (an) into the moral and political tendency of the religion called Roman Catholic. [By Rev. T. Potts.] 8vo. Pp. 165. London, 1790

INQUIRY (an) into the moral, social, and intellectual condition of the industrious classes of Sheffield. Part I. The abuses and evils of charity, especially of medical charitable institutions. [By George Calvert Holland, M.D.] 8vo. Pp. 132. London, 1839

INQUIRY (an) into the nature and design of baptism. . . . [By Rev. —— Cornish, minister at Sherborne, Dorsetshire.] 8vo. [*Brit. Mus.*] London, 1757

INQUIRY (an) into the nature and extent of poetick licence. By N. A. Vigors, Junr. [Rev. Frederick Nolan, LL.D.]. 8vo. [*D. N. B.* vol. 41, p. 95.] London, 1810

INQUIRY (an) into the nature and form of the books of the ancients; with a history of the art of bookbinding, from the times of the Greeks and Romans to the present day: interspersed with bibliographical references to men and books of all ages and countries. Illustrated with numerous engravings. By John Andrews Arnett [John Hannett]. 12mo. Pp. iv. 212. [*Bodl.*] London, 1837

INQUIRY (an) into the nature, cause and cure of the present epidemick fever; together with some general observations concerning the difference betwixt nervous and inflammatory fevers, and the method of treating each. In a letter to a physician. [By John Barker, M.D.] 8vo. [*Brit. Mus.*] London, 1742

INQUIRY (an) into the nature of Zemindary tenures in the landed property of Bengal, etc. By J. G. [James Grant] late Serrishtehdar of Bengal. 4to. Pp. ii. 101. [*Lincoln's Inn Lib.*] London, 1810

INQUIRY (an) into the opinions of the learned Christians, both ancient and modern, concerning the generation of Jesus Christ, . . . Now first published by the editor of *Benj. Ben Mordecai's Seven letters to Elisha Levi* [Henry Taylor]. 4to. London, 1777

INQUIRY (an) into the origin and consequences of the public debt. By a person of distinction [Alexander Montgomery, tenth Earl of Eglinton]. 8vo. London, 1754

Signed: A. M. Mistakenly attributed to Patrick Murray, Lord Elibank.

INQUIRY (an) into the origin and manner of creating Peers. [By Richard West.] 8vo. [Moule's *Bibl. Herald.* No. 452.] London, 1719

Ascribed also to Sir Richard Steele.

INQUIRY (an) into the origin of the human appetites and passions . . . [By Rev. John Barr.] 8vo. Lincoln, 1747

INQUIRY (an) into the origin, progress, and present state of slavery. . . . By a member of the Society of Universal Goodwill, in London and Norwich [—— Murray]. 8vo. [*Brit. Mus.*] London, 1789

INQUIRY (an) into the original of our ideas of beauty and virtue; in two treatises, in which the principles of the late Earl of Shaftesbury are explain'd and defended, against [Bernard de Mandeville] the author of the *Fable of the bees*, and the ideas of moral good and evil are establish'd, according to the sentiments of the ancient moralists. . . . [By Francis Hutcheson, senior.] 8vo. [*Brit. Mus.*] London, 1725

INQUIRY (an) into the past and present relations of France and the United States of America. [By Robert Walsh.] 8vo. Pp. 87. [*Mon. Rev.* lxv. 326.] London, 1811

INQUIRY (an) into the plans, progress, and policy of the American Mining Companies. [By Benjamin Disraeli, later Earl of Beaconsfield.] Third edition, with . . . additions. 8vo. [*Brit. Mus.*] London, 1825

INQUIRY (an) into the powers committed to the Assemblies of this Church, and the nature of deposition from the holy ministry; occasioned by the conduct and procedure of the Assembly 1752. By the author of the Queries in the *Scots Magazine* for July 1752 [John Adams, of Falkirk]. With an introduction by another hand [John Maclaurin, of Glasgow]. 8vo. Glasgow, 1754

INQUIRY (an) into the powers of ecclesiastics, on the principles of Scripture and reason. [By Thomas Gordon, of Kirkcudbright.] 8vo. Pp. 270. London, 1776

Entered also under "Enquiry"; but the above is the correct title.

INQUIRY (an) into the reasonableness and consequences of an union with Scotland; containing a brief deduction of what hath been done, designed or proposed, in the matter of the union, during the last age. . . . [By William Paterson, founder of the Bank of England.] 8vo. London, 1706

Prefatory letter signed: Lewis Medway.

INQUIRY (an) into the remarkable instances of history, and Parliament records, used by the author [Edward Stillingfleet] of The unreasonableness of a new separation on account of the oaths, whether they are faithfully cited and applied. [By Robert Brady, M.D.] 4to. [*D. N. B.* vol. 6, p. 193.] London, 1691

INQUIRY (an) into the revenue, credit, and commerce of France; in a letter to a member of the present Parliament. [By G. Turner.] 8vo. Pp. 64. London, 1742

This pamphlet is properly given as "An enquiry . . ." See above.

INQUIRY (an) into the right of appeal from the Chancellor, or Vice-Chancellor, of the University of Cambridge, in matters of discipline; addressed to a Fellow of a College. To which is added an appendix [by Thomas Francklin. By Thomas Chapman, D.D.]. 8vo. Pp. 79. [*Cat. Lond. Inst.* ii. 147.] London, 1751

This was followed by "A further inquiry . . ." See above.

INQUIRY (an) into the Scripture meaning of the word Satan, and its synonimous terms, the Devil, or the Adversary, and the Wicked-*one*; wherein also, the notions concerning devils, or demons, are brought down to the standard of Scripture; the whole interspersed with remarks on various terms, passages, and phrases in the Old and New Testaments; and undertaken with a view to illustrate the Scriptures, and to separate the Word of God from the doctrines and traditions of men. [By Thos. Barker, M.A., Minister at Lyndon, Rutlandshire.] 8vo. Pp. 117. [*Brit. Mus.*] London, 1772

INQUIRY (an) into the share which King Charles I. had in the transactions of the Earl of Glamorgan, afterwards Marquis of Worcester, for bringing over a body of Irish rebels to assist that king, in the years 1645 and 1646; in which Mr Carte's imperfect account of that affair, and his use of the MS. Memoirs of the Pope's Nuncio, Rinuccini, are impartially considered. . . . [By Thomas Birch, D.D.] 8vo. Pp. viii. 343. London, 1747

The author's name appears in the second edition, published in 1756.

INQUIRY (an) into the spirit and tendency of [Robert Sandeman's] Letters on Theron and Aspasio; with a view of The law of nature, and an inquiry into Letters on the law of nature. [By Robert Riccaltoun.] 12mo. [Watt's *Bibl. Brit.*] London, 1762

INQUIRY (an) into the state of the ancient measures, the Attick, the Roman, and especially the Jewish; with an appendix concerning our old English money, and measures of content. [By George Hooper, D.D.] 8vo. [M'Culloch's *Lit. of Pol. Econ.* p. 134; Green's *Bibl. Somers.* ii. 499.] London, 1721

INQUIRY (an) into the state of finance of Great Britain, in answer to Mr Morgan's Facts. [By Nicholas Vansittart, Baron Bexley.] 8vo. [*Lond. Lib. Cat., Supp.*] London, 1796

INQUIRY (an) into the state of the nation at the commencement of the present administration. [By Charles James Fox and Henry Brougham, Lord Brougham.] Third edition. 8vo. Pp. xviii. 209. [*Brit. Mus.*] London, 1806

INQUIRY (an) into the theories of history, with special reference to the principles of the Positive philosophy. [By William Adam, mineralogist.] 8vo. Pp. 441. [*Lond. Lib. Cat.*] London, 1862

INQUIRY (an) into the true spirit and intent of the Ten-year Divinity-statute; with observations on the conduct of Dr Burrows . . . in degrading the Cambridge Bachelors of Divinity below the Masters of Arts. . . . [By Samuel Perry.] 8vo. [*Brit. Mus.*] London, 1825

INQUIRY (an), on the grounds of Scripture and reason, into the rise and import of the Eucharistic symbols. [By Alexander Knox.] 8vo. Pp. 93. [Martin's *Cat.*] Dublin, 1824

INQUIRY (an) what is the one true faith, and whether it is so professed by all Christian sects. [By Ralph Thicknesse.] 8vo. 1829

INQUIRY (an) whether Popery is a proper subject of toleration, in Protestant states. [By Thomas Reader.] 8vo. [*Brit. Mus.*] London [1780?]

INQUIRY (an) whether the disturbances in Ireland have originated in tithes, or can be suppressed by a commutation of them. By S. N. [Thomas Elrington, Bishop of Fearns.] 8vo. Pp. 62. [*Bodl.*] Dublin, 1822

The author has given the finials of his name.

INQUIRY (an) whether the study of the ancient languages be a necessary branch of modern education? Wherein, by the way, some observations are made on a late performance [by Patrick Clason], intitled, Essays on the origin of colleges, of the custom of lecturing in Latin, etc. [By John Gillies.] 8vo. Pp. xiv. 66. [*J. Maidment.*] Edinburgh, 1769

INQUISITION (the); a letter addressed to the Hon. Sir John Hippisley, Bart., M.P., Recorder of Sudbury, etc. By a Catholic Christian [John Milner, D.D., Bishop]. 8vo. Pp. 27. London, 1816

INQUISITION (an) after blood. To the Parliament in statu quo nunc., and to the army regnant; or any other, whether royallist, Presbyterian, Independent or leveller, whom it may concern. [By James Howell.] 4to. Pp. 13. [*Bodl.*] 1649

INQUISITION (the) examined. By an impartial reviewer [Thomas O'Connor]. 8vo. [Cushing's *Init. and Pseud.* i. 136.] New York, 1825

INQUISITOR (the); a play, in five acts, as performed at the Theatre-Royal in the Hay-market. [By Thomas Holcroft.] 8vo. Pp. 74. [*D. N. B.* vol. 27, p. 118.] London, 1798

INRICHMENT (the) of the weald of Kent; or, a direction to the husbandman, for the true ordering, manuring and inriching of all the grounds within the wealds of Kent and Sussex, and may generally serue for all the grounds in England, of that nature. . . . Painfully gathered for the good of this iland, by a man of great eminence and worth [Gervase Markham]. 4to. Pp. 23. [*Bodl.*] London, 1625

Epistle dedicatory signed: R. J.

INSANABILIA; an essay upon incurables; handling that case, what shall people do under their griefs, when there is no curing of them? [By Cotton Mather.] 12mo. Pp. 48. [*G. Brinley's Amer. Lib.*] Boston, 1714

INSANITY and crime; a medico-legal commentary on the case of G. V. Townley. By the editors of *The Journal of Mental Science* [Charles A. L. Robertson and Henry Maudsley]. 8vo. [*Brit. Mus.*] London, 1864

INSCRIPTIONS from the burying-ground in Salem, Mass. By R. L. Midgley [David Pulsifer]. 8vo. [Cushing's *Init. and Pseud.* i. 193.] Boston, 1837

INSCRIPTIONS (the) upon the tombs, grave-stones, &c., in the Dissenters' burial-place, near Bunhill-Fields. [Ascribed to Richard Rawlinson, LL.D.] 8vo. [Lowndes' *Bibl. Man.* p. 311.] London, 1717

INSCRUTABLE. [A novel.] By Esmé Stuart [Miss Amélie Claire Leroy]. 8vo. Pp. 223. [*Lond. Lib. Cat.*] London, 1894

INSECT architecture. [By Rev. James Rennie, M.A.] 12mo. Pp. xii. 420. [*D. N. B.* vol. 48, p. 18.] London, 1830

The Library of entertaining knowledge.

INSECT life; souvenirs of a naturalist. . . . Translated from the French of J. Henri Fabre, by the author of *Mademoiselle Mori* [Margaret Roberts]. . . . 8vo. Pp. xii. 320. [*Brit. Mus.*] London, 1901

INSECT (the) hunters; or entomology in verse. [By Edward Newman, F.L.S.] 8vo. Pp. viii. 86. [*Bodl.*] London [1857]

INSECT miscellanies. [By Rev. James Rennie, M.A.] 12mo. Pp. xii. 414. London, 1831

The Library of entertaining knowledge.

INSECT stories. By Mary Muller [Lenore E. Mulets]. 8vo. [*Amer. Cat.*] Chicago, 1903

INSECT stories. By Max Vernon [Vernon Lyman Kellogg]. 8vo. [*Amer. Cat.*] New York, 1908

INSECT transformations. [By Rev. James Rennie, M.A.] 12mo. Pp. xii. 420. London, 1830

The Library of entertaining knowledge.

IN-SECURITIE (the) of princes considered in an occasional meditation [in verse] upon the King's [Charles I.] late sufferings and death. [By William Somner.] 4to. [*Brit. Mus.*] [London] 1648

INSIDE; a chronicle of Secession. By George F. Harrington [Rev. Wm. Mumford Baker]. 8vo. [Cushing's *Init. and Pseud.* i. 126.] New York, 1866

INSIDE and out; or, an interior view of the New York State prison. By one who knows [W. A. Coffey]. 8vo. [Cushing's *Init. and Pseud.* i. 218.] New York, 1823

INSIDE out; a curious book. By a singular man [Samuel W. Francis, M.D.]. 8vo. [Cushings' *Init. and Pseud.* i. 268.] New York, 1862

INSIDE Paris during the siege. By an Oxford Graduate [Hon. Denis A. Bingham]. 8vo. London, 1871

INSIDE the bar. See "Market Harborough."

INSIGNIFICANT (an) woman. By W. Heimburg [Bertha Behrens]; from the German by M. S. Smith. 8vo. New York, 1891

INSIGNIFICANTS (the); a comedy of five acts. [By Phanuel Bacon.] 8vo. [*D.N.B.* vol. 2, p. 371.] London, 1757

INSINUATING (the) bawd, and the repenting harlot. Written by a harlot at Tunbridge. [Verse. By Edward Ward.] Fol. [*Brit. Mus.*] London [1698]

INSPECTOR (the). [By Sir John Hill, M.D.] 12mo. 2 vols. [*Bodl.*] London, 1753

"The Inspector" first appeared in March 1751, in the *London Daily Advertiser*.

INSPECTOR (the) in the Shades; a new dialogue in the manner of Lucian. [By John Kennedy, M.D.] 8vo. Pp. 22. [*Manch. Free Lib.*] London, 1752

A satire directed against Sir John Hill, M.D.

INSPECTOR (the); or, select literary intelligence for the vulgar A.D. 1798, but correct A.D. 1801, the first year of the XIXth century. [By William Hales, D.D., rector of Killesandra, and Fellow of Trin. Coll., Dublin.] 8vo. Pp. xii. xviii. 259. [Watt's *Bibl. Brit.*] London, 1799

INSPIRATION (the) of the New Testament asserted, the integrity of the sacred writers vindicated, and the method of salvation by a Redeemer confirmed; in answer to a book of Mr [Thomas] Chubb's, entitled The true Gospel of Jesus Christ asserted . . . By Phileleutherus Christianus [Thomas Broughton]. 8vo. [*Brit. Mus.*] London, 1739

INSTINCT and mind. By Philaletheia [Charles Paynter, Commander in R.N.]. 8vo. Pp. 22. [*Brit. Mus.*] Plymouth, 1868

INSTITUCION (the) of a gentleman. [By Nicholas Grimald or Grimbald?] 4to. [*D. N. B.* vol. 23, p. 250.] London, 1555

INSTITUTE (the); a heroic poem. [By Thomas Pringle.] 12mo. London, 1811

INSTITUTES of experimental chemistry; being an essay towards reducing that branch of natural philosophy to a regular system. By the author of *The elaboratory laid open*, etc. [Robert Dossie]. 8vo. 2 vols. London, 1759

INSTITUTES of health. [By Dr Cleveland.] 8vo. [*Brit. Mus.*] London, 1761

INSTITUTION (the) and observance of the Sabbath considered. [By Rev. George Holden, M.A.] 12mo. Pp. 98. [*Brit. Mus.*] London, 1826

INSTITUTION (the) of Christian religion, written in Latine by Maister John Calvine, and translated into Englishe accordyng to the author's last edition, by T. N. [Thomas Norton]. Whereunto is added a table, to fynde the principall matters entreated of in thys boke, conteyning by order of common places, the summe of the whole doctrine taught in the same. Fol. B.L. [*W.*] London, 1562

INSTITUTION (an) of fluxions; containing the first principles, the operations, with some of the uses and applications of that admirable method, according to the scheme prefix'd to his Tract of quadratures, by its first inventor, Sir Isaac Newton. [By Humphrey Ditton.] 8vo. [Arber's *Term Cat.* iii. 481.] London, 1705

INSTITUTION (the) of Kaiserswerth on the Rhine, for the practical training of Deaconesses. . . . [By Florence Nightingale.] 8vo. [*Brit. Mus.*] London, 1851

INSTITUTION (the) of the Order of the Garter. [By Gilbert West.] 4to. Pp. 64. [Baker's *Biog. Dram.*] London, 1742

INSTITUTIONES horologicæ; or, a physico-mathematical theory of clock-work. [By Benjamin Martin.] 8vo. London, 1764

INSTRUCTED (an) historical account of the settlement of the Episcopal congregation of Dundee in 1727, and of the intrusion there [of Mr D. Fife] in 1743; being a full reply to a late pamphlet by James Dundass, An apology for diocesan Episcopacy, and a defence of the independency of the [Episcopal] Church of Scotland. . . . [By J. Raitt, Bishop of the district of Brechin.] 8vo. [*Brit. Mus.*] [Dundee?] 1744

INSTRUCTION and advice to girls on their first going to service. [By Mary Hoare.] 12mo. [Smith's *Cat. of Friends' Books*, i. 955.] N.P. 1826

INSTRUCTION (an) to judges and lawyers, that they may act and judge as the judges did of old, and that [they] may see how they are degenerated from them that judged at the first; and that in reading this thorow, they may see what hath been lost, and how they may be restored by the power of the Lord into that which the judges were in at the first, and that without money or reward justice might be done. . . . G. F. [George Fox]. 4to. Pp. 40. London, N.D.

Signed at the end: P. M.

INSTRUCTIONS and admonitions to the poor children, educated in the schools founded by Sir John Cass, Knt., in the ward of Portsoken, given at their going out apprentice or to service. [By John Whally.] 8vo. [*Bodl.*] London, 1763

INSTRUCTIONS and regulations for the formations and movements of the cavalry. . . . [Drawn up by Sir David Dundas.] 8vo. [*Brit. Mus.*] London, 1797

Other editions appeared in 1799 and 1807.

INSTRUCTIONS for a young nobleman; or, the idea of a person of honour: done out of [the] French [of J. Trotti de la Chétardie, by Ferrand Spence]. 8vo. Pp. 84. [*Brit. Mus.*] London, 1683

The translator's dedication is signed: F. S.

INSTRUCTIONS for collecting and preserving insects, particularly moths and butterflies; illustrated with a copper-plate . . . [By William Curtis.] 8vo. [Watt's *Bibl. Brit.*] London, 1771

INSTRUCTIONS for collecting and preserving zoological subjects. . . . [Signed: W. S. *i.e.* William Swainson.] 8vo. [*Brit. Mus.*] Liverpool, 1820

INSTRUCTIONS for history; with a character of the most considerable historians, ancient and modern: out of the French [of René Rapin] by John Davies, of Kidwelly. 8vo. [Arber's *Term Cat.* i. 525.] London, 1680

INSTRUCTIONS for making unfermented bread; with observations. By a Physician [George Darling, M.D.]. Sixteenth edition. 8vo. [*Bodl.*] London, 1849

INSTRUCTIONS for meditation and mental prayer. By a priest of the English Church [William Henry Lewthwaite, afterwards a Roman Catholic]. 8vo. [Gillow's *Bibl. Dict.*] Leeds, 1851

INSTRUCTIONS for oratory. [By Obadiah Walker.] 8vo. [Bliss' *Cat.* ii. 39.] Oxford, 1682

INSTRUCTIONS for particular states. [By John Gother.] 12mo. Pp. 360. [*Brit. Mus.*] N.P. 1689

INSTRUCTIONS for preparing abstracts of title. [By Henry Moore, solicitor.] 8vo. [F. Boase's *Mod. Eng. Biog. Supp.* vol. 6, col. 238.] London, 1832

INSTRUCTIONS for right spelling, and plain directions for reading and writing true English, etc. . . . By G. F. and E. H. [George Fox and Ellis Hookes]. Enlarged by A. S. 12mo. [Smith's *Cat. of Friends' Books*, i. 673.] London, 1706

INSTRUCTIONS for the education of a daughter. By [François de Salignac de la Mothe Fénelon] the Archbishop of Cambray, author of *Telemachus*. To which is added, A small tract of instruction for the conduct of ladies of the highest rank; with suitable devotions annexed [by Joachim Trotti de la Chétardie]. Done into English, and revis'd by Dr George Hickes. 8vo. [Arber's *Term. Cat.* iii. 546.] London, 1707

INSTRVCTIONS for the increasing of mulberie trees and the breeding of silke-wormes, for the making of silke in this kingdome: . . . [To the reader, signed: W. S. *i.e.* William Stallenge.] 4to. No pagination. [*Pollard and Redgrave.*] London, 1609

INSTRUCTIONS for the sword exercise, for the Yeomanry Cavalry. [By Henry Angelo.] 12mo. London, 1836

INSTRUCTIONS for the whole year; three parts, for festivals. [By John Gother.] 12mo. [Darling's *Cyclop. Bibl.*] N.P. 1696

INSTRUCTIONS from Rome in favour of the Pretender; inscribed to the most elevated Don Sacheverellio and his brother Don Higginisco; and which all Perkinites, Non-jurors, High-flyers, Popish-desirers, wooden-shoe admirers, and absolute non-resistance drivers are obliged to pursue and maintain (under pain of his Unholinesses damnation) in order to carry on their intended subversion of a government fixed upon Revolution principles. [By Daniel Defoe.] 8vo. [Wilson's *Life of Defoe.*] London, N.D.

INSTRUCTIONS given to the Guild of St John the Evangelist, Upper Norwood, in the course of the year 1876. By W. F. B. [William Fairbairn Latrobe Bateman, M.A.]. 8vo. London, 1897

INSTRUCTIONS on solid piety, on confessions of devotion and on the frequentation of the Sacraments. By the Rev. Father Boone, S.J. Translated from the French by a member of the same Society [George Porter]. 12mo. Pp. 93. [*De Backer.*] London, 1852

INSTRUCTIONS to a celebrated Laureat; alias the progress of curiosity; alias a birth-day ode; alias Mr Whitbread's brew-house. By Peter Pindar, Esq. [John Wolcot, M.D.]. Third edition. 4to. Pp. iv. 42. London, 1787

INSTRUCTIVE narratives from real life. [Translated from the French of Jean Nicolas Bouilly.] 12mo. London, 1814

INSTRUCTIVE (the) picture-book; or, lessons from the vegetable world. By the author of *The heir of Redclyffe* [Charlotte Mary Yonge]. Fol. Edinburgh [1858]

INSTRUCTOR clericalis; the first part, directing clerks both in the court of King's Bench and Common Pleas, in the abbreviation and contraction of words (and thereby the speedy reading of precedents), in the filling up and suing our writs of first process, in drawing declarations, making up issues, ingrossing records, entring judgments, and suing our executions: also pleas and demurrers, etc. . . . [The address to the reader signed: R. G. *i.e.* Robert Gardiner.] The sixth edition, with large and necessary additions. 8vo. Pp. 488. In the Savoy, 1721

—— Volume the second; being a collection of select and useful precedents of declarations in the King's Bench and Common Pleas; in actions upon the case for slander, misfesance, malefesance, nonfesance, assumpsit, deceit, nusance, etc. and on several statutes, both private and popular. . . . By R. G. [Robert Gardiner] a clerk of the court of Common-Pleas. The fifth edition corrected and enlarged. 8vo. Pp. 491. In the Savoy, 1724

INSTRUCTOR clericalis. The third part; being a collection of choice and useful precedents for pleadings, both in the Kings-Bench and Common-Pleas. . . . By R. G. [Robert Gardiner] a clerk of the court of Common-Pleas. The third edition, with additions. 8vo. Pp. 538. In the Savoy, 1713

—— Part IV.; being a continuance of bars and other pleadings from the third part. Wherein the head of covenant is continued; together with a review, either by precedent or reference, of all the pleadings extant, relating to the same. . . . The second edition. By R. G. [Robert Gardiner] a clerk of the court of Common Pleas. 8vo. Pp. xvi. 483. In the Savoy, 1717

—— The fifth and last part, being a continuance of bars, and other pleadings, from the fourth part; wherein the bars and pleadings in debt, detinue, quare impedit, replevin, trespass, trover, and waste, are continued either by precedents of, or references to, all the pleadings extant respecting the same. . . . The second edition, corrected. By R. G. [Robert Gardiner] a clerk of the court of Common Pleas. 8vo. 2 vols. In the Savoy, 1722

INSTRUCTOR (the); or, young man's best companion: containing spelling, reading, writing, and arithmetic. . . . By George Fisher, accomptant [Mrs —— Slack]. The thirty-first edition. 12mo. [*Bodl.*] London, 1810

INSTRUMENTAL music in Christian worship; has it, or has it not, the sanction of New Testament Scripture? An inquiry . . . by a Free Church minister [Rev. John Mackenzie, of Ratho]. 12mo. Edinburgh, 1866

INSUFFICIENCY (the) of the light of nature; exemplified in the vices and depravity of the heathen world. Including some strictures on Paine's Age of reason. [By John Helton.] 8vo. [Smith's *Cat. of Friends' Books*, i. 77, 931.] London, 1797

INSURANCE guide and handbook. [By Cornelius Walford, actuary.] 8vo. London, 1857

The second edition (1867) bears the author's name.

INSURGENT (the) chief. [A romance.] By Gustave Aimard [Ollivier Gloux]. Translated from the French. 8vo. London, 1876

INSURGENT (the) chief; or, O'Halloran: an Irish historical tale of 1798. By Solomon Secondsight, author of *The wilderness*, etc. [James MacHardy, M.D.]. 12mo. 3 vols. [*D.N.B.* vol. 35, p. 108.] London, 1824

This work (sometimes wrongly attributed to Thomas Berkeley Greaves) first appeared in Philadelphia with the title "O'Halloran, or the insurgent chief . . ."

INSURRECTION (the) in Poland. By a recent traveller [Charles Henry Pearson]. 8vo. London [1855 ?]

INSURRECTION (the) of the 3rd of July 1803. By H. B. C. [Henry Brereton Cody, or Code]. 8vo. [O'Donoghue's *Poets of Ireland*, p. 40.] Dublin, 1803

INTELLECTUAL electricity; or, novum organum of vision. . . . By a rational mystic [William Belcher, M.D.]. 8vo. London [1800 ?]

INTELLECTUAL physicks; an essay concerning the nature of being, and the progression of existence. [By Thomas Pownall, governor of South Carolina.] 4to. [*D. N. B.* vol. 46, p. 268.] Bath, 1795

INTELLIGENCER (the). [By Thomas Sheridan and Dean Swift.] 8vo. Pp. 217. Printed at Dublin; London, reprinted 1729

20 Numbers. The 1st, 3rd, 5th, 7th, part of 8th, 9th, 10th, 15th, and 19th, are by Swift; the rest by Sheridan.

INTEMPERANCE; an ethical poem, in three parts. By J. K. C. [Rev. James Casey]. 8vo. [O'Donoghue's *Poets of Ireland.*] Dublin, 1877

INTEMPERATE indulgence in intoxicating liquors, the bane of this country; a sermon. By a minister of the Church of Scotland [John Pollock]. Preached to his parishioners in October 1792; now published by particular desire, and principally addressed to the lower classes of his countrymen. 12mo. Glasgow, 1797

INTER flumina; verses written among rivers. [By Arthur Middlemore Morgan.] 8vo. Oxford, 1883

A later edition (1885) bears the author's name.

INTERCEPTED (an) epistle from a person in Bath [Edward Mangin, M.A.] to his friend in London. 8vo. [Green's *Bibl. Somers.* i. 334.] Bath, 1815

INTERCEPTED (an) letter from J. T., Esq., written at Canton to his friend in Dublin. [By John Wilson Croker.] 8vo. [Courtney's *Secrets.*] Dublin, 1804

INTERCEPTED letters; or, the two-penny post-bag: to which are added Trifles, reprinted. By Thomas Brown, the younger [Thomas Moore]. Sixth edition. 8vo. Pp. xvi. 109. London, 1813

INTERCOURSES (the) of divine love betwixt Christ and the Church; or, the believing soul, as metaphorically expressed by Solomon in the second chapter of the Canticles: opened and improved in several lecture-sermons. . . . By J. C. [John Collings, D.D.]. 4to. [*D. N. B.* vol. 11, p. 356.] London, 1676

INTERDICT (the); a novel. [By Mrs T. F. Steward.] 12mo. 3 vols. [*Brit. Mus.*] London, 1840

INTEREST (the) and claims of the Church and nation of Scotland in the settlement of religion in India, and the necessity of appearing for them at this time. . . . By a North-British Protestant [Archibald Bruce, minister at Whitburn]. 8vo. Pp. 52. [*New Coll. Lib.*] Edinburgh, 1813

INTEREST (the) and trade of Ireland considered. [By Robert Wilson, of Dublin.] 8vo. Dublin, 1731

INTEREST (the) of England consider'd with respect to its manufactures, and East-India callicoes imported, printed, painted, stained, and consumed therein; or, an essay shewing from whence the decay of trade, the melting of coin, the scarcity of silver, the increase of poor do proceed. [By Henry Elking.] 8vo. [*W.*] London, 1720

INTEREST (the) of England in the matter of religion, unfolded in the solution of these three questions. 1. Q. Whether the Presbyterian party should in justice or reason of state be rejected and depressed, or protected and incouraged. II. Q. Whether the Presbyterian party may be protected and incouraged, and the Episcopal not deserted nor disobliged. III. Q. Whether the upholding of both parties by a just and equal accommodation, be not in itself more desireable and more agreeable to the state of England, then the absolute exalting of the one party, and the total subversion of the other. Written by J. C. [John Corbet, B.A., Gloucester]. 8vo. Pp. 130. [Wood's *Athen. Oxon.* iii. 1265.] London, 1660

Wrongly ascribed to J. Constantine.

INTEREST (the) of England in the present war with Holland. By the author of *The Dutch usurpation* [William de Britaine]. 4to. [*Brit. Mus.*] London, 1672

INTEREST (the) of England in the preservation of Ireland humbly presented to the Parliament of England by G. P. Esq. [George Philips]. 4to. Pp. 28. [*Athen. Cat.* p. 243.] London, 1689

INTEREST (the) of England stated; or, a faithful and just account of the aims of all parties now contending: distinctly treating of the designments of The Roman Catholick. The Royalist. The Presbyterian. The Anabaptist. The Army. The late Protector. The Parliament. . . . [By John Fell, D.D.] 4to. Pp. 16. [*Brit. Mus.*] N.P. 1659

INTEREST (the) of Great Britain consider'd; or, the herring fishing propos'd as the most rational expedient for paying our national debts. [By Henry Elking.] 8vo. Pp. 30. [*Brit. Mus.*] London, 1723

INTEREST (the) of Great Britain considered, with regard to her colonies, and the acquisitions of Canada and Guadaloupe. . . . [By Benjamin Franklin.] The second edition. 8vo. Pp. 58. [Rich's *Bibl. Amer.* i. 133.] London, 1761

INTEREST (the) of Great Britain steadily pursued; in answer to a pamphlet [by the Earl of Chesterfield and Edmund Waller], entitl'd, The case of the Hanover forces impartially and freely examined. [By Horatio Walpole, Lord Walpole.] Part I. 8vo. Pp. 63. [Coxe's *Memoirs of Sir Robert Walpole*, i. 87.] London, 1743

Replies to the above were "A vindication of a late pamphlet . . ." and "A further vindication . . ."

INTEREST (the) of Hanover steadily pursued since the A[cession]. By Broad-bottom [Philip Dormer Stanhope, Earl of Chesterfield]. 8vo. [*D. N. B.* vol. 54, p. 28.] London, 1743

A continuation of "The case of the Hanover forces in the pay of Great Britain considered."

INTEREST of money a legalised robbery, and has been the ruin of all nations and is ruining England. . . . By R. V. [James Harvey]. 8vo. [*Gladstone Lib. Cat.*] Liverpool, 1875

INTEREST (the) of Scotland considered, with regard to its police in imploying of the poor, its agriculture, its trade, its manufactures, and fisheries. [By Patrick Lindesay, Lord Provost of Edinburgh.] 8vo. [*Nat. Lib. of Scot.*] Edinburgh, 1733

Attributed also to William Seton, of Pitmeddin.

INTEREST (the) of Scotland in three essays, viz. I. Of the true original and indifferency of Church-government. II. Of the union of Scotland and England into one monarchy. III. Of the present state of Scotland. [By William Seton, Jun., of Pitmeddin.] 8vo. Pp. 119. [Mitchell and Cash's *Scot. Top.* i. 11.] Edinburgh, 1700

INTEREST (the) of the Church defended against the attempts of Papists and others; being the remarkable account of the late rebuilding Winlaton chapel, in the bishoprick of Durham. [By Jonathan Story.] 4to. [*Upcott*, i. 614.] London, reprinted, 1721

INTEREST (the) of the merchants and manufacturers of Great Britain in the present contest with the Colonies stated and considered. [By William Knox.] 8vo. London, 1774

INTEREST (the) of the princes and states [of Europe]. [By Slingsby Bethel.] 8vo. Pp. 354. [Arber's *Term Cat.* i. 525.] London, 1680

The second edition (1681), enlarged, bears the author's name. See also "The present interest of England. . . ."

INTEREST (the) of the Whigs, with relation to the Test Act; in a letter to a friend. [By Rev. James Peirce.] 8vo. [Darling's *Cyclop. Bibl.*] London, 1718

INTEREST (the) of these United Provinces; being a defence of the Zeelanders choice: wherein is shewne, I. That we ought unanimously to defend our selves. II. That if we cannot, it is better to be under England than France, in regard of religion, liberty, estates, and trade. III. That we are not yet come to that extremity, but we may remaine a republick; and that our compliance with England is the onely meanes for this. . . . By a wellwisher to the reformed religion, and the wellfare of these countries [Joseph Hill, B.D.]. 4to. No pagination. Middleburg, 1673

INTERESTING adventures of a hackney coach, as related by the coachman. . . . [By H. Beauchamp.] 8vo. London, 1813

INTERESTING collection of curious anecdotes, scarce pieces, and genuine letters; in which some obscure, but important, historical facts are cleared up and set in a just light. By a gentleman formerly of Brazennose College, Oxford [Charles Manfield?]. 8vo. [*Brit. Mus.*] London, 1790

INTERESTING details of the operations of the American fleet in the Mediterranean [1804]. By W. E. [William Eaton]. 8vo. [Cushing's *Init. and Pseud.* i. 86.] Springfield, Mass., 1805

INTERESTING (an) event. By M. A. Titmarsh [W. M. Thackeray]. 12mo. Pp. 16. [*Ashley Library.*] London, 1849

INTERESTING memoirs. By a Lady [Susanna Harvey Keir]. Fourth edition. 2 vols. 8vo. [Evans' *Amer. Bibl.* vol. 8, p. 306.] New York, 1792

INTERESTING particulars of Napoleon's deportation for life to St Helena. . . . [By William Hone?] 8vo. London, 1816

INTERIOR (the) life. By H. W. S. [Hannah Whitall Smith]. 8vo. Pp. 93. [*Brit. Mus.*] London [1886]

INTERIOUR (the) Christian; or, the interiour conformity which Christians ought to have with Jesus Christ. [By Jean de Bernières Louvigny.] Translated from the French. 8vo. [Barbier's *Dictionnaire.*] Antwerp, 1684

Material derived from the author's writings was edited by François d'Argentan, a Capucin monk.

INTERLINEAR Hebrew Psalter, printed so as to distinguish the servile letters from the radical; with a closely literal English translation under each word. [By Samuel Prideaux Tregelles, LL.D.] 12mo. Pp. 240. [*D. N. B.* vol. 57, p. 171.] London, 1852

INTERMEDIATE (the) state; a poem. [By Susanna Neale.] 8vo. London, 1867

INTERNAL evidences of Christianity deduced from phrenology. By Medicus, member of the Edinburgh Phrenological Society [John Epps, M.D.]. 12mo. [*D. N. B.* vol. 17, p. 382.] Edinburgh, 1827

A second edition was issued in 1836.

INTERNAL (the) management of a country bank; in a series of letters on the functions and duties of a bank manager. By Thomas Bullion [George Rae]. 12mo. [*Brit. Mus.*] [London] 1850

INTERNATIONAL copyright with Great Britain. [By T. H. Carter.] 8vo. Boston, 1878

INTERNATIONAL correspondence by means of numbers. [By Charles Stewart, M.A.] 8vo. [*Brit. Mus.*] London, 1874

INTERNATIONAL (an) spy; the secret history of the Russo-Japanese war. By Monsieur A. Y. [Allen Upward]. 8vo. [*Amer. Cat.*] New York, 1905

INTERPRETATION (the) of dreames, digested into five books, by that ancient philosopher, Artemidorus. Rendred into English [by Robert Wood]. The fourth edition, newly corrected. B.L. 12mo. [*Brit. Mus.*] London, 1644

Signed: R. W.
Many later editions were issued.

INTERPRETATION (the) of the composition between the University [of Cambridge] and King's College. By a member of the Senate [John Rustat Crowfoot]. 8vo. [*Camb. Univ. Lib.*] Cambridge, 1846

INTERPRETATION (an) of the sacred Scriptures of the N.T., in the ancient Eastern manner, from the authority of the critics, interpreters, and commentators, and collations of copies and versions. [By David Macrae, M.A., licentiate of the Church of Scotland.] 8vo. No pagination. London, 1798

This is the first part of what appeared later (1799) as "A revised translation and interpretation . . ." (See later.)

INTERPRETER (the); wherin three principall termes of State much mistaken by the vulgar [viz. Puritan, Protestant, Papist] are clearely unfolded. [In verse. By Rev. Thomas Scott, B.D., Utrecht.] 8vo. [*D. N. B.* vol. 51, p. 68.] N.P., 1622

INTERRUPTED. [A tale.] By Pansy [Mrs Isabella Alden, *née* Macdonald]. 8vo. Pp. 443. Boston [1885]

INTERRUPTED (the) story; or, the boy and his pony. By G. J. F. [George James Foster]. 8vo. [Cushing's *Init. and Pseud.* ii. 56.] London, 1871

INTERRUPTED (the) wedding; a Hungarian tale. By the author of *Mary Powell* [Anne Manning, later Mrs Rathbone]. 8vo. [*Brit. Mus.*] London, 1864

INTERVENING (the) sea. [A novel.] By David Lyall [Mrs Burnett Smith, *née* Annie Swan]. 8vo. Pp. 160. London [1906]

INTERVIEW (the); a companion volume to *Enquire within.* [By Robert Kemp Philp.] 8vo. Pp. xii. 222. [Boase and Courtney's *Bibl. Corn.* ii. 493.] London [1856]

Re-issued in 1867 as "A journey of discovery all around our house," which was the title of the first article in the original work.

INTERVIEWS (the) of great men; their influence on civilization; from the meeting of Diogenes and Alexander, to the final interview of Count Cavour and Victor Emmanuel. . . . By the author of *Heroines of our time*, etc. [Joseph Johnson]. 8vo. Pp. viii. 312. [*Nat. Lib. of Scot.*] London [1862]

INTIMATE story of the origin of railways. By W. D. [Waynman Dixon.] 8vo. Pp. 22. [*Brit. Mus.*] Darlington, 1925

INTO an unknown world; a novel. By John Strange Winter [Mrs Arthur Stannard, *née* Henrietta E. V. Palmer]. 8vo. Pp. 312. London, 1897

INTO Morocco. By Pierre Loti [Louis M. J. Viaud, captain in the French Navy]; translated from the French. 8vo. [*Brit. Mus.*] London, 1890

INTRIGUING (the) milliners and attornies clerks; a mock-tragedy, in two acts: as it was designed to be acted at the Theatre-Royal in Drury-Lane. By a gentleman [—— Robinson, of Kendal]. 12mo. [*Gent. Mag.* vii. 770.] London, 1740

INTRODUCTIO; an introduction to the holy understanding of the glasse of righeousness: wherin are vttered many notable admonitions and exhortations to the good-life, also sundry discreet warnings to beware of destruction, and of wrong-conceiuing and misunderstanding or censuring of any Sentences. Sett forth by H[enry] N[iclas], and by him perused anew, and expressed more playnly. 12mo. [*Pollard and Redgrave.*] [1565?]

INTRODUCTION (an) into the Greeke tongue, in most plaine manner, delivering the principall matters of the grammar thereof, so farre forth as may helpe toward the understanding of the Greeke Text of the holy gospel; composed for their sakes which understand not Latine, and yet are desirous to have some competent knowledge in the original Sacred Scripture. [By Edmund Reeve.] 4to. London, 1650

INTRODUCTION to a natural system of anatomy, physiology, pathology, and medicine; to which is added a general view of natural history. By the author of *Kalogynomia* [Thomas Bell]. 8vo. London, 1825

INTRODUCTION (an) to a system of the laws and principles of matter, proceeding upon an inquiry into the relations of heat and attraction; illustrating the existence of a principle calculated to account for the various phenomena of nature. [By William Hay.] 8vo. Pp. xv. 64. Edinburgh, 1821

INTRODUCTION to a treatise on the state of the currency at the present time, 1824. [By Rev. Richard Cruttwell, LL.B., rector of Spexhall, Suffolk.] 8vo. [*W.*] Halesworth, 1824

INTRODUCTION (an) to astrology. By Montelion [John Phillips]. [Lowndes' *Bibl. Man.* p. 1854.] London, 1661

Attributed also to Thomas Flatman.

INTRODUCTION (an) to English grammar; intended also to assist young persons in the study of other languages. [By Edmund Philip Bridel, LL.D.] 8vo. [*Brit. Mus.*] London, 1797

INTRODUCTION (an) to general history and chronology. . . . [By John Gilderdale, B.D.] 4to. [*Camb. Univ. Lib.*] London, 1833

INTRODUCTION (an) to logick, scholastick and rational. [By Edward Bentham.] 8vo. Pp. 129. [*Bodl.*] Oxford, 1773

INTRODUCTION (an) to Mr James Anderson's Diplomata Scotiæ; to which is added notes, taken from various authors, and original manuscripts. By Thomas Ruddiman, M.A. [Translated from the Latin of Ruddiman by Roger Robertson, of Ladykirk.] 8vo. Pp. 232. [*Nat. Lib. of Scot.*] Edinburgh, 1773

INTRODUCTION (an) to practical organic chemistry; with references to the works of Davy, Brande, Liebig, etc. [By Caroline Frances Cornwallis.] 8vo. [*D. N. B.* vol. 12, p. 233.] London, 1843

Small books on great subjects. No. IV.

INTRODUCTION (an) to religious knowledge; being a sequel to the Lessons on Christian evidences. [By Richard Whately, D.D.] 12mo. [*Brit. Mus.*] London, 1849

INTRODUCTION to Sally. By the author of *Elizabeth and her German garden* [Countess von Armin, afterwards Countess Russell]. 8vo. Pp. 325. London, 1926

INTRODUCTION (an) to the Books of the Old and New Testament, by A. Schumann; translated from the German by the author of the *People's dictionary of the Bible* [John R. Beard, D.D.]. 8vo. Pp. viii. 337. [*Manch. Free Lib.*] London, 1849

INTRODUCTION to the [Roman] Catholic faith. By an English Dominican [Thomas Worthington]. 8vo. Pp. 152. [*D. N. B.* vol. 63, p. 44.] London, 1709

Wrongly attributed to Ambrose Burgis.

INTRODUCTION (an) to the controversy on the disputed verse of St John, as revived by Mr Gibbon. [By Bishop Thomas Burgess.] 8vo. [Darling's *Cyclop. Bibl.* (*Subjects*), p. 1722.] Salisbury, 1835

INTRODUCTION (an) to the doctrine of fluxions, and defence of the mathematicians against the objections of [Bishop Berkeley] the author of the Analyst, so far as they are designed to affect their general methods of reasoning. [By Thomas Bayes.] 8vo. [*N. and Q.* 1860, p. 10.] London, 1736

INTRODUCTION (an) to the doctrine of fluxions. [By John Rowe.] Revised by several gentlemen well skilled in the Mathematics. 8vo. [*Brit. Mus.*] London, 1751

INTRODUCTION (an) to the evidences of Christianity. By a Fellow of the Royal Society [James Orchard Halliwell]. 8vo. Pp. iv. 152. London, 1859

100 copies printed for presentation.
"The Rev. A. Dyce with the kind regards of the author, J. O. Halliwell." In the Dyce collection.

INTRODUCTION (an) to the geometrical analysis of the ancients; containing a dissertation on that analysis, its application to the demonstration of theorems, and to the solution of problems; with a collection of propositions for the exercise of beginners. . . . [By Michael Fryer.] 8vo. Pp. 62. [*W.*] London, 1810

The author corrected and added to this work in preparation for a second edition which was never required; this copy is now in the Library of the Royal Society.

INTRODUCTION (an) to the history and antiquities of Scotland. [Translated from the Latin of Walter Goodal by William Tytler.] 8vo. Pp. 228. [*Aberdeen Pub. Lib.*] London, 1769

INTRODUCTION (an) to the history and study of chess. . . . To which is added the Analysis of chess of A. D. Philidor [François André Danican]. The whole simplifyed, and arranged. . . . By an amateur. 8vo. Cheltenham, 1804

See "Analysis of the game of chess."

INTRODUCTION (an) to the history of America; containing the history of Columbus, an account of the discovery and settlement of North America, geography of the United States, history of the American War, Declaration of Independence, General Washington's Circular Letter, etc. . . . [Compiled by John M'Culloch.] 12mo. Pp. 207. [Evans' *Amer. Bibl.* vii. 130.] Philadelphia, 1787

INTRODUCTION (an) to the history of France. [Signed: T. A. P. *i.e.* Thomas Alder Pope.] 8vo. [*Brit. Mus.*] London, 1860

INTRODUCTION (an) to the history of the Dutch republic for the last ten years, reckoning from the year 1777. [By James Harris, 1st Earl of Malmsbury.] 8vo. [*Gent. Mag.* Nov. 1820, p. 466.] London, 1788

INTRODUCTION (an) to the history of the Inquisition. . . . [By Rev. Samuel Bourn, *secundus*, minister at Crook.] 8vo. [Sparke's *Bibl. Bolt.* p. 29.] London, 1735

INTRODUCTION (an) to the history of the successive revisions of the Book of Common Prayer. [By James Parker, M.A.] 8vo. [*Bodl.*] Oxford, 1877

INTRODUCTION to the holy understanding of the glasse of righteousnesse. See "Introductio . . . ."

INTRODUCTION (an) to the knowledge and practice of thoro' bass; humbly inscrib'd to the Right Honourable Lord Colvill. By A. B. [A. Bayne]. Fol. [*D. Laing.*] Edinburgh, 1717

INTRODUCTION (an) to the knowledge of funguses. [Signed: B. M. F. *i.e.* B. M. Forster.] 12mo. [Jackson's *Lit. of Botany.*] London, 1820

INTRODUCTION (an) to the Latin tongue on the Eton plan; with notes . . . and additional forms, with a more strict application of the auxiliary signs. [By William Belcher.] 12mo. [*Edin. Univ. Lib.*] London, 1816

INTRODUCTION (an) to the law of tenures. [By Sir Matthew Wright.] 8vo. [*Brit. Mus.*] London, 1729

Later editions (1730, etc.) bear the author's name.

INTRODUCTION (an) to the law relative to trials at Nisi Prius. By a learned Judge [Sir Francis Buller]. 8vo. [*Brit. Mus.*] London, 1768

Later editions (1772, 1775, etc.) bear the author's name.

INTRODUCTION (an) to the life and writings of G[ilber]t, Lord Bishop of S[aru]m; being a third letter to his Lordship, occasioned by his Introduction to the third volume of the History of the Reformation. . . . By the author of the two former letters [George Sewell]. 8vo. Pp. 70. London, 1714

Letter signed: G. S.

INTRODUCTION (an) to the literary history of the fourteenth and fifteenth centuries. [By Charles Philpot.] 8vo. [Lowndes' *Bibl. Man.* p. 1860.] London, 1798

Ascribed also to Rev. John Logan.

INTRODUCTION (an) to the metres of the Greek tragedians. By a member of the University of Oxford [James Burton, D.D.]. Second edition. 8vo. [*Camb. Univ. Lib.*] Oxford, 1824

INTRODUCTION (an) to the reading of the Holy Bible. By a lady [Lady —— Mayne]. 12mo. [*Brit. Mus.*] London, 1775

The title of an earlier edition (1770) begins "An abridgment of the sacred history . . ." See above.

INTRODUCTION (an) to the school of Shakspeare. [By William Kenrick.] 8vo. [Wilson's *Shaksperiana*, p. 64.] London [1774]

INTRODUCTION (an) to the scanning of the Greek metres. . . . By W. B. [W. Bruce]. 12mo. [*Brit. Mus.*] Belfast, 1823

INTRODUCTION (an) to the skill of musick; in two books. First, A brief and plain introduction to musick, both for singing and for playing on the violl. By J. P. [John Playford]. Second, The art of setting or composing of musick in parts . . . formerly published by Dr Tho. Campion. . . . 8vo. London, 1655

INTRODUCTION (an) to the study of fungi. By Uncle Matt [Mordecai Cubitt Cooke]. 8vo. London, 1895

INTRODUCTION (an) to the study of Gothic architecture. [By John Henry Parker.] 8vo. Pp. 240. [*Bodl.*] Oxford, 1849

INTRODUCTION (an) to the study of philosophy. . . . By a gentleman educated at Yale College [Samuel Johnson, D.D.]. 8vo. [Evans' *Amer. Bibl.* ii. 241.] New London, Conn., 1743

INTRODUCTION (an) to the study of Shakespeare and Milton. [By James A. Melville, teacher.] 8vo. Pp. 140. London [1884]

Presentation copy from the author.

INTRODUCTION (an) to the study of the Pipe Rolls. [By Hubert Hall.] 8vo. [Gross's *Sources of Eng. History.*] London, 1884

INTRODUCTION (an) to the study of the Greek classic poets; designed principally for the use of young persons at school and college. By Henry Nelson Coleridge, Esq., M.A., late Fellow of King's College, Cambridge [assisted by his wife, Sara Coleridge]. Part I. containing—I. General introduction. II. Homer. 12mo. Pp. 239. [*W.*] London, 1830

"Especially in Mr H. Coleridge's 'Introduction to the study of the Classical Authors' a little work of peculiar interest, because in truth it contains the contributions of two minds—the one that of an elegant classical scholar—the other, one of the strongest as well as most refined of female intellects."—*Edin. Rev.* vol. 108, p. 530.

INTRODUCTION (an) to the study of the law of Scotland. By a member of the Faculty of Advocates [James Starke]. 12mo. [*Nat. Lib. of Scot.*] Edinburgh, 1832

INTRODUCTION (an) to the study of the social sciences. By the author of *Outlines of social economy* [William Ellis]. 8vo. Pp. viii. 118. [*Edin. Univ. Lib.*] London, 1849

INTRODUCTION (an) to the theory of the human mind. By J. U., author of *Clio* [James Usher, of Shaftesbury]. 8vo. Pp. xvi. 96. [*New Coll. Lib.*] London, 1761

INTRODUCTION (an) to the use of the globes, divided into short lessons. . . . [Signed: W. F. *i.e.* William Field.] 8vo. [*Brit. Mus.*] Warwick, 1815

Earlier editions were issued in 1798 and 1801.

INTRODUCTION (an) to theosophy; or, the science of the "mystery of Christ," that is of Deity, nature and creature (Col. i. 15-20): embracing the philosophy of all working powers of life, magical and spiritual; and forming a practical guide to the sublimest purity, sanctity and evangelical perfection: also to the attainment of divine vision, and all holy angelical arts, potencies, and other prerogatives of the regeneration. [Compiled by Christopher Walton.] Vol. I. (complete in itself). 12mo. [*New Coll. Lib.*] London [1854]

Wrongly attributed to J. Fortescue.

INTRODUCTION (an) to universal history, for the use of schools. [By Horace Hayman Wilson.] 12mo. [*Brit. Mus.*] London, 1831

INTRODUCTORY (an) discourse to a larger work, designed hereafter to be published, concerning the miraculous powers which are supposed to have subsisted in the Christian Church, from the earliest ages, through several successive centuries; tending to shew, that we have no sufficient reason to believe, upon the authority of the primitive fathers, that any such powers were continued to the Church, after the days of the apostles. . . . [By Conyers Middleton.] 4to. Pp. 75. [*Brit. Mus.*] London, 1747

INTRODUCTORY (an) handbook to the language of the Bemba People (Awemba). By W. G. R. [W. Govan Robertson]. 8vo. Pp. xxii. 545. [*Brit. Mus.*] London, 1904

INTRODUCTORY lessons on Christian evidences. [By Richard Whately, D.D.] Third edition. 12mo. London, 1843

INTRODUCTORY lessons on mind. By the author of *Lessons on reasoning*, *Lessons on morals*, etc. [Richard Whately, D.D., Archbishop of Dublin]. 12mo. [*Brit. Mus.*] London, 1859

INTRODUCTORY lessons on morals. By the author of *Lessons on the British Constitution* [Richard Whately, D.D.]. 12mo. Pp. 207. London, 1855

INTRODUCTORY lessons on the British Constitution. [By Richard Whately, D.D., Archbishop of Dublin.] 12mo. London, 1854

INTRODUCTORY lessons on the history of religious worship; being a sequel to the Lessons on Christian evidences, by the same author. [By Richard Whately, D.D.] 12mo. 2 parts. [*D. N. B.* vol. 60, p. 428.] London, 1849

Each part has a separate pagination.

INTRODUCTORY remarks respecting the imperial gallon and diagonal table. [By Henry Goodwyn, of Blackheath.] 4to. [*Camb. Univ. Lib.*] London, 1823

INTRODUCTORY remarks to a Narrative of the irruptions of Kafir hordes into the Eastern Province of the Cape of Good Hope, A.D. 1834-5. By the Editor of the *Grahams Town Journal* [Hon. Robert C. Godlonton]. 8vo. Graham's Town, 1835

Author's attestation.

INTROITS and hymns; with some anthems. [By Rev. William Upton Richards, M.A.] 12mo. London, 1852

INTROITS, hymns, responses, and antiphons. [By Rev. Richard Collins, M.A.] 12mo. Leeds, 1873

INTROITS; or, Ante-communion Psalms for the Sundays and Holy-days throughout the year. [By John Henry Alexander.] 8vo. Philadelphia, 1844

INTROSPECTION. [A novel. By John Morgan Matthew.] 12mo. 4 vols. [Upcott and Shoberl's *Biog. Dict.* p. 228.] London [178—?]

INTRUDER (the). [Essays in the style of the *Spectator*. By Charles Winchester, advocate, Aberdeen.] 8vo. Aberdeen, 1802

INTRUSIONS (the) of Peggy. By Anthony Hope [Sir Anthony Hope Hawkins]. 8vo. [*Lit. Year Book.*] London, 1902

INVADERS; a story of the "Hole-in-the-wall" country. By John Lloyd [Jacque Lloyd Morgan]. 8vo. [*Amer. Cat.*] New York, 1910

INVALID (the); with the obvious means of enjoying health and long life. By a nonagenarian, editor of the *Spiritual Quixote*, *Columella*, etc. [Rev. Richard Graves, B.A.]. 8vo. Pp. x. 147. [Green's *Bibl. Somers.* ii. 446.] London, 1804

INVALIDITY (the) of lay-baptism proved from Scripture, and confirmed by the doctrine of Catholick antiquity, and of the Church of England. [By Thomas Blackhall, M.A.] 8vo. Pp. 76. London, 1730

INVALID'S (the) hymn-book. [By Charlotte Elliott.] 12mo. [Julian's *Dict. of Hymnology.*] Dublin, 1840

INVALID'S (an) pastime; an offering to the weeping and the weary. [By E. Jarman.] 8vo. Pp. xii. 228. [*Nat. Lib. of Scot.*] London, N.D.

INVASION (the). [A novel.] By the author of *The collegians*, etc. [Gerald Griffin]. 12mo. 4 vols. [*Camb. Univ. Lib.*] London, 1832

INVASION (the) of England, told twenty years after. By an old soldier [William Francis Butler]. 8vo. London, 1885

INVENTION (an) of engines of motion lately brought to perfection, whereby may be dispatched any work now done in England or elsewhere. . . . By Samuel Hartlib [but really by Cressy Dymock]. 4to. London, 1651

INVENTORIES of records illustrating the history of the Burgh of Aberdeen. [By Peter John Anderson, LL.B.] 4to. Pp. 60. [*Aberd. Univ. Lib.*] Aberdeen, 1890

INVENTORY of worke done for the State, by his Majestie's printer in Scotland [Evan Tyler] Dec. 1642—Oct. 1647. [Edited by Thomas Thomson.] 4to. [Martin's *Cat.*] Edinburgh, 1815

INVESTIGATION (an) into principles, etc., in English and Italian. [By George Baldwin.] 4to. Pp. 720. [*W.*] London [1801]

INVESTIGATION (an) of the cause of the present high price of provisions. By the author of the *Essay on the principle of population* [Thomas Robert Malthus]. 8vo. [*D.N.B.* vol. 36, p. 4.] London, 1800

INVESTIGATION (an) of the native rights of British subjects. [By John Davidson.] 8vo. London, 1734

Presentation copy from the author to Francis Plowden.

INVESTIGATION (an) of the principles of the rules for determining the measures of the areas and circumferences of circular plane surfaces, and the capacities and bulks of certain spherical and cylindrical vessels and solids. By the author of *A new theory of gravitation*, etc. [Joseph Denison]. 12mo. [*Edin. Univ. Lib.*] London, 1844

INVESTIGATOR (the), containing the following tracts: I. On ridicule. II. On Elizabeth Canning. III. On naturalization. IV. On taste. [By William Whitehead.] 8vo. [*Brit. Mus.*] London, 1762

The first two essays were previously published in 1753.

INVESTIGATOR (the); or, universal criterion of knowledge: explaining the mysterious phenomena of nature from the commencement to the conclusion of time. [By Edward Dunn.] 8vo. [*Brit. Mus.*] London, 1797

INVESTING Uncle Ben's legacy; a tale of mining and matrimonial speculations. By "Old Boomerang" [John Richard Houlding]. 8vo. [Kirk's *Supp.*] Melbourne, 1876

INVESTOR'S (an) notes on American railroads. [By John Swann.] 8vo. [*Lib. Journ.* xiv. 59.] New York, 1886

INVIOLABLE (the) sanctuary. By George Birmingham [Dr James Owen Hannay]. 8vo. Pp. 370. London, 1912

INVISIBLE (the) gentleman. By the author of *Chartley the fatalist*, etc. [—— Dalton]. 12mo. 3 vols. [*Brit. Mus.*] London, 1833

INVISIBLE (the) pickpocket; records of a city detective. By James Macgovan [William C. Honeyman]. 8vo. Pp. 256. London, 1922

INVISIBLE (the) spy. By Explorabilis [Mrs Eliza Haywood, *née* Fowler]. Second edition. 12mo. 2 vols. [*Brit. Mus.*] London, 1759

INVITATION (the); or, urbanity, a poem: for the benefit of a Sunday school. By the author of *Wensleydale* [Thomas Maude]. 8vo. Pp. 56. London, 1791

INVITATION (an) to peace: or, Toby's preliminaries to Nestor Ironsides, set forth in a dialogue between Toby and his kinsman. [By John Arbuthnot, M.D.] 8vo. [*Brit. Mus.*] London, 1713

INVOCATION (an) to melancholy; a [poetical] fragment. [By Henry Headley.] 4to. Pp. 15. Oxford, 1785

INVOLUNTARY (the) prophet. [A novel.] By the author of *Brambletye House*, etc. [Horace Smith]. 8vo. [*Brit. Mus.*] London, 1835

INWARD (the) and spiritual warfare, and the false pretence of it; and a distinction between the true liberty and the false: and how God hath anointed the ministers of Christ and his Church, and they have the anointing in them; and shepherds, husbandmen, fisher-men, and trades-men made prophets and apostles, to preach the word of God, and set forth his glory. . . . By G. F. [George Fox]. 4to. [Smith's *Cat. of Friends' Books*, i. 689.] 1690

INWARD (the) light. By Asyncritus [John Eliot Howard]. 8vo. [Cushing's *Init. and Pseud.* ii. 20.] London, 1839

INWARD (the) light. By Henry Fielding [Henry Fielding Hall]. 8vo. London, 1908

INWARD (the) testimony of the Spirit of Christ to his outward revelation, in opposition to the Deist, Socinian and prophane, who deny both; to the formalist, who denies his inward, and to the enthusiast who denies his outward testimony to it. . . . By the author of *The private Christian's witness* [Sir David Hamilton, M.D.]. 8vo. [Darling's *Cyclop. Bibl.*] London, 1701

IO triumphe! A song of victory on our glorious entry into Cabul; to which is added the Massacre of Cabul. [By Charles J. Cruttwell.] 8vo. [*Bodl.*] London, 1842

IONICA. [Poems. By William Johnson, later William Johnson-Cory, assistant master at Eton.] 8vo. Pp. iv. 116. London, 1858

IOPHON; an introduction to the art of writing Greek Iambic verses. By the writer of *Nuces* and *Lucretilis* [William Johnson, later Johnson-Cory]. 12mo. Pp. 47. [*Camb. Univ. Lib.*] London, 1873

A later edition was issued in 1891.

IPHIGENEIA; or, the sail! the seer!! and the sacrifice!!! A classical burlesque. [By Edward Nolan.] Performed at the Music Room, Oxford, by the S. John's College amateurs, during Commemoration, 1866. 8vo. [*Bodl.*] Oxford, 1866

IPHIGENIA; a tragedy, in four acts. [By John Yorke, of Gourthwaite, Yorkshire.] 8vo. Pp. 49. [Martin's *Cat.*] 1783

IPHIGENIA in Aulis; a tragedy, from the Greek of Euripides, adapted to the modern stage. By John William Calcraft [John William Cole]. 12mo. [O'Donoghue's *Poets of Ireland.*] Dublin, 1847

IPHIGENIA in Tauris; a tragedy. By Goethe. [Translated by William Taylor.] 8vo. [Lowndes' *Bibl. Man.*] Norwich, 1793

IRAD and Adah; a tale of the Flood; to which will be added Lyrical poems, principally sacred, including translations of several Psalms of David. By the author of *The Widow of Nain* [Thomas Dale, M.A.]. 8vo. London, 1821

The author's name appears in the second edition, 1822.

IRAS; a mystery. By Theo Douglas [Mrs H. D. Everett]. 8vo. Pp. 281. [*Lit. Year Book.*] Edinburgh, 1896

IRELAND; a satire. To the different grand juries of Ireland and to the men who constitute them, each and all, the following lines are "respectfully" inscribed by one who wishes what he dares not hope—their improvement. [By Rose Lambart Price.] Second edition. 8vo. [Boase and Courtney's *Bibl. Corn.* ii. 527.] London, 1824

IRELAND and its rulers; since 1829. Part the first. [By Daniel Owen Madden.] 12mo. Pp. 357. London, 1843

—— Part the second. 12mo. Pp. 333. London, 1844

—— Part the third. 12mo. Pp. 344. London, 1844

Ascribed also to Richard Robert Madden, M.D., and to John Wiggins.

IRELAND and the Earl of Shrewsbury; an answer to his Lordship's Letter. By W. D. [William Dudley]. 12mo. Pp. 32. Manchester, 1841

IRELAND from sea to sea; a practical handbook to Galway, Achill, and the West of Ireland. . . . [By Charles Slegg Ward.] 8vo. [*Brit. Mus.*] Dublin, 1896

IRELAND in 1829; or, the first year's administration of the Duke of Northumberland. By the author of *A sketch of the Marquess of Anglesey's administration* [Rev. E. Tighe Gregory]. . . . 8vo. Pp. 48. Dublin, 1830

IRELAND in 1831; letters on the state of Ireland. [By Colonel John Fox Burgoyne.] 8vo. Pp. 48. [*Bodl.*] London, 1831

Presentation copy "From the author Colonel John Fox Burgoyne."

IRELAND ninety years ago; being a new and revised edition of *Ireland sixty years ago.* [By the Hon. John Edward Walsh, LL.D.] 12mo. Pp. 172. Dublin, 1876

See the earlier edition below.

IRELAND preserv'd; or, the siege of London-derry: a tragi-comedy. Written by a gentleman who was in the town during the whole siege [Colonel John Michelborne]. 8vo. [Baker's *Biog. Dram.*] Dublin, 1738-9

First edition, 1708.

IRELAND profiting by example; or, the question whether Scotland has gained or lost by an union with England, fairly discussed. [By Colonel —— Tittler.] 8vo. Dublin, 1799

IRELAND sixty years ago. [By the Right Hon. John Edward Walsh, LL.D.] 12mo. Dublin, 1849

See a later edition above ("Ireland ninety years ago.")

The author's name is given in an edition of 1911.

IRELAND; the political tracts of Menenius [Digby Pilot Starkey, LL.D.]. Second edition. 8vo. [*Brit. Mus.*] Dublin, 1849

IRELANDS advocate; or, a sermon preached vpon Novemb. 14. 1641. to promote the contributions by way of lending, for the present reliefe of the Protestant party in Ireland, in the parish church of St Stephens, Coleman Street, London, by the pastor there [John Goodwin]. 4to. [*Brit. Mus.*] London, 1641

IRELAND'S botch and Scotch rulers. By Mr Ellem [William Charles Hennessy, barrister]. 8vo. [O'Donoghue's *Poets of Ireland.*] Dublin, 1886

IRELAND'S case briefly stated; or, a summary account of the most remarkable transactions in that kingdom since the Reformation. By a true lover of his king and country [Hugh Reilly]. 12mo. 2 parts. Pp. 146. [*Bodl.*] N.P. 1695

Each part has a separate title, but the pagination is continuous.

IRELAND'S disease; notes and impressions. By Philippe Daryl [Paul Grousset]. Author's English version. 8vo. Pp. x. 342. [*Brit. Mus.*] London, 1888

IRELAND'S hour. [By Henry Grant.] 8vo. London, 1850

Acknowledgment of authorship is made by the writer in a subsequent work, "The ballot."

IRELAND'S mirror, exhibiting a picture of her present state, with a glimpse of her future prospects. [Signed: D. T. *i.e.* Denis Taaffe.] [*D. N. B.* vol. 55, p. 284.] Dublin, 1795

IRENARCH; or, Justice of the Peace's manual: addressed to the gentlemen in the Commission of the peace for the county of Leicester. By a gentleman of the Commission [Ralph Heathcote, D.D.]. 8vo. [Watt's *Bibl. Brit.*] London, 1774

The third edition bears the author's name.

IRENE; a poem. By Alexandre de Comyn [Charles Thomas Browne]. 8vo. [O'Donoghue's *Poets of Ireland.*] London, 1844

IRENE Floss; and other poems. By Cecil Linker [Harriette S. Smith, later Mrs Bainbridge]. 8vo. [*Lib. Journ.* ix. 94.] London, 1878

IRENE; or, the lonely manor. By Karl Detlef [Caroline Bauer]. 8vo. [Cushing's *Init. and Pseud.* i. 80.] New York, 1882

IRENE'S vow. By Bertha M. Clay [Charlotte M. Braeme]. 8vo. New York, 1887

IRENICON (the); or, peaceable consideration of Christs peaceful kingdom on earth abridged. . . . [By William Sherwin.] 4to. Pp. 48. [*Brit. Mus.*] [1674]

Part of his *Prodromos*, 1674, with separate register and pagination. No separate title-page.

IRIS (the); a journal of literature and science. [By Frederick Lawrence.] 8vo. Nos. 1, 2, and 3 [pp. 72]. [Guildford] 1841

No more published.

IRIS; the romance of an opal ring. By M. B. M. T. [Mrs Mary B. M. Toland]. 8vo. [Cushing's *Init. and Pseud.* ii. 143.] Philadelphia, 1879

IRISH Amy. By L. E. G. [Lucy Ellen Guernsey]. 8vo. [Cushing's *Init. and Pseud.* i. 110.] Philadelphia, 1854

IRISH (the) bar sinister; new edition in four chapters. By Matthew Stradling (author of *Cheap John's auction*) [Martin Francis Mahony]. 8vo. Pp. 136. London, 1872

IRISH (an) Catholic Whig to his fellow countrymen in the United States. [By Charles O'Gorman.] 8vo. [Cushing's *Init. and Pseud.* i. 138.] Providence, R.I., 1852

IRISH chiefs; or the harp of Erin: a poem. By an Irish gentleman [David Stewart Erskine, Earl of Buchan]. 4to. London, 1811

IRISH (the) Church. [By Sir William George Granville Vernon Harcourt.] 8vo. N.P., N.D.

IRISH (the) Church is not the Irish question; a cruise among the Liberals, Radicals, and others. By "Technical Education" [George Shepherd, C.E.] . . . 8vo. [*Brit. Mus.*] London, 1868

IRISH common law reports. . . . [By William Harris Falcon.] 8vo. Dublin, 1852

IRISH (the) compendium . . . containing the . . . titles . . . of all the nobility of Ireland. . . . [By Francis Nichols.] Second edition. 8vo. London, 1727

IRISH convict reform; the intermediate prisons a mistake. [By C. B. Gilson.] 8vo. [*Gladstone Lib. Cat.*] Dublin, 1863

IRISH cottages. By Martin Doyle [Ross Hickey]. 12mo. [*W.*] Dublin, 1830

IRISH (an) cousin. [A novel.] By Geilles Herring [Edith Œ. Somerville] and M. Ross [Violet Martin]. 8vo. 2 vols. London, 1889

IRISH diamonds. [Papers on Irish life and character. By John Smith, Irish journalist.] 12mo. Pp. 183. London, 1847

IRISH (the) difficulty; addressed to his countrymen. By an Englishman [Rev. Frederick W. Robertson, M.A., of Brighton]. 8vo. London, 1848

IRISH (the) dove; or, faults on both sides. [By Mrs Percival.] 12mo. Dublin, 1849

IRISH (the) ecclesiastical register, for the year 1817; containing the dignities and benefices, the names of the beneficed clergy, and of the curates assistant, throughout the several dioceses: carefully compiled from the records in the first-fruits' office. [Preface signed: J. C. E. *i.e.* J. C. Erck.] 12mo. Pp. 132. [*Bodl.*] Dublin, 1817

IRISH education; a letter on the Government scheme of education for Ireland, addressed to the Dissenting ministers who have expressed their approbation of that scheme. By a clergyman of the Church of Scotland [Charles John Brown, D.D.]. 8vo. Glasgow, 1832

IRISH (the) excursion. [A novel. By Mrs —— Colpoys.] 12mo. 4 vols. [S. J. Brown's *Ireland in fiction.*] London, 1801

IRISH fallacies and English facts; being an appeal to the common sense of the British public on the subject of the convict system, etc. By Scrutator [Charles Pennell Measor]. 8vo. Pp. iv. 76. London [1863]

IRISH (the) flora; comprising the phænogamous plants and ferns. [By Lady —— Kane.] 12mo. [*D. N. B.* vol. 58, p. 421.] Dublin, 1833

IRISH folk-lore; traditions and superstitions of the country, with humorous tales. By Lageniensis [Rev. John O'Hanlon, M.R.I.A.]. Pp. x. 312. [*Lib. Journ.* iii. 270.] Glasgow, 1871

IRISH (the) footman's poetry; or, George the rvnner, against Henry the walker, in defence of Iohn the swimmer: being a sur-rejoinder to the rejoinder of the rusty ironmonger, who endeavoured to defile the cleare streames of the water-poet's Helicon. The author, George Richardson, an Hibernian pedestrian. [By John Taylor, the water-poet.] 4to. Pp. 9. [*Bodl.*] 1641

IRISH (the) heiress. [A novel. By Mrs F. C. Patrick.] 8vo. [S. J. Brown's *Ireland in fiction.*] London, 18—

IRISH history for English readers; from the earliest times to the close of the year 1885. By William Stephenson Gregg [Frances Mabel Robinson]. 8vo. Pp. 217. [*Brit. Mus.*] New York, 1886

IRISH (the) Home-Rule Convention; thoughts for a Convention. By A. E. [George William Russell]. 8vo. Dublin, 1917

IRISH (the) Hudibras . . . [By Walter Jones, B.A., M.P. for Sligo.] 8vo. [O'Donoghue's *Poets of Ireland.*] Dublin, 1750

IRISH (the) Hudibras; or, Fingallian Prince: taken from the sixth book of Virgil's Ænæids, and adapted to the present times [by James Farewell]. 8vo. Pp. 156. [*Bodl.*] London, 1689

IRISH land and Irish rights. By an Ulster landlord [Hugh De F. Montgomery]. 8vo. Pp. 41. [*Brit. Mus.*] London, 1881

IRISH life in the castles, the courts and the country. [By Isaac Butt.] 12mo. 3 vols. [*Brit. Mus.*] London, 1840

IRISH local legends. [Thirty stories.] By Lageniensis [Rev. John O'Hanlon, M.R.I.A.]. 8vo. Pp. xi. 144. [*Brit. Mus.*] Dublin, 1896

IRISH (an) lover. By the author of *Without a God* [E. J. Byrne]. 8vo. Pp. 271. [S. J. Brown's *Ireland in fiction.*] London, 1914

IRISH (the) massacre set in a clear light; wherein Mr [Richard] Baxter's account of it in the History of his own life, and the abridgment thereof by Dr Calamy, are throughly consider'd, and the royal martyr fully vindicated. . . . [By Thomas Carte.] The second edition, with additions. 4to. [*Camb. Univ. Lib.*] London, 1715

IRISH (the) middleman; a true story of a Scotch settler. By Outis [Richard Grant White]. 8vo. London, 1892

IRISH (an) midsummer-night's dream. By John Bickerdyke [Charles Henry Cook]. 8vo. [*Lit. Year Book.*] London, 1884

IRISH national poems and songs. By Henry O'Cuirc [Henry Quirke]. 8vo. [O'Donoghue's *Poets of Ireland.*] London, 1822

IRISH nationality in 1870. By a Protestant Celt [Robert Macdonnell]. Second edition. 8vo. Pp. 83. [*Brit. Mus.*] Dublin, 1870

IRISH (the) on the prairies; and other poems. [By Rev. Thomas Ambrose Butler, Romish priest.] 8vo. [O'Donoghue's *Poets of Ireland.*] [St Louis, *c.* 1865]

IRISH (the) orphan in a Scottish home. By the author of *The way home*, etc. [Mrs Margaret F. Barbour]. 8vo. London, 1866

IRISH (the) Poor Law medical system. By Dispensarius [D. Toler T. Maunsell, M.D.]. 8vo. Dublin, 1870

IRISH priests and English landlords. [A tale.] By the author of *Hyacinth O'Gara* [George Brittaine]. 12mo. Pp. 249. [*Brit. Mus.*] Dublin, 1830

IRISH Protestant letters. By R. R. B. [Robert Redman Belshaw]. 8vo. [Cushing's *Init. and Pseud.* ii. 14.] New York, 1855

IRISH pursuits of literature, in A.D. 1798, and 1799; consisting of I. Translations, II. Second thoughts, III. Rival translations, IV. The monstrous republic, V. Indexes. [By William Hales, D.D.] 8vo. [*Brit. Mus.*] Dublin, 1799

IRISH (the) question. By W. Hart Westcombe [Samuel J. MacMullan]. 8vo. [*Lond. Lib. Cat.*] London, 1886

IRISH (the) question; Home Rule. By Leodiensis Hibernicus [James Kavanagh, of Leeds]. 8vo. [1886?]

IRISH rebels. [A novel.] By Alexander Macarthur [Lily Macarthur, later Mrs Nicchia]. 8vo. Pp. 219. [S. J. Brown's *Ireland in fiction.*] London [1893]

IRISH (the) salmon question socially, economically and commercially considered. By a naturalist and an epicure [William Bullen]. 8vo. [*Brit. Mus.*] London, 1863

IRISH (the) Scripture-reader. [By Miss E. Colthurst.] [S. J. Brown's *Ireland in fiction.*] [*c.* 1840]

IRISH (an) sept [viz. the Macnamara clan]; their character and struggle to maintain their lands in Clare. By a member of the sept [Lewis Macnamara]. 8vo. London, 1896

IRISH songs and guard-room rhymes. By Henry O'Cuirc [Henry Quirke]. 8vo. [O'Donoghue's *Poets of Ireland.*] London, 1881

IRISH State papers; a letter to . . . the Marquis of Clanricarde, suggesting that a portion of the Treasury Fund . . . should be applied to editing and printing the State papers. . . . By Historicus Hibernicus [William Bullen]. 8vo. London, 1863

IRISH stew; or, a taste of something spicy and suitable to the time; being an attempt to solve the Main(e) question relating to the disputed territory to the west of St George's Channel. By Corney the Rhymer [Terence M. Hughes]. Edited by Lord B——. Sixth edition. 8vo. [O'Donoghue's *Poets of Ireland.*] London, 1845

A collection of comic songs.

IRISH stories. By E. Owens Blackburne [Elizabeth Owens Blackburne Casey]. 8vo. London, 1893

IRISH (the) valet; a comedy. [By Charles Henry Wilson.] 8vo. [Brown's *Books on Ireland*, i. 174.] London, 1871

IRISH (the) widow; in two acts, as it is performed at the Theatre Royal in Drury-Lane. [By David Garrick.] The third edition. 8vo. [Baker's *Biog. Dram.*] London, 1772

IRISHMAN (the). By an Irishwoman [Anna Perrier]. 8vo. Pp. 79. [*Bodl.*] London, 1866

IRISHMAN (the). By Owen Roe [Eugène Davis]. London, 189—

IRISHMAN (the); a novel. By Oliver Blyth [John Weldon]. 8vo. Pp. 302. London, 1920

IRISHMAN (the) in London; or, the happy African: a farce, in two acts [and in prose. By William Macready]. 8vo. [*Brit. Mus.*] London, 1793

IRISHMAN (an) looks at his world. By George A. Birmingham [James Owen Hannay, D.D.]. 8vo. Pp. 307. [*Brit. Mus.*] London, 1919

IRISHMAN'S (the) gratitude; an amusing story [in verse], reprinted from a volume entitled Brighter days for working men. [By Rev. William Glenn, B.A.] 8vo. London [1877]

IRISHMEN all. By George A. Birmingham [James Owen Hannay, D.D.]. 8vo. Pp. 234. Edinburgh, 1913

IRISHMEN and Irish women. By the author of *Hyacinth O'Gara*, etc. [George Brittaine]. 12mo. Pp. 219. [*Brit. Mus.*] Dublin, 1831

IRON (the) chain and the golden. By A. L. O. E. [A Lady of England *i.e.* Charlotte Maria Tucker]. 8vo. Edinburgh, 1891

IRON (the) question, considered in connection with theory, practice, and experience; with special reference to "The Bessemer process." By Joseph Hall [Rev. James Everett, Wesleyan]. 8vo. London, 1857

IRON (the) question vindicated, and the reviewers reviewed. By an observer [Rev. James Everett, Wesleyan]. 8vo. [*Brit. Mus.*] London, 1857

IRON scrap; or, the issue of an old shoe-heel. By Joseph Hall [Rev. James Everett, Wesleyan]. 8vo. London, 1864

IRON (the) shroud; or, Italian revenge. [By William Mudford.] 12mo. [*Brit. Mus.*] London [1840?]

IRON (the) stair; a romance of Dartmoor. By "Rita" [Mrs W. Desmond Humphreys, *née* Eliza M. J. Gollan]. 8vo. London, 1916

IRON times with the guards. By an O. E. [Old Etonian, *i.e.* Geoffrey Fildes, barrister]. 8vo. Pp. 373. [*N. and Q.*, Dec. 1920.] London, 1918

IRONICON (an); a reply to An eirenicon by the Rev. E. B. Pusey, D.D., Regius Professor of Hebrew, etc. Faithfully and fearlessly addressed to him and to all sorts and conditions of men in the British Empire who call themselves Christians; with an appendix and notes. By an Anglo-Saxon [Captain M. N. Coombs]. 8vo. [Green's *Bibl. Somers.* i. 22.] Bath, 1866

IRONMASTER (the). [A novel.] By Georges Ohnet [Georges Hénot]. Translated from the French. . . . 8vo. [*Brit. Mus.*] London, 1884

IRONMASTER'S (the) daughter. [A novel.] By Bertha M. Clay [Charlotte M. Braeme]. 8vo. London, 1906

IRRATIONALE (the) of speech. By a minute philosopher [Charles Kingsley]. Reprinted from *Fraser's Magazine*, 1859. 8vo. [*Brit. Mus.*] London, 1864

Signed: C. K. The same work appeared under the title, "Hints to stammerers."

IRRATIONALISM (the) of infidelity; being a reply to [Francis Newman's] Phases of faith. [By John N. Darby.] 8vo. Pp. xvi. 384. London, 1853

IRREGULAR (an) ode; addressed to the Hon. William Pitt. [By J. N. Puddicombe.] 4to. [*Mon. Rev.* lxx. 235, 383.] 1784

The second edition has the author's name, and the title "Ode," etc.

IRREGULARITIE (the) of a private prayer in a publick congregation; in a letter to a friend. [By Richard Sherlock, D.D.] 8vo. [*Bodl.*] 1674

IRRELAGH ; or, the last of the chiefs : an Irish tale. By the author of *Loyalty*, etc. [Miss E. Colthurst]. 8vo. [O'Donoghue's *Poets of Ireland.*] London, 1849

IRRESPONSIBLE Kitty. By Curtis Yorke [Mrs W. S. Richmond Lee, *née* —— Jex Long]. 8vo. [*Lond. Lib. Cat.*] London, 1906

IRWELL ; and other poems. By A. [Joseph Anthony]. 12mo. Pp. vi. 58. [*N. and Q.* 1869, p. 168.] London, 1843

IS all well with England? A question. By Marie Corelli [Caroline Cody]. 16mo. Pp. 30. [*Brit. Mus.*] London [1917]

IS cheap sugar the triumph of free trade? A letter to the Right Hon. Lord John Russell. By Jacob Omnium [Matthew James Higgins]. Second edition. 8vo. Pp. 19. London, 1847

A second letter, with the same title, was published in 1848 ; and, in the same year, there appeared a "Third letter to Lord John Russell," *q.v.*

IS educational reform wanted? and what? [By Montagu Burrows, Professor of History.] 8vo. [*Bodl.*] Oxford, 1859

IS "eternal" punishment endless? . . . By an orthodox minister of the Gospel [Rev. James Morris Whiton]. 8vo. [Cushing's *Init. and Pseud.* i. 219.] Boston, 1876

IS Free Trade a mistake? Dedicated to the production of England, both capital and labour. By Don't Care [D. Nickerson]. 8vo. Pp. 27. [*Brit. Mus.*] Southsea, Hampshire, 1887

IS God unknowable? [By Rev. John B. Dalgairns.] 8vo. N.P. private print, 1872

Metaphys. Soc. papers, No. 27.

IS it a blot? A novel. By the author of *The cream of a life* [Charles Phillips]. 8vo. 3 vols. London, 1867

IS it a sin? An inquiry into the lawfulness of complying with the rule of the National Board relative to religious instruction. [By Humphrey Lloyd, D.D., D.C.L.] 8vo. [*D. N. B.* vol. 33, p. 426.] Dublin, 1860

IS it right for a Christian to marry two sisters? By a member of the Society of Friends [Jonathan Pim]. 12mo. Pp. xiii. 86. [Smith's *Cat. of Friends' Books.*] Dublin, 1863

IS it Shakespeare? The great question of Elizabethan literature answered. . . . By a Cambridge Graduate [Rev. Walter Begley, B.A.]. 8vo. Pp. xii. 387. [*Brit. Mus.*] London, 1903

IS it true? Tales curious & wonderful. Collected by the author of *John Halifax, Gentleman* [Dinah Maria Mulock, later Mrs Craik]. 8vo. Pp. vii. 218. London, 1872

IS Liberal policy a failure? By Expertus [Rev. Malcolm MacColl, M.A.]. 8vo. London, 1870

IS man a free agent? The law of suggestion. By Santanelli [James Hawthorne Loryea]. 8vo. [*Amer. Cat.*] Lansing, Michigan, 1902

IS our prosperity a delusion? Our national debt and currency. By a Boston merchant [Amos W. Stetson]. 8vo. [Cushing's *Init. and Pseud.* ii. 132.] Boston, 1864

Signed : A. W. S.

IS Russia wrong? A series of letters by a Russian lady [O. K., *i.e.* Olga Kiryeeva, later Madame Novikova]. . . . 8vo. London, 1878

IS salvation by water baptism the doctrine of the Church of England? A letter to the Very Rev. Ov [Hugh] M'Neile, occasioned by his letter . . . entitled Baptism doth save. By Biblicus [Rev. William Thorn]. 8vo. [*Brit. Mus.*] London, 1852

Attributed also to Joshua Wilson, barrister.

IS sanctification perfect here below? On Romans i.-viii. [By Richard Govett.] 12mo. London, 1875

IS Shakespeare dead? From my autobiography. By Mark Twain [Samuel L. Clemens]. 8vo. Pp. 154. London, 1909

IS that all? [A novel.] [By Harriet Waters Preston.] 8vo. Pp. 244. [*Lib. Journ.* i. 193.] London, 1877

IS the Bible the only rule ; or, doubts and queries respectfully addressed to the Rev. R. Green Armytage. . . . By a Lancaster idolater [John Lingard, D.D.]. 8vo. Pp. 29. [Gillow's *Bibl. Dict.*] Lancaster, 1839

IS the Bible the Word of God? Or, a remonstrance on behalf of Protestantism. [By Robert William Mackay.] 8vo. [*Brit. Mus.*] London, private print, 1856

IS the Bible true? Seven dialogues between James White and Edward Owen, concerning the Essays and reviews. By the author of *Essays on the Church* [Robert Benton Seeley]. 8vo. Pp. 124. [*D. N. B.* vol. 51, p. 193.] London, 1862

The title of the edition issued in 1866 reads : "Is the Bible true? Seven dialogues by a layman."

IS the Pope God's vicegerent? What saith the Word of God? By the late chaplain of the workhouse of the parish of St George's-in-the-East [William Henry Foy]. 8vo. [*Brit. Mus.*] London [1872]

IS the Vicar of Brompton a Tractarian? A question for the parishioners. By a layman [Arthur Ellis]. 8vo. Pp. iv. 16. [*Brit. Mus.*] London, 1855

Preface signed: A. E.

IS the world prepared for peace? [By David Pae.] 8vo. [Edinburgh] 1855

IS there a God? By "Inconoclast" [Charles Bradlaugh]. 8vo. Pp. 8. London [1861]

IS there just reason for seceding from the Church of Scotland? By a member of the Established Church [Rev. Peter Brotherston]. 8vo. [*New Coll. Lib.*] Edinburgh, 1843

IS there not a cause? A letter to Col. Greville-Nugent on the Disestablishment of the Irish Church, with a vindication of Mr Gladstone's consistency. By Scrutator [Malcolm MacColl]. 8vo. [*Gladstone Lib. Cat.*] London, 1868

IS this religion? Or, a page from the book of the world. By the author of *May you like it* [Charles B. Tayler]. 8vo. Pp. 295. London, 1826

ISAAC Bickerstaff's letter to the tongue-loosed Doctor [Henry Sacheverell. By Richard Steele]. 8vo. Pp. 23. [F. Madan's *Sacheverell bibliography*, in the *Bibliographer*, vol. 4.] London, 1713

ISAAC Comnenus; a play. [By Sir Henry Taylor, K.C.M.G.] 8vo. [*Nat. Lib. of Scot.*] London, 1827

ISAAC Eller's money. [A novel.] By Mrs Andrew Dean [Mrs Cicely Sidgwick]. 8vo. Pp. 240. [*Brit. Mus.*] London, 1889

ISAAC Letterman's daughter; a story of the Daggle-mop. By the author of *Earth's many voices* [Elizabeth M. A. F. Saxby]. 8vo. [*Brit. Mus.*] London [1899]

ISABEAU'S hero; a story of the Revolt of the Cevennes. By Esmé Stuart [Miss Amélie Claire Leroy]. 8vo. [*Lond. Lib. Cat.*] London, 1882

ISABEL Trivethoe; a poem. By C. A. R. [Caroline Alice Roberts]. 8vo. [*Lib. Journ.* v. 54.] London, 1878

ISABELLA of Milan; the intimate story of her life in Milan, told in the letters of her Lady-in-Waiting. By Christopher Hare [Mrs Marion Andrews]. 8vo. Pp. 320. [*Lond. Lib. Cat.*] London, 1911

ISABELLA; or, the morning: and other poems. [By Sir Charles Hanbury Williams.] 8vo. [*D.N.B.* vol. 61, p. 379.] London, 1740

ISAGOGE ad Dei providentiam; or, a prospect of Divine providence. By T. C. [Thomas Case, M.A.]. 8vo. [*New Coll. Lib.*] London, 1672

ISEULTE. By the author of *Vera*, *Hôtel du Petit St Jean*, etc. [Charlotte Louisa Hawkins Dempster]. 8vo. Pp. viii. 363. London, 1875

ISHMAEL. [A novel.] By the author of *Lady Audley's secret* [Mrs John Maxwell, *née* Mary Elizabeth Braddon]. 8vo. 3 vols. London [1884]

ISIDORA; or, the adventures of a Neapolitan: a novel. By the old author in a new walk, author of *The Pope and the Colonnas*, etc. [J. R. Best]. 12mo. 3 vols. London, 1841

ISKANDER; or, the hero of Epirus; a romance. By Arthur Spenser [Rev. Samuel Rowe, M.A.]. 12mo. 3 vols. London, 1819

ISLAM. By A. H. A. [Andrew Hilliard Atteridge]. Reprinted . . . from the *Dublin Review*. 8vo. [*Brit. Mus.*] London, 1878

ISLAND (the). By Whyte Thorne [Richard Whiteing]. 8vo. London, 1888

ISLAND (the) camp. By Captain Ralph Bonehill [Edward Stratemeyer]. 8vo. [*Amer. Cat.*] New York, 1904

ISLAND (the) choir; or, the children of the child Jesus. [By James Millard, M.A.] 8vo. [*Bodl.*] London, 1847

ISLAND (the) home; or, the young cast-aways. Edited by Christopher Romaunt [James F. Bowman]. 8vo. Pp. 461. [Cushing's *Init. and Pseud.* i. 131.] Boston, 1852

ISLAND Magee witches. [By Samuel M'Skimin.] 8vo. Belfast, 1822

ISLAND (the) minstrel. By H. Fitzherbert [Herbert Baskett]. 12mo. [Gilbert and Godwin's *Bibl. Hantonensis*, p. 7.] London, 1842

ISLAND (the) mystery. [A novel.] By George A. Birmingham [James Owen Hannay, D.D.]. 8vo. London, 1918

ISLAND (the) of innocence; a poetical epistle to a friend. By Peter Pindar, Esq. [John Wolcot, M.D.]. Part the first. 4to. Pp. 17. London, 1802

ISLAND (the) of life. By a clergyman [Rev. Frederick Gardiner]. 8vo. [Cushing's *Init. and Pseud.* ii. 233.] Boston, 1850

ISLAND (the) of St Marguerite; an opera, in two acts, and first performed at the Theatre Royal, Drury Lane, on Friday, November 13, 1789. [By Hon. John St John.] 8vo. Pp. 32. [Baker's *Biog. Dram.*] London, 1790

ISLAND (the) of seven shadows. [A novel.] By Roma White [Blanche Oram, later Mrs Winder]. 8vo. Pp. 318. London, 1898

ISLAND (the) of sorrow. [An Irish historical romance.] By George Gilbert [Miss M. L. Arthur]. 8vo. Pp. 384. London, 1903

ISLAND (the) of the Saints. By Julius von Rodenberg [Julius Levy]. 8vo. [Cushing's *Init. and Pseud.* i. 253.] London, 1861

ISLAND (the) on the mere; a Cheshire tale. By the author of *The legacy of an Etonian* [Robert William Blessington, M.A.]. 8vo. [*Brit. Mus.*] Cambridge, 1847

ISLAND (the) Pharisees. By John Sinjohn [John Galsworthy]. 8vo. [*Amer. Cat.*] New York, 1904

ISLAND (the) Princess; a story of six weeks—and afterwards. By Theo Gift [Mrs Theodora H. Boulger, *née* Havers]. 8vo. Pp. 270. [*Lit. Year Book.*] London, 1893

ISLAND (the) Princess; or, the generous Portugal: a comedy acted at the Theater Royal by His Majesties servants. [By John Fletcher.] 4to. [Arber's *Term Cat.* i. 525.] London, 1669

ISLAND (an) refuge; Casco Bay in 1676. By James Otis [James Otis Kaler]. 8vo. Pp. 107. [Kirk's *Supp.*] Boston, 1895

ISLANDERS (the); a poem. . . . By Edward Kane [Kathleen Knox]. 8vo. [O'Donoghue's *Poets of Ireland.*] London, 1888

ISLANDERS (the) and their crown; an allegory. By W. T. C. W. [W. T. C. Wilkinson]. 12mo. [Kirk's *Supp.*] London, 1874

ISLANDS (the) of desire; a novel. By Diana Patrick [Mrs Desemea Newman Wilson]. 8vo. Pp. 320. [*Who's Who in Lit.*] London [1920]

ISLE (the) of dreams. By Fiona Macleod [William Sharp]. 8vo. [*Lit. Year Book.*] Portland [U.S.A.] 1905

ISLE of Man; a complete history of the Isle of Man. [By John Seacome.] 8vo. [Harrison's *Bibl. Mon.*] N.P. [*c.* 1741]

ISLE (the) of Man guide; containing an historical sketch, and descriptive views of the Island. . . . [By Samuel Haining.] 8vo. Pp. 20. Douglas, 1824

ISLE (the) of Man; or, the legall proceedings in Manshire against sinne. By R. B. [Richard Bernard, rector of Batcombe]. 8vo. [Green's *Bibl. Somers.* ii. 168.] London, 1627

ISLE (the) of May; a sketch: addressed to J. S. [By Thomas S. Muir.] 8vo. Edinburgh, private print, 1868

ISLE (the) of Thanet; with historical and descriptive notes. By "Rambler" [Arthur Montifiore]. 8vo. London, 1893

ISLE (the) of Pines; or, a late discovery of a fourth island in Terra Australis Incognita; being a true relation of certain English persons, who, in the dayes of Queen Elizabeth, making a voyage to the East India, were cast away, and wracked upon the island, near to the coast of Terra Australis Incognita, and all drowned, except one man and four women, whereof one was a negro. And now lately Anno Dom. 1667, a Dutch ship called the Amsterdam, Cornelius Van Sloetten, captain, driven by foul weather there, by chance have found their posterity (speaking good English) to amount to ten or twelve thousand persons, as they suppose. The whole relation follows, written, and left by the man himself a little before his death, and declared to the Dutch by his grandchild. [By Henry Neville.] 4to. [*N. and Q.* 1861, p. 212.] London, 1668

ISLE (the) of unrest; a novel. By Henry Seton Merriman [Hugh Stowell Scott]. 8vo. Pp. 352. [*Lond. Lib. Cat.*] London, 1909

ISLE (the) of Wight; a poem, in three cantos. [By Henry Jones.] 8vo. Pp. 44. [*Brit. Mus.*] Newport, Isle of Wight, 1782

ISLE Raven. [A novel.] By Owen Rhoscomyl [Owen Vaughan]. 8vo. [*Lit. Year Book.*] London, 1908

ISLES of the sea; or, Young America homeward bound. By Oliver Optic [Wm. T. Adams]. 8vo. [Kirk's *Supp.*] Boston, 1877

ISLINGTON; a poem: addressed to Mr Benjamin Stap. To which are subjoined several other poetical essays, by the same author [John Nichols]. 4to. [Watt's *Bibl. Brit.*] London, 1763

ISLINGTON-WELLS; or, the three-penny-academy: a poem. [By Richard Ames.] 4to. [Dobell's *Cat.*] London, 1691

ISMAEL and Cassander; or, the Jew and the Greek. By M. E. M. J. [Margaret Elizabeth Mary Jones]. 8vo. [*Nat. Lib. of Scot.*] London, N.D.

ISMAY'S children. [A novel.] By the author of *Hogan, M.P.*, etc. [May Laffan, later Mrs Hartley]. 8vo. 3 vols. [*Camb. Univ. Lib.*] London, 1887

ISMEER; or, Smyrna and its British hospital in 1855. By a lady [Martha Nicol]. 8vo. [*Nat. Lib. of Scot.*] London, 1856

ISMENIA and the Prince; or, the royal marriage: being a sequel to *The history of Prince Titi.* [By the Hon. Mrs Stanley.] 12mo. London, 1736

This was followed by "Pausanias and Aurora."

ISOBEL Burns (Mrs Begg); a memoir. [By Robert Burns Begg.] 8vo. Paisley, 1894

ISOLDA; or, good King Stephen; an historical and romantic drama, in five acts. By the author of *Griselda*, etc. [John Watkins, LL.D.]. 8vo. [*Nat. Lib. of Scot.*] London, 1848

Attributed also to Alfred Bate Richards.

ISOLINA; or, the actor's daughter. [By Ann Susan Horner.] 8vo. Philadelphia, 1873

ISRAEL; a juvenile poem. . . . By Serena [Sarah Leigh Pike]. 8vo. 2 vols. [Green's *Bibl. Somers.* iii. 190.] Bath, 1795

ISRAEL defended; or, the Jewish exposition of the Hebrew prophecies, applied by the Christians to their Messiah. By Isaac Orobio. Translated from the French [by Grace Aguilar]; and printed expressly for the use of young persons of the Jewish faith. 12mo. [*W.*] London, 1838

Not published.
The translator's preface signed: G. A.

ISRAEL in Egypt; or, the Books of Genesis and Exodus. Illustrated by existing monuments. [By William Osburn.] 8vo. Pp. xxxi. 437. London, 1854

ISRAEL vindicated. . . . [By George Houston.] 8vo. New York, 1820

ISRAELITISH (the) question, and the comments of the Canaan journals thereon. [A burlesque. By Henry Duff Traill, D.C.L., barrister.] 8vo. [Boase's *Mod. Eng. Biog.*] London, 1876

ISRAEL'S fast; upon the VIIth of Joshua. By H. B. [Henry Burton]. 4to. [*Brit. Mus.*] N.P. 1628

ISRAEL'S greater faith contrasted with "Zion's Watch Tower" doctrine. [By William D. Forsyth.] 8vo. Pp. 38. [*Brit. Mus.*] Rochdale [1909]

ISRAEL'S lamentation after the Lord; or, a discourse, wherein every well-wisher to Zion is excited and directed how to lament after the Lord with prayers and tears, to maintain the ordinances of God, or God's presence with his ordinances amongst us. Being some meditations upon 1 Sam. 7. 2. [By Oliver Heywood.] 8vo. Pp. 143. [*Bodl.*] London, 1683

The address: To all mourners in Zion, etc., signed: O. H.

ISRAEL'S true emancipator, exhibited in a letter to the Rev. Dr Adler, chief Rabbi of the Jewish Congregations of Great Britain and Ireland. . . . By E. H. C. M. [Editor of the *Hebrew Christian's Magazine*, Nathan Davis]. 8vo. [*Brit. Mus.*] London, 1852

ISRAEL'S wanderings; or, the Scuths, the Saxons, and the Kymry: tracing both the "Kelticand the Scandinavian" elements in the British from Palestine. By "Oxonian" [Rev. William Metcalfe Holme Milner, M.A.]. 8vo. London [1881]

ISSACHAR the strong ass overburdened; or, the groans of Britannia from the Pitt: a poem descriptive of the times. [Signed: J. M. *i.e.* J. Maxwell.] 8vo. [Paisley? 1795?]

ISSY and her lovers. By Nellie [Ellen Marsh]. 8vo. [Cushing's *Init. and Pseud.* i. 202.] London [1850?]

ISTHMUS (the) of Suez. [A poem. By Edward W. B. Nicholson, M.A.] 8vo. [*Bodl.*] Oxford, 1871

IT; a comic perennial, in prose and verse. Edited and illustrated by Alfred Crowquill [Alfred Henry Forrester]. 8vo. Pp. 96. London, N.D.

IT came to pass. [A novel.] By Curtis Yorke [Mrs W. S. Richmond Lee, *née* —— Jex-Blake]. 8vo. [*Lond. Lib. Cat.*] London, 1915

IT might have been; a novel. By the author of *Tit for tat* [Mrs Jane Grace Smith]. 8vo. 3 vols. [*Brit. Mus.*] London, 1876

IT would be so; a vision. By Solomon Second-sight [James MacHenry, M.D.]. 8vo. [*D. N. B.* vol. 35, p. 108; O'Donoghue's *Poets of Ireland.*] Dublin, 1811

Incorrectly attributed to Thomas Berkeley Greaves.

ITALIAN (the) biography of Sir Robert Dudley, Knt., known in Florentine history as Il Duca di Nortombria. . . . [By Rev. Vaughan Thomas.] 8vo. [*Brit. Mus.*] Private print [1849]

ITALIAN (the) bride; a play in five acts [and in verse. By S. Yates Levy]. 12mo. [*Brit. Mus.*] Savannah, private print, 1856

ITALIAN (the) captain; a drama, in five acts. [By Ichabod H. Wright.] 8vo. Pp. 95. [*Nat. Lib. of Scot.*] London, 1847

ITALIAN (the) convert; newes from Italy of a second Moses: or, the life of Galeacius Caracciolus, the noble Marquesse of Vico; containing the story of his admirable conversion from Popery, and forsaking of a rich marquesdom for the Gospels sake. Written first in Italian [by Niccolò Balbani] thence translated into Latin by Reverend [Theodore] Beza; and for the benefit of our people put into English, and now published by W. C. [William Crashaw]. 12mo. [*Brit. Mus.*] London, 1639

ITALIAN (the) crisis; a letter addressed to the British Houses of Parliament and to the English nation. By W. A. F. [Lieut. Col. William Augustus Fyers], C.B., R.B. 8vo. [*Camb. Univ. Lib.*] London, 1859

ITALIAN games at cards, and Oriental games. Arranged by Aquarius [Lowis D'A. Jackson]. 12mo. Pp. 61. [*Brit. Mus.*] London, 1890

ITALIAN grammar. By Luigi Mariotti [Antonio Carlo N. Gallenga]. 8vo. [Cushing's *Init. and Pseud.* i. 184.] London, 1858

ITALIAN (the) Heloise; a series of original letters, versified in imitation of the Abelard and Heloise of Pope. By the author of *The Tuileries* [J. M. Richardson]. 12mo. [*Brit. Mus.*] London, 1824

ITALIAN highways and byways from a motor car. By Francis Miltoun [Milburg Francisco Mansfield]. 8vo. [*Amer. Cat.*] Boston, 1909

ITALIAN love. See "Eunuchism displayed."

ITALIAN lyrists of to-day; translations [together with bibliographical and biographical notes] by G. A. G. [George Arthur Greene, M.A.]. 8vo. [O'Donoghue's *Poets of Ireland*, Appendix.] London, 1893

ITALIAN pictures drawn with pen and pencil. By the author of *Spanish pictures*, etc. [Samuel Manning, D.D.]. 8vo. Pp. 216. London [1872]

ITALIAN portraits in Engadine frames. By G. E. X. [Mrs Lydia Ethel F. Painter]. 8vo. [*Amer. Cat.*] Wausau, Wis., 1905

ITALIAN (the) schoole-master; contayning rules for the perfect pronouncing of th' Italian tongue; with familiar speeches, and certain phrases taken out of the best Italian authors. . . . Set forth by Clau: Hollyband [Claude Desainliens], Gent. . . . 8vo. [*Brit. Mus.*] London, 1608

ITALIAN tales; tales of humour, gallantry, and romance, selected and translated from the Italian [by Thomas Roscoe]. 8vo. [*Brit. Mus.*] London, 1824

ITALIAN (the) wife; a tragedy [in five acts, and in verse. By Thomas Doubleday]. 8vo. [*Edin. Univ. Lib.*] Edinburgh, 1823

ITALIANS (the). [A novel.] By Florentine [Mrs Frances Elliot]. 8vo. 3 vols. London, 1875

ITALIANS (the); or, the fatal accusation: a tragedy. With a preface; containing the correspondence of the author with the committee of Drury Lane theatre; P. Moore, Esq., M.P.; and Mr Kean. By the author of *The philosophy of nature* [Charles Bucke]. 8vo. Pp. 112. London, 1819

Preface signed: C. B.

ITALY; a poem. The first part. [By Samuel Rogers, banker.] 12mo. [Courtney's *Secrets*, p. 124.] London, 1822

Part second (1828) as well as later editions of the whole, bears the author's name.

ITALY and her Capital. By E. S. G. S. [Emily S. G. Saunders]. 8vo. [*Brit. Mus.*] London, 1868

See, below, "Italy revisited."

ITALY and its comforts; a manual of tourists. By Valery [Antoine Claude Pasquin]. 8vo. [*Brit. Mus.*] London [1841]

ITALY and the Italians in the nineteenth century; or, letters on the civil, political & moral state of that country. . . . By a Foreign officer in the British Service [André Vieusseux]. 8vo. Pp. viii. 271. [*Brit. Mus.*] London, 1821

An edition in 2 vols. issued in 1824 bears the author's name.

ITALY as it is; or, narrative of an English family's residence for three years in that country. By the author of *Four years in France* [Henry Beste Digby]. 8vo. Pp. xii. 441. London, 1828

ITALY; general views of its history and literature in reference to its present state. By L. Mariotti [Antonio C. N. Gallenga]. 12mo. 2 vols. London, 1841

ITALY in 1848. By L. Mariotti [Antonio C. N. Gallenga]. 8vo. Pp. xii. 499. [*Edin. Univ. Lib.*] London, 1851

ITALY, past and present. By L. Mariotti [Antonio C. N. Gallenga]. 8vo. 2 vols. London, 1848

ITALY revisited; a series of pictures: sequel to *Italy and her Capital*. By E. S. G. S. [Emily S. G. Saunders]. 8vo. Pp. ix. 207. London, 1884

ITALY; with sketches of Spain and Portugal. By the author of *Vathek* [William Beckford]. 8vo. 2 vols. London, 1834

ITEM against sacriledge; or, sundry queries concerning tithes. Collected . . . by one that hath no propriety in tithes [Samuel Clark, minister of St Bennet Fink]. 4to. [Bliss' *Cat.* p. 62.] London, 1653

ITER boreale; attempting somthing [*sic*] upon the successful and matchless march of the Lord General George Monck, from Scotland to London, the last winter, &c. Veni, vidi, vici. [Verse.] By a rural pen [Robert Wild, D.D.]. 4to. Pp. 20. [*Brit. Mus.*] London, 1660

Another edition, with a different imprint, appeared in the same year.

ITER Carolinum; being a succinct relation of the necessitated marches, retreats, and sufferings of his Majesty Charles the I., from January 10. 1641. till the time of his death 1648. Collected by a daily attendant upon his sacred Majesty, during all the said time [Sir Edward Walker]. 4to. [*Bodl.*] London, 1660

ITER Helveticum; being a journal of the doings of a cabinet (so called) of five fellow travellers in Switzerland. . . . [By William Anderton Brigg.] 8vo. Pp. 89. [*Brit. Mus.*] Keighley, private print, 1887

ITER lunare; or, a voyage to the moon; containing some considerations on the nature of that planet; the possibility of getting thither: with other pleasant conceits about the inhabitants, their manners and customs. [By David Russen, of Hythe.] 8vo. [Arber's *Term Cat.* iii. 687.] London, 1703

ITER Lusitanicum; or, the Portugal voyage: with what memorable passages interven'd at the shipping, and in the transportation of her most sacred Majesty Katherine, Queen of Great Britain, from Lisbon to England. Exactly observed

By him that was eye-witnesse of the same,
Who though he publish this, conceals his name.
Plus valet unus oculatus testis
Quam mille auriti. Aug.
Carmina secessum; scribentis et otia quærunt;
Me mare, me venti, me fera jactat hyems.
Verses ask time, and leisure, but I'me tost
With windes, and waves, and with cold winters blast.

By S. H., a Cosmopolite [S. Hinde, or Hynde]. 4to. Pp. 38. [*Bodl.*] London, 1662

ITINERANT traders of London; with notices of the remarkable places given in the background. [By Sir Richard Phillips, publisher.] 4to. London [1805]

See the note to "A biographical class-book . . ."

ITINERARY of a traveller in the wilderness. [By Mrs Ann Taylor, *née* Hinton.] 8vo. Boston, 1825

ITINERARY (the) of Azariah Frijolity; or, what becomes of old barbers. [By William A. Augustine.] 8vo. Pp. 232. [*Brit. Mus.*] Carey, Ohio [1911]

ITINERARY (an) of Launceston, Cornwall; containing some account of its antiquities, compiled from various sources. . . . [By Mrs Anne Gibbons, *née* Trelawny.] 8vo. Pp. 74. [Boase and Courtney's *Bibl. Corn.*] Launceston, 1865

"IT'S all real true"; the story of a child's difficulties. By Eglanton Thorne [Emily Charlton]. 8vo. Pp. 160. London [1881]

IVAN. By Marie Emery [Madame Vandenbussche]. 8vo. [Cushing's *Init. and Pseud.* i. 90.] New York, 1873

IVAN de Biron; or, the Russian court in the middle of last century. By the author of *Friends in council*, etc. [Arthur Helps]. 8vo. [*D. N. B.* vol. 25, p. 372.] London, 1874

IVANHOE; a historical drama, founded on the celebrated romance . . . by the author of *Waverley*. . . . [By Daniel Terry.] 8vo. Pp. 76. [*Brit. Mus.*] Edinburgh, 1823

IVANHOE; a romance. By the author of *Waverley*, etc. [Sir Walter Scott, Bart.]. 8vo. 3 vols. Edinburgh, 1820

IVANHOE; or, the Jewess: a drama founded on the romance of Ivanhoe. By John William Calcraft [John William Cole]. 12mo. [*Camb. Univ. Lib.*] Edinburgh, 1823

I'VE been thinking. . . . [By Mrs Catherine Crowe, *née* Stevens.] 8vo. London [1850?]

IVO and Verona; or, the snowdrop. [By Mary Ann Dyson.] 12mo. [Courtney's *Secrets*, p. 67.] London, 1842

IVON. By the author of *Aunt Agnes* [Selina Gaye]. 8vo. London, 1866

IVORS. By the author of *Amy Herbert*, etc. [Elizabeth Missing Sewell]. 8vo. 2 vols. London, 1856

IVORY, apes, and peacocks. By Israfel [Miss —— Hudson]. 8vo. Pp. 274. London, 1899

IVORY (the) box. [A novel.] By John Strange Winter [Mrs Arthur Stannard, *née* Pearl Teresa Richards]. 8vo. London, 1909

IVY'S armour. [A tale.] By the author of *Katie, the fisherman's little daughter* [Emma S. Pratt]. 8vo. Pp. 199. London [1883]

IWANOWNA; or, the maid of Moscow: a novel. . . . By the author of the *Clergyman's widow*, etc. [Barbara Hofland]. 12mo. 2 vols. [*Brit. Mus.*] London, 1813

IZA; a story of life in Russian Poland. By Grace Ramsay [Kathleen O'Meara]. 8vo. London, 1877

IZA'S story. [A novel.] By Grace Ramsay [Kathleen O'Meara]. 8vo. 3 vols. [*Brit. Mus.*] London, 1869

IZRAM; a Mexican tale; and other poems. By Charlotte Elizabeth [Charlotte Elizabeth Brown, afterwards Mrs Phelan, and subsequently Mrs Tonna]. 12mo. [*D. N. B.* vol. 57, p. 34.] London, 1826

J

J. Ramsay MacDonald, 1923-1925. By Iconoclast [Mary Agnes Hamilton]. 8vo. Pp. 191. [*Brit. Mus.*] London, 1925

JABEZ Murdock; an Irish story. By Banna Borka [T. Fitzpatrick, LL.D.]. 8vo. 2 vols. [S. J. Brown's *Ireland in fiction*, p. 90.] Dublin, 1887

J'ACCUSE. By a German [Dr Richard Grelling]. Translated by Alexander Grey. 8vo. London, 1915

Attributed also to —— Spitteler.

This work treats of the origin of the Great War.

JACK and I in Lotus Land. By the author of *The lady of the decoration* [Mrs Frances Caldwell Macaulay, *née* Little]. 8vo. [*Amer. Cat.*] London, 1922

JACK and Mrs Brown; and other stories. By the author of *Blindfits* [Elizabeth Taylor]. 8vo. [*Brit. Mus.*] Edinburgh, 1879

JACK and the tanner of Wymondham; a tale of the time of Edward the Sixth. By the author of *Mary Powell* [Anne Manning, later Mrs Rathbone]. 8vo. Pp. 118. [*Brit. Mus.*] London, 1854

JACK Arcombe; the story of a waif. By Glance Gaylord [Warren Ives Bradley]. 8vo. [Cushing's *Init. and Pseud.* i. 111.] Boston, 1868

JACK Ariel; or, life on board an Indiaman. By the author of *The Post Captain* [John Dix afterwards Ross]. Second edition. 12mo. 3 vols. London, 1847

JACK ashore. [By Lieutenant the Hon. Edward G. G. Howard.] 12mo. 3 vols. [*D. N. B.* vol. 28, p. 13.] London, 1840

JACK Beresford's yarn. By Harry Collingwood [William J. C. Lancaster]. 8vo. Pp. 402. [*Lit. Year Book.*] London, 1896

JACK Brag. By the author of *Sayings and doings*, etc. [Theodore Edward Hook]. 12mo. 3 vols. [*Brit. Mus.*] London, 1837

JACK Frenchman's defeat [at the Battle of Oudenarde]; being an excellent new song. . . . [By Jonathan Swift.] s. sh. Fol. B.L. [*Brit. Mus.*] [London, 1708?]

JACK Frenchman's lamentation; an excellent new song. . . . [By Jonathan Swift.] s. sh. Fol. [*Brit. Mus.*] [London, 1708?]

JACK Frost and Betty Snow; with other tales for wintry nights and rainy days. [Dedication signed: J. M. and: C. C., *i.e.* J. Mill Chanter and Charlotte Chanter]. 12mo. [*Brit. Mus.*] London, 1858

JACK Frost Christmas stories. By Alix [Alice Brooks]. 8vo. [*Amer. Cat.*] Baltimore, 1905

JACK Gordon, Knight-errant, Gotham, 1883. By Barclay North [W. C. Hudson]. 8vo. Pp. iv. 247. [*Brit. Mus.*] London [1890]

JACK Hornet; or, the march of intellect. By the author of *The adventures of an Irish gentleman* [John Gideon Millingen]. 12mo. 3 vols. [*Brit. Mus.*] London, 1845

JACK Junk; or, the sailor's cruize on shore; a humorous poem, in four cantos, with a glossary. By the author of *The sailor boy*, etc. [William Henry Ireland]. 12mo. [*D.N.B.* vol. 29, p. 36]. London, 1814

JACK Junk; or, The tar for all weathers: a romance of the sea. By the author of *Richard Parker* [Thomas Peckett Prest]. 8vo. [*Brit. Mus.*] London [1857]

JACK Lorimer's holidays. By Winn Standish [Walter Leon Sawyers]. 8vo. [*Amer. Cat.*] Boston, 1909

JACK Malcolm's Log. [By Frederick Chamier.] 8vo. London, 1846

JACK Mason, the old sailor. By Theodore Thinker [Francis Channing Woodworth]. 8vo. [Cushing's *Init. and Pseud.* i. 282.] New York [1840?]

JACK Morning's treasure. By Frank Bailey [Bailey Millard]. 8vo. [*Amer. Cat.*] New York, 1909

JACK o' th' beach; a story for boys. By Morice Gerard [John Joseph Teague]. 8vo. Pp. 160. [*Lit. Year Book.*] London, 1897

JACK; or, the story of a pocket-book. By the author of *The boys of Highfield*, etc. [H. Frederick Charles]. 8vo. Pp. 125. [*Brit. Mus.*] London [1884]

Attributed also to C. F. Higginson.

JACK Pudding; or, a minister made a black-pudding: presented to Mr R. Farmer, parson of Nicholas Church in Bristol. By W. E. [William Erbury]. 4to. [Smith's *Bibl. Anti-Quak.* p. 179.] London, 1654

JACK Sheppard; a drama in four acts [and in prose]. By John Baldwin Buxtone [who dramatised the material of William F. Ainsworth's novel]. 8vo. [*Brit. Mus.*] London, 1837

JACK the fire-dog. By Aunt Lily [Lily F. Wesselhoeft]. 8vo. London, 1911

JACK the giant-killer. By the author of *The comic Latin grammar* [Percival Leigh]; with illustrations by John Leech. 8vo. [*Brit. Mus.*] London, 1844

JACK the Giant Killer; a Christmas masque. By the author of *Blue Beard*, etc. [Joseph A. Atkinson. In verse]. 8vo. Pp. 16. [*Brit. Mus.*] Manchester [1865?]

JACK, the hunchback. By James Otis [James Otis Kaler]. 8vo. [Kirk's *Supp.*] New York, 1892

JACK Webster; a Christian soldier. By E. S. B. [Redna Scott]. 8vo. Pp. 175. [*Brit. Mus.*] London [1899]

JACKDAW (the) of Rheims. By Thomas Ingoldsby [Richard Harris Barham, B.A.]. With twelve illustrations, printed in colours. 4to. Pp. 43. [*Brit. Mus.*] London, 1870

JACKE Drvms entertainement; or, the comedie of Pasqvil and Katherine. [By John Marston, B.A.] 4to. Ff. 36 London, 1616

A satire on Ben Jonson, attributed by R. Simpson to Marston.

JACK'S mate. [A novel.] By M. B. Cox [Noel West]. 8vo. Pp. 320. London, 1899

JACKSON'S recantation; or, the life & death of the notorious high-way-man, now hanging in chains at Hampstead. . . . [By Richard Head.] 4to. No pagination. [*Bodl.*] London, 1674

"This book was written by Richard Head, a bookseller in London."—MS. note by Wood.

JACOB; a poem. By E. S. G. S. [Emily S. G. Saunders]. Obl. 8vo. Pp. 46. [*Brit. Mus.*] London, 1889

JACOB Faithful. By the author of *Peter Simple*, etc. [Captain Frederick Marryat]. 12mo. 3 vols. [*Brit. Mus.*] London, 1834

JACOB Jennings, the Colonist; or, the adventures of a young Scotchman in South Africa. By Janet Gordon [Mrs Janet Hardy, *née* Walker]. 8vo. Pp. 191. [Scott's *Fasti* (second edition), ii. 20.] Edinburgh, 1884

JACOB Winterton's inheritance. [A story.] By the author of *My brother Jack* [Emilie Searchfield]. 8vo. Pp. 159. [*Brit. Mus.*] London, 1892

JACOB wrestling with God, and prevailing; or, a treatise concerning the necessity and efficacy of faith in prayer: wherein divers weighty questions and cases of conscience about praying in faith, are stated and resolved. . . . By one who hath obtained mercy to be a minister of, and sufferer for, the Gospel of Jesus Christ in this hour of temptation [Thomas Taylor]. 8vo. Pp. 196. [*Aberdeen Pub. Lib.*] London, 1663

JACOBINISM; a poem. [By Rev. John Clarke Hubbard]. 4to. [*Gent. Mag.* lxxv. i. 679.] London, 1801

JACOBITE (the); a romance. . . . By Harry Lindsay [Harry Lindsay Hudson]. 8vo. Pp. xi. 338. [*Lit. Year Book.*] London, 1898

JACOBITE (the) conventicle; a poem. [By Richard Ames.] 4to. [*Bodl.*] London, 1692

JACOBITE (the) curse; or, excommunication of King George and his subjects; with some reflections on the same: to which is added, a poem on the Protestant succession. By a lover of the Protestant religion, his countrey, and the Protestant succession [William Wright, minister of Kilmarnock]. 4to. [Wodrow's *Corresp.* i. 624.] Glasgow, 1714

JACOBITE loyalty; or, a letter to North-British Jacobites, about their taking the oaths to King George and the government. [By Patrick Coupar, minister of Pittenweem.] 4to. [Scott's *Fasti.*] Edinburgh, 1724

JACOBITE'S (the) hopes reviv'd by our late tumults and addresses; or, some necessary remarks upon a new and modest pamphlet of Mr Lesly's against the government, entituled, The good old cause: or, lying in truth, &c. [By Benjamin Hoadly.] 8vo. London, 1710

JACOBITE'S (the) journal. By John Trott-Plaid, Esq. [Henry Fielding]. Fol. No. 1-49. [*Brit. Mus.*] London, 1747-8

JACOBITISM (the), perjury, and Popery of High-Church priests. [By John Toland.] 8vo. Pp. 16. [Darling's *Cyclop. Bibl.*] Edinburgh, 1710

JACOB'S Ladder; consisting of fifteene degrees or ascents to the knowledge of God by the consideration of his creatures and attributes. By H. I. [Henry Isaacson]. 12mo. [*D. N. B.* vol. 29, p. 61.] London, 1638

JACOB'S letter; and other stories. By Rowland Grey [Lilian Kate Rowland Brown]. 8vo. Pp. 330. [*Lond. Lib. Cat.*] London, 1889

JACQUELINE. [A novel of English country life.] By John Ayscough [Monsignor Francis Bickerstaffe-Drew]. 8vo. [*Lond. Lib. Cat.*] London, 1918

JACQUELINE. By Théodore Bentzon [Madame Maria Therèse Blanc]; translated from the French. 8vo. [*Lit. Year Book.*] New York, 1893

JACQUELINE; a story of the Reformation in Holland. By Janet Gordon [Mrs Janet Hardy, *née* Walker]. 8vo. [Scott's *Fasti* (second edition), ii. 20.] Edinburgh, 1872

JACQUELINE; a tale. [By Samuel Rogers.] A new edition. 8vo. London, 1814

A later edition gives the author's name.

JACQUES. [A tale of married life.] By George Sand [Madame Amandine L. A. Dudevant]; translated from the French. 8vo. [Haynes' *Pseud.*] New York, 1847

JACQUES Bonhomme; John Bull on the Continent; from my letter-box. By Max O'Rell [Paul Blouet]. 8vo. [*Lit. Year Book.*] London, 1889

JACQUES Bonneval; or, the days of the dragonnades. By the author of *Mary Powell* [Anne Manning, later Mrs Rathbone]. 8vo. Pp. 208. [*Brit. Mus.*] London [1868]

JAIL-BIRDS; or, the secrets of the cells. By Lindon Meadows [Rev. Charles Butler Greatrex]. 8vo. Pp. 143. [*Brit. Mus.*] London [1881]

JAMAICA and its Governor during the last six years. By a Fellow of the Royal Geographical Society [Sir John Peter Grant]. 8vo. [*Brit. Mus.*] London, 1871

JAMAICA as it was, as it is, and as it may be; an authentic narrative of the negro insurrection of 1831. . . . By a retired military Officer [Bernard Martin, senior]. 8vo. London, 1835

JAMAICA enslaved and free. [By Benjamin Luckock.] 12mo. [*Lib. of Col. Inst.* Supp. I. 569.] London, 1868

JAMAICA under the Apprenticeship System. [By the Marquess of Sligo.] 8vo. [*Lib. of Col. Inst.*, Supp. I. 566.] London, 1838

JAMES. [A novel.] By W. Dane Bank [William Henry Williamson]. 8vo. [*Brit. Mus.*] London, 1914

JAMES Chalmers of New Guinea—missionary, pioneer, martyr. By Cuthbert Lennox [John S. Napier]. 8vo. Pp. xv. 208. London, 1902

JAMES Daryll. [A tale.] By Ruth Elliott [Lillie Peck]. Second edition. 8vo. [*Brit. Mus.*] London, 1877

JAMES Dwight Dana. (From the *American Journal of Science.*) [Signed: E. S. D. *i.e.* Edward S. Dana.] 8vo. Pp. 28. [*Brit. Mus.*] [New York, 1895]

JAMES Francis Edward, the Old Pretender. By Martin Haile [Marie Halle]. 8vo. London, 1907

JAMES Gordon's wife; a novel. [By Ellen Clutton-Brock]. 8vo. 3 vols. London, 1871

Testimony from a friend of the author.

JAMES Griffin's adventures in Alaska. By Harry Dee [Harry Edward Dankoler]. 8vo. [*Amer. Cat.*] Milwaukee, 1904

JAMES Merle; an autobiography. Edited [but rather wholly written] by William Black [novelist]. 8vo. Glasgow, 1864

JAMES Ogilvy's experiment. [A temperance tale.] By M. C. Ramsay [Mary Ramsay Calder]. 8vo. Pp. 150. [*Lit. Year Book.*] London, 1906

JAMES Skinner; a memoir. By the author of *Charles Lowder* [Maria Trench]. 8vo. [*Brit. Mus.*] London, 1883

JAMES Veal; or, the man who conquered himself. By the author of *George Wallis and his friends* [Rev. Jonathan L. Stackhouse, M.A.]. 8vo. Pp. 64. London [1869]

JAMES Wallace; a novel. By the author of *Mount-Henneth*, etc. [Robert Bage]. 12mo. London, 1788

JAN Oxber; a novel. By Orme Agnus [John C. Higginbotham]. 8vo. [*Lond. Lib. Cat.*] London, 1903

JANE; a social incident. [A novel.] By Marie Corelli [Caroline Cody]. 12mo. Pp. 148. [*Brit. Mus.*] London, 1897

JANE Austen and her works. By Sarah Tytler [Henrietta Keddie]. 8vo. Pp. viii. 386. [*Lit. Year Book.*] London [1880]

JANE Eyre; an autobiography. Edited by Currer Bell [Charlotte Brontë]. 8vo. 3 vols. [Courtney's *Secrets*, p. 61.] London, 1847

JANE Lomax; or, a mother's crime. By the author of *Brambletye House*, etc. [Horace Smith]. 12mo. 3 vols. London, 1838

JANE Lowe, the wise woman; and the seventh son. By S. W. [Miss S. Warren]. 12mo. [*Brit. Mus.*] London [1862]

JANE Rutherford; or, the miners' strike. By a friend of the people [Sarah Jane Mayne]. 12mo. Pp. 286. [*Bodl.*] London, 1854

JANE Seton, the witch of Edinburgh; or, the king's advocate: a historical drama, in five acts. [By W. D. Baldie.] 8vo. [*Brit. Mus.*] Margate, 1878

JANET; a poor heiress. By Sophie May [Rebecca Sophia Clarke]. 12mo. [Cushing's *Init. and Pseud.* ii. 96.] Boston, 1883

JANET Delille. [A novel.] By E. N. Leigh Fry [Ella Napier Lefroy]. 8vo. 2 vols. London, 1894

JANET Doncaster. [By Millicent Garrett Fawcett.] [*Lib. Journ.* iii. 125.] London, 1878

JANET; or, glances at human nature: the second of a series of tales on the passions. By the author of *Misrepresentation* [Julia Rattray Waddington]. 8vo. 3 vols. [*Nat. Lib of Scot.*] London, 1839

JANET Pytt; or, love for love: a Weymouth story of the fifteenth century. [By John Benjamin Kerridge.] 12mo. Pp. 64. [Mayo's *Bibl. Dors.* p. 251.] Weymouth [1864]

JANET'S home. [By Annie Keary.] 8vo. 2 vols. [*Nat. Lib. of Scot.*] London, 1863

JANI Anglorum facies altera; rendered into English by Redman Westcot [Adam Littleton]. Fol. [*Brit. Mus.*] London, 1683

JANI Anglorum facies nova; or, several monuments of antiquity touching the great councils of the kingdom and the court of the kings immediate tenants and officers, from the first of William the First, to the forty ninth of Henry the Third, reviv'd and clear'd. . . . [By William Atwood.] 8vo. Pp. 266. [*Brit. Mus.*] London, 1680

Ascribed also to George Selden.

JANITA'S cross. By the author of *St Olave's* [Eliza Tabor, later Mrs Stephenson]. 8vo. 3 vols. London, 1864

JANUS on Sion; or, past and to come. By Christian Emanuel, Esq. [George Ensor]. 8vo. Pp. 139. [*Douce Cat.*] London, 1816

Ascribed also to Sir William Drummond, but with less probability.

JANUS; or, the Edinburgh Literary Almanack. [By John G. Lockhart and Professor John Wilson]. 8vo. Edinburgh, 1876

JAPAN. By Pierre Loti [Capt. Julien Viaud]; translated from the French by Laura Ensor. 8vo. [*Lit. Year Book.*] London, 1915

JAPAN, old and new. By Clive Holland [Charles J. Hankinson]. 8vo. Pp. 302. [*Lond. Lib. Cat.*] London, 1907

JAPANESE blossoms. By Onoto Watanna [Mrs Winnifred Eaton Babcock]. 8vo. [*Amer. Cat.*] New York, 1906

JAPANESE chronological tables. Compiled by E. M. S. [E. M. Satow]. 4to. Pp. 54. Yedo, private print, 1874

JAPANESE ideas of London and its wonders, its inhabitants, and their manners and customs; described in a letter to his wife at Yokohama. By a Japanese scout [really S. Cockburn]. 8vo. [*Brit. Mus.*] London, private print [1873]

JAPANESE (a) nightingale. By Onoto Watanna [Mrs Winnifred Eaton Babcock]. 8vo. New York, 1904

JAPANESE (a) romance. By Clive Holland [Charles J. Hankinson]. 8vo. Pp. 338. [*Lond. Lib. Cat.*] London, 1904

JAPANESE (a) victory; and other stories. By Clive Holland [Charles J. Hankinson]. 8vo. London, 1896

JAPHET, in search of a father. By the author of *Peter Simple*, etc. [Captain Frederick Marryat]. 12mo. 3 vols. [*Brit. Mus.*] London, 1836

JE ne parle pas francais. [A tale.] By Katherine Mansfield [Mrs J. Middleton Murry, *née* Kathleen Beauchamp]. 4to. Pp. 25. [*Who's Who in Lit.*] London, 1919

JE ne sçai quoi; or, a collection of letters, odes, etc., never before published. By a lady [Anne B. Poyntz]. 8vo. London, 1769

JEALOUS (the) husbands; a comedy; with the Humours of Sir John Twyford, acted in the Theatre Royal. [A new edition of "The rambling justice; or, the jealous husbands," by John Leanerd, 1678.] 4to. [*Brit. Mus.*] London, 1679

JEALOUSY; a novel. By the author of *Five years in the East*, etc. [Richard N. Hutton]. 8vo. 3 vols. [*Brit. Mus.*] London, 1849

JEAN Berny, sailor. By Pierre Loti [Capt. Julien Viaud]; translated from the French. 8vo. Pp. 312. [*Brit. Mus.*] New York, 1893

JEAN de Kerdren; from the French of Philippe St Hilaire [Madame Jeanne Schultz] by Mrs Waugh. 8vo. Pp. 229. New York, 1893

JEAN Keir of Craigeil. [A novel.] By Sarah Tytler [Henrietta Keddie]. 8vo. Pp. 334. London, 1900

JEAN of the Lazy A. By B. M. Bower [B. M. Sinclair]. 8vo. Pp. 255. [*Eng. Cat.*] London, 1918

JEANIE Wilson, the lily of Lammermoor. By J. D. [Rev. James Dodds, minister in Dunbar]. 8vo. [*Brit. Mus.*] Edinburgh, 1876

JEANIE'S quiet life. By the author of *St Olave's*, etc. [Eliza Tabor, later Mrs Stephenson]. 8vo. 3 vols. London, 1868

JEANNE d'Arc. By C. M. Antony [Catherine Mary Antony Woodcock]. 8vo. London, 1908

JEANNE de Rentaille; Ketchen. [Two tales.] By E. W. L. C. [E. W. L. Cawston]. 8vo. Pp. 122. [*Brit. Mus.*] London, private print, 1896

JEANNETTE Isabelle; a novel. [By George Valentine Cox, M.A.] 8vo. 3 vols. [*Bodl.*] London, 1837

JEANNETTE'S cisterns. [A tale.] By Lynde Palmer [Mary Louise Parmlee, later Mrs A. Peebles]. 8vo. [Cushing's *Init. and Pseud.* i. 224.] Boston, 1881

JEANNIE; or, the flower of Glenburnie. By Isaline [Janet de la Touche]. 8vo. [Cushing's *Init. and Pseud.* i. 139.] London, 1879

JEAN'S opportunity. By Howe Benning [Mrs Mary H. Henry]. 8vo. [Cushing's *Init. and Pseud.* i. 34.] New York, 1899

JEHOIADAHS justice against Mattan, Baals priest; or, the Covenanters justice against idolators: a sermon preacht upon occasion of a speech utter'd upon Tower-Hill; wherein you may find his likeness to Mattan rather then to Christ. His place in John ii. 48 charg'd upon himself. . . . By J. H. [Joshua Hoyle, D.D.], minister of the Gospel. 4to. [*Brit. Mus.*] London, 1645

JEHOVAH unveiled; or, the God of the Jews. [By William Skinner, of Kirkcaldy.] 8vo. London, 1819

JEHOVAH'S ancient people, city, and land. [Signed: W. M. *i.e.* Rev. William Marsh.] 8vo. [*Brit. Mus.*] Dublin [1863]

JEHU'S looking-glass; or, true and false zeal delineated. By R. D. [Richard de Courcy]. 12mo. Edinburgh, 1772

JEM Allen; or, Danger Cove. [A Cornish tale. By Mary C. Phillpotts, later Mrs Herbert.] 12mo. London [1875]

JEM Bunt; a tale of the land and the ocean. By "The old sailor" [Matthew Henry Barker, R.N.]. 8vo. Pp. 280. [*Nat. Lib. of Scot.*] London, N.D.

JEM Morrison, the fisher boy. By Ruth Buck [Mrs Joseph Lamb]. 8vo. [*Nat. Lib. of Scot.*] London [1862]

JEMIMA. By Adelaide [Elizabeth Bogart]. 12mo. New York [1860?]

JEMIMA Placid; or, the advantages of good nature. . . . [By Dorothy Kilner.] 12mo. [*Brit. Mus.*] London [1780]

JENNIE Juneiana; talks on women's topics. By Jennie June [Mrs Jane Cunningham Croly]. 8vo. [Cushing's *Init. and Pseud.* i. 144.] Boston, 1864

JENNIE June's American cookery-book, containing upwards of twelve hundred . . . receipts. . . . [By Mrs Jane Cunningham Croly.] 8vo. New York, 1867

JENNIE of "The Prince's"; a novel. By B. H. B. [Mrs Bertha H. Buxton, *née* Leupold]. 8vo. 3 vols. [*D. N. B.* vol. 8, p. 105.] London, 1876

JENNIE; or, the flower of Glenburnie. By Isaline [Janet de la Touche]. 8vo. [*Lib. Journ.* v. 54.] London, 1879

JENNY Dear. [A novel.] By the author of *A Fellow of Trinity* [Mrs Frances Marshall]. 8vo. Pp. 240. [*Lond. Lib. Cat.*] London [1894]

JENNY Essenden. [A novel. By Miss A. R. Weekes.] 8vo. London, 1922

JENNY (the) Lind mania in Boston; or, a sequel to Barnum's Parnassus. By Asmodeus [Thaddeus W. Meighan]. 8vo. [Cushing's *Init. and Pseud.* i. 20.] Boston, 1850

JENNY Wren up to date; and other poems. By Marcus Whitethorn [M. A. Pilley]. 8vo. London, 1903

JENNY Wren's boarding-house; a story of news-boy life in New York. By James Otis [James Otis Kaler]. 8vo. Pp. 173. [Kirk's *Supp.*] Boston, 1893

JENSEN'S Fair Isle; translated from the German by a Shetlander [Miss Irvine]. 8vo. Kirkwall, 1881

JEPHTHA; an oratorio. [By Rev. John Hoadly, LL.D.] 8vo. [*D. N. B.* vol. 27, p. 22.] London, 1737

JEPHTHA; an oratorio, or sacred drama as it is performed at the Theatre Royal in Covent Garden. [By Thomas Morell.] Set to musick by Mr Handel. 4to. [*Brit. Mus.*] London [1751?]

JEPHTHA; or, the vow: a tragedy, by [George] Buchanan; translated from the Latin by C. C. [Charles Chorley, newspaper editor]. 12mo. Pp. 48. [Boase and Courtney's *Bibl. Corn.*] Truro, 1854

JEPTHA; a dramatic poem. By a lady [Mrs —— Salmon]. 8vo. London, 1846

JEREMIAS redivivus; or, an elegiacall lamentation on the death of our English Josias, Charles the First, King of Great Britaine, etc., publiquely murdered by his Calvino-judaicall subjects. [Ascribed to Walter Mountacute.] 4to. [*Brit. Mus.*] [London] 1649

JERICHO (the) road; a story. . . . By the author of *Helen's Babies* [John Habberton]. 8vo. [*Brit. Mus.*] London [1877]

JERKS in from short-leg. By Quid [Robert Allan Fitzgerald]. Illustrated by W. H. Du Bellew, Esq. 4to. Pp. iii. 137. [*Camb. Univ. Lib.*] London, 1866

JERNINGHAM; or, the inconsistent man. [A novel. By Sir John William Kaye.] 12mo. 3 vols. [*Brit. Mus.*] London, 1836

JEROME; a novel. By Annabel Gray [Mrs Anne Cox]. 8vo. 3 vols. [*Lit. Year Book.*] London, 1891

JEROME Leaster, of Roderick Leaster and Co. By Litere [Lillian Sommers]. 8vo. New York, 1890

JEROVEAM'S wife; and other poems. [By Robert W. Barbour, M.A.] 8vo. Pp. vii. 138. [*New Coll. Lib.*] London, 1879

JERPOINT. By Matthew Stradling [Martin Francis Mahony]. 8vo. 3 vols. [Cushing's *Init. and Pseud.* i. 275.] London, 1875

JERRY; and other stories. By "The Duchess" [Mrs Argles, later Mrs Hungerford, *née* Margaret Hamilton]. 8vo. Pp. 195. [Cushing's *Init. and Pseud.* i. 84.] Philadelphia, 1889

JERRY; or, the sailor-boy ashore. By Walter Aimwell [William Simonds]. 8vo. [Cushing's *Init. and Pseud.* i. 8.] New York, 1885

JERRY'S family; a story of a street waif in New York. By James Otis [James Otis Kaler]. 8vo. Pp. 195. [Kirk's *Supp.*] New York [1895]

JERSEY (the) boys. By Darley Dale [Francesca M. Steele]. 8vo. [*Lond. Lib. Cat.*] London [1878]

JERSEY (a) witch. By Hilarion [Campbell Mackellar]. 8vo. Pp. 265. [*Brit. Mus.*] London, 1892

JERUBBAAL; or, a vindication of the "Sober testimony against sinful complyances. . . ." [By Rev. Thomas Douglas, M.D.] 4to. [Calamy's *Nonconf. Mem.*, Palmer's ed. i. 171.] London, 1668

The title of the work defended begins "Μαρτύριον Χριστιανόν, or a Christian's sober testimony. . . ." It was published in 1664.

JERUSALEM. By Pierre Loti [Captain Julien Viaud]. Translated from the French by W. P. Baines. 8vo. Pp. 220. [*Brit. Mus.*] London, 1915

JERUSALEM. By T. [William Henry Trenwith]. 8vo. [Cushing's *Init. and Pseud.* i. 278.] Philadelphia, 1866

JERUSALEM and Babel; or, the image of both churches, etc. See "The image of bothe churches."

JERUSALEM as it is. By a converted Jew [Paul Hershon]. 12mo. Manchester, 1857

JERUSALEM (the) Bishopric; reprinted from the *Christian Monthly Magazine and Review*. [By Alexander M'Caul, D.D.] 8vo. [Darling's *Cyclop. Bibl.*] London, 1845

JERUSALEM destroyed; or, the history of the siege of that city by Titus, abridged from Flavius Josephus: together with some brief notices of the Jews since their dispersion to the present period. By the author of *Lily Douglas*, etc. [Miss —— Grierson]. 12mo. [*Brit. Mus.*] Edinburgh, 1826

JERUSALEM (the) sinner saved; or, good news for the vilest of men, being an help for despairing souls: shewing that Jesus Christ would have mercy in the first place offered to the biggest sinners. . . . [By John Bunyan.] 12mo. Pp. xi. 131. London, 1774

JERUSHY in Brooklyn. By Jerushy Smith of Smithville [Anna Olcott Commelin]. 8vo. Pp. 84. New York, 1893

JESHURUN. . . . An elementary paper on our British Israelitish origin. . . . [Signed: E. C. D. *i.e.* Mrs E. Clayton Daubeney.] 8vo. Pp. 24. [*Brit. Mus.*] London [1886]

JESMOND (the) mystery. By Headon Hill [Francis Edward Grainger]. 8vo. [*Lond. Lib. Cat.*] London, 1919

JESS & Co. [A tale.] By J. J. B. [John Joy Bell]. 8vo. Pp. 286. London, 1904

JESSAMINE. By Marion Harland [Mary Virginia Hawes, later Mrs Terhune]. 8vo. Pp. 387. [Kirk's *Supp.*] New York, 1891

JESSICA'S first prayer. By the author of *Bede's charity*, etc. [Sarah Smith]. 12mo. London, N.D.

JESSICA'S mother; a sequel to *Jessica's first prayer.* By Hesba Stretton [Sarah Smith]. 8vo. Pp. 116. London, 1904

See the note to "Alone in London."

JESSIE Dearlove; a story. By Esmé Stuart [Amélie Claire Leroy]. 8vo. [*Lond. Lib. Cat.*] London, 1885

JESSIE Melville; or, the double sacrifice: an Edinburgh tale. [By David Pae.] 8vo. Edinburgh, 1856

JESSIE; or, trying to be somebody. By Walter Aimwell [William Simonds]. 8vo. [Cushing's *Init. and Pseud.* i. 8.] New York, 1885

JESSIE Wills; or, how to save the lost. By "Pansy" [Mrs Isabella Alden, *née* Macdonald]. 8vo. Boston, 1870

JESSY Allan, the lame girl. [A tale. By Grace Kennedy.] Twelfth edition. 12mo. [*D. N. B.* vol. 30, p. 421.] Edinburgh, 1853

JEST (the). [A novel.] By Marjorie Bowen [Gabrielle Vere Campbell, later Madame Constanza Gabrielle Vere Long]. 8vo. Pp. 285. [*Lit. Year Book.*] London, 1922

JEST-BOOK (a). By Mark Allerton [William Ernest Cameron, LL.B.]. 8vo. London, 19—

JESTERS. [A novel.] By "Rita" [Mrs W. Desmond Humphreys, *née* Eliza M. J. Gollan]. 8vo. Pp. 252. [*Lit. Year Book.*] London, 1921

JESTER'S (the) window. [A novel.] By Keble Howard [John Keble Bell]. 8vo. Pp. 280. [*Brit. Mus.*] London, 1907

JESTER'S (the) windows. [A novel.] By Clive Holland [Charles J. Hankinson]. 8vo. [*Lond. Lib. Cat.*] London, 1891

JESTS to make you merie. Written by T. D. [Thomas Dekker] and George Wilkins. 4to. [Lowndes' *Bibl. Man.*] London, 1607

JESUIT (the). [By Carl Spindler.] 12mo. 3 vols. London, 1832

JESUIT (the) in India; addressed to all who are interested in the Foreign Missions. [Signed: W. S. *i.e.* William Strickland, Miss. Ap., S.J.] 12mo. Pp. 227. [Sommervogel's *Dictionnaire.*] London, 1852

JESUIT (the); or, a woman's fall: a tale of real life. By Aylmar de Malton [Hardinge Ivers]. 8vo. Pp. vi. 120. [*Brit. Mus.*] London, 1867

JESUIT (the); or, the history of Anthony Babington, Esq.: an historical novel. By the authoress of *More ghosts*, etc. [Mrs F. C. Patrick]. 12mo. 3 vols. [Watt's *Bibl. Brit.*] London, 1799

JESUIT (the); or, the man of the Morgue. By Ekal Gaolg [J. A. Lake Gloag]. 8vo. Pp. vi. 328. Glasgow [1876]

JESUIT (the) unmask'd; or, some remarks on a letter in the *Daily Post* of January the 31st, which relates to the murder of K. Charles: in which letter, this blasphemous position is advanced, viz., that the murderers of K. Charles were more wicked and inexcusable than the murderers of Jesus Christ! . . . [By Caleb Fleming, D.D.] 8vo. London, 1737

Signed: A Protestant.

JESUIT-CABAL (the) farther opened; or, a defence of the Reverend Dr Chapman's late charge, against the cavils of a declamatory remarker. [By John Chapman.] 4to. Pp. 46. [Orme's *Bibl. Bib.*] London, 1747

JESUITES (the) Catechisme; or, examination of their doctrine; published in French [by Étienne Pasquier] in this present yeare 1602, and now translated into English [by William Watson?] [*Pollard and Redgrave.*] 4to. 1602

JESUITES (the) intrigues; with the private instructions of that Society to their emissaries: the first, translated out of a book privately printed at Paris; the second, lately found in manuscript in a Jesuites closet, after his death. . . . [By Henry Compton.] 4to. Pp. 62. [*Bodl.*] London, 1669

JESUITES (the) policy to suppress monarchy, proved out of their own writings that the Protestant religion is a sure foundation and principle of a true Christian. Written by a person of honor [Charles Stanley, Earl of Derby]. 4to. Pp. 27. London, 1678

The same work, with only a portion of the address "To all supreme powers," and with two addresses "To the reader" (the first, dated 1668, and not written by the author), appeared with the author's name, in 1671, bearing the following title:—"The Protestant religion is a sure foundation and principle of a true Christian, and a good subject, a great friend to humane society; and a grand promoter of all virtues, both Christian and moral." From the second address to the reader, as well as from the title-page of another copy, of the same date, both in the Bodleian Library, we learn that the edition of 1671 is the second one. Of the title or date of the first edition, or whether or not it was anonymous, nothing has been ascertained.

JESUITICAL policy and iniquity exposed; a view of the constitution and character of the Society of Jesus, as it existed prior to 1773; and as it now exists. . . . An essay. . . . [By R. C. Mather.] 12mo. Pp. iv. 43. Glasgow, 1831

Acknowledgment by author in a presentation copy.

JESUITS (the); a historical sketch. [By Edward William Grinfield.] 12mo. [*Brit. Mus.*] London [1851]

JESUITS (the) downefall threatned against them by the secular priests for their wicked lives, accursed manners, hereticall doctrine and Machiavellian policie; together with the life of Father Parsons, an English Jesuite. [By Thomas James, D.D.] 4to. [Bliss' *Cat.* ii. 8.] Oxford, 1612

JESUITS' (the) gospel according to Saint Ignatius Loyola. [By John Sergeant?] Fol. London, 1679

JESUITS in conflict; or, historic facts illustrative of the labours and sufferings of the English Mission and Province of the Society of Jesus in the times of Queen Elizabeth and her successors. . . . By a member of the Society of Jesus [Henry Foley]. First series. 8vo. [*Brit. Mus.*] London, 1873

JESUITS' (the) loyalty, manifested in three several treatises lately written by them against the Oath of Allegiance; with a preface shewing the pernicious consequences of their principles to civil government; also three other treatises concerning the reasons of the penal laws, viz. 1. The execution of justice in England, not for religion, but for treason [by Lord Burghley]. 2. Important considerations, by the secular priests [by William Watson]. 3. The Jesuits reasons unreasonable [by Edward Stillingfleet, D.D.]. 4to. [*Mendham Collection Cat.* p. 290.] London, 1677

JESUITS (the) miracles; or, new Popish wonders; containing the Straw, the Crowne, and the Wondrous Child, with the confutation of them and their follies. [Address to the reader signed: R. P. *i.e.* Robert Pricket.] 4to. No pagination. [*Bodl.*] London, 1607

JESUITS (the) morals; collected by a Doctor of the colledge of Sorbon in Paris, who hath faithfully extracted them out of the Jesuits own books, which are printed by the permission and approbation of the superiours of their Society. Written in French [by Nicolas Perrault], and exactly translated into English [by Ezerel Tonge, D.D.]. Fol. Pp. 392. London, 1670

JESUITS (the). [A volume by William Waterworth] reviewed. By Οὖτις [Rev. James Charles Ward]. Part I. 8vo. [*Brit. Mus.*] London, 1852

No more published.

JESUITS (the); their foundation and history. By B. N. [Benjamin Neave]. 8vo. 2 vols. London, 1879

JESUS Christ the mediator between God and men; an advocate for us with the Father; and a propitiation for the sins of the world. [By Martin Tomkins, dissenting minister.] 8vo. Pp. viii. 171. [Darling's *Cyclop. Bibl.*] London, 1732

JESUS; his opinions and character: the New Testament studies of a layman [George Foster Talbot]. 8vo. Pp. ix. 471. [*Brit. Mus.*] Boston, 1883

JESUS, Maria, Joseph; or, the devout pilgrim, of the ever blessed Virgin Mary, in his holy exercises, affections and elevations upon the sacred mysteries. Published for the benefit of the pious Rosarists. By A. C. and T. V. [Arthur Anselm Crowther, O.S.B., and Thomas Vincent Faustus Sadler, O.S.B.]. . . . 12mo. Pp. 648. [Gillow's *Bibl. Dict.*] Amsterdam, 1657

Another edition was issued in 1663.

JESUS (the) of history. [By Sir Richard Davies Hanson.] 8vo. Pp. xx. 426. [*D. N. B.* vol. 24, p. 312.] London, 1869

JESUS of Nazareth; a tragedy. By George Barlow [James Hinton]. 8vo. Pp. 188. London, 1896

JESUS, the carpenter of Nazareth. By a layman [Robert Bird]. Second edition, revised. 8vo. Pp. xii. 498. [*Brit. Mus.*] London, 1891

JESUS the Messiah. [By Charles Tilstone Beke.] 8vo. [*Brit. Mus.*] London, 1872

JESU-WORSHIP confuted; or, certain arguments against bowing at the name Jesus: proving it to be idolatrous and superstitious, and so utterly unlawfull: with objections to the contrary fully answered. By H. B. [Henry Burton]. 4to. [*Bodl.*] London, 1660

JETHRO; a system of lay agency in connexion with Congregational Churches. [By John Campbell, D.D.] 8vo. [*Camb. Univ. Lib.*] London, 1839

JETHRO Bacon of Sandwich. By J. S. of Dale [Frederick J. Stimson]. 8vo. [*Amer. Cat.*] New York, 1902

JETS and flashes. By Erratic Enrique [Henry Clay Lukens]. 12mo. New York, 1883

JETSAM. [A tale.] By Owen Hall [H. H. Lusk]. 8vo. Pp. viii. 280. [*Lond. Lib. Cat.*] London, 1897

JETSAM; occasional verses. By K. [E. E. Kellett]. 8vo. Pp. 151. Cambridge, 1897

JETTA; or, Heidelberg under the Romans: translated from the German of George Taylor [Professor Adolph Hausrath]. 8vo. 2 vols. [*Brit. Mus.*] London, 1886

JETTISON and general average; notes on the judgment in Dickinson and others *v.* Jardine and others. . . . By D. M. T. [John T. Danson]. 8vo. Pp. 25. [*Brit. Mus.*] Liverpool, 1868

JEW (the). [A novel. By Carl Spindler; translated from the German.] 12mo. 3 vols. London, 1832

JEW (the). By Adolf Meyer [Meyer Aaron Goldschmidt]. 8vo. London, 1845

JEW (the); a poem. By Frederick Cerny [Frederick Guthrie, Ph.D.]. 8vo. London, 1863

JEW (the) and the vintner; a true story. [By Joseph Harry Deeble.] Second edition. 8vo. Pp. 17. [Boase and Courtney's *Bibl. Corn.* i. 112.] [Falmouth] 1853

JEW (the) of Chamant; or, the modern Monte Cristo: a romance of crime. By Ivan Trepoff [George Hatfield Dingley Gossip]. 8vo. Buffalo, N.Y., 1898

JEW (the) of Venice; a comedy, as it is acted at the Theatre in Little-Lincolns-Inn-Fields, by His Majesty's servants. [By George Granville, Lord Lansdowne.] 4to. [Baker's *Biog. Dram.*] London, 1701

Altered from Shakspeare's "Merchant of Venice."

JEW (the) our Lawgiver. [By Thomas Carlyle, advocate.] 8vo. Pp. 15. [G. C. Boase's *Cath. Apost. Lit.*] London, 1853

JEW-DE-BRASS. By Paul Pindar [Thomas C. Newby; a satirical poem]. 8vo. London [1850]

JEWEL (the) and the star. [Poems.] [Preface signed: C. S. *i.e.* Charles Stanley, Plymouthist in Sheffield.] 4to. London, 1855

JEWEL (a) of a girl. By the author of *Queenie*, etc. [May Crommelin]. 8vo. 3 vols. London, 1879

JEWEL (the) of joye. [By Thomas Becon.] 8vo. [*Brit. Mus.*] London [1553]

JEWEL (the) of Ynys Galon. [A novel of Welsh life.] By Owen Rhoscomyl [Owen Vaughan]. 8vo. [*Lit. Year Book.*] London, 1895

JEWEL (the) sowers; a novel. [By Edith Allonby.] 8vo. London, 1904

The author is said to have died in despair of finding a publisher.

JEWELRY and the precious stones. By Hipponax Roset [Joseph Rupert Paxton]. 8vo. [Cushing's *Init. and Pseud.* i. 253.] Philadelphia, 1856

JEWESS (the); a tale from the shores of the Baltic. By the author of *Letters from the Baltic* [Elizabeth Rigby, afterwards Lady Eastlake]. 8vo. [*Brit. Mus.*] [London] 1843

JEWISH fairy tales and fables. By Aunt Naomi [Mrs M. J. Landa, *née* Gordon]. 8vo. Pp. 107. London, 1908

JEWISH literature and modern education; or, the use and misuse of the Bible in the schoolroom. By the author of *The pilgrim and the shrine*, etc. [Edward Maitland]. 8vo. Pp. iv. 97. [*Brit. Mus.*] London, 1872

Preface signed: E. M. Previously printed for private circulation.

JEWISH (the) maiden; a novel. By the author of *Ambition*, etc. [Miss M. G. Lewis]. 12mo. 4 vols. [*Lit. Gazette*, xiv. 256.] London, 1830

JEWISH (the) nation; containing an account of their manners and customs, rites and worship, laws and polity. [By George Stokes.] A new edition. 12mo. Pp. 467. London [1860]

JEWISH (the) naturalization considered, with respect to the voice of the people, its own self-inconsistency, and the disingenuity of its advocates. [By George Coningesby, D.D.] 8vo. N.P., 1753

JEWISH philosophers encountered and confuted. [By Rev. Thomas Collis.] 8vo. [*Leslie's Cat.* 1843 (399).] 1725

JEWISH (the) twins. By Aunt Friendly [Mrs Sarah S. Baker, *née* Tuthill]. 12mo. [Cushing's *Init. and Pseud.* i. 108.] London, 1861

JEWS (the) and the fallacies of the Talmud; the arguments against the Talmud touching the Ten Commandments. By H. D. and A. S. [Henry Ducat, and Aaron Sternberg]. 12mo. Pp. 100. Manchester, 1861

J. F. DIDASCALIAE; discourses on several places of the Holy Scriptures, publikely delivered on sundrie occasions, unto an English congregation of believers in Amsterdam. [By John Ferret.] The first part. 8vo. [*Brit. Mus.*] [Amsterdam] 1643

JILL-ALL-ALONE. [A novel.] By "Rita" [Mrs W. Desmond Humphreys, *née* Eliza M. J. Gollan]. 8vo. Pp. 336. [*Lit. Year Book.*] London, 1914

JILT (the); a novel. By the author of *Cousin Geoffrey*, etc. [Mrs Yorick Smythies, *née* Gordon]. 12mo. 3 vols. [*Brit. Mus.*] London, 1844

JILTED! or, my uncle's scheme; a novel. [By William Clark Russell.] 8vo. [*Lib. Journ.* v. 121.] London, 1875

JIM. [A novel.] By Ismay Thorn [Edith Caroline Pollock]. 8vo. [*Brit. Mus.*] London, 1893

JIM Blake's tour from Clonave to London; illustrated with sketches by E. N. [Erskine Nicol], A.R.A. Photographed by G. W. Wilson; preface and notes by A. A. [Adam Anderson, M.R.I.A.]. 4to. Dublin, private print, 1867

JIM o' the Pan's [James Redfern's] journey to London with the new Poor-Law to mend. By a collector [James Faringdon]. 8vo. [*Brit. Mus.*] Huddersfield, 1842

JIM of the Ranges. [A novel of Australian life.] By G. B. Lancaster [Edith Lyttleton]. 8vo. Pp. 374. [*Brit. Mus.*] London, 1910

JIM the parson. [A tale.] By Agnes Ray [Mrs E. Bedell Benjamin]. 8vo. [*Amer. Cat.*] New York, 1891

JIM the penman; the life-story of one of the most astounding criminals that ever lived. By Dick Donovan [Joyce E. P. Muddock]. 8vo. Pp. 378. [*Lit. Year Book.*] London, 1901

JIMMY; a novel. By John Strange Winter [Mrs Arthur Stannard, *née* Henrietta E. V. Palmer]. 8vo. Pp. 306. London, 1903

JIMMY Swan, the joy traveller. By Hugh Foulis [Neil Munro]. 8vo. Pp. vi. 312. [*Brit. Mus.*] Edinburgh, 1917

JIMMY; the tale of a little black bear. By May Wynne [Mabel Wynne Knowles]. 8vo. Pp. 128. [*Lit. Year Book.*] London, 1910

JINGLES; or, original rhymes for children. By Mary Pelham [Dorothy Kilner]. 12mo. Pp. 60. [*Brit. Mus.*] London, 1808

JITNY and the boys. By Bennet Copplestone [F. Harcourt Kitchin]. 8vo. Pp. 311. London, 1918

JOAN and Mrs Carr. [A novel.] By "Rita" [Eliza M. J. Gollan, later Mrs W. Desmond Humphreys]. 8vo. Pp. 158. [*Lit. Year Book.*] London, 1901

JOAN of Arc. By Mark Twain [Samuel Langhorne Clemens]. 8vo. [*Lit. Year Book.*] London, 1896

JOAN of Arc; a poem *not* awarded the Vice-Chancellor's prize. By Robert Blake [Robert Hely Thompson]. 8vo. London, 1876

JOAN of Arc; a prize poem, recited in Rugby School, June 19, 1846. [By F. T. Conington.] 8vo. Pp. 11. [*Brit. Mus.*] Rugby, 1846

JOAN of Overbarrow. [A novel.] By Anthony P. Wharton [Alister McAllister]. 8vo. Pp. 360. [*Brit. Mus.*] London, 1922

JOAN the curate. By Florence Warden [Mrs George E. James, *née* Florence Alice Price]. 8vo. Pp. 315. London, 1898

JOAN the maid, deliverer of England and France; a story of the fifteenth century. By the author of *Chronicles of the Schönberg-Cotta family*, etc. [Mrs Elizabeth Charles, *née* Rundle]. 8vo. London, 1879

JOAN Vellacot; a novel. By Esmé Stuart [Amélie Claire Leroy]. 8vo. 3 vols. [*Lond. Lib. Cat.*] London, 1888

JOANNA and his reverence. [A novel.] By Max Baring [Charles Messent]. 8vo. [*Lit. Year Book.*] London, 1910

JOANNA of Naples. [A novel.] By the author of *Miriam* [Louisa Jane Park, later Mrs Hall]. Second edition. 8vo. [*Brit. Mus.*] Boston 1838

JOANNA; or, learning to follow Jesus. By Mabel [Mary P. Hazen]. 12mo. [Cushing's *Init. and Pseud.* i. 180.] New York, 1871

JOANNA Traill, spinster. [A novel.] By Annie E. Holdsworth [Mrs Lee-Hamilton]. 8vo. [*Lond. Lib. Cat.*] London, 1894

JOAN'S jolly vacation. [A tale.] By Emilia Elliott [Caroline Emilia Jacobs]. 8vo. [*Amer. Cat.*] Philadelphia, 1909

JOB; or, the Gospel preached to the patriarchs: being a paraphrase on the last ten chapters of the book of Job. By the widow of a clergyman of the Church of England [Mrs Walter Birch]. 8vo. [*Nat. Lib. of Scot.*] London, 1838

JOB paraphrased; a poem. [By M. Porteous.] 12mo. Maybole, 1854

IOB'S pietie; or, the patterne of a perfect man: containing an absolute historie of all the excellencies which ought to be in a perfect man, and being drawne from diuine writ, may serve as a patterne for euery reasonable bodie, whether reall or representatiue, being eyther mightie or meane, rich or poore. . . . R[ichard] H[umphreys]. 4to. [*Pollard and Redgrave.*] London, 1624

JOCABELLA; or, a cabinet of conceits; whereunto are added epigrams, and other poems. By R. C. [Robert Chamberlain]. 12mo. [*Pollard and Redgrave.*] London, 1640

JOCASTA; and The famished cat. By Anatole France [Jacques Anatole Thibault]; translated from the French. . . . 8vo. Pp. 264. [*Lond. Lib. Cat.*] London, 1912

JOCELYN; a tale. By John Sinjohn [John Galsworthy]. 8vo. Pp. 318. [*Brit. Mus.*] London, 1898

JOCELYN Erroll. [A novel.] By Curtis Yorke [Mrs W. S. Richmond Lee, *née* Jex-Long]. 8vo. Pp. 286. [*Lond. Lib. Cat.*] London, 1899

JOCK. [A tale of Scottish life.] By Quintin M'Crindle [Rev. David C. Stewart, M.A., of Currie]. 8vo. Pp. 158. Paisley, 1916

JOCK o' th' Beach; a tale for boys. By Morice Gerard [John Jessop Teague]. 8vo. London, 1896

JOCKEY (the) Club; or, a sketch of the manners of the age. [By Charles Pigott.] 8vo. 3 parts. [*Brit. Mus.*] London, 1792

JOCKEY'S downfall; a poem on the late total defeat given to the Scotish Covenanters, near Hamilton Park, June 22, 1679, by His Majesties forces, under the command of His Highness the Duke of Monmouth, etc. Written by the author of *The satyr against hypocrites* [John Philipps]. Fol. S. sh. [*Bodl.*] London, 1679

The author's name in the handwriting of Wood.

JOCO-PERIO; strange news, of a discourse between two dead giants, expressed in an epigram . . . composed by occasion of a scurrilous pamphlet, intituled, A dialogue between Colbrant and Brandamore. . . . Thereto is added an antidote against all ill news whatsoever. [By] G. W. [George Wither]. 8vo. [*Brit. Mus.*] London, 1661

JOE and the geologist; a short story in the Cumberland dialect. Revised by the author [Alexander Craig Gibson]. 8vo. [*Camb. Univ. Lib.*] Carlisle, 1866

JOE and the Howards; or, armed with eyes. By Carl [Charles S. Newhall]. 8vo. Boston [1875?]

JOE Baker on the one Church. [A tale. By Mrs Gertrude Parsons, *née* Hext.] 12mo. [*Brit. Mus.*] London, 1853

JOE Blake. [A tale.] By E. S. B. [Redna Scott]. 8vo. Pp. 95. [*Brit. Mus.*] London [1900]

JOE Crupper, Bus Conductor. By Thomas Le Breton [T. Murray Ford]. . . . 8vo. Pp. 228. [*Brit. Mus.*] London [1925]

JOE Fulwood's trust. [A tale.] By Silvergren [Eliza Metergard]. 8vo. Pp. 144. [*Lond. Lib. Cat.*] Edinburgh [1883]

JOE Miller's jests; or, the wit's vade-mecum: being a collection of the most brilliant jests, the politest repartees, the most elegant bons mots, and most pleasant short stories in the English language; first carefully collected in the company, and many of them transcribed from the mouth of the facetious gentleman whose name they bear, and now set forth and published by his lamented friend and former companion, Elijah Jenkins, Esq. . . . [By John Mottley.] 8vo. [*Gent. Mag.* Feb. 1821, p. 124.] London, 1739

The second and third editions were also published in 1739, the fourth in 1740, the fifth in 1742, and the sixth in 1743. The collection has been frequently reprinted since. In the list of English dramatic writers appended to Whincop's *Scanderbeg*, published in 1747, it is stated, under Mottley's name, that "the book that bears the title of Joe Miller's jests was a collection made by him from other books, and a great part of it supplied by his memory from original stories recollected in his former conversations." Joe Miller himself was a comic actor, who made his first appearance at Drury Lane Theatre on the 30th April 1715, in "The constant couple"; he died on the 16th of August 1738.

JOE; or, a crisis in Dr Mundum's school; a fiscallegory. By Mark Gordon [Richard Marcus Gordon Dill]. 8vo. Pp. 23. Weybridge [1903]

A political pamphlet issued in defence of Mr Joseph Chamberlain's fiscal policy.

JOE Wayring at home; or, the adventures of a fly-rod. By Harry Castlemon [Charles Austin Fosdick]. 8vo. Pp. 413. [*Brit. Mus.*] Philadelphia [1886]

JOE Wilson's ghost. By John [or rather Michael] Banim. 8vo. [*Brit. Mus.*] London [1870]

A reprint of "The ghost-hunter." (1863).

JOEL Collier redivivus; an entirely new edition of that celebrated author's Musical travels; containing, among a variety of interesting particulars, a faithful account of his many ingenious experiments, valuable discoveries, and inestimable inventions, for the improvement of students, and the advancement of science in this country! . . . [By Alexander Bicknell, the latter part by Peter Beckford.] 12mo. Pp. 84. [*Bodl.*] London, 1818

Ascribed also to Thomas Day, of Annesley, in Surrey, and to George Veal.

JOEL Dorman Steele, teacher and author. By Mrs George Archibald [Mrs George Archibald Palmer, *née* Anna Campbell]. 8vo. [*Amer. Cat.*] New York, 1900

JOE'S oddities; a poetical exhibition. [By Thomas Bedford, vicar of St Paul's, Bedford.] Printed for the author's benefit. 4to. [*Bodl.*] Bedford, 1791

JOE'S place. [A novel.] By John Rosslyn [John William Ross]. 8vo. [*Amer. Cat.*] Philadelphia, 1902

JOESSA. [A novel.] By Ivar Jonnson [C. A. Tibbetts]. 8vo. [*Amer. Cat.*] New York, 1901

JOEY at the fair. By James Otis [James Otis Kaler]. 8vo. [Kirk's *Supp.*] New York, 1906

JOHANNES Godartius. Of insects; done into English and methodized, with the addition of notes. By M. L. [Martin Lister]. 4to. [*Brit. Mus.*] York, 1682

JOHN; a model for Volunteer Captains. [An ironical poem. By Joseph Lewis.] 4to. Pp. 12. Stroud, 1798

JOHN and I. [By Matilda Betham Edwards.] 8vo. [*Brit. Mus.*] London, 1862

JOHN Arnold. [A novel.] By the author of *Mathew Paxton*, etc. [William Wilson, minister of Etal]. 8vo. 3 vols. [M'Guffie's *Priests of Etal.*] London, 1862

Incorrectly attributed to Mrs Oliphant (the author's sister), and to W. Mitchell.

JOHN Beal of Hingham, and one line of his descendants. By N. B. S. [Nathaniel Bradstreet Shurtleff]. 8vo. [Cushing's *Init. and Pseud.* i. 257.] Boston 1865

JOHN Bon and Mast Person. [By —— Luke, a physician.] B. L. 4to. [*W.*] London, 1548, reprinted, London [1807]

This dialogue is a satire on the real presence; by it, the printers were brought into much trouble and narrowly escaped being sent to prison: most of the copies were destroyed. Of the reprint, only two hundred and fifty copies were struck off.

JOHN Brown. By Listener [Joseph Edgar Chamberlin]. 8vo. [*Amer. Cat.*] New York, 1899

JOHN Brown's trouble, and the good that came of it. By a clergyman's daughter [Emma F. Lloyd]. 12mo. [*Brit. Mus.*] London [1863]

Signed: E. F. L.

JOHN Bryant; or, the stag-hunt. By E. S. B. [Colonel Edwyn Sherard Burnaby]. 8vo. [*Brit. Mus.*] London, 1868

JOHN Bull & Co.; the great Colonial branches of the firm. By Max O'Rell [Paul Blouet]. 8vo. [*Brit. Mus.*] London, 1894

JOHN Bull and his island. By Max O'Rell [Paul Blouet]. 8vo. London, 1885

JOHN Bull as a national symbol, his disappearance from German war caricature; "Jock" the Scotsman as the new butt of the Bosche. [Extracts from *The Graphic* signed: J. M. B. *i.e.* J. M. Bulloch.] 8vo. [*Brit. Mus.*] [London, 1916]

JOHN Bull as he was, is, and ought to be . . . A poem. By Peter Pindar, jun. [C. F. Lawler]. 8vo. [O'Donoghue's *Poets of Ireland.*] London, 1814

JOHN Bull in America; or, the new Munchausen. [By James Paulding.] 12mo. Pp. xix. 327. [*Bodl.*] London, 1825

JOHN Bull in his senses; being the second part of *Law is a bottomless-pit.* Printed from a manuscript found in the cabinet of the famous Sir Humphrey Polesworth. [By John Arbuthnot, M.D.] 8vo. [*D. N. B.* vol. 2, p. 65.] Edinburgh, 1712

JOHN Bull, junior. By Max O'Rell. Or, French as she is traduced; enlarged from "Drat the boys." By the author of *John Bull and his island* [Paul Blouet]. 12mo. Pp. xii. 168. [*Brit. Mus.*] London, N.D.

JOHN Bull still in his senses; being the third part of *Law is a bottomless-pit.* Printed from a manuscript found in the cabinet of the famous Sir Humphrey Polesworth: and publish'd, (as well as the two former parts) by the author of the *New Atalantis* [John Arbuthnot, M.D.]. 8vo. Pp. 47. [*D. N. B.* vol. 2, p. 65.] London, 1712

JOHN Bull's atonement; a sequel to the Europa school fight. [By Rev. Henry William Pullen.] 8vo. [*Brit. Mus.*] Winterton, 1871

JOHN Bull's last will and testament, as it was drawn by a Welch attorney: with a preface to the Ar[chbisho]p of C[anterbu]ry. By an eminent lawyer of the Temple [John Arbuthnot, M.D.]. The second edition, corrected by the author's own hand. 8vo. Pp. 24. London, 1713

The preface is signed: Philonomus Eleutherus.

JOHN Bull's scientific (?) "man-machine"; or, American common-sense *versus* Huxley's paradoxical nonsense. By a West-Yankee elf [L. A. Wood]. 8vo. [Cushing's *Init. and Pseud.* i. 305.] Louisville, 1871

JOHN Bull's triumph over his unnatural countrymen; or, the land-holders and the contractors in the dumps. . . . By Peter Pindar, jun. [C. F. Lawler]. 8vo. [O'Donoghue's *Poets of Ireland.*] London, 1814

JOHN Bull's womankind. By Max O'Rell [Paul Blouet]. 8vo. [*Brit. Mus.*] London, 1884

JOHN Buncle, Junior, gentleman. [By Rev. Thomas Cogan, M.D.] 12mo. Pp. 280. [*D. N. B.* vol. 11, p. 222.] London, 1776

JOHN Bunyan. By the author of *Mark Rutherford* [William Hale White]. 8vo. [*Brit. Mus.*] London, 1905

JOHN Carew's daughter. . . . By Ray Cunningham [Frances Browne Arthur]. 8vo. Stirling [1897]

JOHN Charaxes; a tale of the Civil War in America. By Peter Boylston [George Ticknor Curtis]. 8vo. Pp. 289. [Kirk's *Supp.*] Philadelphia, 1889

JOHN Dane. By M. A. D. [Mrs Mary Andrews Denison]. 8vo. [Cushing's *Init. and Pseud.* i. 75.] Boston, 1874

JOHN Denton's friends. By Crona Temple [Miss —— Corfield]. 8vo. Pp. 184. London, 1885

JOHN Drayton; a history of the early life and development of a Liverpool engineer. [By William Wilson, minister at Etal.] 8vo. [M'Guffie's *Priests of Etal.*] London, 1851

Wrongly attributed to Mrs Margaret O. Oliphant (sister of the author). [Courtney's *Secrets*, p. 67.]

JOHN, Earl of Gowrie; a tragedy. [By Robert Brown of Newhall.] 8vo. Pp. 67. Edinburgh, 1825

JOHN Falconer Cryptomenysis patefacta. . . . [Bibliography of the writings of the Falconer family. By Thomas Falconer, County Court Judge.] 8vo. [*Brit. Mus.*] London, private print, 1866]

JOHN Forster. By one of his friends [Percy Hetherington Fitzgerald]. 8vo. Pp. 79. [*Brit. Mus.*] London, 1903

JOHN Gentleman, tramp. [A novel.] By Hermione [Jessie A. N. Forbes]. 8vo. London, 1892

JOHN Gilpin's journey to Edmonton. [A ballad. By William Cowper.] 32mo. [*Brit. Mus.*] London [*c.* 1800]

Other anonymous editions were entitled "The diverting history of John Gilpin . . ."; "Gilpin's rig . . ."; "The history of John Gilpin . . . ," and "The journey of John Gilpin. . . ."

JOHN Grantley's conversion. [A novel.] By Tasma [Jessie Huybers, later Mrs Fraser, later Madame Couvrier]. 8vo. [*Lit. Year Book.*] London, 1890

The author took her pseudonym from Tasmania, where her early life was spent.

JOHN Greenleaf, minister. By Julian Warth [Mrs Julia Warth Parsons]. 8vo. [Cushing's *Init. and Pseud.* ii. 154.] Boston, 1888

JOHN Greswold. By the author of *Paul Ferroll*, etc. [Mrs Archer Clive, *née* Caroline Wrigley]. 8vo. 2 vols. D. N. B. vol. 11, p. 104.] London, 1864

JOHN Gutenberg, first master-printer; his acts, and most remarkable discourses, and his death. [A tale. From the German of Franz Dingalstadt] by C. W. 4to. [*Brit. Mus.*] London, 1860

JOHN Halifax, gentleman. By the author of *The head of the family*, etc. [Dinah Maria Mulock, later Mrs Craik]. 8vo. 3 vols. London, 1856

JOHN Harvey; a tale of the twentieth century. By Anon Moore [James M. Galloway]. 8vo. [*Amer. Cat.*] New York, 1897

JOHN Hatherton. [A tale.] By the author of *Effie's friends* [Lady Augusta M. Noel]. 12mo. Pp. 122. [*Brit. Mus.*] London, 1865

JOHN Helsby's wife; a novel. By Effie Adelaide Rowlands [E. Maria Albanesi]. 8vo. Pp. 288. [*Brit. Mus.*] London [1920]

JOHN Herring; a West-of-England romance. By the author of *Mehalah* [Rev. Sabine Baring-Gould]. 8vo. 3 vols. [*Brit. Mus.*] London, 1883

JOHN Holbrook's lessons. [A tale.] By M. E. P. [Mary E. Palgrave]. 8vo. Pp. 159. [*Brit. Mus.*] London [1880]

JOHN Holdsworth, chief mate; a story. By the author of *Jilted* [William Clark Russell]. 8vo. 3 vols. London, 1875

JOHN Hopkins's notions on political economy. By the author of *Conversations on chemistry*, *Political economy*, etc. [Mrs Jane Marcet]. 8vo. [*D. N. B.* vol. 36, p. 123.] London, 1833

JOHN Hvighen van Linschoten his Discours of voyages into yᵉ Easte and Weste Indies; diuided into foure bookes. Translated out of Dutch by W. P. [William Philip or Phillip]. Fol. [*Brit. Mus.*] London, 1598

JOHN Hunter at Earl's Court, Kensington, 1764-1793. [Introductory note signed: J. J. M. *i.e.* John Jones Merriman.] 8vo. [*Brit. Mus.*] London, 1881

JOHN Huss; or, the Council of Constance: a poem, with historical and descriptive notes. [By William Beattie, M.D.] 12mo. Pp. x. 118. [*Bodl.*] London, 1829

JOHN in Patmos; a poem. By one of the old living poets of Great Britain [Rev. William Lisle Bowles]. 8vo. [*Brit. Mus.*] London, 1832

A later edition (1835) has the title: "St John in Patmos; or the last Apostle. . . ."

JOHN Inglesant; a romance. [By Joseph Henry Shorthouse.] 8vo. 2 vols. [*D. N. B.* Second Supp. vol. 3, p. 509.] London, 1882

The preface to the edition of 1881 is signed: J. H. S.

JOHN Jack. [A tale.] By Lynde Palmer [Mary Louise Parmlee, later Mrs A. Peebles]. 8vo. [Cushing's *Init. and Pseud.* i. 224.] Boston, 1869

JOHN Jasper's secret; a sequel to Charles Dickens' unfinished novel The mystery of Edwin Drood. [By Henry Morford and others.] 8vo. Pp. 408. [*Brit. Mus.*] Philadelphia [1871]

JOHN Jones, an original Welsh character: his history, adventures, and witty sayings. [By Rev. John Davies, of Carmarthen.] 8vo. Pp. 60. [*Bibl. Celt.*, 1910.] Carmarthen, 1910

JOHN justified; a reply to The fight in Dame Europa's School, shewing that "there are always two sides to every question." [By Colonel Charles William Grant.] 109th edition. 12mo. [Green's *Bibl. Somers.* i. 286.] Bath, 1871

JOHN Knox. [A biography.] By Marion Harland [Mrs Mary Virginia Terhune, *née* Hawes]. 8vo. [Kirk's *Supp.*] London, 1900

JOHN Knox and his times. By the author of *The story of Martin Luther*, etc. [Elizabeth Warren]. 8vo. London, 1867

Some copies bear the author's name.

JOHN Lyon; or, from the depths. [A tale.] By Ruth Elliott [Lillie Peck]. 8vo. Pp. viii. 495. [*Brit. Mus.*] London [1904]

JOHN Marchmont's legacy. By the author of *Lady Audley's secret*, etc. [Mary Elizabeth Braddon, later Mrs John Maxwell]. Third edition. 8vo. 3 vols. London, 1863

JOHN Merridew; a romance. By Frederick Arthur [Col. Frederick Arthur Heygate Lambert]. 8vo. London, 1911

JOHN Millington Synge; a few personal recollections, with biographical notes. [By John Masefield.] 8vo. [*Lond. Lib. Cat.*] Letchworth, 1916

JOHN Montcalm. [A novel.] By Morice Gerard [John Jessop Teague, M.A.]. 8vo. [*Lit. Year Book.*] London, 1908

JOHN o' London's little books. Edited by John o' London [Wilfrid Whitton]. 16mo. [*Brit. Mus.*] London [1924, etc.]

JOHN of Gerisau. By John Oxenham [William Arthur Dunkerley]. 8vo. [*Brit. Mus.*] London, 1902

JOHN Oldcastle's [Wilfrid Meynell's] guide for literary beginners. Obl. 8vo. [*Lit. Year Book.*] London [1884]

The title of an earlier edition (1880) begins: "Journals and journalism. . . ." See below.

JOHN Orlebar, clk. By the author of *Culmshire folk* [James Franklin Fuller, architect, Dublin]. 8vo. [*Lib. Journ.* iv. 99.] London, 1878

JOHN Physiophilus's specimen of the natural history of the various Orders of monks. [Translated from the Latin, attributed to Ignace de Borne.] [*N. and Q. Feb.* 1869. p. 169.] London, 1783

Attributed also to P. A. M. Broussonet.

JOHN Pottle, the farmer's man. By Ann Jane [Mrs Ann Jane Morgan]. 12mo. Pp. 32. [*W.*] London [1850?]

JOHN Pringle, printer and heretic. [A tale. By Miss J. K. Grant.] 8vo. Pp. 101. [Cushing's *Anon.*] Paisley, 1883

JOHN Remington, martyr. [A story.] By "Pansy" [Mrs Isabella Alden, *née* Macdonald]. 8vo. Pp. viii. 298. [Haynes' *Pseud.*] London, 1892

JOHN Roxenburgh; or, from socialism to individualism. By New Car [John Arthur Burridge and Florence Burridge]. 8vo. Pp. 272. [*Brit. Mus.*] London [1912]

JOHN Savile of Haysted; a tragedy, in five acts. By the author of *Feudal Times*, etc. [Rev. James White]. 8vo. London, 1847

JOHN Search's past words; with a letter . . . to the . . . Bishop of London. [By Rev. Thomas Binney.] 8vo. [*Edin. Univ. Lib.*] London, 1839

JOHN Sevier as a Commonwealth-builder. . . . By Edmund Kirke [James Robert Gilmore]. 8vo. [Cushing's *Init. and Pseud.* i. 158.] New York, 1887

JOHN Sherman and Dhoya. [A novel.] By Ganconagh [William Butler Yeats]. 8vo. [S. J. Brown's *Ireland in fiction*, p. 258.] London, 1891

JOHN Ship, mariner; or, by dint of valor. By Knarf Elivas [Frank Savile]. 8vo. New York, 1898

JOHN Smith, gentleman adventurer. By Charles Harcourt [Charles Harcourt Ainslie Forbes Lindsay]. 8vo. [*Amer. Cat.*] Philadelphia, 1907

JOHN Topp, pirate. [A novel.] By Weatherby Chesney [Cecil J. Cutcliffe Hyne]. 8vo. [*Brit. Mus.*] London, 1901

JOHN Varney's widow. [A story.] By "Mignon" [Mrs —— Baseley]. 8vo. Manchester [1904]

JOHN Wesley in company with High Churchmen. By an old Methodist [Rev. H. W. Holden]. 8vo. Pp. xii. 158. London, 1869

The authorship is not indicated in the body of the book, but some copies bear the writer's name impressed on the back.

JOHN Wesley; or, the theology of conscience. [By Robert Brown.] 8vo. London, 1868

JOHN Winter; a story of harvests. By Edward Garrett [Mrs Mayo, *née* Isabella Fyvie]. 8vo. Pp. 320. [*Brit. Mus.*] London [1890]

JOHN-A-DREAMS; a tale. [By Julian Russell Sturgis.] 8vo. [*Brit. Mus.*] Edinburgh, 1878

JOHNNY Derrivan's travels. [Sketches of Irish life. By Rev. George Brittaine, of Kilcormack, Ardagh.] 8vo. Pp. 36. [S. J. Brown's *Ireland in fiction*, p. 36.] Dublin [1833]

JOHNNY Gibb of Gushetneuk, in the parish of Pyketillim; with glimpses of the parish politics about A.D. 1843. [By William Alexander, LL.D.] Second edition. 8vo. Pp. viii. 272. [Robertson's *Aberd. Bibl.*] Aberdeen, 1871

JOHNNY Lewison; a novel. By A. E. Jacomb [Agnes E. Jacomb Hood]. 8vo. Pp. 404. [*Lit. Year Book.*] London, 1909

JOHNNY Ludlow. [A novel. By Mrs Ellen Wood.] 8vo. [*Brit. Mus.*] London, 1875

JOHNNY Robinson; the story of the childhood and schooldays of an "intelligent artisan." By "The journeyman engineer," author of *Some habits and customs of the working classes* [Thomas Wright]. 8vo. 2 vols. London, 1868

JOHNNY'S Bible. . . . [By Rev. Herbert Edwards.] 12mo. [Boase and Courtney's *Bibl. Corn.*] Penzance [1875]

JOHN'S [John Hunt's] birthday . . . Aug. 28, 1875; a birthday ode. By E. L. B. [Edward Leman Blanchard]. 8vo. [Cushing's *Init. and Pseud.* i. 24.] London, 1875

JOHN'S letter to Dame Europa, expostulating against being called a coward. [By Sampson Sandys, clerk of Chancery.] 12mo. Pp. 24. [*Brit. Mus.*] London, 1871

JOHNSON and Boswell; rambling remarks on the author of "The Rambler" and his biographer. By W. A. C. [William Alexander Clouston]. 8vo. Pp. 34. [Beveridge's *Dunf. Bibl.*] Dunfermline, 1873

JOHNSON and Garrick. [By Sir Joshua Reynolds.] 8vo. Pp. 15. [Martin's *Cat.*] London, 1816

Two hundred copies were printed for private distribution by Lady Thomond, niece of the author. The following note is from Croker's edition of Boswell's Life of Johnson (vol. iv. p. 169). "Sir Joshua Reynolds wrote two dialogues, in illustration of this position; in the first of which, Johnson *attacks* Garrick, in opposition to Sir Joshua, and in the other, *defends* him against Gibbon. They were originally published in a periodical work, but are preserved in Miss Hawkins' *Memoirs*, vol. ii. p. 110. Lord Farnborough has obligingly communicated to the editor the evidence of the late Sir George Beaumont who had received copies of them from Sir Joshua himself, both of their authenticity, and of their correct imitation of Johnson's style of conversation; and the editor has therefore given them a place in the Appendix."

JOHNSON (the) protocol and international good neighborhood. By Pontoosuc [Ensign Hosmer Kellogg]. 8vo. [*Lib. Journ.* vii. 209.]
Pittsfield, Mass., 1869

JOINED to an idol; a novel. By G. S. M. [Mrs G. S. Morgan]. 8vo.
London, 1872

JOINERIANA; or, the book of scraps. [By Samuel Paterson.] 12mo. 2 vols. [Lowndes' *Bibl. Man.* p. 1224.]
London, 1772

JOINT compositions. [By Franklin and Henry Lushington.] 8vo.
Private print [1840?]

JOINTS in our armour. By a minister of the United Presbyterian Church [Robert Rutherford, M.A.]. Second edition. 8vo. Pp. 63. [Small's *History of the Congregations of the U.P. Church*, i. 589.] Edinburgh, 1884

JOINT-TESTIMONIE (the) of the ministers of Devon, whose names are subscribed; with their reverend brethren the ministers of the Province of London, unto the truth of Jesus; with a breif confutation of the errors, heresies, and blasphemies of these times, and the toleration of them, in pursuance of the Solemn League, and Covenant of the three nations. [By Rev. George Hughes, vicar of St Andrews, Plymouth.] 4to. [Davidson's *Bibl. Devon.* p. 94.]
London, 1648

Signed by 73 of the Clergy of Devon.

JOKEBY; a burlesque on Rokeby: a poem in six cantos. By an amateur of fashion [John Roby, banker in Rochdale]. To which are added, occasional notes, by our most popular characters. 12mo. London, 1813

JOLLY good times; or, child life on a farm. By P. Thorne [Mrs Mary Prudence Smith, *née* Wells]. 8vo. [Cushing's *Init. and Pseud.* i. 283.]
Boston, 1875

JOLLY-BOAT (the); or, perils and disasters illustrating courage, endurance, and heroism in the merchant-marine service. Edited by Lieutenant Warneford, R.N., author of *Tales of the coast guard*, etc. [William Russell]. 8vo. 2 vols. London, 1865

IONAH'S contestation abovt his govrd; in a sermon delivered at Pauls Crosse, Septemb. 19. 1624. By R. V. [Robert Vase]. 4to. [*Pollard and Redgrave.*]
London, 1625

JONAS Brand. [A novel.] By Jane Valentine [Nellie J. Meeker]. 8vo. [*Amer. Cat.*] New York, 1901

JONAS Fisher; a poem in brown and white. [By James Carnegie, Earl of Southesk.] 12mo. [*Brit. Mus.*]
London, 1875

JONAS King, missionary to Syria and Greece. By F. E. H. H. [F. E. H. Haines]. 12mo. Pp. 372. [*Brit. Mus.*]
New York [1879]

JONAS redux; or, a divine warning-piece shot from the fort-royal of Nineveh, to all cities, countries, kingdoms and empires; to exhort them to be careful how they do admit of the dominion of sin within their respective territories, lest they fall into the like danger. [By Sir Henry Iänson.] 4to. [Wood's *Athen. Oxon.* iv. 139.]
London, 1672

JONATHAN and his Continents; rambles through American society. By Max O'Rell [Paul Blouet]. 8vo. [*Lit. Year Book.*] London, 1889

JONATHAN'S home. By Alan Dale [Alfred J. Cohen]. 8vo. [*Amer. Cat.*]
Boston, 1885

JONQUILLE; or, the Swiss smuggler. By T. Combe [Mlle Adèle Huguenin]. Translated from the French by B. L. Tollemache. 8vo. Pp. 283. [*Brit. Mus.*] London, 1891

JORDAN (the) and its valley, and the Dead Sea. [By William Henry Davenport Adams.] 8vo. [*Brit. Mus.*]
London, 1871

JORROCKS'S jaunts and jollities; or, the hunting, shooting, racing, driving, sailing, eating, eccentric, and extravagant exploits of that renowned sporting citizen, Mr John Jorrocks, of St Botolph Lane and Great Coram Street. [By Robert Smith Surtees.] With twelve illustrations by Phiz [Hablot K. Browne]. 8vo. Pp. 358.
London, 1838

Published originally in the *New Sporting Magazine* between July 1831 and September 1834.

JOSEPH; a poem, in nine books. Translated from the French of M. Bitaubé, member of the Royal Academy of Sciences and Belles Lettres of Berlin [by William Beloe]. 12mo. 2 vols. [Lowndes' *Bibl. Man.*]
London, 1783

JOSEPH and Benjamin; a conversation. Translated from a French manuscript [by William Playfair]. 8vo. [Ilmy's *Bibl. of Egypt and the Soudan*, ii. 122.]
London, 1787

JOSEPH and his brethren; a Scriptural drama: in two acts. By H. L. Howard [Charles Jeremiah Wells]. 8vo. Pp. v. 252. [*N. and Q.*, Feb. 1870, p. 154.]
London, 1824

JOSEPH Anstey; or, the patron and the protégé: a story of chequered experiences in life, from youth upwards. By D. S. Henry [Henry Dircks]. 8vo.
London [1863]

JOSEPH in jeopardy. [A novel.] By Frank Danby [Mrs Julia Frankau]. 8vo. Pp. 398. [*Lond. Lib. Cat.*] London, 1912

JOSEPH Jenkins; or, leaves from the life of a literary man. By the author of *Random recollections*, etc. [James Grant, journalist]. 12mo. 3 vols. [*Bodl.*] London, 1843

JOSEPH Mazzini; a memoir. . . . By E. A. V. [Mrs Emilie Ashurst Venturi]. 8vo. [*Brit. Mus.*] London, 1875

JOSEPH Redhorn. By J. J. B. [John Joy Bell]. 8vo. London, 1908

JOSEPH Rushbrook; or, the poacher. By the author of *Peter Simple* [Captain Frederick Marryat]. 12mo. 3 vols. [*Brit. Mus.*] London, 1841

JOSEPH the book-man; a heroi-comic poem in five cantos, depicting some of the humours of life in "Scotia's darling seat": together with a few moral and humorous pieces. By a Gent. [Alexander Anderson]. 12mo. Pp. 154. Edinburgh, 1821

JOSEPH the captive, Joseph the ruler. By the author of *Doing and suffering* [Charlotte Bickersteth, later Mrs Wheeler]. 8vo. Pp. 50. London [1866]

JOSEPH the Jew; a tale founded on facts. By the author of *Mary Mathieson* [Mrs —— Scott]. 8vo. [*Nat. Lib. of Scot.*] Edinburgh, 1857

JOSEPH the Jew; the story of an old house. By Cousin Virginia [Virginia Wales Johnson]. 8vo. [Kirk's *Supp.*] New York, 1875

JOSEPH II. and his court. By Louise Mühlbach [Mrs Clara Müller Mundt]. 8vo. [Cushing's *Init. and Pseud.* i. 199.] New York, 1893

JOSEPH'S little coat. [A tale. By Mrs Frances Marshall.] 8vo. London, 1890

IOSEPH'S party-colovred coat, containing a comment on part of the II. chapter of the I. Epistle of S. Paul to the Corinthians. Together with severall sermons. . . . By T. F. [Thomas Fuller]. 4to. Pp. 190. [*Brit. Mus.*] London, 1640

JOSH Billings' [Henry Wheeler Shaw's] old farmer's allminax, 1870-79. 8vo. [*Amer. Cat.*] New York, 1902

JOSH Billing's [Henry Wheeler Shaw's] spice-box, crammed with droll yarns. 4to. New York, 1881

JOSHUA; a sacred drama. [By Thomas Morell.] . . . Set to musick by Mr Handel. 4to. [*Brit. Mus.*] London, 1754

JOSHUA Haggard's daughter; a novel. By the author of *Lady Audley's secret*, etc. [Mary Elizabeth Braddon, later Mrs John Maxwell]. 8vo. 3 vols. [*Brit. Mus.*] London, 1876

JOSHUAD (the); a poem, in thirteen books: with notes. [By Rev. Johnson Grant, M.A.] 8vo. Pp. viii. 451. [Dobell's *Private prints*, p. 66.] London, 1837

JOSIAH. By the author of *Gideon* [Lady Harriet Howard]. 8vo. London, 1842

JOSIAH Allen's wife as a P.A. and P.I. Samantha at the Centennial. By the author of *My opinions and Betsy Bobbet's* [Marietta E. Holley]. 8vo. Pp. 580. [*Brit. Mus.*] Hartford, Conn., 1878

JOSIAH in New York; or, a coupon from the Fresh Air Fund. By James Otis [James Otis Kaler]. 8vo. Pp. 259. [Kirk's *Supp.*] Boston, 1893

JOSIAH'S alarm; and Abel Perry's funeral. By Josiah Allen's wife [Marietta E. Holley]. 8vo. Pp. 85. Philadelphia, 1895

JOTS. By Guy Thorne [Cyril A. E. Ranger-Gull]. 8vo. Pp. 192. [*Lond. Lib. Cat.*] Bristol, 1897

JOTTING (the) book; a political and literary experiment. By an amateur [James Hall, advocate]. I. — Progressive thoughts on the practical working of the House of Commons before and since the Reform bill; intended as an argument for the genuine finality of that measure; being extracts from the diary of a resolute optimist in all that regards the constitution of England. 12mo. [*Nat. Lib. of Scot.*] London, 1839

The author's name appears in the second edition.

JOTTINGS and sketches at home and abroad. By Australian Silverpen [H. Glenny]. 8vo. Belfast, 1888

JOTTINGS en route to Coomassie, with a map. By an Officer [William Toke Doonar]. 8vo. [*Brit. Mus.*] London, 1874

JOTTINGS from the diary of the sun. [By Matilda Horsburgh.] 8vo. Pp. 96. [*Nat. Lib. of Scot.*] Edinburgh [1868]

JOTTINGS of a 75 days' cruise in the West Indies. By a Rover [Joseph Davies, of Warrington]. 8vo. 2 parts. [*Brit. Mus.*] London, 1887

JOTTINGS of a truth-seeker. . . . [By Arthur Guthrie.] 8vo. Pp. viii. 118. 1887

JOTTINGS of an invalid in search of health, comprising a run through British India, and a visit to Singapore and Java : a series of letters. . . . By Tom Cringle [William Walker]. 8vo. Pp. viii. 273. [*Brit. Mus.*] Bombay, 1865

JOTTINGS on the parish of Fintray [in Aberdeenshire. By Rev. J. Catto]. 8vo. [Mitchell and Cash's *Scot. Top.* p. 51.] Fintray, 1901

JOURNAL (a) kept during a summer tour, for the children of a village school. By the author of *Amy Herbert*, etc. [Elizabeth Missing Sewell]. 8vo. 3 parts. London, 1852

JOURNAL (a), kept on a journey from Bassora to Bagdad ; over the little desert, to Aleppo, Cyprus, Rhodes, Zante, Corfu ; and Otranto, in Italy ; in the year 1779. By a gentleman, late an officer in the service of the Honourable East-India Company [C. Eversfield]. . . . 8vo. [Wrangham's *Cat.* p. 229.] Horsham, 1784

JOURNAL of a deputation sent to the East by the Committee of the Malta Protestant College in 1849. [By Adair Crawford, M.D.] 8vo. [*Brit. Mus.*] London, 1855

JOURNAL (the) of a disappointed man. By W. N. P. Barbellion [Bruce Frederick Cummings]. 8vo. Pp. 322. [*Brit. Mus.*] London, 1919

JOURNAL of a few months' residence in Portugal, and glimpses of the South of Spain. [By Mrs Dorothy Quillinan, *née* Wordsworth.] 12mo. 2 vols. [*Preface to E. Quillinan's poems.*] London, 1847

JOURNAL (the) of a modern lady ; in a letter to a person of quality. By the author of *Cadenus and Vanessa* [Jonathan Swift]. 8vo. Pp. 23. [*Brit. Mus.*] London, 1729

JOURNAL (the) of a naturalist. [By John Leonard Knapp.] 8vo. [*Brit. Mus.*] London, 1829

JOURNAL of a ramble in Scotland. [By Charles Lessingham Smith.] 8vo. Pp. xi. 130. [Dobell's *Private prints*, p. 98.] Cheltenham, 1835

JOURNAL of a regimental officer during the recent campaign in Portugal and Spain, under Lord Viscount Wellington. With a correct plan of the battle of Talavera. [By Lieut.-Col. W. Hawker, 14th Light Dragoons.] 8vo. Pp. 137. [*Mon. Rev.* lxiii. 334.] London, 1810

JOURNAL of a residence in Chili. By a young American [Isaac F. Coffin]. 1817-9. 8vo. [Cushing's *Init. and Pseud.* i. 312.] Boston, 1823

JOURNAL of a soldier [Capt. —— Pococke] of the 71st or Glasgow Regiment, Highland Light Infantry, from 1806 to 1815 [in South America]. 12mo. [Edwards' *Cat.*] Edinburgh, 1819

JOURNAL of a steam voyage down the Danube to Constantinople. [By Robert Snow.] 8vo. [Martin's *Cat.*] London, 1842

JOURNAL (a) of a summer's excursion, by the road of Montecasino to Naples, and from thence over all the southern parts of Italy, Sicily, and Malta, in the year 1772. [By William Young.] 12mo. [Martin's *Cat.*] [*c.* 1774]

JOURNAL of a tour and residence in Great Britain, during the years 1810 and 1811, by a French traveller ; with remarks on the country, its arts, literature, and politics, and on the manners and customs of its inhabitants. [By Louis Simond.] 8vo. 2 vols. Edinburgh, 1815

JOURNAL of a tour from Boston to Savannah, thence to Havana. By a citizen of Cambridge-port [Daniel Nason]. 8vo. [Cushing's *Init. and Pseud.* i. 58.] Cambridge, Mass., 1849

JOURNAL of a tour from London to Elgin, made about 1790 in company with Mr Brodie, younger brother of Brodie of Brodie. By R. L. W. [R. L. Willis]. 12mo. [Sinton's *Bibl. of Hawick.*] Edinburgh, 1897

JOURNAL of a tour in Germany, through the Tyrol, the Salzkammergut, the Danube, Hungary, etc., during the months of August, September and October. [By Frederick John, fifth Lord Monson.] 12mo. Pp. 230. [*W.;* Martin's *Cat.*] [London, 1839]

JOURNAL (a) of a tour in Italy. [By Lady Murray or Lady Clanwilliam.] 12mo. 5 vols. [*Brit. Mus.*] London, private print [1836 ?]

JOURNAL of a tour in Persia, during the years 1824 & 1825. By R. C. M. [Robert Cotton Money]. 8vo. Pp. 256. [*Brit. Mus.*] London, 1828

JOURNAL of a tour in the "Indian Territory" performed by order of the . . . Board of Missions of the Protestant Episcopal Church. . . . By their Secretary [Rev. N. Sayre Harris]. 8vo. New York, 1844

JOURNAL of a tour made by a party of friends, in the autumn of 1825, through Belgium, up the Rhine to Franckfort and Heidelberg, and across the eastern side of France, and Paris. By T. B. [Thomas Brightwell]. 8vo. Pp. 88. [*W.;* Martin's *Cat.*] Norwich, 1828

JOURNAL of a tour made by Señor Juan de Vega, the Spanish minstrel of 1828-9, through Great Britain and Ireland, a character assumed by an English gentleman [Charles Cochrane]. 8vo. 2 vols. [*Nat. Lib. of Scot.*] London, 1830

JOURNAL of a tour; or, three autumn days in Perthshire. [By James Brebner, Rector of Harris Academy in Dundee.] 8vo. Dundee, private print, 1874

JOURNAL of a tour round the Southern coasts of England. [By John Henry Manners, Duke of Rutland.] 8vo. Pp. 236. [Mayo's *Bibl. Dors.* p. 10.] London, 1805

JOURNAL of a tour [by Henry Tattam and Miss Platt] through Egypt, the Peninsula of Sinai, and the Holy Land in 1838, 1839. [By Miss —— Platt.] 8vo. 2 vols. [*Brit. Mus.*] London, private print, 1841, 1842

JOURNAL of a tour through North and South Wales, the Isle of Man, etc. [By John Henry Manners, Duke of Rutland.] 8vo. Pp. 389. London, 1805

JOURNAL of a tour through parts of Germany, Holland, and France. [By John Potter.] 8vo. London [1780?]

JOURNAL of a tour through the Highlands of Scotland during the summer of 1829. [By Beriah Botfield.] 12mo. Pp. xvi. 376. [Martin's *Cat.*] Norton Hall, 1830

JOURNAL of a tour through the Netherlands to Paris in 1821. By the author of *Sketches and fragments*, etc. [Marguerite Gardiner, Countess of Blessington]. 8vo. [*Edin. Univ. Lib.*] London, 1822

JOURNAL of a tour through the Northern Counties of Scotland and the Orkney Isles, in autumn 1797; undertaken with a view to promote the knowledge of the Gospel of Jesus Christ. [By James Haldane.] Second edition. 12mo. [*D. N. B.* vol. 24, p. 14.] Edinburgh, 1798

JOURNAL of a tour to Scotland. [By Rev. Frederick Charles Spencer.] 8vo. Pp. 131. [Martin's *Cat.*] Oxford, 1816

JOURNAL of a tour to the Northern parts of Great Britain. [By John Henry Manners, Duke of Rutland.] 8vo. Pp. 300. [*Bodl.*] London, private print, 1813

JOURNAL of a very young lady's tour from Canonbury to Aldborough, through Chelmsford, Sudbury, and Ipswich, and back through Harwich, Colchester, etc., Sept. 13-21, 1804. Written hastily on the road, as circumstances arose. [By Anne Susanna Nichols. In verse.] 8vo. Pp. 16. [*W.;* Martin's *Cat.*] London, 1804

JOURNAL (a) of a voyage round the world, in his Majesty's ship Endeavour [under the command of Captain James Cook] in the years 1768, 1769, 1770, and 1771; undertaken in pursuit of natural knowledge, at the desire of the Royal Society; containing all the various occurrences of the voyage. . . . To which is added, a concise vocabulary of the language of Otahitee. [By Sir Joseph Banks.] 4to. Pp. 137. London, 1771

JOURNAL of a voyage up the Nile in 1848-9. By an American [Francis Lister Hawks, D.D.]. 8vo. [Allibone's *Dict.* i. 804.] New York, 1850

JOURNAL of a walk from Boston to Washington. By the pedestrian [Edward Payson Weston]. 8vo. [Cushing's *Init. and Pseud.* i. 226.] New York, 1862

JOURNAL of a week in Holland, in the summer of 1824. [By Jonathan Gray.] 8vo. Pp. 16. [Martin's *Cat.*] Hull, 1825

JOURNAL (the) of a West Indian proprietor [Matthew Gregory Lewis]. 8vo. [*D. N. B.* vol. 33, p. 194.] London, 1834

JOURNAL (the) of a young man of Massachusetts [Benjamin Waterhouse, M.D.] captured at sea by the British, May 1813. 8vo. [Cushing's *Init. and Pseud.* i. 313.] Boston, 1816

JOURNAL (the) of an African cruiser; sketches of the Canaries, Cape de Verdes, Liberia, Madeira, Sierra Leone, etc. [By Horatio Bridge, U.S.N.] 12mo. Aberdeen, 1848

An edition of 1853, New York, has the author's name.

JOURNAL of an excursion from Troy, New York, to General Carr's headquarters. By one of the party [William H. Young]. 8vo. [Cushing's *Init. and Pseud.* i. 217.] Troy, N.Y., 1871

JOURNAL of an excursion to Antwerp during the siege of the citadel in December 1832. By Captain the Honble. C. S. W. [Charles Stuart Wortley]. 8vo. Pp. vi. 262. [*Manch. Free Lib.*] London, 1833

JOURNAL (the) of an exile. [By Thomas Alexander Boswell.] 12mo. 2 vols. [*Nat. Lib. of Scot.*] London, 1825

JOURNAL of an expedition overland from Auckland to Taranaki, by way of Rotorua Taupo, and the West Coast; undertaken in the summer of 1849-50, by his Excellency the Governor-in-Chief of New Zealand [Sir George Grey. Written by his assistant private secretary, G. S. Cooper]. 12mo. [*W.*] Auckland, 1851

JOURNAL of an expedition to the Court of Morocco in the year 1846. [By Sir John H. D. Hay.] 8vo. [*Brit. Mus.*]
Cambridge, private print, 1848

JOURNAL of an officer in the commissariat department of the army; comprising a narrative of the campaigns under his Grace the Duke of Wellington, in Portugal, Spain, France, and the Netherlands, in the years 1811, 1812, 1813, 1814, & 1815; and a short account of the army of occupation in France during the years 1816, 1817, & 1818. [By John Edgecombe Daniel.] 8vo. [*Nat. Lib. of Scot.*] London, 1820

JOURNAL (the) of Arthur Stirling; the valley of the shadow. [By Upton B. Sinclair.] 8vo. Pp. xvi. 356. [*Brit. Mus.*] New York, 1903

JOURNAL (a) of eight days' journey from Portsmouth to Kingston-upon-Thames; through Southampton, Wiltshire, etc.; with miscellaneous thoughts, moral and religious, in a series of sixty-four letters, addressed to two ladies of the partie. . . . By a gentleman of the partie [Jonas Hanway]. 4to. Pp. vi. 361. [Dobell's *Private prints*, p. 232.] London, 1756

JOURNAL of excursions through the most interesting parts of England, Wales, and Scotland, during the summers and autumns of 1819, 1820, 1821, 1822 and 1823. [By Elizabeth Selwyn.] 12mo. Pp. 256. [Dobell's *Private prints*, p. 162.]
Private print [1824]

JOURNAL (the) of Llewellin Penrose, a seaman. [By Rev. John Eagles.] 8vo. 4 vols. [*Nat. Lib. of Scot.*]
London, 1815

JOURNAL (a) of meditations for every day in the year, gathered out of divers [Roman Catholic] authors; written first in Latine by N. B. [Nathaniel Bacon, alias Richard Strange, S.J.], and newly translated into English by E. M. [Edward Mico, alias Harvey], in the year of our Lord, 1669. 12mo. Pp. 481. [*Camb. Univ. Lib.*]
N.P., 1669

The name of the compiler is sometimes wrongly given as Robert Southwell, and that of the translator as Edward Meredith. Later editions appeared in 1674 and 1687.

JOURNAL of Mr James Hart, one of the ministers of Edinburgh, and one of the Commissioners deputed by the Church of Scotland to congratulate George I. on his accession to the throne, in the year 1714. [Edited by Principal John Lee.] 4to. [*W.*; Martin's *Cat.*] Edinburgh, 1832

JOURNAL (a) of sentimental travels in the southern provinces of France. [By William Combe.] 8vo. [*Book Prices Current*, 1922.] London, 1821

JOURNAL of six weeks' adventures in Switzerland, Piedmont, and on the Italian Lakes. By W. L. and H. T. [William Longman, publisher, and Henry Trower]. 8vo. [*D. N. B.* vol. 34, p. 123.] London, private print, 1856

JOURNAL (a) of the expedition to Carthagena; in answer to a pamphlet entitled An account of the expedition to Carthagena. [By Tobias George Smollett?] 8vo. Pp. 59. [*Brit. Mus.*]
London, 1744

JOURNAL of the heart. Edited by the authoress of *Flirtation* [Lady Charlotte Bury]. 12mo. Pp. viii. 323. [*Brit. Mus.*] London, 1830

JOURNAL of the Lady Beatrix Graham, sister of the Marquis of Montrose. [A novel. By Charlotte M. Yonge.] 8vo. Pp. viii. 253. [Dobell's *Private prints*, p. 231.] 1870

JOURNAL (a) of the plague year; being observations or memorials of the most remarkable occurrences, as well publick as private, which happened in London during the last great visitation in 1665. Written by a citizen who continued all the while in London. Never made publick before. [By Daniel Defoe.] 8vo. Pp. 287.
London, 1722

Signed: H. F.

JOURNAL of the movements of the British Legion [in Spain]. By an Officer [Major John Richardson]. 8vo. [*Brit. Mus.*] London, 1836

JOURNAL of the proceedings in the detection of the conspiracy formed by some white people, in conjunction with negro and other slaves, for burning the City of New York . . . and murdering the inhabitants. By the Recorder of the City of New York [Daniel Horsmanden]. 8vo. [Cushing's *Init. and Pseud.* i. 248.]
New York, 1744

JOURNAL (a) of the siege of Lathom House in Lancashire, defended by Charlotte de la Tremouille, Countess of Derby, against Sir Thomas Fairfax and other Parliamentarian officers. [By Captain Edward Chisenhall, of Chisenhall.] 4to. 1644

JOURNAL of three years' travels through different parts of Great Britain in 1795, 1796 and 1797. [By John Henry Manners, fifth Duke of Rutland.] 8vo. [*Brit. Mus.*]
London, private print, 1805

JOURNAL (a) relating to the Birmingham riots. By a young lady [M. Russell]. 8vo. Birmingham, 1791

JOURNAL through the counties of Berwick, Roxburgh, Selkirk, Dumfries, Ayr, Lanark, East, West, and Mid Lothians, in the year 1817. . . . By W. G. [William Glover], Haddington. 8vo. Pp. xiii. 294. [Mitchell and Cash's *Scot. Top.*] Edinburgh, 1818

JOURNAL written on board of His Majesty's Ship *Cambridge*, from January 1824 to May 1827. By the Rev. H. S. [Hugh Salvin, chaplain]. 8vo. Newcastle, private print, 1829

JOURNALIST (the); a novel. By H. Ogram Matuce [Charles Francis Keary.] 8vo. [*Lond. Lib. Cat.*] London, 1898

JOURNALS and journalism; with a guide for literary beginners. By John Oldcastle [Wilfrid Meynell]. Second edition. 8vo. Pp. 151. [*Lit. Year Book.*] London, 1880

Another edition begins: "John Oldcastle's guide. . . ." See above.

JOURNALS of the ocean, and other miscellaneous poems. By a seaman [Lieut. —— Weaver]. 8vo. [Cushing's *Init. and Pseud.* i. 263.] New York, 1826

JOURNEY (a) across South America, from the Pacific Ocean to the Atlantic Ocean. By Paul Marcoy [Laurent Saint Cricq; translated from the French by E. Rich]. 4to. [*Brit. Mus.*] London, 1873

JOURNEY (a) from Aleppo to Damascus; with a description of those two capital cities, and the neighbouring parts of Syria: to which is added, an account of the Maronites inhabiting Mount Libanus, etc., collected from their own historians. . . . [By John Green.] 8vo. London, 1736

JOURNEY (a) from Philadelphia to New York. By Robert Slender, stocking weaver [Philip Freneau]. 8vo. [Evans' *Amer. Bibl.* vol. 7, p. 117.] Philadelphia, 1787

JOURNEY (the) home; an allegory. By the author of *The dark river* [Edward Monro]. 8vo. [*Brit. Mus.*] London, 1854

The dark river is not anonymous.

JOURNEY (a) into Spain. [Translated from the French of Antoine de Brunel.] 8vo. Pp. 247. [*Brit. Mus.*] London, 1670

Freely translated and abridged from the "Voyage d'Espagne, curieux, historique et politique, fait en l'annèe 1655," Paris, 1665, 4to, which is anonymous. Wrongly attributed to Aarsens de Sommeldyck.

JOURNEY (a) into the country; being a dialogue between an English Protestant Physitian and an English Papist, wherein the proper state of the Popish Controversy is discoursed. . . . [By Charles Creamer.] 4to. Pp. 38. London, 1675

JOURNEY (a) into the interior of the earth. By Jules Verne. [Translated from the French by Fred. A. Malleson, M.A.] 8vo. London [1876]

JOURNEY of Charles the Tenth from Saint Cloud to Cherbourg; or, an authentic and interesting detail of what happened, from day to day, to him and his suite, from the time they left Saint Cloud up to the moment of his embarking for that hospitable country, Old England. [By Vicomte J. J. de Naylies.] From the French by M. A. 8vo. Pp. 68. Paris, 1830

JOURNEY (a) of discovery all round our house; or, the interview: a companion volume to *Enquire within upon everything*. [By Robert Kemp Philp.] The thirty-second thousand. 8vo. Pp. vi. 378. [Boase and Courtney's *Bibl. Corn.* ii. 494.] London, 1867

The original work appeared in 1856 under the title of "The interview."

JOURNEY (the) of Dr Robert Bongout and his lady to Bath: performed in the year 177—. [By Dr Robert Bragg.] 8vo. [*Brit. Mus.*] London, 1778

JOURNEY (the) of John Gilpin, how he went farther than he intended, and came home safe at last. [A ballad. By William Cowper.] 8vo. [*Brit. Mus.*] London [1784]

Other anonymous editions were entitled "The diverting history of John Gilpin . . ."; "Gilpin's rig . . ."; "The history of John Gilpin . . .," and "John Gilpin's journey. . . ."

JOURNEY (a) of life in long and short stages. By Frank Foster [Daniel Puseley]. 8vo. Pp. 451. [*D. N. B.* vol. 47, p. 53.] London [1866]

JOURNEY (a) overland to India, partly by a route never gone before by any European. . . . By Donald Campbell [Stephen Cullen Carpenter]. 4to. London, 1795

JOURNEY (a) round my chamber. [By Xavier de Maistre.] Translated from the French. 12mo. [*Brit. Mus.*] London, 1818

JOURNEY (a) through Egypt. . . . By M. Granger [M. Tourtechot]; translated from the French by J. R. Forster. 8vo. [*Brit. Mus.*] London, 1773

JOURNEY (a) through England; in familiar letters from a gentleman here, to his friend abroad. Containing what is curious in the counties of Norfolk, Suffolk, Essex, Kent, Sussex, Surrey, Berkshire, Middlesex, London, Buckinghamshire, Bedfordshire, Hertfordshire, Hampshire, Wiltshire, Dorsetshire, Devonshire, Oxfordshire, Worcestershire, . . . [By John Macky.] The fourth edition, with large additions. 8vo. 2 vols. [*Bodl.*] London, 1724

JOURNEY (a) through every stage of life, described in a variety of interesting scenes drawn from real characters. By a person of quality [Mrs Sarah Scott]. 12mo. 2 vols. [Brydges' *Cens. Lit.* iv. 292.] London, 1754

JOURNEY (a) through Scotland; in familiar letters from a gentleman here, to his friend abroad: being the third volume, which compleats Great Britain. By the author of *The journey through England* [John Macky]. 8vo. Pp. xxix. 340. [*Bodl.*] London, 1723

JOURNEY (a) through Sweden, containing a detailed account of its population, agriculture, commerce, and finances; to which is added an abridged history of the Kingdom. . . . Written in French by a Dutch officer [—— Drevon], and translated into English by W. Radcliffe. 8vo. [*Edin. Univ. Lib.*] Dublin, 1790

JOURNEY (a) through Switzerland. [By Elizabeth Cavendish, Duchess of Devonshire.] [*D. N. B.* vol. 9, p. 344.] 1796

JOURNEY (a) through the Austrian Netherlands. . . . [By John Macky.] 8vo. [*Brit. Mus.*] London, 1725

JOURNEY (a) to Brighton; supposed to be written by the author of the *Excursion to Weymouth* [James Cecil, first Marquis of Salisbury]. 8vo. [London, 1800?]

JOURNEY to England; with some account of the manners and customs of that nation: written at the command of a nobleman in France. Made English. [Written by William King, LL.D., of Christ Church, Oxford.] 8vo. Pp. 35. [*Brit. Mus.*] London, 1700

JOURNEY (a) to Glasgow; or, the young South country weaver. [By Henry Duncan, D.D., of Ruthwell.] 8vo. [*D. N. B.* vol. 16, p. 166.] Edinburgh, 1821

JOURNEY (a) to Hell; or, a visit to the Devil. In two parts. By the author of *The London Spy* [Edward Ward]. 8vo. [Arber's *Term Cat.* iii. 687.] London, 1700

JOURNEY (a) to London, in the year 1698; after the ingenuous method of that made by Dr Martin Lister to Paris, in the same year, etc. Written originally in French, by Monsieur Sorbiere; and newly translated into English. [Really written entirely by William King, LL.D. of Christ Church, Oxford, as a satire on Dr Lister.] The second edition corrected. 8vo. Pp. 34. [Arber's *Term Cat.* iii. 687.] London, 1699

JOURNEY (a) to nature. [By J. P. Mowbray.] 8vo. [*Amer. Cat.*] New York, 1901

JOURNEY (a) to the Highlands of Scotland; with occasional remarks on Dr Johnson's Tour. By a lady [Mary Anne Hanway]. 8vo. Pp. xvi. 163. London [1777]

JOURNEY (a) to the Simplon, by Lausanne; and to Mount Blanc, through Geneva. By the author of *Letters from Paris in* 1791-2, etc. [Rev. Stephen Weston, B.D.]. 8vo. [*Brit. Mus.*] London, 1818

JOURNEY (a) to the Western Islands of Scotland. [By Samuel Johnson, LL.D.] Pp. 384. London, 1775

Many later editions bear the author's name.

JOURNEY (a) to the world in the moon, etc. By the author of *The true-born Englishman* [Daniel Defoe]. 4to. Pp. 4. [Lee's *Defoe*, p. 69.] Printed at London, and re-printed at Edinburgh, 1705

JOURNEY (a) to the world underground. By Nicholas Klimius [Baron Ludwig de Holberg]; translated from the original. 12mo. Salisbury, 1742

Another translation appeared at London in 1755.

JOVI Eleutherio; or, an offering to liberty. [By Glocester Ridley, LL.B.] 4to. Pp. 27. [*Bodl.*] London, 1745

JOVIAL (the) crew; a comic opera. [By Edward Roome. Adapted from a play by Richard Brome.] 8vo. [*Brit. Mus.*] London, 1731

JOVIALL (the) crew; or, the devill turn'd ranter: being a character of the roaring ranters of these times, represented in a comedie. . . . Written by S. S. [Samuel Sheppard] Gent. 4to. [Lowndes' *Bibl. Man.* pp. 553, 2165, and 2378]. London, 1651

JOVIAN; or, an answer to [Rev. Samuel Johnson's] Julian the apostate. By a minister of London [George Hickes, D.D.] 8vo. [*D. N. B.* vol. 26, p. 353.] London, 1683

This reply was written at the request of Archbishop Sancroft.

JOY and health. By Martellius [H. W. Sheppard]. 8vo. London, 1892

JOY; and other poems. By A. de Younge [Miss A. Watson]. London [*c.* 1860]

JOY; or, the light of Cold-house Ford. By the author of *Queenie* [May Crommelin]. 8vo. 3 vols. [*Brit. Mus.*] London, 1884

JOYCE; a novel. By Curtis Yorke [Mrs W. S. Richmond Lee, *née* —— Jex-Long]. 8vo. Pp. 277. [*Brit. Mus.*] London, 1918

JOYFUL (the) news of opening the Exchequer to the Goldsmiths of London, and their creditors. . . . [By Thomas Turnor.] Fol. [Arber's *Term Cat.* i. 525.] London, 1677

IOYFVLL (the) receyuing of the Queenes most excellent Maiestie into hir Highnesse citie of Norvvich; the things done in the time of hir abode there; and the dolor of the citie at her departure: wherein are set downe diuers orations in Latine, pronounced to hir Highnesse by Sir Robert Wood knight, now maior of the same citie, and others: and certaine also deliuered to hir Maiestie in vvriting: euery of thē turned into English. [By Bernard Garter.] 4to. No pagination. B. L. [*Bodl.*] London [1578?]

The epistle dedicatory signed: B. G.

JOYFULL tidings to the begotten of God in all; with a few words of counsell unto Friends concerning marriage. W. S. [William Smith of Besthorp]. 4to. [Smith's *Cat. of Friends' Books.*] 1664

JOYS and sorrows; where to find, and how to exchange them: comprising Agnes, or, a word for woman; conjugal responsibility; Dan Darwin's home, . . . and other poems. By the authoress of *Amy of the Peak* [Jane M. Bingham]. 8vo. [Smith's *Cat. of Friends' Books*, i. 270.] London, N.D.

JUBAL; a poem, in six cantos. By M. E. M. J. [Margaret Elizabeth Mary Jones], author of *Waldenberg*. 8vo. Pp. viii. 112. [*N. and Q.* 1857, p. 71.] London, 1839

JUBILEE days; an illustrated record of the humorous features of the World's Peace Jubilee. [Edited by Thomas Bailey Aldrich and William Dean Howells.] 8vo. Boston, 1872

JUBILEE essays; a plea for an unselfish life. By Spriggs [Rev. Edward Payson Tenney]. 8vo. [Cushing's *Init. and Pseud.* i. 273.] Boston, 1862

JUBILEE (a) garland from the banks o' Ugie. [By Robert Grant.] 12mo. [*Aberd. Free Lib.*] Peterhead, 1887

JUBILEE (the) guide to Jersey. By a modern Troubadour [Patrick O'Carroll]. 8vo. Pp. 47. [O'Donoghue's *Poets of Ireland.*] Jersey, 1887

JUCKLINS (the); a novel. By the Arkansan traveller [Opie P. Read]. 8vo. Pp. 291. [Kirk's *Supp.*] Chicago, 1896

JUDÆA capta; an historical sketch of the siege and destruction of Jerusalem by the Romans. By Charlotte Elizabeth [Mrs Charlotte Elizabeth Tonna, *née* Browne]. 8vo. Pp. 296. [*D. N. B.* vol. 57, p. 34.] London, 1845

JUDAEO-CHRISTIAN (the) theory of "The Cosmos," of the ages, and more particularly of "The Kingdom of the heavens." . . . [By Rev. Francis John Bodfield Hooper.] 8vo. [*Brit. Mus.*] London [1875]

JUDAH Pyecroft, Puritan; a romance of the Restoration. By Harry Lindsay [Harry Lindsay Hudson]. 8vo. [*Lit. Year Book.*] London, 1902

JUDAH'S lion. By Charlotte Elizabeth [Mrs Charlotte Elizabeth Tonna, *née* Browne]. 8vo. Pp. 433. London, 1843

JUDAS his thirty pieces not received, but sent back to him for his own bag; who hath betrayed the Lord of glory, and sold his Master, and crucified Christ afresh, and put him to open shame, and now liveth wantonly upon the earth, and hath killed the just: being something by way of answer to a letter that was sent to John Reynes, merchant of London, from Robert Rich, in Barbadoes, which was for the distribution of a certain sum of money to saeven Churches, as he calls them. . . . [By John Bolton.] 4to. Pp. 16. [Smith's *Cat. of Friends' Books*, i. 38, 294.] N.P., 1668

JUDAS Iscariot; a poem. By C. W. G. [Colonel Charles William Grant]. 8vo. Bath, 1885

JUDAS Macchabaeus; a sacred drama. [By Thomas Morell.] . . . Set to musick by Mr Handel. 4to. [*Brit. Mus.*] London [1746]

JUDAS'S younger brother manifested; or, the false charge of Francis Bugg, the apostate with his sham-dialogue, discovered to be malice, in his preface to his, and B. L. vicar of Banbury's late defaming book, entituled Quakerism drooping. By J. L. [John Love, Junr.]. 4to. [Smith's *Cat. of Friends' Books*, ii. 131.] London, 1704

JUDDOO'S triumph. . . . By a disciple of the Unitarian mission [Jogut Chunder Gangooly]. 8vo. Calcutta, 1857

JUDEA in her desolation, from the Babylonian captivity to the destruction of Jerusalem by the Romans. . . . [By Hannah W. Richardson.] 12mo. [Smith's *Cat. of Friends' Books.*] Philadelphia, 1866

JUDGE (the); a novel. By Rebecca West [Cecily Fairfield]. 8vo. Pp. 430. [*Brit. Mus.*] London [1922]

JUDGE Burnham's daughters. By Pansy [Mrs Isabella (Macdonald) Alden]. 8vo. Pp. 339. London [1888]

JUDGE not; or, Hester Power's girlhood. By E. L. Llewellyn [Mrs Lydia H. Sheppard]. 8vo. [Cushing's *Init. and Pseud.* ii. 90.] Boston, 1867

JUDGED by his words; an attempt to weigh a certain kind of evidence respecting Christ. [By Thomas Gribble]. 8vo. Pp. 331. [*Bodl.*] London, 1870

IVDGEMENT (the) of a most reverend and learned man from beyond the seas concerning a threefold order of bishops; with a declaration of certaine other waightie points, concerning the discipline and governement of the chvrch. [By Theodore Beza. Translated by John Field.] 8vo. No pagination. [*Brit. Mus.*] N.P. [1580]

"And to make Episcopacy shake and to incline the people to change the government of the Church by Bishops into that of Elders, this year [1580] the said disaffected procured the translation into English of Beza's discourse of Bishops in Latin, done as was thought by [John] Field, one of the chief Puritan ministers."—Strype's *Annals*, folio ed., vol. 2. p. 629; 8vo. ed., vol. 2. pt. ii. p. 335.

JUDGEMENT (the) of Martin Bucer concerning divorce; writt'n to Edward the sixt, in his second book of the Kingdom of Christ, and now Englisht [by John Milton]; wherin a late book [by J. Milton] restoring the doctrine and discipline of divorce, is heer confirmed and justify'd by the authoritie of Martin Bucer. To the Parliament of England. 4to. [*W.*] London, 1644

JUDGEMENT (the) of the Ancient Jewish Church. See "The judgment . . . ."

IVDGEMENT (the) of the apostles, and of those of the first age, in all points of doctrine questioned betweene the Catholikes and Protestants of England, as they are set downe in the 39. articles of their religion. By an old student in Diuinitie [Richard Broughton]. 8vo. Pp. 404. [Gillows' *Bibl. Dict.* i. 319.] At Doway, 1632

The epistle dedicatorie signed: R. B. which has been misread as Robert Brerely.

JUDGEMENT (a) of the comet, which became first generally visible to us in Dublin, December xiii., about 15 minutes before 5 in the evening Anno Dom. 1680. By a person of quality [Edward Wetenhall, D.D.]. 4to. Pp. 53. [*Bodl.*] Dublin, 1672

JUDGES' (the) cave; a romance of the days of the Regicides, 1661. By Margaret Sidney [Mrs Harriett Mulford Lothrop, *née* Stone]. 8vo. [Cushing's *Init. and Pseud.* i. 267.] Boston, 1900

JUDGES' expenses on circuit in 1707. [By Stacey Grimaldi.] From *The Legal Observer.* 8vo. [*Brit. Mus.*] [London, 1838]

JUDGING for ourselves; or, free-thinking the great duty of religion: display'd in two lectures delivered at Plaisterers'-Hall. By P. A. [Peter Annet], minister of the Gospel. 8vo. [*D. N. B.* vol. 2, p. 9.] London, 1739

Included in "A Collection of tracts of a certain Free Enquirer. . . ."

JUDGMENT (the); a vision [in verse]. By the author of *Percy's masque* [James Abraham Hillhouse]. 8vo. [*Brit. Mus.*] New York, 1821

JUDGMENT and mercy for afflicted souls; or, meditations, soliloquies, and prayers. By Francis Quarles. A new edition; with a biographical and critical introduction, by Reginalde Wolfe, Esq. [Thomas Frognall Dibdin, D.D.]. 8vo. Pp. lxiv. 332. [*Camb. Univ. Lib.*] London, 1807

"The year 1807 was one of unusual occupation with me. At its close, I edited a small volume of great moral and devotional excellence, written by the well-known Francis Quarles, about the middle of the seventeenth century, under the title of 'Judgment and mercy for afflicted souls, or meditations, soliloquies, and prayers.' It was edited under the feigned name of Reginald Wolfe, Esq.—a King's printer in the reign of Henry VIII., and contained a biographical and critical introduction. . . .

"The book was printed by Gosnall, upon miserable paper, having a black and red title-page; and is now so scarce, that I know not where a copy may be found."—Dibdin, *Reminiscences of a literary life*, i. 258.

IVDGMENT (the) of a catholicke English-man, living in banishment for his religion: written to his priuate friend in England: concerninge a late booke [by King James I.] set forth, and entituled; Triplici nodo, triplex cuneus, or, an apologie for the oath of allegiance. Against two breves of Pope Pavlvs V. to the Catholickes of England; & a letter of Cardinall Bellarmine to M. George Blackwell, Arch-priest. Wherin, the said oath is shewed to be vnlawfull vnto a Catholicke conscience; for so much, as it conteyneth sundry clauses repugnant to his religion. [By Robert Parsons.] 4to. Pp. 128. [Oliver's *Collections.*] St Omer, 1608

JUDGMENT (the) of an anonymous writer, concerning these following particulars. I. A law for disabling a Papist to inherit the Crown. II. The execution of penal laws against Protestant dissenters. III. A bill of comprehension. All briefly discussed in a letter sent from beyond the seas to a Dissenter, ten years ago. [By George Hickes, D.D.] Second edition. 4to. Pp. 30. [*Bodl.*] London, 1684

A new impression, with a preface by Cavel the publisher of the pamphlet, was published in 1674, under the title, "A letter sent from beyond the seas," *q. v.*

Ascribed also to Sir Roger L'Estrange. [*Nat. Lib. of Scot.*]

IVDGMENT (the) of an vniversity-man concerning M. William Chillingvvorth his late pamphlet, in answere to Charity maintayned. [By William Lacey, a Jesuit.] 4to. Pp. 158. [*Bodl.*] [St Omer?] 1639

JUDGMENT (the) of Archbishop Cranmer concerning the peoples right to, and discreet use of the H. Scriptures. [By Edward Gee.] 4to. Pp. 16. [*D. N. B.* vol. 21, p. 107.] London, 1689

JUDGMENT (the) of Babylon the Great and the introduction of the Glorious Millennium. By Amariah [M. Pendreich] a member of the Free Church of Scotland. 12mo. Pp. xii. 253. Edinburgh, 1876

JUDGMENT (the) of Dr Prideaux, in condemning the murder of Julius Cæsar, by the conspirators as a most villainous act, maintain'd; and the sophistry in the London journals of December the 2d, and 9th, expos'd. With some political remarks on the Roman government. [By Matthew Tindal.] 8vo. [*Brit. Mus.*] London, 1712

JUDGMENT (the) of God; a romance, from the German of E. Werner [Elizabeth Bürstenbinder]. 8vo. Pp. 162. New York [1889]

JUDGMENT (the) of Hercules; a poem. . . . [By William Shenstone.] 8vo. Pp. 35. [*Manch. Free Lib.* p. 642.] London, 1741

JUDGMENT (the) of King James the First, and King Charles the First, against non-resistance, discovered by their own letters, and now offered to the consideration of Dr Sacheverell and his party. [By John Toland.] 8vo. [*Brit. Mus.*] London, 1710

JUDGMENT (the) of Non-conformists about the difference between grace and morality. [By Richard Baxter.] 4to. N.P. 1678

Reprinted in Baxter's Collected works.

JUDGMENT (the) of Non-conformists of the interest of reason in matters of religion; in which it is proved, against Make-bates, that both Conformists and Non-conformists, and all parties of true Protestants are herein really agreed, though unskilful speakers differ in words. [By Richard Baxter.] 4to. London, 1676

Reprinted in Baxter's Collected works.

JUDGMENT (the) of Non-conformists of things indifferent commanded by authority, as far as the subscribers are acquainted with it; written to save the ignorant from the temptations of diabolism, (described 2 Tim. 3. 3. and 1 Joh. 3. 10. 12. 15. Joh. 8. 44). [By Richard Baxter.] 4to. N.P., 1676

JUDGMENT (the) of Paris; an English burletta, in two acts, as it is performed at the Theatre Royal in the Haymarket. [By Ralph Schomberg.] 8vo. [Green's *Bibl. Somers.* i. 462.] London, 1768

JUDGMENT (the) of the ancient Jewish Church against the Unitarians, in the controversy upon the Holy Trinity and the divinity of our blessed Saviour; with a table of matters, and a table of texts of Scripture occasionally explain'd. By a Divine of the Church of England [Peter Allix]. 8vo. Pp. xxii. 460. London, 1699

In the second edition (Oxford, 1821) the author's name is given.

JUDGMENT (the) of the Bishops of France concerning the doctrine, the government, the conduct and usefulness of the French Jesuits. [By Nathaniel Elliot, *alias* Sheldon, S.J.] 8vo. [Sommervogel's *Dictionnaire.*] London [1763]

JUDGMENT (the) of the Church of England in the case of lay-baptism, and of Dissenters baptism. [By William Fleetwood, D.D.] 8vo. Pp. 50. [*Bodl.*] London, 1712

JUDGMENT (the) of the Fathers, concerning the doctrine of the Trinity, opposed to Dr G. Bull's Defence of the Nicene Creed. [By Thomas Smalbroke.] 4to. [*D. N. B.* vol. 41, p. 282.] London, 1695

JUDGMENT (the) of the foreign Reformed Churches concerning the rites and offices of the Church of England; shewing there is no necessity of alterations. In a letter to a member of the House of Commons. [By John Willis, D.D., of Trinity College, Oxford.] 4to. Pp. 60. [*Bodl.*] London, 1690

The Epistle dedicatory is signed: N. S. the last letters of the author's names.

JUDGMENT (the) of whole kingdoms and nations concerning the right, power and prerogative of kings, and the rights, properties and privileges of the people, etc. [This tract, erroneously attributed to John, Lord Somers, has been assigned to Daniel Defoe and to John Dunton.] 8vo. [Lowndes' *Bibl. Man.*, *s.v. Somers.*] London, 1771

JUDGMENT on Alexander and Caesar; and also on Seneca, Plutarch, and Petronius; translated out of the French [of René Rapin, by John Dancer]. 8vo. [*Bodl.*] London, 1672

See also "The comparison of Plato and Aristotle."

JUDICIAL (the) Committee of the Privy Council, and the petition for a Church Tribunal in lieu of it. A letter by an Anglican layman [Edward Bellasis]. 8vo. Pp. 16. [*D. N. B.* vol. 4, p. 131.] London, 1850

This was followed by a second letter "Convocations and Synods. . . ."

JUDICIAL history of Upper Burma. [By George F. Travers-Drapes.] 8vo. [*Lond. Lib. Cat.*] Bangalore, 1888

Reprinted from *The Mandalay Herald.*

JUDICIUM discretionis; or, a just and necessary apology for the peoples judgement of private discretion, exhibited against the arrogant pretences and imperious suggestions of Tannerus, Valentia, Bellarmine, with other advocates of the papal tyrany; and tendred to the consideration of all those, who would secure themselves against antichristian impostures and delusions. [By John Wilson, or Willson.] 8vo. Pp. 111. [Calamy's *Nonconf. Mem.*, ed. Palmer, i. 326.] London, 1667

"The gift of Mr Wilson, the author."

JUDITH; a chronicle of Old Virginia. By Marion Harland [Mary Virginia Hawes, later Mrs Terhune]. 8vo. [Kirk's *Supp.*] New York, 1887

JUDITH; an oratorio, or sacred drama; in three acts and in verse. By W—— H——, [William Higgins], Esq. 8vo. [O'Donoghue's *Poets of Ireland.*] London, 1733

JUDITH, Esther, and other poems. . . . By a lover of the fine arts [Maria Gowan, later Mrs Brooks]. 8vo. [Allibone's *Dict.*] Boston, 1820

JUGGLER (the). [A tale.] By Charles Egbert Craddock [Mary Noailles Murfree]. 8vo. Pp. 405. [Kirk's *Supp.*] London, 1898

JUGGLERY. By X. [Gerrit Smith]. 8vo. Peterborough, 1867

JUICE (the) of the grape; or, wine preferable to water: a treatise wherein wine is shewn to be the grand preserver of health, and restorer in most diseases. . . . By a Fellow of the College [Peter Shaw, M.D.]. 8vo. Pp. xii. 56. [*Bodl.*] London, 1724

JU-JITSU; what it really is. By Apollo [W. Bankier]. 8vo. London, 1904

JULIA; a poetical romance. By the editor of the *Essay on the character, manners and genius of women* [William Russell, LL.D.]. 8vo. [Watt's *Bibl. Brit.*] London, 1773

JULIA and I in Canada. By the author of *Daphne in the Fatherland* [Anne Topham.] 8vo. Pp. 304. [*Brit. Mus.*] London, 1913

JULIA de Gramont. By the Right Honourable Lady H—— [Cassandra, Lady Hawke]. 8vo. 2 vols. [Park's *Walpole*, iv. 397.] London, 1788

JULIA de Roubigné; a tale: in a series of letters, published by the author of *The man of feeling*, and *The man of the world* [Henry Mackenzie]. Third edition. 12mo. 2 vols. London, 1782

JULIA Domna; a play. By Michael Field [Katherine H. Bradley and Edith Emma Cooper]. 8vo. [*Catholic Who's Who.*] Edinburgh, 1903

JULIA Howard. By Mrs Martin Bell [Mrs Bell Martin]. 8vo. [Cushing's *Init. and Pseud.* i. 33.] New York, 1850

JULIA Ingrand; a tale of Catholicism in Peru. From the Spanish of Martin Palm, by J. W. D. [James William Duffy]. 8vo. 3 vols. London, 1877

The translator's full name is given in a subsequent edition (1878).

JULIA of England; a novel. [By Mrs Norris.] 12mo. 4 vols. [*Biog. Dict.* 1816.] 1808

JULIA; or, last follies. [By Rev. William Beloe.] 4to. Pp. 41. [Martin's *Cat.*] London, 1798

JULIA Ried. [A story.] By Pansy [Mrs Isabella Macdonald Alden]. 8vo. Pp. 288. London [1888]

JULIAN (the) and Gregorian year; or, the difference betwixt the old and new-stile: shewing that the Reformed Churches should not alter their old-stile, but that the Romanists should return to it. [By John Willis, D.D.] 4to. [*Bodl.*] London, 1700

JULIAN Mortimer. By Harry Castlemon [Charles A. Fosdick]. 8vo. [Cushing's *Init. and Pseud.* i. 52.] New York, 1888

JULIAN; or, scenes in Judea. By the author of *Letters from Palmyra and Rome* [Rev. William Ware]. 8vo. Pp. 448. [*Bodl.*] London, 1860

JULIAN the Apostate; and other poems. By D. M. P. [David Morrison Panton]. 4to. Pp. viii. 47. [*Brit. Mus.*] Cambridge, 1891

JULIAN the Apostate; being a short account of his life; and the sense of the primitive Christians about his succession; and their behaviour towards him: together with a comparison of Popery and Paganism. [By Rev. Samuel Johnson, rector of Corrington.] 8vo. Pp. 172. London, 1682

For a reply, see "Jovian . . ."

JUMBLES of jottings from a quiet life. [By Alexander Macdonald.] 8vo. Aberdeen, 1894

JUMPING (the) frog. By Mark Twain [Samuel Langhorne Clemens]. 8vo. [*Lit. Year Book.*] London, 1870

JUMPS in Jura. [By Alexander Russell, editor of the *Scotsman.*] 12mo. [Mitchell and Cash's *Scot. Top.* i. 75.] Edinburgh, 1856

JUNCTION Road United Presbyterian Church, Leith; a sketch of its history from its origin in 1822. . . . By one of the Elders [John Russell]. 4to. Pp. 64. Edinburgh, 1896

From private information.

JUNE; a love story. By Mrs Forrester [Mrs —— Bridges]. 8vo. [*Amer. Cat.*] New York, 1887

JUNGLE larks. By "Gar" [Raymond H. Garman]. 4to. [*Amer. Cat.*] Chicago, 1903

JUNIOR (the) captain. By Elsie Jeannette Oxenham [Elsie Jeannette Dunkerley]. 8vo. Pp. 392. [*Brit. Mus.*] London [1923]

JUNIOR (the) clerk; a tale of city life. By Old Merry [Edwin Hodder]. 8vo. [*Lit. Year Book.*] New York, 1893

JUNIOR (the) Dean; a novel. By Alan St Aubyn [Mrs Frances Marshall]. 8vo. 3 vols. [*Lond. Lib. Cat.*] London, 1891

JUNIUS. Sir Philip Francis denied; a letter addressed to the British nation. [By Olivia Wilmot Serres.] 8vo. [*W.*] London, 1817

The letters are here claimed for the author's uncle, the Rev. James Wilmot, D.D.

JUNIUS discovered. By P. T. Esq. [Philip Thicknesse]. 8vo. [Green's *Bibl. Somers.* ii. 514.] London [1789]

In this pamphlet, the authorship is assigned to John Horne Tooke.

JUNIUS proved to be Burke; with an outline of his biography. [By Patrick Kelly.] 8vo. [*Lond. Lib. Cat.*] London, 1826

JUNIUS unmasked; or, Lord George Sackville proved to be Junius. . . . By Atticus Secundus [Joseph Bolles Manning]. 8vo. [Cushing's *Init. and Pseud.* i. 21.] Boston, 1828

JUNIUS'S Letters; the author mystery solved. By Vicarius [Rev. John Samuels]. 8vo. Pp. 46. London, 1903

JURA cleri; or, an apology for the rights of the long-despised clergy; proving, out of antient, and modern records, that the conferring of revenues, honours, titles, priviledges, and jurisdiction upon ecclesiasticks is consistent with Scripture, agreeable to the purest primitive times, and justified by the vsance, and practise of all nations. By Philo-Basileus Philo-Clerus [William Carpender]. 4to. Pp. 96. [Wood's *Fasti Oxon.* ii. 171.] Oxford, 1661

JURA coronæ; His Majesties royal rights and prerogatives asserted, against papal usurpations, and all other anti-monarchical attempts and practices: collected out of the body of the municipal laws of England. [By John Brydall.] 8vo. Pp. 147. [*Bodl.*] London, 1680

JURA populi Anglicani; or, the subjects right to petition set forth; occasioned by the case of the Kentish petitioners. With some thoughts on the reasons which induced those gentlemen to petition, and of the Commons' right of imprisoning. [By Lord John Somers.] 8vo. [Wilson's *Life of Defoe*, i. 412.] London, 1701

JURE divino; a satyr, in twelve books. By the author of *The true-born Englishman* [Daniel Defoe]. Fol. London, 1706

JURE divino; or, an answer to all that hath or shall be written by republicans against the old English constitution. Part the first, in five chapters, viz. Chap. I. Of monarchy in general, of the English monarchy in particular, the king's power from God only. Chap. II. Power not from the people. Chap. III. Kings are the lawmakers. Chap. IV. Kings of England have no equal, England allows no co-ordination. Chap. V. A short account of the English constitution. [By Henry Gandy, M.A., nonjuring Bishop.] 4to. [*Bodl.*] London, 1707

JURIDICAL letters; addressed to the Right Hon. Robert Peel, in reference to the present crisis of law reform. By Eunomus [John James Park, LL.D.]. 8vo. [*Nat. Lib. of Scot.*] London, 1830

JURISDICTION and practice of the Court of great sessions of Wales, upon the Chester circuit; with preface and index. [By Charles Abbot, first Lord Colchester.] 8vo. Pp. xl. 134. London, 1795

JURISDICTION (the) of the Chancery as a Court of Equity researched, and the traditionall obscurity of its commencement cleared; with a short essay on the judicature of the Lords in Parliament upon appeals from Courts of Equity. [By Roger Acherley.] 8vo. [*Brit. Mus.*] London, 1733

JURISDICTION of the Church over Universities [in Scotland. By Rev. Anstruther Taylor, of Carnbee]. 8vo. [Scott's *Fasti.*] Edinburgh, 1844

JURISDICTION (the) of the Court-leet; exemplifyed in the articles which the jury or inquest for the king in that court is charged and sworn, and by law enjoined, to enquire of and present: together with approved precedents of presentments and judgments in the leet and a large introduction. . . . [By Joseph Ritson.] 8vo. Pp. xxviii. 36. London, 1791

JUS academicum; or, a defence of the peculiar jurisdiction which belongs of common right to Universities in general, and hath been granted by Royal Charters, confirm'd in Parliament, to those of England in particular. . . . By a person concern'd [John Colbatch, D.D.]. 4to. Pp. 44. [*Bodl.*] London, 1722

The author's name is in the handwriting of Rawlinson.

JUS Anglorum ab antiquo; or, a confutation of an impotent libel against the government by King, Lords, and Commons, under pretence of answering Mr Petyt, and the author of "Jani Anglorum facies nova." With a speech, according to the answerer's principles, made for the Parliament at Oxford. [By William Atwood.] 8vo. Pp. 31. [Watt's *Bibl. Brit.*] London, 1681

The speech has separate title and pagination [pp. 27]. See also "Jani Anglorum facies nova."

JUS (the) of Presbyterie; or, a treatise evidently proving, by Scripture, all true ministers or embassadors of the Gospel, to be endued with Divine power from on high, do personate Christ, and are to be heard and esteemed accordingly. [By Clement Writer.] Second edition. 12mo. Pp. 94. [London] 1655

JUS populi; or, a discourse wherein clear satisfaction is given, as well concerning the right of subiects as the right of princes: shewing how both are consistent, and how they border one upon the other; as also, what there is divine, and what there is humane in both. . . . [By Henry Parker, of Lincoln's Inn.] 4to. Pp. 68. [Jones' *Peck*, i. 40.] London, 1644

JUS populi divinum; or, the people's right to elect their pastors; made evident by Scripture, confirmed from antiquity and judgment of foreign Protestant Churches and divines since the Reformation, as also from Books of Discipline, Acts of General Assemblies, and sentiments of our best writers in the Church of Scotland, etc. By a minister of the Church of Scotland [John Currie, minister at Kinglassie]. 8vo. Pp. xv. 164. [*New Coll. Lib.*] Edinburgh, 1727

JUS populi vindicatum; or, the peoples right to defend themselves and their covenanted religion vindicated: wherein the Act of defence and vindication, which was interprised Anno 1666, is particularly justified: the lawfulnesse of private persons defending their lives, libertyes and religion, against manifest oppression, tyranny and violence, exerced by magistrats supream and inferiour, contrare to solemne vowes, covenants, promises, declarations, professions, subscriptions, and solemne engadgments, is demonstrated by many arguments: being a full reply to the first part of the Survey of Naphtaly [by Bishop Andrew Honyman] &c. By a friend to true christian liberty [Sir James Stewart, of Goodtrees]. 8vo. 1669

JUS primatiale; or, the ancient right and preheminency of the see of Armagh, above all other archbishopricks in the kingdom of Ireland, asserted by O. A. T. H. P. [Oliver Plunkett]. 8vo. Pp. 75. [*Trin. Coll. Dub. Lib.* p. 121.] 1672

The initials represent "Oliverus Armachanus totius Hiberniæ Primus."

JUS regium; or, the King's right to grant forfeitures and other revenues of the Crown . . . [By Lord John Somers?] 4to. [*D. N. B.* vol. 55, p. 228.] London, 1701

JUS regum; or, a vindication of the regall power against all spirituall authority exercised under any form of ecclesiasticall government. . . . [By Henry Parker.] 4to. Pp. 38. [Thomason's *Coll. of Tracts*, i. 377.] London, 1645

JUST about a boy. By El Comancho [Walter S. Phillips]. 8vo. New York, 1899

JUST (a) account upon the Account of truth and peace. [By Ezekiah Woodward.] 4to. [Thomason's *Coll. of Tracts*, ii. 140.] London, 1656

JUST (a) and lawful trial of the teachers & professed ministers of England, by a perfect proceeding against them; and hereby they are righteously examined and justly weighed, and truly measured and condemned out of their own mouths, and judged by their own professed rule, viz. the Scriptures; and hereby are proved to disagree, and be contrary to all the ministers of Christ in former ages. . . . By a friend to England's Common-wealth, for whose sake this is written and sent abroad. E. B. [Edward Burrough]. 4to. Pp. 25. London, 1657

JUST (a) and lawful tryal of the Foxonian chief priests, by a perfect proceeding against them; . . . and being brought to the bar of justice, their own ancient testimonies have judged them guilty, and to be no Christians of Christ's making. [By Thomas Crisp.] 8vo. Pp. 130. [*Bodl.*] London, 1697

JUST (a) and modest vindication of the proceedings of the two last Parliaments [of Charles II. By Algernon Sidney, Lord John Somers, and Sir William Jones]. 4to. Pp. 48. [*D.N.B.* vol. 53, p. 228.]

Incorrectly attributed to Robert Ferguson "the Plotter."

JUST (a) and modest vindication of the Scots design, for the having established a colony at Darien; with a brief display how much it is their interest to apply themselves to trade, and particularly to that which is foreign. [By Robert Ferguson, the Plotter.] 8vo. [Ferguson's *Memoir*, p. 333.] N.P. 1699

Wrongly ascribed to James Hodges.

JUST (the) and necessary apologie of Henrie Airay, the late Reverend Provost of Queenes Colledge in Oxford, touching his suite in law for the rectorie of Charleton. [Edited by Christopher Potter.] 12mo. [*W.*] London, 1621

At the end is an Attestation signed: T. W. [Thomas Wilson] with separate pagination.

JUST and sober remarks on some parts and passages of the Overtures concerning Kirk-Sessions, etc.; compiled and printed anno. 1719, and laid before the R. Presbytry of Glasgow March 2d 1720. By J. C. [James Clark] one of the ministers of the Gospel at Glasgow. 8vo. [Scott's *Fasti.*] N.P. 1720

JUST (a) and sober vindication of the Observations upon [commemorating] the thirtieth of January and twenty-ninth of May. By J. G. G. [John Gailhard, Gentleman]. 4to. Pp. 73. [*New Coll. Lib.*] London, 1694

JUST (a) and solemn protestation of the Lord Mayor, Aldermen, etc. of London, against two ordinances of 18 and 20 Dec., for the choosing Common Councell men. . . . [By William Prynne.] 4to. [*Brit. Mus.*] 1648

IUST (a) apologie for the gesture of kneeling in the act of receiving the Lord's Supper; against the manifold exceptions of all opposers in the churches of England and Scotland; wherein this controversie is handled fully, soundly, plainly, methodically. [By Thomas Paybody.] 4to. [*New Coll. Lib.*] London, 1629

JUST (a) apology for His Sacred Majestie; or, an answer to a late lying and scandalous pamphlet, intitled, "Behold two letters," one from the Pope to the Prince of Wales, and the answer. . . . By E. L. [Sir Edward Lake]. 4to. Pp. 8. London, 1642

JUST as I am; a novel. By the author of *Lady Audley's secret*, etc. [Mary Elizabeth Braddon, later Mrs John Maxwell]. 8vo. 3 vols. London [1880]

JUST as it was. [A novel.] By John Strange Winter [Mrs Arthur Stannard, *née* Henrietta E. V. Palmer]. 8vo. Pp. 299. London, 1905

JUST (a) censure of Francis Bugg's Address to the Parliament against the Quakers; published by, and in behalf of the said people. [By William Penn.] 8vo. [Smith's *Cat. of Friends' Books*, i. 46; ii. 318.] London, 1699

JUST (a) correction and inlargement of a scandalous Bill of the Mortality of the malignant clergie of London and other parts of the Kingdome which have been justly sequestred from their pastorall charges . . . since . . . 1641 to this present yeare 1647. . . . By J. V. [John Vicars]. 4to. [*Brit. Mus.*] London, 1647

JUST (a) defence and vindication of Gospel ministers and Gospel ordinances against the Quakers many false accusations, slanders, and reproaches. In answer to John Horwood his Letter, and E. B. [Edward Burrough] his book, called "A just and lawful tryal of the Ministers and teachers of this age, and several others: proving the Ministers calling and maintenance just and lawful, and the doctrine of perfection by free justification, preached by them, agreeable to the Scriptures. . . . By a lover of Gospel ministers and Gospel ordinances [John Gaskin]. 4to. Pp. 320. [Smith's *Anti-Quak.* p. 197.] London, 1660

Signed: J. G.

JUST (a) defence of Charles I. . . . [By Rev. William Baron.] 8vo. London, 1699

JUST (a) discharge to Dr Stillingfleet's vnjvst charge of idolatry against the Church of Rome; with a discovery of the vanity of his late defence, in his pretended Answer to a book entituled Catholicks no idolaters by way of dialogue between Evnomivs, a conformist & Catharinvs, a non-conformist. The first [second and third] part. Concerning the charge of idolatry, etc. [By Thomas Godden, really Tylden.] 8vo. Pp. 529. Paris, 1677

JUST measures; in an Epistle of peace and love to such professors of truth as are under any dissatisfaction about the present order practis'd in the Church of Christ. By G. P. [George Penn]. 12mo. Pp. 21. N.P. 1692

JUST (the) measures of the pious institution of youth, represented according to the maxims of the Gospel, in several essayes. [By George Monro, M.A.] 12mo. 2 vols. [*Brit. Mus.*] Edinburgh, 1700

A second edition, corrected and enlarged, was issued at London, 1711.

JUST ourselves. By Mrs George Norman [Mrs George Blount]. 8vo. Pp. 286. [*Catholic Who's Who.*] London, 1916

JUST reflections upon a pamphlet [by Hugh Clark], entitled, A modest reply to a letter from a friend to Mr John M'millan. Part I. Containing reflections on the reply to the preface; wherein the preface prefixed to the printed letter is defended against the unreasonable clamour of the adversary. . . . By one of the ministers of this present Church [G. Hamilton]. 4to. Pp. 48. N.P. 1712

—— Part II. Containing reflections on the reply to the letter it self; wherein the answers to the queries are examined, and found unsatisfactory: the replyer's arguments, for vindicating Mr John M'millan and other separatists, are weighed, and found light: . . . By the author of the former part [G. Hamilton]. Written in May, anno 1710. 4to. Pp. 68. Edinburgh, 1712

JUST (a) reprimand to Daniel de Foe; in a letter to a gentleman in South Britain. [By James Clark, minister of the Tron Church, Glasgow.] 4to. Pp. 8. [*D. Laing.*] N.P. N.D.

"JUST saved;" or, out of the pit. By R. C. L. [R. C. Lepper]. 12mo. N.P. 1907

JUST (the) scrutiny; or, a serious enquiry into the modern notions of the soul. I. Consider'd as breath of life, or a power (not immaterial substance) united to body, according to the H. Scriptures. II. As a principle naturally mortal, but immortaliz'd by its union with the baptismal spirit, according to Platonisme lately Christianiz'd. . . . By W. C. [William Coward, M.D.]. 8vo. Pp. 221. [Abbot's *Lit. of a future life.*] London [*c.* 1704]

JUST sixteen; a volume of stories. By Susan Coolidge [Sarah Chauncey Woolsey]. 8vo. [Kirk's *Supp.*] Boston, 1889

JUST (the) steward. [A novel.] By Richard Dehan [Clotilde Graves]. 8vo. [*Lond. Lib. Cat.*] London, 1922

JUST (a) view of the constitution of the Church of Scotland, and of the proceedings of the last General Assembly in relation to the deposition of Mr Gillespie. [By John Hyndman, D.D.] 8vo. Pp. 36. [*Nat. Lib. of Scot.*] Edinburgh, 1753

JUST (a) view of the principles of the Presbytery of Relief; being an answer to a pamphlet [by Rev. Thomas Bennett], entitled, Terms of communion of the Scots Methodists, generally known by the specious denomination of The presbytery of Relief. By a lover of the truth in Fife [William Campbell, minister in Dysart]. Second edition. 8vo. [Struthers' *Hist. of the Relief Church* (1843), p. 571.] Edinburgh, 1778

JUST (a) vindication of learning; or, an humble address to the High Court of Parliament in behalf of the liberty of the press. By Philopatris [Charles Blount]. 4to. [*D. N. B.* vol. 5, p. 244.] London, 1679

The writer drew largely on the material in Milton's *Areopagitica.*

JUSTICE (the) and equity of assessing the net profits of the land for the relief of the poor. . . . By a Norfolk clergyman [Samuel Hobson]. 12mo. [*Brit. Mus.*] Norwich [1838]

JUSTICE (the) and expediency of the plan contained in a report addressed by the Right Hon. H. Labouchere, to the Chancellor of the Exchequer, on the subject of the present affairs of Edinburgh and Leith, dated Board of Trade 18th January 1836, examined and considered. By an Edinburgh burgess of 1786 [John Gladstone]. 8vo. Edinburgh, 1836

JUSTICE (the) and policy of the late Act of Parliament for making more effectual provision for the government of Quebec, asserted and proved. . . . [By William Knox.] 8vo. [Jaggard's *Index*, ii.] London, 1774

JUSTICE (the) and utility of penal laws for the direction of conscience examined; in reference to the Dissenters late application to Parliament: addressed to a member of the House of Commons. [By John Fell, Dissenting minister.] 8vo. Pp. 128. [*Nat. Lib. of Scot.*] London, 1774

Signed: Phileleutheros. Also assigned to Joseph Fownes.

JUSTICE for India; a letter to Lord Palmerston. By a plain speaker [—— Redfern]. 8vo. [*Brit. Mus.*] London, 1858

JUSTICE in all its branches; or, a collection of the rules of Scripture that teach men to do justly. [By Samuel Wright, D.D.] 8vo. [*Brit. Mus.*] London, 1731

JUSTICE (the) of our cause in the present war, in respect of what is peculiar to the English, in the matter of civil right. [By Edward Stephens.] 4to. [*Bodl.*] N.P., N.D.

JUSTICE (the) of the present establish'd law, which gives the successor in any ecclesiastical benefice, on promotion, all the profits from the day of avoidance, justified; and a proposal that hath been offered for making an alteration in it, in favour of the predecessor, fully examined and shown to be contrary to charity, justice, the good of the Church, and interest even of those ministers themselves, for whose sake this alteration is pretended to be endeavoured. . . . [By Humphrey Prideaux, D.D.] 4to. Pp. 60. [*Bodl.*] London, 1703

Signed: A. B.

JUSTICE (the) of the present war against the French. . . . By J. E. [Jonathan Ellis]. 8vo. [Cushing's *Init. and Pseud.* i. 85.] Newport, R. I., 1755

JUSTICE revived; being the whole office of a countrey justice; briefly and yet more methodically than ever yet extant. By E. W. [Edmund Wingate] of Grayes Inn, Esq. 12mo. [Wood's *Athen. Oxon.* iii. 426.] London, 1661

JUSTICES (the) of peas; the boke of iustyces of peas, etc. See Boke (the) of iustyces of peas.

JUSTIFIABLE Conformity; a few hints to Protestant Dissenters. . . . By a Dissenter [John Herford]. 8vo. Pp. 16. London, 1834

JUSTIFICATION; a poem. By the author of *The Diaboliad* [William Combe]. 4to. [*Brit. Mus.*] London, 1777

JUSTIFICATION by faith alone. [By Rev. John Berridge, M.A.] 12mo. [Kinsman's *Cat.* No. 25.] London, 1762

JUSTIFICATION justified; or, the whole doctrine of justification stated as sound Protestants and the holy Scriptures do state it; whereby several fundamental truths, always own'd by the Church of England since its Reformation from Popery, are vindicated from the errors and exceptions of Mr William Sherlock. . . . By S. R. [Samuel Rolle]. 8vo. [Calamy's *Nonconf. Mem.* ed. Palmer, i. 298.] London, 1674

JUSTIFICATION (the) of a sinner; being the main argument of St Paul's Epistle to the Galatians. [By John Croll. Translated from the Latin by Thomas Lushington.] Fol. [Wood's *Athen. Oxon.* iii. 530.] London, 1650

JUSTIFICATION of Mr Murdoch M'Kenzie's nautical survey of the Orkney Islands and Hebrides; in answer to the accusations of Doctor [James] Anderson. [By John Clerk, of Eldin.] 8vo. Pp. 55. [*W.*] Edinburgh, 1785

JUSTIFICATION (a) of the present war against the United Netherlands; wherein the declaration of His Majesty is vindicated, and the war proved to be just, honourable, and necessary; the dominion of the sea explained, and His Majesties rights thereunto asserted; . . . By an Englishman [Henry Stubbe, M.A., Oxford]. 4to. Pp. 80. [*D. N. B.* vol. 55, p. 117.] London, 1672

JUSTIFICATION of the proceedings of the House of Commons in the last session of Parliament. [By Sir Humphrey Mackworth?] Fol. Pp. 23. 1701

JUSTIFICATION (a) of two points now in controversy with the Anabaptists concerning Baptisme: with a brief answer to Master Tombes arguments, in his exercitation about Infants Baptisme. . . . By T. B. [Thomas Bakewell]. 8vo. Pp. ii. 30. [Whitley's *Bapt. Bibl.* i. 22.] London, 1646

JUSTIFIED (a) sinner. [A novel.] By Ernest Wilding [Joseph Fitzgerald Molloy]. 8vo. Pp. viii. 330. London, 1897

JUSTIFYING faith; or, that faith by which the just do live . . . describ'd in a discourse on 1 John 5, 12. By the author of *Summum bonum, or, an explication of the Divine goodness*, etc. [Clement Elys]. 12mo. [*Bodl.*] London, 1679

JUSTINA; a play: translated from the Spanish [El mágico prodigioso] of Calderon de la Barca, by J. H. [Denis Florence M'Carthy]. 8vo. [O'Donoghue's *Poets of Ireland.*] London, 1848

JUSTIN'S lovers. By Violet Vane [Mrs Jane L. Howell]. 8vo. [Cushing's *Init. and Pseud.* i. 292.] New York, 1878

JUSTO Ucundono, Prince of Japan. By Philalethes [Rev. John E. Blox]. 8vo. [Cushing's *Init. and Pseud.* i. 230.] Baltimore, 1854

JUSTORUM semita; or, the path of the just: a history of the lesser holydays of the present English kalendar. [By James Augustine Stothert.] 8vo. Edinburgh, 1844

JUSTORUM semita; or, the path of the just: a history of the saints and holydays of the present English kalendar. [By James Augustine Stothert.] 8vo. Pp. xlvi. 254. Edinburgh, 1843

JUTHOO and his Sunday-school. By a native Brahmin [Joguth Chunder Gangooly]. 8vo. [Cushing's *Init. and Pseud.* i. 201.] Boston, 1861

JUVENALIAD (the); a satire. [By George Wallis.] 4to. [*Mon. Rev.* l. 232, 484.] London, 1774

In Baker's *Biog. Dram.*, the title is given as "The Juveniliad," and the date 1773.

JUVENALIS redivivus; or, the first satyr of Juvenal taught to speak plain English: a poem. [By Thomas Wood, D.C.L.] 4to. [Wood's *Athen. Oxon.* iv. 557.] N.P. 1683

JUVENAL'S tenth and thirteenth satires, translated [in verse] by E. L. L. S. [Edmund Lewis Lenthal Swift, barrister]. 8vo. Dublin, 1818

JUVENILE conversations on the botany of the Bible; illustrative of the power, wisdom and goodness of God. [By C. MacNab.] 8vo. 2 parts. Edinburgh, 1850-1

JUVENILE (the) culprits. By the author of *The juvenile moralists* [George Mogridge]. 12mo. [*Brit. Mus.*] Wellington, Salop, 1829

JUVENILE delinquency. [By Edward Rushton.] 8vo. [*Brit. Mus.*] London, 1842

JUVENILE delinquency; its causes and cure. By a county magistrate [Hugh Barclay, sheriff of Perth]. 8vo. Edinburgh, 1850

JUVENILE indiscretions; a novel. By the author of *Anna, or the Welsh heiress* [Mrs A. M. Bennet]. 12mo. 5 vols. [Watt's *Bibl. Brit.*] London, 1786

JUVENILE (the) museum; or, child's library of amusement and instruction. By "Quiet George" [George Frederick Pardon]. 8vo. [*Olphar Hamst.*] London [1849]

JUVENILE (the) moralists. By the author of *The juvenile culprits* [George Mogridge]. 12mo. [*Brit. Mus.*] Wellington, Salop, 1829

JUVENILE (the) olio, or mental medley; consisting of original essays, written by a father [William Mavor] chiefly for the use of his children. 12mo. [*Brit. Mus.*]. London, 1796

JUVENILE performances in poetry. By a student in the University of Edinburgh [Charles Kerr, Abbotrule]. 8vo. Pp. 112. [*D. Laing.*] Edinburgh, 1788

JUVENILE poems. [By Chandos Lees.] 8vo. London, 1815

JUVENILE poems; a sequel to *Original poems.* By the author of *Affection's gift* [Mary Anne Hedge]. Third edition. 12mo. London, 1823

JUVENILE poems. By a student of the University of Glasgow [William Hamilton Drummond]. 8vo. [*D.N.B.* vol. 16, p. 52.] Glasgow [1795]

JUVENILE poems. By the author of *Rimes* [John Pinkerton]. 8vo. N.P. [*c.* 1785]

JUVENILE poems on several occasions. By a gentleman of Oxford [—— Griffin, of Edmund Hall]. 12mo. Oxford, 1764

JUVENILE poems on several occasions. By J. J. [J. Jenkins]. 8vo. [*Brit. Mus.*] Waterford, 1773

JUVENILE (the) poetical moralist. [By Elizabeth Tuck.] 8vo. Frome, 1821

JUVENILE (the) scrap-book. [By Mrs William Ellis, *née* Sarah Stickney.] 8vo. [*Brit. Mus.*] London, 1844

JUVENILE (the) speaker; or, dialogues and miscellaneous pieces in prose and verse. . . . By the author of *The polite reasoner* [Mary Weightman]. 12mo. London, 1787

JUVENILE (the) Tatler. By a Society of young ladies. . . . [Signed: E. F. *i.e.* Lady Eleanor Fenn.] 12mo. [*Brit. Mus.*] London, 1789

JUVENILIA; a collection of miscellaneous poems. By H. G. [Hamilton Geale]. 8vo. [O'Donoghue's *Poets of Ireland.*] Dublin, 1838

JUVENILIA; essays on sundry æsthetical questions. By Vernon Lee [Violet Paget]. 8vo. 2 vols. [*Lond. Lib. Cat.*] London, 1887

K

K. Lamity's Texas tales. [By John Sturgis Bonner.] 8vo. [*Amer. Cat.*] Austin, Texas, 1905

K. N. pepper and other condiments. By Jacques Maurice [James W. Morris]. 8vo. [Cushing's *Init. and Pseud.* i. 185.] New York, 1859

KABALA (the) of numbers; a handbook of interpretation. By "Sepharial" [Walter Gorn Old]. 8vo. Pp. 168. [*Brit. Mus.*] London, 1910

KABALISTIC astrology; or, your fortune in your name. By Sepharial [Walter Gorn Old]. 8vo. Pp. vi. 73. [*Brit. Mus.*] London [1895]

KAESO; a tragedy of the first century. By Nathanael Hurd [Blomfield Jackson]. 8vo. Pp. 113. [*Brit. Mus.*] London, 1889

KAINER; or, the usurer's doom: a German tale, translated by the author of *Industry and laziness* [Frederick Bolingbroke Ribbans]. 8vo. Pp. 64. [*Brit. Mus.*] London, 1881

KAISERWERTH; the Deaconess Institution of Rhenish Westphalia; its origin and fields of labour: translated from the German by A. N. [A. Northey]. 8vo. London, 1883

KALEIDOSCOPE (the). [By Harriet Warner Ellis.] 8vo. [Kirk's *Supp.*]

KALOOLAH; or, journeyings to the Djebel Kumri; an autobiography of Jonathan Romer; edited [or rather written] by William Starbuck Mayo, M.D. 8vo. New York, 1849

KAMA (the) Sutra of Vatsyayana. Translated from the Sanscrit [by Sir Richard Burton and F. F. Arbuthnot]. 8vo. 7 parts. [Penzer's *Bibl. of Burton.*] Benares, private print, 1883

KANSAS and its constitution. By Cecil [Sidney George Fisher]. 8vo. [Cushing's *Init. and Pseud.* i. 53.] Boston, 1856

KAPÉLION (the), or poetical ordinary; consisting of great variety of dishes in prose and verse; recommended to all those who have a good taste or keen appetite. By Archimagírus Metaphoricus [William Kenrick, LL.D.]. To be continued occasionally. 8vo. [*D. N. B.* vol. 30, p. 16.] London, 1720

KARL Krinken, his Christmas stocking. By the authors of *The wide, wide world*, etc. [Susan and A. B. Warner]. 12mo. London, 1857

KARMATH; an Arabian tale. By the author of *Rameses, an Egyptian tale* [Edward Upham, bookseller, F.S.A., mayor of Exeter]. 12mo. [*Nat. Lib. of Scot.*] London, 1827

KASIDAH (the) of Haji Abdu 'l-Yazdi; [a poem] translated and annotated by his friend and pupil F. B. [Sir Richard Francis Burton, who really composed the whole work]. Second edition. 4to. [*D. N. B.* First Supp. vol. 1, p. 355.] London, 1894

KATE Carnegie and those ministers. By Ian Maclaren, author of *Beside the bonnie brier bush*, etc. [John Watson, D.D., Liverpool]. 8vo. [*Lit. Year Book.*] London, 1896

KATE Comerford; or, sketches of garrison life. By Teresa A. Thornet [Mrs Anna Holloway]. 8vo. [*Lib. Journ.* xii. 178.] Philadelphia, 1881

KATE Coventry; an autobiography: edited [or rather written] by George John Whyte Melville. 8vo. [*Brit. Mus.*] London, 1856

KATE Hamilton; or, profession and principle. [A tale.] By Rosa Gaythorne [Rhoda Haddock]. 8vo. Bilston, 1859

KATE Jameson and her friends. By Joy Allison [Mary A. Cragin]. 12mo. [Cushing's *Init. and Pseud.* i. 10.] Boston, 1872

KATE Kennedy; a novel. By the author of *Wondrous strange*, etc. [Mrs C. J. Newby]. 12mo. 2 vols. London, 1865

KATE Peyton; or, jealousy. [A drama. By Charles Reade.] 8vo. Pp. 84. Private print [1869?]

Afterwards issued with the author's name.

KATE Temple's mate. By the author of *Clary's Confirmation*, etc. [Frances E. Reade]. 8vo. Pp. 160. [*Brit. Mus.*] London, 1899

KATE Walsingham. By [Elizabeth Youatt] the editor of *The Grandfather* by the late Ellen Pickering. 12mo. 3 vols. London, 1848

KATHARINE Ashton. By the author of *Amy Herbert*, etc. [Elizabeth Missing Sewell]. 8vo. 2 vols. [*Brit. Mus.*] London, 1854

KATHARINE Blythe. [A novel.] By Katharine Lee [Katharine Lee Jenner]. 8vo. 3 vols. [*Lond. Lib. Cat.*] London, 1886

KATHARINE Walton; or, the rebel of Dorchester: an historical romance of the Revolution in Carolina. By the author of *Richard Hurdis*, etc. [William Gilmore Simms, LL.D.]. 8vo. [*Brit. Mus.*] Philadelphia, 1851

KATHERINE; a tale. [By Mrs Barbara Hofland, *née* Wreaks.] 12mo. 4 vols. London, 1828

KATHERINE and her sisters. [A novel.] By the author of *The discipline of life*, etc. [Lady Emily C. M. Ponsonby]. 8vo. 3 vols. [*Brit. Mus.*] London, 1861

KATHERINE Evering. By the author of *Mr Arle* [Emily Jolly]. 8vo. [*Nat. Lib. of Scot.*] Edinburgh, 1857

Vol. II. of *Love in light and shadow*, *q.v.*

KATHERINE Morris; an autobiography. [By Frances West Atherton, later Mrs Pike.] 8vo. Boston, 1858

KATHERINE Walton; or, the rebel of Dorchester: an historic romance of the Revolution in Carolina. [By William Gilmore Simms.] 8vo. [*Brit. Mus.*] Philadelphia, 1851

KATHERINE'S trial. By Holme Lee, author of *Kathie Brande*, etc. [Harriet Parr]. 8vo. Pp. 282. [*Brit. Mus.*] London, 1873

KATHIE Brande; a fireside history of a quiet life. By Holme Lee, author of *Thorney Hall*, etc. [Harriet Parr]. 12mo. 2 vols. [*Brit. Mus.*] London, 1856

KATHLEEN. [A novel.] By the author of *Raymond's heroine* [Isabella Harwood]. 8vo. [*Brit. Mus.*] London, 1869

KATHLEEN Clare; her book, 1637-41. [A novel.] Edited [but rather written] by D. G. MacChesney. 8vo. Pp. vi. 286. [*Brit. Mus.*] Edinburgh, 1895

KATHLEEN O'Neil; a grand national melodrama, in three acts. [By Mary Balfour.] 8vo. [S. J. Brown's *Books on Ireland*, i. 175.] Belfast, 1814

KATHLEEN; or, the secret marriage. By the author of *The Hebrew maiden* [Clara Reeve]. 8vo. Pp. iv. 636. London [1842]

ΚΑΘΟΛΙΚΩ (τῷ) Stilingfleeton; or, an account given to a Catholick friend of Dr Stilingfleet's late book against the Roman Church: together with a short postil upon his text, in three letters. By I. V. C. [John Vincent Cane]. 8vo. [Gillow's *Bibl. Dict.* i. 393.] Bruges, 1672

KATIE Stewart; a true story. [By Mrs Oliphant.] 8vo. [Courtney's *Secrets*, p. 68.] Edinburgh, 1853

KATIE, the fisherman's little daughter. [A tale. By Miss Emma S. Pratt.] 8vo. [*Brit. Mus.*] London [1878]

KATRINA; a poem. By Timothy Titcomb, Esquire [Josiah Gilbert Holland, M.D.]. 8vo. [Cushing's *Init. and Pseud.* i. 284.] New York, 1892

KATTY the Flash. [An Irish novel.] By Sydney Starr [Fannie Gallaher]. 8vo. [S. J. Brown's *Ireland in Fiction*, p. 94.] Dublin, 1880

KATY of Catoctin; or, the chain-breakers: a national romance. By "Gath" [George Alfred Townsend]. 8vo. [Cushing's *Init. and Pseud.* i. 111.] New York, 1886

KATYDID'S poems. [By Catherine Slaughter, later Mrs M'Kinnlay.] 8vo. Montgomery, Alabama, 1887

KATY'S story, and other poems and tales. By Edith May [Anna Drinkwater]. 4to. [*Brit. Mus.*] Philadelphia, 1855

KEANE Malcombe's pupil; a story. [By Mrs B. L. Adams.] 8vo. [*Brit. Mus.*] London, 1874

KEEKIAD (the); a poem. [By John Maclaurin, Lord Dreghorn.] 8vo. Pp. 24. [Edinburgh, 1840?]

KEELY and his discoveries; aerial navigation. By Mrs H. O. Ward [Mrs Clara Jessup Moore]. 8vo. [*Amer. Cat.*] New York, 1895

KEEP my secret. [A novel.] By G. M. Robins [Mrs Louis Baillie Reynolds]. 8vo. [*Lit. Year Book.*] London, 1892

KEEPERS (the) of the gate. [A novel.] By Sydney C. Grier [Hilda Caroline Gregg]. 8vo. Pp. 336. [*Lit. Year Book.*] Edinburgh, 1911

KEEPER'S travels in search of his master. [By Edward Augustus Kendall.] 12mo. [*Gent. Mag.* Dec. 1842, p. 671.] London, 1798

KEEPING house; a story on home management. By the author of *A letter for you* [Mrs Jane M. King]. 8vo. Pp. 119. [*Brit. Mus.*] London, 1910

KEEPING the vow. . . . By the author of *Joined to an idol* [Mrs Morgan Morgan]. 8vo. Pp. 337. [*Brit. Mus.*] London, 1882

KEEPSAKE (a) for the young; a book of amusement. By Aunt Friendly [Mrs Sarah S. Baker, *née* Tuthill]. 8vo. [Kirk's *Supp.*] London, N.D.

KEITH Deramore. [A novel.] By the author of *Miss Molly* [Beatrice May Butt]. 8vo. Pp. 383. [*Brit. Mus.*] London, 1894

KELROY; a novel. . . . By a lady of Pennsylvania [Rebecca Rush]. 8vo. Philadelphia, 1812

KELSO records; being traditions and recollections of Kelso. By John Mason. [This volume contains "A particular account of the town of Kelso," by Ebenezer Lazarus (*i.e.* Robert Mason).] 8vo. Pp. 205. [*Brit. Mus.*] Edinburgh, 1839

KELSO (the) souvenir; or, selections from her scrap-book [of poems]. . . . By a lady [Mrs John Ballantyne]. 12mo. Edinburgh, 1832

Private information.

KELSO tracts. [Forty-six in all. By Horatius Bonar, D.D.] 8vo. London, 1851

KELTIC (the) Journal and Educator. [By the Rev. Ulick J. Bourke.] Seven parts. 4to. Pp. 56. [*Manch. Free Lib.*] Manchester [1867]

KELVINGTON; a tale for the turf and the table. By "Whitebelt" [Alfred White]. 8vo. Pp. xii. 234. [*Brit. Mus.*] London, 1883

KEMPTON-WACE (the) letters. [By Jack London and Anna Strunsky.] 8vo. New York, 1903

KENELM Chillingley; his adventures and opinions. By the author of *The Caxtons* [Sir Edward G. E. Lytton Bulwer-Lytton, Baron Lytton]. 8vo. 3 vols. London, 1873

KENILWORTH; a musical drama founded on the celebrated romance . . . by the author of Waverley. . . . [By Daniel Terry.] 8vo. Pp. 62. [*D. N. B.* vol. 56, p. 84.] Edinburgh, 1823

KENILWORTH; a romance. By the author of *Waverley*, etc. [Sir Walter Scott, Bart.]. 8vo. 3 vols. Edinburgh, 1821

KENNAQUHAIR; a narrative of Utopian travel. By Theophilus MacCrib [Henry Boyle Lee]. 8vo. [*Lond. Lib. Cat.*] London, 1872

KENNEL diseases. By Ashmont [Dr Joseph Frank Perry]. 8vo. [*Amer. Cat.*] Boston, 1903

KENNEL secrets; how to breed, exhibit and manage dogs. By Ashmont [Dr Joseph Frank Perry]. 8vo. Boston, 1893

KENNETH, my King. By Virginia Madison [Sallie A. Brock, later Mrs Putnam]. 8vo. [Cushing's *Init. and Pseud.* i. 181.] New York, 1875

KENNETH; or, the rear guard of the grand army. By the author of *Scenes and characters*, *Kings of England*, etc. [Charlotte Mary Yonge]. 8vo. Oxford, 1850

KENSINGTON garden. [By Thomas Tickell.] 4to. Pp. 32. [*D. N. B.* vol. 56, p. 381.] London, 1722

KENSINGTON Gardens in 1830; a satirical trifle. By the author of *Écarté* [John Richardson]. 8vo. [*Brit. Mus.*] London, 1830

KENT Fielding's ventures. By Marion Thorne [Ida T. Thurston]. [*Amer. Cat.*] Boston, 1896

KENTISH (the) curate; or, the history of Lamuel Lyttleton. [A romance. By Henry Lemoine.] 12mo. 4 vols. [*D. N. B.* vol. 33, p. 28.] London, 1786

KENTISH (the) traveller's companion; in a descriptive view of the towns, villages, remarkable buildings and antiquities situated on or near the road from London to Margate, Dover, and Canterbury. [By Thomas Fisher, bookseller of Rochester.] 12mo. [Smith's *Bibl. Cant.* p. 80.] Canterbury, 1776

KENTUCKIAN (the) in New York; or, the adventures of three Southerners. By a Virginian [William A. Carruthers]. 12mo. 2 vols. [*Brit. Mus.*] New York, 1834

KERNEL (the) and the husk; letters on spiritual Christianity. By the author of *Philochristus* and *Onesimus* [Edwin A. Abbott, D.D.]. 8vo. [*Lond. Lib. Cat.*] London, 1887

KERNEL (the) further discussed; or, the [Scottish Church] Convocation resolutions based on an erroneous doctrine. [By Thomas Myles, minister in Aberlemno.] 8vo. [*New Coll. Lib.*] Edinburgh, 1844

KERNEL (the) of the controversy; or, the [Scottish] Church question brought to a point. [By Thomas Myles, minister in Aberlemno.] 8vo. Edinburgh, 1843

Wrongly attributed to Thomas Inglis.

KERNWOOD; or, after many days; a historical romance. By L'Inconnue [Mrs L. Virginia French, *née* Smith]. 8vo. Louisville, 1868

KESTELL of Greystone. [A novel.] By Esmé Stuart [Amélie Claire Leroy]. 8vo. 3 vols. [*Lond. Lib. Cat.*] London, 1890

KETTLE (the) abusing the pot; a satirical poem. By Black Dwarf [Thomas Jonathan Wooler]. Seventh edition. 8vo. London, 1820

These verses relate to the dispute between George IV. and Queen Caroline.

KETTLE (the) Club: Christmas tales for children. By Cousin Virginia [Virginia W. Johnson]. 8vo. [Cushing's *Init. and Pseud.* i. 296.] 8vo. Boston, 1866

KETTNER'S book of the table; a manual of cooking . . . [By Eneas Sweetland Dallas.] 8vo. [*Brit. Mus.*] London, 1877

KEY (a); being observations and explanatory notes upon the travels of Lemuel Gulliver. By Signor Corolini [Jonathan Swift]. . . . Translated from the Italian original. 12mo. Pp. 17. [*Brit. Mus.*] Dublin, 1727

KEY (the) of Heaven. [By John Hugh Owen, S.J.] 12mo. [Oliver's *Collections*, p. 153.] London, 1670

A Romish prayer-book.

KEY (the) of knowledge not found in the University Library of Cambridge; or, a short answer to a foolish, slanderous pamphlet, entituled, A gagg for the Quakers, which wants the author's name to it; but he is known chiefly to be Thomas Smith . . . Keeper of the said Library in Cambridge. . . . By a friend to them that hate iniquity, G. W. [George Whitehead]. 4to. Pp. 16. [Smith's *Anti-Quak.* p. 405.] London, 1660

KEY (a) opening a way to every common understanding, how to discern the difference betwixt the religion professed by the people called Quakers, and the perversions, misrepresentations and calumnies of their several adversaries. . . . [By William Penn.] 8vo. Pp. 37. [Smith's *Cat. of Friends' Books*, ii. 306.] London, 1693

KEY (the) that fits the lock. By Lizabeth [Kathryn Wallace]. 8vo. [*Amer. Cat.*] Girard, Kansas, 1903

KEY (a) to a delicate investigation. By Esculapius [Samuel Ferrand Waddington, M.D.]. 8vo. [*D. N. B.* vol. 58, p. 411.] London, 1812

KEY (the) to astrology; containing a complete system of genethliac astrology. By Raphael [R. C. Smith], the astrologer of the nineteenth century. Second edition. 12mo. Pp. 108. London, 1896

Attributed also to J. Palmer.

KEY (a) to cooking that will unlock many kitchen mysteries. [By Mrs Helen Nitsch.] 12mo. London, 1887

KEY (the) to fortune in new lands; and handbook of the "Explorer's Test Case." . . . By W. B. L. [William Barry Lord]. 8vo. [*Brit. Mus.*] London [1869]

KEY (a) to open Scripture metaphors. Book I., containing sacred philologic, or the tropes in Scripture reduced under their heads, with a brief explication of each; partly translated, and partly compil'd, from the works of the learned. By T. D. [Thomas Delaune]. Books II. III., containing a practical improvement (paralel-wise) of several of the most frequent and useful metaphors, allegories, and express similitudes of the Old and New Testaments. By B. K. [Benjamin Keach]. Fol. [Arber's *Term Cat.* i. 457.] London, 1681

KEY (a) to the chronology of the Hindus; in a series of letters, in which an attempt is made to facilitate the progress of Christianity in Hindostan, by proving that the protracted numbers of all oriental nations, when reduced, agree with the dates given in the Hebrew text of the Bible. [By Alexander Hamilton.] 8vo. 2 vols. [*Camb. Univ. Lib.*] Cambridge, 1820

KEY (a) to the Fragment. By Amias Riddinge, B.D.; with a preface. By Peregrine Smyth, Esq. [By William King, LL.D.] 8vo. Pp. viii. 46. [Bartholomew's *Cat. of Camb. Books.*] London, 1751

KEY (a) to the King's Cabinet; or, animadversions upon the three printed speeches, of Mr Lisle, Mr Tate, and Mr Brown, spoken at a common-hall in London, 3. July 1645: detecting the malice and falshood of their blasphemous observations made upon the King and Queenes letters. [By Dr Thomas Browne, Student of Christ Church, Oxford.] 4to. Pp. 53. [*Bodl.*] Oxford, 1645

The author's name is in the handwriting of Barlow.

KEY (a) to the knowledge of Church history [ancient]. [By Mary F. B. Pownall.] Edited by John Henry Blunt, M.A. 8vo. Pp. vi. 164. [*Bodl.*] London, 1869

KEY (a) to the lock; a comedy, in two acts, performed at the Hay Market. [By James J. Foord.] 8vo. [Baker's *Biog. Dram.* iii. 475.] London, 1788

KEY (a) to the lock; or, a treatise proving, beyond all contradiction, the dangerous tendency of a late poem, entituled, The rape of the lock, to government and religion. By Esdras Barnivelt, Apoth. [By Alexander Pope.] Third edition. . . . 8vo. Pp. 32. [Lowndes' *Bibl. Man.*] London, 1718

"Written by Pope himself." "(First ed. in 1715.)"—MS. note in the handwriting of Dyce.

Ascribed also to John Arbuthnot, M.D., and to A. Hill.

KEY (a) to the Memoirs of the affairs of Scotland. [By David Craufurd.] 8vo. London, 1714

KEY (a) to the Missal. [By Christopher Tootell, Roman Catholic Priest.] 8vo. [Gillow's *Bibl. Dict.*] London, 1698

KEY (a) to the mystery of the [Book of the] Revelation; whereby all its dark meanings, being reduced to one regular system, are easily accounted for and explained. [By —— Taylor.] 8vo. London, 1785

KEY to the New practical arithmetic. By a practical teacher [Benjamin Greenleaf]. 8vo. [Cushing's *Init. and Pseud.* i. 238.] Boston, 1867

KEY to the New Testament; giving an account of the several books, their contents, their authors, and of the times, places, and occasions, on which they were respectively written. [By Dr Thomas Percy, Bishop of Dromore.] 12mo. [*D. N. B.* vol. 44, p. 439.] London, 1779

KEY (a) to the plot, by reflections on the Rebellion; shewing how, as in matter of right, it was rais'd by the revolters against their own most peculiar principles; so, by providence, it turns towards the reverse of their design; by precluding the like monstrous attempts to perpetuity, and curing many separate evils. . . . In a letter from a countryman in Scotland to a courtier in London. [By Francis Grant, Lord Cullen.] 8vo. Pp. viii. 78. [*Nat. Lib. of Scot.*] London, 1716

KEY (a) to the Prophet Isaiah. [By Rev. John Martin Butt.] 12mo. [*Brit. Mus.*] Newbury, 1823

KEY (a) to the Psalms; being an explanation of words, allusions, and sentences in them. By the Rev. W. C. [William Cole]. 8vo. [*Brit. Mus.*] Cambridge, 1788

KEY (a) to the Scripture character of Jesus Christ; or the doctrine of the ancient existence of his glorious soul in union with his Deity clearly proved . . . from revelation. . . . By a free enquirer after truth [Rev. William Ashdowne, Unitarian]. 8vo. [*Brit. Mus.*] London, 1784

KEY (a) (with the whip) to open the mystery & iniquity of the poem [by John Dryden] called, Absalom and Achitophel; shewing its scurrilous reflections upon king and kingdom. [By Christopher Nesse.] 4to. Pp. 40. [*Bodl.*] N.P. 1682

See Vol. I., p. 6, footnote.

KEYNOTES. By George Egerton [Mrs Egerton Clairmonte]. 8vo. [*Lit. Year Book.*] London, 1892

A collection of short tales.

KEYNOTES of the Bible. By S. T. [Thomas Smith, D.D.]. 12mo. Pp. viii. 181. Edinburgh, 1862

Later editions give the author's name.

KEYS (the) of the Creeds. [By Edward Maitland.] 8vo. [*Brit. Mus.*] London, 1875

KEYS to the universe. By Vernon Lee [Violet Paget]. 8vo. [*Lond. Lib. Cat.*] London [1898]

KEYSTONE (a) of Empire; Francis Joseph of Austria. By the author of *The martyrdom of an Empress* [Margaret Cunliffe Owen]. 8vo. Pp. 330. [*Brit. Mus.*] London, 1903

KEZIAH in search of a friend; a story for school-girls. By Noel Hope [Sarah L. Morewood]. 8vo. London, 1908

KHEDIVES and Pashas; sketches of contemporary Egyptian rulers and statesmen. By one who knows them well [Charles Frederick Moberly Bell]. 12mo. [*D. N. B.*, Second Supp. vol. i. p. 130.] London, 1884

KICK (a) for a bite; or, review upon review; with a critical essay on the works of Mrs S. Rowson, in a letter . . . By Peter Porcupine [William Cobbett]. 8vo. [Cushing's *Init. and Pseud.* i. 238.] Philadelphia, 1796

KICKLEBURYS (the) on the Rhine. By Mr M. A. Titmarsh [William Makepeace Thackeray]. 12mo. London, 1851

KIDDLE-A-WINK (the); or, ghostly stories on the Western Coast, comprising Gualmara, or the house of bitterness; a tale of love; and a life lost. By Francis Derrick [Frances Eliza Millet Notley, later Mrs Thomas]. 8vo. Pp. 146. [*Lit. Year Book.*] London, 1864

Another edition of the following entry.

KIDDLE-A-WINK (the); or, the three guests. By the author of *Patience Caerhydon*, etc. [Frances E. M. Notley, later Mrs Thomas]. 8vo. Pp. 359. London [1875]

KIDNAPPED; or, Lewis Lloyd's adventures in Virginia. By Ascott R. Hope [Ascott Robert Hope Moncrieff]. 8vo. Pp. 128. [*Lit. Year Book.*] London [1883]

KIDNAPPING (the) of Ettie. [A novel.] By Brown Linnet [Ella Tomlinson]. 8vo. Pp. 312. London, 1902

KILLARNEY; a poem. By an officer in the army [Joseph Atkinson]. 4to. [*Brit. Mus.*; O'Donoghue's *Poets of Ireland.*] Dublin, 1750

KILLARNEY'S lakes and fells. By F. M. Allen [Edmund Downey]. 8vo. [*Lit. Year Book.*] London, 1901

KILLARNEY sketches; in verse. By Fitz-Erin [Rev. J. Fitzgerald Day]. 8vo. [O'Donoghue's *Poets of Ireland.*] Dublin, 1862

KILLINCHY; or, the days of [the Rev. John] Livingston [there, after 1629. By James Meikle]. 12mo. Pp. 156. [S. J. Brown's *Ireland in fiction.*] Belfast, 1839

KILLING is murder; or, an answer to a treasonus [*sic*] pamphlet [by Col. Edward Sexby and Col. Silius Titus], entituled "Killing no murder." [By Michael Hawke.] 4to. London, 1657

KILLING noe murder; with some additions briefly discourst in three questions, fit for publick view. . . . By William Allen [Col. Edward Sexby and Col. Silius Titus]. 4to. [*Eng. Hist. Rev.* 1902, p. 308, article by Professor Terry.] London [really Holland] 1657

KILLVILLAIN; a catechetical ode. By the late Tyro Trimstave, M.D.; with a preface and notes by Cosmo Caustic, Gent. [By Christopher Reid.] 12mo. [*J. Maidment.*] Edinburgh, 1835

KILTS and Philibegs! The northern excursion of Geordie, Emperor of Gotham [King George IV.] and Sir Willie Curt-his; a serio-tragico-comico-ludicro-aquatico burlesque gallimaufry. . . . [By William Hone, publisher?] 8vo. London [1822]

Another edition, published later in the same year, begins "The northern excursion of Geordie . . ."

KIMBOLTON Castle; and Lady Jane Grey: two dramatic sketches. By Armar Greye [Mrs Maria Greer]. 8vo. Pp. 100. London, 1871

KIMBOLTON Park; a poem. [By Rev. Benjamin Hutchinson, rector of Holywell.] 8vo. [*N. and Q.* July 1864, p. 18.] London, 1765

KINCAID'S widow. [A novel. By Henrietta Keddie.] 8vo. London, 1895

KIND (a) caution to prophane swearers. By a minister of the Church of England [Josiah Woodward, D.D.]. 4to. [*Bodl.*] London, 1704

No title-page.

KIND (a) invitation to the people called Quakers, to the due consideration of some important truths; in a letter and twenty questions, sent long since to their second-days meeting, and now to them all: to both which, an answer from their present yearly meeting, 1697, is desired. [By Edward Stephens.] 4to. Pp. 8. [*Bodl.*] N.P., N.D.

Invitation signed: E. S., and dated 31 August, 1696.

KIN-DA-SHON'S wife; an Alaskan story. By Rachel Penn [Mrs Eugenia S. Willard]. 8vo. [*Amer. Cat.*] Chicago, 1900

KINDE-HARTS dreame; containing five apparitions, with their inuectives against abuses raigning: deliuered by seuerall ghosts vnto him to be publisht after Piers Penilesse Post had refused the carriage. By H. C. [Henry Chettle]. 4to. B. L. [Lowndes' *Bibl. Man.*] London [1593]

KINDNESS and cruelty; or, the grateful ogre. By Alfred Crowquill [Alfred Henry Forrester]. 8vo. [*D. N. B.* vol. 20, p. 6.] London [1859]

KINDNESS to animals. By Charlotte Elizabeth [Mrs Charlotte Elizabeth Tonna, *née* Browne]. 12mo. Pp. 108. London, N.D.

KING Alfred's jewel. [A drama, in verse.] By the author of *Mors et victoria* [Mrs Katrina Spencer Trask]. 8vo. London, 1908

KING (the) and Isabel. [A novel.] By the author of *The adventures of John Johns* [Frederick Carrel]. 8vo. Pp. 306. [*Brit. Mus.*] London, 1909

KING (the) and the angel: a drama. By Ross Neil [Isabella Harwood]. 8vo. [*Lond. Lib. Cat.*] London, 1874

KING (the) and the Church vindicated and delivered; or, the prime minister convicted of counselling to the crown a violation of the coronation oath: in an address to the House of Lords, and in a plain, solemn, and faithful appeal to his grace the Lord Archbishop of Canterbury. By a minister of the Church of Ireland [The Hon. and Rev. Arthur P. Perceval]. 8vo. Pp. 51. [*Camb. Univ. Lib.*] London, 1833

Ascribed also to Robert J. M'Ghee.

KING (the) and the countess; a romance. [By Stephen Watson Fullom.] 12mo. 3 vols. [*Nat. Lib. of Scot.*] London, 1849

KING Arthur; not a love story. By the author of *John Halifax, gentleman* [Mrs Craik, *née* Dinah M. Mulock]. 8vo. [*Brit. Mus.*] London, 1886

KING Charles the First; an historical tragedy, written in imitation of Shakespeare: as it is acted at the Theatre Royal in Lincoln's-Inn-Fields. [By William Havard.] 8vo. [*D. N. B.* vol. 25, p. 173.] London, 1737

KING Charles the First no man of blood, but a martyr for his people; or, a sad and impartiall enquiry whether the King or Parliament began the warre, which hath so much ruined and undon the kingdom of England? and who was in the defensive part of it? [By Fabian Philipps.] 4to. Pp. 66. [*D. N. B.* vol. 45, p. 169.] 1649

KING Charles I. vindicated from the charge of plagiarism brought against him by Milton; and Milton himself convicted of forgery, and a gross imposition on the public. To the whole is subjoined the judgment of several learned and impartial authors concerning Milton's political writings. [By William Lauder, M.A.] 8vo. Pp. 64. [*Bodl.*] London, 1754

The fly title is "The grand impostor detected."

KING Charles the First's Bishops no puritans. [By J. Collier.] 8vo. [Leslie's *Cat.* 1843.] N.P. 1713

KING Charls his starre; or, astrologie defined, and defended by Scripture, &c.; with the signification of the comet seen Decemb. 1652, as it hath relation to his Majesty, Charles King of Scotland. By Θ 4 $\underline{1000}$ I S A'10 2. [Arise Evans.] 8vo. Pp. 46. [*Bodl.*] 1654

The author's name is in the handwriting of Wood.

KING Coal's levee; or, geological etiquette, with explanatory notes; and the council of the metals. [By John Scafe.] Fourth edition; to which is added, Baron Basalt's Tour. 12mo. Pp. 119. [Green's *Bibl. Somers.* i. 300.] Bath, 1820

KING Edward the Fourth. [By Thomas Heywood.]

See "The first and second partes of . . ."

KING Edward VII.; his life and reign: the record of a noble career. By Edgar Sanderson and Lewis Melville [Lewis Samuel Benjamin]. 8vo. 6 vols. [*Brit. Mus.*] London, 1910

KING Edward the Third, with the fall of Mortimer, Earl of March; an historicall play. [In five acts. By J. Bancroft?] 4to. [*Brit. Mus.*] London, 1691

The dedication is by W. Mountfort.

KING Gab's story-bag, and the wonderful stories it contained. By Heraclitus Grey, author of *Armstrong Magney*, etc. [Charles Marshall]. 8vo. Pp. 206. [Cushing's *Init. and Pseud.* i. 120.] London [1869]

KING George's right asserted, and the Church of England vindicated from the charge of schism. [By Gilbert Nelson, surgeon.] 8vo. London, 1717

KING George's title asserted; or, a letter . . . shewing the lawfulness of the oaths required for the present Government. [By Richard Venn.] 8vo. [*Brit. Mus.*] London, 1715

Signed: A. B.

KING Glumpus; an interlude, in one act [and in verse. By John Barrow]. 12mo. London, private print, 1837

Incorrectly attributed to Wm. M. Thackeray.

KING Henry VIII.'s scheme of Bishopricks; with illustrations of his assumption of Church property. [By Henry Cole.] 8vo. [W. D. Macray's *Cat.*] London, 1838

KING Henry the Second: an historical drama. [By Sir Arthur Helps.] 8vo. Pp. 182. [*Brit. Mus.*] London, 1843

KING Henry the VII.; or, the Popish impostor: a tragedy, as it is acted by his Majesty's servants at the Theatre Royal, in Drury-Lane. [By Charles Macklin.] 8vo. [Baker's *Biog. Dram.*] London, 1746

KING Henry the Third; part the first: an historical play in five acts. By the author of *An essay on the Oxford tracts* [John Sibbald Edison]. 8vo. Pp. 122. [*Bodl.*] London, 1840

KING (the) in the country; a dramatic piece, in two acts: acted at the Theatres-Royal, at Richmond and Windsor, 1788. [By Francis Godolphin Waldron.] 8vo. Pp. 28. [Baker's *Biog. Dram.*] London, 1789

KING (a) in the lists. [A novel.] By May Wynne [Mabel Wynne Knowles]. 8vo. Pp. 251. [*Lit. Year Book.*] London, 1922

KING James his welcome to London; with Elizaes tombe and epitaph, and our kings triumph and epitimie: lamenting the ones decease and reioycing at the others accesse. Gaudia cum lachrymis iungamus, seria ludis. Written by J. F. [John Fenton]. 4to. [Lowndes' *Bibl. Man.*] London, 1603

KING Lear; or, the undutiful children: a tale in twelve chapters. [By Susannah Beever.] 8vo. Pp. 61. [*Bodl.*] London, 1870

KING Leopold's soliloquy; a satire. By Mark Twain [Samuel Langhorne Clemens]. 8vo. London, 1907

KING Noanett; a story of Old Virginia and the Massachusetts Bay. By J. S. of Dale [Frederick Jessup Stimson]. 8vo. Pp. 327. [*Lond. Lib. Cat.*] Boston, 1896

KING (the) of a day; a romance. By May Wynne [Mabel Wynne Knowles]. 8vo. Pp. viii. 294. [*Brit. Mus.*] London, 1918

KING (the) of Kerisal. [A novel.] By Mayne Lindsay [Mrs —— Clarke]. 8vo. [*Lit. Year Book.*] London, 1907

KING of the Castle. By Keble Howard [John Keble Bell]. 8vo. [*Lit. Year Book.*] London, 1922

KING (the) of the Commons; a drama. By the author of *The Earl of Gowrie* [Rev. James White of Bonchurch]. 8vo. Pp. 100. [*Brit. Mus.*] London, 1846

KING (the) of the dead; a weird romance. By Frank Aubrey [Frank Atkins]. 8vo. London, 1903

KING (the) of the Golden River; or, the black brothers: a tale. [By John Ruskin.] 8vo. [*W.*] London, 1851

KING (the) of the Hurons. [A tale.] By the author of *The first of the Knickerbockers* [P. Hamilton Myers]. 12mo. [Kirk's *Supp.*] Philadelphia, 1850

KING (the) of the Jews; a sacred drama. By K. P. [the Grand Duke Constantine]; translated from the Russian by Victor E. Marsden. 8vo. Pp. 170. London, 1914

KING (the) of the Peak: a romance. By the author of *The cavalier*, etc. [William Bennett, solicitor]. 12mo. 3 vols. London, 1823

Dedication signed: Lee Gibbons.

Mistakenly attributed to Thomas Roscoe, junr.

KING (the) of the sea. By Ned Buntline [Edward Z. C. Judson]. 8vo. [Cushing's *Init. and Pseud.* i. 43.] New York, 1868

KING, or knave? [A novel.] By the author of *Hilda and I*, etc. [Mrs Hartley]. 8vo. 2 vols. [*Camb. Univ. Lib.*] London, 1877

KING Pepin's campaign; a burlesque opera. [By William Shirley, dramatist.] 8vo. [*Lond. Lib. Cat.*] London [1755]

KING Pippin; a story. . . . By Mrs Gerard Ford [Mrs Vevey Stockley]. 8vo. Pp. 278. London, 1896

KING Poppy; a story [in verse] without an end. [By Edward Robert Bulwer Lytton, Baron Lytton.] Pp. ix. 276. [Dobell's *Private prints*, pp. 101 and 234.] N.P. [1874]

Published later, with the author's name.

KING Richard the Third revived; containing a memorable petition and declaration contrived by himself and his instruments, whiles Protector, in the name of the three estates of England, to importune and perswade him to accept the kingship and crown of England, by their joynt election, as if he were unwilling to undertake, or accept, though he most ambitiously aspired after them, by the bloudy murthers of K. Henry 6. Edward 5. and sundry others, before his coronation. . . . [By William Prynne.] 4to. [Thomason's *Coll. of Tracts*, ii. 175.] London, 1657

KING Robert Bruce; or, the battle of Bannockburn. By the author of *The Scottish village* [Charles Winchester]. 8vo. London, 1833

KING Sham; and other atrocities in verse. By Peter Punever [Laurence N. Greenleaf]. 12mo. [Haynes' *Pseud.*] New York, 1868

KING Solomon's wives; or, the phantom mines. By Hyder Ragged [Andrew Lang, LL.D.]. 8vo. London, 1887

A burlesque imitation of *King Solomon's mines*, by Ryder Haggard.

KING Stephen's watch; a tale, founded on fact. By the author of the *Heroic epistle to Sir William Chambers, Knt.* [William Mason]. 8vo. London, 1782

KING Stork and King Log; a study of modern Russia. By Stepniak [Sergie Michaelovitsh Kravchinsky]. 8vo. 2 vols. [*Lond. Lib. Cat.*] London, 1895

KING (the) waits. [A romance relating to General Monk.] By Morice Gerard [John Jessop Teague]. 8vo. Pp. 288. [*Lond. Lib. Cat.*] London, 1921

KING William and Queen Mary conquerors; or, a discourse endeavouring to prove that their Majesties have on their side, against the late king, the principal reasons that make conquest a good title; shewing also how this is consistent with that declaration of Parliament, King James abdicated the government, etc. . . . [By Charles Blount.] 4to. Pp. 59. [Lathbury's *Nonjurors*, p. 74.] London, 1693

KING William's affection to the Church of England examin'd. [By Daniel Defoe.] The fifth edition. 4to. Pp. 30. [Wilson's *Life of Defoe.*] London, 1703

Ascribed also to John, Lord Somers.

KINGDOM (the); a descriptive and historical handbook to Fife, . . . edited by "Kilrounie" [John R. Russell]. 8vo. Pp. iv. 140. [Mitchell and Cash's *Scot. Top.*] Cupar, Fife [1882]

KINGDOM (the) and Church of Hawaii; a historical sketch. . . . By a friend of the Hawaiian Church Mission [George Edward Biber]. 8vo. [*Brit. Mus.*] London, 1865

Signed: G. E. B.

KINGDOM (the) of Christ; or, hints on the principles, ordinances, and constitution of the Catholic Church: in letters to a member of the Society of Friends. By a clergyman of the Church of England [Frederick Denison Maurice]. 12mo. [*Bodl.*] London [1837-8]

KINGDOM (the) of content. [A novel.] By "Pan" [Leslie Beresford]. 8vo. Pp. 278. [*Brit. Mus.*] London, 1918

KINGDOM (the) of Foigue. By a "herd loon" [Charles Horne]. 8vo. Aberdeen, 1903

KINGDOM (the) of God; containing a brief account of its properties, trials, privileges, and duration. By the author of *Impressions of the heart* [Lady Colquhoun, *née* Janet Sinclair]. 8vo. Edinburgh, 1835

KINGDOM (the) of God the good news, not individual salvation only. [By David Ker, of the Catholic Apostolic Church.] 8vo. Pp. 31. Edinburgh, 1879

KINGDOM (the) of heaven; the revelation of a divine purpose. . . . By ΣΑΕΡΔΝΑ [= Andreas (reversed), *i.e.* Andrew Anderson, photographer in Dunfermline]. 8vo. Pp. 390. London, 1891

KINGDOM (the) of Judah. By the author of *The wide, wide world* [Susan Warner]. 8vo. Pp. 260. London, 1878

KINGDOM (the) of waste lands. [A novel.] By Sydney C. Grier [Hilda C. Gregg]. 8vo. Pp. 318. [*Lond. Lib. Cat.*] Edinburgh, 1917

KINGHORN; a tour by Tom, Dick, and Harry; in which is given the historical, geographical, and statistical account of the ancient and royal burgh. By an heritor [—— Dempster]. 4to. Edinburgh, 1863

KING'S (the) army. By Annie Gray [Annie Grayjones]. Fourth edition. 8vo. Pp. 206. London, 1912

KING'S (the) army; and other stories. By Legude Palmer [Mary Louise Parmlee, later Mrs A. Peebles]. 8vo. [Haynes' *Pseud.*] London [1891]

KINGS at arms. [A historical novel.] By Marjorie Bowen [Gabrielle Vere Campbell, later Madame Long]. 8vo. Pp. 319. London, 1918

KINGS (the) [Charles I.] cause rationally, briefly, and plainly debated, as it stands de facto; against the irrationall, groundlesse misprisions of a still deceived sort of people. [By John Doughty, of Merton College, Oxford.] 4to. Pp. 41. [*Bodl.*] 1644

KING'S College and Mr [F. D.] Maurice. No. 1. The facts. By a barrister of Lincoln's Inn [J. M. Ludlow]. 8vo. [Bartholomew's *Camb. Books.*] London, 1854

KING'S College buildings [in Aberdeen]; a descriptive account. By R. S. R. [Robert Sangster Rait, M.A.]. 8vo. Pp. 20. [*Aberd. Pub. Lib.*] Aberdeen, 1895

KING'S Cope; a novel. [By Ellen Wallace.] 8vo. 3 vols. [*Nat. Lib. of Scot.*] London, 1849

KING'S daughter. [A tale.] By Pansy [Mrs Alden, *née* Isabella Macdonald]. 8vo. Pp. 320. [*Lit. Year Book.*] London, 1904

KING'S (the) diadem. [A tale.] By Annie Gray [Annie Grayjones]. 8vo. Pp. 185. London [1890]

KING'S (the) disguise. [By John Cleveland.] 4to. [*Brit. Mus.*] [London, 1646]

A poem on Charles I.

KING'S (the) English. By H. W. F. and F. G. F. [Henry Watson Fowler and Francis George Fowler]. 8vo. Pp. x. 370. [*Camb. Univ. Lib.*] Oxford, 1906

KING'S (the) folly and the Queen's revenge; the true story of a Court scandal. By Viva Vox [Henry Charles John Lingham. Verse]. Pp. 59. [*Brit. Mus.*] Melbourne [1900?]

KING'S (the) garden. By W. L. M. Jay [Mrs Julia L. M. Woodruff]. 8vo. [Haynes' *Pseud.*] New York, 1902

The pen-name is based on the reversed initials of the true name.

KING'S (the) gift. By Cousin Annie [Annie M. Barnes]. 8vo. [*Amer. Cat.*] Philadelphia, 1903

KING'S (the) grant of privilege for sole printing common law-books, defended, and the legality thereof asserted. [By Richard Atkyns.] 4to. [*Brit. Mus.*] London, 1669

KING'S (the) guide; a romance. By Naunton Covertside [Naunton Davies]. 8vo. Pp. 360. London, 1901

KING'S (the) highway; some more helpful verse. By John Oxenham [William Arthur Dunkerley]. 12mo. Pp. 94. [*Lit. Year Book.*] London, 1916

KINGS (the) Majesties [Charles I.] letter to the Queen concerning the differences betwixt the English and the Scots, and the great distractions within the City of London &c.; with certain proposals to the kingdome of England: perused and examined by a perfect copy, and published for general satisfaction of all His Majesties subjects. [By Thomas Wilson.] 4to. [*Brit. Mus.*] London, 1648

KING'S (the) mark. By Walter D. Dunlap [Sylvanus Cobb, jun.]. 8vo. [Cushing's *Init. and Pseud.* ii. 46.] New York, 1895

KING'S (a) masquerade. [A novel.] By May Wynne [Mabel Wynne Knowles]. 8vo. [*Lit. Year Book.*] London, 1910

KING'S (the) mirror. [A novel.] By Anthony Hope [Sir Anthony Hope Hawkins]. 8vo. Pp. viii. 311. [*Brit. Mus.*] London, 1899

KING'S (the) most gratious messages for peace, and a personal treaty; published for his people's satisfaction, that they may see and judge, whether the foundation of the Commons declaration, touching their votes of no farther addresse to the king, (viz. His Majesties aversenesse to peace) be just, rationall and religious. [By Edward Symmons.] 4to. Pp. 138. [Watt's *Bibl. Brit.*] N.P. 1648

KINGS of England; a history for young children. [By Charlotte Mary Yonge.] Third edition. 12mo. Pp. vii. 284. London, 1851

KINGS of Israel and Judah; their history explained to children: being a continuation of "Lines left out." By the author of *Peep of day*, etc. [Mrs Thomas Mortimer]. 8vo. Pp. xii. 415. London, 1872

KINGS (the) of the East; a romance of the near future. By Sydney C. Grier [Hilda C. Gregg]. 8vo. [*Lit. Year Book.*] Edinburgh, 1900

KINGS of the hunting-field. . . . By "Thormanby" [W. Willmott Dixon]. 8vo. Pp. xii. 471. [*Brit. Mus.*] London, 1899

KINGS of the rod, rifle, and gun. By "Thormanby" [W. Willmott Dixon]. 8vo. 2 vols. [*Brit. Mus.*] London, 1901

KINGS of the Turf; memoirs and anecdotes of distinguished owners, backers, trainers, and jockeys who have figured on the British Turf. . . . By "Thormanby" [W. Willmott Dixon]. 8vo. Pp. viii. 378. [*Brit. Mus.*] London, 1898

KING'S (the) own. By the author of *The naval officer* [Captain Frederick Marryat]. 12mo. 3 vols. [*Brit. Mus.*] London, 1830

KING'S (the) prerogative and the subject's priviledges asserted according to the laws of England; together with observations on the laws and government of most of the kingdoms and states of the universe. By J. N. [Rev. John Nalson, LL.D.] 8vo. Pp. 151. [*Bodl.*] London, 1684

KING'S (the) right of indulgence in spiritual matters, with the equity thereof, asserted. By a person of honour, and eminent minister of state, lately deceased [Arthur Annesley, Earl of Anglesey]. 4to. Pp. 75. [Jones' *Peck*, i. 90.] London, 1688

KING'S (a) romance; the story of Milan and Natalie, first King and Queen of Servia. By Frances A. Gerard [Geraldine P. Fitzgerald]. 8vo. London, 1903

KING'S (the) secret. By the author of *The lost heir* [Tyrone Power]. Second edition. 12mo. 3 vols. [*Bodl.*] London, 1831

KING'S (the) servants. I. Faithful in little. II. Unfaithful. III. Faithful in much. By Hesba Stretton [Sarah Smith], author of *Jessica's first prayer*, etc.. 8vo. Pp. viii. 200. London, 1873

See note to "Alone in London."

KING'S (the) service; a story of the Thirty Years' War. By the author of *The Spanish brothers* [Deborah Alcock]. 8vo. [*Brit. Mus.*] London [1885]

KING'S (the) signet. By Morice Gerard [John Jessop Teague]. 8vo. Pp. 248. [*Lond. Lib. Cat.*] London, 1919

KING'S (the) story book. [The parables of our Lord explained.] . . . By Mark Evans [Paul Tidman]. 8vo. [Cushing's *Init. and Pseud.* ii. 55.] London, 1880

KING'S (the) talisman; or, the lion of Mount Hor: an Eastern romance. By Walter D. Dunlap [Sylvanus Cobb, jun.]. 8vo. [Cushing's *Init. and Pseud.* ii. 46.] New York, 1899

KING'S (a) tragedy. [A novel.] By May Wynne [Mabel Wynne Knowles]. 8vo. [*Lit. Year Book.*] London, 1905

KINGSBRIDGE and Salcombe . . . historically and topographically depicted. [By Abraham Hawkins.] 12mo. [Davidson's *Bibl. Devon.*]. Kingsbridge, 1819

KINGSFORD. [A novel.] By the author of *Son and heir*, etc. [Frances West Atherton Pike]. 8vo. [*Nat. Lib. of Scot.*] London, 1867

Attributed also to Emily Spender.

KINGSTONIAN poems. By the inventor of the art of printing in dry colours [William Kingston]. 8vo. [*Brit. Mus.*] London, 1835

KINGSWELLS; lines. [By Alexander Edmond.] 8vo. [Robertson's *Aberd. Bibl.*] Aberdeen, 1876

KINGSWESTON Hill; a poem. [By Thomas Hobhouse.] 4to. [Watt's *Bibl. Brit.*] London, 1784

The second edition has the author's name.

KINGUSSIE and Upper Speyside; a descriptive guide to the district, with map of Badenoch. [By George A. Crerar.] 8vo. [P. J. Anderson's *Bibl. of Inverness*, p. 196.] Kingussie [1910]

KINK (the). [A novel.] By Lynn Brock [Alister McAllister]. 8vo. Pp. 290. [*Brit. Mus.*] New York [1927]

KINKAID (the) venture. By "Fleeta" [Kate W. Hamilton]. 8vo. [*Amer. Cat.*] Philadelphia, 1900

KINNEARS (the); a Scottish story. [By Henrietta Keddie.] 8vo. 3 vols. London, 1852

KINSFOLK and others. [A novel.] By the author of *Mademoiselle Mori* [Miss Margaret Roberts]. 8vo. [*Brit. Mus.*] London, 1891

KINSMEN (the); or, the Black Riders of Congàree. By the author of *The partisan*, etc. [William Gilmore Simms, LL.D.]. 12mo. [*Brit. Mus.*] New York, 1841

KINTAIL Place; a tale of the Revolution. By the author of *Dorothy* [Margaret Agnes Colville, later Mrs Paul]. 8vo. [*Brit. Mus.*] London, 1886

KIRK patronage the people's privilege. [By Thomas Gillespie, LL.D.] 12mo. Cupar, 1636 [for 1836]

KIRK (the), the poets, and the critics. [By William Cadenhead.] 8vo. [*Aberd. Pub. Lib.*] Aberdeen, 1874

KIRKCUMDOON. By Rev. Peter Ponder [Rev. William Bell]. 8vo. Pp. 152. [*New Coll. Lib.*] Edinburgh, 1875

KIRKHOLME Priory; or, modern heroism: a tale. By the author of *The ransom* [Laura Jewry]. 12mo. London, 1847

KIRKIAD (the); or, golden age of the Church of Scotland. Canto I. [By Archibald Bruce, minister at Whitburn.] 8vo. [Anderson's *Scottish Nation.*] Edinburgh, 1774

KIRK-O-FIELD; a tragedy, in four acts. By Robert Blake [Robert Hely Thompson]. 12mo. [*Brit. Mus.*] Omagh, Tyrone [1895]

Reprinted from the *Tyrone Constitution.*

KIRKS and kirk-yards; an essay on the singular respect and veneration shewn to the human body after death, and on the growing evil of profaning kirks and kirk-yards. . . . By a ruling elder of the [Episcopal] Church of Scotland [Robert Forbes, Bishop of Moray]. 8vo. [Memoir prefixed to his "Lyon in Mourning" (*Scot. Hist. Society Publications*).] [Edinburgh ?] 1767

KIRKSTEAD! or, the pleasures of shooting; a poem. [By Major Richard Ellison.] 12mo. [*Brit. Mus.*] London [1837]

KIRSTY Macintosh's scholars. [By William M. Philip.] 8vo. Aberdeen, 1882

KIRSTY o' the Mill Toun. By the author of *Mona Maclean* [Margaret Todd, M.D.]. 8vo. Pp. 64. [*Brit. Mus.*] Edinburgh, 1896

KIRSTY'S Prince; a story of Holyrood. By Crona Temple [Miss —— Corfield]. 8vo. Pp. 120. [*Brit. Mus.*] London [1896]

KIRWAN'S [Rev. Nicholas Murray's] letter to Dr Cote, on Baptism, with Dr Cote's reply. 12mo. [Cushing's *Init. and Pseud.* i. 158.] New York, 1849

KISHOGE (the) papers [in verse]. By Bouillon de Garçon [Michael Joseph Barry]. 8vo. [O'Donoghue's *Poets of Ireland.*] Dublin [1860?]

New edition, 1872 (London).

KISMET. [An Egyptian novel.] By Dudu [Julia Constance Fletcher]. 8vo. [Ilmy's *Bibl. of Egypt.*] Boston, 1875

Afterwards published (London, 1877) as "A Nile novel. By George Fleming."

KISS (the) of Isis. By Arthur Amyand [Col. Andrew C. P. Haggard]. 8vo. [*Brit. Mus.*] London, 1900

KISS (the) of peace; or, England and Rome at one on the doctrine of the Holy Eucharist: an essay, in two parts. By a Fellow of * * * College, Cambridge [Gerard Francis Cobb]. 8vo. Pp. xx. 172. London, 1867

A second edition, published in 1868, has the author's name.

KISS (the) of the enemy; a novel. By Headon Hill [Frank E. Grainger]. 8vo. Pp. 320. [*Lond. Lib. Cat.*] London, 1904

KISSES; being an English translation, in verse, of the Basia of Joannes Secundus Nicolaius of the Hague; accompanied with the original Latin text: to which is added, an essay on the life and writings of Secundus. Ornamented with a frontispiece representing the origin of kisses, and a likeness of Secundus from a painting by Scorellius. [By John Nott, M.D.] 8vo. [*Gent. Mag.* xcv. 2, 566.] London, 1775

KISSING; its origin and species. By a disciple [Harriet Anne De Salis]. 8vo. [*Brit. Mus.*] London [1873]

KIT-CATS (the); a poem. [By Sir Richard Blackmore.] 8vo. [Lowndes' *Bibl. Man.* p. 1280.] London, 1718

KITCHEN (the) garden. . . . By Eugene Sebastian Delamer [Rev. Edmund Saul Dixon, M.A.]. 8vo. [Kirk's *Supp.*] London, 1855

KITE (the); an heroi-comical poem, in three canto's. [By Phanuel Bacon.] 4to. [*D. N. B.*] London, 1729

KITE (a) story; a birthday festival. By G. L. V. [Mrs Gertrude Lefferts Vanderbilt]. 8vo. [Cushing's *Init. and Pseud.* i. 291.] New York, 1871

KITTY Costello. [A novel.] By Mrs Alexander [Mrs Annie F. Hector, *née* French]. 8vo. Pp. 320. [*Brit. Mus.*] London, 1906

KITTY Fagan; a romance of pit life. By Ramsay Guthrie [Rev. John George Bowran]. 8vo. Pp. 280. [*Meth. Who's Who.*] London, 1900

KITTY Fairhall. [A novel.] By John Halsham [G. Forrester Scott]. 8vo. London, 1901

KITTY in Fairyland. By Phyllis Dare [Phyllis Dones]. 4to. Pp. viii. 120. [*Brit. Mus.*] London, 1914

KITTY the rag. By the author of *Peg the rake* [Mrs W. Desmond Humphreys, *née* Eliza M. J. Gollan]. 8vo. [*Brit. Mus.*] London, 1896

KITTYLEEN. By Sophie May [Rebecca Sophia Clarke]. 8vo. [Cushing's *Init. and Pseud.* i. 185.] Boston, 1880

KITTY'S engagement; a novel. By Florence Warden [Florence Alice Price, later Mrs George E. James]. 8vo. Pp. 312. London, 1895

KITTY'S rival; a story. By Sydney Mostyn [William Clark Russell]. 8vo. 3 vols. [*Brit. Mus.*] London, 1873

Κλεὶς εὐαγγελίου τοῦ μυστικοῦ; or, a key to the doctrines contained in this book . . . with some additions. By W. S. [William Sherwin], minister of the gospel. 4to. [*Brit. Mus.*] London, 1672

The first letter in the title is mistakenly printed X.

KLOSTERHEIM; or, the masque. By the English opium-eater [Thomas De Quincey]. 8vo. [*D. N. B.* vol. 14, p. 391.] Edinburgh, 1832

KLYTIA; a story of Heidelberg Castle. By George Taylor [Professor Adolf Hausrath]; from the German. 8vo. [*Brit. Mus.*] London, 1883

KNAPSACK (the); a collection of fugitive poems. By a soldier [Sergeant —— Walker]. 8vo. Pp. 132. Kingston [Canada] 1853

KNAPSACK ballads. By Uncle Nic [G. A. Thompson]. 8vo. Chicago, 1903

KNAVE (the) in graine, new vampt; a witty comedy acted at the Fortune. . . . Written by J. D. [John Day?], Gent. 4to. London, 1640

KNAVE (the) of clubbes; or, 'tis mery when Knaves mete. [By Samuel Rowlands.] 4to. Pp. 48. [Hart's *Index Expurg. Angl.* p. 47.] London, 1600

Dedication signed: S. R.

Reprinted by Percy Jacobin in 1843, and by the Hunterian Club, 1872.

KNAVE (the) of harts. Haile fellow, well met. [By Samuel Rowlands.] 4to. Pp. 48. London, 1612

Reprinted by the Hunterian Club, 1874.

KNAVERY in all trades; or, the Coffee House: a comedy. . . . [By John Tatham.] 4to. [*D. N. B.* vol. 55, p. 384.] London, 1664

KNAVERY unmasked; or, the confessions of a celebrated dacoit. By an Indian detective [R. Reid]. 8vo. [*Calc. Imp. Lib.*] Calcutta, 1891

KNAUES (the) of spades and diamonds, with new additions. [By Samuel Rowlands.] 4to. [*Christie-Miller Cat.*] N.P. [1612]

KNEELING (the) Christian. By the author of *How to live the victorious life* [Albert Ernest Richardson]. 8vo. Pp. 148. [*Brit. Mus.*] London [1924]

KNICKERBOCKER days. By Harris Tweed [Frederick Watson, M.A.]. 8vo. Pp. 170. London, 1912

KNICKNACKS from an editor's table. [By Lewis Gaylord Clark.] 8vo. [Cushing's *Init. and Pseud.* i. 86.] New York, 1853

KNIGHT (the). [By William Meston.] 8vo. Pp. v. 111. [Robertson's *Aberd. Bibl.*] N.P. 1723

Dedication "To somebody," signed: Quidam.

A third edition was published at London in 1728, with the title, "The knight of the Kirk: or, the ecclesiastical adventures of Sir John Presbyter."

KNIGHT (a) among ladies. [A novel.] By J. E. Buckrose [Mrs Falconer Jameson]. 8vo. [*Lit. Year Book.*] London, 1922

KNIGHT (the) and the lady; a domestic legend of the reign of Queen Anne. By Thomas Ingoldsby [Rev. Richard Harris Barham, B.A.]. Fol. [*Brit. Mus.*] London, 1886

KNIGHT (a) at heart. [A novel.] By Owen Oliver [Sir Joseph Albert Flynn]. 8vo. Pp. 318. [*Brit. Mus.*] London [1925]

KNIGHT (the) of Dumbleton foil'd at his own weapons; or, an answer to a scandalous pamphlet, entituled The Church of England secured, the Toleration Act enervated, and the dissenters ruined and undone: addressed by way of letter to Sir Richard Cocks, Bart., in which the many vile reflections of that writer upon the clergy of the Established Church, are confuted, and his gross sophistications, quibbles, and blunders, fully exposed. By a gentleman, and no knight [Zachary Grey]. 8vo. [*Bodl.*] London, 1723

KNIGHT (a) of evil. By Dick Donovan [Joyce E. P. Muddock]. 8vo. Pp. 318. [*Lond. Lib. Cat.*] London, 1905

KNIGHT (the) of Snowden; or, the Saxon and the Gael. By M. C. H. [Mrs M. C. Haldane]. 8vo. Pp. 248. Paisley, 1902

KNIGHT (a) of Spain. By Marjorie Bowen [Gabrielle Margaret Vere Campbell, later Madame Long]. 8vo. Pp. 320. [*Lit. Year Book.*] London, 1912

KNIGHT (the) of the burning pestle. [By Francis Beaumont, and John Fletcher.] 4to. No pagination. London, 1613

The first edition.

KNIGHT (the) of the Kirk; or, the ecclesiastical adventures of Sir John Presbyter. [By William Meston.] Third edition. 8vo. London, 1728

See also "The knight" above.

KNIGHT (the) of the Rose; an allegorical narrative. . . . By the author of *The adventures of the six princesses of Babylon*, etc. [Lucy Peacock]. 12mo. [*Brit. Mus.*] London, 1793

KNIGHT (a) of the twentieth century; a novel. By Arthur Forbes [Rev. Forbes Phillips, vicar of Gorleston]. 8vo. London, 1898

KNIGHT (the) of the White Feather. By "Tasma" [Madame Couvreur, *née* Jessie Huybers]. 8vo. 2 vols. London, 1892

The authoress took her pen-name from Tasmania, where she spent her early years.

KNIGHT (a) on wheels. By Ian Hay [John Hay Beith, M.A.]. 8vo. Pp. 320. [*Lond. Lib. Cat.*] London, 1914

KNIGHTAGE (the) of Great Britain and Ireland. [By J. and Sir John B. Burke.] 12mo. [*Brit. Mus.*] London, 1841

KNIGHTED by the Admiral; or, the days of the Great Armada. By Crona Temple [Miss —— Corfield]. 8vo. [*Brit. Mus.*] London, 1890

KNIGHT-ERRANT (the); a novel. By Edna Lyall [Ada Ellen Bayly]. 8vo. 3 vols. [*Lit. Year Book.*] London, 1887

KNIGHTS (the). [By John Hookham Frere. Translated from the Greek of Aristophanes.] 4to. Pp. 89. Malta, 1839

No title-page.

See also "Aristophanes" in Vol. I.

KNIGHT'S excursion companion; excursions from London. [By James Thorne.] 8vo. London, 1851

KNIGHTS in fustian. [A novel.] By Caro. Brown [Caro. Virginia Krout]. 8vo. [*Amer. Cat.*] Boston, 1900

KNIGHT'S (the) motto. By Walter D. Dunlap [Sylvanus Cobb, junr.]. 8vo. [Cushing's *Init. and Pseud.* ii. 46.] London, 1904

KNIGHTS (the) of Rosemullion. [A tale.] By Esmé Stuart [Amélie Claire Leroy]. 8vo. Pp. 218. [*Lond. Lib. Cat.*] London, 1897

KNIGHTS of the Grail; Lohengrin; Galahad. By Norley Chester [Emily Underdown]. 8vo. London, 1907

KNIGHTS (the) of St John; with the Battle of Lepanto and the Siege of Vienna. [By Augusta Theodosia Drane.] 8vo. Pp. x. 282. [*Brit. Mus.*] London, 1858

Preface signed: E. H. T. [E. Healy Thomson].

KNIT by felony. [A novel.] By E. Livingston Prescott [Edith Katherine Spicer-Jay]. 8vo. Pp. 352. [*Lit. Year Book.*] London, 1903

KNITTERS in the sun. [A series of short stories.] By Octave Thanet [Alice French]. 8vo. [Haynes' *Pseud.*] Boston, 1887

KNITTING work; a web of many textures. By Ruth Partington [Benjamin Poore Shillaber]. 8vo. [Cushing's *Init. and Pseud.* i. 225.] Boston, 1859

KNOT (a) of fooles. [A satire, in verse. By Thomas Brewer.] 4to. [Thomason's *Coll. of Tracts*, ii. 201.] [London] 1658

KNOT (the) unty'd; or, the Association disbanded. [By Robert Ferguson, "the Plotter."] 4to. [*Brit. Mus.*] London, 1682

KNOW your own mind; a comedy [in five acts, and in prose], performed at the Theatre-Royal in Covent-Garden. [By Arthur Murphy.] 8vo. [*Brit. Mus.*] London, 1778

KNOWLEDGE (the) of divine things from revelation, not from reason or nature: wherein the origin and obligation of religious truths are demonstrated; arguments of Deists, moralists, &c. proved to have no foundation in nature or reason. . . . By a gentleman of Brazen-nose College, Oxford; now of the diocese of Chester [John Ellis, D.D.]. 8vo. Pp. xxiv. 440. London, 1743

The edition of 1771 is not anonymous.

KNOWLEDGE (the) of medals; or instructions for those who apply themselves to the study of medals, both ancient and modern. From the French [of Louis Jobert. Translated by Roger Gale]. Pp. 215. [*Bodl.*] London, 1697

KNOWLEDGE (the) of things unknown; shewing the effects of the planets and other astronomical constellations, with the strange events that befall men, women and children born under them. . . . [By —— Godfridus.] 8vo. [*Brit. Mus.*] London, 1743

Earlier editions, including the first, *c.* 1530, were not anonymous.

KNOX Rannoch's prophecy. . . . By Mark Meldrum [Rev. Alex. Webster]. 8vo. Aberdeen [*c.* 1895]

KNUTSFORD (the) mystery. [A novel.] By Dick Donovan [Joyce E. P. Muddock]. 8vo. Pp. 320. [*Lond. Lib. Cat.*] London, 1906

KODAK (the) woman. [A novel.] By Bertha M. Clay [Mrs Charlotte M. Braeme, *née* Law]. 8vo. Pp. 318. Chicago [1895]

KOHELETH; a novel. By S. A. Lewis [Lewis Austin Storrs]. 8vo. New York, 1897

KONINGSMARKE, the long Finne; a story of the new world. [By James Kirk Paulding.] 8vo. 3 vols. [*Bodl.*] New York, 1823

KOREA, and the ten lost tribes of Israel; with Korean, Japanese, and Israelitish explanations. . . . [By N. Macleod.] Obl. fol. [*Brit. Mus.*] Yokohama, 1879

KORMAK; an Icelandic romance of the tenth century. [Translated by William Leighton.] 8vo. [Cushing's *Anon.*] Boston, 1861

KOSMOGONIA; a glance at the old world, in which are set forth certain missing links of the Darwinian chain. By Lake-Elbe [Archibald Bleloch, M.D.]. 4to. Pp. 71. Edinburgh, 1878

KOSSUTH and "The Times." By the author of *The revelations of Russia* [Charles Frederick Henningsen]. Fourth edition. 8vo. [*Brit. Mus.*] London, 1851

KULU; its beauties, antiquities, and silver mines; including a trip over the snowy range and glaciers. By the author of *Notes on the mineral wealth of India* [John Calvert, C.E.]. 8vo. [*Brit. Mus.*] Calcutta, 1871

The "Notes," privately printed, are not anonymous.

KUZZILBASH (the): a tale of Khorasan. [By James Baillie Fraser.] 12mo. 3 vols. [*Bodl.*] London, 1828

KYZIE Dunlee; a golden girl. By Sophie May [Rebecca Sophia Clarke.] 8vo. Pp. 80. [Haynes' *Pseud.*] Boston, 1895

L

L. A. SENECA the philosopher, his book of consolation to Marcia; translated into an English poem [by Sir Ralph Freeman]. 4to. Pp. 46. [*Bodl.*] London, 1635

Address to the reader signed: Philophrastes.

L. ANNÆUS Seneca's Troas; a tragedy, translated from the Latine by J. T. [J. Talbot]. 4to. Pp. 44. [Mayor's *Bibliographical clue to Latin literature*, p. 135.] London, 1686

LA GAVIOTA; the sea-gull; or, the lost beauty. By Fernan Caballero [C. F. J. Arrom de Ayala]. 12mo. Philadelphia, 1877

LA SCAVA; or, some account of an excavation of a Roman town on the hill of Chatelet, in Champagne, between St Dizier and Joinville, discovered in the year 1772; to which is added, a journey to the Simplon, by Lausanne, and to Mont Blanc through Geneva. By the author of *Letters from Paris in* 1791-2, etc. [Stephen Weston, B.D.]. 8vo. [*Brit. Mus.*] London, 1818

LA STREGA; and other stories. By "Ouida" [Louise de la Ramée]. 8vo. [*Brit. Mus.*] London, 1899

LABOR rewarded; the claims of labor and capital conciliated; or, how to secure to labor the whole products of its exertions. By one of the idle classes [William Thompson, of Cork and Rosscarberry]. 8vo. Pp. viii. 127. [*Edin. Univ. Lib.*] London, 1827

LABORIOUS days; leaves from the Indian record of Sir Charles Alfred Elliott . . . Lieutenant-Governor of Bengal. [By Francis B. H. Skrine.] 8vo. [*Calc. Imp. Lib.*] Calcutta, 1892

LABOUR and live; a story. [By Mrs Ellen Epps, *née* Elliott.] 8vo. [*Brit. Mus.*] London, 1848

LABOUR and profits. By Boyd Cable [Ernest Andrew Ewart]. 8vo. Pp. 96. [*Brit. Mus.*] London, 1925

LABOUR defended against the claims of capital. . . . By a labourer [Thomas Hodgskin]. 12mo. [*Brit. Mus.*] London, 1825

LABOURERS in the vineyard; dioramic sketches in the lives of eminent Christians. By M. H., author of *The story of a red velvet Bible*, etc. [Matilda Horsburgh]. . . . 8vo. Pp. 174. Edinburgh, 1863

LABOURING (the) classes in Ireland; an inquiry as to what beneficial changes may be effected in their condition by the legislature, the landowner and the labourer respectively. By Martin Doyle, author of *Hints to small farmers*, etc. [Ross Hickey]. 12mo. Pp. vi. 78. Dublin, 1846

LABOURING (the) classes of England. . . . By an Englishman [William Dodd]. 8vo. [Cushing's *Init. and Pseud.* ii. 53.] Boston, 1847

LABOURING (the) persons remembrancer; or, a practical discourse of the labour of the body; with suitable devotions. [By Francis Lee, M.D., Fellow of St John's College, Oxford.] 8vo. Pp. 51. [*Bodl.*] Oxford, 1690

LABOURS (the) of idleness; or, seven nights' entertainments. By Guy Penseval [George Darley, B.A.]. 8vo. [O'Donoghue's *Poets of Ireland.*] London, 1826

LABRADOR; a poetic epistle. By G. C. [George Cartwright], Esq. 8vo. [*Brit. Mus.*] Doncaster, 1785

LABYRINTHS (the) of life; a novel. By Mrs Thomson [Miss Harriot Pigott]. 12mo. London, N.D.

LABYRINTHVS Cantvariensis; or, Doctor Lawd's labyrinth; beeing an ansvver to the late Archbishop of Canterbvries Relation of a conference between himselfe and Mr Fisher, etc. Wherein the true grounds of the Roman Catholiqve religion are asserted, the principall controuersies betvvixt Catholiques and Protestants throughly examined, and the Bishops meandrick vvindings throughout his vvhole vvorke layd open to publique veivv. By T. C. [Thomas Carwell, alias Thorold]. Fol. [Lowndes' *Bibl. Man.* p. 1317; Jones' *Peck*, i. 222.] Paris, 1658

A later edition of this work bears the title "Lawd's *Labyrinth. . . .*" *q.v.*

LA CHANCE (the) mine mystery. By S. Carleton [Susan Carleton Jones]. 8vo. Pp. 304. [*Amer. Cat.*] New York, 1920

LACHRYMAE lachrymarum; or, the distillation of teares shede for the vntymely death of the incomparable Prince Panaretus [Henry Prince of Wales. By Joshua Sylvester]. 16 leaves. 4to. [*Bodl.*] London, 1612

LACHRYMAE musarum ; the tears of the muses : exprest in elegies ; written by divers persons of nobility and worth, upon the death of the most hopefull, Henry Lord Hastings, onely sonn of the Right Honourable Ferdinando Earl of Huntingdon, heir-generall of the high-born Prince George Duke of Clarence, brother to King Edward the fourth. Collected and set forth by R. B. [Richard Brome]. 8vo. Pp. 98. [*British Bibliographer*, iv. 134 ; Scott's *Dryden*, xi. 93.] London, 1649

LACIS ; practical instructions in filet brodé. By Carita [Mrs Isabel A. Simpson]. 8vo. [*Lond. Lib. Cat.*, *Supp.*] London, 1909

LACKINGTON'S Confessions rendered into narrative. By Allan Macleod [Henry Lemoine]. 12mo. [*D. N. B.* vol. 33, p. 28.] London, 1804

LACONIA ; or, legends of the White Mountains. By an old mountaineer [J. P. Scribner ?]. 8vo. [Cushing's *Init. and Pseud.* i. 212.] Boston, 1856

LACONICS ; or, the best words of the best authors. [Collected by John Timbs.] Fifth edition. 12mo. 3 vols. [*W.*] London, 1834

LAD (the) from London. . . . By Ascott R. Hope [Ascott Robert Hope Moncrieff]. 8vo. Pp. 120. London [1896]

LAD (a) of the O'Friels. By "Mac" [Seumas M'Manus]. [S. J. Brown's *Ireland in fiction.*] London, 1903

LADBROOKE and its owners. By S. H. A. H. [Sydenham Henry Augustus Harvey]. 4to. Pp. xvi. 398. [*Brit. Mus.*] Bury St Edmunds, 1914

LADDER (a) of tears ; a novel. By George Colmore [Mrs Gertrude Colmore Dunn, later Mrs Baillie Weaver]. 8vo. Pp. 334. London, 1904

LADDIE. By the author of *Miss Toosey's mission* [Evelyn Whitaker]. 8vo. Pp. 92. [*Amer. Cat.*] London, 1894

LADENSIUM αὐτοκατάκρισις, the Canterburians' self-conviction ; or, an evident demonstration of the avowed Arminianisme, Poperie, and tyrannie of that faction, by their owne confessions ; with a postscript to the personat Jesuite Lysimachus Nicanor, a prime Canterburian. [By Robert Baillie.] 4to. [*Nat. Lib. of Scot.*]
Written in March, and printed in Aprile, 1640

LADIES (the) a second time assembled in Parliament ; (a continuation of "The Parliament of ladies" ;) their votes, orders, and declarations. [By Henry Neville.] 4to. Pp. 12. [*D.N.B.* vol. 40, p. 259.] N.P. 1647

LADIES (the) ! A shining constellation of wit and beauty. By E. Barrington [L. Adams Beck]. 8vo. Pp. 268. [*Brit. Mus.*] London, 1922

LADIES' (the) calling ; in two parts. By the author of *The whole duty of man* [Richard Allestree, D.D.] 8vo. Pp. 261. Oxford, 1673

See the note to "The art of contentment."

LADIES' (the) defence ; or, the bride-woman's counsellor answered : a poem, in a dialogue between Sir John Brute, Sir William Loveall, Melissa, and a parson. [By Mary, Lady Chudleigh.] 8vo. [Green's *Bibl. Somers.* iii. 276.] London, 1701

LADIES' (the) dispensatory ; containing the natures, vertues, and qualities of all herbs, and samples usefull in physick. [By Leonard Sowerby.] 8vo. Pp. 532. [Watt's *Bibl. Brit.*] London, 1651

LADIES' fair and frail ; sketches of the demi-monde during the eighteenth century. By Tivoli [Horace William Bleackley]. 8vo. [*Amer. Cat.*] New York, 1909

LADIES' (the) friend ; being a treatise on the virtues and qualifications which are the brightest ornaments of the fair sex. . . . [Translated from the French anonymous treatise of Pierre Joseph Boudier de Villemert.] 12mo. Pp. 107. Newhaven [Conn.] 1789

LADIES' (the) handbook. [By Mrs M. A. G. Gascoyne.] 4to. [*Brit. Mus.*] London [1846]

LADIES' (the) library. Written by a lady [Mary Wray, granddaughter of Jeremy Taylor and wife of Sir Cecil Wray ?] and published by Sir Richard Steele. 12mo. 3 vols. [*W.*] London, 1714

LADIES' (the) monitor ; being a series of letters, first published in Bengal on . . . female apparel, tending to favour a regulated adoption of Indian costume. . . . By the author of *A vindication of the Hindoos* [Charles Stuart]. 8vo. London, 1809

LADIES' Museum. [Edited by Mrs Charlotte Lennox.] 8vo. 2 vols. [Lowndes' *Bibl. Man.*] London, 1760-1

LADIES' (the) New-year's gift ; see "The lady's New-year's gift. . . ."

LADIES (the) of Bever Hollow; a tale of English country life. By the author of *Mary Powell* [Anne Manning, later Mrs Rathbone]. 8vo. 2 vols. London, 1858

LADIES (the) of Lovel-Leigh. By the author of *Margaret and her bridesmaids*, etc. [Mrs Julia Stretton]. 8vo. 3 vols. [*D. N. B.* vol. 36, p. 219.] London, 1862

Incorrectly attributed to Mrs Marsh-Caldwell; by others to Henrietta Keddie.

LADIES' (the) school across the water; or, how came John to be neutral? A forgotten chapter, edited by a graduate of Dame Europa's school. [By John Edward Field, M.A., Worcester College.] 12mo. Pp. 19. [*Bodl.*] London [1871]

LADIES' (the) subscription; a dramatic performance. [By John Cleland.] 8vo. [*Brit. Mus.*] London, 1755

LADIES' (the) visiting-day; a comedy, as it was acted at the theatre in Lincolns-Inn-Fields, by his Majesties servants: with the addition of a new scene. By the author of *The reformed wife* [Charles Burnaby]. 4to. Pp. 52. [Baker's *Biog. Dram.*] London, 1701

LADY Alice; or, the new Una: a novel. [By Jedediah Vincent Huntington.] 12mo. 3 vols. [*Nat. Lib. of Scot.*] London, 1849

LADY Alimony, or the Alimony Lady; an excellent pleasant new comedy. [By Thomas Lodge, M.D., and Robert Greene?] 4to. [*Brit. Mus.*] London, 1659

LADY (the) and the dressmaker; or, a peep at fashionable folly. By a Bluenose [George E. Fenety]. 8vo. [Cushing's *Init. and Pseud.* i. 37.] St Johns, New Brunswick, 1842

LADY (the) and the pye . . . and the plum-cakes. By Z. [Hannah More]. 8vo. [*Brit. Mus.*] London, 1800

LADY (the) and the Saints. [By W. F. Patterson.] 8vo. London, 1839

LADY (the) Annabetta; a novel. By the authoress of *Constance* and *Rosabel* [Mrs Katherine Thomson]. 12mo. 3 vols. [*Bodl.*] London, 1837

LADY Anne's trustee; and other stories. By Florence Warden [Florence Alice Price, later Mrs George E. James]. 8vo. Pp. 320. London, 1907

LADY (the) "Arabella Stuart"; a poem. By E. S. L. [Elizabeth Susan Law, later Lady Colchester]. 8vo. Pp. 126. [Dobell's *Cat.*] London [1836?]

LADY Audley's secret. [A novel. By Mary E. Braddon, later Mrs John Maxwell.] 8vo. [*Brit. Mus.*] London, 1879

LADY Augusta Stanley. Reminiscences by the author of *The Schönberg-Cotta family* [Mrs Charles, *née* Elizabeth Rundle]. 8vo. Pp. 64. [*Brit. Mus.*] London, 1893

LADY Beatrix and the forbidden man. [By M. A. Ross.] 8vo. Pp. viii. 300. [*Brit. Mus.*] London, 1902

LADY Beauty; or, charming to her latest day: a novel. By Alan Muir [Rev. Hayes Robinson]. 8vo. 2 vols. [*Lond. Lib. Cat.*] London, 1882

A later edition (1891) has the title, "Charming to her latest day."

LADY Bell; a story of last century. By the author of *Citoyenne Jacqueline* [Henrietta Keddie]. 8vo. 3 vols. [*Brit. Mus.*] London, 1873

LADY Blanche; and other poems. By "Ida" [Mrs Ida L. White]. 8vo. [O'Donoghue's *Poets of Ireland.*] Belfast, 1824

LADY Bluebeard. [A novel.] By the author of *Zit and Xoe* [Henry Curwen, journalist]. 8vo. 2 vols. Edinburgh, 1888

LADY Bountiful. By George A. Birmingham [James Owen Hannay, D.D.]. 8vo. Pp. 240. [*Lit. Year Book.*] London, 1921

LADY Branksmere. [A novel.] By the author of *Phyllis*, etc. [Mrs Margaret Argles, later Mrs Hungerford]. 8vo. 3 vols. [*Brit. Mus.*] London, 1886

LADY Castlemaine's divorce. By Bertha M. Clay [Charlotte M. Braeme]. 8vo. New York, 1887

LADY Clara's rival. By Bertha M. Clay [Charlotte M. Braeme]. 8vo. London, 1915

LADY Damer's secret; a novel. By Bertha M. Clay [Charlotte M. Braeme]. 8vo. New York, 1886

LADY Diana's pride. By Bertha M. Clay [Charlotte M. Braeme]. 8vo. New York, 1887

LADY Dobbs. By the author of *Estelle* [Emily Marion Harris]. 8vo. 2 vols. London, 1890

LADY (the) Drusilla. By Q. [Thomas Parnell]. 8vo. London, 1887

LADY Ella; or, the story of Cinderella in verse. By the authoress of *Hymns and scenes of childhood* [Jane E. Leeson]. 12mo. Pp. 151. [Julian's *Dict. of Hymnology.*] London, 1847

LADY Fanny. By Mrs George Norman [Mrs George Blount]. 8vo. Pp. 328. [*Catholic Who's Who.*] London, 1911

LADY Flavia. By the author of *Lord Lynn's wife* [John Berwick Harwood]. 8vo. 3 vols. [*Brit. Mus.*] London, 1865

LADY (the) forger; an original play. [By Frederick John Melville.] 8vo. Pp. 54. [*Brit. Mus.*] London, 1906

LADY Gay and her sister. By Mrs George Archibald [Anna Campbell, later Mrs George Archibald Palmer]. 8vo. Boston, 1898

LADY Geraldine Seymour; a tale. [By Mrs Fawkes, daughter of Thomas Maitland, Lord Dundrennan.] 8vo. [*Cat. Phil. Inst. Edin.* p. 104.] London, 1852

LADY Glastonbury's boudoir; or, the history of two weeks. By the author of *The new Utopia* [Augusta Theodosia Drane]. 8vo. Pp. iv. 279. [*D. N. B.* First Supp. vol. 2, p. 156.] London, 1883

LADY Good-for-nothing. By "Q" [Sir Arthur T. Quiller-Couch]; a man's portrait of a woman. 8vo. Pp. 506. London, 1910

LADY Granard's nieces; a novel. [By Jane Vaughan Pinkney.] 8vo. 3 vols. [*Nat. Lib. of Scot.*] London, 1848

LADY Gwendolyn's dream. By Bertha M. Clay [Charlotte M. Braeme]. 8vo. New York, 1887

LADY (the) Herbert's gentlewomen. By Silverpen [Eliza Meteyard]. 8vo. 3 vols. [Kirk's *Supp.*] London, 1882

LADY Hetty; a story of Scottish and Australian life. [By John Service, D.D.] 8vo. 3 vols. London, 1875

LADY Huntworth's experiment; an original comedy, in three acts. By Richard Claude Carton [Richard Claude Critchott]. 8vo. Pp. 81. [*Brit. Mus.*] London [1904]

LADY Hutton's ward. By Bertha M. Clay [Charlotte M. Braeme]. 8vo. Chicago, 1888

LADY (a) in black; a novel. By Florence Warden [Florence Alice Price, later Mrs George E. James]. 8vo. Pp. 266. London, 1897

LADY (the) in furs. By Florence Warden [Mrs George E. James, *née* Florence Alice Price]. 8vo. London, 1922

LADY (a) in grey. By G. Ohnet [Georges Hénot]. Translated from the French. 8vo. [*Lond. Lib. Cat.*] London, 1905

LADY Jane and the smallholders. By M. E. Francis [Mrs Francis Blundell, *née* Mary Evans Sweetman] and Margaret Blundell. 8vo. London, 1924

LADY Jane Grey and her times. By George Howard, Esq. [Lieut. Francis C. Laird, R.N.]. 8vo. London, 1822

LADY Jane Grey; Inez, or the Bride of Portugal. [Tragedies.] By Ross Neil [Isabella Harwood]. 8vo. [*Lond. Lib. Cat.*] London, 1871

LADY Jean's son; a novel. By Sarah Tytler [Henrietta Keddie]. 8vo. Pp. 284. [*Brit. Mus.*] London, 1897

LADY Jean's vagaries; a novel. [By Henrietta Keddie.] 8vo. London, 1896

LADY Jennifer. By John Strange Winter [Mrs Arthur Stannard, *née* Henrietta E. V. Palmer]. 8vo. London, 1908

LADY Jenny's trials. By Mignon [Mrs —— Baseley]. 8vo. Manchester, 1899

LADY Joan's companion. By Florence Warden [Florence Alice Price, later Mrs George E. James]. 8vo. Pp. 332. London, 1901

LADY Ju. By Charles Aver [Charles Wesley Keyworth, B.A.]. 8vo. Pp. 136. [*Methodist Who's Who.*] London, 1911

LADY Julia's emerald. By Katharine Wylde [Helen Hester Colvill]. 8vo. [*Lit. Year Book.*] London, 1908

LADY (the) knife-thrower. [A novel. By Henry Llewellyn Williams.] 8vo. [*Brit. Mus.*] London [1890]

LADY Lee. [A novel.] By Florence Warden [Florence Alice Price, later Mrs George E. James]. 8vo. [*Brit. Mus.*] London, 1908

LADY Livingston's legacy; a novel. By the author of *Lady Flavia*, etc. [John Berwick Harwood]. 8vo. 3 vols. London, 1874

LADY Lowater's companion. By the author of *St Olave's*, etc. [Eliza Tabor, later Mrs Stephenson]. 8vo. 3 vols. [*Lond. Lib. Cat.*] London, 1884

LADY Lynette. By the author of *In the gloaming* [Herbert Herbert]. 8vo. London, 1903

LADY Macbeth; a study. [By M. Leigh Noel, later Mrs M. L. Elliott.] 12mo. Pp. iv. 87. [*Brit. Mus.*] London, 1884

LADY Madalina. . . . By the author of *My mother's diamonds* [Maria J. Greer]. . . . 8vo. [*Brit. Mus.*] London [1882]

LADY (the) married. By the author of *The lady of the decoration* [Frances Little, Mrs Fanny C. Macauley]. 8vo. Pp. 240. [*Amer. Cat.*] London, 1917

LADY Mary Wortley Montagu and her times. By George Paston [Emily Morse Symonds]. 8vo. [*Lond. Lib. Cat.*] London [1907]

LADY Mary Wortley Montagu: her life and letters, 1689-1762. By Lewis Melville [Lewis S. Benjamin]. 8vo. Pp. 320. [*Brit. Mus.*] London [1925]

LADY Molly of Scotland Yard. By Baroness Orczy [Mrs Montagu Barstow]. 8vo. Pp. 352. [*Lit. Year Book.*] London, 1910

LADY Moreton's governess. By Mignon [Mrs —— Baseley]. 8vo. London, 1903

LADY Nancye. [A novel.] By "Rita" [Mrs W. Desmond Humphreys, *née* Eliza M. J. Gollan]. 8vo. 3 vols. [*Brit. Mus.*] London, 1887

LADY (the) of fashion. By the author of *The history of a flirt* [Lady Charlotte Susan Maria Bury]. 8vo. 3 vols. [*Brit. Mus.*] London, 1856

LADY (the) of Glynne. By the author of *Margaret and her bridesmaids* [Mrs Julia Cecilia Stretton]. 8vo. 3 vols. [*D. N. B.* vol. 36, p. 219.] London, 1857

Wrongly attributed to Mrs Anne Marsh-Caldwell, or to Henrietta Keddie.

LADY (the) of Karani; a true tale of the war in the Crimea in 1854-55. [By M. A. Biddulph, Major, Royal Artillery.] 12mo. Private print, N.D.

LADY (the) of Las Cruces. By Christian Reid [Frances Fisher, later Mrs James M. Tiernan]. 8vo. [Kirk's *Supp.*] New York [1896?]

LADY (the) of limited income; a tale of English country life. By the author of *Mary Powell* [Anne Manning]. 8vo. 2 vols. London, 1872

LADY (the) of Lyons; or, love and pride: a play in five acts, as performed at the Theatre Royal, Covent Garden. By the author of *Eugene Aram*, etc. [Edward George Earle Lytton Bulwer-Lytton, Lord Lytton]. 8vo. Pp. x. 72. London, 1843

Preface signed: E. L. B.

LADY (the) of Lyte. By Graham Hope [Miss Jessie Hope]. 8vo. [*Lit. Year Book.*] London, 1906

LADY (the) of Provence; or, humbled and healed: a tale of the first French Revolution. By A. L. O. E., author of *Rescued from Egypt*, etc. [Charlotte M. Tucker]. 8vo. Pp. 400. [*Brit. Mus.*] London, 1871

LADY (the) of St Luke's. By Mark Allerton [William Ernest Cameron, LL.B.]. 8vo. [*Lit. Year Book.*] London, 1919

LADY (the) of the decoration. [A novel. By Frances Little, later Mrs Frances Caldwell Macauley.] 8vo. [*Amer. Cat.*] New York, 1907

LADY (the) of the night. By Benjamin Swift [William Romaine Paterson]. 8vo. Pp. 320. [*Lit. Year Book.*] London, 1912

LADY (the) of the valley; an Essex legend, in three parts. [Dedication signed: J. H. D. *i.e.* Rev. J. H. Davies.] Colchester, 1875

LADY (the) Paramount. By Sidney Luska [Henry Harland]. 8vo. [*Lond. Lib. Cat.*] New York, 1902

LADY Rodway's ordeal. By Florence Warden [Florence Alice Price, later Mrs George E. James]. 8vo. Pp. 319. London, 1909

LADY Rose; a tale. By Crona Temple [Miss —— Corfield]. 12mo. London, 1879

LADY (a) skipper. By Androshus [Captain W. J. Ward]. 8vo. [*Camb. Univ. Lib.*] N.P., N.D.

LADY Suffolk and her circle. By Lewis Melville [Lewis S. Benjamin]. 8vo. [*Jewish Year Book.*] London, 1924

LADY Susan, and not the Cardinal. By Lucas Cleeve [Mrs Howard Kingscote, *née* Adelina G. I. Wolff]. 8vo. Pp. 320. [*Brit. Mus.*] London, 1910

LADY Sylvia; a novel. By Lucas Cleeve [Mrs Howard Kingscote, *née* Adelina G. I. Wolff]. 8vo. London, 1904

LADY Temple's grandchildren. By H. F. E. [Evelyn Everett Green]. 8vo. London, 1883

LADY Val's elopement. By John Bickerdyke [Charles H. Cook]. Pp. 396. [*Lit. Year Book.*] London, 1899

LADY Valworth's diamonds. By the author of *Phyllis*, etc. [Mrs Margaret Argles, later Hungerford]. 8vo. Pp. 188. [*Brit. Mus.*] London, 1886

LADY Varley. By Derek Vane [Mrs B. Eaton-Back]. 8vo. [*Lit. Year Book.*] London, 1914

LADY Verner's flight. By "The Duchess" [Mrs Margaret Argles, later Mrs Hungerford]. 8vo. Pp. 310. New York, 1893

LADY (the) with the garnets. [A novel.] Translated [from the German of E. Marlitt, *i.e.* Eugenie John]. 8vo. Pp. 318. London, 1886

LADY (the) with the rubies; translated from the German of E. Marlitt [Eugenia John]. 8vo. Pp. 370. Chicago [1895]

LADYE (the) chace; a ballad. By the author of *Christian ballads* [Bishop Arthur Cleveland Coxe, D.D.]. 12mo. Philadelphia, 1877

LADY'S (the) assistant, for regulating and supplying her table, containing one hundred and fifty select bills of fare, properly disposed for family dinners . . . with upwards of fifty bills of fare for suppers. . . . [By Mrs Sarah Mason.] 8vo. [Watt's *Bibl. Brit.*] London, 1773

LADY'S (a) diary. [By Anna Brownell Murphy, later Mrs Jameson.] 8vo. [*Brit. Mus.*] London, 1824

The title of a subsequent edition (1826) is "The diary of an ennuyée."

LADY'S (a) diary of the siege of Lucknow; written for the perusal of friends at home. [By Mrs G. Harris.] 12mo. [*Brit. Mus.*] London, 1858

LADY'S (the) dressing room. To which is added, I. A poem on cutting down the old thorn at Market Hill. II. Advice to a parson. III. An epigram on seeing a worthy prelate go out of church in the time of divine service to wait on his grace the D. of D. By the Rev. Dr S—t [Jonathan Swift, D.D.]. Second edition. 4to. Pp. 20. London, 1732

LADY'S (the) every-day book; a practical guide in the elegant arts and daily difficulties of domestic life. By the author of *Enquire within*, etc. [Robert Kemp Philp]. 8vo. Pp. iv. 363. London, 1875

LADY'S (the) mile. By the author of *Lady Audley's secret*, etc. [Mary Elizabeth Braddon, later Mrs John Maxwell]. Fourth edition. 8vo. 3 vols. [*Brit. Mus.*] London, 1866

LADY'S (a) narrative [of a residence in India. By Lady Alicia E. Scott], 1834. 8vo. [*Brit. Mus.*] London, private print, 1874

LADY'S (the) new-years gift; or, advice to a daughter, under these following heads; viz. religion, husband, house and family; servants, behaviour and conversation, friendships. . . . [By George Savile, Marquis of Halifax.] Second edition, corrected. 12mo. Pp. 170. [*Bodl.*] London, 1688

Afterwards published in a volume of "Miscellanies." London, 1717.

LADY'S (a) ride across Spanish Honduras. By Maria Soltera [Mary Lester]. 8vo. Pp. 319. [*Brit. Mus.*] Edinburgh, 1884

Reprinted from *Blackwood's Magazine*.

LADY'S (a) tour round Monte Rosa; with visits to the Italian valleys in 1850-58. [By Mrs Henry Warwick Cole.] 8vo. [*Brit. Mus.*] London, 1859

Attributed also to Mrs —— Freshfield.

LADY'S (the) triumph; a comi-dramatic opera: as it is now perform'd at the Theatre in Lincoln's-Inn-Fields. . . . By E. S. [Elkanah Settle]. 12mo. Pp. 63. [Baker's *Biog. Dram.*] London, 1718

LADY'S (a) visit to Manilla and Japan. By Anna D'A. [Anna D'Almeida]. 8vo. [*Bodl.*] London, 1863

LÆLIUS and Hortensia; or, thoughts on the nature and objects of taste and genius, in a series of letters to two friends. [By John Stedman, M.D.] 8vo. Edinburgh, 1782

LAGONELLS. [A tale.] By the author of *Darmayne* [Florence Emily Ashley]. 8vo. [Kirk's *Supp.*] London, 1872

Signed: F. E. A.

LAHORE as it is and was. [By Thomas Henry Thornton and J. K. Kipling.] 12mo. Lahore, 1876

LAIDLAW'S wife. By Florence Warden [Florence Alice Price, later Mrs George E. James]. 8vo. London, 1911

LAIRD (the) and his friends. . . . [By Malcolm Stark.] 8vo. [*Brit. Mus.*] London, 1895

LAIRD (the) o' Cockpen. [A novel.] By "Rita" [Mrs W. Desmond Humphreys, *née* Eliza M. J. Gollan]. 8vo. 3 vols. [*Lit. Year Book.*] London, 1891

LAIRD (the) o' Glenalmond; or, the nightingale's trill [and other verses. By Graham Mercer, of Redgorton]. 8vo. Private print, N.P. [*c.* 1875]

LAIRD (the) of Coul's ghost, etc. [By Mrs Betty Stuart.] [Martin's *Cat.*] London [*c.* 1810]

Printed for private distribution by Sir James Stuart of Coltness.

LAIRD (the) of Darnick Tower. By J. H. [John Heiton]. 8vo. [Edinburgh, private print] 1858

LAIRD (the) of Logan; anecdotes and tales illustrative of the wit and humour of Scotland. [By John Donald Carrick.] 8vo. [*Aberd. Pub. Lib.*] Edinburgh, 1878

LAIRD (the) of Norlaw; a Scottish story. By the author of *Margaret Maitland*, etc. [Mrs Oliphant]. 12mo. 3 vols. London, 1858

LAITY (the) in Synod [of the Scottish Episcopal Church]; a letter to the Right Reverend Bishop Suther. [By John Ligertwood, advocate.] 8vo. [*Aberd. Pub. Lib.*] Aberdeen, 1870

LAKE (the); and other poems. [By Rev. John Dawson Hull, B.A. of Killaney.] 12mo. [O'Donoghue's *Poets of Ireland.*] London, 1846

LAKE breezes. [A story for boys.] By Oliver Optic [William Taylor Adams]. 8vo. [Kirk's *Supp.*] New York, 1878

LAKE Land, English and Scottish. By S. B. H. [S. B. Hancock]. 12mo. [Green's *Bibl. Somers.* i. 243.] Bath, 1864

LAKE lore; or, an antiquarian guide to some of the ruins and recollections of Killarney. By A. B. R. [Arthur Blennerhassett Rowan]. 12mo. [*Gent. Mag.* 1861, p. 565.] Dublin, 1853

LAKE (the) of the Red Cedars; or, will it live? By Y. N. L. [Rev. Timothy Horton Ball]. 8vo. [*Amer. Cat.*] Crown Point, Indiana, 1880

The writer has given the last letters of his names.

LAKE (the) of the woods; a tale illustrative of the twelfth chapter of Romans. By A. L. O. E., authoress of *Christian love and loyalty*, etc. [Charlotte M. Tucker]. 8vo. Pp. 215. [*Brit. Mus.*] Edinburgh [1867]

LAKE Zaisan and the Black Irtysh; freely translated from the Russian of the *Turkestan Gazette*. By P. M. [P. Mosa]. 8vo. [*Calc. Imp. Lib.*] Simla, 1878

LAKERS (the); a comic opera, in three acts. [By James Plumptre.] 8vo. Pp. xv. 61. [*Gent. Mag.* 1832, p. 369.] London, 1798

LALAGE'S lovers. [A novel.] By George A. Birmingham [James Owen Hannay, D.D.]. 8vo. Pp. 305. [*Lond. Lib. Cat.*] London, 1911

LAMBETH Palace and its associations; supplementary chapter: Mediæval life among the old palaces of the primacy. [By John Cavis Brown.] 8vo. Edinburgh, N.D.

LAMBKIN'S remains. By H. B. [Joseph Hilaire Pierre Belloc]. 12mo. [*Lond. Lib. Cat.*] Oxford, 1900

LAMBS (the) of Christ fed with the sincere milk of the Word. By the author of *Christianity in short* [Clement Ellis]. 12mo. [*Bodl.*] London, 1692

LAMBS (the) officer is gone forth with the Lambs message, which is the witnesse of God in all consciences, to call them up to the bar, the judgement of the Lamb, in this his day which is come; to all the parish clerks, vicars, curates, and professors in England, Ireland, and Scotland, and elsewhere in the whole Christendom; for you all to come up to the Lambs bar, in this his day; . . . G. F. [George Fox]. 4to. [Smith's *Cat. of Friends' Books*, i. 658.] London, 1659

LAMB'S (the) warre against the man of sinne; the end of it, the manner of it, and what he wars against; his weapons, his colours, and his kingdom. . . . [By James Nayler.] 4to. [Smith's *Cat. of Friends' Books*, ii. 227.] London, 1657

LAME (a) dog's diary. By Seumas Macnaughton [Sarah Macnaughton]. 8vo. London, 1914

LAMENT (a) for England's Queen [Charlotte] . . . and other poems. [By Charles P. N. Wilton.] 8vo. [*Brit. Mus.*] London, 1818

LAMENTABLE newes from the North; also strange newes from Leicester, how Colonell Lunsford, Captain Legg, and Mr Hastings have appeared in a warlike manner. . . . [By William Jenkinson.] 4to. [Thomason's *Coll. of Tracts*, i. 131.] London, 1642

LAMENTABLE vision of the devout hermit. [Edited by W. Yates.] Fol. [Martin's *Cat.*] Manchester, 1816

LAMENTACION of a Christian against the Citie of London. Made by Roderico More [Henry Brinkelow]. 12mo. No pagination. B.L. [*Brit. Mus.*] [London, 1542]

LAMENTATION (a) of England for John Jvele, Bishop of Sarisburie, who deceased the 22 of September, 1571. By W. Ph. [William Phiston]. [Lowndes' *Bibl. Man.*] London, 1571

For an account of this tract, see Brydges' *British Bibliographer*, i. 567-9.

LAMENTATION (a) over England, from a true sight . . . of the lamentable wickedness of such rulers, priests, and people that are erred . . . from the way of God. . . . By M. W. [Morgan Watkins]. 4to. [*Brit. Mus.*] [London] 1644

LAMENTATION (a) over thee, O London, with thy rulers and people, who hast slighted the day of thy visitation, and resisted the Spirit of the Lord, and despised his counsel, and evil intreated and persecuted his servants, messengers, and children; and now must receive thy reward at the hand of the Lord. [Signed: R. C. *i.e.* Richard Crane.] 4to. [Smith's *Cat. of Friends' Books*, i. 461.] London, 1665

LAMENTATION (a) over Zion, on the declaration of the Church. By W. L. [William Lamboll, junior]. 8vo. [Evans' *Amer. Bibl.* vol. 4, p. 18.] Wilmington [U.S.A.] 1765

LAMENTATIONS (the) of Jeremiah, literally translated with a paraphrase and commentary [by John Udall?]. 4to. [Lowndes' *Bibl. Man.*] London, 1593

LAMENTATIONS (the) of the porter-vat, which exploded of the drug-gripes, 17th October 1814: a poem. By Peter Pindar, Esq. [John Wolcot, M.D.]. Dedicated, without permission, to the London porter brewers and consumers. Second edition. 8vo. Pp. 23. London, N.D.

LAMIA; a confession. [By Mrs Robert Cartwright.] 8vo. 2 vols. [*Brit. Mus.*] London, 1850

LAMP (the) of life; a grandmother's story. By the author of *Etymology made easy* [Fanny Elizabeth Bunnett]. 12mo. Pp. 101. [*Olphar Hamst.*] London, 1857

LAMP (the) of life; poems. [By John A. Langford.] 12mo. [*Brit. Mus.*] Birmingham, 1856

"LAMP (a) unto my feet." By M. Bidder [Mrs Horace Porter]. 8vo. London, 1902

LAMPETER. By Philip Sidney [George Eyre Evans]. 8vo. Aberystwith [1902]

LAMPLIGHTER (the). [By Maria S. Cummins.] Illustrated by John Gilbert. 8vo. Pp. 396. [*Brit. Mus.*] London, 1863

LAMPLUGH Club, by a looker-on; intended to assist in preserving a faithful record of the dialect of the neighbourhood of Whitehaven. [By William Dickinson, of Workington.] 12mo. Pp. 12. Whitehaven, 1858

LAMPS of the law and lights of the Gospel; or, the titles of some spiritual, polemical, and metaphysical new books. [By Thomas Blount, barrister.] 8vo. [*D. N. B.* vol. 5, p. 254.] London, 1658

LAMPS of the Temple; crayon sketches of the men of the modern pulpit. [By Rev. Edwin Paxton Hood?] Third edition. 8vo. London, 1856

See another edition below.

LAMPS of the Temple; examples of eloquence of the modern pulpit; edited by "Elmo" [Thomas W. Handford]. 8vo. [*Amer. Cat.*] Chicago, 1894

LAMPS (the) of the Temple; shadows from the lights of the modern pulpit. [By Rev. Edwin Paxton Hood?] 8vo. London, 1852

See another edition above.

LANCASHIRE and the Empire. By "Imperialist" [James Rochfort Maguire]. 8vo. [*Col. Inst. Lib.* Supp. I. 482]. London, 1896

LANCASHIRE (the) dialect; or the whimsical adventures and misfortunes of a Lancashire clown: a new edition, with great improvements. By Tim Bobbin, Esq. [John Collier]. 12mo. York, N.D.

LANCASHIRE (the) Levite rebuk'd; or, a vindication of the Dissenters from Popery, superstition, ignorance, and knavery, unjustly charged on them by Mr Zachary Taylor in his book entituled, "The Surey imposter"; in a letter to himself. By an impartial hand [John Carrington, of Lancaster]. . . . 8vo. London, 1698

Signed: N. N.

Another pamphleteer who engaged in this controversy was Thomas Jollie.

LANCASHIRE needles and thread; or, the history of Birtley sewing-class. By A. E. G. [A. E. Greenhill]. 8vo. London [1860?]

LANCASHIRE tales. By Ab-o-th'-yate [Benjamin Brierley]. 8vo. London [1868?]

LANCASHIRE'S valley of Achor is England's doore of hope. . . . [By John Angier, of Denton.] 4to. [*D. N. B.* vol. 1, p. 418.] London, 1643

LANCELOT Ward, M.P.; a love story. By George Temple [Charles J. G. Rampini, Sheriff of Shetland]. 8vo. Pp. 311. [*Nat. Lib. of Scot.*] Edinburgh, 1884

LANCES (the) of Lynwood. By the author of *The little duke*, etc. [Charlotte Mary Yonge]. With illustrations by J. B. 8vo. London, 1855

LAND (the) after the war; a business proposition. By G. C. P. [George Cawkwell Phillips]. 8vo. Pp. 54. [*Brit. Mus.*] London [1915]

LAND and labour in Australia. By a Port Philip squatter [Gideon S. Lang]. 8vo. [*Lond. Lib. Cat.*] Melbourne, 1845

LAND and sea tales. By the Old Sailor, author of *Tough yarns*, etc. [Matthew Henry Barker]. Illustrated by George Cruikshank. 8vo. 2 vols. [*Brit. Mus.*] London, 1836

LAND (the) assessment and landed tenures of Canara. By C. F. C. [Captain Frederick Chamier, R.N.]. 8vo. Mangalore, 1853

LAND at last. [A novel. By Edmund Yates and Mrs Cashel Hoey.] 8vo. London, 1866

LAND for the million to rent; addressed to the working classes of England. By H. M. [Rev. Henry Moule, M.A.?]. 8vo. London, 1870

LAND (the); its inherent capabilities, and how to secure their full development. . . . By G. C. P. [George Cawkwell Phillips]. 8vo. Pp. xviii. 126. [*Brit. Mus.*] London [1913]

"LAND o' the leal." By the author of *Comin' thro' the rye*, etc. [Helen Mathers, later Mrs Henry Reeves]. 8vo. Pp. iv. 177. [*Brit. Mus.*] London, 1878

LAND (the) of Ararat; or, up the roof of the world. By a special correspondent [Alexander Macdonald]. 8vo. Pp. xvi. 348. [*Brit. Mus.*] London, 1893

LAND (the) of Arthur; its heroes and heroines. By Marie Trevelyan [Mrs Paslieu]. 8vo. London, 1895

LAND (the) of darkness; along with some further chapters in the experiences of the little pilgrim. [By Mrs Margaret Oliphant.] 8vo. Pp. 238. London, 1888

A mother's meditations on the loss of a son; afterwards published with the writer's name.

LAND (the) of liberty; an allegorical poem, in the manner of Spenser: in two cantos, dedicated to the people of Great Britain. [By John Tait, W.S.] 4to. [*Nat. Lib. of Scot.*] London, 1775

LAND (the) of long ago. By Eliza Calvert Hall [Mrs Eliza Caroline Obenchain]. 8vo. Pp. viii. 295. [*Amer. Cat.*] Boston, 1909

LAND (the) of love; a romance. By Sidney Luska [Henry Harland]. 8vo. [*Lond. Lib. Cat.*] Philadelphia, 1887

LAND (the) of Niniveh; a fragment addressed to the farmers. . . . By a friend to husbandry [Sir John Sinclair, Bart.]. Fol. [*Brit. Mus.*] [1795?]

LAND (the) of promise; being an authentic and impartial history of the rise and progress of the new British Province of South Australia. . . . By one who is going [John Stephens]. 8vo. [*Camb. Univ. Lib.*] London, 1839

LAND (the) of promise; or, my impressions of Australia. By the author of *Golden dreams and waking realities* [William Shaw]. 8vo. London, 1854

LAND (the) of the Mammoth; or, a boy's Arctic adventures three hundred years ago. By the author of *The Realm of the Ice King* [Thomas Frost]. 8vo. [*Nat. Lib. of Scot.*] London [1877]

LAND (the) of the sky. By Christian Reid [Frances C. Fisher, later Mrs James N. Tiernan]. 8vo. [Kirk's *Supp.*] New York, 1875

LAND (the) of the Sphinx. By Georges Montbard [Charles Augustus Lopez]. 8vo. London, 1894

LAND (the) of the sun. By Christian Reid [Mrs James N. Tiernan, *née* Frances C. Fisher]. 12mo. [Kirk's *Supp.*] New York, 1894

LAND (the) of vision; or glimpses of the past, the present, and the future. [By James Flamank.] 8vo. Pp. 315. London, 1835

LAND (the) question answered from the Bible. [By J. Murdoch.] 8vo. [1883]

LAND (the) question; whose is the land? . . . A dialogue. By W. Welsh [William Baxter]. 12mo. [Glasgow, 1870]

LAND (the) smaller. [A novel.] By F. M. Allen [Edmund Downey]. 8vo. [*Lit. Year Book.*] London, 1893

LAND (the) we love; our military wilderness and the way out of it. By Vivian Grey [Elliott E. Mills]. 8vo. [*Brit. Mus.*] Oxford, 1905

LAND-LAW (the) of the future. By Capricornus [George Ranken]. 8vo. Pp. 64. Sydney, N.S.W., 1877

LANDLORDISM in Wales. [By T. J. Hughes]: with an appendix by Stuart Rendel, M.P. 8vo. Pp. 58. London, 1887

LANDLORDS' landlords; or, the self-elected League Land Surveyors of England. [By Charles Sturgeon.] 8vo. [*Brit. Mus.*] London [1869]

LANDMARKS of history; ancient history from the earliest times to the Mahometan conquest. By the author of *Kings of England*, etc. [Charlotte Mary Yonge]. 8vo. London, 1852

—— Middle ages: from the reign of Charlemagne, to that of Charles V. By the author of *Kings of England*, etc. [Charlotte Mary Yonge]. 8vo. Pp. viii. 310. London, 1853

—— Modern history: from the Reformation to the fall of Napoleon. By the author of the *Heir of Redclyffe*, etc. [Charlotte Mary Yonge]. 8vo. Pp. iv. 579. London, 1857

LANDON Decroft; a socialistic novel. . . . By Laon Ramsey [Ramsden Balmforth]. 8vo. Pp. xii. 207. London [1886]

LANDS of the Moslem. By El Mukattem [Rev. Howard Crosby, D.D.]. 8vo. New York, 1881

LANDSCAPE and figure composition. By Sidney Allan [Sadakichi Hartmann]. 4to. [*Amer. Cat.*] New York, 1910

LANDSCAPE; how to copy it in black-lead pencil. [Signed: E. D. H. *i.e.* Elizabeth Deacle Holt.] 8vo. [*Brit. Mus.*] London [1877]

LANDSCAPES, churches, and moralities. By the author of *The recreations of a country parson* [Andrew K. H. Boyd, D.D.]. 8vo. London, 1874

LANDSCAPES in verse, taken in spring. By the author of *Sympathy* [Samuel Jackson Pratt]. 4to. [*N. and Q.* 1855, p. 429.] London, 1785

LANDSEER'S dogs and their stories. By Sarah Tytler, author of *Papers for thoughtful girls*, etc. [Henrietta Keddie]. With six chromographs after paintings by Sir Edwin Landseer. 4to. Pp. 149. London, 1877

LAND-TEMPEST (the); or, a paper-pellet, much in a mouthful, a long answer to a short question. . . . By W. P. [William Prynne]. 4to. London, 1644

LANETON parsonage; a tale for children, on the practical use of a portion of the Church catechism. By the author of *Amy Herbert*, etc. [Elizabeth Missing Sewell]. 12mo. 3 parts. London, 1846-49

LANGDALES (the) of Langdale End; a tale. By the author of *Valeria* [Eleanor Lloyd]. 8vo. [*Brit. Mus.*] London, 1879

LANGLEY school. By the author of *The kings of England* [Charlotte Mary Yonge]. Reprinted from "The magazine for the young." 12mo. London, 1850

LANG-SHAN (the) fowl: its history and characteristics. [By C. W. Gedney.] 8vo. Pp. 122. London, 1889

LANGUAGE: its connection with the present condition and future prospects of man. By a Heteroscian [Rowland G. Hazard.] 12mo. Pp. 153. [Smith's *Cat. of Friends' Books*, Supp. p. 184.] Providence, Rhode Island, 1836

LANGUAGE (the) of flowers. [Translated from the French of C. de la Tour, *i.e.* L. Aimé Martin.] 12mo. London, 1834

LANGUAGE (the) of the walls, and a voice from the shop-windows; or, the mirror of commercial roguery. By one who thinks aloud [James Dawson Burn]. 8vo. Leeds, 1855

LANTERN (the) of luck. [A novel.] By Hudson Douglas [Robert Aitken]. 8vo. Pp. 377. [*Brit. Mus.*] New York, 1909

LANTY and the ghost; a new and original recitation. By the author of *The land we love the best* [T. E. Sherlock]. 8vo. [O'Donoghue's *Poets of Ireland.*] Barnet [London, 1885?]

Signed: T. E. S.

LAPIDARIUM septemtrionale; or, a description of the monuments of Roman rule in the North of England. [Edited by John Collingwood Bruce, LL.D.] Fol. [*Brit. Mus.*] Newcastle-on-Tyne, 1875

LAPSE (the) of the Bishop. By Guy Thorne [Cyril A. E. Ranger-Gull]. 8vo. Pp. 303. [*Lit. Year Book.*] London, 1920

LAPSED, but not lost: a story of Roman Carthage. By the author of *Chronicles of the Schönberg-Cotta family* [Mrs Charles]. 8vo. Pp. 308. London, 1877

LAPSUS calami. [Poems.] By J. K. S. [James Kenneth Stephen]. 8vo. Pp. viii. 188. [*Brit. Mus.*] Cambridge, 1891

LAQUEI ridiculosi; or, springes for woodcocks: in two books. By H. P. [Henry Parrot]. 8vo. Pp. 252. [Lowndes' *Bibl. Man.*] London, 1613

Some copies have not the author's initials.

LARA; a tale. [By Lord Byron.] Jacqueline; a tale. [By Samuel Rogers.] 8vo. Pp. 123. London, 1814

LARGE additions to Common sense; addressed to the inhabitants of America . . . To which is added and given, An appendix to Common sense. . . . [By Thomas Paine.] 8vo. Philadelphia, 1776

Previous editions were entitled "Common sense . . ." and "Additions to Common sense. . . ."

LARGE (a) review of the Summary view [by Sir John Cooke] of the articles exhibited against [Thomas Watson] the Bp. of St David's, and of the proofs made thereon. [By Robert Ferguson.] 4to. Pp. 439. [*Brit. Mus.*] N.P. 1702

LARGER (a) and new description of the parish of Linkinhorne in the County of Cornwall. . . . By W. H. [William Harvey]. 12mo. Pp. 28. [Boase and Courtney's *Bibl. Corn.*] 1728

LARRAMYS (the). [A novel.] By Gerard Ford [Mrs Vevey Stockley]. 8vo. Pp. 326. Edinburgh, 1899

LARRY Hudson's ambition. [A tale.] By James Otis [James Otis Kaler]. 8vo. [Kirk's *Supp.*] Boston, 1906

LASH (a) at enthusiasm; in a dialogue founded on real facts, between Mrs Clinker and Miss Martha Steady. [By Sir Richard Hill.] 8vo. [R. Green's *Anti-Methodist Publications*, p. 122.] Shrewsbury, 1774

LASH (the) in the British army, forty years since. By an eye-witness [Alexander Clark]. 8vo. Aberdeen, 1880

LASH (a) to the Old Seceder, merited by his Remarks on a speech addressed to the Synod of Ross. [By Rev. Donald M'Kenzie, minister of Fodderty.] 8vo. [*New Coll. Lib.*] Inverness, 1812

LASS (a) and her lover. By Leslie Keith [Grace Leslie Keith Johnston]. 8vo. Pp. 260. [*Lit. Year Book.*] London, 1907

LASSES and lads. By Theo. Gift [Mrs Dora Henrietta Boulger]. 8vo. [*Brit. Mus.*] London, 1888

LASSIE. By the author of *Laddie* [Evelyn Whitaker]. 8vo. Pp. 201. [*Amer. Cat.*] London, 1901

LAST (the) Aldini. [An Italian tale.] By George Sand [Madame Amandine L. A. Dudevant]: translated from the French. 8vo. [*Amer. Cat.*] Philadelphia, 1840

LAST (the) and heavenly speech and glorious departure of John Viscount Kenmuir. [By Samuel Rutherfurd, or Rutherford.] 8vo. Pp. 28. Edinburgh, 1703

LAST (the) at school; and other tales. By Aunt Fanny [Fanny Barrow]. 4to. [Haynes' *Pseud.*] London [1887]

LAST (the) autumn at a favourite residence; with other poems. By a lady [Mrs Rose Lawrence, of Wavertree Hall, Liverpool]. 8vo. Pp. 104. London, 1828

LAST (the) bell tolls; monody on the death of the Princess Louise. By the author of *Keep your temper* [Miss H. St A. Kitching]. 4to. London, 1832

LAST (the) chance; a tale of the Golden West. By Rolf Boldrewood [Thomas Alexander Browne]. 8vo. Pp. 462. [*Lond. Lib. Cat.*] London, 1906

LAST (the) Christian; an epic poem. By a successor of man [J. A. Flynn]. 8vo. [O'Donoghue's *Poets of Ireland.*] Dover, 1833

LAST (the) David; and other poems. [By Charles J. Pickering.] 8vo. Pp. 123. London, 1883

LAST (the) day; a poem. By Ram Sharma [Naba Krisna Ghosa]. 8vo. [*Calc. Imp. Lib.*] Calcutta, 1886

LAST (the) days of Aurelian; or, the Nazarenes of Rome: a romance. By the author of *Zenobia*, *Queen of the East* [William Ware, Unitarian minister]. 12mo. 2 vols. [*Brit. Mus.*] London, 1838

LAST (the) days of Mary Stuart: a novel. [By Emily Finch.] 12mo. 3 vols. [*Camb. Univ. Lib.*] London, 1841

LAST days of Pekin; from the French of Pierre Loti [Louis M. J. Viaud]. 8vo. [*Brit. Mus.*] London, 1902

LAST (the) days of Pompeii. By the author of *Pelham*, *Eugene Aram*, etc. [Sir Edward Bulwer-Lytton, afterwards Lord Lytton]. 12mo. 3 vols. London, 1834

LAST (the) daze of Pompeii; an antiquarian muddle. By Messrs J. W. Hogo-Hunt & J. F. Sunavill [John William Houghton and James Frank Sullivan]. 12mo. N.P., N.D.

LAST (a) diary of the Great War. By Samuel Pepys, Jun. [R. A. Bennett and R. A. Freeman]. . . . 8vo. Pp. 307. London, 1919

LAST (the) Earl of Desmond; a historical romance of 1599-1603. [By Rev. Charles Bernard Gibson, M.R.I.A.] 12mo. 2 vols. [S. J. Brown's *Ireland in fiction.*] Dublin, 1854

LAST (the) efforts of afflicted innocence; being an account of the persecution of the Protestants of France; and a vindication of the Reformed religion from the aspersions of disloyalty and rebellion, charg'd on it by the Papists. [By Pierre Jurien.] Translated out of French [by Walter Vaughan]. 8vo. Pp. 289. London, 1682

LAST (the) French hero. By Alexander Sue-Sand fils [Lieut.-Gen. Sir Edward Hamley Bruce]. 8vo. [Cushing's *Init. and Pseud.* ii. 141.] Edinburgh, 1879

LAST (the) green leaf; a ballad. The words and part of the melody by T. H. B. [Thomas Haynes Bayly]. Fol. London [1830]

LAST (the) guinea; a poem. [By John Fowler.] Third edition. 12mo. [*Nat. Lib. of Scot.*] Edinburgh, 1759

LAST (a) hope. By Esmé Stuart [Amélie Claire Leroy]. 8vo. [*Lond. Lib. Cat.*] London, 1885

LAST (the) hope. By Henry Seton Merriman [Hugh Stowell Scott]. 8vo. Pp. 124. [*Brit. Mus.*] London [1913]

LAST (the) house in London. By Crona Temple [Miss —— Corfield]. 8vo. [*Brit. Mus.*] London, 1890

LAST (the) King of Ulster. [By Edmund Getty.] 8vo. 3 vols. [S. J. Brown's *Ireland in fiction.*] London, 1841

LAST (the) link. [A novel.] By Morice Gerard [Rev. John Jessop Teague]. 8vo. Pp. 320. [*Lond. Lib. Cat.*] London, 1911

LAST (a) love; from the French of Georges Ohnet [Georges Hénot]; translated by A. D. Vandam. 8vo. Pp. 347. [*Brit. Mus.*] London, 1890

LAST (the) man. By the author of *Frankenstein* [Mrs Mary W. Shelley]. 8vo. 3 vols. [Courtney's *Secrets*, p. 60.] London, 1826

LAST (the) meeting; a story. By Arthur Penn [James Brander Matthews]. 8vo. [Cushing's *Init. and Pseud.* i. 227.] London, 1887

LAST (the) million [viz. the American army for the Great War]. By Ian Hay [John Hay Beith]. 8vo. Pp. xxxv. 271. [*Brit. Mus.*] London [1919]

LAST (the) monarch of Tara. [A tale of Ireland in the sixth century.] By Eblana [Miss Teresa J. Rooney]. 8vo. Pp. 311. [S. J. Brown's *Ireland in fiction.*] London, 1887

LAST (the) of her line. By the author of *St Olave's*, etc. [Eliza Tabor, later Mrs Stephenson]. 8vo. 3 vols. [*Brit. Mus.*] London, 1879

LAST (the) of the Barons. By the author of *Rienzi* [Edward G. E. L. Bulwer-Lytton, Baron Lytton]. 12mo. 3 vols. [*Lond. Lib. Cat.*] London, 1843

LAST (the) of the cavaliers. [By Rose Piddington.] 12mo. 3 vols. [London] 1859

LAST (the) of the Grenvilles; a story of modern seafare. By Bennet Copplestone [F. Harcourt Kitchin]. 8vo. Pp. 308. [*Brit. Mus.*] London, 1918

LAST (the) of the Incas; a tale of the Pampas; translated from the French of Gustave Aimard [Olivier Gloux, by Sir F. C. Lascelles Wraxhall]. 8vo. [*Lit. Year Book.*] London, 1862

LAST (the) of the Lairds; or, the life and opinions of Malachi Mailings, Esq. of Auldbiggings. By the author of *Annals of the parish*, etc. [John Galt]. 8vo. [*Nat. Lib. of Scot.*] Edinburgh, 1826

LAST (the) of the Mohicans; a narrative of 1757. By the author of *The red rover*, etc. [James Fenimore Cooper]. 8vo. Pp. vi. 346. [Allibone's *Dict.*] London, 1850

LAST (the) of the Mortimers; a story in two voices. By the author of *Margaret Maitland*, etc. [Mrs Margaret Oliphant]. 8vo. 3 vols. [*Brit. Mus.*] London, 1862

LAST (the) of the old squires; a sketch. By Cedric Oldacre, of Sax-Normanbury, sometime of Christ Church, Oxon [Rev. John Wood Warter]. 8vo. [*Brit. Mus.*] London. 1854

LAST (the) of the Plantagenets; an historical romance, illustrating some of the public events, and domestic and ecclesiastical manners of the fifteenth and sixteenth centuries. [By William Heseltine.] 8vo. [*Brit. Mus.*] London, 1829

LAST pages from a journal; with other papers. By Mark Rutherford [William Hale White]. 8vo. Pp. 321. [*Lond. Lib. Cat.*] London, 1915

LAST poems. By Laurence Hope [Mrs Malcolm H. Nicolson]. 8vo. [*Lond. Lib. Cat.*] London, 1905

LAST (the) prior of St Antony (in Roseland). [By E. D. Longlands, afterwards Mrs Drewe.] 12mo. Pp. 80. [Boase and Courtney's *Bibl. Corn.* i. 121.] Truro, 1857

LAST (the) refuge; a Sicilian romance. By Stanton Page [Henry B. Fuller]. 8vo. [*Amer. Cat.*] Boston, 1900

LAST (the) regret; or, the power of divine regeneration: a poem, illustrative of truths of inspiration assailed in a work entitled Essays and reviews. By a soldier of the Cross [William Robertson Aikman]. 8vo. [*Bodl.*] London, 1861

LAST (the) search after claret in Southwark; or, a visitation of the vintners in the mint, with the debates of a committee of that profession thither fled to avoid the cruel persecution of their unmerciful creditors: a poem. . . . [By Richard Ames.] 4to. [Dobell's *Cat.*] London, 1691

LAST (the) sentence. [A novel.] By Maxwell Gray [Mary Gleed Tuttiett]. 8vo. 3 vols. [*Lond. Lib. Cat.*] London, 1893

LAST (the) stroke; a detective story. By Laurence L. Lynch [Emma M. Murdoch, later Mrs Van Deventer]. 8vo. Pp. vii. 319. [*Brit. Mus.*] London [1897]

LAST (the) supper; or, Christ's death kept in remembrance. By the author of the *Morning and evening sacrifice*, etc. [Thomas Wright, minister of Borthwick]. 12mo. [*Nat. Lib. of Scot.*] Edinburgh, 1828

LAST (the) survivor of the ancient English hierarchy, T. Goldwell, Bishop of St Asaph. [Signed: T. F. K. *i.e.* Thomas Francis Knox.] 8vo. [*Brit. Mus.*] London [1876]

LAST (y^e) sweet thing in corners. . . . By F. I. D. [Mrs Florence I. Duncan]. 8vo. [Kirk's *Supp.*] Philadelphia, 1880

LAST (the) three sermons preached in the church of Looe, Cornwall, by the late perpetual curate of East and West Looe [Richard William Barnes]. 8vo. [Boase and Courtney's *Bibl. Corn.* i. 14.] Truro, 1850

LAST verses. By Susan Coolidge [Sarah Chauncey Woolsey]. 8vo. [Kirk's *Supp.*] Boston, 1906

LAST (the) will and testament of the Earl of Pembroke. [A satire. By Sir Charles Sedley.] Fol. [*Brit. Mus.*] London [1650]

LAST (the) words of Thomas Carlyle . . . . Edited by J. C. A. [Jane Carlyle Aitken]. 8vo. [Cushing's *Init. and Pseud.* ii. 3.] Edinburgh, 1882

LASTING (the) resentment of Miss Keasu Lwan Wang; a Chinese tale, translated from the original by Sloth [Robert Thom]. 4to. [Cushing's *Init. and Pseud.* ii. 138.] Canton, 1839

LATE (the) apology in behalf of the Papists re-printed and answered, in behalf of the Royallists. [By William Lloyd, D.D., Bishop of Worcester.] 4to. Pp. 48. [*Brit. Mus.*] London, 1667

Attributed also to Charles, Earl of Derby, and to Roger Palmer, Earl of Castlemaine.

LATE (the) Assembly of Divines Confession of Faith examined, as it was presented by them unto the Parliament; wherein many of their excesses and defects, of their confusions and disorders, of their errors and contradictions are presented both to themselves and others. [By William Parker.] 8vo. [*Brit. Mus.*] London, 1651

LATE (the) censors deservedly censured; and their spurious litter of libels against Dr Greenfield, and others, justly expos'd to contempt; by the following answer to all, but especially the last, intituled, A reply to the reasons against the censors of the College of Physicians, etc. humbly offer'd to the perusal of Dr {Thomas Burwell, Richard Forbes, William Daws, Thomas Gill} the late censors, and to the expiring censure of Dr Charles Goodal. By Lysiponius Celer, M.D.L. [Johann Groenevelt, M.D.]. 4to. [*W.*] London, 1698

LATE (the) converts exposed; or, the reasons of Mr Bays [Dryden]'s changing his religion, considered in a dialogue. Part the second. With reflections on the life of St Xavier; Don Sebastian King of Portugal. . . . [By Thomas Brown.] 4to. [*Nat. Lib. of Scot.*] London, 1690

For the first part, see "The reasons of Mr Bays . . ."

LATE (a) dialogue betwixt a civilian and a divine, concerning the present condition of the Church of England. [By George Gillespie.] 4to. Pp. 42. Scott's *Fasti*, new edition, i. 58.] London, 1644

LATE (the) election [for Cork]; containing a full report of its proceedings. . . . By a Reporter [—— O'Leary]. 8vo. [*Brit. Mus.*] Cork, 1830

LATE (the) excise scheme dissected; or, an exact copy of the late bill, for repealing several subsidies, and an impost, now payable on tobacco, etc. with all the blanks filled up, as they probably would have been, if the bill had passed into a law; and proper observations on each paragraph. . . . [By William Pulteney, afterwards Earl of Bath.] 8vo. Pp. viii. 80. London, 1734

LATE (the) John Wilkes's catechism of a ministerial member. . . . [By William Hone.] 8vo. [*Brit. Mus.*] London, 1817

LATE laurels. By the author of *Wheat and tares* [Sir Henry Stewart Cunningham]. 8vo. 2 vols. [*Camb. Univ. Lib.*] London, 1864

LATE (a) letter from Sir Thomas Fairfax's army, now in Truro, relating the severall passages in the treaty . . . communicated to both Houses of Parliament, 16 March 1645. [Signed: J. R. *i.e.* John Rushworth.] 4to. [*Brit. Mus.*] London, 1645

LATE (the) "Newes from Brussells" [by Marchamont Nedham] unmasked, and His Majesty vindicated from the base scandal and calumny therein fixed on him. [By John Evelyn.] 4to. [*D.N.B.* vol. 18, p. 82.] London, 1660

LATE (the) occurrences in North America, and policy of Great Britain considered. [By John Dickinson, farmer.] 8vo. Pp. 44. Boston, 1766

LATE (the) payment of weekly wages considered in connexion with Sunday trading in London. By a layman [William Rivington]. 8vo. [*Olphar Hamst*, p. 179.] London, 1854

LATE (the) pretence of a constant practice to enter the Parliament as well as provincial writ in the front of the Acts of every Synod; consider'd and disprov'd, in a letter to the author of that assertion; with a certificate from the register of York. [By Charles Trimnell, D.D.] 4to. [*Brit. Mus.*] London [1701]

LATE (the) pretence of a constant practice to enter the Parliament as well as provincial writ in the front of the Acts of every Synod, further consider'd and disprov'd, in a second letter to the author of that assertion; occasion'd by a second letter of that author: with a postscript in answer to the postscript of that second letter. [By Charles Trimnell, D.D.] 4to. London [1701]

Continuing his contention, the writer published "An answer to a third letter. . . ." See above.

LATE (the) proceedings and votes of the Parliament of Scotland; contained in an address delivered to the King, signed by the plurality of the members thereof, stated and vindicated. [By —— Ferguson.] 4to. Pp. 63. Glasgow, 1689

LATE (the) regulations respecting the British colonies on the continent of America, considered; in a letter from a gentleman in Philadelphia to his friend in London. [By John Dickinson.] 8vo. [Allibone's *Dict.*] London, 1766

LATE (the) religious commotions in New-England considered; an answer to the Reverend Mr Jonathan Edward's sermon, entitled, The distinguishing marks of a work of the Spirit of God. . . . By a lover of truth and peace [Charles Chauncy]. 8vo. Pp. 60. [Evans' *Amer. Bibl.* vol. 2, p. 232.] Boston, 1743

LATE repentance. By Clara Vance [Mrs Mary Andrews Denison]. 8vo. [Kirk's *Supp.*] New York, 1889

LATE (the) Rev. Thomas Streatfield, of Chart's Edge. [A memoir.] By L. E. L. [Lambert B. Larking]. 4to. [*Brit. Mus.*] [London, 1861]

No separate title-page.

LATE (the) Revolutions and present state of these nations. By Socrates Christianus [Edward Stephens, Nonjuror]. 4to. Pp. 14. N.P., 1689

LATE (the) tryal and conviction of Count Tariff. [By Joseph Addison.] 8vo. [*Biog. Brit.* i. 51.] London, 1713

LATER autumn leaves. [Poems.] By Thomas Brevior [Thomas Shorter]. 12mo. [*Brit. Mus.*] London, 1896

LATER magic. By Professor Hoffmann [Angelo John Lewis]. 8vo. [*Lit. Year Book.*] London, 1904

LATER poems. By Julio [Joseph Sykes, M.A.]. 8vo. Pp. viii. 189. [*Bodl.*] London, 1871

LATER years. By the author of *The old house by the river* [William Cowper Prime]. 8vo. [Allibone's *Dict.*] New York, 1867

LATEST (the). [A tale.] By Renniks de Dnayrrah [Harry and Ed. Skinner]. 8vo. Pp. 320. London, 1900

The pseudonym is the reversed spelling of the names of the two authors.

LATEST (the) form of infidelity examined; a letter to Mr Andrews Norton, occasioned by his "Discourse before the Association of the Alumni of the Cambridge Theological School. . . ." By an Alumnus of that School [George Ripley]. 8vo. [Cushing's *Init. and Pseud.* ii. 5.] Boston, 1839

LATEST news from Italy. By Luigi Mariotti [Antonio Gallenga]. 8vo. [*Brit. Mus.*] London, 1847

LATHAMS (the). A tale. [By Fairleigh Owen.] 8vo. [*Brit. Mus.*] Glasgow, 1858

LATHE (the) and its uses; or, instruction in the art of turning wood and metal: including a description of the most modern appliances for the ornamentation of plane and carved surfaces. . . . [By Rev. James Lukin, of Stetchworth.] Copiously illustrated. 8vo. Pp. v. 284. London [1868]

The preface to the 3rd edition, published in 1871, has the author's initials: J. L.

LATIN and English poems. By a gentleman of Trinity College, Oxford [Benjamin Loveling]. 12mo. Pp. 179. [*N. and Q.* 1922, p. 269.] London, 1741

Wrongly attributed to William Loveling.

LATIN (the) dedication of the Honourable Mr Alexander Hume-Campbell, with a literal translation thereof by Cardinal Alberoni; and the same translation again versified by another hand [George Douglas, of Friershaw]. 4to. [*D. Laing.*] London, 1724

LATIN (the) genius. By Anatole France [Jacques Anatole Thibault]: translated from the French by Wilfrid Jackson. 8vo. London, 1923

LATIN (the) odes of Mr [Thomas] Gray, in English verse [translated by Edward Burnaby Greene], with an ode [signed: E. B. G.] on the death of a favourite spaniel. 4to. [*Brit. Mus.*] London, 1775

LATIN (a) phrase book. . . . By a teacher [Henry White Pickering]. 8vo. [Cushing's *Init. and Pseud.* ii. 143.] Boston, 1836

LATIN (the) play at a Catholic school. . . . By an "Ancient Actor" [Edward Bellasis, barrister]. 8vo. [*Brit. Mus.*] London [1883]

LATIN (a) Quarter courtship; and other stories. By Sidney Luska [Henry Harland]. 8vo. [*D. N. B.* Second Supp. vol. 2, p. 214.] London, 1890

LATIN (a) syntax and first reading book; being an adaptation of Broeder's Little Latin grammar, to the Eton syntax, etc. [Signed: T. K. A. *i.e.* Rev. Thomas Kerchever Arnold.] 12mo. [*W.*] London, 1836

LATIN without tears; or, *one* word a day. By the author of *Peep of day*, etc. [Mrs Thomas Mortimer]. 4to. Pp. 336. [*Brit. Mus.*] London, 1877

LATINÆ grammaticæ curriculum; or, a progressive grammar of the Latin language, for the use of all classes in schools. [By Benjamin Hall Kennedy, D.D.] 12mo. [*Bodl.*] London, 1844

LATTE (il); an elegy. [By Edward Jerningham.] 4to. Pp. 11. [*D. N. B.* vol. 29, p. 346.] London, 1767

LATTER (a) day romance. By Mrs Murray Hickson [Mrs Sidney A. P. Kitcat]. 8vo. [*Bookman*, Jan. 1923, p. 185.] London, 1893

LATTER day (a) saint; being the story of Ethel Jones, related by herself. [By Thomas Wharton.] 8vo. [Cushing's *Init. and Pseud.* ii. 80.] New York, 1884

LAUDABLE (the) life and deplorable death of Prince Henry; together with some other poems in honor of King James, Prince Charles and Princesse Elizabeth. By J. M. [James Maxwell] Master of Artes. 4to. [*W.*] London, 1612

LAUDER and her lovers ; a novel of the north. By Deas Cromarty [Mrs Robert A. Watson, *née* Elizabeth S. Fletcher]. 8vo. [*Lit. Year Book.*] London, 1902

LAUGHABLE jokes, comic stories, and old-time songs. By the Rolling-mill man [John W. Kelly]. 8vo. [*Amer. Cat.*] 8vo. New York, 1900

LAUGHABLE (a) poem ; or, Robert Slender's [Philip Freneau's] journey from Philadelphia to New York by way of Burlington. . . . 12mo. [Foley's *Amer. Books.*] Philadelphia, 1809

LAUGHING eyes. By Arrah Leigh [Mrs H. C. Hoffman]. 8vo. New York, 1885

LAUGHING (a) philosopher in the middle of the nineteenth century. By Alfred Crowquill [Alfred H. Forrester]. 8vo. [*Lit. Year Book.*] Philadelphia, 1889

LAUGHTER and tears. [Short stories for the young.] By Marion J. Brunowe [Mary Josephine Browne]. 8vo. Pp. 173. [*Amer. Cat.*] St Louis, Mo., 1897

LAUGHTER (the) of Peterkin ; a re-telling of old tales of the Celtic wonder-world. By Fiona Macleod [William Sharp]. 8vo. Pp. 288. [*Lond. Lib. Cat.*] London, 1897

LAUGHTON priory. [A novel.] By Gabrielli [Mrs Mary Meeke]. 12mo. 4 vols. London, 1809

LAUNCHING away ; or, Roger Larksway's strange mission. . . . By J. R. H. Hawthorn [John Richard Houlding]. 8vo. Pp. 319. London, 1882

LAURA ; a novel. By the author of *The Independent* [Andrew Macdonald]. 12mo. 2 vols. London [1790]

LAURA Huntley ; a story for girls. . . . By a New England lady [Maria J. B. Browne]. 8vo. [Cushing's *Init. and Pseud.* ii. 105.] Boston, 1850

LAURA Linwood ; or, the price of an accomplishment. By the author of *The White Cross* [C. J. Ingham Sarson] . . . 8vo. [*Brit. Mus.*] London, 1875

LAURA ; or, an anthology of sonnets (on the Petrarchan model) and elegiac quatorzains, English, Italian, Spanish, Portuguese, French, and German ; original and translated. By C. L. [Capel Lofft, senr.]. 12mo. 5 vols. [*D. N. B.* vol. 34, p. 71.] London, 1815

LAURA Temple ; a tale for the young. [By Anne Bowman.] 8vo. Pp. 231. [*Bodl.*] London, 1853

LAURA ; the toyes of a traveller, or the feast of fancie, divided into 3 parts. By R. T. [Robert Tofte] gent. of London. 4to. [*W.*] Printed for Valentine Simmes, 1597

LAURA'S dream ; or, the moonlanders : a poem. [By Mrs Helesina Trench.] 8vo. Pp. 47. [O'Donoghue's *Poets of Ireland; D. N. B.* vol. 57, p. 190.] London, 1816

LAURE ; the story of a blighted life. By L. C. H. [Laura Carter Holloway]. 8vo. [Cushing's *Init. and Pseud.* i. 124.] Philadelphia, 1872

LAUREAD (the) ; a literary, political, and naval satire. By the author of *Cavendish* [William Johnson Neale]. In four books. Book the first. Second edition. 8vo. [*Brit. Mus.*] London, 1833

No more published.

LAUREAT (the) ; a poem inscribed to the memory of Charles Churchill. [By E. B. Greene.] 4to. [*W.*] London, 1765

LAUREL (the) ; a poem on the Poet-Laureat. [By Robert Gould.] 8vo. [*Brit. Mus.*] London, 1685

A satire on John Dryden.

LAUREL (the) bush ; an old-fashioned love story. By the author of *John Halifax, Gentleman* [Dinah Maria Mulock, later Mrs Craik]. 8vo. Pp. 205. London, 1877

LAUREL (the) wreath ; being a collection of original poems, moral, comic, and divine. By W. P. [William Perfect, surgeon]. 12mo. 2 vols. London, 1766

LAURISTONS. By John Oxenham [William Arthur Dunkerley]. 8vo. Pp. 332. [*Lit. Year Book.*] London [1910]

LAURUS nobilis ; chapters on art and life. By Vernon Lee [Violet Paget]. 8vo. Pp. vii. 315. [*Brit. Mus.*] London, 1909

LAUSUS and Lydia, with Madam Bonso's three strings to her bow ; or, three bows to her string ! ! ! A comedy in three acts and in prose. By A. B. C. [Sarah Lawrence]. 8vo. [*Brit. Mus.*] London, 1806

LAUTERDALE ; a story of two generations. [By J. Fogerty.] 8vo. 3 vols. [*Brit. Mus.*] London, 1873

LAVINIA. By the author of *Lorenzo Benoni* and *Doctor Antonio* [Giovanni Ruffini]. 8vo. 3 vols. [*Nat. Lib. of Scot.*] London, 1860

LAW (the) ; a monthly magazine of legal matters. . . . [By Frederick G. M. Wetherfield, besides other contributors.] 8vo. Vol. I. [*Brit. Mus.*] London, 1875

LAW (the) against bankrupts; or, a treatise wherein the statutes against Bankrupts are explained, by several cases, resolutions, judgments, and decrees, both at common law and in Chancery. . . . By T. G. [Thomas Goodinge], Serjeant-at-Law. 8vo. [Arber's *Term Cat.* ii. 478.] London, 1693

LAW and lawyers; curious facts and characteristic sketches. [By D. Laing Purves.] 8vo. Pp. 154. [*Nat. Lib. of Scot.*] Edinburgh [1868]

LAW (the) and lawyers laid open, in twelve visions; to which is added, Plain truth, in three dialogues, between Truman, Skinall, Dryboots, three Attorneys, and Season, a Bencher. [By J. A. Purves.] 12mo. Pp. xlviii. 269. London, 1737

LAW and lawyers; or, sketches and illustrations of legal history and biography. [By Archer Polson.] 12mo. 2 vols. [*Brit. Mus.*] London, 1840

Attributed also, but more doubtfully, to James Grant.

LAW (the) and practice in bankruptcy, as founded on the recent statute; with forms. By John Frederick Archbold. Second edition, with considerable additions by an Equity barrister [John Flather]. 12mo. 2 parts. [*Brit. Mus.*] London, 1827

Many other editions followed.

LAW (the) and the Gospel clearly demonstrated, in six sermons. . . . [By Rev. John Tyler.] 12mo. Norwich, Conn., 1815

LAW (the) and the testimony. By the author of *The wide, wide world* [Susan Warner]. 8vo. Pp. viii. 840. [*Brit. Mus.*] London, 1853

LAW (the) bringers. [A novel.] By G. B. Lancaster [Edith Lyttleton]. 8vo. Pp. 396. [*Brit. Mus.*] London, 1913

LAW (the) given at Sinai. [A poem. By Thomas Dawes, barrister.] 4to. Pp. 7. [Sabin's *Dict.*] Boston, 1777

LAW is a bottomless-pit; exemplify'd in the case of The Lord Strutt, John Bull, Nicholas Frog, and Lewis Baboon, who spent all they had in a law-suit. Printed from a manuscript found in the cabinet of the famous Sir Humphry Polesworth. [By John Arbuthnot, M.D.] Second edition. 8vo. [*D. N. B.* vol. 2, p. 65.] London, 1712

LAW lyrics. [By Robert Bird.] Second edition, enlarged. 12mo. [*Brit. Mus.*] Paisley, 1887

Followed by "More law lyrics" (1898).

LAW, not justice. [A novel.] By Florence Warden, author of *The House on the Marsh* [Mrs George E. James, *née* Florence Alice Price]. 8vo. Pp. 330. London, 1906

LAW (the) of Chili as to the marriage of non-Catholics. By an advocate [Henry Good]. 8vo. [Cushing's *Init. and Pseud.* ii. 4.] Valparaiso, 1880

LAW (the) of duty; a suggested moral text-book, based on the ethical and religious teaching of Dr James Martineau: prepared for Indian students. [By T. E. Slator.] 8vo. [*Brit. Mus.*] Madras, 1889

LAW (the) of evidence; wherein all the cases that have yet been printed in any of our law books or tryals, and that in any wise relate to points of evidence, are collected and methodically digested under their proper heads. . . . By a late learned Judge [Sir Geoffrey or Jeffrey Gilbert]. 8vo. Pp. 243, 74. In the Savoy, 1717

LAW (the) of executions. By S. C. [Samuel Carter, barrister-at-law]. 8vo. [*Brit. Mus.*] London, 1706

LAW (the) of laws: or, the golden rule of the Gospel. By a corresponding member of the Society for propagating Christian knowledge [Elisha Smith, M.A.]. Second edition. With an appendix. 8vo. [*Bodl.*] London, 1719

LAW (the) of mercy; a poetical essay on the punishment of death, with illustrative notes. [By Thomas Hancock, M.D.] 8vo. [Smith's *Cat. of Friends' Books*, i. 89.] London, 1819

LAW (the) of obligations and conditions; or, an accurate treatise wherein is contained the whole learning of the law concerning bills, bonds, conditions, statutes, recognizances and defeasances; as also declarations on special conditions, and the pleadings thereon. . . . By T. A., of Grays-Inn, Esq. [Thomas Ashe]. 8vo. Pp. 578. [*Brit. Mus.*] London, 1693

The dedication is signed: J. A.

LAW (the) of physicians, surgeons, and apothecaries; containing all the statutes, cases at large, arguments, resolutions and judgments concerning them. [By T. Cunningham.] 8vo. [Clarke's *Law Cat.*] London, 1768

LAW (the) of Replevins . . . now first published from the original manuscript . . . Wrote by a late learned Judge [Sir Geoffrey Gilbert]. 8vo. [*Brit. Mus.*] Dublin, 1755

LAW (the) of the corner. By Leo Versor [Professor George Lyon Turner]. 8vo. London, 1896

The pseudonym is a Latin rendering of "Lion turner."

LAW (the) of the Sabbath of perpetual obligation; in answer to the Letter to Dr Candlish, "The Jewish Sabbath and Sunday"; being a letter to his friend, by a country minister [Alexander Dunlop]. . . . 8vo. [*New Coll. Cat.*] Edinburgh, 1847

LAW (the) of the Territories [in the United States. Two essays. By Charles Edward Fisher]. 8vo. Pp. 127. Philadelphia, 1859

The author subscribes himself: Cecil, in the second essay.

LAW (the) of truth; or, the obligations of reason essential to all religion. To which are prefixed, some remarks supplemental to a late tract [by the same author], entitled, Divine rectitude. [By John Balguy, vicar of Northallerton.] 8vo. Pp. xxiii. 48. London, 1733

LAW (the) of uses and trusts . . . together with a treatise of dower. [By Sir Geoffrey Gilbert.] 8vo. [*Brit. Mus.*] In the Savoy, 1734

A second edition was issued in 1741.

LAW (the) of values; an exposition of the primary causes of stock and share fluctuations. By Sepharial [Walter Gorn Old]. 8vo. Pp. 80. [*Brit. Mus.*] London [1918]

LAW Reform Association proposal. [By Jeremy Bentham.] 8vo. [*Brit. Mus.*] London [1830]

LAW, religion, and education; considered in three essays. . . . [By Francis Grant, afterwards Lord Cullen?] 8vo. [*Nat. Lib. of Scot.*] Edinburgh, 1715

In fact, only two essays were printed.

LAW (the) scrutiny; or, attornies' guide. [By Andrew Blair Carmichael.] 8vo. [O'Donoghue's *Poets of Ireland.*] Dublin, 1807

A satire; sometimes wrongly attributed to the Rev. Richard Frizelle, and to William Norcott.

LAW (the) students' and practitioners' commonplace book of law and equity. . . . By a barrister [Charles Erdman Petersdorff]. 4to. [*Brit. Mus.*] London, 1871

LAW (the) student's guide. By a member of Gray's Inn [P. Brady Leigh]. 12mo. [Lowndes' *Bibl. Man.* p. 1323.] London, 1827

LAW (the) student's statute remembrancer. [By George Nichols Marcy.] 8vo. [*Bodl.*] N.P., N.D.

The third edition (London, 1870), enlarged, has the author's name.

LAWD'S Labyrinth; being an answer to the late Archbishop of Canterbury's Relation of a conference between himself and Mr Fisher. . . . By T. C. [Thomas Carwell, *alias* Thorold, S.J.]. Fol. Paris, 1668

This is a later edition of "Labyrinthus Cantuarensis. . . ." (1658): see above.

LAWES (the) of Virginia now in force; collected out of the Assembly records and digested into one volume. . . . [By Francis Moryson.] Fol. [*Brit. Mus.*] London, 1662

LAWES (the) subversion; or, Sir John Maynards case truly stated; being a perfect relation of the manner of his imprisonment upon pleasure, for the space of five moneths, by the House of Commons. . . . By J. Howldin [Major Sir John Wildman]. 4to. [*D. N. B.* vol. 61, p. 235.] [London] 1648

LAWFUL prejudices against an incorporating Union with England; or, some modest considerations on the sinfulness of this Union, and the danger flowing from it to the Church of Scotland. [By James Webster, minister of the Tolbooth Church, Edinburgh.] 4to. [Lee's *Defoe*, i. 133.] Edinburgh, 1707

LAWFULNES (the) and unlawfulnes of an oath or covenant, set downe in short propositions agreeable to the law of God and man, and may serve to rectifie the conscience of any reasonable man. . . . [By Joseph Hall, Bishop of Norwich.] 4to. [Madan's *Oxford Books*, ii. 290.] Oxford [? rather London] 1643

The Epistle dedicatory is signed: Jos: Exon.

This is a re-issue, with another title, of "Certain irrefragable propositions. . . . By J. H." London 1639.

LAWFULNES (the) of obeying the present government [after the execution of Charles I.], and acting under it; proposed by one that loves all Presbyterian lovers of truth and peace [Francis Rous, senior]. 4to. [Thomason's *Coll. of Tracts*, ii. 711.] London, 1649

Another edition, enlarged, was published in the same year, with a modified title. In reply, there were evoked "An enquiry after further satisfaction concerning a change of government beleeved to be unlawfull. . . ." "A second part of the Religious Demurrer . . . an answer to a tract called The lawfulnesse of obeying the present government," and "The grand case of conscience stated, about submission to the present power. . . ."

LAWFULNES (the) of tithes demonstrated to the convincing of such of the Quakers as pretend conscience against the payment of them; or, a demonstration for liberty of conscience to the Quakers in the payment of their tithes. By W. J. [William Jeffery]. 4to. [Smith's *Anti-Quak.* p. 253.] London, 1676

LAWFULLNESS (the) and necessitie of observing the anniversary fasts and festivals of the Church maintain'd, particularly of Christmass. 1. From the law of nature, and Gods positive law to the Jews. 2. From the power the Church has to appoint ceremonies. 3. From the practice of the Church. 4. From the advantages of their observation. 5. From the libertie which the opposers take to themselves. 6. From the sentiments of the learned reformers. 7. From the weakness of the objections against them. [Preface signed: R. C. *i.e.* Robert Calder.] 8vo. Pp. 58. [*Nat. Lib. of Scot.*] N.P. 1710

LAWFULNESS (the) and necessity of the ministers their reading the Act of Parliament, for bringing to justice the murderers of Captain John Porteous. [By Rev. George Logan.] 8vo. Pp. 49. [Scott's *Fasti*, vol. 1.] Edinburgh, 1737

LAWFULNESS (the) and right manner of keeping Christmas: shewed in a familiar conference between a Churchman and a Dissenter. [By Robert Watts, LL.D.] 8vo. [*Bodl.*] London, 1710

LAWFULNESS (the) of breaking faith with heretics proved to be an established doctrine of the Church of Rome; in a letter to Mr G. H. [George Hay, Roman Catholic Bishop, Edinburgh. By William Abernethy Drummond, Bishop of the Scottish Episcopal Church, Edinburgh]. 8vo. Pp. iv. 52. Edinburgh, 1788

Advertisement signed: W. A. D.

LAWFULNESS (the) of taking the new Oaths asserted. [By Henry Maurice, D.D.] 4to. [*Brit. Mus.*] London, 1689

LAWFULNESS (the) of the religious clause of some burgess-oaths, asserted in several remarks upon some notes of sermons, delivered lately at a certain occasion, by some brethren, who therein attempted publickly to shew the unlawfulness thereof. [By Ralph Erskine, M.A.] 8vo. Pp. 88. [M'Kerrow's *Hist. of the Secession*, p. 844.] Glasgow, 1747

LAWLES (the) tythe-robbers discovered, who make tythe-revenue a mock-mayntenance, being encouraged thereunto by the defect of law and justice about ministers maintenance. [By Richard Culmer.] 4to. [*D. N. B.* vol. 13, p. 286.] London, 1655

LAW-POWER; or, the law of relation, written in the heart of Ministers and people by the finger of God, is mighty, through Him, to prevaile with both, to live as a people separated to their God, and from the world, specially at the Lords Table. [By Hezekiah Woodward.] [*McAlpin Coll. Cat.*] London, 1656

"Directions to binder," give indication of authorship.

LAW-PRIEST (the); or, Quibus dissected; in a series of letters to a friend. By Rusticus [George Maxwell]. 8vo. [*Brit. Mus.*] Spalding, 1797

LAWRENCE the martyr; scenes in our parish. By a country parson's daughter [Mrs Elizabeth Holmes]. 12mo. Bristol [1830?]

LAWRIE Todd's hints to merchants, married men, and bachelors. [By Grant Thorburn.] 8vo. [Cushing's *Init. and Pseud.* i. 284.] New York, 1847

LAWRIE Todd's notes on Virginia. [By Grant Thorburn.] 8vo. [Cushing's *Init. and Pseud.* i. 284.] New York, 1848

LAWS (the) and judicatures of Scotland, vindicated from the calumnies and false reasonings contained in a late pamphlet [by Patrick Haldane], entitled, The case of the forfeited estates in Scotland, consider'd: in a letter to a noble L—d. [By Sir David Dalrymple, Lord Hailes.] 8vo. Pp. 56. Edinburgh, 1718

The author's name is in the handwriting of Dr David Laing.

LAWS (the) and policy of England, relating to trade, examined by the maxims and principles of trade in general; and by the laws and policy of other trading nations. By the author of the *Treatise on the Police of France*, etc. [Sir William Mildmay]. 4to. Pp. 125. [*Brit. Mus.*] London, 1765

LAWS (the) and practice of whist. By Cœlebs, M.A. [Edward A. Carlyon]. 12mo. Pp. 82. [Boase and Courtney's *Bibl. Corn.* i. 59.] London, 1851

LAWS (the) and principles of whist stated and explained, and its practice illustrated on an original system. . . . By "Cavendish" [Henry Jones]. Twenty-fourth edition, revised and greatly enlarged. 8vo. Pp. xii. 306. [*D. N. B.* First Supp. vol. 3, p. 46.] London, 1901

LAWS (the) of écarté adopted by the Turf Club; with a treatise on the game. By "Cavendish," author of *The laws and principles of whist*, etc. [Henry Jones]. 8vo. Pp. 62. [*Brit. Mus.*] London, 1878

LAWS (the) of Leflo. [A novel.] By the author of *Miss Molly* [Beatrice May Butt]. 8vo. Pp. v. 181. [*Lond. Lib. Cat.*] London, 1911

LAWS of nature; a comedy. . . . [By Thomas Lodge, B.A., and Robert Greene?] 4to. [*D. N. B.* vol. 34, p. 61.] London [1600?]

LAWS (the) of nature defended by Scripture. . . . [By Robert Sandeman.] 8vo. Edinburgh, 1760

LAWS (the) of Paradise, given forth by Wisdom to a translated spirit. [By Jane Lead; edited by F. Lee.] 8vo. [*Brit. Mus.*] London, 1695

LAWS (the) of picquet; with a treatise on the game. By "Cavendish" [Henry Jones]. 8vo. [*D. N. B.* First Supp. vol. 3, p. 46.] London, 1896

LAWS (the) of poetry, as laid down by the Duke of Buckinghamshire in his Essay on poetry, by the Earl of Roscommon in his Essay on translated verse, and by the Lord Lansdowne on Unnatural flights in poetry: explain'd and illustrated. [By Charles Gildon.] 8vo. Pp. 351. [*Manch. Free Lib.*] London, 1721

LAWS (the) of Rubicon bézique, adopted by the Portland and Turf Clubs. . . . By "Cavendish" [Henry Jones]. Second edition. 8vo. Pp. 50. [*D.N.B.* First Supp. vol. 3, p. 46.] London, 1892

LAWS (the) of taxation; being a concise treatise of all the Acts of Parliament . . . relating to the taxes of England. . . . [Signed: G. J. *i.e.* Giles Jacob.] 8vo. [*Brit. Mus.*] [London] 1720

LAWS (the) relating to horses; considered as the subject of property, sale, hire, wages, etc. [By Henry Jeremy.] 8vo. [*Brit. Mus.*] London, 1825

LAWS (the) respecting Commons and Commoners, comprising the law relative to the rights and privileges of both Lords and Commoners; and in which the law relative to the inclosing of commons is particularly attended to, as collected from the several statutes, reports, and other books of authority, up to the present time. . . . Third edition, corrected. By the author of the *Laws of landlord and tenant*, etc. [James Barry Bird]. 8vo. Pp. iv. 108. [*Brit. Mus.*] London, 1817

LAWS (the) respecting highways and turnpike roads. . . . By the author of *The laws of landlord and tenant* [James Barry Bird]. 8vo. [*Brit. Mus.*] London, 1801

LAWS (the) respecting landlords, tenants, and lodgers, laid down in a plain, easy, and familiar manner, and free from the technical terms of the law; with many practical directions concerning leases, assignments, surrenders, agreements, covenants, repairs, waste, etc.; demand and payment of rent, distress, and ejectment, as collected from the several reports and other books of authority up to the commencement of the present Easter term, 1794. . . . [By James Barry Bird.] 8vo. Pp. 118. [*Brit. Mus.*] London, 1794

LAWS (the) respecting masters and servants. . . . By the author of *The laws respecting landlords and tenants* [James Barry Bird]. 8vo. [*Brit. Mus.*] London, 1795

LAWS (the) respecting parish matters; containing the several duties of churchwardens, overseers, constables, etc. with an appendix. By the author of the *Laws of landlord and tenant* [James Barry Bird]. 8vo. [*Brit. Mus.*] London, 1795

LAWS (the) respecting tithes; comprising all the cases and statutes on the subject. . . . Third edition, enlarged. [By James Barry Bird.] 8vo. [*Brit. Mus.*] London, 1805

LAWS (the) respecting travellers and travelling; comprising all the cases and statutes relative to that subject: including the using of hired horses, robbery, accidents, obstructions, etc. upon the road. Third edition, with additions. By the author of the *Laws of landlord and tenant*, etc. [James Barry Bird]. 8vo. Pp. 72. [*Brit. Mus.*] London, 1819

LAWS (the) respecting wills, testaments, and codicils, and executors, administrators, and guardians. . . . Fourth edition, corrected and enlarged. [By James Barry Bird.] 8vo. Pp. 132. [*Brit. Mus.*] London, 1802

LAVVYER (the) of Lincolnes-inne [William Prynne] reformed; or, an apology for the army: occasioned by ix queries, upon the printed charge of the army, against the xi members, and the papers thereto annexed; submitted to the publique consideration of all lovers of justice, truth, parliaments, army and their native countrey. By the author of *The case of the kingdome*, etc. [Marchamont Nedham]. 4to. [*Bodl.*] N.P. 1647

LAWYER (the) outlaw'd; or, a brief answer to Mr Hunts Defence of the charter. With some useful remarks on the Commons proceedings in the last Parliament at Westminster. In a letter to a friend. [By Sir Roger L'Estrange.] 4to. [Watt's *Bibl. Brit.*] [London] 1683

LAWYER'S advice to his son. [By Mark Hildesley.] 8vo. [Lowndes' *Bibl. Man.* p. 1323.] London, 1685

LAWYERS and legislators; or, notes on the American Mining Companies. [By Benjamin Disraeli, later Earl of Beaconsfield.] 8vo. [*Brit. Mus.*] London, 1825

LAWYERS and their victims; a satire [in verse]. . . . By Lindon Meadows [Rev. Charles Butler Greatrex]. Second edition. 8vo. Pp. 31. [*Brit. Mus.*] London [1885]

LAWYER'S (the) fortune; or, love in a hollow tree: a comedy. [By William Grimston, Viscount Grimston.] Second edition. 4to. Pp. 68. [*Dyce Cat.* i. 357.] London [1705]

LAWYER'S (a) idle hours. By Frank Myrtle [C. Augustus Haviland]. 8vo. [*Amer. Cat.*] New York, 1902

LAWYERS (the) investigated; in a series of letters addressed to the Right Honourable E— D—, Sir S. S. S—he, Sir W. M—d. etc. By W. G. [William Gardner] of Richmond; and the lawyers' letters in reply, with other needful vouchers. 8vo. Pp. viii. 92. [*Bodl.*] Brentford, 1771

LAWYERS (the) light: or, a due direction for the study of the law; for methode, choyce of bookes moderne, selection of authours of more antiquitie, application of either, accommodation of diuers other vsefull requisits; all tending to the speedy and more easie attayning of the knowledge of the common law of this kingdome. . . . Written by the reverend and learned professor thereof, I. D. [Sir John Doderidge, or Dodderidge, or Doddridge]. To which is annexed, for the affinitie of the subiect, another treatise [by Francis, Lord Bacon], called The use of the law. 4to. Pp. 119. London, 1629

The use of the law has a separate title and pagination [pp. 93].

LAWYERUS bootatus & spurratus; or, the long vacation: a poem. By a student of Lincolns-Inn [Richard Ames]. 4to. [Arber's *Term Cat.* ii. 381.] London, 1691

LAY baptism invalid; or, an essay to prove that such baptism is null and void; especially to those who knew that 'twas administer'd to them, in opposition to the divine right of the apostolical succession. By a lay hand [Roger Lawrence]. 8vo. Pp. xxx. 85. [Lathbury's *Hist. of the Nonjurors.*] London, 1708

LAY (the) Christian's obligation to read the Holy Scriptures. [By Nicholas Stratford, D.D. 4to. [Watt's *Bibl. Brit.*] London, 1687

Several other editions were issued.

LAY (a) from Cornwall for the Jubilee of Queen Victoria. [Signed: H. S. S. *i.e.* Henry Sewell Stokes.] 8vo. Pp. 4. Bodmin, 1887

LAY (the) monastery; consisting of essays, discourse, etc. publish'd singly under the title of the Lay monk: being the sequel of the Spectators. Second edition. [By Sir Richard Blackmore and John Hughes.] 12mo. [Lowndes' *Bibl. Man.* p. 1326.] London, 1714

Originally published, Monday, Wednesday, and Friday, in single papers in 40 numbers, No. 1, 16 Nov. 1713, No. 40, 15 Feb. 1714. All the Friday's papers are by Hughes.

LAY nonconformity further justify'd: containing a reply to a late pamphlet, entitled, The layman's pleas for separation from the Church of England, answer'd. . . . [By Rev. John Norman, minister in Portsmouth.] 8vo. [*Brit. Mus.*] London, 1718

See the following entry.

LAY nonconformity justified; in a dialogue between a gentleman of the town in communion with the Church of England, and his Dissenting friend in the country. [By Rev. John Norman.] 8vo. Pp. 56. [*Brit. Mus.*] London, 1716

A seventh edition appeared in 1728. See also the previous entry.

LAY (the) of a graduate. [By William Beattie, M.D., Cockermouth.] 8vo. London, 1820

LAY (a) of Lochleven. By Will o' ye West [William Forsyth]. 8vo. Pp. 108. Glasgow, 1887

LAY (the) of St Aloys; a legend of Blois. By Thomas Ingoldsby [Rev. Richard Harris Barham]. Fol. [*Brit. Mus.*] London, N.D.

LAY (the) of St Odille. . . . By Thomas Ingoldsby [Rev. Richard Harris Barham]. 8vo. [*Brit. Mus.*] London, 1915

LAY (the) of the Beanmhòr: a song of the Sudreyar. [By Alex. Nicolson, M.A., Sheriff-Substitute of Kirkcudbright.] 8vo. Pp. 32. Dunedin, 1867

Presentation copy from the author.

LAY (the) of the clock; and other poems. By J. B. [John Brown, of Horncastle], author of *Neddy and Sally; or, the statute-day*. 8vo. [*Camb. Univ. Lib.*] Horncastle, 1861

LAY (the) of the last angler; or, a tribute to the Tweed at Melrose, at the end of the season of 1867. By a sexagenarian [the Hon. and Rev. Robert Liddell, M.A.]. 8vo. Pp. 58. [Dobell's *Private prints*, p. 105.] Kelso, 1867

LAY (the) of the last minstrel travesty. [By O. Neville.] 8vo. [*Biog. Dict.* 1816.] 1811

LAY (a) of the [Aberdeen] Links. [By George Davidson, bookseller]. 8vo. [Robertson's *Aberd. Bibl.*] [Aberdeen, 1856]

LAY (the) of the old church clock. [By Thomas Hingston Harvey.] 8vo. Pp. 4. [*Brit. Mus.*] [Truro, 1851]

LAY (the) of the poor fiddler; a parody on the Lay of the last minstrel, with notes and illustrations. By an admirer of Walter Scott [John Roby, banker in Rochdale]. 12mo. [*N. and Q.* 1858, p. 257.] London, 1814

LAY (the) of the Reedwater minstrel, illustrated with notes historical and explanatory; addressed to Matthew Forster, of Broomyholme, Esq. by a son of Reed [Robert Roxby]. 4to. Pp. 43. [*Bodl.*] Newcastle, 1809

LAY (the) of the Scottish fiddle; a poem, in five cantos: supposed to be written by W— S— Esq. [Sir Walter Scott]. [By James Kirke Paulding.] First American, from the fourth Edinburgh edition. 8vo. Pp. xvi. 222. London, 1814

LAY (the) of the Turings; a sketch of the family history, feebly conceived and imperfectly executed: now dedicated to the Chief with the sincerest respect and affection, by H. M'K. [Henry M'Kenzie, vicar of St Martin-in-the-Fields]. 4to. Pp. 76. [Martin's *Cat.*] N.P. [1849]

The notes to the Lay are by R. F. T. [Robert Fraser Turing].

LAY (the) of the Unitarian Church. [By Henry Arthur Bright, M.A.] 8vo. London [*c.* 1870]

LAY (a) preacher's reminiscences of rural Christianity. By V. D. M. [T. R. Hooper]. 8vo. London, 1907

LAY sermons. By a member of the Legislature [William Edward Baxter, M.P.]. 8vo. Pp. iv. 235. [*D. N. B.* First Supp. vol. 1, p. 146.] London, 1865

LAY sermons from *The Spectator*. By C. M. E. [Emma Marie Caillard]. 8vo. Pp. 306. London, 1909

LAY-FOLKS' (the) mass-book. [By Benjamin Francis Conn Costelloe.] 8vo. London [1896]

LAYING (the) on of hands upon baptized believers, as such, proved an ordinance of Christ. . . . By B. K. [Benjamin Keach]. 12mo. [*Brit. Mus.*] London, 1698

LAYMAN'S (a) account of his faith and practice as a member of the Episcopal Church [in Scotland. By John Niven, of Thornton]. 8vo. [Grub's *Hist. of the Episc. Church in Scotland*, vol. 4, p. 121, foot-note.] Edinburgh, 1801

Wrongly attributed to Bishop John Skinner.

LAYMANS (the) answer to the laymans opinion. [Signed: W. D. *i.e.* William Darrell]; in a letter to a friend. 4to. Pp. 12. [*Brit. Mus.*] London, 1687

LAYMAN'S (a) apology. . . . By Sherlock [Solomon Southwick]. 8vo. [Cushing's *Init. and Pseud.* i. 266.] Albany, New York, 1834.

LAYMAN'S (a) faith; being a review of the principal evidences of the truth of the Christian religion, interspersed with several curious observations. By a free-thinker and a Christian [John Mawer, M.A.]. 8vo. Pp. xviii. 64. [Davies' *Mem. of the York Press*, p. 182.] Newcastle upon Tyne, 1732

LAYMAN'S (a) faith, doctrines and liturgy. By a layman [Thomas Crowther Brown]. 8vo. [Smith's *Cat. of Friends' Books*, i. 327.] London, 1866

LAYMAN'S (the) letter to [Benjamin Hoadly] the Bishop of Bangor; or, an examination of His Lordship's Preservative against the non-jurors; of the Vindication of the realm and Church of England; of the Nonjurors seperation (*sic*) from publick assemblies, examin'd, by Dr Bennet; and of all other late discourses occasion'd by the charge of perjury, rebellion, and schism, imputed to the body of the people. [By John Shute Barrington, Viscount Barrington]. 4to. Pp. 44. London, 1716

LAYMAN'S (a) letters to [Thomas Sherlock] the author of the Trial of the witnesses. [By Augustus William and Julius Charles Hare.] [*Preface to "Guesses at truth."*] 1824

The fourth letter is by Julius.

LAYMAN'S (a) letters to the Rev. William Cunningham, of Trinity College parish, in reference to his Letter to the Dean of Faculty. [By Alexander Peterkin.] 8vo. [*New Coll. Lib.*] Edinburgh, 1839

LAYMAN'S (the) manual . . . drawn out of Holy Scripture, the Roman ritual, the Catechism ad parochos, etc. By C. T. [Christopher Tootell], clergyman of the Roman Catholic Church. 12mo. [Gillow's *Bibl. Dict.*] [London] 1698

See also below, "The Layman's ritual."

LAYMAN'S (the) opinion [on passive obedience] sent in a private letter to a considerable divine of the Church of England. [Signed: W. D. *i.e.* William Darrell.] 4to. Pp. 8. [Jones' *Peck*, p. 77.] N.P. 1687

LAYMAN'S (a) reply to Professor G. A. Smith's Modern criticism and the preaching of the Old Testament. [By William Logie.] 8vo. Glasgow, 1902

LAYMAN'S (the) ritual; containing practical methods of Christian duties. By C. T. [Christopher Tootell]. 12mo. 1698

See also above, "The Layman's manual."

LAYMAN'S (the) second letter to [Benjamin Hoadly] the Bishop of Bangor; or an examination of his Lordship's sermon before the King, and of Dr Snape's Letter to his Lordship. [By John Shute Barrington, Viscount Barrington.] 8vo. [*Brit. Mus.*] London, 1717

LAYMAN'S (the) sermon upon the late storm, held forth at an honest coffee-house conventicle; not so much a jest as 'tis thought to be. [By Daniel Defoe.] 4to. [Wilson's *Life of Defoe.*] 1704

LAYMAN'S (a) story; or, the experiences of John Laicus and his wife in a country parish. [By Lyman Abbott, D.D.] 8vo. [Kirk's *Supp.*] New York, 1873

LAYMAN'S (the) test; or, the true minister of the Church of England. [By Arthur Benoni Evans, D.D.] 8vo. [*Brit. Mus.*] London, 1830

LAYMAN'S (a) thoughts about union; expressed in a letter to the Rev. James Begg, D.D. [By Walter Brown.] 8vo. Glasgow, N.D.

LAYMAN'S (the) vindication of the Convocation's charge against [Benjamin Hoadly] the Bishop of Bangor; being some animadversions on the Report reported. . . . By the author of the *Bulwork* [sic] *storm'd* [Edward Hart]. 8vo. [*Brit. Mus.*] London, 1717

LAYS and ballads from English history etc. By S. M. [Menella Bute Smedley]. 12mo. Pp. vi. 184. London [1856]

LAYS and legends of Kent. By the author of *The Sea-wolf* [John Brent]. Second edition. 8vo. Canterbury, 1841

Presentation copy from the author.

LAYS and legends of the North of Ireland. By Cruck-a-leaghan [Dugald MacFadyen] and Slievegallion [David Hepburn, who edited the whole collection]. 8vo. [O'Donoghue's *Poets of Ireland.*] [Glasgow?] 1884

LAYS and lyrics. [With music.] By Hugh Conway [Frederick John Fargus]. 4to. [*Brit. Mus.*] London, 1887

LAYS and lyrics of the blessed life; consisting of Light from the Cross, and other poems. By Marianne Farningham [Mary Anne Hearne, of Farningham]. 12mo. Pp. xii. 270. [*Lit. Year Book.*] London, 1860

LAYS from an Australian lyre. By Austral [Mrs James Glenny Wilson]. 8vo. Pp. vii. 120. London [1882]

LAYS from the Cimbric lyre; with various verses. By Goronva Camlan [Rowland Williams, D.D.]. 8vo. [B. M. Pickering's *Cat.*] London, 1846

LAYS of a lazy lawyer. By Al-So [Alexander Somers, solicitor in Manchester]. 8vo. London, 1891

LAYS of a lifetime; the record of one departed. [By Mrs Mary Noel Meigs]. 4to. [*Brit. Mus.*] New York, 1857

This dedication is signed: M. N. M.

LAYS of a pilgrim. [By Frederick Wright.] 8vo. [Cushing's *Init. and Pseud.*] Brockville, Con., 1864

LAYS of a Subaltern. By "The Subaltern" [Andrew Alexander Irvine]. 8vo. [*Brit. Mus.*] London, 1895

LAYS of ancient Greece and Rome; with Forfel's Saga. By W. R. [William Richardson]. 8vo. Pp. 126. [*Glas. Univ. Lib.*] Glasgow, 1878

LAYS of early years, etc. [By Jane Bragg.] 12mo. [Smith's *Cat. of Friends' Books*, i. 104.] London, 1839

LAYS of Erin. [By Miss E. Colthurst.] 8vo. [O'Donoghue's *Poets of Ireland.*] 1839

LAYS of home. [By John Dix Ross.] Bristol, 1840

LAYS of Ind; poems illustrative of English life in India. By "Aliph Cheem" [Major Walter Yeldham]. 8vo. [*Lond. Lib. Cat.*] London, 1897

LAYS of Leix. By Slieve-Margy [William O'Neill, Irish merchant]. 12mo. Pp. 100. [S. J. Brown's *Guide to books on Ireland*, p. 81.] Dublin, 1903

LAYS of memory, sacred and social. By a mother and son [E. and R. M. Benson]. 8vo. London, 1856

LAYS of past days. By the author of *Provence and the Rhone* [John Hughes, A.M.]. 8vo. London, 1850

The dedication to Miss Mitford is signed: J. H.

LAYS of Poland. By the author of *The Sea-wolf* [John Brent]. 12mo. Pp. 48. London, 1836

LAYS of the better land. By a Catholic priest [Rev. Thomas O'Sullivan]. 12mo. [O'Donoghue's *Poets of Ireland.*] Dublin, 1862

LAYS of the Church, and other verses; intended chiefly for young persons. By the author of *Kind words* and other poems, etc. [Frederick George Lee]. 12mo. [*Bodl.*] London, 1851

Verses signed: F. G. L.

LAYS of the deer forest; with sketches of olden and modern deer hunting, traits of natural history in the forest, traditions of the Clans, miscellaneous notes. By John Sobieski and Charles Edward Stuart [John Hay Allan and Charles Stuart Hay Allan]. 8vo. 2 vols. [*Brit. Mus.*] Edinburgh, 1848

LAYS of the dragon-slayer. By Maxwell Gray [Mary Gleed Tuttiett]. 8vo. [*Lit. Year Book.*] London, 1893

LAYS of the Land League. By T. D. S. [Timothy Daniel Sullivan]. 12mo. [O'Donoghue's *Poets of Ireland.*] Dublin, 1887

LAYS of the Luri; and other rimes. By Una [Jane Dunn Sutherland]. 8vo. Pp. 36. Keighley, 1885

LAYS of the Minnesingers or German Troubadours of the twelfth and thirteenth centuries, illustrated by specimens of the cotemporary lyric poetry of Provence and other parts of Europe; with historical and critical notices, and engravings from the MS. of the Minnesingers in the King's Library at Paris, and from other sources. [By Edgar Taylor and Sarah Austin.] 8vo. Pp. vi. 326. [*N. and Q.*, Sept. 1855, p. 207.] London, 1825

The "Advertisement" begins thus:—Though this little work is sent into the world anonymously, it may be proper to state that it is the joint production of two authors: one of whom (the writer of this notice) is answerable for the arrangement, and for what may be called the critical department of the book; while he resigns the poetic department, with few and trifling exceptions, to his associate, to whom the reader will correctly attribute whatever is most worthy of his perusal.

LAYS of the moonlight men. By Barney Bradey [William Theodore Parkes, Irish journalist]. 8vo. [O'Donoghue's *Poets of Ireland.*] London, 1898

LAYS of the sea; and other poems. By Peronne [Mrs Theodora E. Lynch, *née* Foulks]. 12mo. Pp. xiv. 285. [*Brit. Mus.*] London, 1846

A larger edition was published in 1860.

LAYS of the sea-side; a rhythmical rendering of sea-side stories and incidents. By Aliph Cheem [Major Walter Yeldham]. 8vo. Pp. 232. [*Brit. Mus.*] London, 1887

LAYS of the seven half-centuries; for St Paul's School's three hundred and fiftieth anniversary, 1859. [Signed: H. K. *i.e.* Herbert Kynaston.] 8vo. Pp. 22. [*Brit. Mus.*] [London, 1859]

LAYS on land. By Ismael Fitzadam, formerly able seaman on board the —— Frigate, and author of *The harp of the desert, containing the battle of Algiers*, etc. [John Macken]. 8vo. Pp. viii. 167. [O'Donoghue's *Poets of Ireland.*] London, 1821

LAYTON (the) court mystery. By? [Anthony Berkeley Cox]. 8vo. Pp. 316. [*Brit. Mus.*] London, 1925

LAZARILLO; or, the excellent history of Lazarillo de Tormes, the witty Spaniard, both parts. The first [by Hurtado de Mendoza], translated by D. Rowland; the second [by Juan de Luna], gather'd out of the chronicles of Toledo, and done into English. 8vo. [Arber's *Term Cat.* i. 316.] London, 1678

An earlier edition appeared in 1653.

LAZARUS; a tale of the earth's great miracle. By Lucas Cleeve [Mrs Howard Kingscote, *née* Adelina G. I. Wolff]. 8vo. Pp. 371. [*Lit. Year Book.*] London, 1897

LAZARUS redivivus; or, a discovery ot the trials and triumphs that accompany the work of God in and about his people: with an essay, tending to clear up those mistakes men have about it. Laid open in several sermons. [By Nicolas Blaikie.] 8vo. Pp. 256. [*D. Laing.*] London, 1671

The epistle to the reader is signed: N. B.

This work has also been attributed to Nathanael Blakey.

LAZARUS'S sores lick'd. [By Edmund Hall, M.A.] 4to. London, 1650

An attack on Lazarus Seaman.

LAZY thoughts of a lazy girl. By Jenny Wren [Jane Atkinson]. 8vo. Pp. 108. [*Amer. Cat.*] London, 1891

LE FORESTER; a novel. By the author of *Arthur Fitz-Albini* [Sir Samuel Egerton Brydges]. 12mo. 3 vols. London, 1802

LEAD me into temptation. [A novel.] By Frank Heller [Gunnar Serner]. Translated by R. E. Lee. 8vo. Pp. 277. [*Brit. Mus.*] New York [1927]

LEADEN (the) casket. By Averil Beaumont [Mrs Margaret Hunt]. 8vo. 3 vols. [Cushing's *Init. and Pseud.* i. 32.] London, 1880

LEADENHENDRIE; or, the chase of Fearn. [By Rev. David Harris.] 8vo. [*And. Jervise.*] Edinburgh, 1847

LEADERS of men; a book of biographies specially written for youth. By H. A. Page, author of *Golden lives*, etc. [Alexander Hay Japp, LL.D.]. 8vo. Pp. 405. London, 1880

LEADERS (the) of public opinion in Ireland. [By William Edward Hartpole Lecky, M.A.] 8vo. Pp. 308. London, 1861

The revised and enlarged editions issued in 1871, and afterwards, give the author's name.

LEADERS (the) of the old Bar of Philadelphia. By H. B. [Horace Binney]. 8vo. [Cushing's *Init. and Pseud.* i. 25.] Philadelphia, 1866

LEADIN' (the) road to Donegal; and other stories. By "Mac" [James MacManus]. 8vo. Pp. x. 248. [S. J. Brown's *Ireland in fiction.*] London [1895]

LEADING cases done into English [verse]. By an apprentice of Lincoln's Inn [Sir Frederick Pollock]. 8vo. [*Brit. Mus.*] London, 1876

An enlarged edition appeared in 1892.

LEAF (a) omitted out of the Record report; or, some remarks upon the present state of the records; contained in a letter addressed to a member of Parliament. [By John Bruce, F.S.A.] 8vo. London, 1837

LEAFLESS (a) spring; after the German of Ossip Schubin [Lola Kirschner]. 8vo. Pp. 295. [Kirk's *Supp.*] Philadelphia, 1893

LEAFLETS. [Poems.] By M. E. C. W. [Mackenzie Edward Charles Walcott, D.D.]. 8vo. [*Brit. Mus.*] London, 1872

LEAGUE (the) of life. [A novel.] By Morice Gerard [Rev. John Jessop Teague]. 8vo. Pp. 114. [*Lit. Year Book.*] London, 1909

LEAH'S mistake. By Arrah Leigh [Mrs H. C. Hoffman]. 8vo. New York, 1886

LEAL (a) lass; a novel. By Basil [Richard Ashe King, M.A.]. 8vo. 2 vols. [Cushing's *Init. and Pseud.* ii. 16.] London, 1888

LEANDER and Hero; a tragedy [in five acts and in verse. By Thomas Horde]. 8vo. [*Brit. Mus.*] London, 1769

LEAN'NORA; a supernatural though sub-pathetic ballad . . . after the German of G. A. Bürger. By H. Y. Snekul [Henry Clay Lukens]. 4to. [*Brit. Mus.*] Philadelphia, 1870

For other renderings of the ballad, see "Lenore" and "Bürger's Lenore."

LEAP Year; addressed to the bachelor members of Her Majesty's Rifle Corps. By a Spinster [Mrs E. J. Lean]. 8vo. [*Brit. Mus.*] London, 1860

LEARNED (a) and exceeding well compiled vindication of liberty of religion; written by Junius Brutus [Johannes Crellius] in Latine, and translated into English by N. Y. who desires, as much as in him is, to do good unto all men, &c. 12mo. [*W.*] [London] 1646

LEARNED (a) and necessary argument to prove that each subject hath a propriety in his goods; shewing also the extent of the kings prerogative in impositions upon the goods of merchants exported and imported, out of and into this kingdome. Together with a remonstrance presented to the kings most excellent majesty, by the honourable House of Commons, in the parliament holden Anno Dom. 1610. Annoq; Regis Jacobi, 7. By a late learned judge of this kingdome [Sir James Whitelocke]. 4to. Pp. 66. [Hargrave's *State tryals*, vol. xi. pp. 29, 52; *N. and Q.* July 1860]. London, 1641

The work has also been ascribed to Sir Henry Yelverton and to William Hakewill of Lincoln's Inn.

LEARNED (a) comment upon Dr Hare's excellent sermon preach'd before the D. of Marlborough, on the surrender of Bouchain. By an enemy to peace [Jonathan Swift]. 8vo. [*Camb. Hist. of Eng. Lit.*] London, 1711

LEARNED (a) dissertation upon Dumpling; its dignity, antiquity, and excellence; with a word upon Pudding. . . . addressed to A. P., Esq. [Ambrose Philips. By Thomas Gordon]. Fifth edition. 12mo. Pp. iv. 25, viii. [*Brit. Mus.*] London, 1726

A satirical imitation of Philip's pretentious style of writing.

LEARNED (a) dissertation upon old women, male and female, spiritual and temporal, in all ages. . . . [By Thomas Gordon.] 12mo. N.P. 1720

LEARNED (the) maid; or, whether a maid may be a scholar: a logick exercise written in Latine by that incomparable virgin Anna Maria à Schurman of Utrecht. [Translated by Clement Barksdale.] [Bliss' *Cat.*] London, 1659

The dedication is signed: C. B.

LEARNED (a) summary upon the famous poeme (The first and second weeke) of William of Saluste, Lord of Bartas; wherein are discovered all the excellent secrets in metaphysicall, physicall, morall, and historicall knowledge. Translated out of French by T. L. D. M. P. [Thomas Lodge, Doctor Medicus, Physicus]. Fol. [*Camb. Univ. Lib.*] London, 1637

LEARNING (the) of foreign languages. . . . By an Ex-teacher [Charles Cuthbert Brydon]. 8vo. Pp. 20. [*Brit. Mus.*] Manchester, 1898

LEARNING (the) of the beasts; a fable: for the year 1795. [By William Jones, of Nayland.] 8vo. [*Bodl.*] N.P., N.D.

LEARNING to act. [By George Mogridge.] 12mo. [*Brit. Mus.*] London [1846]

LEARNING to think. [By George Mogridge.] 12mo. London [1846]

LEATHER (the) Hill farm. By Henley I. Arden [Henrietta Knight]. 8vo. London [1891]

LEATHER stocking and silk; or, Hunter John Myers and his times: a story of the valley of Virginia. [By John Esten Cooke.] 12mo. Pp. 408. [Wegelin's *Bibl. of J. E. Cooke.*] New York, 1854

LEAVEN for dough-faces; or, three score and ten parables touching slavery. . . . By a former resident of the South [Darius Lyman, junr.]. 8vo. [Cushing's *Init. and Pseud.* i. 104.] Cincinnati, 1856

LEAVES. [Poems, including translations from Latin and German.] By J. N. [John Nichol, B.A., Professor]. 8vo. Pp. viii. 163. [Dobell's *Private prints*, p. 131.] Edinburgh, private print, 1854

LEAVES blown together. [Verse.] By Lottie [Charlotte Walker]. 12mo. [Cushing's *Init. and Pseud.* i. 174.] London [1865]

LEAVES from a diary in Lower Bengal, 1862-70. By "C. S. (Retired)" [Arthur H. Clay]. 8vo. London, 1896

LEAVES from a garden. By the author of *Leaves from a life* [Mrs Jane Ellen Panton]. 8vo. Pp. 311. [*Brit. Mus.*] London, 1910

LEAVES from a journal. [Preface signed: P. R. Patrick Robertson, Lord Robertson.] 4to. Pp. 34. N.P. private print, 1844

LEAVES from a life. [By Mrs Jane Ellen Panton.] 8vo. [*Brit. Mus.*] London, 1908

LEAVES from a physician's journal. [By D. E. Smith.] 8vo. [Cushing's *Init. and Pseud.* i. 234.] New York, 1867

LEAVES from a Sabbath-school teacher. [By Robert Frame.] 8vo. [Cushing's *Init. and Pseud.* i. 259.] London, 1859

LEAVES from a trooper's diary. [By John A. B. Williams.] 8vo. [Cushing's *Init. and Pseud.* i. 287.] Philadelphia, 1869

LEAVES from an Indian jungle, gathered during thirteen years of a jungle life in the Central Provinces, the Deccan, and Berar. [By Captain Alexander Inglis R. Glasfurd.] 8vo. Bombay, 1903

LEAVES from an old log; Péhe Núe, the tiger whale of the Pacific. By Captain Barnacle [Charles M. Newell]. 8vo. [*Lib. Journ.* iv. 208.] Boston, 1877

LEAVES from Elim. [Religious poems.] By Marianne Farningham [Mary Anne Hearne, of Farningham]. 12mo. [*Lit. Year Book.*] London [1873]

LEAVES from life. By L. N. R., author of *The book and its story* [Mrs Lydia N. Ranyard]. 4to. London, 1855

LEAVES from Margaret Smith's journal in the Province of Massachusetts Bay, 1678-9. [Edited or rather written by John Greeley Whittier.] 8vo. [*Brit. Mus.*] Boston, 1849

LEAVES from my journal during the summer of 1851. By a Member of the late Parliament [Lord Robert Grosvenor, Baron Ebury]. With illustrations. 8vo. London, 1852

LEAVES from my writing-desk; being tracts on the question, What do we know? By an old student [Rev. John Barling]. 8vo. [Cushing's *Init. and Pseud.* ii. 167.] London, 1872

LEAVES from our cypress and our oak. [Poems. By Francis Davis.] 4to. [O'Donoghue's *Poets of Ireland.*] London, 1863

LEAVES from Sherwood Forest. By January Searle [George Searle Phillips]. 8vo. London, 1850

LEAVES from the backwoods. [By Mary Ann Walker.] 8vo. Pp. 174. Montreal, 1861

LEAVES from the Christian Remembrancer. [By Charlotte Elliott.] 12mo. 8vo. [*D. N. B.* vol. 17, p. 266.] London, 1871

LEAVES from the country-side; an episode. By the author of *Leaves from a life* [Mrs Jane Ellen Panton]. 8vo. Pp. 318. [*Brit. Mus.*] London, 1914

LEAVES from the diary of a dreamer. [By Henry Theodore Tuckerman.] 8vo. Pp. viii. 165. [*Brit. Mus.*] London, 1853

LEAVES from the diary of a law-clerk. By the author of *Recollections from the diary of a police-officer* [William Russell]. 8vo. Pp. 295. [*Brit. Mus.*] London [1857]

LEAVES from the diary of an army surgeon, 1861-2. [By Thomas T. Ellis.] 8vo. [Cushing's *Init. and Pseud.* i. 19.] New York, 1863

LEAVES from the diary of an Officer of the Guards. [By Lieut.-Col. Sir John Cowell Stepney, Coldstream Guards.] 12mo. [*Brit. Mus.*] London, 1854

LEAVES from the journal of a Custom-house officer. By "Waters" [William Russell]. 8vo. [*Brit. Mus.*] London, 1868

LEAVES from the Lime-Walk. By one of the Trinity undergraduates [William Copeland Borlase]. 8vo. Oxford, 1867

LEAVES from the memorandum-book of A. Crowquill [Alfred Henry Forrester]. Obl. 4to. 4 parts. [*D.N.B.* vol. 20, p. 6.] London, 1834-5

LEAVES from the note-book of a New York detective; the private record of J. B. [James Brampton]. 8vo. [Cushing's *Init. and Pseud.* ii. 105.] New York, 1865

LEAVES from the scrap-book of an awkward man [Frederick L. Slous]. 8vo. [Cushing's *Init. and Pseud.* i. 551.] London, 1844

LEAVING the manse; a Disruption tale. By Kezia [Mrs M. H. Roberton, Pulteneytown]. 8vo. Pp. 128. [Mowat's *Bibl. of Caithness*, p. 80.] Edinburgh, 1893

LEBANON leaves; metrical soliloquies on passages of Holy Scripture. By the author of *Tendrils inverse* [Ebenezer Palmer, the publisher]. 8vo. Pp. 275. London, 1867

The second edition (1880), enlarged, (pp. 374) gives the author's name.

LECTURE notes on human physiology, . . . [By Rev. Thomas Allen Blyth. B.A.] 8vo. Oxford [1881]

LECTURE (a) on bees and bee-keeping. [By Charles Tite, of Yeovill.] 8vo. [Green's *Bibl. Somers.* iii. 318.] [Yeovill] 1878

LECTURE (a) on future punishment. By J. J., Philomath [John Jenkins]. 12mo. Pp. 26. [Boase and Courtney's *Bibl. Corn.*] Penzance, 1866

LECTURE (a) on maintaining good works. By Philomath [Joseph Jenkins]. 12mo. Pp. 28. [*Brit. Mus.*] Penzance, 1866

LECTURE (a) on the generation, increase, and improvement of the human species. . . . [By James Graham, M.D.] 12mo. Pp. 71. [*Brit. Mus.*] London [1780?]

LECTURES. By Burton Holmes [Elias Burton]. 8vo. 10 vols. [*Amer. Cat.*] Michigan, 1903

LECTURES delivered at the monthly parochial meeting in S. John's School-room, Keswick. [By Rev. Frederick Myers.] 8vo. 2 vols. Private print, 1840-8

Writer's acknowledgment of authorship.

LECTURES explanatory of the Diatesseron; or, the life of our Lord and Saviour Jesus Christ, collected from the four Evangelists. [By John David Macbride, D.C.L.] 8vo. Pp. vi. 232. [*Bodl.*] Oxford, 1824

LECTURES on French history, from the restoration of the Bourbons to the fall of Louis Philippe. By J. S. [Joseph Sykes, A.M.]. 8vo. Pp. 95. [*Bodl.*]. Brighton, 1863

LECTURES on law, prepared principally from Kent. By a lawyer [John Fine], for the use of his sons. 8vo. [Kirk's *Supp.*] Albany, New York, 1852

LECTURES on miracles, selected from the New Testament. By the author of *Lectures on parables*, etc. [Mary Jane Mackenzie]. 8vo. London, 1823

LECTURES on parables, selected from the New Testament. By the author of *Geraldine* [Mary Jane Mackenzie]. The second edition. 8vo. Pp. xv. 319. London, 1822

LECTURES on poetry, read in the schools of Natural Philosophy at Oxford, by Joseph Trapp, A.M. . . . Translated from the Latin, with additional notes [by William Bowyer and William Clarke of Buxted; edited by Bowyer]. 12mo. [Nichols' *Lit. Anec.* ii. 148.] London, 1742

LECTURES on polarized light, delivered before the Pharmaceutical Society of Great Britain; and in the Medical School of the London Hospital. [By Jonathan Pereira, M.D.] 8vo. [*D.N.B.* vol. 46, p. 2.] London, 1843

LECTURES on prayer. By a country pastor, author of *Lectures on the Scripture revelations of a future state*, etc. [Richard Whately, D.D., Archbishop of Dublin]. 12mo. Pp. viii. 194. [*D. N. B.* vol. 60, p. 428.] London, 1860

LECTURES on some of the Scripture Parables. By a country pastor, author of *Scripture revelations respecting a future state* [Richard Whately, D.D., Archbishop of Dublin]. 8vo. Pp. viii. 266. [*D. N. B.* vol. 60, p. 427.] London, 1859

LECTURES on the characters of our Lord's apostles, and especially their conduct at the time of his apprehension and trial. By a country pastor, author of *Lectures on the Scripture revelations respecting a future state* [Richard Whately, D.D.]. 12mo. London, 1851

LECTURES on the Church Catechism, delivered in Eton College Chapel. [By Rev. Dr E. C. Hawtrey, Provost of Eton.] 12mo. [Martin's *Cat.*] Paris, 1845-7

LECTURES on the Creed of Pope Pius IV., or, the Trent Confession of Faith. [By Humphrey Shuttleworth.] 12mo. London, 1785

LECTURES on the Epistle to the Colossians, delivered . . . 1891. By F. E. R. [F. E. Raven]. 8vo. Pp. 78. [*Brit. Mus.*] London, 1891

LECTURES on the First Epistle of John. By F. E. R. [F. E. Raven]. 8vo. Pp. 91. London, 1891

LECTURES on the history of England. By a lady [Mrs Frances A. Trevelyan]. 8vo. [*Brit. Mus.*] Littlemore, Oxford, 1850

LECTURES on the history of the Turks in its relation to Christianity. By the author of *Loss and gain* [John Henry Newman]. 12mo. Pp. xi. 287. [*Bodl.*] Dublin, 1854

LECTURES on the mountains; or, the Highlands and Highlanders as they were and as they are. [Address signed: W. G. S. *i.e.* William Grant Stewart.] First series. 12mo. Pp. xii. 301. London, 1860

LECTURES on the mountains; or, the Highlands and Highlanders of Strathspey and Badenoch as they were and as they are. [By William Grant Stewart.] Second series. 12mo. Pp. xii. 334. London, 1860

LECTURES on the Nyáya philosophy of Gautama. . . . By J. R. B. [James Robert Ballantyne]. 8vo. [*D. N. B.* vol. 3, p. 82.] Mirzapore, 1850

LECTURES on the Scripture revelations respecting good and evil angels. By a country pastor, author of *Lectures on the Scripture revelations respecting a future state* [Richard Whately, D.D.]. 12mo. [*D. N. B.* vol. 60, p. 428.] London, 1851

LECTURES on the Second Coming. By J. N. D. [John Nelson Darby]. 8vo. London, 1865

LECTURES on the seven sentences uttered by our blessed Lord on the Cross. [By Rev. Francis Edward Paget.] 12mo. London, 1839

LECTURES read at a mechanics institute in the country. [Preface signed: C. B. *i.e.* Charles Bathurst, M.A.] 8vo. Pp. vii. 392. London, 1854

LECTURES [by William Jesse] supposed to have been delivered by [Soame Jenyns] the author of a *View of the internal evidence of the Christian religion*, to a select company of Friends. 8vo. [*Brit. Mus.*] London, 1787

LECTURES to ladies on practical subjects. [By Frederick Denison Maurice.] 8vo. London, 1855

LECTURES upon the XII Articles of our Christian Faith [by John Baker]; also a briefe and clear confession of the Christian Faith written by that learned and godly martyr J. H. [John Hooper], sometime Bishop of Gloucester. 12mo. [*Brit. Mus.*] London, 1584

LECTURES (the) used by the Manchester Unity of the Independent Order of Oddfellows, sanctioned . . . June 1846. [By George Jacob Holyoake.] 12mo. Pp. 64. London, 1846

LEEDLE Yawcob Strauss; and other poems. [By Charles Follen Adams.] 12mo. [Kirk's *Supp.*] Boston, 1878

LEES (the) of Blendon Hall; an autobiography. By the author of *Alice Wentworth*, etc. [Noell Radecliffe]. 8vo. 3 vols. London, 1859

LEFT alone; and other stories. By Hesba Stretton [Sarah Smith]. 8vo. Pp. 152. London, 1904

See the note to "Alone in London."

LEFT behind; or, ten days a newsboy. By James Otis [James Otis Kaler]. 12mo. [Kirk's *Supp.*] New York, 1885

LEFT in charge; being the story of my great responsibility. By Austin Clare [Miss W. M. James]. 8vo. [*Lit. Year Book.*] London [1878]

LEFT in charge. . . . By Clara Morris [Clara Morris Harriott]. 8vo. London, 1904

LEFT on Labrador; or, the cruise of the schooner-yacht "Curlew." By Wash [Charles Asbury Stephens]. 12mo. [Kirk's *Supp.*] Boston, 1872

LEGACIE (a) left to Protestants, containing eighteen controversies. [By Thomas Bayly, D.D.?] 12mo. [*D.N.B.* vol. 3, p. 450; *Brit. Mus.*] Dowa, 1654

Preface signed: T. B.

LEGACY (a); being the life and remains of John Martin, schoolmaster and poet. Written and edited by the author of *John Halifax, gentleman* [Dinah Maria Mulock, later Mrs Craik]. 2 vols. 8vo. [*Brit. Mus.*] London, 1878

LEGACY (the) of an Etonian [Robert William Blessington, M.A.]; edited by Robert Nolands, sole executor. 8vo. [Bartholomew's *Camb. Books.*] Cambridge, 1846

LEGACY (the) of an octogenarian. By Obadiah Oldpath [James Robinson Newhall]. 8vo. [*Amer. Cat.*] New York, 1897

LEGACY (a) of hate. [A novel.] By Theo Douglas [Mrs H. D. Everett]. 8vo. Pp. vi. 297. [*Lit. Year Book.*] London, 1899

LEGACY (a) to farmers; or, some words between an Anti-Corn-Law delegate and an agriculturist. By Γηγενής [Richard Cruttwell]. 8vo. [*Brit. Mus.*] Halesworth [1849]

LEGACY (a) to the world; or, essays to promote practical Christianity. By a civil magistrate [Hamon L'Estrange, junior]. 8vo. [*Brit. Mus.*] London, 1762

LEGAL (a) argument on the Statute 1st William and Mary, chapter 18, intituled "An Act for exempting their Majesties' Protestant Subjects, dissenting from the Church of England, from the penalties of certain laws." By a barrister-at-law of Lincoln's Inn [Thomas Denman, later Lord Denman]. 8vo. Pp. 75. [*Bibliographer*, vol. v.] London, 1812

LEGAL considerations on the Regency, as far as it regards Ireland. [By John Reeves.] 8vo. Pp. 26. [*Brit. Mus.*] London, 1789

LEGAL (the) judicature in Chancery stated; with remarks on a late book [by Philip Yorke, Earl of Hardwicke, Lord Chancellor] intitled, A discourse of the judicial authority belonging to the Master of the Rolls in the High Court of Chancery. [By Samuel Burroughs.] 8vo. [Bishop Warburton's *Works*, i. 8.] London, 1727

In this reply to Lord Chancellor Hardwicke, Burroughs was assisted by William (afterwards Bishop) Warburton.

LEGAL lyrics; or, metrical illustrations of the Law of Scotland. By Quizdom Rumfunidos [George Outram]. 8vo. Pp. 32. [Martin's *Cat.*] N.P. 1871

LEGAL provisions for the poor; or, a treatise of the common and statute laws concerning the poor. [By Samuel Carter.] 12mo. [*Lincoln's Inn Cat.*] London, 1710

LEGAL reform in Scotland proposed; in a letter to the Right Hon. Francis Jeffrey, Lord Advocate of Scotland. [By David Dakers Black.] 8vo. Pp. 15. [*Andrew Jervise.*] Edinburgh, 1731

Signed: V. S. N. the initial letters of Virtus sola nobilitas, the notarial docquet of D. D. B.

LEGAL songs and verses. By an old contributor to Maga [Charles Neaves, Lord of Session]. 12mo. [*Nat. Lib. of Scot.*] Edinburgh, 1869

LEGALITY (the) of the court held by His Majesties ecclesiastical commissioners, defended; their proceedings no argument against the taking off penal laws & tests. [By Henry Care.] 4to. [*Camb. Univ. Lib.*] London, 1688

LEGALITY (the) of the present academical system of the University of Oxford asserted against the new calumnies of the Edinburgh Review. By a member of Convocation [Vaughan Thomas, B.D., vicar of Yarnton]. 8vo. 2 parts. Oxford, 1831-2

LEGEND. By Clemence Dane [Winifred Ashton]. 8vo. [*Bodl.*] London, 1919

LEGEND lays of Ireland. By Lageniensis [Rev. Canon John O'Hanlon]. 8vo. [O'Donoghue's *Poets of Ireland.*] Dublin, 1870

LEGEND (the) of a summer day; a northern dream [in verse]. By E. L. H. [Ellen Louisa Harvey]. 8vo. [*Brit. Mus.*] London, 1861

LEGEND (a) of Argyle; or, 'Tis a hundred years since. [By David Carey.] 8vo. 3 vols. London, 1821

LEGEND (the) of Bab's Oak, "Will o' the Wisp" [in verse. By W. G. Pidduck]. 4to. Pp. 22. Canterbury, 1884

LEGEND (a) of Bennetsfield; and Ippack of Ordhill. By Steven Ravenfoot [John Sinclair]. 8vo. Inverness, 1863

LEGEND (the) of Captaine Iones, relating his adventure to sea, his first landing, and strange combate with a bear; his furious battell with his sixe and thirty men against the army of eleven kings, with their overthrow and deaths; his relieving of Kemper castle; his strange and admirable sea-fight with sixe huge gallies of Spain, and nine thousand souldiers; his taking prisoner, and hard usage; lastly, his setting at liberty by the king's command, and return for England. [By David Lloyd, D.D., Dean of Bangor.] 4to. Pp. 44. [*Bodl.*] London, 1648

In the *Athen. Oxon.* vol. ii. col. 331, 2d. ed., this work is said to have been printed in 1656, in 8vo, with commendatory verses by other writers. These verses are not in this edition, which Wood does not seem to have seen.

LEGEND (the) of Cosmo; a tale. By Basil [Richard Walker?]. 12mo. [*Brit. Mus.*] London, 1860
Signed: W.

LEGEND (the) of Fair Rosamund. [A poem.] By W. Avon [Rev. William Kenrick, LL.D.]. 8vo. Birmingham, 1772

LEGEND (a) of Fyvie Castle. [By Mrs —— Gordon, of Fyvie.] 8vo. [Mitchell and Cash's *Scot. Top.* i. 52.] Banff [1885?]

LEGEND (the) of Genevieve; with other tales and poems. By Delta [David Macbeth Moir, chemist]. 8vo. Edinburgh, 1825

LEGEND (the) of Hob-or-Nob. By Reuben Lingerlong [James M. Carpenter]. 8vo. [*Amer. Cat.*] New York, 1870

LEGEND (the) of Jubal; and other poems. By George Eliot [Marian Evans, later Mrs Cross]. 8vo. Pp. 242. Edinburgh, 1874

LEGEND (a) of Killarney. [By Thomas Haines Bayly.] 8vo. [*D. N. B.* vol. 3, p. 451.] London, 1828

LEGEND (the) of Maandoo. By the author of *Prometheus' daughter* [James Abbot]. Second edition. 8vo. [*Camb. Univ. Lib.*] London, 1893

LEGEND (the) of Madame Krasinska. By Vernon Lee [Violet Paget]. 8vo. [*Lit. Year Book.*] Washington, 1903

LEGEND (the) of Mary, Queen of Scots, [by Thomas Wenman?] and other ancient poems; now first published from MSS. of the sixteenth century: with an introduction, notes, and an appendix [by John Fry, of Bristol]. 8vo. Pp. xix. 159, xviii. [*Brit. Mus.; Dyce Cat.* ii. 60.] London, 1810
Introduction signed: J. F.

LEGEND (the) of Naworth; a poem. By O. B. C. [Owen Blayney Cole]. 8vo. [O'Donoghue's *Poets of Ireland.*] Dublin, 1846

LEGEND (a) of Polecat Hollow; an American story. By Tobe Hodge [Charles MacIlvaine]. 8vo. [Kirk's *Supp.*] London, 1882

LEGEND (a) of Reading Abbey. By the author of *The camp of refuge* [Charles Macfarlane]. 12mo. London, 1845

LEGEND (the) of St Cuthbert; with the antiquities of the church of Durham. By B. R. Esq. [Robert Hegge, M.A.]. 8vo. Pp. 93. [*Bodl.*] London, 1663
An edition was published at Sunderland in 1816, with an account of the author, by John Brough Taylor.

LEGEND (the) of St Mungo, done into metre by the poet Keelivine [A. D. Robertson, artist]. 4to. Glasgow [private print] 1869

LEGEND (a) of St Nicholas. By W. C. [William Cadenhead]. 8vo. [Robertson's *Aberd. Bibl.*] [Aberdeen, 1860?]

LEGEND (the) of St Nicholas; a Christmas fantasy. [By George Nevill.] 8vo. [*Aberd. Pub. Lib.*] Aberdeen, 1912

LEGEND (a) of St Swithin; a rhyme for rainy weather. [By George Davidson, bookseller.] Illustrations by John Faed. 4to. [Mitchell and Cash's *Scot. Top.* i. 48.] Aberdeen, 1861

LEGEND (the) of Sour Lake. By M. J. Y. [Mrs Maud J. Young, *née* Fuller]. 8vo. [Cushing's *Init. and Pseud.* i. 311.] Houston, 1864

LEGEND (the) of the chapel of St Thomas of Acon, commonly called Mercers' chapel; [in verse] with an historical introduction. By I. C. [Isabella Golding Clark]. 8vo. Pp. cxix. 408. [*Brit. Mus.*] London, 1865

LEGEND (the) of the velvet cushion; in a series of letters to my brother Jonathan, who lives in the country. By Jeremiah Ringletub [John Styles, D.D.]. 8vo. London, 1815

LEGENDÆ Catholicæ; a lytle boke of seyntlie gestes. [Edited by William Barclay David Donald Turnbull.] 12mo. Pp. xviii. 257. Edinburgh, 1840
Forty copies printed. In a copy of this book which appeared in the sale catalogue of Mr Horne's Library, May 1854, the following note was written on the fly-leaf:—"Printed by me, previous to my *public* profession of Catholicism, with a view to ridicule the absurd inconsistencies of Puseyism."—W. B. D. D. Turnbull. The name was however signed in Mr Turnbull's peculiar hand, and the cataloguer being probably unable to read it made to be inserted in the catalogue "W. Maskell." The volume was consequently withdrawn from the sale, but was sold about two years afterwards in another sale.

LEGENDARY history of New York. By John Tripod [Rev. George Blagden Bacon]. 8vo. [Kirk's *Supp.*] New York, 1870

LEGENDARY tales [in verse]; with a few illustrative notes. [By Rev. Luke Aylmer Conolly.] 8vo. Pp. 50. [O'Donoghue's *Poets of Ireland.*] Belfast, 1813

LEGENDS (the) and commemorative celebrations of St Kentigern, his friends, and disciples; translated from the Aberdeen Breviary and the Arbuthnott Missal, with an illustrative appendix [by William Stevenson, D.D.]. 4to. Pp. viii. 168. Edinburgh, private print, 1872

LEGENDS and lyrics. By Miss Mary Berwick [Adelaide Anne Procter]. 8vo. [Cushing's *Init. and Pseud.* i. 34.] London, 1858

LEGENDS, ballads, etc. [By James Abbott, Captain in the Bengal Artillery.] 4to. Pp. 132. Calcutta, 1854

LEGENDS from fairy land; narrating the history of Prince Glee and Princess Trill, the cruel persecutions and condign punishment of Aunt Spite, the adventures of the great Tuflongbo, and the story of the Blackcap in the giant's well. By Holme Lee [Harriet Parr] author of *Kathie Brande*, etc. 8vo. Pp. vi. 239. London, 1860

LEGENDS from the Lothians. By Robert Steuart [Miss E. H. Letham]. 8vo. Kilmarnock, 1899

LEGENDS of Connaught; tales, etc. By the author of *Connaught in* 1798 [Matthew Archdeacon, teacher]. 8vo. Pp. xv. 406. [S. J. Brown's *Ireland in fiction.*] Dublin, 1829

LEGENDS of England and Wales, in humorous verse. By Edward Johns [R. J. Edwards, of Ruthin]. 8vo. Pp. 104. [*Brit. Mus.*] London, 1903

LEGENDS of Florence; collected from the people and retold. By Hans Breitmann [Charles Godfrey Leland]. 2nd series. 8vo. Pp. 278. [*Amer. Cat.*] New York, 1896

LEGENDS of London; tales of an antiquary, chiefly illustrative of the manners, traditions, and remarkable localities of ancient London. By the author of *Chronicles of London Bridge* [Richard Thomson]. New edition. 8vo. 3 vols. [*Brit. Mus.*] London, 1832

LEGENDS of Mount Leinster: Three months in Kildare-Place; Bantry and Duffrey traditions; The library in Patrick-St. By Harry Whitney, Philomath [Patrick Kennedy]. 8vo. Pp. ii. 283. Dublin, 1855

—— Tales and sketches. By Harry Whitney [Patrick Kennedy]. 8vo. London [1856]

LEGENDS of St Augustine, St Anthony, and St Cuthbert, painted on the stalls in Carlisle Cathedral. [Edited by C. G. Vernon Harcourt.] 8vo. [*Brit. Mus.*] Carlisle, 1868

LEGENDS of Strathisla, Inverness-shire, and Strathbogie; and a walk from Keith to Rothiemay. By R. S. [R. Sim]. Third edition. 12mo. Elgin, 1862

LEGENDS of the Braes o' Mar. [By John Grant, of Glencairn.] 8vo. Aberdeen, 1861

A later edition appeared in 1876.

LEGENDS of the conquest of Spain. By the author of *The sketch book* [Washington Irving]. 12mo. New York, 1835

LEGENDS of the land of lakes. By George Francis [George Francis Thomas]. 8vo. [Kirk's *Supp.*] Chicago, 1884

LEGENDS of the library at Lilies. By the Lord and Lady there [George Grenvile, Lord Nugent, and Lady Nugent]. 12mo. 2 vols. London, 1832

The address to the reader signed: G.

LEGENDS of the North. The guidman o' Inglesmill, and The fairy bride; with glossary and introductions, historical and legendary. [By Dr Patrick Buchan.] 4to. Pp. 88. [*And. Jervise.*] Edinburgh, 1873

LEGENDS of the Revolution. By Darppil [George Lippard]. 8vo. [Cushing's *Init. and Pseud.* i. 78.] Philadelphia, 1847

Published also with the author's correct name, and a fuller title, "Washington and his Generals; or, legends of the Revolution. . . ." [*Brit. Mus.*]

LEGENDS of the Rhine and of the Low Countries. By the author of *Highways and by ways* [Thomas Colley Grattan]. 12mo. [*Brit. Mus.*] London, 1832

LEGENDS of the saints; or, stories of faith and love [in verse. By Monica Healy]. 8vo. [O'Donoghue's *Poets of Ireland.*] Dublin, 1869

LEGENDS of the sea. By H. E. Chevalier [Edward I. Sears, Irish-American journalist]. 8vo. [O'Donoghue's *Poets of Ireland.*] New York, 1863

LEGENDS, traditions, and history of the Rhine. By George St George [Joseph Snowe]. 8vo. [Cushing's *Init. and Pseud.* ii. 134.] London, 1839

LEGIONARIES; a story of the Great Raid. By Henry Scott Clarke [Millard F. Cox, lawyer]. 8vo. [*Amer. Cat.*] Indianapolis, 1899

LEGION'S humble address to the Lords. [By Daniel Defoe.] Fol. S. sh. [Lee's *Defoe*, p. 55.] [London] 1704

LEGION'S memorial to the Commons. [By Daniel Defoe.] 4to. 2 leaves. [Lee's *Defoe*, p. 22.] [London] 1701

LEGION'S nevv paper; being a second memorial to the gentlemen of a late House of Commons, with Legion's humble address to His Majesty. [By Daniel Defoe.] 4to. Pp. 20. [Lee's *Defoe*, p. 27.] London, 1702

LEGIONS of the dawn; a novel. By Allan Reeth [G. H. Davis]. 8vo. London, 1908

LEGISLATION. [Signed: E. D. H. *i.e.* Edward Dykes Hayward.] 8vo. [*Brit. Mus.*] London [1859]

LEGISLATIVE (the) authority of the British Parliament, with respect to North America, and the privileges of the Assemblies there, briefly considered. By J. M. [Jasper Mauduit], of the Inner Temple. 8vo. [*Brit. Mus.*] London, 1766

LEGISLATIVE biography; or, an attempt to ascertain the merits and principles of the most admired orators of the British Senate. . . . By Anthony Pasquin [John Williams]. 8vo. [*Brit. Mus.*] London, 1795

LEGISLATIVE (the) power is Christs peculiar prerogative; proved from the ninth of Isaiah, verses 6, 7. By W. A— [William Aspinwall]. 12mo. Pp. 52. [Whitley's *Bapt. Bibl.* i. 63.] London, 1656

LEICESTER gaol. By A. Balance, Esq., of the Middle Temple [Thomas Binney, D.D.]. 8vo. [*D. N. B.* vol. 5, p. 58]. London, 1841

This pamphlet condemned the imprisonment of William Baines for non-payment of church rates.

LEICESTER (the) militia in South Africa. [By Major G. H. P. Burne.] Obl. 8vo. [1902]

LEICESTER Square, old and new. [By John Camden Hotten.] Arranged by E. D. Atwell. 8vo. [*Lond. Lib. Cat.*] London [1874]

LEICESTERS Commonwealth. . . . See Laycester's Commonwealth. . . .

LEILA Ada, the Jewish convert. [By Osborn W. T. Heighway.] 8vo. [Allibone's *Dict.*] London [1850]

LEILA; or, the siege of Granada; and Calderon the Courtier. By the author of *Rienzi*, etc. [Edward G. E. Lytton Bulwer Lytton, Baron Lytton.] 8vo. [*Brit. Mus.*] London, 1838

LEILA Vane's burden. [A novel.] By Effie Adelaide Rowlands [E. Maria Albanesi]. 8vo. Pp. 138. [*Brit. Mus.*] London [1911]

LEILA'S diary. [By Osborn W. T. Heighway.] 8vo. [Allibone's *Dict.*] London, 1852

LEISURE (the) hour improved; or, moral miscellanies, in prose and verse, original and selected. [By Robert Barnard.] 8vo. [Smith's *Cat. of Friends' Books*, i. 193.] Ironbridge, 1809

LEISURE hours; a series of occasional poems. [By George Lunt.] 12mo. [*Brit. Mus.*] Boston, 1826

LEISURE hours; a series of poems, original and translated. By Zeta [Rev. James Griffiths, of Wilmslow]. 8vo. London, 1870

LEISURE hours at sea; being a few miscellaneous poems. By a midshipman of the United States Navy [William Leggatt]. 12mo. [*Brit. Mus.*] New York, 1825

LEISURE hours in town. By the author of *The recreations of a country parson* [Andrew K. H. Boyd, D.D.]. 8vo. Pp. vi. 382. London, 1862

LEISURE hours of a busy life. . . . [By Andrew Tod, Edinburgh.] [1886?]

LEISURE hours; or, desultory pieces in prose and verse. By E. L. [Mrs Lydia Lillybridge Simons, Missionary in Burma]. 8vo. Pp. 320. Calcutta, 1846

LEISURE hours; or, entertaining dialogues, between persons eminent for virtue and magnanimity: the characters drawn from ancient and modern history, designed as lessons of morality for youth. By Priscilla * * * * [Priscilla Wakefield]. 12mo. 2 vols. [Smith's *Cat. of Friends' Books*, ii. 848.] London, 1794

Republished in 1796 with the name of the authoress.

LEISURE hours; or, poems on various subjects. . . . [Preface signed: T. B. *i.e.* Rev. Thomas Baker]. 8vo. Pp. 124. Newcastle, 1837

LEISURE moments in the camp and in the guard room. By a veteran British officer [J. F. Neville]. 12mo. [*Brit. Mus.*] York, 1812

Signed: J. F. N.

LEISURE moments; or, letters and poems, etc. By a lady [M. E. Dunch]. 12mo. [Cushing's *Init. and Pseud.* ii. 85.] Greenwich, 1826

LEIXLIP Castle; a romance of the penal days of 1690. By Emslibie de Celtis [Miss M. L. O'Byrne]. 8vo. Pp. xiv. 649. [*Brit. Mus.*] Dublin, 1883

LELIA. [A novel.] By George Sand [Madame Amandine L. A. Dudevant]; translated from the French. 8vo. [Haynes' *Pseud.*] Boston, 1833

LEMMATA proverbialia. [Compiled by William Stirling, M.P.] 4to. Title; 12 leaves. [*W.*] Londini, 1851

Printed in red, on one side only. Only ten copies printed, one on vellum, and nine on paper.

A collection of one hundred and forty-four proverbs in different languages, viz. Latin, English, French, Spanish, German, etc.

LENA; or, the silent woman. [A novel.] By the author of *The King's cope*, etc. [Ellen Wallace]. 8vo. 3 vols. [*Brit. Mus.*] London, 1852

LENDING a hand; or, help for the working classes: chapters on some vexed questions of the day. [By Charlotte Bickersteth, later Mrs Wheeler.] 8vo. [*Nat. Lib. of Scot.*] London, 1866

LENORE; a tale; from the German of G. A. Bürger [by Henry James Pye]. 4to. London, 1796

See also "Lean'nora," and "Bürger's Lenore."

LENT; meditations and a litany for each day in Lent. [By Mrs Edward Howley Palmer.] 12mo. London, 1851

LENT lilies; a tale. By the author of *Mrs Maitland*, etc. [Mrs Gertrude Parsons, *née* Hext]. 12mo. Pp. 58. [Boase and Courtney's *Bibl. Corn.* ii. 426.] London, N.D.

LENTEN (a) litany. By Mr C—d [William Coward?]. 8vo. [*Brit. Mus.*] London, 1698

LENTEN (the) monitor to Christians, in pious thoughts, moral reflections, and devout aspirations on the Gospels. . . . By P. B. [Pacificus Baker], O.S.F. Third edition. 12mo. Pp. xii. 432. [Gillow's *Bibl. Dict.*] London, 1769

Other editions have modifications of the title.

LENTIAD (the); or, Peter the Pope, and his pioneers the Puseyites pommelled and pounded with a Hudibrastic cudgel,

A tale in rhymes
For Lenten times,

By a beefeater, domestic chaplain to Fill Potts [Rev. John Allan, minister of Union Church, Aberdeen]. 12mo. Pp. 264. London, 1853

An enlarged edition, with the author's name as editor, was published in 1863.

LEO; a tale. By M. J. H. [Miss Josephine Hannan]. 8vo. London, 1883

LEO and Dick; or, seeds of kindness. By C. E. S. [but rather C. E. I. *i.e.* Miss C. E. Irvine]. 8vo. Pp. 128. [Kirk's *Supp.*] London [1884]

LEOLINE and Sydanis; an heroic romance of the adventures of amourous princes; together with sundry affectionate addresses to his mistresse under the name of Cynthia. By Sir F. K. [Francis Kinaston]. 4to. [Lowndes' *Bibl. Man.*] London, 1642

LEON; and the lesson he learned. By the author of *Dreams and deeds* [Louisa Emily Dobrée]. 8vo. [Kirk's *Supp.*] London, 1886

LEON de Beaumanoir; or, the twin-born. By Aemilia Julia [Emily Julia Black]. 8vo. [*Camb. Univ. Lib.*] London, 1865

LEON Tolstoy; a biographical and critical study. By Thomas Sharnol [Thomas Sharper Knowlson]. 8vo. [*Lond. Lib. Cat.*] London [1910?]

LEONARD Harlowe; or, the game of life. By "Waters" [William Russell]. 8vo. [*Nat. Lib. of Scot.*] London, 1862

LEONARD, the lion-heart. By the author of *The heir of Redclyffe*, etc. [Charlotte Mary Yonge]. 12mo. Pp. 54. London, 1856

LEONI; a legend of Italy. By J. R. [John Ruskin]. 8vo. [*Ashley Library.*] London, 1868

LEONIDAS; a poem. [By Richard Glover.] 12mo. [Watt's *Bibl. Brit.*] London, 1737

In the fifth edition [1770], the work was increased from 9 to 12 Books.

LÉONIE Vermont; a story of the present time. By the author of *Mildred Vernon* [Hamilton Murray]. 12mo. 3 vols. London, 1849

LEONORA; a love story. [By Mrs Nisbet.] 12mo. 3 vols. [*Brit. Mus.*] London, 1848

LEONORA; an elegy on the death of a young lady. [By John Nott, M.D.] 4to. [*Brit. Mus.*] 1775

LEOPARD (the) and the Liby. [A historical romance.] By Marjorie Bowen [Gabrielle Vere Campbell, later Madame Long]. 8vo. Pp. 288. [*Lond. Lib. Cat.*] London, 1920

LEOPARD (the) cats o' Aberdeen. [By Sir Wm. D. Geddes.] 8vo. Aberdeen, 1892

LEOPOLD; or, the bastard. [By Henry Whitfield.] 12mo. 2 vols. London, 1804

LEPER (the) of the city of Aoste. Translated from the French [of Xavier de Maistre] by H. M. Williams. 8vo. [*Brit. Mus.*] London, 1817

LESCAR, the universalist. By the author of *Artiste*, etc. [Maria M. Grant]. 8vo. 3 vols. London, 1874

LESLEY'S guardians. [A novel.] By Cecil Horne [Mrs Augusta Webster, *née* Davies]. 8vo. 3 vols. [*D. N. B.* vol. 60, p. 115.] London, 1864

LESLIE (the) stories; the secret of success. By Mrs Madeline Leslie [Harriet Newell Baker]. 8vo. [Kirk's *Supp.*] Boston, 1865

LESLIE'S scholarship; or, the secret of success. By the author of *The old brown book and its secret* [H. Frederick Charles]. 12mo. London [1877]

LESS (the) familiar Kipling and Kiplingana. By G. P. Monkshood [William James Clarke]. 8vo. Pp. 168. [*Brit. Mus.*] London, 1917

LESSER'S daughter. [A novel.] By Mrs Andrew Dean [Mrs Cicely Sidgwick]. 12mo. Pp. 190. [*Brit. Mus.*] London, 1894

LESSON in story; Pansy's lesson-book for boys and girls. [By Mrs Isabella M. Alden.] 12mo. Boston, 1878

LESSONS at the Cross. By Samuel Hartley [Rev. Samuel Hopkins]. 8vo. [Kirk's *Supp.*] Boston, 1853

The second edition, published the same year, gives the author's real name.

LESSONS for children; in three parts. [By Mrs E. Fenwick.] 12mo. London, 1809

LESSONS for government; or, the deliverance of a people. [By Benjamin Wills, surgeon.] 8vo. Pp. 56. Croydon [1800?]

LESSONS for little children, from the history of the Church. By C. A. R. [Catherine Anne Rowland]. 8vo. London, 1870

LESSONS for the day; being the first and second chapters of the Book of Preferment. [By Horace Walpole, Earl of Orford.] 8vo. [*Brit. Mus.*] London, 1742

A political parody.

LESSONS for the heart; selected from the best examples, for the improvement of young persons. By the authors of *The odd volume* [Misses Corbett]. 12mo. [*Brit. Mus.*] Edinburgh, 1836

LESSONS in life; a series of familiar essays. By Timothy Titcomb [Josiah Gilbert Holland]. 8vo. [Allibone's *Dict.*] New York, 1882

LESSONS in love. By Henry Hayes [Ellen Warner Olny, later Mrs Kirk]. 8vo. [Kirk's *Supp.*] Philadelphia, 1883

LESSONS of middle age: with some account of various cities and men. By the author of *The recreations of a country parson* [Andrew K. H. Boyd, D.D.]. 8vo. Pp. vi. 384. London, 1868

LESSONS of virtue; or, the book of happiness. . . . By the author of *Keeper's travels*, etc. [Edward Augustus Kendall]. 12mo. Pp. 174. [*Brit. Mus.*] London, 1801

LESSONS on early Church history, from the conclusion of the Acts of the Apostles to the establishment of Christianity under Constantine. By the author of *The Spanish brothers* [Deborah Alcock]. 8vo. Pp. xii. 175. [Kirk's *Supp.*] London, 1879

LESSONS on shells. . . . By the author of *Lessons on objects* [Elizabeth Mayo]. 8vo. [*Brit. Mus.*] London, 1838

LESSONS on the [English] Liturgy. By a Churchman [Rev. Edward Rupert Humphreys, LL.D.]. 12mo. London, 1861

LESSONS on the phenomena of industrial life, and the conditions of industrial success. [By William Ellis.] 8vo. [*Edin. Univ. Lib.*] London, 1854

LESSONS on the truth of Christianity; being an appendix to the fourth book of Lessons. [By Richard Whately, D.D., Archbishop of Dublin.] 12mo. [*Brit. Mus.*] Dublin, 1850

LESSONS to a young prince, by an old statesman, on the present disposition in Europe to a general revolution. [By Rev. David Williams.] Seventh edition. To which is added, a lesson on the mode of studying and profiting by "Reflections on the French Revolution," by Edmund Burke. 8vo. Pp. iv. 182. [*Manch. Free Lib.*] London, 1791

LESSONS worth learning, for boys. By Old Humphrey [George Mogridge]. 12mo. Pp. 108. London [1851]

LEST we forget. [Thoughts suggested by the Jubilee celebrations of 1897.] By J. R. C. [John R. Crawford]. 8vo. Pp. 126. [*Brit. Mus.*] London, 1897

LESTERRE Durant. [A novel.] By the author of *Miss Molly* [Beatrice May Butt]. 8vo. 2 vols. [*Lond. Lib. Cat.*] Edinburgh, 1886

L'ESTRANGE no Papist nor Jesuite; discussed in a short discourse between Philo-L'Estrange and Pragmaticus. [By Roger L'Estrange.] 4to. London, 1681

LET Erin remember. [An Irish romance.] By May Wynne [Mabel Wynne Knowles]. 8vo. Pp. 312. [S. J. Brown's *Ireland in fiction.*] Dublin, 1908

LET justice be done. By Mark Allerton [William Ernest Cameron, M.A., LL.B.]. 8vo. Pp. 352. [*Lit. Year Book.*] London, 1914

LET the roof fall in. [A novel.] By Frank Danby [Mrs Julia Frankau]. 8vo. Pp. 476. [*Lond. Lib. Cat.*] London, 1910

LET them say! [A novel.] By Frances Hammond [Frances A. Croal]. 8vo. [*Lit. Year Book.*] London, 1913

LET us keep the feast; a manual for the Holy Communion. [By Mary M. Davidson.] 12mo. Pp. 155. Edinburgh, 1892

The second edition (1896) gives the author's name.

LET us keep the feast; or, the Thanksgiving day. Brief thoughts and advice. . . . By one of the clergy of Bath [Rev. William N. Tilson Marsh, M.A.]. 8vo. [Green's *Bibl. Somers.* i. 340.] Bath [1840?]

LET well alone. [A tale.] By the author of *The widow's son*, etc. [Jane Alice Sargant]. 12mo. Pp. 196. London, 1851

LET well alone; or, removal of blemishes from Church and State. By Alazon [Richard William Barnes]. 8vo. Pp. 197. [Boase and Courtney's *Bibl. Corn.* i. 14.] London, 1860

LETTER (a) about a motion in Convocation, to the Reverend Dr Thomas Brett, LL.D. rector of Betteshanger in Kent. [By White Kennett, D.D.] 8vo. [Newton's *Life of Kennett*, p. 208.] London [1712]

LETTER (a) addressed to Dr Priestley. By Justinophilus [Rev. Samuel Badcock]. 8vo. [*D. N. B.* vol. 46, p. 362.] Exeter, 1782

LETTER (a) address'd to every honest man in Britain, and most respectfully submitted to the serious and patriotal perusal of the Ministry; demonstrating that not only the honour, the interest, but even the preservation of Great Britain, absolutely calls for a speedy and vigorous war with Spain if Britain cannot, by amicable means, and without any farther delay, obtain ample satisfaction for the damages she has already received from the Spaniards, and full security for her trade for the future. . . . By Mr F—r—n [C. Ferguson]. 8vo. Pp. vii. 50. London, 1738

Letter signed: C. F—n.

LETTER (a) addressed to Joseph John Gurney, on the subject of his publication, entitled, Observations on the peculiarities of the Society of Friends, &c. By a true Quaker [William Singleton]. No. 1. 8vo. [Smith's *Cat. of Friends' Books*, ii. 577.] Nottingham, 1824

LETTER (a) addressed to Lord Ebrington, relating to the stag-hunting establishment of the county of Devon. [By Lord Graves.] 4to. [Davidson's *Bibl. Devon.* p. 8.] Exeter, 1814

LETTER (a) addressed to Mr Orde, upon the education of the people. By Melantius [Robert Stearne Tighe]. 8vo. [*Brit. Mus.*] Dublin, 1787

LETTER (a) addressed to the Catholic clergy of England, on the appointment of bishops. By a layman [Sir John Courtenay Throckmorton, Bart.]. 8vo. [*Brit. Mus.*] London, 1790

LETTER (a) addressed to the Dean and Chapter of Norwich. By Ebenezer Tom-Tit [Charles Smith, minor canon of Norwich]. 8vo. [*Bodl.*] Norwich, 1824

LETTER (a) addressed to the delegates from the several congregations of Protestant Dissenters who met at Devizes on September 14, 1789. [By George Isaac Huntingford, D.D., Bishop of Hereford.] 8vo. Pp. 27. [*Bodl.*] Salisbury, 1789

LETTER (a) addressed to the Earl of Winchelsea and Nottingham on the Catholic question. [By D. Moner.] 8vo. Pp. 15. [*Bodl.*] London, 1829

LETTER (a) addressed to the editor of the Gentlemen's Magazine . . . on the much misunderstood subject of tithes. By S. T. B., a freeholder of the County of Somerset [Rev. John Noble Shipton, rector of Hinton Bluett]. 8vo. [Green's *Bibl. Somers.* ii. 124.] Bristol, 1831

LETTER (a) addressed to the heritors or landed proprietors of Scotland, holding their lands of subject superiors, or mediately of the Crown. By Scoto-Britannus [James Grant, advocate]. 8vo. [*Brit. Mus.*] Edinburgh, 1790

LETTER (a) addressed to the honest Reformers of Scotland; with remarks on the Poors' Rates, Corn Bill, religious establishment, right of property, equality of ranks, and revolution. [By John Maxwell, M.P. for Renfrew.] 8vo. [Watt's *Bibl. Brit.*] Glasgow, 1818

LETTER (a) addressed to the Hon. and Rev. Baptist W. Noel, occasioned by his statement and illustration of certain great principles of action, in the speech delivered by him at the anniversary of the British and Foreign Bible Society. . . . By Fiat Justitia [Rev. Thomas Binney, D.D.]. 8vo. Pp. 48. [*Brit. Mus.*] London, 1831

LETTER (a) addressed to the Hon. Charles James Fox, in consequence of his speech in the House of Commons on the character of the late . . . Francis, Duke of Bedford. [By John Bowles.] Second edition. 8vo. London [1802]

LETTER (a) addressed to the magistrates in the County of Buckingham, upon their intended revision of the parochial assessments. . . . By a civilian [James Howe]. 8vo. [*Brit. Mus.*] London, 1856

LETTER (a) addressed to the Rev. R. W. Jelf, D.D. canon of Christ Church, in explanation of No. 90, in the series called the Tracts for the times. By the author [John Henry Newman]. 8vo. Pp. 30. Oxford, 1841

Letter signed: J. H. N.

LETTER (a) addressed to the Rev. W. Dalton. By a Dissenter [Rev. Stephenson Hunter, Principal of Caermarthen College]. 12mo. Pp. 12. [Simm's *Bibl. Staff.* p. 239.] London, 1832

LETTER (a) addressed to the Right Hon. Sir Robert Peel . . . on the political aspect of Popery. By Britannicus [Rev. Benjamin Richings]. 8vo. [*Brit. Mus.*] London, 1837

LETTER (a) addressed to two great men [William Pitt and the Duke of Newcastle] on the prospect of peace; and on the terms necessary to be insisted upon in the negociation. [By John Douglas, D.D.] 8vo. Pp. 56. [*D. N. B.* vol. 15, p. 339.] London, 1760

This pamphlet excited great attention; though generally attributed to William Pulteney, Earl of Bath, the actual instigator, it was really written by John Douglas, D.D., Bishop of Salisbury.

LETTER (a) asserting the lawfulness of informing against the vitious and profane before the courts of immorality. [By Rev. George Meldrum.] 4to. [Scott's *Fasti.*] Edinburgh, 1701

LETTER (a) ballancing the necessity of keeping a Land Force in time of peace, with the dangers that may follow on it. [By John, Baron Somers.] 4to. [Arber's *Term Cat.* iii. 635.] London, 1697

This was one of several anonymous pamphlets issued in the controversy roused by John Trenchard's "Argument" regarding Standing Armies. Daniel Defoe intervened with "Some reflections," and a "Confutation" of the Ballancing Letter was written by the Rev. Samuel Johnson. Trenchard followed with "A letter . . . to the author of the Ballancing Letter," and "A short history of Standing Armies in England" (1698), *q.v.*

LETTER (a) by a delegate to the General Assembly to Dr M. on the subject of the Earl of Aberdeen's Bill for removing doubts as to the powers of the Church courts to adjudicate exclusively on the qualification and fitness of presentees to the particular parishes to which they are named by patrons. . . . By C. G. [Charles Gibbon, minister at Lonmay]. 8vo. Pp. 16. Aberdeen, 1840

LETTER by a forreyner [John Dayman, Sheriff of Cornwall] on Blundell's School. 8vo. Tiverton [1819]

LETTER (a), by authority, on the Royal Military College at Sandhurst. [By Colonel George Walter Prosser.] 8vo. [*Brit. Mus.*] London [1848]

Signed: Z.

LETTER (a), commercial and political, addressed to the Rt. Honble. William Pitt; in which the real interests of Britain, in the present crisis, are considered, and some observations are offered on the general state of Europe. Second edition, corrected and enlarged. By Jasper Wilson, Esq. [James Currie, M.D.]. 8vo. Pp. 72. [*D. N. B.* vol. 13, p. 342.] London, 1793

LETTER (a) concerning allegiance. Written by [Henry Compton, D.D.] the Lord Bishop of L—n [London] to a clergyman in Essex, presently after the Revolution: never before published. . . . 8vo. [*Cat. Lond. Inst.* ii. 32.] London, 1710

LETTER (a) concerning enthusiasm, to my Lord —— [Somers. By Robert Hunter, governor of Jamaica]. 8vo. Pp. 84. [Nichol's *Lit. Anec.* i. 339; vi. 89.] London, 1708

Ascribed also to Swift, and to the Earl of Shaftesbury (Anthony Ashley Cooper).

LETTER (a) concerning libels, warrants, and the seizure of papers, with a view to some late proceedings and the defence of them by the majority. [By John Almon.] Second edition. 8vo. [*W.*] London, 1764

LETTER (a) concerning the Council of Trent. By N. N. [Sylvester Jenks, D.D.]. 12mo. Pp. 264. [Gillow's *Bibl. Dict.* iii. 618.] N.P. 1686

LETTER (a) concerning the free British fisheries; with draughts of a herring-buss and nets, and the harbour and town of Peterhead. [By F. Grant.] 8vo. [Mitchell and Cash's *Scot. Top.*] London, 1750

LETTER (a) concerning the necessity of learning for the priesthood. [By Rev. Samuel Madden, D.D.] 8vo. [*Brit. Mus.*] Dublin, 1733

LETTER (a) concerning the overtures about Kirk-sessions and Presbyteries, which were transmitted by the Commission of the General Assembly, November xi. 1719. [By William Dunlop, Professor of divinity.] 8vo. [Wodrow's *Correspondence*, i. 35.] Edinburgh, 1720

LETTER (a) concerning the present state of physick, and the regulation of the practice of it in this kingdom; written to a Doctor here in London. [By Christopher Merrett, M.D.] 4to. Pp. 65. [*W.*] London, 1665

Signed: T. M.

LETTER (a) concerning the present state of the Church of Scotland and the consequent danger to religion and learning from the arbitrary and unconstitutional exercise of the Law of Patronage. [By James Oswald, D.D., of Methven.] 8vo. [Scott's *Fasti.*] Edinburgh, 1767

LETTER (a) concerning the Remarks upon the considerations of trade, by [Daniel Defoe] the author of the 4th Essay at removing national prejudices. [By William Black, advocate.] 4to. Pp. 4. N.P., N.D.

LETTER (a) concerning the Ten Pound Court, in the City of New York. By Mercer [James Cheetham]. 8vo. [Cushing's *Init. and Pseud.* i. 192.] New York, 1800

LETTER (a) concerning the true state of the question between the non-jurant and jurant-ministers of the Church of Scotland. [By James Hog.] 8vo. Pp. 22. [*Nat. Lib. of Scot.*] [Edinburgh, 1718]

No title-page.

LETTER (a) concerning the two first chapters of Luke; addressed to an editor of the Improved Version. [By William Taylor, of Norwich.] 8vo. Pp. 122. [*Brit. Mus.*] 1810

LETTER (a) concerning the use and method of studying history. By the author of *Letters concerning mind* [John Petvin]. 8vo. London, 1753

LETTER (a) concerning toleration; humbly submitted. . . . [By John Locke. Translated from the Latin by William Popple.] 4to. Pp. 61. [*D.N.B.* vol. 34, p. 34.] London, 1689

Various editions were issued afterwards.

A reply was made [by Jonas Proast) in "The argument" of the "Letter concerning toleration. . . ." (1690). This evoked from "Philanthropus" [John Locke himself] "A second letter concerning toleration . . ." (1690), and "A third letter for toleration . . ." (1692). Another reply [by Thomas Long] appeared (1689) in "The letter for toleration deciphered . . ."

LETTER (a), containing an account of some antiquities between Windsor and Oxford; with a list of the several pictures in the School-gallery adjoyning to the Bodlejan Library. [Edited by Thomas Hearne.] 8vo. Pp. 48. [*Upcott*, i. 584.] N.P. 1725

LETTER containing an account of the unfortunate difference between Sir Cuthbert Shafto of Bavington and his Lady. [By Sir Robert Heron.] 8vo. N.P. 1797

LETTER containing remarks upon a pamphlet [by the author himself] concerning the necessity of erecting an Academy at Glasgow. [By Rev. William Thom, minister in Govan.] 8vo. [Thom's *Collected works.*] Glasgow, 1763

LETTER (a) containing some loose hints on the means and the expediency of providing an establishment for the Roman Catholic religion in Ireland. [By Theobald M'Kenna.] 8vo. Pp. 32. [*Bodl.*] Dublin, 1801

LETTER (a) containing some reflections on His Majesties Declaration for liberty of conscience. Dated the fourth of April, 1687. [By Gilbert Burnett, D.D.] 4to. Pp. 8. [*Bodl.*]

No title-page.

Ascribed also to Daniel Defoe [Lee's *Defoe*].

LETTER (a) containing some remarks on the two papers, writ by his late Majesty King Charles the Second, concerning religion. [By Gilbert Burnett, D.D.] 4to. Pp. 8. [*Bodl.*] N.D.

No title-page.

LETTER (a) describing the ride to Hulne Abbey, from Alnwick in Northumberland. [By Thomas Percy, Bishop of Dromore.] 8vo. [Anderson's *Brit. Top.*] [London, 1765]

LETTER (a) desiring a just and merciful regard of the Roman Catholicks of Ireland. [By Rev. Peter Walsh.] S.sh. fol. [*Brit. Mus.*] [Dublin? 1662]

Signed: P. W., and addressed to the Marquess of Ormond.

LETTER (a) desiring information of the Conference at the Dean of St Paul's [between Edward Stillingfleet and Thomas Godden, *vere* Tylden] mentioned in the Letter to Mr G. [By Edward Meredith, S.J.] 4to. [Gillow's *Bibl. Dict.* vol. 4, p. 565.] London, 1687

LETTER I. to Lord Althorp, on the ruinous consequences of an oligarchical system of government. [Signed: T. V. *i.e.* T. Veitch.] 8vo. [*Brit. Mus.*] London, 1831

LETTER (the) for toleration deciphered, and the absurdity and impiety of an absolute toleration demonstrated. . . . [By Thomas Long.] 8vo. [Arber's *Term Cat.* ii. 618.] London, 1689

See above, "A letter concerning toleration. . . ." [by John Locke].

LETTER (a) for you; and other readings for mothers' meetings. By J. M. K. [Mrs Jane M. King]. 8vo. Pp. 192. [*Brit. Mus.*] London [1898]

LETTER (a) from a blacksmith to the ministers and elders of the Church of Scotland, in which the manner of public worship there is pointed out; its inconveniences and defects considered, and methods for removing them humbly proposed. A new edition, prefaced by a brief account of some late publications on the leading points at issue between Protestant Dissenters and the Church of England. By the editor [John Witherspoon, D.D.?]. 8vo. Pp. 68. London, 1791

The first edition (1759), signed "A. T., blacksmith," ostensibly a resident in Inverary, is generally ascribed to Dr John Witherspoon; but this letter is not included in his collected works; the names of Henry Horne (Lord Kames) and John Horne have also been suggested, though less confidently. Several editions were issued at various places, with different dates (1761, 1766, 1816, 1826, etc.).

LETTER (a) from a brother at London to the Society belonging to the Tabernacle at Norwich. [By William Cudworth?] 12mo. [*Brit. Mus.*] Norwich, 1754

LETTER (a) from a by-stander to a Member of Parliament; wherein is examined what necessity there is for the maintenance of a large regular land-force in this island; what proportions the revenues of the crown have born to those of the people, at different times from the Restoration to his present Majesty's accession; and whether the weight of power in the regal or popular scale now preponderates. [By Corbyn Morris.] 8vo. [M'Culloch's *Lit. of Pol. Econ.* p. 328.] London, 1741

LETTER (a) from a cavalier in Yorkshire to a friend. [By John Austin.] 4to. [*D. N. B.* vol. 2, p. 264.] [London] 1648

LETTER from a Churchman to his friend in Newhaven. . . . [By John Bowden, D.D.] 8vo. Newhaven, Conn., 1808

LETTER (a) from a city minister to a Member of the high and honourable court of Parliament, concerning present affairs; being a vindication of the Church of England clergy, for their owning and praying for K. William & Q. Mary. [By Daniel Whitby, D.D.] 4to. Pp. 19. London, 1689

LETTER (a) from a clergyman, giving his reasons for refusing to administer baptism in private, by the public form, as desired by a gentleman of his parish. [By Rev. Caleb Parfect.] 8vo. Pp. 56. London, 1763

LETTER (a) from a clergyman in the city to his friend in the country, containing his reasons for not reading the Declaration [of Indulgence of James II. By George Savile, Marquis of Halifax]. 4to. Pp. 8. [*Brit. Mus.*] [London, 1688]

LETTER (a) from a clergyman of the Established Church in Ireland [John Gast, D.D., Archdeacon of Glendaloch] to those of his parishioners who are of the Popish communion. 8vo. Dublin, 1767

LETTER (a) from a clergyman [Rev. Richard Hardy] to one of his parishioners who was inclined to turn Methodist. 8vo. [*Brit. Mus.*] London, 1753

LETTER (a) from a country clergyman to his brother in the neighbourhood, touching some reproaches cast upon the Bishops. [By William Wake, D.D.] 4to. Pp. 8. [*Cat. Lond. Inst.* ii. 187.] London, 1702

LETTER (a) from a country divine to his friend in London, concerning the education of the Dissenters in their private academies, in several parts of this nation. . . . [By Samuel Wesley, sen.] 4to. [*D. N. B.* vol. 60, p. 315.] London, 1703

The publication of this pamphlet embittered the feelings of the Nonconformists, whose case was chiefly presented by Samuel Palmer; Wesley next wrote a "Defence" (1704) and a "Reply" (1707) both with his name. See "A defence of the dissenters' education. . . ."

LETTER (a) from a country gentleman, to a Member of Parliament, on the present state of public affairs; in which the object of the contending parties, and the following characters are particularly considered; the Dukes of Norfolk, Portland, and Northumberland; the houses of Devonshire and Russel; the Lords Thurlow, Camden, Loughborough, Kenyon, and North; Mr Pitt,—Mr Fox,—Mr Burke,—Mr Sheridan; Mrs Fitzherbert, and his royal Highness the Prince of Wales. [By William Combe.] The seventh edition, with additions. 8vo. Pp. 79. [*D. N. B.* vol. 11, p. 431.] London, 1789

LETTER (a) from a country gentleman, to his friend in the city ; shewing the reasons which induce him to think that Mr W—r [Webster] is not the author of the answer to the Essay for peace, &c. [By Sir Francis Grant, Lord Cullen.] Fol. Pp. 4. [*D. N. B.* vol. 22, p. 386.] N.P. [1704]

LETTER (a) from a Dissenter to a Member of Parliament, with a view to secure . . . some relief. [By Rev. Samuel Rosewell, M.A.] 8vo. London, 1716

Signed : George English.

LETTER (a) from a Dissenter to the author of the Craftsman ; occasioned by his paper of the 27 of Oct. last. [By Rev. Daniel Neal.] 8vo. Pp. 31. [Darling's *Cyclop. Bibl.*] London, 1733

LETTER (a) from a Dissenting minister [Joshua Toulmin], addressed separately to three gentlemen. . . . 8vo. [*Brit. Mus.*] [London *c.* 1800]

LETTER (a) from a field officer at Madras [Sir George Dallas] . . . on the conversion of Hindoos to Christianity. 8vo. [*D. N. B.* vol. 13, p. 396.] London, 1813

LETTER (a) from a foreign minister in England, to Monsieur Pettecum, containing the true reasons of the late changes in the Ministry, and the calling a new Parliament ; and therefore fit to be perus'd by all the electors. Translated from the French original. [By Sir Robert Walpole.] 8vo. Pp. 15. [*Bodl.*] London, 1710

LETTER (a) from a freeholder to the rest of the freeholders of England, and all others who have votes in the choice of Parliament-men. [By Samuel Johnson, chaplain to William, Lord Russell.] 4to. Pp. 8. [1689?]

No title-page.

LETTER (a) from a Freeman of South Carolina [William Henry Drayton] to the Deputies of North America, assembled in the High Court of Congress at Philadelphia. 4to. Pp. 47. [Evans' *Amer. Bibl.* vol. 5, p. 24.] Charles-Town, 1774

LETTER (a) from a friend in the city to a Member of Parliament anent patronages. [By Rev. George Meldrum.] 4to. [*New Coll. Lib.*] Edinburgh, 1703

LETTER (a) from a friend in the country, to his friend in London. [By William Gibson, Quaker.] 8vo. Pp. 16. [*Bodl.*] London, 1717

LETTER (a) from a friend in the North, with special reference to the effects of disunion upon slavery. [By Ebon C. Ingersoll.] 8vo. Philadelphia, 1866

LETTER (a) from a friend to Mr John Mackmillan, wherein is demonstrate the contrariety of his principles and practices to the Scripture, our Covenants, Confession of faith, and practice of Christ, and the primitive Christians ; containing also remarks on his and Mr John Mackniely's printed protestation, declinature and appeal, . . . [By Thomas Linning.] 4to. Pp. 17. [*New Coll. Lib.*] N.P. [1712]

No title-page. Ascribed to James Webster by Currie, in his Essay on separation, p. 28 ; but Webster wrote the preface only.

LETTER (a) from a gentleman at Edinburgh . . . containing an account of the . . . late conference of ministers at Edinburgh, concerning the Act of Parliament for bringing to justice the murderers of Captain John Porteous. [Signed : P. R. *i.e.* Patrick Grant, advocate.] 8vo. Pp. 40. Edinburgh, 1737

LETTER (a) from a gentleman at Halifax, to his friend in Rhode-Island, containing remarks upon a pamphlet [by Stephen Hopkins] entitled, The rights of colonies examined. [By Martin Howard, afterwards Chief Justice of North Carolina.] 8vo. Pp. 22. [*Bodl.*] Newport, 1765

LETTER (a) from a Gentleman at R—e [Rome] to a friend in L—n [London]. [Against the Pretender and his supporters. By Thomas John Strickland, Bishop of Namur.] 8vo. [*D. N. B.* vol. 55, p. 53.] N.P. 1718

LETTER (a) from a gentleman in Boston to a Unitarian clergyman in that city. [By Lewis Tappan.] Boston, 1828

LETTER (a) from a gentleman in Boston to Mr George Wishart, one of the ministers of Edinburgh, concerning the state of religion in New England. [By Charles Chauncy, D.D.] 8vo. [Sabin's *Dictionary.*] Edinburgh, 1742

LETTER (a) from a gentleman in Edinburgh [Rev. Robert Elliott] to a lady in London. [Containing verses on the quarrel between Mr James Stuart and Mr Stevenson.] 8vo. [*Brit. Mus.*] [Edinburgh, 1821]

LETTER (a) from a gentleman in Edinburgh to his friend in the country, occasioned by the late theatrical disturbances. [By Allan Ramsay, junior, artist.] 12mo. [Lowe's *Theat. Lit.* p. 275.] Edinburgh, 1766

LETTER (a) from a gentleman in London, to his friend in Pensylvania; with a satire; containing some characteristical strokes upon the manners and principles of the Quakers. [By William Smith, Provost of the College of Philadelphia.] 8vo. Pp. 26. [Smith's *Anti-Quak.* p. 406.] London, 1756

LETTER (a) from a gentleman in Scotland to his friend in England, against the Sacramental Test. . . . [By Charles Leslie.] Second edition, corrected. 4to. Pp. 32. [*W.*] London, 1708

LETTER (a) from a gentleman in the city to a minister in the country. [By Rev. Robert Wylie, Hamilton.] 4to. [*Nat. Lib. of Scot.*] [Edinburgh, 1703]

LETTER (a) from a gentleman in the city to his friend in the country, concerning the threaten'd prosecution of the Rehearsal, put into the news-papers. [By Charles Leslie.] 4to. Pp. 4.

No title-page.

Letter dated January, the 18. 1708.

LETTER (a) from a gentleman in the city, to his kinsman in the country, concerning the Quakers. [By Benjamin Coole.] 4to. [Smith's *Cat. of Friends' Books*, i. 450.] London, 1705

Signed: Eclea-Nobj-moni—an anagram of the author's name.

LETTER (a) from a gentleman in the country, to his friends in London, upon the subject of the penal laws and tests. [By William Penn?] 4to. [Smith's *Cat. of Friends' Books*, ii. 304.] 1687

LETTER (a) from a gentleman in the English House of Commons, in vindication of his conduct with regard to the affairs of Ireland, addressed to [Thomas Burgh] a member of the Irish Parliament. [By Edmund Burke.] 8vo. Pp. 58. [*Bodl.*] London, 1780

LETTER (a) from a gentleman in the North, to a minister who has not intimated the Act of Parliament for the more effectual bringing to justice the murderers of Captain John Porteous. . . . [By Alexander M'Laggan, minister at Little-Dunkeld.] 8vo. Pp. 24. N.P. 1737

The author's name is given in the handwriting of Dr David Laing. The pamphlet has also been attributed to Alex. Howe, minister at Tarves.

LETTER from a gentleman in town to his friend in the country; regarding Keeley, the theatre, and other matters connected with the drama in Edinburgh. [By W. H. Logan.] 8vo. [Edinburgh, June 7, 1834]

Signed: H. M.

LETTER (a) from a gentleman to a member of Parliament; concerning toleration. [By Rev. James Ramsay, of Eyemouth.] 4to. Pp. 13. [*Nat. Lib. of Scot.*] Edinburgh, 1703

LETTER (a) from a gentleman to his friend, a subscribing minister in the North of Ireland. [By Rev. James Duchal, D.D., of Antrim.] 12mo. Pp. 16. [Witherow's *Lit. Presb. in Ireland*, ii. 15.] Dublin, 1731

LETTER (a) from a gentleman [Francis Plumer] to his nephew at Oxford. 8vo. [*Brit. Mus.*] London, private print, 1772

The letter is mainly a criticism of Burke's Essay on the sublime and beautiful.

LETTER (a) from a gentlewoman in the country, to [Benjamin Hoadly] the Lord Bishop of Bangor. [By Mrs Katherine Willis.] 8vo. Pp. 15. [*Bodl.*] London [1717]

Signed: E. S. (the final letters of the writer's name).

LETTER (a) from a grower of long combing wool to the manufacturers of that valuable staple. [By Thomas Cheplin?] 8vo. [*Brit. Mus.*] London, 1782

LETTER (a) from a Jesuit in Paris [but really by Rev. John Nalson, LL.D.] . . . shewing the most effectual way to ruine the government and Protestant religion. 4to. Pp. 11. [*D. N. B.* vol. 40, p. 30.] London, 1679

Signed: D. P.

LETTER (a) from a Jesuite; or, the mysterie of equivocation. [By Joannes Armondus de Hess.] 4to. [*Camb. Univ. Lib.*] [Dublin] 1670

LETTER (a) from a lady at Madrass [Jane Smart] to her friends in London, giving an account of the visit made by the Governor of that place [Mr Benyon] with his lady and others to the Nabob. . . . 8vo. [*Brit. Mus.*] London, 1743

LETTER (a) from a lady to her daughter, on the manner of passing Sunday rationally and agreeably. [By Mrs Mary Wiseman.] 8vo. [*Brit. Mus.*] London, 1788

LETTER (a) from a lady [Mrs Charlotte MacCarthy] to the Bishop of London. . . . 8vo. London, 1768

LETTER (a) from a lay-man in communion with the Church of England, tho' dissenting with her in some points. To the Right Revd. the Lord Bishop of ——. [By John Shute Barrington, Viscount Barrington.] 4to. Pp. 28. London, 1714

LETTER (a) from a layman in the country . . . concerning the Act of Parliament for bringing to justice the murderers of Captain John Porteous. [By H. Webster.] 8vo. Pp. 36. [*New Coll. Lib.*] [Edinburgh] 1737

Signed: Y. Z.

LETTER (a) from a layman to a lay-deacon, of the Kirk of Scotland; containing the reasons of his dissenting from the Presbyterain (*sic*), and joining the Episcopal communion: wherein some doctrines in the Westminster Confession and Catechism are examined; as also, an enquiry into the validity of Presbyterian ordination, with observations on their worship, discipline, etc. . . . [By Duncan Innes, shoemaker in Edinburgh.] 8vo. Pp. 51. [*D. Laing.*] N.P. 1749

The address to the reader is signed: D. I.

LETTER (a) from a London minister to Lord Fleetwood. [By Matthew Poole.] 4to. Pp. 6. [*Bodl.*] London, 1659

Signed: M. P. The author's name is in the handwriting of Wood.

LETTER (a) from a lover of Zion and her believing children, to his intangled friend; discovering the mystery of national church covenanting under the New Testament. [By John Glas or Glass, founder of the "Glassites."] 8vo. [*Nat. Lib. of Scot.*] Edinburgh, 1728

LETTER (a) from *** a magistrate in the countrey, to *** his friend: giving a new historical account of designs, through the Christian world, for reforming manners therein; discovering how it's not the publick's fault that the laws against immoralities are not execute in Scotland; removing difficulties which seem to impede those, at whom this glorious workappears to stick, here; and thereupon rousing up such from their lethargie, which, otherwise, will be fatal, both to themselves, the Church and the kingdom: . . . [By Sir Francis Grant, Lord Cullen.] 4to. Pp. 22. [*D.N.B.* vol. 22, p. 386.] Edinburgh, 1701

LETTER (a) from a magistrate to Mr William Rose, of Whitehall, on Mr Paine's Rights of men. [By the Hon. John Saint John.] 8vo. [*Brit. Mus.*] London, 1791

LETTER (a) from a Member of Parliament to a friend in the country, concerning the sum of 115,000l. granted for the service of the Civil List. [By William Pulteney, afterwards Earl of Bath.] 8vo. Pp. 30. [*Brit. Mus.*] London, 1729

LETTER (a) from a Member of Parliament to his friend in the country; giving an account of the proceedings of the Tackers, upon the occasional and Self-denying Bills, the Act of Security in Scotland, and other occurrences in the last session of Parliament. [By Sir Humphry Mackworth.] The second edition. 4to. Pp. 8. [*D. N. B.* vol. 35, p. 189.] London, 1704

LETTER (a) from a Member of Parliament to his friend in the country; giving his reasons for opposing the farther extension of the excise laws; and shewing, that had the late attempt succeeded, it had been destructive of parliament, and fatal to the constitution. [By William Pulteney, afterwards Earl of Bath.] 8vo. Pp. 28. London [1733]

LETTER (a) from a Member of Parliament to his friend in the country, upon the motion to address his Majesty to settle 100,000l. per annum on his Royal Highness the Prince of Wales, &c. in which the antient and modern state of the civil list, and the allowance to the heir-apparent, or presumptive, of the crown, are particularly consider'd. [By William Pulteney, afterwards Earl of Bath.] 8vo. Pp. 60. London, N.D.

LETTER (a) from a Member of Parliament to his friends in the country, concerning the duties on wine and tobacco. [By Sir Robert Walpole.] 8vo. London, 1733

LETTER (a) from a Member of Parliament to one of his constituents on the late proceedings of the House of Commons in the Middlesex elections; with a postscript, containing some observations on [Jeremiah Dyson's] The case of the late election for the County of Middlesex considered. [By Constantine John Phipps, Lord Mulgrave.] 8vo. [Park's *Walpole*, iv. 345.] 1769

LETTER (a) from a member of the Boston Bar to an avaricious landlord. [By Abby H. Folsom.] 8vo. Boston, 1851

LETTER (a) from a Member of the House of Commons in Ireland, to a member of the House of Commons in England, concerning the Sacramental Test. [By Jonathan Swift, D.D.] 4to. Pp. 28. [Reid's *Hist. of the Presb. Ch. in Ireland*, iii. 126.] London, 1709

LETTER (a) from a Member of the House of Commons to a gentleman without doors, relating to the Bill of Peerage lately brought into the House of Lords; together with two speeches for and against the bill, supposed to be spoke in the House of Commons. [By Robert Molesworth, Viscount Molesworth.] 4to. Pp. 36. [Moule's *Bibl. Herald*, p. 305.] London, 1719

LETTER (a) from a Member of the House of Commons to his friend in the country, relating to the Bill of commerce, with a true copy of the Bill, and an exact list of all those who voted for and against engrossing it. [By Daniel Defoe.] 8vo. [Wilson's *Life of Defoe.*] London, 1713

LETTER (a) from a member of the Marine Society; shewing the piety, generosity, and utility of their design, with respect to the sea-service, at this important crisis: addressed to all true friends of their country. [By Jonas Hanway.] Fifth edition, with several additions. 8vo. Pp. 117. [*D. N. B.* vol. 24, p. 314.] London, 1757

LETTER from a merchant in London to his nephew in North America, relative to the present posture of affairs in the colonies. [By Josiah Tucker.] 8vo. [Rich's *Bibl. Amer.* i. 156.] London, 1766

LETTER (a) from a merchant to a Member of Parliament, relating to the danger Great Britain is in of losing her trade by the great increase of the naval power of Spain; with a chart of the Mediterranean Sea annexed. [By R. Williams, Philomath.] 8vo. Pp. 6 and map. [*Athen. Cat.*] London, 1718

LETTER (a) from a merchant who has left off trade . . . in which the case of the British and Irish manufacture of linnen, threads, and tapes is fairly stated. [By David Bindon.] 8vo. London, 1738

LETTER (a) from a minister of an united parish in the city of London to his parishioners, on occasion of a collection to be made therein for the support of the Society for the Propagation of the Gospel in Foreign Parts. [By William Best, D.D.] 4to. London, 1742

LETTER (a) from a minister of the Church of England to Mr Peter Dowley, a dissenting teacher of the Presbyterian or else Independent perswasion. [By Edward Wells, D.D., rector of Bletchley.] 8vo. Pp. 45. [*Bodl.*] Oxford, 1706

LETTER (a) from a minister of the Church of England [James Wetmore] to his dissenting parishioners, shewing the . . . dangerous consequences of separating from the Established Episcopal Church. By a Missionary from the Hon. Society for propagating the gospel. 12mo. Pp. 28. [Evans' *Amer. Bibl.* vol. 2, p. 49.] New York [1732]

LETTER (a) from a new member of the House of Commons to the Right Hon. George Canning on the probable safety in resuming case payments. [By —— Callaghan.] 8vo. Pp. 150. [*W.*] London, 1819

LETTER (a) from a noble-man abroad to his friend in England. [By George Granville, Lord Lansdowne.] 8vo. Pp. 8. London, 1722

LETTER (a) from a nobleman in London to his friend in the country, written some months ago; now published for the common good. [By George Savile, Marquess of Halifax.] 4to.

No title-page. Dated 8 of Feb., 1689.

LETTER (a) from a Parliament man to his friend, concerning the proceedings of the House of Commons, this last sessions, begun the 13th of October, 1675. [By Anthony Ashley Cooper, Earl of Shaftesbury.] 4to. [*Brit. Mus.*] [London] 1675

Signed: T. E.

LETTER (a) from a parochial bishop to a prelatical gentleman in Scotland, concerning the government of the Church; wherein the controversie anent Bishops, and Presbyterian ordinations, is set in a true light, and distinctly handled. . . . [By John Willison, minister of Dundee.] 8vo. [Scott's *Fasti; D. N. B.* vol. 62, p. 27.] Edinburgh, 1714

LETTER (a) from a parson [Rev. William Myers, vicar of Walton, in Suffolk] to a captain in Suffolk [Philip Thickness]; to which is annexed a specimen of the Captain's veracity, religious principles, party, etc. . . . 8vo. [Green's *Bibl. Somers.* ii. 509.] London, 1756

LETTER (a) from a patriot in retirement to the Right Hon. William Pitt, upon the resigning of his employment. [By the Hon. Thomas Hervey.] 8vo. London, 1761

LETTER (a) from a person abroad, to a lady in Scotland. [By William Mercer.] 4to. [*Nat. Lib. of Scot.*] Edinburgh, 1785

LETTER (a) from a person of honour in the country, written to the Earl of Castlehaven; being observations and reflections upon his Lordship's Memoires concerning the wars of Ireland. [By Arthur Annesley, Earl of Anglesey.] 8vo. Pp. 75. [*Bodl.*] London, 1681

LETTER (a) from a person of quality in the North to a friend in London, concerning Bishop Lake's late declaration of his dying in the belief of the doctrine of passive obedience, as the distinguishing character of the Church of England. [By Mrs Eyre.] 4to. [*McAlpin Coll. Cat.*] London, 1689

LETTER (a) from a person of quality to his friend in the country. [By Anthony Ashley Cooper, 1st Earl of Shaftesbury.] 4to. Pp. 34. [Watt's *Bibl. Brit.*] N.P. 1675

Ascribed also to John Locke.

LETTER (a) from a physician in town to a friend in the country on the subject of inoculation, in which the reasons for the practice are considered and enforced. . . . [By Daniel Cox, M.D.] 8vo. [Watt's *Bibl. Brit.*] London, 1757

LETTER (a) from a Presbyterian minister in the countrey to a Member of Parliament and also of the Commission of the Church, concerning toleration and patronages. [By John Bannatyne, minister at Lanark.] 4to. Pp. 19. [*New Coll. Lib.*] N.P. 1703

LETTER (a) from a Protestant Dissenting minister to the clergy of the Church of England, occasioned by the alarming growth of Popery in this kingdom; wherein several late Popish publications are considered. [By Caleb Fleming.] 8vo. Pp. 78. [Wilson's *Hist. of Diss. Ch.* ii. 288.] London, 1768

LETTER (a) from a Protestant gentleman to a lady revolted to the Church of Rome. [By Anthony Horneck.] 12mo. Pp. 181. [*Bodl.*] London, 1678

"Lib: T. L. ex dono Dni Anth. Horneck authoris."—MS. note by Barlow. Reprinted in Four tracts, 1697.

LETTER (a) from a Rector [Rev. William Stanley Goddard, D.D.] to his curate, on the subject of the Bible Society. 8vo. [*Camb. Univ. Lib.*] London, 1817

LETTER (a) from a Right Honourable person [William Pitt, Earl of Chatham, on his resigning the seals] and the answer to it [by William Beckford] translated into verse [by Philip Francis, D.D.]. . . . 4to. Pp. 26. [*Brit. Mus.*] London, 1761

Attributed also to Arthur Murphy.

LETTER from a Society in Glasgow, who are not yet touched with a taste for literature. . . . [By Rev. William Thom.] 8vo. Glasgow [1763?]

Reprinted in Collected works.

LETTER (a) from a student at Oxford to a friend in the country, concerning the approaching Parliament; in vindication of His Majesty, the Church of England and university. [By White Kennett, D.D.] 4to. Pp. 22. [*Bodl.*] London, 1681

LETTER (a) from a Trinitarian [Thomas Foster Barham] to a Unitarian. . . . 12mo. [Boase and Courtney's *Bibl. Corn.* i. 12.] Penzance, 1811

LETTER (a) from a Trinitarian [Joshua Leavitt] to a Unitarian. . . . 8vo. [Cushing's *Init. and Pseud.* ii. 146.] Greenfield, Mass., 1820

LETTER (a) from a trooper in Flanders to his comerade; shewing that Luxemburg is a witch, and deals with the Devil. [By John Sergeant?] 4to. London, 1695

LETTER (a) from a true and lawfull Member of Parliament, and one faithfully engaged with it from the beginning of the war to the end; to one of the Lords of his Highness Councell, upon occasion of the last Declaration, shewing the reasons of their proceedings for securing the peace of the Commonwealth, published on the 31th of October 1655. [By Edward Hyde, Earl of Clarendon.] 4to. Pp. 71. [*D. N. B.* vol. 28, p. 388.] N.P. 1656

Ascribed to Sir Henry Vane by Barlow.

LETTER (a) from a venerated nobleman [William Wentworth, Earl of Fitzwilliam] recently retired from this country, to the Earl of Carlisle: explaining the causes of that event. 8vo. Pp. 29. [*Bodl.*] Dublin, 1795

This was followed by a Second letter, bearing the author's name.

LETTER (a) from a Virginian to the Members of the Congress to be held at Philadelphia on the first of September, 1774. [By Jonathan Boucher.] 8vo. Pp. 31. [Evans' *Amer. Bibl.* vol. 5, p. 12.] [New York] 1774

LETTER (a) from a Welsh freeholder [Thomas Pennant] to his representative. 8vo. London, 1784

LETTER from Abel Knockdunder, Lieutenant, H. P. [Andrew Shortrede, printer in Edinburgh] to Mr Luke Tinto, haberdasher in Glasgow, containing strictures on the proceedings of the Association for promotion of the fine arts in Scotland. 8vo. Pp. 40. Edinburgh, 1840

LETTER (a) from an absented member to a friend at Westminster, shewing his reasons for retiring into the country upon the present situation of the affairs of Great Britain. [By Sir William Windham.] 8vo. Pp. 26. London, 1739

LETTER (a) from an aged and retired citizen of Boston [Harrison Gray Otis] to [William Hayden] a member of the House of Representatives of Massachusetts. . . . 8vo. [Cushing's *Init. and Pseud.* ii. 4.] Boston, 1848

LETTER (a) from an American [William Bingham] now resident in London, on the restraining proclamation. 8vo. [Cushing's *Init. and Pseud.* ii. 7.] London, 1784

LETTER (a) from an American woman [Mrs H. C. Tracy Cutler, M.D.] to Lord Palmerston. 8vo. [Cushing's *Init. and Pseud.* i. 14.] New York, 1862

LETTER (a) from an author, to a Member of Parliament, concerning literary property. [By William Warburton, D.D.] 8vo. Pp. 27. [*Bodl.*] London, 1747

LETTER (a) from an ex-M.P. [William Peter, M.A.] to his late constituents; containing a short review of the Acts of the Whig Administration. 8vo. [*D. N. B.* vol. 45, p. 66.] London, 1835

LETTER (a) from an English traveller at Rome to his father, of the 6th of May, 1721. O. S. [By William Godolphin, Marquis of Blandford.] 4to. Pp. 8. [*Bodl.*] [1721]

No title-page.

LETTER (a) from an Irish dignitary to an English clergyman, on the subject of tithes in Ireland. [By Thomas Lewis O'Beirne, D.D.] 8vo. [*D. N. B.* vol. 41, p. 305.] London, 1807

Reprinted, with the addition of some observations and notes, suggested by the present state of the momentous question. Dublin, 1822, 8vo.

LETTER (a) from an Irish emigrant, giving an account of the commotions in Ireland. [By Thomas Ledlie Birch.] 8vo. [Cushing's *Init. and Pseud.* ii. 79.] Philadelphia, 1799

LETTER (a) from an officer at New York to a friend in London [on the affairs of America. By Thomas Roch]. 8vo. London, 1777

LETTER (a) from an officer, retired, to his son in Parliament. [By M. J. Home.] 8vo. Pp. 38. [*Bodl.*] London, 1776

LETTER from an old Proctor to a young one, containing serious advice for the discharge of his duty. . . . [By Terence Cavenagh.] 12mo. Pp. 36. [Bradshaw's *Coll. of Irish Books.*] Dublin, 1733

LETTER (a) from Athens, addressed to a friend in England. [By Charles Kelsall.] 4to. Pp. 95. London, 1812

"This 'Letter' was written by Charles Kelsall."—MS. note by Dyce.

LETTER (a) from Britannicus [Thomas Robe] in praise of the Queen [Caroline]. Fol. [*Brit. Mus.*] London, 1732

LETTER (a) from Candor [Charles, Lord Camden?] to the Public Advertiser. Second edition. 8vo. Pp. 54. London, 1764

Signed: Candor, Gray's Inn.

LETTER (a) from Captain Tom to the mobb, now rais'd for Dr Sacheverel. [By Daniel Defoe.] 8vo. Pp. 8. [*Bibliographer*, vol. 4, p. 174.] London, 1710

LETTER (a) from Cataline, to the surviving members of the constitutional and other societies of the year 1794; or, symptoms of the times. By a barrister [Isaac Espinasse]. 8vo. Pp. 28. [*New Coll. Lib.*] London, 1810

LETTER (a) from Dionysius [Sir Richard Cox] to the renowned Triumvirate [on the Money Bill in the Irish House of Commons.] 8vo. [*Camb. Univ. Lib.*] Dublin, 1754

See also "The proceeding of the . . . House of Commons of Ireland vindicated."

LETTER (a) from Dr P— [William Payne, D.D.] to the Bishop of R— in vindication of his sermon on Trinity Sunday. 4to. Pp. 25. London, 1696

The Latin and Greek quotations are unpaged. There is, in addition, a postscript of 30 pages.

LETTER (a) from E. C. [Earl of Cromarty] to E. W. [Earl of Wemyss] concerning the Union. [By George Mackenzie, Earl of Cromarty.] 4to. Pp. 16. N.D.

No title-page.

LETTER (a) from Edinburgh to Dr Sherlock, rectifying the Committee's notions of sincerity; defending the whole of the B. of Bangor's doctrine: and maintaining that religion, not a profession of it, is religion; that the gospel, not a corruption of it, is the gospel; that Christ, not the Church, is Christ: in which is an apology for the English Dissenters: with a word or two relating to Mr Toland. By Gilbert Dalrymple, D.D. [Gerard Legh]. 8vo. Pp. 51. [*New Coll. Lib.*] London [1718]

LETTER (a) from H. G—g, Esq. [Henry Goring], one of the gentlemen of the Bedchamber to the Young Chevalier, and the only person of his retinue that attended him from Avignon, in his late journey through Germany and elsewhere; containing many remarkable and affecting occurrences which happened to the P— [Prince] during the course of his mysterious progress. 8vo. [A. Lang, in *Bibliographica*, iii. 414.] London, 1750

LETTER (a) from Holland touching liberty of Conscience. [Signed: C. D. W. *i.e.* Cornelius de Witt.] 4to. [*Brit. Mus.*] [London] 1688

LETTER (a) from Irenopolis to the inhabitants of Eleutheropolis; or, a serious address to the Dissenters of Birmingham. By a member of the Established Church [Samuel Parr, LL.D.]. Second edition. 8vo. Pp. 40. [Watt's *Bibl. Brit.*] Birmingham, 1792

LETTER (a) from J. K. L. [James Warren Doyle, Roman Catholic Bishop of Kildare and Leighlin] to Archbishop Magee, in reply [to his charge to the clergy of his archdiocess, 1822]. 12mo. [Dublin, 1822]

Dated Oct. 29, 1822.

LETTER (a) from Mercurius Civicus to Mercurius Rusticus. [Attributed to Samuel Butler.] [*Somers' Tracts*, vol. iv.] 1643

LETTER (a) from Mr J. Burdett, who was executed on Friday, Febr. 1. at Tyburn, for the murder of Captain Falkner, to some attorneys clerks of his acquaintance; written six days before his execution. [By William Fleetwood, D.D.] 8vo. Pp. 23. [*Bodl.*] London, 1717

Signed: J. B.

LETTER (a) from Mr Reason, to the high and mighty Prince the Mob. [By James Donaldson.] 4to. [*Nat. Lib. of Scot.*] [Edinburgh, 1706]

No title-page.

In a MS. note in an old hand on one of the copies in the Nat. Lib., this work is ascribed to Defoe.

LETTER (a) from one of the country party to his friend of the court party. [By Rev. James Webster.] 4to. Pp. 24. N.P. [1704]

Dated March 1704. It was handed about to a few leading men in the time of the parliament, 1704, but not sold publicly till December 3d. of that year.

LETTER (a) from one of the special constables in London on the late occasion of their being called out to keep the peace. [By Sir Arthur Helps.] 8vo. London, 1848

LETTER (a) from Paris, concerning some new electrical experiments made there. [Signed: T. N. *i.e.* John Turberville Needham.] 4to. [*Brit. Mus.*] London, 1746

LETTER (a) from Peter Wilkins [Cyrus Redding] to Isaac Tomkins [Henry, Lord Brougham]. 8vo. Pp. 24. [Boase and Courtney's *Bibl. Corn.*] London, 1839

LETTER (a) from Phocion [Alexander Hamilton] to the citizens of New York on the politics of the times. 8vo. [Cushing's *Init. and Pseud.* i. 234.] Philadelphia, 1784

LETTER (a) from Ralph Anderson Esq. [Robert Heron] to Sir John Sinclair, Bart., M.P. &c., on the necessity of an instant change of Ministry, and an immediate peace: in order to renew the circulation of coin, to revive public and private credit, and to save the British constitution from utter ruin. 8vo. Edinburgh, 1797

LETTER (a) from Sir R—S—[Sir Robert Sibbald] to Dr Archibald Pitcairn. 8vo. Pp. 39. Edinburgh, 1709

LETTER (a) from South Carolina, giving an account of . . . that Province, . . . written by a Swiss gentleman [Capt. Thomas Nairn], to his friend in Bern. 8vo. [*Brit. Mus*]. London, 1710

LETTER from Sydney, the principal town of Australia, edited by Robert Gouger; together with a system of colonisation. [By Edward Gibbon Wakefield, Colonial statesman.] 12mo. [*D. N. B.* vol. 58, p. 450.] London, 1829

LETTER (a) from the anonymous author [Philip Francis, D.D.] of the Letters versified to the anonymous writer of the Monitor. 4to. [*Brit. Mus.*] London, 1761

Attributed also to Arthur Murphy.

LETTER (a) from [John Trenchard, edited by Walter Moyle] the author of the *Argument against a standing army*, to [John, Lord Somers] the author of the Ballancing letter. 4to. Pp. 15. London, 1697

See the note to "A letter ballancing the necessity . . ."

LETTER (a) from [Simon Patrick, D.D.] the author of the *Friendly debate*, to [Samuel Parker] the author of A discourse of ecclesiastical polity. 4to. [*Brit. Mus.*] London, 1671

LETTER (a) from the Borders of Scotland, concerning somewhat of agreement between a Scotch General Assembly and an English Provincial Convocation. By an Episcopal divine [White Kennett, D.D.?]. 4to. 1702

LETTER (a) from the cocoa-tree to the country gentleman. [By Philip Francis ?] 8vo. London, 1762

LETTER (a) from the country containing some remarks concerning the National Covenant and Solemn League; in answer to a late pamphlet [by James Webster], entituled, Lawful prejudices against an incorporating Union with England. [By William Adam, minister at Humby.] 4to. Pp. 12. [*Nat. Lib. of Scot.*] Edinburgh, 1707

LETTER (a) from the Dublin apothecary [Charles Lucas] to the Cork surgeon [A. Litten] on the subject of an invasion of Ireland by the French. 8vo. [*Brit. Mus.*] Dublin, 1759

LETTER (a) from the facetious Dr Andrew Tripe, at Bath, to his loving brother, the profound Greshamite, shewing that the scribendi cacoethes is a distemper arising from a redundancy of biliose salts. . . . [By William Wagstaffe, M.D., of Bath]. Second edition. 8vo. [*Brit. Mus.*] London, 1719

LETTER (a) from the facetious Doctor Andrew Tripe, at Bath, to the venerable Nestor Ironside. . . . [By William Wagstaffe, M.D., of Bath]. 8vo. [*Brit. Mus.*] London, 1714

LETTER (a) from the king. [By —— Wasborough.] 8vo. Pp. 64. [*Bodl.*] London [1820]

Letter signed: Montague Williams.

LETTER (a) from the Leaguer before Colchester to the Committee at Derby House, of a great fight between the Lord Fairfax and the forces in Colchester. [Signed: J. R. *i.e.* John Rushworth.] 4to. [*Brit. Mus.*] London, 1648

LETTER (a) from the Lord Vi[scoun]t B[olingbro]ke [Henry St John, Lord Viscount Bolingbroke], to the Revnd Dr S[wif]t, D[ea]n of St P[atric]k's: written at Calais, on Tuesday the 29th of March, O. S., which was found with the master of the vessel who convey'd his Lordship thither from Dover. Fol. Pp. 7. London, 1715

LETTER (a) from the man in the moon, to Mr Anodyne Necklace; containing an account of a robbery committed in hell, and the breaking open the devil's cabinet, carrying off his hocus-pocus bag and juggling-box, &c. with several copies of private commissions to his agents in London, and memorandums of pensions, disbursements, &c. pay'd to pretended reformers, for secret services. [By Captain Anstruther, of Spencerfield.] 8vo. Pp. 38. London, 1725

LETTER (a) from the man in the moon to the author of the True born Englishman. [By Daniel Defoe.] 4to. Pp. 4. [Lee's *Defoe*, p. 70.] London, printed; Edinburgh, reprinted, 1705

LETTER (a) from the minister of W—d, in Leicester-shire, to his parishioners; containing a vindication of infant baptism; and a perswasive to frequent Communion. [By Edward Moises.] Pp. 50. [*Bodl.*] Nottingham, N.D.

LETTER (a) from the [Rev. John Pierpont] pastor of Hollis Street Society to his parochial friends; with their reply. [By Edmund Jackson.] . . . 8vo. Boston, 1841

LETTER (a) from the prince of the infernal legions, to a spiritual lord on this side the great gulf; in answer to a late invective epistle levelled at his Highness, containing many material and intertaining observations, worthy to be perused not only by his many friends (witness the late earthquakes) but likewise by his few enemies in London, Westminster, and ten miles around. [By John Campbell, LL.D.] 8vo. London, 1751

LETTER (a) from the Right Honourable L—t G—l B—gh [Lieutenant-General Thomas Bligh] to the Right Honourable W—m P—tt [William Pitt], Esq. Se—y of S—e [Secretary of State]: together with His Majesty's instructions for the late expedition to the coast of France. 8vo. [*Cat. Lond. Inst.* ii. 192]. London, 1758

LETTER (a) from [Henry Joseph Johnston] the vindicator of the Bishop of Condom to [William Clagett] the author of a late Discourse concerning the sacrament of Extreme Unction. 4to. Pp. 4. [*Aberdeen Pub. Lib.*] London, 1687

LETTER (a) from Xo-ho, a Chinese philosopher at London, to his friend Lien Chi at Pekin. [By Horace Walpole, Earl of Orford.] 8vo. [*D. N. B.* vol. 59, p. 173.] London, 1757

LETTER (a) in answer to divers curious questions concerning the religion, manners, and customs of the countreys of Muley Arxid, King of Tafiletta; also their trading to Tombutum for gold; and divers other remarkable particulars. By Mons. A* * * [A. Charant]. Englished out of French. 12mo. Pp. 71. [Playfair and Brown's *Bibl. of Morocco.*] London, 1671

LETTER (a) in answer to one suspected to have been written by a stranger, assisted by the Jacobin priests of the West Riding. By the Enquirer [William Atkinson, M.A.]; . . . 8vo. [*Brit. Mus.*] Bradford, 1801

LETTER (a) in defence of our present [English] Liturgy. [By Rev. Henry Piers, vicar of Bexley.] 8vo. London, 1750

LETTER (a) in reference to his late pamphlet. By an old Etonian [Sir Alexander Malet]. 8vo. [Gilbert and Godwin's *Bibl. Hanton*, p. 44.] London, 1828

LETTER (a) in reply to some objections advanced, against The whole counsel of God. By Abiezer [Adolphus Kent]. 12mo. Pp. 22. Bath, 1845

LETTER (a) in reply to some remarks on Soul, spirit and mind, Hades and Gehenna . . . By Abiezer [Adolphus Kent]. 12mo. Pp. 48. Bath, 1845

LETTER (a) in vindication of the Answer to the Queries concerning schism and toleration; with some additional quotations, out of our English divines. [By Henry Gandy, M.A., Nonjuring Bishop.] 4to. Pp. 14. [*D. N. B.* First Supp. vol. ii. p. 269.] London, 1701

LETTER (a) in vindication of The whole counsel of God from sundry objections proposed by . . . Plymouth Brethren. By Abiezer [Adolphus Kent]. 12mo. Pp. 38. Bath, 1845

LETTER (a) intended for the Manchester Guardian, now . . . recommended to the ladies of the Anti-Corn-Law League. By a fellow-townsman [J. Bridge]. [*N. and Q.* Feb. 1869, p. 168.] Manchester, 1843

LETTER (a) lately sent by a reverend Bishop [Joseph Hall] from the Tower to a private friend [H. S.]. 4to. [*Lond. Lib. Cat.*] London, 1642

LETTER (a) most respectfully addressed to (Mrs Church) a most respectable Old Lady. By "A Friend of the family" [Joseph Hambleton]. 8vo. [*Brit. Mus.*] London, 1850

Signed: J. H.

LETTER (a) occasioned by the Second letter to Dr Burnet, written to a friend. [By Gilbert Burnet.] 4to. [London, 1685]

No title-page. Also incorporated in his *Collection of several tracts*, 1685.

LETTER (a) of a Catholic man beyond the seas, written to his friend in England . . . touching the imputation of the death of Henry the IIII., late King of France, to priests, Jesuits, or Catholike doctrine. [By Thomas Owen, S.J.] 8vo. [Gillow's *Bibl. Dict.* v. 225.] [St Omer] 1610

Signed: T. A., the Latinised name of "Owen" being "Audoenus."

LETTER (a) of a Catholicke man (subscribing himself T. A. [Thomas Ashe]), including another of P. Coton, priest, of the Society of Jesus, to the Queene Regent of France. Translated out of French. . . . 8vo. [Gillow's *Bibl. Dict.* i. 73.] Douay, 1610

LETTER (a) of a clergyman to his parishioners; being an expostulatory address on their breach of the Sabbath and neglect of all religion. [Signed: J. C. *i.e.* Rev. John Courtarey.] Fol. [*Brit. Mus.*] [1810?]

LETTER (a) of a gentleman to his friend, shewing that the Bishops are not to be judges in Parliament in cases capital. [By Denzil, Lord Holles.] 8vo. Pp. 119. [*D. N. B.* vol. 27, p. 166.] N.P. 1679

LETTER of a Unitarian [Admiral James Gifford] to the minister of St James's Church, Jersey. 8vo. St Hilier, 1845

LETTER (a) of abuse to D—d G—k [David Garrick. By David Garrick himself]. 8vo. London, 1757

Attributed also to George Colman. [*Cushing.*]

LETTER (a) of advice to a friend upon the modern argument of the lawfulness of simple fornication, half-adultery, polygamy. [By Charles Leslie?] 4to. [*Brit. Mus.*] London, 1696

LETTER (a) of advice to a young gentleman at the University; to which are subjoined directions for young students. [By Rev. James Bentham, senior?] 8vo. Pp. 37. London, 1751

LETTER (a) of advice to a young gentleman [Lord Lanesborough] leaving the University, concerning his behaviour and conversation in the world. By R. L. [Richard Lingard]. 12mo. Pp. 60. [*D. N. B.* vol. 33, p. 324.] London, 1670

An edition of 1671 bears the author's name.

LETTER (a) of advice to the Churches of the Non-conformists in the English nation; endeavouring their satisfaction in that point, who are the true Church of England? [By Cotton Mather.] 4to. Pp. 20. [Dexter's *Cong. Bibl.*] London, 1700

Signed: Philalethes.

LETTER (a) of advice to the farmers, land-labourers, and country tradesmen in Scotland, concerning roups of growing corn, and of tacks. [By William Thom, minister of Govan.] 8vo. Pp. 26. [*Nat. Lib. of Scot.*] Glasgow, 1771

LETTER (a) of advice to the Protestant Dissenters. [By Sir Michael Foster.] 8vo. [*D. N. B.* vol. 20, p. 60.] London, 1720

LETTER (a) of an Independent to his honoured friend Mr Glyn, recorder of London. [By Thomas Swadlin, D.D.] 4to. Pp. 9. [*Bodl.*] N.P. 1645

LETTER (a) of consolation and counsel to the good people of England, especially of London and Westminster, occasioned by the late earthquakes. By a layman [Thomas Gordon]. 8vo. [*Cat. Lond. Inst.* ii. 518.] London, 1750

LETTER (the) of credit. [A tale.] By the author of *The wide, wide world* [Susan Warner]. 8vo. Pp. 733. [*Brit. Mus.*] New York, 1882

LETTER (a) of due censure and redargution to Lieut. Coll. John Lilburne, touching his triall in October last. [Signed: H. P. *i.e.* Henry Parker.] 4to. [Thomason's *Coll. of Tracts*, i. 801.] London, 1650

LETTER (a) of enquiry to the Reverend Fathers of the Society of Jesus. Written in the person of a dissatisfied Roman Catholick [by James Taylor]. 4to. Pp. 44. [Mendham's *Collection*, p. 295.] London, 1689

LETTER (a) of free advice to a young clergyman. [By Rev. John Clubbe.] 8vo. [*Athen. Cat.*] Ipswich, 1765

LETTER (a) of inquiry to ministers of the Gospel . . . on slavery. By a northern presbyter [Nathan Lord, D.D.]. 8vo. [Cushing's *Init. and Pseud.* i. 206.] Boston, 1854

LETTER of Jack Downing to Mr Dwight, of the New York Daily Advertiser. [By Seba Smith.] 8vo. [*Lond. Lib. Cat.*] London, 1835

Wrongly ascribed to C. A. Davis.

LETTER (a) of love to the young, convinced of that blessed everlasting way of truth and righteousnesse, now testified unto by the people of the Lord (call'd Quakers) of what sex, age, and rank soever, in the nations of England, Ireland, and Scotland, with the Isles abroad. . . . [By William Penn.] 4to. Pp. 7. N.P. [1669]

Signed: W. P.

LETTER (a) of remarkes upon Jovian By a person of quality [William Atwood]. 4to. Pp. 15. [*Bodl.*] London, 1683

Ascribed also to Arthur Annesley, Earl of Anglesea [*Ant. à Wood*].

LETTER (a) of remonstrance, addressed to . . . J. C. Barrow. By a Protestant father [John Pulman, barrister]. 8vo. Kensington, 1859

Signed: J. P.

LETTER (a) of resolution concerning Origen and the chief of his opinions; written to the learned and most ingenious C. L. Esquire, and by him published. [By George Rust, Bishop of Dromore.] 4to. Pp. 136. [*Brit. Mus.*] London, 1661

LETTER (a) of resolution concerning the doctrines of the Trinity. . . . [By Stephen Nye, B.A.] 4to. [*D. N. B.* vol. 41, p. 282.] London [1691 ?]

LETTER (a) of several French ministers fled into Germany upon the account of the persecution in France, to such of their brethren in England as approved the King's Declaration touching liberty of conscience. Translated from the . . . French [by William Wake, D.D.]. 4to. [*Brit. Mus.*] [London, 1688]

LETTER (a) of thanks from a young clergyman to the Reverend Dr Francis Hare, Dean of Worcester, for his visitation sermon at Putney. [By Joseph Butler, LL.D., Bishop of Durham.] 8vo. Pp. 38. [Hearne's *List of pamphlets on the Bangorian Controversy.*] London, 1719

LETTER (a) of thanks from my Lord W * * * * * n to the Bishop of Asaph [Fleetwood], in the name of the Kit-Cat-Club. [By Jonathan Swift, D.D.] 8vo. Pp. 14. [*Bodl.*] N.P. 1712

LETTER (a) of thanks from the author of *Sure-footing* [John Sergeant] to his answerer Mr J. T. [John Tillotson]. 8vo. Pp. 131. [*Bodl.*] Paris, 1666

Signed: J. S.

Author's name in the handwriting of Barlow.

LETTER (a) of thanks to Mr Benja. Bennet, for his moderate rebuke of the author of an insolent pamphlet [by Zachary Grey], entituled, Presbyterian prejudice display'd, etc.; in which the great candour and distinguish'd moderation of that worthy Presbyterian teacher are set forth, and his polite language and flowers of rhetorick put in one view, for the diversion and satisfaction of the reader. By one who is neither Jacobite, nor republican, Presbyterian, nor Papist [Zachary Grey, LL.D.]. 8vo. Pp. 42. [*Bodl.*] London, 1723

LETTER (a) of thanks to the Right Honourable the Earl of Nottingham, for his late excellent Defence of the Christian faith; with some observations on the late attempts to corrupt the Christian worship. [By Thomas Manningham, D.D.] [Nichols' *Lit. Anec.* i. 207.] 1721

LETTER (a) offered to *The Times* [on Governor Eyre's case] and placed by it among its "rejected addresses." [By Charles Chorley, journalist.] 8vo. Pp. 16. [Boase and Courtney's *Bibl. Corn.*] Truro, 1868

Signed: Timothy Tugmutton.

LETTER (a) on administrative reform. By Jacob Omnium [Matthew James Higgins]. 8vo. [Haynes' *Pseud.*] London, 1855

LETTER (a) on American history. [By William Bradford Reed, LL.D.] 8vo. [Allibone's *Dict.*] Philadelphia, 1847

LETTER (a) on American slavery. . . . By an American [Sidney Edwards Morse]. [Cushing's *Init. and Pseud.* i. 13.] New York, 1847

LETTER (a) on army reform. By Jacob Omnium [Matthew James Higgins]. 8vo. [Haynes' *Pseud.*] London [1855?]

LETTER (a) on Biblical interpretation. (The Kingdom of Heaven). [Signed: H. M. L. *i.e.* Hill Mussenden Leathes.] 8vo. [*Brit. Mus.*] London [1875]

LETTER (a) on Canada in 1806 and 1817. . . . By E. M. [E. Magrath]. 12mo. [Haynes' *Pseud.*] 1853

LETTER (a) on certain statements contained in some late articles in The old Church Porch [by William J. E. Bennett] entitled "Irvingism," addressed to a minister. [By John Bate Cardale.] 8vo. Pp. 73. [Boase's *Cath. Apost. Lit.* p. 9.] London [1855]

LETTER (a) on family worship; reprinted from the Evangelical Magazine. [By John Hayden, Congregational minister, High Wycombe.] 12mo. Pp. 12. [*Brit. Mus.*] London [1853]

Signed: J. H.

[LETTER on Irish affairs. By Right Hon. Sir William Henry Gregory, K.C.M.G.] 8vo. Pp. 20. [*H. R. Tedder.*] [London, 1881]

No title-page. Headed "Confidential," and beginning "To ——: I said to you a few months ago." Only a few copies printed for private circulation.

LETTER (a) on medical reform. By a provincial hospital-surgeon [John Smith Soden]. 8vo. [Green's *Bibl. Somers.* iii. 16.] London, 1834

LETTER (a) on reading and preaching; a short treatise on elocution. By a Devonshire Rector [Rev. Joseph Limebear Harding, B.A., of Littleham, Bideford]. 8vo. Exeter, 1877

LETTER (a) on Shakspeare's authorship of the Two noble kinsmen; a drama commonly ascribed to John Fletcher. [By William Spalding.] 8vo. Pp. 111. Edinburgh, 1833

Signed: W. S.

LETTER (a) on South American affairs to Mr Monroe. By an American [Henry M. Brackenridge]. 8vo. [Cushing's *Init. and Pseud.* i. 13.] Baltimore, 1818

LETTER (a) on the Belgic Revolution, June, 1831; its origin, causes, and consequences. [By Silvain Van de Weyer.] 8vo. [Martin's *Cat.*] London, 1831

LETTER (a) on the genius and dispositions of the French government, including a view of the taxation of the French empire. By an American recently returned from Europe [Robert Walsh]. Fifth edition. 8vo. Pp. iv. 252. Philadelphia printed; London reprinted, 1810

LETTER on the government scheme of education for Ireland; addressed to the dissenting ministers who have expressed their approbation of that scheme. [By Charles J. Brown, D.D.] 8vo. [*New Coll. Lib.*] Glasgow, 1832

LETTER (a) on the Lord's Supper. By a member of the Society of Friends [Mary Stacey]. 12mo. [Smith's *Cat. of Friends' Books*, i. 222; ii. 619.] London, 1836

LETTER (a) on the nature and effects of the tread-wheel, as an instrument of prison labour and punishment, addressed to the Right Hon. Robert Peel, M.P., His Majesty's principal secretary of state for the home department, etc., etc. With an appendix of notes and cases. By one of his constituents and a magistrate of the county of Surrey [John Ivatt Briscoe]. 8vo. Pp. vi. 174. [*Bodl.*] London, 1824

LETTER (a) on the recent church-rate contest in Tavistock. [By R. Sleeman.] 8vo. [Davidson's *Bibl. Devon.* p. 52.] Plymouth [1833]

LETTER (a) on the recent judgment in the case of Gorham *v.* the Bishop of Exeter: with an appendix on Baptism. [By Rev. Charles Stephen Grueber.] 8vo. [Green's *Bibl. Somers.* ii. 456.] Taunton, 1850

Signed: G.

LETTER (a) on the state of the War [in the United States]. By one recently returned from the enemy's country [Edward Alfred Pollard]. 8vo. [Cushing's *Init. and Pseud.* ii. 112.] Richmond, 1865

LETTER (a) on the subject of the British & Foreign Bible Society; addressed to the Rev. Dr Gaskin. By an old friend of the Society for promoting Christian knowledge [Rev. William Ward, rector of Mile End, near Colchester]. 8vo. Pp. 63. [*Bodl.*] London, 1810

LETTER (a) on the wool question; to which is annexed a second letter on tithes, addressed to Lords Holland and Rosslyn. By "The old enquirer" [Rev. William Atkinson]. 8vo. Bradford, 1816

LETTER (a) on "Uncle Tom's cabin." By the author of *Friends in council*, etc. [Sir Arthur Helps]. 8vo. [*Brit. Mus.*] Cambridge [Mass.] 1852

LETTER (a) out of Lancashire to a friend in London, giving some account of the late tryals there; together with some seasonable and proper remarks upon it. . . . [By Thomas Wagstaffe, A.M.] 4to. Pp. 16. [Fishwick's *Lancashire Lib.* p. 372; *Bodl.*] N.P. 1694

LETTER (a) out of Suffolk to a friend in London; giving some account of the last sickness and death of Dr William Sancroft, late Lord Archbishop of Canterbury. [By Thomas Wagstaffe, A.M.] 4to. Pp. 39. [*Bodl.*] London, 1694

LETTER (a) out of the country, to [Sir John St Leger] the author of The Managers pro and con, in answer to his account of what is said at Child's and Tom's in the case of Dr Sacheverell, article by article. [By Joseph Trapp.] 8vo. Pp. 40. London, 1710

Only the preface was written by Joseph Trapp, as he states in the MS. contents of the volume which contains it, and which belonged to him.

LETTER (a) relative to the affairs of the poor of Frome-Selwood, in Somersetshire . . . with notes and observations on the extinction of pauperism. . . . [By Thomas Bunn.] 8vo. Pp. 158. [Green's *Bibl. Somers.* ii. 208.] Frome, 1834

LETTER (a) respectfully addressed to [John Randolph] the Lord Bishop of London, after a perusal of the charge delivered at his Lordships primary visitation, in 1810. By an Episcopalian [—— Lake, D.D.]. Second edition. 8vo. Pp. 64. London, 1811

LETTER (a) respecting disestablishment and disendowment, addressed, by permission, to the Right Honourable and Right Reverend Lord Arthur C. Hervey, D.D., Lord Bishop of Bath and Wells. By one of the Clergy [Rev. Philip Barker]. 8vo. [Green's *Bibl. Somers.* ii. 422.] Wells, 1885

LETTER (a) respecting Shetland to the . . . Highland Society of Scotland, in answer to one lately addressed to them, entitled, A letter by the Landholders of Shetland. [By Rev. —— Saville.] 8vo. [Mitchell and Cash's *Scot. Top.*] Edinburgh, 1803

Signed: Vindicator.

LETTER (a) respecting the [General] Assembly [of the Church of Scotland]. [By Robert Wylie, minister at Hamilton.] 4to. [*New Coll. Lib.*] N.P. 1708

LETTER (a) sent from a gentleman to Mr Martin, Member for Worcester. [By Lionel Copley?] 4to. London, 1642

LETTER (a) sent from beyond the seas to one of the chief ministers of the Non-conforming party; by way of reply to many particulars which he sent to the author in a letter of news. Useful for these distempered times. By a lover of the established government both of Church and state [George Hickes, D.D.]. 4to. Pp. 35. 1674

The letter is dated Saumur. May 7. 1674. A second edition appeared in 1684, with the title:—The judgment of an anonymous writer, *q.v.*

The letter has been frequently ascribed to Edward Hyde, Earl of Clarendon, and was received as his, when it first appeared; but the date of the letter, compared with the date of Clarendon's death at Rouen (Dec. 3. 1683) shows that it could not have been written by the Chancellor.

LETTER (a) sent to a friend containing some reflections upon a late book, intituled The Roman Church vindicated, and M. S. convicted of a false witnesse against her. . . . By J. S. [Joshua Stopford], B.D. 4to. [*Brit. Mus.*] [London] 1675

LETTER (a) sent to an honourable gentleman in way of satisfaction concerning some slanderous reports lately raised against the Bishops and the rest of the Clergie. [By Joseph Hall, D.D.] 4to. [Thomason's *Coll. of Tracts*, i. 18.] London, 1641

LETTER (a) sent to General Monk, to St Albons the 29 of January; wherein the antient government of England, founded upon Magna Charta and the Petition of Rights is vindicated. . . . [Letter signed: H. N. *i.e.* Henry Nichols.] 4to. [*Camb. Univ. Lib.*] London, 1659

LETTER (a) sent to the Hono^{ble} W. Lenthal, Esq. concerning Sir T. Fairfax's routing of the enemy in the West, near Bodman March 8, 1645. . . . [Signed: J. R. *i.e.* John Rushworth.] 4to. Pp. 8. London, 1645

LETTER (a) sent to the Hon. W. Lenthal . . . of the fight between His Excellency's the Lord Fairfax forces at Maidstone, and the Kentish forces, June 1, 1648. [By John Rushworth.] 4to. [*Brit. Mus.*] London, June 3, 1648

LETTER (a) sent to the Hon. W. Lenthall, Esq. . . . of the late fight at Colchester. . . . [Signed: J. R. *i.e.* John Rushworth.] 4to. [*Brit. Mus.*] London, 1648

LETTER (a) sent to the King [Charles II.] from M. F. [Margaret Fell, Quakeress]. 4to. [Smith's *Cat. of Friend's Books.*] N.P. [1666]

LETTER (a) shewing why our English Bibles differ so much from the Septuagint, though both are translated from the Hebrew original. [By Thomas Brett, LL.D.] 8vo. Pp. 71. [Nichol's *Lit. Anec.* i. 407.] London, 1743

Signed: T. B.

Reprinted in Bp. Watson's Collection of theological tracts.

LETTER (a), stating the true site of the ancient colony of Camulodunum. [By Sir Richard Colt Hoare.] 8vo. [Martin's *Cat.*] Shaftesbury, 1827

LETTER (a) to a Bishop concerning lectureships. By F. T. Assistant-Curate at ——, and Joint-lecturer of St —— [Thomas Francklin, D.D.]. 8vo. [*Brit. Mus.*] London, 1768

LETTER (a) to a Bishop, concerning some important discoveries in philosophy and theology (3rd ed.). Some thoughts concerning religion, natural and revealed, and the manner of understanding Revelation; tending to shew that Christianity is indeed very near, as old as the Creation. [By Duncan Forbes.] Fourth edition. 12mo. Pp. 132. [*Bodl.*] London, 1747

LETTER (a) to a Bishop concerning the present settlement, and the new oaths. [By Thomas Comber, D.D., Dean of Durham.] 4to. Pp. 36. [*Bodl.*] London, 1689

Attributed also to Edward Gee.

LETTER (a) to a Bishop [Dr Lowth]; occasioned by the late petition to Parliament for relief in the matter of subscription. [By John Sturges, LL.D.] 8vo. Pp. 62. [Nichols' *Lit. Anec.* ix. 545.] London, 1772

LETTER (a) to a brother in Christ, on liberty of ministry. [By George V. Wigram.] 12mo. Pp. 12. London, N.D.

LETTER (a) to a child. By the author of *A book for the cottage* [Maria Charlesworth]. 16mo. 12 parts. [*Brit. Mus.*] London, 1849-55

LETTER (a) to a clergyman [on ordained and voluntary religious ministrations. By John Wesley]. 12mo. [Green's *Wesley Bibliography*, p. 54.] Dublin, 1748

Signed: J. W.

LETTER (a) to a clergyman in the country, concerning the choice of members, and the execution of the Parliament-writ, for the ensuing convocation. [By Francis Atterbury, D.D.] 4to. Pp. 10. [*Bodl.*] London, 1701

No title-page.

LETTER (a) to a clergy-man in the country, concerning the votes of the Bishops in the last session of Parliament, upon the Bill against occasional conformity. [By Benjamin Hoadly, D.D.] 4to. Pp. 32. [*Bodl.*] London, 1704

LETTER (a) to a clergyman of the diocese of Durham [Henry Phillpotts], in answer to his second letter to the author of the Remarks on the Bishop of Durham [Barrington]'s charge. [By John Lingard, D.D.] 12mo. Pp. 62. [*Bodl.*] Newcastle upon Tyne, 1808

LETTER (a) to a clergyman, relating to his sermon on the 30th Jan. By a lover of truth [G. Coade, junr., merchant at Exeter]. [*N. and Q.* July 16, 1859, p. 58; May 6, 1854, p. 425.] 1746

The second edition is not anonymous.

LETTER (a) to a college friend relative to some late transactions of a literary society at Exeter. With a postscript. [By Rev. Richard Polwhele]. 8vo. [Davidson's *Bibl. Devon.* p. 28.] London, 1798

LETTER (a) to a Convocation-man concerning the rights, powers, and priviledges of that body. [By Sir Bartholomew Shower.] 4to. Pp. 68. [*Brit. Mus.*] London, 1697

LETTER (a) to a country clergyman [Thomas Sikes] occasioned by his Address to Lord Teignmouth, President of the British and Foreign Bible Society. By a suburban clergyman [John Owen, M.A., curate of Fulham]. 8vo. Pp. 61. London, 1805

LETTER (a) to a country clergyman [Rev. John Tucker, B.D.] on his Serious appeal to the Bible, from a resident member of the University [of Oxford, viz. Rev. John David Macbride, D.C.L.]. 8vo. Pp. 23. [*Brit. Mus.*] Oxford, 1829

LETTER to a county member on the means of securing a safe and honourable peace. [By Henry Beeke, D.D.] 8vo. [*Biog. Dict.* 1816.] 1798

LETTER (a) to a Deist, concerning the beauty and excellency of moral virtue, and the support and improvement which it receives from the Christian revelation. By a country clergyman [John Balguy]. The second edition. To which is added a postscript. 8vo. [*Brit. Mus.*] London, 1730

LETTER (a) to a Deist, in answer to several objections against the truth and authority of the Scriptures. [By Edward Stillingfleet, D.D.] 8vo. Pp. 135. [*Bodl.*] London, 1677

LETTER (a) to a Dissenter, upon occasion of His Majesties late gracious Declaration of Indulgence. [By George Savile, Marquis of Halifax.] 4to. Pp. 7. [Jones' *Peck*, i. 74.] [1687]

No title-page.
Signed: T. W. *i.e.* The Writer.

LETTER (a) to a Dissenting minister, containing remarks on the late Act for the relief of His Majesty's subjects, professing the Popish religion; with some strictures on the appeal from the Protestant Association to the people of Great Britain; also, extracts from several acts of Parliament. . . . By a lay-dissenter [John Stevenson]. 8vo. [*European Mag.* vii. 213.] 1780

LETTER (a) to a friend. By the author of *Remarks on two particulars of a refutation of Calvinism* [Joseph Holden Pott]. 8vo. Pp. 24. [*Brit. Mus.*] London, 1818

LETTER (a) to a friend, concerning a French invasion to restore the late King James to his throne; and what may be expected from him, should he be successful in it. [By William Sherlock, D.D.] 4to. Pp. 30. [*Manch. Free Lib.*] London, 1692

LETTER (a) to a friend, concerning his changing his religion. [Signed: R. D. *i.e.* Rowland Davies.] 4to. [*Brit. Mus.*] London, 1692

LETTER (a) to a friend concerning Mr [Robert] Calder's late paper entitled "A return" etc. and the continuation thereof. [By Rev. John Anderson.] 4to. [*Nat. Lib. of Scot.*] Glasgow, 1712

LETTER (a) to a friend concerning some of Dr Owens principles and practices; with a postscript to the author [Sam Parker] of the late Ecclesiastical Polity and an Independent catechism. [By George Vernon, M.A., chaplain of All Souls.] 4to. Pp. 78. [*D. N. B.* vol. 58, p. 275.] London, 1670

LETTER (a) to a friend concerning the Infallibility of the Church of Christ. [By Richard Challoner, D.D., Romish Bishop]; in answer to a late pamphlet [by J— R—] intituled, An humble address to the Jesuits, by a dissatisfied Roman Catholic. 12mo. [*D. N. B.* vol. 9, p. 445; Gillow's *Bibl. Dict.* i. 454.] London, 1743

LETTER (a) to a friend concerning the Oath of Abjuration. [By George Ridpath.] 4to. [*Nat. Lib. of Scot.*] [London, 1712]

No title-page.

LETTER (a) to a friend containing a few heads for consideration, on subjects that trouble the Church [viz. Irvingism]. By Charlotte Elizabeth [Mrs Charlotte Elizabeth Tonna, *née* Browne]. 8vo. Pp. 16. [*D. N. B.* vol. 57.] London, 1831

LETTER (a) to a friend, containing diverse remarks concerning the sacrament of the Lord's Supper; with some hints at the Scriptural-rules for administration of, and admission to the same. [By James Hog, minister at Carnock.] 12mo. Pp. 98. [*New Coll. Lib.*] Edinburgh, 1706

LETTER (a) to a friend [in Hudibrastic verse] containing some matters relating to the Church. By a Cornish vicar [Robert Stephen Hawker, M.A.]. 8vo. Pp. 16. [Cushing's *Init. and Pseud.* i. 67.] London, 1857

LETTER (a) to a friend [from Margaret Evanson], containing some observations on Mr [Thomas] Falkner's Critique on the Dissonance [by Edward Evanson.] . . . 12mo. [*Brit. Mus.*] London, 1811

LETTER (a) to a friend, containing some quaeries about the new Commission for making alterations in the Liturgy, Canons, &c. of the Church of England. [By William Jane.] 4to. Pp. 4. [Wood's *Athen. Oxon.* iv. 644.] [London, 1689]

No title-page.
Ascribed also to William Sherlock, D.D.

LETTER (a) to a friend, giving a concise but just representation of the hardships and sufferings the town of Boston is exposed to and must undergo, in consequence of the late Act of the British Parliament. . . . By T. W., a Bostonian [Charles Chauncy]. 12mo. Pp. 35. [Evans' *Amer. Bibl.* vol. 5, p. 16.] Boston, 1774

LETTER (a) to a friend, giving an account how the Treaty of Union [between Scotland and England] has been received here; and wherein are contained answers to the most material objections against it, with some remarks upon what has been written by Mr H. [Hodges] and Mr R. [Ridpath]. [By Sir John Clerk, of Penicuik.] 4to. Pp. 44. Edinburgh, 1706

Incorrectly attributed to Daniel Defoe.

LETTER (a) to a friend, giving an account of all the treatises that have been publish'd with relation to the present persecution against the [Episcopal] Church of Scotland. [By Alexander Monro, D.D.] 4to. [*Nat. Lib. of Scot.*] London, 1692

LETTER (a) to a friend in a slave state. By a citizen of Pennsylvania [Charles Ingersoll]. 8vo. [Cushing's *Init. and Pseud.* i. 59.] Philadelphia, 1862

LETTER (a) to a friend, in answer to a letter written against Mr Lowth, in defence of Dr Stillingfleet. [By Samuel Grascome.] 4to. Pp. 30. [*Bodl.*] London, 1688

LETTER (a) to a friend in Italy; and verses occasioned on reading Montfaucon. [By Edward Clarke, M.A.] 4to. Pp. 22. [*Bodl.*] London, 1755

LETTER (a) to a friend in Lancashire, occasioned by a report, concerning injunctions, and prohibitions, by authority; relating to some points of religion, now in debate. [By Benjamin Hoadly.] 8vo. London, 1714

LETTER (a) to a Friend, in reply to the question, What is vegetarianism? [By William Bennett.] 12mo. [Smith's *Cat. of Friends' Books*, i. 247.] London, 1849

LETTER (a) to a friend in the country, attempting the solution of the scruples & objections of a conscientious or religious nature commonly made against the new way of receiving the small-pox. By a minister in Boston [Cotton Mather, D.D.]. 8vo. Pp. 13. [Evans' *Amer. Bibl.*] Boston, 1721

LETTER (a) to a friend in the country, concerning the proceedings of the present Convocation. [By Edmund Gibson, Bishop of London.] 4to. Pp. 8. [1701]

No title-page.

LETTER (a) to a friend in the country on the publication of Thurloe's State Papers, in which is contained an impartial account of the author and the book, and several particulars relating to British history are examined and set in a true light. [By John Campbell, LL.D.] 8vo. Pp. 70. [Lowndes' *Bibl. Man.* p. 2682.] London, 1742

LETTER (a) to a friend; in which is shewn the inviolable nature of publick securities. By a lover of his country [Arthur Ashley Sykes, D.D.]. 8vo. Pp. 40. [Disney's *Memoir of Sykes*, p. 12.] London, 1717

LETTER (a) to a friend; in which the Occasional Conformists are proved to be guilty of schism and hypocrisy: in answer to some arguments produc'd to the contrary in a late pamphlet, intituled, The rights of Protestant dissenters, etc. [By William Buckridge, of Corpus Christi College.] 4to. Pp. 38. [*Bodl.*] Oxford, 1704

LETTER (a) to a friend, occasioned by a French pamphlet [entitled, Lettres de M. L'Abbé au Sr Kennicott, Anglois] lately published against Doctor Kennicott, and his collection of the Hebrew MSS. [By Benjamin Kennicott himself.] 8vo. Pp. 33. [*D. N. B.* vol. 31, p. 21.] London, 1772

Mistakenly attributed to George Harbin.

The "Lettres de M. L'Abbé," really written by J. A. Dumay, were translated [by W. Stevens] into English as "Letters of Mr the Abbot of ——" [see *infra*]; a new and enlarged translation by the same writer was published in 1773.

LETTER (a) to a friend, occasioned by a rhapsody, delivered in the Old Jewry by a reverend bookseller [Samuel Chandler, D.D.], at the shutting-up his evening entertainment for the last winter session. [By Rev. Abraham Taylor.] 8vo. Pp. 41. [*Brit. Mus.*] London, 1729

LETTER (a) to a friend, occasioned by Epistola objurgatoria, etc., by S. P. Y. B. [By William King, LL.D., St Mary Hall, Oxford.] 4to. [*D. N. B.* vol. 31, p. 168.] London, 1744

LETTER (a) to a friend, occasioned by the surrender of Mons. [By Edward Wetenhall, D.D.] 4to. [Watt's *Bibl. Brit.*] London, 1691

LETTER (a) to a friend [Mr —— Bignell, of Banbury] on the late Revolution in France. [By Francis Eyre.] 8vo. London, 1791

LETTER (a) to a friend on the mineral customs of Derbyshire; in which the questions relative to the claim of the duty of lot on Smitham is occasionally considered. By a Derbyshire working miner [Anthony Tissington]. 8vo. Pp. 43. [Gough's *Brit. Topog.* i. 293.] London, 1766

LETTER (a) to a friend on the Test Act. By a Christian believer, philanthropist, and North Briton [Alexander Dalrymple]. 8vo. Pp. 37. [*Bodl.*] London, 1790

LETTER (a) to a friend, reflecting on some passages in a Letter [by John Sargeant] to the D. of P. [Edward Stillingfleet, Dean of St Paul's] in answer to the arguing part of his first letter to Mr G[odden]. [By Clement Ellis, M.A.] 4to. Pp. 31. [*Bodl.*] London, 1687

LETTER (a) to a friend relating to the present Convocation at Westminster. [By Humphrey Prideaux.] 4to. Pp. 27. [Boase and Courtney's *Bibl. Corn.* ii. 528.] London, 1690

LETTER (a) to a friend respecting commerce, free ports, and London docks. [By William Vaughan.] 8vo. [Watt's *Bibl. Brit.*] London, 1795

LETTER (a) to a friend, tending to prove: I. That valid ordination ought not to be repeated; II. That ordination by Presbyters is valid. With an appendix. By R. A. [Richard Alleine, M.A.]. [Calamy's *Nonconf. Mem.* Palmer's ed. iii. 158.] 1661

LETTER to a friend touching Gods providence about sinful actions. In answer to a letter entituled, The reconcileableness of God's prescience, etc. and to the postscript of that letter. By "J. T." [John Troughton]. 8vo. Pp. 80. [*Bodl.*] London, 1678

LETTER (a) to a friend, upon the subject of infant baptism. By a chaplain in the Navy [Rev. Henry P. Beloe]. 8vo. [*Brit. Mus.*] Plymouth, 1877

LETTER (a) to a friend; with a poem called "The Ghost of Werter." By a Lady [Lady Eglantine Wallace]. . . . 4to. [*Brit. Mus.*] London, 1787

Signed: E. W.

LETTER (a) to a friend; with two poems sacred to the memory of the late R. R. Dr Thomas Rattray of Craighall, Bishop of Edinburgh. [By Thomas Drummond, D.D.] 4to. Pp. 12. Edinburgh, 1743

The author was ancestor of Sir W. Drummond of Logiealmond.

LETTER (a) to a gentleman at Edinburgh, a ruling elder of the Church of Scotland, concerning the proceedings of the last General Assembly, with respect to doctrine chiefly. [By Rev. Gabriel Wilson.] 8vo. Pp. 27. [*New Coll. Lib.*] London, 1721

LETTER (a) to a gentleman, containing a detection of errors in a print [by Charles Leslie] intituled, The snake in the grass. Wherein that author giveth his remarks upon the Marrow of modern divinity, lately re-printed. [By Rev. James Hog, of Carnock.] 12mo. Pp. 23. [*New Coll. Lib.*] Edinburgh, 1719

LETTER (a) to a gentleman elected a knight of the shire to serve in the present parliament. [By Thomas Wagstaffe, A.M.] 4to. Pp. 20. [*Bodl.*] [London, 1694]

No title-page.

LETTER (a) to a gentleman [George Paton] from his friend in Orkney, containing the true causes of the poverty of that country. [By Thomas Hepburn, minister at Birsay, later at Athelstanford.] 8vo. Pp. 44. [*Bodl.*] London, 1760

LETTER (a) to a gentleman in Edinburgh; wherein the proposal made to the last General Assembly for having Dr Johnston's Paraphrase of the Psalms taught in the schools as a proper sacred lesson betwixt Castalio's Dialogues and Buchanan is considered. . . . [By John Love, rector of Dalkeith Academy.] 4to. Pp. 22. [*Scottish N. and Q.* 1895, p. 67.] Edinburgh, 1740

Signed: Philo-Buchananus.

LETTER (a) to a gentleman in the country, containing the representation of the Commission of the G. Assembly, to their Excellencies the Lords Justices. With some remarks upon it, concerning the shutting up the Episcopal Meeting-houses. [By J. Smith.] 8vo. Pp. 20. [*Nat. Lib. of Scot.*] Edinburgh, 1724

LETTER (a) to a gentleman in the Massachusetts General Assembly, concerning taxes to support religious worship. [By Rev. Isaac Backus.] 8vo. Pp. 22. [Dexter's *Cong. Bibl.* No. 3613.] [Boston] 1771

Signed: A countryman.

LETTER (a) to a gentleman of Leicestershire, shewing, out of the publicke writings which have passed betwixt his Majestie and his two Houses of Parliament, that, all the overtures which have beene made for peace and accommodation have proceeded from His Majestie onely; and, that the unsuccessefulnesse of the late treatie is not to be imputed to His Majesty, but to them alone. [By Peter Heylin.] 4to. Pp. 29. [*Bodl.*] 1643

LETTER (a) to a lady, concerning the due improvement of her advantages of celibacie, portion, and maturity of age and judgment: which may serve indifferently for men under the same circumstances. [By Edward Stephens of Cherington.] Pp. 8. [*Bodl.*] N.P., N.D.

LETTER (a) to a lady concerning the new Play House. [By Jeremy Collier.] 8vo. Pp. 16. [*Bodl.*] London, 1706

LETTER (a) to a lady, furnishing her with Scripture testimonies against the principal points and doctrines of Popery. [By Charles Barecroft.] 4to. [Mendham's *Collection*, p. 16.] London, 1688

LETTER (a) to a lady in France on the supposed failure of a National Bank. . . . [By Thomas G. Cary.] 8vo. Boston, 1843

LETTER (a) to a lady, on card-playing on the Lord's Day. [By Robert Bolton, LL.D., Dean of Carlisle.] 8vo. [Green's *Bibl. Somers.* i. 314.] London, 1748

LETTER (a) to a lady on the mode of conducting herself during pregnancy. . . . [By Sarah Brown.] 8vo. [*Brit. Mus.*] London, 1877

LETTER (a) to a lady; wherein the canonical authority of St Matthew's Gospel is defended; the Bishop of London's third pastoral letter vindicated; and the misrepresentations and forgeries contain'd in a late pamphlet, . . . are laid open to the meanest capacity. [By Brampton Gurdon? or Richard Biscoe?] 8vo. Pp. 118. [*Brit. Mus.*] London, 1732

LETTER (a) to a layman, on the subject of the Rev. Mr Theophilus Lindsey's proposal for a reformed English Church, upon the plan of the late Dr Samuel Clarke. [By Joseph Priestley, LL.D.] 8vo. Pp. 29. [*D. N. B.* vol. 46, p. 367.] London, 1774

LETTER (a) to a Lord [Bishop Hoadly], in answer to his late book entitled, A plain account of the nature and end of the sacrament of the Lord's Supper. [By Patrick Delany, D.D., Dean of Down.] 8vo. Pp. 32. [*Bodl.*] Dublin printed; London reprinted 1736

LETTER (a) to a Lover of the Gospel [Dr Joseph Priestley], occasioned by his Appeal to . . . Professors of Christianity on the following subjects, viz. 1. The use of reason in matters of religion. 2. The power of man to do the will of God. . . . [By Thomas Reader.] 12mo. [*Brit. Mus.*] London, 1772

See, above, "An appeal to the serious. . . ."

LETTER (a) to a Member of Parliament [on mines]. [By John Binning.] 4to. Pp. 4. N.D.

No title-page.

LETTER (a) to a Member of Parliament, containing a proposal for bringing in a bill to revise, amend or repeal certain obsolete statutes, commonly called the Ten Commandments. [By John Hildrop, D.D.] 8vo. [*D. N. B.* vol. 26, p. 386.] London, 1738

A satire, directed against the irreligion of the times. This tract, on its first appearance, was generally ascribed to Dean Swift: it is included in the second volume of Hildrop's miscellaneous works, published by himself in 1754.

LETTER (a) to a Member of Parliament; occasioned by a Letter to a Convocation-man [by Sir Bartholomew Shower], concerning the rights, powers, and privileges of that body. . . . [By William Wright, recorder of Oxford.] 4to. Pp. 72. [*Bodl.*] London, 1697

LETTER (a) to a Member of Parliament, on the case of the Protestant Dissenters; and the expediency of a general repeal of all penal statutes that regard religious opinions. [By Alexander Geddes, LL.D.] 8vo. Pp. 37. [*D. N. B.* vol. 21, p. 100.] London, 1787

LETTER (a) to a Member of Parliament, shewing how probably the credit of the nation may be speedily raised. . . . By T. H. [Thomas Houghton]. 4to. Pp. 7. London, 1697

LETTER (a) to a Member of Parliament, stating the necessity of an amendment in the laws relating to the woollen manufactory, so far as respects the wages of the spinners. [By John Kirby.] 8vo. Ipswich, 1787

LETTER (a) to a Member of Parliament upon the 19th article of the treaty of union between the two kingdoms of Scotland and England. [By George Mackenzie, Earl of Cromarty.] 4to. [*D. N. B.* vol. 35, p. 147.] N.P. 1706

LETTER (a) to a Member of Parliament, wherein the power of the British Legislature and the case of the Colonies [in America] are briefly and impartially considered. [By William Knox.] 8vo. [*D. N. B.* vol. 31, p. 337.] London, 1764

LETTER (a) to a member of the Convention. [By William Sherlock.] 4to. Pp. 4. [Somers' *Tracts* (ed. Scott) x. 185.] N.P. [1689]

LETTER (a) to a member of the Convocation of the University of Oxford, containing the case of a late Fellow elect of University College in that University. [Signed: C. U. *i.e.* Charles Usher.] 4to. Pp. 31. London, 1699

LETTER (a) to a Member of the Hon. House of Commons of Ireland [proposing a scheme for regulating the Corporation of the city of Dublin. By James Grattan]. 8vo. [*Camb. Univ. Lib.*] Dublin, 1760

This was followed by "A second letter . . ."

LETTER (a) to a Member of the House of Commons, concerning the Bishops lately in the Tower, and now under suspension. [By Henry Maurice, D.D.] 4to. Pp. 10. [*Bodl.*] London, 1689

LETTER (a) to a Member of the House of Commons concerning the proceedings against [Thomas Watson] the Bishop of St David's. [By Gilbert Burnet, Bishop of Salisbury.] 4to. [Clarke and Foxcroft's *Life of Bp. Burnet*, Appendix.] [London, 1699]

LETTER (a) to a member of the Senate of the University of Cambridge. By the author of *Discourses to academic youth* [Edward Pearson, B.D.]. 8vo. Pp. 30. [*Camb. Univ. Lib.*] Cambridge, 1799

Signed: E. P.

LETTER (a) to a Methodist. By a presbyter of the diocese of Maryland [Rev. Norris M. Jones]. 8vo. [Cushing's *Init. and Pseud.* i. 239.] Baltimore, 1844

LETTER (a) to a minister from his friend concerning communicating, occasioned by the late Overture of the Synod of Glasgow and Air upon that subject. [By Rev. Thomas Randall.] 8vo. Pp. 90. [*New Coll. Lib.*] Glasgow, 1749

LETTER (a) to a minister, giving advice how to act under temptations. [By Samuel Mather.] 8vo. Pp. 24. [*Bodl.*] London, 1721

LETTER (a) to a minister in the Presbytry of Edinburgh, explaining the passage of a sermon misconstructed by some. [By James Clark, minister at Glasgow.] S. Sh. N.P. [1704]

Dated April 15. 1704.

LETTER (a) to a Minister of State, respecting taxes on knowledge. [By Francis Place.] 8vo. Pp. 16. [*W.*] London, 1831

LETTER (a) to a minister of the Church of Scotland; shewing the unreasonableness of extending Chapter VII. of the Form of process to probationers; that this is contrary to Scripture rules, and must have dismal effects. [By John Maclaurin, minister in Glasgow.] 8vo. Pp. 79. [Struthers' *History of the Relief Church*, p. 558.] Glasgow, 1747

LETTER (a) to a minister of the Gospel, concerning the Parish of Bathgate. [By the Rev. James Kid.] 12mo. Pp. 64. [*New Coll. Lib.*] N.P. 1720

LETTER (a) to a missionary priest. By Socrates Christianus [Edward Stephens], concerning the qualifications requisite for that service, and the usual performance thereof, and the authority by which he acts. . . . 4to. Pp. 15. [*Bodl.*] N.P., N.D.

Letter dated 23 Aug. 1700.

LETTER (a) to a modern defender of Christianity; to which is added, a tract on the ground and nature of Christian redemption. [By John Payne.] 12mo. Pp. vi. 93, xxiii. [Darling's *Cyclop. Bibl.*] London, 1771

LETTER to a Neapolitan from an Englishman, 1815. [By Henry Richard Vassal Fox, Lord Holland.] 8vo. Pp. vi. 40. London, 1818

LETTER (a) to a noble Duke, on the incontrovertible truth of Christianity; the second edition, corrected; to which is now added a postscript. [By Charles Leslie.] 8vo. Pp. 117. [*Brit. Crit.* xxxiv. 424.] London, 1808

LETTER (a) to a noble Lord, concerning the late expedition to Canada. [By Jeremiah Dummer, graduate of Harvard College.] 12mo. Pp. 26. [Sabin's *Dictionary.*] London, 1712

LETTER (a) to a noble Lord, from the author of *Objections to the project of creating a Vice-Chancellor of England* [Sir Samuel Romilly]. 8vo. [*D. N. B.* vol. 49, p. 191.] London, 1813

LETTER (a) to a noble Lord; or, a faithful representation of the Douglas cause: containing many curious and essential anecdotes, among which are the rise of the family of Douglas, and a true character of the late Duke of that name. [By Andrew Henderson.] 8vo. [Lowndes' *Bibl. Man.* p. 665.] London, 1768

LETTER (a) to a nobleman, containing considerations on the laws relative to dissenters, and on the intended application to Parliament for the repeal of the Corporation and Test Acts. By a layman [Sir George Colebrooke, Bart.]. 8vo. Pp. 192. [*Camb. Univ. Lib.*] London, 1790

LETTER (a) to a non-conformist minister of the Kirk, shewing the nullity of the Presbyterian mission or authority to preach the Gospel. [Re-edited by Robert Calder.] 8vo. Pp. 32. London, 1705

First printed in 1677.

LETTER (a) to a non-resident friend, upon subscription to the Thirty-nine Articles of matriculation. By a senior member of convocation [Benjamin Parsons Symons, D.D., Warden of Wadham]. 8vo. Pp. 8. [*Bodl.*] Oxford [1840?]

No title-page.

The author's name is in the handwriting of Dr Bliss.

LETTER to a non-resident member of the Cambridge Camden Society on the present position of that body. By C. A. S. [C. A. Swainson]. 12mo. Pp. 18. [Bowes' *Cat. of Camb. Books.*] Cambridge, private print, 1845

LETTER (a) to a patriot senator, including the heads of a Bill for a constitutional representation of the people. [By Sir William Jones.] 8vo. [Nichols' *Lit. Anec.* viii. 136.] London, 1783

LETTER (a) to a person lately join'd with the people called Quakers; in answer to a letter wrote by him. [By John Wesley.] 8vo. Pp. 16. [Smith's *Anti-Quak.* p. 447.] London, 1748

LETTER (a) to a person of honor, on the evil spirit of Protestants. [By William Wright, S.J.] 4to. [Sommervogel's *Dictionnaire.*] N.P. 1622

LETTER (a) to a person of honour, concerning the blackbox. [By Robert Ferguson.] 4to. Pp. 8. [Somers' *Tracts*, *ed.* Scott, viii. 187.] [London, 1680]

LETTER (a) to a person of honour, concerning the Kings disavovving the having been married to the D. of M. [Duke of Monmouth]'s mother. [By Robert Ferguson.] 4to. Pp. 23. N.P., N.D.

Letter dated London, June the 10th. 1610 [1680].

LETTER (a) to a person of quality, concerning fines received by the church at its restoration; wherein, by the instance of one of the richest cathedrals, a very fair guess may be made at the receipts and disbursements of all the rest. By a prebend of the church of Canterbury [Peter Du Moulin, D.D.]. 4to. Pp. 8. N.P. 1668

Signed: P. D. M.

LETTER to a person of quality who took offence at Dr Stillingfleet's Mischief of separation. [By Rev. John Howe.] 4to. [*D. N. B.* vol. 28, p. 86.] London, 1681

LETTER (a) to a person of scrupulous conscience about the time of keeping Christmas, according to the new stile; to which is added, a dialogue between a clergyman and his parishioners, familiarly explaining the reason and expediency of the new style. [By Rev. W. Parker.] 12mo. Pp. 23. [*Bodl.*] London, 1753

LETTER (a) to a philosopher [John Stuart Mill] in reply to some recent attempts to vindicate Berkeley's Theory of vision. [By Samuel Bailey.] 8vo. [*D. N. B.* vol. 2, p. 410.] London, 1843

LETTER (a) to a physician on the domestic management of invalids in a mild winter climate. By a clergyman [Rev. Peter Leopold Dyke Acland, M.A.]. 8vo. [Kirk's *Supp.*] Oxford, 1866

LETTER (a) to a political economist; occasioned by an article in the Westminster Review on the subject of value. By the author of the *Critical dissertation on value therein reviewed* [Samuel Bailey]. 8vo. London, 1826

Authorship declared in Bury edition (1881) of "Essays on opinions."

LETTER (a) to a private Christian, wherein it is plainly demonstrated that the believer's receiving the law as the law of Christ, is the only effectual method for attaining Gospel holiness and persisting therein, and for escaping the dangerous rocks of Antinomianism. [By James Hog, minister at Carnock.] 12mo. Pp. 16. [*New Coll. Lib.*] [Edinburgh, 1722]

LETTER to a Professor of Anthropology. [By George Tyrrell, S.J.] 8vo. N.P. 1904

LETTER (a) to a Protestant gentleman, upon the subject of Absolution and Indulgencies, and in vindication of the Catholic Church against the charges of ignorance, bigotry and intolerance. By a Catholic layman [Charles Fox Larkin, surgeon]. 8vo. Pp. 31. [Gillow's *Bibl. Dict.*]
Newcastle-upon-Tyne, 1828

LETTER (a) to a Quaker in Norfolk, proving that water baptism is the ordinance our Saviour (who came down from heaven to instruct us in the way thither) has appointed for one of the means of salvation; without which, according to the terms of the Gospel, we cannot enter into that kingdom. [By Philip Bedingfield, of Burnham-Thorpe, Norfolk.] 8vo. Pp. 40. [Smith's *Anti-Quak.* p. 69.]
Norwich, N.D.

LETTER to a retired officer, on the opinions and sentence of a general court martial, held at the Horse Guards, Nov. 27, 1795, and on many subsequent days, for the trial of Col. John Fenton Cawthorne, of the Westminster regiment of Middlesex militia. [By William Combe.] 4to. Pp. 39.
London, 1796

LETTER (a) to a reverend gentleman in Oxford, on the subject of drinking healths. [By Peter Browne, Bishop of Cork and Ross.] 8vo. [*D. N. B.* vol. 7, p. 54.] London, 1722

LETTER (a) to a Roman Catholick. [By John Wesley, M.A.] 12mo. Pp. 12. Dublin, 1750

The third edition has the author's name.

LETTER (a) to a Scots clergyman [Robert Wallace, D.D., Edinburgh] lately ordained, concerning his behaviour in the Judicatures of the Church. By a lover of truth, liberty and charity, and an enemy to violent measures on all hands [J. Dudgeon]. 8vo. Pp. 27. [*New Coll. Lib.*]
Edinburgh, 1735

LETTER (a) to a student at a foreign University, on the study of divinity. By T. P., S.C.T. [Thomas Phillips, S.J., Senior Canon of Tongres]. 8vo. Pp. 126. [*D. N. B.* vol. 45, p. 216.]
London, 1756

The third edition (1765) bears a different title: "The study of sacred literature fully stated and considered, in a discourse to a student in divinity."

LETTER (a) to a Tory friend, upon the present critical situation of our affairs; wherein every objection of the disaffected to the present government is fully answered; the fond distinction of a king *de facto*, absolutely refuted; and His Majesty King George demonstrated to be King of Great-Britain, &c. *de jure*, in the strongest sense of the words. [By Samuel Squire, D.D., archdeacon of Bath, afterwards Bishop of St David's.] 8vo. Pp. 75. [*Bodl.*; Green's *Bibl. Somers.* iii. 279.]
London, 1746

LETTER (a) to a Whig neighbor, on the approaching State election. By an old Conservative [John Gorham Palfrey, D.D.]. 8vo. [Cushing's *Init. and Pseud.* i. 211.] Boston, 1855

LETTER (a) to a young divine; containing directions for composing and delivering of sermons. By J. R. [J. Prince], Presbyter of the Church of England. 8vo. [Arber's *Term Cat.* ii. 618.] London, 1692

LETTER (a) to a young gentleman. By a tutor, and Fellow of a college in Oxford [Edward Bentham, D.D., Fellow of Oriel]. 8vo. Pp. 31.
N.P. 1748

LETTER (a) to a young gentleman in prison. By Eubulus [John Martin, Baptist minister]. 8vo. Pp. 31. [*Brit. Mus.*] London, 1791

LETTER (a) to a young gentleman, lately enter'd into holy orders. By a person of quality [Jonathan Swift, D.D.]. 8vo. Pp. 31. [*Camb. Hist. of Eng. Lit.*] London, 1721

Signed: A. B.

LETTER (a) to a young man who has just entered College, from an older one who has been through [William P. Atkinson]. 8vo. [Cushing's *Init. and Pseud.* ii. 163.] Boston, 1849

LETTER (a) to a young officer, written in the year 1776, by an officer in the British Army [Major Edward Drewe]. 4to. [Evans' *Amer. Bibl.* vol. 5, p. 372.]
New York, 1778

LETTER (a) to Adam Smith, LL.D. on the life, death, and philosophy of his friend David Hume. By one of the people called Christians [George Horne, Bishop of Norwich]. 12mo. [*D. N. B.* vol. 27, p. 357.] London, 1782

LETTER (a) to Alexander Bannerman, Esq., M.P., in apology for the opposition made by the inhabitants of Aberdeen and the North of Scotland to his University Bill. By Philologus [Robert Cruickshank]. 8vo. Pp. 28. [Anderson's *Aberd. Univ. Bibl.* p. 453.]
Aberdeen, 1835

LETTER (a) to Alexander Shaw, Esq., baker, Dean of Guild of the royal Burgh of Inverness, on the powers and duties of the Dean of Guild. By M. [Kennedy MacNab]. [Anderson's *Inverness Bibl.* p. 135.]
[Inverness] 1861

LETTER (a) to all the proprietors of Drury-Lane Theatre (excepting Peter Moore and others who are, or have been concerned in the management thereof). . . . [By Samuel James Arnold.] 8vo. [Lowe's *Theat. Lit.* p. 97.] London, 1818

LETTER (a) to an English Member of Parliament, from a gentleman in Scotland, concerning the slavish dependencies which a great part of that nation is still kept under, by superiorities, wards, reliefs, and other remains of the feudal law, and by clanships and tithes. [By Rev. John Willison of Dundee.] 8vo. Pp. 39. [*Memoir*, prefixed to his collected works.] Edinburgh, 1721

Wrongly ascribed to John Ker, of Kersland, and to William Logan, of Logan.

LETTER (a) to an Honourable Brigadier-General [Lord George Townshend], Commander-in-Chief of H.M. Forces in Canada. [By Charles Lee.] 8vo. London, 1760

Ascribed also to "Junius."

LETTER (a) to an inhabitant of the parish of St Andrew's, Holbourn, about new ceremonies in the church. [By William Fleetwood, D.D.] 8vo. Pp. 31. [*Camb. Univ. Lib.*] London, 1717

LETTER (a) to an officer of the army, on travelling on Sundays. [By Robert Bolton, LL.D., Dean of Carlisle.] 8vo. Pp. 50. [*Lond. Lib. Cat.*] London, 1747

LETTER to Anne, Duchess of York, a few months before her death. [By George Morley, Bishop of Winchester.] [*D. N. B.* vol. 39, p. 76.] N.P. 1681

LETTER (a) to Anonymus, in answer to his Three letters to Dr Sherlock about Church-communion. [By William Sherlock, D.D.] 4to. Pp. 58. London, 1683

Signed: W. S.

LETTER (a) to Archdeacon Wilberforce on supremacy. By a Yorkshire clergyman [Francis Orpen Morris, B.A., rector of Numburnholme, Hayton, Yorkshire]. 8vo. Pp. 32. London, 1854

LETTER (a) to Basil Montague, upon his "Examination of some Observations [made in the House of Commons] on a passage in Dr Paley's Moral . . . philosophy"; with some remarks upon Dr Paley's explanation of that passage. By Juvenis [R. G. Arrowsmith]. 8vo. [*Brit. Mus.*] London, 1810

LETTER (a) to Bishop Horsley on his opinion concerning Antichrist. By a country clergyman [Thomas Zouch, D.D., Prebendary of Durham]. 8vo. [*D. N. B.* vol. 63, p. 414.] London, 1801

LETTER (a) to Bourchier Cleeve, Esq., concerning his calculations of taxes; from the author of the *Calculations of taxes paid by a family of each rank, degree or class* [Joseph Massie]. 8vo. Pp. 49. [M'Culloch's *Lit. of Pol. Econ.* p. 331.] London, 1757

LETTER (a) to Caleb D'Anvers, Esq.; concerning the state of affairs in Europe as published in the Craftsman, January 4, 1728-9. By John Trott, yeoman [Henry St John, Lord Bolingbroke]. 8vo. Pp. 35. London, 1730

LETTER (a) to children and young persons. [By Josiah Townsend.] 12mo. [*Brit. Mus.*] London, 1806

LETTER to Cibber. [By Lord John Hervey.] 8vo. [Leslie's *Cat.* 1843, p. 407.] London, 1742

LETTER (a) to Courtney Melmoth, Esq. [Samuel Jackson Pratt], with some remarks on two books, called Liberal opinions, and The pupil of pleasure. By Euphrasia [Clara Reeve]. 8vo. [Haynes' *Pseud.*; Green's *Bibl. Somers.* i. 347.] London, 1777

LETTER (a) to Daniel K. Sandford, Esq., Professor of Greek in the university of Glasgow, in answer to the strictures of the Edinburgh Review on the open colleges of Oxford. By a member of a close college [Augustus William Hare]. 8vo. Pp. viii. 73. [*MS. note on the Dyce copy.*] Oxford, 1822

LETTER (a) to David Garrick, Esq.; occasioned by the intended representation of The minor at the Theatre Royal in Drury Lane. [By Abraham Portal.] 8vo. Pp. 48. [Nichol's *Lit. Anec.* ii. 725.] London, 1760

Wrongly attributed to the Rev. Martin Madan.

LETTER (a) to David Garrick, Esq., on his conduct as principal manager and actor at Drury-Lane. [By Rev. David Williams.] 8vo. Pp. 39. [*Bodl.*] London, 1772

LETTER (a) to Dean Swift, Esq., on his Essay upon the life, writings and character of Dr J. Swift. By the author of the *Observations on Lord Orrery's remarks, &c.* [Dr Patrick Delany]. 8vo. Pp. 51. London, 1755

Signed: The Observer.

LETTER (a) to Dion [Bp. Berkeley], occasion'd by his book call'd Alciphron, or the minute philosopher. By the author of the *Fable of the bees* [Bernard Mandeville]. 8vo. Pp. 70. London, 1732

LETTER (a) to Dr Adams, D.C.L., shewing Purgatory inseparably connected with prayers for the dead. . . . By Alethphilos [Rev. Joseph Rathbone, R. C. priest]. 8vo. Pp. 24. [Gillow's *Bibl. Dict.*] Isle of Wight, 1840

LETTER to Dr [afterwards Sir William] Blackstone. By [Sir William Meredith] the author of *The question stated.* 8vo. Pp. 60. [*Camb. Univ. Lib.*] London, 1770

LETTER (a) to Dr Bvrnet. Occasioned by his late Letter to Mr Lowth. [By Simon Lowth.] 4to. [*D. N. B.* vol. 34, p. 216.] London, 1685

No title-page.

LETTER (a) to Dr Calamy; shewing, that Mr Archdeacon Echard has done the part of a faithful historian, in branding Mr Edmund Calamy (the Doctor's grandfather) as a promoter of rebellion, and an incendiary to posterity. [By Thomas Lewis?] 8vo. Pp. 28. London [1718?]

The letter is signed: Anonymus Londinensis.

Ascribed also to Matthias Earbery. [*Nat. Lib. of Scot.*]

LETTER (a) to Dr E. S. [Edward Stillingfleet] concerning his late letter to Mr G[odden], and the account he gives in it of a conference between Mr G. and himself. From one who was present at the conference [Edward Meredith]. 4to. [Jones' Peck, p. 128.] London, 1687

Ascribed also to John Sergeant. [*Queen's Coll. Cat.* p. 218.]

LETTER (a) to Dr [James] Fordyce, in answer to his sermon on the delusive and persecuting spirit of Popery. [By Joseph Berington, Catholic priest.] 8vo. [*Brit. Mus.*] London, 1779

LETTER (a) to Dr Formey, F.R.S., Professor of philosophy, and perpetual secretary of the Royal Academy of sciences and belles lettres of Berlin, &c. By J. B. [James Beezley]. 8vo. [Smith's *Cat. of Friends' books*, i. 67, 232.] London, 1776

Signed: Philalethes, London, 15th of 9th mo. 1766.

LETTER (a) to Dr [Samuel] Hallifax upon the subject of his Three discourses preached before the University of Cambridge, occasioned by an attempt to abolish subscription to the Thirty-nine Articles. [By Samuel Blackhall, B.D., rector of Loughborough.] 4to. Pp. iv. 31. [*European Mag.* xxi. 408.] London, 1772

LETTER (a) to Dr Henry Halford Jones [Josiah Gilbert Holland] . . . concerning his habit of giving advice to everybody, and his qualifications for the task. By Carl Benson [Charles Astor Bristed]. 8vo. [Kirk's *Supp.*] New York, 1864

LETTER (a) to Dr Houldsworth, occasioned by his sermon . . . concerning the resurrection of the same body. . . . By the author of a *Defence of Mr Locke's Essay of human understanding* [Mrs Catherine Cockburn]. 8vo. [*D. N. B.* vol. 11, p. 183.] London, 1726

LETTER (a) to Dr Jeune, in vindication of the handbill distributed at the doors of the Sheldonian Theatre. [By Rev. Charles P. Golightly, M.A.] 8vo. [*D. N. B.* vol. 22, p. 101.] Oxford, 1861

LETTER (a) to Dr [Samuel] Mather, occasioned by his disingenuous reflexions upon a certain pamphlet [by Charles Chauncy] entitled, Salvation for all men. . . . [By John Clarke, D.D.] 4to. Pp. 9. [Evans' *Amer. Bibl.* vol. 6, p. 161.] Boston, 1782

LETTER (a) to Dr Parr, occasioned by his republication of Tracts by Warburton and a Warburtonian [Bishop Richard Hurd. By Robert Lucas, D.D.]. 8vo. [Simms' *Bibl. Staff.* p. 240.] London, 1790

LETTER (a) to Doctor [Joseph] Priestley; occasioned by his late address to the subscribers to the Birmingham library. By somebody, M. S. [John Clutton, M.A.] 8vo. Pp. 44. [*Bodl.*] Birmingham, 1787

LETTER (a) to Dr Priestley respecting his late publication of Mr Wesley's letters. By Philalethes [John Wesley?]. 8vo. [Lowndes' *Bibl. Man.*] London, 1791

LETTER (a) to Doctor [Thomas] Randolph . . . occasioned by a charge delivered by him . . . in vindication of the reasonableness of requiring subscription to Articles of Religion. By a member of the Church of England [Nicholas Carter, D.D.]. 8vo. [*Brit. Mus.*] London, 1772

See the note to "The Confessional. . . ."

LETTER (a) to Dr Samuel Johnson; occasioned by his late political publications; with an appendix, containing some observations on a pamphlet lately published by Dr Shebbeare. [By Joseph Towers, LL.D.]. 8vo. Pp. 78. [*Bodl.*] London, 1775

LETTER (a) to Dr Sherlock, in vindication of that part of Josephus's History, which gives an account of Iaddus the high-priest's submitting to Alexander the Great while Darius was living: against the answer to the piece intituled, Obedience and submission to the present government. [By William Lloyd, D.D.] 4to. Pp. 33. London, 1691

LETTER (a) to Dr [Edward] Synge, in answer to his letter, entitled, "Dr Synge's defence of himself against the unjust aspersions thrown upon him in a late pamphlet, entitled, A reply to a Vindication of a Letter published in a pamphlet [by Ralph Lambert, Dean of Down] called, "Partiality detected," etc. [By P. Percivale.] 4to. [Watt's *Bibl. Brit.*] London, 1711

LETTER (a) to Dr Troy, titular Archbishop of Dublin, on the coronation of Bonaparte by Pope Pius the Seventh. [By Thos. Lewis O'Beirne, D.D., Bishop of Meath.] 8vo. [*D. N. B.* vol. 41, p. 304.] Dublin, 1805

Signed: Melanchthon.

LETTER (a) to Dr W[illiam] Payne regarding non-resistance and non-juring. [By Samuel Grascome.] 4to. [London, 1689]

This evoked "An answer to a printed letter to Dr W. P. concerning non-resistance. . . ." [Signed: W. P. 1690.]

LETTER (a) to Dr Waterland, containing some remarks on his Vindication of Scripture; in answer to a book [by Matthew Tindal], intituled, Christianity as old as the creation: together with the sketch or plan of another answer to the said book. [By Conyers Middleton, D.D.] 8vo. Pp. 67. [Darling's *Cyclop. Bibl.*] London, 1731

LETTER (a) to Dr [Daniel] Waterland, occasioned by his Remarks [published anonymously] on Dr [Samuel] Clarke's Exposition of the Church Catechism. [By Rev. Thomas Emlyn.] 8vo. [*D. N. B.* vol. 17, p. 359.] London, 1730

LETTER (a) to Dr [Richard] Watson King's Professor of Divinity in the University of Cambridge. [By W. Vincent.] 8vo. [Bartholomew's *Camb. Books*, p. 263.] London, 1780

LETTER (a) to Dr [Richard] Whately, the Lord Archbishop of Dublin, on the effect which his work, "Elements of logic" has had, in retarding the progress of English metaphysical philosophy. By a follower of Locke [Benjamin Humphrey Smart]. 8vo. Pp. 31. London, 1851

LETTER (a) to Earl Fitzwilliam, demonstrating the real tendency of the proceedings of the late York meeting for taking into consideration the transactions at Manchester on Aug. 16 last. . . . By a member of no party [Arthur Henry Kenney, D.D.]. 8vo. London, 1819

LETTER (a) to Earl Grey, on his renunciation of the English monarchy. By one of His Majesty's servants [The Hon. Arthur Philip Perceval]. 8vo. [*Nat. Lib. of Scot.*] London, 1832

LETTER (a) to Earl Stanhope on the subject of the Test; as objected to in a pamphlet recommended by his Lordship, entitled "The right of Protestant Dissenters to a complete toleration asserted." [By Charles Hawtrey, M.A.] 8vo. [Nichols' *Lit. Anec.* ix. 569.] London, 1790

Ascribed also to Rev. Charles Hawkins, vicar of Bampton, Oxfordshire.

LETTER (a) to Edmund Burke, Esq., controverting the principles of American government, laid down in his lately published speech on American taxation, delivered in the House of Commons on the 19th of April 1774. [By John Cartwright, major, Nottinghamshire militia.] 8vo. [*W.*] London, 1775

Signed: Constitutio.

LETTER (a) to Edmund Burke, Esq., occasioned by his speech in Parliament, February 11, 1780. [By Allan Ramsay, junr.] 8vo. Pp. 38. [*Nat. Lib. of Scot.*] London, 1780

Signed: Steady.

LETTER (a) to Edmund Burke, Esq., on the latter part of the report of the Select Committee of the House of Commons, on the state of justice in Bengal; with some curious particulars, and original anecdotes, concerning the forgery committed by Maharajah Nundcomar Bahadar, on the proof of which he lost his life. [By Captain Joseph Price.] 8vo. Pp. 227. [*Brit. Mus.*] London, 1782; reprinted, 1783

LETTER (a) to Edward Copleston, D.D., Provost of Oriel College, Oxford, occasioned by his Inquiry into the doctrines of necessity and predestination. By Philalethes Cantabrigiensis [Thomas Turton, D.D., Bishop of Ely]. 8vo. [*D. N. B.* vol. 57, p. 377.] London, 1822

Bishop Copleston replied in "Remarks upon the objections. . . ."

LETTER (a) to Eusebia; occasioned by Mr Toland's letters to Serena. [By William Wotton, B.D.] 8vo. Pp. 75. [*Brit. Mus.*] London, 1704

LETTER (a) to Father Lewis Sabran Jesuite, in answer to his Letter to a peer of the Church of England; wherein the postscript to the answer to Nubes testium is vindicated, and F. Sabran's mistakes further discovered. [By Edward Gee, M.A.] 4to. Pp. 8. [*Bodl.*] London, 1688

LETTER (a) to Francis Jeffrey, editor of the Edinburgh Review. By an Anti-Reformist [John Hope, Lord Justice Clerk]. 8vo. Edinburgh, 1811

Attestation by Henry, Lord Cockburn.

LETTER (a) to [his brother] Francis Plowden, Esq., Conveyancer of the Middle Temple, on his work intitled "Jura Anglorum." By a Roman Catholic clergyman [Robert Plowden, S.J.]. 8vo. Pp. 230. [Sommervogel's *Dictionnaire;* Oliver's *Collections.*] London, 1794

LETTER (a) to General Monck, in answer to his of the 23th of January, directed to Mr Rolle, to be communicated to the gentlemen of the county of Devon. By one of the excluded Members of Parliament [Richard Morris]. 4to. Pp. 8. [*Bodl.*] London, 1659

Signed: R. M.

The author's name is in the handwriting of Wood.

Ascribed also to Sir William Morice of Werrington. [Davidson's *Bibl. Devon.*, p. 89.]

LETTER (a) to George Hardinge, Esq., on the subject of a passage in Mr Steven's preface to his impression of Shakespeare. [By Rev. John Collins, of Ledbury, Herefordshire.] 4to. Pp. iii. 48. [Boase and Courtney's *Bibl. Corn.* p. 82.] London, 1777

LETTER (a) to George Keith, concerning the salvability of the heathen; together with a testimony to the same doctrine, as long held, and not newly taken up, out of several former books of him that writ it. By his respectful neighbour, J. H. [John Humphrey, vicar of Frome]. 4to. Pp. 26. [Smith's *Anti-Quak.* p. 241.] London, 1700

LETTER (a) to George Washington. By Jasper Dwight [William Duane]. 8vo. [Cushing's *Init. and Pseud.* i. 85.] Philadelphia, 1796

LETTER (a) to Governor Johnstone on [East] Indian affairs. [By Nathaniel Brassey Halhed.] 8vo. Pp. 50. [*D. N. B.* vol. 24, p. 42.] London, 1783

Signed: Detector.

LETTER (a) to Granville Sharp, Esq., respecting his remarks on the two last petitions in the Lords Prayer. From a country clergyman [Charles Dunster]. 12mo. [*Gent. Mag.* lxxxvi. 1, 472.] London, 1807

LETTER (a) to Her Grace the Duchess of Devonshire. [By William Combe.] A new edition. 4to. Pp. 16. [*Bodl.*] London, 1727

LETTER to Her Most Gracious Majesty the Queen, upon the Papal question; with an address to the electors of the United Kingdom. By one of the people [William Glover, M.D.]. 8vo. Pp. 50. [*Nat. Lib. of Scot.*] Edinburgh, 1851

LETTER (a) to Henry Brougham, Esq., on his Durham speech, and three Articles in the Edinburgh Review. [By Rev. Thomas Rennell, D.D.] 8vo. London, 1823

LETTER (a) to His Excellency the Marquis of Wellesley . . . on the state of Ireland. By a Representative Peer [Charles John Gardiner, Earl of Blessington]. 8vo. [*Camb. Univ. Lib.*] London, 1822

LETTER (a) to His Grace the Archbishop of Canterbury [William Howley] occasioned by a late meeting in support of the Society for the Propagation of the Gospel in Foreign Parts. [By James Robert Hope-Scott, B.C.L.] 8vo. [*D. N. B.* vol. 27, p. 330.] London, 1838

LETTER (a) to His Grace the Archbishop of Canterbury [William Howley] on the right of the Convocation to tax the clergy for the service of the Church. [By Francis Charles Massingberd.] 8vo. [*Brit. Mus.*] London, 1835

LETTER (a) to His Grace the Duke of Buccleugh, on national defence; with some remarks on Dr [Adam] Smith's chapter on that subject in his book entitled "An enquiry into the nature and causes of the wealth of nations." [By Alex. Carlyle, D.D., of Inveresk.] 8vo. Pp. 72, 10. [*Autobiography of Alex. Carlyle.*] London, 1778

LETTER (a) to His Grace [William Cavendish, the seventh] Duke of Devonshire; Chancellor of the University of Cambridge [about an offer of a collection of ancient Greek works of art]. [By John Howard Marsden, B.D.] 8vo. Pp. 15. [*Brit. Mus.*] Private print [London, 1863]

Signed: A member of the Senate.

LETTER (a) to His Grace the Duke of Grafton, First Commissioner of His Majesty's Treasury. [By John Wilkes.] 8vo. Pp. 35. [*W.*] London, 1767

LETTER to His Grace the Duke of Wellington, K.T. upon the state of the English navy, in comparison with that of other navies. By a Flag officer [Rear-Admiral E. Hawker]. 8vo. Pp. 42. London, 1840

LETTER to his Grace the Duke of Wellington, on the state of the times. [By Alexander Marjoribanks.] Second edition. 8vo. Pp. 15. [*W.*] Edinburgh, 1830

Signed by the author in MS.

LETTER (a) to his most excellent Majesty King William III., shewing 1. The original foundation of the English monarchy: 2. The means by which it was removed from that foundation: 3. The expedients by which it has been supported since that removal: 4. Its present constitution, as to all its integral parts: 5. The best means by which its grandeur may be for ever maintained. [By William Stephens, B.D.] The third edition. 4to. [*Cat. Lond. Inst.* ii. 559.] London, 1699

LETTER (a) to his parishioners, on the disturbances which have lately occurred. By a country pastor [Richard Whately, later Archbishop of Dublin]. 12mo. London, 1820

LETTER (a) to His Royal Highness the Prince Regent on the ultimate tendency of the Roman Catholic claims. By the author of the *Vindication of the reign of George III.* [William Hunter, barrister]. Second edition. 8vo. Pp. 52. [*Brit. Mus.*] London, 1812

LETTER (a) to His Serene Highness Prince Edward of Saxe-Weimar, from [the Duke of Manchester] a Spectator of part of the [Franco-German] campaign of 1870. 4to. Pp. 59. [Dobell's *Private prints*, p. 117.] Private print, 1871

LETTER (a) to Hull Barton . . . By his friend Notus Nemini [George W. Ogden]. 8vo. [Cushing's *Init. and Pseud.* i. 512.] New Bedford [U.S.A.] 1823

LETTER (a) to Isaac Bickerstaff, Esq., occasion'd by the Letter to the Examiner. [By Sir William Cowper, first Earl Cowper.] 8vo. Pp. 16. [*Cat. Lond. Inst.* ii. 577.] London, 1710

The Letter to the Examiner was written by Bolingbroke.

LETTER (a) to Isaac Tomkins, Gent. author of the Thoughts upon the aristocracy, from Mr Peter Jenkins [Henry Brougham, Lord Brougham and Vaux]. Seventh edition, with a postscript. 8vo. Pp. 16. [*Quarterly Review*, vol. liii. p. 546.] London, 1835

LETTER (a) to J. O. [giving an account of Madame J. M. Guyon]. By J. M. [Josiah Martin]. 4to. Pp. 12. [*Brit. Mus.*] N.P. [1727]

LETTER (a) to James Bunter, Esq., on religious tracts, and the ignorance of the English and Irish Roman Catholics. By R. T. [Rev. Richard Towers, Romish priest]. 8vo. [Green's *Bibl. Somers.*] Taunton, 1824

LETTER to James Moncrieff, Esq. advocate, chairman of the Pantheon meeting. By a friend of the people [Rev. George Tod]. 8vo. Pp. 21. Edinburgh, 1820

LETTER (a) to John [Kaye], Bishop of Bristol, respecting an additional examination of students in the University of Cambridge. By Philograntus [James Henry Monk]. 8vo. [Bartholomew's *Camb. Books*, p. 170.] London, 1822

For a reply, see "A letter to Philograntus. . . ."

LETTER (a) to John Bull Esq. from his second cousin Thomas Bull, author of the first and second letters to his brother John. [By William Jones, of Nayland.] 8vo. Pp. 49. [*Brit. Mus.*] London, 1793

LETTER (a) to John Burridge Cholwich, Esq., one of His Majesty's justices of the peace for the county of Devon, upon the subject of the resolutions submitted by him to the magistrates of the said County, assembled at the Michaelmas quarters sessions, 1812. [By Joseph Davie Bassett.] 8vo. [Davidson's *Bibl. Devon.* p. 7.] Exeter, 1813

LETTER (a) to John Buxton, of Shadwell, on the contests relative to the ensuing election for the County of Norfolk. [By Rev. —— Potter.] 8vo. [*Brit. Mus.*] N.P. 1768

LETTER to John Murray, Esq., "touching" Lord Nugent; in reply to a letter from his Lordship, touching an article in the Quarterly Review. By the author of that article [Robert Southey]. 8vo. Pp. 96. [*Dyce Cat.* i. 257.] London, 1833

Ascribed also to Isaac D'Israeli.

LETTER (a) to John Philip Kemble, Esq., involving strictures on a recent edition of Ford's Dramatic Works. [Written chiefly by the Rev. J. Mitford.] 8vo. [*W.*; Lowndes' *Bibl. Man.*] London, 1811

LETTER (a) to [Major] John Scott-Waring, in refutation of his "Observations on the East India Company"; with strictures on his conduct towards the missionaries. [By Rev. John Owen, rector of Paglesham.] 8vo. Pp. 84. London, 1808

LETTER (a) to John Trot-Plaid, Esq.; author of the Jacobite Journal, concerning Mr Carte's General history of England. By Duncan MacCarte, a highlander [Samuel Squire, D.D.]. 8vo. Pp. 36. [*Bodl.*] London, 1748

LETTER (a) to John Wilkinson, on his resignation of membership in the Society of Friends. By the author of *The truth vindicated* [Henry Martin]. 12mo. [Smith's *Cat. of Friends' books*, i. 222.] London, 1836

LETTER (a) to Jonas Hanway, Esq., in which some reasons are assigned, why houses for the reception of penitent women who have been disorderly in their lives ought not to be called Magdalen-houses. [By Nathaniel Lardner, D.D.] 8vo. [Wilson's *Hist. of Diss. Ch.* i. 104.] London, 1758

LETTER (a) to Joseph Gurney Bevan; containing observations on the ministry and discipline of the people called Quakers. [By George Brown, of Shields.] 8vo. [Smith's *Cat. of Friends' books*, i. 79.] London, 1804

LETTER to Joshua Spencer, Esq. occasioned by his Thoughts on an union. By a barrister [William Johnson]. 8vo. [Watt's *Bibl. Brit.*] London, 1798

LETTER (a) to Junius [on the election of John Wilkes as M.P. for Middlesex]. By [Nathaniel Forster] the author of the *Answer to the "Question stated . . ."* [by Sir William Meredith]. 4to. Pp. 15. [*D. N. B.* vol. 20, p. 20.] London, 1769

See the "Answer to The question stated . . ." and "The question stated . . ." which began the controversy; also "A letter to Dr Blackstone . . ."

LETTER to Lord Brougham, on the elective franchise. By B. M. [Barclay de Mounteney, gentleman of the Privy Chamber to William IV.]. 8vo. Pp. 15. London, 1839

LETTER (a) to Lord Brougham on the subject of American slavery. By an American [Robert Baird, D.D.]. 8vo. [Cushing's *Init. and Pseud.* ii. 6.] London, 1836

LETTER (a) to Lord Chatham, concerning the present war of Great Britain against America; reviewing, candidly and impartially, its unhappy cause and consequence; and wherein the doctrine of Sir William Blackstone, as explained in his Commentaries on the laws of England, is opposed to ministerial tyranny, and held up in favour of America. . . . By a gentleman of the Inner Temple [Matthew Dawes]. 8vo. N.P. [1776]

Signed: M. D.

LETTER (a) to Lord Dufferin and Clandeboye on the subject of the Irish branch of the United Church. By a clergyman [Rev. Skeffington Armstrong]. 8vo. [Kirk's *Supp.*] London, 1868

LETTER (a) to Lord Dunfermline, on the Scottish freehold movement. By a political freethinker [Rev. William B. Nivison, minister at Kirtle]. 8vo. [Scott's *Fasti.*] Edinburgh, 1857

LETTER (a) to Lord John Russell, in favour of urging the revival of Convocation at the present crisis in the Church of England. By Lucius [James Blatch Piggot Dennis]. 8vo. Pp. 15. [*Camb. Univ. Lib.*] London, 1850

LETTER (a) to Lord John Russell, on the operation of the Established Church Bill, with reference to the interests of the Principality of Wales. By the author of *An essay on the causes which have produced Dissent from the Established Church in Wales* [Arthur James Johnes]. 8vo. Pp. 28. [*Brit. Mus.*] London, 1836

LETTER (a) to Lord John Russell on the present state of affairs in Gibraltar. By a merchant [C. Blake]. 8vo. [*Gladstone Lib. Cat.*] London, 1855

LETTER to Lord John Russell on the Reform Bill. [By Robert Benton Seeley.] 8vo. [Darling's *Cyclop. Bibl.*] London, 1831

LETTER (a) to Lord John Russell, relative to some allusions in his Lordship's speech concerning the appropriation of the revenues of the Irish Church. By Lucius [James Blatch Piggot Dennis]. 8vo. Pp. 15. [*Gent. Mag.* 1861, p. 462.] London, 1848

LETTER to Lord Mahon on the ministerial changes of 1801 and 1804. [By the Hon. Colonel Grey.] 8vo. Pp. 24. [Martin's *Cat.*] London, 1852

LETTER (a) to Lord Viscount Beauchamp, upon the subject of his "Letter to the first Belfast Company of Volunteers in the province of Ulster." [By Charles Coote, first Earl of Bellamont.] 8vo. [*Cat. Lond. Inst.* ii. 148.] London, 1783

LETTER (a) to **** ****, M.D. heretofore of **** **** College in the University of O****d. [By George Wilmot.] 8vo. Pp. 16. [*Bodl.*] London, 1752

Signed: Olim Oxoniensis.

LETTER (a) to Major Alexander Hamilton. . . . By a citizen of these [United] States [Uzab Ogden]. 8vo. [Cushing's *Init. and Pseud.* ii. 31.] New York, 1800

LETTER to members of the Church, and inhabitants of the parish of Teviothead. By their late pastor [Rev. James Duncan]. 8vo. [Sinton's *Bibl. of Hawick.*] Hawick, 1853

LETTER (a) to Messrs Coke, Curwan, & Co., with a postscript and notes on their injustice in expecting the reduction of national interest to keep up war rents. . . . [By Thomas Lowndes.] 8vo. Dover, 1823

LETTER (a) to Monsieur Van B— De M— at Amsterdam; written Anno 1676. [By Denzil, first Baron Hollis.] 4to. [*Cat. Lond. Inst.* ii. 551.] [1676]

LETTER (a) to Mr Caleb D'Anvers, Esq., on his Proper reply to a late scurrilous libel [by Sir William Yonge] entitled "Sedition and defamation display'd." [By John, Lord Hervey.] 8vo. Pp. 52. [*D. N. B.* vol. 26, p. 296.] London, 1731

LETTER (a) to Mr Fleetwood; occasioned by his late Essay on miracles. [By Benjamin Hoadly, D.D.] 4to. Pp. 29. [*Bodl.*] London, 1702

LETTER (a) to Mr Francis Melvil, one of the Presbyterian teachers in Aberdeen, in vindication of the English Liturgy, against his unjust charges; to which are added, some considerations concerning set forms of prayers, episcopacy, schism, etc. By a citizen of Aberdeen [William Gordon]. 8vo. Pp. vi. 120. [*Nat. Lib. of Scot.*] London, 1718

LETTER (a) to Mr G. [Thomas Godden] giving a true account of a late conference at the D. of P. [Dean of St Paul's]. [Signed: E. S. *i.e.* Edward Stillingfleet.] 4to. Pp. 8. [*Bodl.*] London, 1687

LETTER (a) to Mr Harwood, wherein some of his evasive glosses, false translations, and blundering criticisms, in support of the Arian heresy, contained in his Liberal translation of the New Testament, are pointed out and confuted. [By William Julius Mickle.] 8vo. Pp. 56. [*D. N. B.* vol. 37, p. 336.] London, 1768

LETTER (a) to Mr How, by way of reply to his Considerations of the preface to an Enquiry into the occasional conformity of Dissenters. By the author of the said preface and enquiry [Daniel Defoe]. 4to. Pp. 34. [Wilson's *Life of Defoe.*] London, 1701

Signed: D. F.

LETTER (a) to Mr John Dick [D.D.]. . . . Containing some observations on his sermon [against William MacGill, D.D.] which he calls The conduct and doom of false teachers. [By James Purves.] 12mo. Pp. 30. [*New Coll. Lib.*] Berwick, 1788

LETTER to Mr John Goodwin, shewing that he hath condemned himself of iniquity; together with problemes concerning religion. By P. D. [Sir Francis Nethersole]. 4to. [Watt's *Bibl. Brit.*] London, 1642

LETTER (a) to Mr Joseph Houlcroft, Churchwarden of Pennington. [By Richard Guest.] 8vo. Pp. 16. Manchester, 1821

LETTER (a) to Mr [William] Law, occasion'd by reading his treatise on Christian perfection; with a copy of verses, address'd to the same author. [By William Duncombe.] 8vo. London, 1728

LETTER (a) to Mr Mason; on the marks of imitation [in poetry. By Richard Hurd, D.D.]. 8vo. Pp. 76. [*Brit. Mus.*] Cambridge, 1757

LETTER (a) to Mr Miles Prance, in relation to the murther of Sir Edmondbury Godfrey. [By John Farwell.] Fol. S. sh. [*Bodl.*] London [1682]

Letter signed: Truman.

LETTER (a) to Mr Robert Burscough, in answer to his Discourse of schism. . . . [By Samuel Stoddon.] 8vo. Pp. 115. [Dredge's *Devon. Bibl.* p. 86.] London, 1700

LETTER (a) to Mr Sanxy, surgeon in Essex-Street, occasioned by his very singular conduct in the prosecution of Miss Butterfield. [By Rev. Joseph Robertson.] 8vo. [Nichol's *Lit. Anec.* iii. 501.] London, 1775

LETTER (a) to Mr Secretary Trenchard, discovering a conspiracy against the laws and ancient constitution of England; with reflections on the present pretended plot. [By Robert Ferguson.] 4to. Pp. 44. [*D. N. B.* vol. 18, p. 353.]

No title-page.

Signed: A. B. October the 9th, 1694.

LETTER (a) to Mr [Richard B. B.] Sheridan on his conduct in Parliament. [By Rev. Charles Edward Stewart, Rector of Reed, in Suffolk.] 8vo. [*Lond. Lib. Cat.*] Bury St Edmunds, 1794

This was followed by "A second letter . . ." from the same writer.

LETTER (a) to Mr Speaker Lenthall, shewing that it were better to comply with His Maiesties offers and desires of peace, then to pursue the destruction of this land, in the continuance of this unnatural warre. [By Sir Philip Warwick.] 4to. Pp. 14. [*Bodl.*] 1646

LETTER (a) to Mr Thomas Blackwell, Professor of Divinity . . . with other papers concerning the observation of Christmas and the other festivals of the Church. By W. G. [William Gordon], citizen of Aberdeen. 8vo. Pp. 35. [Robertson's *Aberd. Bibl.*] Edinburgh, 1722

LETTER (a) to Mr T[homas] Chubb, occasioned by his late book intitled, "The true Gospel of Jesus Christ asserted." By R. P. [Richard Parker]. 8vo. Pp. 88. [*Brit. Mus.*] London, 1739

LETTER (a) to Mr Timothy Goodwin [publisher], to be communicated to his friend, L. M. [L. Molesworth, *pseud.* of Daniel Defoe], author of the "Narrative of Count Patkul." By Aylmer Salt. 8vo. [Lee's *Life of Defoe.*] London, 1717

See also "A short narrative of the life and death of John Rhimholdt, Count Patkul . . ."

LETTER (a) to Mr Whitbread, on the duty of rescinding the resolutions which preceded the impeachment of Lord Viscount Melville. [By James Sedgwick, barrister-at-law.] 8vo. Pp. 38. [*Bodl.*] London, 1806

LETTER (a) to my class: addressed to young women attending a Sunday School. By a clergyman's wife [Mrs S. E. Mapleton]. 12mo. Leeds, 1859

Signed: S. E. M.

LETTER (a) to my Lord Chief Justice Holt on the noise of a plot. [By Robert Ferguson (the "Plotter").] 4to. [*D. N. B.* vol. 18, p. 353.] N.P. 1694

LETTER (a) to my Lords the Bishops, on occasion of the present Bill for the preventing of adultery. [By Maurice Morgan.] 8vo. [*Brit. Mus.*] London, 1779

LETTER (a) to my mediæval friends, and to my Protestant brethren of the Church of England. By John Henry Trueman [Rev. George Thomas Horn, M.A.]. 8vo. Oxford [1877]

LETTER (a) to my neighbours. By a country curate [Rev. George Wheeler, of Shipton, Moyne, Gloucestershire]. 8vo. [Green's *Bibl. Somers.* i. 132.] Bath, 1830

LETTER (a) to Napoleon III. on slavery in the Southern States. By a creole of Louisiana [Eugène Musson]; translated from the French. 8vo. [Cushing's *Init. and Pseud.* i. 70.] London, 1862

LETTER (a) to Norman Sievwright, M.A.; in vindication of the Episcopal clergy of Scotland from his charge of innovations in politics and religion. [By Rev. John Skinner, Langside.] 8vo. Pp. 140. [*Brit. Mus.*] Aberdeen [1767]

LETTER (a) to Peter Burrowes, Esq., on the present state of the Catholic interests. [By W. Jephson Baker.] 8vo. [*Camb. Univ. Lib.*] Dublin, 1816

LETTER to Phileleutheros Orielensis [Rev. John Davison] on his notable discoveries in Kett's Elements, etc. [By Frederick Nolan.] 8vo. [Lowndes' *Bibl. Man.* p. 1268.] Oxford, 1804

LETTER (a) to Philip Thicknesse, Esq., in reply to a charge brought by him against a noble Earl of Great Britain. [By Rev. John Hawkins.] 8vo. Pp. 39. [Green's *Bibl. Somers.* ii. 514.] Worcester, 1786

LETTER (a) to Philograntus [James Henry Monk, D.D., in reply to his Letter regarding the students at the University of Cambridge]. By Eubulus [Samuel Butler, D.D., of Shrewsbury]. 8vo. [*Camb. Hist. of Eng. Lit.* vol. 14, p. 594.] London, 1822

LETTER (a) to Professor Edwards A. Park. . . . By a Catholic layman [—— Cole]. 8vo. [Cushing's *Init. and Pseud.* ii. 28.] Boston, 1844

LETTER (a) to Prof. F. Max Müller on the Sacred Books of China, Part I. [translated by James Legge]. By Inquirer [A. P. Happer]. 8vo. Pp. 26. [*Brit. Mus.*] Shanghai, 1880

LETTER (a) to Protestant Dissenters concerning their conduct in the ensuing elections; formerly published in the year 1722. [By John Shute Barrington, first Viscount Barrington.] 8vo. Pp. 11. London, 1733

LETTER (a) to R— H— [Richard Hughes, M.D.] on his joining the Irvingites. . . . By E. P. [Ebenezer Palmer], Sen. 12mo. [*Brit. Mus.*] London, private print, 1839

LETTER (a) to R. M. Beverley from an Undergraduate of the University of Cambridge. [By W. Forsyth.] 8vo. Pp. 28. Cambridge, 1833

LETTER (a) to R. M. Beverley, in defence of his strictures on the University of Cambridge. By an undergraduate [Hugh Ford Bacon]. 8vo. Pp. 29. [Bowes' *Camb. Books.*] Cambridge, 1834

LETTER (a) to Ralph Wardlaw, D.D.; being a reply in brief to the most important positions in his treatise on The nature and extent of the Atonement of Christ. By a Preacher of the Gospel [Peter Hately Waddell, D.D.]. 8vo. Glasgow, 1844

LETTER (a) to Rev. Alexander Ewing, Congregational Chapel, Thurso. By a member of the establishment [James Traill Calder]. 8vo. Pp. 38. [Mowat's *Caithness Bibl.* p. 33.] Thurso, 1827

LETTER to Rev. Nehemiah Adams, occasioned by his sermon entitled, "Injuries done to Christ." By an Unitarian [Henry Ware, D.D.]. 8vo. [Cushing's *Init. and Pseud.* i. 147.] Boston, 1841

LETTER (a) to Richard Hill, Esq. [later, Sir Richard Hill]. Containing some remarks on that gentleman's Five letters to the Rev. J. Fletcher. By J. M. [John Murlin]. 12mo. Pp. 42. [Osborn's *Method. Lit.* p. 145.] Bristol, 1775

LETTER (a) to Robert Harley, Esqr., in favour of the Scots Act for an African Company. [By Robert Ferguson (the "Plotter").] 8vo. [*D.N.B.* vol. 18, p. 353.] London [1698?]

LETTER (a) to Robert Heron, Esq. [John Pinkerton]; containing a few brief remarks on his Letters of literature. By one of the barbarous blockheads of the lowest mob, who is a true friend to religion and a sincere lover of mankind [William Pettman]. 8vo. Pp. vi. 34. [*Bodl.*] London, 1786

LETTER (a) to Robert Moss and Thomas Gooch, and the rest of the ministers who, in a late petition to the House of Lords, stiled themselves the Clergy in and about London. To which is added the copy of a paper entitled, 1. The petition of the London Clergy to the House of Lords against the Quakers Bill. 2. The Lords protest on rejecting the said petition. 3. The Lords protest against the Quakers Bill. By Joshua Freeman [Arthur Ashley Sykes]. 8vo. Pp. 70. [Disney's *Memoir of Sykes*, p. xvi.] London, 1722

LETTER (a) to Robert Wallace, of Kelly, in reply to his late Appeal to the people of Scotland on the subject of reform in the law. By a member of the Faculty of Advocates [Benjamin Bell]. 8vo. [*Brit. Mus.*] Edinburgh, 1837

LETTER (a) to Robert [Plumer] Ward, Esq., M.P. [in reply to his View of the relative situations of Mr Pitt and Mr Addington. By John Adolphus, barrister]. 8vo. [*D. N. B.* vol. 1, p. 141.] London, 1804

LETTER (a) to Samuel Johnson, LL.D. [By John Wilkes.] 8vo. [*Brit. Mus.*] [London] 1770

A bitter address, evoked by Johnson's anonymous "False alarm."

LETTER (a) to Scripturista [Rev. William Hart], containing some remarks on his Answer to Paulinus's three questions. . . . [By Joseph Bellamy, D.D.]. 8vo. [Evans' *Amer. Bibl.* vol. 3, p. 247.] New Haven, Conn. 1760

LETTER (a) to Sir George Murray, G.C.B. H.M.'s principal secretary of state for the colonies, relative to the deportation of lecesne and escoffery from Jamaica. [By William Burge, Q.C.] 8vo. Pp. xii. 577. [*Athen. Cat.*] London, private print, 1829

LETTER (a) to Sir J. B. [Jacob Bancks], by birth a S— [Swede], but naturaliz'd, and now a M—r of the present P—t: concerning the late Minehead doctrine, which was establish'd by a certain free Parliament of Sweden, to the utter enslaving of that kingdom. [By William Benson, Sheriff of Wilts.] 8vo. Pp. 40. [*Brit. Mus.*] London, 1711

First published under the title of "The history or present state of Sweden," *q.v.* In the same year, there followed "A second letter. . . ."

LETTER (a) to Sir John Sinclair, Bart., on the necessity of an instant change of ministry. By Ralph Anderson [Robert Heron]. 8vo. [*D. N. B.* vol. 26, p. 252.] Edinburgh, 1797

LETTER (a) to Sir Phil. Jen. Clerke, chairman of the committee of the House of Commons, to whom the petition of Benjamin Lacam, sole proprietor of New harbour in Bengal, was referred. [By Captain Joseph Price.] 8vo. Pp. 144. [*Nat. Lib. of Scot.*] London, 1783

LETTER (a) to Sir Richard Brocas, Lord Mayor of London, on the erection of a new theatre in Goodsman's Fields. By a citizen [Isaac Maddox or Madox, D.D.]. 8vo. London, 1730

Attributed also to Francis Hare.

LETTER (a) to Sir Richard R. Vyvyan, Bart., M.P. for the county of Cornwall, on the nature and use of credit and currency. By one of his constituents [Henry Boase]. 8vo. Pp. 49. [Boase and Courtney's *Bibl. Corn.* i. 29.] Penzance, 1826

LETTER (a) to Sir Robert Peel on the endowment of the Roman Catholic Church of Ireland. By the Knight of Kerry [Maurice Fitz-gerald]. 8vo. Pp. 14. [*Camb. Univ. Lib.*] London, 1845

LETTER (a) to Sir Thomas Dyke Acland, Bart., M.P., upon Mr Wilmot Horton's pamphlet respecting the claims of the Roman Catholics. [By Francis Huyshe.] 8vo. [*Brit. Mus.*] London, 1826

LETTER (a) to Sir Thomas Osborn, one of His Majesties Privy Council, upon the reading of a book [by Slingsby Bethel] called, The present interest of England stated. [By George Villiers, second Duke of Buckingham.] 4to. Pp. 16. [*Cat. Lond. Inst.* ii. 551.] London, 1672

LETTER (a) to Sir William Meredith, upon the subject of subscription to the liturgy and Thirty-nine Articles of the Church of England. By an Englishman [John Jebb, M.D.]. 4to. [Jebb's *Works*, i. 223.] London, 1772

LETTER (a) to Stephen Clarke, rector of Burythorpe in Yorkshire, in answer to his Short vindication of the clergy's right to tithes. By one of the people called Quakers [Joseph Besse]. 8vo. [Smith's *Cat. of Friends' Books*, i. 60.] London, 1740

LETTER (a) to T—— P——, Esq.; from the author of *Siris* [George Berkeley, D.D., Bishop of Cloyne] containing some farther remarks on the virtues of tar-water, and the methods for preparing and using of it. . . . 8vo. [*W.*] London, 1744

LETTER (a) to the absentee landlords of the South of Ireland, on the means of tranquillising their tenantry and improving their estates. [By John Wiggins.] 8vo. [*Brit. Mus.*] London, 1822

The substance of this pamphlet, by a land agent, was reproduced in 1824, as "South of Ireland; hints to Irish landlords. . . ." A further contribution from the same pen is "The case of the landed interest fairly stated, . . ." 1827.

LETTER (a) to the admirers of Chatterton. By the author of *An essay on light reading* [Edward Mangin]. 8vo. [*Olphar Hamst*, p. 127; Green's *Bibl. Somers.* i. 335.] Bath, 1838

LETTER (a) to the American Peace Society. . . . By a member of the Committee of Peace in Paris [George M. Gibbs]. 8vo. [Cushing's *Init. and Pseud.* i. 188.] Paris, 1842

LETTER (a) to [John Potter] the Archbishop of Canterbury, concerning the validity of lay Baptism. [By Archibald Campbell, Bishop of Aberdeen.] 8vo. [*Scot. Episc. Lib.* p. 40.] London, 1738

LETTER (a) to the Archbishop of Canterbury [William Howley] on the right of the Convocation to tax the clergy for the service of the Church. [By Francis Charles Massingberd.] 8vo. [*Brit. Mus.*] London, 1835

LETTER (a) to the author of a book called A candid and impartial sketch of the life and Government of Pope Clement XIV. [By John Milner, D.D.] 8vo. Pp. 32. London, 1785

The "Candid and impartial sketch" was most probably written by Charles Plowden, *alias* Simons, S.J.

LETTER (a) to [Dr James Knight] the author of a book entitled, The true Scripture-doctrine of the most holy and undivided Trinity continued and vindicated, etc. [By Samuel Clarke, D.D.] 8vo. [*Bodl.*] N.P. 1719

LETTER (a) to [Rev. William Atkinson] the author of A candid inquiry into the democratic schemes of the Dissenters. [By Edward Parsons, Congregationalist.] 8vo. [*Brit. Mus.*] Leeds, 1801

Signed: Vindex.

LETTER (a) to the author [Thomas Chapman, D.D.] of A further enquiry into the right of appeal from the Chancellor or Vice chancellor of the University of Cambridge, in matters of discipline. [By John Smith, M.A. of King's College, Cambridge.] 8vo. [*Bodl.*] London, 1752

LETTER (a) to the author of a late epistolary dissertation; wherein all his objections to Mr Warburton's interpretation of the command to Abraham to offer up his son Isaac are considered. By L. U. P—, A.M. [Thomas Edwards]. 8vo. [Darling's *Cyclop. Bibl.* 1027.] London, 1744

LETTER (a) to the author of a late pamphlet, entitled, A letter to the Right Reverend the Lord Bishop of London; occasion'd by disputing with a Quaker: containing the answers which the writer of that letter might and ought to have given to the Quaker, upon the several heads in dispute. [By —— Harris, of Tollesbury, Essex.] 8vo. Pp. 59. [Smith's *Anti-Quak.* p. 40.] London, 1737

LETTER (a) to [Dr Edward Fowler] the author of a late paper, entituled A vindication of the divines of the Church of England, &c.; in defence of the History of passive obedience. [By George Hickes, D.D.] 4to. Pp. 161. [*D. N. B.* vol. 26, p. 354.] N.P. 1689

As the "History of passive obedience" and its "Continuation" were both written by Abednego Seller, it has been held that he wrote also this "Defence."

LETTER (a) to the author of a "Letter to a young lady." [By John Roabard, M.D.] 8vo. London, 1764

LETTER (a) to the author [James Beezly] of a Letter to Dr Formey; in which some of the prevailing sentiments of that worthy body of men called Quakers, as they stand in Mr Robert Barclay's Apology, and as they are touched upon in that letter, are freely discussed, and their apprehended natural tendency manifested. [By Rev. Samuel Newton, of Norwich.] 8vo. Pp. 84. [Smith's *Anti-Quak.* p. 43, 336.] London, 1767

LETTER (a) to [John Clarke] the author of a Letter to Dr Mather. . . . By one of the readers [Samuel Mather, D.D.]. 8vo. Boston, 1733

LETTER (a) to [Rev. —— Potter] the author of a Letter to Mr [John] Buxton [on a Parliamentary election in Norfolk]; in which it is proved that the design of that Letter has been entirely misunderstood. . . . [By Samuel Cooper, D.D.] 8vo. [*Brit. Mus.*] N.P. 1768

LETTER (a) to [John Mainwaring] the author of a pamphlet, entitled Remarks on the Pursuits of literature; in a letter to the author, dated Cambridge, May 1, 1798, containing observations on "The remarks." By a country gentleman, formerly of the University of Cambridge [Thomas James Mathias]. 8vo. Pp. 28. [*Dyce Cat.* ii. 66.] London, 1798

LETTER to [Rev. George Logan] the author of a pamphlet, intituled, The lawfulness and necessity of ministers, their reading the Act of Parliament for bringing to justice the murderers of Captain John Porteous. [By Rev. George Wishart, of Tron Church, Edinburgh.] 8vo. Pp. 35. [*New Coll. Lib.*] Edinburgh, 1737

LETTER (a) to [Dr Thomas Tenison] the author of a sermon entituled, A sermon preached on the funeral of her late Majesty Queen Mary, of ever blessed memory. [By Thomas Ken, D.D.] 4to. Pp. 8. [*Bodl.*] N.P., N.D.

The letter is dated 1695.

LETTER (a) to [Strickland Gough] the author of An enquiry into the causes of the decay of the Dissenting Interest; containing an apology for some of his inconsistences, with a plea for the Dissenters and the liberty of the people. To which is added a short epistle to . . . Mr [Strickland] Gough, occasioned by his taking orders in the Church of England. [By Abraham Taylor.] 8vo. Pp. 40. [*Brit. Mus.*] London, 1730

LETTER (a) to [George Rous] the author of An essay on the Middlesex Election [of John Wilkes]: in which his objections to the power of expulsion are considered, and the nature of representation in Parliament examined. [By Sir William Meredith?] 4to. London, 1770

LETTER (a) to [William S. Powell, D.D.] the author of an Observation on the design of establishing annual examinations at Cambridge. [By —— Lambert.] 8vo. Pp. 37. [Queen's *Coll. Cat.* p. 728.] Cambridge, 1774

Ascribed also to Ann Jebb.

LETTER (a) to [Henry Dodwell, junr.] the author of Christianity not founded on argument. By a young gentleman of Cambridge [Rev. Henry Etough, rector of Therfield, Hertfordshire]. 8vo. Pp. 43. [Darling's *Cyclop. Bibl.*] London, 1742

LETTER to [A. Clark?] the author of Hints to the clergy of the Established Church. . . . By a Kentish clergyman [Rev. Montague Pennington]. 8vo. [*Brit. Mus.*] London, 1814

LETTER (a) to [Roger Lawrence] the author of Lay baptism invalid; to which is annexed the judgment of the Reformation in France, extracted out of the Acts of their publick synods; as also those of Mr Calvin, and other Genevans, concerning the invalidity of lay-baptism. By a priest of the Church of England, and rector of a church in the city of London [Luke Milbourn, formerly chaplain at Hamburgh, Rotterdam, and Harwich]. 8vo. [Kennet's *Wisdom*, p. 264.] Printed for H. Clements, 1713

LETTER (a) to [Roger Lawrence] the author of Lay baptism invalid, wherein the Popish doctrine of Lay baptism is censured and condemned. [By Thomas Brett, LL.D.] 8vo. [*D. N. B.* vol. 6, p. 286.] London, 1711

In reply to this Joseph Bingham wrote his "Scholastical history of lay baptism."

LETTER (a) to [John Lingard, D.D.] the author of Remarks on a charge delivered by Shute [Barrington], Bishop of Durham, at the ordinary visitation of that diocese in the year 1806. By a clergyman of the diocese of Durham [Henry Phillpotts, D.D.]. 12mo. Pp. iv. 42. [*Bodl.*] Newcastle upon Tyne, 1807

LETTER (a) to the author of Some considerations on the Act to prevent clandestine marriages. With a postscript occasioned by the Enquiry [by —— Stebbing] into the force and operation of the annulling clauses in a late Act for the better preventing clandestine marriages, with respect to conscience. By a country clergyman [William Dodwell]. 8vo. [Watt's *Bibl. Brit.*] London, 1755

LETTER (a) to the author of the Calculations in the White-Hall Evening-Post, relating to South-sea stock, shewing the mistakes in the said calculations; and, these being rectified, what the present value of South-sea stock is. . . . By a member of the House of Commons [Archibald Hutcheson]. Fol. Pp. 15. [*Bodl.*] London, 1720

LETTER (a) to [Francis Blackburne] the author of the Confessional, containing remarks on his preface to the first edition. [By Gloucester Ridley.] 8vo. [*Brit. Mus.*] London, 1768

See note to "The Confessional. . . ."

LETTER (a) to [William Warburton, D.D.] the author of The Divine legation of Moses. [By Robert Lowth, D.D.] 8vo. [*D. N. B.* vol. 34, p. 214.] London, 1766

LETTER (a) to [John Witherspoon, D.D.] the author of the Ecclesiastical characteristicks. . . . [By Andrew Moir.] 8vo. Edinburgh, 1755

LETTER (a) to [G. Turner] the author of the Enquiry into the revenue, credit, and commerce of France; wherein the former and present state of the power and commerce of that kingdom are fully consider'd. . . . By a Member of Parliament [—— Monice]. 8vo. Pp. 72. London, 1742

Attestation of authorship in contemporary handwriting.

LETTER (a) to the author of The expediency and necessity of revising and improving the public Liturgy; being a modest enquiry, what is that form or manner which Christians ought to observe in their private and public prayer, as taught and commanded in Scripture. [By Richard Moseley.] 8vo. Pp. 52. [*Brit. Mus.*] London, 1750

LETTER (a) to the author of the late Letter out of the countrey, occasioned by a former Letter to a member of the House of Commons [by Henry Maurice, D.D.], concerning the Bishops lately in the Tower, and now under suspension. [By Thomas Wagstaffe, A.M.] 4to. Pp. 8. [*Bodl.*] [London, 1690]

No title-page.

LETTER (a) to [John Toland] the author of the Memorial of the state of England. [By William Stephens, B.D.] 4to. Pp. 32. London, 1705

The authorship is acknowledged in a MS. letter on the back of the title-page of the Bodleian copy.

LETTER (a) to the author of the Observations on the Review of Mr [James] Hunter's Letter to the Commissioners of Supply for the County of Haddington. [By Robert Brown, of Markle.] 8vo. Pp. 60. Haddington, 1805

LETTER (a) to the author of the proposal for the establishment of public examinations [at Cambridge]. [By Mrs Anne Jebb.] 8vo. Pp. 11. [Disney's *Memoirs of Jebb*, *Jebb's works*, i. 81.] Cambridge, 1774

LETTER (a) to [Thomas James Mathias the [anonymous] author of The pursuits [of literature]. By a country gentleman, formerly of the University of Cambridge [John Mainwaring]. 8vo. London, 1798

LETTER (a) to the author of the Queries [regarding the case of Captain John Porteous] unmasked. [By Rev. Robert Wallace, D.D., Edinburgh.] 8vo. [*New Coll. Lib.*] Edinburgh, 1737

LETTER (a) to [Sir William Meredith] the author of The question stated. By another Member of Parliament [Sir William Blackstone]. 8vo. Pp. 24. [*Bodl.*] London, 1769

LETTER (a) to [Jonathan Swift] the author of the Short view of the state of Ireland. By the author of *Seasonable remarks* [John Browne]. 12mo. Dublin, 1728

LETTER (a) to the author of the Vindication of Mr Nation's sermon; in which the importance of faith, in matters of religion, and particularly as to the doctrine of the deity of our Saviour, is considered: and the assembly of the United ministers of Devon and Cornwall is further defended. To which is added A second letter to Mr Nation. . . . [By Rev. John Enty, Dissenting minister at Exeter.] 8vo. Pp. 70. [Boase and Courtney's *Bibl. Corn.* i. 143.] London, 1732

There is, in addition, "A postscript; being a third letter to Mr Nation," London, 1732, pp. 71-87.

LETTER (a) to the author [Henry Dodwell, sen.,] of the Vindication of the deprived Bishops, in reply to his reasons for the validity of the lay-deprivation of the Bishops by the statute of 1 Eliz. c. 1. [By Edward Stephens.] 4to. Pp. 4. [*Bodl.*] N.P., N.D.

LETTER (a) to the author of Unitarianism defended. By a young Wesleyan [Robert W. Clegg]. 8vo. [Smale's *Whitby authors.*] Whitby, 1849

LETTER (a) to the authors of Divine Analogy, and The minute philosopher, from an old officer [Rev. Philip Skelton]. 8vo. [*D. N. B.* vol. 52, p. 334.] London, 1744

The authors are Bishops Peter Browne and George Berkeley.

LETTER (a) to [William Fleetwood] the Bishop of Ely upon the occasion of his suppos'd late charge (Aug. 7th, 1716) . . . against frequent communion. . . . By Philalethes [Matthew Earbery]. Second edition. 4to. London, 1717

LETTER (a) to [Henry Phillpotts], the Bishop of Exeter, on the decision of the Judicial Committee of the Privy Council in the Gorham case. By a Layman [Sir Edward Hall Alderson]. 8vo. Pp. 14. [*Brit. Mus.*] London, private print, 1850

This was followed, in 1851, by "A second letter."

LETTER (a) to [Beilby Porteus] the Bishop of London. By a layman [Richard Gough]. 8vo. [Nichols' *Lit. Anec.* vi. 319.] London, 1799

LETTER (a) to [Edmund Gibson] the Bishop of London, occasioned by the abuse of a passage in his Lordship's pastoral letter. By a presbyter of the Church of England [William Asplin]. 8vo. Pp. 39. [Darling's *Cyclop. Bibl.*] London, 1730

Signed: W. A.

Ascribed also to W. Austin. [*Brit. Mus.*]

LETTER (a) to [Charles James Blomfield] the Bishop of London on the present state of the Society for promoting Christian knowledge in the metropolis and its suburbs. [By Rev. Edward William Grinfield.] 8vo. Pp. 19. [*Athen. Cat.*] London, 1834

LETTER (a) to [Richard Bagot] the Bishop of Oxford, containing strictures upon certain parts of Dr Pusey's Letter to his Lordship. By a clergyman of the diocese [Rev. Charles Pourtales Golightly, M.A.]. 8vo. [*D. N. B.* vol. 22, p. 100.] Oxford, 1840

LETTER (a) to [Thomas Burgess] the Bishop of St Davids, on some extraordinary passages in a charge delivered to the clergy of his diocese in September 1813. By a lay seceder [George Wilson Meadley]. [*Gent. Mag.* 1819, p. 208.] London, 1814

LETTER (a) to [Gilbert Burnet] the Bishop of Salisbury occasioned by his son's Letter to the Earl of Halifax. [By Daniel Burgess, M.A.] 8vo. [*D. N. B.* vol. 7, p. 309.] London, 1715

LETTER (a) to [John Douglas] the Bishop of Salisbury on his late charge to the clergy of his diocese. By a Dissenter [Henry Wansey]. 8vo. Pp. 26. [*Brit. Mus.*] Salisbury, 1798

Signed: H. W.

LETTER (a) to the Bishops, on the application of the Protestant Dissenters to Parliament for a repeal of the Corporation and Test Acts; including strictures on some passages in the Bishop of Gloucester's sermon, on January 30, 1788. [By Joshua Toulmin, D.D.] 8vo. Pp. 45. [*Bodl.*] London, 1789

LETTER (a) to the Church of England, pointing out some popular errors of bad consequence. By an old friend and servant of the Church [William Jones, F.R.S.]. 8vo. [Watt's *Bibl. Brit.*] London, 1798

LETTER (a) to the citizens of Charleston, embracing strictures. . . . By Expositor [Aaron W. Leland]. 8vo. [Cushing's *Init. and Pseud.* i. 95.] Charleston, S.C., 1818

LETTER (a) to the clergy and laity of the Protestant Episcopal Church in the diocese of New York. By Pacificator [Murray Hoffman]. 8vo. [Cushing's *Init. and Pseud.* i. 223.] New York, 1850

LETTER (a) to the clergy, ministers and Protestant Christians . . . of Great Britain on the deplorable spiritual condition of the metropolis. By the editor of the *London City Mission Magazine* [Rev. Robert Ainslie]. 8vo. [*Brit. Mus.*] London, 1841

LETTER (a) to the clergy of the Church of England, in the county of Northumberland. By a Christian [William Hewetson]. 8vo. [Smith's *Cat. of Friends' Books*, i. 54.] Printed in 1732

LETTER (a) to the clergy of the Church of England; on occasion of the commitment of [Francis Atterbury] the Right Reverend the Lord Bishop of Rochester to the Tower of London. By a clergyman of the Church of England [Zachary Pearce]. 4to. Pp. 20. [*Bodl.*] London, 1722

LETTER (a) to the clergy of the county of Norfolk; in which the necessity for the abolition of tithes is plainly proved, and the propriety of other plans is fully evinced. By no tithe gatherer [Rev. Samuel Cooper]. 8vo. [*Gent. Mag.* 1800, p. 177.] Norwich, 1773

LETTER (a) to the clergy of the Deanery of Cary. By their Rural Dean [Rev. Roger Frankland]. 8vo. [Green's *Bibl. Somers.* ii. 410.] Southampton, 1816

LETTER (a) to the clergy upon the speech of the Rt. Rev. [Edward Stanley] the Lord Bishop of Norwich in the House of Lords, 26 May, 1840. By a priest of the Church of England [William Maskell, M.A.]. 8vo. [*D. N. B.* vol. 36, p. 413.] London, 1840

LETTER (a) to the Commissioners of Landlord and Tenant Inquiry, on the state of the law in respect of the building and occupation of houses in towns in Ireland. [By Charles Haliday, M.R.I.A.] 8vo. [*D. N. B.* vol. 24, p. 45.] Dublin, 1844

LETTER (a) to the commoners in Rockingham Forest; wherein is briefly and plainly shewn, the right of common they are intitled to [in] the forest; and a method propos'd by which they may preserve their rights. . . . By a commoner [William Gould, rector of Weldon]. 8vo. Pp. 18. [*Upcott.*] Stamford, 1744

LETTER (a) to the congregation of the [Episcopal] chapel at Old Deer. [By Rev. John Skinner, bishop of Aberdeen.] 8vo. [Robertson's *Aberd. Bibl.*] Aberdeen, 1798

LETTER (a) to the Country Spectator, in reply to the author of his ninth number. . . . By a Professor of Music [Edward Miller, Mus.Doc.]. 8vo. [*D. N. B.* vol. 37, p. 406.] Doncaster, 1792

LETTER (a) to the Craftsman on the game of chess; occasioned by his paper of the fifteenth of this month. [By John Hervey, Lord Hervey.] 8vo. Pp. 29. London, 1733

LETTER (a) to the D. of P. [Edward Stillingfleet, Dean of St Paul's] in answer to the arguing part of his first letter to Mr G. [Godwin *alias* Godden]. [By John Sergeant.] 8vo. [Jones' Peck, p. 127.] London, 1687

LETTER to the Dean of the Faculty of Advocates, relative to a plan which has been proposed for reporting the decisions of the Court of Session. By a member of the Faculty [Robert Hannay]. 8vo. Pp. 16. [*Nat. Lib. of Scot.*] Edinburgh, 1823

LETTER (a) to the Deists. [By Humphrey Prideaux, D.D. ?] 8vo. London, 1696

LETTER (a) to the deputies of Protestant Dissenting congregations, in and about the cities of London and Westminster; on their intended application to Parliament for the repeal of the Corporation and Test Acts. [By Stephen Addington.] 8vo. Pp. viii. 35. [*Bodl.*] London [1787]

LETTER (a) to the Dissenters. [By Daniel Defoe.] 8vo. Pp. 48. [Lee's *Defoe*, p. 151.] London, 1713

LETTER (a) to the Dissenters. [By Daniel Defoe.] 8vo. Pp. 27. [Wilson's *Life of Defoe*, iii. 424; Lee's *Defoe*, p. 196.] London, 1719

LETTER (a) to the Duke of Devonshire, Chancellor of the University of Cambridge. [By Rev. John Howard Marsden.] 8vo. Pp. 15. [*Brit. Mus.*] Private print, 1863

Signed: A member of the Senate.

LETTER (a) to the Duke of Gloucester, in vindication of the University of Cambridge from the calumnious attacks of R. M. Beverley. [By A. Watson.] 8vo. [Bartholomew's *Camb. Books.*] Cambridge, 1833

LETTER (a) to the Duke of Grafton [Augustus Henry Fitzroy], with notes. [By William Augustus Miles.] To which is annexed, a complete exculpation of M. de la Fayette from the charges indecently urged against him by Mr Burke in the House of Commons on the 17th of March, 1794. 8vo. [*Brit. Mus.*] London, 1794

LETTER (a) to the Duke of Richmond, anent his losses in the sale of his salmon, and on other fish-trading and free-trading matters. By a brother fish-dealer from the far north [—— Anderson]. 8vo. Pp. 10. [*W.*] London, 1844

Signed: The originator of the Shetland Fishery Company.

LETTER (a) to the Duke of Wellington on the propriety and legality of creating Peers for life; with precedents. [By Sir Nicholas H. Nicolas.] Second edition. 8vo. Pp. 56. [*Brit. Mus.*] London, 1830

LETTER (a) to the Duke of Wellington on the reasonableness of a Church reform, and its fitness to the present times. By a minister of the Establishment [Henry Card, D.D.]. 8vo. [*Brit. Mus.*] London, 1830

LETTER (a) to the Duke of Wellington upon the actual crisis of the country, in respect to the state of the navy. By a flag-officer [Rear Admiral Hawker]. 8vo. London, 1838

Attributed also to Sir Charles Napier.

LETTER (a) to the Dutch merchants in England. [By Sir James Marriott, LL.D.] 8vo. [*D. N. B.* vol. 36, p. 198.] London, 1759

LETTER (a) to the Earl of Arundel and Surrey on the Bull "In cœnâ Domini." By the editor of the *Bull*, as published for the National Club [George Edward Biber, LL.D.]. 8vo. Pp. 20. [*Bodl.*] London, 1848

LETTER (a) to the Earl of Bute. [By John Almon.] 8vo. [Watt's *Bibl. Brit.*] London, 1771

LETTER (a) to the Earl of Chatham [William Pitt] on the Quebec Bill. [By Sir William Meredith.] 8vo. [*D. N. B.* vol. 37, p. 272.] London, 1774

LETTER (a) to the Earl of Fingal. By the author of the *Letter to Mr Canning* [Thomas Lewis O'Beirne, D.D.]. 8vo. Pp. 73. [*D. N. B.* vol. 41, p. 305.] Dublin, 1813

Assigned also to G. Spencer.

LETTER (a) to the Earl of Lauderdale, containing strictures on His Lordship's Letters to the peers of Scotland. By John Gifford, Esq. [John Richards Green]. 8vo. Pp. 179. [*Brit. Mus.*] London, 1795

LETTER to the Earl of Leicester on the recent discovery of the Roman cloaca, or sewer, at Leicester: with some thoughts on Jewry Wall. [By John Throsby.] 4to. Pp. 39. [*Upcott*, i. 547.] Leicester, 1793

LETTER (a) to the Earl of Liverpool on the proposed annexion of the King's Library to that of the British Museum. By one of the people [Thomas Frognall Dibdin ?]. 8vo. [*Brit. Mus.*] London, 1824

LETTER (a) to the Earl of O—d [Oxford], concerning the Bill of Peerage. By Sir R—d S—le [Sir Richard Steele]. 8vo. Pp. 32. [Moule's *Bibl. Herald.* p. 304.] London, 1719

LETTER (a) to the Earl of Radnor upon the oaths, dispensations, and subscription to the xxxix. Articles at the University of Oxford. By a resident member of Convocation [Edward Hawkins, D.D., Provost of Oriel]. 8vo. Pp. 26. [*Bodl.*] Oxford, 1835

The author's name is in the handwriting of Dr Bliss.

LETTER (a) to the Earl of Shelburne . . . from a noble Earl of Ireland [Charles Coote, Earl of Bellamont], respecting the legislative rights of Ireland. Second edition. 8vo. [*Lond. Lib. Cat.*] London, 1783

LETTER (a) to the Earle of Pembrooke concerning the times, and the sad condition both of prince and people. [By James Howell.] 4to. Pp. 12. [Bliss' *Cat.*] 1647

Attributed also to Thomas Herbert.

LETTER (a) to the editor of the Christian Instructor, by the author of *The Word made flesh; or, the true humanity of God in Christ demonstrated from the Scriptures* [Thomas Carlyle, advocate]. 8vo. Pp. 15. [G. C. Boase's *Lit. of Cath. Apost. Church.*] Edinburgh, 1830

LETTER (a) to the editor of the Colombo Observer on Temperance Societies. [By Rev. B. Bailey.] 8vo. Colombo, 1835

LETTER to the editor of the Edinburgh Review, in reply to the Rev. Mr Goode. By the author of the articles on church rates that appeared in 134th and 141st numbers of the Edinburgh Review [John Allen]. 8vo. Pp. iv. 32. [*W.*] London, 1840

LETTER (a) to the editor of the Edinburgh Weekly Journal, from Malachi Malagrowther, Esq. [Sir Walter Scott, Bart.] on the proposed change of currency, and other late alterations, as they affect, or are intended to affect, the kingdom of Scotland. Second edition. 8vo. Pp. 60. Edinburgh, 1826

LETTER (a) to the editor [or rather, Lord Bolingbroke, the author] of the Letters on the spirit of patriotism. . . . [By William Warburton, D.D.] 8vo. [*Brit. Mus.*] London, 1749

LETTER (a) to the editor of The Times, in reply to his strictures on the Bishop of London's Letters on the present neglect of the Lord's Day. By Christianus [Thomas F. Dibdin]. 8vo. [*Brit. Mus.*] London, 1830

LETTER (a) to the editor of the Yorkshire Gazette, on the subject of Mr Fawkes's Address to the nobility, gentry, and clergy of the county of York. By a Yorkshire freeholder [John Courtney]. 8vo. Pp. 31. [*Brit. Mus.*] York, 1822

LETTER (a) to the electors of Westminster. From a Conservative [John Lettsom Elliot]. 8vo. [*Camb. Univ. Lib.*] [London] 1847

LETTER (a) to the electors of Westminster. From a Protectionist [John Lettsom Elliot]. 8vo. Pp. 84. [*Camb. Univ. Lib.*] London, 1848

LETTER (a) to the electors of Westminster. From an Aristocrat [John Lettsom Elliot]. 8vo. Pp. 100. [*Camb. Univ. Lib.*] London, 1850

LETTER (a) to the Episcopal clergy in Scotland; being the sincere and humble advice of an unknown friend. [By George Garden, D.D. ?] 4to. Edinburgh [1703]

LETTER (a) to the Examiner. [By Henry St John, Viscount Bolingbroke.] 8vo. Pp. 16. N.P. 1710

LETTER (a) to the farmers and tithe-payers of Suffolk, on the history, evils, and injustice of the tithe-system. . . . By Peter Ploughman [Nicholas Hankey Smith]. 8vo. [*Brit. Mus.*] Ipswich [1832]

LETTER (a) to the fatal triumvirate; in answer to that pretended to be written by Dr Byfield: and shewing reasons why Dr Woodward should take no notice of it. [By John Harris, D.D.] 8vo. Pp. 23. [*Bodl.*] London, 1719

LETTER (a) to the female members of our Society, from one of themselves [S. J. J. Fox]. 8vo. [*Brit. Mus.*] London, 1873

LETTER (a) to the first Belfast Company of Volunteers, in the province of Ulster. By a member of the British parliament [Francis Ingram Seymour Conway, Viscount Beauchamp]. 8vo. [*Cat. Lond. Inst.* ii. 148.] London, 1783

LETTER to the freeholders and electors in the counties and burghs of Scotland on Parliamentary reform; with a plan of reform congenial to the law of Scotland and not materially affecting private rights. By the author of *Letter to the landholders on the Hypothec Bill* [Walter Ferrier]. 8vo. Pp. 35. [*W.*] Edinburgh, 1831

Signed: A country voter.

LETTER (a) to the freeholders of the county of York [on the Catholic question]. By an English Catholic [the Hon. Edward Robert Petre]. 8vo. [Gillow's *Bibl. Dict.*] Leeds, 1826

LETTER (a) to the friends of F. T. Gray. By a proprietor [Lewis Glover Pray]. 8vo. [Cushing's *Init. and Pseud.* ii. 125.] Boston, 1842

LETTER (a) to the Governors of the Charter-House, in reply to certain allegations . . . by the Rev. H. H. Hale. . . . [By Redmond W. Pilkington.] 8vo. London, 1834

LETTER (a) to the Guildry [of Aberdeen] on the present state of their affairs, and on the late extraordinary conduct of the Lord Provost, Magistrates, and Council. By a Guild brother [Alexander Bannerman]. 8vo. [Robertson's *Aberd. Bibl.*] Aberdeen, 1835

LETTER (a) to the Harbour Trustees of the city of Aberdeen. [By Alexander Bannerman.] 8vo. [Robertson's *Aberd. Bibl.*] Aberdeen, 1826

LETTER (a) to the heritors, farmers, and inhabitants of the county of Edinburgh; to the Lord Provost, magistrates, and town-council; the heritors and inhabitants of the city of Edinburgh; and to the heritors and inhabitants of the town of Leith: concerning the establishment of an additional imposition, by raising all the tolls in the neighbourhood of the city; and exacting new tolls at the Water-gate and Wester-road to Leith. By a citizen [Hugo Arnot, advocate]. 8vo. Pp. 27. Edinburgh, 1775

LETTER (a) to the Hon. Daniel Webster, on the causes of the destruction of the steamer "Lexington." By a traveller [Henry Russell Cleveland]. 8vo. [Cushing's *Init. and Pseud.* i. 285.] Boston, 1840

LETTER (a) to the Honourable Daniel Webster, on the political affairs of the United States. By Marcellus [Noah Webster]. 8vo. [Cushing's *Init. and Pseud.* i. 183.] Philadelphia, 1837

LETTER (a) to the Hon. Josiah Quincy on the law of libel. By a member of the Suffolk Bar [Harrison Gray Otis]. 8vo. [Cushing's *Init. and Pseud.* i. 191.] Boston, 1823

LETTER (a) to the Honourable Mr Horace Walpole, concerning the dispute between Mr Hume and Mr Rousseau. [By Ralph Heathcote, D.D.] 12mo. Pp. 23. [Nichol's *Lit. Anec.* iii. 541.] London, 1767

LETTER (a) to the Hon. Samuel Eliot. By Hancock [Franklin Dexter]. 8vo. [Cushing's *Init. and Pseud.* i. 126.] Boston, 1851

LETTER (a) to the Honourable Sir David Dalrymple, Lord Hailes, on his Remarks on the history of Scotland. [By Patrick Murray, fifth Lord Elibank.] 12mo. Pp. 51. Edinburgh, 1773

LETTER to the Honourable the Lord Provost, respecting the proposed Statute Labour Bill for Glasgow. By a citizen [James Cleland, LL.D.]. 8vo. Pp. 36. Glasgow, 1819

LETTER (a) to the Honourable the Lords Commissioners of trade and plantations; wherein the grand concern of trade is asserted and maintained, with an attempt to prove that our nobility, gentry and clergy are more nearly concern'd in trade in its success and consequences than even the merchant or trader himself. By an impartial hand [George Coad, Junr., of Exeter]. 8vo. Pp. viii. 143. [*W.*] London, 1747

LETTER (a) to the Hon. Thomas Erskine; containing some strictures on his View of the causes and consequences of the present war with France. By John Gifford [John Richards Green]. 8vo. Pp. 171. [*Gladstone Lib. Cat.*] London, 1797

LETTER (a) to the Hon. W. Lenthal, Esq. . . . concerning Sir T. Fairfax's proceedings in Cornwal, since his advance from Torrington and Launceston to Bodman. . . . [Signed: J. R. *i.e.* John Rushworth.] 4to. [*Brit. Mus.*] London, 1645

LETTER (a) to the human race. By a brother [Robert Manning]. 12mo. Pp. 91. [*Brit. Mus.*] London, 1840

LETTER (a) to the independent electors of Westminster, in the interest of Lord Hood and Sir Cecil Wray. [By Sir Cecil Wray, Bart.] 8vo. [London, 1784]

LETTER (a) to the infamous Tom Paine, in answer to his Letter to General Washington. By Peter Porcupine, author of *The bone to gnaw for democrats*, etc. [William Cobbett]. 8vo. Pp. 23. Philadelphia printed; London reprinted, 1797

LETTER (a) to the inhabitants of Edinburgh, on the new Police Bill. [By Henry Cockburn, Lord Cockburn.] 8vo. Pp. 68. [*Brit. Mus.*] Edinburgh, 1822

Signed: A fellow-citizen.

LETTER (a) to the inhabitants of Great Britain and Ireland; to stir them up to all necessary preparations to meet a perfidious enemy, who intend to invade our land and attack our liberties. By a lover of his king and country [Samuel Hayward]. 8vo. [*Mon. Rev.* xiv. 359.] London, 1756

LETTER (a) to the inhabitants of Salcombe-Regis. [By Thomas William Christie.] 8vo. [Davidson's *Bibl. Devon.* p. 106.] Sidmouth, 1851

LETTER (a) to the inhabitants of Sheffield on a subject which has lately made, and is likely to make, much noise in the town and neighbourhood; or, a short peal on the new bells. . . . [By Rev. George Smith, M.A., curate of the parish church, Sheffield.] 12mo. [*N. and Q.* 1869, p. 169.] Sheffield, 1799

Signed: L. L. A portion of it appeared in the *Country Spectator*, Gainsborough, 1792-3, over the signature: Leonard Lovechurch.

LETTER (a) to the inhabitants of Spital-Fields, on the character and views of our modern reformers. By a member of the Spital-Fields Benevolent Society [Irving Brock]. 8vo. [*Edin. Univ. Lib.*] London, 1817

LETTER (a) to the inhabitants of Whitby, particularly addressed to the middle class, on the decline of the town. [By John Watkins.] 12mo. Pp. 28. [Smales' *Whitby authors*, p. 149.] Whitby, 1838

LETTER (a) to the jurors of Great Britain; occasioned by an opinion of the Court of Kings Bench, read by Lord Chief Justice Mansfield, in the case of the King and Woodfall, and said to have been left by his Lordship with the Clerk of Parliament. [By George Rous.] 8vo. [*European Mag.* xli. 503.] London, 1771

LETTER (a) to the King [George III.] on the state of the Established Church of England. [By John Rippingham.] 8vo. [*Brit. Mus.*] London, 1808

LETTER to the law practitioners of Scotland on the attorney-tax. By an attorney [William Muir, S.S.C.]. 8vo. Edinburgh, 1833

LETTER (a) to the Lay-expositor, concerning his exposition of the orthodox system of civil rights and church-power, &c.; in which the merits of his system are examined and stated. . . . By the author of the *Comment on Mr Warburton's Alliance between Church and State* [Caleb Fleming]. 8vo. Pp. 26. [*Bodl.*] London, 1749

LETTER (a) to the laymen of the Scotch Episcopal Church. By a Scotch Episcopalian [H. Robertson]. 8vo. Pp. 8. [*D. Laing.*] Edinburgh, 1848

LETTER (a) to [Fidelio], the learned author of the Queries; being a detection of several errors . . . in a pamphlet entituled, Answers to the Queries. [By —— Lindsay.] 8vo. Pp. 43. [*New Coll. Lib.*] Edinburgh, 1737

LETTER (the) to the learned author of the Queries, unmasked; presented to the view of the author. [By Robert Wallace, minister in Edinburgh.] 8vo. Pp. 24. Edinburgh, 1737

The author's name is in the handwriting of Dr David Laing.

LETTER (a) to the learned Dr [John] Woodward. By Dr Byfielde [John Freind, M.D.]. 8vo. Pp. 51. [*Camb. Univ. Lib.*] London, 1719

A satire upon Woodward's State of physic and diseases, 1718, 8vo.

LETTER (a) to the learned Mr Henry Dodwell; containing some remarks on a (pretended) demonstration of the immateriality and natural immortality of the soul, in Mr Clark's Answer to his late Epistolary discourse, &c. The second edition, corrected. [By Anthony Collins.] 8vo. Pp. 16. [*Brit. Mus.*] London, 1709

In other editions the title is varied.

LETTER (a) to the Livery of London relative to the duties and office of Sheriff. By William Mavor [Sir Richard Phillips]. 12mo. [*Bibliographer*, vol. 4, p. 168.] London, 1808

LETTER (a) to the Liverymen of the Worshipful Company of Carpenters. [By J. Simmons.] 8vo. London, 1825

LETTER (a) to [Henry Dundas] the Lord Advocate of Scotland. [By Hugo Arnot.] 4to. [*Nat. Lib. of Scot.*]

Dated Edinburgh, Nov. 18, 1777, and signed: Eugene.

LETTER to the Lord Advocate, on the procedure in the Court of Session and jury trials. By a member of Court [John Archibald Murray, Lord Murray]. With an appendix. . . . 8vo. Pp. 69. [*Nat. Lib. of Scot.*] Edinburgh, 1850

The Letter is signed: J. A. M.; and the appendix has a separate pagination.

LETTER (a) to the Lord Advocate [Francis Jeffrey] on the Scotish Reform Bill. [By James Dennistoun.] 8vo. Pp. 31. [*Brit. Mus.*] Edinburgh, 1832

Signed: A Conservative.

LETTER (a) to [William Nicholson] the Lord Bishop of Carlisle, concerning one of his predecessors, Bishop Merks; on occasion of a new volume for the Pretender [by George Harbin], intituled, The hereditary right of the Crown of England asserted. [By White Kennett, D.D.] Third edition. 8vo. Pp. 24. [Newton's *Life of Kennett*, p. 209.] London, 1713

Signed: W. K., dated Octob. 28, 1713. This letter, with other two which followed (the last in 1717), occupies a prominent place in the controversy which had been raised.

LETTER (a) to the Lord Bishop of Ripon on the subject of Dr Hook's sermon preached before Her Majesty, entitled Hear the Church. By one of the clergy [Rev. John William Gowring, B.A.]. 8vo. Pp. 16. [*Brit. Mus.*] London, 1838

LETTER (a) to [Richard Hurd] the Lord Bishop of Worcester, on his strictures on Archbishop Secker and Bishop Lowth, in his life of Bishop Warburton. [By Ralph Churton.] 8vo. [*Brit. Mus.*] Oxford, 1796

Attributed also, with less reason, to Thomas Wintle, and to Samuel Parr.

LETTER (a) to the Lord Marquis of Buckingham, Knight of the most noble Order of the Garter, &c.; chiefly on the subject of the numerous emigrant French priests and others of the Church of Rome, resident and maintained in England at the public expence; and on the spirit and principles of the Romish Church, sacred and political. Second edition (first printed in October 1796). By a layman [Thomas James Mathias]. 8vo. Pp. 39. [*Brit. Mus.*] London, 1797

LETTER (a) to the Lord Mayor, merchants, and others of the City of London [about peace with France]. From an old servant [Ralph Heathcote]. Second edition. 8vo. [*Lond. Lib. Cat.*] London, 1762

LETTER (a) to the Lord Mayor [Sir John Barnard], occasioned by his Lordship's nomination of five persons disqualified by Act of Parliament, to serve the office of Sheriffs; in which the nature and design of the Corporation Act is impartially considered. [By Samuel Chandler, D.D.] 8vo. [*Brit. Mus.*] London, 1738

A second edition was issued in the same year.

LETTER (a) to the Lord Primate on intra-mural burial. [By Rev. William Hale, M.A., archdeacon of London?] 8vo. London [1854]

LETTER (a) to the Lord Provost, Magistrates, and Town Council of Aberdeen on the present condition of city matters. [By Alexander Walker.] 8vo. [Robertson's *Aberd. Bibl.*] Aberdeen, 1874

LETTER (a) to the Lord Viscount B[olingbro]ke, occasion'd by his treatment of a deceased friend [Alexander Pope]. 8vo. [By William Warburton, Bishop of Gloucester.] [*Brit. Mus.*] [London, 1749]

On a duplicate slip is written in MS., "He denied it."

LETTER (a) to the Lords, upon the matter of the Occasional Bill. By Roger [Rev. William Stephens]. 8vo. London, 1704

LETTER (a) to the Managers and Directors of the Royal Institution, Edinburgh. By Roger Roundrobin, Esq. [Patrick Gibson, artist]. 8vo. Edinburgh, 1826

LETTER (a) to the Marquis of Clanricarde explanatory of the defects in the Cause Petition system as a mode of instituting Equity suits in Ireland. . . . [By William Bullen.] 12mo. [*Brit. Mus.*] London, 1862

LETTER (a) to the Members of both Houses of Parliament, on the Dissenters' petitions, and on church grievances. By a late Fellow of All Souls College, Oxford [The Hon. and Rev. Arthur Philip Perceval]. 8vo. Pp. 56. [*Camb. Univ. Lib.*] 8vo. Pp. 56. London, 1834

LETTER (a) to the members of the Cambridgeshire Farmers' Association. By their secretary [George J. Twiss]. 12mo. [Bowes' *Camb. Books*]. Cambridge, 1835

LETTER (a) to the members of the congregation of St James' Chapel, Edinburgh, with reference to certain resolutions which have been entered into by some of the members of the vestry of that chapel. By a member of the congregation [Joseph Moule]. 8vo. Pp. 9. Edinburgh, 1842

LETTER (a) to the Members of the House of Commons, respecting the petition for relief in the matter of Subscription. By a Christian Whig [Richard Watson, D.D.]. Second edition. To which is added a second letter. 8vo. [Bartholomew's *Camb. Books*, p. 262.] London, 1772

LETTER (a) to the members of the Legislature of Pennsylvania, on the removal of the deposits from the Bank of the United States. By Mr William Penn [Stephen Colwell]. 8vo. [Cushing's *Init. and Pseud.* i. 227.] Philadelphia, 1834

LETTER (a) to the members of the Oxford Union. By Philodikaios [Richard Smith, of Balliol College]. 12mo. Pp. 10. Manchester, 1868

LETTER to the members of the Senate on the subject of the subscription required of medical graduates in the University. [By John Haviland.] 8vo. [Bartholomew's *Camb. Books.*] [Cambridge, 1833]

LETTER (a) to the ministers of the Synod of Ulster. By Amicus [Benjamin M'Dowell, D.D.]. 8vo. Pp. 15. [Witherow's *Presb. Lit. in Ireland.*] [Belfast] 1807

LETTER (a) to [Thomas Gother] the misrepresenter of Papists; being a vindication of that part of the Protestant preface to the Wholesome advices from the Blessed Virgin, &c. which concerns the Protestants charity to Papists, and a layman's writing it. . . . By the same layman who translated the Wholesome advices, &c. and made the preface to them [James Taylor]. 4to. Pp. 16. [*Bodl.*] London, 1687

LETTER (a) to the Moderate brethren. By a friend [Robert Lundin Brown]. 8vo. Pp. 16. [*New Coll. Lib.*] Edinburgh [1842]

LETTER (a) to the moderator of the New Hampshire Association. By Timothy [Thomas Worcester]. 8vo. [Cushing's *Init. and Pseud.* i. 283.] Boston, 1812

LETTER (a) to the Moral Philosopher [Dr Thomas Morgan]; being a vindication of a pamphlet, entitled, The immorality of the Moral Philosopher. [By Joseph Hallet.] 8vo. Pp. 38. [*Bodl.*] London, 1737

LETTER (a) to the most noble Thomas, Duke of Newcastle, on the dangers arising from Popery and disaffection; occasioned by the seizing of certain papers in a Popish chapel in the north-west highlands of Scotland. [By Michael Hughes.] 8vo. Pp. 30. [*D. Laing.*] London, 1747

LETTER (a) to the most reverend [John Potter] the Lord Archbishop of Canterbury, concerning the validity of lay-baptism; and of the baptisms of those who never had episcopal baptism nor ordination. [By the Hon. Archibald Campbell, Scottish episcopal Bishop.] 8vo. Pp. 66. [*Bodl.*] London, 1738
Signed: Philalethes.

LETTER (a) to the most reverend the Lord Archbishop of Canterbury, on the present opposition to any further reformation. [By John Disney, D.D.] 8vo. Pp. 23. London, 1774

LETTER (a) to the nobility, gentry, and landholders, of the county of Mayo, on the waste or misapplication of the county cess, or acre money; containing an account of an histro, comico, politico farce, performed in front of the Court-house in Castlebar, on Tuesday, the 16th of Oct., 1821. To the great surprise of a crowded audience, by a political bear. [By Benjamin Pemberton.] 8vo. Pp. iii. 47. [*Bodl.*] N.P. 1822

LETTER (a) to the Norfolk militia, upon the proceedings of ancient nations, when engaged in war. By a dumpling-eater [Rev. Thomas Stona, M.A.]. 8vo. [*Lond. Lib. Cat.*] London, 1759

LETTER (a) to the parishioners of St B[otolph], A[ldgate], recommending parochial communion at the approaching feast of Easter; and a conscientious payment of their accustom'd offerings. [Signed: S. B. *i.e.* Samuel Brewster.] 8vo. Pp. 16. [*Bodl.*] London, 1701

LETTER (a) to the parishioners of Walcot on the affairs of the parish. By the rector [Thomas Dehany Bernard]. 8vo. Bath, 1886

LETTER to the Peers, from a Peer's son, on the duty and necessity of immediate legislative interposition in behalf of the Church of Scotland, as determined by considerations of constitutional law. [By George Douglas Campbell, Marquis of Lorne, later Duke of Argyle.] 8vo. Pp. 101. [*New Coll. Lib.*] Edinburgh, 1842

LETTER (a) to the people of Aberdeen [regarding religious observances. By the Rev. —— Aitken]. 8vo. [*Aberd. Pub. Lib.*] Aberdeen, 1791

LETTER (a) to the people of England, occasion'd by the falling away of the clergy from the doctrines of the Reformation. [By Jonathan Warne.] 8vo. Pp. 39. [*Brit. Mus.*] London, 1735

Signed: Paulinus.

Attributed also to Robert Seagrave.

LETTER (a) to the people of England on the present situation and conduct of national affairs. Letter I. [By John Shebbeare, M.D.] Fourth edition. 8vo. Pp. 58. [*Brit. Mus.*] London, 1756

This letter was followed by five, if not seven others, from the same writer, on political and economic subjects.

LETTER (a) to the people of Great Britain and Ireland [concerning the Rebellion in 1745. By Rev. Daniel Noble, Dissenting minister]. 8vo. Pp. 34. London, 1746

LETTER (a) to the people of Ireland. By M. B. Draper (*sic*) [Jonathan Swift, D.D.]. 8vo. Pp. 16. Dublin, 1729

Letter signed: Publicola.

LETTER (a) to the people of Lancashire, concerning the future representation of the commercial interest. [By Sir James Phillips Kay-Shuttleworth, M.D.] 8vo. [*D. N. B.* vol. 30, p. 251.] Manchester, 1831

LETTER to the people of Laurencekirk, on occasion of presenting the King's charter, by which that village is erected into a free and independent Burgh of Barony; to which are subjoined, An abridgement of two letters published by Sir Richard Cox, containing an account of the establishment and progress of industry in his village near Corke in Ireland; —— the Guardian, No. 9; —— and, The clause of erection of Laurencekirk into a Burgh of Barony. [By Francis Garden, Lord Gardenstone.] 8vo. [*D. N. B.* vol. 20, p. 408.] Edinburgh, 1780

LETTER (a) to the people of the United States. . . . By John A. Than [John A. Lynch]. 8vo. [Cushing's *Init. and Pseud.* ii. 144.] Washington, 1872

LETTER (a) to the people, to be left for them at the booksellers: with a word or two of the Band-Box Plot. [By Sir Thomas Burnet, barrister.] 8vo. [*D. N. B.* vol. 7, p. 411.] London, 1710

LETTER (a) to the President of Harvard College. . . . By a member of the Corporation [Samuel Atkins Eliot]. 8vo. [*Brit. Mus.*] Cambridge, Mass., 1849

LETTER (a) to the President of the United States; from a refugee [Frederick Augustus Porter Barnard]. 8vo. [Cushing's *Init. and Pseud.* i. 249.] New York, 1863

LETTER (a) to the Prime Minister and the First Lord of the Admiralty from a Captain in the Royal Navy [James Manderson], on the extension of the naval establishments of the country. . . . 4to. Pp. 50. [*Brit. Mus.*] London, 1810

LETTER to the Prince of Wales, on the subject of the debts contracted by him since 1787. [By William Augustus Miles.] 8vo. [*D. N. B.* vol. 37, p. 380.] London, 1795

Thirteen editions were required.

LETTER (a) to the proprietors and directors of East India stock; together with an epistle dedicatory to Robert Gregory, Esq. chairman of the Court of Directors. . . . [By Captain Joseph Price.] 8vo. Pp. iii. 25. [*Brit. Mus.*] London, 1782; reprinted, 1783

LETTER (a) to the proprietors of East India stock, on the subject of Lord Clive's Jaghire, occasioned by his Lordship's Letter on that subject. [By John Dunning, Lord Ashburton.] 8vo. [*Brit. Mus.*] London, 1764

LETTER (a) to the proprietors of [East] India stock, relative to the critical situation of their affairs. [By E. Poulet?] 8vo. London, 1767

LETTER (a) to the Protestant Dissenting ministers, who lately solicited Parliament for further relief. [By John Butler, D.D., Bishop of Oxford, and afterwards of Hereford.] 8vo. Pp. 39. [*Brit. Mus.*] London, 1772

LETTER (a) to the "Public Advertiser." . . . [By John Dunning, Lord Ashburton?] 8vo. London, 1764

Ascribed also to Sir Philip Francis.

LETTER (a) to the public, containing the substance of what hath been offered in the late debates upon the subject of . . . clandestine marriages. [By S. Martin?] 8vo. London, 1753

LETTER (a) to the public meeting of the friends to the repeal of the Test and Corporation Acts, at the London Tavern, on February the 13th, 1790, from a lay Dissenter [Richard Sharp]. 8vo. Pp. 15. London, 1790

LETTER (a) to the publick on the present posture of affairs [in Ireland. By Gorges Edmond Howard]. 8vo. [*Brit. Mus.*] Dublin, 1754

Two other letters followed.

LETTER (a) to the publisher of the Quarterly Review, and of A dissertation on the course and probable termination of the Niger. By the author of that dissertation [Lieut. Gen. Sir Rufane Donkin]. 8vo. Pp. 58. London, 1829

LETTER (a) to the Queen, on the state of the Monarchy. By a Friend of the People [Henry Brougham, Lord Brougham]. 8vo. Pp. 46. [Thomas's *Bibl. List.* p. 11.] London, 1838

LETTER (a) to the rate-payers of Bodmin on the use to be made of the (old) Poor-House. . . . By a foe to ignorance [Henry Mudge, surgeon]. 8vo. [Boase and Courtney's *Bibl. Corn.*] Bodmin, 1840

LETTER (a) to the real and genuine Pierce Dod, M.D., actual physician of St Bartholomew's Hospital; plainly exposing the low absurdity or malice, of a late spurious pamphlet, falsely ascrib'd to that learned physician. . . . By Dod Pierce, M.S. [Dr Barrowby and Dr Schomberg, Junr.?]. 8vo. [*W.*] London, 1746

LETTER to the Reforming gentleman. [By Rev. Wm. Atkinson.] 8vo. Bradford, 1817

LETTER (a) to the representatives of Scotland in Parliament, respecting the state of our law, and the jurisdiction and duties of the Court of Session. By a Scottish barrister [John Borthwick]. 8vo. [*Nat. Lib. of Scot.*] Edinburgh, 1830

LETTER (a) to the representatives of the General Court, from the town of New Bedford. By a citizen [James B. Congdon]. 8vo. [Cushing's *Init. and Pseud.* i. 57.] New Bedford, 1847

LETTER (a) to the Reverend Andrew Croswell; occasioned by his Brief remarks on the satyrical drollery last Commencement Day. . . . By Simon the Tanner [Rev. Thomas Prentice]. 8vo. Pp. 42. [Cushing's *Init. and Pseud.* ii. 138.] Boston, 1771

LETTER (a) to the Rev. Andrew Thomson [D.D.], minister of St George's Church, on the respect due to national feeling. By Lucius [Joseph Hume, advocate]. The second edition. . . . 8vo. [*New Coll. Lib.*] Edinburgh, 1817

LETTER (a) to [Samuel Webster] the reverend author of the Winter-evening conversation on original sin; from one of his candid neighbours [Joseph Bellamy, D.D.]. 8vo. [Cushing's *Init. and Pseud.* ii. 111.] Boston, 1758

LETTER (a) to the Rev. Caleb Evans [in reply to his Scripture doctrine of the deity of the Son of God and Holy Spirit. By Edward Harwood]. 12mo. Pp. 28. [Whitley's *Bapt. Bibl.* i. 185.] 1766

LETTER (a) to the reverend clergy of both universities, concerning the Trinity and the Athanasian Creed; with reflections on all the late hypotheses. . . . [By Matthew Tindal.] 4to. [M'Lachlan's *Nonconformist Library*, p. 76.] 1694

Part of Third collection of tracts, 1695.

LETTER (a) to the Rev. Dr Adams of Shrewsbury; occasioned by the publication of his sermon, entitled, A test of true and false doctrines. By the author of *Pietas Oxoniensis* [Sir Richard Hill]. 8vo. Pp. 56. [*D. N. B.* vol. 26, p. 406.] London, 1770

Letter signed: Philalethes.

LETTER (a) to the Rev. Dr Bennet, rector of St Giles, Cripplegate, upon this question: Whether the people call'd Quakers, do not the nearest, of any other sect in religion, resemble the primitive Christians in principles and practice? Very necessary to be consider'd in this age. . . . By Aristobulus [Thomas Woolston]. 8vo. [Smith's *Cat. of Friends' Books*, i. 52.] London, 1720

LETTER (a) to the Rev. Dr Clark, rector of St James', Westminster. From the author of the *Scripture doctrine of the Holy Trinity, the Eucharist*, &c. [James Knight, D.D.]. Occasion'd by some passages in a Letter from Dr Clark to Dr Wells. 8vo. Pp. 51. [*Bodl.*] London, 1714

LETTER (a) to the Revd. Dr Cobden, rector of St Austins and St Faith's, and of Acton, and chaplain in ordinary to His Majesty, containing an exact copy of a pastoral epistle to the Protestant Dissenters in his parishes, with remarks thereon; wherein the guilt of our separation is endeavoured to be removed from the door of the Doctor; and some friendly advice tender'd to him. By a parishioner of the Doctor's [Caleb Fleming, D.D.]. 8vo. Pp. 38. London, 1738

LETTER (a) to the Rev. Dr Codex [Edmund Gibson], on the subject of his modest instruction to the Crown, inserted in the Daily Journal of Feb. 27th 1733. From the second volume of Burnet's History. [By William Arnall.] 8vo. Pp. 36. [Chalmers' *Biog. Dict.*; *D. N. B.* vol. 1, p. 203.] London, 1734

LETTER (a) to the Rev. Dr Conyers Middleton, occasioned by his late Free enquiry. [By John Wesley.] 8vo. London, 1749

LETTER (a) to the Rev. Dr Edmund Law, occasioned by his Discourse on the nature and end of death, and his appendix concerning the use of the word "Soul" in Scripture. . . . [By the Rev. John Bristed.] 8vo. Pp. 37. London, 1760

LETTER (a) to the Rev. Dr Edward Tenison, concerning some citations made from his Grace the Arch-Bishop of Canterbury's Preliminary discourse to the Apostolical Fathers, in a paper lately published, intituled, A letter to the Reverend the Prolocutor: being an answer to a Paper, &c. By the author of that Letter [Thomas Herne, M.A.]. 8vo. Pp. 22. [*Brit. Mus.*] London, 1718

LETTER (a) to the Rev. Dr Francis Atterbury; occasion'd by the doctrine lately deliver'd by him in a funeral-sermon on 1 Cor. 15. 19. August 30. 1706. [By Benjamin Hoadly.] 8vo. Pp. 16. [*Brit. Mus.*] London [1706]

LETTER (a) to the Reverend Dr Goddard [on his sermon at the installation of the Bishop of London]. By a layman [Thomas Sanden, M.D.]. 8vo. Chichester, 1815

LETTER (a) to the Rev. Dr Henry Sacheverell, on occasion of his sermon, and late sentence pass'd on him by the Honourable House of Lords. By a Cambridge-gentleman [—— Rawson]. 8vo. [Kennett's *Wisdom*, p. 30.] London, 1710

LETTER (a) to the Rev. Dr Inglis, author of An examination of Professor Stewart's Short statement of facts relative to the election of Mr Leslie. By a minister of the Church of Scotland, author of *A letter to Principal Hill on Professor Leslie's case* [Andrew Thomson, D.D.]. 8vo. Edinburgh, 1806

LETTER to the Revd. Dr [Robert] Lowth occasioned by his Letter to the author of The divine legation of Moses. [By John Brown, D.D.] 8vo. Pp. 44. [Kinsman's *Cat.* p. 25.] Newcastle-on-Tyne, 1766

LETTER (a) to the Rev. Dr Lowth, prebendary of Durham; in vindication of the conduct of the Fellows of New College in Oxford, in their late election of a Warden of Winchester. [By John Bridle, D.D., rector of Hardwick.] 8vo. London, 1758

Signed: O. W.

LETTER (a) to the Rev. Dr M. [Dr Thomas Morell] on the question of electing aliens into the vacant places in Eton College. By the author of *The extract* [Thomas Ashton, D.D.]. 4to. [Nichols' *Lit. Anec.* iii. 89.] London, 1771

LETTER (a) to the Rev. Dr [Thomas] Mangey; occasioned by his sermon on Christmas-day, entitled, Plain notions of our Lord's divinity. By Phileleutherus Cantabrigiensis [Thomas Herne, M.A.]. 8vo. [*Brit. Mus.*] London, 1719

This was followed in the same year, by "A second letter . . . on the eternal existence of our Lord. . . ."

LETTER (a) to the Rev. Dr [Thomas] Nowell; containing some remarks on certain alterations and additions in the second edition of his Answer to Pietas Oxoniensis. By the author of *Pietas Oxoniensis* [Sir Richard Hill]. 8vo. Pp. 45. London, 1769

LETTER (a) to the Rev. Dr Priestley. By an undergraduate [George Horne, D.D.]. 8vo. [*Brit. Mus.*] Oxford, 1787

LETTER (a) to the Rev. Dr Richard Watson, King's Professor of divinity in the University of Cambridge. [By William Vincent, D.D., Dean of Westminster.] 8vo. [Nichols' *Lit. Anec.* ix. 128; *D. N. B.* vol. 58, p. 363.] London, 1780

LETTER (a) to the Rev. Dr [John] Rogers, on occasion of his eight sermons, concerning the necessity of divine revelation; and the preface prefix'd to them. . . . [By Anthony Collins.] 8vo. Pp. 144. [*Brit. Mus.*] London, private print, 1727

LETTER (a) to the Rev. Dr Rutherforth, Archdeacon of Essex, &c.; occasioned by his Second vindication of the right of Protestant churches to require the clergy to subscribe to an established confession of faith and doctrines. From the examiner of the first [Benjamin Dawson, LL.D., rector of Burgh]. 8vo. Pp. 67. [*Brit. Mus.*] London, 1767

This was preceded by two similar examinations of Dr Rutherforth's argument. . . . See also "The Confessional. . . ."

LETTER (a) to the Rev. Dr Samuel Chandler, from the writer of the *History of the man after God's own heart* [Archibald Campbell]. 8vo. [*N. and Q.* 29th Sept. 1855, p. 255; *D. N. B.* vol. 8, p. 342.] 1762

LETTER (a) to the Rev. Dr Sherlock, one of the Committee of Convocation, appointed to draw up a representation concerning [Benjamin Hoadly] the Bishop of Bangor's Preservative and sermon; comparing the dangerous positions and doctrines contained in the Doctor's sermon, preach'd November 5th, 1712, with those charged upon the Bishop in the late report of the Committee. [By Arthur Ashley Sykes.] 8vo. Pp. 27. London, 1717

Signed: A. V.

LETTER (a) to the Rev. Dr S—k—y [Stukeley], on the first part of his Medallic history of Carausius, emperor of Britain, his ill grounded opinions and most extraordinary assertions therein contained. [By John Kennedy.] 4to. Pp. 9. [*Bodl.*] N.P., N.D.

LETTER (a) to the Rev. Dr [Andrew] Snape; wherein the authority of the Christian priesthood is maintain'd, the uninterrupted succession of bishops from the Apostles days is lineally deduced; and the cavils of hereticks and fanaticks are answer'd. By a curate of Wilts [William Fleetwood, D.D.]. 8vo. Pp. 68. [*New Coll. Lib.*] London, 1718

Signed: S. T.

LETTER (a) to the Rev. Dr Thomas Leland, Fellow of Trinity College, Dublin; in which his late Dissertation on the principles of human eloquence is criticized; and the Bishop of Gloucester's idea of the nature and character of an inspired language, as delivered in his Lordship's Doctrine of grace, is vindicated from all the objections of the learned author of the Dissertation. [By Richard Hurd, D.D.] 8vo. Pp. 80. [Nichols' *Lit. Anec.* ii. 433.] London, 1764

LETTER (a) to the Rev. Dr [Joseph] Trapp; occasioned by a late pamphlet, entituled, The true spirit of the Methodists, &c., supposed to be written by the Doctor himself: wherein T. S—y's [Story's] charge of Deism in the Congratulatory letter, against the Four sermons, is further enforced, and fully confirmed, out of the Reply to Mr Seagrave's Answer. . . . By T. S—y, Esq. [Richard Finch]. 8vo. [Smith's *Cat. of Friends' Books*, i. 609-10.] London, 1740

This afterwards formed part of a volume entitled, "Tracts,—By Richard Finch."

LETTER (a) to the Rev. Dr [Josiah] Tucker in reply to An apology for the present Church of England . . . occasioned by the Petition for abolishing subscriptions. [By Rev. John Bristed.] 8vo. Gloucester, 1772

LETTER (a) to the Rev. Dr [Daniel] Waterland concerning the nature and value of sincerity; with some remarks on his treatment of it, in a late treatise, entitled The importance of the doctrine of the Holy Trinity asserted. [By Phillips Glover.] 8vo. Pp. 31. [Darling's *Cyclop. Bibl.*] London, 1734

LETTER (a) to the Rev. Dr Waterland, occasioned by his late writings in defence of the Athanasian hypothesis. By Philanthropus Oxoniensis [Thomas Morgan, M.D.]. 8vo. Pp. 27. [*D. N. B.* vol. 39, p. 35.] London, 1722

LETTER (a) to the Rev. Frederick T. Gray . . . at the "Bullfinch Street Church." By a proprietor of said Church [Benjamin B. Mussey]. 8vo. [Cushing's *Init. and Pseud.* i. 241.] Boston, 1842

LETTER (a) to the Rev. George Harris, containing an examination of the arguments adduced in his lectures to prove the non-existence of the devil. [By James Barr, D.D.] 8vo. Pp. 51. [*New Coll. Lib.*] Liverpool, 1820

The letter is signed: Aliquis.

LETTER (a) to the Rev. Henry Budd . . . in consequence of his having adopted, in his recent work on infant baptism, the Socinian view of the Lord's Supper. By a friend [John Dennis]. 8vo. London, 1828

Attestation of authorship by an intimate friend.

LETTER (a) to the Rev. Henry Hart Milman, M.A. reputed author of a History of the Jews, in the fifth, sixth, and seventh volumes of the Family Library: deprecating the republication of that work. By "one who is also an elder" [Richard Mant, D.D., Bishop of Down and Connor]. 8vo. Pp. 22. [*Bodl.*] Oxford, 1830

See note to "The history of the Jews."

LETTER (a) to the Rev. Hugh Blair, D.D., one of the ministers of Edinburgh; on the improvement of psalmody in Scotland. [By James Beattie, LL.D.] 12mo. Pp. 31. N.P. 1778

Not published. Reprinted at Edinburgh in 1829, with the author's name.

LETTER (a) to the Rev. Hugh M'Neile, A.M., rector of Albury, Surrey ; in reply to objections to the present miraculous manifestations in the Church. . . . By a member of the Church of England [William Tarbet]. 12mo. Pp. 46. Liverpool, 1832

The writer afterwards joined the Catholic Apostolic Church.

LETTER (a) to the Rev. James Ibbetson, D.D., occasioned by a third edition of his Plea for the subscription of the clergy to the Thirty-nine Articles of religion ; in which the present scheme of petitioning the Parliament for relief in the matter of subscription is occasionally defended. By a clergyman of the Church of England [Rev. John Firebrace]. 8vo. [*Mon. Rev.* xlv. 403, 405.] London, 1771

LETTER to the Rev. John Cumming, D.D., on the subject of his lecture entitled God in science. [Signed: W. D. *i.e.* W. Davidson.] 8vo. Pp. 47. London, 1851

Presentation copy with the author's name.

LETTER (a) to the Reverend John Martin ; occasioned by his intended speech on the repeal of the Test and Corporation Acts. By no reverend Dissenter [—— Allum, of Southwark]. 8vo. Pp. 32. [*Bodl.*] London, N.D.

LETTER (a) to the Rev. John Smith, D.D., containing a few strictures on his Life of St Columba. [Signed: A. C. *i.e.* Alexander Cameron, Bishop of Maximianopolis.] 8vo. Edinburgh, 1798

LETTER (a) to the Rev. John Tod Brown. [By Henry Beveridge, advocate, of Inzievar.] 8vo. [Beveridge's *Dunfermline Bibl.*] Dunfermline, 1839

Signed: A Church extensionist.

LETTER (a) to the Rev. John Wesley, occasioned by his Calm address to the American Colonies. By a lover of truth and the British constitution [Caleb Evans, D.D.]. 12mo. [Whitley's *Bapt. Bibl.* i. 198.] London, 1775

Signed: Americanus.

LETTER (a) to the Rev. Josiah Tucker, Dean of Gloucester, occasioned by his Apology for the present Church of England. [By William Hopkins, B.A., Vicar of Bolney.] 8vo. [*D. N. B.* vol. 27, p. 339.] London, 1772

See also "A letter to the Rev. Dr Tucker. . . ."

LETTER (a) to the Reverend Master of Trinity College in Cambridge, editor of a new Greek and Latin Testament. [By Richard Bentley.] The second edition. 4to. Pp. 23. [Bartholomew's *Bentley Bibliography*, p. 23.] London, 1721

Signed: Philalethes.

LETTER (a) to the Rev. Mr Bate, rector of St Paul, Deptford ; occasioned by his book, intitled, Infidelity scourged, or Christianity vindicated, &c. . . . By the author of *Free and impartial thoughts*, etc. [Richard Finch]. 8vo. [Smith's *Cat. of Friends' Books*, i. 62, 610.] London, 1746

LETTER (a) to the Rev. Mr Brydges, rector of Croscombe, occasion'd by a sermon preach'd at that place, by Mr [Samuel] H[ill], Archdeacon of W[ell]s ; being a vindication of the Dissenters. By a student of the Temple [Jonathan Bleuman]. 8vo. [Green's *Bibl. Somers.* ii. 204; *D. N. B.* vol. 26, p. 421.] London, 1715

LETTER (a) to the Reverend Mr Dean Swift, occasioned by a satyre said to be written by him [but really by Thomas Gordon], entitled A dedication to a great man concerning dedications. . . . By a sparkish pamphleteer of Button's Coffee-house [Dr John Arbuthnot]. Pp. 11. [*Camb. Hist. of Eng. Lit.*] N.P. [1719]

LETTER (a) to the Reverend Mr George Whitefield. By Canonicus [Rev. Charles Chauncy]. 8vo. [Evans' *Amer. Bibl.* vol. 2, p. 232.] Boston, 1743

This was followed by "A second letter. . . ."

LETTER (a) to the Rev. Mr George Whitefield, publickly calling upon him to vindicate his conduct or confess his faults. By K. L. [Charles Chauncy, D.D.]. 8vo. [Evans' *Amer. Bibl.*] Boston, 1745

LETTER (a) to the Rev. Mr James Adams at Kinnaird ; occasion'd by his Survey of Professor Campbel's Oration. [By Robert Lyon.] 8vo. Edinburgh, 1734

Signed: Anti-Tindalian.

LETTER (a) to the Rev. Mr James Fisher, minister of the Gospel in the Associate congregation at Glasgow: containing remarks upon his Review of a pamphlet intituled, A serious enquiry into the burgess oaths of Edinburgh, Perth and Glasgow: wherein the fallacy of the reviewer's reasoning is discovered, and the Enquiry is further confirmed. By the author of the foresaid enquiry [Andrew Stevenson]. 12mo. Pp. 40. [*New Coll. Lib.*] Edinburgh, 1747

The letter is signed: A—w S—n.

LETTER (a) to the Reverend Mr James Grant at his chapel in Skinners-Close, Ed. [Edinburgh. By Rev. William Abernethy - Drummond, afterwards Bishop]. 8vo. Pp. 8. [*New Coll. Lib.*] Edinburgh, 1748

Signed : Philalethes.

LETTER (a) to the Rev. Mr Jebb, with relation to his declared sentiments about the unlawfulness of all religious addresses to Christ Jesus. [By Robert Findlay, D.D.] 8vo. [Orme's *Bibl. Bib.*] London, 1778

Signed : Philalethes.
A second letter was appended to "Remarks on Mr [Theophilus] Lindsey's Dissertation upon praying to Christ. . . ."

LETTER (a) to the Rev. Mr John Stirling, Principal of the University of Glasgow, relating to Mr John Elder's case, now before the venerable Assembly. [By David Dickson, M.D.] 4to. Pp. 8. N.P. [1711]

No title-page.

LETTER (a) to the Rev. Mr John Wesley, in answer to his late [anonymous] pamphlet entitled, Free thoughts on the present state of public affairs. [By Joseph Towers, LL.D.] 8vo. [*Brit. Mus.*] London, 1771

LETTER (a) to the Rev. Mr John Wesley ; in vindication of the doctrines of absolute . . . election, particular redemption, etc. [By Anne Dutton.] 8vo. Pp. 88. [*Brit. Mus.*] London, 1742

LETTER (a) to the Rev. Mr [William] Law, on the cause between the English Universities and [Benjamin Hoadly] the Bishop of Bangor. [By Nicholas Amhurst.] 8vo. London, 1719

LETTER (a) to the Rev. Mr [Edmund] Massey, occasioned by his late wonderful sermon against inoculation. [By Charles Maitland, surgeon.] 8vo. [*Brit. Mus.*] London, 1822

Controversial pamphlets were continued on both sides.

LETTER (a) to the Rev. Mr [Thomas] Pyle, occasion'd by his exceptions against Mr Law's First letter to the Bishop of Bangor ; to which is annex'd, a postscript in answer to Mr Pyle's challenge. By P. F. Minister of the Church of England [P. Fuller]. 8vo. London, 1718

LETTER (a) to the Rev. Mr [Henry] Stebbing ; being remarks upon his late book relating to sincerity : with a postscript concerning the authority of the Church. By a Christian [Rev. George Legh, LL.D.]. 8vo. Pp. 28. [*New Coll. Lib.*] London, 1718

LETTER to the Rev. Mr T. Warton, on his late edition of Milton's juvenile poems. [By Rev. Samuel Darby, M.A., rector of Whatfield.] 8vo. [*N. and Q.* 1862, p. 451.] London, 1785

LETTER (a) to the Rev. Mr Thomas Carte, author of the Full answer to the Letter from a Bystander : in which several important and interesting facts respecting the revenues and civil government of England are elucidated. By a gentleman of Cambridge [Corbyn Morris]. Second edition. 8vo. [*Camb. Univ. Lib.*] London, 1744

LETTER (a) to the Rev. Mr Tong, Mr Robinson, Mr Smith, & Mr Reynolds ; occasion'd by the late differences amongst the Dissenters : wherein is consider'd the regard Dissenters ought to pay to human forms in matters of faith ; with some general remarks on their late book. . . . By a layman [Samuel Saunders]. 8vo. [*New Coll. Lib.*] London, 1719

LETTER (a) to the Rev. Mr [John Wesley. By George Fisher [Rev. Mr —— Baily, of Cork]. 8vo. Cork, 1750

LETTER (a) to the Rev. Mr William Holmes of Antrim, concerning his Impartial reflections upon Mr [James] Duchal's Remarks upon an Answer to a Letter from a gentleman to a subscribing minister. By H. B. [Hugh Blair], of Belfast, layman. 8vo. [Witherow's *Lit. of Presb. in Ireland*, ii. 23.] Belfast, 1732

LETTER (a) to the Rev. Mr William Warburton, A.M. occasioned by some passages in his book entituled, The divine legation of Moses demonstrated. By a gentleman of Lincolns-Inn [Philip Carteret Webb]. 8vo. Pp. 63. [Nichols' *Lit. Anec.* ii. 280.] London, 1742

LETTER (a) to the R-v-r-nd Pr-nc-p-l H-ll [Hill] on some of the proceedings of the last G-n-rl Ass-mbly of the Ch-rch of Sc-tl-nd. [By Andrew Thomson, D.D., of St George's Church.] 8vo. Pp. 40. [*New Coll. Lib.*] Edinburgh, 1803

LETTER (a) to the Rev. Principal Hill, on the case of Mr John Leslie, professor of mathematics in the University of Edinburgh. By the author of *Two letters to Principal Hill*, etc. [Andrew Thomson, D.D.]. 8vo. [*New Coll. Lib.*] Edinburgh, 1805

LETTER (a) to the Rev. Professor Campbell; whereto is subjoin'd remarks on his Vindication of the Apostles from enthusiasm, and on his preface thereto; wherein is shown the Apostles and disciples of our Lord did not reckon him an impostor, betwixt his death and resurrection or after. . . . By W. S., M. P. [William Stewart, minister at Perth]. 8vo. Pp. 74. [*New Coll. Lib.*] Glasgow, 1731

LETTER (a) to the Rev. Richard Warner. [By Rev. Thomas Falconer, A.M., M.D.] 8vo. [*Brit. Mus.*] Bath, 1804

LETTER to the Rev. Richard Watson. [By W. Vincent.] 8vo. [Bartholomew's *Camb. Books.*] London, 1780

LETTER to the Rev. Robert Burns, D.D., F.S.A. and the Rev. William Hamilton, D.D. occasioned by their late publications, entitled, The Gareloch heresy tried, and Remarks on certain opinions recently propagated, respecting universal redemption, &c. By a lay member of the Church of Scotland [Thomas Carlyle, advocate]. 12mo. Pp. 12. [Boase's *Cath. Apost. Lit.*] Greenock, 1830

LETTER (a) to the Rev. Robert S. Candlish. By a parishioner of St George's parish, Edinburgh [James Bryce, D.D.]. 8vo. [*New Coll. Lib.*] Edinburgh [1841]

LETTER (a) to the Rev. the President and Fellows of Sion College, upon occasion of the address lately presented to the Bishop of London. [By Arthur Ashley Sykes, D.D.] 8vo. Pp. 37. [Disney's *Memoir of Sykes*, p. xx.] London, 1736

LETTER (a) to the Rev. the Prolocutor; being an answer to a paper, advertised as published in the Post-Boy of April 3d, 1718, intituled, A letter from the Prolocutor, to the Reverend Dr Edward Tenison, Arch-Deacon of Carmarthen. By a gentleman of Cambridge [Thomas Herne, M.A.]. 8vo. Pp. 39. [*Brit. Mus.*] London, 1718

LETTER (a) to the Rev. the Vice-Chancellor of the University of Oxford on the present state of theology in the Universities and the Church of England, and on the causes of existing scepticism and infidelity. By Clericus [Rev. Augustus Clissold]. 8vo. [*W.*] Oxford, 1856

LETTER (a) to the Rev. Thomas Coke, LL.D. and Mr Henry Moore; to which is added an appeal and remonstrance to the people called Methodists. [Attributed to J. A. Colet.] 8vo. [Lowndes' *Bibl. Man.* p. 2876.] London, 1792

LETTER (a) to the Rev. Thomas Fothergill, A.M. Fellow of Queen's College, Oxford, relating to his sermon preached before that University 30th Jan. 1753, upon the reasonableness and uses of commemorating King Charles's martyrdom. [By Ralph Heathcote, D.D.] 8vo. [Nichols' *Lit. Anec.* iii. 536.] London, 1753

LETTER (a) to the Rev. W. J. E. Bennett. . . . I. It being a reply to a note of his on auricular confession, and to be found in his work on the Eucharist, annexed to p. 145. II. Shewing the infallibility and divine origin of the Catholic Church in communion with the see of Rome. By Verax, a Catholic layman [M. D. Talbot]. 8vo. [*Brit. Mus.*] London, 1847

LETTER (a) to the Rev. Walter F. Hook, M.A., on his Inaugural discourse. By an Observer [Rev. William Vevers, Wesleyan]. 8vo. Pp. 32. [Osborn's *Method. Lit.* p. 193.] Leeds, 1837

LETTER (a) to the Rev. William Cockburne. . . . By one of the Magistrates of the Public Office in Great Marlborough Street [Philip Neve]. 8vo. London, 1804

LETTER (a) to the reviewers, occasioned by their account of a book called Memoirs containing the lives of several ladies of Great Britain. . . . [By Thomas Amory.] 8vo. London, 1755

The "Memoirs" is also anonymous: see the entry.

LETTER (a) to the Rt. Hon. and Hon. the Members of both Houses of Parliament regarding the doctrines of the Established Church. By the author of *An apology of an Officer for withdrawing from the profession of arms* [Thomas Thrush]. 8vo. Pp. 14. [*Brit. Mus.*] Harrogate, 1836

LETTER (a) to the Right Honourable Baron Brougham and Vaux, Lord High Chancellor of Great Britain, on the proposed suppression of one of the Colleges of Aberdeen. By Ignotus [Rev. Robert Cruickshank]. 8vo. Pp. 60. [Anderson's *Aberd. Univ. Bibl.* p. 451.] Aberdeen, 1833

LETTER to the Right Hon. Benjamin Disraeli [in verse. By Edward James Mortimer Colliers]. 8vo. [*D. N. B.* vol. 11, p. 373.] London, 1869

LETTER (a) to the Right Hon. Charles James Fox on . . . his conduct upon the charges made by Mr Paull against the Marquis of Wellesley. . . . By a lover of consistency [James Paull, M.P., himself]. 8vo. [*D. N. B.* vol. 44, p. 99.] London, 1806

LETTER (a) to the Right Hon. Charles James Fox upon the dangerous and inflammatory tendency of his late conduct in Parliament; in which the principles, the duties, and the composition of minorities are particularly considered. By the author of the first letter [Richard Bentley, jun.]. 8vo. [*Brit. Mus.*] London, 1793

LETTER (a) to the Right Hon. Charles Jenkinson. [By John Almon.] 4to. [Watt's *Bibl. Brit.*] London, 1781

LETTER (a) to the Right Honourable Charles Jenkinson, Esq. . . . animadverting on the late mutinies in the Highland Regiments. By the translator of the *Caledonian bards* [John Clark, F.S.A.]. Second edition. 8vo. Pp. 31. [*Brit. Mus.*] Edinburgh, 1780

LETTER (a) to the Right Hon. E. G. Stanley. . . . By an emigrant [Adam Thom]. 8vo. Montreal, 1854

LETTER (a) to the Right Honourable Earl Grey, occasioned by his Lordships speech in the House of Lords, on moving the second reading of his bill for abrogating the declarations contained in the 25th and 30th of Charles II., commonly called "The test against Popery." By a clergyman of the diocese of Durham [Thomas Le Mesurier, B.D.]. 8vo. Pp. 54. [*Bodl.*] Durham, 1819

Attributed also to Henry Phillpotts, afterwards Bishop of Exeter. [*D. N. B.*]

LETTER (a) to the Right Hon. Earl Grey, on the obligation of the coronation oath. By one of His Majesty's chaplains [Hon. Arthur Philip Perceval]. 8vo. Pp. 16. London, 1833

LETTER (a) to the Right Hon. Edmund Burke. [By Sir Brooke Boothby.] 8vo. [*Brit. Mus.*] London, 1791

LETTER (a) to the Rt. Hon. Edmund Burke, in reply to the insinuations in the ninth report of the select committee, which affect the character of Mr Hastings. By J. S. [Major John Scott, later John Scott Waring]. 4to. Pp. 44. [*Bodl.*] London, 1783

LETTER (a) to the Right Hon. Edmund Burke, on the present state of Ireland. [By John Philpot Curran.] 8vo. [*Camb. Univ. Lib.*] Dublin, 1795

Authorship attested by a contemporary hand.

LETTER (a) to the Right Honourable George Canning on his proposed motion in favour of Catholic Emancipation. [By Thomas Lewis O'Beirne, D.D., Bishop of Meath.] 8vo. Pp. 67. [*D. N. B.* vol. 41, p. 305.] London, 1812

LETTER (a) to the Right Hon. George Canning, M.P. on the origin and continuation of the war with America. By Ulysses [Samuel Collcton Graves]. 8vo. [*Biog. Dict.* 1816, p. 433.] London, 1814

LETTER (a) to the Right Hon. George Canning on the principle and the administration of the English poor laws. By a select vestryman of the parish of Putney, under the 59 Geo. 3, Cap. 12. [Rev. William Carmalt]. 8vo. Pp. 109. London, 1823

LETTER to the Rt. Hon. George Grenville occasioned by his publication of the speech he made in the House of Commons on the motion for expelling Mr Wilkes, Friday, February 3, 1769; to which is added a Letter on the public conduct of Mr Wilkes first published November 1, 1768, with an appendix. [By John Almon.] 8vo. [*W.*] London, 1769

LETTER (a) to the Right Honourable Henry Dundas, of Melville, Esq., Lord-Advocate of Scotland. [By Hugh Arnot.] 4to. [*Cat. of Lond. Inst.* ii. 512.] Edinburgh, 1777

LETTER (a) to the Rt. Hon. Henry Dundas on the situation of the East-India Company. [By the Right Hon. George Tierney.] 4to. [*Brit. Mus.*] London, 1791

LETTER (a) to the Right Hon. Henry Erskine, Lord Advocate of Scotland, relative to the Act of Parliament for regulating the police of Edinburgh. [By Robert Forsyth, advocate.] 8vo. Pp. 30. Edinburgh, 1806

Signed: Civis.

LETTER (a) to the Right Hon. John Musgrove, Lord Mayor of London . . . [on the office of Coroner. By William Payne]. 8vo. London, 1851

LETTER (a) to the Right Hon. Lord Holland, on foreign politics. [By Lord John Russell.] Second edition. 8vo. Pp. 47. [*Brit. Mus.*] London, 1819

Later editions give the author's name.

LETTER to the Right Hon. Lord John Russell, M.P., on the constitutional defects of the University and Colleges of Oxford; with suggestions for a Royal Commission of inquiry into the Universities. By a member of the Oxford Convocation [Rev. Charles Adolphus Row]. 8vo. Pp. iv. 59. London, 1850

LETTER (a) to the Right Hon. Lord John Russell . . . on the present state of affairs in Gibraltar. [By Charles Blake.] 8vo. [*Brit. Mus.*] London, 1855

Signed: A merchant.

LETTER to the Right Hon. Lord Lyndhurst, on the appointment of Sheriffs in Ireland, under the Earl of Mulgrave. By a barrister [Henry H. Joy]. 8vo. London, 1838

LETTER (a) to the Right Hon. Lord Viscount H—e [Howe] on his naval conduct in the American war. [By Joseph Galloway.] 8vo. Pp. 50. [Rich's *Bibl. Amer.* i. 275.] London, 1779

LETTER (a) to the Right Hon. Lord Viscount Howick, on the subject of the Catholic bill. By the author of *Unity the bond of peace*, *The influence of Christianity on the military and moral character of a soldier*, etc. [J. Symons, B.D., rector of Whitburn, Durham]. 8vo. Pp. 41. [*Brit. Crit.* xxix. 316.] London, 1807

The works named are not anonymous.

LETTER (a) to the Right Hon. Lord Viscount Melville, Secretary of state, and keeper of His Majesty's signet, for Scotland. By a member of the honourable Society of Writers to the Signet [William Jamieson]. 8vo. Pp. vii. 138. [*Edin. Univ. Lib.*] Edinburgh, 1814

LETTER (a) to the Right Hon. my Lord Chief Justice Holt, occasioned by the noise of a plot. [By Robert Ferguson.] 4to. Pp. 31. N.P., N.D.

Letter dated August 22. 1694. No title-page. Included by Ferguson in his list of his own tracts in Smith MS. xxxi. p. 30.

LETTER (a) to the Right Hon. Robert Peel, M.P. for the University of Oxford, on the pernicious effects of a variable standard of value, especially as it regards the condition of the lower orders and the poor laws. By one of his constituents [Rev. Edward Copleston, D.D., Bishop of Llandaff]. Second edition. 8vo. [*D. N. B.* vol. 12, p. 175.] Oxford, 1819

LETTER (a) to the Right Hon. Robert Peel, on the courts of law in Scotland. [By James Bridges.] 8vo. Pp. 75. [*Nat. Lib. of Scot.*] Edinburgh, 1823

LETTER (a) to the Right Hon. Robert Peel, on the subject of the London University. By Christianus [Rev. George D'Oyly, D.D.]. 8vo. London, 1828

LETTER (a) to the Right Hon. Sir John Sinclair, Bart. on the subject of his remarks on Mr Huskisson's pamphlet. By a country gentleman [William Kingsman, of Petworth]. 8vo. [*N. and Q.* 1867, p. 292.] London, 1811

LETTER (a) to the Right Honourable Sir Robert Peel . . . on the political aspect of Popery. By Britannicus [B. Richings]. 8vo. Pp. 34. [*Brit. Mus.*] London, 1837

LETTER (a) to the Right Hon. Sir R—— W—— [Robert Walpole], &c. upon the present posture of affairs; wherein, amongst other things, the Convention will be set in a clear light. . . . By Caleb Danvers, Esq. [Nicholas Amhurst, or Amherst]. 8vo. Pp. 30. London, 1739

LETTER (a) to the Right Hon. the Earl of . . . concerning the affair of Elizabeth Canning. By a clergyman. [Really by Allan Ramsay, artist.] 8vo. [*Brit. Mus.*] London, 1753

LETTER (a) to the Right Honourable the Earl of Eldon on the justice and expediency of removing the Catholic disabilities. By a Protestant Layman [James Whishaw, Barrister]. 8vo. Pp. 16. [*Brit. Mus.*] London, 1829

LETTER (a) to the Right Hon. the Earl of Minto. By Rusticus [William Scott, of Teviot Bank]. 8vo. [Sinton's *Bibl. of Hawick.*] Hawick, 1832

LETTER (a) to the Right Hon. the Earl of Nottingham; occasioned by a late motion made by the Archdeacon of London, at his visitation, for the city clergy to return their thanks to his Lordship for his Answer to Mr Whiston. By a curate of London [Arthur Ashley Sykes, D.D.]. Second edition. 8vo. Pp. 40. [Disney's *Memoir of Sykes*, p. xv.] London, 1721

LETTER (a) to the Right Hon. the Lord B——y [Blakeney]; being an inquiry into the merits of his defence of Minorca. [By Israel Mauduit.] 8vo. [*Mon. Rev.* xvii. 245.] London, 1757

LETTER (a) to the Right Hon. the Lord Brougham and Vaux, etc. on the late decision of the Earldom of Devon. [By Sir Thomas Christopher Banks.] 8vo. [*Gent. Mag.* Feb. 1855, p. 207.] London, 1831

LETTER (a) to the Right Hon. the Lord Chancellor, concerning the mode of swearing, by laying the hand upon, and kissing the Gospels. By a Protestant [Rev. David Wilson, Presbyterian minister in London]. . . . 8vo. Pp. 40. [*New Coll. Lib.*] London, 1768

LETTER (a) to the Right Hon. the Lord-Chief-Justice King, on his Lordship's being designed a Peer. [By Henry Gally, D.D.] 4to. [*Camb. Univ. Lib.*] London, 1725

LETTER (a) to the Right Hon. the Lord Mayor, on the state of the country . . . and his Lordship's duty at the present crisis. [By Anthony Robinson.] 8vo. London, 1799

LETTER (a) to the Right Hon. the Lord Mayor, the worshipful aldermen, and the Common Council, the merchants, citizens and inhabitants of the City of London. . . . From an old servant [George Heathcote]. 8vo. [*Brit. Mus.*] London, 1762

LETTER (a) to the Right Hon. the Lord North, Chancellor of the University of Oxford, concerning subscription to the xxxix Articles, and particularly the undergraduate subscription in the University. By a member of Convocation, [generally supposed to be George Horne, D.D., president of Magdalen College]. With a preface and notes by the editor [Vaughan Thomas, D.D.]. 8vo. Pp. xxi. 48. [*Bodl.*] Oxford, 1834

The editor's name is in the handwriting of Dr Bliss. The first edition was published in 1773.

Ascribed also to Thomas Patten, D.D.

LETTER (a) to the Right Hon. the Lord * * *, occasion'd by a pamphlet, just publish'd, entitled, Thoughts on the affairs of Ireland, with an account of the expulsion of A—r J—s N—ll, Esq.; late surveyor and engineer-general, from the Hon. the H—se of C-mm-ns in that kingdom. By M. B., Drapier [Jonathan Swift, D.D.]. 8vo. Pp. 26. [*Brit. Mus.*] London, 1754

The "Drapier" issued other letters.

LETTER (a) to the Right Honourable the Lord Provost of Edinburgh, on the seat-rents of the City Churches, etc. By a member of the Presbytery of Edinburgh [Alex. Lockhart Simpson, D.D., minister at Kirknewton]. 8vo. Pp. 26. [Scott's *Fasti.*] Edinburgh, 1834

LETTER (a) to the Right Hon. the Lord Provost of Edinburgh, relative to the election of a professor of logic in the University of Edinburgh. [By Alexander Peterkin, Sheriff-substitute of Orkney.] 8vo. Pp. 9. [Edinburgh, 1836]

Signed: Alumnus Edinensis.

LETTER (a) to the Right Hon. T. Spring Rice, Chancellor of Her Majesty's Exchequer . . . containing a new principle of currency, and plan for a national system of banking. By a Liverpool merchant [John Hall]. 8vo. [*Brit. Mus.*] London, 1837

LETTER (a) to the Right Hon. William Pitt, on the influence of the stoppage of issues on specie at the Bank of England, on the prices of provisions, and other commodities. The second edition, corrected. By Walter Boyd, Esq. M.P. [William Combe]. 8vo. Pp. viii. 112. [*Bodl.*]. London, 1811

LETTER (a) to the Right Hon. William Wickham, chief secretary to His Excellency the Lord Lieutenant of Ireland, and one of His Majesty's most honourable Privy Council, etc. on the subject of Mr Scully's advice to his Catholic brethren. By a yeoman [Sir William Cusack Smith, second Baronet]. Third edition, with additions. 8vo. Pp. 65. [*Brit. Mus.*] Dublin, 1803

LETTER to the Right Hon. Willoughby Bertie, by descent Lord Norreys, High Steward of Abingdon and Wallingford; in which his Lordship's candid and liberal treatment of the new Earl of Mansfield is fully vindicated. [By Dr Lind.] 8vo. Pp. xi. 86. [Rich's *Bibl. Amer.* i. 472.] London, 1778

LETTER (a) to [Dr William Warburton] the Right Rev. author of The divine legation of Moses demonstrated; in answer to the appendix to the fifth volume of that work: with an appendix, containing a former literary correspondence. By a late professor in the University of Oxford [Robert Lowth, D.D.]. Second edition. 8vo. Pp. 136. [*Brit. Mus.*] London, 1766

LETTER (a) to the Right Reverend Bishop Hobart, occasioned by the strictures on Bible Societies contained in his late charge to the Convention of New York. By a Churchman of the diocese of New York [William Jay]. 8vo. [Cushing's *Init. and Pseud.* i. 57.] New York, 1822

LETTER (a) to the Right Rev. Dr William Cleaver, Lord Bishop of Chester; on the subject of two sermons addressed by him to the clergy of his diocese: comprehending also a vindication of the late Bishop Hoadly. [By Robert Edward Garnham.] 8vo. Pp. 43. London, 1790

LETTER (a) to the Right Rev. Doctor Wiseman, on transubstantiation. By Herman Heinfetter [Frederick Parker], author of *Rules for ascertaining the sense conveyed in ancient Greek manuscripts*, etc. 12mo. Pp. 15. [*Brit. Mus.*] London, 1848

LETTER (a) to the Right Rev. Father in God, Shute [Barrington], Lord Bishop of Landaff, from a petitioner [Benjamin Thomas]. 8vo. Pp. 51. Marlborough, 1774

LETTER (a) to the Right Rev. John [Kaye], Bishop of Bristol, respecting an additional examination of students in the University of Cambridge, and the different plans proposed for that purpose. By Philograntus [James Henry Monk, D.D., later Bishop of Gloucester]. 8vo. Pp. 63. [*D. N. B.* vol. 38, p. 175.] London, 1822

LETTER (a) to the Right Rev. Levi Silliman Ives, of the Protestant Episcopal Church in the State of Carolina, occasioned by his late address to the Convention of his diocese. By a Protestant Episcopalian [William Jay]. 8vo. Pp. 32. [Cushing's *Init. and Pseud.* ii. 125.] New York, 1847

LETTER (a) to the Right Rev. Lewis [Bagot], by divine permission, Lord Bishop of Norwich, requesting his Lordship to name the prelate, to whom he referred, as "contending strenuously for the general excellence of our present authorised translation of the Bible." [By Robert Edward Garnham.] 8vo. Pp. 18. [*Camb. Univ. Lib.*] London, 1789

Letter signed: Terræ Filius.

LETTER (a) to the Right Reverend Richard [Beadon] Lord Bishop of Bath and Wells. By the author of *An essay on light reading* [Edward Mangin]. 8vo. [Green's *Bibl. Somers.* i. 334.] Bath, 1819

LETTER (a) to the Right Rev. Richard [Bagot], Lord Bishop of Oxford, on certain passages in his recent charge. By a Churchman [Rev. Robert Wood Kyle]. 8vo. [*Mendham Collection Cat. Supp.*, p. 18.] London, 1842

LETTER (a) to the Right Rev. Samuel [Horsley], Lord Bishop of St David's, on the charge he lately delivered to the clergy of his diocese. By a Welch freeholder [David Jones, of Llandovery]. 8vo. Pp. 31. [Murch's *Dissenters*, p. 518; *Mon. Rev.* iv. 349.] London, 1790

LETTER (a) to the R. R. the Archbishops and Bishops of England; pointing out the only sure means of preserving the Church from the dangers that now threaten her. By an upper-graduate [Alexander Geddes, LL.D.]. 8vo. Pp. 25. [*Brit. Mus.*] London, 1790

LETTER (a) to the Right Rev. [Edmund Law] the Lord Bishop of Carlisle; containing a few remarks on some passages of his Lordship's pamphlet, entitled, Considerations on the propriety of requiring a subscription to articles of faith. [By Joseph Cornish.] 8vo. Pp. 78. [Murch's *Dissenters*, p. 341.] London, 1777

LETTER (a) to the Right Rev. [Robert Clayton] the Lord Bishop of Clogher, occasioned by his lordship's Essay on spirit. . . . [By Richard Moseley.] 8vo. London, 1752

LETTER (a) to the Right Rev. [William Warburton] the Lord Bishop of Gloucester, in which The divine legation of Moses is vindicated, as well from the misapprehensions of his Lordship's friends, as the misrepresentations of his enemies; and in which his Lordship's merits as a writer are clearly proved to be far superior to the encomiums of his warmest admirers. [By Rev. Samuel Cooper.] 8vo. [*Mon. Rev.* xxxv. 423.] London, 1766

LETTER (a) to the Right Rev. the Lord Bishop of London [Beilby Porteus], humbly suggesting a further consideration of a passage in the Gospel of St Matthew [xviii. 7]. [By Charles Dunster, M.A., rector of Petworth, Sussex.] 8vo. Pp. 78. [Darling's *Cyclop. Bibl.*] London, 1804

LETTER (a) to the Right Reverend the Lord Bishop of Oxford, occasioned by a book . . . entitled, The Christian plan exhibited in the interpretation of Elohim, by Walter Hodges. . . . [By Richard Moseley.] 8vo. [*Brit. Mus.*] London, 1752

Signed: Philo Christus.

LETTER (a) to the Right Rev. the Lord Bishop of O[xfor]d [Robert Lowth]; containing some animadversions upon a character given of the late Dr Bentley; in a letter from a late professor in the University of Oxford, to [William Warburton] the Right Rev. author of The divine legation of Moses demonstrated. By a member of the University of Cambridge [Richard Cumberland, LL.D.]. The second edition. 8vo. Pp. 46. [*Bodl.*] London, 1767

Ascribed also to Gregory Sharpe, LL.D.

LETTER (a) to the Roman Catholic clergy of Ireland, on the primary doctrine of revealed religion, and the purity of the early Irish Church. By Catholicus Verus [Andrew Carmichael]. 8vo. London, 1824

LETTER (a) to the Roman Catholic priests of Ireland, on the expediency of reviving the canonical mode of electing Bishops by Dean and Chapter. . . . By C. O. [Rev. Cæsar Otway, B.A.]. 8vo. [*Brit. Mus.*] Dublin, 1814

LETTER (a) to the Roman Catholics of the city of Worcester [England] from the chaplain of said Society; stating the motives which induced him to relinquish their communion and become a member of the Protestant Church. [By Charles H. Wharton, D.D.] 8vo. [Cushing's *Init. and Pseud.* i. 54.] Philadelphia, 1784

LETTER (a) [about George Whitefield] to the Second Church and congregation in Scituate. Written by their Rev. pastor [Rev. Nathaniel Eells]. 8vo. [Cushing's *Init. and Pseud.* ii. 144.] Boston, 1745

LETTER (a) to the Secretary of the Treasury [W. H. Crawford] on the commerce and currency of the United States. By Aristides [William P. Van Ness]. 8vo. [Cushing's *Init. and Pseud.* i. 19.] New York, 1819

LETTER (a) to the seven incorporated trades of Aberdeen. [By William Clyne.] 8vo. [Robertson's *Aberd. Bibl.*] Aberdeen, 1828

LETTER (a) to the seven Lords of the committee appointed to examine Gregg. [By John Oldmixon.] 8vo. Pp. 24. London, 1711

LETTER (a) to the so-called "Boston Churches," which are in truth only parts of one Church. By a member of the same [Rev. George Frederick Simmons]. 8vo. [Cushing's *Init. and Pseud.* i. 99.] Boston, 1846

LETTER (a) to the Society for promoting Christian knowledge; occasioned by two recent publications respecting the British and Foreign Bible Society. [By William Van Mildert, D.D., Bishop of Durham.] 8vo. Pp. 48. [*Bodl.*] London, 1805

LETTER (a) to the Society of the Dilettanti on the works in progress at Windsor. By Mela Britannicus [Charles Kelsall]. 8vo. [*Gladstone Lib. Cat.*] London, 1827

LETTER (a) to the Speaker of the House of Commons, of the late fight at Colchester; and how the suburbs were fired. . . . [Signed: J. R. *i.e.* John Rushworth.] 4to. [*Brit. Mus.*] London, 1648

LETTER (a) to the superiours, (whether Bishops or priests) which approve or license the Popish books in England, particularly to those of the Jesuits order, concerning Lewis Sabran, a Jesuit. [By Edward Gee.] 4to. [*Brit. Mus.*] London, 1688

LETTER (a) to the Times newspaper; containing observations on Mr George Robins's El Dorado, at the Cape of Good Hope, by Sam Sambox (A. Caper). [By Captain Duncan Campbell.] 8vo. Pp. 46. London, 1843

LETTER (a) to the Tories. [By George, Lord Lyttleton.] 8vo. [*D. N. B.* vol. 34, p. 373.] London, 1747

Signed: J. H., June 19, 1747.

This publication was deemed of so much importance that Horace Walpole wrote (anonymously also) "A letter to the Whigs, occasion'd by the Letter to the Tories," and added later "A second and third letter to the Whigs." Edward Moore's poem, "The trial of Selim the Persian for divers high crimes and misdemeanours," is a defence of Lyttleton.

LETTER (a) to the Trustees of the British Museum on the condition of the national collection of invertebrata. By Philocosmos [Hamlet Clark]. 8vo. [*Gladstone Lib. Cat.*] London, 1865

LETTER (a) to the two hundred and ninety-three electors of the City of Exeter who voted for T. Northmore, Esq., at the late general election, June 18th. . . . By Phileleutherus Devoniensis [Thomas Northmore]. 8vo. [*Brit. Mus.*] Exeter, 1818

LETTER to the Very Rev. E. B. Ramsay, M.A., Dean of Edinburgh, on the Scottish Episcopal Society, or the threefold obligations of a Churchman. By X. B. [George Oliver]. 8vo. Pp. 34. Edinburgh, 1847

LETTER (a) to the Very Rev. William Cockburn, D.D., Dean of York, occasioned by his late Remarks upon the charge of [C. J. Blomfield] the Lord Bishop of London. [By William Maskell.] 8vo. Pp. 8. London, 1842

Signed: W. M., a beneficed priest of the diocese of Salisbury.

LETTER (a) to the women of England on the injustice of mental subordination; with anecdotes. By Anne Frances Randall [Mrs Mary Robinson, *née* Darby]. 8vo. [Watt's *Bibl. Brit.*] London, 1799

LETTER (a) to the working classes of Aberdeen, showing the deep interest they have in the union of King's and Marischal Colleges. By a lover of truth [George B. Bothwell]. Second edition. 8vo. Pp. 24. [Anderson's *Aberd. Univ. Bibl.* p. 470.] Aberdeen, 1859

LETTER (a) to the working men of England. From one of themselves [C. Penrhyn Aston]. 8vo. [Cushing's *Init. and Pseud.* i. 218.] London, 1866

LETTER (a) to the young men of the Society of Friends. By one of themselves [Theodore Compton]. Third thousand. 12mo. [Smith's *Cat. of Friends' Books*, i. 105.] London, 1840

LETTER (a) to Theophilus Lindsey, A.M.; occasioned by his late publication of An historical view of the state of the Unitarian doctrine and worship. By a layman [Thomas Kynaston]. 8vo. Pp. iv. 192. [*Bodl.*] London, 1785

Written at the special request of Miss Tucker, daughter of the author of "The light of nature pursued."

LETTER (a) to Thomas Bannerman, Esq., on the Aberdeen Committee on Education and their "Interim report." By Philologus [Robert Cruickshank]. 8vo. Pp. 36. [Anderson's *Aberd. Univ. Bibl.* p. 453.] Aberdeen, 1835

LETTER (a) to Thomas Burnet, Esq.; showing that he hath used the same fidelity in printing a letter of Dr Beach's in the life of Bishop Burnet, as the editors of Bishop Burnet's History of his own times have exemplified in the publication thereof: with a specimen of some of the castrations in that history. [By Philip Beach.] 8vo. Pp. xii. 64. [Darling's *Cyclop. Bibl.*] London, 1736

LETTER (a) to Thomas Burnett, Esq; occasion'd by his to the Earl of Hallifax. [By Robert Whatley.] 8vo. Pp. 19. [*Bodl.*] London, 1715

LETTER (a) to Thomas Chalmers, D.D., on the present position of the Free Church of Scotland. By a Free Church Presbyterian [Rev. James Wright, Original Seceder]. 8vo. Edinburgh, 1844

Information from a friend of the author.

LETTER (a) to Thomas Erskine, containing strictures on his View of the causes . . . of the War with France. By John Gifford [John Richards Green]. 8vo. [*Lond. Lib. Cat.*] London, 1797

LETTER (a) to Thomas Erskine, Esq., Advocate, containing remarks on his late work, entitled The unconditional freeness of the Gospel. By a minister of the Church of Scotland [Rev. James Buchanan, D.D.]. 8vo. Pp. 23. Edinburgh, 1828

LETTER (a) to Thomas Moore, Esq., on the subject of Sheridan's School for scandal. [By Edward Mangin.] 8vo. [Green's *Bibl. Somers.* i. 334.] Bath, 1826

LETTER to Thomas Prior, Esq., containing some farther remarks on the virtues of tar-water. . . . [By Rev. George Berkeley, D.D., Bishop of Cloyne.] 8vo. [*D.N.B.* vol. 4, p. 352.] Dublin, 1714

LETTER (a) to W. Manning, Esq., M.P., on the causes of the rapid and progressive depreciation of West India property. [By Charles Bosanquet.] Second edition. 8vo. Pp. 56. [*D.N.B.* vol. 5, p. 412.] London [1807]

LETTER to W. Manning on the proposition submitted to the consideration of Government, for taking the duties of the Muscovado sugar ad valorem. [By Charles Bosanquet.] 8vo. [*D.N.B.* vol. 5, p. 412.] London [1807?]

LETTER (a) to W. W. [Dr William Warburton] occasioned by some passages in his book intituled, The divine legation of Moses demonstrated. By a gentleman of Lincoln's Inn [Philip Carteret Webb]. 8vo. [*D. N. B.* vol. 60, p. 108.] London, 1742

LETTER (a) to William Augustus Miles, Esq., containing some observations on a letter addressed by him to His Royal Highness the Prince of Wales. By Philopolites [William Pettman]. 8vo. Pp. 32. [*D. N. B.* vol. 37, p. 380.] London, 1808

LETTER to William Clay, Esq., M.P.; containing strictures on his late pamphlet, on the subject of joint stock banks; with remarks on his favourite theories. By Vindex [—— Hannay, of Marylebone bank]. 8vo. Pp. 36. London, 1836

LETTER (a) to Wm. Huskisson, Esq., M.P., on his late publication. By a proprietor of Bank stock [Peter Carey]. 8vo. Pp. vi. 42. [*W.*] London, 1811

LETTER (a) to William Pitt, containing some new arguments against the abolition of the slave trade. By Britannicus [Francis Randolph, D.D.]. 8vo. London, 1804

LETTER (a) to William Pitt, Esq; concerning the fifteen new regiments lately voted by Parliament: wherein some of the general arguments, together with his in particular, for opposing the motion to address His Majesty, are fairly answered, and the case itself is shortly and plainly stated. [By the Hon. Thomas Hervey.] 8vo. Pp. 39. [*Brit. Mus.; D. N. B.* vol. 26, p. 290.] London, 1746

LETTER (a) to William Rae, Esq., Sheriff depute of the county of Edinburgh, on the public execution of criminals. [By Sir George Stewart Mackenzie, Bart.] Pp. 21. [*Edin. Univ. Lib.*] [Edinburgh, 1815]

The letter is signed: M., and acknowledged in a letter from the author to Sir Henry Jardine.

LETTER (a) to William W. Whitmore, Esq., M.P.; pointing out some of the erroneous statements contained in a pamphlet by Joseph Marryat, Esq., M.P., entitled A reply to the arguments contained in various publications, recommending an equalization of the duties on East and West India sugars. By the author of a pamphlet entitled *East and West India sugar* [Zachary Macaulay]. 8vo. Pp. 38. [*Brit. Mus.*] London, 1823

LETTER (the) torn in pieces; or, a full confutation of Ludlow's suggestions, that King Charles I. was an enemy to the state. By the author of two papers formerly published, viz. *The vindication of the honour of King Charles the First;* and the *Earnest call to the people of England, etc.* [Edmund Elys]. . . . 4to. Pp. 8. [*Bodl.*] London, 1692

The author's name is in the handwriting of Wood.

LETTER (a) touching a colledge of maids, or, a Virgin-Society. Written Aug. 12. 1675. [By Clement Barksdale.] 8vo. No pagination. [*Bodl.; D. N. B.* vol. 3, p. 216.]

No title-page. Signed: B. C.
The author's name is in the handwriting of Wood.

LETTER (a) touching the late Rebellion, and what means led to it; and of the Pretender's title: showing the duty and interest of all Protestants to be faithful to King George. . . . By Philalethes [Whitelocke Bulstrode]. 8vo. [Watt's *Bibl. Brit.*] London, 1717

LETTER (a) unto a person of honour & quality containing some animadversions upon [George Morley] the Bishop of Worcester's letter. [By Edward Bagshaw, junr.] 4to. Pp. 13. [*Camb. Univ. Lib.*] London, 1662

Signed: D. E.
See, next, "A letter with animadversions upon the animadverter . . ."; also, "A second letter . . ."

LETTER (a) upon law. . . . By a member of the Bar [George Lunt]. 8vo. [Cushing's *Init. and Pseud.* ii. 97.] Boston, 1835

LETTER (a); whearin, part of the entertainment vntoo the Queens Maiesty, at Killingwoorth Castl, in Warwik Sheer, in this soomers Progress. 1575. is signified: from a freend officer attendant in Coourt, vntoo his freend a citisen, and merchaunt of London. [By Robert Laneham.] 8vo. Pp. 91. B. L. [*Bodl.*] N.P., N.D.

LETTER (a), wherein the scriptural grounds and warrants for the reformation of churches by way of Covenant, are succinctly considered and cleared; in opposition to some, who of late have too boldly (and yet without censure), vented their heterodox notions against our solemn and sacred national Covenants. By a welwisher to a covenanted reformation [James Hog]. 12mo. Pp. 16. [*Nat. Lib. of Scot.*] Edinburgh, 1727

LETTER (a) with animadversions upon the animadverter [Edward Bagshaw, junr.] on the Bishop of Worcester's [George Morley's] Letter. By J. C. [John Collop, M.D.]. 4to. Pp. 14. [*Camb. Univ. Lib.*] London, 1661

LETTER (a) writ by Segdirboeg, [George Bridges] in answer to five written by Mr Samuel Webber, upon the decay of the woollen manufactories in Great Britain and Ireland; also to his scheme to prevent that iniquitous traffick for the future, by an universal registry. . . . 8vo. Pp. 20. London, 1739

Segdirboeg, reversed, becomes Geo. Bridges.

LETTER (a) writ in the year 1730, concerning the question, whether the Logos supplied the place of a human soul in the person of Jesus Christ; to which are now added two postscripts. . . . [By Nathaniel Lardner, D.D.] 8vo. Pp. xii. 218. [*D. N. B.* vol. 32, p. 150.] London, 1759

The letter is signed: Philalethes.

LETTER (a) writ to an atheistical acquaintance, upon his turning Papist in his old age. By a person of honour [Francis Boyle, Viscount Shannon]. 4to. Pp. 27. [*Bodl.*] London, 1691

LETTER (the) writers; or, a new way to keep a wife at home: a farce, in three acts, as it is acted at the theatre in the Hay-market. Written by Scriblerus Secundus [Henry Fielding]. 8vo. Pp. 48. London, 1731

Later editions give the author's name.

LETTER (a) written by a french Catholicke gentleman [Philippe De Mornay, Seigneur du Plessis Marly], conteyning a briefe aunswere to the slaunders of a certaine pretended Englishman [L. d'Orleans. . . . Translated from the French]. 4to. Pp. 90. [*Brit. Mus.*] London, 1589

LETTER (a) written by a lady [Susannah Hopton] to a Romish priest [Henry Turberville] upon her return from the Church of Rome to the Church of England. . . . [John Austin's *Devotions*, *ed.* Hickes, Preface, p. xxvii.]

LETTER (a) written by G. L. [Rev. George Leyburn, D.D.] to Mr And. Knigh. [Andrew Knightley] and Mr Tho. Med. [Thomas Medcalfe]. 12mo. Pp. 5. [Douai, 1656]

LETTER (a) written out of the countrey to a person of quality in the city, who took offence at the late sermon of Dr Stillingfleet, Dean of S. Pauls, before the Lord Mayor. [By John Howe, M.A.] 4to. [*D. N. B.* vol. 28, p. 86.] London, 1680

LETTER (a) written to a friend, concerning Popish idolatrie. [By Herbert Croft, D.D., Bishop of Hereford.] 12mo. [*D. N. B.* vol. 13, p. 107.] London, 1674

Reprinted in 1679.

LETTER (a) written to a friend in Wilts [Thomas Gore, of Alderton] upon occasion of a late ridiculous pamphlet; wherein was inserted a pretended prophecy of Thomas à Becket. By T. T. [Thomas Tully]. 4to. [Watt's [*Bibl. Brit.*] London, 1666

LETTER (a) written to a gentleman in the country, touching the Dissolution of the late Parliament, and the reasons thereof [May 3, 1653]. By N. LL. [John Hall of Durham]. 4to. London, 1653

The writer has given the final letters of his names.

LETTER (a) written to Dr [Gilbert] Burnet, giving an account of Cardinal Pool's secret powers; from which it appears that it was never intended to confirm the alienation that was made of the Abbey-Lands: to which are added, Two breves that Card. Pool brought over, and some other of his letters that were never before printed. [Signed: W. C. *i.e.* Sir William Coventry.] 4to. Pp 40. [*Brit. Mus.*] London, 1685

LETTER (a) written to Dr Samuel Turner, concerning the Church and the revenues thereof. [By John Fountaine.] 4to. Pp. 8. [*Bodl.*] N.D.

No title-page.

LETTER (a) written upon the discovery of the Plot. [By Gilbert Burnet, D.D.] 4to. Pp. 45. [*Bodl.*] London, 1678

LETTER-BAG (the) of the Great Western; or, life in a steamer. By the author of *The sayings and doings of Samuel Slick* [Thomas C. Haliburton]. 12mo. London, 1840

LETTERS [from Europe]. By A. C. B. [Amos C. Barstow]. 8vo. [Cushing's *Init. and Pseud.* i. 23.] New York, 1873

LETTERS. By a farmer [J. M'Cully]. 8vo. Belfast, 1787

LETTERS about missuses. By a maid of all work [Horace Mayhew]. 8vo. London, 1854

LETTERS about the Hudson river and its vicinity; written in 1835 and 1836. By a citizen of New York [Freeman Hunt]. 8vo. [Cushing's *Init. and Pseud.* i. 59.] New York, 1836

LETTERS addressed to a Baptist clergyman, on the doctrine of endless punishment. By a layman [D. N. Prime]. 12mo. Pp. 146. [Eddy's *Universalism in America*, ii. 567.] Boston, 1859

LETTERS addressed to Caleb Strong, Esq., late Governor of Massachusetts, showing war to be inconsistent with the laws of Christ and the good of mankind. [By Rev. R. Whelpley.] 8vo. [Sabin's *Dictionary.*] New York; reprinted in London, 1818

LETTERS addressed to Lord Grenville and Lord Howick, upon their removal from the Councils of the King, in consequence of their attempting the total repeal of the Test laws now in force, with respect to His Majesty's army and navy. By a Protestant [Edward Cooke]. 8vo. Pp. 37. [*Camb. Univ. Lib.*] London, 1807

LETTERS addressed to Mrs P. Latouche. By Melantius [Robert Stearne Tighe]: containing a state of the orphan-houses of England, Ireland, Zeland, and Holland. 8vo. [*Brit. Mus.*] Dublin, 1793

LETTERS addressed to Soame Jenyns, Esq.; containing strictures on the writings of Edward Gibbon, Esq., Dr Priestley, Mr Theophilus Lindsay, etc., and an abstract of Dr Priestley's Account current with Revelation. [By John Young.] The second edition, with a preface, or what may be called, the Reviewers reviewed. 12mo. Pp. xxxvi. 340. London, 1791

Signed: Simplex.
The first edition was published in 1786.

LETTERS addressed to the Archbishop of Canterbury. . . . By a Catholic priest [Rev. Peter Gandolphy]. 8vo. [Cushing's *Init. and Pseud.* i. 29.] London, 1813

LETTERS addressed to the Friends of Freedom and the Union. By Hampden [John Bloomfield Jervis, LL.D.]. 8vo. [Cushing's *Init. and Pseud.* i. 126.] New York, 1856

LETTERS addressed to the minister. By a freeholder north of Trent [William Hutchinson, Esq.]. 8vo. [Cushing's *Init. and Pseud.* ii. 60.] London, 1798

LETTERS addressed to the Right Hon. William Pitt . . . pointing out the inequality, oppression, and impolicy of the taxes on coal. . . . [By Henry Grey Macnab, M.D.] 4to. [*Brit. Mus.*] London, 1793

LETTERS addressed to the yeomanry of the United States . . . on funding and banking systems. By an American farmer [George Logan]. 8vo. [Cushing's *Init. and Pseud.* ii. 6.] Philadelphia, 1793

Wrongly attributed to A. Hamilton, and to H. S. Crevecœur.

LETTERS addressed to the youth of the Unitarian Congregation at Tenterden, intended as an exposure of the . . . Rev. J. Exall. . . . [By John Dobell.] 12mo. Pp. 130. Cranbrook, 1814

LETTERS, admonitory and argumentative, from J. H. [Jonas Hanway], merchant, to J. S—t, merchant, in reply to . . . a pamphlet entitled, Further considerations in the Bill, etc. 8vo. [*D. N. B.* vol. 24, p. 313.] London, 1753

LETTERS against non-intrusion, addressed to a friend; with an appendix on the causes and probable consequences of that movement. [By Rev. John I. Adamson, minister at Thornton.] 8vo. [Scott's *Fasti.*] Edinburgh, 1843

LETTERS and dissertations. By the author of *Analysis A. P. on the disputes between Great Britain and America* [Thomas Crowley]. 12mo. Pp. 130. [Rich's *Bibl. Amer.* i. 307.] 1782

LETTERS and essays, in prose and verse. [By Richard Sharp, M.P.] 8vo. Pp. viii. 268. [*D. N. B.* vol. 51, p. 414.] London, 1834

The author's name is given in the third edition.

LETTERS and miscellaneous papers, by Barré Charles Roberts, student of Christ Church, Oxford; with a memoir of his life. [Edited by Grosvenor Bedford.] 4to. Pp. 370. [Martin's *Cat.*] London, 1814

LETTERS and observations written in a short tour through France and Italy. By a gentleman [William Beckford]. 8vo. [*Brit. Mus.*] Salisbury, 1786

The ascription has been questioned. [Courtney's *Secrets*, p. 17.]

LETTERS and poems, amorous and gallant. [By William Welsh.] 8vo. Pp. 120. London, 1692

"Humfredi Hody ex dono autoris Domini Welsh. He was afterwards Parliament-man for the county of Worcester."—MS. note on the Bodleian copy.

LETTERS and remains of the Lord Chancellor Bacon; collected by Robert Stephens, Esq., late Historiographer-Royal. [With an historical introduction. Edited by J. Locker.] 4to. [*W.*] London, 1734

LETTERS and reminiscences of the Rev. J. Mitford; with a sketch of his correspondent's [E. Jesse's] life. By C. M. [Mrs M. C. Houstoun]. 8vo. Pp. vii. 285. [*Brit. Mus.*] London, 1891

LETTERS and tracts on the choice of company and other subjects. [By Robert Bolton, LL.D., Dean of Carlisle.] Second edition. 8vo. [*Brit. Mus.*] London, 1762

LETTERS as from a father to his once prodigal son. [By Emmett Skidmore.] 12mo. [Smith's *Cat. of Friends' Books*, ii. 579.] N.P. 1836

LETTERS by a British Commoner. No. II. The dangers of England and duties of Englishmen. A letter addressed to the electors of Great Britain. By "a British Commoner" [Edward Rupert Humphreys, LL.D., headmaster of the Cheltenham Grammar School]. 8vo. Pp. 48. [*W.*] London, 1855

LETTERS by Historicus [Sir William George Granville Vernon Harcourt] on some questions of international law. Reprinted from The Times, with considerable additions. 8vo. [*Brit. Mus.*] Cambridge, 1863

LETTERS concerning Confessions of Faith and subscriptions to Articles of religion in Protestant Churches; occasioned by the perusal of The Confessional [by Rev. Francis Blackburne]. [By Thomas Balguy.] 8vo. [*Brit. Mus.*] London, 1768

LETTERS concerning education, addressed to a gentleman entering at the University. [By Peter Williams, M.A.] 8vo. [Watt's *Bibl. Brit.*] London, 1785

LETTERS concerning mythology. [By Thomas Blackwell, LL..D, Principal of Marischal College, Aberdeen.] 8vo. Pp. iv. 411. [*Brit. Mus.*] London, 1748

LETTERS concerning poetical translations, and Virgil's and Milton's Arts of verse. etc. [By William Benson, M.A.] 8vo. Pp. 83. [*Brit. Mus.*] London, 1739

LETTERS concerning taste. [By John Gilbert Cooper.] 8vo. Pp. 143. [*D. N. B.* vol. 12, p. 136.] London, 1755

LETTERS concerning the general health. By a householder [Samuel Miles Hopkins]. 8vo. [Cushing's *Init. and Pseud.* i. 133.] New York, 1805

LETTERS concerning the love of God, between [Mary Astell] the author of the *Proposal to the ladies* and Mr John Norris. . . . Published by J. Norris, M.A., rector of Bemerton near Sarum. 8vo. London, 1695

LETTERS concerning the persecution of the Episcopal clergy in Scotland. [First letter by Thomas Morer, the second and third by Bishop John Gage, the fourth by Alexander Monro, D.D.] 4to. [*New Coll. Lib.*] 1689

LETTERS concerning the present state of Poland, with the Manifesto of Vienna, Petersburgh, and Berlin. [By John Lind, M.D.] 8vo. [*Lond. Lib. Cat.*] London, 1773

Separate pagination for each letter.

LETTERS concerning the present state of the Church of Scotland, and the consequent danger to religion and learning, from the arbitrary and unconstitutional exercise of the law of patronage. [By James Oswald, D.D.] 8vo. Pp. iv. 49. Edinburgh, 1767

The author's name is in the handwriting of Dr David Laing.

LETTERS concerning the present state of the French nation. . . . [By Arthur Young, F.R.S.] 8vo. [*Brit. Mus.*] London, 1769

LETTERS concerning the religion essential to man, as it is distinct from what is merely an accession to it: in two parts. By the author of *The world unmask'd; or, the state of souls separated from their bodies* [Marie Huber]. Translated out of the French. 12mo. Pp. xx. 206. London, 1738

LETTERS containing observations on colonial policy, particularly as applicable to Ceylon. . . . [By Sir Robert J. W. Horton, Bart.] London, 1839

This is a reprint of "Letters on colonial policy." . . . Colombo, 1833. See below.

LETTERS, conversations and recollections of Samuel Taylor Coleridge. [Collected and edited by Thomas Allsopp.] 8vo. 2 vols. [Lowndes' *Bibl. Man.*] London, 1836

LETTERS describing a tour through part of South Wales. By a pedestrian traveller [Comte Armand B. L. Maudet de Penhouet]. With views, designed and etched by the author. 4to. Pp. ii. 74. London, 1797

The author's name is in the handwriting of Douce.

LETTERS describing the character and customs of the English and French nations; with a curious essay on travelling; and a criticism on Boileau's Description of Paris. [By Béat Louis Muralt.] Translated from the French. 8vo. Pp. viii. 312. London, 1726

LETTERS descriptive of the Virginia Springs. By Peregrine Prolix [Philip H. Nicklin]. 8vo. [Cushing's *Init. and Pseud.* i. 241.] Philadelphia, 1837

LETTERS developing the character and view of the Hartford Convention. By one of the Convention [Harrison Gray Otis]. 8vo. [Cushing's *Init. and Pseud.* i. 216.] Washington, 1820

LETTERS for literary ladies; to which is added an Essay on the noble science of self-justification. [By Maria Edgeworth.] 8vo. 3 parts. [*Brit. Mus.*] London, 1795

LETTERS for the people. By Lynceus [Frederick Starr, junr.]. 8vo. [Cushing's *Init. and Pseud.* i. 176.] New York, 1853

LETTERS from a cat, published by her mistress . . . for the amusement of little children. By H. H. [Helen Hunt, later Mrs Jackson]. 8vo. Pp. 89. [*Brit. Mus.*] Boston [1880]

LETTERS from a Chinese official [on] Western civilisation. [By Goldsworthy L. Dickinson.] 8vo. London, 1907

LETTERS from a farmer in Pennsylvania to the inhabitants of the British Colonies. [By John Dickinson, President of the State of Delaware.] 8vo. Pp. 146. [Evans' *Amer. Bibl.* vol. 4, p. 173.] Boston, 1768

LETTERS from a father [David Thurston, D.D.] to a son, an apprentice. 8vo. [Cushing's *Init. and Pseud.* ii. 58.] Portland, Maine, 1858

LETTERS from a father to a son on revealed religion. [By Henry S. Sutton?] 8vo. London, 1855

LETTERS from a father to his son, a student of divinity. [By James Paton, D.D., minister of Craig.] 12mo. Pp. 107. Edinburgh, 1796

LETTERS from a gentleman in the north of Scotland to his friend in London; containing the description of a capital town in that northern country, with an account of some uncommon customs of the inhabitants; likewise an account of the Highlands, with the customs and manners of the Highlanders. . . . [By Captain Edward Burt or Birt.] 8vo. 2 vols. [*Nat. Lib. of Scot.*] Dublin, 1755

A new edition with notes [by Robert Jamieson, advocate], was published in 1815.

LETTERS from a gentleman to his friend in the country, occasioned by the late theatrical disturbances. [By Allan Ramsay, junior.] 12mo. Pp. 16. Edinburgh, 1766.

See also "Letters on the present disturbances. . . ."

LETTERS from a lady [Anne Carter] to her sister, during a tour to Paris. . . . 12mo. [*Brit. Mus.*] London, 1814

LETTERS from a lady who resided some years in Russia, to her friend in England; with historical notes. [By Mrs Vigor, *née* Rondeau]. 8vo. Pp. viii. 207. [Nichols' *Lit. Anec.* iii. 209.] London, 1775

LETTERS from a landscape painter [Charles Lanman]. 8vo. [Cushing's *Init. and Pseud.* i. 164.] Boston, 1845

LETTERS from a late eminent prelate [Dr William Warburton, Bishop of Gloucester] to one of his friends [Richard Hurd, D.D., Bishop of Worcester]. Second edition. 8vo. Pp. 510. [*W.*] London, 1809

LETTERS from a mother to her children on various important subjects. By Mary Pelham [Dorothy Kilner]. 12mo. [*Brit. Mus.*] London [1780]

LETTERS from a mourning city. . . . By Puck Munthe [Axel Munthe]. Second edition. 8vo. Pp. 221. [*Brit. Mus.*] London, 1899

LETTERS from a mystic of the present day. [By Rev. Rowland William Corbet.] 8vo. London, 1883

Later editions give the author's name.

LETTERS from a Persian in England, to his friend at Ispahan. [By Sir George Lyttelton, first Baron Lyttelton.] Second edition. 12mo. [*Brit. Mus.*] London, 1735

LETTERS from a Portuguese nun to an officer in the French army. Translated [from the French of C. J. Dorat] by W. R. Bowles. 12mo. London, 1808

For the titles of other editions, see "Love without affectation . . ." (1709); "Five love letters . . ." (1678).

LETTERS from a self-made merchant to his son. [By George Horace Lorimer.] 8vo. Pp. 328. [*Brit. Mus.*] London, 1902

LETTERS from a silent study. By John Oliver Hobbes [Mrs Pearl Mary Teresa Craigie]. 8vo. Pp. vi. 236. London, 1904

LETTERS from a theatrical scene-painter. [By T. W. Erle.] Two series. 12mo. Private print, 1859-62

Presentation copies from the author.

LETTERS from a tutor to his pupils. [By William Jones, F.R.S.] 8vo. [Watt's *Bibl. Brit.*] London, 1780

LETTERS from a work-house boy; with a short account of the writer. By the author of *Hints for the improvement of early education*, etc. [Louisa Hoare]. 12mo. Pp. 91. [Smith's *Cat. of Friends' Books*, i. 95.] London, 1826

LETTERS from a young officer [J. M. Matthew] under Cornwallis, on the operations of the army to the capture of Bangalore. 4to. Pp. 60. London, 1793

LETTERS from a young painter abroad to his friends in England: adorned with copper plates. [By John Russell.] Second edition. 8vo. 2 vols. [Lowndes' *Bibl. Man.*] London, 1750

"These letters have been ascribed to Sir Joshua Reynolds."—MS. note by Douce.

LETTERS from abroad; or, scraps from New Zealand, Australia, and America. By H. B. T. [H. B. Tucker]. 8vo. Glasgow, 1884

LETTERS from abroad to kindred at home. By the author of *Hope Leslie*, etc. [Catherine Maria Sedgwick]. 12mo. 2 vols. [*Brit. Mus.*] New York, 1841

LETTERS from Academicus [Charles Crawford] to Eugenius; on various subjects. 8vo. [*Camb. Univ. Lib.*] London, 1773

LETTERS from Altamont in the capital to his friends in the country. [By Rev. Charles Jenner, junior.] 8vo. [Nichols' *Lit. Anec.* ix. 563.] London, 1764

LETTERS from America. [By Rev. Harry Jones.] 12mo. [New York] 1870

LETTERS from an absent brother; containing some account of a tour through parts of the Netherlands, Switzerland, Northern Italy, and France, in the summer of 1823. [By Daniel Wilson, D.D.] Second edition. 2 vols. 8vo. [*D. N. B.*, vol. 62, p. 89.] London, 1824

Several editions were issued.

LETTERS from an afflicted husband. [By Hall Jackson Kelley.] 8vo. [Cushing's *Init. and Pseud.* ii. 4.] Palmer, Mass., 1851

LETTERS from an American farmer. [By Hector St John Crevecœur.] 8vo. [Cushing's *Init. and Pseud.* i. 14.] Philadelphia, 1794

LETTERS from an Armenian in Ireland, to his friends at Trebisond, etc. Translated [but rather wholly written] in the year 1756 [by Robert Hellen]. 8vo. Pp. 122. [*Brit. Mus.*] London, 1757

Attributed by others to Viscount Edmund Sexton Pery.

LETTERS from an Egyptian Kafir on a visit to England in search of a religion. [By Samuel Bailey.] 8vo. London, 1837

The authorship of this fiction is revealed in the Preface to the Bury edition.

LETTERS from an elder to a younger brother, on the conduct to be pursued in life. [By William Hussey.] 12mo. Pp. 128. [Watt's *Bibl. Brit.*] London, 1809

LETTERS from an English traveller in Spain, in 1778, on the origin and progress of poetry in that kingdom; with occasional reflections on manners and customs; and illustrations of the romance of Don Quixote: adorned with portraits of the most eminent poets. [By Sir John Talbot Dillon.] 8vo. Pp. x. 322. [*D. N. B.* vol. 15, p. 85.] London, 1781

LETTERS from an English traveller [Rev. Martin Sherlock]; translated from the French original printed at Geneva and Paris, with notes: a new edition, revised and corrected. 8vo. Pp. xv. 190. [*Manch. Free Lib.*] London, 1780

LETTERS from an officer in the Guards [George Edward Ayscough] to his friend in England, containing some accounts of France and Italy. 8vo. [*Camb. Univ. Lib.*] London, 1778

LETTERS from an old man [Count Carl Gustav Tessin] to a young Prince [afterwards Gustavus III. King of Sweden]; with the answers: translated from the Swedish [by J. Berkenhout]. . . . 12mo. 2 vols. [*Brit. Mus.*] London, 1756

A second edition was issued in 1759.

LETTERS from an Oregon ranch. By "Katharine" [Louise G. Stephens]. 8vo. [*Amer. Cat.*] Chicago, 1905

LETTERS from an unknown friend. By the author of *Charles Lowder* [Maria M. Trench]. . . . 8vo. Pp. viii. 140. [*Brit. Mus.*] London, 1884

LETTERS from Aristarchus to Philemon. . . . [By Chauncy Lee.] 8vo. [Cushing's *Init. and Pseud.* ii. 9.] New Haven, Conn., 1833

LETTERS from Barbary, France, Spain, Portugal, etc. By an English officer [Lieut.-Col. Alexander Jardine]. 8vo. 2 vols. [*Brit. Mus.*] London, 1788

See also "Letters from Morocco."

LETTERS from Buenos Ayres and Chili, with an original history of the latter country. By the author of *Letters from Paraguay* [Joan Constance Davie]. 8vo. [*Brit. Mus.*] London, 1819

LETTERS from Cambridge, illustrative of the studies, habits, and peculiarities of the University. [By Ernest Sylvanus Appleyard.] 8vo. [*Camb. Univ. Lib.*] London, 1828

LETTERS from Catalonia, and other parts of Spain. By Rowland Thirlmere [John Walker]. 8vo. 2 vols. [*Lond. Lib. Cat.*] London, 1905

LETTERS from Cicero [Joseph Galloway, Speaker of the House of Commons in Pennsylvania] to Cataline the Second [Charles James Fox]; with corrections and explanatory notes. 8vo. [Cushing's *Init. and Pseud.* i. 57.] London, 1781

LETTERS from Cicero [Joseph Galloway, Speaker of the House of Commons, in Pennsylvania] to the Right Hon. Lord Viscount H[ow]e, occasioned by his speech in the H[ous]e of C[ommon]s. 8vo. London, 1781

LETTERS from Cockney lands. [By William Harrison Ainsworth.] 12mo. [Allibone's *Dict.* vol. i.] London, 1827

LETTERS from Edinburgh, written in the years 1774 and 1775; containing some observations on the diversions, customs, manners and laws of the Scotch nation, during a six months residence in Edinburgh. [By Capt. Edward Topham.] 8vo. Pp. xv. 383. [*Brit. Mus.*] London, 1776

Reprinted with the author's name.

LETTERS from Eliza [Mrs Elizabeth Draper] to Yorick [Laurence Sterne]. 12mo. Pp. 70. [*Brit. Mus.*] London, 1775

LETTERS from England. By Don Manuel Alvarez Espriella, translated from the Spanish [but really written by Robert Southey]. 12mo. 3 vols. [*Brit. Mus.*] London, 1807

LETTERS from Europe. By Aunt Esther [Mrs John A. Smith]. 8vo. [Cushing's *Init. and Pseud.* i. 93]. Chicago, 1870

LETTERS from Europe during a tour through Switzerland and Italy in the years 1801 and 1802. Written by a native of Pennsylvania [Joseph Sansom]. 8vo. 2 vols. [*Supp.* to Smith's *Cat. of Friends' Books*, p. 297.] Philadelphia, 1805

This work was issued again in 1808, with the title: "Travels from Paris, through Switzerland and Italy, in 1801-02."

LETTERS from Felicia to Charlotte. [By Mrs Collyer.] 12mo. [*Gent. Mag.* xcviii. i. 184.] London, 1750

In *Mon. Rev.*, ii. 229, the title is given as—"Felicia to Charlotte, or letters from a young lady in the country, to a friend in town." Vol. II. London, 1750, 12mo.; and it is stated that the first volume was published about four years earlier.

LETTERS from Fleet Street. [By Armiger Barclay, and Mrs Marguerite Barclay.] 8vo. Pp. 262. London, 1911

A later edition gives the authors' names.

LETTERS from France and Italy. By Anthony Rowley [Arthur Guthrie]. 8vo. [*Amer. Cat.*] Chicago, 1909

LETTERS from Futtehgurh. By Rose C. M. [Rose C. Monckton]. 8vo. [*Brit. Mus.*] Clifton, 1858

LETTERS from Harold's Cross. [By Rev. R. Burton.] 12mo. Dublin, 1850

LETTERS from head-quarters; or, the realities of the war in the Crimea. By an officer on the staff [Hon. Somerset John Gough Calthorpe]. Second edition. 12mo. 2 vols. [*Bodl.*] London, 1857

"Great part contributed by Lord Alfred Paget."—W.

LETTERS from Hell. By E. Levi [L. A. Constant]. Translated by J. M. Wheeler. 8vo. [*Gladstone Lib. Cat.* (*Lib. Club*).] London [1884]

LETTERS from Hell. By M. Rowel [Valdemar Adolph Thisted. Translated from the Danish]. 8vo. 2 vols. London, 1866

Another translation, by L. W. J. S., with a preface by Dr George Macdonald, was published in 1884.

LETTERS from his late Majesty [George III.] to the late Lord Kenyon, on the Coronation Oath; with his Lordship's Answers, etc. [Edited by Henry Phillpotts, Bishop of Exeter.] 4to. Pp. 45. [Lowndes' *Bibl. Man.*] London, 1827

LETTERS from Hofwyl, on the educational institutions of De Fellenberg. . . . [By Mrs Louisa M. Barwell.] 8vo. [*D. N. B.* vol. 3, p. 350.] London, 1842

LETTERS from India and Kashmir, 1870. [By J. Duguid]. 8vo. London, 1874

LETTERS from Ireland MDCCCXXXVII. By Charlotte Elizabeth [Mrs Charlotte Elizabeth Tonna]. 12mo. Pp. iv. 436. [*Brit. Mus.*] London, 1838

LETTERS from Italy and Vienna. [By William Rind, M.A.] 8vo. [Boase's *Mod. Eng. Biog.* Supp. vol. 6, col. 297.] London, 1852

LETTERS from Italy, describing the manners, customs, antiquities, paintings, &c. of that country, in the years 1770 and 1771, to a friend residing in France. By an English woman [Lady Anna Riggs Miller]. 8vo. 3 vols. [*N. and Q.* 1865, p. 192.] London, 1776

LETTERS from Jamaica "the land of streams and woods." [By Charles J. G. Rampini, Sheriff of Shetland.] 8vo. Pp. 182. [*Nat. Lib. of Scot.*] Edinburgh, 1873

LETTERS from John Chinaman. [By Goldsworthy Lowes Dickinson.] 8vo. Pp. 62. [*Lond. Lib. Cat.*] London, 1902

LETTERS from Juliet, Lady Catesby, to her friend Lady Henrietta Campley. Translated from the French of M. J. Riccoboni [by Mrs Francis Brooke, *née* Moore]. Sixth edition. 12mo. [*Brit. Mus.*] London, 1780

LETTERS from London; observations of a Russian during a residence in England of ten months. . . . [By John Badcock.] 8vo. [*D. N. B.* vol. 2, p. 382.] London, 1816

LETTERS from Lothario to Penelope. [By Rev. Charles Jenner.] 12mo. 2 vols. [Nichol's *Lit. Anec.* ix. 563.] London, 1770

LETTERS from Lusitania; and other compositions in prose and verse. By T. C. B. [T. C. Button, afterwards T. C. Alton]. 8vo. Windsor, 1876

LETTERS from Madras, during the years 1836-39. By a lady [Mrs Julia Charlotte Maitland, *née* Barrett]. 8vo. Pp. xii. 300. [*Bodl.*] London, 1843

LETTERS from Minorca, describing the constitution, government, produce, antiquities, and natural history of that island. . . . [By John Armstrong, engineer.] 12mo. Pp. xvii. 248. [*Brit. Mus.*] Dublin, 1782

Earlier editions (1752, 1756) with the title "The history of the island of Minorca . . ." are not anonymous.

LETTERS from Morocco. . . . By an English officer [Lieut.-Colonel Alexander Jardine, R.A.]. 8vo. 2 vols. [Cushing's *Init. and Pseud.* i. 91.] London, 1790

See also "Letters from Barbary. . . ."

LETTERS from Nahant, historical, descriptive, and miscellaneous. [By William W. Wheildon.] 8vo. Pp. 48. [Allibone's *Dict.*] Charlestown, S.C., 1842

LETTERS from Orinda [Mrs Katherine Philips, *née* Fowler] to Poliarchus [Sir Charles Cotterel]. 8vo. Pp. 246. [*Dyce Cat.* ii. 155.] London, 1705

LETTERS from Oxford, with notes. By Ignotus [Ven. Arthur Blennerhasset Rowan, D.D.]. 8vo. [*D. N. B.* vol. 49, p. 335.] Dublin, 1843

LETTERS from Palestine, descriptive of a tour through Gallilee and Judæa; with some account of the Dead Sea, and of the present state of Jerusalem. [By Thomas R. Joliffe.] 8vo. Pp. viii. 251. London, 1819

LETTERS from Palmyra, by Lucius Manlius Piso, to his friend Marcus Curtius, at Rome; now first translated and published. [By Rev. William Ware.] 12mo. 2 vols. [*Nat. Lib. of Scot.*] London, 1838

LETTERS from Paris, during the summer of 1791. (And in the summer of 1792.) [By Stephen Weston, B.D.] 8vo. 2 vols. [*Brit. Mus.*] London, 1792-93

LETTERS from Portugal and Spain, written during the march of the British troops under Sir John Moore; with a map of the route, and appropriate engravings. By an officer [Sir Robert Ker Porter]. 8vo. Pp. 320. [Lowndes' *Bibl. Man.*] London, 1809

LETTERS from Portugal, on the late and present state of that kingdom. [By Lieutenant Blanket.] 8vo. Pp. 66. [*W.*] London [1777]

LETTERS from Portugal, Spain, and France, during the memorable campaigns of 1811, 1812 and 1813; and from Belgium and France in the year 1815. By a British officer [James Hope, of the Gordon Highlanders]. 8vo. Pp. 307. [*Brit. Mus.*] Edinburgh, 1819

LETTERS from Portugal, Spain, Sicily, and Malta, in 1812, 1813, and 1814. By G. A. F. H. B. [George A. F. H. Bridgeman, second Earl of Bradford]. 8vo. Pp. 248. [Simms' *Bibl. Staff.* p. 79.] London, private print, 1875

Only a few copies printed.

LETTERS from Queensland. By *The Times* special correspondent [Flora L. Shaw, later Lady Lugard]. 8vo. [*Lib. of Coll. Inst.* i. 151.] London, 1893

LETTERS from Rome, A.D. 138. By the author of *Clouds and sunshine*, etc. [F. Townsend]. 12mo. Pp. 239. New York, 1854

LETTERS from Rome on the [Vatican] Council. By Quirinus [Lord John E. E. Acton]. Reprinted from the Allgemeine Zeitung; authorized translation. 8vo. Pp. xxii. 856. [*D. N. B.* Second Supp. vol. 1, p. 10.] London, 1870

Wrongly attributed to Dr I. I. Döllinger.

LETTERS from Scandinavia, on the past and present state of the northern nations of Europe. [By William Thomson, LL.D.] 8vo. 2 vols. [*Brit. Mus.*] London, 1796

LETTERS from Sicily; containing some account of the political events in that Island, during the spring of 1849. [By Mary Charlton, later the Marchesa Pasqualine.] 8vo. [*Brit. Mus.*] London, 1850

LETTERS from Simkin the Second [Captain Ralph Broome] to his brother Simon in Wales; dedicated, without permission, to the ancient and respectable family of the Grunters. 8vo. [*Camb. Univ. Lib.*] London, 1796

Directed against Edmund Burke. See also "Strictures on Mr Burke's Two letters. . . ."

LETTERS from Simpkin the Second [Captain Ralph Broome] to his dear brother in Wales, containing an humble description of the trial of Warren Hastings in Westminster Hall. Second edition. 12mo. London, 1792

LETTERS from Snowdon, descriptive of a tour through the Northern counties of Wales; containing the antiquities, history, and state of the country: with the manners and customs of the inhabitants. [By Joseph Cradock, F.R.S.] 8vo. Pp. 218. [*Bodl.*] London, 1770

LETTERS from South Africa, reprinted from *The Times*, July-Oct. 1892. [By Flora Louisa Shaw, afterwards Lady Lugard.] 8vo. Pp. 116. London, 1892

LETTERS from Spain. By Don Leucadio Doblado [Joseph Blanco White, M.A., of Oriel]. 8vo. [*Bodl.*] London, 1822

LETTERS from Spain, 1863 to 1866. By a resident there [—— La Corte]. 8vo. London, 1868

LETTERS from Spain in 1856 and 1857. [By John Leycester Adolphus, barrister.] 8vo. [*D.N.B.* vol. 1, p. 142.] London, 1858

LETTERS from Switzerland and Italy. [By John Carne.] 8vo. [*Brit. Mus.*] London, 1834

LETTERS from Switzerland, 1833. [By Philip Henry Stanhope, Earl Stanhope.] 8vo. Pp. 160. Carlsruhe, 1834

Unpublished.

LETTERS from Sylvius [Hugh Williamson] to the freemen inhabitants of the United States. 8vo. [Cushing's *Init. and Pseud.* ii. 142.] New York, 1787

LETTERS from the army in the Crimea, written during the years 1854, 1855, & 1856. By a staff-officer who was there [Sir Anthony Coningham Stirling]. 8vo. Pp. xlviii. 496. N.P., N.D.

For private circulation only.

"Bodl. Lib. By will of the author, the late Sir Anthony Coningham Stirling."—MS. note on Bodleian copy.

LETTERS from the Bahama Islands, written in 1823-4. [By Miss Hart.] 12mo. [Rich's *Bibl. Amer.* ii. 196.] Philadelphia, 1827

LETTERS from the beloved city. To S. B. from Philip [Beste]. 8vo. London, 1904

LETTERS from the Cape of Good Hope in reply to Mr Warden. [By Barry Edward O'Meara, surgeon.] 8vo. [*Brit. Mus.*] London, 1817

Preface signed: C—.

LETTERS from the Cardinal Borgia and the Cardinal of York. [Edited by Sir John Coxe Hippisley, Bart.] 4to. [Martin's *Cat.*] London, 1799, 1800

LETTERS from the Continent. By a clergyman's wife [Mrs Margaret Fison]. 8vo. London, 1846

LETTERS from the Crimea. By a Subaltern officer [Arthur Brooksbank, 38th Regiment]. 12mo. London, 1873

LETTERS from the Danube. By the author of *Gisella*, etc. [John Palgrave Simpson, M.A.]. 12mo. 2 vols. London, 1847

LETTERS from the Duchess de Crui and others, on subjects moral and entertaining; wherein the character of the fair sex, with their rank, importance, and consequence, is stated, and their relative duties in life are enforced. By a lady [—— Walker]. 8vo. 5 vols. [Dr Macknight's *Cat.*] London, 1776

LETTERS from the Earl of Peterborough to General Stanhope, in Spain, from the originals at Chevening. [Edited by Lord Viscount Mahon.] 8vo. Pp. 51. [Martin's *Cat.*] London, 1834

Not published, and only fifty copies printed.

LETTERS from the East, written in 1750 . . . containing observations on the productions of nature, monuments of art, and manners of the inhabitants. [By —— Hill.] 8vo. 2 vols. London, 1753

LETTERS from the forty-fourth Regiment M.V.M., 1862-63. By Corporal [Zenas T. Haines]. 8vo. [Cushing's *Init. and Pseud.* i. 67.] New York, 1863

LETTERS from the Highlands in 1883. [By Alexander Innes Shand, advocate.] Reprinted from *The Times.* 8vo. [*Brit. Mus.*] London, 1884

LETTERS from the Highlands; or, two months among the salmon and the deer. By James Conway [James Conway Walter]. 8vo. Pp. viii. 142. London, 1859

A later edition (1859) enlarged, bears a different title: "Forays among salmon and deer."

LETTERS from the Inspector [Sir John Hill, M.D.] to a lady, with the genuine answers: both printed verbatim from the originals. 8vo. Pp. 48. [*Bodl.*] London, 1752

The letters are signed: J. H. and the answers: D.

LETTERS from the Irish Highlands of Connemara. By a family party [Mrs Henry Wood, *née* Ellen Price]. 8vo. Pp. xviii. 359. London, 1825

LETTERS from the kingdom of Kerry in the year 1845. [By Mrs Lydia Jane Fisher.] 8vo. [*Camb. Univ. Lib.*] Dublin, 1847

LETTERS from the Mediterranean. By H. W. [H. Watson]. 8vo. N.P. private print [1876]

LETTERS from the mountains; being the real correspondence of a lady, between the years 1773 and 1807 [Mrs Anne Grant, *née* Macvicar]. Fourth edition. 12mo. 3 vols. [*Brit. Mus.*] London, 1809

LETTERS from the North of Italy; addressed to Henry Hallam, Esq. [By William Stewart Rose.] 8vo. 2 vols. [Courtney's *Secrets*, p. 22.] London, 1819

Introduction signed: W. S. R.

LETTERS from the Old World. By a lady of New York [Mrs Sarah Haight]. 12mo. 2 vols. [*Brit. Mus.*] New York, 1840

LETTERS from the Red Beech; six letters by a layman [Alex. Taylor Innes, LL.D.] to a minister of the Free Church of Scotland, on the Canon, the pulpit, and criticism. 4to. Pp. 23. [*New Coll. Lib.*] Edinburgh [1880]

A pamphlet on the case of Professor W. Robertson Smith.

LETTERS from the Right Honourable W. E. [William Eden, afterwards Baron Auckland] on the late political arrangement, to the Earl of Carlisle. . . . 8vo. Pp. 58. [*Brit. Mus.*] London, 1786

LETTERS from the shores of the Baltic. [By Elizabeth Rigby, afterwards Lady Eastlake.] 8vo. [Courtney's *Secrets*, p. 63.] London, 1844

A reprint of "A residence on the shores of the Baltic," *q.v.*

LETTERS from the South and West [of the United States]. By Arthur Singleton, Esq. [Henry Cogswell Knight]. 8vo. [*Brit. Mus.*] Boston, 1824

LETTERS from the South [United States], written during an excursion in the summer of 1816. By the author of *John Bull*, etc. [James Kirke Paulding]. 12mo. 2 vols. [*Brit. Mus.*] New York, 1817

LETTERS from the spirit world. [By Lord Carlingford.] 8vo. N.P. private print, 1904

LETTERS from Virginia; translated from the French [but really written in English, by George Tucker]. 12mo. [*Brit. Mus.*] Baltimore, 1816

LETTERS from Washington, on the Constitution and laws; with sketches of some of the prominent characters of the United States. . . . [By George Watterston.] 12mo. [*Brit. Mus.*] Washington, 1818

Signed: S—.

LETTERS from X. [Signed: J. S. *i.e.* J. Stuart.] 8vo. Pp. 127. [*Brit. Mus.*] London, 1893

LETTERS from Yorick [Laurence Sterne] to Eliza [Mrs Draper]; a new edition. 12mo. Pp. 104. [*Dyce Cat.* ii. 331.] London, 1775

LETTERS from Zilia to Aza; taken from the French. [By Col. Beaver.] 4to. Pp. ii. 70. [*Bodl.*] Dublin, 1853

LETTERS illustrative of Italian scenery and antiquities; suggested during a tour on the Continent performed in the summer of 1817. [Signed: R. C. M. *i.e.* R. C. Marsden.] 12mo. Pp. 101. [Dobell's *Private prints*, p. 118.] N.P. 1821

LETTERS in answer to some queries, concerning the genuine reading of the Greek text, 1 Tim. iii. 16. [By —— Mawers.] 8vo. [Leslie's *Cat.* p. 1843.] 1758

LETTERS in answer to two propositions advanced by Dr W. J. M. in favour of Teetotalism. By Delta [Edwin Toby Caulfield, Lieut. R.N.]. 12mo. Pp. 87. [Green's *Bibl. Somers.* i. 95.] Bath, 1840

LETTERS in defence of the British and Foreign Bible Society, addressed to a friend in the country. . . . [By David Brown, Bookseller.] 8vo. [*New Coll. Lib.*] Edinburgh, 1826

Signed: Amicus.

LETTERS in proof of a particular Providence, addressed to Dr Hawkesworth. [By —— Caulfield.] 8vo. London, 1777

LETTERS in the Devonshire dialect. By Nathan Hogg [Thomas Baird]. 8vo. [Davidson's *Bibl. Devon.* p. 13.] Exeter, 1847

LETTERS lately published in the Diary, on the subject of the present disputes with Spain, under the signature of Verus [Sir James Bland Burges]. 8vo. Pp. 101. [*Mon. Rev.* iii. 475.] London, 1790

LETTERS, literary and political, on Poland; comprising observations on Russia and other Sclavonian nations and tribes. [By Christianus Lach Szyrma.] 8vo. [*Brit. Mus.*] Edinburgh, 1823

LETTERS (the) of a betrothed. [By Marguerite A. Power.] 8vo. [*Olphar Hamst*, p. 59.] London, 1858

The letters are signed either: Honoria N—, or simply: Honoria.

LETTERS of a Hampshire Conservative on points of the London Government Bill. [By Edward Edwards, librarian.] 8vo. London, 1884

LETTERS of a lady of quality to a Chevalier. [By Mrs Eliza Haywood.] 8vo. [*D. N. B.* vol. 25, p. 315.] London, 1724

LETTERS of a man of God [W. B. Sississon]; with preface by H. N. [H. Newton]. 8vo. London, 1879

LETTERS of a man of the times to the citizens of Baltimore. [By John Pendleton Kennedy.] 8vo. [Allibone's *Dict.*] Baltimore, 1836

LETTERS of a sentimental idler, from Greece, Turkey, Egypt, Nubia, and the Holy Land. [By Henry Harewood Leech.] 8vo. [Cushing's *Init. and Pseud.* i. 265.] London, 1866

LETTERS of a son to his self-made father. By Charles Eustace Merriman [Wilder Dwight Quint and George Tilton Richardson]. 8vo. Boston, 1904

LETTERS of a traveller. By George Sand [Madame A. A. L. Dudevant]. Translated by Eliza A. Ashurst; edited by Matilda M. Hays, author of *Helen Stanley*. 8vo. Pp. 321. [*Lit. Year Book.*] London, 1847

LETTERS of Abelard and Heloise; to which is prefix'd a particular account of their lives, amours, and misfortunes. . . . Translated from the French [by John Hughes]. 12mo. London, 1722

Later editions have the translator's name.

LETTERS of advice touching the choice of knights and burgesses for the Parliament, and directed to all those counties, cities and boroughs of this kingdome, to whom the choice of such knights, and burgesses do appertaine; that for prevention of the publike ruine now threatened, they may be more carefull to make good elections now and hereafter, then they have been heretofore. . . . [By George Wither.] 4to. Pp. 26. [*Bodl.*] London, 1646

LETTERS of affaires, love and courtship. By Monsieur de Voiture. English'd by J. D. [John Davies]. Pp. 370. London, 1657

LETTERS of Algernon Sydney in defence of civil liberty. . . . [By Benjamin Watkins Legh.] 8vo. [Cushing's *Init. and Pseud.* i. 278.] Richmond, Va., 1830

LETTERS of an American, mainly on Russia and revolution: edited [but rather written] by W. S. L. [Walter Savage Landor]. 8vo. [Green's *Bibl. Somers.* i. 304.] London, 1854

LETTERS of an architect [Joseph Woods] from France, Italy, and Greece. 8vo. [Cushing's *Init. and Pseud.* i. 18.] London, 1828

LETTERS of an English traveller to his friend in England, on the "Revivals of Religion" in America. [By Orville Dewey.] 12mo. [*Brit. Mus.*] Boston, 1828

LETTERS (the) of an Englishman. [By Charles Whibbley]. 8vo. 2 vols. [*Brit. Mus.*] London, 1911-12

Reprinted from the *Daily Mail.* The author's name is given in a later edition (1915).

LETTERS of an Italian nun. [By William Combe?] 8vo. London, 1789

LETTERS of Atticus. [By Richard, Viscount Fitzwilliam.] 12mo. Pp. 65. [Martin's *Cat.*] 1811

LETTERS of Atticus, printed in the *London Journal* in 1729 and 1730, on various subjects; with an introduction. [By Thomas Cooke, of Braintree, Essex.] 8vo. [*Brit. Mus.*] London, 1731

LETTERS (the) of Britannicus on important questions relating to the tea industry in the Province of Assam: reprinted from *The Englishman.* [By Gustavus Septimus Judge.] 8vo. [*Calc. Imp. Lib.*] Calcutta, 1886

LETTERS (the) of Brutus to certain celebrated political characters. [By Henry Mackenzie.] 8vo. [*W.*] Edinburgh, 1791

LETTERS (the) of Cardinal Manning; with notes by John Oldcastle [Wilfrid Meynell]. 8vo. [*Brit. Mus.*] London, 1892

LETTERS of certain Jews to M. de Voltaire, containing an apology for their own people, and for the Old Testament, with critical reflections. [By the Abbé Anthony Guénée.] Translated by the Rev. Philip Lefanu, D.D. 8vo. 2 vols. [*Brit. Mus.*] Dublin, 1777

LETTERS (the) of Civis [Sir Henry Russell] on Indian affairs, 1842-49. 8vo. [Cushing's *Init. and Pseud.* i. 60.] London, 1850

LETTERS of Clericus [Charles Plowden, S.J.] to Laicus [—— Blair, an apothecary]. 8vo. [Oliver's *Collections*, p. 168.] London, 1815

LETTERS of Crito on the causes, objects, and consequences of the present war. [By John Millar.] Second edition. 12mo. [*Nat. Lib. of Scot.*] Edinburgh [1796]

LETTERS of Curtius. [By John Thompson.] 8vo. [Cushing's *Init. and Pseud.* i. 72.] Richmond, Va., 1804

LETTERS of Daniel Hardcastle [Richard Page] to the editor of *The Times* journal, on the subject of the Bank restriction. . . . 8vo. [Cushing's *Init. and Pseud.* i. 126.] London, 1819

LETTERS (the) of Detector [Nathaniel Brassey Halhed] on the seventh and eighth reports of the Select Committee, and the India Registration Bill. 8vo. [Cushing's *Init. and Pseud.* ii. 44.] London, 1783

LETTERS (the) of Fabius in 1788, on the Federal Constitution, and in 1797 on the present situation of public affairs. [By John Dickinson.] 8vo. [Cushing's *Init. and Pseud.* i. 98.] Wilminston, Delaware, 1797

LETTERS of Fabius to the Right Hon. William Pitt, on his proposed abolition of the Test in favour of the Roman Catholics of Ireland. [By John Ireland, D.D., Dean of Westminster.] 8vo. [*D. N. B.* vol. 29, p. 31.] London, 1801

These letters were previously published in Wm. Cobbett's paper "The Porcupine."

LETTERS of friendship to those clergymen who have lately renounced Communion with the Ministers and Churches of Christ in general. . . . [By Joseph Huntingdon, D.D.] 8vo. Pp. 134. [Evans' *Amer. Bibl.* vol. 6, p. 79.] Hartford [Conn.] 1780

LETTERS of George Sand [Madame Amandine A. L. Dudevant], translated and edited by R. L. de Beaufort. . . . 8vo. 3 vols. [*Brit. Mus.*] London, 1886

LETTERS (the) of Guatimozin. [By Frederick Jebb.]

See "Guatimozin's Letters."

LETTERS of Henry and Frances [Richard Griffith and his wife, Elizabeth Griffith]. 8vo. [Watt's *Bibl. Brit.*] London, 1755

LETTERS (the) of her mother to Elizabeth. [By W. R. H. Trowbridge.] 8vo. Pp. 159. London, 1901

Attributed also to Mrs Clayton Glyn.

LETTERS of Hiberno-Anglus; containing strictures on the conduct of the present Administration in Ireland. [By Sir John Joseph Dillon.] 8vo. [Watt's *Bibl. Brit.*] London, 1812

LETTERS (the) of Hierophilus [John MacHale, Roman Catholic Archbishop of Tuam] on the education of the poor of Ireland, &c. 8vo. [*D. N. B.* vol. 35, p. 106.] Dublin, 1821

LETTERS of Hierophilos [John MacHale, R.C. Archbishop of Tuam] to the English people, on the moral and political state of Ireland. . . . 8vo. [Cushing's *Init. and Pseud.* i. 129.] London, 1822

LETTERS of importance, wherein are contained some serious queries upon several very interesting points . . . directed to the ensuing Venerable Synod of Ulster. . . . By Pistophilos Philecclesia [Benjamin M'Dowell, D.D., minister in Dublin]. 12mo. Pp. 52. [Witherow's *Lit. Presb. in Ireland*, ii. 145.] Belfast, 1775

LETTERS (the) of Indophilus [Sir Charles Edward Trevelyan, K.C.B.] to *The Times*. With additional notes. 8vo. [*D. N. B.* vol. 57, p. 209.] London [1857]

LETTERS of J. L. Guez. de Balzac; translated into English according to the last edition by W. T. [William Tirwhyt], Esq. 4to. [Watt's *Bibl. Brit.*] London, 1634

LETTERS of Jack Downing, Major, Downingville Militia, second brigade, to his old friend, Mr Dwight of the New-York *Daily Advertiser.* [By Seba Smith.] 12mo. [*W.*] New York, 1834

Second English edition with three additional letters, London, 1835, 12mo.

LETTERS of Jonathan Oldstyle, Gent. [By Washington Irving.] 8vo. [Allibone's *Dict.*] New York, 1824

LETTERS of Junius, with preliminary dissertations and copious notes. By Atticus Secundus [John M'Diarmid]. 12mo. [Lowndes' *Bibl. Man.* p. 1242.] Edinburgh, 1822

LETTERS (the) of Junius. [Published in the *Public Advertiser* from January 1769 to January 1772. The first letter is dated 21 January 1769, and the last January 21, 1772.]

Newbery published a spurious and surreptitious edition of the first fifteen letters under the title of *The Political Contest* in August 1769. A second and a third edition of this were published; and a second part, containing a continuation to September 1769, was also issued. Almon also published an edition in 1769. Fuller series of the letters were afterwards collected, and several spurious editions were published in 1770 and 1771. The first authorized and acknowledged edition, printed by H. S. Woodfall, printer of the *Public Advertiser*, was published in 1772, 2 vols. sm. 8vo. This is the true Woodfall edition, although the following edition is very generally so called:—Junius, including Letters by the same writer under other signatures (now first collected) . . . with a Preliminary Essay [by J. Mason Good, M.D.]. London, 1812, 3 vols. 8vo; second edition. London, Printed by G. Woodfall, 1814, 3 vols. 8vo. A new edition by John Wade was published in Bohn's Standard Library in 1850, 2 vols. sm. 8vo. Many other editions have been published, but it is not necessary to mention them here.

The secret of the authorship of these letters which puzzled the men of the last century still remains unsolved, and it may be added that with our present information it is practically insoluble. Almost every public man of the time has been supposed by some one to be the author, and yet one and all of these men have died and made no sign. It is therefore more than probable that the true author has never been so much as suspected. Mr Charles Dilke, late editor of the *Athenæum*, by far the most acute critic who has investigated the subject, believed Junius to have been a middle-class man, and an old newspaper correspondent. Junius himself writes of long experience of the world, and most of those to whom the authorship has been attributed were far advanced in life, but in those cases, such as that of Sir Philip Francis, where the supposed writer was young, this has been treated as a ruse of the writer to throw inquirers off the scent. The question of the authorship, always a difficult one, has been immensely complicated since 1812, when the edition containing Dr Mason Good's Essay was published by G. Woodfall. In this edition a large number of letters, never before attributed to the author of Junius, were printed as his without the slightest authority, and what was worse the writer or writers of these letters were referred to without explanation as Junius. Thus it was confidently stated that Junius wrote a year or two before his first letter appeared, and that such and such a person could not have been Junius because he died before Junius ceased to write, although the true Junius may really have ceased to write long before. Mr Wade follows this bad precedent in his edition, and the following is a good instance of the confusion thus introduced into the question. He writes of Lord Chesterfield, "Besides the old earl died when Junius was in full career" (Junius, ed. 1850, vol. ii. p. xxix.). Now the earl died on March 24, 1773, and the last letter of Junius appeared in the January of the previous year. It has been supposed that as Mason Good's edition was published by Woodfall it has some special authority, but in fact George Woodfall and Good had no information as to authorship that was not open to the whole world. Mr Dilke annihilated the authority of this edition in his trenchant articles in the *Athenæum*, reprinted in his posthumous *Papers of a Critic*. He showed that the dates affixed to the Private Letters of Junius are nearly all conjectural, although these dates are treated as if they were affixed by Junius himself, and arguments are founded upon them. In spite of many groundless rumours that have been recorded, it appears pretty certain that many if not all of the chief actors in the scenes criticised by Junius did not know who he really was. The Duke of Sussex learned from his mother that George III. was to the last uninformed as to the authorship. Mr Wade makes a very remarkable statement as to the king's knowledge, for he writes: "That George III. was authentically in possession of the secret soon after will be presently shown, and that the king knowing Francis to be the author accounts for the fact that he was the only person, with the exception of Mr Burke, who would speak to him on his unexpected return from India; his Majesty being among the few who were aware of the kind of subject that had reappeared in his dominions, and unwilling perhaps to afford fuel for a new Junian warfare." Those who have any conception of George III.'s character will probably hold that the fact of the king's coming forward to receive Francis proves that he did not connect him with the authorship of Junius. Wraxall tells us that both Lord North and Lord Temple protested their ignorance of the author. H. S. Woodfall knew sufficient to be able to say that such a one could not be Junius, but he died without the slightest knowledge of who he really was.

The following is a list of the persons to whom the authorship has at different times been attributed, with the names of those who have publicly advocated these claims, or failing such advocacy the names of those who have mentioned various claimants. The names are numbered, and at the end of the list I have made a few notes on some of the more important facts relative to some of the claimants.

1. ADAIR, JAMES, M.P., Serjeant-at-law, Recorder of London, died 1798. Allibone.

2. BARRÉ, Lieut.-Colonel ISAAC, M.P. 1848. John Britton. Britton supposes that Barré was assisted by Lord Shelburne and Dunning (afterwards Lord Ashburton). As early as 1813 an opinion was expressed in the *Morning Herald* that the Earl of Shelburne was Junius, and that he was assisted by Barré and Dunning.

3. BENTINCK, WILLIAM HENRY CAVENDISH, mentioned in George Coventry's *Critical Enquiry*, 1825.

4. BOYD, HUGH M'AULAY, b. 1746, d. 1791. 1798-1800. L. D. Campbell in edition of Boyd's *Miscellaneous Works*. John Almon, the publisher, is said to have been the first to attribute the Letters to Boyd, and this was in 1769. 1800. George Chalmers (appendix to the Supplemental Apology). 1817. Chalmers, *The author of J. ascertained.*

5. BURKE, Right Hon. EDMUND, b. 1728, d. 1797. 1771. *Genuine Letters, with Anecdotes of the Author* (Piccadilly edition). 1813. John Roche. 1826. *Junius proved to have been Burke.* [By Patrick Kelly.]

6. BURKE, WILLIAM. 1859. Jellinger Cookson Symons.

7. BUTLER, JOHN, Bishop of Hereford, d. 1802. 1814. Mentioned in Dr Mason Good's Essay.

8. CAMDEN, CHARLES, Lord, b. 1713, d. 1794. Wade, Allibone.

9. CHATHAM, WILLIAM PITT, Earl of, b. 1708, d. 1778. 1809. *Another guess at Junius* [attributed to Rev. —— Fitzgerald]. 1831. Benjamin Waterhouse (New York), 1833. John Swinden. 1837. Anon., *Who was Junius?* 1857. William Dowe (New York).

10. CHESTERFIELD, PHILIP DORMER STANHOPE, Earl of, b. 1695, d. 24 March 1773. 1821, 1850, 1851. William Cramp. In 1851 Mr Cramp published Facsimile Autograph Letters of Junius, Lord Chesterfield, and Mrs C. Dayrolles, showing that the wife of Mr Solomon Dayrolles was the amanuensis employed.

11. DE LOHNE, JOHN LEWIS, b. 1745 (or 1742), d. 1807. 1816. Thomas Busby, Mus.D.

12. DUNNING. See *Barré*.

13. DYER, SAMUEL, b. 1725, d. 1772. Mentioned in Dr Mason Good's Essay, and in George Coventry's *Critical Enquiry*, 1825.

14. FLOOD, HENRY, b. 1732, d. 1791. 1814. Mentioned in Dr Mason Good's Essay.

15. FRANCIS, Sir PHILIP, b. 1740, d. 1818. 1816. John Taylor, *Junius Identified.* 1822. Atticus Secundus. 1850. Sir Fortunatus Dwarris. Dwarris was of opinion that the Letters were not the work of one hand, but were probably written by many of those to whom they have been attributed, and that Sir Philip Francis received pay and was the chief contributor. 1867. *Memoirs of Sir Philip Francis, K.C.B.* By Joseph Parkes and Herman Merivale, 2 vols. 8vo. 1871. *Handwriting of Junius professionally investigated* by Charles Chabot, with preface and collateral evidence by the Hon. Edward Twisleton.

16. FRANCIS, PHILIP, D.D., d. 1773. 1813. John Taylor, *A Discovery of the Author of the Letters of Junius.*

17. GIBBON, EDWARD, b. 1737, d. 1794. 1819. Anon., *Junius unmasked.* 1909. James Smith (Australian.)

18. GLOVER, RICHARD, author of *Leonidas*, b 1712, d. 1785. 1813. Richard Duppa.

19. GRATTAN, HENRY, b. 1750, d. 1820. 1861. R. Perry. Almon (*Junius*, 1806, i. xxii.) says that it was supposed by some that Grattan and Maclean were joint authors.

20. GREATRAKES, WILLIAM. Mentioned in Wraxall's *Memoirs of his own Time*, and in George Coventry's *Critical Enquiry*, 1825. John Britton supposed him to have been the amanuensis employed by Junius.

21. GRENVILLE, GEORGE, Prime Minister, b. 1712, d. 1770. Wade, Allibone.

22. GRENVILLE, JAMES, Lord of the Treasury, d. 1783. Wade, Allibone.

23. HAMILTON, WILLIAM GERARD ("Single-Speech" Hamilton), b. 1729, d. 1796. There is a letter in the *Public Advertiser* of November 30, 1771, addressed to William Junius Singlespeech, Esq. Mentioned in Mason Good's Essay.

24. HOLLIS, JAMES. Wade, Allibone.

25. HOLLIS, THOMAS, b. 1720, d. 1774. Mentioned in George Coventry's *Critical Enquiry*, 1825.

26. JONES, Sir WILLIAM, b. 1746, d. 1794. Mentioned in George Coventry's *Critical Enquiry*, 1825.

27. KENT, JOHN. He wished to pass as Junius. He died after a lingering illness on 22d January 1773.

28. LEE, General CHARLES, b. 1731, d. 1782. 1803. General Lee is said to have asserted in confidence that he was Junius. 1807, 1808, 1813. Thomas Girdlestone, M.D.

29. LLOYD, CHARLES, Secretary to George Grenville. 1814. Mentioned in Dr Mason Good's Essay. 1825. Mentioned in George Coventry's *Critical Enquiry*. 1828. E. H. Barker. (Dr Parr was a believer in Lloyd's claim.)

30. LYTTELTON, THOMAS, 2nd Lord, b. 1744, d. 1779. *Quarterly Review*, vol. 90, p. 91 (David Trevena Coulton).

31. MACLEANE, LAUGHLIN, b. 1727 or 1728, d. 1777. Mentioned by Almon (1806) as supposed to be joint-author with Grattan. 1816. Galt in his *Life of West.* Also Sir David Brewster in various publications.

32. PORTLAND, WILLIAM, Duke of, b. 1738, d. 1809. 1816. *Letters to a Nobleman* [by A. G. Johnston].

33. POWNALL, Governor THOMAS, b. 1722, d. 1805. 1854. Fred. Griffin (Boston, Mass.).

34. RICH, Lieut.-Col. Sir ROBERT, Bart. 1853. Francis Ayerst, *The Ghost of Junius.*

35. ROBERTS, JOHN. Mentioned in Mason Good's Essay as having died July 13, 1772, before Junius (?) discontinued writing.

36. ROSENHAGEN, Rev. PHILIP. 1814. Mentioned in Mason Good's Essay. Hardly worth noticing.

37. SACKVILLE, GEORGE, Viscount (Lord George Sackville, afterwards Germaine), b. 1716, d. 1785. 1822. Charles Butler's *Reminiscences.* 1825. George Coventry. 1828. *Junius unmasked:* by Atticus Secundus [Joseph Bolles Manning], Boston, U.S. Also attributed to John Elwyn. 1843. John Jaques.

38. SHELBURNE, Earl of. See *Barré*.

39. STUART, Dr GILBERT, b. 1742, d. 1786, 1799. *Scots Magazine* (No. xi., p. 734). Mentioned in George Coventry's *Critical Enquiry*, 1825.

40. TEMPLE, RICHARD, Earl, b. 1711, d. 1779. 1831. Isaac Newhall (Boston, U.S.). 1852. W. J. Smith, *Grenville Correspondence*, vol. iii. Lady Temple is supposed to have been her husband's amanuensis.

41. TOOKE, JOHN HORNE, b. 1736, d. 1812. 1789. Philip Thicknesse. 1813. Rev. John Brickdale Blakeway. 1828. John A. Graham, LL.D., New York. 1829. *Junius's Posthumous Works, with Life of Horne Tooke* [by J. Bellows], (New York). 1904. *Junius's Letters: the author mystery solved*, by Vicarius [Rev. J. Samuels].

42. WALPOLE, (HORATIO), Earl of Orford, b. 1717, d. 1797. Sir Charles Grey. George Coventry takes some little pains to show the groundlessness of the ascription.

43. WEDDERBURN, ALEXANDER (Lord Loughborough and Earl of Rosslyn), b. 1733, d. 1805. Wraxall's *Memoirs of his own Time*.

44. WILKES, JOHN, b. 1727, d. 1797. 1770. *Address to Junius*.

45. WILMOT, JAMES, D.D., b. 1726, d. 1807. 1813, 1817. Olivia Wilmot Serres.

46. WRAY, DANIEL, Deputy Teller of the Exchequer, b. 1701, d. 1783. 1830. James Falconar, jun.

To these names may be added a Captain Allen; Bickerton, an eccentric Oxonian; William Combe, the author of *Doctor Syntax*; an utterly unknown Mr Jones; the Rev. Edmond Marshall, Vicar of Charing; and Thomas Paine. The Letters have actually been attributed to George III., and in 1819 a pamphlet was published at Oxford under the title of "Junius with his visor up," in which the claims of Snett, the comedian, are jokingly set forth.

The name "Allibone" in the above list refers to Mr Allibone's *Dictionary of English Literature*, which contains a very excellent article on Junius, and a full list of the claimants.

4. Boyd has been described as "an admirer of Junius, and vain enough to wish to be thought the author." He is one of the supposed authors whose claims are considered by Sir Nathaniel Wraxall, Memoirs of his own Time, 1836, ii. 93-4).

5. Burke made three distinct denials, which have been recorded, one to Lord Townshend, another to Sir William Draper (which satisfied that gentleman), and the third to Dr Johnson when he said, "I could not if I would, and I would not if I could."

7. Bishop Butler was originally secretary to the Rt. Hon. Bilson Legge, Chancellor of the Exchequer, and it is reported that Wilkes at one time suspected him to be the author.

10. Chesterfield was old and infirm, and Mr Dilke points out that when the Letters were appearing he wrote to the Bishop of Waterford—"I am prodigiously old, and every month of the Calendar adds at least a year to my age. My hand trembles to that degree that I can hardly hold my pen. My understanding stutters and my memory fumbles" (*Papers of a Critic*, ii. 142).

11. A sufficient answer to the claim set up for De Lohne is that, according to his own account, he came to England for the first time in 1769.

13. Malone persisted in saying that if the Letters were not written by Burke, they were at least written by some person who had received great assistance from Burke in composing them, and he was strongly inclined to fix the authorship of them upon Dyer. It was reported that upon Dyer's death Burke secured and suppressed all the papers which he had left behind him. Dyer is referred to in Malone's *Life of Dryden* as "a man of excellent taste and profound erudition, whose principal literary work, under a Roman signature, when the veil with which for near thirty-six years it has been enveloped shall be removed, will place him in a high rank among English writers, and transmit a name now little known with distinguished lustre to posterity."

15. Sir Philip Francis was not suspected until after the publication of the 1812 edition, which contained the Miscellaneous Letters. Mr Wade writes, "Had the public never known any edition of the Letters except that revised by Junius himself, it is probable that the author would have remained even unsuspected. But the "Private Letters," numbers 61 and 62, and the "Miscellaneous Letters," subscribed Veteran, Scotus, and Nemesis, afforded a clue of which an ingenious inquirer [John Taylor] availed himself." (*Junius* (H. G. Bohn, 1850), vol. ii. p. xxxi. Oddly enough Taylor first supposed that Dr Francis, Sir Philip's father, was the author, and as Mr Dilke remarks, he supported his theory by quotations from that scholar's editions of Horace and Demosthenes. When, however, a few years later he put aside the father in favour of the son, all these elaborate proofs were forgotten. The coincidences that have been brought forward in favour of Sir Philip Francis have convinced a large number of distinguished men, and it may be safely said that at one time the general opinion was in his favour. Charles Butler held that the external evidence was all in favour of Francis, and the internal evidence all against him; and to harmonize these conflicting evidences, he supposes Francis to have been the amanuensis of Junius, and several other writers have held this same opinion. It must, however, be borne in mind that Mr Dilke, by means of his searching criticism, cleared away at least half of the evidence which was supposed to tell in favour of Francis. The strongest point against Francis is this, that he and his friend Dubois did all in their power to make the public believe that he was the author, and yet had he really been such, nothing would have been easier than for him to leave behind him some evidence which would have settled the matter. This he never did.

18. Glover is one of those mentioned by Wraxall, who says that the son of the poet assured him that "he had not the least reason to suppose or to believe that his father composed the Letters of Junius" (*Memoirs of his own Time*, 1836, ii. 97).

19. Almon, the publisher, wrote a letter of inquiry to Grattan and received the following reply:—"Sir, —I frankly assure you that I know nothing of Junius, except that I am *not* the author. When Junius began I was a boy, and knew nothing of politics or the persons concerned in them. I am, Sir, *not Junius*, but your very good wisher and obedient servant, H. Grattan.—Dublin, November 4, 1805."

20. Greatrakes was private secretary to the Earl of Shelburne. His claim appears to be almost entirely based on the fact that he died suddenly on his way from Bristol to London, and was buried there, with the Junian motto, *Stat Nominis Umbra*, inscribed upon his tombstone.

21. As Grenville died some time before the Letters were discontinued, his claim does not deserve much consideration. Moreover, Junius positively asserted that he had no personal knowledge of Grenville.

23. Hamilton's claim at one time had many supporters. Fox said that though he would not back him against the field, he would back him against any single horse. Wraxall wrote as follows to the same effect, "Throughout the various companies in which from 1775 down to the present time I have heard this mysterious question agitated, the great majority concurred in giving to Hamilton the merit of composing the Letters under examination." Commenting on this passage Mrs Piozzi wrote that she was of the same opinion that Hamilton was the man, and added "N. Seward said, 'How the arrows of Junius were sure to wound, and likely to stick.' 'Yes, sir,' replied Dr Johnson, 'yet let us distinguish between the venom of the shaft and the vigour of the bow.' At which expression Mr Hamilton's countenance fell in a manner that to *me* betrayed the author. Johnson repeated the expression in his next pamphlet, and Junius *wrote no more*." Wraxall's opinion loses much of its force from his subsequent confession that Taylor's book had converted him to a belief in the claims of Francis. One

reason for attributing the Letters to Hamilton was found in the following anecdote. One day when in company with the Duke of Richmond he alluded to the purport of one of the letters as though he had just read it. No such letter did appear on that day, although it did appear on the day after. The inference was that Hamilton must have been the author, but Dr Mason Good's explanation was that Hamilton was a friend of H. S. Woodfall, and may have seen the MS. before the letter was printed. Against the supposition that Hamilton was the author there are the following facts:—1. that he solemnly denied the charge in his last illness; 2. that Woodfall repeatedly declared that neither Burke nor Hamilton was the writer; and 3. that Hamilton was Chancellor of the Exchequer in Ireland from September 1769 to April 1774, during the very period when all the Letters of Junius appeared.

30. The "wicked" Lord Lyttelton's claims are almost too absurd for a moment's consideration. Mr Dilke annihilated them in the *Athenæum*, and his article is reprinted in *Papers of a Critic*, vol. ii. Mr Thoms proved by the date of one of Lyttelton's letters that he was abroad in November 1771, when Junius must have been in London. (*Notes and Queries*, 1st Series, vol. xi., March 17, 1855.)

36. Wraxall knew Rosenhagen, and refers to him as a frequent visitor at Lord Shelburne's, but he did not consider his claim as entitled to serious refutation. Rosenhagen was a schoolfellow of H. S. Woodfall, who repeatedly declared that he was not Junius.

37. A very fair case was made out for Lord Sackville, and Charles Butler, who devoted considerable attention to the subject, was inclined to think that he was the author. Sir William Draper divided his suspicions between Burke and Lord George Sackville, and on Burke's unequivocal denial he transferred them wholly to Sackville, who was (it is said) at times suspected by H. S. Woodfall. Dr Sidney Swinney asked Sackville if he were the author, and Junius mentions the fact in a private letter to Woodfall. This has been supposed by some to be sufficient evidence that Junius and Sackville were one and the same man. Wraxall knew Sackville intimately, and frequently conversed with him on the subject of the authorship. "He always declared himself ignorant of the author, but he appeared to be gratified and flattered by the belief or imputation lighting on himself." (*Memoirs of his own Time*, 1836, vol. ii. p. 90.)

38. Lord Shelburne (then Marquis of Lansdowne) denied the authorship a week before his death in 1804, and his son the second Marquis believed that his father did not know who the author was.

42. Sir Charles Grey started the theory in a pamphlet which he sent from India to Lord Holland, but according to Dilke the pamphlet was suppressed on the advice of Lord Holland, as it ran counter to the popular ascription to Francis. Subsequently the substance of the claim was given in a letter from Sir Charles to the editor of Walpole's Letters, which was published in the edition of 1840. Mr Dilke said that it was by no means the wildest conjecture he had heard, and he then proceeded to show the possibility of Walpole's friend Mason having been the author. The reasons given are curious and worthy of further investigation, although Mr Dilke did not assert that his advocacy of Mason's claims was actually in earnest. (See *Papers of a Critic*, vol. ii. p. 158.)

43. Wraxall writes that "during many years of my life, notwithstanding the severity with which Wedderburn is treated by 'Junius,' I nourished a strong belief, approaching to conviction, that the late Earl of Rosslyn, then Mr Wedderburn, was himself the author of these Letters" (*Memoirs of his own Time*, 1836, vol. ii. p. 97).

44. It was only for a short time that anyone supposed Wilkes to be the author. He always repudiated the claim, and on one occasion he said "Would to Heaven I could have written them."

45. Probably no one but Mrs Serres (and she was an impostor) believed in Wilmot's claim, although "Vathek" Beckford is said to have expressed an opinion in his favour. Wilmot was curate of Kenilworth during several years commencing in 1770, and habitually resided there in the discharge of his professional duties.

LETTERS of literature. By Robert Heron, Esq. [John Pinkerton]. 8vo. [Nichols' *Lit. Anec.* viii. 159; Courtney's *Secrets*, p. 197.] London, 1785

LETTERS of Major Jack Downing [Seba Smith] to Mr Dwight, of the *New York Daily Advertiser.* [By Charles Augustus Davis.] 8vo. [Cushing's *Init. and Pseud.* i. 83.] London, 1835

LETTERS of Marcus [William P. Van Ness] and Philo-Cato [Matthew L. Davis] addressed to De Witt Clinton. 8vo. [Cushing's *Init. and Pseud.* i. 232.] New York, 1810

LETTERS of Marius; or, reflections upon the Peace, the East India Bill, and the present crisis. [By Thomas Day, barrister and philanthropist.] 8vo. [Watt's *Bibl. Brit.*] London, 1784

LETTERS of Mary Lepel, Lady Hervey; with a memoir and illustrative notes [by Rt. Hon. John Wilson Croker]. 8vo. [*W.*] London, 1821

LETTERS of Mr ——, the Abbot of ——, ex-Professor of the Hebrew language in the University of —— to Mr Kennicott [Benjamin Kennicott, D.D.], of the Royal Society in London, etc. Translated from the French [of J. A. Dumay, by William Stevens]. 12mo. [*D. N. B.* vol. 31, p. 21.] London, 1772

Kennicott at once replied, anonymously, in "A letter to a friend, occasioned by a French pamphlet . . ." See above.

LETTERS of Observator [Rev. John Evans], and the Rev. Eugene Egan, in 1835-36, on the free circulation of the Scriptures, etc. 8vo. [Mendham's *Collection* (*Supp.*), p. 12.] Whitchurch, Salop, 1837

LETTERS (the) of one; a study in limitations. By Charles Hare Plunkett [Arthur Christopher Benson]. 8vo. [*Camb. Univ. Lib.*] London, 1907

LETTERS (the) of one of the Commons of Great Britain on the subject of Mr [Warren] Hastings' impeachment, as first published in the *Gazeteer*; together with a letter addressed to the editor of that paper. . . . [By Dr —— Lawrence.] 8vo. London, 1790

Contemporary attestation of authorship.

LETTERS of Orellana, an Irish Helot, to the seven Northern Counties not represented in the national assembly of delegates, held at Dublin, October 1784, for obtaining a more equal representation of the people in the Parliament of Ireland. Originally published in the *Belfast News-letter.* [By William Drennan, M.D., Belfast.] 8vo. Pp. 75. [*Manch. Free Lib.*] Dublin, 1785

LETTERS of Papinian; in which the conduct, present state, and prospects of the American Congress are examined. [By Charles Inglis, Bishop of Nova Scotia.] 8vo. Pp. vi. 86. New York, printed; London, reprinted, 1779

The letters are five in number, and signed: Papinian.

LETTERS of Peregrine Pickle. [By George P. Upton.] 8vo. [Cushing's *Init. and Pseud.* i. 234.] Chicago, 1869

Reprinted from the *Chicago Tribune.*

LETTERS of Philopatris [Thomas Burgess, D.D., Bishop of St David's] to Dr Phillimore. I. On the political and anti-social evils of the Roman Catholic system. II. On religious liberty, and Roman Catholic merit, as pleas for admission to political power. III. On the unreformed Church. IV. On the same subject. V. With Sir Humphrey Lynde's contrast between the Reformed Church of England, and the unreformed Church of Rome: Proving by the confession of all sides, that the Protestant's religion is safer. . . . [The first part.] 8vo. Pp. 42. London, 1819

—— to Dr Phillimore on the Roman Catholic petition, and on Mr Wix's proposal of union between the Churches of England and of Rome. Part the second. 8vo. Pp. 38. London, 1819

—— on Lord Grey's Bill for abrogating the declarations against Transubstantiation & Popery, required by Stat. 25 & 30 of Ch. II. 8vo. Pp. 26. London, 1819

The letters are collected from the *Morning Post*, and consist of the 11th, 12th, 13th, 14th and 15th of the Letters addressed to Dr Phillimore.

LETTERS (the) of Publicola, from the *Weekly Dispatch*, with notes and emendations. By Publicola [D. J. Williams]. 8vo. Pp. 192. London, 1840

Presentation copy, with the author's own signature.

LETTERS of Publicola; or, a modest defence of the Established Church. By a member of it [Rowley Lascelles]. 8vo. Pp. 103. [*D. N. B.* vol. 32, p. 157.] Dublin, 1816

Originally published in the *Patriot*, a Dublin newspaper. See also "Letters of Yorick," a later edition of the same work.

LETTERS of religion between Theophilus and Eugenio. [By Sir Richard Blackmore.] 4to. London, 1729

LETTERS (the) of Runnymede. [By Benjamin Disraeli, afterwards Lord Beaconsfield.] 8vo. Pp. xx. 234. [*Brit. Mus.*] London, 1836

LETTERS (the) of Rusticus [Edward Newman, F.L.S.] on the natural history of Godalming; extracted from the *Magazine of Natural History*, the *Entomological Magazine*, and the *Entomologist.* 8vo. London, 1849

LETTERS of Scævola, on the dismissal of His Majesty's late Ministers. [By John Allen.] 8vo. 2 parts. [*Brit. Mus.*] London, 1807

LETTERS of Shahcoolen, a Hindu philosopher residing in Philadelphia, to his friend, El Hassan, an inhabitant of Delhi. [By Samuel Lorenzo Knapp.] 8vo. [Cushing's *Init. and Pseud.* i. 266.] Boston, 1802

LETTERS of Silas Standfast to his friend Jotham. [By George Stillman Hillard, LL.D.] 8vo. [Cushing's *Init. and Pseud.* i. 273.] Boston, 1853

LETTERS (the) of Simpkin the Second, poetic recorder of all the proceedings upon the trial of Warren Hastings, Esq. in Westminster Hall. [By Ralph Broome.] 8vo. Pp. viii. 224. [*Camb. Univ. Lib.*] London, 1789

"These Letters were originally published in the *World*, where they will be continued next year, and are now re-published and corrected by their author, with ten additional letters, which include the whole impeachment, from its commencement in February 1788, to the close of the proceedings in this year."—Printed note on title-page.

LETTERS of Terry Finnegan to the Hon. T. D. M'Gee. [By James M'Carroll.] 8vo. [Cushing's *Init. and Pseud.* i. 102.] Toronto, 1864

LETTERS (the) of the British spy. [By William Wirt.] 12mo. [Rich's *Bibl. Amer.* ii. 60.] 1812

First printed in Baltimore.

LETTERS of the late Lord Lyttelton. [Edited by William Combe.] New edition. 12mo. [*Brit. Mus.*] London, 1806

LETTERS of the Right Honourable Lady M--y W---y M----e [Mary Wortley Montague]; written during her travels in Europe, Asia and Africa, to persons of distinction, men of letters, &c. in different parts of Europe. . . . 8vo. 3 vols. [*Brit. Mus.*] London, 1763

LETTERS of the Southern Spy [Edward Alfred Pollard] in Washington and elsewhere. 8vo. [Cushing's *Init. and Pseud.* i. 272.] Baltimore, 1861

LETTERS of the Swedish Court, written chiefly in the early part of the reign of Gustavus III.; to which is added an appendix, containing an account of the assassination of that monarch. . . . [By Mrs Julia Smith.] 12mo. Pp. x. 282. [*Gent. Mag.* Feb. 1835, p. 211.] London, 1809

LETTERS (the) of Tim Tunbelly [William A. Mitchell] on the Tyne, Newcastle, etc. Vol. I. 8vo. Newcastle, 1823

No more published.

LETTERS (the) of Valens (which originally appeared in the *London Evening Post*); with corrections, explanatory notes, and a preface by the author [William Burke, assisted by Richard Burke]. 8vo. [*Brit. Mus.*] London, 1777

LETTERS (the) of Valerius [William Combe] on the state of parties, the war, the volunteer system, and most of the political topics which have lately been under public discussion; originally published in *The Times*. 8vo. [*Brit. Mus.*] London, 1804

LETTERS of "Verax" [Henry Dunckley, M.A., editor of the Manchester Examiner and Times]. (Reprinted from the *Manchester Weekly Times*.) 8vo. Pp. viii. 260. [*Lib. Journ.* iii. 163.] Manchester, 1878

LETTERS (the) of Verax on the currency; reprinted from the *Manchester Gazette* and the *Manchester Courier*. [By Dr Edward Carbutt.] 8vo. Pp. viii. 40. [*Brit. Mus.*] Manchester, 1829

LETTERS of Verus to the native Americans. [By Timothy Pickering.] 8vo. [Cushing's *Init. and Pseud.* i. 293.] Philadelphia, 1797

LETTERS (the) of Vetus, from March 10 to May 10, 1812. [By Captain Edward Stirling, father of John Stirling.] 8vo. [*Brit. Mus.*] London, 1812

Sometimes attributed to Charles Marsh.

These letters, six in number, appeared originally in *The Times*. A second part, containing letters No. VII. to No. XV., was published in November 1812.

LETTERS of Warren Hastings to his wife, transcribed in full from the originals in the British Museum; annotated by Sydney C. Grier [Hilda C. Gregg]. 8vo. [*Brit. Mus.*] London, 1905

LETTERS of yesterday. By J. W. [Rev. James Wood, of Edinburgh]. 8vo. London, 1907

Attestation of authorship from a friend of the writer.

LETTERS of Yorick; or, a good-humoured remonstrance in favour of the Established Church. By a very humble member of it. In three parts. . . . [By Rowley Lascelles.] 8vo. Pp. 377. [*D. N. B.* vol. 32, p. 157.] Dublin, 1817

This is a later edition of "Letters of Publicola." (See above.)

LETTERS of Zeno, addressed to the citizens of Edinburgh, on Parliamentary representation; and, particularly, on the imperfect representation for the city of Edinburgh and the other burghs of Scotland. A new edition, with considerable enlargements, by the author [Thomas M'Grugar]. 12mo. Pp. 60. Edinburgh, 1783

These letters appeared originally in the Edinburgh newspapers of December 1782 and January 1783.

LETTERS on a journey to Bombay, through Syria and Arabia, in 1834-35. [By Alexander S. Finlay.] 8vo. Pp. 176. [*Edin. Univ. Lib.*] Glasgow, private print, 1837

LETTERS on ancient history; exhibiting a summary view of the history, geography, manners and customs of the Assyrian, Babylonian, Median, Persian, Egyptian, Israelitish, and Grecian nations. . . . By a lady [Anne Wilson]. 8vo. Glasgow, 1809

LETTERS on army reform [including four reprinted from *The Times*]. By Jacob Omnium [Matthew James Higgins]. 8vo. [*D. N. B.* vol. 26, p. 371.] London [1855]

LETTERS on baptismal regeneration. By Defensor [Samuel Fuller]. 8vo. [Cushing's *Init. and Pseud.* ii. 43.] New York, 1852

LETTERS on capital punishments, addressed to the English judges. By Beccaria Anglicus [Richard Wright, Unitarian Baptist minister of Wisbeach]. 8vo. London, 1807

LETTERS on Catholic loyalty; originally published in the *Newcastle Courant*. [Signed: J. L. *i.e.* John Lingard, D.D.] 8vo. Pp. 36. [Gillow's *Bibl. Dict.*] Newcastle, 1807

LETTERS on certain statements contained in some late articles in the "Old Church Porch," entitled "Irvingism." [By John Bate Cardale, solicitor.] 8vo. [Boase's *Cath. Apost. Lit.*] London, 1855-57

LETTERS on chess; an account of some of the principal works on the game, with remarks: translated from the German of C. K. Vogt by U. Ewell [W. Lewis]. 8vo. [*Van der Linde.*] London, 1848

LETTERS on chivalry and romance. [By Richard Hurd, D.D.] 8vo. Pp. 120. [Moule's *Bibl. Herald.* No. 592.] London, 1762

LETTERS on Christian Baptism, addressed to Mr Charles Leckie. By a Baptist [David Macallan]. 8vo. [*Aberd. Pub. Lib.*] Aberdeen, 1840

LETTERS on Christian education. By a mother [Mrs Mary Hooker Cornelius]. 8vo. [Cushing's *Init. and Pseud.* i. 103.] New York, 1830

LETTERS on Christian missions. By a layman of the Church of England [Julius P. Cæsar]. 8vo. [Cushing's *Init. and Pseud.* i. 88.] Calcutta, 1858

Signed: J. P. C.

LETTERS on Church government. [By —— Clinch.] 8vo. [Lowndes' *Brit. Lib.* p. 391.] Dublin, 1812

LETTERS on Church [of England] matters. By D. C. L. [Alexander James Beresford Hope]. Reprinted from the *Morning Chronicle;* Nos. I. to XI. 8vo. [*Brit. Mus.*] London, 1851-55

No more published.

LETTERS on Church questions. By Vigilans [Rev. Charles Valentine Le Grice]. 8vo. [Boase and Courtney's *Bibl. Corn.*] Truro, 1845

LETTERS on Church subjects in the West of Cornwall. By Civis [Rev. Charles Valentine le Grice]. 8vo. [Boase and Courtney's *Bibl. Corn.*] Truro, 1844

LETTERS on colonial policy, particularly as applicable to Ceylon. By Philalethes [Sir Robert John Wilmot Horton, Bart., M.A., M.P., Governor of Ceylon]. 8vo. Pp. 20. [*Brit. Mus.*] Colombo, 1833

Republished in 1839 at London as "Letters containing observations on colonial policy. . . ."

LETTERS on confederation, botheration and political transmogrification. By Barney Rooney [William Garvie]. 8vo. [Cushing's *Init. and Pseud.* i. 253.] Halifax, Nova Scotia, 1865

LETTERS on Convocation. By A. H. E. [Sir Arthur Hallam Elton]. 8vo. [Green's *Bibl. Somers.* ii. 384.] Bristol, 1852

LETTERS on different subjects, in four volumes; amongst which are interspers'd the adventures of Alphonso, after the destruction of Lisbon. By the author of *The unfortunate mother's advice to her absent daughters* [Lady Sarah Pennington]. 8vo. London, 1766-67

A letter, forming part of the preface, is signed: S. P.

LETTERS on Disestablishment. By Criticus [Rev. William Spark, minister at Kirkwall]. 8vo. Kirkwall, 1875

LETTERS on education, addressed to a friend. [By Rev. Joseph Dear.] 12mo. [Green's *Bibl. Somers.* i. 142.] Bath, 1828

Signed: Philomathes.

LETTERS on emigration. By a gentleman lately returned from America [—— Hodgkinson]. 8vo. [*Cat. Lond. Inst.* ii. 542.] London, 1794

LETTERS on England. By Victoire, Count de Soligny; translated from the original MS. [Really written in English by Peter George Patmore.] 8vo. [*Brit. Mus.*] London, 1823

LETTERS on free trade, etc. By a working man [Alexander Ewen]. 8vo. [*Brit. Mus.*] Aberdeen, 1877

LETTERS on godly and religious subjects; the result of a correspondence showing the difference between true Christianity and religious apostasy. By Onesimus [Garnet Terry]. Second edition. 12mo. 2 vols. [*Brit. Mus.*] London, 1808

LETTERS on golf. By a parish minister [Rev. Alex. Lawson, B.D., Elgin]. 8vo. [Scott's *Fasti.*] Elgin, 1889

LETTERS on happiness, addressed to a friend. By the authoress of *Letters to my unknown friends* [Sydney Warburton]. 12mo. [*Brit. Mus.*] London, 1850

LETTERS on history, addressed to a beloved god-child. By the author of *Affection's gift* [Mary Anne Hedge]. 12mo. London, 1820

Signed: M. A. H.

LETTERS on infant education. [By Alexander Leslie.] 8vo. Peterhead, 1823

LETTERS on infidelity. By the author of a *Letter to Doctor Adam Smith* [George Horne, D.D.]. 8vo. Pp. iii. 301. [*Bodl.*] Oxford, 1784

LETTERS on international relations before and during the war of 1870. By *The Times* correspondent at Berlin [Carl Abel]. 8vo. 2 vols. [*Camb. Univ. Lib.*] London, 1871

LETTERS on Irish national education. By James [T. Adair]. 8vo. Dublin, 1875

LETTERS on liberty and slavery; an answer to . . . Negro slavery defended by the Word of God. By Philanthropos [Rev. Morgan John Rhees]. 8vo. [Cushing's *Init. and Pseud.* ii. 120.] New York, 1798

LETTERS on life. By Claudius Clear [Rev. Sir William Robertson Nicoll, LL.D.]. 8vo. [*Lit. Year Book.*] London, 1901

LETTERS on literature. By Photius, Junior [W. Sherlock, a Dublin barrister]. 8vo. 2 vols. [*N. and Q.* 1863, p. 134.] Brussels, 1836

LETTERS on Lord Byron. By Sir Cosmo Gordon [Sir Samuel Egerton Brydges]. 8vo. [Cushing's *Init. and Pseud.* i. 118.] London, 1824

LETTERS on materialism and Hartley's Theory of the human mind; addressed to Dr Priestley, F.R.S. [By Rev. Joseph Berington.] 8vo. [Gillow's *Bibl. Dict.* i. 192.] London, 1776

LETTERS on military education. By Jacob Omnium [Matthew James Higgins]. 8vo. Pp. viii. 155. [*Brit. Mus.*] London, 1856

These seven letters appeared originally in *The Times.*

LETTERS on miscellaneous and domestic subjects, intended for the use of the writer's family and a few select friends. [By Benjamin Oakley.] 8vo. Pp. 384. [Martin's *Cat.*] London, 1812

LETTERS on Mr Hume's History of Great Britain. [By Daniel MacQueen, D.D.] 8vo. Pp. 328. [*Nat. Lib. of Scot.*] Edinburgh, 1756

LETTERS on political liberty, addressed to a member of the English House of Commons on his being chosen into the committee of an associating county. [By Rev. David Williams.] 8vo. [*D. N. B.* vol. 61, p. 392.] London, 1782

LETTERS on practical subjects, from a clergyman of New England [William Buell Sprague, D.D.] to his daughter. 8vo. [Cushing's *Init. and Pseud.* ii. 34.] Hartford, Conn., 1822

LETTERS on prejudice. [By Arthur H. Kenny, D.D.] Vol. I. In which the nature, causes, and consequences of prejudice in religion are considered; with an application to the present times. Vol. II. In which the influence of prejudice in religion is considered, as it is connected with the general estimate of the pulpit divinity of the last century. 8vo. 2 vols. London, 1822

In *N. and Q.* 1853, p. 143, this work is ascribed to Mary Kenny; but the authorship is assigned as above, on the authority of a MS. note by Mr Laing.

LETTERS on primitive Christianity. . . . [By Rev. John Walker (T.C.D.), B.D.] 8vo. Dublin, 1820

LETTERS on public-house licensing; shewing the errors of the present system; (originally printed in *The Times* newspaper) together with a proposal for their cure. By a magistrate for Middlesex [John Thomas Barber Beaumont]. 8vo. Pp. 31. [*Gent. Mag.* 1841, p. 97.] London, 1816

Reprinted in the *Pamphleteer*, vii. 107.

LETTERS on religious persecution. By a Catholic layman [Mathew Carey]. Fourth edition. 8vo. [Cushing's *Init. and Pseud.* i. 52.] Philadelphia, 1827

LETTERS on responsible government. By Legion [Robert Baldwin Sullivan]. 8vo. [Cushing's *Init. and Pseud.* i. 170.] Toronto, 1844

LETTERS on several subjects. By the late Sir Thomas Fitzosborne, Bart. [William Melmoth, Junr.]. Published from the copies found among his papers. Second edition. 8vo. Pp. xiv. 192. [*Brit. Mus.*] London, 1747

A second volume was published in 1749. Later editions give the author's real name.

LETTERS on several subjects, from a preceptress to her pupils. . . . [By Charlotte Palmer.] 8vo. [Cushing's *Init. and Pseud.* i. 123.] London, 1797

LETTERS on slavery, addressed to the pro-slavery men of America. . . . By O. S. Freeman [Edward Coit Rogers]. 12mo. [Cushing's *Init. and Pseud.* i. 106.] Boston, 1855

LETTERS on slavery. By X. [William Ware]. 8vo. [Cushing's *Init. and Pseud.* i. 310.] London, 1832

LETTERS on some of the events of the Revolutionary War. [By the Hon. and Rev. Richard Boyle Bernard, rector of Glankeen, diocese of Cashel.] 8vo. Pp. 16, 416. London, 1817

LETTERS on some questions of International Law. By Historicus [Sir William G. G. Vernon Harcourt]. 8vo. [Haynes' *Pseud.*] London, 1863

LETTERS on South American affairs to Mr Monroe. By an American [Henry M. Brackenridge]. 8vo. [Cushing's *Init. and Pseud.* i. 13.] 1818

LETTERS on spiritual subjects and divers occasions, sent to relatives and friends. By one who has tested that the Lord is gracious [Mrs Anne Dutton]. 8vo. [*Brit. Mus.*] London, 1748

LETTERS on the Bank of England; with a prospectus of a new Joint-stock Banking Company. By a Liverpool merchant [John Hall]. 8vo. [*Brit. Mus.*] London, 1836

LETTERS on the cholera morbus; containing ample evidence that this disease, under whatever name known, cannot be transmitted from the persons of those labouring under it to other individuals. . . . By a Professional Man of thirty years' experience [J. Gillkrest]. . . . 8vo. [*Brit. Mus.*] London, 1831

LETTERS on the Church. By an Episcopalian [Richard Whately, D.D.]. 8vo. Pp. iv. 192. [*D. N. B.* vol. 60, p. 425.] London, 1826

LETTERS on the compilation of a Judicial Code. [By P. M. Wynch.] 8vo. [*Calc. Imp. Lib.*] Calcutta, 1832

LETTERS on the constitution, government and discipline of the Christian Church; humbly submitted to the ensuing General Assembly of the Church of Scotland. [By Rev. John Brown, of Haddington.] 12mo. Pp. 108. [*New Coll. Lib.*] Edinburgh, 1767

LETTERS on the corn-laws, and on the rights of the working classes . . . shewing the injustice, and also the impolicy of empowering those among a people who have obtained the proprietary possession of the lands of a country, to increase artificially the money value of their exclusive estates. By H. B. T. [James Deacon Hume, of the Board of Trade]. 8vo. Pp. 48. [*W.*] London, 1835

LETTERS on the corn-trade; containing considerations on the combinations of farmers, and the monopoly of corn; also remarks on the trade, as connected with the manufactures and general interests of the community. . . . [By Joseph Storrs Fry.] 8vo. [Smith's *Cat. of Friends' Books*, i. 820.] Bristol, 1816

LETTERS on the crimes of George III. By an American officer in the service of France [John Skey Eustace]. 8vo. [Cushing's *Init. and Pseud.* i. 14.] Paris, 1794

LETTERS on the culture of the vine, fermentation, and the management of wine in the cellar. By "Maro" [Hon. William Macarthur]. 8vo. [*Sydney Lib.*] Sydney, 1844

LETTERS on the drama. [By John Penn, of Stoke Park.] 8vo. [*Brit. Mus.*] London, 1796

LETTERS on the drama. By Jonathan Oldstyle, Gent. [Washington Irving]. 8vo. [Cushing's *Init. and Pseud.* i. 466.] New York, 1802

LETTERS on the Eastern [United] States. [By William Tudor.] 8vo. [Allibone's *Dict.* vol. iii.] Boston, 1821

LETTERS on the education of young children. By S. G. O. [Lord Sidney Godolphin Osborne]. 12mo. Pp. 39. [*Brit. Mus.*] Edinburgh, 1866

LETTERS on the eloquence of the pulpit. [By Rev. John Langhorne.] 8vo. Pp. 75. [*Athen. Cat.*] London, 1765

LETTERS on the English nation; by Batista Angeloni, a Jesuit who resided many years in London: translated from the original Italian by the author of *The Marriage act: a novel* [John Shebbeare, M.D.]. Second edition with corrections. 8vo. 2 vols. [Watt's *Bibl. Brit.*] London, 1756

The Jesuit was a fictional character.

LETTERS on the evidences of Christianity addressed to Hindus. By Philalethes [Rev. John Murray Mitchell, LL.D.]. 12mo. Pp. v. 179. Calcutta, 1837

Later editions give the name of the author.

LETTERS on the evidences of faith and the impregnable security of believers in Christ . . . also, a letter from Luther to Erasmus. By a layman [R. Hunt]. 8vo. [*Brit. Mus.*] London, 1826

LETTERS on the evidences of the Christian religion. By an inquirer [William Cuninghame, of Lainshaw]. New edition. 12mo. Pp. xii. 132. [Watt's *Bibl. Brit.*] London, 1804

The first edition appeared in 1802, at Serampore, as "Twelve letters. . . ."

LETTERS on the female mind, its powers and its pursuits. [By Lætitia Matilda Hawkins.] 12mo. 2 vols. London, 1799

LETTERS on the great political questions of the day. By Ismaël [Christopher A. M. Harris]. 8vo. London, 1852

LETTERS on the herring-fishing in the Moray Firth. By the author of *Poems written in the leisure hours of a journeyman mason* [Hugh Miller]. 8vo. Pp. 50. Inverness, 1829

LETTERS on the high price of bullion, in the autumn of 1812; shewing the necessity of circulating bank tokens at their intrinsic value; and of repressing local tokens. [By Sir William Scott, afterwards Lord Stowell.] 8vo. Pp. 58. [*Bodl.*] London, 1813

The letters are signed: Chrysal.

LETTERS on the Ilbert Bill controversy. By Gamin De Bon Accord [W. Forbes Mitchell]. 8vo. [*Calc. Imp. Lib.*] Calcutta, 1885

LETTERS on the impediments which obstruct the trade and commerce of the City and Port of Bristol, which appeared in Felix Farley's *Bristol Journal* under the signature of Cosmo [John Matthew Gutch]. 8vo. Pp. 114. [Cushing's *Init. and Pseud.* i. 68.] Bristol, 1823

LETTERS on the importance, duty, and advantages of early rising; addressed to heads of families, the man of business, the lover of nature, the student, and the Christian. [By A. C. Buckland.] Third edition. 12mo. Pp. xii. 204. [*Bodl.*] London, 1820

LETTERS on the improvement of the mind; addressed to a young lady. [By Hester Chapone.] 12mo. 2 vols. [Watt's *Bibl. Brit.*] London, 1774

LETTERS on the internal political state of Spain during 1821-3; extracted from the private correspondence of the author, and founded upon authentic documents, now published for the first time. By G. G. D. V[audoncourt]. 8vo. [*W.*] London, 1825

LETTERS on the kind and economic management of the poor, chiefly as regarding incorporated Poor Houses; with copious tables of actual expenditure, etc. [By Major Edward Moor.] 8vo. [*W.*] Woodbridge, 1825

These letters are republished from the *Ipswich Journal* and are signed "A. B.," "C. D.," "E. F." etc.

LETTERS on the late Catholic Bill, and the discussions to which it has given rise; addressed to British Protestants, and chiefly Presbyterians in Scotland. By a Scots Presbyterian [Thomas M'Crie, D.D., senior]. 8vo. [*New Coll. Lib.*] Edinburgh, 1807

LETTERS on the management of hounds. By Scrutator [K. W. Horlock]. 8vo. [*Brit. Mus.*] London, 1852

LETTERS on the moral and religious duties of parents. By a clergyman [Otis A. Skinner]. 12mo. Pp. 156. [Eddy's *Universalism in America*, ii. 546.] Boston, 1844

LETTERS on the natural history and internal resources of the State of New York. By Hibernicus [De Witt Clinton]. 12mo. Pp. 224. [Cushing's *Init. and Pseud.* i. 129.] New York, 1822

LETTERS on the new theatre. By a father [David Hale]. 8vo. [Cushing's *Init. and Pseud.* i. 58.] London, 1827

LETTERS on the origin and progress of the New Haven theology. From a New England minister to one at the South. [By Bennet Tyler, D.D.] 12mo. Pp. iv. 180. [Cushing's *Init. and Pseud.* i. 203.] New York, 1837

LETTERS on the political condition of the Gold Coast since the exchange of territory between the English and Dutch Governments on January 1, 1868. . . . By "Africanus" [B. Horton]. 8vo. [*Lib. of Coll. Inst.*, Supp. I. 404.] London, 1870

LETTERS on the present disturbances in Great Britain and her American provinces. [By Allan Ramsay, Junr.] 8vo. [Rich's *Bibl. Amer.* i. 471.] London reprinted, 1777

Originally printed in the *Public Advertiser* under the signatures of "Marcellus" and "Britannicus."

LETTERS on the present state and probable results of theological speculations in Connecticut. By an Edwardean [Joseph Harvey]. 8vo. [Cushing's *Init. and Pseud.* ii. 51.] Colchester, Conn., 1832

LETTERS on the present state of Newfoundland, and on federation. By an "Outsider" [Rev. Dr Howley]. 8vo. Pp. 39. [*Brit. Mus.*] St John's, Newfoundland, 1869

LETTERS on the prophecies, selected from eminent writers. By J. Smith, gentleman [Charles Baring]. 8vo. [*N. and Q.* 1869, p. 169.] London, 1810

LETTERS on the proposed united Banks of England; with remarks on the exportation of gold, and the principle of currency. By a Liverpool merchant [John Hall]. 8vo. [*Brit. Mus.*] London, 1837

LETTERS on the purchase system. By Jacob Omnium [Matthew James Higgins]. 12mo. Pp. ii. 89. [Haynes' *Pseud.*] London, 1857

LETTERS on the Rebellion, to a citizen of Washington, from a citizen of Philadelphia [Benjamin Rush]. 8vo. [Cushing's *Init. and Pseud.* i. 59.] Philadelphia, 1862

LETTERS on the Rev. D. T. K. Drummond's Remarks on the Archbishop of Canterbury's Letter. [Signed: A. B. C. *i.e.* A. B. Campbell, of Skerrington.] 8vo. Pp. 32. [*New Coll. Lib.*] Edinburgh, 1845

LETTERS on the royal veto. By Fidelis [Dr John Power, Bishop of Waterford]. Second edition; carefully revised by the author. 8vo. Pp. 26. [*Bodl.*] Waterford, 1809

These letters were first published in the newspaper called the *Shamrog*, printed at Waterford.

LETTERS on the Spanish aggression at Nootka. By Verus [Sir James Bland Burgess Lamb, Bart., D.C.L.]. 8vo. [Cushing's *Init. and Pseud.* i. 293.] London, 1790

LETTERS; on the spirit of patriotism, on the idea of a patriot king, and on the state of parties at the accession of King George the First. [By Henry St John, Viscount Bolingbroke.] 8vo. [*Brit. Mus.*] London, 1749

LETTERS on the state of education in Ireland, and on Bible Societies; addressed to a friend in England. By J. K. L. [James Warren Doyle, R.C. Bishop of Kildare and Leighlin]. 8vo. Pp. 60. [*Bodl.*] Dublin, 1824

LETTERS on the state of Ireland; addressed by J. K. L. [James Warren Doyle, R.C. Bishop of Kildare and Leighlin] to a friend in England. 8vo. Pp. viii. 364. Dublin, 1825

LETTERS on the state of religion in some parts of the Highlands of Scotland, and the means of propagating the Gospel there. By some late travellers. [Three letters, signed: M'G. *i.e.* William M'Gavin.] 12mo. Pp. 26. [*New Coll. Lib.*] [Glasgow, 1818]

LETTERS on the subject of subscription to the Liturgy and Thirty-nine Articles of the Church of England: first printed in the Whitehall *Evening Post* under the signature of Paulinus; now reprinted, with notes and additions. Humbly dedicated to the members of the Honourable House of Commons, and the two Universities, by the author [John Jebb, M.D., F.R.S.]. 8vo. Pp. 56. London, 1772

LETTERS on the subject of the Catholics, to my brother Abraham, who lives in the country. By Peter Plymley [Sydney Smith]. Eleventh edition. 8vo. Pp. 175. [*D. N. B.* vol. 53, p. 123.] London, 1808

LETTERS on the subject of the concert of princes, and the dismemberment of Poland and France. (First published in the *Morning Chronicle* between July 20, 1792 and June 25, 1793.) With corrections and additions by a calm observer [Benjamin Vaughan]. 8vo. Pp. lx. 231. [*W.*] London, 1793

Attributed by some to James Currie, M.D., Liverpool.

LETTERS on the subject of Union, addressed to Messrs Saurin and Jebb. [By Sir William Cusack Smith.] 8vo. Dublin, 1799

LETTERS on the utility and policy of employing machines to shorten labour, occasioned by the late disturbances in Lancashire; with hints for the improvement of our woollen trade. . . . [By Thomas Bentley.] 8vo. Pp. 40. London, 1780

Attributed also to John Kay.

LETTERS on the West India question. By a Presbyter [Henry Duncan, D.D., Ruthwell]. 8vo. [*D. N. B.* vol. 16, p. 166.] London, 1830

LETTERS on the wool question; to which are annexed Letters on tithes, addressed to Lords Holland, and Rosslyn. [By Rev. William Atkinson.] 8vo. Bradford, 1817

LETTERS on Theron and Aspasio, addressed to the author [James Hervey. By Robert Sandeman]. Third edition. With two prefaces, and two appendixes, containing an account of the progress of the controversy, and of the principal pieces that have been wrote against the Letters. 8vo. 2 vols. Edinburgh, 1762

LETTERS philological, theological, and harmonological to Hugh Hart on his embracing and preaching the Sabellian heresy. [By William Henderson.] 8vo. [Robertson's *Aberd. Bibl.*] Aberdeen, 1838

LETTERS philosophical and divine concerning the love of God between [Mary Astell] the author of *The Proposal to the ladies* and Mr J[ohn] Norris . . . 8vo. London, 1694

In the edition of 1695, there are omitted from the title the words "philosophical and divine."

LETTERS reprinted from the *Weekly Dispatch* [on London Government]. By Nemesis [James Beal]. 8vo. [*Gladstone Lib.* (*Liberal Club*).] London, 1876

LETTERS respecting the performances at the Theatre Royal, Edinburgh; originally addressed to the editor of the *Scots Chronicle*, under the signature of "Timothy Plain," and published in that paper during the years 1797, 1798, 1799, and 1800. [By Moncrieff Threepland, advocate.] 12mo. Pp. v. 284. [*Nat. Lib. of Scot.*] Edinburgh, 1800

The author's name is also given as Stewart Threipland [Lowe's *Theat. Lit.*]

LETTERS supposed to have passed between M. de St Evremond and Mr Waller; collected and published by the editor of the *Letters between Theodosius and Constantia* [John Langhorne, D.D.]. 8vo. 2 vols. [*D. N. B.* vol. 32, p. 102.] London, 1769

LETTERS to a Dissenting minister of the Congregational Independent denomination; containing remarks on the principles of that sect, and the author's reasons for leaving it and conforming to the Church of England. By L. S. E. [Rev. Michael Augustus Gathercole]. 8vo. [*Brit. Mus.*] London [1834]

The author has given the finials of his name.

Satirical replies to these letters by Robert M. Beverley and others.

LETTERS to a friend on the present condition of things in the Church of God. . . . By C. H. M. [Charles H. Mackintosh]. 8vo. [*Brit. Mus.*] London [1892]

LETTERS to a friend under affliction. [By Maria Louisa Charlesworth.] 8vo. [*Brit. Mus.*] London, 1849

LETTERS to a nobleman from a gentleman travelling through Holland, Flanders and France. [By J. Shaw.] 8vo. [Bliss' *Cat.* p. 265.] 1709

LETTERS to a nobleman, on the conduct of the war in the middle Colonies. [By Joseph Galloway.] 8vo. Pp. viii. 101. London, 1779

The author afterwards (1781) issued "A reply to the Observations of Lieutenant-General Sir William Howe. . . ."

LETTERS to a nobleman, proving a late prime minister [the Duke of Portland] to have been Junius; and developing the secret motives which induced him to write under that and other signatures; with an appendix, containing a celebrated case published by Almon in 1768. [By Andrew Gregory Johnston.] 8vo. [*Lond. Lib. Cat.*] London, 1816

LETTERS to a Peer concerning the honour of Earl Marshal. [By John Anstis.] 8vo. [*Brit. Mus.*] London, 1706

Only the first letter was published, signed: N. S. (the last letters of his name).

LETTERS to a Protestant divine in defence of Unitarianism. By another barrister [Reader Wainewright]. Second edition, with two additional letters. 8vo. Pp. xxxvi. 439. [*Brit. Mus.*] London, 1824

LETTERS to a wife. By the author of *Cardiphonia* [Rev. John Newton]. 8vo. 2 vols. [*W.*] 1793

LETTERS to a young Christian. By S. J. [Mrs Sarah Tappan, *née* Jackson Davis]. 8vo. [Cushing's *Init. and Pseud.* i. 140.] New York, 1851

LETTERS to a young nobleman upon various subjects, particularly on government and civil liberty; wherein occasion is taken to remark on the writings of some eminent authors upon those subjects. . . . [By George Pitt, Baron Rivers.] 8vo. [*Brit. Mus.*] London, 1784

LETTERS to a young planter; or, observations on the management of a sugar plantation: to which is added, the planter's kalendar. Written in the Island of Grenada, by an old planter [Lieut. Gordon Turnbull]. 8vo. [Rich's *Bibl. Amer.* i. 330, 335.] N.P. 1785

LETTERS to Alexander Bannerman, Esq., Epistles 1, 2, 3. By a lover of facts [Joseph Robertson, LL.D.]. 8vo. [*Aberd. Pub. Lib.*] Aberdeen, 1832

LETTERS to an aged mother. . . . By a clergyman [Thomas Vowler Short, D.D., Bishop of St Asaph]. 8vo. [*D. N. B.* vol. 52, p. 155.] London, 1841

LETTERS to "an anti-pluralist"; shewing the incompetency of Church courts to entertain the question of pluralities; proving the union of teaching, in schools, colleges, and universities, with the ministrations of religion, to be sanctioned by the word of God; the example of Prophets and Apostles; the law of the state and practice of the Church, from the Reformation downwards to the present hour. [By Alexander Fleming, M.A., minister of Neilston.] 8vo. Pp. 68. Edinburgh, 1826

Presentation copy from the author to Sir Henry Jardine.

LETTERS to an Episcopalian on the origin, history, and doctrine of the Book of Common Prayer. By Augustin Bede [Henry Major]. 8vo. [Cushing's *Init. and Pseud.* ii. 16.] Baltimore, 1860

LETTERS to an universalist; containing a review of the controversy between Mr Vidler, and Mr Fuller, on the doctrine of universal salvation. By Scrutator [Charles Jerram, A.M.]. 8vo. Clipstone, 1802

LETTERS to and from Henrietta, countess of Suffolk, and her second husband the Hon. George Berkeley, from 1712 to 1767; with historical, biographical and explanatory notes [by Rt. Hon. John Wilson Croker]. 8vo. 2 vols. [*W.*] London, 1824

LETTERS to and from Rome in the years A.D. 61, 62, and 63; selected and translated by C. V. S. [Sir Richard Davies Hanson]. 8vo. Pp. viii. 69. London, 1873

LETTERS to Atticus. [By Richard, Viscount Fitzwilliam.] 12mo. Pp. 65. [Martin's *Cat.*] N.P. 1811

LETTERS to children. By Uncle Bob [Robert W. Blew]. 8vo. [Cushing's *Init. and Pseud.* ii. 19.] Memphis, Tenn., 1875

LETTERS to Christian women. . . . Thoughts on the Zulu war. By a Cornishwoman [Ellen J. Pearce]. 8vo. Pp. 8. [Boase and Courtney's *Bibl. Corn.*] Penryn [1875]

LETTERS to Dr Clarke concerning liberty and necessity, from a gentleman of the University of Cambridge [Richard Bulkeley]; with the Doctor's answers to them. 8vo. [*Aberdeen Pub. Lib.*] London, 1717

Part of "A collection of papers which passed between the late learned Mr Leibnitz, and Dr Clarke," pp. 403-416.

LETTERS to Dolly. By Keble Howard [John Keble Bell]. 8vo. Pp. 256. [*Lit. Year Book.*] London, 1902

LETTERS to eminent hands. [Literary criticism.] By "I" [Gleeson White]. 8vo. Pp. 74. Derby, 1892

LETTERS to Eusebia; occasioned by Mr Toland's Letters to Serena. [By William Wotton.] 8vo. [Arber's *Term Cat.* iii. 688.] London, 1705

LETTERS to friends the Lord has given me. [By Harriet Perfect.] 8vo. London, 1870

LETTERS to His Majesty King George the Fourth. By Captain Rock [Roger O'Connor]. [*Brit. Mus.*] London, 1828

Ascribed also to Michael J. Whitty.

LETTERS to J. E. Gordon, M.P., shewing, 1. The true nature of the evils of the country. 2. The inadequacy of the remedy hitherto proposed. 3. The only true remedy. . . . By M. S. G. [Tresham Dames Gregg]. 8vo. [*Brit. Mus.*] London, 1832

The author has given the finials of his names.

LETTERS to John H. Hopkins, D.D. . . . By an Episcopalian [Lucius Manlius Sargent]. 8vo. [Cushing's *Init. and Pseud.* ii. 54.] Windsor, Vermont, 1836

LETTERS to living artists. [By Joseph W. Gleeson White.] 8vo. Pp. 168. London, 1891

LETTERS to Lord Althorp . . . on his proposed change of the tithe system, and the working of the Poor Laws. . . . [Signed: E. N. *i.e.* Eardley Norton.] 8vo. [*Brit. Mus.*] London, 1883

LETTERS to Lord Viscount Milton; to which is added a sermon to electors and men in office. [By Rev. William Atkinson, M.A.] 8vo. Bradford [Yorks], 1821

LETTERS to Mr J. Brounfield, minister of the Independent congregation in Whitby. By Vindex [Francis Gibson]. 8vo. [Smale's *Whitby Authors.*] Whitby, 1790

LETTERS to my son. [By Winifred James.] 8vo. Pp. xi. 169. [*Brit. Mus.*] London, 1910

LETTERS to my unknown friends. By a lady [Sydney Warburton]. 12mo. Pp. vii. 277. [*Brit. Mus.*] London, 1846

Later editions omit "By a lady" from the title-page.

LETTERS to Parliament-men, in reference to some proceedings in the House of Commons, during the last session, continuing to the latter part of June, 1701; being one concerning the redress of grievances; another, concerning the Bill for prevention of bribery in corporations; a third, concerning the Dissenter's conformity upon occasion of an office; a fourth, concerning the Bill about the succession; a fifth, concerning comprehension. By a lover of peace and the publick good [John Humphrey]. 4to. Pp. 31. [*Bodl.*] London, 1701

Each letter is signed: J. H.

LETTERS to Punch; Among the witches; and other humorous papers. By Artemus Ward [Charles Farrar Browne]. 12mo. [Cushing's *Init. and Pseud.* i. 303.] London [1875]

LETTERS to Richard Heber, Esq., containing critical remarks on the series of novels beginning with "Waverley," and an attempt to ascertain their author. [By John Leycester Adolphus.] 8vo. [*Brit. Mus.*] London, 1821

LETTERS to Sir Walter Scott, Bart. on the moral and political character and effects of the visit to Scotland in August 1822, of his majesty King George IV. [By James Simpson.] 8vo. Pp. iv. 170. [*Brit. Mus.*] Edinburgh, 1822

LETTERS to Sir William Seton. . . . [By James Edmond.] 8vo. [Robertson's *Aberd. Bibl.*] Aberdeen, 1840

LETTERS to 'Squire Pedant. By Lorenzo Altisonant [Samuel K. Hoshour]. 8vo. [Kirk's *Supp.*] Cincinnati, 1850

LETTERS to the authors of the Plain Tracts for critical times. By a layman [John Sibbald Edison, barrister]. 12mo. Pp. xii. 256. London, 1839

LETTERS to the Editor [contributed to various newspapers] from 1864 to 1889. By the author of *Leisure hours of a busy life* [Andrew Tod, of Edinburgh]. 8vo. Pp. 160. Haddington, 1890

LETTERS to the editor of *The Times* journal, on the affairs and conduct of the Bank of England; the introduction of British silver money into the Colonies; and generally, on the currency of the United Kingdom, both paper and metallic: with notes and an appendix. By Daniel Hardcastle [Richard Page]. 8vo. Pp. viii. 310. [*Gent. Mag.* 1841, p. 441.] London, 1826

LETTERS to the electors of President and Vice-President of the United States. By a citizen of New York [Edmond Charles Genet]. 8vo. [Cushing's *Init. and Pseud.* i. 59.] New York, 1808

LETTERS to the Hon. Horace Mann. . . . By Clericus Hampdenensis [Dorus Clarke, D.D.]. 8vo. [Cushing's *Init. and Pseud.* i. 34.] Boston, 18—

LETTERS to the Hon. James T. Morehead, on Transylvania University. . . . By William Pitt [Robert Wickliffe, junr.]. 8vo. [Cushing's *Init. and Pseud.* i. 235.] Smithland, Kentucky, 1837

LETTERS to the inhabitants of the British Colonies. By a Pennsylvania farmer [John Dickinson]. 8vo. [Cushing's *Init. and Pseud.* i. 227.] Boston, 1767

LETTERS to the inhabitants of Wigan, occasioned by . . . Mr Fawel's discourse on the divinity of Jesus Christ. [By J. H. *i.e.* Rev. John Holland, H. T. *i.e.* Harry Toulmin, and others.] 12mo. 5 parts. [*Brit. Mus.*] [Wigan?] 1791

LETTERS to the Joneses. By Timothy Titcomb, Esquire [Josiah Gilbert Holland]. 8vo. [Cushing's *Init. and Pseud.* i. 284.] New York, 1864

LETTERS to [Matthew Wood] the Lord Mayor; with an appendix containing an analysis and new classification of the state of the representation of the New House of Commons. [By Major John Cartwright.] 8vo. London, 1817

LETTERS to the Marquis of Hastings, on the Indian press; with an appeal to reason and the British Parliament, on the liberty of the press in general. By a friend to good government [Capt. Francis Romeo]. 8vo. [*Calc. Imp. Lib.*] London, 1824

LETTERS to the members, patrons, and friends of the Branch American Tract Society in Boston. By the Secretary of the Boston Society [Rev. Seth Bliss]. 8vo. [Cushing's *Init. and Pseud.* i. 264.] Boston, 1858

LETTERS to the mob. By Libertas [Hon. Mrs Caroline E. S. Norton]. Reprinted from the *Morning Chronicle.* 8vo. Pp. 21. [Lowndes' *Bibl. Man.* p. 1707.] London, 1848

LETTERS to the people of Great Britain, respecting the present state of their public affairs. [Signed: J. F. *i.e.* John Fenwick.] 8vo. [*Brit. Mus.*] London [1795]

LETTERS to the people of the United States. By Concivis [G. H. Belden]. 8vo. [Cushing's *Init. and Pseud.* i. 65.] New York, 1849

LETTERS to the Protestants and Dissenters of the Isle of Wight, on the one, ancient, holy, and only Catholic religion. . . . By Alethphilos [Joseph Rathbone, R. C. priest]. 8vo. Pp. 30. [Gillow's *Bibl. Dict.*] Isle of Wight, 1839

LETTERS to the Rt. Hon. Edmund Burke. By J. S. [Major John Scott, later Scott-Waring]. 8vo. Pp. 40. [*Bodl.*] London, 1783

LETTERS to the Right Honorable Henry Dundas on his inconsistency as the Minister of India. By Asiaticus [Major John Scott Waring?]. 8vo. London, 1792

LETTERS to the Right Honourable the Lord K—— on the rights of succession to Scottish peerages; with an appendix. . . . [By Ephraim Lockhart.] 8vo. [*Brit. Mus.*] London, 1830

The second edition, issued the same year, contains additional material, and differs in the title: "A disquisition on the right of jurisdiction in peerage successions. . . ." (See above.)

LETTERS to the Right Rev. John Hughes, Roman Catholic Bishop of New-York. Three series. To which are added, the decline of Popery, and its causes; and the difference between Protestantism and Popery. By Kirwan [Nicholas Murray, D.D.]. 8vo. Pp. viii. 266. [*Nat. Lib. of Scot.*] Edinburgh, 1851

LETTERS to the Right Reverend [William Nicolson] the Ld. Bishop of Carlisle; occasioned by some passages in his late book of the Scotch Library, wherein Robert the Third is beyond all dispute freed from the imputation of bastardy. . . . [By Thomas Rymer.] 8vo. London, 1702

There are three letters in all, each having a separate title and pagination. Letter II. contains An historical deduction of the alliances between France and Scotland, whereby the pretended old league with Charlemagne is disproved. The letter was published at London, has no date, and contains pp. 100. Letter III. contains a third vindication of Edward the Third, which was published at London in 1706, and contains pp. 14.

LETTERS to the stranger in Reading. By Detector [Rev. Henry Gauntlett]. 8vo. Pp. vii. 217. [*Bodl.*] London, 1810

The same work was issued with a varied title, "The stranger in Reading. . . ."

LETTERS to *The Times* on the principal Pre-Raphaelite pictures of 1854 [viz. Holman Hunt's "The Light of the World" and "The Awakening Conscience"]; from [John Ruskin] the author of *Modern Painters*. 8vo. Pp. 9. [Dobell's *Private prints*.] Private print, 1876

LETTERS to the Yeomanry. . . . By A. Y. [Arthur Young]. 8vo. [*Brit. Mus.*] London, 1797

Also given more fully as "National danger, and the means of safety. . . ."

LETTERS to W. E. Channing on the existence and agency of fallen spirits. [By Rev. William Shedd.]. 8vo. Boston, 1828

LETTERS to William Wilberforce, Esq., M.P., on the doctrine of hereditary depravity. By a layman [Thomas Cogan, M.D.]. 8vo. Pp. 172. [*Camb. Univ. Lib.*] London, 1799

LETTERS to working people on the new poor law. By a working man [John Lash Latey]. . . . 12mo. Pp. 108. [*Manch. Free Lib.*] London, 1841

LETTERS to young mothers. By Uncle Jerry [Mrs Anne Porter, *née* Emerson]. 8vo. [Cushing's *Init. and Pseud.* i. 144.] Boston, 1854

LETTERS to young people, single and married; re-written by an English editor after Timothy Titcomb [Josiah Gilbert Holland]. 8vo. Pp. x. 208. London [1874]

See the New York edition "Titcomb's letters. . . ."

LETTERS (the) which never reached him. [A novel] translated from the German [of the Baroness Elizabeth von Heyking]. 8vo. [*Brit. Mus.*] London, 1904

LETTERS writ by a Turkish spy, who lived five and forty years undiscovered at Paris; giving an impartial account to the Divan at Constantinople, of the most remarkable transactions of Europe; and discovering several intrigues and secrets of the Christian courts (especially of that of France): continued from the year 1637, to the year 1682. Written originally in Arabick, translated into Italian, from thence into English, and now published with a large historical preface and index to illustrate the whole, by the translator of the first volume. [By Giovanni Paolo Marana.] Twenty-sixth edition. 12mo. 8 vols. [*D.N.B.* vol. 37, p. 366.] London, 1770

This work was begun in 1685-88, when four volumes were published (Paris and Amsterdam) in French; the substance of these formed Vol. I., in English, of the Letters by a Turkish spy; possibly Marana may have written the remainder; but Mrs Manley affirmed that her father, Roger Manley, wrote the first two (the best) volumes, while Dunton stated that most of the Letters were composed by a hack writer named South, under Dr Robert Midgley, who held the copyright, and may thus be regarded as the editor.

LETTERS written by his Excellency Hugh Boulter, D.D., Lord Primate of all Ireland, &c. to several ministers of State in England, and some others; containing an account of the most interesting transactions which passed in Ireland from 1724 to 1738. [Edited by Dr Wall, Boulter's nephew.] 8vo. 2 vols. [*W.*] Oxford, 1769-70

LETTERS written during a captivity of upwards of six years in France. By an officer of His Majesty's late ship *Wolverene* [M. Miller, Lieutenant in R.N.]. 12mo. [*Brit. Mus.*] London, 1814

LETTERS written during a four days' tour in Holland, in the summer of 1834. [By Mrs H. Gunn; edited by her father, Dawson Turner, to whom they are addressed.] 12mo. Pp. vii. 127. [Martin's *Cat.*] 1834

LETTERS written for the Post, and not for the Press. [By John, first Earl Russell.] 8vo. [*Edin. Univ. Lib.*] London, 1820

LETTERS written from Colombia, during a journey from Caracas to Bogota. . . . [By John Hankshaw.] 8vo. [*Edin. Univ. Lib.*] London, 1824

LETTERS written from France and the Netherlands, in the summer of 1817. [By John Merritt.] Pp. 67. [*Brit. Mus.*] Liverpool [1817]

LETTERS written from the Continent, during a six weeks' tour, in 1818; afterwards published in the *York Chronicle*. [By Jonathan Gray.] 8vo. Pp. 119. [Martin's *Cat.*] York, 1819

LETTERS written from Tivoli and Rome, in 1863. By a lady [Janet Moyes]. 12mo. Pp. 62. Edinburgh, 1866

Each letter is signed: Gianetta.

LETTERS written in 1816 on infant education, etc. . . . [By James Nicol, of Strichen.] 8vo. Peterhead, 1823

LETTERS written in 1725, to the Rev. Dr Samuel Clarke, relating to an argument advanced by the Doctor, in his Demonstration of the being and attributes of God, in proof of the unity of the Deity: with the Doctor's answers. [By Anthony Atkey.] 8vo. London, 1745

LETTERS written to and for particular friends on important occasions. . . . [By Samuel Richardson.] 12mo. [*Edin. Univ. Lib.*] London, 1750

LETTICE Arnold; a tale. By the author of *Emilia Wyndham*, etc. [Mrs Anne Marsh, later Marsh-Caldwell]. 8vo. [*D. N. B.* vol. 36, p. 219.] London, 1850

LETTICE Lisle. By the author of *Stone Edge* [Lady Frances Parthenope Verney]. With three illustrations. 8vo. Pp. viii. 328. London, 1870

LETTING (the) of hvmovrs blood in the head-vaine; with a new morissco, daunced by seauen satyres, upon the bottome of Diogines tubbe. [Preface signed: S. R. *i.e.* Samuel Rowlands.] 4to. Pp. 85. London, 1600

Reprinted in 1815, with a preface and notes by Sir Walter Scott; and by the Hunterian Club, in 1874. See also "Humours ordinarie."

LETTRE (the) de cachet; a tale. The Reign of terror; a tale. [By Mrs Catherine Gore.] 8vo. Pp. 406. [*Brit. Mus.*] London, 1827

LEUCOTHOE; a dramatic poem [in three acts. By Isaac Bickerstaffe]. 8vo. [*Brit. Mus.*] London, 1756

LEVEE (the); a farce, as it was offer'd to, and accepted for representation by the master of the Old-House in Drury-Lane, but by the inspector of farces denied a licence. [By John Kelly.] 8vo. Pp. 42. [Baker's *Biog. Dram.*] London, 1741

LEVEL (the) track. By Curtis Yorke [Mrs W. S. Richmond Lee, *née* —— Jex-Long]. 8vo. [*Lond. Lib. Cat.*] London, 1919

LEVELLERS (the) levell'd; or, the independents conspiracie to root out monarchie: an interlude, written by Mercurius Pragmaticus [Marchamont Nedham]. 4to. Pp. 14. [*Brit. Mus.*] 1647

LEVIA Pondera; an essay-book. By John Ayscough [Monsignor Francis Bickerstaffe-Drew]. 8vo. Pp. 380. [*Lit. Year Book.*] London, 1913

LEVVDE (a) apologie of pryuate Masse, sedyciously spred abroade in wrytynge without name of the authour; as it seemeth, against the offer and protestacion made in certaine sermons by the reuerende father Bishop of Salesburie: with a learned and godly answere to the same Apologie. [By Thomas Cooper, Bishop of Lincoln.] B. L. 159 leaves. [*Christie Miller Cat.*] London, Mens. Nouemb. 1562

Other copies of the same edition bear a different title: see "An apologie of priuate Masse sediciously spredde abroade. . . ."

LEWELL pastures. By the author of *Sir Frederick Derwent*, etc. [Rosa Mackenzie Kettle]. 8vo. 2 vols. London, 1854

The authoress preferred to be called Mary Rosa Stuart Kettle.

LEWES (the) library society; a poem. [By John Button.] 4to. [*Camb. Univ. Lib.*] London, 1804

LEWESDON Hill; a poem. [By William Crowe, LL.D.] 4to. Pp. 28. [W. D. Macray's *Cat.*] Oxford, 1788

LEWIE; or, the bended twig. By Cousin Cicely [L. Lermont]. 8vo. [Cushing's *Init. and Pseud.* i. 57.] Auburn, New York, 1853

LEWIS Baboon turned honest, and John Bull politician; being the fourth part of Law is a bottomless-pit: printed from a manuscript found in the cabinet of the famous Sir Humphry Polesworth; and publish'd (as well as the three former parts and appendix) by the author of *The New Atalantis* [John Arbuthnot, M.D.]. 8vo. [*Edin. Univ. Lib.*] London, 1712

LEX custumaria; or, a treatise of copy-hold estates, in respect of the
{ lord,
{ copy-holder: wherein the nature of customs in general, and of particular customs, grants and surrenders, and their constructions and expositions in reference to the thing granted or surrendred, and the uses or limitations of estates are clearly illustrated. . . . By S. C., barister at law [Samuel Carter]. Second edition, with additions. 8vo. Pp. 392. [*Brit. Mus.*] London, 1701

LEX parliamentaria; or, a treatise of the law and custom of the Parliaments of England. By G. P., Esq. [George Petyt]. With an appendix of a case in Parliament between Sir Francis Goodwyn and Sir John Fortescue, for the knights place for the county of Bucks, 1 Jac. 1. From an original French manuscript, translated into English. 8vo. Pp. 320. [*Brit. Mus.*] London, 1690

Another edition was published in 1747.

LEX Rex; a short digest of the principal relations between Latin, Greek, and Anglo-Saxon sounds. . . . [Signed: W. G. R. *i.e.* William Gunyon Rutherford.] Pp. 55. [*Brit. Mus.*] Westminster, 1884

LEX, Rex; the law and the prince: a dispute for the just prerogative of king and people, containing the reasons and causes of the most necessary defensive wars of the kingdom of Scotland, and of their expedition for the ayd and help of their dear brethren of England; in which their innocency is asserted, and a full answer is given to a seditious pamphlet, intituled, Sacrosancta regum majestas, or the sacred and royall prerogative of christian kings; under the name of J. A., but penned by Jo. Maxwell, the excommunicate P. Prelat. With a scripturall confutation of the ruinous grounds of W. Barclay, H. Grotius, H. Arnisæus, Ant. de Domi. P. Bishop of Spalato, and of other late anti-magistratical royalists; as, the author of Ossorianum, D. Fern, E. Symmons, the doctors of Aberdeen, etc. [By Samuel Rutherford.] 4to. London, 1644

After the Restoration of the monarchy in 1660, copies of this treatise were publicly burnt by the hangman at the crosses in Edinburgh and St Andrews; the author was also deprived of his offices in St Andrews, and summoned to appear for trial on a charge of treason; his death, however, speedily supervened.

LEX talionis; a sermon [on Jud. 1/7]. . . . By I. R. [John Rawlinson], D.D. 4to. Pp. 29. [*Brit. Mus.*] [London, 1620]

LEX talionis; or, the author of Naked truth [Herbert Croft] stript naked. [First ascribed to Dr Peter Gunning, Bishop of Chichester, afterwards of Ely; afterwards to Dr William Lloyd, Dean of Bangor; but, on better grounds, it is ascribed to Rev. Philip Fell, Fellow of Eton College.] 4to. [*Biog. Brit.* iv. 464.] London, 1676

LEX terræ; a discussion of the law of England, regarding claims of inheritable rights of peerage. [By Sir Samuel Egerton Brydges.] 8vo. [*W.*] Geneva, 1831

LEX vadiorum; the law of mortgages; wherein is treated the nature of mortgages, and the several sorts of proviso's in the same deed, or by deed absolute; defeazance, demise and redemise; or by covenant, and otherwise. . . . [By Samuel Carter.] 8vo. Pp. 223. London, 1706

The second edition, published in 1728, has the author's name.

LEXICON Balatronicum; a dictionary of British slang, University wit, and pickpocket eloquence. By a member of the Whip Club [Francis Grose], assisted by Hell-fire Dick. [Edited by Dr Howson Clarke, of Gateshead.] 8vo. [*W.*] London, 1811

Earlier editions appeared as "A classical dictionary of the vulgar tongue."

LEXICON (a) of New Testament Greek. [By Theodore Jones.] 8vo. London, 1877

LEXICON of the thoughts in the English language. Part I. [By Nicholas Littleton, M.R.C.S.] 4to. Pp. 68. [*Brit. Mus.*] London, 1854

No more published.

LEXIPHANES; a dialogue; imitated from Lucian, and suited to the present times: with a dedication to Lord Lyttleton, a preface, notes, and postscript: being an attempt to restore the English tongue to its ancient purity, and to correct, as well as expose, the affected style, hard words, and absurd phraseology of many late writers, and particularly of our English Lexiphanes, the Rambler. [By Archibald Campbell, purser in the Royal Navy.] 8vo. [*Brit. Mus.*] London, 1767

A satire on Dr Samuel Johnson and his style. Another edition was issued in 1774.

LEYCESTERS commonwealth; conceived, spoken and published with most earnest protestation of all dutifull good will and affection towards this realm; for whose good onely, it is made common to many. [By Robert Persons, or Parsons?] 4to. Pp. 182. Printed 1641

'Leicester's commonwealth' was written by Parsons, the Jesuit, from materials with which he is said to have been furnished by Lord Burghley. It was first published abroad in 8vo in 1584, under the title of 'A dialogue between a scholar, a gentleman and a lawyer'; and was previously handed about in England under the name of 'Parsons's Black Book.'—MS. note in Bodelian copy, by Malone.

It is to be observed, however, that Parsons disclaimed authorship, and the denial is otherwise confirmed [*D. N. B.* vol. 43, p. 418].

LIA; a tale of Nuremberg. By Esmé Stuart [Amélie Claire Leroy]. 8vo. [*Lond. Lib. Cat.*] London, 1883

LIAR (the); or, a contradiction to those who in the titles of their bookes affirmed them to be true when they were false: although mine are all true, yet I term them lyes—veritas veritatis. [By John Taylor, the water-poet.] 4to. [*Brit. Mus.*] 1641

LIBBIE Marsh's three eras. By the author of *Mary Barton*, etc. [Mrs Eliza Cleghorn Gaskell]. 8vo. Pp. 24. London, 1855

LIBEL (a) on Dr D—ny [Delany] and a certain great Lord. By Dr Sw—t [Jonathan Swift, D.D.]. Occasion'd by a certain epistle. To which is added, I. An epistle to his Excellency John Lord Carteret, by Dr D—ny. II. An epistle on an epistle; or, a Christmas-box for Dr D—ny. III. Dr Sw—t's proposal for preventing the children of poor people being a burthen to their parents or country, and for making them beneficial to the public. The second edition. 8vo. Pp. 32. [*Camb. Hist. of Eng. Lit.*]
Printed at Dublin, and reprinted at London, 1730

LIBELLER (the) characteriz'd by his own hand; in answer to a scurrilous pamphlet [by R. H.], intituled, The character of a Quaker. . . . [Signed: T. R. *i.e.* Thomas Rudyard.] 4to. [*Brit. Mus.*] London, 1671

LIBER amoris; or, the new Pygmalion. [By William Hazlitt.] 12mo. [*Brit. Mus.*] London, 1823

LIBER librorum; its structure, limitations and purpose. [By Henry Dunn.] 8vo. [*Lib. Journ.* vi. 190.] London, 1867

LIBER redivivus; or, the booke of the Universall Kirke reopened. [By David Aitchison, Archdeacon of Argyll.] 12mo. [*New Coll. Lib.*] Glasgow, 1839

LIBER cccxxxiii., the book of lies, which is also falsely called Breaks. . . . [By Aleister Crowley.] 12mo. Pp. 130. [*Brit. Mus.*] London, 1913

LIBERAL (the); verse and prose from the South. [By Lord Byron, P. B. Shelley, Leigh Hunt and others.] Volume the first. 8vo. London, 1822

—— Volume the second. 8vo. London, 1823

LIBERAL (a) critique on the present Exhibition of the Royal Academy; being an attempt to correct the national taste. . . . By Anthony Pasquin [John Williams]. 8vo. [*Brit. Mus.*] London, 1794

LIBERAL despotism. By the author of *Liberal misrule in Ireland* [James Herman De Ricci]. 8vo. [*Gladstone Lib. Cat.*] London [1884]

LIBERAL (the) mis-leaders. [By George Stronach, M.A.] 4to. No pagination. [*Nat. Lib. of Scot.*] Edinburgh and London [1880]

A political pamphlet, directed against the Gladstone Government.

LIBERAL misrule in Ireland. [By James Herman De Ricci.] 8vo. London [1882?]

LIBERAL opinions, upon animals, man, and Providence; in which are introduced anecdotes of a gentleman. . . . By Courtney Melmoth [Samuel Jackson Pratt]. 8vo. 6 vols. [*Brit. Mus.*] London, 1775-77

LIBERAL vacillation. By the author of *Liberal misrule in Ireland* [James Herman De Ricci]. 8vo. [*Gladstone Lib. Cat.*] Bedford [1883]

LIBERALITY; or, memoirs of a decayed macaroni: a poetical narrative. By [Christopher Anstey] the author of *The new Bath guide.* Third edition. 4to. Pp. iv. 12. [Green's *Bibl. Somers.*] Bath [1788?]

LIBERALITY; or, the decayed macaroni: a sentimental piece. [By Christopher Anstey.] 4to. [Cunningham's *Lives*, viii. 120.] Bath, 1788

LIBERATIONISTS (the) unmasked. . . . By an ex-dissenting minister [Rev. Robert Christison]. 8vo. [*Brit. Mus.*] Leeds, 1874

LIBERATUS triumphans; a poem, occasion'd by the glorious victory obtain'd near Odenard by the forces of the Allies under the command of John, Duke of Marlborough, on the 1st of July, 1708. [By Charles Gildon.] Fol. Pp. 20. London, 1708

LIBERTIES (the), usages, and customes of the city of London; confirmed by especiall Acts of Parliament, with the time of their confirmation; also divers ample and most beneficiall charters granted by King Henry the 6th, King Edward the 4th, and King Henry the 7th, not confirmed by Parliament as the other charters were. . . . [Collected by Sir Henry Calthrop, Knight.] 4to. Pp. 25. [*Bibliographer*, i. 152.] London, 1642

Another edition was published in 1674.

LIBERTINE (the). [A novel.] By Charlotte Dacre [Mrs Byrne]. Third edition. 12mo. 4 vols. [*Brit. Mus.*] London, 1807

LIBERTINE'S (the) choice; or, the mistaken happiness of the fool in fashion. [A poem. By Edward Ward.] 4to. [*Brit. Mus.*] London, 1704

LIBERTY; a poem on the independence of America. [By St George Tucker.] 4to. [Evans' *Amer. Bibl.* vol. 7, p. 272.] Richmond, Va., 1788

LIBERTY and common-sense to the people of Ireland, greeting. [By Henry Brooke.] 8vo. [*Camb. Univ. Lib.*] Dublin, 1760

LIBERTY (the) and independency of the Kingdom and Church of Scotland asserted from antient records. [By Sir Robert Sibbald.] 4to. [*Brit. Mus.*] Edinburgh, 1702

Later editions bear the author's name.

LIBERTY and pasture. By H. C. A. [H. C. Anstey]. 8vo. London [1899]

LIBERTY and property vindicated, and the St—pm—n [Stamp man, viz. Jared Ingersoll] burnt; a discourse . . . made on burning the effigy. . . . By a friend to the liberty of his country [Benjamin Church]. 4to. Pp. 11. [Evans' *Amer. Bibl.* vol. 4, p. 6.] [Hartford, Connecticut, 1765]

LIBERTY chastised; or, patriotism in chains: a tragi— comi— political farce. By Paul Tell-truth, Esq. [George Saville Carey]. 8vo. [*Brit. Mus.*] London, 1768

LIBERTY, civil and religious. By a friend to both [Thomas Bowdler, M.A.]. 8vo. Pp. 73. [*Nat. Lib. of Scot.*] London, 1815

LIBERTY Hall; an original drama, in four acts. By Richard Claude Carton [Richard Claude Critchett]. 8vo. Pp. 76. [*Brit. Mus.*] London [1901]

LIBERTY Hall; or, a test of good fellowship: a comic opera, in two acts [and in prose], as it is performed with the greatest applause at the Theatre-Royal in Drury-Lane. [By Charles Dibdin, sen.] 8vo. [*Brit. Mus.*] London, 1785

LIBERTY of conscience asserted and vindicated. By a learned country-gentleman [George Care?]. Humbly offered to the consideration of the Lords and Commons in this present Parliament. 4to. Pp. 27. London, 1689

This work bears the initials G. C. but it is by no means certain that Care was the author.—Note in *Bodl. Cat.*

LIBERTY of conscience asserted; or, a looking-glass for persecutors; being a plain deduction from scripture-history of the original grounds and pretences for persecution. By H. C. [Henry Care?]. 4to. [Mendham's *Collection Cat.*] London, 1687

LIBERTY of conscience; or, the sole means to obtaine peace and truth: not onely reconciling His Majesty with His subjects, but all Christian states and princes to one another, with the freest passage for the Gospel. [By Henry Robinson.] 4to. Pp. 62. [Whitley's *Bapt. Bibl.* i. 16; Thomason's *Coll. of Tracts*, i. 316.] 1644

LIBERTY of conscience, the magistrates interest; or, to grant liberty of conscience to persons of different perswasions in matters of religion, is the great interest of all kingdoms and states, and particularly of England; asserted and proved. By a Protestant, a lover of peace, and the prosperity of the nation [Sir Charles Wolseley, Bart.]. 4to. Pp. 22. [Whitley's *Bapt. Bibl.* i. 93.] London, 1668

This is the second part of the following.

LIBERTY of conscience upon its true and proper grounds asserted & vindicated; proving that no prince, nor state, ought by force to compel men to any part of the doctrine, worship, or discipline of the Gospel. Written by a Protestant, a lover of truth and the peace and prosperity of the nation [Sir Charles Wolseley, Bart.]. 4to. Pp. 54. [Whitley's *Bapt. Bibl.* i. 93.] London, 1668

LIBERTY (the) of Episcopal Dissenters in Scotland truly stated. [By Daniel Defoe.] 4to. [Wilson's *Life of Defoe.*] London, 1703

LIBERTY (the) of prayer asserted, and guarded from licentiousness. By a minister of the Church of England [Benjamin Jenks, M.A.]. 8vo. [Arber's *Term. Cat.* iii. 688.] London, 1695

LIBERTY (the) of the spirit and of the flesh distinguished; in an address to . . . the people called Quakers. . . . By an unworthy member of that community [John Rutty]. 8vo. [Smith's *Cat. of Friends' Books.*] Philadelphia, 1759

LIBERTY (the), property, and religion of the Whigs; in a letter to a Whig: occasion'd by some discourse upon the Reverend Dr Sacheverell's sermons on Palm-Sunday, and 29th of May, 1713. [By William Robertson, M.A.] 8vo. Pp. 24. London, 1713

LIBERTY without licentiousness; in two letters to a friend. [By William Taylor, Associate minister of Renton.] 8vo. Pp. 60. [*New Coll. Lib.*] Paisley, 1792

LIBERTY'S last squeak; containing an elegiac ballad, an ode to an informer, an ode to jurymen, and crumbs of comfort for the grand informer. By Peter Pindar, Esq. [John Wolcot, M.D.]. 4to. Pp. 30. London, 1795

LIBRA; an astrological romance. By Eleanor Kirk [Mrs Ellen Maria Easterbrooke Ames]. 8vo. Pp. 269. [Cushing's *Init. and Pseud.* i. 158.] New York, 1896

LIBRARY (the); a poem. [By George Crabbe.] 4to. Pp. 34. [Nichols' *Lit. Anec.* viii. 90.] London, 1781

LIBRARY (the); an epistle from a bookseller to a gentleman, his customer; desiring him to discharge his bill. [By Charles Marsh.] 4to. [Nichols' *Lit. Anec.* iii. 647.] [London] 1766

LIBRARY (the) of a bibliomaniac. [By Almon W. Griswold.] 8vo. [Cushing's *Init. and Pseud.* i. 35.] New York, 1880

LIBRARY (the); or, moral and critical magazine, for the year 1761 [and 1762]. By a Society of Gentlemen. [Edited and principally written by Andrew Kippis, D.D.] 8vo. 2 vols. [*W.*] London, 1761-2

Some of the papers are assigned to the Rev. John Alexander.

LIBRETTO (a); containing The armoury, The illuminated saltier, The holier Rood, and The London season. By P. S. G. [Rev. Peter Southmead Glubb, B.D.]. 8vo. Private print, 1875

LICHT frae the smiddy o' Saunders Dinwuddie. [By Rev. Charles Marshall, F. C. minister, Dunfermline.] 8vo. [Beveridge's *Dunfermline Bibl.*] Edinburgh, 1880

LICIA; or, poemes of love, in honour of the admirable and singular vertues of his lady, to the imitation of the best Latin poets, and others: whereunto is added the Rising to the crowne of Richard the Third. [By Giles Fletcher.] 4to. Pp. 80. [*D. N. B.* vol. 19, p. 301.] N.P., N.D.

The Epistle dedicatorie, and to the reader are dated, the first, Sept. 4, 1593, and the last, Septemb. 8, 1593.

To W. H. Allnutt, Esq., of the Bodleian Library, I am indebted for the information that this work was printed at Cambridge, by John Legate; and that the emblematical figures in the title-page are from Queen Elizabeth's Prayer Book [A booke of Christian prayers] printed by John Daye in 1569, 1578, 1581, and by Richard Yardley, and Peter Short, for the assignes of Richard Day 1590, in which last edition these very four figures are wanting.—J. L.

LIE (the) circumspect; a novel. By Rita [Eliza M. J. Gollan, later Mrs W. D. Humphreys]. 8vo. [*Lit. Year Book.*] London, 1902

LIEUTENANT (the); a story of the Tower. By the author of *Estelle* [Emily Marion Harris]. 8vo. Pp. vi. 383. [*Camb. Univ. Lib.*] London, 1882

LIEUTENANT (the) and the crooked midshipman; a tale of the ocean. By a naval officer, author of *Cutting out ashore*, etc. [Augustus Collingridge]. 12mo. 2 vols. London, 1844

Author's acknowledgment.

LIEUTENANT (a) at eighteen. By Oliver Optic [William T. Adams]. 8vo. Pp. 483. [Kirk's *Supp.*] Boston, 1895

LIEUTENANT (a) of the King; a novel. By Morice Gerard [John Jessop Teague, M.A.]. 8vo. Pp. 312. [*Lit. Year Book.*] London, 1904

LIEUT.-COLONEL John Lilb[urne] tryed and cast; or, his case and craft discovered: wherein is shewed the grounds and reasons of the Parliaments proceeding, in passing the act of banishment against him, and wherefore since his coming over hee hath been committed to the Tower by the Parliament. . . . [By Sir Arthur Heselrig.] 4to. Pp. 164. [*Brit. Mus.*] London, 1653

LIEUTENANT'S (the) daughters; or, the little mother. . . . [By James Anthony Froude.] 8vo. [Courtney's *Secrets*, p. 102.] London, 1874

LIFE (the). [A novel.] By Victoria Cross [Miss Vivian Cory]. 8vo. Pp. 220. [*Amer. Cat.*] London, 1912

LIFE; a dream. From the Spanish of Don Pedro Calderon de la Barca [by Malcolm Cowan]. 12mo. Pp. 106. Edinburgh, 1830

LIFE; a poem. By the author of *Emmanuel* [Miss E. Colthurst]. 12mo. [*Brit. Mus.*] Cork, 1835

LIFE (the), adventures, and many and great vicissitudes of fortune of Simon [Fraser], Lord Lovat. . . . [By Archibald Arbuthnot.] 12mo. [*Brit. Mus.*] London, 1746

LIFE (the), adventures, and pyracies of the famous Captain Singleton; containing an account of his being set on shore at Madagascar, his settlement there, with a description of the place and inhabitants. . . . [By Daniel Defoe.] 8vo. London, 1720

LIFE among my ain folk. By the author of *Johnny Gibb of Gushetneuk* [William Alexander, LL.D., journalist]. 8vo. Edinburgh, 1890

LIFE among the Close Brethren. . . . [By Dr —— Murdoch.] 8vo. London, 1890

LIFE among the Germans. By an American student-girl [Emma Louisa Parry]. 8vo. [*Amer. Cat.*] Boston, 1887

LIFE amongst the Modocs; unwritten history. By Joaquin Miller [Cincinnatus Heine Miller]. 8vo. Pp. viii. 400. [Cushing's *Init. and Pseud.* i. 194.] London, 1873

LIFE (the) and actions of Jesus Christ, from his birth to his resurrection; by way of question and answer, for the edification of children and youth. Part I. By a lover of Christ [Rev. John Collett Ryland, the elder]. 12mo. [*D. N. B.* vol. 50, p. 517.] London, 1766

LIFE (the) and actions of Lewis Dominique Cartouche, who was broke alive upon the wheel at Paris, Nov. 28, 1721, N.S.; relating at large his remarkable adventures, desperate enterprises, and various escapes: with an account of his behaviour under sentence, and upon the scaffold, and the manner of his execution. Translated from the French. [By Daniel Defoe.] 8vo. Pp. 88. [Lee's *Defoe*, p. 214.] London, 1722

LIFE and adventures in the South Pacific. By a roving printer [—— Jones]. 8vo. [Cushing's *Init. and Pseud.* ii. 254.] New York, 1861

LIFE (the) and adventures of a Cheap Jack. By one of the Fraternity [William Green]. 8vo. [*Brit. Mus.*] London, 1876

LIFE (the) and adventures of Arthur Clenning. By the author of *Recollections of ten years in the valley of the Mississippi*, etc. [Timothy Flint]. 12mo. 2 vols. [*Brit. Mus.*] Philadelphia, 1828

LIFE (the) and adventures of Chickasan the Scout. [By L. H. Naron.] 8vo. [*Amer. Cat.*] Chicago, 1865

LIFE (the) and adventures of common sense; an historical allegory. [By Herbert Lawrence, surgeon.] 8vo. 2 vols. [*Bodl.*] London, 1769

LIFE (the) and adventures of Dick Diming. By Priam [Charles James Collins]. 8vo. [*Brit. Mus.*] London, 1854

LIFE (the) and adventures of Dr Dodimus Duckworth, A.N.Q.; to which is added the History of a steam Doctor. . . . By the author of *A Yankee among the Nullifiars* [Asa Greene]. 8vo. 2 vols. [Allibone's *Dict.*] New York, 1833

LIFE (the) and adventures of John Nicol, mariner. [Edited by John Howell.] 8vo. Pp. viii. 215. [*And. Jervise.*] Edinburgh, 1822

It is stated, in the postscript, which is signed: J. H. that the narrative was taken down from Nicol's "own mouth."

LIFE (the) and adventures of Lazarillo de Tormes, written by himself; translated from the original Spanish [of Diego Hurtado de Mendoza]. 8vo. [Arber's *Term Cat.* iii. 571.] London, 1707

LIFE and adventures of Major Roger Sherman Potter. By Pheleg Van Truesdale [Frederic Colburn Adams]. 8vo. [Kirk's *Supp.*] New York, 1858

LIFE (the) and adventures of Mr Francis Clive. [By Mrs Phebe Gibbes.] 12mo. 2 vols. [*Mon. Rev.* xxx. 243.] London, 1764

LIFE (the) and adventures of Mrs Christian Davies, the British Amazon, commonly called Mother Ross; who served as a foot-soldier and dragoon in several campaigns under King William and the late Duke of Marlborough. . . . [By Daniel Defoe.] The second edition. 8vo. 2 parts. [Lee's *Defoe.*] London, 1741

Each part has a separate pagination.

LIFE (the) and adventures of Ned Buntine. By Will Wildwood [Frederick Eugene Pond]. 8vo. [Cushing's *Init. and Pseud.* i. 307.] Cincinnati, 1888

LIFE (the) and adventures of Paul Plaintive, Esq., an author; compiled from original documents, and interspersed with specimens of his genius, in prose and poetry. By Martin Gribaldus Swammerdam (his nephew and executor). [By William Mudford.] 12mo. 2 vols. [*Brit. Mus.*] London, 1811

LIFE (the) and adventures of Peter Porcupine, with a full and fair account of all his authoring transactions: being a sure and infallible guide for all enterprising young men who wish to make a fortune by writing pamphlets: to which is added, his will and testament. By Peter Porcupine himself [William Cobbett]. 12mo. Pp. 57. Glasgow, 1798

LIFE (the) and adventures of Peter Wilkins, a Cornishman; relating particularly, his shipwreck near the South Pole; his wonderful passage thro' a subterraneous cavern into a kind of new world; his there meeting with a gawry or flying woman, whose life he preserv'd, and afterwards married her. . . . By R. S. a passenger in the *Hector* [Robert Paltock, or Pultock]. 12mo. 2 vols. [Boase and Courtney's *Bibl. Corn.* ii. 420.] London, 1751

Introduction signed: R. P.

LIFE (the) and adventures of Rupert Calderford. By "Mardale" [Richard H. Holme]. 8vo. [*Brit. Mus.*] London, 1904

LIFE (the) and adventures of Simon Seek; or, Canada in all shapes. By Maple Knot [Ebenezer Clemo]. 8vo. [Cushing's *Init. and Pseud.* i. 158.] Montreal, 1858

LIFE (the) and adventures of Sir Bartholomew Sapskull, Baronet, nearly allied to most of the great men of the three kingdoms. By Somebody [William Donaldson]. 12mo. 2 vols. [*Mon. Rev.* xxxix. 83.] London, 1768

LIFE and adventures of the Marchioness Urbino in England, Spain, Turkey, Italy, France, and Holland. [By Dorothy Noake.] 8vo. London, 1735

LIFE (the) and adventures of the Old Lady of Threadneedle Street [the Bank of England]; containing an account of her numerous intrigues with various eminent statesmen of the past and present times: written by herself. [By William Reid, political economist.] 8vo. Pp. 62. [*Brit. Mus.*] London, 1832

LIFE (the) and adventures of Thomas Titmouse; and other stories. By Peter Parley [Samuel Griswold Goodrich], author of the *Wanderers by sea and land.* 12mo. Pp. 64. [*Brit. Mus.*] London [1860?]

LIFE and adventures, songs, services, and speeches of Private Miles O'Reilly, 47th Regiment New York Volunteers [Charles Graham Halpine]. 8vo. [Cushing's *Init. and Pseud.* i. 219.] New York, 1864

LIFE and anecdotes of Jemmy Wood, the eccentric banker, merchant and draper of Gloucester. [Compiled by Charles H. Savory.] 8vo. [*Brit. Mus.*] London [1883]

LIFE (the) and character of Marcus Portius Cato Uticensis; collected from Plutarch in the Greek, and from Lucan, Salust, Lucius Florus, and other authors in the Latin tongue: designed for the readers of Cato, a tragedy. [By Lewis Theobald.] 4to. Pp. 24. [*D. N. B.* vol. 56, p. 118.] London, 1713

Prepared when Joseph Addison's drama was immensely popular.

LIFE (the) and character of Sir William Temple, Bart. Written by a particular friend [his sister, Lady Giffard, *née* Martha Temple]. 8vo. [*Brit. Mus.*] London, 1728

LIFE (the) and character of that eminent and learned prelate, the late Dr Edw. Stillingfleet, Lord Bishop of Worcester; together with some account of the works he has publish'd. [By Dr Timothy Goodwin.] 8vo. Pp. 149. [*Bodl.*] London, 1710

The author, after practising as physician in Leyden, took holy orders at Oxford, was appointed chaplain to Stillingfleet, and became a prebendary of Canterbury.

"When this book first came out, Dr Timothy Goodwin . . . was said to be the author; which I rather believe, than that it was done (as it hath been suggested) by Mr Spinckes, a non-juror."—MS. note by Hearne, to whom the copy belonged.

LIFE (the) and character of the late Lord Chancellor Jefferys. [By A. Moore.] 8vo. Pp. 47. [Green's *Bibl. Somers.* ii. 531.] London, 1725

LIFE (the) and character of William Penn. [By Edmund Rack.] 12mo. [*Brit. Mus.*] London, 1777

LIFE (the) and correspondence of Francis Bacon, Viscount St Albans, Lord Chancellor of England, "The wisest, brightest, meanest of mankind." [By J. F. Foard.] 12mo. Pp. xxiv. 568. London, 1861

LIFE and correspondence of M. G. Lewis; with many pieces never before published. [By Margaret Harries, later Mrs Baron-Wilson.] 8vo. 2 vols. [*Brit. Mus.*] London, 1839

LIFE (the) and daring exploits of Thomas Cochrane, tenth Lord Dundonald. [By Rev. John M'Gilchrist.] 8vo. [*Brit. Mus.*] London, 1861

LIFE (the) and death of Dr Martin Luther, the passages whereof have bin taken out of his owne and other godly and most learned mens writings, who lived in his time. [By Thomas F. Hayne.] 4to. [*Brit. Mus.*] London, 1641

LIFE (the) and death of Jack Strawe. [A drama. By George Peele?] 4to. [*D. N. B.* vol. 44, p. 228.] London, 1593

LIFE (the) and death of Jamie Fleeman, the Laird of Udny's Fool. [By Dr J. B. Pratt.] 8vo. Aberdeen, 1904

LIFE (the) and death of John Fisher, Bishop of Rochester; selected from several ancient records by Thomas Bayly [but really written by Richard Hall, of Christ's College, Cambridge]. 12mo. [*D. N. B.* vol. 19, p. 63.] London, 1740

LIFE (the) and death of Major Clancie, the grandest cheat of this age. . . . [Dedication signed: E. S. *i.e.* Elkanah Settle.] 8vo. Pp. 150. [*D. N. B.* vol. 51, p. 275.] London, 1680

LIFE (the) and death of Mother Shipton . . . strangely preserved amongst other writings belonging to an old monastery in York-shire, and now published for the information of posterity. . . . [Signed: R. H. *i.e.* Richard Head.] 4to. B. L. [*Brit. Mus.*] London, 1684

LIFE (the) and death of Mr Henry Jessey, late preacher of the Gospel of Christ in London; vvho, having finished his testimony, was translated the 4th day of September, 1663. . . . E[dward] W[histon]. 8vo. [Whitley's *Bapt. Bibl.*] N.P. 1671

LIFE (the) and death of Mr John Rowe, of Crediton in Devon. [By Theophilus Gale.] 8vo. [Davidson's *Bibl. Devon.* p. 193.] London, 1673

LIFE (the) and death of Mr Tho: Wilson, minister of Maidstone, in the county of Kent, M. A. [By George Swinock, or Swinnock, M.A.] 12mo. Pp. 99. [Smith's *Bibl. Cant.*] 1672

The address to the Christian reader signed: G. S. Reprinted in 1831, with the author's name.

LIFE (the) and death of Pomponius Atticus, written by his contemporary and acquaintance, Cornelius Nepos; translated out of his fragments, together with observations political and moral thereupon [by Sir Matthew Hale]. 8vo. Pp. 242. [*Lincoln's Inn Cat.* p. 548.] London, 1677

LIFE (the) and death of Sam, in Virginia. By a Virginian [—— Gardner]. 8vo. [Cushing's *Init. and Pseud.* i. 296.] Richmond, Va., 1856

LIFE (the) and death of Silas Barnstarke; a story of the seventeenth century. By Talbot Gwynne [Josepha Gulston]. 8vo. London, 1852

LIFE (the) and death of Sir Henry Vane, Kt.; or, a short narrative of the main passages of his earthly pilgrimage; together with a true account of his purely Christian, peaceable, spiritual, gospel-principles, doctrine, life, and way of worshipping God, for which he suffered contradiction and reproach from all sorts of sinners. . . . [By George Sikes.] 4to. Pp. 162. 1662

LIFE (the) and death of Sir Thomas Moore, Lord High Chancellour of England. Written by M. T. M. [Magister Thomas More] and dedicated to the Queens Most Excellent Maiestie. [Really written by Cresacre More.] 4to. Pp. 432. N.P., N.D.

Printed abroad about 1627. The epistle dedicatory is signed: M. C. M. E.

See a discussion on the authorship in the Preface, by the Rev. Joseph Hunter, to the edition published at London by Pickering, in 1828.

LIFE (the) and death of that judicious divine, and accomplish'd preacher, Robert Harris, D.D., late President of Trinity Colledge in Oxon. . . . By W. D. his dear friend and kinsman [William Durham]. 8vo. Pp. 119. [*Bodl.*] London, 1660

"Writt by Will: Durham."—Wood.

LIFE (the) and death of that renowned John Fisher, Bishop of Rochester; comprising the highest and hidden transactions of Church and state, in the reign of King Henry the 8th; with divers morall, historicall, and politicall animadversions upon Cardinall Wolsey, Sir Thomas Moor, Martin Luther, with a full relation of Qu: Katharines divorce: carefully selected from severall ancient records by Tho: Baily, D.D. [By Richard Hall, D.D.] 8vo. Pp. 261. [*Bodl.*] London, 1655

"The true and genuine author was Rich. Hall, D.D. 'Twas only published, with some alterations, by Dr Baily. See Athen. Oxon. Vol. I. col. 487."—MS. note on Bodleian copy.

LIFE (the) and death of that Reverend divine and excellent historian, Doctor Thomas Fuller. [By John Fell, D.D.] 12mo. Pp. 106. [*Bibliographer*, vol. 4, p. 117.] Oxford, 1662

This is practically the same as an issue in 1661 with a slightly different title ("The life of that Reverend divine and learned historian, Dr Thomas Fuller.")

LIFE (the) and death of the English rogue, or his last legacy to the world. [Abridged from a larger work by Richard Head and Francis Kirkman, entitled "The English rogue described in the life of Meriton Latroon.] . . ." 4to. [Arber's *Term Cat.* i. 526.] London, 1679

Preface signed: R. H.

LIFE (the) and death of the godly man, exemplified in a sermon preached Nov. 12. 1676, at the funeral of that pious and faithful minister of Christ, Mr Thomas Wadsworth. By R. B. [Robert Bragge]. 4to. Pp. 32. [*Bodl.*] London, 1676

LIFE (the) and death of the most blessed among women, the Virgin Mary. . . . [By John Taylor, the water-poet.] 12mo. [*Brit. Mus.*] London, 1622

LIFE (the) and death of Thomas Tregosse, late minister of the Gospel at Milor and Maybe in Cornwall. . . . [By Theophilus Gale.] 8vo. Pp. 66. [Whitley's *Bapt. Bibl.* i. 99.] 1672

LIFE (the) and death of Thomas Woolsey, Cardinal; once Arch Bishop of York, and Lord Chancellour of England. Containing, 1. The original of his promotion, and, the way he took to obtain it. 2. The continuance in his magnificence. 3. His negotiations concerning the peace with France and the Netherlands. 4. His fall, death, and burial; wherein are things remarkable for these times. Written by one of his own servants, being his gentleman usher [George Cavendish]. 8vo. Pp. 175. [*Bodl.*] London, 1667

The epistle dedicatory signed: N. D.
The first edition was printed in 1641, 4to.

LIFE (the) and death of William Lawd, late archbishop of Canterburie, beheaded on Tower Hill, Friday, the 10th of January, 1644. By E. W. [Edmund Waller?]. 4to. London, 1645

LIFE and death of William Longbeard, the most famous and witty English traitor, borne in the city of London: accompanied with manye other most pleasant and prettie histories. By T. L. [Thomas Lodge] of Lincolns Inne, Gent. 4to. [Lowndes' *Bibl. Man.*] London, 1593

LIFE and death; or, Christ's and Satan's regimes. [Signed: W. D. F. *i.e.* William D. Forsyth.] 8vo. Pp. 79. [*Brit. Mus.*] Rochdale [1913]

LIFE (the) and defence of the conduct and principles of the venerable and calumniated Edmund Bonner, Bishop of London, in the reigns of Henry VIII., Edward VI., Mary, and Elizabeth; in which is considered the best mode of again changing the religion of this nation. By a Tractarian British critic [George Townsend, M.A.]. Dedicated to the Bishop of London. 8vo. [*D. N. B.* vol. 57, p. 104.] London, 1842

An ironical work.

LIFE (the) and doctrine of Martin Luther. [By Edward Lovel, D.D.] 8vo. [Gillow's *Bibl. Dict.* iv. 334.] [1620?]

LIFE (the) and doctrines of our Saviour Jesus Christ; with short reflections for the help of such as desire to use mental prayer. . . . Two parts. By H. M. [Henry More, *alias* Telman, *alias* Parr], of the Societie of Jesus. 8vo. Pp. 236, 218. [Gillow's *Bibl. Dict.* vol. 5, p. 98.] Gant, 1656

Previously issued (Antwerp, 1649) in Latin. A later English edition appeared in London, 1880.

LIFE (the) and errors of John Dunton, with the lives and characters of more than a thousand contemporary divines and other persons; to which are added Dunton's Conversation in Ireland; selections from his other genuine works, and a portrait of the author. [Edited by John Bowyer Nichols.] 8vo. 2 vols. [*Brit. Mus.*] London, 1818

Signed: J. B. N.
The pagination is continued throughout.

LIFE (the) and experiences of a Warwickshire labourer, with his own thoughts on the agricultural strike. [By T. Burgess.] 12mo. Warwick, 1872

LIFE (the) and exploits of Baron Munchausen. . . . [By Rudolf Eric Raspe.] 12mo. Glasgow, 1827

See footnote on p. 177, col. 1.

LIFE (the), and extraordinary adventures of James Molesworth Hobart, *alias* Henry Griffin, *alias* Lord Massey, the Newmarket Duke of Ormond, etc., involving a number of well-known characters. . . . By N. Dralloc [John Collard]. 12mo. 2 vols. London, 1794

LIFE (the) and extraordinary adventures of the Chevalier John Taylor; written from authentic materials, and published by his son, John Taylor, oculist. [A fabrication, by Henry Jones.] 12mo. 2 vols. [Lowndes' *Bibl. Man.* p. 2596.] London, 1761

LIFE (the) and genius of Goethe. [By Dr George Bancroft.] 8vo. [Cushing's *Anon.*] Boston, 1824

LIFE (the) and gests of S. Thomas Cantilupe, Bishop of Hereford, and some time before L. Chancellor of England. Extracted out of the authentique records of his canonization as to the maine part, Anonymus, Matt. Paris, Capgrave, Harpsfeld, and others. Collected by R. S., *S.J.* [Richard Strange, Jesuit]. 8vo. [Dodd's *Church History*, iii. 313; Oliver's *Collections.*] Gant, 1674

LIFE (the) and history of a pilgrim. . . . By G. W. [George Wollaston]. 8vo. Dublin, 1753

A London edition gives the author's name.

LIFE (the) and history of Belisarius, who conquer'd Africa and Italy; with an account of his disgrace. . . . [By John Oldmixon.] 8vo. [*Brit. Mus.*] London, 1713

LIFE (the) and humours of Falstaff. By C. S. [C. Short]. 8vo. [Jaggard's *Shakespeare Bibl.*] London, 1829

LIFE (the) and labours of the pious Robert Nelson. [By Charles F. Secretan.] 8vo. [*D. N. B.* vol. 40, p. 212.] London [1864]

LIFE and letters in the Italian Renaissance. By Christopher Hare [Mrs Marion Andrews]. 8vo. Pp. 326. [*Lond. Lib. Cat.*] London, 1915

LIFE and letters of Dr [John] Radcliffe. [By William Pittis.] 8vo. [Lowndes' *Bibl. Man.*] London, 1736

Other editions bear varying titles: "Dr [John] Radcliffe's life," etc.

LIFE and letters of John Lingard, 1771-1851. By Martin Haile [Marie Hallé] and Edwin Bonney. 8vo. Pp. 414. London, 1911

LIFE (the) and letters of Laurence Sterne. By Lewis Melville [Lewis Samuel Benjamin]. 8vo. 2 vols. [*Lit. Year Book.*] London, 1911

LIFE (the) and letters of Louis Moreau Gottschalk. By Octavia Hensel [Mrs Mary Alice Ives Seymour]. 8vo. [*Lib. Journ.* viii. 83.] Boston, 1870

LIFE (the) and letters of Madame Bonaparte. By Lemoine [Eugene Lemoine Didier]. 8vo. [Cushing's *Init. and Pseud.* i. 170.] New York, 1879

LIFE (the) and letters of Sydney Dobell; edited by E. J. [Emily Jolly]. 8vo. 2 vols. [*Brit. Mus.*] London, 1878

LIFE (the) and letters of William Beckford of Fonthill, author of "Vathek." By Lewis Melville [Lewis Samuel Benjamin]. 8vo. Pp. 408. [*Lit. Year Book.*] London, 1910

LIFE (the) and letters of William Cobbett in England and America; based upon hitherto unpublished family papers. . . . By Lewis Melville [Lewis Samuel Benjamin]. 8vo. 2 vols. [*Brit. Mus.*] London, 1913

LIFE and light. [By Ellen and Thomas Badley or Bodley.] 8vo. Private print, 1893

LIFE and memorable actions of many illustrious persons of the Eastern nations. [By John Morgan.] 12mo. London, 1739

LIFE (the) and memorials of Saint Teilo. [By John Hobson Matthews, of Cardiff.] 8vo. Pp. 16. Preston, 1893

LIFE (the) and miracles of S. Wenefride. [Translated from the Latin of Robert, Prior of Shrewsbury, by John Flood, S.J., *alias* Alford, *alias* Griffiths.] [*Brit. Mus.*] N.P. 1712

This is an amended reprint of "The admirable life . . ." St Omer, 1635.

LIFE (the) and miracles of St Winifrede [by Robert, Prior of Shrewsbury], together with her litanies; with some historical observations made thereon. [By William Fleetwood, Bishop of Ely.] 8vo. Pp. 128. [*Camb. Univ. Lib.*] London, 1713

See also "The admirable life of St Wenefride. . . ."

LIFE (the) and opinions of Sir Richard Maltravers, an English gentleman of the seventeenth century. [By Henry Augustus Dillon-Lee, Viscount Dillon.] 8vo. 2 vols. [*Edin. Univ. Lib.*] London, 1822

LIFE and opinions of the celebrated George Buchanan. By the author of the *Lives of George Wishart, the Regent Moray*, etc. [John Parker Lawson, M.A.]. 12mo. Pp. 285. Edinburgh, 1829

LIFE (the) and opinions of Tristram Shandy, Gentleman. [By Laurence Sterne, D.D.] 8vo. 9 vols. London, vols. 1-2, 1760; 3-4, 1761; 5-6, 1762; 7-8, 1765; 9, 1767.

LIFE (the) and particular proceedings of the Rev. Mr George Whitefield. By an impartial hand [Josiah Tucker, Dean of Gloucester]. 8vo. Pp. 96. London, 1739

LIFE (the) and posthumous works of Arthur Maynwaring, Esq.; containing several original pieces, and translations in prose and verse, never before printed. [By John Oldmixon.] To which are added, several political tracts written by him, before and after the change of the ministry. 8vo. Pp. xviii. 358. [*Bodl.*] London, 1715

Dedication signed: J. O.

LIFE (the) and reign of Edward I. By the author of *The greatest of the Plantagenets* [Robert Benton Seeley]. 8vo. Pp. xvi. 352. [*D. N. B.* vol. 51, p. 193.] London, 1872

The second edition of *The greatest of all the Plantagenets* (1861). The work has been mistakenly attributed to Edmund Clifford.

LIFE (the) and reign of King Richard the Second. By a person of quality [Sir Robert Howard]. . . . 12mo. Pp. 240. [Arber's *Term Cat.* i. 552.] London, 1681

LIFE (the) and reigne of King Charls or, the pseudo-martyr discovered; with a late reply to an invective remonstrance against the Parliament and present government; together with some animadversions on the strange contrariety between the late kings publick declarations, protestations, imprecations, and his pourtraiture, compared with his private letters, and other of his expresses not hitherto taken into common observation. [By John Milton.] 8vo. Pp. 228. [*Bodl.*] London, 1651

LIFE (the) and remains of Wilmot Warwick; edited by his friend, Henry Vernon. [By George Wightwick.] 8vo. Pp. 326. London, 1828

LIFE and scenery in Missouri; reminiscences of an Irish missionary priest [John O'Hanlon]. 8vo. Pp. xii. 292. [*Brit. Mus.*] St Louis, 1890

LIFE (the) and strange surprizing adventures of Mr D— De F—, of London, hosier . . . in a dialogue between him, Robinson Crusoe, and his man Friday. . . . [By Charles Gildon.] 8vo. Pp. xviii. 48. [*Brit. Mus.*] London, 1719

LIFE (the) and strange surprizing adventures of Robinson Crusoe, of York, mariner; who lived eight and twenty years, all alone in an un-inhabited island on the coast of America, near the mouth of the great river of Oroonoque; having been cast on shore by shipwreck, wherein all the men perished but himself: with an account how he was at last as strangely deliver'd by pyrates. Written by himself. [By Daniel Defoe.] 8vo. London, 1719

LIFE (the) and strange, unparallel'd, and unheard-of voyages and adventures of Ambrose Gwinet, formerly well known to the public as the Lame Beggar man; written by himself. [Really by Isaac Bickerstaffe.] Second edition. 8vo. [*Brit. Mus.*] London, 1770

LIFE (the) and times of Conrad the squirrel. . . . By the author of *Effie's friends* [Lady Augusta Noel]. 8vo. Pp. 118. [*Brit. Mus.*] London, 1872

LIFE (the) and times of Cranmer. By the author of *Three experiments of living*, etc. [Mrs Hannah F. Lee, of Boston]. 12mo. [*Brit. Mus.*] Boston, 1841

LIFE and times of Francis the First, King of France. [By Sir James Bacon, barrister.] 8vo. 2 vols. [*Brit. Mus.*] London, 1829

LIFE (the) and times of Girolamo Savonarola; illustrating the progress of the Reformation in Italy, during the fifteenth century. [By John Abraham Heraud.] 12mo. [*Brit. Mus.*] London, 1843

LIFE (the) and times of John Kettlewell; with details of the history of the Non-jurors. By the author of *Nicholas Ferrar, his household and his friends* [Jane F. M. Carter]. . . . 8vo. Pp. xvii. 273. London, 1895

LIFE and times of Martin Luther. By the authoress of *Three experiments of living* [Mrs Hannah F. Lee, of Boston]. 8vo. Pp. 80. [*Brit. Mus.*] Bristol, 1839

LIFE (the) and times of Selina [Shirley], Countess of Huntingdon. By a member of the houses of Shirley and Hastings [Aaron Crossley Hobart Seymour]. 8vo. 2 vols. [*New Coll. Lib.*] London, 1839

LIFE (the) and times of Sir Philip Sydney. By S. M. D. [Mrs Sarah Matilda Davis]. 12mo. [Cushing's *Init. and Pseud.* i. 75.] Boston, 1859

LIFE (the) and travels of John Pemberton. Compiled for the "American Friends' Library," by W. H., Junr. [William Hodgson]. 12mo. [Smith's *Cat. of Friends' Books*, ii. 282.] London, 1844

LIFE (the) and troubles of Mr Bowser. By "M. Quad" [Charles B. Lewis]. 8vo. [*Amer. Cat.*] New York, 1902

LIFE (the) and wonderful adventures of Totty Testudo; an autobiography. [By Mrs Frances Wylde.] 8vo. Edinburgh, 1873

LIFE (the) and work of the seventh Earl of Shaftesbury. By Old Merry [Edwin Hodder]. 8vo. [Cushing's *Init. and Pseud.* i. 212.] London, 1886

LIFE (the) and works of John Raphael Smith. By Frank Danby [Mrs Julia Frankau]. 8vo. [*Lit. Year Book.*] London, 1902

LIFE (the) and writings of Major Jack Downing, of Downingville. [By Seba Smith.] Second edition. 12mo. [*Brit. Mus.*] Boston, 1834

LIFE (the) and writings of Philip, Duke of Wharton. . . . By Lewis Melville [Lewis Samuel Benjamin]. 8vo. Pp. 336. [*Lit. Year Book.*] London, 1913

LIFE (the) and writings of St Peter. By the author of *Essays on the Church*, etc. [Robert B. Seeley]. 8vo. [*D. N. B.* vol. 51, p. 193.] London, 1873

LIFE (the) and writings of Sir Walter Raleigh. From the *Edinburgh Review*. [By Macvey Napier.] 8vo. Pp. 98. [*D. Laing.*] Edinburgh, 1840

LIFE (the) and writings of Solomon, King of Israel. [By Peter Perring Thoms.] 12mo. Pp. 106. [*Brit. Mus.*] London [1848]

LIFE assurance; objections answered. [By R. A. Sim.] 8vo. Pp. 56. Edinburgh [1888]

LIFE before him. [By Oliver Bell Bunce.] 8vo. New York, 1860

LIFE (the) boat; a poem. . . . By a member of the Humane Society [John Davis, LL.D.]. [Cushing's *Init. and Pseud.* i. 189.] N.P., N.D.

LIFE book (the) of a labourer; essays. By a working clergyman [Rev. Erskine Neale]. Second edition. 12mo. [*D. N. B.* vol. 40, p. 141.] London, 1850

LIFE by the fireside. By the author of *Visiting my relations*, etc. [Mary Ann Kelty]. 8vo. [*Brit. Mus.*] London, 1853

LIFE (the), character, and genius, of Ebenezer Elliott, the corn law rhymer. By January Searle, author of *Leaves from Sherwood Forest*, etc. [George Searle Phillips]. 12mo. Pp. 184. London, 1850

See also "Memoirs of Ebenezer Elliott."

LIFE (the), character and service of General G. B. M'Clellan. By Peter Boylston [G. Ticknor Curtis]. 8vo. London, 1887

LIFE (the), confessions, and adventures of Alfred Teufel. By "Arrelsee" [R. L. C., *i.e.* Robert L. Cope]. 8vo. [*Camb. Univ. Lib.*] Doylestown, Pa., 1867

LIFE doubled by the economy of time. By the author of *How a penny became a thousand pounds* [Robert Kemp Philp]. 8vo. Pp. 100. [Boase and Courtney's *Bibl. Corn.* ii. 493.] London [1859]

LIFE (the) everlasting; a reality of romance. By Marie Corelli [Caroline Cody]. 8vo. Pp. v. 436. [*Brit. Mus.*] London, 1911

LIFE (a) for a life. By the author of *John Halifax, Gentleman*, etc. [Dinah Maria Mulock, later Mrs Craik]. 8vo. 3 vols. London, 1859

LIFE in a crack regiment. By Baron von Schlicht [Count von Baudissin]. 8vo. London, 1904

LIFE in a French village. By L. G. Seguin [Mrs Strahan, wife of the Publisher]. 12mo. London, 1879

LIFE in a man-of-war. By a fore-top-man [Henry James Mercier, and William Gallop]. 8vo. [Cushing's *Init. and Pseud.* ii. 60.] Philadelphia, 1841

LIFE in a rebel prison; or, the experience of a prisoner of war. [By C. M. Erskine.] 8vo. [Cushing's *Init. and Pseud.* ii. 124.] Philadelphia, 1883

LIFE in a Swiss chalet . . . a tale. By H. W. [H. Whately?]. 8vo. London, 1878

LIFE in Algoma; or, three years of a clergyman's life and Church work in that diocese. By H. N. B. [Harold Nelson Burden]. 8vo. Pp. 167. [*Brit. Mus.*] London, 1894

LIFE in Arcadia. By a Son of the Soil [Joseph Smith Fletcher]. 8vo. [*Amer. Cat.*] New York, 1896

LIFE in California during a residence of several years; also an account of the Indians of Alta-California. By an American [Alfred Robinson]. 8vo. [Cushing's *Init. and Pseud.* i. 13.] New York, 1846

LIFE in Danbury. By the Danbury newsman [James Montgomery Bailey]. 12mo. [Cushing's *Init. and Pseud.* i. 77.] Boston, 1877

LIFE in Dixie's Land; or, South in Secession-time. By Edmund Kirke [James Roberts Gilmore]. 8vo. [*Nat. Lib. of Scot.*] London, 1863

LIFE in featherland. By M. M. W. [M. M. Esdaile]. 4to. Pp. 139. [*Brit. Mus.*] Paisley [1891]

LIFE in Feejee; or, five years among the cannibals. By a lady [Mrs Mary Davis Wallis, *née* Cook]. 8vo. [Cushing's *Init. and Pseud.* i. 162.] Boston, 1851

LIFE in heaven; there, faith is changed into sight, and hope is passed into blissful fruition. By the author of *Heaven our home* [William Branks]. Fifteenth thousand. 8vo. Pp. viii. 264. [*Brit. Mus.*] Edinburgh, 1863

LIFE in India; or, the English in Calcutta. [By Mrs —— Monkland.] 8vo. 3 vols. London, 1828

LIFE in Mexico, during a residence of two years in that country. By Madame C. de la B.ı [Calderon de la Barca]. With a preface, by W. H. Prescott, author of *The history of Ferdinand and Isabella of Spain*. 8vo. [Cushing's *Init. and Pseud.* i. 48.] London, 1843

LIFE in New York. By the author of *The old white Meeting-house* [Samuel Irenaeus Prime, D.D.]. 12mo. [Allibone's *Dict.*] New York, 1851

LIFE in New York. Edited [or rather written] by O. Hum & Co. [Frederick Saunders]. 8vo. [Cushing's *Init. and Pseud.* i. 134.] New York, 1839

LIFE in Normandy; sketches of French fishing, farming, cooking, natural history and politics drawn from nature. [By W. F. Campbell, edited by John Francis Campbell.] 8vo. 2 vols. Edinburgh, 1863

LIFE in our villages. By the *Daily News* Special Commissioner [G. F. Millin]. 8vo. [*Brit. Mus.*] London, 1891

LIFE in the cloister; or, faithful and true. By the author of *The world and the cloister*, etc. [Agnes M. Stewart]. Second edition. 8vo. Pp. 224. [*Brit. Mus.*] Edinburgh, N.D.

The first edition appeared in 1865, at London.

LIFE in the eagle's nest; a tale of Afghanistan. By A. L. O. E. [Charlotte Maria Tucker]. 8vo. Pp. 222. [*Lit. Year Book.*] London [1883]

LIFE in the far west; or, the adventures of a hoosier [Adolphus M. Hart]. 8vo. [Cushing's *Init. and Pseud.* i. 133.] New York, 1860

LIFE in the Ghetto: or, the Jewish physician. [By Charlotte Bickersteth, later Mrs Ward.] 8vo. London, 1872

LIFE in the low parts of Manchester; a midnight visit. . . . By Junius Junior [Joseph Johnson]. 8vo. Pp. 16. Manchester [1861]

LIFE in the Mofussil; or, the civilian in Lower Bengal. By an Ex-civilian [G. Graham]. 8vo. 2 vols. London, 1878

LIFE in the saddle; or, the cavalry scout. By Ned Buntline [Edward Z. C. Judson]. 8vo. [Cushing's *Init. and Pseud.* i. 43.] New York, 1877

LIFE in the sick-room; essays. By an invalid [Harriet Martineau]. 12mo. Pp. xv. 221. [*D. N. B.* vol. 36, p. 313.] London, 1844

LIFE in the South [United States]; from the commencement of the war [between North and South]. By a blockaded British subject [Sarah L. Jones]. Being a social history of those who took part in the battles, from a personal acquaintance with them in their own homes; from the spring of 1860 to August 1862. 8vo. 2 vols. [Sabin's *Dictionary.*] London, 1863

Attributed also to Catherine Cooper Hopley.

LIFE in the tent; or, travels in the desert and Syria, in 1850. By a young pilgrim [Anne Hindley, daughter of C. Hindley, Esq., M.P. for Ashton, and afterwards wife of Henry Woods, Esq. M.P.]. 12mo. [*N. and Q.* Feb. 1869, p. 167.] London [1850?]

LIFE in the walls, the hearth, and the eaves. [By Miss A. C. Chambers.] 12mo. [*Brit. Mus.*] London, 1874

LIFE in the white bear's den. By A. L. O. E. [Charlotte Maria Tucker]. 8vo. Pp. 219. [*Lit. Year Book.*] London [1884]

LIFE insurance. By Philanthropos John [Thomas Barber Beaumont]. 8vo. [*D. N. B.* vol. 4, p. 61.] London, 1814

LIFE (a) interest. [A novel.] By Mrs Alexander [Mrs Alexander Hector, *née* Annie French]. 8vo. Pp. 382. [*Lit. Year Book.*] London, 1896

LIFE is life; and other tales and episodes. By Zack [Gwendoline Keats]. 8vo. Pp. 328. [*Brit. Mus.*] Edinburgh, 1898

LIFE (the), labours, and travels of the Rev. Robert Newton, D.D. By a Wesleyan Preacher [Rev. Thomas Jackson]. 12mo. Pp. 184. [Osborn's *Method. Lit.* p. 149.] London, 1855

A larger edition was also published in the same year: see "The life of the Rev. Robert Newton, D.D."

LIFE lectures. By the author of *Alpha* [Edward Nichols Dennys]; being lectures on the religion of life, etc. 8vo. [*Brit. Mus.*] London, 1871

LIFE (the) line of the lone one; or, autobiography of the world's child. [By Warren Chase.] 8vo. [Cushing's *Init. and Pseud.* i. 383.] Boston, 1857

LIFE lines; or, God's work in a human being. By F. J. P. [Mrs Frances Julia Pakenham]. 8vo. [Cushing's *Init. and Pseud.* i. 222.] London, 1862

LIFE lost or saved; words of affectionate counsel. By S. D. [Selina Ditcher]. 12mo. [Cushing's *Init. and Pseud.* i. 75.] London, 1866

LIFE (the) of a beauty; a novel. By the author of *The jilt*, etc. [Mrs Yorick Smythies, *née* Gordon]. 12mo. 3 vols. [*Brit. Mus.*] London, 1846

LIFE (the) of a boy. By the author of *The panorama of youth* [Mary R. Stockdale]. 12mo. [*Brit. Mus.*] London, 1821

LIFE (the) of a conspirator; being a biography of Sir Everard Digby by one of his descendants . . . the author of *A life of Archbishop Laud*, etc. [Thomas Longueville]. 8vo. Pp. ix. 306. [*Brit. Mus.*] London, 1895

LIFE (the) of a lawyer. Written by himself. [By Sir James Stewart.] 12mo. Pp. 421. London, 1830

LIFE (the) of a prig. By a prig [Thomas Longueville]. 8vo. [*Brit. Mus.*] London, 1880

LIFE (the) of a sailor. By a Captain in the navy [Frederick Chamier]. 12mo. 3 vols. [*Bodl.*] London, 1832

LIFE (the) of a satirical puppy called Nim. . . . By T. M. [Thomas May ?]. 8vo. Pp. 118. [*Brit. Mus.*] London, 1657

LIFE (the) of a soldier; a narrative of twenty-seven years' service in various parts of the world. By a Field officer [Ross Lewin]. 12mo. 3 vols. [*Nat. Lib. of Scot.*] London, 1834

LIFE (the) of a sportsman. By Nimrod [Charles James Apperley]. With thirty-six coloured illustrations, by Henry Alken. 8vo. Pp. 414. [*Brit. Mus.*] London, 1842

LIFE (the) of a travelling physician, from his first introduction to practice; including twenty years' wanderings through the greater part of Europe. [By Sir George William Lefevre, M.D.] 8vo. 3 vols. [*D. N. B.* vol. 32, p. 399.] London, 1843

LIFE (the) of a vagrant [Josiah Basset]; or, the testimony of an outcast to the value and truth of the Gospel. Fifth edition, enlarged and improved. Edited by the author of the *Hebrew martyrs*, etc. [John Waddington]. 12mo. [*W.*] London, 1856

LIFE of Abraham Newland, Esq.; late principal Cashier at the Bank of England; with some account of that great national establishment. . . . [By John Dye Collier.] 12mo. [Watt's *Bibl. Brit.*] London, 1808

LIFE of Adam Wallace and Walter Mill, Martyrs; with an essay on the establishment of the Scottish Reformation. By the author of the *Life of George Wishart* [John Parker Lawson]. 12mo. [*Nat. Lib. of Scot.*] Edinburgh, 1827

LIFE (the) of Alexander Hamilton. By Anthony Pasquin [John Williams]. 8vo. [Cushing's *Init. and Pseud.* i. 225.] Boston, 1804

LIFE (the) of Andrew Jackson, President of the United States. [By Seba Smith.] 12mo. [*Brit. Mus.*] Philadelphia, 1834

LIFE of Antony Ashley Cooper, first Earl of Shaftesbury. [By Benjamin Martyn; revised by Dr Gregory Sharpe and Dr Andrew Kippis.] 4to. [Martin's *Private Prints.*] [*c.* 1790]

LIFE (the) of Archbishop Laud. By "A Romish Recusant" [Thomas Longueville]. 8vo. [*Brit. Mus.*] London, 1894

LIFE (the) of Armelle Nicolas, commonly called the good Armelle; a poor maid servant in France, who could not read a letter in a book, and yet was a noble and happy servant of the King of kings. [Translated by James Gough.] 8vo. [Smith's *Cat. of Friends' Books*, i. 853.] Bristol, 1772

LIFE of Automathes. [By John Kirkby.] 8vo. London, 1745

LIFE of Beato Angelico da Fiesole, of the Order of Friar Preachers; translated by a member of the same Order [Charles F. Palmer] from the French of E. Cartier. 8vo. [Boase's *Mod. Eng. Biog.* vol. 6, col. 348.] London, 1865

LIFE (the) of Bishop [Johann] Spangenberg . . . Bishop of the Unity of the Brethren: from the German of Charles F. Ledderhose . . . [Translated by the Rev. Godfrey Clemens.] 8vo. Pp. v. 118. London, 1855

LIFE (the) of blessed Alphonsus Rodriguez, lay-brother of the Society of Jesus. By a lay-brother of the same Society [Henry Foley]. 8vo. Pp. xxiii. 220. [*Bodl.*] London, 1873

LIFE of Bonaparte, First Consul of France, from his birth to the Peace of Luneville. . . . [By Louis Dubroca.] 8vo. [*Brit. Mus.*] London, 1802

LIFE of Captain John Smith, the founder of Virginia. By Frank Cooper [William Gilmore Simms]. 12mo. [Cushing's *Init. and Pseud.* i. 67.] New York, 1846

LIFE of Columbus. By the author of *Friends in Council* [Sir Arthur Helps]. 8vo. [*Brit. Mus.*] London, 1892

LIFE (the) of Daniel Defoe. [By George Chalmers.] 4to. [*D. N. B.* vol. 9, p. 446.] London, 1785

LIFE (the) of Dr [John] Barclay. [By Sir George Ballingall, M.D.] 8vo. Pp. xix. [Edinburgh, 1827]

LIFE (the) of Dr James Usher, late Lord Archbishop of Armagh, and primate of all Ireland; collected from the best authorities. [By Rev. Joseph D'Arcy Sirr, B.A.] 8vo. Pp. lxii. [*Bodl.*] Dublin, 1815

LIFE (the) of Dr Oliver Goldsmith; written from personal knowledge, authentic papers, and other indubitable authorities. . . . [By Thomas Percy, D.D., Bishop of Dromore.] 8vo. Pp. 50. London, 1774

The authorship has been questioned.

LIFE (the) of Dr Thomas Morton, late Bishop of Duresme; begun by R. B. [Richard Baddeley], secretary to his Lordship, and finished by J. N., D.D., [Joseph Naylor] his Lordship's chaplain. 8vo. Pp. ix. 189. [Davies' *Mem. of the York Press*, p. 102.] York, 1669

LIFE (the) of Donna Olimpia Maldachini, who governed the Church during the time of Innocent the X., which was from the year 1644 to the year 1655: written in Italian by Abbot Gualdi [Gregorio Leti]; and faithfully rendered into English [by Henry Compton, Bishop of London]. 8vo. Pp. 214. [Wood's *Athen. Oxon.* iv. 576.] London, 1677

LIFE (the) of Edmund Kean. [By Byran Waller Procter.] 12mo. 2 vols. [Jaggard's *Index*, ii.] London, 1835

LIFE (the) of Edward II. with the fates of Gavestone and the Spencers: a poem in three canto's. To which (for the better understanding of the whole) is prefix'd an account of that Princes reign, from Dr Echard and others. Done from a manuscript. [By Sir Francis Hubert.] 12mo. Pp. 146. [*Bodl.*] London, 1721

LIFE (the) of Edwin Forrest. By Colley Cibber [James Rees]. 8vo. [Cushing's *Init. and Pseud.* i. 57.] Philadelphia, 1874

LIFE (the) of Elisha Tyson, the philanthropist. By a citizen of Baltimore [John S. Tyson]. 8vo. [Cushing's *Init. and Pseud.* i. 58.] Baltimore, 1825

LIFE (the) of Elizabeth, Queen of Bohemia, daughter of King James VI. of Scotland. By a lady [Jane Webster, of St Andrews]. 4to. [*New Coll. Lib.*] London, 1857

LIFE (the) of Emily Davison. By George Colmore [Mrs Baillie Weaver]. 8vo. [*Brit. Mus.*] London, 1913

LIFE (the) of Enoch again revived, in which Abels offering is accepted, and Cains mark known, and he rejected, through the opening of the inward mystery of creation, by the first Mover and Former thereof, who is the onely wise invisible God, to whom be the glory and praise in and over all his works. . . . [Signed: W. B. *i.e.* William Bayly.] 4to. Pp. 27. [Smith's *Cat. of Friends' Books*, i. 216.] London, 1662

LIFE of Francis of Lorrain, Duke of Guise [translated from the French, by F. S., *i.e.* Ferrand Spence]. 12mo. [*Brit. Mus.*] London, 1682

LIFE (the) of Francis Xavier; abridged from Father Bohours. [By J. Morgan, of Wellen, Kent.] 8vo. London, 1864

LIFE (the) of Friedrich Schiller; comprehending an examination of his works. [By Thomas Carlyle.] 8vo. Pp. vi. 352. London, 1825

LIFE (the) of Galileo Galilei; with illustrations of the advancement of experimental philosophy. [By Col. John Elliott Drinkwater, afterwards Bethune.] 4to. [*Brit. Mus.*] London, 1829

See also "Life of Keppler."

LIFE (the) of General the Right Honourable Sir David Baird, Bart. G.C.B. K.C. &c. &c. [By Theodore Edward Hook.] 8vo. 2 vols. [*D. N. B.* vol. 27, p. 275.] London, 1832

LIFE of General Thomas J. Jackson. By an Ex-Cadet [James Dabney MacCabe]. 8vo. [Kirk's *Supp.*] Richmond, Va., 1863

LIFE of George Lesley. [By Sir David Dalrymple, Lord Hailes.] 4to. [*Nat. Lib. of Scot.*] N. P. [1786]

Included in the author's "Annals of Scotland," vol. iii.

LIFE (the) of . . . George Thomson. By one of his nephews [John E. H. Thomson, D.D.]. 8vo. Edinburgh, 18—

LIFE of George Washington, studied anew. By Col. Frederic Ingham [Edward Everett Hale]. 12mo. [Cushing's *Init. and Pseud.* i. 137.] New York, 1887

LIFE of George Wishart, of Pitarrow, the martyr. [By John Parker Lawson, M.A.] 12mo. Pp. xxiii. 244. [*Nat. Lib. of Scot.*] Edinburgh, 1827

LIFE (the) of God in the soul of man; or, the nature and excellency of the Christian religion, with the methods of attaining the happiness which it proposes: also an account of the beginnings and advances of a spiritual life. [By Henry Scougal.] With a preface, by Gilbert Burnet, now Lord Bishop of Sarum. The fifth edition, carefully corrected; to which is added a table. 8vo. Pp. 152. [*D. N. B.* vol. 51, p. 120.] London, 1707

The first edition appeared in 1677: many others have followed.

LIFE (the) of Gustavus Adolphus, King of Sweden. . . . [By Deborah Alcock.] 12mo. [Bayly's *Life of D. Alcock.*] Bath [1857]

LIFE (the) of Hannah More; with a critical review of her writings. By the Rev. Sir Archibald Mac Sarcasm, Bart. [William Shaw, D.D., rector of Chelvy]. 8vo. Pp. viii. 208. [Green's *Bibl. Somers.* iii. 97.] Bristol, 1802

LIFE (the) of Harriot Stuart; written by herself [rather by Charlotte Ramsay, later Mrs Lennox]. 12mo. [Courtney's *Secrets*, p. 44.] London, 1751

LIFE (the) of Haydn, in a series of letters written at Vienna; followed by the life of Mozart, with observations on Metastasio, and on the present state of music in France and Italy. Translated from the French of L. A. C. Bombet. With notes by the author of *The sacred melodies* [Thomas Gardiner]. 8vo. Pp. xv. 496. London, 1817

"The letters were really written by Giuseppe Carpani, and are translated from his work entituled 'Le Haydine.' Le Chevalier Beyle published them as his own, under the pseudonym of Bombet." L. Alex. César Beyle.—Note in *Bodl. Cat.*

LIFE of Henri Perreyve, by A. Gratry; translated by the author of *A Dominican artist* [Henrietta Louisa Farrer, later Mrs Sidney Lear]. 8vo. Pp. xvi. 233. [*Brit. Mus.*] London, 1872

LIFE of Henry VIII. and his six wives. By Frank Forester [Henry William Herbert]. 12mo. [Kirk's *Supp.*] Philadelphia, 1886

LIFE (the) of Henry VIII., by Mr William Shakespear; in which are interspersed historical notes, moral reflections and observations, in respect to the unhappy fate Cardinal Wolsey met with. Adorned with several (6) copperplates. By the author of the *History of the life and times of Cardinal Wolsey* [Joseph Grove]. 8vo. [Lowndes' *Bibl. Man.* p. 2282.] London, 1758

LIFE (the) of Henry St John, Lord Viscount Bolingbroke. [By Oliver Goldsmith.] 8vo. Pp. 112. [*Brit. Mus.*] London, 1770

LIFE of Her Most Gracious Majesty the Queen [Victoria]. . . . By Sarah Tytler [Henrietta Keddie]. . . . 4to. 2 vols. [*Lit. Year Book.*] London [1883-5]

LIFE of Hippolyte Flandrin, a Christian painter of the nineteenth century. [By Henrietta Louisa Farrer, later Mrs Sidney Lear.] 8vo. [*Brit. Mus.*] London, 1875

LIFE of Hugh Peters. [By William Harris, D.D., nonconformist minister.] 8vo. [Watt's *Bibl. Brit.*] London, 1751

LIFE (the) of James Crichton of Clunie, commonly called the Admirable Crichton. [By Francis Douglas.] 8vo. [*Brit. Mus.*] [Aberdeen, 1760]

LIFE of James Renwick, the last of the Scottish Martyrs. By the author of the *History of the Covenanters* [William Sime]. 12mo. Pp. 180. [*Nat. Lib. of Scot.*] Edinburgh, 1838

LIFE (the) of James II. late King of England: containing an account of his birth, education, religion, and enterprizes, both at home and abroad, in peace and war, while in a private and publick capacity, till his dethronment; with the various struggles made since for his restoration; the state of his court at St Germains, and the particulars of his death. . . . [By David Jones.] 8vo. Pp. 420. [Arber's *Term Cat.* iii. 688.] London, 1702

LIFE of Jean Paul F. Richter, compiled from various sources; together with his autobiography, translated from the German. [By Mrs Eliza Lee, *née* Buckminster.] Second edition. 8vo. [*Nat. Lib. of Scot.*] London, 1849

LIFE (the) of Jesus, according to his original biographers; with notes. By E. Kirke [James Roberts Gilmore]. 12mo. [Kirk's *Supp.*] Boston, 1867

LIFE (the) of Jesus, critically examined by Dr David Friedrich Strauss; translated from the fourth German edition [by Marian Evans, later Mrs Cross]. 8vo. 3 vols. [*Brit. Mus.*] London, 1846

LIFE (the) of Jesus, for young people. By the editor of *Kind words* [Benjamin Clarke]. 8vo. [*Brit. Mus.*] London, 1868

LIFE (the) of Jesus, written for the young. By G. J. F. [George James Foster]. 12mo. [Cushing's *Init. and Pseud.* ii. 56.] Kingland, 1866

LIFE (the) of Joan of Arc. By Anatole France [Jacques Anatole Thibault]; translated by Winifred Stephens. 8vo. 2 vols. [*Lond. Lib. Cat.*] London, 1909

LIFE (the) of John Buncle Esq.; containing various observations and reflections made in several parts of the world, and many extraordinary relations. [By Thomas Amory.] 12mo. 4 vols. London, 1770

Published in 1825, 3 vols, with the author's name.

LIFE of John Bunyan. By the author of *Mark Rutherford* [William Hale White]. 8vo. [*Brit. Mus.*] London, 1905

LIFE of John Calvin, the Genevan Reformer. By the author of the *Life of Martin Luther* [William Sime]. 12mo. Edinburgh, 1823

LIFE (the) of John Calvin, "the man of Geneva"; for young persons. By the author of *The story of Martin Luther*, and *The story of Ulrich Zwingle* [Elizabeth Warren]. 12mo. [*Brit. Mus.*] London [1864]

LIFE (the) of John De Wycliffe. By the author of *The story of Martin Luther* [Elizabeth Warren]. 8vo. London [1865]

LIFE (the) of John [Dalrymple] Earl of Stair; containing his birth and education; his negotiations at Warsaw, Paris and the Hague; the articles of the Union, and of the Peace of Utrecht; his magnificent entry into Paris, with his speeches and memorials to the French king and regent: with a full account of all the battles and sieges, particularly that of Dettingen, in which his Lordship was engaged; the spring of the Rebellions 1715, 1719, and 1745.... [By Andrew Henderson.] 12mo. Pp. 257. [*Bodl.*] London, N.D.

LIFE (the) of John Eliot, the apostle of the Indians, including notices of the principal attempts to propagate Christianity in North America, during the seventeenth century. [By John Wilson, D.D., Bombay.] 12mo. Pp. 300. [*New Coll. Lib.*] Edinburgh, 1828

LIFE of John Erskine of Dun. 1508-1591. By Scoto-Britannico [Mary Webster of St Andrews]. 8vo. Pp. x. 95. [*New Coll. Lib.*] Edinburgh, 1879

LIFE (the) of John Gay, author of The Beggar's opera, etc. [Signed: E. C. *i.e.* Edmund Curll.] 8vo. London, 1733

LIFE of John Knox, the Scottish Reformer. [By William Sime.] 12mo. Edinburgh [1820?]

LIFE (the) of John Milton; containing, besides the history of his works, several extraordinary characters of men and books, sects, parties and opinions. [By John Toland.] 8vo. [*D. N. B.* vol. 56, p. 441.] London, 1699

LIFE (the) of John Wesley. . . [By Robert Benton Seeley.] 8vo. [*Brit. Mus.*] London, 1856

LIFE (the) of John Wickliff; with an appendix and list of his works. [By Patrick Fraser Tytler.] 8vo. Pp. vii. 207. [*Nat. Lib. of Scot.*] Edinburgh, 1826

LIFE (the) of John Wilkes . . . in the manner of Plutarch. [By Joseph Cradock.] Second edition, revised and corrected. 8vo. [*Brit. Mus.*] London, 1773

LIFE of Joseph, the son of Israel; in eight books: chiefly designed to allure young minds to a love of the sacred Scriptures. [By J. Macgowan.] 12mo. [Wilson's *Hist. of Diss. Ch.* i. 453.] London, 1803

LIFE of [Johann] Keppler. [By Col. John Elliott Drinkwater, later Bethune.] 4to. [*Brit. Mus.*] [London, 1833]

No title-page: extracted from "Eminent persons . . ." pub. by Soc. for Diff. Useful Knowledge.

LIFE of King William IV. [By Cyrus Redding.] 8vo. [*D. N. B.* vol. 47, p. 371.] London, 1837

Hastily written before the King's death.

LIFE (the) of Lady Guion, written by herself in French; now abridged, and translated in English, exhibiting her eminent piety, charity, meekness, resignation, fortitude, and stability; her labours, travels, sufferings and services, for the conversion of souls to God. . . . [By James Gough.] 8vo. 2 vols. [Smith's *Cat. of Friends' Books*, i. 853.] Bristol, 1772

LIFE of Lady Jane Grey and of Lord Guildford Dudley, her husband. By Edward Baldwin [William Godwin]. 8vo. Pp. vii. 107. [*Brit. Mus.*] London, 1824

LIFE (the) of Lady Warner of Parham, in Suffolk, in religion called Sister Clare of Jesus. Written by a Catholic Gentleman, N. N. [Edward Carisbrick *alias* Neville, S.J.]. 8vo. Pp. 376. [Sommervogel's *Dictionnaire.*] 1692

LIFE (the) of Leo XIII. By John Oldcastle [Wilfrid Meynell]. 8vo. London [1887]

LIFE (the) of Lewis [of Bourbon], late Prince of Condé, digested into annals; with many curious remarks on the transactions of Europe for this last sixty years. [By Pierre Coste]; done out of French. 8vo. [Arber's *Term Cat.* ii. 452, 634.] London, 1693

LIFE (the) of Lord Somers. [By David Jardine.] 8vo. [*Brit. Mus.*] London, 1833

Library of Useful Knowledge.

LIFE of Louise, Countess of Albany. By Vernon Lee [Violet Paget]. 8vo. [*Brit. Mus.*] London, 1884

LIFE (the) of Lucilio (alias Julius Cæsar) Vanini, burnt for atheism at Thoulouse; with an abstract of his writings; being the sum of the atheistical doctrine taken from Plato, Aristotle, Averroes, Cardanus and Pomponatus's philosophy; with a confutation of the same. . . . Translated from the French [of David Durand] into English. 8vo. Pp. vi. 110. London, 1730

LIFE (the) of Luther. By A. L. O. E. [Charlotte M. Tucker]. Taken chiefly from D'Aubigné's "History of the Reformation." 12mo. Pp. 71. London [1873]

LIFE (the) of Madame Louise de France, daughter of Louis XV; known also as the mother Térèse de St Augustin. By the author of *Tales of Kirkbeck* [Henrietta Louisa Farrer, later Mrs Sidney Lear]. 8vo. Pp. xi. 291. London, 1869

LIFE (the) of Mansie Wauch, tailor in Dalkeith: written by himself. [By David Macbeth Moir.] 12mo. Pp. viii. 374. [*Nat. Lib. of Scot.*] Edinburgh, 1828

LIFE of Martin Luther. [By William Sime.] 12mo. Edinburgh [1820?]

LIFE (the) of Martin Van Buren. By David Crockett [Augustine Smith Clayton]. 8vo. [Cushing's *Init. and Pseud.* ii. 38.] Philadelphia, 1835

LIFE (the) of Mary Magdalene, Saint. By Vernon Lee [Violet Paget]. 8vo. [*Brit. Mus.*] London, 1904

LIFE (the) of Mary, Queen of Scots. [By James Grant.] 12mo. [*Brit. Mus.*] Elgin, 1828

LIFE of Mary, Queen of Scots, translated from the French [of P. Le Pesant de Bois Guibert], with notes, by James Freebairn. 8vo. [*W.*] Edinburgh, 1725

LIFE (the) of Mirabeau. By S. G. Tallentyre [Miss E. Beatrice Hall]. 8vo. [*Lit. Year Book.*] London, 1908

LIFE (the) of Mr Thomas Firmin, late citizen of London. Written by one of his most intimate acquaintance [Stephen Nye]. . . . 8vo. 2 parts. London, 1698

MS. note: This book was written by Mr Nye as he told me himself, July 10, 1706. [*McAlpin Coll.*]

LIFE (the) of Mother Shipton; a new comedy [in five acts and in prose]. . . . Written by T. T. [Thomas Thompson, dramatist]. 4to. [*Brit. Mus.*] London [1660?]

LIFE (the) of Mr Anthony à Wood, historiographer of the most famous University of Oxford; with an account of his nativity, education, works, etc. [By Richard Rawlinson, D.D.] 8vo. [Martin's *Cat.*] London, 1711

LIFE (the) of Mr [Blaise] Paschal; with his Letters relating to the Jesuits: translated into English by W. A. [William Andrews, of Wedmore]. 8vo. 2 vols. [*Brit. Mus.*] London, 1744

LIFE (the) of Mr Thomas Betterton, the late eminent tragedian; wherein the action and utterance of the stage, bar, and pulpit, are distinctly consider'd. . . . [By Charles Gildon.] To which is added, The amorous widow, or the wanton wife; a comedy, written by Mr Betterton, now first printed from the original copy. 8vo. Pp. xiv. 176. [*Bodl.*] London, 1710

The amorous widow has a separate title and pagination [pp. 87].

LIFE of my heart. [A novel.] By Victoria Cross [Miss Vivian Cory]. 8vo. Pp. 320. [*Amer. Cat.*] London, 1914

LIFE (the) of Napoleon; a Hudibrastic poem, in fifteen cantos. By Dr Syntax [William Combe], embellished with engravings by George Cruickshank. 8vo. London, 1815

LIFE (the) of Napoleon Buonaparte, Emperor of the French: with a preliminary view of the French Revolution. By the author of *Waverley*, etc. [Sir Walter Scott]. 8vo. 9 vols. Edinburgh, 1827

LIFE (the) of [Admiral] Nelson; with original anecdotes, notes, etc. By the Old Sailor, author of *Tough yarns*, etc. [Matthew Henry Barker, R.N.]. 8vo. Pp. 486. [*Brit. Mus.*] London, 1867

LIFE (the) of Oliver Cromwell. By Frank Forester [Henry William Herbert]. 8vo. [Kirk's *Supp.*] Philadelphia, 1886

LIFE (the) of Oliver Cromwell, Lord Protector of the Common-wealth of England, Scotland, and Ireland; impartially collected from the best historians, and several original manuscripts. [By Rev. Isaac Kimber.] Third edition, with additions. 8vo. Pp. xvi. 423. [*Brit. Mus.*] London, 1731

This work has also been ascribed to Edmund Gibson (Bishop of London), and to Sir Thomas Pengelly.

LIFE (the) of our Lord and Saviour Jesus Christ, from the Latin of St Bonaventure; newly translated for the use of members of the Church of England. [Introduction signed: F. O. *i.e.* Frederick Oakeley, M.A.] 8vo. Pp. xlvi. 282. [*Brit. Mus.*] London, 1844

LIFE (the) of our Lord and Saviour Jesus Christ; gathered out of the famous Doctor S. Bonaventure, and other devout Catholike writers: augmented and enriched with many most excellent and goodly documents. By J. H. [John Heigham]. Third edition. 12mo. Pp. 815. [Gillow's *Bibl. Dict.*] N.P. 1634

LIFE (the) of our Lord Jesus Christ [By A. Lloyd.] 8vo. Pp. xi. 247. [*Brit. Mus.*] London, 1916

The author's name, though not given within the book itself, appears on the cover.

LIFE (the) of [Thomas] Paine. By the editor of the *National* [George Jacob Holyoake]. 8vo. Pp. 54. [*Brit. Mus.*] London, 1851

LIFE (the) of Paris. By Whyte Thorne [Richard Whiteing]. 8vo. London, 1900

LIFE of Patrick Hamilton, abbot of Ferme, the first Scottish martyr; with discussions on the ecclesiastical and literary state of Scotland before the Reformation. By the author of the *Life of George Wishart*, etc. [John Parker Lawson, M.A.]. 12mo. Edinburgh, 1828

LIFE of Patrick Hamilton, the proto-martyr of Scotland. By a lady [Mary Webster]. 4to. Pp. 118. St Andrews, 1880

Authorship attested by a friend of the writer.

LIFE of Paul Jones. By Edward Hamilton [Captain Alexander Slidell, afterwards Mackenzie]. 8vo. [Cushing's *Init. and Pseud.* ii. 72.] Aberdeen, 1848

LIFE (the) of Paul Jones; from original documents in the possession of John Henry Sherburne. . . . [Abridged, with a preface by Benjamin D'Israeli, later Earl of Beaconsfield.] 8vo. [*Brit. Mus.*] London, 1825

LIFE (the) of Pauline Markham. Written by herself. [By Richard Grant White ?] 18mo. [Foley's *Amer. Authors.*] New York, 1871

LIFE (the) of Petrarch, collected from "Mémoires pour la vie de F. Pétrarque" by J. F. P. A. de Sade. [By Mrs Susannah Dobson.] 8vo. 2 vols. [*Bibl. Lind.*] London, 1775

The third and later editions give the lady's name.

LIFE of Prince Talleyrand; accompanied with a portrait. [A translation from the anonymous French original of Charles Maxime de Villemarest.] 8vo. 4 vols. [*Brit. Mus.*] London, 1834-6

LIFE of Queen Victoria. By Grace Greenwood [Mrs Sarah Jane Lippincott, *née* Clarke]. 8vo. [Cushing's *Init. and Pseud.* i. 120.] Boston, 1884

LIFE (the) of Raffaelle Sanzio da Urbino. By the author of the *Life of Michael Angelo* [Richard Duppa]; and, The characters of the most celebrated painters of Italy, by Sir Joshua Reynolds. 8vo. [*D. N. B.* vol. 16, p. 243.] London, 1816

LIFE of Rama, the son of Dasaratha, King of Ajodya. . . . Completed by R. N. C. [Robert Needham Cust]. 8vo. [Cushing's *Init. and Pseud.* ii. 25.] London, 1854

LIFE of Reginald Pole. By Martin Haile [Marie Hallé]. 8vo. London, 1910

LIFE of Rev. Samuel Rutherford. [By Thomas Murray, F.A.S.E.] 12mo. Pp. xii. 383. Edinburgh [1827]

Issued in 1828 with a new title-page, a dedication, and the author's name.

LIFE (the) of Richard Cobden; with a faithful likeness, from a photograph, by Eastham, of Manchester. [By James Ewing Ritchie.] Fol. Pp. 17. [*Bodl.*] London [1865]

LIFE (the) of Richard Nash, of Bath, Esq.; extracted principally from his original papers. [By Oliver Goldsmith.] 8vo. Pp. 234. [Green's *Bibl. Somers.* i. 371.] London, 1762

LIFE (the) of Robert, Earl of Leicester, the favourite of Queen Elizabeth: drawn from original writers and records. [By Samuel Jebb, M.D.] 8vo. [*Brit. Mus.*] London, 1727

LIFE of Robert Gray, Bishop of Cape Town. [By Henrietta L. Farrer, later Mrs Sidney Lear.] . . . 8vo. 2 vols. [*Brit. Mus.*] London, 1876

LIFE of Robert Rudolf Suffield. [By Rev. C. Hargrave.] 8vo. London, 1893

LIFE (the) of St Aldegunda, from the French of F. Binetti [translated by Henry Hawkins, S.J.]. 12mo. [Oliver's *Collections*; Sommervogel's *Dictionnaire.*] Paris, 1632

LIFE (the) of St Antony, originally written in Greek by St Athanasius, Bishop of Alexandria; faithfully translated out of the Greek by D. S. [Edward Stephens, late of Cherington, in the county of Gloucester, sometime barrister-at-law of the Middle Temple]. To which the lives of some others of those holy men are intended to be added, out of the best approved authors. 8vo. Pp. 96. [Walton's *Biog. of William Law*, p. 637]. London, 1697

LIFE of St Augustine of Canterbury, Apostle of the English; with some account of the Early British Church. [By Rev. Francis Oakeley, M.A.] 12mo. Pp. 271. London, 1845

LIFE (the) of St Catharine of Sweden. By J. F. [John Falkner, S.J.]. 12mo. [Gillow's *Bibl. Dict.*] St Omer, 1635

LIFE (the) of St Charles Borromeo. [By Mrs Harriet Diana Thompson, *née* Calvert.] 8vo. Pp. 249. London, 1858

LIFE (the) of St Dunstan. By W. R. [William Robinson, barrister, LL.D.]. 4to. [*Brit. Mus.*] London, 1844

LIFE (the) of St Elizabeth. By H. H. [Henry Hawkins, S.J.]. 4to. Pp. 415. [Oliver's *Collections;* Sommervogel's *Dictionnaire.*] Paris, 1632

LIFE (the) of S. Francis de Sales, Bishop and Prince of Geneva. By the author of *A Dominican artist* [Henrietta Louisa Farrer, later Mrs Sidney Lear]. 8vo. Pp. 272. [*Brit. Mus.*] London, 1871

LIFE (the) of S. Francis de Sales; written in French by Mons. Marsollier, and done into English from the second edition [by William Henry Coombes]. 8vo. Pp. 332. London, 1737

The edition of 1812 gives the translator's name.

LIFE (the) of S. Francis of Assisi from the "Legenda Sancti Francisci" of S. Bonaventura. By the author of *The life of S. Teresa* [Elizabeth Lockhart]. 8vo. [*Brit. Mus.*] London, 1868

LIFE (the) of St Ignatius, Founder of the Society of Jesus. Written in French . . . by Dominique Bonhours, and translated into English by a person of quality [John Dryden ?]. 8vo. Pp. 403. London, 1686

LIFE of St Ignatius of Loyola. [Translated from the Latin of Peter Ribadeneira, by Michael Walpole, S.J.] 12mo. [Oliver's *Collections;* Sommervogel's *Dictionnaire.*] St Omer, 1616

LIFE (the) of S. John Francis Regis, of the Society of Jesus. Written in French by F. William Daubenton, of the same Society: translated into English by C * * * M * * * [Cornelius Murphy, S.J.]. 8vo. Pp. viii. 368. [Sommervogel's *Dictionnaire.*] London, 1738

LIFE (the) of St Mary Magdalene of Pazzi, a Carmelite nunn; newly translated out of Italian by the Reverend Father Lezin de Sainte Scholastique, Provincial of the Reformed Carmelites of Touraine. At Paris, for Sebast. Cramoisy in St James's Street, at the Sign of Fame. 1670; and now done out of French [by Thomas Smith, S.T.B.] . . . 4to. Pp. 134. London, 1687

LIFE (the) of Saint Teresa. By the author of *Devotions before and after holy communion* [Maria Trench]. 8vo. Pp. xxiv. 344. [*Brit. Mus.*] London, 1875

LIFE (the) of St Teresa, of the Order of Our Lady of Mount Carmel. [By Elizabeth Lockhart.] . . . 8vo. [*Brit. Mus.*] London, 1865

LIFE (the) of Samuel Morley. By Old Merry [Edwin Hodder]. 8vo. [*Brit. Mus.*] London, 1887

LIFE (the) of Sethos; taken from private memoirs of the ancient Egyptians. Translated from a Greek manuscript into French [by Jean Terrasson], and now faithfully done into English from the Paris edition by Mr Lediard. 8vo. 2 vols. [*Dyce Cat.* ii. 356.] London, 1732

LIFE (a) of Shelley. By Fiona Macleod [William Sharp]. 8vo. [*Lit. Year Book.*] London, 1887

LIFE (the) of Sir Francis Bernard, Baronet, late Governor of Massachusets' Bay. [By his son, Sir Thomas Bernard.] 8vo. Pp. 211. [Martin's *Cat.*] London, 1790

LIFE (the) of Sir Henry Gage. [By Edward Walsingham, secretary to Lord Digby.] 4to. [Watt's *Bibl. Brit.*] Oxford, 1645

LIFE (the) of Sr Henry Walton, sometime Provost of Eaton College. [By Izaak Walton.] 8vo. Pp. 79. [*Brit. Mus.*] London, 1670

LIFE of Sir Julius Cæsar, Knt. Judge of the High Court of Admiralty, Master of the Rolls, Chancellor of the Exchequer, and a Privy Councellor to Kings James, and Charles, the First; with memoirs of his family and descendants. [By Edmund Lodge.] 4to. [*Brit. Mus.*] London, 1810

LIFE (the) of Sir Kenelm Digby. By one of his descendants [Thomas Longueville]. 8vo. [*Brit. Mus.*] London, 1896

LIFE (the) of Sir Thomas Gresham, founder of the Royal Exchange. . . . [By Charles Macfarlane.] 12mo. London, 1845

LIFE (a) of Sir Titus Salt, Bart.; with an account of Saltaire, in Airedale. [By Abraham Holroyd.] 8vo. [Anderson's *Brit. Top.*] Saltaire, 1871

A small edition (12mo), with a different title ("Saltaire and its founder"), gives the author's name.

LIFE of Sir William Wallace. [By J. Carrick ?] Third edition. 12mo. London and Glasgow, 1849

The preface signed: J. C.

LIFE (the) of Sir William Wallace; or, Scotland five hundred years ago. [By —— Hutchison.] 8vo. [Cushing's *Anon.*] Glasgow, 1858

LIFE (the) of Sister Rosalie, Sister of Charity [Jeanne Marie Rendu]. By the author of *Tales of Kirkbeck* [Henrietta Louisa Farrer, afterwards Lear]. 18mo. [*Brit. Mus.*] London, 1858

LIFE (the) of Stonewall Jackson, from official papers. By a Virginian [John Esten Cooke]. 8vo. [Cushing's *Init. and Pseud.* i. 296.] Richmond, Va., 1863

Wrongly assigned to John M. Donald.

LIFE (the) of Tamerlane the Great; with his wars against the great Duke of Moro, the King of China, the great Turk . . . and some others. [By Samuel Clarke, Minister of St Bennet Fink.] 4to. Pp. 61. [*Brit. Mus.*] London, 1653

LIFE (the) of that eminent comedian, Robert Wilks, Esq. [By Edmund Curll.] 12mo. [*Brit. Mus.*] London, 1733

LIFE (the) of that incomparable man, Faustus Socinus, Senensis, described by a Polonian Knight [Samuel Przipcovius]; whereunto is added an excellent discourse which the same author would have premised to the works of Socinus; together with a catalogue of his works [translated from the Latin by John Biddle]. 8vo. [Wallace's *Antitrinitarian Biography*, iii. 186.] London, 1653

LIFE (the) of that most illustrious Prince Charles V. late Duke of Lorrain and Bar, Generalissimo of the imperial armies; rendred into English [by —— Wilson] from the copy lately printed at Vienna. Written by a person of quality, and a great officer in the imperial army [J. de La Brune]. 8vo. London, 1691

The dedication signed: Wilson.

LIFE (the) of that Reverend divine and learned historian, Dr Thomas Fuller. [By John Fell, D.D.] 12mo. Pp. 106. [*Brit. Mus.*] London, 1661

An issue in the following year has the title "The life and death of that Reverend divine and excellent historian. . . ." See above.

LIFE (the) of the Apostle St Paul; written in French by the famous Bishop of Grasse [Antoine Godeau], and now Englished by a person of honour [Edward, Lord Vaux]. 12mo. Pp. 358. [*Camb. Univ. Lib.*] London, 1653

LIFE (the) of the blessed Virgin Mary. By B. D. [B. Dingley, really John Falkner, or Falconer, S.J.]. 12mo. [*D. N. B.* vol. 18, p. 162.] St Omer, 1632

LIFE (the) of the celebrated Jean Bart, a naval commander in the service of Louis XIV. From the French [of Adrien Richer] by the Rev. Edward Mangin, M.A., author of an *Essay on light reading*, etc. 8vo. [Green's *Bibl. Somers.* i. 334.] London, 1828

LIFE of the celebrated Lord Brougham. By Landor Praed [George Jacob Holyoake]. 8vo. [*Brit. Mus.*] London, 1868

LIFE of the celebrated Regent Moray, patron of the Scottish reformation, who was assassinated 23d Jan. 1570; including an account of the contention between the Queen Regent and the Lords of the Congregation. By the author of the *Life of George Wishart*, etc. [John Parker Lawson]. 12mo. Edinburgh, 1828

LIFE (the) of the celebrated Sir Francis Drake, the first English navigator. [By John Campbell, LL.D.] Reprinted from the *Biographia Britannica* [with additional notes by Dr A. Kippis]. 8vo. Pp. 58. [*Brit. Mus.*] London, 1828

LIFE of the Chevalier Bayard. By Frank Cooper [William Gilmore Simms]. 12mo. [Cushing's *Init. and Pseud.* i. 67.] New York, 1848

LIFE (the) of the Countess of Dunois, author of *The ladies travels into Spain*, written by herself, by way of answer to Mon. Saint Evremond; containing withal a modest vindication of the female sex . . . made English from the original [really written by the Countess Henriette J. de Murat]. 8vo. [Arber's *Term Cat.* iii. 94.] London, 1698

LIFE (the) of the Dvtches of Svffolke; as it hath beene divers and sundry times acted, with good applause. [By Thomas Drue.] 4to. [London] 1631

LIFE (the) of the Emperor Julian; translated [by Anne Williams] from the French [of Jean Philippe René de la Bleterie], and improved, with coins, notes, and genealogical tables. 12mo. Pp. ix. 346. [*Manch. Free Lib.*] London, 1746

"LIFE" (the) of the Ettrick Shepherd anatomized; in a series of strictures on the Autobiography of James Hogg, prefixed to the first volume of the *Altrive tales*. By an old dissector [James Browne, LL.D.]. 8vo. Pp. 48. Edinburgh, 1832

LIFE (the) of the famous Cardinal, Duke de Richlieu, principal Minister of State to Lewis XIII., King of France and Navarr. [By Jean Le Clerc.] 8vo. 2 vols. [Arber's *Term. Cat.* ii. 557.] London, 1695

LIFE (the) of the famous Jean Baptiste Colbert, late Minister and Secretary of State to Lewis XIV. Done into English from a French copy [by Gatien Courtilz de Sandras] printed at Cologne. 8vo. [*Brit. Mus.*] London, 1695

LIFE (the) of the holy and venerable Mother Suor Maria Maddelena de Patsi, a Florentine lady and religious of the Order of the Carmelites; written in Italian by the Rev. Priest Signor Vincentio Puccini, who was sometymes her ghostly Father. Now translated into English [by George Gregory Brown, O.S.B.]. 12mo. [Gillow's *Bibl. Dict.* i. 320.] Bruxelle, 1619

LIFE (the) of the holy mother S. Teresa, foundress of the reformation of the discalced Carmelites, according to the primitive rule: divided into two parts. The second containing her foundations. [By Abraham Woodhead.] 4to. Pp. 326. [*D.N.B.* vol. 62, p. 400.] 1671

LIFE (the) of the Lady Warner; in which the motives of her embracing the Roman Catholick faith, quiting her husband and children to become a Poor Clare at Gravling, her rigorous life, and happy death are declar'd. The third edition, to which is added an abridgment of the life of her sister-in-law Mrs Elizabeth Warner, in religion Sister Mary Clare. Written by a Catholick gentleman [Edward Scarisbrick, *alias* Neville, S.J.]. 8vo. Pp. 376. [*D. N. B.* vol. 40, p. 215.] London, 1696

The epistle dedicatory signed: N. N.
A fourth edition appeared in 1858.

LIFE (the) of the Lady Warner, of Parham in Suffolk, in religion call'd Sister Clare of Jesus: in which are specify'd the occasion and motives of her conversion to the Roman Catholick faith . . . together with her excellent devotions, and pious practices, and most happy death. Written by a Catholick gentleman [Edward Scarisbrick, *alias* Neville, S.J.]. 8vo. [Gillow's *Bibl. Dict.* p. 482.] [St Omers] 1691

LIFE (the) of the late Earl of Barrymore; including a history of the Wargrave theatricals, and original anecdotes of eminent persons. By Anthony Pasquin, Esq. [John Williams]. Third edition, corrected and much enlarged. 8vo. Pp. 119. [*Brit. Mus.*] London, 1793

LIFE (the) of the late famous comedian, Jo. Hayns; containing his comical exploits and adventures, both at home and abroad. [By Thomas Brown.] 8vo. Pp. 63. [*Bodl.*] London, 1701

The dedication signed: Tobyas Thomas.

LIFE (the) of the late Hon. Robert Price, Esq., one of the Justices of Her Majesty's Court of Common Pleas. [By Edmund Curll?] 8vo. London, 1734

LIFE (the) of the learned Sir Thomas Smith, Kt., Doctor of the Civil Law, principal Secretary of State to King Edward the Sixth and Queen Elizabeth; wherein are discovered many singular matters relating to the state of learning, the reformation of religion, and the transactions of the kingdom, during his time. . . . [By John Strype.] 8vo. [*W.*] London, 1698

LIFE of the Lord Jesus Christ; with his discourses to his disciples according to Saint Matthew, rendered from the original documents. By "Light" [Holden Edward Sampson]. 8vo. [*Amer. Cat.*] Londville, Ga., 1904

LIFE (the) of the most Hon. and vertuous Lady, the Lady Magdalen Viscountesse Montague; written in Latin . . . by Richard Smith, Doctour of Divinity . . . and now translated into English by C. F. [John Cuthbert Fursdon, O.S.B.]. 4to. Pp. 48. [Gillow's *Bibl. Dict.*] [Douai?] 1627

LIFE (the) of the most learned Father Paul [Pietro Sarpi], of the Order of the Servie; Covncellour of state to the most Serene Republicke of Venice, and authour of the "Covnsell of Trent." [By Fulgentio Micanzio.] Translated out of Italian by a person of quality [John Saint-Amard]. 8vo. Pp. vii. 204. [*Brit. Mus.*] London, 1651

LIFE (the) of the Renfrewshire bard, Robert Tannahill, author of Jessie, the flow'r o' Dumblane—The braes o' Gleniffer, etc. [By William M'Laren, weaver, Paisley.] Attached to the work is an address delivered at the celebration of the birth of Burns, in the year 1805. [By the same author.] 8vo. Pp. 40. [*D. Laing.*] Paisley, 1815

The Address has a separate pagination. At the end of the Life, there is a short poem, entitled, Lines to the memory of Robert Tannahill. [By Robert Allan.] It is dated, Kilbarchan, June 1810.

LIFE (the) of the Rev. and learned Mr John Sage, wherein also some account is given of his writings, both printed and in manuscript; and some things are added towards the clearing the ancient government of the Church of Scotland from the mistakes of a late author. [By John Gillan.] 8vo. Pp. 79. [*Brit. Mus.*] London, 1714

The late author referred to is Sir James Dalrymple, in his Collections concerning the Scottish history preceding the death of King David I. in the year 1153.

LIFE (the) of the Rev. Dr John Barwick, D.D. sometime Fellow of St John's College in Cambridge; and immediately after the Restoration successively Dean of Durham and St Paul's. Written in Latin by his brother Dr Peter Barwick, formerly Fellow of the same College, and afterwards physician in ordinary to King Charles II. Translated into English by the editor of the Latin Life [Hilkiah Bedford]. . . . 8vo. [*Camb. Univ. Lib.*] London, 1724

LIFE (the) of the Rev. Legh Richmond. . . . By S. B. W. [Stephen B. Wickins]. 8vo. [Cushing's *Init. and Pseud.* i. 300.] New York, 1842

LIFE (the) of the Rev. Mr Geo. Trosse, late minister of the Gospel in the city of Exon, who died Jan. 11, 1712-3 in the 82d year of his age, &c. To which is added the sermon preached at his funeral. By J. H. [Joseph Hallet]. 8vo. [Davidson's *Bibl. Devon.* p. 201.] Exon, 1714

LIFE (the) of the Rev. Robert Newton, D.D. By a Wesleyan Preacher [Rev. Thomas Jackson]. 8vo. Pp. 427. [Osborn's *Method. Lit.* p. 123.] London, 1855

A smaller edition ("The life, labours, and travels of the Rev. Robert Newton, D.D.") was published in the same year.

LIFE of the Rev. Sir James Stonhouse, Bart., M.D.; with extracts from his correspondence. [By William Alexander Greenhill.] 12mo. Pp. viii. 263. [*Brit. Mus.*] Oxford, 1844

LIFE (the) of the Right Rev. Dr White Kennett, late Lord Bishop of Peterborough; with several original letters of the late archbishop of Canterbury, Dr Tennison, the late Earl of Sunderland, Bishop Kennett, &c.; and some curious original papers and records, never before publish'd. [By Rev. William Newton.] 8vo. Pp. xi. 288. [Nichol's *Lit. Anec.* i. 257.] London, 1730

LIFE (the) of the Right Rev. Father in God, Edw. Rainbow, D.D. late Lord Bishop of Carlisle. [By Jonathan Banks]; to which is added, a sermon preached at his funeral by Thomas Tully, his Lordships chaplain. . . . 8vo. Pp. 112. [*Bodl.*] London, 1688

LIFE (the) off the 70. Archbishopp off Canterbury [Dr Matthew Parker] presentlye sittinge englished and to be added to the 69. lately sett forth in Latin. [By John Josselin.] 8vo. [Lowndes' *Bibl. Man.*] Imprinted 1574

"The true author of this life (which is a translation from the Latin that is in very few copies of the London edition, and wholly omitted in the Hanover edition) was John Josselin. It is a very great rarity. The marginal notes were done by some Puritan."—MS. note by Hearne.

LIFE (the) of the valiant and learned Sir Walter Raleigh, Knight; with his tryal at Winchester. [By John Shirley, A.M.] 8vo. Pp. 243. [*Bodl.*] London, 1677

The author's name is in the handwriting of Wood.

LIFE (the) of Theodore Agrippa D'Aubigné; containing a succinct account of the most remarkable occurrences during the civil wars of France in the reigns of Charles IX. Henry III. Henry IV. and in the minority of Lewis XIII. [By Mrs Sarah Scott.] 8vo. Pp. xv. 451. [Brydges' *Cens. Lit.* iv. 292.] London, 1772

LIFE (the) of Thomas Day, Esq., author of Sandford and Merton. [By —— Wilkie, of Ladythorn.] 12mo. Pp. 8. [Martin's *Cat.*] Berwick, 1836

LIFE (the) of Thomas Dermody [Irish poet. By J. G. Raymond]. 8vo. 2 vols. [O'Donoghue's *Poets of Ireland*, p. 55.] London, 1806

LIFE (the) of Thomas Egerton, Lord Chancellor of England. [By Francis Henry Egerton, Earl of Bridgewater.] Fol. Pp. 59. [Martin's *Cat.*] [*c.* 1793]

LIFE of Thomas Harrison Burder, M.D.; with extracts from his correspondence. [Preface signed: *a*, *i.e.* William Alexander Greenhill.] 12mo. Pp. vi. 206. [*Brit. Mus.*] London, 1845

LIFE (the) of Thomas Hobbes, part written by himself; since his death, finished by Dr R. B. [Richard Blackbourne, M.D.]. 8vo. [Arber's *Term Cat.* i. 538.] London, 1681

LIFE (the) of Thomas Ken, Bishop of Bath and Wells. By a layman [John Lavicount Anderdon]. 8vo. London, 1851

Ascribed also to F. A. Clarke.

LIFE (the) of Thomas Pain [*sic*], the author of the Rights of man; with a defence of his writings. By Francis Oldys, A.M. of the University of Philadelphia [George Chalmers]. 8vo. Pp. 125. [*D. N. B.* vol. 43, p. 79; also vol. 9, p. 445.] London, 1791

LIFE (the) of Thomas Paine. [Abridged by H. Mackenzie from the Life written by G. Chalmers under the pseudonym of Francis Oldys.] 8vo. [*Brit. Mus.*] [London, 1793]

LIFE (the) of Thomas Paine. By the editor of *The National* [William James Linton]. 8vo. [*Brit. Mus.*] London, 1840

LIFE (the) of Thomas Wanless, peasant. [By Alex. Johnstone Wilson.] 8vo. [Robertson's *Aberd. Bibl.*] Manchester [1885]

LIFE of Ulrich Zuinglius . . . with a biographical sketch of J. Ecolampadius. By the author of *The history of the Reformation*, etc. [William Sime]. 12mo. [*Brit. Mus.*] Edinburgh, 1827

LIFE (the) of Van Amburgh, the brute-tamer; with anecdotes. . . . By Ephraim Watts, brute-tamer [Richard Henry Horne]. 12mo. [*D. N. B.* vol. 27, p. 358.] London [1838]

LIFE (the) of Virgil. [Preface signed: G. D. *i.e.* George Darley.] 12mo. [*Brit. Mus.*] London, 1825

LIFE of Voltaire. By S. G. Tallentyre [E. Beatrice Hall]. 8vo. 2 vols. Pp. 750. [*Amer. Cat.*] London, 1903

LIFE (the) of William Bedell, D.D. Bishop of Kilmore, in Ireland. [By Gilbert Burnet, D.D.] 8vo. Pp. 259. London, 1685

LIFE (the) of William Cowper; with selections from his correspondence. [By Robert Benton Seeley.] 12mo. [*D. N. B.* vol. 51, p. 193.] London, 1855

LIFE of William M'Kinley. By Marshall Everett [Henry Neil]. 8vo. [*Amer. Cat.*] Chicago, 1901

LIFE (the) of William Makepeace Thackeray. By Lewis Melville [Lewis Samuel Benjamin]. 8vo. 2 vols. [*Lit. Year Book.*] London, 1899

LIFE on the Great Hydropathium. By Don T. B. Leevitt, of Chickomango, Ohio, U.S. [James Mudie Spence, F.R.G.S.]. [Boase's *Mod. Eng. Biog.* vi. col. 599.] New York, 1877

LIFE on the Lakes; being tales and sketches collected during a trip to the Pictured Rocks of Lake Superior. [By Thomas Bangs Thorpe.] 12mo. 2 vols. [Foley's *Amer. Authors.*] New York, 1839

LIFE on the Mississippi. By Mark Twain [Samuel Langhorne Clemens]. 8vo. London, 1883

LIFE or death in India under the Zemindary system. [By Florence Nightingale.] Fol. Pp. 2. [*Lond. Lib. Cat.*] London [1874]

LIFE; or, the adventures of William Ramble, Esq.; with three frontispieces, designed by Ibbetson, highly engraved, and two new and beautiful songs, with the music by Pleyel and Sterkel. By the author of *Modern times; or, the adventures of Gabriel Outcast* [John Trusler, LL.D.]. 12mo. 3 vols. [*Brit. Mus.*] London, 1793

LIFE out of death; a romance. [By Nathaniel Cartwright, of Manchester.] 8vo. 3 vols. [*Lib. Journ.* i. 376.] London, 1876

LIFE (the) sentence; an entirely new novel. By Victoria Cross [Miss Vivian Cory]. 8vo. Pp. 220. [*Amer. Cat.*] London, 1912

LIFE stories of famous children; adapted from the French. By the author of *Spenser for children* [M. H. Towry]. 8vo. Pp. 116. [*Brit. Mus.*] London, 1886

LIFE (the) story of Dinah Kellow. By Christopher Hare [Mrs Marion Andrews]. 8vo. Pp. 320. [*Lond. Lib. Cat.*] London, 1901

LIFE the accuser. By the author of *A superfluous woman* [Emma Brooke]. 8vo. Pp. 296. [*Brit. Mus.*] London, 1897

LIFE, the day for work; exemplified in a brief memoir. . . . By J. B. [Rev. John Baylie]. 12mo. [*Brit. Mus.*] London, 1854

LIFE the modeller. [A novel.] By C. Gasquoine Hartley [Mrs Walter Gallichan]. 8vo. Pp. 328. [*Lond. Lib. Cat.*] London, 1899

LIFE (the), times, and travels of Abraham. By a Master of Arts of Trinity College, Cambridge [Rev. Robert Allen]. 8vo. [Kirk's *Supp.*] Cambridge, 1875

LIFE (the), travels, and adventures of Christopher Wagstaffe, gentleman, grandfather to Tristram Shandy. [By John Dunton]. . . . 8vo. 2 vols. [*Brit. Mus.*] London, 1762

LIFE, travels and books of A. von Humboldt; with an introduction by Bayard Taylor. [By Richard Henry Stoddard.] 12mo. [Foley's *Amer. Authors.*] New York, 1859

LIFE underground, in the Church tower, the woods, and the old keep. By the author of *Life in the walls*, etc. [Miss A. C. Chambers]. 12mo. [*Brit. Mus.*] London, 1873

LIFE, ventures, and funny hoaxes of P. T. Barnum, the Yankee showman, in all his ups and downs in fortune and failure. [By Henry Llewellyn Williams.] 8vo. Pp. 30. [*Brit. Mus.*] London, 1889

LIFE (the), voyages, and adventures of George Alexander Lovatt [George A. Elliston]. 8vo. Pp. 34. York [1820]

LIFE (the), writings, opinions and times of . . . Lord Byron. . . . By an English gentleman, in the Greek military service, and comrade of his Lordship. . . . [By Matthew Iley, the publisher?]. 8vo. 3 vols. [Chew's *Byron in England.*] London, 1825

Attributed also to J. M. Millingen.

LIFE work; or, the link and the rivet. By L. N. R., author of *The Book and its story*, and *The missing link* [Mrs Lydia N. Ranyard]. 8vo. Pp. 343. London, 1861

LIFE'S (a) arrears. [A novel.] By Florence Warden [Florence Alice Price, later Mrs George E. James]. 8vo. Pp. 334. London, 1908

LIFE'S (a) assize; a novel. By F. G. Trafford [Mrs Charlotte E. L. Riddell]. 8vo. 3 vols. [*D. N. B.* Second Supp. vol. 3, p. 193.] London, 1871

LIFE'S battle lost and won; or, Robert Joy's victory. By the author of *Christian manliness*, etc. [Rev. S. S. Pugh]. 8vo. Pp. 190. London [1894]

LIFE'S blue and gray. [Poems.] By Hazel Hinckle [Clara V. Fleharty]. 8vo. [*Amer. Cat.*] Chicago, 1900

LIFE'S compass. [A novel.] By Priscilla Craven [Mrs William Teignmouth Shore]. 8vo. Pp. 404. [*Amer. Cat.*] London, 1908

LIFE'S (a) idylls; and other poems. By Hugh Conway [Frederick John Fargus]. 8vo. Pp. ix. 144. [*Lit. Year Book.*] Bristol, 1887

LIFE'S (a) love. By the author of *Heiress of the Blackburnfoot* [Miss —— Urquhart]. 8vo. 2 vols. [*Brit. Mus.*] London, 1866

LIFE'S painter of variegated characters in public and private life; with political strokes on the ticklish times. By G. P. [George Parker], Librarian of the College of wit and humour. 8vo. [O'Donoghue's *Poets of Ireland.*] Dublin, 1786

Sketches, in prose and verse, of Dublin society.

LIFE'S problems. [By Sir Rutherford Alcock.] Second edition, revised and enlarged. 8vo. Pp. xiv. 266. [*D. N. B.* First Supp. vol. 1, p. 30.] London, 1861

LIFE'S progress through the passions; or, the adventures of Natura. By the author of *The fortunate Foundlings* [Eliza Heywood]. 12mo. London, 1748

LIFE'S questionings. [A novel.] By Benjamin Swift [William Romaine Paterson]. 8vo. [*Brit. Mus.*] London, 1906

LIFE'S remorse; a novel. By the author of *Molly Bawn*, etc. [Mrs Margaret Argles, later Mrs Hungerford]. 8vo. 3 vols. [*Brit. Mus.*] London, 1890

LIFE'S shop-window. [A novel.] By Victoria Cross [Miss Vivian Cory]. 8vo. [*Amer. Cat.*] London, 1908

LIFE'S sunny side. By W. L. M. Jay [Julia Matilda Louisa Woodruff]. 8vo. [*Amer. Cat.*] New York, 1886

LIFE'S Testament; Songs from the Hill of the seven echoes. By W. B. [William Blocksidge]. 8vo. Pp. 40. [*Brit. Mus.*] N.P. private print [1914]

LIFE'S (a) trouble; a story of the nineteenth century. By Melville Gray [Mary Ethel Granger]. 8vo. Pp. 143. [*Brit. Mus.*] London, 1886

LIFE'S vicissitudes; or, the Norrice family: a tale. [By C. L. Smith.] 8vo. Pp. 153. London, 1863

LIFE'S working creed; twenty sermons. By John Ackworth [Frederick R. Smith, M.A.]. 8vo. [*Methodist Who's Who.*] London, 1909

LIFE-SAVERS (the); a story of the United States life-saving service. By James Otis [James Otis Kaler]. 8vo. Pp. iii. 327. [Kirk's *Supp.*] London [1902]

LIFE-SCENES in the Reign of Terror. [By Rev. Washington Frothingham.] 8vo. [Kirk's *Supp.*] New York, 1865

LIGAN; a collection of tales and essays. By W. D. [William Dunne]. 8vo. Philadelphia, 1857

LIGHT after darkness. [Verse.] By M. E. G. [Mary Ethel Granger]. 8vo. London, 1885

LIGHT (the) and dark of the Rebellion [in the United States. By Charles Edwards Lester]. 8vo. [Kirk's *Supp.*] Philadelphia, 1855

LIGHT and darkness; or, fate's shadow. By Lizzie Petit [Mrs P. C. Cutler]. 8vo. [Cushing's *Init. and Pseud.* ii. 119.] New York, 1883

LIGHT and rest; or, the confessions of a soul seeking and finding. . . . [By Samuel Borton Brown.] 8vo. Pp. 184. London [1881]

LIGHT and shade. [A tale.] By Mrs Madeline Leslie [Mrs Harriet Newell Baker, *née* Woods]. 8vo. [Kirk's *Supp.*] Boston, 1864

LIGHT and shade; pictures of London life: a sequel to *The bitter cry of outcast London.* [By William C. Preston.] 8vo. Pp. 164. [*Gladstone Lib. Cat.*] London, 1885

Attributed also to Rev. Andrew Mearns.

LIGHT at eventide. [By Miss L. M. F. Phillips.] 8vo. Oxford [1870?]

LIGHT (the) dragoon. By the author of *The subaltern*, etc. [George Robert Gleig, D.D.]. 8vo. 2 vols. London, 1844

"Advertisement" signed: G. R. G.

LIGHT (a) for the line; or, the story of Thomas Ward, a railway workman. By the author of *English hearts and English hands*, etc. [Catherine Marsh]. 12mo. London, 1858

LIGHT from the sun of righteousness, discovering and dispelling darkness; or, the doctrines, and some of the corrupt principles of the people called Quakers, briefly and plainly laid open and refuted. . . . By H. G. [Henry Grigg]. 8vo. Pp. 95. [Smith's *Anti-Quak.* p. 205.] 1672

LIGHT horse. By Jacob Omnium [Matthew Jacob Hfggins]. 8vo. Pp. 47. [*Brit. Mus.*] London, 1855

LIGHT in darkness; a short account of a blind deaf-mute [viz. Eliza Cooter. By Sarah Robinson]. 8vo. [*Brit. Mus.*] London, 1859

LIGHT in darkness; or, Christ discovered in his true character. By a Unitarian [Rev. William Leonard Gage, M.A.]. 12mo. [Cushing's *Init. and Pseud.* ii. 147.] Boston, 1864

LIGHT in the cloud; or, Christ alone exalted. By the author of *The faithful witness*, etc. [John Ross M'Duff, D.D.]. 8vo. Pp. 151. London, 1859

LIGHT in the dwelling; or, a harmony of the four Gospels; with very short and simple remarks, adapted to reading at family prayers, and arranged in 365 sections, for every day of the year. By the author of *The peep of day*, etc. [Mrs Thomas Mortimer]. Revised and corrected by a clergyman of the Church of England [Rev. Thomas Mortimer, B.D.]. 8vo. Pp. xxiv. 814. London, 1846

LIGHT (the) in the robber's cave. By A. L. O. E., authoress of *The young pilgrim*, etc. [Charlotte M. Tucker]. 8vo. Pp. 223. London, 1862

LIGHT (the) in the upper storey. By Florence Warden [Florence Alice Price, later Mrs George E. James]. 8vo. Pp. 304. [*Brit. Mus.*] London, 1917

LIGHT (the) Keepers. [A tale.] By James Otis [James Otis Kaler]. 8vo. [Kirk's *Supp.*] Boston, 1906

LIGHT (the) of Christ exalted; or, the more excellent way briefly set forth; being an apology for leaving the Methodists, and joining the Society of Friends; addressed to the sincere and devout among the Methodists. By J. S. [Joseph Sutton]. 12mo. [Smith's *Cat. of Friends' Books*, i. 102; ii. 687.] London, 1835

LIGHT (the) of Egypt. By Zanoni [Thomas H. Burgoyne]. 8vo. 2 vols. [*Amer. Cat.*] Denver, Col., 1900

LIGHT (the) of life; dedicated to the young. By the author of *The female visitor to the poor*, etc. [Maria Louisa Charlesworth]. 8vo. [*Brit. Mus.*] London, 1850

LIGHT (the) of nature pursued. By Edward Search, Esq. [Abraham Tucker]. 8vo. [*Brit. Mus.*] London, 1768-77

LIGHT (the) of other days. [A novel]. By Mrs Forrester [Mrs —— Bridges]. 8vo. 2 vols. [*Amer. Cat.*] London, 1894

LIGHT (the) of other days seen through the wrong end of an opera-glass. By Willert Beale [Walter Maynard]. 8vo. 2 vols. [*Lond. Lib. Cat.*] London, 1890

LIGHT (the) of Provence; a dramatic poem. By J. S. of Dale [Frederic J. Stimson]. 8vo. [*Lond. Lib. Cat.*] New York, 1917

LIGHT (the) of the conscience. By the author of *The life of S. Francis de Sales*, etc. [Henrietta Louisa Farrer, later Mrs Sidney Lear]. With an introduction by the Rev. T. T. Carter, M.A. 8vo. Pp. xii. 239. London, 1876

LIGHT (the) of the morning; or, clear shining after rain. By Amy Lothrop [Anna B. Warner]. 8vo. [Cushing's *Init. and Pseud.* ii. 174.] New York, 1887

LIGHT (the) of the West; or, a historical sketch of the Protestant Church in Ireland, from the second to the nineteenth century. By a Graduate of Cambridge [Rev. Rupert James Rowton, M.A.]. 8vo. London, 1869

LIGHT (the) of the world; a most true relation of a pilgrimess, M. A. B. [Madame Antoinette Bourignon], travelling towards eternity. . . . Written originally in French, and now translated into English. . . . 8vo. [*Brit. Mus.*] London, 1696

LIGHT (the) of truth and pleasure of light; in four books. [By Rev. Michael Smith.] 12mo. Pp. 292. [Eddy's *Universalism in America*, ii. 513.] Milledgeville, Georgia, 1827

LIGHT on the after life. By A. B. O. W. [A. B. O. Wilberforce]. 8vo. Pp. 46. London, 1917

LIGHT (a) on the broom; verses. By William Dara [William A. Byrne]. 8vo. [O'Donoghue's *Poets of Ireland.*] Dublin, 1901

LIGHT on the foothills. By Heather B. [Heather Bellairs]. 8vo. Pp. 124. [*Brit. Mus.*] London [1927]

LIGHT on the path; a treatise written for the personal use of those who are ignorant of the Eastern wisdom, and who desire to enter within its influence: written down by M. C. [Mabel Collins], Fellow of the Theosophical Society. New edition, with notes by the author. 8vo. [*Brit. Mus.*] London, 1888

LIGHT on the pathway. By L. B. E. [Mrs L. B. Earle]. 8vo. London, 1890

LIGHT reading at leisure hours; or, an attempt to unite the proper objects of gaiety and taste, in exploring the various sources of rational pleasure, the fine arts, poetry, sculpture, painting, music, dancing, fashionable pastimes, lives, memoirs, characters, anecdotes, etc. [By Edward Mangin.] 12mo. Pp. 464. [Green's *Bibl. Somers.* i. 333.] London, 1805

Sometimes wrongly attributed to Charles M'Cormick.

LIGHT (a) shining out of darknes; or, occasional queries submitted to the judgment of such as would enquire into the true state of things in our times. The whole work is revised by the authour, the proofs Englished, and augmented with sundry material discourses concerning the ministry, tythes, &c.; with a brief apologie for the Quakers, that they are not inconsistent with a magistracy. [By Henry Stubbe, Student of Christ Church.] 4to. Pp. 192. [*Bodl.*] London, 1659

Attributed also to Sir Harry Vane.

LIGHTED (the) candles. [A novel]. By Priscilla Craven [Mrs William Teignmouth Shore]. 8vo. Pp. 408. [*Amer. Cat.*] London, 1909

LIGHTED (the) valley; or, the closing scenes of the life of a beloved sister [viz. Abby Bolton]. By one of her sisters [Miss R. Bolton]. 8vo. [Cushing's *Init. and Pseud.* i. 215.] New York, 1850

LIGHTER days with Troddles. By R. Andom [Alfred Wilson Barrett]. 8vo. [*Lit. Year Book.*] London, 1907

LIGHTER (the) side of Irish life. By George A. Birmingham [James Owen Hannay, D.D.]. 8vo. [*Lond. Lib. Cat.*] London, 1911

LIGHTER (the) side of school life. By Ian Hay [John Hay Beith, M.A.]. 8vo. Pp. 227. [*Lit. Year Book.*] Edinburgh, 1914

LIGHTHOUSE (the); a sketch, addressed to my landlady in Limbus Patrum. [By Thomas S. Muir.] 8vo. Pp. 68. [Edinburgh, private print, 1864]

No title-page.

Signed: Unda. Authorship acknowledged by the writer.

LIGHTHOUSE Lige; or, Orceola. [A tale.] By "Bruin" [J. F. C. Adams]. 8vo. [Cushing's *Init. and Pseud.* ii. 20.] New York, 1874

LIGHTHOUSE management; the report of the Royal Commissioners on lights, buoys, and beacons, 1861, examined and refuted. By an Englishman [Charles Blake]. 8vo. [*Brit. Mus.*] London, 1861

LIGHTNING Jo. By "Bruin" [J. F. C. Adams]. 8vo. [Cushing's *Init. and Pseud.* ii. 20.] New York, 1875

LIGHTS along the line; a geographical and topographical description of the salubrious city of Southport. . . . By Yrneh Koorbezarg [Henry Grazebrook]. 8vo. Liverpool, 1855

LIGHTS and shadows in a canine life; with sketches of travel. By Ugly's mistress [Mrs Hilliard]. 8vo. [*Brit. Mus.*] London, 1871

LIGHTS and shadows in an hospital. By Alice Terton [Alice Terrot, afterwards Mrs Boulton]. 8vo. London, 1902

LIGHTS and shadows of German life. [Tales, freely translated from Zschokke, Pichler, and others; by M. M. M., *i.e.* M. M. Montgomery]. 12mo. 2 vols. [*Brit. Mus.*] London, 1833

LIGHTS (the) and shadows of literary life. By the author of *Consolatio afflictorum*, etc. [Henry Galloway Gill]. 8vo. [*Brit. Mus.*] London, 1878

LIGHTS and shadows of London life. By the author of *Lost Sir Massingberd*, etc. [James Payn]. 8vo. 2 vols. [*Brit. Mus.*] London, 1867

LIGHTS and shadows of London life. By the author of *Random recollections of the Lords and Commons*, etc. [James Grant, journalist]. 12mo. 2 vols. [*Brit. Mus.*] London, 1842

LIGHTS and shadows of Scottish character and scenery. By Cincinnatus Caledonius [John Gordon Barbour, of Bogrie]. 8vo. Pp. xii. 347. [*Bibliographer*, v. 24.] Edinburgh, 1824

LIGHTS and shadows of Scottish character and scenery. Second series. By Cincinnatus Caledonius [John Gordon Barbour], author of *Queries connected with Christianity*. 8vo. Pp. xii. 329. Dumfries, 1825

LIGHTS and shadows of Scottish life; a selection from the papers of the late Arthur Austin. [By Professor John Wilson.] 8vo. Pp. viii. 430. Edinburgh, 1822

LIGHTS and shadows on the sunny side of Skiddaw [in verse]. [By Frances Rolleston.] 12mo. [*Brit. Mus.*] Keswick [1859]

LIGHTS and shadows; or, double acrostics. By the Old Vicar [John Samuel Bewley Monsell, LL.D.]. Third edition. 8vo. Pp. xvi. 127. [Dobell's *Private Prints*, p. 124.] London, 1870

LIGHTS in art; a review of ancient and modern pictures: with critical remarks on the present state, treatment, and preservation of oil paintings. By an artist [George William Novice]. 8vo. Edinburgh, 1865

The second edition (1874) has the author's name.

LIGHTS on the way; some tales within a tale. By the late J. H. Alexander, B.A. [Alexander Hay Japp]; with an explanatory note by H. A. Page [another pseudonym of the author]. 8vo. [*Brit. Mus.; D. N. B.*, Second Supp. vol. 2, p. 363.] London, 1878

LIGHTS, shadows, and reflections of Whigs and Tories. By a country gentleman [William Fletcher, of Dublin]. 8vo. Pp. vi. 237. [*Camb. Univ. Lib.*] London, 1841

LIKE and unlike; a novel. By the author of *Lady Audley's secret* [Mary E. Braddon, later Mrs John Maxwell]. 8vo. [*Brit. Mus.*] London [1887]

LIKE another Helen; the history of the cruel misfortunes and undeserved distresses of a young lady . . . resident at Bengall during the years 1755-57. . . . By Sidney C. Grier [Hilda C. Gregg]. 8vo. Pp. 476. Edinburgh, 1902

LIKE Dian's kiss; a novel. By "Rita" [Mrs W. Desmond Humphreys, *née* Eliza M. J. Gollan]. 8vo. [*Lit. Year Book.*] London, 1885

LIKE father, like son; a novel. By the author of *Lost Sir Massingberd*, etc. [James Payn]. 8vo. 3 vols. [*Brit. Mus.*] London, 1871

First published in *Chambers's Journal* under the title "Bred in the bone."

LIKE his own daughter; a story. By the author of *The Chorister Brothers* [Mrs Disney Leith]. 8vo. Pp. viii. 430. London, 1883

LIKE Lucifer; a novel. By Denzil Vane [F. Du Tertre]. 8vo. 2 vols. [*Brit. Mus.*] London, 1886

LIKE no other love. By Bertha M. Clay [Mrs Charlotte M. Braeme, *née* Law]. 8vo. London, 1886

LIKE stars that fall; a music-hall novel. By Geoffrey Mortimer [Walter M. Gallichan]. 8vo. Pp. 312. [*Brit. Mus.*] London, 1896

LIKE unto Christ. De imitatione Christi, by Thomas à Kempis [translated by James Hain Friswell]. 8vo. [*D. N. B.* vol. 20, p. 278.] London, 1868

LIL Lorimer; a novel. By Theo Gift [Mrs Dora Henrietta Boulger]. 8vo. [*Lit. Year Book.*] London, 1887

LIL of the slums. [A novel.] By Dick Donovan [Joyce Emerson Preston Muddock]. 8vo. [*Brit. Mus.*] London, 1909

LILIAN. [A tale. By Frances Charlotte Armstrong.] 8vo. Pp. 312. [Kirk's *Supp.*] Boston, 1863

LILIAN; a tale of three hundred years ago. [By George E. Sargent.] 12mo. London [1864]

LILIAN and Lili. [A novel.] By the author of *The atelier du Lys* [Margaret Roberts]. 8vo. Pp. 329. [*Brit. Mus.*] London, 1891

LILIAN Gordon. By Nellie Graham [Mrs Annie Dunning, *née* Ketchum]. 8vo. [Haynes' *Pseud.*] Philadelphia, 1867

LILIAN Gray; a poem. By Cecil Home [Mrs Julia Augusta Webster, *née* Davies]. 8vo. [*Brit. Mus.*] London, 1864

LILIAN'S golden hours. By Silverpen [Eliza Metergard]. 8vo. [Haynes' *Pseud.*] London [1857]

LILIAN'S penance. By the author of *Recommended to mercy*, etc. [Mrs Margaret C. Houstoun]. 8vo. 3 vols. [*Brit. Mus.*] London, 1873

LILIAS Carment; for better, for worse. [A novel.] By Gordon Roy [Helen Wallace]. 8vo. [*Brit. Mus.*] London, 1892

LILIES of Florence; and other stories and legends. From the French of George Sand [Madame A. L. A. D. Dudevant]. 8vo. [*Amer. Cat.*] New York, 1887

LILITH and Adam; a poem in four parts. By A. F. Scot [Alex. Hay Japp, LL.D.]. 8vo. Pp. 91. [*Brit. Mus.*] London, 1899

LILLIESLEAF; being a concluding series of passages in the life of Mrs Margaret Maitland, of Sunnyside: written by herself. [By Mrs Margaret O. Oliphant.] 12mo. 3 vols. [Courtney's *Secrets*, p. 67.] London, 1855

LILLIPUT; a dramatic entertainment, as it is performed at the Theatre-Royal in Drury-Lane. [By David Garrick.] 8vo. [Baker's *Biog. Dram.*] London, 1756

Prefatory letter signed: W. C.

LILLIPUT lectures. By the author of *Lilliput levee* [William Brighty Rands]. 8vo. Pp. 155. London, 1871

LILLIPUT legends. By the author of *Lilliput levee* [William Brighty Rands]. 8vo. Pp. vii. i. 215. London, 1872

LILLIPUT levee. [By William Brighty Rands.] With illustrations by J. E. Millais and G. J. Pinwell. 8vo. Pp. 111. London, 1864

LILLIPUT revels. By the author of *Lilliput levee*, etc. [William Brighty Rands]. 8vo. Pp. 147. [*Brit. Mus.*] New York, 1871

LILTS frae the Border. By A. E. M. [A. Eglantine Maxwell]. 8vo. Private print, N.D.

Name on presentation copy by the author.

LILTS o' the lea-rig. [Scots poems.] By a herd loon [Rev. R. H. Calder, M.A., Glenlivet]. 8vo. Pp. 67. Brechin, 1900

LILY; a novel. By the author of *Busy moments of an idle woman* [Mrs Henry King]. 12mo. London, 1855

LILY (the) and the bee; an apologue of the Crystal Palace of 1851. [By Samuel Warren, D.C.L.] 8vo. [*Brit. Mus.*] London, 1854

LILY and the totem; or, Huguenots in Florida, 1562-1570. [By William Gilmore Simms.] Second edition. 8vo. Pp. 470. [Allibone's *Dict.*] New York, 1850

LILY Douglas; a simple story, humbly intended as a pattern for Sabbath scholars. By the author of *Pierre and his family*, etc. [Miss Grierson]. 8vo. [*Brit. Mus.*] Edinburgh, 1821

LILY Gordon, the young housekeeper. By "Cousin Kate" [Catherine Douglas Bell]. 12mo. [Haynes' *Pseud.*] Edinburgh, 1853

LILY Hudson; or, early struggles 'midst continual hope. By Alice Grey [Julia A. Mathews]. 8vo. [Kirk's *Supp.*] New York, 1855

LILY (the) of St Paul's; a romance of Old London. By the author of *Trevethlan* [William Davy Watson, barrister]. 8vo. 3 vols. [*Brit. Mus.*] London, 1852

LILY (the) of the Arno; or, Florence past and present. By Cousin Virginia [Virginia Wales Johnson]. 8vo. [Cushing's *Init. and Pseud.* i. 296.] London [1891]

LILY (the) of the Resurrection. [Easter poems.] By Miriam Lester [Mrs Marian Longfellow Morris]. 12mo. New York, 1885

LIMB (the); an episode of adventure. By XL. [Julian Osgood Field] author of *Aut Diabolus aut nihil.* 8vo. Pp. 466. [*Brit. Mus.*] London, 1896

LIMBO; to which is added Ariadne in Mantua. By Vernon Lee [Violet Paget]. 8vo. [*Brit. Mus.*] London, 1908

LIMBO-MASTIX; that is, a canvise of Limbus Patrum, shewing . . . that Christ descended not in soule to hell to deliver the Fathers from thence. [By Andrew Willet.] 4to. [*D. N. B.* vol. 61, p. 291.] London, 1604

LIME-KILN (the) Club. By "M. Quad" [Charles B. Lewis]. 12mo. [Cushing's *Init. and Pseud.* i. 243.] Chicago, 1887

LIMIT (the); or, nothing personal: a satirical melodrametta by A. D. K. [Knox] and M. A. Y. [Young] performed in King's College. 8vo. [Bartholomew's *Camb. Books.*] Cambridge, 1907

LIMITED; a comedy, in three acts. By Robert Blake [Robert Hely Thompson]. 12mo. Pp. 46. [*Brit. Mus.*] Omagh, Tyrone [1894?]

LIN; or, jewels of the third plantation. By Obadiah Oldpath [James Robinson Newhall]. 8vo. [Cushing's *Init. and Pseud.* i. 214.] Lynn, Mass., 1862

LINA and Gertrude. See "Home plays for ladies."

LINCOLNSHIRE Churches; an account of the Churches in the Division of Holland, in the County of Lincoln, with sixty-nine illustrations. [By Stephen Lewin, architect.] 8vo. [*Brit. Mus.*] Boston, 1843

LINCOLNSHIRE in 1836; displayed in a series of nearly one hundred engravings, with descriptive text. . . . [By Mary Saunders.] 8vo. [*Brit. Mus.*] Lincoln, 1836

LINCOLNSHIRE (the) tragedy; passages in the life of the faire gospeller, Mistress Anne Askew, recounted by ye unworthie pen of Nicholas Moldwarp, B.A., and now first set forth by the author of *Mary Powell* [Anne Manning, later Mrs Rathbone]. 8vo. Pp. vii. 296. London, 1866

LINDA. By A. G. [Agnes Giberne], author of *Maud Grenville*, etc. 8vo. Pp. 159. [*Brit. Mus.*] London, 1866

LINDA Tressel. By the author of *Nina Balatka* [Anthony Trollope]. 12mo. [*Brit. Mus.*] Edinburgh, 1868

Originally published in *Blackwood's Magazine.*

LINDAH; or, the festival: a metrical romance of ancient Scinde, with minor poems. By the author of *The white rose wreath*, etc. [H. E. Burton]. 8vo. [*Camb. Univ. Lib.*] London, 1845

LINDEN rhymes. By Maude [Clotilda Jennings]. 8vo. [Cushing's *Init. and Pseud.* i. 185.] Halifax, N.S., 1854

LINDENBLUMEN; and other stories. By Rowland Grey [Lilian Kate Rowland Brown]. 8vo. [*Lond. Lib. Cat.*] London, 1885

LINDENDALE stories. By Lawrence Lancewood [Daniel Wise, D.D.]. 8vo. 5 vols. [Kirk's *Supp.*] Chicago, 1881

LINDLEY Murray Hoag, and the Society of Friends. By Custos [Thomas Bevan]. 8vo. [Cushing's *Init. and Pseud.* i. 72.] London, 1853

LINE (a) of life; pointing at the immortalitie of a vertuous name. [By Bartholomew Robertson.] 12mo. Pp. 127. [*Bodl.*] [London] 1620

LINE (the) of righteousness and justice stretched over all merchants, &c.; and an exhortation unto all Friends and people whatsoever, who are merchants, tradesmen, husbandmen, or seamen, who deal in merchandize, trade in buying and selling by sea or land, or deal in husbandry, that ye all do that which is just, equal and righteous in the sight of God and man one to another, and to all men. . . . G. F. [George Fox]. 4to. Pp. 8. [Smith's *Cat. of Friends' Books.*] London, 1661

LINE (the) of time; presenting its several joynts in a clear view, from the first to the last Sabbatism. . . . By T. B. [Rev. Thomas Beverley]. 8vo. [Arber's *Term Cat.* ii. 585.] London, 1696

LINE upon line. . . . By the author of *Peep of day* [Mrs Favell Lee Mortimer]. 8vo. [*Brit. Mus.*] London, 1837

LINES [of verse]. By L. C. S. [Mrs Lucy Cummings Smith]. 12mo. Pp. 59. Brighton, 1883

LINES. By W. D. [Wedderburn Dundas]. 8vo. Pp. 286. St Andrews, 1838-39

LINES addressed to a noble Lord [Lord Byron]. . . . By one of the Small Fry of the Lakes [Miss —— Barker]. 8vo. [*Brit. Mus.*] London, 1815

LINES for little lips. H. D. [in monogram. Mrs Henry Davidson, *née* Harriet Miller]. 8vo. Pp. 29. [*Nat. Lib. of Scot.*] Edinburgh, 1856

LINES from the land of streams; a miscellany in prose and verse. By the author of *The Crescent*, etc. [Mrs Mary Anne M'Mullan, *née* Ward]. 8vo. [*Brit. Mus.*] London, 1841

LINES in memory of T. S. Bolitho. [Signed: H. S. S. *i.e.* Henry Sewell Stokes.] 8vo. London [1887]

LINES left out; or, some of the histories left out in "Line upon line." This first part relates events in the times of the Patriarchs and the Judges. By the author of *The peep of day.* [Mrs Thomas Mortimer]. 12mo. Pp. xiv. 391. London, 1862

LINES occasioned by a bright gleam of sunshine, on the 14th Nov. 1817. [By Robert Pierce Gillies.] 4to. Edinburgh, 1817

LINES on the inaugural meeting of the Shelley Society. [By Andrew Lang, LL.D.] 8vo. Private print, 1886

LINES on the lamented death of Sir John Moore. . . . By E. C. [Mrs E. Cockle]. 4to. London, 1810

LINES sacred to the memory of the Reverend James Grahame, author of the "Sabbath," etc. [By Professor John Wilson.] 4to. Pp. 19. ["*Christopher North*"*; a memoir of John Wilson. Compiled by his daughter Mrs Gordon*, i. 168.] Glasgow, 1811

LINES written at Ampthill Park, in the autumn of 1818. [By Henry Luttrell.] 4to. Pp. 46. [*Brit. Mus.*] London, 1819

LINES written at Jerpoint Abbey. [By Samuel Carter Hall: with notes, illustrations inserted, Irish songs with the music, etc. by the editor, S. Grace.] 8vo. [*Brit. Mus.*] London, 1820

LINGUA; or, the combate of the tongue, and the fiue sences for superiority; a pleasant comoedie. [By Thomas Tomkis.] 4to. [*Brit. Mus.*] London, 1607

Many editions followed.

LINGUA tersancta; or, a most sure and compleat allegorick dictionary to the holy language of the Spirit. . . . By W. F. [William Freke] Esq., author of *The New Jerusalem.* 8vo. [*D. N. B.* vol. 20, p. 247.] London, 1703

LINGUA testium; wherein monarchy is proved to be jure divino. By Testis Mundus Catholicus [Edmund Hall, M.A.]. 4to. London, 1651

LINGUAL exercises for advancied vocabularies. [Poems.] By the author of *Recreations* [Siegfried Sassoon]. 8vo. Cambridge, private print, 1925

LINGUISTIC notes on some obscure prefixes and affixes in Greek and Latin. [By Rev. Francis Crawford, LL.D.] 8vo. London, 1882

LINK by link. [A novel.] By Dick Donovan [Joyce E. Preston Muddock]. 8vo. Pp. 318. [*Lit. Year Book.*] London, 1893

LINKED lives; a novel. By George Douglas [Lady Gertrude Georgina Douglas]. 8vo. 3 vols. [*Brit. Mus.*] London, 1876

LINKS (the). [By William Cadenhead.] 8vo. Pp. 4. [*And. Jervise.*] N.P. [1811]

LINKS and clues. By Vita [Lady Welby-Gregory]. 8vo. Pp. xvi. 414. London, 1881

Later editions bear the name of the authoress.

LINKS in Rebecca's life. [A tale.] By "Pansy" [Mrs Isabella (Macdonald) Alden]. 8vo. Pp. 422. [*Lit. Year Book.*] London, 1882

LINKS in the chain. [A novel.] By Headon Hill [Francis E. Grainger]. 8vo. Pp. 302. [*Lond. Lib. Cat.*] London, 1909

LINKS of the Lower House; or, an alphabetical list of the members of the House of Commons. . . . [By William Cobbett?] 8vo. Pp. 32. [*Brit. Mus.*] [London, 1821]

LINNET'S trial; a tale in two volumes. By the author of *Twice lost* [Menella Bute Smedley]. 8vo. London, N.D.

An edition, in one volume, was published in 1871, with the name of the authoress.

LINWOODS (the); or, "Sixty years since" in America. By the author of *Hope Leslie*, etc. [Catherine Maria Sedgewick]. 12mo. 2 vols. [*Brit. Mus.*] New York, 1835

LION (the); a tale of the coteries. [By Henry Fothergill Chorley.] 12mo. 3 vols. London, 1839

LION (the) and the water-wagtail; a mock heroic poem. . . . By Castigator [Charles Dibdin, sen.]. 12mo. [*Brit. Mus.*] London, 1809

LION (the) in the path; an historical romance. By the authors of *Abel Drake's wife* [John Saunders] and *Gideon's rock* [Katherine Saunders]. 8vo. 3 vols. London, 1875

LIONEL and Clarissa; a comic opera, as it is performed at the Theatre-Royal in Covent-Garden. [By Isaac Bickerstaffe.] 8vo. Pp. 76. London, 1768

"The date in my copy is printed MDCXLVIII."—Note by Mr Halkett.

LIONEL Deerhurst; or, fashionable life under the regency. [By Barbara Hemphill.] Edited by the Countess of Blessington. 12mo. 3 vols. London, 1846

LIONEL Lincoln; or, the leaguer of Boston. By the author of the *Spy*, etc. [James Fenimore Cooper]. 12mo. 3 vols. [*Brit. Mus.*] London, 1825

LIONEL Merval; a novel. [By William Bainbridge, barrister.] 8vo. 3 vols. [Boase's *Mod. Eng. Biog.* i. col. 132.] London, 1866

LIONEL Wakefield. By the author of *Sydenham* [W. Massie]. 12mo. 3 vols. London, 1836

LIONEL'S courage; or, Clementine's great peril. By Francis Forrester [Daniel Wise, D.D.]. 8vo. Pp. 291. New York, 1893

LIONESS'S (the) rout. [By Mrs Catherine Ann Dorset?] 8vo. [*Brit. Mus.*] London [1807]

LION-HEARTED. [A novel.] By the author of *The gambler's wife*, etc. [Mrs Elizabeth Caroline Grey]. Second edition. 8vo. 2 vols. [*Brit. Mus.*] London, 1864

LIONS, living and dead; or, personal recollections of the great and gifted. By the author of *Pen and ink sketches of authors and authoresses* [John Dix, afterwards Ross]. 12mo. [*Brit. Mus.*] London, 1852

LION'S (the) masquerade; a sequel to *The peacock at home.* Written by a Lady [Mrs Dorset, *née* Catherine Ann Turner]. 4to. Pp. 26. [*Bibliographer*, v. 19.] London, 1807

LION'S (the) share. By Octave Thanet [Alice French]. 8vo. [*Amer. Cat.*] Indianapolis, Ind., 1907

LIQUOR (the) trades in relation to the national prosperity. [By Thomas Beggs.] 8vo. [*Edin. Univ. Lib.*] London, 1871

LISABEE'S love story. By the author of *John and I*, etc. [Matilda Betham Edwards]. 8vo. 3 vols. [*Lond. Lib. Cat.*] London, 1865

LISBETH; a novel. By Leslie Keith [Grace Leslie Keith Johnston]. 8vo. [*Lit. Year Book.*] London, 1894

LISE Fleuron. [A novel.] By Georges Ohnet [Georges Hénot]. Translated from the French by Lady William G. Osborne. 8vo. 2 vols. [*Brit. Mus.*] London, 1885

LISETTE. [A tale.] By Eglanton Thorne [Emily Charlton]. 8vo. Pp. 128. London [1890]

LISPINGS from low latitudes; or, extracts from the journal of the Hon. Impulsia Gushington. [By Harriot Blackwood, Lady Dufferin.] 4to. Pp. 98. [*Nat. Lib. of Scot.*] London, 1863

LIST (a) of books and manuscripts relating to Orkney and Shetland. . . By W. B. B. [William Balfour Blaikie]. 8vo. [Cursiter's *Books on Orkney and Shetland.*] Kirkwall, 1847

LIST (a) of books recommended to the younger clergy and other students in divinity within the diocese of Chester. [By William Cleaver, Bishop of Chester.] Third edition enlarged. . . . 8vo. [*Brit. Mus.*] Oxford, 1808

LIST (a) of convicted Recusants in the reign of King Charles II. [Edited by Joseph S. Hansom.] 8vo. London, 1909

Signed: J. S. H.

LIST of County Court Judges. [By Thomas Falconer.] 8vo. [*Brit. Mus.*] London [1865]

LIST of English books printed not later than the year 1600. [By Henry Pyne.] 8vo. 2 parts. [*Brit. Mus.*] [London] private print, 1874-8

LIST (a) of hall-marks 1756-1900. By W. H. [W. Horsman]. 8vo. [*Brit. Mus.*] [London, 1898]

LIST of manuscript books in the collection of David Laing, LL.D. [By Walter Macleod.] 8vo. Pp. 135. [Edinburgh, 1879]

Only 24 copies printed.

LIST of natural flies, taken by trout, &c., in the streams of Ripon. [By Michael Theakston.] 12mo. [Westwood's *Bibl. Pisc.*] London, 1854

LIST (a) of printed service books, according to the ancient uses of the Anglican Church. [By Francis Henry Dickinson.] 8vo. [*Brit. Mus.;* Green's *Bibl. Somers.* ii. 366.] London, 1850

LIST (a) of the absentees of Ireland, and the yearly value of their estates and incomes spent abroad; with observations on the present state and condition of that kingdom. [By Thomas Prior.] 8vo. Pp. 85. [*Bodl.*] Dublin, 1729

LIST of the Deans of Guild of Aberdeen from 1436 to 1875, with contemporary matters added; meant to form a local leaflet in the history of Scotland. By one of them [Alexander Walker]. 8vo. [Mitchell and Cash's *Scot. Top.* i. 35.] Aberdeen, private print, 1875

LIST (a) of the knights and burgesses who have represented the county and city of Durham in Parliament. [Edited by Sir Cuthbert Sharp.] 4to. Pp. 41. [Martin's *Cat.*] Durham, 1826

LIST of the members of the Society of Antiquaries, from 1717 to 1796. [By Richard Gough.] 4to. [*W.*] 1798

LIST (a) of the rare plants found in the neighbourhood of Tunbridge Wells. [By Thomas Furley Forster?] 8vo. [*Brit. Mus.*] London [1801?]

LIST (a) of two hundred Scoticisms. With remarks. [By James Beattie, LL.D.] 12mo. Pp. 18. Aberdeen, 1779

This is the first edition of Dr Beattie's work, which was published at Edinburgh in 1787 under the title, "Scoticisms arranged in alphabetical order, designed to correct improprieties of speech and writings." [Robertson's *Aberd. Bibl.*]

LIST (a) of various editions of the Bible, and parts thereof, in English, from the year 1526 to 1776. A manuscript list of English Bibles, copied from one compiled by the late Mr Joseph Ames, presented to the Lambeth Library by Dr Gifford, hath furnished some part of this publication; late discoveries of several learned gentlemen [particularly Dr Andrew C. Ducarel] have supplied the rest. 8vo. Pp. 73. [*D. N. B.* vol. 16, p. 85; Martin's *Cat.*] London, 1778

LIST (a), or catalogue of all the mayors and bayliffs, lord mayors and sheriffs, of the most ancient, honourable, noble, and loyall city of Yorke, from the time of King Edward the First, untill this present year, 1664, being the 16th year of the most happy reign of our most gratious sovereign lord King Charles the Second. . . . [By Christopher Hildyard.] 4to. Pp. 67. [Boyne's *Yorkshire Lib.* p. 42.] York, 1664

Reprinted at London in 1715.

LISTENER (the). [By Caroline Fry, afterwards Mrs Wilson.] 12mo. 2 vols. London, 1830

Other editions were issued with the author's name.

LISTENER (the) in Oxford. By the author of *Christ our example*, etc. [Caroline Fry, later Mrs Wilson]. Second edition. 12mo. Pp. vi. 182. London, 1840

LISTS of officers of King's College. Aberdeen, 1495-1860. By P. J. A. [Peter John Anderson, LL.B., Librarian]. 4to. [*Aberd. Univ. Lib.*] Aberdeen, 1893

LISTS of subjects for courses of sermons. [By Rev. Frederick A. G. Eichbaum.] 8vo. [*Brit. Mus.*] London, 1880

LITERÆ sacræ; or, the doctrines of moral philosophy and Scriptural Christianity compared. [By A. Norman.] 8vo. London, 1825

LITERAL (a) translation of St Paul's Epistle to the Romans, on definite rules of translation. By Herman Heinfetter [Frederick Parker]. 12mo. 2 parts. [*Brit. Mus.*] London, 1842

LITERAL (a) translation of selected passages of Holy Scripture, on definite rules of translation, and an examination of certain doctrines connected with them. By Herman Heinfetter, author of *Rules for ascertaining the sense conveyed in ancient Greek manuscripts*, etc. [Frederick Parker]. 12mo. Pp. 19. [*Brit. Mus.*] London, 1850

LITERAL (a) translation of the Apostolical Epistles and Revelation, with a concurrent commentary. [By William Heberden, junior.] 8vo. Pp. 578. [*Brit. Mus.*] London, 1839

LITERAL (a) translation of the eight last Books of the New Testament, on definite rules of translation, and an English version of the same. By Herman Heinfetter, author of *Rules for ascertaining the sense conveyed in ancient Greek manuscripts*, etc. [Frederick Parker]. 12mo. Pp. vi. London, May 1st, 1854

The work is unpaged beyond the preface.

LITERAL (a) translation of the Epistles of John and Jude, on definite rules of translation. By Herman Heinfetter, author of *Rules for ascertaining the sense conveyed in ancient Greek manuscripts*, etc. [Frederick Parker]. 12mo. Pp. 40. London, 1849

LITERAL (a) translation of the Epistles of Paul the Apostle to the Corinthians, on definite rules of translation, and an English version of the same. By Herman Heinfetter, author of *Rules for ascertaining the sense conveyed in ancient Greek manuscripts*, etc. [Frederick Parker]. 12mo. Pp. 3, xviii. London, October 1st, 1851

The work is unpaged beyond the preliminary matter.

LITERAL (a) translation of the Epistles of Paul the Apostle to the Thessalonians, Timothy, Titus, and Philemon, on definite rules of translation; and an English version of the same, as also of the Epistles of Paul the Apostle to the Galatians, Ephesians, Philippians, and Colossians. By Herman Heinfetter, author of *Rules for ascertaining the sense conveyed in ancient Greek manuscripts*, etc. [Frederick Parker]. 12mo. London, 1850

LITERAL (a) translation of the Saxon Chronicle. [By Anna Gurney.] 8vo. [Smith's *Cat. of Friends' Books*, i. 878.] Norwich, 1819

LITERAL (a) translation of the Vatican manuscripts eleven last Epistles of Paul the Apostle, on definite rules of translation, and an English version of the same, followed by the Authorized English version collated with the above-named English version. By Herman Heinfetter, author of *Rules for ascertaining the sense conveyed in ancient Greek manuscripts*, etc. [Frederick Parker]. 8vo. Pp. 582. London, 1862

LITERAL translations from the German. By A. A. [Arthur Anderson]. 8vo. Aberdeen, 1884

LITERARY bye-hours; a book of instructive pastime. By H. A. Page [Alexander Hay Japp]. 8vo. Pp. 232. [*D. N. B.* Second Supp. vol. 2, p. 363.] London, 1881

LITERARY (the) character, illustrated by the history of men of genius, drawn from their own feelings and confessions. By the author of *Curiosities of literature* [Isaac D'Israeli]. 8vo. Pp. viii. 336. London, 1818

Published subsequently with the author's name.

LITERARY cookery, with reference to matter attributed [by J. P. Collier] to Coleridge and Shakespeare, a letter addressed to *The Athenæum* [by a Detective], with a P.S. containing some remarks upon the refusal of that journal to print it. [By Andrew Edmund Brae, of Leeds.] 8vo. [*Olphar Hamst*, p. 5.] London, 1855

LITERARY (a) curiosity; a sermon in words of one syllable only. By a Manchester layman [Rev. J. Gill]. [*N. and Q.* 1869, p. 167.] Manchester, 1860

LITERARY (the) examiner; consisting of the Indicator, a review of books, and miscellaneous pieces in prose and verse. [By J. H. Leigh Hunt.] 8vo. Pp. 412. London, 1823

LITERARY hearthstones; studies of the home-life of certain writers and thinkers. By Marion Harland [Mary Virginia Hawes, later Mrs Terhune]. 8vo. [Kirk's *Supp.*] London, 1899

LITERARY (the) history of the New Testament; comprising a critical enquiry into the authorship, chronological order, characteristic features, internal evidence, and general scope of the sacred documents. [By Josiah Conder, D.D.] 8vo. [*D. N. B.* vol. 12, p. 3.] [London] 1845

LITERARY (the) history of the Troubadours; containing their lives, extracts from their works, and many particulars relative to the customs, morals and history of the twelfth and thirteenth centuries: collected and abridged from the French of M. de Saint-Pelaie, by the author of the *Life of Petrarch* [Mrs Susannah Dobson]. 8vo. [*Camb. Univ. Lib.*] London, 1779

LITERARY ideals in Ireland; nationality and cosmopolitanism in literature. By A. E. [George Russell]. 8vo. [*Brit. Mus.*] London, 1899

LITERARY (a) journal; or, a continuation of the memoirs of literature. [By Michael de La Roche.] 8vo. 3 vols. [*Queen's Coll. Lib.* p. 898.] London, 1730

LITERARY (the) life. By William Shepard [William Shepard Walsh]. 8vo. [Cushing's *Init. and Pseud.* ii. 137.] New York, 1883

LITERARY memoirs of living authors of Great Britain, arranged according to an alphabetical catalogue of their names; and including a list of their works, with occasional opinions upon their literary character. [By David Rivers, Dissenting minister, Highgate.] 8vo. 2 vols. [*D. N. B.* vol. 49, p. 32.] London, 1798

LITERARY memorials. By the author of *Four years in France* [Henry Digby Beste]. 8vo. [*Brit. Mus.*] London, 1829

LITERARY (the) Quixote; or, the beauties of [Richard] Townley versified. [By John Sotwell.] 4to. Pp. 16. [Harrison's *Bibl. Monensis.*] Douglas, Isle of Man [1791]

LITERARY (the) what-not; or, New Year's offering for 1871, consisting of original papers in prose and verse. [By T. B. Lawrence.] 8vo. [*Calc. Imp. Lib.*] Calcutta, 1870

LITERATURE (the) and curiosities of dreams; a common-place book of speculations concerning the mystery of dreams and visions. . . . By Frank Seafield [Alexander H. Grant], M.A. 8vo. 2 vols. [*Aberd. Quatercent. Studies*, vol. 19, p. 360.] London, 1865

LITERATURE and its professors. By Q. [Thomas Purnell]. 8vo. [Cushing's *Init. and Pseud.* i. 243.] London, 1867

LITERATURE (the) of Bengal; being an attempt to trace the progress of the national mind . . . as reflected in the nation's literature. . . . By Ar Cy Dae [Rames Chandra Datta]. 8vo. Calcutta, 1877

LITERATURE (the) of Society. By Grace Wharton [Mrs Katharine Thomson, *née* Byerley]. 8vo. 2 vols. [Cushing's *Init. and Pseud.* i. 306.] London, 1862

LITERATURE (the) of the rail. . . . [By Samuel Phillips, LL.D.]. 8vo. [*Brit. Mus.*] London [1851]

LITERATURE (the) of the ten principal food-fishes of the North Sea. By P. P. C. H. [P. P. C. Hoek]. 8vo. London, 1903

LITERATURE (the) relating to New Zealand. [Prefatory note signed: J. C. *i.e.* J. Collier.] 8vo. Pp. 236. [*New Coll. Lib.*] Wellington, 1889

LITHOBOLIA; or, the stone-throwing devil: being an account of the various actions of infernal spirits at Great Island, in New England. By R. C. [Richard Chamberlaine]. 4to. [*Brit. Mus.*] London, 1698

LITTLE Ada; or, the three new years. By H. L. H. [H. L. Henry]. 8vo. [Cushing's *Init. and Pseud.* i. 123.] Philadelphia, 1871

LITTLE Amy's birthday and other tales; a story book for autumn, written for young children by Mrs Harriet Myrtle [Mrs Lydia Falconer Miller]. 8vo. Pp. 131. London, 1846

LITTLE Ann. By the author of *Tip-cat* [Evelyn Whitaker]. 8vo. [*Amer. Cat.*] London, 1857

LITTLE Annie's first Bible-lessons. By Nellie Graham [Mrs Annie Dunning, *née* Ketchum]. 8vo. [Haynes' *Pseud.*] Philadelphia, 1861

LITTLE Apple-Blossom. By C. E. K. [Caroline E. Kelly, later Mrs Davis]. 8vo. [Cushing's *Init. and Pseud.* i. 156.] Boston, 1863

LITTLE Arthur's history of England. By M. C. [Lady Maria Callcott, *née* Graham]. 8vo. [*Brit. Mus.*] London, 1835

LITTLE (the) aunt. [A novel.] By John Strange Winter [Mrs Arthur Stannard, *née* Henrietta Eliza Vaughan Palmer]. 8vo. Pp. 304. London, 1904

LITTLE (a) beast book. By Israfel [Miss —— Hudson]. 8vo. Pp. 120. London, 1902

LITTLE Ben. By Mignon [Mrs Baseley]. 8vo. Manchester, 1901

LITTLE Benjamin; or, truth discovering error: being a clear and full answer unto the letter subscribed by forty-seven ministers of the Province of London. . . . By J. R. [John Reading, D.D.], a reall lover of all those who love peace and truth. 4to. [*D. N. B.* vol. 47, p. 364.] London, 1648

LITTLE Bill, and other stories. By Margaret Vandergrift [Margaret Thomson Janvier]. 8vo. [Kirk's *Supp.*] Philadelphia, 1875

LITTLE (the) black devil. [A novel.] By Martin Edwardes [E. L. Murphy]. 8vo. Pp. 190. [S. J. Brown's *Ireland in fiction*, p. 82.] Dublin, 1910

LITTLE Bluebird, the girl missionary. By John Strathesk [John Tod, of Lasswade]. 12mo. Pp. 95. Edinburgh, 1884

LITTLE Bob. [A novel.] By Gyp [Sibylle Gabrielle de Mirabeau, Comtesse de Martel de Janville]. 8vo. Pp. 196. [*Lit. Year Book.*] London, 1900

LITTLE (a) book about Great Britain. By Azamat-Batuk [Nicolas Leon Thieblin]. 12mo. [*Brit. Mus.*] London, 1870

Reprinted from the *Pall Mall Gazette*, with additional material.

LITTLE (a) book for young persons. . . . By G. J. F. [George James Foster]. 8vo. Pp. 81. [*Brit. Mus.*] London, 1884

LITTLE (a) book of ballads; edited by E. V. U. [Edward Vernon Utterson]. 8vo. Pp. 72. [*Dyce Cat.*] Newport [U.S.A.] 1836

A selection from *Songs and ballads*, in black letter, in the possession of Edward Vernon Utterson, and presented by him to the Roxburgh Club.

LITTLE (the) book of family prayer; with an introduction on family prayer. [Signed: W. L. D. *i.e.* W. L. Dickinson.] 12mo. London, 1870

LITTLE (a) book of family verse. By W. A. B. [William Adams Brown, D.D.]. 8vo. [*Amer. Cat.*] New York, private print, 1906

LITTLE (a) book of nature. By Fiona Macleod [William Sharp]. 12mo. [*Lit. Year Book.*] Edinburgh, 1909

LITTLE (the) Book (see the tenth chapter of Revelation); or, a close and brief elucidation of the 13th, 14th, 15th, 16th, 17th, and 18th chapters of Revelations. By Eben-ezer—"Hitherto hath the Lord helped us," (Sam. vii. 12)—High Peak, Derbyshire [Rev. Ebenezer Aldred, Unitarian minister of Great-Hucklow, Co. Derby]. 8vo. Pp. 74. [Martin's *Cat.*] London, 1811

Introduction, pp. 61. First supplement, pp. 4. Second supplement, Sheffield, 1816, pp. 128.

LITTLE Bo-Peep. By Susan Coolidge [Sarah C. Woolsey]. 8vo. [Kirk's *Supp.*] Boston, 1901

LITTLE (the) boy who lived on the hill. By Annie Laurie [Winifred Black]. 8vo. Pp. 80. New York, 1895

LITTLE (the) boy's companion. . . . By T. K. A. [Thomas Kerchever Arnold]. 8vo. [*Brit. Mus.*] London, 1838

LITTLE (a) boy's story; translated from the French by Howard Glyndon [Laura C. Redden, later Mrs Searing]. 8vo. [*Brit. Mus.*] Boston, 1870

LITTLE bricks. By Darley Dale [Francesca M. Steele]. New edition. 8vo. [*Lond. Lib. Cat.*] London, 1890

LITTLE (the) brother; a story of tramp life. By Josiah Flynt [Josiah F. Willard]. 8vo. [*Amer. Cat.*] New York, 1902

LITTLE (the) brother to the bear; and other animal stories. By Peter Rabbit [William Joseph Long]. 8vo. [*Amer. Cat.*] Boston, 1905

LITTLE (the) brown girl; a story. . . . By Esmé Stuart [Amélie Claire Leroy]. 8vo. Pp. 254. [*Lond. Lib. Cat.*] London, 1905

LITTLE brown seed. By Mrs George Archibald [Anna Campbell, later Mrs George Archibald Palmer]. 8vo. [*Amer. Cat.*] Chicago, 1891

LITTLE (the) brown teapot. [A tale.] By "Brenda" [Mrs Castle Smith]. 8vo. Pp. 192. [*Brit. Mus.*] London, 1901

LITTLE (the) budget, for little folks. By Old Humphrey [George Mogridge]. 12mo. [*Brit. Mus.*] London [1852]

LITTLE bullets from Batala. By A. L. O. E. [Charlotte Maria Tucker]. 8vo. Pp. 159. [*Lit. Year Book.*] London [1880]

LITTLE (the) camp on Eagle Hill. By the author of *The wide wide world*, etc. [Susan Warner]. 8vo. Pp. 380. London, 1863

LITTLE (the) captain; a temperance tale. By Lynde Palmer [Mrs Mary L. Peebles, *née* Parmlee]. 12mo. [Haynes' *Pseud.*] London, 1867

LITTLE (a) catechism, with little verses and little sayings, for little children. By Mr J. M. [Rev. John Mason], author of *The midnight cry*. 12mo. [*Brit. Mus.*] London, 1693

LITTLE (the) child's book of divinity; or, Grandmamma's stories about Bible doctrines. By the author of *Morning and night watches*, etc. [John Ross M'Duff, D.D.]. Second edition. 12mo. Pp. 79. London, 1855

LITTLE (the) chronicle of Magdalena Bach. [The life of J. S. Bach, purporting to be written by his wife, but really by Esther Meynell.] 8vo. Pp. 183. [*Brit. Mus.*] London, 1925

LITTLE (a) cockney; a story for girls. By S. G. [Selina Gaye]. 8vo. Pp. 187. London, 1903

LITTLE (the) colonel. [A tale.] By Mina Doyle [Mrs Charles W. Young]. 8vo. Pp. 278. London, 1902

LITTLE (the) colonist; or, King Penguin Land. By Theo. Gift [Theodora Havers, later Mrs Boulger]. 8vo. Pp. viii. 164. [*Lit. Year Book.*] London [1890]

LITTLE (a) country girl. By Susan Coolidge [Sarah Chauncey Woolsey]. 8vo. [Kirk's *Supp.*] Boston, 1885

LITTLE cousins; or, Georgie's visit to Lotty. By Brenda [Mrs Castle Smith]. 8vo. Pp. 176. [*Brit. Mus.*] London [1880]

LITTLE (the) creoles; or, the history of Francis and Blanche; a domestic tale: by the author of *Montague Park* [A. Selwyn]. 8vo. Pp. 71. [*Brit. Mus.*] London [1820]

LITTLE (the) crown; a compendium from "The crown of Jesus"; containing the devotions and instructions most frequently required. [By Rev. Robert Rodolph Suffield.] 8vo. Pp. xii. 272. London [1870]

LITTLE Daniel; a story of a flood on the Rhine; and other tales. By the author of *The basket of flowers*, etc. [Johann C. von Schmid]. 12mo. Pp. 126. London [1822]

LITTLE Derwent's breakfast. [Poems.] By a Lady [Emily Trevenen]. 8vo. Pp. viii. 84. [Courtney's *Secrets*, p. 16.] London, 1839

LITTLE doctor; or, the magic of nature. By Darley Dale [Francesca M. Steele]. 8vo. [*Lond. Lib. Cat.*] London, 1892

LITTLE (the) doings of some little folks. By Chatty Cheerful [William Martin]. 8vo. Pp. 176. [*Brit. Mus.*] London [1885]

LITTLE (the) duke; or, Richard the Fearless. By the author of *The heir of Redclyffe*, etc. [Charlotte Mary Yonge]. With illustrations, drawn and lithographed by J. B. 8vo. London, 1854

LITTLE Ella, and the Fire king; and other tales. [Preface signed: M. W. *i.e.* Mary Williams.] With illustrations by Henry Warren. 12mo. Pp. 118. [*W.*] Edinburgh, 1861

LITTLE (the) emigrant; a tale, interspersed with moral anecdotes and instructive conversations, designed for the perusal of youth. By the author of *The adventures of the six princesses of Babylon*, etc. [Lucy Peacock]. 12mo. Pp. ii. 203. London, 1799

LITTLE Empress Joan. By the author of *Aunt Tabitha's waifs*, etc. [Madeline Bonavia Hunt]. 8vo. Pp. viii. 276. [*Brit. Mus.*] London [1880]

LITTLE fables for little folks. [By John Henry Brady.] 8vo. [*Brit. Mus.*] London, 1835

LITTLE Fadette; a tale of French country life. By George Sand [Madame A. L. A. Dudevant]; translated from the French. 8vo. [*Brit. Mus.*] London, 1895

LITTLE (the) farm. By "Home Counties" [John W. Robertson Scott]. 8vo. Pp. xvi. 136. [*Brit. Mus.*] London, 1905

LITTLE fishers and their nets. By Pansy [Mrs Isabella (Macdonald) Alden]. 8vo. Pp. viii. 375. [*Lit. Year Book.*] London, 1887

LITTLE Flaggs, the almshouse foundling. By the author of *Myself and my relatives* [Annie J. Robertson]. 8vo. [*Brit. Mus.*] London, 1864

LITTLE (a) fleet. By Jack B. Yeats. [With verses by John Masefield.] 12mo. [Williams' *Bibl. of Masefield.*] London [1909]

LITTLE (the) Florentine. [A tale.] By H. N. W. B. [Mrs Harriet Newell (Woods) Baker]. 12mo. [Kirk's *Supp.*] Boston, 1870

LITTLE folk life. By Gail Hamilton [Mary Abigail Dodge]. 12mo. [Kirk's *Supp.*] New York, 1872

LITTLE folks in feathers and fur, and others in neither. By Olive Thorne Miller [Mrs Harriet Miller, *née* Mann]. 8vo. [Kirk's *Supp.*] New York, 1879

LITTLE (the) fool; a novel. By John Strange Winter [Mrs Arthur Stannard, *née* Henrietta Eliza V. Palmer]. 8vo. London, 1889

LITTLE (the) foundling. [A tale.] By Harriet Myrtle [Lydia Falconer Miller]. 8vo. [Kirk's *Supp.*] London, 1836

LITTLE Freddie feeding his soul. By Say Putnam [Anna A. Pratt, later Mrs Peerless]. 8vo. [Cushing's *Init. and Pseud.* i. 243.] New York, 1869

LITTLE Freddie; or, friends in need. By H. F. E. [Evelyn Everett Green]. Pp. 184. [*Brit. Mus.*] London [1882]

LITTLE (the) freeholder; a dramatic entertainment, in two acts. [By David Dalrymple, Lord Hailes.] 8vo. Pp. 63. [*Nat. Lib. of Scot.*] London, 1790

LITTLE Frida; a tale of the Black Forest. [By Matilda Horsburgh, later Mrs H. Douglas.] 8vo. Edinburgh, 1914

LITTLE (a) gate of tears; a romance of the Island of Guernsey. By Austin Clare [Miss W. M. James]. 8vo. Pp. 326. [*Lond. Lib. Cat.*] London, 1906

LITTLE (the) gentlemen in green; an American fairy story. By Una Savin [Mrs George Hughes Hepworth]. 8vo. [Cushing's *Init. and Pseud.* i. 261.] Boston, 1875

LITTLE Gervaise. [A story.] By John Strange Winter [Mrs Arthur Stannard]; and other stories by Frances E. Crompton, Olive Molesworth, and E. M. Green. 8vo. London [1898]

LITTLE (the) girl beautiful. By May Wynne [Mabel Wynne Knowles]. 8vo. Pp. 192. [*Brit. Mus.*] London [1919]

LITTLE (the) gods of Grub Street; a satire. [By Eric Mackay.] 8vo. London, 1896

LITTLE Goldie; a story of woman's love. By Hattie Hateful [Mrs Sumner Haydn]. 8vo. New York, 1884

LITTLE (the) gray man. By Jane Wardle [Mrs Oliver Max Hueffer]. 8vo. Pp. 334. London, 1910

LITTLE (the) green man. [A fairy story.] By F. M. Allen [Edmund Downey]. 8vo. Pp. 152. [*Brit. Mus.*] London [1895]

LITTLE (a) green world; a village comedy without a plot and without a problem. By J. E. Buckrose [Mrs Falconer Jameson]. 8vo. Pp. 350. [*Lit. Year Book.*] London, 1909

LITTLE (the) grey mouse. By Florence Warden [Florence Alice Price, later Mrs George E. James]. 8vo. Pp. 311. London, 1915

LITTLE hand and muckle gold; a study of to-day. By X. L., the author of *Aut Diabolus aut nihil* [Julian Osgood Field]. 8vo. 3 vols. [*Brit. Mus.*] Edinburgh, 1889

LITTLE Harry's troubles; a story of gipsy life. . . [By Mrs Richardson, of Bristol.] 8vo. Edinburgh, 1866

LITTLE heather-blossom. From the German of Emmy von Rothenfels [Emilie von Ingersleben]. 8vo. New York, 1891

LITTLE helpers. By Margaret Vandergrift [Margaret Thomson Janvier]. 8vo. [Kirk's *Supp.*] Philadelphia, 1882

LITTLE Henry and his bearer. [By Mary Martha Butt, later Mrs Sherwood.] 12mo. [Courtney's *Secrets*, p. 51.] London, 1814

LITTLE (the) hermit; or, the German Robinson Crusoe. . . . By the author of *The basket of flowers* [Johann Christoph von Schmid]. 12mo. London, 1853

LITTLE Hodge. By the author of *Ginx's baby* [John Edward Jenks, M.P.]. 8vo. [*Brit. Mus.*] London, 1872

LITTLE homespun. By Ruth Ogden [Mrs Frances Otis Ide]. 8vo. New York, 1897

LITTLE Ike Templin, and other stories. By Philemon Perch [Robert Malcolm Johnston]. 8vo. [Cushing's *Init. and Pseud.* i. 228.] Boston, 1894

LITTLE Indabas. [Short tales of South African life.] By J. Mac. [James MacManus]. 8vo. London, 1900

LITTLE Jessie's dream; a juvenile operetta. Written and composed by L. M. [L. M'Hale]. 8vo. London, 1889

LITTLE Jessie's work. [By Sarah Maria Fry.] 12mo. [*Brit. Mus.*] London, 1857

LITTLE Joan; a novel. By John Strange Winter [Mrs Arthur Stannard, *née* Henrietta E. V. Palmer]. 8vo. [*Lit. Year Book.*] London, 1903

LITTLE Joanna. By Kamba Thorpe [Mrs Elizabeth Whitfield Bellamy]. 8vo. [Cushing's *Init. and Pseud.* i. 283.] New York, 1876

LITTLE Joe. . . By James Otis [James Otis Kaler]. 8vo. [Kirk's *Supp.*] Boston, 1898

LITTLE journeys to ancient sanctuaries [in Colorado]. By Ben Boston [Harry Byron Magill]. 8vo. [*Amer. Cat.*] Boston, 1908

LITTLE Kate and Jolly Jim. [By Alice Gray.] 12mo. London, 1865

LITTLE King Rannie, the missing heir of Camberley; a novel. By M. E. Winchester [M. E. Whatham]. 8vo. Pp. 493. London, 1899

LITTLE King Richard. By Maud Carew [Florence M. King]. 8vo. Pp. 258. London, 1905

LITTLE (the) King; the story of the childhood of Louis XIV., King of France. [By Edwin Caskoden.] 8vo. [*Amer. Cat.*] New York, 1910

LITTLE Lady Maria. [A novel.] By the author of *A Fellow of Trinity* [Mrs Frances Marshall]. 8vo. [*Brit. Mus.*] London, 1893

LITTLE (a) lady of lavender. By Baynton Foster [Theodora C. Elmslie]. 8vo. [*Amer. Cat.*] New York, 1894

LITTLE ladyship. By May Wynne [Mabel Wynne Knowles]. 8vo. Pp. 186. [*Lit. Year Book.*] London, 1921

LITTLE (the) lame lord; or, the child of Cloverlea. By Baynton Foster [Theodora C. Elmslie]. 8vo. [*Amer. Cat.*] New York, 1898

LITTLE (the) lame prince and his travelling cloak; a parable for young and old. By the author of *John Halifax, Gentleman* [Dinah Maria Mulock, later Mrs Craik]. With twenty-four illustrations by J. M'L. Ralston. 8vo. Pp. 169. [*Lond. Lib. Cat.*] London, 1875

LITTLE (a) lass and lad. . . . [A tale.] By Sarah Tytler [Henrietta Keddie]. 8vo. Pp. 310. [*Lit. Year Book.*] London, 1896

LITTLE laughs over the lives of musicians; Handel, Rossini, Haydn, Beethoven. By "Marcus" [Howard Marcus Strong]. 8vo. [*Amer. Cat.*] Springfield, Mass., 1907

LITTLE lessons for little folks. By Aunt Elmina [Mrs Elmina D. Slenker]. 8vo. New York, 1886

LITTLE lessons for little housekeepers. By E. H. [Emily Huntington]. 8vo. [Cushing's *Init. and Pseud.* i. 122.] New York, 1875

LITTLE (the) lexicon; or, multum in parvo of the English language; to which is added a table of terms and phrases from the French, Italian and Spanish languages. [By Samuel Maunder.] 8vo. [*W.*] London [1825]

LITTLE Lisette. By the author of *Louis Michaud*, etc. [Mrs Mary E. Gellie]. 12mo. [Kirk's *Supp.*] London, 1872

LITTLE (the) Loo; a story of the South Sea. By Sydney Mostyn [William Clark Russell]. 8vo. 3 vols. [*Brit. Mus.*] London, 1878

LITTLE (a) love affair; or, an infatuation. By "Gyp" [Comtesse de Martel de Janville]. 8vo. Pp. 199. [*Brit. Mus.*] New York, 1897

LITTLE (a) lower than the angels. By Berkley Aikin [Fanny Aikin Kortwright]. 8vo. [*Brit. Mus.*] London, 1874

LITTLE (a) maid of Arcady. By Christian Reid [Frances C. Fisher, later Mrs James M. Tiernan]. 8vo. Pp. 284. [Kirk's *Supp.*] Philadelphia, 1893

LITTLE (the) maid of Concord Town; a historical romance of the American Revolution. By Margaret Sidney [Mrs Harriett Mulford Lothrop, *née* Stone]. 8vo. [Kirk's *Supp.*] Boston, 1898

LITTLE (a) manual of the [Romanist] poore man's dayly devotion; collected out of severall pious and approved authors. By W. C. [William Clifford]. 12mo. Pp. 429. [*D. N. B.* vol. 11, p. 82.] London, 1687

Earlier editions were issued on the Continent.

LITTLE (the) manuall of devout [Roman Catholic] prayers and exercises, collected and translated out of divers authors, by R. R. [Richard Rowlands, *alias* Verstegan]. 12mo. [Gillow's *Bibl. Dict.*] Antwerp [*c.* 1590]

LITTLE Meg's children. By Hesba Stretton [Sarah Smith]. 8vo. Pp. 160. London, 1869

See note to "Alone in London."

LITTLE memoirs of the eighteenth century. By George Paston [Emily Morse Symonds]. 8vo. Pp. 400. [*Lond. Lib. Cat.*] London, 1901

LITTLE memoirs of the nineteenth century. By George Paston [Emily Morse Symonds]. 8vo. Pp. 386. 2 vols. [*Lond. Lib. Cat.*] London, 1902

LITTLE Minnie; or, good out of evil. . . . By N. D'anvers [Nancy Meugens, later Mrs —— Bell]. 8vo. Pp. viii. 194. [*Brit. Mus.*] London [1890]

LITTLE Minnie's troubles. By N. D'anvers [Mrs Nancy Bell, *née* Meugens]. 8vo. [*Brit. Mus.*] London, 1876

LITTLE Miss Dorothy. By Martha James [Martha Claire Douglas]. 8vo. [*Amer. Cat.*] Boston, 1900

LITTLE Miss Fairfax; a novel. By Kenner Deene, author of *The schoolmaster of Alton* [Charlotte Smith]. 12mo. 3 vols. London, 1867

LITTLE Miss Prim; a novel. By Florence Warden [Florence Alice Price, later Mrs George E. James]. 8vo. Pp. 296. [*Brit. Mus.*] London, 1898

LITTLE Miss Primrose. By the author of *St Olave's*, etc. [Eliza Tabor, later Mrs Stephenson]. 8vo. 3 vols. [*Brit. Mus.*] London, 1880

LITTLE Miss Wardlaw. By Kate Thorne [Louisa M. Gray]. 8vo. London, 1889

LITTLE Miss Weesey's brother. By Penn Shirley [Sarah J. Clarke]. 8vo. [*Amer. Cat.*] 1893

LITTLE Miss Weesey's sister. By Penn Shirley [Sarah J. Clarke]. 8vo. [*Amer. Cat.*] 1890

LITTLE (the) moorland princess. [A novel.] By E. Marlitt [Eugenie John]; from the German. 8vo. Pp. 387. [*Lond. Lib. Cat.*] London [1881]

LITTLE (a) more than kin. [A novel.] By Patricia Wentworth [Mrs —— Dillon, *née* D. O. Ellis]. 8vo. Pp. 316. London, 1911

LITTLE Mr Bouncer and his friend, Verdant Green. By Cuthbert Bede [Rev. Edward Bradley]. 8vo. [*Brit. Mus.*] London [1873]

LITTLE Mr Thimblefinger and his queer country. . . . By Uncle Remus [Joel Chandler Harris]. 8vo. [Cushing's *Init. and Pseud.* i. 249]. Boston, 1891

LITTLE Mrs Lee. [A novel.] By Margaret Hope [Mrs M. Z. Hadwen]. 8vo. London, 1914

LITTLE (the) museum keepers. By "Silverpen" [Eliza Meteyard]. 8vo. Pp. 160. [*Lit. Year Book.*] Edinburgh, 1863

Chambers's Library for young people. Second series.

LITTLE Nettie's journey. By A. K. C. [Antoinette K. Crichton]. 8vo. London, 1877

LITTLE night-cap letters. By Aunt Fanny, author of the six *Night-cap books* [Mrs Frances E. Barrow, *née* Mease]. 8vo. Pp. 174. [Kirk's *Supp.*] Edinburgh, 1868

LITTLE Nin; a story for the young. By Victor Meredith Bell [Virge Reese Phelps]. 4to. Pp. 199. Boston, 1896

LITTLE (the) nurse of Cape Cod. By Amy Lothrop [Anna Bartlett Warner]. [Kirk's *Supp.*] London, 1863

LITTLE (the) ones of Innisfail. [A story. By Miss E. Colthurst.] 8vo. [S. J. Brown's *Ireland in fiction*, p. 54.] London [*c.* 1850]

LITTLE (the) pastoral of a Scottish Bishop, in which he setteth forth briefly dyvours of the sorrows which haf of late years fallen to his lot. [By John Davidson, writer, Aberdeen.] With two illustrations. Fourth edition. 8vo. Pp. 4. [*And. Jervise.*] Aberdeen, N.D.

LITTLE Paul and the Frisbie school. By Margaret Sidney [Mrs Lothrop, *née* Harriet Mulford Stone]. 8vo. Pp. 206. [Kirk's *Supp.*] Boston, 1893

LITTLE (the) peace-maker; discovering foolish pride the make-bate; or some animadversions on Proverbs 13, 10. In a dialogue between Eumenus, quiet, and Thermos, hot and hasty. [By Rev. Charles Morton.] 12mo. Pp. 86. [*Brit. Mus.*] London, 1674

LITTLE (the) people of Japan. By Mary Muller [Lenore E. Mulets]. 8vo. [*Amer. Cat.*] Chicago, 1903

LITTLE people of the snow. By Mary Muller [Lenore E. Mulets]. 8vo. [*Amer. Cat.*] Chicago, 1900

LITTLE people whom the Lord loved. By E. E. F. [Elizabeth E. Flagg]. 8vo. New York, 1871

LITTLE Peter; a Christmas morality for children of any age. By Lucas Malet [Mrs William St Leger Harrison, *née* Mary Kingsley]. 4to. [*Brit. Mus.*] London, 1909

LITTLE pieces; verse and prose. By Quilp, Jr. [William H. Halstead]. 8vo. [Cushing's *Init. and Pseud.* i. 244.] Norfolk, Virginia, 1868

LITTLE Pierre. By Anatole France [Jacques Anatole Thibaut]; a translation by J. Lewis May. 8vo. Pp. 297. [*Brit. Mus.*] London, 1921

LITTLE (the) pilgrim. By Alfred Crowquill [Alfred Henry Forrester]. 4to. Pp. 12. [*Lit. Year Book.*] London, N.D.

LITTLE (a) pilgrim in the Unseen. [By Mrs Margaret O. Oliphant.] 8vo. [*D. N. B.* First Supp. vol. 3, p. 232.] London, 1886

LITTLE pitchers. By Sophie May [Rebecca Sophia Clarke]. 8vo. [Kirk's *Supp.*] Boston, 1882

LITTLE place. By Esmé Stuart [Amélie Claire Leroy]. 8vo. [*Lond. Lib. Cat.*] London, 1885

LITTLE (a) plain English, addressed to the people of the United States, on the treaty negociated with his Britannic Majesty, and on the conduct of the President relative thereto; in answer to "The letters of Franklin." . . . By Peter Porcupine, author of *Observations on Dr Priestley's Emigration to America*, etc. [William Cobbett]. 8vo. Pp. 111. Philadelphia, printed; London, reprinted, 1795

LITTLE poems of a poeticule. By Antaeus [William Joseph Ibbett]. 4to. Pp. 35. [*Brit. Mus.*] London, 1893

LITTLE (the) princess, and other stories. By Aunt Hattie [Mrs Harriet Newell Baker, *née* Woods]. 8vo. [Kirk's *Supp.*] New York, 1874

LITTLE Prudy stories. By Sophie May [Rebecca Sophia Clarke]. 8vo. 6 vols. [Kirk's *Supp.*] Boston, 1864-6

LITTLE Ray and her friends. By Ruth Elliott [Lillie Peck]. 12mo. [Cushing's *Init. and Pseud.* i. 89.] London [1877]

LITTLE (the) red shop. By Margaret Sidney [Mrs Harriett Mulford Lothrop, *née* Stone]. 8vo. [Kirk's *Supp.*] Boston [1885?]

LITTLE Rie and the rosebuds. [By Jean Ingelow.] 12mo. [*Brit. Mus.*] London, 1867

LITTLE Rosy's voyage round the world. . . . Adapted from the French of P. J. Stahl [Pierre Jules Hetzel]. 8vo. [*Brit Mus.*] London, 1869

LITTLE Saint Hilary. By Barbara Yechton [Lyda Farrington Krausé]. 8vo. New York, 1893

LITTLE Serena in a strange land. By the author of *Christie Redfern's troubles* [Margaret Murray Robertson]. 8vo. [*Brit. Mus.*] London, 1881

LITTLE (a) ship. By "Taffrail [Henry Taprell Dorling]. 8vo. Pp. vi. 337. [*Brit. Mus.*] London, 1919

LITTLE Sister Snow. By the author of *The lady of the decoration* [F. Little]. 8vo. Pp. 114. [*Brit. Mus.*] London, 1911

LITTLE (a) sister to the wilderness. [A tale.] By Lilian Bell [Mrs A. H. Bogue]. 8vo. Pp. x. 186. London, 1895

LITTLE Sisters of Pity. The dunce of the village. Christina's opportunities [and other stories]. By Ismay Thorn [Edith Caroline Pollock]. 8vo. Pp. 126. London [1892]

LITTLE (the) soldier. By Rosalie Gray [Mrs D. H. Mann]. 8vo. [Kirk's *Supp.*] New York, 1880

LITTLE star; and other poems. By A. M. W. [Miss A. M. Wright]. 8vo. [O'Donoghue's *Poets of Ireland.*] Bath, 1864

LITTLE (the) step-daughter. [A tale.] By the author of *The atelier du Lys* [Margaret Roberts]. 8vo. Pp. 265. [*Brit. Mus.*] London [1887]

LITTLE stories about women. By George Fleming [Julia Constance Fletcher]. 8vo. Pp. 244. [*Brit. Mus.*] London, 1897

LITTLE Sunshine; a tale for very young children. By the author of *A trap to catch a sunbeam*, etc. [Mrs Matilda Anne Mackarness]. 8vo. Pp. vi. 72. London, 1861

LITTLE Sunshine's holiday; a picture from life. By the author of *John Halifax, Gentleman* [Dinah Maria Mulock, later Mrs Craik]. Second edition. 8vo. Pp. 277. London, 1871

LITTLE (a) thing. By Nellie Graham [Mrs Annie Dunning, *née* Ketchum]. 12mo. [Haynes' *Pseud.*] Philadelphia, 1868

LITTLE things. [By Henrietta Wilson.] Thirteenth thousand. 12mo. [*Brit. Mus.*] Edinburgh, 1852

LITTLE threads; or, tangle-thread, silver thread, and golden thread. By the author of *Little Susy* [Mrs Elizabeth Prentiss *née* Payson]. 8vo. [Kirk's *Supp.*] London, 1864

LITTLE Tich; a book of travels and wanderings. By Little Tich [Harry Ralph]. 8vo. Pp. 135. [*Brit. Mus.*] London, 1911

LITTLE Tom; or, the boy that fought a good fight. [Signed: G. J. F. *i.e.* George Jarvis Foster.] 12mo. [*Brit. Mus.*] London, 1871

LITTLE Tommy. [A tale.] By Huldah Herrick [Miss Sarah Endicott Ober]. 8vo. Boston, 1884

LITTLE Tommy; a remarkable instance of the teaching of the Holy Spirit. [By Sarah Bass, afterwards Mrs Thompson.] 12mo. [Smith's *Cat. of Friends' Books*, i. 203.] Brighton, 1856

LITTLE Tommy Tucker. By Susan Coolidge [Sarah C. Woolsey]. 12mo. [Kirk's *Supp.*] Boston, 1900

LITTLE Toss. By Captain Carnes [M. J. Cummings]. 8vo. [Cushing's *Init. and Pseud.* i. 50.] Boston, 1872

LITTLE (a) tour in Ireland; being a visit to Dublin, Galway, Connamara, Athlone, Limerick, Killarney, Glengarriff, Cork, etc. By an Oxonian [Samuel Reynolds Hole]. With illustrations by John Leech. 8vo. Pp. viii. 220. [*Brit. Mus.*] London, 1859

LITTLE (the) traveller. . . . By the editor of *The Christmas Tree* [George Frederick Pardon]. 8vo. [*Brit. Mus.*] London, 1857

LITTLE (a) treatise of baile and mainprize. Written by E. C., Knight [Sir Edward Coke], and now published for the general good. Second edition. 4to. [*Cat. Lond. Inst.* ii. 132.] London, 1637

LITTLE (a) treatise vppon the firste verse of the 122 Psalm; stirring vp vnto carefull desiring & dutifull labouring for true Church gouernement. By R. H. [Robert Harrison]. 8vo. B.L. No pagination. [*Bodl.*] N.P. 1583

LITTLE Tu'penny. By the author of *John Herring* [Rev. Sabine Baring-Gould]. 8vo. [*Brit. Mus.*] London, 1887

LITTLE Turning-aside. By Barbara Yechton [Lyda Farrington Krausé]. 8vo. New York, 1898

LITTLE (the) vanities of Mrs Whittaker; a novel. By John Strange Winter [Mrs Henrietta E. V. Stannard, *née* Palmer]. 8vo. Pp. vi. 299. [*Lit. Year Book.*] London, 1904

LITTLE (the) vesper-book. . . . By a priest of the congregation of the most holy Redeemer [Rev. J. H. Cornell]. 12mo. [Cushing's *Init. and Pseud.* i. 240.] Baltimore, 1860

LITTLE village folk. By A. B. Romney [A. Beatrice Rambaut]. 8vo. Pp. 224. [*Lond. Lib. Cat.*] London, 1899

LITTLE walks in London. By Yveling Rambaud [Frédéric Gilbert]. Drawings by John Leech. 8vo. Pp. xvii. 57. [*Lib. Jour.* iv. 99.] London, 1875

LITTLE (the) water-cress sellers. [By Sarah Maria Fry.] 12mo. [*Brit. Mus.*] London [1854]

LITTLE (the) white cot. By Roselinda [Rose C. King, later Mrs White]. 12mo. [Cushing's *Init. and Pseud.* i. 253.] Boston, 1872

LITTLE women; a story for girls. By the author of *Good wives*, etc. [Louisa May Alcott]. 8vo. Pp. iv. 283. [*Brit. Mus.*] London [1871]

LITTLE (a) worldling. By L. L. Worth [Mrs Mary Wolcott Ellsworth]. 8vo. [Cushing's *Init. and Pseud.* i. 297.] New York, 1890

LITTLECOTE. [By Vernon Watney.] Second edition. 4to. [*Lond. Lib. Cat.*] [Private print] 1900

LITURGIA domestica; or, services for every morning and evening of the week from the Book of Common Prayer, for the use of families. To which are appended sentences, prayers, and hymns for the commemoration of the seasons of the Church. . . . [Arranged by Arthur H. D. Acland, M.A.] 12mo. Pp. xv. 226. [*Brit. Mus.*] Oxford, 1840

LITURGICAL (the) Considerator considered; or, a brief view of Dr Gauden's Considerations touching the Liturgy of the Church of England; wherein the reasons by him produced for imposing the said Liturgy upon all, are found to be so weak, his defence of things offensive in it so slight, the arguments against the Liturgy, by himself afforded, are so strong, that some, who upon his Majesties Declaration did incline to the Liturgy, are now further from it, by reading his wordy discourse about it. The second edition. By G. F. [Giles Firmin], as firm and loyal a subject to His Majesty, as the Considerator is. 4to. Pp. 24, 39. [*Brit. Mus.*] London, 1661

LITURGICAL (a) discourse of the holy sacrifice of the Mass. . . . Collected by A. F., the least of Friar Minors [Richard Angelus Mason]. 8vo. [Gillow's *Bibl. Dict.*] N.P. 1670

LITURGICAL (the) discourse of the holy sacrifice of the Masse, by omission of controversial questions, abridged. . . . By A. F. the author [Richard Angelus Mason, O.S.F.]. 12mo. Pp. 424. N.P. 1675

Another edition of this Abridgment was published in 1768 as "Holy altar and sacrifice explained. . . ."

LITURGY and loyalty asserted and recommended in two sermons preach'd on the 13th of May, 1711. By T. R. [Thomas Rattray, afterwards Bishop of Edinburgh]. 12mo. Pp. 56. [*New Coll. Lib.*] N.P. 1711

LITURGY (the) and other divine offices of the [Catholic Apostolic, or Irvingite] Church. [Mainly prepared by John Bate Cardale, S.S.C.] 8vo. Pp. 18. 374. [Edinburgh] 1861

LITURGY (the) [of the Church of England] catechetically explained. . . . By E. A. M. [Mrs E. A. Maddock?]. 12mo. 3 vols. [*Brit. Mus.*] Winchester, 1839-40

LITURGY (a), collected principally from the [English] Book of Common Prayer, for the use of the First Episcopal Church in Boston, together with the Psalter or Psalms of David. [By James Freeman, D.D.] 4to. [Evans' *Amer. Bibl.* vol. 6, p. 344.] Boston, 1785

This work was really prepared for Unitarian use.

LITURGY compiled from the [English] Book of Common Prayer, reformed according to the plan of the late Dr Samuel Clarke [by Theophilus Lindsey]; together with a collection of psalms and hymns, for public worship. [By Thomas Porter, Unitarian minister.] 12mo. Pp. iv. 106, 213, viii. Plymouth, 1791

LITURGY (the) explained (in question and answer), so far as it is used in the morning and evening services of the Lord's Day: compiled from several authors for the use of schools. [By —— Howes.] 12mo. Pp. 28. [*Bodl.*] Yarmouth, N.D.

LITURGY (a) for the use of the [Unitarian] Mint-Meeting in Exeter. [By Joseph Bretland.] 8vo. Pp. 192. [*Brit. Mus.*] Exeter, 1792

LITURGY (the) in Rome; Feasts and functions of the Church; the ceremonies of Holy Week. By M. A. R. T. [Mildred A. R. Tuker]. 8vo. [*Brit. Mus.*] London, 1897

LITURGY (the) of the ancients represented, as near as well may be, in English forms; with a preface concerning the restitution of the most solemn part of the Christian worship in the Holy Eucharist to its integrity and just frequency of celebration. [By Rev. Edward Stephens, sometime barrister-at-law.] 4to. Pp. 24. [*Brit. Mus.*] London, 1696

LITURGY (the) of the Church of England, a manual of Christian doctrine and spiritual devotion; a sermon extracted from the *Christian Observer* for July 1844. [By Thomas Hartwell Horne.] 8vo. London, 1844

From a list of his works appended to the *Reminiscences*.

LITURGY (the) of the Church of England illustrated, with its history from the period of its compilation. By the author of the *History of the Reformation in Scotland* [William Sime]. 12mo. Edinburgh, 1838

LITURGY (the) of the Church of England, in its ordinary service, reduced nearer to the standard of Scripture; to which are prefixed, reasons for the proposed alterations. . . . Revised and published by the author of the *Appeal to the common sense of all Christian people*, etc. [William Hopkins, B.A.]. 12mo. Pp. xii. 116. [*Brit. Mus.*] London, 1763

LITURGY (a) on the universal principles of religion and morality. [By Rev. David Williams.] 8vo. Pp. xii. 121. [*Brit. Mus.*] London, 1776

LIVE boys in the Black Hills; or, the young Texan gold-hunters. By Arthur Morecamp [Thomas Pilgrim]. 8vo. [Cushing's *Init. and Pseud.* i. 198.] Boston, 1880

LIVE boys; or, Charley and Nasho in Texas. . . . By Arthur Morecamp [Thomas Pilgrim]. 8vo. Pp. 308. [*Lib. Journ.* iv. 136.] Boston, 1879

"LIVE soberly"; a sermon preached to the First Church in Brookline. By the pastor [Frederick Henry Hedge]. 8vo. Boston, 1867

LIVE (a) woman in the mines; a play. By the Old Block [Alonzo Delano]. 8vo. [Cushing's *Init. and Pseud.* i. 210.] New York, 1857

LIVELY (the) oracles given to us; or, the Christian's birth-right and duty, in the custody and use of the Holy Scripture. By the author of *The whole duty of man* [Richard Allestree, D.D.]. Third edition. 8vo. Oxford, 1679

See note to "The art of contentment."

LIVERPOOL a few years since. By an old stager [Rev. James Aspinall, M.A.]. 8vo. Liverpool, 1852

LIVERPOOL (the) magistrates, and the open licensing system. [By Thomas Chilton.] 12mo. Liverpool, 1878

LIVERY (the) rake, and country lass; an opera, as it is perform'd by the company of comedians of his majesty's revels, at the new theatre in the Hay-market. [By Edward Phillips.] With the musick prefix'd to each song. 8vo. Pp. 35. [*D. N. B.* vol. 45, p. 199.] London, 1733

LIVES and characters of illustrious persons who died in the years 1711, 12, 13, 14 and 15. [Generally attributed to John Le Neve.] 8vo. 3 vols. [Lowndes' *Bibl. Man.* p. 1372.] London, 1713-14

LIVES (the) and characters of the English dramatick poets; also an exact account of all the plays that were ever yet printed in the English tongue . . . with remarks and observations on most of the said plays. First begun by Mr [Gerard] Langbain, improv'd and continued down to this time, by a careful hand [Charles Gildon]. 8vo. Pp. 182. London, 1699

LIVES and legends of the English Bishops and Kings, mediæval monks, and other later saints. By N. D'Anvers [Nancy Meugens, later Mrs Nancy Bell]. 4to. [*Brit. Mus.*] London, 1904

LIVES I have known. [By Annie Umbers.] 8vo. London, 1911

LIVES in a Lowland parish. [By Charles Edward Green, publisher.] 4to. Pp. 118. [*In memoriam notice*, by Lord Guthrie.] Edinburgh, 1906

LIVES made sublime by faith and works. By the author of *Doing good; or, the Christian in walks of usefulness* [Rev. Robert Steel]. 8vo. Pp. 328. [*Brit. Mus.*] London [1862]

Other editions have the author's name.

LIVES of Adam Wallace and Walter Mill, martyrs, with an essay on the establishment of the Scottish reformation. By the author of the *Life of George Wishart* [John Parker Lawson]. 12mo. Pp. xvi. 272. Edinburgh, 1827

LIVES (the) of alchemystical philosophers; with a critical catalogue of books in occult chemistry, and a selection of the most celebrated treatises on the theory and practice of the Hermetic art. [By Francis Barrett.] 8vo. Pp. iv. 384, ii. [Gardner's *Roscicrucian Books*, p. 9.] London, 1815

See, below, the title of another edition (1814), "The lives of the adepts in alchemystical philosophy. . . ."

LIVES (the) of all the Roman emperors, being exactly collected from Iulius Cæsar, unto the now reigning Ferdinand the Second; with their births, governments, remarkable actions, & deaths. [By Richard Brathwayt.] 12mo. Pp. 384. London, 1636

The epistle dedicatory is signed: R. B.

LIVES of British physicians. [By William Macmichael.] 12mo. Pp. vi. 341. [*Brit. Mus.*] London, 1830

LIVES of certain Fathers of the Church in the fourth century; for the instruction of the young. [By Henrietta Louisa Farrer, later Mrs Sidney Lear.] Edited by the Rev. Wm. J. E. Bennett, M.A. 8vo. 2 vols. London, 1847-50

LIVES (the) of Cleopatra and Octavia. By the author of *David Simple* [Sarah Fielding]. 4to. [Watt's *Bibl. Brit.*] London, 1757

LIVES (the) of eminent Conservative statesmen. By Mark Rochester [William Charles Mark Kent]. 8vo. Pp. 264. [*Brit. Mus.*] London, 1866

A later edition of "The Derby Ministry. . . ." (1859).

LIVES of eminent persons; consisting of Galileo [by J. Drinkwater Bethune], Kepler [by the same], Newton [translated and adapted from the French of Biot by Sir Howard Elphinstone], Mahomet [by John Arthur Roebuck, M.P.], Wolsey [by Mrs A. E. Thomson], Sir E. Coke [by Ed. Plunkett Burke], Lord Somers [by David Jardine], Caxton [by —— Stephenson], Blake [by John Gorton], Adam Smith [by William Draper], Niebuhr [by Mrs Austen], Sir C. Wren [by Henry Bellenden Ker], and Michael Angelo [by Thomas Roscoe]. 8vo. [*W.*] London, 1833

LIVES of good servants. By the author of *Mary Powell* [Anne Manning, later Mrs Rathbone]. 8vo. Pp. viii. 148. [*Brit. Mus.*] London, 1857

LIVES (the) of Holy Confessors, translated from the Italian of F. Peter Maffaeus [by Henry Hawkins, S.J., whose initials, "H. H." are given]. 4to. [Oliver's *Collections;* Sommervogel's *Dictionnaire.*] Paris, 1636

LIVES (the) of Jonathan and Virginia [in verse]. By Boswell [W. B. Johnson, of Virginia]. 12mo. Pp. 120. [Cushing's *Init. and Pseud.* i. 38.] Philadelphia, 1873

LIVES (the) of Mrs Ann H. Judson, Mrs Sarah B. Judson, and Mrs Emily C. Judson, missionaries in Burmah. . . . By Fanny Forester [Mrs Emily Chubbuck Judson]. 8vo. [*Calc. Imp. Lib.*] London, 1860

LIVES of St Alphonsus Liguori, St Francis de Girolamo, St John Joseph of the Cross, St Pacificus of San Severino, and St Veronica Giuliani; whose canonization took place on Trinity Sunday, May 26, 1839. [By Nicholas Wiseman, D.D.] 12mo. [Mendham's *Collection*, p. 330.] London, 1839

LIVES (the) of St John the Baptist, the twelve Apostles, and of St Paul. Adapted for the use of the young. By a lady [Ann Ritchie, afterwards wife of Dr John Smythe Memes]. 12mo. Pp. 74. [*And. Jervise.*] Edinburgh, 1824

LIVES (the) of saints; collected from authentick records of Church history; with a full account of the other festivals throughout the year. . . . [By Charles Fell, D.D.] 4to. 4 vols. [*D. N. B.* vol. 18, p. 292.] London, 1729

Incorrectly attributed to Bishop Challoner. Another edition was published in 1750.

LIVES (the) of saints, gathered out of . . . Peter Ribadaneyra . . . D. Alfonsus Villegas, and other authenticall authors. Translated out of Italian into English, and conferred with the Spanish by W. and E. Kin, B. [W. and Edward Kinsman, brothers]. 8vo. 2 vols. [Gillow's *Bibl. Dict.*] Doway, 1610-14

The following is a different edition.

LIVES (the) of saints, with other feasts of the Roman Calendar: written in Spanish by the Rev. Fr. Peter Ribadaneyra, priest of the Society of Jesus, and translated into English by W. P. [Hon. William Petre], Esquire. Fol. Pp. 1036. [Gillow's *Bibl. Dict.* vol. 5, p. 297.] St Omers, 1669

Another edition "corrected and amended" [by Thomas Coxon] was published in London in 1720.

LIVES of Scottish poets, by the Society of Ancient Scots, re-established A. D. 1770. [By Joseph Robertson.] 12mo. 3 vols. [*Nat. Lib. of Scot.*] London, 1821-2

LIVES (the) of the adepts in alchemystical philosophy, with a critical catalogue of the books in this science. . . . [By Francis Barrett.] 8vo. London, 1814

The edition published in 1815 bears a slightly different title: "The lives of alchemystical philosophers. . . ." See above.

LIVES of the British Reformers, from Wicliffe to Fox. [By George Stokes.] 8vo. London [1853]

This work was afterwards amalgamated with "The Lollards."

LIVES (the) of the English Bishops from the Restauration to the Revolution; with an account of the most remarkable publick transactions in which they were concern'd: containing the lives of the following prelates, viz. Dr Juxon, Dr Sheldon, Dr Sandcroft, Dr Glemham, Dr Griffith, Dr Barrow, Dr Lloyd, Dr Morgan, Dr Lloyd, Dr Creighton, Dr Ken, Dr Ironside, Dr Goulston, Dr Brideoake, Dr Carleton, etc. etc. Design'd to vindicate them from the aspersions of the Bishops Burnet, Kennet, and others; from the dreams of Rapin, and the vile history of the Stuarts. [By Nathaniel Salmon, LL.B., a Non-juror.] 8vo. [*N. and Q.* 1854, p. 175.] London, 1733

LIVES of the most eminent literary and scientific men of France. [By Mrs Mary W. Shelley.] 8vo. 2 vols. London, 1838-9

LIVES of the most eminent literary and scientific men of Great Britain. [By Samuel Astley Dunham, LL.D.] 8vo. 3 vols. London, 1836-8

Lardner's *Cabinet Cyclopædia*, Nos. 84, 93, and 106.

LIVES of the most eminent literary and scientific men of Italy, Spain, and Portugal. [By Sir David Brewster, Mrs Mary W. Shelley, James Montgomery, and others.] 12mo. 2 vols. [*W.*] London, 1835-7

Lardner's *Cabinet Cyclopædia.*

LIVES (the) of the most eminent modern painters who have lived since or were omitted by Mons. De Piles. By J. B. [James Burgess]. 8vo. [Lowndes' *Bibl. Man.* p. 1865.] London, 1754

LIVES (the) of the poets of Great Britain and Ireland to the time of Dean Swift, compiled from ample materials scattered in a variety of books. . . . In four [five] volumes. By Mr [Theophilus] Cibber. [Really by Robert Shiells and others.] 12mo. [*Brit. Mus.; D.N.B.* vol. 10, p. 363.] London, 1753

Cibber revised the whole work, which includes a few lives by himself.

LIVES of the poets-laureate. By Vaughan Dayrell [Wiltshire Stanton Austin, and J. Ralph]. 8vo. London, 1853

LIVES (the) of the Right Hon. Francis North, Baron Guilford (*sic*), Lord Keeper of the Great Seal under King Charles II. and King James II.; the Hon. Sir Dudley North, Commissioner of the Customs and afterwards of the Treasury to King Charles II.; and the Hon. and Rev. Dr John North, Master of Trinity College Cambridge, and Clerk of the Closet to King Charles II. By the Hon. Roger North. A new edition, with notes and illustrations, historical and biographical [by H. Roscoe]. 8vo. 3 vols. [*W.*] London, 1826

LIVES (the) of the three Normans, Kings of England: William the First, William the Second, and Henrie the First. Written by J. H. [John Hayward]. . . . 4to. Pp. 314. [*Manch. Free Lib.*] London, 1613

LIVES (the) of those eminent antiquaries John Leland, Thomas Hearne, and Anthony à Wood; with an authentick account of their respective writings and publications, from original papers. . . . [Edited and partly written by William Huddesford, keeper of the Ashmolean Library.] 8vo. 2 vols. [*Upcott*, ii. 1090.] Oxford, 1772

LIVES (the) of two cats; from the French of Pierre Loti [Louis M. J. Viaud]. 8vo. [*Lond. Lib. Cat.*] London, 1902

LIVES that came to nothing. By John Garrett Leigh [John Lee]. 8vo. Pp. 128. [*Brit. Mus.*] London, 1895

LIVING (the) among the dead; a story founded on facts. By the author of *Blenham*, etc. [Mrs Ellen Epps, *née* Elliott]. 8vo. [*Brit. Mus.*] London, 1860

LIVING and serving. By Holme Lee [Harriet Parr]. 8vo. 3 vols. [*Lond. Lib. Cat.*] London, 1883

LIVING (the) and the dead. By a country curate [Erskine Neale, vicar of Exning, Newmarket]. 12mo. 2 series. London, 1827-9

LIVING (a) epitaph. [A novel.] By George Colmore [Gertrude Colmore Dunn, later Mrs Baillie Weaver]. 8vo. Pp. 276. [*Brit. Mus.*] London, 1890

LIVING (the) female writers of the South [United States]. Edited by the author of *Southland writers* [Ida Raymond, *i.e.* Mary T. Tardy]. 8vo. [Cushing's *Init. and Pseud.* i. 248.] Philadelphia, 1872

LIVING jewels; diversities of Christian character suggested by precious stones, with biographical examples. By A. L. O. E. [Charlotte M. Tucker]. 8vo. Pp. vii. 1. 188. London, 1868

LIVING on a little while. By Caroline French Benton [Caroline Benedict Burrell]. 8vo. [*Amer. Cat.*] Boston, 1908

LIVING or dead; a novel. By Hugh Conway [Frederick John Fargus]. 8vo. 3 vols. [*Lit. Year Book.*] London, 1886

LIVING Paris and France; a guide to manners, monuments . . . and the life of the people; and a handbook for travellers. By Alb [Mrs Richard Whiteing]. 8vo. Pp. xvi. 464. [*Camb. Univ. Lib.*] London, 1886

LIVING (a) picture of London, for 1828, and stranger's guide through the streets of the metropolis; shewing the frauds, the arts, the snares and wiles of all descriptions of rogues that every where abound; with suitable admonitions, precautions, and advice how to avoid or defeat their attempts. . . . By Jon Bee, Esq. [John Badcock] author of *A dictionary of the varieties of life*, etc. 12mo. Pp. x. 312. [*Bodl.*] London, N.D.

LIVING (the) questions of the age. By an American citizen [James Barr Walker]. 12mo. [*Brit. Mus.*] Philadelphia, 1869

LIVING (the) remnant; and other Quaker tales. By K. K. K. [F. O'Brien]. 8vo. Pp. 168. London, 1900

LIVING too fast. By Oliver Optic [William T. Adams]. 8vo. Pp. 250. [Kirk's *Supp.*] Boston, 1876

LIVING waters. By A. L. W. [Alice L. Williams]. 8vo. Boston, 1889

LIVING (the) Word; or, Bible truths and lessons. By J. C. P. [James C. Parsons]. 8vo. [Cushing's *Init. and Pseud.* i. 222.] Boston, 1872

LIVING words; addresses, etc. Edited by J. F. G. [J. F. Govan]. 4to. Edinburgh, 1895

LIVINGSTONES (the); a story of real life. [By Mrs H. E. Dalrymple.] 8vo. 3 vols. [*Camb. Univ. Lib.*] London, 1851

LIVONIAN tales. The disponent. The wolves. The Jewess. By the author of *Letters from the Baltic* [Elizabeth Rigby, afterwards Lady Eastlake]. 8vo. Pp. v. 178. [*Brit. Mus.*] London, 1846

LIVRE des Anglois; or, register of the English Church at Geneva under the pastoral care of Knox and Goodman, 1555-9. [Edited by Prof. Alex. F. Mitchell.] 8vo. [*New Coll. Lib.*] [Edinburgh, 1885]

Signed: A. F. M.

LIZ'S shepherd. [A story.] By the author of *A Fellow of Trinity* [Mrs Frances Marshall]. 8vo. [*Brit. Mus.*] London, 1891

LIZZIE Leigh; and other tales. By the author of *Mary Barton* [Mrs Elizabeth C. Gaskell]. 8vo. [*Brit. Mus.*] London, 1855

LIZZIE Weston's mission. By A. L. W. [Anna Letitia Waring]. 8vo. [*Brit. Mus.*] Boston [1864]

LLANDAFF; a poem. [By James Mullin, M.D.] 8vo. [O'Donoghue's *Poets of Ireland.*] Cardiff [1889?]

LLANDRINDOD legends and lyrics. By "Ladyloft" [John Hutchinson]. 8vo. [*Lit. Year Book.*] Brecon, 1895

LLEWELLEN; or, the vale of Plinlimmon. [By Mrs Grace Buchanan Stevens.] 12mo. 3 vols. [*Brit. Mus.*] Edinburgh, 1818

LLOYD'S encyclopædic dictionary. [By Rev. Robert Hunter, LL.D.] 8vo. 7 vols. [*D. N. B.* First Supp. vol. 3, p. 15.] London, 1895

First issued in 1889 as "An encyclopædic dictionary."

LOAD (the) of chips. By H. N. W. B. [Mrs Harriet Newell Baker, *née* Woods]. 8vo. [Kirk's *Supp.*] Boston, 1870

LOANS by private individuals of Great Britain to foreign states, shewn to be entitled to protection, or indemnity, by the principles on which states are founded, laid down by public jurists, and by the law of the land. [By Rev. T. J. Bramly.] 8vo. Pp. iv. 106. London, 1845

LOCAL antiquarian notes; being sketches of an ancient Druidical circle near Bolton, with extracts and remarks on the customs of the old English Druids. . . . [By Joseph D. Greenhalgh.] 8vo. Pp. 34. [Sparkes' *Bolton Bibl.*] Bolton, 1874

LOCAL guide of British Guiana. . . . [By Richard Hildreth.] 8vo. Pp. clvi. 828. [Sabin's *Dictionary.*] Demarary, 1843

LOCAL humbugs. By the Baron of Leys [W. K. Leask]. 8vo. [Aberdeen, 1884]

LOCAL issues; joint stock banks and Bank of England notes, &c. contrasted. By a merchant [—— Breed, of Liverpool]. 8vo. Pp. 16. London, 1834

LOCAL (a) lion; a story of a false estimate. By Austin Clare [Miss W. M. James]. 8vo. Pp. 384. [*Lond. Lib. Cat.*] London, 1891

LOCAL (the) loans of England and Wales. [By Cornelius Neale Dalton, M.A.] 8vo. London, 1883

LOCAL loiterings and visits in the vicinity of Boston [U.S.A.]. By a looker-on [John Dix Ross]. 12mo. [*Brit. Mus.*] Boston, 1846

LOCAL (the) rights and interests of farm labourers. By Equitas [John Theodore Dodd, M.A.]. 8vo. Leamington [1875]

LOCAL (the) tradesman; a multum in parvo on men and things written and compiled by the author of *British valour* [Elijah J. S. Norton]. 4to. [*Brit. Mus.*] London [1888]

LOCH Etive and the sons of Uisnach. [By Robert Angus Smith, Ph.D.] 8vo. Pp. xi. 376. London, 1879

LOCH (the) Leven angler. By an Ex-President of the Kinross-shire Fishing Club [Rev. Robert Burns Begg]. 12mo. Kinross, 1874

LOCHANDHU; a tale of the eighteenth century. [By Sir Thomas Dick Lauder, Bart.] 12mo. 3 vols. Edinburgh, 1825

The introductory address is signed: Charles Montague Montgomery.

LOCHENBRECK [in Kirkcudbright. By J. C. Mackenzie]. 12mo. Castle Douglas, 1881

LOCHIEL; or, the field of Culloden; a romance. [By David Carey.] 8vo. 3 vols. [P. J. Anderson's *Inverness Bibl.* p. 156.] London, 1820

LOCHLÊRE; a poem [imitating Early English. By W. Marshall]. 8vo. [*Brit. Mus.*] London, 1877

LOCHLOMOND (the) expedition, 1715; reprinted and illustrated with original documents [by James Dennistoun, advocate]. 8vo. Pp. vi. 62. Glasgow, 1834

The original tract is in the National Library of Scotland, and consists of 14 pages, including the title, which is as follows:—The Loch-Lomond expedition with some short reflections on the Perth manifesto . . . Glasgow, Printed 1715. It is dated, "Dumbarton, October 15, 1715." The author's name is unknown. The copy is believed to be unique.

LOCKE and Sydenham. [By John Brown, M.D.] 8vo. Pp. 35. Edinburgh, 1835

LOCOMOTIVE sketches. [By William Bromwell.] 8vo. Philadelphia, 1854

LOCUST'S (the) years. [A novel.] By M. Hamilton [Mrs Churchill Luck]. 8vo. Pp. 254. [*Lond. Lib. Cat.*] London, 1919

LODGE (a) in the wilderness. [By John Buchan, M.A.] 8vo. [*Lond. Lib. Cat.*] Edinburgh, 1906

LODORE. By the author of *Frankenstein* [Mary W. Shelley]. 12mo. 3 vols. [Courtney's *Secrets*, p. 60.] London, 1835

LOG (the) cabin; or, the world before you. [A tale.] By the author of *Three experiments of living.* [Mrs Hannah F. Lee]. 12mo. [*Brit. Mus.*] London, 1844

LOG (the) of a Privateersman. [A naval romance.] By Harry Collingwood [William J. C. Lancaster]. 8vo. [*Lond. Lib. Cat.*] London, 1896

LOG (the) of Commodore Rollingpin. [By John Hanson Carter.] 8vo. [Cushing's *Init. and Pseud.* i. 253.] New York, 1874

LOG (the) of the "Flying Fish." By Harry Collingwood [William J. C. Lancaster]. 8vo. [*Lond. Lib. Cat.*] London, 1887

LOG (the) of the scarlet house. By Kythe Wylwynne [Miss M. E. F. Hyland]. 8vo. London, 1905

LOG (the) of the Water Lily (four-oared Thames gig) during a rowing excursion on the Rhine, and other streams of Germany. By an Oxford man and a Wykehamist [Robert Blackford Mansfield]. 8vo. Pp. iv. 59. London, 1852

LOGAN; a family history. [By John Neal.] 8vo. Philadelphia, 1822

LOGAN'S loyalty. [A novel.] By Sarah Tytler [Henrietta Keddie]. 8vo. [*Lit. Year Book.*] London, 1900

LOGIC for the million; a familiar exposition of the art of reasoning. By a Fellow of the Royal Society [James William Gilbart, F.R.S.]. 12mo. [*Camb. Univ. Lib.*] London, 1851

Later editions give the author's name.

LOGICK; or, the art of thinking; in which, besides the common, are contained many excellent new rules for directing reason and acquiring of judgment. In four parts. . . . [By Antoine Arnauld and Pierre Nicole.] Printed many times in French and Latin, and now, for publick good, translated by several hands. 8vo. [Arber's *Term Cat.* ii. 618.] London, 1685

LOGICK (the) primer; some logical notions to initiate the Indians in the knowledge of the rule of reason, especially for the instruction of such as are teachers among them. Composed by J. E. [John Eliot] for the use of the praying Indians. 12mo. [*Brit. Mus.*] [Cambridge, Mass.?] 1672

LOGIC Town. [A novel.] By Sarah Tytler [Henrietta Keddie]. 8vo. London, 1887

ΛΟΓΟΙ εὔκαιροι; essayes and observations, theologicall and morall, wherein many of the humours and diseases of the age are discovered. . . . By a student of theologie [Rev. William Master, M.A.]. [*D. N. B.* vol. 37, p. 24.] London, 1654

ΛΟΓΟΜΑΧΙΑ; or, the conquest of eloquence; containing two witty orations as they may be read in Ovid's Metamorphoses, Lib. XIII. By P. K. [Patrik Ker]. 12mo. [*Brit. Mus.*] London, 1689

ΛΟΓΟΥ θρησκεία; or, a seasonable recommendation and defence of reason in the affairs of religion; against infidelity, scepticism, and fanaticisms of all sorts. [By Joseph Glanvill.] 4to. Pp. 36. [*Bodl.*] London, 1670

LOGROÑO; a metric drama, in two acts [and in verse]. . . . By Frederick Cerny [Frederick Guthrie, Ph.D.]. 8vo. London, 1877

LOHENGRIN retold from Wagner. By Norley Chester [Emily Underdown]. 8vo. [*Lond. Lib. Cat.*] London, 1892

LOIS Weedon husbandry as it is. By the author of *A word in season to the farmer* [Rev. Samuel Smith, M.A.]. 8vo. [Boase's *Mod. Eng. Biog.* vol vi. col. 585.] London, 1856

LOITERER (the); a periodical work. [Conducted by James Austen, St John's College, Oxford, who was also the chief contributor.] 8vo. 2 vols. [Lowndes' *Bibl. Man.* p. 1385.] Oxford, 1790

LOITERINGS among the lakes of Cumberland and Westmoreland. By the author of *Wanderings in the Isle of Wight* [George Mogridge]. 12mo. [*Brit. Mus.*] London [1849]

LOITERINGS in pleasant paths. . . . By Marion Harland [Mary Virginia Hawes, later Mrs Terhune]. 8vo. Pp. vii. 435. [Kirk's *Supp.*] New York, 1880

LOLLARDS (the); a tale, founded upon the persecutions which marked the early part of the fifteenth century. By the author of *The witch-finder*, etc. [Thomas Gaspey]. 8vo. Pp. viii. 399. [*Camb. Univ. Lib.*] London [1859]

LOLLARDS (the); or, some account of the witnesses for the truth in Great Britain, from A.D. 1400 to A.D. 1546: with a brief notice of events connected with the early history of the Reformation. [By George Stokes.] 8vo. Pp. xii. 360. London [1880]

This work was afterwards amalgamated with "Lives of the British Reformers," by the same author.

LOMBARD (a) street mystery; a novel. By Muirhead Robertson [Henry Johnson]. 8vo. London, 1888

LOMOND (the) hills; a poem. [By —— Brunton.] 12mo. [Mitchell and Cash's *Scot. Top.*] Cupar-Fife, 1877

Attributed also to G. Gulland.

LONDINI quod reliqvvm; or, Londons remains: in Latin and English. [By Simon Ford, D.D., vicar of Old Swinford, Worcestershire.] 4to. Pp. 16. [*Bodl.*] London, 1667

LONDINUM triumphans; or, an historical account of the grand influence the actions of the City of London have had upon the affairs of the nation for many ages past: shewing the antiquity, honour, glory and renown of this famous city; the grounds of her rights, privileges and franchises; the foundation of her charter; the improbability of a forfeiture, and impossibility of a legal seizure. . . . [By William Gough.] 8vo. Pp. 373. [*Upcott*, ii. 678.] London, 1682

The dedication is signed: W. G. Some copies have the author's name on the title-page.

LONDON; a poem, in imitation of the third satire of Juvenal. [By Samuel Johnson, LL.D.] Fol. Pp. 19. [Simms' *Bibl. Staff.* p. 251.] London, 1738

Wrongly assigned to Captain Charles Johnson.

LONDON and its eccentricities in the year 2023; or, revelations of the dead alive. By the author of *Boyne Water*, etc. [John Banim]. 8vo. Pp. 376. [*Brit. Mus.*] London, 1845

LONDON and its hospitals; being a short account of ten. . . . [By Beatrice Clugston.] 8vo. [Glasgow] 1866

LONDON; being an accurate history and description of the British metropolis and its neighbourhood, to thirty miles extent, from an actual perambulation. By David Hughson, LL.D. [Dr Edward Pugh]. 8vo. 6 vols. [*Upcott*, ii. 659.] London, 1806

LONDON bigger than old Rome; or, an essay upon old Rome, wherein 'tis plainly demonstrated that its extent did not exceed that of new Rome, against Justus Lipsius, Vossius, and their followers; and that it never was so big as London is now. By a person of quality [—— de Souligné]. 4to. Pp. 12. [*Brit. Mus.*] London, 1701

The author treated the same subject more fully in "A comparison between old Rome . . . and London . . ." (1709), which re-appeared in 1710 as "Old Rome and London compared. . . ."

LONDON (the) citizen exceedingly injured; or, a British inquisition display'd, in an account of the unparallel'd case of a citizen of London, bookseller to the late Queen, who was in a most unjust and arbitrary manner sent on the 22d of March last, 1738, by one Robert Wightman, a mere stranger, to a private mad house. . . . [By Alexander Cruden.] 8vo. Pp. 60. London, 1739

Author's name in the handwriting of Dr David Laing.

LONDON (a) cobweb. [A novel.] By Christian Lys [Percy James Brebner]. 8vo. Pp. 197. [*Brit. Mus.*] London, 1892

LONDON cries and public edifices. By Luke Limner [John Leighton]. 8vo. [Cushing's *Init. and Pseud.* i. 171.] London, 1847

See also "London out of town. . . ."

LONDON (the) distiller. . . . From "The art of distillation." [By John French, M.D.] 4to. London, 1667

LONDON in 1914; its stones and commercial landmarks. [By Herbert Fry.] 8vo. Pp. 270. London, 1914

LONDON in the olden time; or, tales intended to illustrate the manners and superstitions of its inhabitants from the twelfth to the sixteenth century. [By Miss H. Laurence.] 8vo. 2 series. London, 1825

LONDON legends. By Paul Pindar, Gent. [John Yonge Akerman]. 12mo. 2 vols. [*Camb. Univ. Lib.*] London, 1842

In 1853 there appeared an edition with the author's name, and with the title "Legends of Old London."

LONDON medical practice; its sins and shortcomings. . . . [By Samuel Dickson, M.D.] 8vo. [*Brit. Mus.*] London, 1860

LONDON; or, interesting memorials of its rise, progress and present state. By Sholto & Reuben Percy, brothers of the Benedictine monastery, Mont Benger [Thomas Byerley and Joseph Clinton Robinson]. 12mo. 3 vols. [*Brit. Mus.*] London, 1824

LONDON; or, the gift revoked: a fairy tale. [By Alicia Lefanu, granddaughter of Sheridan.] 8vo. [*Gent. Mag.* lxxv. 1, 152.] London, 1805

LONDON out of town; or, the adventures of the Browns by the sea-side. By Luke Limner, Esq. [John Leighton]. 12mo. [Cushing's *Init. and Pseud.* i. 171.] London [1847]

See also "London cries. . . ."

LONDON pageants. I. Accounts of fifty-five royal processions and entertainments. . . . II. A bibliographical list of Lord Mayors' pageants. [By John Gough Nichols, F.S.A.] 8vo. [*Brit. Mus.*] London, 1831

LONDON preachers. By Thornton Wells [T. Williams]. 8vo. [*Lib. Journ.* v. 188.] London, 1879

LONDON pride; a comedy . . . [Signed: A. D. A. *i.e.* A. D. Ainslie.] 8vo. [*Brit. Mus.*] London [1870]

LONDON railways; a contribution to the Parliamentary papers of the session. By a middle-aged citizen [R. Russell]. 8vo. [*Brit. Mus.*] London, 1867

LONDON scenes and London people; anecdotes, reminiscences, and sketches of London City, past and present. By "Aleph" [William Harvey, of Islington]. 8vo. [*Brit. Mus.*] London, 1863

LONDON (the) Spy; for the month of November, 1698. Part I., third edition. By the author of the *Trip to Jamaica* [Edward Ward]. Fol. Pp. 16. London, 1702

Parts 1 to 12 form the first vol.

The second volume consists of 6 parts, 1699 and 1700.

LONDON tales; or, reflective portraits. [By Mrs Regina Maria Roche, *née* Dalton.] 12mo. [*D. N. B.* vol. 49, p. 71.] London, 1814

LONDON (the) Terræ filius; or, the satyrical reformer: being droll reflections on the vices and vanities of both sexes. To be continu'd. By the author of *The London Spy* [Edward Ward]. 8vo. 6 numbers. [*Brit. Mus.*] London, 1707-8

Each number has a separate pagination.

LONDON town; sketches of London life and character. By Marcus Fall [Richard Dowling]. 8vo. 2 vols. [*Camb. Univ. Lib.*] London, 1880

LONDON voices. By Keble Howard [John Keble Bell]. 8vo. Pp. 310. [*Lond. Lib. Cat.*] London, 1913

LONDON (the) way. By Mark Allerton [William Ernest Cameron, LL.B.]. 8vo. [*Brit. Mus.*] London, 1908

LONDONER'S (a) log-book, 1901-1902. By the author of *Collections and recollections* [George William Erskine Russell]. 8vo. Pp. 314. [*Brit. Mus.*] London, 1902

LONDONS charitie stilling the poore mans cry; providing places and provision, by the care of the Corporation appointed by Parliament. By S. H. [Samuel Hartlib]. . . . 4to. London, 1649

LONDONS charity inlarged, stilling the orphans cry, by the liberality of the Parliament in granting two houses, by Act, and giving a thousand pound towards the work for the imployment of the poor, and education of poor children. . . . By S. H. [Samuel Hartlib], a well-wisher to the nations prosperity and the poors comfort. 4to. [*Brit. Mus.; D. N. B.* vol. 25, p. 173.] London, 1650

LONDONS dove; or, a memoriall of the life and death of Maister Robert Dove, citizen and merchant-taylor of London. . . . [By Anthony Nixon.] 4to. [*D. N. B.* vol. 41, p. 75.] London, 1612

LONDON'S gate to the Lord's Table. [By Edward Fisher.] 12mo. [*D. N. B.* vol. 19, p. 56.] London, 1647

Dedication signed: E. F.

LONDON'S glory. . . . By Harry Helicon, Esq. [Joshua West]. 8vo. [*Brit. Mus.*] London, 1789

LONDON'S humourous side. By a cynical citizen [A. Leonard Summers]. 8vo. Putney, 1903

LONDONS ioyfull gratulation and thankfull remembrance for their safeties. Presented to . . . the Earle of Essex and . . . Robert, Earle of Warwicke. [By Thomas Jordan. Verse.] 4to. 4 leaves. [*Christie-Miller Cat.*] London, 1642

LONDONS love, to the royal Prince Henrie, meeting him on the river of Thames, at his return from Richmonde, with a worthie fleete of her cittizens. . . . [By Anthony Munday.] 4to. [*Brit. Mus.*] London, 1610

LONDON'S lure; an anthology in prose and verse. By Helen and Lewis Melville [Helen and Lewis S. Benjamin]. 12mo. [*Brit. Mus.*] London, 1909

LONDON'S peril. By F. M. Allen [Edmund Downey]. 8vo. Pp. 96. [*Lond. Lib. Cat.*] London, 1900

LONDONS resurrection, poetically represented, and humbly presented to his most sacred Majesty. [By Simon Ford, D.D.] 4to. Pp. 22. London, 1669

This is an English translation of "Londini renascentis imago poetica. Ad serenissimum Britanniarum monarcham Carolum II." Londini, 1668. 4to. Both works are by Ford. The author's name in the Bodleian copy is in the handwriting of Richard Gough.

LONDON'S river. By Joseph Conrad [Joseph Conrad Korzeniowski]. 4to. Pp. 18. [*Lit. Year Book.*] London, private print, 1919

Originally printed in the *London Magazine.*

LONDONS triumph. [A description of the Lord Mayor's show.] By T. B. [Thomas Brewer?]. 8vo. [*D. N. B.* vol. 6, p. 296.] London, 1656

LONE (the) cottage; or, "who's the stranger?" A romance. By the author of *The Hebrew maiden, Fatherless Fanny*, etc. [Clara Reeve]. 8vo. [*Brit. Mus.*] London, 1845

LONELINESS and leisure; a record of the thoughts and feelings of advanced life. By the author of *Visiting my relations* [Mary Ann Kelty]. 8vo. Pp. vii. 248. [*Brit. Mus.*] London, 1866

The preface is signed: M. A. K.

LONELY (the) island; a narrative for young people. [By Mrs Julia Cecilia Wilkins, afterwards Stretton.] 8vo. [F. Boase's *Mod. Eng. Biog.* vol. 6, col. 641.] London, 1852

LONELY (a) lassie. By Sarah Tytler [Henrietta Keddie]. 8vo. Pp. 224. London, 1905

LONELY (a) life. [A novel. By Miss —— Veitch.] 8vo. London [1881?]

LONELY (a) maid. By "The Duchess" [Mrs Hungerford, *née* Margaret Hamilton]. 8vo. Pp. 262. [*Brit. Mus.*] London, 1876

LONELY (the) man of the ocean; a tale [in verse]. By the author of *The feast of Belshazzar* [Thomas Wilson, of Adelaide]. 12mo. Adelaide, 1856

LONELY (the) road. By A. E. Jacomb [Agnes E. Jacomb Hood]. 8vo. [*Lit. Year Book.*] London, 1911

LONESOME (a) lassie. By Raymond Jacberns [Georgina I. Selby Ash]. 8vo. Pp. 134. [*Lit. Year Book.*] London, 1902

LONESOME (a) trail. By B. M. Bower [Bertha M. Sinclair]. 8vo. [*Amer. Cat.*] Chicago, 1909

LONEWOOD Corner; a countryman's horizons. By John Halsham [Forrester Scott]. 8vo. London, 1907

LONG ago; a year of child life. By Ellis Gray [Louisa T. Cragin]. 12mo. [Cushing's *Init. and Pseud.* i. 120.] Boston, 1878

LONG ago. [Poems based on the fragments of Sappho.] By Michael Field [Katharine Bradley and Edith E. Cooper]. 8vo. Pp. 132. [*Catholic Who's Who.*] London, 1889

LONG (the) desiderated knowledge of the life and personality of Shakespeare. . . . By Clelia [Charles Downing]. 8vo. Pp. 32. [*Brit. Mus.*] London [1892]

LONG engagements; a tale of the Affghan Rebellion. [By Sir John William Kaye.] 8vo. Pp. 320. [*D. N. B.* vol. 30, p. 253.] London, 1846

LONG (a) history of a certain session of a certain Parliament, in a certain kingdom [*i.e.* Ireland, in 1713. By Dr Richard Helsham and Dr Patrick Delany]. 12mo. Pp. viii. 130. [Dublin?] 1714

Authors' names given in a contemporary hand.

LONG (a) lane. By the author of *Cherry-blossom*, etc. [Catherine March]. 8vo. [*Brit. Mus.*] London [1893]

LONG livers; a curious history of such persons of both sexes who have liv'd several ages and grown young again; with the rare secret of rejuvenescency of Arnold de Villa Nova . . . as how also to prepare the universal medicine. By Eugenius Philalethes, F.R.S. [Robert Samber, who really translated the work from Harouet de Longeville]. 8vo. Pp. lxiv. 199, viii. [*Brit. Mus.*] London, 1722

LONG (a) love; a vacation idyll, and other sketches. By Tom Palatine [Thomas Nash]. 8vo. Pp. 167. Manchester, 1881

LONG (the) pack; a Northumbrian tale, an hundred years old. [By James Hogg.] 12mo. Pp. 24. Newcastle, 1817

LONG (the) Parliament dissolved. [By Denzil, Lord Hollis.] 4to. Pp. 23. [*Bodl.*] N.P. 1676

LONG (the) Parliament revived; or, an act for continuation, and the not dissolving the Long Parliament (call'd by King Charles the First, in the year 1640) but by an Act of Parliament: with undeniable reasons deduced from the said act to prove that that Parliament is not yet dissolved. Also, Mr Will. Prynne his five arguments fully answered: whereby he endeavours to prove it to be dissolved by the king's death, &c. By Tho. Phillips, Gent., a sincere lover of his king and country. [Really by Sir William Drake.] 4to. Pp. 22. [Thomason's *Coll. of Tracts*, ii. 344.] London, 1661

In a note by Wood, it is stated that Drake was impeached for writing the above seditious pamphlet, and that he acknowledged himself to be the author of it. Wood has altered the date to 1660.

LONG resistance and ultimate conversion. [By —— Douglas.] 8vo. Pp. xii. 308. [*Bodl.*] London, 1868

LONG (the) road. By John Oxenham [William Arthur Dunkerley]. 8vo. Pp. 256. [*Lond. Lib. Cat.*] London, 1912

LONG (a) shadow. By B. M. Bower [Bertha M. Sinclair]. 8vo. [*Amer. Cat.*] Chicago, 1909

LONG Tom, otherwise Thomas Long. [A tale in verse. By Frances Mary Sutcliffe.] 8vo. [*Brit. Mus.*] London, 1836

LONG (the) trick. By "Bartimeus" [Lewis Anselm Da Costa Ricci]. 8vo. Pp. 300. [*Lond. Lib. Cat.*] London, 1918

LONG (a) vacation ramble in Norway and Sweden. By X and Y (two unknown quantities) [John Willis Clark, and J. W. Dunning]. 8vo. [Bartholomew's *Camb. Books.*] Cambridge, 1857

LONGBEARD, Lord of London; a romance. [By Charles Mackay, LL.D.] 12mo. 3 vols. [*Nat. Lib. of Scot.*] London, 1841

LONG-BOW (the) of the past; the rifle for the future: addressed to the rising generation of the British Empire. By H. Britannicus [Robert Potts, M.A.]. Second edition, corrected and enlarged. 8vo. Pp. 36. [Bowes' *Camb. Books.*] Cambridge, 1860

LONGFELLOW (the) collector's handbook; a bibliography of first editions. [By W. E. Benjamin, the publisher.] 12mo. Pp. 56. New York, 1885

LONGLEAT. [A novel.] By Elleray Lake [Mrs David Armstrong]. 8vo. 3 vols. London, 1870

LONGSWORD, Earl of Salisbury; an historical romance. [By Thomas Leland, D.D.] 8vo. 2 vols. London, 1762

Hesitatingly ascribed also to Dr John Leland. [*D. N. B.* vol. 33, p. 18, and *Brit. Mus.*]

LONGUS, Daphnis and Chloe; a pastoral novel [translated by Rev. Charles Valentine Le Grice]. 8vo. [Boase and Courtney's *Bibl. Corn.*] Penzance, 1803

LONGWOODS (the) of the Grange. By the author of *Adelaide Lindsay* [Mrs Anne Marsh, later Marsh-Caldwell]. 8vo. 3 vols. London, 1853

LOOK at home; or, a short and easy method with the Roman Catholics. [By Rev. Charles P. Golightly, M.A.] 8vo. [*D. N. B.* vol. 22, p. 100.] Oxford, 1837

"LOOK before you leap." [By Matthew Carey.] 8vo. Philadelphia, 1835

LOOK before you leap; a novel. By Mrs Alexander [Mrs Alexander Hector, *née* Annie French]. Revised edition. 8vo. Pp. 373. [*Lit. Year Book.*] London, 1882

LOOKE on me, London; I am an honest English-man. . . . [Signed: R. I. *i.e.* Richard Johnson.] 4to. B.L. [*Brit. Mus.*] London, 1613

LOOKE to it; for, Ile stabbe ye. [Signed: S. R. *i.e.* Samuel Rowlands.] 4to. Pp. 47. London, 1604

Reprinted by the Hunterian Club, 1872.

LOOKER-ON (the); a periodical paper. By the Rev. Simon Olive-branch, A.M. [William Roberts, barrister-at-law]. Third edition. 12mo. 4 vols. London, 1795

Begun March 10, 1792, and ended Feb. 1, 1794. Folio. Six papers are by the Rev. James Beresford; two by Mr Chalmers of Throgmorton Street: and some pieces of poetry by Mrs Opie.

LOOKING ahead; a tale of adventure. [By Alfred Morris]; *not* by the author of "Looking backward" [Edward Bellamy]. 8vo. Pp. iv. 264. [*Brit. Mus.*] London [1892]

LOOKING-UP; or, Nanny West and her grandam. By F. C. A. [Frances Charlotte Armstrong]. 8vo. [Cushing's *Init. and Pseud.* i. 3.] London, 1874

LOOKING-GLASS (the); a true history of the early years of an artist [William Mulready], calculated to awaken the emulation of young persons of both sexes, in the pursuit of every laudable attainment, particularly in the cultivation of the fine arts. By Theophilus Marcliffe [William Godwin]. 12mo. [Courtney's *Secrets*, p. 202.] London, 1805

A facsimile reprint appeared in 1885.

LOOKING-GLASS (a) for loyalty; or, the subject's duty to his sovereign: being the substance of several sermons preached by a person who always looked upon his allegiance as incorporated into his religion [John Higham]. 8vo. [Arber's *Term. Cat.* i. 526.] London, 1675

LOOKING-GLASS (a) for rich people, and people in prosperity; shewing how they may improve their riches to the greatest advantage: or, a plea for the poor. [By Andrew Gardner, merchant in Edinburgh.] 12mo. [*Nat. Lib. of Scot.*] Edinburgh, 1727

LOOKING-GLASS (a) for schismaticks; or, the true picture of fanaticism: in a summary view of the principles of the rebels of Forty-one, taken from their sermons, pamphlets, speeches in Parliament, remonstrances, declarations, petitions, votes, orders, and ordinances. By a gentleman of the University of Cambridge [Zachary Grey, LL.D.]. 8vo. Pp. xxii. 116. [*Bodl.*] London, 1725

LOOKING-GLASS (a) for the clergy; or, some traits of the false prophets, particularly maintenance by force: in reply to a pamphlet lately published by George Markham, vicar of Carleton; entitled "Truth for the seekers." [By Thomas Scantlebury.] 8vo. [Smith's *Cat. of Friends' Books*, i. 76; ii. 541.] London, 1797

Signed at the end: A. L. M.

LOOKING-GLASS (a) for the fanaticks; or, the true pictures of fanaticism. By a gentleman of the University of Cambridge [Zachary Grey, LL.D.?]. 8vo. London, N.D.

LOOKING-GLASS (a) for the Jews; wherein they may clearly see that the Messiah is come, by the prophets in the Old Testament (above sixteen hundred years since) and the manifest testimonies since: and also, they may see their own blindness and ignorance of their own prophets, and of the Messiah unto this day; by which, my desire is they may turn to him, that their eyes may be opened, that they may see him whom they have pierced. By G. F. [George Fox]. To which is added a paper writ formerly to the Jews who assemble in Bevers-Marks, London, to be read and considered by them; with a few queries for them to answer. By G. W. [George Whitehead]. 8vo. Pp. 78. 1674

LOOKING-GLASS (a) for the Quakers; in two columns; wherein they may in part see themselves, and may also be seen by others. The first column is, what they formerly published against the Papists; and the other column is, what they published on their behalf, when uppermost. By Phil. Anglus [Joseph Pennyman]. The second edition. . . . 4to. Pp. 16. London, 1689

LOOKING-GLASS hours. By "Rita" and "Alien" [Mrs W. Desmond Humphreys, and Mrs L. A. Baker]. 8vo. [*Lit. Year Book.*] London, 190—

LOOKING-GLASS (the) of conscience. By I. F. [John Falconer, or Falkner, S.J.]. 12mo. [*D. N. B.* vol. 18, p. 162.] St Omer, 1632

LOOKING-GLASSE (a) for all lordly prelates; wherein they may cleerely behold the true divine originall and laudable pedigree whence they are descended; together with their holy lives and actions laid open in a double parallell, the first, betweene the divell; the second, betweene the Iewish high-priests, and lordly prelates; and by their double dissimilitude from Christ, and his Apostles. [By William Prynne.] 4to. Pp. 104. [Wood's *Athen. Oxon.*] 1636

LOOKING-GLASSE (a) for the Parliament, wherein they may see the face of their unjust, illegal, and rebellious practices; argued between two Judges, the one remaining an exile, the other a prisoner for his allegiance to his King and country. [By David Jenkins.] 4to. [Thomason's *Coll. of Tracts*, i. 589.] London, 1648

Preface signed: D. J. and: R. H.

"LOOKING unto Jesus"; a narrative of the brief race of a young disciple. By her mother [Judith Towers Grant]. 8vo. Pp. ix. 164. [*Nat. Lib. of Scot.*] London, 1854

The preface is signed: J. T. G.

LOOSE hints upon education, chiefly concerning the culture of the heart. [By Henry Home, Lord Kames.] Second edition. 8vo. [*D. N. B.* vol. 27, p. 234.] Edinburgh, 1782

LOOSE leaves for a scrap-book. By the author of *Dashwood's letters* [W. Copeland]. 8vo. Pp. 31. London, 1833

LOOSE leaves from the portfolio of a late patriot prisoner [Thomas Jefferson Sutherland] in Canada. 8vo. [Cushing's *Init. and Pseud.* i. 165.] New York, 1840

LOOSE leaves of Craven history. [By William Harbutt Dawson.] First series. Pp. viii. 222. London [1891]

The second series, 1906, has the editor's name.

LOOSE (a) rein. [A sporting novel.] By "Wanderer" [Elim H. d'Avigdor]. 8vo. [*Lond. Lib. Cat.*] London, 1887

LOOSE remarks on certain positions to be found in Mr Hobbes's Philosophical rudiments of government and society; with a short sketch of a democratical form of government; in a letter to Signior Paoli. [By Catherine Macaulay, afterwards Mrs Graham.] 8vo. Pp. 39. London, 1767

The name of the author appears on the title-page of the second edition, published in 1769.

LOOSING (the) of the lion's whelps; and other stories. By John Oxenham [William Arthur Dunkerley]. 8vo. Pp. 346. [*Brit. Mus.*] London, 1917

LORA; a romance in verse. By Paul Pastnor [J. Buckham]. 8vo. Philadelphia, 1881

LORA, the major's daughter. [A novel.] By W. Heimburg [Martha Behrens]; translated from the German. . . . 8vo. Pp. 325. [Cushing's *Init. and Pseud.* i. 128.] New York, 1889

LORD and Lady Russell; a drama. By Ross Neil [Isabella Harwood]. 8vo. [*Lond. Lib. Cat.*] London, 1876

LORD Bacon's confession; a statement of the facts. By W. H. D. [William Hepworth Dixon]. 8vo. [*Brit. Mus.*] London, private print, 1861

LORD Bantam. By the author of *Ginx's baby* [John Edward Jenkins, M.P.]. 8vo. 2 vols. [*Brit. Mus.*] London, 1872

LORD Beaconsfield, K.G., as a writer; from a political point of view. . . . By J. A. P. [John Alfred Pitman]. 8vo. Pp. 51. Beverley [1899]

LORD (the) Bishop of London's [John Robinson's] Letter to his clergy defended, wherein the constant worship of Son and Holy Spirit, with the Father, during the first ages, is set forth. . . . By a believer [Thomas Mangey]. 8vo. [*Brit. Mus.*] London, 1719

LORD Bishops none of the Lords Bishops; or, a short discourse wherein is proved that prelaticall jurisdiction is not of divine institution, but forbidden by Christ himselfe as heathenish, and branded by his apostles for anti-christian. . . . [By William Prynne.] 4to. [*Brit. Mus.*] November, 1640

LORD Bridgnorth's niece. [A novel.] By J. C. Ayrton [Mary Frances Chapman]. 8vo. [Cushing's *Init. and Pseud.* ii. 10.] London, 1862

LORD Brokenhurst; or, a fragment of winter leaves: a tragic tale. By the author of *Mary De-Clifford* [Sir Samuel Egerton Brydges]. 12mo. Pp. 108. [*Brit. Mus.*] Paris, Genève, London, 1819

LORD Broke's wife; and other stories. By John Strange Winter [Mrs Henrietta Eliza Vaughan Stannard, *née* Palmer]. 8vo. Pp. 115. [*Brit. Mus.*] London, 1901

LORD Brougham's Local Courts Bill examined. By H. B. Denton [Edgar Taylor]. 8vo. London, 1833

LORD Byron vindicated; or, Rome and her pilgrim. [Verse.] By "Manfred" [Elliott W. Preston]. 4to. Pp. xxxi. 147. [*Brit. Mus.*] London, 1876

LORD Castlemain's and Robert Pugh's Apology in behalf of the Papists, re-printed and answered. [By Dr William Lloyd, Bishop of St Asaph.] 4to. [*D. N. B.* vol. 33, p. 438.] London, 1667

This reply is also attributed to Charles, Earl of Derby. A fourth edition, corrected, was issued in 1675.

LORD (the) Chief Justice Herbert's account examin'd. By W. A., barrister-at-law [William Atwood]. Wherein it is shown that those authorities in law whereby he would excuse his judgment in Sir Edward Hales his case, are very unfairly cited, and as ill applied. 4to. Pp. 72. [*Brit. Mus.*] London, 1689

LORD Darlington's wooing. [A novel.] By Bertha M. Clay [Charlotte M. Braeme]. 8vo. London [1906]

LORD Elsmere's wife. By Bertha M. Clay [Charlotte M. Braeme]. 8vo. New York [1889]

LORD Elwyn's daughter. [A novel.] By the author of *In a grass country* [Caroline Emily Cameron]. 8vo. Pp. 220. [*Brit. Mus.*] London, 1889

LORD Erlistoun; Alwyn's first wife; The water cure; The last house in C— Street. [Tales.] By the author of *John Halifax, Gentleman* [Mrs Craik, *née* Dinah M. Mulock]. 12mo. Leipzig, 1864

LORD Fitzwarine. By "Scrutator" [K. W. Horlock]. 8vo. 3 vols. [*Nat. Lib. of Scot.*] London, 1860

LORD (the) George Digby's cabinet and Dr Goff's negotiations; together with His Majesties, the Queens, and the Lord Jermin's, and other letters, taken at the battel at Sherborn in Yorkshire about the 15th of October last; also observations upon the said letters. [By Thomas May.] 4to. [*D. N. B.* vol. 37, p. 144.] London, 1646

LORD Harry Bellair; a tale of the last century. By the author of *Mary Powell* [Anne Manning, later Mrs Rathbone]. 8vo. 2 vols. London, 1874

LORD (the) H—'s speech in the House of Lords, on the first Article of the impeachment of Dr Henry Sacheverell. [By John Thompson, Lord Haversham.] 8vo. Pp. 16. [*Brit. Mus.*] London, 1710

LORD have mercie upon us; or, a plaine discovrse declaring that the plague of warre, which now wasts this nation, tooke its beginning in and from the citie of London, and from thence also hath received both increase and nourishment, to the infection and destruction of the rest of the kingdome. . . . [By Peter Heylin.] 4to. Pp. 49. 1643

LORD (the) High Steward of England; or, an historical dissertation on the origin, antiquity, and functions of that officer: shewing the difference between him and the King's Chief Justiciar, and the Steward of the King's houshold, and explaining the offices of the two latter: with remarks on the antient and modern modes of trying peers. . . . [By Sambroke Nicolas Russell.] 8vo. [*Brit. Mus.*] London, 1776

LORD Jim; a tale. By Joseph Conrad [Joseph Conrad Korzeniowski]. 8vo. Pp. 454. [*Lond. Lib. Cat.*] Edinburgh, 1900

LORD John Russell and Mr Macaulay on the French Revolution. [By Philip Henry Stanhope, Earl Stanhope.] 8vo. Pp. 42. London, 1833

LORD Lisle's daughter. By Bertha M. Clay [Charlotte M. Braeme]. 8vo. Chicago [1890]

LORD London; a romance of to-day. By Keble Howard [John Keble Bell]. 8vo. Pp. 300. [*Brit. Mus.*] London, 1913

LORD Loudoun's campaign, 1745. By D. M. R. [D. Murray Rose]. 8vo. [*Brit. Mus.*] [London, 1900]

LORD Lynne's choice. By Bertha M. Clay [Charlotte M. Braeme]. 8vo. New York, 1885

LORD Lynn's wife. [By John B. Harwood.] 8vo. 2 vols. London, 1864

LORD (the) Mayor of London; a sketch of the origin, history, and antiquity of the office. [By Theophilus Charles Noble.] 12mo. [*Brit. Mus.*] London [1860]

LORD (the) Mayor's fool. [By Charles Robert Forrester.] 8vo. [*D. N. B.* vol. 20, p. 7.] London, 1840

LORD (the) Mayor's visit to Oxford, in the month of July, 1826; written at the desire of the party, by the chaplain to the Mayoralty [Robert Crawford Dillon, D.D.]. 8vo. Pp. vi. 157. London, 1826

The unconscious humour of this account was so effectively shown by Theodore Hook that the author made every endeavour to suppress it.

LORD Morcar of Hereward; a romance of the times of William the Conqueror. [By Julia S. H. Pardoe.] 12mo. 4 vols. [*Brit. Mus.*] London, 1829

LORD Nial. By J. M. M. [J. M. Moore]. 8vo. New York, 1834

LORD (the) of Latimer Street; a novel. By Jane Wardle [Oliver Madox Hueffer]. 8vo. Pp. viii. 470. London, 1907

LORD of my life. [A novel.] By "Rita" [Mrs W. Desmond Humphreys, *née* Eliza M. J. Gollan]. 8vo. [*Lond. Lib. Cat.*] London, 1901

LORD (a) of the creation. By the author of *Ethel* [Marian James]. 8vo. [*Nat. Lib. of Scot.*] Edinburgh, 1857

LORD (the) of the forest and his vassals; an allegory. [Signed: C. F. H. *i.e.* Cecil Frances Humphreys, later Mrs Alexander.] 8vo. [*Brit. Mus.*] London, 1848

LORD (the) of the manor; a comic opera, as it is performed at the Theatre Royal in Drury Lane. [By Lieutenant-General John Burgoyne.] 8vo. [Baker's *Biog. Dram.*] London, 1781

LORD Petworth's daughter. [A novel.] By Florence Warden [Florence Alice Price, later Mrs George E. James]. 8vo. [*Brit. Mus.*] London, 1912

LORD Quare's visitor. [A novel.] By Florence Warden [Florence Alice Price, later Mrs George E. James]. 8vo. Pp. 320. London, 1915

LORD Seaforth's campaign, 1715. [By D. Murray Rose.] 8vo. Pp. 30. [*Brit. Mus.*] [1895?]

LORD Selborne's [Roundell Palmer's] Letter to the *Times* (on the Public Worship Regulation Bill); and an answer paragraph by paragraph. By a layman [Basil Montagu Pickering]. 8vo. [*Brit. Mus.*] London, 1874

Signed: B. M. P.

LORD Shrewsbury's miraculous virgins. [By Rev. Joseph Mendham.] Reprinted from the *Church of England Quarterly Review*. 8vo. [*Mendham Collection Cat.* p. 205.] London, 1843

LORD Spencer's library: a sketch of a visit to Althorp, Northamptonshire. [By Samuel Timmins.] 8vo. [*D. Laing.*] N.P., N.D.

Signed: S. T. Printed for private circulation. Reprinted by permission from *The Birmingham Daily Post*, 16 April, 1870.

LORD Ulswater; a novel. By the author of *Lord Lynn's wife*, etc. [John B. Harwood]. 8vo. 3 vols. [*Nat. Lib. of Scot.*] London, 1867

LORDS (the) and Commons first love to, zeale for, and earnest vindication of their injuriously accused and impeached Members, and violated priviledges; manifested by their owne printed declarations, petitions, votes, in the case of the Lord Kimbolton, Mr Denzill Hollis, and some other Members, impeached by the Kings atornie, Mr Herbert, (by the Kings owne speciall command) of high treason, in Ianuary 1641: with a paralell of Cromwells plot, in bringing the army to London, with Henry Jermins and Percyes. . . . [By William Prynne.] 4to. Pp. 19. London, 1647

LORDS and ladies. By the author of *Margaret and her bridesmaids*, etc. [Mrs Julia Stretton]. 8vo. 3 vols. [*D. N. B.* vol. 36, p. 219.] London, 1866

This and other works have been erroneously attributed to Mrs Marsh-Caldwell, or to Henrietta Keddie.

LORDS (the) and the Franchise Bill. [By Alexander Ewan.] 8vo. Aberdeen, 1884

LORD'S (the) body. [A treatise on the Lord's Supper. By the Rev. Clement Prynder, M.A.] 12mo. Pp. 155. London, 1881

An edition of 1884 has the author's name.

LORD'S (the) controversy with England. By W. W. [William Wileman]. 8vo. [Cushing's *Init. and Pseud.* ii. 153.] London, 1880

LORDS day (the); or, a succinct narration compiled out of the testimonies of H. Scripture and the reverend ancient fathers, and divided into two books. . . . [By Thomas Young.] 8vo. Pp. 409. [*Bodl.*] London, 1672

The Epistle dedicatory is signed: Theophilus Philokuriaces Loncardiensis.

LORDS (the) day the Sabbath day; or, a briefe answer to some materiall passages in a late treatise of the Sabbath day. [By William Prynne.] Second edition. 4to. [*Brit. Mus.*] [London] 1636

Signed: A. Attributed also to Richard Byfield. [*D. N. B.*]

LORDS (the) day vindicated; or, the first day of the week the Christian Sabbath: in answer to Mr Bampfield. By G. T. [George Trosse], a well-wisher to truth and concord. 12mo. Pp. 142. [Calamy's *Nonconf. Mem. Palmer's ed.* vol. 2, p. 108.] London, 1692

LORDS (the) Lieutenants and High Sheriffs of Oxford, 1086-1868. [By John Mariott Davenport.] 8vo. [W. D. Macray's *Cat.*] Oxford, private print [1868]

LORDS (the) loud call to England; being a true relation of some late various and wonderful judgments, or handy-works of God, by earthquake, lightening, whirlwind, great multitudes of toads and flyes; and also the striking of divers persons with sudden death, for what causes let the man of wisdome judge. . . . Published by H. J. [Henry Jersey], a servant of Jesus the Christ, and a lover of peace and holiness. 4to. Pp. 44. [Hart's *Index Expurg. Angl.* p. 179.] London, 1660

LORD'S (the) movements in relation to the Assembly; readings and addresses, 1924. [By J. Taylor.] 8vo. Pp. 152. [*Brit. Mus.*] London [1925]

LORDS (the) of life. By Bessie Dill [L. Beith Dalziel]. 8vo. London, 1901

LORD'S (the) prayer, illustrated by the Lord's life. By A. T. M. [A. T. Meugens]. 12mo. London, 1894

LORD'S (the) purse-bearers. By Hesba Stretton [Sarah Smith]. 8vo. Pp. 141. London, 1883

See note to "Alone in London."

LORD'S table (the); whether it is to be spread like a table in an inne for all comers? That it ought not so be done is here maintained. [By Hezekiah Woodward.] 4to. London, 1656

See note at end of his "Law-Power," 1656.

LORENZINO di Medici, and other poems. [By William Roscoe.] 8vo. [*Brit. Mus.*] London, 1797

LORENZO Benoni; or, passages in the life of an Italian: edited by a friend. [By Giovanni Ruffini.] 8vo. Pp. vi. 505. [*Nat. Lib. of Scot.*] Edinburgh, 1853

LORENZO of "The Merchant of Venice": his character . . . a phantasie. By Launcelot Cross [Frank Carr, merchant]. 8vo. Pp. 52. [*Brit. Mus.*] London, 1885

LORENZO; or, the tale of redemption. [A poem. By John Roby, banker in Rochdale.] 8vo. London, 1819

Later editions bear the author's name.

LORGNETTE (the); or, studies of the towns. By an opera-goer [Donald Grant Mitchell]. 8vo. [Haynes' *Pseud.*] New York, 1832

LORIN Mooruck; and other Indian stories. By George Truman Kercheval [Winnifred Jennings]. 8vo. Boston, 1888

LOS Cerritos. By Frank Lin [Mrs Gertrude Franklin Atherton]. 8vo. New York, 1889

LOSS and gain. [By John Henry Newman, D.D.] 8vo. Pp. 386. [*D. N. B.* vol. 40, p. 349.] London, 1848

LOSS and gain; or, great fortunes. By Nellie Graham [Mrs Annie Dunning, *née* Ketchum]. 8vo. [Haynes' *Pseud.*] Philadelphia, 1878

LOSS (the) of the "Flying Fish"; aerial and submarine peril. By Harry Collingwood [William J. C. Lancaster]. 8vo. [*Lond. Lib. Cat.*] London, 1886

LOST—a sweetheart. By John Strange Winter [Henrietta E. V. Palmer, later Mrs Arthur Stannard]. 8vo. [*Brit. Mus.*] London, 1903

LOST; and other tales for children: adapted from the French by the author of *Tyborne* [Frances Magdalen Taylor]. 8vo. [*Brit. Mus.*] London [1885]

LOST and won; or, the love test. By the author of *The maid's husband* [Mrs Henrietta C. Jenkins]. 12mo. [*Brit. Mus.*] London, 1846

LOST at the winning-post; a novel. By H. L. H., author of *A heart twice won* [Harriet Lydia Stevenson]. 8vo. 2 vols. [*Brit. Mus.*] London, 1867

LOST (a) battle. [By Eleanor C. Price.] 8vo. 2 vols. Edinburgh, 1878

LOST (the) battle; and Victory. By the author of *The little bugler of Kassassin* [Mrs —— Ballard]. 8vo. London [1884]

LOST (the) blue diamond of the Stuarts. [A novel.] By Lewis Ramsden [A. Lisle Dowding]. 8vo. London [1904]

LOST (the) bride; or, the price of silence. By Clara Augusta [Winifred Winthrope]. 8vo. [Cushing's *Init. and Pseud.* ii. 32.] New York, 1889

LOST (the) brooch; or, the history of another month: a tale for young people. By the author of *The fairy bower* [Mrs Harriet Mozley]. 8vo. 2 vols. [*Brit. Mus.*] London, 1841

LOST, but found. By Aunt Hattie [Mrs Harriet Newell Baker, *née* Woods]. 12mo. [Kirk's *Supp.*] Boston, 1868

LOST by a head; a play. [By M. Tertius Collins.] 8vo. [*Birm. Free Lib.*] Birmingham [1850]

LOST (a) cause; a novel. By Guy Thorne [Cyril A. E. Ranger-Gull]. 8vo. Pp. 320. [*Lond. Lib. Cat.*] London, 1905

LOST (the) dog; and other stories. By Ascott R. Hope [Ascott Robert Hope Moncrieff]. 8vo. Pp. 128. [*Lit. Year Book.*] London [1892]

LOST (the) earldom; a tale of Scotland's reign of terror. By Cyril Grey [A. Balfour Symington]. 8vo. Pp. 330. London, 1914

LOST (the) farm. . . . [By Maria Frances Dickson.] 8vo. London, 1836

LOST (the) father; or, Cecilia's triumph: a story of our own day. By Daryl Holme [David Herbert]. 8vo. [*Nat. Lib. of Scot.*] Edinburgh, 1870

In the preface, the author states that this work is a "transference" of Julie Gourand's *Cécile, ou la petite sœur.*

LOST (the) fisherman; a legend of Auchmithie. [By William Durie.] 12mo. Pp. 8. [*And. Jervise.*] [Montrose, 1848]

LOST for love; a novel. By the author of *Lady Audley's secret*, etc. [Mary Elizabeth Braddon, later Mrs John Maxwell]. 8vo. 3 vols. London, 1874

LOST Gip. By Hesba Stretton, author of *Jessica's first prayer*, etc. [Sarah Smith]. 8vo. Pp. 154. London, 1873

See the note to "Alone in London."

LOST (the) Greenland; or, Uncle Philip's conversations . . . about the lost colonies of Greenland. [By Francis Lister Hawks.] 12mo. [Allibone's *Dict.*] New York, 1844

LOST (the) heir; and The prediction. [By Tyrone Power.] 12mo. 3 vols. [*Nat. Lib. of Scot.*] London, 1830

LOST (the) home. [Poems. By Thomas Matthews Blagg.] 8vo. [*Brit. Mus.*] London, 1899

LOST (a) illusion. [A novel.] By Leslie Keith [Grace Leslie Keith Johnstone]. 8vo. [*Lit. Year Book.*] London, 1891

LOST in Blunderland; the further adventures of Clara. By Caroline Lewis [M. H. Temple, Stafford Ransome, and Harold Begbie]. 8vo. Pp. 166. London, 1903

A political skit against A. J. Balfour, in imitation of Lewis Carroll's *Alice in Wonderland.*

LOST in the crowd; or, better broke than kept. By the author of *Recommended to mercy* [Mrs Margaret Houstoun]. 8vo. 3 vols. [*Brit. Mus.*] London, 1882

LOST in the jungle; a story for girls. By May Wynne [Mabel Wynne Knowles]. 8vo. Pp. 222. [*Lit. Year Book.*] London, 1921

LOST (a) inheritance. [A novel.] By Scott Graham [Hazelton Black]. 8vo. Pp. 342. [*Brit. Mus.*] London [1912]

LOST (the) jewel: a tale. By A. L. O. E., authoress of *The Claremont tales*, etc. [Charlotte M. Tucker]. 8vo. Pp. iv. 290. London, 1860

LOST (the) key. By the author of *The little watercress sellers* [Sarah Maria Fry]. 12mo. London [1855]

LOST (the) lady; a tragy comedy. [By Sir William Berkeley.] Fol. Pp. 53. [*Bodl.*] London, 1639

LOST (the) laird; a novel. By Dick Donovan [Joyce E. P. Muddock]. 8vo. [*Brit. Mus.*] London, 1898

LOST (the) lamb. By Faith Latimer [Mrs John A. Miller]. 8vo. [Cushing's *Init. and Pseud.* i. 166.] New York, 1884

LOST (the) lawyer. By George A. Birmingham [James Owen Hannay, D.D.]. 8vo. Pp. 242. [*Lond. Lib. Cat.*] London, 1921

LOST (a) life. By Mignonette [Emily H. Moore]. 8vo. [Cushing's *Init. and Pseud.* i. 193.] New York, 1871

LOST (the) lode. By Christian Reid [Mrs Frances C. Fisher Tiernan]. 8vo. [Kirk's *Supp.*] New York, 1892

LOST (a) love; a novel. By Ashford Owen [Annie C. Ogle]. 8vo. London, 1920

LOST Maggie; or, a basket of roses. By M. E. Winchester [M. E. Whatham]. 8vo. Pp. 126. [*Amer. Cat.*] London [1885]

LOST (the) manuscripts of a Blue Jacket. [A series of letters from Germany. By A. Mainwaring.] 8vo. London, 1859

LOST (the) naval papers. By Bennet Copplestone [F. Harcourt Kitchin]. 8vo. Pp. 300. London, 1918

LOST (the) principle; or, sectional equilibrium. By Barbarossa [John Scott]. 8vo. [Cushing's *Init. and Pseud.* i. 30.] Richmond, 1860

LOST (a) reputation. [A novel. By Olive M. Birrell.] 8vo. Pp. vi. 273. [*Brit. Mus.*] London, 1887

LOST (the) ship. [A novel.] By the author of *Cavendish* [William Johnson Neale]. 8vo. [*Brit. Mus.*] London, 1860

LOST Sir Massingberd; a romance of real life. [By James Payn.] 8vo. 2 vols. [*Brit. Mus.*] London, 1864

LOST (the) son; and the Glover's daughter. By Stephen Yorke [Mary Linskill]. 8vo. [*Lond. Lib. Cat.*] London, 189—

LOST (a) summer. [A novel.] By Theo Douglas [Mrs H. D. Everett]. 8vo. Pp. 352. [*Lit. Year Book.*] London, 1907

LOST to the world. By Arrah Leigh [Mrs H. C. Hoffman]. 8vo. New York, 1885

LOST (the) tribes; a tale of Irish life. By George A. Birmingham [James Owen Hannay, D.D.]. 8vo. Pp. 331. [*Lit. Year Book.*] London, 1914

LOST (the) trinket. By the author of *The harvest of a quiet eye* [Rev. John Richard Vernon, M.A.]. 8vo. [*Brit. Mus.*] London, 1886

LOST (the) Venus of Knidos. [By J. Bell.] 8vo. London, 1888

LOST (the) witness; or, the mystery of Leah Paget. By Lawrence L. Lynch [Emma M. Murdoch, later Mrs F. Van Deventer]. 8vo. [*Lond. Lib. Cat.*] London, 1890

LOTHAIR'S children. By H. R. H. [Campbell Mackellar]. 8vo. Pp. 265. [*Brit. Mus.*] London, 1890

A sequel to Lord Beaconsfield's "Lothair."

LOTOS (a) eater in Capri. By Alan Walters [H. A. W. Miller]. 8vo. London, 1893

LOTTERIES of circumstance. [A novel.] By the author of *Marcia in Germany* [Sybil Spottiswoode]. 8vo. [*Lond. Lib. Cat.*] London, 1914

Published also, in 1915, under the title of "Chronicles of a German town."

LOTTERY (the). By St Denis le Cadet [E. Denison]. 8vo. Baltimore, 1815

LOTTERY (the); a farce, as it is acted at the Theatre-Royal in Drury-Lane, by his Majesty's servants: with the musick prefixed to each song. [By Henry Fielding.] 8vo. Pp. 31. [*Bodl.*] London, 1732

LOTTIE of the mill. By W. Heimburg [Bertha Behrens]. 8vo. [*Lib. Jour.* ix. 164.] Philadelphia, 1882

LOTTIE Wilde's picnic. . . . By Grandmother Hope [Mrs Henry Gally Knight]. 8vo. [Cushing's *Init. and Pseud.* i. 475.] New York, 1867

LOTTIE'S wooing. By Darley Dale [Francesca M. Steele]. 8vo. Pp. 371. [*Lond. Lib. Cat.*] New York, 1893

LOTTY'S visit to Grandmamma; a story for the little ones. By Brenda [Mrs Castle Smith]. 8vo. [*Brit. Mus.*] London, 1877

LOTUS leaves from Africa and Covent Garden. By Israfel [Miss Hudson]. 8vo. Pp. 240. London, 1908

LOUD (a) cry for help to the struggling Church of Scotland; being a letter from an elder in Glasgow, to the several members of Kirk-sessions thro' the land; proper to be read, and seriously considered, before the election of members to the next General Assembly. [By John Maclaurin, M.A.] 8vo. Pp. 32. [Struthers' *Hist. of the Relief Church*, p. 558.] Glasgow, 1752

Signed: X. Y., Tallow-chandler. Dated "from my shop in the Candleriggs, Jan. 15th, 1753."

LOUGH Fea. [By Evelyn Philip Shirley.] 4to. [Anderson's *Brit. Top.*] Private print, 1859

A description of the manor in County Monaghan.

LOUIE Atterbury. [A tale.] By the author of *Rutledge*, etc. [Mrs Sidney S. Harris]. 8vo. [*Nat. Lib. of Scot.*] London, 1866

LOUIE'S last term at St Mary's. By the author of *Rutledge*, etc. [Mrs Sidney S. Harris]. 8vo. [*Brit. Mus.*] London, 1871

LOUIS Michaud; or, the little French Protestant. By M. E. B. [Mrs Mary E. Gellie]. 12mo. [Kirk's *Supp.*] London, 1868

LOUIS Norbert; a twofold romance. By Vernon Lee [Violet Paget]. 8vo. Pp. 304. [*Lond. Lib. Cat.*] London, 1914

LOUISA of Prussia and her times. By Louise Mühlbach [Mrs Clara Müller Mundt]. Translated from the German. 8vo. [*Amer. Cat.*] New York, 1872

LOUISA; or, the bride. By the author of the *Fairy bower* [Mrs Harriet Mozley]. 8vo. Pp. 302. London, 1842

LOUISA; or, the cottage on the moor. [By Elizabeth Helme.] 12mo. 2 vols. [Watt's *Bibl. Brit.*] London, 1787

LOUISE Maximilienne, Countess of Albany. By Vernon Lee [Violet Paget]. 8vo. [*Brit. Mus.*] London, 1884

LOUNGER'S (the) common-place book; or, miscellaneous collections in history, criticism, biography, poetry & romance. [By Jeremiah Whitaker Newman.] Third edition. 8vo. 4 vols. [*W.*] London, 1805-7

The title of the fourth volume is, "A new volume of the Lounger's common-place book, etc."

LOUSIAD (the); an heroi-comic poem. Five cantos. By Peter Pindar, Esq. [John Wolcot, M.D.]. 4to. [*D. N. B.* vol. 62, p. 293.] London and Dublin, 1787-95

Each canto was published separately, at varying intervals: several editions of the earlier portions were required, and considerable additions were made to these.

LOVABLE (a) crank; or, more leaves from the roses. By Barbara Yechton [Lydia Farrington Krause]. 8vo. New York, 1898

LOVAT and Lily; a pastoral. By C. Edine [John Moffat]. 12mo. [*Nat. Lib. of Scot.*] Edinburgh, 1854

LOVE. [A novel.] By the author of *Elizabeth and her German garden* [Mary Annette, Countess Russell]. 8vo. Pp. 408. [*Brit. Mus.*] London, 1925

LOVE. By the authoress of *Flirtation*, etc. [Lady Charlotte Maria Bury]. 8vo. 3 vols. [*Brit. Mus.*] London, 1837

LOVE à la mode; a comedy, as it was lately acted with great applause at Middlesex House. Written by a person of honour [T. Southland]. 4to. 48 leaves. London, 1663

LOVE à la mode; a comedy. [By Charles Macklin.] 12mo. [*Brit. Mus.*] Dublin, 1786

LOVE; a poem. By the author of *Corn Law rhymes* [Ebenezer Elliott]. Third edition. 8vo. [*Brit. Mus.*] London, 1831

LOVE (the) affairs of Amaryllis. [A novel.] By Dorothea Baird [Mrs H. B. Irving]. 8vo. London, 1908

LOVE (the) affairs of some famous men. By the author of *How to be happy though married* [Rev. Edward J. Hardy, M.A.]. 8vo. [*Lond. Lib. Cat.*] London, 1897

LOVE among the gamins; and other poems. By Peleg Arkwright [David L. Proudfit]. 4to. [Haynes' *Pseud.*] New York [1877]

LOVE among the lions. . . . By F. Anstey [Thomas Anstey Guthrie]. 8vo. [*Lit. Year Book.*] London, 1898

LOVE and a cottage. [A novel.] By Keble Howard [John Keble Bell]. 8vo. Pp. xii. 241. [*Lond. Lib. Cat.*] London, 1903

LOVE and a sword; a tale of the Afridi war. By Kennedy King [George Douglas Brown, M.A.]. 8vo. Pp. 346. London, 1899

LOVE and ambition. By the author of *Rockingham* [Count de Jarnac]. 8vo. 3 vols. [*Nat. Lib. of Scot.*] London, 1851

LOVE and hate; or, the court of Charles I.: a historical drama, in four acts. By C. C. [Charles Coghlan]. 8vo. London, 1857

LOVE and honour; a dramatick poem, taken from Virgil. [By Thomas Delamayne.] 12mo. [*Brit. Mus.*] London, 1742

LOVE and lordship. [A novel.] By Florence Warden [Florence Alice Price, later Mrs George E. James]. 8vo. Pp. 402. London, 1906

LOVE and madness; a story too true: in a series of letters between parties whose names would perhaps be mentioned were they less known, or less lamented. [By Rev. Sir Herbert Croft, LL.B.] A new edition. 12mo. Pp. viii. 298. [*D. N. B.* vol. 13, p. 108.] London, 1780

The "names" have been given as Mr Hackman and Miss Reay.

LOVE and patriotism: or, the extraordinary adventures of M. Duportail. . . . [Translated from the "Vie du Chevalier de Faublas" of J. B. Louvet de Couvray.] 12mo. [*Brit. Mus.*] Philadelphia, 1797

LOVE and pride. By the author of *Sayings and doings*, etc. [Theodore Edward Hook]. 12mo. 3 vols. [*D. N. B.* vol. 27, p. 275.] London, 1833

LOVE and quiet life; Somerset idylls. By Tom Cobbleigh [Walter Raymond]. 8vo. [*Aberd. Pub. Lib.*] London, 1894

LOVE and the Freemason. By Guy Thorne [Cyril A. E. Ranger-Gull]. 8vo. Pp. 281. [*Lond. Lib. Cat.*] London, 1916

LOVE and the King. By Lucas Cleeve [Mrs Howard Kingscote, *née* Wolf]. 8vo. Pp. 318. London, 1906

LOVE and the lodger. [A novel.] By Priscilla Crowen [Mrs William Teignmouth Shore]. 8vo. Pp. 304. [*Amer. Cat.*] London, 1909

LOVE and the philosopher. [A novel.] By Marie Corelli [Caroline Cody]. 8vo. Pp. 248. [*Brit. Mus.*] London, 1923

LOVE and the soul-hunters. [A novel.] By John Oliver Hobbes [Mrs Reginald Walpole Craigie, *née* Pearl Teresa Richards]. 8vo. London, 1902

LOVE and truth; in two modest and peaceable letters, concerning the distempers of the present times: written from a quiet and conformable citizen of London, to two busie and factious shop-keepers in Coventry. [By Isaak Walton.] 4to. Pp. 40. [*Bodl.*] London, 1680

The letters are signed: R. W.

LOVE and twenty; a novel. By John Strange Winter [Mrs Henrietta E. V. Stannard, *née* Palmer]. 8vo. Pp. 316. London, 1905

LOVE and valour, celebrated in the person of the author, by the name of Adraste [or rather, Vital d'Audignier]; or, the divers affections of Minerva. One part of the unfained story of the true Lisander and Caliste, translated out of the French by W. B. [W. Barwick]. 4to. London, 1638

LOVE at a loss; or, most votes carry it: a comedy. By the author of *The fatal friendship* [Catherine Trotter, afterwards Mrs Cockburn]. 4to. [*Manch. Free Lib.*] London, 1701

LOVE at a venture; a comedy. . . . By the author of *The gamester* [Mrs Susanna Centlivre, *née* Carroll]. 4to. [*Brit. Mus.*] London, 1706

LOVE at first sight; a ballad farce, of two acts, as performed at the Theatre-Royal in Drury-Lane. [By Thomas King.] 8vo. [Baker's *Biog. Dram.*] London, 1763

LOVE at seventy. [A novel.] By Albert Ross [Linn Boyd Porter]. 8vo. [*Amer. Cat.*] New York, 1894

LOVE betray'd; or, the agreable disappointment: a comedy, as it was acted at the theatre in Lincolns-Inn-Fields. By the author of *The ladies visiting-day* [Charles Burnaby]. 4to. Pp. 61. London, 1703

LOVE conquers pride. By Arrah Leigh [Mrs H. C. Hoffman]. 8vo. New York, 1885

LOVE elegies. [By John Lettice.] 4to. London, 1760

LOVE elegies; written in the year 1732. [By James Hammond.] Fourth edition. 4to. Pp. 31. [Lowndes' *Bibl. Man.*] London [1757]

LOVE elegies, written in the year 1770. [By G. Birch, of Remenham, Berkshire.] 4to. London, 1775

LOVE (a) elegy. By Cuthbert Cudgel, Esq. [Thomas Houston?]. 12mo. [*Brit. Mus.*] Newcastle, 1800

LOVE (a) epistle, in verse; written at Paris. By the author of *The marriage act*, etc. [John Shebbeare, M.D.]. Second edition. 4to. [*Brit. Mus.*] London, 1756

LOVE (the) epistles of Aristænetus; translated from the Greek into English metre [by Nathaniel Brassey Halhed and Richard Brinsley Sheridan]. 8vo. Pp. xvi. 174. London, 1771

Preface signed: H. S., the initials of Halhed and Sheridan. Later editions give the names of the translators.

LOVE finds a way; a romance. By May Wynne [Mabel Wynne Knowles]. 8vo. Pp. 188. [*Lit. Year Book.*] London, 1920

LOVE for a day. By Bertha M. Clay [Charlotte M. Braeme]. 8vo. New York, 1884

LOVE for a key. [A novel.] By George Colmore [Mrs Gertrude Colmore Dunn, later Mrs Baillie Weaver]. 8vo. Pp. 190. [*Lond. Lib. Cat.*] London, 1897

LOVE given o're; or, a satyr against the pride, lust and inconstancy, &c. of woman. [In verse. By Robert Gould.]4to. Pp. 12. [*Brit. Mus.*] London, 1683

LOVE gone astray. By Albert Ross [Linn Boyd Porter]. 8vo. Pp. 297. [*Amer. Cat.*] New York, 1896

LOVE (the) hater. By Guy Thorne [Cyril A. E. Ranger-Gull]. 8vo. Pp. 304. [*Lit. Year Book.*] London, 1921

LOVE in a little town. By J. E. Buckrose [Mrs Falconer Jameson]. 12mo. Pp. 296. [*Lit. Year Book.*] London, 1920

LOVE in a mist; a farce now acting at the city-theatre in Dublin, with great applause. [By John Cunningham.] 8vo. Pp. 34. [Baker's *Biog. Dram.*] Dublin printed; London reprinted, 1747

LOVE in a mist; and kindred verse. By the author of *Random rhymes of a Vectensian* [C. J. Arnell]. 8vo. Pp. 58. [*Brit. Mus.*] Newport, Isle of Wight [1920]

LOVE in a village; a comic opera, as it is performed at the Theatre Royal in Covent-Garden. [By Isaac Bickerstaffe.] The eleventh edition. 8vo. Pp. ii. 73. [*Brit. Mus.*] London, 1765

LOVE in a wood; or, the country squire. By G. J. [Giles Jacob]. 12mo. [Baker's *Biog. Dram.*] London, 1714

LOVE in idleness. By Henry Hayes [Ellen Warner Olney, later Mrs Kirk]. [Kirk's *Supp.*] Philadelphia, 1877

LOVE in idleness; a volume of poems. [By Henry C. Beeching, J. W. Mackail, and J. B. B. Nichols.] 8vo. [*Brit. Mus.*] London, 1883

LOVE in it's extasie; or, the large prerogative: a kind of royall pastorall written long since, by a gentleman student at Æton, and now published. [By William Peaps.] 4to. [Baker's *Biog. Dram.*] London, 1649

LOVE in June; a pastoral comedy. . . . By Keble Howard [John Keble Bell]. 8vo. Pp. 317. [*Lond. Lib. Cat.*] London, 1905

LOVE in light and shadow. Vol. 1. Sister Anne. By the author of *Ethel* [Miss M. James]. Vol. 2. Katherine Evering. By the author of *Mr Arle* [Emily Jolly]. 8vo. 2 vols. [*Brit. Mus.*] Edinburgh, 1857

LOVE in our village; a novel. By Orme Agnus [John C. Higginbotham]. 8vo. [*Lond. Lib. Cat.*] London, 1900

LOVE in the backwoods. By John Philip Vartey [Langdon Elwyn Mitchell]. 8vo. New York, 1897

LOVE in the city; a comic opera: as it is performed at the Theatre Royal in Covent-Garden: the words written, and the music compiled by the author of *Love in a village* [Isaac Bickerstaffe]. Second edition. 8vo. [Baker's *Biog. Dram.*] London, 1767

LOVE in the East; or, adventures of twelve hours: a comic opera, in three acts, written by the author of the Strangers at home, as performed at the Theatre-Royal, Drury-Lane. [By James Cobb.] 8vo. Pp. 81. [Baker's *Biog. Dram.*] London, 1788

The dedication to Thomas Linley, Esq. is signed: J. C.

LOVE in the lists; a pension comedy. By K. L. Montgomery [Kathleen and Letitia Montgomery]. 8vo. Pp. 318. London, 1905

LOVE in the purple. [A novel.] By Morice Gerard [Rev. John Jessop Teague]. 8vo. Pp. 288. [*Lit. Year Book.*] London, 1910

LOVE in the Suds; a town eclogue: being the lamentation of Roscius [David Garrick] for the loss of his Nyky [Isaac Bickerstaffe]. . . . [By William Kenrick, LL.D.] Fol. [*D. N. B.* vol. 31, p. 18.] London, 1772

LOVE laughs at locksmiths. [A drama.] By Arthur Griffinhoof, of Turnham Green [George Colman, junior]. 8vo. London, 1808

Another edition of 1808 has the author's name.

LOVE laughs last. [A novel.] By Stephen G. Tallentyre [E. Beatrice Hall]. 8vo. Pp. 347. [*Lond. Lib. Cat.*] Edinburgh, 1919

LOVE lyrics. By Torquil Argestoile [Aylmer Cecil Strong]. 8vo. Edinburgh, 1920

LOVE (a) match. By Mrs Alexander [Mrs Alexander Hector, *née* Annie French]. 8vo. [*Brit. Mus.*] New York, 1894

LOVE (a) match. By Walter D. Dunlap [Sylvanus Cobb, jun.]. 8vo. [Cushing's *Init. and. Pseud.* ii. 46.] New York, 1894

LOVE (the) of a lifetime. By Carroll Winchester [Mrs Caroline G. Curtis]. 8vo. [Cushing's *Init. and Pseud.* i. 308.] Boston, 1883

LOVE (the) of an obsolete woman. [By Mrs Clara L. Roberts.] 8vo. London, 1897

LOVE (the) of an uncrowned Queen; Sophie Dorothea, Consort of George I., and her correspondence with Königsmarck. By W. H. De Winton [William Henry Wilkins]. 8vo. 2 vols. [*Lond. Lib. Cat.*] London, 1900

LOVE of fame, the universal passion; in seven characteristical satires. [By Edward Young, LL.D.] Second edition, corrected and enlarged. 8vo. Pp. 175. [*Brit. Mus.*] London, 1728

Originally published separately, in folio, under the title of "The universal passion."

LOVE (the) of Jesus; or, visits to the blessed Sacrament for every day of the month. By Omega [Rev. Daniel Gilbert]. 12mo. London, 1865

An edition of 1869 bears the author's name.

LOVE (the) of long ago; and other stories. By Marie Corelli [Caroline Cody]. 8vo. Pp. v. 271. [*Brit. Mus.*] London, 1920

LOVE (the) of order; a poetical essay, in three cantos. [By Richard Graves.] 4to. [Nichol's *Lit. Anec.* iii. 133; Green's *Bibl. Somers.* ii. 444.] London, 1773

LOVE (the) of our country; a poem, with historical notes. . . . By a curate from Snowdon [Rev. Evan Evans]. 8vo, Carmarthen, 1772

LOVE (the) of Philip Hampden. [A novel.] By John Strange Winter [Mrs Henrietta E. V. Stannard, *née* Palmer]. 8vo. Pp. 310. London, 1906

LOVE (the) of pleasure inconsistent with reason, and with the peculiar spirit of Christianity; a sermon. . . . By a preacher of the Gospel [John Mackenzie, D.D., of Portpatrick]. 8vo. Pp. viii. 36. [Scott's *Fasti.*] Edinburgh, 1770

LOVE (the) of the sovle; made by G. M. [Gregory Martin]: whereunto are annexed certaine Catholike questions to the Protestants, with a new addition of a catalogue of the names of Popes and other professors of the ancient Catholike faith; and a challenge to Protestants to shew (if they can) a like catalogue of the names of the professors of the Protestant faith. 12mo. Pp. 79. [*Bodl.*] 1619

The "Catalogue" has a separate title and pagination.

LOVE one another; a tub lecture preached at Watford in Hartfordshire at a Conventicle on the 25th of December last [1642]. By John Alexander, a joyner [John Taylor, the Water poet]. 4to. [*Brit. Mus.*] [London, 1642]

LOVE only lent. By Roof Roofer [Rufus Randell]. 8vo. Pp. 95. [*Brit. Mus.*] London [1896]

LOVE poems and sonnets. By Owen Innsly [Lucy White Jennison]. 8vo. [Cushing's *Init. and Pseud.* i. 137.] Boston, 1881

LOVE (the) poems of Louis Barnaval [Charles De Kay]; edited, with an introduction, by Charles De Kay. 8vo. [Cushing's *Init. and Pseud.* i. 30.] New York, 1883

LOVE (the) seekers. [A novel.] By Lucas Cleeve [Mrs Howard Kingscote, *née* Adelina G. I. Wolff]. 8vo. [*Lit. Year Book.*] London, 1912

LOVE songs, and other poems. By Owen Innsly [Lucy White Jennison]. 8vo. [*Lib. Journ.* vii. 66.] New York, 1902

LOVE sonnets. By Evelyn Douglas [John E. Barlas]. 8vo. Pp. 72. Chelmsford, 1889

LOVE sonnets of a hoodlum. [By Wallace Irwin.] 8vo. San Francisco, 1902

LOVE (the) sonnets of Proteus. [By Wilfrid Scawen W. Blunt.] 8vo. Pp. x. 120. London, 1881

The first edition (1875) has a different title ("Proteus sonnets and songs").

LOVE (a) story. By a Bushman [Major —— Christie, Post-master in N. S. Wales]. 8vo. [Barton's *Lit. in N. S. Wales*, p. 111.] Sydney, 1841

LOVE (the) story of a Mormon. By Winifred Graham [Mrs Theodore Cory]. 8vo. Pp. 318. London, 1911

LOVE that casteth out fear; Muriel and her father. By Eglanton Thorne [Emily Charlton]. 8vo. [*Brit. Mus.*] London, 1891

LOVE (the) that lasts. [A novel.] By Florence Warden [Florence Alice Price, later Mrs George E. James]. 8vo. Pp. 344. London, 1900

LOVE (the) that loves alway. By E. Owen Blackburne [Elizabeth Owen Blackburne Casey]. 8vo. 3 vols. [*Lond. Lib. Cat.*] London, 1881

LOVE the avenger. By the author of *All for greed* [Marie Pauline Rose, Baroness Blaze De Bury]. 8vo. 3 vols. [*Brit. Mus.*] London, 1869

The dedication is signed: A. A. A.

LOVE the debtor. By Basil [Richard Ashe King]. 8vo. 3 vols. [*Brit. Mus.*] London, 1882

LOVE, the magnet. By "Pan" [Leslie Beresford]. 8vo. Pp. vi. 306. [*Brit. Mus.*] London [1916]

LOVE the pilgrim. By the author of *Queenie* [Miss May Crommelin]. 8vo. 3 vols. [*Brit. Mus.*] London, 1886-8

LOVE (the) thief. By Marjorie Bowen [Madame Gabrielle Vere Campbell Long]. 8vo. [*Lond. Lib. Cat.*] London, 1922

LOVE thy neighbour as thyself; or, the story of Mike the Irish boy. By Cousin Kate [Catherine D. Bell]. 12mo. [*Lit. Year Book.*] London, 1871

LOVE to the lost; and a hand held forth to the helpless to lead out of the dark; wherein is plainly held out divers particular things as they are learned of Christ. . . . By one . . . who was called in derision . . . a Quaker [James Nayler]. 4to. [Smith's *Cat. of Friends' Books.*] [London] 1665

Signed: J. N.

LOVE triumphant. By R. L. Paget [Frederick L. Knowles]. 8vo. [*Amer. Cat.*] Boston, 1904

LOVE triumphant over reason. [A poem. By Thomas B. Hamilton, Earl of Haddington.] 4to. Edinburgh, 1708

LOVE will firde out the way; an excellent comedy. By T. B. [James Shirley]. As it was acted with great applause by her Majesties servants, at the Phœnix in Drury Lane. 4to. [Baker's *Biog. Dram.*] London, 1661

This is a republication of "The constant maid."

LOVE without affectation; in five letters from [Mariana d'Alcoforado] a Portuguese nun to a French Cavalier, done into English verse from the newest edition, lately printed at Paris. To which is added, a prefatory discourse of the nature and use of such epistles in general, with the excellency of these in particular. . . . 8vo. [Arber's *Term Cat.* iii. 645.] London, 1709

For the titles of other editions, see "Five love letters . . ." (1678), "Letters from a Portuguese nun . . ." (1808), "Love-letters of a Portuguese nun . . ." (1901).

LOVE-CONQUEST (the); or, the little strength of Philadelphia. . . . [By Richard Roach, B.D.] 8vo. London, 1774

LOVED beyond words. [Poems.] By George Barlow [James Hinton]. 8vo. Pp. 227. London, 1885

LOVE-KNOTS. By the author of *Ursula's love-story*, etc. [Mrs Gertrude Parsons, *née* Hext]. 8vo. 3 vols. London, 1881

LOVE-LETTERS [in verse]. By a violinist. [By George Eric Mackay.] 12mo. Pp. 125. [*Brit. Mus.*] London, 1884

Later editions give the author's name, with other poems.

LOVE-LETTERS between a noble-man [Ford, Earl Grey] and his sister [Countess of Berkeley]. [By Aphra Behn.] 8vo. Pp. 296. [Arber's *Term Cat.* iii. 688.] London, 1693

Letters signed "Philander" and "Silvia."

LOVE-LETTERS from a nobleman to his sister; mixt with the history of their adventures. The second part, by the same hand [Aphra Behn]. 8vo. Pp. 405. London, 1693

The epistle dedicatory is signed: A. B.

LOVE-LETTERS (the) of a faithless wife. By Lucas Cleeve [Mrs Howard Kingscote, *née* Georgina A. I. Wolff]. 8vo. [*Lit. Year Book.*] London, 1911

LOVE-LETTERS (the) of a Fenian. [Verse.] By May Shorsa [May Wilson Slater]. 8vo. [O'Donoghue's *Poets of Ireland.*] Dublin, 1861

LOVE-LETTERS of a Portuguese nun [Mariana Alcoforado]. English version by R. H. 8vo. Pp. 96. London, 1901

See above, "Love without affectation."

LOVE-LETTERS of eminent persons; edited by Charles Martel [Thomas Delf]. Second edition. 8vo. [*Brit. Mus.*] London, 1859

LOVE-LETTERS of Mrs Piozzi written when she was eighty, to W. A. Conway. [Edited by William Andrew Chatto.] 8vo. London, 1843

LOVELL'S whim. By Shirley Smith [Ella J. Curtis]. 8vo. [Cushing's *Init. and Pseud.* i. 259.] New York, 1889

LOVELS (the) of Arden; a novel. By the author of *Lady Audley's secret*, etc. [Mary Elizabeth Braddon, later Mrs John Maxwell]. 8vo. 3 vols. [*Brit. Mus.*] London, 1871

LOVELY Mrs Pemberton. By Florence Warden [Florence Alice Price, later Mrs George E. James]. 8vo. Pp. 310. London, 1901

LOVER (the). By Marmaduke Myrtle, Gent.; to which is added, The reader. [Both by Sir Richard Steele.] 12mo. [*Brit. Mus.*] London, 1789

LOVER and husband; a novel. By Ennis Graham [Mrs Mary Louisa Molesworth]. 8vo. 3 vols. London, 1870

LOVER (a) at forty. [A novel.] By Gerald Cumberland [C. Fred Kenyon]. 8vo. Pp. 336. London, 1922

LOVER (a) true. By Rita [Mrs W. Desmond Humphreys, *née* Eliza J. M. Gollan]. 8vo. [*Lit. Year Book.*] London, 1901

LOVER (the) upon trial, and a voice. By the author of *Olivia*, etc. [Augusta Louisa, Lady Lyons]. 8vo. Pp. 248. [*Brit. Mus.*] London, 1853

LOVERS and friends; or, modern attachments: a novel. By Anne of Swansea [Anne Hatton], author of *Conviction*, etc. 12mo. 5 vols. [*Brit. Mus.*] London, 1821

LOVERS' (the) battle; a comedy in rhyme. By Richard Dehan [Miss Clotilde Graves]. 8vo. [*Camb. Univ. Lib.*] London, 1911

LOVER'S (a) fate and a friend's counsel. By Anthony Hope [Sir Anthony Hope Hawkins]. 8vo. [*Lit. Year Book.*] London, 1894

LOVERS in exile. By the author of *The letters that never reached him* [Baroness Elizabeth von Heyking]. 8vo. Pp. 344. London, 1914

Adapted by the authoress from her original German novel "Ille mihi," and translated by E. Andrews.

LOVERS' knots. By Marjorie Bowen [Madame Gabrielle Margaret Vere Campbell Long]. 8vo. Pp. 256. London, 1912

LOUERS made men; a masque presented in the hovse of the right honorable the lord Haye, by diuers of noble qualitie, his friends; for the entertaynment of Monsieur Le Baron de Tovr, extraordinarie ambassador for the French king, on Saterday the 22. of Febrvary. 1617. [By Ben Jonson.] 4to. No pagination. [*Bodl.*] N.P. 1617

LOVERS (the) of Mademoiselle. By Clive Holland [Charles J. Hankinson]. 8vo. Pp. 350. [*Lond. Lib. Cat.*] London, 1913

LOVER'S (a) quarrel; or, the county ball. . . . [By Mrs Yorick Smythies, *née* Gordon.] 8vo. 3 vols. [*Brit. Mus.*] London, 1858

LOVES and death of Lady Sarah; a lay of the Orkney Isles. By Skraemur [W. T. Dennison]. 8vo. [Cursiter's *Lit. of Orkney and Shetland.*] Kirkwall, 1872

LOVE'S artifice; or, the perplexed squire: a farce of two acts [and in prose. By John Wignell]. 8vo. [*Brit. Mus.*] [York, 1762]

LOVE'S contrivance; or, le medecin malgre lui: a comedy, as it is acted at the Theatre Royal in Drury-Lane. [By Susanna Centlivre.] 4to. Pp. 67. [Baker's *Biog. Dram.*] London, 1703

LOVE'S depths. [A novel.] By G. Ohnet [Georges Hénot]; translated from the French by Frederick Rothwell. 8vo. Pp. 320. [*Lond. Lib. Cat.*] London, 1899

LOVE'S empire; a romance. [By T. Dowden.] 8vo. 3 vols. [*Brit. Mus.*] London, 1883

LOVE'S guerdon; a romance of the West Country. By Conrad Carroder [Walter John Tripp]. 8vo. Pp. 302. 1900

LOVE'S labour lost . . . regained; a continuation of Shakespeare's play. [By Major —— Browne.] 8vo. London, 1841

LOVE'S legend. By Henry Fielding [Henry Fielding-Hall]. 8vo. [*Lond. Lib. Cat.*] London, 1914

LOVE'S looking-glass; a volume of poems. [Those signed "B." are by Henry C. Beeching; "M." by J. W. Mackail; and "N.," J. B. B. Nichols.] 8vo. Pp. viii. 169. London, 1891

LOVE'S memorials. [Poems. By Theodore Wratislaw.] 4to. [*Brit. Mus.*] Rugby, 1892

LOVE'S messages. By M. S. C. [Mary S. Cobb]. 8vo. [*Amer. Cat.*] New York, 1897

LOVE'S moods. [A poem.] By Ælian Prince [Frank Carr]. 12mo. Pp. 104. [*Brit. Mus.*] London [1884]

LOVES (the) of an apothecary. [By Frederick Greenwood.] 8vo. Pp. vi. 198. [*Camb. Univ. Lib.*] London, 1854

LOVES (the) of Clitophon and Leucippe; a most elegant history, written in Greeke by Achilles Tatius, and now Englished [by Anthony Hodges]. 8vo. [*Brit. Mus.*] Oxford, 1638

LOVES (the) of Jonathan and Virginia [in verse]. By Boswell [W. B. Johnson]. 8vo. [Cushing's *Init. and Pseud.* i. 470.] Philadelphia, 1873

LOVES (the) of Othniel and Achrah; translated from the Chaldee [rather, wholly written by William Tooke, senior]. 8vo. [*D. N. B.* vol. 57, p. 49.] London, 1769

LOVES of the plants. [By Erasmus Darwin.] 8vo. [Courtney's *Secrets*, p. 122.] London, 1789

LOVES (the) of the poets. By "Le petit homme rouge" [Ernest Alfred Vizetelly]. 8vo. [*Lit. Year Book.*] London, 1915

LOVES (the) of the poets. By the author of the *Diary of an ennuyée* [Mrs Anna B. Jameson]. 8vo. 2 vols. London, 1829

LOVE'S offering. [Poems.] By James Hinton [George Barlow]. 8vo. [*Camb. Univ. Lib.*] London, 1883

LOVE'S progress. By the author of *The recollections of a New England housekeeper*, etc. [Mrs C. Gilman]. 12mo. [*Brit. Mus.*] New York, 1840

LOVE'S provocations; being extracts taken, in the most unmanly and unmannerly manner, from the diary of Miss Polly C——. By Cuthbert Bede [Rev. Edward Bradley, B.A.]. 8vo. [*D. N. B.* First Supp. vol. 1, p. 251.] London, 1855

LOVE'S revenge; a dramatic pastoral in two interludes [in verse]. [By Rev. John Hoadly, LL.D.] 8vo. [*D. N. B.* vol. 27, p. 22.] London, 1734

Later editions were issued in 1737 and 1745.

LOVE'S sacrifice; or, the rival merchants: a play, in five acts [chiefly in verse]. By the author of *The Provost of Bruges* [George W. Lovell]. 8vo. [*Brit. Mus.*] London, 1829

LOVE'S sentinel. By Florence Warden [Florence Alice Price, later Mrs George E. James]. 8vo. London, 1913

LOVE'S shadows. [A novel.] By Effie Adelaide Rowlands [E. Maria Albanesi]. 8vo. Pp. 245. [*Brit. Mus.*] London [1920]

LOVE'S side street. [A novel.] By "Pan" [Leslie Beresford]. 8vo. Pp. 319. [*Lit. Year Book.*] London, 1920

LOVE'S tribute; a sonnet sequence. By James Whitehead [Dr C. J. W. Dixon]. 8vo. [Sinton's *Bibl. of Hawick.*] Edinburgh, 1904

LOVES triumph; a play. [By Mary Frere.] 8vo. Pp. vi. 120. London, 1869

Authorship acknowledged by the writer.

LOVE'S victim; or, the queen of Wales: a tragedy, as it was acted at the Theatre in Lincolns-Inn-Fields, by his Majesty's servants. [By Charles Gildon.] 4to. Pp. 49. [Baker's *Biog. Dram.*] London, 1701

LOVE-TOKEN (a) for children. By the author of *The Linwoods* [Catherine Maria Sedgwick]. 8vo. [*Brit. Mus.*] London, 1838

LOVICE. [A novel.] By "The Duchess" [Mrs Margaret Hamilton Hungerford, formerly Mrs Argles]. 8vo. Pp. 315. [*Amer. Cat.*] Philadelphia, 1897

LOVING and loth; a novel. By the author of *Rosa Noel* [Bertha de Jongh]. 8vo. 3 vols. London, 1875

LOVING and serving. [A novel.] By Holme Lee [Harriet Parr]. 8vo. 3 vols. [Haynes' *Pseud.*] London, 1883

LOVING (the) ballad of Lord Bateman. [By William M. Thackeray; with etchings by George Cruikshank.] 12mo. [*Brit. Mus.*] London, 1839

LOVING (a) salutation to the seed of Abraham among the Jewes; where ever they are scattered up and down upon the face of the earth; and to the seed of Abraham among all people upon the face of the earth; which are all out of the way, wandering up and down from mountaine to hill, seeking rest and finding none. . . . By M. F. [Margaret Fell]. 4to. Pp. 37. [Smith's *Cat. of Friends' Books.*] London, 1657

LOW-CHURCH-MEN (the) vindicated from the unjust imputation of being no-Church-men; in answer to a late pamphlet, entitled The distinction of High-Church and Low-Church distinctly consider'd, &c.; with a fair state of the case of moderation. [By John Hancock, D.D., prebendary of Canterbury.] 8vo. Pp. 40. [*Brit. Mus.*] London, 1705

LOWER (the) depths; a play in four acts. By Maxim Gorki [Aleksyei M. Pyeshkov]. Translated from the original Russian by Laurence Irving. 8vo. Pp. 191. [*Brit. Mus.*] London [1912]

LOWER Eatington; its Manor House and Church. By E. P. S. [Evelyn Philip Shirley]. 8vo. Private print, 1869

LOWER slopes; reminiscences of excursions round the base of Helicon: poems. By Cecil Power [Charles Grant Blairfindie Allen]. 8vo. [*D. N. B.* First Supp. vol. 1, p. 38]. London, 1894

LOWLY (the) estate. [By David Grayson.] 8vo. London, 1910

LOWLY (a) lover. By Florence Warden [Florence Alice Price, later Mrs George E. James]. 8vo. Pp. 320. London, 1899

LOWLY mantle and armour wearers; an illustrated natural history reader. By N. D'Anvers [Nancy R. E. Bell, *née* Menghens]. 8vo. [*Brit. Mus.*] London [1883]

LOYAL. [A novel. By Mrs George William Godfrey.] 8vo. 3 vols. London, 1872

LOYAL (a) address to the Queen's most gracious Majesty. [By Francis Barham.] 8vo. [Boase and Courtney's *Bibl. Corn.* p. 11.] [London, 1840]

Signed: Δ.

LOYAL (the) and impartial satyrist; containing eight miscellany poems. . . . [By Thomas Rogers.] 4to. Pp. 30. [*Brit. Mus.*] London, 1694

The Epistle dedicatory is signed: S. S., the last letters of the author's names.

LOYAL heart; or, the trappers. By Gustave Aimard [Ollivier Gloux]; translated from the French by William Robson. 8vo. [*Brit. Mus.*] London, 1858

LOYAL (the) hussar; and other stories. By Alan St Aubyn [Mrs Frances Marshall]. 8vo. Pp. 356. [*Lond. Lib. Cat.*] London, 1901

LOYAL (a) little maid; a story of Mar's Rebellion. By Sarah Tytler [Henrietta Keddie]. 8vo. [*Lit. Year Book.*] London, 1899

LOYAL (a) little maid. By Elizabeth Schuyler [Edith Robinson]. 8vo. Boston, 1885

LOYAL (a) song of the royall feast, kept by the prisoners in the Towre in August last, with the names, titles and characters of every prisoner. By Sir F. W., Knight and Baronet, prisoner [Sir Francis Wortley]. A broadside. [*Bodl.*] N.P., N.D.

The author's name is in the handwriting of Wood, who says that it was published about 1647.

LOYAL (a) tear dropt on the vault of our late martyred sovereign; in an anniversary sermon on the day of his murther. [By Joseph Glanvil, F.R.S.] 4to. [Green's *Bibl. Somers*, i. 206.] [Bath] 1667

LOYALISTS (the); an historical novel. By the author of *Letters to a young man*, etc. [Mrs Jane West]. 12mo. 3 vols. [*Brit. Mus.*] London, 1812

LOYALISTS (the) reasons for his giving obedience, and swearing allegiance to the present government; as being oblieged thereto, by (it being founded on) the laws of God, nature, nations, and civil; and seing, hereby, justice preceeds advantage, and right possession, and rule precedents. . . . By F. G. Gent. [Francis Grant, Lord Cullen]. 8vo. Pp. 113. [*Nat. Lib. of Scot.*] Edinburgh, 1689

LOYALL (the) convert. [By Francis Quarles.] 4to. Pp. 20. [*N. and Q.* 1858, pp. 201, 299, 440.] Oxford, 1643

LOYALTY; a poem. By the author of *Futurity* [Miss —— Colthurst]; with explanatory notes. 8vo. [*Brit. Mus.*] Cork, 1858

LOYOLA and the early Jesuits. By Stewart Rose [Caroline Rose Erskine, Countess of Buchan]. 8vo. [*Lond. Lib. Cat.*] London, 1870

LOYS, Lord Berresford; and other tales. By the author of *Phyllis* [Margaret Argles, later Mrs Hungerford]. 8vo. 3 vols. [*Brit. Mus.*] London, 1883

LUCA della Robbia; with other Italian artists. By Leader Scott [Mrs Lucy Baxter]. 8vo. [*Brit. Mus.*] London, 1883

LUCIANUS redivivus; or, dialogues on men, manners, and opinions. [By Andrew Beckett.] 8vo. [Kinsman's *Cat.* p. 25.] London, 1811

LUCIDA intervalla; miscellaneous poems. . . . Written at Finsbury and Bethlem. By the Doctor's patient extraordinary [James Carkesse]. 4to. Pp. 68. [*Brit. Mus.*] N.P. 1679

LUCIEN Greville. By a Cornet in the Hon. East India Company's service [Thomas L. Pettigrew]. With etchings by George Cruikshank. 12mo. 3 vols. [*Brit. Mus.*] London, 1833

LUCIE'S mistake. By W. Heimburg [Bertha Behrens]. 8vo. New York, 1890

LUCIFER and Mammon; an historical sketch of the last and present century, with characters, anecdotes, etc. [By Joseph Moser.] 8vo. Pp. 296. [Watt's *Bibl. Brit.*] London, 1793

LUCIFER'S lacky; or, the devil's new creature: being the true character of a dissembling Brownist. . . . [By John Taylor, the Water poet.] 4to. London, 1641

LUCILE. By Owen Meredith, author of *The wanderer*, etc. [Edward Robert Bulwer-Lytton, Earl of Lytton]. 8vo. Pp. vi. 361. [*Brit. Mus.*] London, 1860

LUCILLA; an experiment. By Alice Spinner [Mrs Augusta Zelia Fraser]. 8vo. 2 vols. London, 1895

LUCILLA; or, the reconciliation. By the author of *The twin sisters*, etc. [Elizabeth Sandham]. 12mo. 2 vols. [*Brit. Mus.*] London, 1819

LUCILLE Belmont; a novel. [By Alex. Baillie Cochrane.] 8vo. 3 vols. London, 1849

LUCINA sine concubitu; a letter humbly address'd to the Royal Society; in which is proved by most incontestible evidence, drawn from reason and practice, that a woman may conceive and be brought to bed without any commerce with man. [By Sir John Hill, M.D.] Third edition. 8vo. [*Brit. Mus.*] London, 1750

This pamphlet is signed: Abraham Johnson.

LUCINDA; a drama. [By Rev. Charles Jenner.] 8vo. [Watt's *Bibl. Brit.*] London, 1770

LUCINDA; a novel. By Anthony Hope [Sir Anthony Hope Hawkins]. 8vo. [*Lit. Year Book.*] London, 1920

LUCINDA; or, the self-devoted daughter. [By Thomas Manti.] 8vo. [*European Mag.* i. 209.] London, 1782

LUCIUS Carey; or, the mysterious female of Mora's Dell: an historical tale. By the author of *The weird woman* [H. Coates]. 12mo. 4 vols. [*Brit. Mus.*] London, 1831

LUCIUS Davoren; or, publicans and sinners: a novel. By the author of *Lady Audley's secret*, etc. [Mary Elizabeth Braddon, later Mrs John Maxwell]. 8vo. 3 vols. London, 1873

LUCIUS; or, the Roman convert; a tale: to which is added Giannetto's courtship, or the usage of Belmonte; a drama: and Perolla, or the revolt of Capua; a tragedy. [By James Marshall.] 12mo. Pp. viii. 482. [*Nat. Lib. of Scot.*] Edinburgh, 1860

LUCK (the) of Ladysmede. [A novel. By William Lucas Collins.] 8vo. 2 vols. [*D. N. B.* vol. 11, p. 381.] Edinburgh, 1860

LUCK (the) of the lanes. By John Barnett [John Reginald Stagg]. 8vo. Pp. viii. 256. [*Brit. Mus.*] London, 1907

LUCK (the) of the Napiers. [A novel.] By John Strange Winter [Mrs Arthur Stannard, *née* Henrietta E. V. Palmer]. 8vo. Pp. 314. London, 1911

LUCKLESS (the) Black. [Verses.] By Hippopolis [James Macdonald Horsburgh]; with four illustrations by WHO [William H. Overend]. 8vo. Pp. 18. [*Brit. Mus.*] London, private print, 1892

LUCKLESS (the) drave; and other poems. By the author of *Verses in memory of Dunbar Collegiate Church* [George Miller, of Dunbar, bookseller]. 8vo. Pp. 72. [Couper's *Millers of Haddington.*] Edinburgh, 1820

LUCKY (the) chance; or, an alderman's bargain: a comedy, as it is acted at the Theatre Royal. By Mrs A. B. [Aphra Behn]. 4to. [Arber's *Term Cat.* ii. 618.] London, 1687

LUCKY (the) discovery; or, the tanner of York: a ballad opera, as it is acted at the Theatre Royal in Covent Garden. [By John Arthur.] 8vo. [*W.*] London [1738?]

An edition was published at York, having the preface signed with the author's name.

LUCKY Mr Loder. [A novel.] By Guy Thorne [Cyril A. E. Ranger-Gull]. 8vo. Pp. 319. [*Brit. Mus.*] London, 1918

LUCKY (the) number; a novel. By Ian Hay [John Hay Beith]. 8vo. [*Lit. Year Book.*] London, 1923

LUCRETIA; a tragedy in five acts and in verse. Translated [by Sir Arthur Rumbold]. . . . 8vo. [*Brit. Mus.*] London, 1848

LUCRETIA; or, the children of night. By the author of *Rienzi*, etc. [Edward George Earle Lytton Bulwer-Lytton, Lord Lytton]. Second edition. 12mo. 3 vols. London, 1847

LUCRETIA; or, the heroine of the nineteenth century. . . . [By Francis Edward Paget, rector of Elford.] 8vo. [*Nat. Lib. of Scot.*] London, 1868

"LUCTOR et emergo"; being an historical essay on the state of England at the Peace of Ryswyck, 1697. By Marjorie Bowen [Gabriella Margaret Vere Campbell]. 8vo. Pp. 32. [*Brit. Mus.*] Newcastle-upon-Tyne, 1925

LUCUBRATIONS. By a Lady [Charlotte Harwood]. 12mo. [Upcott and Shoberl's *Biog. Dict.*] London, 1786

LUCUBRATIONS; consisting of essays, reveries, &c. in prose and verse. By the late Peter of Pontefract [Rev. Richard Graves]. 12mo. [Green's *Bibl. Somers.* ii. 445.] London, 1786

On the title-page is an engraving of a lamp, with the motto "Languescit."

LUCUBRATIONS during a short recess. By —— —— Esq.; Member of Parliament for the county of —— [Sir John Sinclair, Bart.]. 8vo. Pp. 65. [*Life*, i. 93.] London, 1782

A second edition, corrected, was issued in 1783 with the author's name.

LUCUBRATIONS (the) of Gaffer Greybeard; containing many curious particulars relating to the manners of the people in England, during the present age; including the present state of religion, particularly among the Protestant dissenters: in a series of letters, on a plan entirely new. [By Robert Sanders.] 12mo. 2 vols. [Nichol's *Lit. Anec.* ii. 730.] London, 1773

LUCUBRATIONS (the) of Humphrey Ravelin, Esq., late Major in the * * regiment of infantry. [By George Proctor.] 8vo. Pp. 414. London, 1823

LUCUBRATIONS (the) of Isaac Bickerstaff Esq. [Sir Richard Steele]. 8vo. 4 vols. [*Brit. Mus.*] London, 1710

LUCUBRATIONS on the epigram,

'Ει μεν ἠν μαθειν ἀ δει παθειν,
Και μη παθειν, καλον ἠν το μαθειν.
'Ει δε δει παθειν ἀδ' ἠν μαθειν,
Τι δει μαθειν; χρη γαρ παθειν.

[By James Gregory, M.D.] 8vo. [*D. Laing.*] Edinburgh, 1808

LUCULLUS; or, palatable essays. By the author of *The Queen's Messenger*, etc. [Major Herbert Byng Hall]. 8vo. [*Brit. Mus.*] London, 1878

Attributed also, but on questionable grounds, to Eustace E. Grenville Murray.

LUCY Bettesworth. By George Bourne [George Sturt]. 8vo. Pp. xi. 280. [*Brit. Mus.*] London, 1913

LUCY Clare; and the Babes in the casket. [By Mary Maria Butt, later Mrs Sherwood.] 8vo. Pp. 234. [*Brit. Mus.*] Edinburgh, 1882

An earlier edition of the first part is "The history of Lucy Clare."

LUCY Crofton. By the author of *Margaret Maitland*, etc. [Mrs O. Oliphant]. 8vo. Pp. 317. [*Brit. Mus.*] London, 1860

LUCY Fitzadam; an autobiography. [By Edward Whitaker.] 8vo. [*Brit. Mus.*] London, 1872

LUCY Gelding; a tale of land and sea. By Willa West [Mary S. F. Slocum]. 8vo. [Cushing's *Init. and Pseud.* i. 305.] Chicago, 1862

LUCY Hardinge; a second series of Afloat and ashore. [By James Fenimore Cooper.] 8vo. 3 vols. [Allibone's *Dict.*] London, 1844

LUCY Herbert. By Estelle [Mrs Piper]. 8vo. [Cushing's *Init. and Pseud.* i. 93.] Boston, 1863

LUCY Meridyth. By the author of *An art-student in Munich* [Anna Mary Howitt, later Mrs Watts]. 8vo. [*Brit. Mus.*] London [1866]

LUCY [Sara] Sampson; or, the unhappy heiress: a tragedy in five acts, translated from the German [of Gotthold Ephraim Lessing] by a citizen of Philadelphia [David Rittenhouse]. 8vo. Pp. 88. Philadelphia, 1789

LUCY, the factory girl; or, the secret of the Tontine Close. . . . [By David Pae.] 8vo. [*Nat. Lib. of Scot.*] Edinburgh, 1860

LUCY'S Christmas box; or, how Georgie found his cousin. [By J. Lockhart.] 8vo. Pp. 64. [*Brit. Mus.*] London, 1884

LUDLOW no lyar; or, a detection of Dr Hollingworth's disingenuity in his second defence of King Charles I., and a further vindication of the Parliament of the 3d of Novemb. 1640, with exact copies of the Pope's letter to K. Charles the First, and of his answer to the Pope: in a letter from General Ludlow, to Dr Hollingworth. . . . [By Slingsby Bethell?] 4to. Pp. xx. 63. Amsterdam, 1692

LUDOVICO Ariosto; his satyres, in seven famous discourses; in English by Garuis Markham [but really translated by Robert Tofte]. 4to. [*Brit. Mus.*] London, 1608

See another translation: "The satires of Ludovico Ariosto. . . ." (1759).

LUDUS amoris. By Benjamin Swift [William Romaine Paterson]. 8vo. [*Brit. Mus.*] London, 1910

LUDUS mathematicus; or, the mathematical game, explaining the description, construction, and use of the numericall table of proportion. . . . By E. W. [Edmund Wingate]. 12mo. Pp. 76. [*Bodl.*] London, 1654

LUDUS scacchiae; a satyr, with other poems. By R. G. [Robert Gould]. 8vo. Pp. 62. [Lowndes' *Bibl. Man.*] London, 1675

Ascribed also to R. Goodridge. [*Bodl.*]

LUDUS scacchiae; chesse-play: a game both pleasant, wittie and politicke, with certaine briefe instructions thereunto belonging: translated out of the Italian [of Diamo da Odemira] into the English tongue [by J. Rowbothum]. . . . 4to. [*Brit. Mus.*] London, 1597

A reprint was issued about 1810.

"LUKNON"; light cast on the footprints of Israel. [By Henry Peach Keighley.] 8vo. [*Brit. Mus.*] London, 1880

LULU Reid's pupil. By H. N. W. B. [Mrs Harriet Newell (Woods) Baker]. 8vo. [Kirk's *Supp.*] Boston, 1871

LUMEN de lumine; or, a new magicall light discovered, and communicated to the world. By Eugenius Philalethes [Thomas Vaughan]. 12mo. Pp. 101. [Wood's *Athen. Oxon.* iii. 724.] London, 1651

LUMEN siccum; an essay on the exercise of the intellect in matters of religious belief; addressed to Members of the Society of Friends. [By George Stewardson Brady, surgeon in Sunderland.] Pp. 38. [Supp. to Smith's *Cat. of Friends' Books*, p. 21.] London, 1868

LUMINALIA; or, the festivall of light: personated in a masque at Court by the Queenes Maiestie and her ladies. [By Sir William Davenant?] 4to. [*Pollard and Redgrave.*] London, 1637

LUMLEY the painter. [A novel.] By John Strange Winter [Mrs Arthur Stannard, *née* Henrietta E. V. Palmer]. 8vo. London, 1891

LUNAR observations. [A satire. By Dionysius Thompson.] 8vo. London, 1839

LUPICINE; or, the hermit of St Loup; founded on the French of Charles Chatelanat. By C. S. H. [Charles Sumner Harington, M.A.]. 8vo. [*Brit. Mus.*] London, 1873

LURE (the) of contraband; a novel. By J. Weare Giffard [John W. Price]. 8vo. London, 1920

LURE (the) of fame. [A novel.] By Clive Holland [Charles J. Hankinson]. 8vo. Pp. 238. [*Lond. Lib. Cat.*] London, 1896

LURE (the) of the dim trails. [A novel.] By B. M. Bower [Mrs Bertrand M. Sinclair]. 8vo. [*Amer. Cat.*] New York, 1907

LURED away; or, the story of a wedding-ring. By Bertha M. Clay [Charlotte M. Braeme]. 8vo. Pp. 189. New York [1889]

LURIDA lumina. [A poem.] By the author of *Jonas Fisher* [James Carnegie, Earl of Southesk]. 8vo. Pp. 52. [*Brit. Mus.*] Edinburgh, private print, 1876

LUSCAR Knowes. By J. M. [John Miller, builder in London]. Pp. 9. [Beveridge's *Dunf. Bibl.*] Dunfermline, 1873

LUSHAIS (the), 1873 to 1889. [By Capt. H. K. Browne.] Fol. [*Calc. Imp. Lib.*] Shillong, 1889

LUSORIUM (the); a collection of convivial songs, etc. [By William O'Brien.] 12mo. [O'Donoghue's *Poets of Ireland.*] London, 1783

LUSORIUM (the); a collection of facetiæ. By Harry Lusus, Esq. [William O'Brien]. 12mo. [O'Donoghue's *Poets of Ireland.*] London, 1798

LUSUS fortunæ; the play of fortune; continually acted by the severall creatures on the stage of the world; or, a glance at the various mutability, inconstancie, and uncertainty of all earthly things, from a consideration of the present times. By T. F. [Thomas Forde]. 8vo. Pp. 108. [*Brit. Mus.*] [London] 1649

LUSUS pueriles. [Poems.] By C. R. S. [Christopher Reynolds Stone]. 8vo. Pp. 55. [*Brit. Mus.*] London, 1901

LUSUS serius; or, serious passe-time: a philosophicall discourse concerning the superiority of creatures under man, translated from the Latin of Michael Meyerus, by J. de la Salle [John Hall, of Durham]. 8vo. [*D. N. B.* vol. 24, p. 71.] London, 1654

LUTHER. Knox. The Inquisition. New England; papers from *The Teacher's Offering*. [By Miss Childs.] 12mo. Pp. 224. [Martin's *Cat.*] Bungay, 1845

LUTHER Miller's ambition. By Lillie Montfort [Eliza Mumford]. 8vo. London, 1883

LUTHERS life, collected from the writinges of him selfe, and other learned Protestants; together with a further shorte discourse, touching Andreas Melanchton, Bucer, Ochine, Carolostadius, Suinglius, Caluine and Beza, the late pretended Reformers of religion: taken from the onely reporte of learned Protestants themselves. By John Brerely [Lawrence Anderton] priest and author of the *Protestants apologie*. 4to. [*The Library*, Sept. 1926, p. 162.] S. Omer, 1624

LUTHER'S words and the word of God. . . . By the author of *What sort of man was Martin Luther?* [William Henry Anderdon]. 8vo. [*Brit. Mus.*] London, 1883

LUX hominum; studies of the living Christ in the world of to-day. By Frederick W. O. Ward [Frederick Harald Williams]. 8vo. Pp. 426. [*Brit. Mus.*] London, 1907

LUX in tenebris; or, a clavis to the Treasury in Broad Street. [By Thomas Fontleroy.] London, 1653

An attack on the Commissioners of Excise.

LUX Mundi in Convocation. [By George Anthony Denison, archdeacon.] 8vo. Pp. 27. [Green's *Bibl. Somers.* ii. 365.] Taunton, 1891

LUX occidentalis; or, Providence display'd in the coronation of King William and Queen Mary, and their happy accession to the crown of England; with other remarks. By T. R., A. M. Oxon. [Thomas Rogers]. 4to. Pp. 28. [Arber's *Term. Cat.* ii. 655.] London, 1689

LUX orientalis; or, an enquiry into the opinion of the Eastern sages concerning the præexistence of souls: being a key to unlock the grand mysteries of Providence, in relation to man's sin and misery. [By Joseph Glanvill.] 8vo. [*Brit. Mus.*] London, 1662

LUX renata [in verse]; a Protestant's epistle, with notes. By the author of *Religio Clerici* [Rev. Edward Smedley, M.A.]. 8vo. Pp. 63. [*Brit. Mus.*] London, 1827

LUXURY no political evil, but . . . proved to be necessary to the preservation and prosperity of States. . . . [By John Trusler, LL.D.] 8vo. [*D. N. B.* vol. 57, p. 268.] London [1780]

LUXURY, pride and vanity, the bane of the British nation; wherein is shewn the prodigality and profuseness of all ranks, and conditions; the transposition of the city to the court, with the tradesmen's expensive manner of living; the encrease of the wine-trade, the decay of the wealth and industry of the people; town and country over-run with false splendor; most of our modern equipage compar'd to the life of man; physicians, and even apothecaries under an absolute necessity of keeping equipages in support of their characters and families, . . . [By Erasmus Jones.] Second edition. [London, 1735]

A manuscript note on the copy in the National Library of Scotland, states that "there have come oute two Editions in 3 days." See also *N. and Q.* 1855, p. 419, from which it appears that the fourth edition was printed within two months of the appearance of the first.

LUZARA; a Pindarique ode, on Prince Eugenius of Savoy, and his late victory over the French and Spaniards, in Italy: most humbly dedicated to His Grace the Duke of Somerset. [By Joseph Harris.] Fol. Pp. 12. London, 1702

LUZETTE; or, good brought out of evil. By Maria [Maria D. Weston]. 8vo. [Cushing's *Init. and Pseud.* ii. 95.] Boston, 1847

LYCHGATE Hall. [A novel.] By M. E. Francis [Mrs Francis Blundell, *née* Margaret E. Sweetman]. 8vo. [*Brit. Mus.*] London, 1904

LYCIDAS; a masque: to which is added Delia, a pastoral elegy, and verses on the death of the Marquis of Carmarthen. [By Thomas Lambe, formerly scholar at Eton College.] 4to. [*N. and Q.* 1855, p. 147.] London, 1762

LYCIDUS; or, the love in fashion: a novel: being an account, from Lycidus to Lysander, of his voyage from the Island of Love. By the author of *The voyage to the Island of Love* [Mrs Aphra Behn]. . . . 8vo. [Arber's *Term Cat.* ii. 217.] London, 1688

LYCORIS; or, the Grecian courtezan: translated from the French [of A. Bret] by a gentleman. 12mo. [*Brit. Mus.*] London, 1761

In a later edition (1779) the title begins "The Grecian courtezan. . . ."

LYDIA. [A novel.] By Sydney Christian [Maria L. Lord]. 8vo. Pp. 280. [*Brit. Mus.*] London, 1893

LYDIA; or, conversion: a sacred drama, inscribed to the Jews. By a clergyman of the Church of England [William Pace]. 8vo. London, 1835

LYDIA; or, filial piety: a novel. By the author of *The marriage act;* and, *Letters on the English nation* [John Shebbeare, M.D.]. 12mo. 2 vols. [*Brit. Mus.*] London, 1755

LYDIA'S heart opened; or, divine mercy magnified in the conversion of a sinner by the Gospel: being the sum of several sermons preached lately by J. S. [James Strong, minister at Ilminster]. 12mo. [Green's *Bibl. Somers.* iii. 293.] London, 1675

LYME Regis; a guide-book. [By Miss F. Stanger Leathes.] 12mo. [*Brit. Mus.*] Lyme Regis, 1886

LYMPSFIELD and its environs; being a series of views, with descriptions, of that village and objects of interest in its vicinity; and The old oak chair, a ballad, with illustrations by George Cruikshank. [By Thomas Streatfield.] 8vo. No pagination. [*Bodl.*] Westerham, 1838

LYNDE Weiss; an autobiography. [By Thomas Bangs Thorpe.] 8vo. Philadelphia, 1854

LYNMOUTH; or, sketchings and musings in North Devon. By a sojourner [Rev. John Gay Copleston]. 8vo. [Davidson's *Bibl. Devon.* p. 132.] London, private print, 1835

LYNN'S (the) Court mystery. [A novel.] By Denzil Vane [F. Du Tertre]. 8vo. Pp. 139. [*Brit. Mus.*] London [1892]

LYON (the) campaign in Missouri; being a history of the First Iowa Infantry, together with a bird's-eye view of the conditions in Iowa preceding the Great Civil War of 1861. By "Ironquill" [Eugene Fitch Ware]. 8vo. Pp. 388. [*Amer. Cat.*] Topeka, Kansas [1908]

LYRA Apostolica. [Contributions of six authors to the *British Magazine*, and reprinted therefrom. Each poem is signed with a letter of the Greek alphabet from alpha to zeta, and the following are the authors' names:— α = John W. Bowden; β = Richard Hurrell Froude; γ = John Keble; δ = John Henry Newman; ϵ = Isaac Williams; ζ = Robert Isaac Wilberforce.] 12mo. Pp. 226. [*W.*] Derby and London, 1836

LYRA Biblica; or, Scriptural lyrics on the New Testament. By W. B. W. [William Burt Whitmarsh]. 8vo. [Kirk's *Supp.*] London, 1873

LYRA consolationis; hymns for the day of sorrow and weariness. [By Mrs —— Bonar.] 8vo. London, 1866

LYRA evangelica; poetical meditations and hymns. [By John James Cummins.] 8vo. [O'Donoghue's *Poets of Ireland.*] London, 1839

An enlarged edition was issued in 1849 as "Hymns, meditations, and poems."

LYRA innocentium; thoughts in verse on Christian children, their ways, and their privileges. [By John Keble, M.A., vicar of Hursley.] Fifth edition. 8vo. Pp. xii. 214. [*D. N. B.* vol. 30, p. 294.] Oxford, 1851

The first edition was published in 1846.

LYRA liturgica; reflections in verse for Holy Days and Seasons. [Signed: F. O. *i.e.* Rev. Frederick Oakeley, M.A.] 12mo. [*Brit. Mus.*] London, 1865

LYRA Nigeriæ. By Adamu [Edward Coker Adams]. 8vo. Pp. xi. 110. London, 1910

LYRA piscatoria; original poems on the nature, habits, and mode of capture of all British fresh-water fishes; on flies, fishing, fishermen, etc. By Cotswold Isys, M.A. [Rev. R. H. Glover]. 8vo. Pp. xvi. 173. London, 1895

LYRA sancta. [Sacred poems.] By A. E. G. [A. E. Greenhill]. 12mo. Pp. 54. Edinburgh, 1863

LYRA sanctorum; lays for the minor festivals of the English Church. [Edited and partly written by William John Deane.] 8vo. [*Brit. Mus.*] London, 1850

A reprint of poems published in the "Ecclesiastic" in the years 1847 and 1848. The Advertisement is signed: W. J. D., Wyck Rissington.

LYRE and lancet; a story in scenes. By F. Anstey [Thomas Anstey Guthrie]. 8vo. Pp. viii. 256. [*Brit. Mus.*] London, 1895

LYRE and star; poems. By the author of *Ginevra* [Francis A. H. Terrell]. 8vo. London, 1883

LYRE (the) of love (a selection of amatory poems). [By Peter L. Caurtier or Courtier.] 12mo. 2 vols. [Bliss' *Cat.* p. 53.] 1806

LYRIC consolations; with the speech of Alderman W. [Wilkes] delivered in a dream, at the King's Bench prison, the evening of his inauguration. [By John Hall-Stevenson.] 4to. [*D. N. B.* vol. 54, p. 239.] London, 1769

LYRIC odes, for the year 1785. By Peter Pindar, Esq., a distant relation of the poet of Thebes, and Laureat to the Royal Academy [John Wolcot, M.D.]. 4to. Pp. 50. [*D. N. B.* vol. 62, p. 293.] London, 1785

LYRIC odes to the Royal Academicians, for 1782. By Peter Pindar, a distant relation of the poet of Thebes [John Wolcot, M.D.]. Fifth edition, enlarged. 4to. Pp. 36. London, 1787

LYRIC (the) works of Horace, translated into English verse; to which are added a number of original poems. By a native of America [Lieut.-Colonel John Parke]. 8vo. Pp. 375. [Evans' *Amer. Bibl.* vol. 7, p. 35.] Philadelphia, 1786

LYRICAL ballads from the German of Schiller, containing "The song of the bell" and other minor poems. By the translator of *Mary Stuart* [Mrs Anne Gibbons, *née* Trelawny]. 8vo. Pp. 38. [*Brit. Mus.*] Devonport, 1868

LYRICAL ballads, with a few other poems. [By William Wordsworth and Samuel Taylor Coleridge.] 12mo. Pp. v. 210. London, 1798

The original edition.

LYRICAL (the) part of the drama of Caractacus, as altered by the author [William Mason]. 8vo. [*Brit. Mus.*] London, 1776

LYRICAL poems; songs, pastorals, roundelays, war-poems, madrigals. By Emily Hawthorne [Mrs Emily Thornton Charles]. 12mo. Philadelphia, 1886

LYRICK (the) poet; Odes and Satyres translated out of Horace into English verse by J. S. [John Smith]. 8vo. [*Brit. Mus.*] London, 1649

LYRICKS (the) of Horace, comprising his odes, epodes, and secular odes, in English verse; with the Latin text revised and subjoined [by John Nott, M.D.]. 8vo. 2 vols. [*D. N. B.* vol. 41, p. 233.] London, 1803

LYRICS. By Christopher Carr [Arthur Christopher Benson]. 8vo. Pp. 189. [*Brit. Mus.*] London, 1895

LYRICS. By Ellis Walton [Mrs F. Percy Cotton]. 8vo. Pp. xi. 60. London, 1895

LYRICS. By J. H. S. [John Henry Scourfield, formerly Philipps]. 8vo. Pp. 79. [Cushing's *Init. and Pseud.* i. 133.] Cheltenham, 1864

LYRICS. By "Nomad" [Adèle Crafton-Smith]. 8vo. Pp. 72. [*Lond. Lib. Cat.*] London, 1899

LYRICS. By Pearl Rivers [Mrs Eliza Jane Nicholson, *née* Poitevent]. 8vo. [Cushing's *Init. and Pseud.* i. 252.] Philadelphia, 1873

LYRICS. By the letter H [Charles Graham Halpine, B.A.]. 8vo. [O'Donoghue's *Poets of Ireland.*] New York, 1854

LYRICS and idylls. By Gerda Fay [Mrs Caroline M. Gemmer]. 8vo. [Cushing's *Init. and Pseud.* i. 100.] London, 1861

LYRICS and landscapes. By Guy Roslyn [Joseph Hatton]. 8vo. [Cushing's *Init. and Pseud.* i. 253.] London, 1878

Ascribed also to George Barnett Smith.

LYRICS and lays. By Pips [William Henry Abbott, junior]. 12mo. Pp. vi. 210. [*Calcutta Imp. Lib.*] Calcutta, 1867

Attributed also to F. F. Wyman.

LYRICS and Philippics. By J. H. P. [John Henry Philipps, later J. H. Scourfield]. 8vo. [*Brit. Mus.*] Middle-Hill Press, private print, 1859

LYRICS and rhymes. By Ab. Original [James Sadler]. 12mo. [*Lib. of Col. Inst.* i. 675.] Adelaide, 1890

LYRICS and sonnets of Ireland. By Conaciensis [Matthew F. Hughes]. 8vo. [O'Donoghue's *Poets of Ireland.*] Dublin, 1871

LYRICS for heart and voice; a contribution to the Hymnal of the future. By Thomas Brevior [Thomas Shorter]. 12mo. [Boase's *Mod. Eng. Biog.* vol. 6, col. 554.] London [1833]

LYRICS for the League. By an old friend of the working-classes [—— Sturgeon]. 8vo. 2 parts. [*Brit. Mus.*] [London, 1867]

LYRICS of a day; or, newspaper poetry. By a Volunteer in the United States service [Henry Howard Brounell]. 12mo. [Kirk's *Supp.*] New York, 1876

LYRICS of the soul; a book of poems. By Marianne Farningham [Marianne Hearne, of Farningham]. 8vo. [*Brit. Mus.*] London, 1908

LYSIMACHIA; a poem. [By Dr —— Glass.] 12mo. Belfast, 1797

LYTTEL (a) booke of nonsense. [Signed: R. D. *i.e.* Randall Davies.] In verse. 8vo. Pp. 153. London, 1912

LYTURGIE (the) of the masse; wherein are treated three principal pointes of faith. 1. That in the sacrament of the Eucharist are truly and really contained the body and bloud of Christ. 2. That the masse is a true and proper sacrifice of the body and bloud of Christ, offered to God by preistes. 3. That communion of the Eucharist to the laity vnder one kind is lawful. The ceremonies also of the masse now vsed in the Catholicke Church, are al of them deriued from the primitiue Church. By Iohn Brereley, preist [Lawrence Anderton]. 4to. Pp. 469. [*The Library*, Sept. 1926.] Colen [or rather Birchley Hall, Lancs.], 1620